CLARK'S
KENTUCKY ALMANAC

AND BOOK OF FACTS

2006

A comprehensive publication with contemporary and historical information, infused with many photos, facts, and archival treasures that make up the rich and exciting history of Kentucky

The
Clark
Group

CLARK'S
KENTUCKY ALMANAC
AND BOOK OF FACTS
2006

ISBN (softcover) 1-883589-68-1
ISBN (hardcover) 1-883589-72-X

Published and distributed by The Clark Group
Printed in the United States of America

To order online, log on to www.kyalmanac.com
To order by telephone, call 1-800-944-3995

The **Clark** Group

Sam Stephens	Editor-in-Chief
Florence S. Huffman	Managing Editor
Robert G. Clark	Publisher & Production Manager
Dea Riley	Marketing & Public Relations
Sid Webb	Photo Editor
Scott Risner	Graphic Design & Production
John A. McGill	Sports Editor
Carla Bryan	Associate Production Manager
Kelly Elliott	Associate Production Manager
Jennifer Kash	Associate Production Manager
Robert Seelbach	Associate Production Manager
Mark Reinhardt	Associate Editor
Robyn Wilkinson	Customer Service Manager
Melissa Anthony	Advertising Manager

Your Safety Comes First.

Your safety shield when weather is at its worst.

Five LIVE Doppler Radars to alert you FIRST.

The early warning you need to stay safe from the storm.

Chief Meteorologist TG Shuck is Lexington's first Certified Broadcast Meteorologist

*By the American Meteorological Society

WKYoT 27 NEWSFIRST

TG Shuck, Marina Jurica, Chris Bailey and Keisha Kirkland

Table of Contents

———:🎗️:———

A **MAN** fell from his horfe, and the fall
for a few minutes deprived him of fenfation ;
on the return of his underftanding, he was
afked how he did ? " Oh," faid he, I begin to
come to my fenfes :" " I congratulate you,"
faid a wag, " for you never had any before."

———:🎗️:———

Note: Until the late 1780s, American publishers practiced the English method of typesetting the
letter "s" as an "f." Source: The Kentucky Almanac 1801, published by John Bradford, Lexington,
Ky. All reproductions of antique Kentucky Almanac's included in this publication are reproduced
with permission of Readex, a division of NewsBank, Inc., and the American Antiquarian Society.

Thomas D. Clark
A Dedication

"The tapestry of Kentucky history is woven from a multiplicity of strands of natural and human elements."
– Thomas D. Clark

Thomas D. Clark will forever be woven into the strands of Kentucky's fabric. How fortunate that the University of Kentucky became his choice for graduate studies in 1928 after journeying from his home in Louisville, Mississippi. His tenure at Kentucky as history professor and chairman of the Department of History lasted for 37 years, teaching and influencing thousands of students, many who have become distinguished historians themselves.

Dr. Clark's many contributions to Kentucky are as permanent as our Constitution. His more than 30 books published and co-authored will forever chronicle the history of Kentucky and its role and influence on the exploration and development of this nation. His rescue of truckloads of state papers with the help of Governor A.B. "Happy" Chandler and the establishment of the Department for Libraries and Archives became one of the most important milestones in the preservation of Kentucky's historical documents.

We are deeply indebted to Dr. Clark for his Foreword, his support and encouragement of this historic revival of the Kentucky Almanac after 150 years.

We hereby dedicate this Premier Edition in loving memory of Thomas D. Clark.

The Clark Group, Lexington, Kentucky

Acknowledgements

Contributing Writers

Kandie Adkinson, Secretary of State's Office
Bill Ambrose, Historian
Bob Arnold, Executive Director, Kentucky Association of Counties (KACO)
Bob Babbage, President, Babbage CoFounder
Ewell Balltrip, Historian
James R. Bean, M.D.
Royal Berglee, Professor, Morehead State University, Dept. of Geology, Gov't & History
Robert Boles, Writer & Producer
Zachary Bortolot, Professor, Morehead State University, Dept. of Geology, Gov't & History
Ed Bowen, President, Grayson-Jockey Club Research Foundation, Inc
Michael Breeding, Americana Productions
Bill Bright, Curator, Kentucky Military History Museum
Ron Bryant, Historian
Anne Butler, Kentucky State University
Jim Carroll, Kentucky Dept. of Parks
Lindy Casebier, Executive Director, Kentucky Office for Arts & Cultural Humanities
Todd Cassidy, Executive Director, Kentucky Film Office
Jerry Cecil, Kentucky's Civilian Aide to the Secretary of the U.S. Army
Robert G. Clark, Publisher
Thomas D. Clark (1903-2005), Kentucky Historian Laureate
Martha Layne Collins, Executive Director, Kentucky World Trade Center
Glen Conner, Professor, Western Kentucky University, State Climatologist Emeritus
Bill Cooke, Museum Director, International Museum of the Horse
Gary Cordner, Ret. Dean, Eastern Kentucky University, College of Justice & Safety
Al Cross, Institute for Rural Journalism & Community Issues
Ron Crouch, Director, Kentucky State Data Center
Stephanie Durst, Kentucky State Fair
Nelson Dawson, Kentucky Historical Society
Megan Diamond, Louisville Bats
Michelle Edwards, Marion County Tourism Commission
Kadie Engstrom, Education Coordinator, The Belle of Louisville
Momfeather Ericksen, Director, Mantle Rock Native Education and Cultural Center
Jan Fletcher, Kentucky Home School Association
Stuart Foster, Professor, Western Kentucky University, and Kentucky State Climatologist
Virginia Fox, Secretary, Kentucky Education Cabinet
Gatewood Galbreath, Attorney & Historian
Jon Gassett, Commissioner, Dept. for Fish & Wildlife Resources
Jerry Gibson, Historian, Journalist
Jerrell Goodpaster, Writer & Hiking Authority

Bill Gordon, Writer, History Professor (Ret.) & Vintner
Rosemary O. Gordan, American Vegetable Grower Magazine
Tolley Graves, Executive Director of the American Saddlebred Museum
Trey Grayson, Secretary of State
John Mark Hack, President, Global Development Partners
Col. Claude E. Hammond
Gwynn Henderson, Kentucky Archaeological Survey
Janet Holloway, Executive Director, Women Leading Kentucky
Charlie Hughes, Poet, Wind Publications
Steve Jones, Professor, Murray State University
Chris Kellogg, Writer
Nancy Jo Kemper, Kentucky Council of Churches
Kentucky Adult Education (CPE)
Thomas J. Kiffmeyer, Professor, Morehead State University, Dept. of Geology, Gov't & History
James Klotter, Professor of History, Georgetown College, and Kentucky State Historian
Robert Lawson, Executive Director, Kentucky Music Hall of Fame
Sylvia Lovely, Executive Director, Kentucky League of Cities
Mark Maloney, Sports Writer
William E. Matthews, Historian & Co-Owner, Back Home in Kentucky
Michael McCall, President, Kentucky Community & Technical College System
John A. McGill, Sports Editor
Christine E. McMichael, Professor, Morehead State University, Dept. of Geology, Gov't & History
Lori Meadows, Kentucky Arts Council
Dr. Lynwood Montell, Author & Professor, Western Kentucky University
Gary O'Dell, Professor, Morehead State University, Dept. of Geology, Gov't & History
Jim Ogle, News Director, WKYT-TV
John Ed Pearce, Journalist & Author
David Pollack, Director, Kentucky Archaeological Survey
Chester Powell, Poet
O. Leonard Press, founder of Kentucky Educational Television
Prichard Committee for Academic Excellence
Diana Ratliff, Shakertown at Pleasant Hill
Billy Reed, Sportswriter, Editor
Robert Rennick, Kentucky Humanities Council
Bob Schulman, Journalist
Patsy Sims, Author
Brandon Slone, Kentucky Military Research Br.
Frederick Smock, Writer
Herb Sparrow, Executive Director, The Group Travel Leader Inc.
Statewide Local Historical Societies, County Judge/Executives and Mayors

Robert L. Stephens (1927-2002), Chief Justice
of the Kentucky Supreme Court & Kentucky
Statesman of the 20th Century
Thomas E. Stephens, Ky Historical Society
Bob Stewart, former Commissioner, Kentucky
Dept. of Travel
Marvin E. Strong, Jr., Secretary, Economic
Development Cabinet
Paul Tenkotte, History Professor, Thomas More
College, Editor of the Northern Kentucky
Encyclopedia

Charles Thompson, Humanities Council
Lisa Thompson, Dept. for Libraries & Archives
James Tidwell, Professor, Kentucky State
University
Lee Todd, Historian & President, University of
Kentucky
John Trowbridge, Historian
Tom Wallace, Author & Sports Authority
Sid Webb, Photo Editor
Paul Wesslund, Kentucky Living Magazine

Special Thanks

Adair Printing Technologies
Ale-8-One
Bill Ambrose
Americana Productions, Michael Breeding
American Saddlebred Museum
Back Home Kentucky Magazine, Bill Matthews
Bell South
Belle of Louisville, LaDonna Miller
Elwood and Elizabeth Breeding, Supporters
Wanda Bertram, Editor
Kimberly N. Bunnell, Supporter
Lisa Clark and Amelia C. Clark, Supporters
Central Bank & Trust, Lexington
Susan Stokely Clary, Supreme Court of Kentucky
Vivian Coles, Editor
Robert Coomer, Photographer
Darklight Imagery, Chris Anderson
Eastern Kentucky University, College of
Justice & Safety
Emporia State University, Kansas
Betty Hall, Photographer
Kaiser Family Foundation
Chris Kellogg, Supporter
Kentucky Alcoholic Beverage Control Board
Kentucky Archaeological Survey
Kentucky Artisan Center at Berea
Kentucky Association of Counties, Cathy Jones
Kentucky Cabinet for Justice & Public Safety
Kentucky Crafted
Kentucky Commerce Cabinet, W. James Host,
Secretary; Randy Fiveash, Commissioner,
Dept. of Tourism; John Nicholson, Kentucky
Horse Park; Jon Vaden, Creative Services;
George Ward, Commissioner, Dept. of Parks;
Kathy Yount & Marge Bateman, Dept. of Tourism
Kentucky Community & Tech. College System
Kentucky Dept. for Fish & Wildlife Resources
Kentucky Dept. of Agriculture
Kentucky Dept. of Libraries & Archives, Jim
Nelson, Richard Belding & Tim Tingle
Kentucky Dept. of Military Affairs and
Military Records & Research Branch,
Evan Miller & Brandon Slone
Kentucky Economic Development Cabinet
Kentucky Education Cabinet, Virginia Fox,
Secretary
Kentucky Education Television (KET)
Kentucky Festivals & Events Association
Kentucky Folk Art Center
Kentucky Geological Survey
Kentucky Golf Association
Kentucky Heritage Council, Diane Comer

Kentucky High School Athletic Association
Kentucky Historical Society, Kent Whitworth,
Kim Lady Smith & Mary Winters
Kentucky Home School Association
Kentucky Hospital Association
Kentucky Humanities Council
Kentucky Living Magazine
Kentucky Museum of Art & Craft
Kentucky Music Hall of Fame
& Museum, Robert Lawson
Kentucky State University, Betsy Morelock
Kentucky State Police
Kentucky Women's State Golf Association
Kentucky World Trade Center
Kindred Trails, Inc.
Lexington Herald-Leader
Lexington Legends
Lexington Public Library
LG&E Energy / KU
Library of Congress
Louisville Bats
McConnell Technology & Training Center
Muhammad Ali Center
National Aeronautics Space Administration
National City Bank, Lexington
Clayton Nichols, The Computer Group
Northern Kentucky University Native American
Studies
Gary O'Dell, Photographer
Candy Parker, Editor
John Perkins, Photographer
Pioneer Times
Plum Lick Publishing, David & Lalie Dick
Prichard Committee for Academic Excellence
Readex, a division of NewsBank, Inc.
Billy Reed, Editor
Kerry Risner, Editor
Mary Seelbach, Supporter
SouthEast Telephone
Sports Information Directors
The Red Mile & U.S. Trotting Association
Tier1 Performance Solutions
University of Kentucky, College of Medicine
University of Kentucky, Special Collections
University of Louisville, School of Medicine
University Press of Kentucky
U.S. Senator Mitch McConnell's Office
U.S. Representative Ben Chandler's Office
U.S. Army Corps of Engineers
U.S. Dept. of Defense
Esther Webb, Editor & Photographer
Winchester - Clark Co. Chamber of Commerce
Wind Publications, Charlie Hughes

A very special thanks to our sponsors and advertisers! (See page 748)

.completely about Kentucky

Seeking an elusive piece of information about Kentucky? Visit *kybiz.com* – your web portal to Kentucky.

kybiz.com is designed to help visitors link with data-rich web sites providing valuable and up-to-date information about Kentucky.

Plus, at *kybiz.com* you'll find exclusive, searchable archives and the current issue of *The Lane Report*, Kentucky's business news source for 20 years.

together

we

Grow • Every day is a new opportunity to give your best performance. At Ashland, our vision is to enable growth and add value to all we touch. Our people and products are hard at work improving processes, solving problems, and helping customers and communities worldwide to grow and succeed.

Foreword

Thomas D. Clark

The tapestry of Kentucky history is woven from a multiplicity of strands of natural and human elements. Throughout extended millennia the surface of the land was shaped by the same powerful forces which bore upon the universe itself. Imprinted on the physical face of Kentucky are the imperishable landmarks of mountains, streams and plains. Lying beneath the surface has rested a rich resource of minerals. It may be true that archeologists, anthropologists, and historians have only a general idea of earliest human occupation of the land. There remains positive evidence of the existence of a primitive stone age human presence, documented by a generous littering of stone artifacts, cliff hieroglyphics, and soot stains of cliff dwellers.

All across primeval Kentucky there spewed up through fissures in the earth chemicals, which created salt licks and salt-ladened streams. Throughout untold ages herbivorous animals gathered at the licks and tramped trails across the land in doing so. The licks and connecting trails in the future played active roles in the settlement of Kentucky, and even in the opening of many of its arterial highways.

By gradual processes of population and economic expansion, and international rivalry, an Anglo-American civilization spread westward. Kentucky was the first state to be hacked out of the vast American frontier. Because of this fact the act of pioneering in the virginal backwoods became precedental in the future spread of American civilization. This fact was reflected in folkways, economies, politics, and international rivalries.

A basic theme in the history of Kentucky pioneering was, and remains, land. With the lingering direct ties of colonial Virginia and with the Atlantic Ocean, plus a modest population, there was little if any adventuring into the back country. A slight breakthrough came in 1671 when colonial Governor William Berkeley made Abraham Wood responsible for exploring areas to the west. General Wood's mission was to determine whether or not a stream beyond the Allegheny Ridge flowed into a great south sea. Wood's men discovered instead the New River and its fall line. This stream became a landmark in future explorations.

General Wood's exploration could hardly be called a major geographical breakthrough. The "dark" western littoral remained undisturbed until 1716 when Governor Alexander Spotswood, stimulated somewhat by Indian legend, led a party of gentlemen trail riders up to a peak ridge in the Blue Ridge Mountains to look into the Shenandoah Valley and speculate on whether or not the river they saw flowed into a northern lake. They drank toasts to all members of the royal family and went home to be knighted into the Order of the Golden Horseshoe.

Gradually during the mid-decades of the eighteenth century the western country came into focus. Many of its rich natural resources were highly visible, and so were the potential profits to be garnered from the trade in Indian goods. It is significant in the opening of Kentucky history that two speculative land and Indian trade companies became active. First, the Loyal Land Company of Virginia sought to establish an imperial-sized claim to western lands. In 1750 that company employed Dr. Thomas Walker, a surveyor (among his other areas of interest), to lead an exploratory party to the southwest and the great webwork of Tennessee River streams. This mounted party traveled down the Buffalo-Indian path, and water courses to stand on April 13, 1750 in the saddle of the gap across the rock spine of the front face of the Appalachian Highlands. The Walker party, however, failed to penetrate the western country deep enough to reach the rich cane lands of the inner bluegrass. They departed the western country up the streams and mountain coves by way of Pound Gap and the great valley to Charlottesville. Dr. Walker's most important contributions to Kentucky history were making

Dr. Thomas Walker Cabin
Source: Ky Dept for Libraries & Archives

a written record of the existence of the great passways through the mountains into the land on the waters of the Ohio and Mississippi river systems, the naming of the gap, the mountain range, and the first river system he visited for the "Bloody" hero of Culloden, the Duke of Cumberland. The final entry in his journal tabulated the number of bears, deer, elk, and turkeys the party slaughtered.

A more aggressive band of speculators were those Virginians and Englishmen who formed the Ohio Company of Virginia. The list of names of members of this company was virtually synonymous with the leadership of colonial Virginia, containing such names as George and Lawrence Washington, Thomas Nelson, John Taylor, Thomas Cresap, Thomas Lee, and others. Their interest in the west was the Indian trade, land, and French and Indian activities. The company employed Christopher Gist, an experienced surveyor, to visit the western river valley in 1750 to discover and describe possible land sites for the establishment of settlements, to observe Indian activities, and to travel down the Ohio River to its fall line. Like Thomas Walker, Christopher Gist kept a rather full journal of his travels. There was one exception, Gist made numerous magnetic compass readings along the way. For twenty-nine days Christopher Gist wandered through the northern and upper rim of present Kentucky. He went up the central branch of the Kentucky River and left the region by way of Pound Gap, never having seen much of the bluegrass area.

With the visitation of the two-company land explorers and the rising tempo of the commercial trading with the western tribes, there came a host of other viewers. In this manner the Kentucky frontier gradually came into focus. After the late fall of 1775, cabins and crude frontier fortresses came into view. As settlements advanced so did the administrative responsibilities of the commonwealth of Virginia. Its General Assembly took the first political step into the region by the creation of Kentucky County late in December 1776. This was the first time the name Kentucky was offi-

cially applied to the region.

At this juncture in Kentucky history, it must be emphasized that land, with its high magnetic attraction, became a central matter of attention. It may well be argued that no other element in Kentucky's history has continu-

George Washington
Source: Ky Historical Society

ously and consistently evoked such a volume of documentation, stirred so much human anxiety and anger, or provoked such a body of litigation and court decisions. From the moment the first wandering land claimant hacked evidence of his claim on a white oak tree, the ill-managed distribution of land warrants or "patents" has meant confusion. Unhappily, Kentucky fell heir to the ancient mode of land marking known as "metes and bounds." It would be folly to call metes and bounds a survey system of precision.

Neither the crown government nor colonial Virginia ordained an orderly plan for land management and disposal. This failure became visible at the end of the French and Indian War as documented in King George's

Proclamation of 1763. King George's proclamation shifted the burden of paying French and Indian war veterans from the exchequer to newly acquired western lands.

Following settlement in 1775, that part of the west in the Ohio Valley became heavily involved in British activities in the American Revolution. The isolated Kentucky settlements were exposed to British-Indian raids and attacks, such as those, which occurred against Ruddell's Station and Martin's Station on the Stoner Fork of the Licking River. Internally Boonesboro, Harrod's Town, and Bryan's Station barely escaped destructive assaults. The major phase of Kentucky in the American Revolution was the campaign that George Rogers Clark and his thin line of militiamen conducted against the western British-Indian posts of Kaskaskia, Cahokia, and Vincennes, and Clark's subsequent drive against the Shawnee-Wyandott villages north of the Ohio. The stunning attack against Kentucky, however, was the woeful defeat of the frontier militia in the Battle of the Blue Licks, August 19, 1782. Ironically, this battle occurred almost a year after Lord Cornwallis surrendered British forces at Yorktown.

No precise date can be stated as to that period when the raw pioneering process ended, and Kentuckians became involved in attending to the affairs of a rapidly expanding population. By the same token, it is doubtful that a full list of

TAKING FIRST VIEW OF "THE BEAUTIFUL LEVEL OF KENTUCKY"

Daniel Boone mural at the Capitol
Source: Ky Dept for Libraries & Archives

frontiersmen and women can be identified as bona fide pioneers in the heroic sense–the most readily sustainable fact that the exploration and settling of the virgin Kentucky frontier was not a single individual achievement.

Because of a historical-literary bit of luck, the name of Daniel Boone became almost synonymous with that of the American westward movement. Without any intent to denigrate that reputation of the old woodsman, faithfulness to the documentary record shows that Kentucky produced a host of pioneers of significant importance. There were Benjamin Logan, James Harrod, Simon Kenton, George Rogers Clark, Michael Bedinger, Isaac Shelby, and a host of others. There were the long-wandering hunter-Indian traders who became sources of first-hand information about the land and environment. Much less noted, but of monumental importance on the Kentucky frontier, were the land speculators who exercised a major influence in the settlement of Kentucky. There are few facts, if any, more fully documented than the omnivorous greed in the claiming of Kentucky lands.

In a much broader historical sense, land has been one of the major economic, political, and social elements in the commonwealth. It has filled that psychological and spiritual niche in the human psyche called "space." Following the opening decades of the nineteenth century, Kentuckians came

Re-enactment of the Battle of Blue Licks
Source: Sid Webb

to place great emphasis on the provincial as giving one an in-born sense of special heritage and belonging.

By 1790, Kentucky farmers and merchant traders had developed a rich commerce in tobacco, hemp, cured meats, lard, whiskey, corn, and small grains. Flatboats were drifted out of creeks and rivers into the main Ohio-Mississippi rivers flatboat trade. The name "Mill Road" was early attached to roads leading to creekbed sites of grain mills. By 1811, and almost miraculously, most of the prime, good, land in central Kentucky had been claimed, the forest cleared away, and cultivated fields and grassy meadows were yielding rich harvests of field crops and herds and droves of livestock.

Equally important was the early development of driving herds of cattle, sheep, and horses over land by way of Cumberland

First Constitution of Kentucky
Source: Ky Dept for Libraries & Archives

Ford and the Atlantic coastal market. Literally thousands of hogs were driven that way. This rising commerce in agricultural products and the use of the western rivers as outlet channels involved the western Virginia counties in deep concern about the Spanish control of the Lower Mississippi, an issue which was to have a bearing on the formation of the Commonwealth of Kentucky.

Between 1775 and 1810, there was a phenomenal increase in the tide of emigration westward. At the same time, there was a growing dissatisfaction with Virginia's administration of its western counties. Involved in this condition was protection against Indian raids, remoteness from the capital in Richmond, and the expense of transporting court cases to the state capital for

Daniel Boone
Ky. Historical Society

adjudication. The most immediate problem in 1784 was protecting the Kentucky settlements against Indian raids. This was the principle subject discussed in the first regional assembly in Danville in 1784. A second meeting (convention) was convened in 1785 in which the suggestion of separation from Virginia and creating an independent state was discussed. Involved in this proposition was a series of issues: the format of self government, sentimentalities regarding the Virginia attachment, the protection of the entangled mass of original land titles, the protection of an established court system, and the great and vexing problem of Spanish control of the lower central river system. Debaters, in convention and through the columns of the newly established *Kentucke Gazette*, discussed all these issues in extensor.

After all the debating in the ten conventions, the first Kentucky Constitution was written in a remarkably short period of time–less than a month. George Nicholas has been called "The Father of the Constitution," and the document reflects rather faithfully the second constitution of Pennsylvania and the one of Virginia. President George Washington temporarily approved the admission to the union of the new commonwealth. The date, June 1, was an arbitrary one. Officially Congress did not approve the admission until its fall session.

The operational government of Kentucky was formed in Lexington on June 4, 1792. Isaac Shelby had been chosen governor. On June 7, following the inaugural ceremony, the General Assembly held its first meeting. In Shelby's first message he admonished legislators to establish a judicial system and, "By your humanity as well as your duty will induce you to pass laws to compel the proper treatment of slaves,

Columns of the *Kentucke Gazette* down to 1794 contained notations of Indian raids in the state. In some instances land surveyors reported that they were hesitant about going into the woods because of these threats. Anthony Wayne's major drive against the

Masthead for the Kentucke Gazette
Source: The Kentucky Gazette, Frankfort

agreeable to the direction of the Constitution." The governor then asked that a revenue system be instituted, and that a permanent seat of government be located at an early date.

Location of the permanent seat of the Kentucky government was a complicated issue caused by sectionalism north and south of the Kentucky River, and competition among various towns and strategic sites. A committee of twenty-one names was selected, and militia officers struck off names until a group of only five was left. During the remainder of 1792 this committee met and considered various sites and finally settled on the Kentucky River village of Frankfort. This place was chosen for several reasons: it was near the center of the population, it was on a navigable stream, there was some political finagling, and some citizens, including General James Wilkinson, made generous contributions of land and building materials for the construction of a state house. There was not unanimous approval of Frankfort as the capital. Between 1793 and 1904 there were recurring efforts to move the capital to Louisville.

northern lake tribes ended in the battle of Fallen Timbers and the subsequent Treaty of Greenville.

A more significant matter, however, was the activities of the British and Indians in the Lake Erie rim, incidents of violation of the freedom of the seas, and a possible threat against the vital port of New Orleans. All these issues were of major public concern. It was as an advocate of embargo of British importations of British goods, and the potential threat on the Great Lakes frontier that Henry Clay attracted national attention as a "Warhawk."

Kentucky became involved in the War of 1812 on both the lakes and gulf fronts. Isaac Shelby in 1812, and in his second term as governor, received permission from the Kentucky General Assembly to leave the state and command the state's militia forces on the Great Lakes front. Overwhelming success in the Battle of the Thames was a veritable "hero maker," as was the Battle of New Orleans. Being a veteran of either of these battlefronts was a carte blanche assurance of political success.

The War of 1812 and its aftermath had tremendous influence in almost every area of life, none more so than being victimized by the great financial panic of 1819, and its lingering problems. This was an era in Kentucky history when the entire economic and political structures were thrown into chaos, wounds were inflicted upon the body politic, ones which required years to heal.

In 1792, Kentucky had approximately 90,000 inhabitants and by 1820 this number had expanded impressively to 220,000 individuals. By the latter date, Kentucky, like Virginia, had become a mother state feeding population into the new developing states, west and south. The white population steadily comprised approximately three-fourths of the numbers, and black slaves approximately a quarter of the total population. The history of slavery in Kentucky was, from the beginning, as indicated in Governor Shelby's address to the first General Assembly, a complex human and economic issue. By 1820, slave labor had ceased to be of major importance when weighed against the expansion of the cotton and sugar growing activities of the gulf coastal South. Stamped indelibly in the annals of Kentucky is the stain of the interstate slave trade, a practice fully documented in the contemporary press, in pamphlets, travel accounts, and anti-slavery literature, plus modern studies of the subject. Three contemporary publications merit consideration: Harriett Beecher Stowe's, Uncle Tom's Cabin; Cassius M. Clay's newspaper, The True American; and Stephen Foster's, My Old Kentucky Home, Good Night, originally

First Lady Suzan Shelby
Source: Ky Historical Society

entitled, Poor Uncle Tom, Goodnight. By 1850, it was reasonably clear that slavery was perhaps a vanishing institution. Kentucky, however, had long been a focal center of critical viewing of the institution, and, subsequently, of the Underground Railway activities. The long stretch of the Ohio River became a line of passage into the land of freedom. Finally, slaves were freed with the ratification of the Thirteenth Amendment of the federal Constitution.

As indicated, the lands in central Kentucky and along the central Tennessee border were highly productive of vital field crops and livestock. Since 1778 the trade, downriver and overland, of these products was profitable. Historically this trade had evolved through the flatboat, steamboat, and opening railway era.

Transported as dead weight, freight was hempen goods, tobacco, small grains, cured meats, and whiskey. A precious material in the interstate trade was salt, refined from numerous licks and sites. This trade was a major factor in the rise of Louisville as a market center, and in tying many Kentucky commercial interests to the Lower South.

During the decades of 1810-1840, Kentucky farmers shaped the image of Kentucky as a prime livestock producing area. The explorers, Thomas Walker and Christopher Gist, penetrated the western wilderness on horseback. So did Daniel Boone and John Findley. The horse, draft and sporting, became a fact in Kentucky history from the beginning. Native cattle were driven west from Virginia, but at an early

Gov. Isaac Shelby
Source: Ky Historical Society

date improved breeds of English stock were imported to graze in blue grass pastures. This was true of hogs, sheep, and later, mules. Central counties, such as Bourbon, Clark, Woodford, Franklin and Fayette, became nationally famous as agriculture, livestock, and sporting horse breeding centers.

In the same degree, Kentucky in the first half of the nineteenth century and in its human ranks, produced an impressive body of political, scientific, and business leaders. No doubt

Dr. Ephraim McDowell
Source: Kentucky Historical Society

but that the confusion which arose over land issues was influential in the development of a distinguished western country bar. The names of lawyers such as George Nicholas, Humphrey Marshall, John Breckinridge, Caleb Wallace, Henry Clay, John J. Crittenden, and a host of others enjoyed national status. In the field of science were Dr. Ephraim McDowell, Dr. Samuel Brown, Dr. Benjamin Dudley, John J. Audubon, the eccentric Constantine Rafinesque, Robert Peter, and Daniel Drake. The Kentucky governors, 1792 to 1865, comprised an interesting collection of personalities. Most of them were appreciable landholders, lawyers, men with military experience, and some with only limited formal educational backgrounds.

Members of the General Assembly, all male, ranged from individuals with reasonably good native qualifications to none at all. All of these facts had a distinct bearing on the course of Kentucky's history.

Just as individuals left their imprints on the first half of the nineteenth century, so did many internal changes – the geographical and geological physical nature of the surface of the state. These features effected the social, economic, cultural, and political actions of the population. In no area was this more distinctly revealed than in the breaking of the natural barriers, and the lacing of the state with a webwork of roads. These ranged from the opening of the road to Cumberland Gap, the road from Maysville south by way of Paris, Lexington, Harrodsburg south to Nashville, Tennessee, and the ancient Midland Trail from Ashland to the Falls of the Ohio. Many of the internal roads followed animal and Indian trails, but by no means all of them. County court order books are filled with the matter of appointing committees to locate the rights of way of roads, their openings, and maintenance. In the steeper mountainous areas many roads were along streambeds.

It may be said that the opening of the modern age of transportation history in Kentucky occurred in 1811 when Nicholas Roosevelt piloted the little sternwheeler New Orleans into Louisville. In time, sternwheel boats plied many of the major Kentucky streams. As a matter of fact, Kentucky administrative and legislative officials became blinded to the dawning of the railway age. In 1831, the Lexington and Ohio Railway Company was chartered to build a line from Lexington to some point below Louisville on the Ohio. It was not until March 1850 that Kentucky really entered the interstate railway age when the Louisville and Nashville Railway was planned to connect the two cities. Four major issues confronted Kentuckians in the decade 1840 to 1850, issues which had lingered since the creation of the state. They were the devisement and support, both financially and academically, of a school program. Slavery, as Governor Shelby indicated in his message to the first Kentucky General Assembly, was a matter of public concern and responsibility. Then there was the highly tangible matter of sharp sectional divisions of an irregular, geographically-shaped, landed commonwealth. Throughout three quarters of a century, the people and officials sought answers to these problems, none of which demanded more imagination and public attention than establishing schools without first creating a basis of fiscal support. From the very opening of the western lands to settlement, there was a realization that some degree of learning was mandatory for success. Timidly, the Virginia General Assembly in May 1781 appropriated three tracts of escheated lands (lands owned by British subjects at the time of the Revolution). There were eighteen thousand acres in the three tracts "donated from this of a public school or seminary of learning." In the body of the act appeared the eloquent dedication of funds from the sale of the lands, "Might some day be a valuable fund for the education of youth, and it being the interest of this commonwealth always to promote and encourage every design which may tend to the improvement of the mind and the diffusion of useful knowledge, even among the most remote citizens, whose situation a barbarous neighborhood and a savage intercourse might otherwise render unfriendly to science." This

Henry Clay
Source: Library of Congress

was the first, and somewhat snobbish, tribute to a need for education even on the wild Kentucky frontier. No mention was made in either the first two Kentucky Constitutions of education. In December 1794, in its second meeting, the Kentucky General Assembly chartered the Kentucky Academy in connection with the state's land grant law, which appropriated to each new county 6,000 acres of unclaimed public lands. This was a noble gesture, which fell far short of achieving its purpose.

Repeatedly up to 1849 citizens and legislators undertook to organize a public school system, and find a painless way to support it. Educational needs were extensively discussed in the constitutional convention of 1849 with no clear academic mandate being written into the new document, this despite all the previous attempts to effect real advancement. It might be a futile endeavor to try and determine which decade in Kentucky's history might be considered a seminal one. Certainly the one 1850-1860 would have to be given serious attention. Statistically this was an age of coming into political and social maturity. Measured objectively and statistically it was not only one of prosperity, but one of rich promise. The land had become highly productive, livestock breeding and production had reached a zenith, and, under the new constitution the financial future of the state appeared brighter. The half century mark (1850) revealed how far Kentucky had advanced in many governmental areas since

1792. The population of 980,405 souls indicated a distinctive increase, despite the fact the opening and operation of the Erie Canal had directed much of the western population flow around Kentucky. Much of Kentucky in

Confederate monument at the Perryville battlefield
Source: Sid Webb

1850 was still a virgin frontier, and basically unproductive of either revenue income or a stable domestic economy. The impact of this condition was to be reflected many times over in sharp regional and cultural differentiations.

It may be true that one of the tragic moments in Kentucky history was centered in the disruptive national issues which threatened the existence of the union of states in the latter half of the 1850s decade. This was reflected in the efforts of the state's leaders such as Henry Clay, John Jordan Crittenden, George D. Prentice, Robert Jefferson Breckinridge and others to find compromises and assurances of national unity. In 1860 Kentucky found itself in a key strategic position geographically, politically, economically, and emotionally. Kentucky had almost everything to lose in the divisive political debates in the issues pertaining to slavery, and in the internal unity of its people

and sections. In this connection, the question of whether Kentucky in 1860 was southern or northern has little pertinence. It was, as it had been formed, a border state caught in a binding political and economic triangle. It occupied a strategic geographical position which was vital to both North and South. It had vital agricultural productive capacity plus a generous blessing of natural resources such as salt, coal, timber, and iron ore. Too, it was tied to both sections by highway, railway, and river connections. In the convulsive moment of secession of the southern states in 1861, Kentucky's leadership was divided over the issue of secession. A strong core of leadership led by such persons as George D. Prentice, Albert Gallatin Hodges, John Jordan Crittenden, and Robert J. Breckinridge temporarily managed to keep Kentucky neutral. Internally, Governor Beriah Magoffin and a substantial body of Kentuckians were pro southern. Kentucky's position of neutrality was quickly violated by both southern and northern forces. Kentucky never seceded. The history of Kentucky's involvement in the Civil War has evoked the production of a modest library of biographies, histories of battles, essays, maps, and edited diaries. There were at lest three strategic battles, and numerous skirmishes, fought in the state. In the full measure of the fundamental meanings of the Civil War in Kentucky is to be reckoned in the sectional and partisan divisions among the people, the disruption of the state's economy, internal strife caused, first, by runaway guerilla activities, disruption of what might have been educational progress, and in the rise of a stifling partisanism in state politics to say nothing of the abuses of constitutional rights of citizens by high-handed military actions.

The post-Civil War period, down to the opening of the twentieth century, was in many respects one of reconstruction. It was an era of recovering markets for Kentucky agriculture, timber, and mineral resources, of expanding an internal system of railroads, of renewing the crusade for expanding the public school system, and of dealing with crime and civil upheavals. One of the most important events in this era was voter approval of the calling of a fourth constitutional convention to revise many of the restrictive elements in the third constitution, to bring Kentucky's government into alignment with the fundamental changes wrought in the nation by adoption of the 13th, 14th, and 15th amendments to the United States Constitution. The four volumes containing the proceedings of the convention mirror the times and issues confronting Kentucky at the close of the nineteenth century. For more than a century the fourth Kentucky Constitution has been a subject of public debate, court decisions, and campaigns to redraft it. The document has been amended numerous times, with the complete rewriting of the judicial article making substantial changes in this division of Kentucky constitutional history.

Source: Sid Webb

During the decade, 1890-1900, there were sharp political divisions over monetary-agrarian-bipartisan matters. Within the Democratic Party there was division over all of the above issues plus the emerging dominance of a strong factional conflict between Senator William Goebel of northern Kentucky and the more conservative pro-Confederate-southern faction in state political control. In 1895 William O. Bradley was elected as Kentucky's first Republican governor. There was that dark political moment in the Democratic Convention in the famous Louisville Music Hall when William Goebel was nominated the party's candidate for the governorship. The Republicans nominated their attorney general, William S. Taylor, as their gubernatorial candidate. The gubernatorial election of 1899 was one of the most hotly contested in Kentucky's gubernatorial history. The popular vote seemed to favor Taylor, the Republican, but the vote was challenged by the Democrats on several grounds. While that debate occurred, Goebel was shot. He died four days later. The assassination of the Democratic candidate for governor, William Goebel, divided the people into angry partisan groups, and, along with the recurring mountain blood feuds, gave the state an image of runaway savagery. The victorious Republican governor-elect William S. Taylor, was unseated after a long, bitter court fight. The young bachelor Democrat lieutenant governor was elevated to the office. In all the bitterness and court trials, three Republicans were tried, and two went to prison. All were later paroled. This crime colored political affairs and Kentucky's image for at least three decades. Beyond this, no one can say beyond all evidentiary support who fired the rifle shot which did so much public damage.

The commonwealth was caught up in a second threat of anarchy. There occurred in the dark-fired tobacco-growing region of the state guerilla warfare, known as the Black Patch War, between the farmers and the tobacco corporate managers over marketing practices and ruinously low prices. It took more than a decade to quell this disturbance.

In the same interval of time there occurred a vigorous campaign to improve the status of education. Teachers colleges were chartered to prepare more effective teachers. At the same time a quasi-public-private campaign was conducted to supplement public efforts. This was to be a major concern throughout the century.

Later, a group of principals who represented school districts which had received less support than was guaranteed them under the "Equal Opportunity Clause" of the 1890 constitution. The Franklin County Circuit Court and the Supreme Court declared the operation of the school system unconstitutional. The Kentucky General Assembly in 1990 enacted the massive House Bill 940. This act outlined the general purpose and a new direction of education in the future. To an encouraging extent the omnibus legislation placed the management of educational management beyond local and state partisan political controls. Fundamentally the Kentucky Education Reform Act (KERA), measured by many criteria, is the most far-reaching piece of social and cultural legislation ever enacted by the Kentucky General Assembly. The test of this lies in the impressive gains Kentucky has made against its traditional bottom rail educational rating, and in several of the national comparative scales.

Gov. Martha Layne Collins
*Source: Kentucky Department of
Libraries & Archives*

In no era did Kentucky make more historical and economic changes in the 20th century than in the area of farming and in the agrarian folkways of rural life. Tobacco, burley and dark leaf, prevailed during the century as Kentucky's leading staple cash crop. The growing and marketing of the leaf underwent at least three crisis stages, and, after, periods of readjustment. Advancements were made in combating plant diseases and parasitic infestations. Tobacco growing and sales reflected the impact of two world wars. But other factors soon affected the fortunes of towns, banks, service enterprises, and even the romantic glow of the crop and its sales. The closing quarter of the twentieth century saw a sharp change in the tobacco industry, a change wrought by revelations that smoking was injurious to personal health. At the close of the century a major question was the survival of tobacco production, and the search for a new staple crop. Generally the major farming activities were shifted to the lands of central and western Kentucky. Farms were mechanized, and plant breeders introduced more productive varieties of grains, soy beans, and hay crops.

A major change in the last half of the twentieth century was the disappearance of the family farm. By mid-twentieth century corporate farms began to appear in Kentucky, producing chickens and hogs. There were even modest adventures in the production of shrimp and catfish. Certainly the state held on to a respectable ranking in the field of livestock production, and to the breeding, sales, and racing of the major breeds of sporting horses. A mid-twentieth century Kentucky underwent far-reaching changes in the fields of civil and human rights.

Historically the state in the 1870s granted full voting privileges to its African American population, but it failed to extend full educational advantages. In 1949 the indefensible Day Law, effective in 1904, was challenged by the NAACP in the lawsuit *Lyman Johnson v. University of Kentucky*. Johnson, a Jefferson County school teacher, won the case permitting him to take graduate courses in the university. The big change, however, came after the United States Supreme Court rendered its decision in 1954 in *Brown v. Board of Education,* which removed racial barriers in the nation's public schools. There were some aftermath disturbances in

Clay, Sturgis, and Louisville. In 1966 Governor Edward T. Breathitt Jr. signed the Kentucky Civil Rights Act into law.

In the industrial areas the mining of coal in both the western and eastern fields was colored by periods of genuine prosperity, and at others, by a sagging national and world economy. The eastern coal field especially, was fraught

No change in the 20th century reached so deep into human lives as the introduction of electric energy, private and public. The passage by the United States Congress in 1933 of the Tennessee Valley Authority (TVA) was to have a marked impact on Kentucky, even though it offered service to only a limited part

"No aspect of Kentucky history and human dedication has been more consistent than the absorbing interest in politics."
Source: Sid Webb

with labor unrest and, on occasion, by violence. The physical mining procedures underwent phenomenal changes by the introduction of machines, which caused marked displacement of human miners. A major change in mining procedures was reflected in the introduction of strip mining procedures, which wrought fundamental changes in the topography of lands in both the eastern and western fields, provoking a fierce reaction from hoards of environmentalists. Documenting the changes are the abandoned coal mining villages, the shrunken ranks of miners, the negation of the "broad-form deed," and the mode of transporting coal.

of the state. The rural electrification laws and the favorable court decisions in the 1940s, that allowed the organization of the Rural Electrification Administration (REA) districts, the building of a network of power lines across the state, and the availability of electricity to every rural home was a revolutionary advance in the Kentucky way of life.

The Federal Aid Highway Act of 1956 in many respects realigned highway development in Kentucky. Slicing across two sections of the state are the arterial limited interstate roads I-75 and I-65, plus links of I-24 and I-71. The Kentucky Highway Authority used the Kentucky bonding power to construct a series of toll roads to be liquidated by use collections. Construction of the Western Kentucky, the Mountain and the Bluegrass turnpikes, plus the eastern Daniel Boone Parkway, made substantial progress in penetrating Kentucky's historical isolated regions, and proved to be a more tightly lacing together of all parts of the state.

The persuasion of Governor Martha Layne Collins that the Japanese Toyota Automobile

Kentucky authors at a reunion at UK (l. to r.)
Ed McClanahan, Bobbie Ann Mason,
James Baker Hall, Gurney Norman, Wendell Berry
Source: Sid Webb

manufacturer locate a plant in Georgetown, plus the Ford Motor Company operation in Louisville, and the General Motors plant in Bowling Green moved Kentucky deeper into the modern industrial world. Not only were main manufacturing plants located in the state, but also there was the major development of satellite supply industries, which were located in various places about the state.

Just as Kentucky underwent changes in its agrarian way of life, in its breaking of isolative physical barriers, and in considerable transitions from a basically rural-agrarian state to an urban service-industrial one, it underwent impressive advances in the areas of the human services and humanities. It would be challenging to fully appraise the advances made in the area of basic medical care. The establishment of a medical school and hospital in the University of Kentucky, and the advancements made in the University of Louisville medical school have been reflected in the advancement of human welfare, and possibly in an expansion of the life span of the populace.

Kentuckians made important advances during the twentieth century in the areas of the liberal arts. During the century an older order of authors passed on and a younger and more expansive one took over. This was the era which produced such significant renascent figures as Elizabeth Madox Roberts, Robert Penn Warren, Elizabeth Chevalier, A.B. Guthrie, Harriette Arnow, Jesse Stuart, James Still, Wendell Berry, Bobbie Ann Mason, and Janice Holt Giles as creative writers. There came on the scene a host of historians and non-fiction writers including John F. Day, William H. Townsend, J. Winston Coleman, Jr., Lowell Harrison, David Dick, Harry Caudill, William Ellis, Charles Roland, Edward (Mack) Coffman, Tracy Campbell, and a host of others.

The creation of the University Press of Kentucky opened a progressive challenge for the publication of regional books. In the last half of the century library expansion and availability in Kentucky went from a limited number of inadequately stocked public libraries, horseback book conveyers, and bookmobiles, to the establishment of local and county libraries. In Frankfort, the severely limited state library system was revitalized. In the closing two centuries the annual Book Fair in Frankfort has increased many-fold the sale and distribution of books.

Kentucky, following the Great Depression, experienced a renaissance of the fine arts in the fields of music, graphics, and sculpture. The state claimed a central role in country music in all its forms in the performing arts in places like Louisville, Owensboro, Bowling Green, Lexington, and Danville.

No aspect of Kentucky history and human dedication has been more consistent than the absorbing interest in politics. This interest has not been solely based in the fundamentals of theoretical functioning democratic principles so much as in the great stone yard of rigid partisanism. John Adair, governor of Kentucky (1820-1824) could march onto the Kentucky political scene in 2005 and not feel completely out of place. He was an active party to partisan bickering, and in almost two centuries few, if any, revisionary changes have occurred.

In spite of all the deterrent features

Governor John Adair
Source: Kentucky Historical Society

Governor William Bradley
Source: Kentucky Historical Society

in the history of Kentucky politics, Kentucky produced a remarkable number of individuals in the twentieth century who rendered major service to the state and nation. During the century a coterie of governors created appreciable images of statesmanship in such areas of governmental reform, civil rights, economic development, education, and interstate relations. Each governor has to be evaluated within the context of his times and the leadership he supplied, not in a popularity poll. At the local levels of government there were officials who achieved reforms in both organization and projection reforms. Nationally Kentuckians became members of the Supreme Court, of diplomatic services, and as leaders in both houses of Congress. There were state legislators who on many occasions exhibited genuine statesmanship.

On the flip side of Kentucky's political history has been the ever-lurking virus of partisanism. Kentucky opened the twentieth century deadlocked in a vicious spasm of partisan hatred, which resulted an image-destroying act of violence. Almost by rote it has opened the twenty-first century a victim of the same witless virus.

Once more, possibly no historian or political analyst could even in the most general terms, state fully the positives and negatives of Kentucky's history. It is safe, however, to assume the costs of failure to take full advantage of

social and environmental influences. They established government entities at all levels, nurtured institutions, tolerated defiances of law, made enormous patriotic responses to state and nation in moments of crises, and glorified the past, without fully developing a knowledge of local and state history.

Cumberland Gap
Source: Kentucky Department of Tourism

opportunities along the way have been considerable when translated in human terms. The wanton waste of opportunity to advance the welfare of human institutions caused by fruitless partisan bickering and neglect has been unconsciously great at times. It is an irony of Kentucky history that in a state, which reveres the name of Henry Clay, the word "compromise" long ago became archaic.

We might stand on the mountain pinnacle towering over Cumberland Gap with the scales of history in hand and ask the question, "How well have Kentuckians fared in their virgin western Eden?" The answer would surely have to be stated in parts. Over two and a half centuries Kentuckians created a vigorous, often colorful mosaic of history. They made a veritable kaleidoscopic response to place, and

Eighteenth-century citizens brought cultural baggage in their move west and a deep-seated love of politics – politics, which bordered on being an all-season pastime. The quests have remained a Kentucky constant. Governors Simon Bolivar Buckner and William O. Bradley might well sit at a table on which rests a bottle of bourbon whiskey and conclude Kentucky politics and Kentucky politicians have changed little since they lived in the Governor's Mansion over a century ago.

Collectively Kentucky has undergone deep fundamental changes which may be best symbolized by the construction of a single generation house, in a new suburban rural community, alongside a decaying tobacco barn, all of this giving a fresh connotation to Stephen Collins Foster's deep spiritual lament.

Did you know?

THE LAND WE KNOW TODAY AS KENTUCKY was the home of Native Americans for millennia before European pioneers traveled into Kentucky. These native peoples built houses, farmed Kentucky's fertile ridgetops and floodplains, raised their children, and buried their dead in cemeteries near their homes. Before Europeans appeared in Kentucky, native communities were decimated by deadly European diseases to which they had no immunity. Direct European contact brought new threats, the greatest of which was settlers who wanted Indian lands.

These sovereign native peoples sought to limit European contact, yet still trade for the items of European technology that they desired. By keeping enough distance between themselves and these newcomers, they felt they could retain their autonomy; deal with Europeans on their own terms; maintain the lifeways of their forefathers; and perform their rituals. As active, equal players in the events on the frontier, Kentucky's native peoples approached situations as any sovereign peoples would — they pursued actions that served their own best interests.

For 20 years, from the late 1730s to 1758, the lower Shawnee Town was the principal village of the Shawnee and home to over 1,500 people. Chiefs Newcommer, Big Hominy, and The Pride, are examples of Kentucky Indian leaders who relied on their own evaluations of situations and worked in the interest of their people during negotiations with the French and English. In their attempt to maintain native lands and cultural traditions, other Native Americans resisted European migration.

Contributed by A. Gwynn Henderson and David Pollack, Kentucky Archaeological Survey.

With $600 million spent on emissions reduction in 2004, our mission is clear.

As one of America's lowest-cost energy providers, LG&E Energy and its subsidiaries generated enough electricity last year to serve more than a million customers. To put that in perspective, that's enough electricity to light up more than 52 million 100-watt lightbulbs 24 hours a day, 365 days a year. Having said that, we've long been recognized as a leader in the energy industry for our environmental efforts and we've already committed to do our part in the future to enhance electric reliability for our customers and cleaner air for all Kentuckians. Last year, we completed a $600 million emissions reduction project and over the next five years we plan to be part of an additional $2.3 billion investment in Kentucky to further reduce emissions, increase hydroelectric generation and add state-of-the-art, coal-fired generation. As a result, we will continue to meet the needs of our customers with safe, reliable and low-cost power and not at the expense of the environment.

LG&E KU

State Profile

Nickname: *The Bluegrass State*
Population - 2000 Census: *4,041,769*
Population – 2005 Estimate: *4,165,814*
Population – 2030 Projection: *4,912,621*
Increase 1990 – 2000 Census: *9.63%*
Geographic Size: *40,395 square miles*
US Census metropolitan areas are within or extend into Kentucky:
Bowling Green; Cincinnati-Middletown (KY-OH-IN), including part of northern Kentucky;
Clarksville (TN)-Hopkinsville; Elizabethtown; Evansville (IN)-Henderson;
Huntington (WV)-Ashland; Lexington-Fayette; Louisville; and Owensboro.
Source: http://www.uky.edu/KentuckyAtlas/kentucky.html

Kentucky Gross State Product (GSP), by Component: 1995, 2000, and 2001 GSP: Current Dollars (In Millions of Dollars)			
Industry	**1995**	**2000**	**2001**
Total Gross State Product	91,472	117,233	120,266
Private industries	78,522	101,566	103,632
Agriculture, forestry, & fishing	1,874	2,681	2,498
Mining	2,426	1,986	2,235
Construction	3,588	5,500	5,635
Manufacturing	25,848	30,891	30,297
Transportation & public utilities	7,574	9,433	9,905
Wholesale trade	5,332	7,502	7,461
Retail trade	8,300	10,947	11,369
Finance, insurance, & real estate	9,979	13,731	14,152
Services	13.599	18,895	20,081
Government	12,950	15,667	16,633

Source: U.S. Census

Cumulative Estimates of the Components of Population Change for Selected States April 1, 2000 to July 1, 2004				
Geographic Area	**Total Population Change***	**Natural Increase**		
		Total	**Births**	**Deaths**
United States	**12,230,802**	**6,901,163**	**17,198,187**	**10,297,024**
Arkansas	79,231	41,362	159,897	118,535
Illinois	293,987	321,232	774,574	453,342
Indiana	157,052	128,284	365,221	236,937
Kentucky	103,637	60,299	230,345	170,046
Missouri	157,935	88,807	322,858	234,051
Ohio	105,866	172,340	637,404	465,064
Tennessee	211,700	96,450	334,641	238,191
West Virginia	7,004	-2,044	87,308	89,352

Source: http://www.census.gov/popest/states/tables/NST-EST2004-04.xls

Kentucky Driven.

In Kentucky, we are driven to help people move forward.

Photo by Doug Prather

STATE PROFILE

State Flag & Symbols

Capital: *Frankfort*

State Seal, *adopted 1942*

State Motto: *"United We Stand, Divided We Fall,"adopted 1942*

Official Latin Motto: *"Deo gratiam habeamus"("Let us be grateful to God"), adopted 2002*

State Flag, *adopted 1962*

State Bird: *Cardinal (Cardinalis cardinalis), adopted 1926*

State Fossil: *Brachiopod, adopted 1986*

State Butterfly: *Viceroy Butterfly (Limenitis archippus), adopted 1990*

State Wild Animal Game Species: *Gray Squirrel (Sciurus carolinensis), adopted 1968*

State Horse: *Thoroughbred (Equus caballus), adopted 1996*

State Fish: *Kentucky Spotted Bass, adopted 1956*

State Fruit: *Blackberry (Rubus allegheniensis), adopted 2004*

State Flower: *Goldenrod (Soldiago gigantea), adopted 1926*

State Rock: *Kentucky Agate, adopted 2000*

State Gemstone: *Freshwater Pearl, adopted 1986*

State Soil: *Crider Soil Series, adopted 1990*

State Mineral: *Coal, adopted 1998*

State Tree: *Tulip Poplar (Lirodendroan tulipifera), adopted 1994*

State Musical Instrument: *Appalachian Dulcimer, adopted 2001*

State Song: *"My Old Kentucky Home"- modern version, adopted 1986/1988*

State Bluegrass Song: *"Blue Moon of Kentucky," adopted 1988*

Source: Kentucky Department for Libraries and Archives

Photo Source: Betty Hall & Sid Webb

SURE, THEIR BACKS ARE STRONG. THEY SUPPORT THOUSANDS OF FAMILIES.

Horses work hard for Kentucky, plowing thousands of jobs and about $4 billion dollars into the state's gross domestic product. They're our state's #1 cash crop – in a state where 30% of the economy is agricultural. They are a key attraction for the Commonwealth's $8 billion tourism industry. They put workers in riding rings, at auction sales, in feed and tack stores, in barns, in pastures, in offices, at race tracks… and in every single county in Kentucky, they help us prosper. Every one of Kentucky's 120 counties suffers a significant loss when the economic impact of the horse industry goes elsewhere. And it is. Other states offer significant incentives for our horse business – our economic lifeblood – to move elsewhere. Tax incentives, boarding incentives, breeding incentives, and racing purse incentives… are stealing the signature industry of Kentucky. And, as it goes, so go our jobs. With the kind of economic benefits and international status that horses have given Kentucky, who can blame other states for becoming competitive? But, we can blame only ourselves if we let this distinctive Kentucky industry slip away. Sure, we're proud of our automotive, food service, distilled spirits and coal industries – and pleased to have the jobs that come with them. But, if Kentucky stands for anything in the world, it has to be our horses. Find out how to keep jobs in Kentucky and to protect its heritage as "Horse Capital of the World."

Visit **www.horseswork.com**– or call toll-free **1-866-771-KEEP (5337)**.

AMERICAN SADDLEBREDS • APPALOOSAS • ARABIANS
DRAFT HORSES • KENTUCKY MOUNTAIN HORSES • MORGANS
MULES • NATURAL GAITED HORSES • PAINT HORSES

Horses work for Kentucky.

PALOMINOS • PONY BREEDS • PINTOS • QUARTER HORSE
ROCKY MOUNTAIN HORSES • STANDARDBREDS
THOROUGHBREDS • WALKING HORSES • WARMBLOODS

KENTUCKY EQUINE KEEP EDUCATION PROJECT

Top News Stories of 2004-2005

Jim Ogle

Several thousand Kentucky residents have served or are serving in the battlefields of Iraq and Afghanistan. While many of those serving are career soldiers with units such as the 101st Airborne Division out of Fort Campbell, thousands of Kentucky families in scores of communities sent their citizen soldiers in the Kentucky National Guard to serve in both Iraq and Afghanistan.

The costs of the guard deployment have been telling for many Kentucky communities. More National Guard soldiers from Kentucky are serving overseas now than at any time during the Gulf War of 1991. For the communities affected, the loss of these soldiers on long deployments have been telling—from doctors, to lawyers, to teachers and business people.

have served more than one deployment.

Kentucky's general election in 2004 was expected to feature a bruising battle over gay marriage (Kentuckians

Sen. Jim Bunning wins a narrow victory
Source: Lexington Herald-Leader

did approve the amendment defining marriage as a union between only men and women), but the race that really took center stage was the election of a U.S. Senator.

Republican Senator Jim Bunning of Southgate had been expected by many observers to coast to re-election with limited opposition. Most major Democrats who had been expected to possibly challenge Bunning dropped out of the race. Democratic State Senator Daniel Mongiardo of Hazard won the Democratic Party's nomination. Initially raising a small portion of the money Bunning had available to him, Mongiardo began combining old-fashioned campaign efforts of physically blitzing the state with aggressive use of the Internet to post policy statements and recruit both

Sgt. David Schrier, Lewisburg
saw his daughter Zoe, who was born July 23, 2004, for the first time on Sunday, Feb 6, 2005
Source: Lexington Herald-Leader

More of those serving have died in deployment than in the Gulf War. Some of the units

WE GREW UP IN KENTUCKY.

SO WE'RE GLAD TO HELP TELL ITS STORY.

Founded in Northern Kentucky, Tier 1 Performance Solutions is proud to have played a role in the creation of the 2006 Kentucky Almanac. We're experts when it comes to the organization and delivery of information—whether you need to train your sales force, spread corporate strategy throughout your organization, or catalogue over a century's worth of state history into a single volume.

Our combination of consulting, customizable software, and development services helps you translate your vision into the knowledge and information your people need to perform.

Tier 1 Performance: we turn your vision into results.

Learning Solutions
· E-Learning
· Classroom Training
· Instructional Design

Change Management
· Communications
· Train the Trainer
· Program Management

Knowledge Management
· Document Management
· Content Management
· Intranets and Portals

Solution Accelerators
· Learning Management Systems
· Content Management Systems
· Document Management Systems

TiER1
PERFORMANCE SOLUTIONS

www.tier1performance.com

5 W 5th St | Covington, KY 41011
859.431.7300

donations and volunteers.

The campaign really seemed to turn when Bunning made a series of statements. First, he joked at a Republican dinner that Mongiardo, an Italian-American, looked like one of Saddam Hussein's sons. When initially asked to apologize to Mongiardo, Bunning refused.

Bunning agreed to participate in only one debate with Mongiardo, but it wasn't face-to-face. Bunning, because of late congressional budget action, was televised from the Washington headquarters of the Republican Party. Mongiardo appeared at the WKYT studios in Lexington on October 11th.

During the debate, Bunning offered his apology for past remarks against Mongiardo, but attacked the state senator for mounting a whisper campaign against him regarding his health. Mongiardo attacked Bunning's record and conservatism.

After the debate, reporters questioned Bunning if he received any electronic help during the debate. He said he "hadn't broken any rules." Later his campaign did admit that it had used a tele-prompter to pass information to Bunning during the debate.

Polling showed a tightening contest as national Democratic leaders began pouring money and appearances of notable Democrats in Kentucky into the race.

On election night, it turned out to be one of the tightest races in the country. Bunning won by 22,652 votes out of 1.7 million votes casts.

Ironically, that margin was three times the one Bunning had over then Rep. Scotty Baesler in his first race for the senate in 1998.

Geoff Davis was elected by a 54 percent to 44 percent margin in the 4th District
Source: Lexington Herald-Leader

Congressman Ben Chandler toured the Tokico Plant in Berea
Source: Sixth District Congressional Office

Kentucky's federal congressional delegation remained overwhelmingly Republican in the 2004 election. Republican Geoff Davis was elected by a

54 percent to 44 percent margin in the 4th District of northern Kentucky that was previously held by Democrat Rep. Ken Lucas who retired that year. Democrats kept the 6th District centered on Lexington with the election of Rep. Ben Chandler to serve a full two-year-term by a 58 percent to 40 percent margin. Chandler had won the seat vacated by Ernie Fletcher who beat Chandler in the governor's race of 2003. In that January 2004 special election, Chandler defeated Republican State Senator Alice Forgy Kerr by a 55 percent to 43 percent margin.

Kentucky Republicans kept their 23-15 advantage in the Kentucky Senate and expanded their numbers in the Kentucky House. They now trail Democrats there by a 43-57 margin. State Senator Bob Leeper of Paducah, who had originally ran and was elected as a Democrat before changing his party affiliation to Republican in 1999, later changed his party again to Independent after he was upset by Republican efforts to seat a candidate for state senate a court ruled ineligible to serve. Republicans now boast a 22-15 edge in the Senate.

In the same election, Kentucky joined scores of other states in passing a constitutional amendment that defined marriage as a union between only men and women.

Political priorities also played a huge roll in the fight over Kentucky's spending priorities—both the general budget for the Commonwealth and 2005 plan for state employees' health care.

Governor Fletcher originally proposed a plan that greatly increased out-of-pocket expenses for state employees. Fletcher said the increases were caused by the skyrocketing cost of coverage combined with the number of people applying for coverage. He said the increases in costs were needed in order for the state to be able to have enough money to pay for health care for all its employees.

Many state workers were outraged by the unexpected increases shown in the Fletcher plan. As the governor stumped the state in support of the effort, he often was greeted by angry state teach-

ers and other employees who objected to the changes.

After much bickering, Fletcher called the General Assembly into a special session on the

Teachers rally at Phoenix Park in Lexington, to protest the governor's health insurance plan
Source: Lexington Herald-Leader

Health Care Plan in October 2004. Kentucky Education Association members applied political pressure on the legislators when they voted to strike on October 27th if a plan they approved wasn't passed by the General Assembly.

Bowing to pressure, legislators approved a compromise proposal that basically adopted the previous year's health care plan with only minor changes.

Legislators and the governor also avoided political problems by agreeing on a budget dur-

Lexington born and read.

At Smiley Pete Publishing, we bring you the latest information
from the vibrant local communities where we live and work
and from the people who make things happen.

ing the 2005 session of the General Assembly. Legislators almost unanimously approved a plan that contained hundreds of new capital projects, gave teachers and school workers a three-percent raise, and gave Governor Fletcher $75-million to hand out to local communities.

Some of the money for the plan came from a three cent per pack increase in Kentucky's cigarette tax. It was the first such increase in the tax in decades. It came on the heels of Lexington passing one of the nation's most stringent "no smoking" laws in the country. Almost all public buildings were included in the plan. Restaurant and bar owners lobbied unsuccessfully for changes in the ordinance. Several other Kentucky communities, including Louisville, have followed Lexington's lead in passing different variations of indoor smoking bans.

The University of Louisville gained significant bragging rights over the University Kentucky during the past year. The football Cardinals finished their last season in Conference USA with a championship and an eventual Top 10 national ranking. It also solidified a move to the Big East Conference and a better chance to be in the hunt for a national football championship. The basketball Cardinals had an up and down regular season that included a blown lead against Kentucky in Freedom Hall as Patrick Sparks hit three crucial free throws in the game's final seconds to give the Wildcats the victory. Rick Pitino and his Cardinals learned much from

their losses as they stormed to the NCAA Final Four before finally closing out their season.

While University of Kentucky football continued it rebuilding efforts, the basketball team surprised skeptics by winning the Southeastern Conference Championship and making it to the NCAA Regional Finals before dropping out. The Cats SEC crown was one of four different titles

UK and U of L football game
Source: Lexington Herald-Leader

Eastern Kentucky University and Tennessee State basketball game
Source: Lexington Herald-Leader

won by the University in the SEC. Men's basketball, soccer, golf and tennis all finished atop the SEC.

Eastern Kentucky University cheered both its men's and women's teams into the NCAA Basketball Tournaments (one of the rare schools to quaify in both championships).

Louisville merged its government during the year, but still wrestled with questions about a rising murder rate in its West End combined with controversy over police behavior. McKenzie Mattingly, a white police officer, shot 19-year-old black criminal suspect Michael Newby to death. Authorities charged Mattingly with murder, reckless homicide and manslaughter in the case. A jury acquitted Mattingly in September.

Sharing in Kentucky's heritage.

Kentucky Power has been a part of Kentucky's history for 85 years. Serving 175,000 customers in 20 eastern counties, we are a part of the rich heritage that makes the region special. And we plan to be here well into the future. By investing millions of dollars in environmental improvements at our power plant, and millions more in our energy delivery system, we are investing in Kentucky, its people and a bright future. When it comes to serving the Commonwealth, *Kentucky Power is there, always working for you.*

AEP

KENTUCKY POWER®

A unit of American Electric Power

Despite the electoral successes of 2004, Governor Fletcher's Republican administration continued to weather a storm of accusations during 2005 over its efforts to hire campaign supporters

Gov. Ernie Fletcher
Source: Lexington Herald-Leader

into state jobs covered by the Commonwealth's merit system.

In what one commentator called "Blackberry Jam," some of the evidence used by a Franklin County Grand Jury to indict Fletcher officials of misdemeanor charges of violating the merit system came from short messages sent back and forth between officials on Blackberry hand-held communication devices.

Fletcher and his campaign supporters said whatever errors that may have been made came about because the merit law was vague, his officials were inexperienced in dealing with the law, and the violations weren't significant. Attorney General Greg Stumbo's office led the investigation after it received a complaint and hundreds of documents from a whistle-blower. Stumbo said it was his responsibility to confront lawbreaking without excuses.

Republicans and the Governor accused Stumbo of a political witch-hunt. It culminated in an August 29th speech before cheering Republicans in the State Capital Rotunda. Fletcher continued his attacks on the Attorney General's inves-

tigation and pardoned everyone who had been charged in the case. Fletcher also announced that he would not pardon himself nor would he give material testimony the next day before the Grand Jury.

As this Almanac goes to press, the investigation, and the political charges, continue.

Bad communication among Federal authorities put the Fletcher administration in an unwanted national spotlight. When former President Ronald Reagan died in June 2004, Fletcher flew to the Washington, DC to attend funeral rites in a decades old plane owned by Kentucky. The plane had problems with its transponder, which shows who and how high the plane is flying. Although the Federal Aviation Administration gave the plane clearance to fly into the Reagan Washington National Airport, the FAA failed to alert other federal agencies of the clearance. Defense officials observed an unidentified intruder aircraft on their radar screens.

They ordered an immediate evacuation of the

**Attorney General Greg Stumbo
at the Fancy Farm Picnic**
Source: Lexington Herald-Leader

U.S. Capitol and other buildings as thousands scrambled for safety. One federal authority said they almost ordered the plane brought down. Congress later held hearings on the problems between the FAA and the National Capital Region Coordination Center.

Well, what about that?

For 120 consecutive years, picnickers and politicians have made their way to the Fancy Farm picnic held the first Saturday of August at St. Jerome's Parish in Fancy Farm.

HISTORY

Dr. James C. Klotter
State Historian

The date that the first human walked on the land that now comprises Kentucky remains unknown to history. Archaeologists indicate that the event took place well over 12,000 years ago. While those early peoples left no written record of their existence, they did likely leave an enduring legacy—Kentucky's name.

Determination of the

Daniel Boone, Cherokee Park, Louisville
Source: Sid Webb

origin and meaning of historical names is difficult—and sometimes impossible. In the case of the word "Kentucky," various interpretations have been given.

One meaning was the "meadow land." To early Indians who lived in the area, Kentucky furnished abundant game, fertile land and pleasant climate. Many tribal nations had long made this land their old Kentucky home. Yet by the time the first European explorers visited the region, this place of

Constitution Square, Danville
Source: Sid Webb

first contact between cultures became a place of death for Native-Americans, as deadly microbes killed thousands. Disease swept over the land, tribal boundaries changed, and other factors intruded to mean that this land once filled with Native-American homes now had few permanent Indian settlements by the 1760s. Several tribes still regarded the region as their hunting ground, however.

As the two cultures met in this middle ground of Kentucky, another of its names grew up: "Dark and Bloody Ground." In the 1750s and the 1760s, land-hungry explorers, such as Christopher Gist and Dr. Thomas Walker, and then Long Hunters, among them Daniel Boone, James Harrod and Simon Kenton, first brought to the East stories of the richness of this seemingly unclaimed land beyond the mountains. A young man who would soon conquer the Northwest Territory, George Rogers Clark, proclaimed "a richer and more beautiful country than this I believe has never been seen in America." Attracted by the promise of what has been called the "Kentucky myth of plenty," eager settlers, imbued with "Kentucky Fever," flocked to the area just as the Revolutionary War broke out. Settlements erected at Harrodsburg in 1774 and Boonesborough and Stanford in 1775 met resistance. Indians fought this intrusion into their happy hunting ground. Bloodshed resulted and filled the first decade of settlement with death and sorrow. Native-Americans, and European settlers and their African-American slaves, all mourned

their losses.

Peace finally did come to Kentucky and another meaning of its name reflected its promise to newcomers. It was "the land of tomorrow." Men and women who had been simply protecting and constructing wilderness homes now turned to building a state. By 1790, these Kentucky counties of Virginia had 73,000 people (16 percent of them slaves) and sought separation from the Mother State. After flirting briefly with independence, Kentucky, in 1792, finally joined the union as the fifteenth state—and first one west of the mountains. Revolutionary war hero Isaac Shelby became its first governor. He would later serve a second term and lead Kentucky forces in battle in the so-called Second American Revolution, the War of 1812.

In the period from 1800 to 1860, Kentucky was one of the most important states in the young republic. In 1840, its population ranked sixth in the nation. A diversified agricultural base gave Kentucky a sound economic foundation: it stood first in hemp production (then used in rope and bagging) and wheat; second in tobacco, corn, hogs and mules; third in flax; and fourth

Abe Lincoln statue
at Hodgenville
Source: Sid Webb

in rye. Its political leadership also gave the state much influence in national circles: John Breckinridge served as the first federal cabinet-level member from west of the Alleghenies; Richard M. Johnson and John Cabell Breckinridge functioned as vice presidents (Breckinridge the youngest ever); President Zachary Taylor, although not a Kentuckian by birth, lived in the state many years (and is buried here); and, of course, the "Great Pacificator," three-time presidential candidate Henry Clay, gained fame for his compromises designed to avert conflict. The state's cultural advancement gave Lex-

Aunt Rachel, "Slave to Her Mistress"
Headstone at Old Mulkey Meeting House
Source: Sid Webb

ington its title as "the Athens of the West," while Louisville's booming river and business trade made it one of the largest cities in the South and West. Overall, Kentucky had a reputation as a forward-looking commonwealth, a place for the ambitious and the eager.

Yet, lurking below the surface of prosperity lay elements that would disrupt the state and nation. For this commonwealth that was the first in the nation to allow people to vote without owning property did not give equal rights to many of those who lived in its borders. Slavery had existed in Kentucky since the earliest settlers came from Virginia, and by 1830 almost one-fourth of the population lived in bondage. The commonwealth had the third highest number of slaveholders among the slave states. Most held only a few slaves—the state ranked third lowest in the average number of slaves. But the voices of those denied human rights, the cries from the slave auction block, the search for freedom by bondsmen such as Henry Bibb and Josiah Henson, showed that the existence of even one person in slavery could "cause the very heart to sicken." If Kentucky had survived earlier crises with the Indians, the British, and political factions, it now had to face the questions of slavery or emancipation, secession or nationalism. Its greatest crisis was yet to come.

The cost of deciding those momentous questions was great. With ties to both North and South, Kentucky knew that war would tear the state apart. Divided sentiment meant divided families fighting each other. Household after household saw one son ride north, another south. For the commonwealth, the conflict became truly "the Brothers' War." As many as 100,000 Kentucky soldiers (23,000 of them African-American) fought for the Union, which the state supported in 1861; perhaps another 40,000 went to the Confederate cause. Of all those men, 30,000 never returned from the battlefield.

Two natives of the state symbolized all the wartime divisions, for both Presidents Abraham Lincoln and Jefferson Davis were born in the commonwealth, less than eight months and eighty miles apart. Both sought to win their home state for their cause. At first the state declared itself neutral, and the land saw three separate entities—the United States, the Confederate States, and Kentucky. But such a stance could not continue, and Kentucky finally abandoned neutrality and remained in the Union. However, disgruntled southern sympathizers formed a rump government, with its capital at Bowling Green. The state soon became a star in both flags. Fighting first broke out in Kentucky in the winter of 1861-1862. Confederate losses ended their control, and the bloody Battle of Perryville in late 1862 marked the Confederacy's high-water mark in Kentucky. After that conflict, the Confederate army made no serious threats to retake Kentucky, and so the excesses that often accompany military rule fell chiefly on the Union side. In addition, Confederates who did enter the state (chiefly the raiders of Gen. John Hunt Morgan) presented a dashing, heroic front to most of the populace. Though only partly correct, such an image contrasted with that of Federal leaders who had to deal with the daily problems that Morgan never faced. Thus the southern cavalier image grew more attractive.

Union policies regarding slavery compounded northern problems. While Lincoln's Emancipation Proclamation did not directly affect Kentucky, ostensibly a loyal state, news of that declaration created resentment among state leaders. Even devoted unionists questioned and criticized the administration's policies, particularly after Kentucky slaves began enlisting in the army in return for their freedom.

The commonwealth slowly turned anti-administration and even prosouthern in sympathy. Soon after the end of hostilities in 1865, a newspaper remarked that Kentucky had waited until after the war to secede. And so it seemed, for the vanquished in war soon became the victors in postwar politics. Since Kentucky did not undergo Reconstruction, ex-Confederates quickly gained power, and for the next three decades dominated Democratic party councils, until Republicans registered their first gubernatorial triumph in 1895. (From then until the 1930s the two parties contested on a reasonably equal basis for major offices, but the effects of the Great Depression and the actions of the New Deal would again make the state solidly Democratic until the later decades of the 20th Century, when a realignment of voting patterns began to emerge.)

Re-enactment of Louis & Clark exploration docked at Louisville
Source: Sid Webb

That same period saw marked changes in the Kentucky character. Despite many problems, the state continued its cultural advances. Kentucky novelists such as James Lane Allen and John Fox Jr. "The Little Shepherd of Kingdom Come", and then later, Elizabeth Madox Roberts, Harriette Arnow, Jesse Stuart and Robert Penn Warren (winner of three Pulitzer Prizes and the nation's first poet laureate) gave the state a firm foundation in regional literature. Newspapermen such as Henry Watterson, the colorful editor of the Louisville *Courier-Journal*, left their imprint on the nation. To a lesser extent, artists—including the nationally known Frank Duveneck and the regionalist Paul Sawyier—and a wide range of those who produced folk art, offered citizens of the commonwealth attractive alternatives.

Yet during the same period, the effects of the war, depression and general stagnation stripped some of the veneer of antebellum prosperity from the land. The postwar introduction of the new burley tobacco increasingly oriented the agrarian economy to one crop and subjected it to its vagaries of price.

Despite Louisville's presence as a supplier of the South, the state did not keep pace with the rapid industrial advancement and urbanization of America. (Not until 1970 would Kentucky have more urban dwellers then rural—a half century after the United States made that transformation.) On top of all this, violence erupted in the form of a dozen or more so-called feuds, giving the state an image it found hard to overcome. The assassination of a governor in 1900, violent farm protests in the Black Patch War, plus later coal-oriented conflicts added to the stereotype. Ironically, Kentucky now ranks very low in those statistics regarding violent crime.

Labor union conflicts, failures of leadership, more than a decade of Prohibition, the Great Depression, and then World War II, all added to the problems that Kentuckians faced. State citizens in search of work migrated to northern cities, the Appalachian area continued poor as the coal industry remain depressed, and the state's financial poverty made educational support difficult.

Slowly some change again came to the Bluegrass State. Improved transportation and additional industry beginning in the 1950s gradually started to reverse population losses. A parks system attracted tourism while bettering recreational facilities for Kentuckians. Coal gained an increasingly important share in the national energy program and prices spiraled upward in the 1970s. The state slowly and basically changed from an agricultural base to an industrial one—by the 21st Century it ranked third among the states in the production of motor vehicles, for example.

Regarding civil rights, Kentucky had adopted a policy of segregation following the Civil War, though it never disenfranchised its black voters, as did the deeper South. The first African-American legislator,

The Kentucky Archaeological Survey conducts a dig at Ashland, home of Henry Clay
Source: Sid Webb

Charles Anderson Jr., took office in the 1930s. Following the 1954 U.S. Supreme Court decision outlawing public school segregation, the state's mostly peaceful integration made it, for a time, a symbol of success and model for the South in the ensuing struggle for equal rights. But later riots in the state soon showed that much of that change was more symbolic than real. Still, Kentucky's passage of the first state Civil Rights Act and the first Fair Housing Act in the South showed that it remained a place of paradox.

Through it all, Kentuckians continued to enjoy the world around them. Hunting and fishing, always popular pastimes, competed with other sports for attention. Indicative of what one writer has called the state's ability to reconcile "red-eye, racing, and religion," the people increasingly supported the breeding and racing of thoroughbreds. Beginning as a small affair in 1875, the Kentucky Derby grew in popularity as the years passed. Newer sports made their appearance and one, basketball, made particularly rapid strides. The state's nationally known teams both divided and bound citizens together.

At times seemingly a part of Kentuckians' recreation, politics continued to attract attention, and the state produced respected and influential statesman. Folksy, personable Alben Barkley ("theVeep") served as senate majority leader under Franklin D. Roosevelt and vice president under Harry Truman, while Fred Vinson represented the state as Chief Justice of the U.S. Supreme Court. Also on the

Henry Clay
Source: Library of Congress

national scene, men such as Earle Clements, John Sherman Cooper, Wendell Ford and Mitch McConnell took leadership positions and left their imprint on national affairs.

On the state homefront, Kentucky had earlier taken a leadership role in the struggle for women's rights, through the efforts of Laura Clay, Madeline McDowell Breckinridge, and others. Once women gained the right to vote in 1920, political involvement followed. Kentucky had one of the first eight women to serve in Congress—Katherine Langley— and one of the first half-dozen women governors in America—Martha Layne Collins.

With party struggles, political scandals and lively election contests continuing to the present, Kentucky politics indicates that the conclusion of Judge James Mulligan's famous poem still reflects reality:

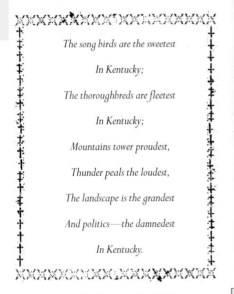

The song birds are the sweetest

In Kentucky;

The thoroughbreds are fleetest

In Kentucky;

Mountains tower proudest,

Thunder peals the loudest,

The landscape is the grandest

And politics—the damnedest

In Kentucky.

And so, in the first decade of the 21st Century, the commonwealth continues to reflect its past, as it looks to the future. It stands exactly in the middle of the states in population, and its 4,041,769 residents (in 2000) rank high in the nation in the percentage of native-born people who still live in the state of their birth. The traditional commonwealth remains a place still tied to the ideals of the family farm, small town life, and a sense of place, but another side of Kentucky reflects all the elements of modern America. This land of contrast still searches to see what it needs to do to achieve its dream to be "the land of tomorrow."

"Well, I never!"

Two natives of the state symbolized all the wartime divisions, for both Presidents Abraham Lincoln and Jefferson Davis were born in the commonwealth, less than eight months and eighty miles apart. Both sought to win their home state for their cause. At first the state declared itself neutral, and the land saw three separate entities—the United States, the Confederate States, and Kentucky. But such a stance could not continue, and Kentucky finally abandoned neutrality and remained in the Union. However, disgruntled southern sympathizers formed a rump government, with its capital at Bowling Green. The state soon became a star in both flags. Fighting first broke out in Kentucky in the winter of 1861-1862. Confederate losses ended their control, and the bloody Battle of Perryville in late 1862 marked the Confederacy's high-water mark in Kentucky.

HISTORY

Anne S. Butler, Ph.D.

Civil Rights

When the newly formed Commonwealth of Kentucky chartered its first Constitution in 1792, it incorporated Article IX, a provision that sanctioned slavery under the rule of law.

Article IX "obliged the owners of slaves to treat them with humanity, to provide for their necessary clothing and provision, and to abstain from all injuries to them extending to life or limb." Another provision enabled the legislature to "pass laws to permit the owners of slaves to emancipate them." Although many citizens opposed the adoption of slave codes for the new state, their political strength was insufficient to stop the migration of slavery into the Commonwealth. Despite the continuing efforts of anti-slavery forces, a second Constitution was adopted in 1799 codifying the practice of slavery and thereby insuring its continuation.

It was the retention of slavery through the end of the Civil War that set the stage for prolonged efforts by African-Americans, both free and enslaved, to secure basic civil liberties. Adoption of slave codes in the Constitutions of 1792, 1799, and 1850, signaled a three-fold aim among most lawmakers and the proslavery factions they represented. The inherent aims of the framers of the constitution were: to protect and promote the interests of slaveholders throughout the southern colonies;

to recognize and support the importance of slavery for commercial interests in the northeast; and to ensure availability of the free labor needed for the country's westward expansion. Codification of chattel slavery not only denied African Americans the basic and inalienable "rights of man," it branded enslaved people as inferior beings.

It took more than a century of protest and ultimately a civil war, and interventions at the federal level, before serious consideration of civil rights for African Americans began to unfold within

Source: Kentucky State University

Martin Luther King with Gov. Ned Breathitt
Source: Kentucky Department of Libraries & Archives

the Commonwealth. Among the enslaved population, however, neither the rule of law nor their status as "chattel property" was strong enough to extinguish the visions and hopes they held for liberty. Thus began individual and collective actions to acquire full access to the democratic ideals and practices governing a civil society. These efforts reached a high-water mark during the Civil War when 24,703 enslaved men in Kentucky joined the war effort both to preserve the union and secure freedom for themselves and their families. This number represented the third largest contingency of African American men in the nation that joined the war effort.

A series of promising steps following the Civil War gave the appearance that both the Nation and the Commonwealth were ready to bestow civil rights to all citizens. Chief among these steps was the abolishment of slavery, in December 1865, through federal ratification of the Thirteenth Amendment. Subsequently, passage of the federal Civil Rights Act of 1866, and adoption of the Fourteenth and Fifteenth Amendments to the United States Constitution, bestowing citizenship to former slaves and voting rights for men, provided small, but significant victories. African Americans would realize, however, that the same proverbial winds bringing positive and progressive changes are often buttressed by winds of resistance.

Whitney Young, Jr.
Source: Kentucky Dept. of Libraries &
Archives

Disparate treatment in public modes of transportation provided a venue for a civil rights protest in Louisville in 1870. While African American women were allowed seats on the inside of street cars, their male companions were not allowed to sit with them. Instead, the men were required to stand on platforms outside the box cars. Filing a suit against this disparate treatment in federal court resulted in a victory for Horace Pierce, Robert and Samuel Clark, each a respected business owner residing in the city. The legal actions of these men resulted in elimination of the offensive practice among all local carriers.

Passage of the federal Civil Rights Act of 1875, also initially provided the appearance of access to a wider spectrum of public accommodations, including the "full enjoyment of the accommodations, advantages, facilities and privileges of inns, public conveyances on land or water, theaters and other places of public amusement." Almost as soon as the Act was published, the response to the bill in Kentucky was negative. One columnist writing for the March 7, 1875, issue of the *Lexington Weekly Press* commented that "The Negro is now endowed with all the political privileges, *miscalled rights*, which it is possible for him or any other man to possess in this country." The columnist made clear his disdain for such legislation and that of many of his readers.

Numerous strategies were designed to stifle or block African American access to the public accommodation measures contained in the 1875 Act. One of the most overt forms of opposition was the passage of a bill in the General Assembly, during its 1891 session, requiring separate coaches for African American and white passengers using interstate railroad transportation. A "separate, but equal" policy widely employed in other southern states would gain a foothold in Kentucky slowing progress in transportation, housing and employment, as well as in educational arenas.

In response to this proposed legislation mandating separate rail cars, a statewide committee was formed to fight against passage of such an unfair bill. Known as the Anti-Separate Coach Movement, the committee was unsuccessful in persuading the General Assembly that such legislation was both retrogressive and in violation of the federal Civil Rights Act. When the case was heard in the U.S. District Court, a ruling was issued on June 4, 1894, declaring the actions of the General Assembly unconstitutional. Ten years later, the "separate but equal" strategy was again imposed by the General Assembly. Passage of its infamous "Day Law," in 1904, ended nearly 40 years of integrated education at Berea College. It was not until almost 50 years later that the "separate but equal" clause was ruled unconstitutional.

Once physical enslavement ended in the Nineteenth Century, the persistence of prejudice and racial discrimination remained a formidable foe throughout most of the first-half of the twentieth century. On March 4, 1964, civil rights activists in Kentucky staged a protest march on the State Capital with renewed demands for open accommodations. They were joined by Dr. Martin Luther King, Jr., Jackie Robinson and other civil rights leaders with state, regional and national profiles. After much ideological struggle, the Kentucky General Assembly, under the leadership of Governor Ned Breathitt, passed the Civil Rights Act of 1966. This Act was hailed as "the strongest and most comprehensive civil rights bill passed by a southern state."

The civil rights being sought by African Americans were intrinsically rights of access to opportunities that held promise of increasing the quality of their lives. These, at a basic level, included: the right to equal educational opportunities and access to public accommodations, the right to vote and participate in governance, the right to purchase land and homes free of segregated restrictions, and the right to testify in courts and to serve as jurors, as well as the right to fair competition in the marketplace. Throughout much of the last part of the twentieth century, African Americans were joined in their quest for civil rights by many other groups who experienced similar inequities.

A KENTUCKY CIVIL RIGHTS TIMELINE

1792 - Kentucky admitted to union; first state constitution establishes legality of slavery.

1794 - Kentucky statute gives free or freed Negroes legal equality to whites.

1798-1799 - Law concerning "Slaves, Free Negroes, Mulattos, and Indians" and second Kentucky Constitution change status of free people of color by placing limitations on their rights, including voting and self-defense.

1855 - Berea College founded by abolitionist Rev. John G. Fee to provide interracial education.

1859 - Fee is forced to close the school and leave Kentucky following John Brown's raid on Harper's Ferry, Va.

1863 - President Abraham Lincoln issues the Emancipation Proclamation, but his native state of Kentucky is unaffected because the proclamation frees slaves only in those states that have seceded from the Union.

1864 - Camp Nelson, S. of Nicholasville, becomes the most important Union recruiting station and training camp for African Americans.

1865 - Slavery ends nationwide, including in Kentucky, after the critical number of states ratify the 13th Amendment to the U.S. Constitution. The first great African-American migration begins.

1866 - Berea College is reestablished by Fee and others, including African Americans from the Camp Nelson refugee camp.

1870 - Members of Quinn Chapel A.M.E. Church in Louisville organize Kentucky's first known protest of racial discrimination, challenging segregation on local streetcars. This action and other early black protests would spark other actions demanding the rights to testify in court against whites, to serve on juries, and to vote.

1896 - In *Plessy v. Ferguson,* U.S. Supreme Court rules that "separate but equal" treatment for blacks and whites under the law is constitutional.

1904 - The Day Law takes effect, segregating both public and private schools across Kentucky.

1908 - U.S. Supreme Court upholds Kentucky's Day Law. Justice John Marshall Harlan again dissents, protesting that the ruling puts racial prejudice ahead of civil liberties.

1914 - The NAACP opens a branch in Louisville to protest lynching and mob violence against blacks and to fight a new housing ordinance reinforcing racial segregation.

1917 - U.S. Supreme Court declares the 1914 Louisville residential segregation ordinance unconstitutional in *Buchanan v. Warley.*

1935 - Charles W. Anderson is the first African American elected to the Kentucky House of Representatives since Reconstruction.

1941 - Louisville sit-in protests segregated library.

1945 - Baseball Commissioner A.B. "Happy" Chandler allows the Dodgers to sign Jackie Robinson as the first African American to play in the modern major leagues. Chandler agrees.

1948 - Lyman T. Johnson files suit against the University of Kentucky for admission.

1949 - UK admits the first black students to its graduate and professional schools.

1950 - The Day Law is amended to allow individual colleges to decide whether to admit African Americans if no comparable course is taught at Kentucky State College.

1954 - U.S. Supreme Court, in *Brown v. Board of Education of Topeka,* abolishes segregated public schools.

1955 - Remaining state colleges opened to all applicants.

1957 - Kentucky High School Athletics Association allows accredited African-American high schools to become members and to participate in state tournaments.

1959 - NAACP Youth Council pickets Louisville's Brown Theater when its management refuses to admit African Americans to see *Porgy and Bess.*

1960 - African Americans in Louisville organize a voter registration campaign to replace city officials, capped by a rally where Dr. Martin Luther King Jr. of the Southern Christian Leadership Conference speaks to thousands.

Young people in Louisville form a chapter of the Congress on Racial Equality and begin demonstrations at downtown businesses.

General Assembly establishes Kentucky Commission on Human Rights and prohibits discrimination in state employment.

1961 - Kentuckian Whitney Young Jr. becomes executive director of the National Urban League.

1963 - Gov. Bert Combs issues a Governor's Code of Fair Practice against segregation in state government and state contracts.

1964 - U.S. Congress passes federal Civil Rights Act. Lack of support in the Kentucky legislature for a strong public accommodations bill leads to a mass march on Frankfort.

1965 - At a major conference on civil rights in Louisville, Gov. Edward Breathitt pledges support for a strong civil rights bill addressing employment as well as public accommodations.

1966 - General Assembly passes the Kentucky Civil Rights Act, and King calls it "the strongest and most comprehensive civil rights bill passed by a Southern state."

1967 - Mae Street Kidd of Louisville is elected to the Kentucky House of Representatives.

Open housing ordinances are passed in Covington and Kenton County, and the Fayette County Fiscal Court bans discrimination in housing in Lexington and the county. One of the first acts of Louisville's new Board of Aldermen is to pass a strong ordinance against housing discrimination, replacing the weaker, voluntary one.

1968 - Georgia Powers of Louisville is elected to the Kentucky Senate. The General Assembly adds housing discrimination to the enforcement section of the state Civil Rights Act. A protest against police mistreatment in Louisville turns violent, and a week of disturbances ends in the arrests of six African Americans—dubbed the "Black Six"—on charges that they conspired to blow up Ohio River oil refineries. After more than two years of demonstrations and court hearings, all charges against the six would be dismissed.

1969 - The Kentucky Commission on Human Rights opens centers in Louisville and Lexington to help African Americans moving into new neighborhoods. A group of black students, inspired by the Black Power movement, takes over a building at the University of Louisville to force changes on campus.

1970 - The Jefferson County Fiscal Court extends enforcement of Louisville's local housing law to the county.

1975 - Cross-district busing to equalize the racial makeup of Louisville's public schools sparks sometimes violent reactions, which eventually subside after two years.

1976 - Correcting a historical oversight, the General Assembly, after a campaign led by Kidd, ratifies the 13th, 14th, and 15th Amendments to the U.S. Constitution—more than 100 years after they became law.

1996 - The state constitution is amended to remove provisions for a poll tax and segregated schools.

Source: Kentucky Educational Television (KET)

Whitney M. Young, Jr. (1921-1971), educator and civil rights leader, lived in a simple two-story wooden house on the campus of the Old Lincoln Institute near Simpsonville (a National Historic Landmark) until he was 15. He spent most of his career working to end employment discrimination in the South and turning the National Urban League from a relatively passive civil rights organization into one that aggressively fought for justice. In 1968, President Johnson honored Young with the highest civilian award. — **MEDAL OF FREEDOM**—

KentuckyHistoricalSociety

Enjoy the sights and sounds that bring Kentucky history to life!

Connections to the Past
Perspective on the Present
Inspiration for the Future

Discover the treasures contained in the 167,000 square foot **Thomas D. Clark Center for Kentucky History** plus two National Historic Register buildings—the 1830s Greek Revival **Old State Capitol** and the 1850s Old State Arsenal, home of the **Kentucky Military History Museum**. All sites are conveniently located on the Kentucky Historical Society's "history campus" in downtown Frankfort, 5 minutes from I-64 exits 58 or 53B.

Explore 12,000 years of Kentucky history, inspiring architecture, exhibits and collections. Trace your family history in the **Martin F. Schmidt Library**, a comprehensive genealogical resource. Shop for the best Kentucky has to offer in the **1792 Store**.

Hours and Admission

Exhibits: Tues.–Sat. (10–5), Sun. (1–5)

Library: Tues.–Sat. (8–4), Sun. (1–5)
Special Collections: Tues.–Fri. (8–4)

Admission (includes all museums and exhibits)
Adults $4, Youth (6-18) $2, Children 5 and under FREE
KHS members FREE   Group rates available
Library and 1792 Store FREE and open to the public
Veterans receive FREE admisstion to the Kentucky Military History Museum
★ Second Sunday of every month FREE ★

100 W. Broadway • Frankfort, KY 40601 • 502-564-1792 • history.ky.gov
an agency of the Kentucky Commerce Cabinet

Kentucky UNBRIDLED SPIRIT

HISTORY

Kentucky History Center

Thomas E. Stephens

The Kentucky Historical Society was founded on April 22, 1836, by 16 "patriotically inclined Kentucky gentlemen," who met in the secretary of state's office at the state capitol (now Old State Capitol) in Frankfort.

Their efforts were in response to a pioneer era letter concerning Daniel Boone that was published two years earlier in the Frankfort Commonwealth. The new society resolved "to collect and preserve authentic information and facts connected with the early history of the State."

KHS was incorporated in Louisville on Feb. 16, 1838. After 11 years in the state's largest city, the society languished, and its sizable collection was incorporated into one of many efforts to establish what would become the Louisville Free Public Library.

The Kentucky Historical Society remained dormant for more than a quarter century until a group of history enthusiasts met to reorganize it on Oct. 31, 1878, in the Capital Hotel in Frankfort. The group obtained a new state charter from the legislature—"secured and held sacred"—that made the society custodian of the state's historical treasures. Two rooms "over the Auditor's Office, in the third story" of the present Old State Capitol Annex were reserved for the society's use.

After another lapse, the Kentucky Historical Society was revived under its state charter in 1896

Opening of the Kentucky History Center
Source: Sid Webb

by Mrs. Jennie Chinn Morton of Frankfort. Working with Gov. J.C.W. Beckham, Mrs. Morton won public printing status for a history journal, the Register of Kentucky State Historical Society, which began publication in January 1903. In his dual role as the state's chief magistrate and KHS president, Gov. Beckham secured, on March 16, 1906, an annual $5,000 state appropriation by the legislature. The act also mandated the publishing of the Register and officially established that Kentucky's governors would serve as the society's presidents ex-officio.

Gov. Augustus E. Willson granted the society four rooms in the newly completed state capitol in 1909, where the collection could grow. The society built on the state's collection of battle flags and portraits of "Governors, statesmen, and other famous men and women of Kentucky." One particular effort was the commissioning of gubernatorial portraits that would later become the KHS Hall of Governors. By this time, KHS had begun to be recognized by state government as the custodian of Kentucky's treasures, received the collection of paintings from the then-abandoned Old State Capitol and began collecting military equipment. KHS also published its first book in 1910, "Kentucky: Mother of Governors," by John Wilson Townsend.

Mrs. Morton died suddenly on Jan. 9, 1920, and

Mrs. Jouett Taylor Cannon was elected secretary-treasurer. She led the society for the next 26 years. One of Cannon's first acts was to move the KHS headquarters. At the behest of Gov. Edwin P. Morrow and Lt. Gov. S. Thruston Ballard, the state sinking fund commissioners had the Old State Capitol repaired and renovated. The building, constructed in 1828-30, would become the society's most enduring symbol and provide space for all of its functions for the next five decades

By 1943, the society's library boasted more than 14,000 books and pamphlets, and the museum contained more than 2,600 items, including the portrait and battle flag collections, sculpture and numerous relics and other items of interest. One important addition during this period was the acquisition of the silver service used on the retired battleship U.S.S. Kentucky, which was arranged by Lt. Gov. Thruston Ballard. Ballard also drummed up support for the society and personally helped rescue precious old state records for the use of genealogists.

In August 1948 the society founded the Kentucky Historical Markers Committee, which in conjunction with the state highway department, began to place markers at significant sites throughout the state. A new state charter that altered the society's functions and titles was enacted in 1960.

The meteoric rise in family history brought the addition of a genealogical quarterly, Kentucky Ancestors, which debuted in July 1965 with Mrs. Anne Walker Fitzgerald as editor. Kentucky Ancestors incorporated the genealogical features formerly in the Register and added others over the years.

KHS expanded into the Old State Capitol Annex—ironically its headquarters in the 1880s—in 1974, and the old capitol entered the first phase of its conversion to a museum. The Kentucky Military History Museum also opened in 1974, in the Old State Arsenal. By 1987, however, the society had been adding to its collections and responsibilities for 13 years in the same space and was almost literally bursting at the seams. It was estimated that more than 90 percent of the museum's collection was in storage, unable to be adequately conserved or displayed. Under the leadership of Director James C. Klotter, KHS secured state funding for a new home, the Kentucky History Center.

Through the assistance of Gov. Brereton Jones, the general Assembly in 1992 approved construction of a Kentucky History Center. The project would eventually grow to $29 million, including $7 million in additional funds raised though the Kentucky Historical Society Foundation Inc. for the permanent exhibit, special equipment and furnishings, technology and landscaping.

KHS also enjoyed a groundswell of public support, in addition to corporate contributions. To celebrate its 10th anniversary in Kentucky, Toyota Manufacturing, USA of Georgetown and Toyota Motor Co. of Japan, donated $1 million to the project.

Opening on April 10, 1999, the history center is a 167,000-square-foot state-of-the-art museum and research library and provides office space and other facilities on a 3.7-acre block shared by the Old Governor's Mansion. It was named The Thomas D. Clark Center for Kentucky History on July 9, 2005, during festivities honoring the life of Thomas D. Clark (1903-2005), the state's former historian laureate.

Located at 100 West Broadway, the History Center is the focal point of the society's campus, which offers numerous learning opportunities to students, historians, genealogists and anyone else interested in Kentucky's past. Programs and activities include the Kentucky Junior Historical Society, the Kentucky Folklife Festival, a museum theatre program and Elderhostels for seniors and also weekend and summertime programs for children. The campus extends northwest to the Old State Capitol and southeast to the Old State Arsenal on Main Street, home to the Kentucky Military History Museum.

The History Center museum's $2.8 million permanent exhibit, A Kentucky Journey, employs a remarkable blend of more than 3,000 historic artifacts, sights and sounds to bring the state's glorious past to present generations. This chronological walk through time boasts life-size environments, state-of-the art technology and 14 interactive displays. Another area, Pure Kentucky, highlights the lives and contributions of famous Kentuckians.

More than 30,000 genealogists and other patrons use the society's research library each year. The facility is an important resource that maximizes both access to and security of the more than 90,000 volumes, microfilm and files in the collection. Tables are equipped for laptop computer use. Internet workstations allow for access to the KHS catalog, commercial databases and the Online Public Access Catalog.

The society's web site, http://history.ky.gov, offers virtually anyone the opportunity to access its services. Online visitors can search the library's more than 80,000 published works via the KHS Research Collections Catalog, browse the manuscript and photographic collections or order genealogical research through the museum shop.

HISTORY

Women in
Kentucky History   Janet Holloway

Women in Kentucky have played an important role in the development of the Commonwealth since they first crossed into the frontier, having a major influence on every sphere of life.

In the field of education Jane Coomes opened the first school at Fort Harrod in 1776. In 1825 Julia Ann Tevis founded the Science Hill Female Academy in Shelbyville, emphasizing science and math as key subjects. In 1902 May Stone and Katherine Pettit founded the Hindman Settlement School in Knott County, being the first of its kind in the country. The school gained regional renown for its academic and cultural programs. In 1987 Jane Stephenson founded the New Opportunity School for Women in Berea to help Appalachian women become better educated.

Women have been at the forefront of spiritual life, with Eldress Nancy Moore leading the Shaker community of South Union in Logan County during the Civil War. Her diaries chronicle a letter to President Abraham Lincoln asking for recognition of Shaker pacifism, which was eventually granted.

Kentucky women raised their voices regarding women's rights and suffrage. Chief among them was Josephine K. Henry, who fought for the passage of The Women's Property Act. She joined Laura Clay, daughter of abolitionist Cassius Clay of Lexington, to organize the Kentucky Equal Rights Association, which in the 1890s successfully lobbied for women's wages to be paid directly to themselves instead of to their husbands and to enable women to make wills, contracts, control real estate, sue and enter into business.

In government Emma Guy Cromwell paved the way as the first woman elected to a state office as state librarian in 1896. Later as secretary of state she became the first woman to serve as acting governor. Her unpopular decision as state treasurer in 1927, requiring banks with state monies to be fully funded, helped to safeguard Kentucky's money during the Depression.

In business, women ran farms, distilled whis-key, navigated the Ohio River, raised cattle and Thoroughbreds, and established retail stores in the 18th and 19th centuries. Julia Dinsmore (1833-1926) ran *The Dinsmore Homestead*, kept a daily journal and was a published poet. Jennie Benedict created benedictine cheese, edited *The Courier-Journal's* "Household" section and published "The Blue Ribbon Cookbook" in 1902. Ruth Booe and Rebecca Gooch started Rebecca-Ruth Candy in Frankfort in 1919.

Mary Todd Lincoln
Source: Sid Webb

Katherine "Katie" Peden stands out as an accomplished 20th century woman, being the first to serve as Kentucky's Commissioner of Commerce (1963), the first nominee to the U.S. Senate and the only woman on the National Advisory Commission on Civil Disorders under President Lyndon B. Johnson.

Kentucky women have excelled in sports, with swimmer Mary T. Meagher winning three gold medals at the Olympic Games in 1984, and Tori Murden being the first American and first woman to row the Atlantic Ocean solo in 1999.

Finally, philanthropy from women has made a difference. Sallie Bingham gave $10 million in 1985 to set up the Kentucky Foundation for Women and seed the Kentucky Women Writers Conference. Lucille Wright, heiress to the Calumet baking powder fortune, created the Lucille Markey Charitable Trust, investing half a billion dollars in medical research and building the Markey Cancer Center at the University of Kentucky. Mary Lucille Caudill Little (1909-2002) contributed more than $21 million to the performing arts and education, founding the Lexington Children's Theatre and Studio Players as well as the Bluegrass Girl Scout Council.

Bill Bright

Military History

The Kentucky Military History Museum is housed in the Old State Arsenal in Frankfort, a fitting site for this collection of military memorabilia including uniforms, weapons, flags and personal items once belonging to members of the state's armed forces.

The building itself is rich in history. It sits high above the Kentucky River, overlooking the capital's downtown area, its fortress-like architecture belying its designated use as an arsenal. It was the third arsenal that the state had, the first having been outgrown and the second having been destroyed by fire in 1836. By 1850 Kentucky's legislature deemed it necessary to have an arsenal once again, so $8,000 was appropriated in order to have one built.

Kentucky Military History Museum
Source: Kentucky Historical Society

The architect for the new arsenal was Frankfort resident Nathanial C. Cook, who had designed several other public buildings in Kentucky including courthouses and churches. His design for the arsenal depicted a striking two-story, red brick building resembling a crenellated castle in the popular Gothic Revival style. Although severely damaged by fire in 1934, the building that we see today is much how Cook designed it to look from the outside.

Upon completion of construction the building became the primary depot for some 12,000 weapons. These weapons would be used to equip Kentucky's troops as well as the local citizenry.

The arsenal also served as a cartridge factory during the Civil War. Indeed, Union troops from Kentucky, Indiana, Ohio and Michigan were all supplied with ammunition made by the ladies of Frankfort. During the 1862 capture of Frankfort by Confederate forces, the cartridge factory ceased operation. However, recent research has proven that after Confederate forces left Frankfort in 1862, the cartridge factory resumed operations and continued to provide ammunition until the end of the war.

Only once in its history did the State Arsenal actually come under fire. That was in 1864 when the Confederates once again tried to capture the capital. Gunners on the arsenal lawn exchanged shots with Confederate cavalrymen on the opposite bank of the Kentucky River, but the attack failed.

After the Civil War the arsenal resumed its function as munitions storehouse, supplying troops of the Kentucky State Guard in several riots, the Spanish-American War, the Mexican Border Campaign and World War I. In 1934 a fire of indeterminate origin gutted the interior of the building and destroyed its contents. The exterior brick walls remained serviceable, and a new interior was constructed.

By the early 1970s the Department of Military Affairs had built a new complex called Boone Center, rendering the State Arsenal redundant. Meanwhile, the Kentucky Historical Society's restoration of the Old State Capitol had displaced the extensive collection of weapons and other military relics once housed there. So, in 1973, officials of both agencies decided to place this collection in the State Arsenal, thus creating the Kentucky Military History Museum.

The museum, jointly operated by the Kentucky Department of Military Affairs and the Kentucky Historical Society, chronicles more than two centuries of military service from the frontier era of the Kentucky Militia through to the present day. Displays include an impressive collection of firearms, edged weapons, artillery, uniforms, flags, photographs, personal items, and other equipment that illustrate the Commonwealth's martial heritage, plus exhibits of the cartridge factory, Kentucky inventors and Medal of Honor recipients.

Kentucky in the War of 1812
William E. Matthews

Kentucky had been a state for only 20 years when the U. S. Congress declared war against Britain in June 1812. Anti-British feelings had been slowly mounting for several years over disputes about U.S. neutrality during the wars between Britain and France and its allies starting back in 1793.

During this period U.S. ships were frequently boarded, their crews impressed, and their cargoes confiscated. Particularly galling to Americans was British insistence on the right to seize British-born citizens aboard U.S. ships.

With Kentuckians already peeved by what was perceived as congressional indifference to blatant British interference with American shipping, their mood for war was heightened by the Nov. 11, 1811, battle at Tippecanoe between Indian followers of Tecumseh and a military detachment under Indiana Territorial Governor William Henry Harrison.

The Congressional Declaration of War in 1812 spurred Kentuckians into action and during the course of the two and a half-year war the Commonwealth provided more than 25,000 regulars, militia and volunteers to the American cause. Almost 20 percent of those who fought the British in the War of 1812 were Kentuckians.

Unlike other states whose troops were mostly used to garrison installations and guard borders, most Kentuckians actually got into combat. Consequently, casualties were high.

> Unlike other states whose troops were mostly used to garrison installations and guard borders, most Kentuckians actually got into combat.

Kentuckians entered the fray full of optimism which was tempered substantially when Detroit was surrendered to the British in August 1812.

In January 1813, 1,300 Kentuckians under the command of Gen. James Winchester attacked the British-guarded town of Frenchtown on the River Raisin. About 1,000 Kentuckians took over the small settlement. On Jan. 22 the British counterattacked and over 500 Kentuckians were captured, more than 100 killed, and many others wounded or missing. Later, Indians massacred as many as 65 badly-wounded Kentuckians left at Frenchtown when the British withdrew.

Defeat at the River Raisin dampened Kentuckians' ardor for war and when Gov. Isaac Shelby asked for 3,000 men to help Harrison, only a few responded.

But the Americans, led by Kentucky Sen. Richard M. Johnson's cavalry regiment, Shelby's 3,500 volunteers and about 120 regulars, won a convincing victory at the Battle of the Thames, routing 3,000

Indians and capturing most of the British regulars. Tecumseh himself was slain during the battle.

The deadliest battle of the war, on Jan. 8, 1815, at New Orleans was, ironically, fought after the warring parties had signed the Treaty of Ghent 15 days before, on Dec. 24, 1815. Kentuckians who fought at the Battle of New Orleans had been placed at the very center of the British attack, and inflicted heavy casualties on the attackers.

After the war, Kentuckians could take pride in helping rid the British from the upper northwest and of being an integral part of the defense of New Orleans.

Among the Kentuckians who distinguished themselves during the War of 1812 were:

John E. King, a general who led the only brigade in the 5th Regiment under the command of William Rennick. He fought under Gen. William Henry Harrison in the Battle of the Thames:

James M. Meade, Woodford County native who was killed at the Battle of the River Raisin. He was one of nine soldiers from Kentucky whose death in battle was honored by having Kentucky counties named after them.

John Montgomery Edmonson, who formed a company of volunteer riflemen and joined Lt. Col. John Allen's 1st Rifle Regiment of the Kentucky militia. He was killed on Jan. 22, 1813, at the Battle of the River Raisin. Edmonson County is named in his honor.

John Simpson, resident of Lincoln County, who served under Col. John Allen in the 1st Rifle Regiment. He was killed in the early stages of the second battle at Frenchtown. Simpson County and also Simpsonville in Shelby County are named after him.

Nathaniel Gray Smith Hart, captain of the Lexington (Ky.) Light Infantry, organized a company of about 100 men to fight the British. After the disastrous defeat at the River Raisin, Hart was taken prisoner. Later, he was killed by Wyandotte Indians. Hart County is named in his honor.

Paschal Hickman, a lieutenant in the Kentucky Militia, was among 65 soldiers massacred by Indians on Jan. 23 following the British-Indian victory at Frenchtown on Jan. 18. Hickman County is named in his honor.

William Russell, who was a member of the Virginia legislature that passed the act separating Kentucky from the Commonwealth of Virginia, distinguished himself in the War of 1812. Russell County is named after him.

(Sources: The Kentucky Encyclopedia, The New History of Shelby County, The Louisville Encyclopedia)

A time to mourn...

AS OF SEPT. 15, 2005,
30 KENTUCKIANS HAVE BEEN KILLED IN IRAQ SINCE 2003.

Michael D. Acklin II	Christopher T. Heflin	Tatjana Reed
Jason E. Ames	Robert L. Henderson II	George S. Rentschler
Gary B. Coleman	James T. Hoffman	Scott C. Rose
Chase Johnson Comley	Jonathan A. Hughes	James A. Sherrill
Robert V. Derenda	Sean M. Langley	Joseph M. Tackett
Nicholas J. Dieruf	Ryan J. Montgomery	Joshua K. Titcomb
Stephen P. Downing II	Deshon E. Otey	Eric L. Toth
Jeffrey C. Graham	Christopher W. Phelps	Jeffery L. Wiener
James William Harlan	Darrin K. Potter	Ronnie D. Williams
Michael Ray Hayes	James E. Powell	David Neil Wimberg

Source: Iraq Coalition Casualty Count, http://icasualties

Kentucky in the Civil War
William E. Matthews

Native son Abraham Lincoln is reported to have said that he "hoped to have God on his side, but I must have Kentucky."

Historian James M. McPherson wrote that the War divided Kentucky "more tragically than any other state; for Kentuckians it was truly a war between and among brothers."

McPherson concludes that it is scarcely an exaggeration to say that the Confederacy would have won the war if it could have gained Kentucky, and, conversely, that the Union's success in retaining Kentucky as a base for invasions of the Confederate heartland gave Mr. Lincoln the state he had to "have," and preserved the United States of America.

In the election of 1860, two of the four candidates were Kentuckians. John C. Breckinridge, Lexington native and former vice president, ran on the Southern Democrat ticket. He was opposed by Republican nominee Abraham Lincoln, an attorney born near Hodgenville. When the ballots were cast, most Kentuckians voted for Tennessean John Bell, whose platform was based on the preservation of the Union. Lincoln received a total of 1,364 votes in Kentucky. Of these only five came from Fayette County, the home of his in-laws.

As Southern states began leaving the Union toward the end of 1860, Kentucky faced turmoil. Democratic Gov. Beriah Magoffin believed in the legality of slavery and secession. Like most Kentucky Democrats, Magoffin thought that Southern rights had been violated.

Following the fall of Fort Sumter, in April, 1861, President Lincoln asked for 75,000 troops to crush the rebellion. Gov. Magoffin replied defiantly, "Kentucky will furnish no troops for the wicked purpose of subduing her sister Southern States." Magoffin turned down a similar request from Confederate President Jefferson Davis, also a native Kentuckian. Many, if not most, Kentuckians longed for Kentucky to stay neutral.

On May 16, 1861, the Kentucky House of Representatives declared that Kentucky should remain neutral, and though the governor and senate approved this policy, hopes of mediation were dashed by the state elections of Aug. 5, 1861, when Southerners boycotted the election, enabling

Troops under command of John Hunt Morgan lured the ALICE DEAN ashore, captured her and used her as a ferry to move from Brandenburgh, Ky. to the Indiana side of the river where they burned her
Source: Back Home in Kentucky Magazine

Unionist candidates to score a sweeping victory.

The first blood to be shed in Kentucky came at Barbourville on Sept. 19, 1861, when troops under the command of Gen. Felix K. Zollicoffer defeated a small Union detachment. Zollicoffer reported that 18 Federalists had been killed while he lost only two men. Local historians, however, document the loss of only one soldier on each side.

The Battle of Barbourville is one of 11 major battles fought in Kentucky, according to the National Park Service. While there were innumerable other skirmishes, such as the one at Sacramento, where Nathan Bedford Forrest first found fame, and Tebbs Bend where John Hunt Morgan's men were repulsed, the Park Service has designated only the following as "major" battles: Barbourville, Camp Wildcat Mountain, Ivy Mountain, Paducah, Cynthiana, Munfordville, Rowletts Station, Columbus-

Belmont, Middle Creek, Richmond and Perryville.

The confrontation at Perryville on Oct. 8-9, 1862, represented the largest concentration of forces on both sides in Kentucky. The Confederates won a tactical victory, but strategically they were overwhelmed. Their invasion of Kentucky was ended, and the hopes of a

Gen. Garfield at the Battle of Pound Gap
Source: Back Home in Kentucky Magazine

Confederate Kentucky were lost forever.

Thinking that Kentucky would be a fertile recruiting ground, the Confederates brought 20,000 rifles into the state, but only about 2,500 Kentuckians signed on. One Southerner complained that Kentuckians were "too well off to fight." The war ended on April 9, 1865, with Robert E. Lee's surrender at Appomattox to Ulysses S. Grant.

The cost to the nation, and especially to Kentucky, was enormous. While precise figures will never be established, more than 100,000 Kentuckians answered Mr. Lincoln's call, while somewhere between 25,000 and 35,000 responded to Jefferson Davis' call. Of these more than 100,000 troops, nearly 30,000 died. It is believed that about 10,000 died in battle; the rest fell victim to disease, accidents and exposure.

It has been said that Kentucky seceded from the Union after the Civil War. Kentucky and Delaware voted against ratification of the 13th amendment, which abolished slavery. But when the amendment was eventually ratified, slavery finally came to a legal end in the two recalcitrant states.

Stuart Sanders, until recently the Director of Interpretation for the Perryville Battlefield Association, writes, "Kentucky's opinion of the Federal government became increasingly antagonistic. Although the Southern Democrats were defeated

in the election of 1860, by 1867 the population had become fiercely Democratic. The 14th Amendment, which protected the civil rights of freemen, and the 15th amendment, which gave the vote to African Americans, was met with hostility. Anger spread into the polls. Many Kentuckians who had served the Confederacy were elected to the state legislature and the U. S. Congress. Simon Bolivar Buckner, a general in the Southern army, was elected governor in 1887."

The Union also had its heroes. Ulysses S. Grant and James A. Garfield, who first found fame at Paducah and Middle Creek respectively, were elected president of the United States.

In Volume III of Kentucky's Civil War 1861-1865, published by Back Home In Kentucky, Civil War researcher Lisa Matthews

Reenactment of the Battle of Sacramento
Source: Back Home in Kentucky Magazine

writes: "It is indisputable that Kentucky played an important, if not integral role in the War. Of the Border States, Kentucky was the most significant because of its river systems and railroads.

"It can also be argued that residents of border states suffered more acutely as brother faced off against brother, neighbor against neighbor. Social events were cancelled, business relationship foundered, and churches split along battle lines that remained entrenched long after the war was over.

"These divisions within families, communities, and regions demonstrate how individual loyalties were tested far beyond traditional bounds."

One Confederate soldier summed up the experience in three mere words when he wrote, after his experience at the Battle of Perryville, "Oh, wretched war!"

Civil War Battleground Sites
William E. Matthews

1861
*Sept. 19 Battle of Barbourville
(Barbourville)
*Oct. 21   Battle of Wildcat Mountain
(near London)
Oct. 23   Battle of Saratoga Springs
(near Eddyville)
*Nov. 8   Battle of Ivy Mountain
(near Prestonsburg)
*Dec. 17   Battle of Rowlett's Station
(near Munfordville)
Dec. 27   Battle of Sacramento
(Sacramento)

1862
*Jan. 10   Battle of Middle Creek
(near Prestonsburg)
*Jan. 19   Battle of Mill Springs
(Nancy)
*July 17 – First Battle of Cynthiana
(Cynthiana)
Aug. 17 – Battle of London
(London)
*Aug. 29-30 – Battle of Richmond
(Richmond)
*Sept. 14-17 – Battle of Munfordville
(Munfordville)
Sept. 19 – Battle of Panther Creek
(near Owensboro)
Sept. 21 – Battle of Woodsonville
(near Munfordville)
Sept. 27 – Battle of Augusta (Augusta)
*Oct. 8 – Battle of Perryville (Perryville)

Dec. 23-Jan. 2 – John Hunt Morgan's
   Christmas Raid into Kentucky
Dec. 30 – Battle of New Haven

1863
Mar. 22 – Battle of Mt. Sterling
Mar. 30 – Battle of Dutton's Hill (near
Somerset)
July 2-26 – John Hunt Morgan's Raid
   through Kentucky, into Indiana, Ohio
July 4 – Battle of Tebb's Bend (near
Campbellsville)
July 4 – Battle of Lebanon (Lebanon)
July 30 – Battle of Irvine

1864
*Mar. 25 – Battle of Paducah
May 30 – John Hunt Morgan begins last
   raid into Kentucky
June 11-12 –Second Battle of Cynthiana

Nov. 8 – Kentucky joins New Jersey and
   Delaware as the only states to cast
   electoral votes for Democratic candidate
   George B. McClellan. Abraham Lincoln is
   re-elected in a landslide.

1865
April 9 – Gen. Robert E. Lee surrenders at
   Appomattox Courthouse in Virginia.
* Designated "major" Civil War sites by the
   National Park Service

Oct. 7 – At 7 P.M., Gen. Buell sends special written orders to Gen. Thomas, in part as follows: 'The 3d corps, Gilbert's, is within 3 ½ miles of Perryville, the calvary being nearer, perhaps 2 ½ miles. From all the information received to-day it is thought the enemy will resist our advances in to Perryville. They are said to have a strong force in and around the place. We expect to attack and carry the place to-morrow. March at 3 o'clock precisely, to-morrow morning, without fail; and if possible get all the canteens filled, and have the men cautioned to use water in the most sparing manner. Every officer must caution his men on this point. ... (From Collins' Historical Sketches, Vol. II, Page 113.)

Kentuckians in Wars & Conflicts

WAR OR CONFLICT	IN ACTION	CASUALTIES
American Revolution	**	**
War of 1812	24,000	1,200
Texas Independence	600*	75*
Mexican War	4,694	612
Civil War		
Union	115,760	12,774
Confederate	35,000-38,000***	10,4000***
Spanish-American War	6,065	89
Mexican Punitive Expedition	2,394	1
WWI	95,575	2,418
WWII	306,362	7,932
Korean Conflict	88,273	1,025
Vietnam Conflict	125,000	1,066
Persian Gulf War	1,321****	6

* = Figures are estimates, no other data available
** = No Figures For Kentuckians in the American Revolution because Kentucky was a part of Virginia; (recall, Kentucky became a state in 1792).
*** = Figures are estimates, there are no authoritative figures for Confederate forces.
**** = Kentucky National Guard only, the deaths are from all branches of service.

KENTUCKY NATIONAL GUARD MOBILIZATIONS AND DEPLOYMENTS SINCE 9/11

(As of 9/1/05)

	OPERATION NOBLE EAGLE	OPERATION ENDURING FREEDOM	OPERATION IRAQI FREEDOM
ARMY	1,265	955	3,405
AIR	0	572	1,038
TOTAL	1,265	1,527	4,443

7,235 Mobilizations since 9/11

Note: these figures include multiple deployments. Two individuals from the air guard have been deployed nine times. Air Guard deployments typically are shorter in duration, from one to six months whereas Army deployments are typically one-year deployments.
Source: Kentucky Department of Military Affairs, Kentucky Military Records and Research Branch
Photo Source: Department of the Navy

Congressional Medal of Honor

John Trowbridge

The Medal of Honor, our country's highest award for military valor, is given only to those who have acted with supreme courage and total disregard for their own safety in the face of the most hazardous conditions.

The Medal is an award that only a comparative handful of men in the world are entitled to wear. It is bestowed by act of Congress and reflects our nation's gratitude to those who, in moments of uncommon risk, offered everything they had in its defense, including life itself.

The medal is but a humble token, a gesture of recognition for sacrifices that cannot be repaid in worldly goods. Of the men and women of all branches of our armed forces who have been awarded the Medal of Honor for 'conspicuous gallantry' while defending our nation, many did not live to have the honor bestowed on them personally. These recipients died in the actions for which they were cited.

To them, 'above and beyond the call of duty,' were not mere words but self-sacrifice in the face of almost certain death. Their reward was the knowledge that they were acting in the tradition of the highest ideals of the military and the United States.

Those who live to wear the medal do so proudly and yet with the spirit of humility befitting true heroes. They share the highest glory of which it is a symbol, yet hold it in solemn trust for comrades less fortunate.

Whether they lived or died, our nation is richer for their actions.

Information gathered from numerous sources including, Center of Military History, The Medal of Honor Society, and The Congressional Record.

WILD BIRDS.

By Nelly Marshall M'Afee

Lo! by the grave of one I loved
I bent in bitter weeping,
When clear in the air there rang the songs
Of birds, where he lay sleeping.
Blithely they sang unheeding on—
Unmoved by my heart's sadness;
The anguished tears that wet the mold
Chilled not their paeans of gladness.
It seemed so strange to me, to see
Mirth and Misery meeting—
And over a lonely grave to hear
Joy and Grief give greeting!
There I knelt in dark despair
My dear dead deploring—
Above me, far in upper air,
The happy birds were soaring.
And e'en as broke my plaintive sobs
Over his precious dust—
While Faith, beside me—weeping, too—
Forgot his solemn trust,

Lo! from the shadowy grasses round,
A gay, glad bird upspringing
Cleft the clouds and heavenward soared,
Softly, sweetly singing.
And close to my wretched heart I clasped
This blessed, bright conviction—
That God's dear love is always near
In every deep affliction.
And just as out of silence then
Broke the song of the little bird,
If we but listen, the "still small voice
Of love is ever heard.
And out of every darkness
That shades our lives on earth,
There is a day of brightness
To which it will give birth;
And so we do observe it—
To faith and duty clinging;
Our hearts, like birds both far and wide,
Will fill all life with singing.

Kentucky Medal of Honor Recipients

Civil War 1861-1865

Army Captain William P. Black
Army Private John C. Callahan
Army Sergeant John S. Darrough
Army Private John Davis
Army Drummer William H. Horsfall
Army Private Aaron Hudson
Army Private Henry B. Mattingly
Army Sergeant Francis M. McMillen
Navy Landsman Daniel Noble
Army Private Oliver P. Rood
Army Sergeant Andrew J. Smith
Army Private William Steinmetz
Army Doctor Mary E. Walker
Army Major John F. Weston
Army Colonel James A. Williamson

Indian Campaigns 1870-1891

Army Second Lieutenant Thomas Cruse
Army First Sergeant William L. Day
Army Corporal John J. Givens
Army Private William M. Harris
Army Captain John B. Kerr
Army Private Franklin M. McDonald
Army Private George D. Scott
Army Sergeant Thomas Shaw
Army Private Thomas W. Stivers
Army Private Thomas Sullivan
Army Saddler Otto E. Voit
Army Sergeant Brent Woods

Actions in Peacetime 1871-1910

Navy Seaman Edward W. Boers
Navy Watertender Edward A. Clary
Navy Quarter Gunner George Holt

Wars of American Expansion 1897-1902

Army Colonel J. Franklin Bell
Army First Lieutenant
  Benjamin F. Hardaway
Army Private James J. Nash

World War I 1917-1919

Army Sergeant Willie Sandlin

World War II 1941-1945

Marine Corps Corporal Richard E. Bush
Army Technical Sergeant Morris E. Crain
Marine Corps Private First Class
  Leonard F. Mason
Marine Corps Reserve Private First Class
  Wesley Phelps
Army Private Wilburn K. Ross
Marine Corps Private First Class
  Luther Skaggs Jr.
Army Staff Sergeant Junior J. Spurrier
Army Sergeant John C. Squires

Korean War 1950-1953

Marine Corps Captain William E. Barber
Marine Corps Private First Class
  William B. Baugh
Army Corporal John W. Collier
Army First Lieutenant Carl H. Dodd
Army Second Lieutenant Darwin K. Kyle
Army Private First Class David M. Smith
Army Private First Class Ernest E. West

Vietnam War 1961-1975

Army Sergeant Charles C. Fleek
Army Staff Sergeant Don Jenkins
Army Private First Class Billy L. Lauffer
Army Sergeant First Class Gary L. Littrell
Army Second Lieutenant
  John J. McGinty III
Army Private First Class David P. Nash
Marine Corps Lance Corporal Joe C. Paul

Source: http://www.medalofhonor.com/KentuckyRecipients.htm

Photo Source: U.S. Army

HISTORY
Lewis & Clark

When Thomas Jefferson had a dream of sending an exploring party into the American West, he asked George Rogers Clark, the hero of the Revolution in the West. Twenty years later George's youngest brother, William, actually did what the author of the Declaration of Independence and future president proposed to George Rogers Clark.

the Spanish in Louisiana. And to the north across the Ohio River, although the American Revolution had ended, the British from their posts in Canada, and ones they still garrisoned in the Northwest Territory, supplied Indians for their continuing war with the Kentuckians.

In March 1801 Thomas Jefferson became the third president of the United States. That same month, a young army officer named Meriwether Lewis accepted Jefferson's invitation to serve as his private secretary.

Kentucky was fast becoming a major state in the young republic, but it was still a western state. It was a major outfitting and recruitment center for pioneers traveling elsewhere and hunters and traders striking out in to the wilderness. Its location and the outdoor talents of young men destined it to be the cradle of the "Corps of Discovery."

Re-enactment of Louis & Clark Discovery exploration docked at Louisville
Source: Sid Webb

In 1783, Kentucky was the West. It was the United States' "First West" — the young nation's first country to be settled beyond the Appalachians. Kentucky became the first western state and a major supplier of settlers for lands that would become future states to the north, south and west.

It was an area of intrigue by foreign powers. The infamous "Spanish Conspiracy" of the 1780s and 1790s witnessed attempts by the Spanish to influence Kentucky politics and possibly separate it from the young United States.

In the 1790s French agents sought to enlist Kentuckians—led by George Rogers Clark—against

An account of a Scotsman's journey across Canada (ending with a recommendation that the British seize control of the Pacific Northwest and monopolize its rich fur trade) prompted Jefferson to activate his long-held plan of sending an exploring party up the Missouri. In early 1803 the expedition began to take shape. Jefferson asked Congress for $2,500 in January for what was called a commercial and scientific undertaking (The final price tag was almost $40,000).

Nine Young Men From Kentucky — Key Figures in the Expedition: William Bratton, private, born in Augusta County, Virginia, on July 29, 1778. He served the Corps primarily as a blacksmith and hunter; **John Colter**, private, was born in Virginia about 1775 and served the expedition primarily as a hunter; **Joseph and Reubin Fields**, privates, both of whom were born in Virginia — Joseph about 1780 and Reubin probably in 1781; **Charles Floyd**, sergeant, was born in Jefferson County in 1782 and was the only man to die during the expedition; **George Gibson**, private, was born in Pennsylvania at an undetermined year, and served the Corps as a marksman, hunter, interpreter and fiddle player; **Nathaniel Pryor**, sergeant, was born in Virginia in 1772 (he was also appointed sergeant in command of a squad); **George Shannon**, private, was born in Pennsylvania in 1785, and served primarily as a hunter. Shannon, with

Meriwether Lewis

another man, became separated from the group on a search for lost horses (in what is now South Dakota) and was found 16 days later, near starvation; **John Shields**, private, was born in Rockingham County, Virginia, in 1769. A blacksmith, gunsmith, carpenter and hunter, he was noted for his skills as an artist and in repairing guns; and **York**, the black slave thought to have been born in Caroline County, Virginia, and "…performed his full share of duties with the other members of the party." **York**, William Clark's companion since childhood, was the first African American to cross the continent from coast to coast.

MERIWETHER LEWIS — Born in 1774 in Albemarle County (near Charlottesville), Virginia, Lewis' father had been a Revolutionary War officer and died when Meriwether was a young boy. Early on he showed a keen interest in the outdoors and, at the age of 20, became an officer in the military.

During 1801-1802 Lewis served as President Thomas Jefferson's personal secretary, and lived and dined at the president's House. In 1802 Jefferson informed Captain Lewis that he would command an expedition to the Pacific.

Upon their return from the expedition, Lewis and Clark were treated as national heroes, and each man was given 1,600 acres of public land as a reward for their accomplishments. Lewis was appointed governor of the Louisiana Territory in 1808. The following year he died, on October 9, of a gunshot wound while en route to Washington. His death occurred at Grinders Stand, an inn along the Natchez Trace. He was buried near the inn, and a monument was erected on his grave in the 1840s. The words etched upon his stone obelisk are now faint and unreadable.

There is considerable mystery about the tragic death of this famous explorer at the age of 33. There is considerable speculation whether he committed suicide, died accidentally, or was murdered. Most historians believe his wounds were self-inflicted because Lewis suffered from melancholic moods, and had been reported drinking heavily prior to the trip.

WILLIAM CLARK — Born in Virginia in 1770, William was the youngest brother of Gen. George Rogers Clark of Revolutionary War fame. When he was 14, his family moved to Louisville, Kentucky.

Clark served in the Kentucky militia and was commissioned a 2nd Lieutenant in the U.S. Army. He fought at the Battle of Fallen Timbers, which ended the threat of the Northwest Indian Confederation. Lewis appointed him co-leader of the expedition, and he and Lewis met at Louisville to prepare for the journey.

Following the expedition, Clark married and settled in St. Louis. There he served as an Indian agent for the Louisiana Territory (1807-1813) and superintendent of Indian Affairs from 1813 until his death in 1838. He frequently interceded with the federal government to obtain more just treatment for the Indians.

Clark named his eldest son Meriwether Lewis Clark. The famed explorer died at the age of 69 and is buried at Bellefontaine Cemetery in St. Louis.

Lewis and Clark put names to the land, and people were lured to those places. As historian Bernard DeVoto put it, 'theirs was the first report on the West, "on the United States over the hill and beyond the sunset. …It satisfied desire, and it created desire: the desire of a westering nation.'"

Summary of "Kentucky and the Lewis & Clark Expedition," reprinted with permission by Back Home in Kentucky, Lewis & Clark Bicentennial Edition.

HISTORICAL SOCIETIES & MUSEUMS

COUNTY	HISTORICAL SOCIETY/MUSEUM	CONTACT	ADDRESS	CITY	ZIP	PHONE
Adair	Adair County Historical Society; Adair Public Library	Lila Ford, President	PO Box 613, 307 Greensburg St	Columbia	42728	(270) 384-2472
Allen	Allen County Historical Society	Rosemary Harper, President	301 N 4th St	Scottsville	42164	(270) 237-3026
Anderson	Anderson County Historical Society		PO Box 212	Lawrenceburg	40342	(502) 839-1815
Ballard	Ballard-Carlisle County Historical Society	Kathleen Rolland, Director	PO Box 279	Wickliffe	42087	(270) 335-3323
Ballard	Barlow House Museum		509 Broadway, Hwy 60	Barlow	42024	(270) 334-3010
Ballard	Wickliffe Mounds		94 Green St, Hwy 60	Wickliffe	42087	(270) 335-3681
Barren	Bell's Tavern Historical Park		Old W Dixie Hwy	Park City	42160	(270) 749-5695
Barren	S Central KY Historical & Genealogical Society		PO Box 157	Glasgow	42142	(270) 651-9114
Barren	South Central Kentucky Cultural Center		200 W Water St	Glasgow	42141	(270) 651-9792
Barron	South Central KY Historical Society		PO Box 157	Glasgow	42142	
Bell	American Association-Middlesboro Museum		Vistor's Center	Middlesboro	40965	
Bell	Bell County Historical Society	Jerry Browning, President	PO Box 1344	Middlesboro	40965	(606) 242-0005
Bell	The Coal House Museum		106 N 20th St	Middlesboro	40965	(606) 248-1075
Bell	The Lost Squadron Museum		1420 Dorchester Ave	Middlesboro	40965	(606) 248-1149
Bllitt	Hartman Cooperage Museum, Jim Beam Distillery		149 Happy Hollow Rd	Clermont	40110	(502) 543-9877
Boone	Big Bone Lick State Park Museum		3380 Beaver Rd	Union	41091	(859) 384-3522
Boone	Boone County Historical Society	Don Clare, Curator	8100 Ewing St	Florence	41042	
Boone	Rabbit Hash Historical Society and Museum		11646 Lower River Rd	Union	41091	(859) 586-6431
Bourbon	Hopewell Museum	Betsy Kephart, Director	800 Pleasant St	Paris	40361	(859) 987-7274
Boyd	Eastern KY Genealogical Society	Mark Meinhart	Box 1544	Ashland	41105	
Boyd	Highlands Museum and Discovery Center	Nancy Smith, Director	1620 Winchester Ave	Ashland	41101	(606) 329-8888
Boyle	Danville/Boyle County Historical Society		Constitution Square	Danville	40422	
Boyle	McDowell House Museum and Apothecary Shop		125 S Second St	Danville	40472	(859) 236-2804
Bracken	Bracken County Historical Society	George Cummins, President	PO Box 307	Brooksville	41004	(606) 735-3337
Breathitt	Breathitt County Historical & Genealogy Society	Nancy E. Herald, President	1024 College Ave	Jackson	41339	(606) 666-7722
Breckinridge	Breckinridge County Historical Society	David W. Hayes, President	PO Box 498	Hardinsburg	40143	(270) 756-2867
Breckinridge	Breckinridge County Historical Society Museum		Main St	Hardinsburg	40143	(270) 756-2347
Bullitt	Bullitt County Genealogy Society	Barbara Bosley, President	PO Box 950	Shepherdsville	40165	(502) 957-3332
Bullitt	Bullitt County History Museum	David Strange, Director	300 S Buckman PO Box 206	Shepherdsville	40165	(502) 921-0161
Bullitt	Mt. Washington Historical Society Museum		434 Riverview Dr	Mt. Washington	40047	(502) 538-7660
Butler	Butler County Hist. and Gen. Society	June	PO Box 435	Morgantown	42261	(270) 526-5971
Butler	Green River Museum		108 N Church St	Woodbury	42288	
Caldwell	Adsmore Museum	Ardell Jarratt, Director	304 N Jefferson St	Princeton	42445	(270) 365-3114
Caldwell	Caldwell County Historical Society	Gale Cherry, President	206 Jefferson St	Princeton	42445	
Caldwell	Caldwell County Railroad Historical Museum		116 Edwards St	Princeton	42445	(270) 365-0582
Calloway	Wrather West Kentucky Museum	Kate Reeves, Manager	100 Wrather Museum Murray State University	Murray	42071	(270) 762-4771
Campbell	Campbell County Historical and Genealogical Society	Kenneth A. Reis, President	19 E Main St	Alexandria	41001	(859) 635-6407
Campbell	Newport Aquarium WAVE Foundation	Doug Allender, Director	1 Aquarium Way	Newport	41071	(859) 491-3467
Campbell	NKU Museum of Anthropology		221 Landrum Acad. Center	Highland Heights	41076	
Carroll	Butler-Turpin Historic Home		1068 Hwy 227	Carrollton	41008	(502) 732-4384
Carroll	Port William Historical Society	Janet Bentley, President	714 Highland Ave	Carrollton	41008	
Carter	Carter County Historical and Genealogical Society	Gladys C. Thomas, President	PO Box 1128	Grayson	41143	
Casey	Bicentennial Heritage of Casey County	Charles R. Jackson, President	147 Wolford Street	Liberty	42539	(606) 787-6194
Christian	Christian County Historical Society		1110 Bethel St	Hopkinsville	42240	
Christian	Don F. Pratt Memorial Museum		Building 5702 Tennessee Ave	Ft. Campbell	42223	(270) 798-4986
Christian	Pennyroyal Area Museum	Donna Stone, Executive Director	217 E 9th St PO Box 1093	Hopkinsville	42241	(270) 887-4270
Clark	Bluegrass Heritage Museum	Jim Pitts	217 S Main St	Winchester	40391	(859) 745-1358

HISTORICAL SOCIETIES & MUSEUMS

COUNTY	HISTORICAL SOCIETY/MUSEUM	CONTACT	ADDRESS	CITY	ZIP	PHONE
Clark	Clark County Historical Society		122 Belmont	Winchester	40391	(859) 744-6616
Clark	Holly Rood Clark Mansion		122 Belmont	Winchester	40962	(606) 598-5507
Clay	Clay County Genealogy and Historical Society		PO Box 394	Manchester	42602	(606) 387-5519
Clinton	Clinton County Historical Society		Rt 4 Box 638	Albany		
Crittenden	Ben Clements Mineral Museum	Bill Frazier, Chairman of the Board	205 N Walker St	Marion	42064	(270) 965-4263
Crittenden	Bobby Wheeler Museum, Crittenden County Historical Society		W Carlisle St	Marion	42064	(270) 965-9657
Crittenden	Crittenden County Historical Society	Myrtle Dunning, Director/Treasurer	PO Box 25	Marion	42064	(270) 965-4666
Daviess	Daviess County Historical Society	Sheila E. Heflin, Director	PO Box 80	Livermore	42301	(502) 684-0211
Daviess	International Bluegrass Music Museum	Gabrielle Gray, Executive Director	207 E Second St	Owensboro	42303	(270) 926-7891
Daviess	Owensboro Area Museum of Science and History	Jeffery Jones, Executive Director	122 E Second St	Owensboro	42303	(270) 687-2732
Edmonson	Edmonson County Historical Society		8621 Brownsville Rd	Brownsville	42210	(270) 597-3140
Elliott	Cultural Heritage Center	Laurell Gorge, Director	Old 7 and 32 PO Box 653	Sandy Hook	41171	(606) 738-5543
Estill	Estill County Historical & Genealogy Society	Diane Rogers, President	PO Box 221	Irvine	40472	(859) 723-3806
Fayette	American Saddlebred Museum	Tolley Graves, Director	4083 Iron Works Pike	Lexington	40511	(859) 259-2746
Fayette	Ashland, The Henry Clay Estate		120 Sycamore Rd	Lexington	40502	(859) 266-8581
Fayette	Aviation Museum of Kentucky	Alice McCormick, Operations Manger	PO Box 4118 4316 Hanger Dr Bldg 13	Lexington	40544	(859) 231-1219
Fayette	Explorium	Sara Holcomb, Director	440 W Short St	Lexington	40507	(859) 258-3253
Fayette	Fayette County Genealogical Society	Debbie Steuert, Director	800 Apache Trl	Lexington	40503	(859) 224-9406
Fayette	Headley-Whitney Museum		4435 Old Frankfort Pk	Lexington	40510	(859) 255-6653
Fayette	Hunt Morgan House		201 N Mill St	Lexington	40507	(859) 233-3290
Fayette	International Museum of the Horse	Bill Cook	4089 Iron Works Pike	Lexington	40511	(859) 233-4303
Fayette	Kentucky Hemp Museum		PO Box 8551	Lexington	40533	(606) 873-8957
Fayette	Kentucky Horse Park		4089 Iron Works Pike	Lexington	40511	(800) 678-8813
Fayette	Lexington History Museum Inc	Ed Houlihan, Director	PO Box 116 215 W Main St	Lexington	40507	(859) 264-0530
Fayette	Mary Todd Lincoln House		578 W Main St	Lexington	40507	(859) 233-9999
Fayette	UK Basketball Museum	Van Florence, Executive Director	PO Box 89	Lexington	40588	(859) 225-5670
Fayette	University of Kentucky Art Museum	Kathy Walsh-Piper, Director	116 Singletary Center Rose and Euclid Aves	Lexington	40506	(859) 257-5716
Fayette	William S Webb Museum of Anthropology	George Crothers, Director	1020A Export St	Lexington	40506	(859) 257-8208
Fleming	Fleming County Historical Society	Brenda Plummer, Director	290 W Water St	Flemingsburg	41041	
Fleming	Fleming County Museum Society		PO Box 24	Flemingsburg	41041	
Floyd	Floyd County Historical and Genealogical Society	Bertha Daniels, Director	PO Box 982	Auxier	41653	
Floyd	Samuel May House	Chris McCrory, Director	1001 Wilkinson Blvd	Prestonsburg	41653	(606) 886-3863
Franklin	Buffalo Trace Distillery Museum	Dr. Anne Butler	103 Jackson Hall, KSU	Frankfort	40601	(502) 223-7641
Franklin	Center of Excellence for the Study of Ky. African Americans			Frankfort	40601	(502) 597-6315
Franklin	Kentucky Historical Society	Kent Whitworth, Executive Director	100 W Broadway	Frankfort	40601	(502) 564-1792
Franklin	Kentucky Military History Museum	Bill Bright, Curator	120 E Main St	Frankfort	40601	(502) 564-3265
Fulton	Fulton County Historical Society	Margaret Adams, President	PO Box 1031	Fulton	42041	(270) 838-6961
Fulton	Warren Thomas Black History Museum		603 Moulton St	Hickman	42050	(270) 236-2535
Gallatin	Gallatin County Historical Society		PO Box 165	Warsaw	41095	
Gallatin	Peak-Corkran House	Jaqueline Mylor, President	PO Box 1241	Warsaw	41095	(859) 567-6941
Garrard	Garrard County Historical Society		208 Danville St	Lancaster	40444	
Grant	Grant County Historical Society	Ruby Miller, Director	PO Box 33	Mason	41054	(859) 824-7181
Graves	Graves County Historical Society		Rt 1 Box 171	Cunningham	42035	
Graves	Western Kentucky Museum		Old Ice House, 120 N 8th St	Mayfield	42066	(270) 247-6971
Grayson	Grayson County Historical Society		PO Box 84	Leitchfield	42755	(270) 230-8989
Grayson	Jack Thomas House, Grayson County Historical Society		122 E Main St	Leitchfield	42755	(270) 230-8989
Green	Green County Historical Society		PO Box 276	Greensburg	42743	

HISTORICAL SOCIETIES & MUSEUMS

COUNTY	HISTORICAL SOCIETY/MUSEUM	CONTACT	ADDRESS	CITY	ZIP	PHONE
Greenup	McConnell House		1023 Riverside Dr	Wurtland	41144	(606) 833-9098
Hancock	Hancock County Agricultural Museum at Lewisport	L R Waitman	Lewisport City Hall	Lewisport	42351	
Hancock	Hancock County Historical Society		PO Box 667	Hawesville	42348	(270) 927-8095
Hancock	Hancock County Museum Inc.		PO Box 605 110 River St	Hawesville	42348	(270) 927-8672
Harden	Ft Duffield Park Civil War Site		US 31W at Salt River Dr	West Point	40177	(502) 922-4574
Hardin	Children's Museum of E town	Angela Wilcox, Director	447 King's Way	Elizabethtown	42701	(270) 360-9696
Hardin	Hardin County Historical Society		209 W Dixie Ave	Elizabethtown	42701	(270) 737-4126
Hardin	Patton Museum of Cavalry and Armor		Off US Hwy 31 W	Ft Knox	40121	(502) 943-8977
Hardin	Schmidt Museum of Coca-Cola Memorabilia	Roy Minagawa, Director	109 Buffalo Creek Dr	Elizabethtown	42701	(270) 234-1100
Hardin	Swopes Cars of Yesteryear Museum		1100 N Dixie Ave	Elizabethtown	42701	(270) 765-2181
Harlan	Harlan County Genealogical Society		PO Box 1498	Harlan	40831	
Harlan	Kentucky Coal Mining Museum	Bobbie Gothard, Curator	PO Box A 231 Main St	Benham	40807	(606) 848-1530
Harrison	Cynthiana-Harrison County Museum	Martha S Barnes, President	PO Box 411 112 S Walnut St	Cynthiana	41031	(859) 234-7179
Harrison	Harrison County Historical Society	Phillip Naff	1490 Ammerman Pk	Cynthiana	41031	(859) 234-5835
Hart	American Cave Museum and Hidden River Cave		119 E Main St	Horse Cave	42749	(270) 786-1466
Hart	Battle for the Bridge Civil War Site		940 S Dixie Hwy	Munfordville	42765	(270) 524-0101
Hart	Hart County Historical Society		PO Box 606	Munfordville	42765	(270) 524-0101
Henderson	Henderson County Historical and Genealogical Society	Netta Mullin, Director	PO Box 303	Henderson	42420	
Henry	Henry County Historical Society	Shirely Sills, Director	PO Box 570	New Castle	40050	
Hickman	Hickman County Museum		RR 1 Box 70	Clinton	42031	
Hopkins	Historical Society of Hopkins County		221 E Clay St	Clinton	42031	(270) 653-6948
Jackson	Jackson County Historical Society	Ken Williams, Director	107 S Union St	Madisonville	42431	(606) 287-7672
Jefferson	Callahan Museum, American Printing House for the Blind		299 Hooten Rd	McKee	40447	(800) 223-1839
Jefferson	Cathedral Heritage Foundation		1839 Frankfort Ave	Louisville	40206	(502) 558-5336
Jefferson	Col. Harland Sanders Museum		429 W Muhammad Ali Blvd	Louisville	40202	(502) 874-8353
Jefferson	Filson Historical Society		1441 Gardiner Ln	Louisville	40213	(502) 635-5083
Jefferson	Frazier Historical Arms Museum	B J Davis, Manager of Education	1310 S Third St	Louisville	40208	(502) 412-2220
Jefferson	Historic Middletown Museum		829 W Main St	Louisville	40202	(502) 254-4303
Jefferson	Jeffersontown Historical Museum		726 Waterford Rd	Louisville	40207	(502) 261-8290
Jefferson	Kentucky Derby Museum	Sherry Srose, COO	10635 Watterson Trail	Jeffersontown	40299	(502) 637-1111
Jefferson	Little Loomhouse, Lou Tate Foundation		704 Central Ave Churchill Downs	Louisville	40208	(502) 367-4792
Jefferson	Louisville Science Center	Scott Alvey, Asst Dir	328 Kenwood Hill Rd	Louisville	40214	(502) 561-6100
Jefferson	Louisville Slugger Museum	Bill Williams	727 W Main St	Louisville	40202	(877) 775-8443
Jefferson	Muhammad Ali Center	Michael Fox, President/CEO	800 W Main St	Louisville	40202	(502) 584-9254
Jefferson	Portland Museum	Nathalie Andrews, Executive Director	144 N Sixth St	Louisville	40202	(502) 776-7678
Jefferson	SW Jefferson County Historical Society		2308 Portland Ave	Louisville	40212	(502) 585-5247
Jefferson	Thomas Edison House		13700 Sandray Blvd	Louisville	40201	(502) 897-2944
Jessamine	Whitehall Historic House, Historic Homes Foundation		729-31 E Washington St	Louisville	40202	(859) 881-9126
Jessamine	Camp Nelson Heritage Park		3110 Lexington Rd	Louisville	40206	(859) 885-4871
Jessamine	Jessamine County Historical Society	George Dean, Director	Ky Hwy 3026/US Hwy 27	Nicholasville	40356	
Johnson	Johnson County Historical Society		504 W Maple St	Nicholasville	40356	
Johnson	Kentucky Highway 23 Country Music Museum		444 Main St	Paintsville	41240	
Johnson	Mountain Homeplace		US Hwy 23	Paintsville	41502	(800) 542-5790
Johnsons	Coal Miner's Museum, Van Lear Historical Society		Paintsville Lake Park	Staffordsville	41256	(606) 297-1850
Kenton	Behringer Crawford Museum	Laurie Risch, Executive Director	78 Miller's Creek Rd	Van Lear	41265	(606) 789-8540
Kenton	Erlanger Historical Society		PO Box 67 1600 Montaague St	Covington	41011	(859) 491-4003
			3313 Crescent Ave	Erlanger	41018	(859) 727-2630

HISTORICAL SOCIETIES & MUSEUMS

COUNTY	HISTORICAL SOCIETY/MUSEUM	CONTACT	ADDRESS	CITY	ZIP	PHONE
Kenton	Kenton County Historical Society	John Boh, Secretary	507 Russell Street	Covington	41011	(859) 341-2802
Kenton	Oldenburg Brewery Archives & Museum		I-75 & Buttermilk Pk	Ft. Mitchell	41011	(859) 341-0461
Kenton	Vent Haven Museum		33 W Maple St	Ft. Mitchell	41011	(859) 341-0461
Kenton	Vent Haven Museum	Lisa Sweasy, Curator	33 W Maple St	Ft. Mitchell	41011	(859) 341-0461
Knott	Knott County Historical and Genealogical Society	David Smith, Director	PO Box 1023	Hindman	41822	(606) 785-5751
Knox	Knox County Historical Society		601 N. Main St.	Barbourville	40906	
Knox	Knox Historical Museum		PO Box 1446 196 Daniel Boone Dr	Barbourville	40906	(606) 546-4300
Larue	Larue County Historical Society		PO Box 361	Hodgenville	42748	
Larue	The Lincoln Museum		66 Lincoln Sq	Hodgenville	42748	(270) 358-3163
Laurel	Col. Sanders Café Museum		688 US 25W & 25E	Corbin	40701	(606) 528-2163
Laurel	Laurel County Historical Society	William Meaders, Director	PO Box 816	London	40743	
Laurel	Mountain Life Museum, Levi Jackson State Park		998 Levi Jackson Mill Rd	London	40744	(606) 878-8000
Lee	Lee County Historical Society	John Wilson	PO Box V	Beattyville	41311	
Leslie	Leslie County Historical Society		PO Box 9	Hyden	40840	(859) 374-7828
Letcher	C.B.Caudill Store/History Center	Gaynell Begley, Proprietor	7822 Hwy 7S	Whitesburg	41858	(606) 633-3281
Letcher	Letcher County Historical & Genealogical Society		PO Box 312	Whitesburg	41858	
Letcher	Zegeer Coal-Railroad Museum		PO Box 4	Jenkins	41537	(606) 832-4676
Lewis	Lewis County Historical Society		PO Box 212	Vanceburg	41179	
Lewis	Vanceburg Depot Museum		615 2nd St	Vanceburg	41179	(606) 796-3044
Lincoln	L & N Depot Museum		1866 Depot St	Stanford	40484	(859) 365-0207
Lincoln	Lincoln County Historical Society	Luzia Foster, President	PO Box 570	Stanford	40484	(606) 365-2536
Livingston	Livingston County Historical Society	Joyce Woodyard, President	PO Box 96	Smithland	42081	(270) 928-4656
Livingston	Livingston County Welcome Center and Museum		117 State St	Smithland	42081	(270) 928-4656
Livingston	Morris Toy Museum		1007 1st St	Smithland	42081	(270) 988-3591
Logan	Auburn Museum	Eloise Haddon, President	433 W Main St	Auburn	42206	(270) 542-4677
Logan	Historic Russellville Visitors' Center-Bibb House Museum and 1817 Saddle Factory Museum		280 E Fourth St	Russellville	42276	(270) 726-4181
Logan	Historic Russellville	Judy Lyne, President	PO Box 853	Russellville	42276	(270) 726-2206
Logan	Shaker Museum at South Union	Tommy Hines, Director	PO Box 177	Auburn	42206	(270) 542-4167
Logan	Shaker Museum at South Union		850 Shaker Museum Rd	South Union	42283	(270) 542-4167
Lyon	Lyon County Historical Society	Mary Katherine Edwards, Director	PO Box 894	Eddyville	42038	
Madison	Berea College Mus . App.Center	Chris Miller, College Curator	CPO 2196	Berea	40404	(859) 985-3373
Madison	Ft Boonesborough State Park/Kentucky River Museum		4375 Boonesboro Rd	Richmond	40475	(859) 527-3131
Madison	Irvinton House Museum		345 Lancaster Ave	Richmond	40475	(859) 626-1422
Madison	Madison County Historical Society	Charles Hay, Director	PO Box 5066	Richmond	40476	
Madison	White Hall State Historic Site		500 White Hall Shrine Rd Box 222	Richmond	40475	(859) 626-9178
Magoffin	Magoffin County Historical Society		515 Nerinx Rd	Salyersville	41465	(606) 349-1607
Marion	Loretto Archives Heritage Room		3350 Burks Springs Rd	Loretto	40037	(270) 865-5811
Marion	Maker's Mark Distillery and Museum	Mary Perry, Director	201 E Main St	Loretto	40037	(270) 865-2099
Marion	Marion County Historical Society	Michael Ragsdale	PO Box 373	Lebanon	40033	(270) 692-4698
Marshall	Marshall County Historical Genealogical Society	Evelynn Cassady, President	PO Box 501	Benton	42025	(502) 527-4749
Martin	Martin County Historical Society	Marsha H Jones, Secretary	2124 Old Main St	Inez	41224	
Mason	Harriet Beecher Stowe Slavery to Freedom Museum		c/o Mason County Museum 215 Sutton	Washington	41056	(606) 759-7411
Mason	Mason County Historical Society		215 Sutton St	Maysville	41056	(606) 564-5865
Mason	Musem County Museum	Sue Ellen Grannis, Curator	2215 Old Main St	Maysville	41056	(606) 564-5865
Mason	Old Washington		533 Madison St	Washington	41096	(606) 759-7411
McCracken	Alben Barkley Museum	Martha Beck	533 Madison St	Paducah	42001	(270) 534-8264

HISTORICAL SOCIETIES & MUSEUMS

COUNTY	HISTORICAL SOCIETY/MUSEUM	CONTACT	ADDRESS	CITY	ZIP	PHONE
McCracken	Market House Museum		PO Box 12 121 Market St Sq	Paducah	42001	(270) 443-7759
McCracken	McCracken County Genealogical and Historical Society		4640 Buckner Ln	Paducah	42001	
McCracken	Metropolitan Hotel Museum	Sharon Poat, Treasurer	446 Kinkead St	Paducah	42003	(270) 443-9229
McCracken	Museum of the American Quilters Society		215 Jefferson St	Paducah	42001	(270) 442-8856
McCracken	Paducah Railroad Museum		3rd and Washington St	Paducah	42001	(270) 442-4032
McCracken	River Heritage Museum	Julie Harris, Director	117 S Water St	Paducah	42001	(270) 575-9958
McCreary	The Tilghman Heritage Foundation		631 Kentucky Ave	Paducah	42003	(270) 575-1870
McCreary	Blue Heron Mining Community		Hwy 742	Stearns	42005	(606) 376-3787
McCreary	McCreary County Historical and Genealogical Society			Whitley City	42653	
McCreary	Stearns Museum		PO Box 400	Stearns	42647	(606) 376-5730
McLean	Forrest's Orphans Museum	Fred Wilhite	PO Box 452	Calhoun	42327	(270) 785-4594
McLean	McLean County Historical & Genealogy Museum		PO Box 10	Calhoun	42327	(270) 273-9760
Menifee	Menifee County Roots		540 Main St Box 34	Frenchburg	40322	(606) 768-3323
Mercer	Harrodsburg Historical Society		PO Box 114	Harrodsburg	40330	(606) 734-5985
Metcalfe	Metcalfe County Historical Society	Kay Harbison, President	PO Box 316	Edmonton	42129	
Monroe	Old Mulkey Meeting House State Historic Site		Box 910	Tompkinsville	42167	(270) 487-8481
Montgomery	Montgomery County Historical Society	Ray F Shear, President	1819 Old Mulkey Rd	Mt. Sterling	40353	(859) 498-0119
Morgan	Memory Hill Foundation	Laberta Potter, President	607 Elmwood Dr	West Liberty	41472	(606) 743-3330
Morgan	Morgan County Historical Society		89 Memory Hill Ln	West Liberty	41472	
Morgan	Morgan County History Museum		Morgan St	West Liberty	41472	(606) 743-2588
Muhlenberg	Duncan Cultural Center		122 S Cherry St	Greenville	42345	(270) 338-2605
Muhlenberg	Everly Brothers Monument		203 N 2nd St	Central City	42330	(270) 754-9603
Muhlenberg	Muhlenberg County Genealogy & Local History Annex	Barry Edwards, Manager	PO Box 758	Greenville	42345	(270) 338-5388
Nelson	Bardstown Civil War Museum	Joe Masterson, Director	310 E Broadway	Bardstown	40004	(502) 349-0291
Nelson	Bardstown Historical Museum	Mary Ellyn Hamilton, Curator	114 N 5th St Spalding Hall	Bardstown	40004	(502) 348-2999
Nelson	Doll Museum			Bardstown	40004	
Nelson	Heaven Hill Distillery Museum	Lynn Grant, Director	1311 Glikey Run Rd	Bardstown	40004	(502) 337-1000
Nelson	Kentucky Railway Museum	Greg Matthews, Executive Director	PO Box 240	New Haven	40051	(502) 549-5470
Nelson	Nelson County Genealogical Roundtable		PO Box 409	Bardstown	40004	(502) 348-5652
Nelson	Oscar Getz Museum	Mary Ellyn Hamilton, Curator	114 N 5th St	Bardstown	40004	(502) 348-2999
Nicholas	Nicholas County Historical Society	Joan Conley, President	PO Box 222 101 Market St	Carlisle	40311	(606) 289-9135
Ohio	Bill Monroe Homeplace	Campbell "Doc" Mercer	PO Box 429 6210 HWY 62	Rosine	42320	(270) 274-9181
Ohio	Fordsville Historical Society Museum		Old Train Depot, 32 Ridge Rd	Fordsville	42343	(270) 298-7452
Ohio	Ohio County Historical Society	JT Boling, Director	Box 44	Hartford	42347	(270) 298-3444
Ohio	Ohio County Historical Society Museum		415 Mulberry St	Hartford	42347	(270) 298-3177
Oldham	Oldham County Historical Society	Nancy Theiss, Director	106 N. Second St.	LaGrange	40031	(502) 222-0826
Owen	Owen County Historical Society	Katie Gibson, President	PO Box 84	Owenton	40359	
Owen	Owen County Historical Society, J.C. Harsough Museum		206 Main St	Owenton	40359	(502) 484-2321
Pendleton	Pendleton County Historical Society		PO Box 130	Falmouth	41040	
Perry	Bobby Davis Museum and Park	Martha Quigley, Director	234 Walnut St	Hazard	41701	(606) 439-4325
Perry	Perry County Historical Society		148 Chester St	Hazard	41701	
Pike	Big Sandy Heritage Center	Everett Johnson, Director	PO Box 1041 773 Hambley Blvd	Pikeville	41501	(606) 218-6050
Pike	Elkhorn City Railroad Museum		100 Pine St	Elkhorn City	41522	(606) 754-8300
Pike	Pike County Historical/Genealogical Society		PO Box 36	Somerset	42502	
Powell	Red River Historical Society	Larry Meadows	220 Powell Road	Clay City	40312	
Pulaski	Mill Springs Battlefield National Historic Landmark		PO Box 814	Somerset	42502	(606) 679-1859
Pulaski	Pulaski County Historical Society		PO Box 36	Somerset	42501	(606) 679-8401

HISTORICAL SOCIETIES & MUSEUMS

COUNTY	HISTORICAL SOCIETY/MUSEUM	CONTACT	ADDRESS	CITY	ZIP	PHONE
Robertson	Robertson County Historical Society	William Wheaton, Past President	PO Box 282	Mt. Olivet	41064	(606) 256-9814
Rockcastle	Bittersweet Cabins Museum	Carol Bryant, Director	Hwy 25	Renfro Valley	40473	(859) 433-3208
Rockcastle	Brush Arbor Appalachian Pioneer Log Village	Jerry Hayes	PO Box 57	Renfro Valley	40473	(606) 256-1000
Rockcastle	Kentucky Music Hall of Fame		2590 Richmond Rd	Renfro Valley	40473	
Rockcastle	Rockcastle County Historical Society	Gary Lewis, V.P.	PO Box 930	Mt. Vernon	40456	
Rowan	Rowan County Historical Society		236 Allen Ave PO Box 60	Morehead	40351	
Russell	Russell County Historical Society	Mary Donna Foley, Director	PO Box 544	Jamestown	42629	
Scott	Georgetown & Scott County Museum	John Toncray, Director	229 E Main St	Georgetown	40324	(502) 863-6201
Scott	Scott County Historical Society	Ann Bevins, Director	119 N Hamilton St PO Box 1064	Georgetown	40324	
Shelby	Shelby County Historical Society	Bill Matthews, Director	104 Bradford Ln PO Box 444	Shelbyville	40066	
Simpson	African American Heritage Center		500 Jefferson St.	Franklin	42134	(270) 586-0099
Simpson	Octagon Hall Museum and Archives		6040 Bowling Green Rd	Franklin	42134	(270) 586-9343
Simpson	Simpson County Archives and Museum		206 N College St	Franklin	42134	(270) 586-4228
Simpson	Simpson County Archives/Historical Society		206 N College St	Franklin	42134	(270) 586-4228
Spencer	Spencer County Historical and Genealogical Society		PO Box 266	Taylorsville	40071	(502) 477-2980
Taylor	Atkinson-Griffith House		Green River Road	Campbellsville	42178	(270) 465-4463
Taylor	Hiestand House Museum Inc	Betty Gorin, Board Member	112 Kensington Way PO Box 4021	Campbellsville	42718	(270) 465-3786
Taylor	Taylor County Historical Society Inc		PO Box 14	Campbellsville	42718	
Todd	Todd County Library		302 E Main St	Elkton	42220	(270) 265-9071
Trigg	Homeplace 1850		Visitors Center, Land Between the Lakes	Golden Pond	42211	(270) 924-2233
Trigg	Trigg County Historical Society		PO Box 1008	Cadiz	42211	(270) 522-6988
Trimble	Preston Plantation		341 Watson Landing Rd & Venard Rd	Milton	40045	(502) 268-5858
Trimble	Trimble County Historical Society	Vicki Ricketts, Director	PO Box 128	Smithfield	42544	
Union	Camp Breckinridge Museum		1116 N Village Sq	Morganfield	42437	(270) 389-1082
Union	Union County Historical Society	Charles Phillips, Director	130 E Geiger	Morganfield	42437	(270) 389-1901
Warren	Barren River Imaginative Museum of Science	Wendell Strode, Executive Director	1229 Center St	Bowling Green	42101	(270) 843-9779
Warren	National Corvette Museum		350 Corvette Drive	Bowling Green	42101	(270) 781-7973
Warren	The Kentucky Museum	Timothy Mullin, Director	1 Big Red Way, Western Kentucky University	Bowling Green	42101	(270) 745-2592
Wayne	Wayne County Historical and Genealogical Society	Phillip Catron, Chairman	PO Box 320	Monticello	42633	
Webster	Providence Museum and Learning Center		500 S Broadway	Providence	42450	
Webster	Webster County Historical and Genealogical Society	Lowell Childress, President	1005 W Main St	Providence	42450	(270) 667-5022
Whitley	Corbin Genealogical Society	Joyce Culver, Director	99 Boone Ave PO Box 353	Corbin	40701	
Whitley	Cumberland Falls State Res Park Blair Museum.	Bret Smitty, Director	7351 Hwy 90	Corbin	40701	(606) 528-4121
Whitley	Cumberland Inn Museum	David Maggard, General Manager	649 S 10th St	Williamsburg	40769	(800) 315-0286
Wolfe	Wolfe County Historical Museum		Main St	Campton	41301	(606) 668-3113
Woodford	Bluegrass Railway Museum	Winfrey Adkins, President	PO Box 27 175 Beasley Dr	Versailles	40383	(859) 873-2476
Woodford	Jouett House, Woodford County Heritage Commission		Craig's Creek Rd	Versailles	40383	(859) 873-7902
Woodford	Midway Museum	David Hume, President	PO Box 4592	Midway	40347	(859) 846-4214
Woodford	Woodford County Historical Society	Danna Estridge, Curator	121 Rose Hill	Versailles	40383	(859) 873-3823
Woodford	Woodford Reserve's Labrot and Graham Distillery		7855 McCracken Pk	Versailles	40383	(859) 879-1812

Source: Kentucky Historical Society and Family Guide to Kentucky Museums and Historic Sites - 2004, published by Back Home in Kentucky Magazine.

Kandie Adkinson

HISTORY
Land Grants

In 1763, the British government declared land would be awarded to veterans of the French and Indian War in lieu of cash. After the Revolutionary War, Virginia expanded the land grant system through its Land Law of 1779. Kentucky, in turn, reaffirmed the system after separation from Virginia. The land grant system is still in use today as a method of appropriating Kentucky land. Structurally, the process has changed very little since its inception.

Kentucky is known as a state-land-state, meaning the Kentucky government has assumed the responsibility for land appropriation within our borders. Other state-land-states include the 13 original colonies as well as Maine, Tennessee, Texas, Vermont, West Virginia and Hawaii. The remaining states are in public domain, meaning the federal government acts as the appropriating agency.

WHAT IS A LAND PATENT?

Patenting refers to the system of land appropriation used in Kentucky to transfer land from the Commonwealth to an individual or group of individuals. All deeds trace back to an original patent recorded in the Kentucky Land Office. Land patenting consists of four steps, all of which must be completed before title is granted.

Step #1: The Warrant (Synonym Certificate, Order)

This document authorizes a survey. It does not specify the exact location of the land. Present-day county court orders (warrants) are to be used within the county in which they are issued.

Patents authorized include those for military service, settlement certificates, preemption claims,

importation warrants or village rights warrants, special acts of the General Assembly such as "for the relief of poor persons," and for seminary funding. It should also be added that warrants can be traded, sold or reassigned, in whole or in part, any-

Source: Kentucky Historical Society

time during the patenting process.

Step #2: The Entry

This record is an intention to file for a patent. Entries are not binding and may be altered or withdrawn if an individual so desires.

Step #3: The Survey (Synonym Plat, Survey Certificate)

The next stage in land patenting is the preparation of the survey depicting the tract and describing metes and bounds. Surveys, like warrants, can also be traded, sold or reassigned.

Step #4: The Grant (Synonym Patent Deed, Patent)

The issuance of the Governor's grant finalizes the land patenting process.

HOW ARE LAND GRANTS FILED?

Time periods and possible land locations play an important role in determining which group or groups of land grants.

• *Virginia Series*

This series generally includes warrants, surveys and grants completed before 1792. Approximately 10,000 patents are filed with this grouping, some of which were authorized by military warrants.

• *Old Kentucky Series*

There are over 7,600 patents filed in this series, some of which were classified as military. In the Old Kentucky grouping, the grant was issued after June 1792.

• *South of Green River Series*

This series was established by a 1795 act of the General Assembly which opened the former military district to settlers meeting certain requirements. The purchaser of the warrant (certificate) had to be 21 years of age or older and a resident on the property in question for one year. An improvement, such as planting a crop or building a cabin was also required. There are over 16,600 patents filed in this series, many of which are located out of the South of Green River area and as far north as Pendleton County.

• *Warrants for Headrights*

Research continues on this series of land grant records. To date, it has not been determined why this grouping of 55 patents was not filed under one of the major series.

• *Tellico Series*

This area of Kentucky was purchased from the Cherokee Indians in 1805. In 1810, the Kentucky General Assembly approved an act appropriating the land under the patent system. There are 590 patents in this series, primarily for land located in southeastern Kentucky.

• *Kentucky Land Warrant Series*

By 1815 the Kentucky Land Office was issuing land patents under three separate series, namely, Old Kentucky, South of Green River and Tellico. This undoubtedly produced an abundance of confusion. By 1815 the Kentucky General Assembly established the Kentucky Land Warrant system which combined all three series. Under this series of 26,080 patents, we see various types of warrants used. Not only were warrants simply purchased in Frankfort, but there are also warrants issued to poor widows and to trustees and commissioners overseeing educational institutions, building roads or constructing bridges.

• *West of Tennessee River Military Claims*

In 1818 land west of the Tennessee River, now known as the Jackson Purchase, was ceded to the United States by the Chickasaw Indians. There were, at that time, numerous Revolutionary War veterans who had settled in the area. In 1820, the Kentucky and advised veterans to apply for patents on land as soon as possible. Four thousand acres of land were donated by the Commonwealth resulting in 242 patents.

• *West of Tennessee River Series (Non-Military)*

Also in 1820, the Kentucky General Assembly approved legislation mandating the mapping of the Jackson Purchase into townships and sections. Lands which were not patented by veterans were ordered sold at public auction if a minimum state price was met. This series contains 9,308 patents.

• *South of Walker's Line Series*

Due to surveying error, the Kentucky Land Office became responsible for patenting lands in a small northern area of Tennessee. The series includes 4,327 patents issued by Kentucky for lands in Tennessee.

• *County Court Order Series*

All series of land patents were combined into one by the 1835 Act of the General Assembly establishing the county court order system. Under this series, counties sold warrants for unappropriated land within their boundaries. Over 70,000 land patents are included in this series.

KEY POINTS TO REMEMBER IN LAND PATENTING

• The only Military Warrants recognized in the Kentucky land grant system were for service in the French and Indian War and the Revolutionary War (by Virginia soldiers).

• Follow the patent through step by step. Study the warrant first, entry if available, survey description and plat and then the grant.

• Microfilm of the original documents is available on a limited basis. Some libraries restrict their holdings to copies of the Land Office Survey and Giant books. The Kentucky Historical Society and the secretary of state's Land Office are the only Frankfort agencies housing complete documentation for the Kentucky land grant records.

• There is no master patent map available. There are, however, several historians on the county level who have accepted the challenge of mapping early land patents within their county or particular area.

• Remember, warrants and surveys could be traded, sold or reassigned anytime during the patenting process.

• Last, but definitely not least, all original records of Kentucky land grants are housed with the Office of Secretary of State in Frankfort. Researchers are invited to inspect the documents anytime during regular working hours. The Land Office will also be happy to work with researchers by phone if there are questions regarding the patent system or need to order copies.

For further information, contact the Land Office, Secretary of State, Capitol Building, Frankfort, KY 40601-3493; (502) 564-3490.

HISTORY

Historical Markers

The Kentucky Historical Highway Marker Program, administered by the Kentucky Historical Society in cooperation with the Kentucky Transportation Cabinet, commemorates historic sites, events and personalities throughout the Commonwealth. Through the program, the wealth of history which is Kentucky's past is made accessible to the public as they travel along the state's roadways – in excerpts which stimulate an interest in the history of local communities. The plaques are on-the-spot history lessons that add drama and interest to the countryside for native Kentuckians as well as tourists. The goal of the Kentucky Historical Highway Marker Program is to connect events and personalities with their place, to bring the past to life and to increase the awareness of what we owe to those who came before us. The subjects of the more than 1,750 markers in Kentucky are varied. There are markers that tell of a duel of honor, a seven-year-old boy who served as a drummer in the Revolutionary War and the 1937 Ohio River flood. Others highlight "moonlight" schools that were established to combat illiteracy, an Indian academy and the first state-supported school for the hearing impaired in the US. Consider these examples:

Grave of Steamboat Captain

(Marker Number: 1778)
County: Jefferson
Location: Bank St., W. of 34th St. at entrance to Portland Cem.
Description: Mary M. Miller of Louisville, a pioneer among women, was issued license as master of a steamboat on inland waters, Feb. 16, 1884, in New Orleans. License authorized her to navigate waters of Quachita, Mississippi, Red, and other western rivers. She and her husband George, a pilot and master, owned steamboat SALINE, built nearby. Died 1894; buried in Portland Cem.

Alice Virginia Coffin (1848-88)

(Marker Number: 1715)
County: Jefferson
Location: Jefferson St., between Preston & Floyd Sts., Louisville
Description: Born on this street, Alice Virginia was one of seven founders of P.E.O., an international philanthropic and educational organization for women. It began as a sorority at the Iowa Wesleyan College, 1869; owns Cottey College in Missouri, and provides monetary assistance for education

Source: *South East Telephone*

of women. Miss Coffin designed P.E.O. seal. Presented by Ky. P.E.O. Chapters.

Ann I. Baker (1873-1931)

(Marker Number: 2137)
County: McCracken
Location: Paducah, 125 Kentucky Avenue
Description: Born in Kansas, Ann Baker came to Paducah in 1899 to work for her father, Henry Baker, at Ayer-Lord Tie Co. (railroad crossties). She retired from there, 1930. Marine Ways named a boat, A.I. Baker, for her. Organized Paducah Business and Professional Women's Club, 1920. Baker was elected president and served three years in

that office. Ann Baker had idea for professional women's club in Paducah. Business Women's Club held first meeting, Sept. 1920, chartered Oct. 1920. Name changed to Paducah Business and Professional Women. Baker also served as first president of Ky. Federation of BPW. She was generous contributor to charitable and welfare institutions.

Louis Dembitz Brandeis, 1856-1941
(Marker Number: 1880)

County: Jefferson
Location: Entrance to Univ. of Louisville Law School, Louisville
Description: U.S. Supreme Court Justice, 1916-1939, born on Center Street (now Armory). Brandeis attended public school in Louisville and later Harvard Law School. Pres. Woodrow Wilson nominated him for Supreme Court, 1916. He actively supported rights of speech and assembly, consumer protection, and women's rights. See over. U.S. Supreme Court Justice - Brandeis was first Jew named to high court. Oliver Wendell Holmes, Jr. was often his ally there. Brandeis championed such causes as low-cost life insurance through savings banks; opposed trusts, monopolies, and "the curse of bigness" in government and business. Brandeis Univ. in Mass. named for him. His ashes interred at Univ. of Louisville Law School.

Anna Mac Clarke (1919-44)
(Marker Number: 1970)

County: Anderson
Location: Courthouse lawn, Lawrenceburg
Description: This Lawrenceburg native was one of the first black women in Ky. to enlist during World War II. She joined Women's Army Auxiliary Corps in 1942, and was commissioned a 1st Lieutenant the next year in newly named Women's Army Corps. While stationed at Douglas Air Field, Arizona, she led fight to desegregate base theater. Presented by Ky. African American Heritage Commission. Anna Mac Clarke (1919-44) - A 1937 graduate of Lawrenceburg's Colored High School, Clarke earned B.A. from Ky. State College. After army enlistment, she became only African American in 15th Officer Training Class at Ft. Des Moines, Iowa. In 1943, she was first black WAAC assigned to duty with an all-white company as platoon commander (4th Co., 3rd Regt.). Buried Woodlawn Hills Cem., Stringtown.

Bellevue, Kentucky
(Marker Number: 1351)
County: Campbell
Location: 24 Fairfield Ave., Bellevue, KY 8
Description: Incorporated March 15, 1870, on part of original land grant to Gen. James Taylor, pioneer, for whose farm this city was named. A general in War of 1812, banker, and statesman, whose farm was an underground railroad station. President of the first town trustees was George D. Allen. Hometown of Anna E. Wolfram, one of Kentucky's first women doctors.

Camp Nelson Refugee Camp
(Marker Number: 1965)
County: Jessamine
Location: Camp Nelson, New US 27 at Hall Rd.
Description: Established in 1863 to house families of African American soldiers, Camp Nelson became the chief center issuing emancipation papers to former slaves. Army's withdrawal from camp in 1866 exposed refugees to violence of white "regulators," who were opposed to presence of freed African Americans. Conditions at Refugee Camp - Many women and children died from disease and exposure to weather in make-shift camp. Brutal expulsion of refugees from camp in winter of 1864 was fatal to many. Only efforts by Rev. John G. Fee and other humanitarian workers improved conditions. A school, a hospital, and permanent housing later served up to 3,000 African Americans in their transition to freedom. Over.

Enid Yandell (1869-1934)
(Marker Number: 2133)
County: Jefferson
Location: Louisville, Jct. 2100 Eastern Parkway & 1400 Cherokee Rd.
Description: Challenged the role of women in the art world as a renowned sculptor. Born 1869 in Louisville and graduated Cinn. Art Acad. in 1889. Gained prominence sculpting caryatids for Woman's Building at 1893 World's Columbian Exposition in Chicago. In 1897, the Tennessee Centennial Exposition chose her to sculpt a 25' Athena in Nashville. Presented by Ky. Foundation for Women and Enid: Generations of Women Sculptors. Renowned Woman Sculptor - Enid Yandell established studios in N.Y. and Paris. Studied with Rodin and MacMonnies. Inducted into National Sculpture Society in 1899 as one of first women

members. She founded Branstock summer art school in Edgartown, Mass. Two noted works in Louisville: Daniel Boone Monument and Hogan's Fountain. Buried in Cave Hill Cem. Presented by the families of David Yandell Wood and Ian Yandell Henderson.

Matthew H. Jouett (1788-1827)
(Marker Number: 1888)
County: Fayette
Location: Georgetown Rd. [US 25] & Nandino Blvd., Lexington
Description: Master portrait painter Matthew Harris Jouett was born in Mercer Co., a son of Capt. Jack Jouett. He graduated from Transylvania and studied law under Judge George M. Bibb. Served in War of 1812 as paymaster of infantry regiment. Vouchers were lost during battle, and Jouett was thrown into debt. After leaving army he abandoned law and devoted himself to art. Matthew H. Jouett (1788-1827) - Jouett was noted for his ability to paint men, women, and children equally well. His portraits reflect unusual ability to memorize faces. Depicted eminent people of era, including Lafayette. Jouett studied briefly with Gilbert Stuart in Boston. Struggled to support large family; paid war debt before he died at farm near Lexington. Judged one of Kentucky's greatest artists.

Murder Branch Massacre
(Marker Number: 189)
County: Menifee
Location: 10 mi. E. of Frenchburg, KY 1274
Description: April 1793, Indians captured 19 women and children of Morgan's Station in Montgomery County. Overtaken north of here by posse. Indians massacred some captives, taking others across Ohio River. Last Indian raid into Kentucky.

Site of Winnie A. Scott Hospital
(Marker Number: 2025)
County: Franklin
Location: Frankfort, 228 E. 2nd St.
Description: The Women's Club Hospital Company, with community support, established a hospital here on Dec. 26, 1915. It was named for Winnie A. Scott, a local teacher instrumental in its founding. The facility was the only Frankfort hospital serving African Americans until desegregation of King's Daughters Hospital in 1959. Presented by Frankfort Civic Organizations and the Ky. African American Heritage Commission.

Sarah Blanding
(Marker Number: 2011)
County: Fayette
Location: Lexington, U of K, Blanding Tower
Description: A 1923 U.K. graduate, Blanding (1898-1985) was President of Kappa Kappa Gamma sorority and Captain of the women's basketball team. After two years as Acting Dean, Blanding was named U.K. Dean of Women in 1925. She also taught political science. Class of 1997. Sarah Blanding - Blanding left U.K. in 1941 to become Dean of the School of Home Economics at Cornell University. In 1946 she became Vassar College's first woman president, a position she held until 1964. In 1968 Blanding Tower was named in her honor. Class of 1997

Source: South East Telephone

Pioneer Spirit (Marker Number: 1209)
County: Fulton
Location: State Line Rd., Fulton-Graves Co. Line
Description: Nearby gravesite of Lucy Flournoy Roberts, believed to be the first woman of French Huguenot lineage to come to this area. Her husband and 25 dependents are also buried here. She was a descendant of one of the founders of Manakintown, Va., a Huguenot settlement. One of many brave women who left family ties to go with their husbands to a new life in the wilderness. Presented by descendants.

To learn more about Kentucky highway markers . . . check out the searchable database at: http://kentucky. gov/kyhs/hmdb/. Also check out Roadside History: A Guide to Kentucky Highway Markers, University Press of Kentucky (2002), 800-839-6855 or http://www.kentuckypress.com.

HISTORY
Milestones & Timeline

Dr. James Klotter

Pre-1750

10000 B.C. or before – First people come to what is now Kentucky

1000-1750 – Late Prehistoric Period, with small villages, trade networks, and developed religions

Late 1600s-1750s – Sporadic contact between Native peoples and European explorers brings disease that kills thousands of Indians

1750-1800

1750 – Thomas Walker and Christopher Gist make separate trips to explore Kentucky

1755 – Mary Ingles taken to Kentucky as captive, probably first English woman in area

1767 – Daniel Boone's first trip to Kentucky

1774 – James Harrod's first attempt at settlement; abandoned later

1775 – Fort Harrod established as first permanent English settlement

1775 – Daniel Boone blazes Wilderness Road

1776 – Kentucky County established as part of Virginia

1778-79 – George Rogers Clark's N.W. Campaign

1780 – Present-day Transylvania University is chartered

1780 – Kentucky County is divided into three counties – Fayette, Jefferson, and Lincoln

1782 – Battle of Blue Licks marks last major conflict between settlers and Native Americans within Kentucky

1784 – John Filson's *Discovery, Settlement, and Present State of Kentucke* appears, with Boone's autobiography in it

1787 – *Kentucke Gazette*, first newspaper, is published

1792 – Kentucky becomes 15th state, with Isaac Shelby as first governor

1798-99 – Kentucky Resolutions passed, support theory of nullification

1799 – Kentucky's second constitution adopted

1800-1850

1800 – Kentucky population is 220,955

1801 – Great Revival changes face of religion

1807 – Thomas Todd of Kentucky is first from the state to be named to U.S. Supreme Court

1807-19 – John James Audubon lives in Kentucky

1808 – Jefferson Davis is born in Kentucky

1808 – Bardstown becomes center of first Catholic diocese west of the mountains

1809 – Dr. Ephraim McDowell performs first ovariotomy operation in world

1809 – Abraham Lincoln born in Kentucky

1811 – New Madrid Earthquake hits West Kentucky

1812-14 – War of 1812

1818 – Jackson Purchase added

1819 – Centre College chartered

1820 – Death of Daniel Boone

1823 – Kentucky School for the Deaf established, first such state-supported school in the U.S.

1824 – Henry Clay runs for president, but loses

1825 – Choctaw Academy for Native Americans revived in Scott County, closes in 1842

1829 – Georgetown College chartered, fifth Baptist college in U.S.

1832 – Henry Clay is defeated for presidency by Andrew Jackson

1836 – Death of Simon Kenton

1836 – Richard M. Johnson of Kentucky is elected vice president of the U.S.

1838 – Kentucky establishes a public school system

1838 – "Trail of Tears," Indian removal west

1842 – Kentucky School for the Blind set up; sixth one in U.S.

1844 – Henry Clay runs for president a third time and loses to James K. Polk

1846-48 – Mexican War

1848 – Zachary Taylor is selected president

1850-1900

1850 – Kentucky population is 982,405, ranking it eighth among the states

1850 – Zachary Taylor dies, is buried in Louisville

1850 – Kentucky's third constitution adopted

1852 – "Uncle Tom's Cabin" appears, is set in Kentucky

1852 – Death of Henry Clay

1853 – "My Old Kentucky Home" is published; becomes state song in 1928

1855 – "Bloody Monday" election-day riots in Louisville kill some 20 people, mostly immigrants

1856 – John C. Breckinridge of Kentucky is elected U.S. vice president

1860 – John C. Breckinridge runs for president, but

loses to Abraham Lincoln

1861 – Kentucky declares itself neutral at start of Civil War, then, in September, officially remains in the union. Supporters of the Confederacy set up a separate government

1862 – Major battles at Mill Springs, Richmond, and Perryville

1865 – Civil War ends; 13th Amendment to the U.S. Constitution officially frees Kentucky slaves

1865 – Current-day University of Kentucky established

1868 – Louisville *Courier-Journal* formed; under editor Henry Watterson it becomes nationally known, continues status under Binghams

1875 – First Kentucky Derby

1870s-1903 – Numerous feuds take place across eastern Kentucky

1887 – Kentucky State University opens

1888 – State Treasurer "Honest Dick" Tate disappears with state funds

1888 – Kentucky Equal Rights Association formed, first in South

1891 – Kentucky's fourth and present constitution adopted

1898 – Spanish-American War

1900-1950

1900 – Assassination of William Goebel in disputed election. Named governor after he was shot.

1900 – Kentucky population is 2,147, 174

1903 – Of 10 books on best seller list, five are written by Kentuckians

1904 – Day Law segregates Berea College, last integrated college in the South

1905-1909 – "Black Patch War" in tobacco fields

1906 – Eastern Kentucky University and Western Kentucky University formed

1911 – Death of Justice John Marshall Harlan

1911 – First "Moonlight School" opened by Cora Wilson Stewart, to help adult illiterates

1912 – Kentucky's last county, McCreary, formed

1917-18 – U.S. involvement in World War I

1918 – Fort Knox established

1918-19 – Great influenza epidemic kills thousands

1920 – Kentucky women get the right to vote

1922 – First woman, Mary Flanery, serves in legislature

1922 – WHAS, state's first radio station, on air

1922 – Morehead State University and Murray State University created

1923 – Last member of Shaker religion in Kentucky dies

1924 – Ashland Oil formed

1925 – Frontier Nursing Service established

1927 – Katherine Langley elected as first woman from Kentucky to serve in Congress

1929 – Great Depression begins

1930s – Labor conflicts in coal fields give "Bloody Harlan" its name

1933 – Thomas Hunt Morgan wins Nobel Prize.

1937 – Great Ohio River flood

1937 – Alben Barkley selected as Majority Leader of U.S. Senate

1941 – Mammoth Cave becomes national park

1941 – Thomas Merton, Kentucky's most famous religious writer, enters Gethsemani monastery

1941-45 – U.S. involvement in World War II

1945-51 – Happy Chandler serves as baseball commissioner

1946 – Fred Vinson of Kentucky named Chief Justice of the U.S.

1948 – University of Kentucky wins the first national basketball championship for the state

1948 – Alben Barkley elected U.S. vice president

1948 – 1st television station in state, WAVE, starts

1950-2003

1950 – Kentucky population is 2,944,806

1950-53 – Korean War

1954 – U.S. Supreme Court declares racial segregation illegal

1955 – Amendment to Kentucky constitution gives 18 year-olds the right to vote

1960 – Sales tax goes into effect

1960s – "War on Poverty"

1961-75 – Vietnam War

1961 – Whitney Young Jr. named head of National Urban League

1964 – Martin Luther King Jr. leads march on Frankfort in support of civil rights

1966 – Kentucky passes Civil Rights Act, first in the South

1968 – Northern Kentucky University formed

1970 – Census shows that the state is more urban than rural for the first time

1975 – Passage of a state amendment that revises the state judicial system

1980 – Opening of Corvette plant in Bowling Green

1980 – Death of Colonel Harland Sanders

1983 – Martha Layne Collins elected as first woman governor

1987 – Opening of Toyota plant near Georgetown

1989 – Kentucky reestablishes lottery

1989 – Death of Kentucky writer and U.S. Poet Laureate Robert Penn Warren

1990 – Kentucky Education Reform Act (KERA) passed

2000 – Kentucky population is 4,041,769

2001 – Worst terrorist attacks in U.S. history, nearly 3,000 killed when four hijacked jets slammed into the twin towers of New York's World Trade Center, the Pentagon and a field in Pennsylvania

2002 – Death of Triple Crown winner Seattle Slew, one of the most successful stallions in horse-racing history

2003 – U.S. invasion of Iraq; Ernie Fletcher elected governor

State Government & Politics

CONSTITUTIONAL OFFICERS

The **Governor** serves as the chief administrator of the state and, in addition to other powers and duties, acts as Commander-in-Chief of state military forces, appoints executive officers and members of boards and commissions, and has the power to grant pardons and commutations.

Ernie Fletcher
Governor

As chief administrator of Kentucky, the Governor ensures that state government provides needed services to the citizens of the Commonwealth at minimum cost to the taxpayers. The Governor's office includes: The **Military Affairs Commission, which** has been a part of the Office of the Governor since 1996, the **Office of the State Budget Director**; Kentucky **Department of Veterans' Affairs; Kentucky Commission on Human Rights; Governor's Office for Local Development; Local Initiatives for a New Kentucky; Department of Military Affairs**; and **Commission on Women**.

Steve Pence
Lt. Governor

The **Lieutenant Governor** is a constitutional officer elected jointly with the Governor. The Lieutenant Governor is to assume the duties and responsibilities of the Office of the Governor should the Governor be impeached or removed from Office, die, fail to qualify, resign, or be unable to discharge the duties of that office. Additional duties of the Lieutenant Governor include serving on various boards and commissions, serving on Kentucky delegations to several interstate compact commissions, and appointing members to various boards.

The **Secretary of State** is the constitutional officer entrusted with filing, maintaining, and preserving the important documents and records of the Commonwealth. The Secretary also keeps the Seal of the Commonwealth and affixes it to all communications and commissions issued in the name of the state. The State Board of Elections administers the election laws of the state and supervises the registration and purgation of voters. The role of the Kentucky Registry of Election Finance is to assure the integrity of the Commonwealth's electoral process.

Trey Grayson
Secretary of State

The **Attorney General**, serves as the Commonwealth's constitutional chief law enforcement officer. They perform a range of legal, investigative, and administrative duties.The Office has five major programmatic areas: **Administrative Services, Criminal Services, Advocacy Services, Civil Services,** the **Uninsured Employers Fund** and the Prosecutor's Advisory Council Services Division, whose duties include: personnel, payroll, fiscal, budget, state and federal grants, and legal education related to the Unified Prosecutorial System.

Greg Stumbo
Attorney General

Jonathan Miller
State Treasurer

The **State Treasurer** manages the Treasury Department, which is the central administrative agency responsible for the receipt and custody of all revenues collected by state government and for writing all checks and disbursing state funds, issuing over 7,500,000 checks each year. The Disbursements and Accounting division receives all funds of the Commonwealth including fees, grants, taxes, federal funds, fees from officials in counties over 75,000 in population, and fees from various boards and commissions. The Abandoned Property program receives unclaimed property reports from holders and potential holders of unclaimed property, collects unclaimed property, pursues the location.

Crit Luallen
State Auditor

The **Auditor of Public Accounts** is the constitutional officer responsible for auditing all state agencies and county governments. The Auditor must examine the management and control of all institutions and public works in which the state has financial interest or legal power. The Auditor must examine the management and control of all institutions and public works in which the state has financial interest or legal power. The Auditor's Office is responsible for assisting state and local officials in establishing and maintaining proper accounting records, internal controls, and administrative controls over public funds.

The **Department of Agriculture** is headed by the **Commissioner of Agriculture**, an elected Constitutional Officer. The department includes the **Office for Consumer and Environmental Protection, Office**

Jim Host
Commerce

of State Veterinarian and **Office for Agricultural Marketing and Product Promotion**. The department develops and manages programs which promote Kentucky produced agricultural products; conducts research and development of new and expanded outlets for Kentucky's agricultural products, agricultural education, agritourism development, farm safety and farmland preservation.

The **Commerce Cabinet's** mission is to capitalize on the natural assets of the Commonwealth and draw from resources in business development, tourism, outdoor attractions, arts, and cultural heritage. The cabinet includes the **Department of Tourism; Department of Parks; Kentucky State Fair Board; Kentucky Horse Park; Department of Fish and Wildlife Resources; Kentucky Arts Council; Kentucky Heritage Council; Kentucky Center for the Arts** and **Office of Arts & Cultural Humanities**.

The **Cabinet for Economic Development** is governed by the Kentucky Economic Development Partnership. The cabinet includes the **Department for Commercialization and Innovation; Department for Existing Business Development; Department for New Business Development; Department of Regional Development; Department of Financial Incentives and Bluegrass State Skills Corporation**.

Gene Strong
Economic
Development

In 1990 the General Assembly reconstituted the **Department of Education** and required the implementation of the Kentucky Education Reform Act. The Department of Education is headed by a Commissioner of Education appointed by the Kentucky Board of Education. The Kentucky Supreme Court's 1989 mandate to equalize funding for public school pupils regardless of economic circumstances or place of birth, created a new mechanism for distributing state support to local school districts. The Support Education Excellence in Kentucky (SEEK)

Richie Farmer
Agriculture

program replaced the Minimum Foundation and Power Equalization programs. The Department includes **Office of Results Planning; Office of Leadership and School Improvement; Office of Supportive Learning Environments; Office of Assessment and Accountability; Office of Academic and Professional Development; Office of Academic and Professional Development**; and **Office of Education Technology**

The **Education Cabinet** was created by combining several departments and offices from the former Education, Arts and Humanities Cabinet and the former Workforce Development Cabinet. The cabinet includes: **Office of Operations and Development**; **Kentucky Authority for Educational Television** (KET); **School Facilities Construction Commission; Kentucky Environmental Education Council; Department for Libraries and Archives; Teachers' Retirement System; Education Professional Standards Board; Office for Career and Technical Education; Department of Vocational Rehabilitation;** and **Department for Employment Services (DES)**. The **Council on Postsecondary Education** serves as the representative agency in matters of postsecondary education and in this role brings a statewide perspective to postsecondary education issues and planning. The council has the responsibility both for guiding the system and serving as an advocate for postsecondary education as a part of the total education enterprise. The agency is also responsible for Adult Education.

Virginia Fox
Education

The Environmental and Public Protection Cabinet is charged with the protection and preservation of land, air and water resources, supervision and regulation of industries providing services to the citizens of the Commonwealth and the administration of rules for the state concerning employer-employee relationships. The cabinet includes

LaJuana Wilcher
Environmental &
Public Protection

Petroleum Storage Tank Environmental Assurance Fund; **Department for Environmental Protection; Department for Natural Resources; Office of Mine Safety and Licensing; Environmental Quality Commission; Kentucky Nature Preserves Commission; Board of Claims; Crime Victims' Compensation Board; Office of Alcoholic Beverage Control (ABC); Office of Financial Institutions; Office of Insurance; Kentucky Horse Racing Authority; Office of Housing, Buildings, and Construction; Public Service Commission; Board of Tax Appeals; Office for Charitable Gaming; Boxing and Wrestling Authority; Department of Labor; and Mine Safety Review Commission.**

The **Finance and Administration Cabinet** is responsible for managing the financial resources of the Commonwealth and providing central administrative services to agencies of state and local government. The Cabinet's duties include construction of state facilities, property management, tax administration and collection, management of the Commonwealth's information technology systems, expenditure control, and state purchasing.

Robbie Rudolph
Finance
& Administration

The Cabinet includes: **Department of Revenue; Kentucky Teachers' Retirement System Board of Trustees; Office of Equal Employment Opportunity and Contract Compliance; Office of General Counsel; Office of Administrative Services; Office of the Controller; Office of Financial Management; Office of Material and Procurement Services; Office of the Customer Resource Center; Office of Policy and Audit; Department for Facilities and Support Services; and Commonwealth Office of Technology (COT).**

The **Health and Family Services Cabinet** is the primary state agency responsible for leadership in protecting and promoting the health and well being of all Kentuckians through the delivery of quality health and human services. The cabi-

James Holsinger
Families & Children

net includes: **Department for Medicaid Services; Department for Mental Health/Mental Retardation Services; Department for Public Health; Department for Community Based Services; Commission for Children with Special Health Care Needs; Office of Certificate of Need; Division of Aging Services; Office of the Inspector General; Administrative Support; Department for Disability Determination Services; Division of Women's Physical and Mental Health; Division of Family Resources and Youth Services Centers; Kentucky Commission on Community Volunteerism and Service; Office of the Ombudsman; Division of Child Abuse and Domestic Violence Services; Office of Legislative and Public Affairs; and Office of Legal Affairs.**

The **Justice and Public Safety Cabinet** Secretary is Lt. Governor Steve Pence. The cabinet has seven departments: **Department of Justice Administration, Department of State Police, Department of Juvenile Justice, Department of Criminal Justice Training, Department of Corrections, Department of Public Advocacy, and Department of Vehicle Enforcement**. The **Department of Justice Administration** manages the **Office of Investigations, Office of Management and Administrative Services, Office of Legal Services, Office of Legislative and Intergovernmental Services, Kentucky State Parole Board, and Kentucky State Medical Examiner (Office of Forensic Technology)**. The cabinet is responsible for the overall administration of the cabinet, provision of legal services, development of legislation, regulation, policy, and coordination of activities within and among the cabinet departments and agencies. The **Kentucky State Police** is the statewide law enforcement agency of the Commonwealth. State Troopers are assigned to 16 regional posts across the State. The Department is responsible for the enforcement of criminal and traffic laws, along with white-collar crime, organized crime, electronic crime, racketeering, and drug-related crime. The State Police also provide protection for the Governor, Lieutenant Governor, their families, and property. The Kentucky State Police is comprised of three divisions: Administrative, Operations, and Technical Services.

The **Personnel Cabinet** is comprised of five appropriation units: General Operations, Public Employees Deferred Compensation Authority, the Workers' Com-

pensation Benefits and Reserve, Government Training, the State Salary and Compensation Fund, and the State Group Health Insurance Fund. The cabinet has an Office of Government Training. The cabinet is comprised of five appropriation units: General Operations, Public Employees Deferred Compensation Authority, the Workers' Compensation Benefits and Reserve, Government Training, the State Salary and Compensation Fund, and the State Group Health Insurance Fund. The responsibilities of this department include recruiting, counseling, testing, and certifying persons for employment with the Commonwealth; maintaining the classification and compensation system; auditing and certifying state payrolls; preparing and maintaining the official personnel and payroll records; and coordinating and implementing employee performance evaluation systems.

Bill Nighbert
Transportation

The Transportation Cabinet is responsible for maintaining and improving transportation services in the Commonwealth. All modes of transportation are addressed by the cabinet, including air transportation, railroads, waterways, public transit, and highways. The cabinet receives funding from the state Road Fund, proceeds from bonds issued by the Kentucky Turnpike Authority, and federal aid apportionments for highways.

The Transportation Cabinet includes the departments of **Administrative Services, Aviation, Vehicle Regulation, Intergovernmental Programs, and Highways**. Additional units include the **Office of Public Affairs; Office of Transportation Operations Center, Office of Budget and Fiscal Management; Office of Transportation Delivery; Office of Legal Services; Office for Business and Occupational Development; Office of Inspector General; Office of Legislative and Intergovernmental Affairs; Office of Personnel Management; Office of Program Planning and Management; Office of Project Development; Office of Construction and Operations; Office of Intermodal Programs; Office of Transportation Enhancements; and Office of Rural and Secondary Roads**.

Erwin Roberts
Personnel Cabinet

Source: 2004-2006 Budget of the Commonwealth, www.osbd.ky.gov.

STATE GOVERNMENT & POLITICS

Governor's & Their Terms

Governor Isaac Shelby
Term: 1792-1796
Party: Jeffersonian Republican
Resident KY County: Lincoln
Election Returns: N/A
Born: 12/11/1750 - Died: 7/18/1826
Occupation(s): Farmer, Surveyor, Soldier

Governor James Garrard
Term: 1796-1804
Party: Jeffersonian Republican
Resident KY County: Bourbon
Election Returns:
James Garrard - 8,390 (39.4%);
Christopher Greenup - 6,745 (31.7%); Benjamin
Logan - 3,995 (18.8%); Thomas Todd - 2,166
(10.2%)
Born: 1/14/1749 - Died: 1/19/1822
Occupation(s): Farmer, Miller, Whiskey Maker,
Solider, Baptist Minister

Governor Christopher Greenup
Term: 1804-1808
Party: Jeffersonian Republican
Resident KY County: Mercer/
Fayette
Election Returns:
Christopher Greenup (Unopposed) 25,917
Born:1750 - Died: 4/17/1818
Occupation(s): Surveyor, Lawyer, Land Speculator

Governor Charles Scott
Term: 1808-1812
Party: Jeffersonian Republican
Resident KY County: Woodford
Election Returns:
Charles Scott - 22,050 (61.3%); John
Allen - 8,430 (23.4%); Green Clay - 5,516 (15.3%)
Born: 4/1739 - Died: 10/22/1813
Occupation(s): Farmer, Miller, Soldier

Governor Isaac Shelby
Term: 1812-1816
Party: Jeffersonian Republican
Resident KY County: Lincoln
Election Returns:
Isaac Shelby - 30,362 70.9%; Gabriel
Slaughter - 12,464 29.1%
Born: 12/11/1750 - Died: 7/18/1826
Occupation(s): Soldier, Farmer

Governor George Madison
Term: 1816
Party: Jeffersonian Republican
Resident KY County: Franklin
Election Returns: George Madison
(Unopposed)
Born: 6/1763 - Died: 10/14/1816
Occupation(s): Soldier, Public Servant

Governor Gabriel Slaughter
Term: 1816-1820
Party: Democratic Republican
Resident KY County: Mercer
Election Returns: Succeeded Gov.
George Madison, who died while
holding office (1816)
Born: 12/12/1767 - Died: 9/19/1830
Occupation(s): Farmer, Soldier

Governor John Adair
Term: 1820-1824
Party: Democratic Republican
Resident KY County: Mercer
Election Returns:
John Adair - 20,493 (32.8%;)
William Logan - 19,947 (32.0%;)
Joseph Desha - 12,419 (19.9%); Anthony Butler
- 9,567 (15.3%)
Born: 1/9/1757 - Died: 5/19/1840
Occupation(s): Farmer, Soldier

Governor Joseph Desha

Term: 1824-1828
Party: Jeffersonian Republican
Resident KY County: Mason
Election Returns:
Joseph Desha - 38,463 (59.5%);
Christopher Tompkins 22,300 (34.5%); William
Russell 3,899 (6.0%)
Born: 12/9/1768 - Died: 10/12/1842
Occupation(s): Farmer, Soldier

Governor Thomas Metcalfe

Term: 1828-1832
Party: National Republican (Whig)
Resident KY County: Nicholas
Election Returns:
Thomas Metcalfe - 38,940 (50.5%);
William T. Barry 38,231 (49.5%)
Born: 3/10/1780 - Died: 8/18/1855
Occupation(s): Stonemason

Governor John Breathitt

Term: 1832-1834
Party: Jacksonian Democrat
Resident KY County: Logan
Election Returns:
John Breathitt - 40,780 (50.9%);
Richard Buckner 39,269 (49.1%)
Born: 9/9/1786 - Died: 2/21/1834
Occupation(s): Surveyor, Lawyer

Governor James Turner Morehead

Term: 1834-1836
Party: Whig
Resident KY County: Warren
Election Returns: Succeeded Gov.
John Breathitt, who died while holding office
(1834)
Born: 5/24/1797 - Died: 12/28/1854
Occupation(s): Lawyer

Governor James Clark

Term: 1836-1839
Party: Whig
Resident KY County: Clark
Election Returns:
James Clark - 38,591 (55.8%)
Matthew Flournoy - 30,576 (44.2%)
Born: 1/16/1779 - Died: 8/27/1839
Occupation(s): Lawyer, Judge

Governor Charles Anderson Wickliffe

Term: 1839-1840
Party: Whig
Resident KY County: Nelson
Election Returns: Succeeded Gov.

James Clark, who died while holding office (1839)
Born: 6/8/1788 - Died: 10/31/1869
Occupation(s): Soldier, Lawyer

Governor Robert P. Letcher

Term: 1840-1844
Party: Whig
Resident KY County: Garrard
Election Returns:
Robert P. Letcher - 54,892 (58.4%);
Richard French - 39,160 (41.6%)
Born: 2/10/1788 - Died: 1/24/1864
Occupation(s): Lawyer

Governor William Owsley

Term: 1844-1848
Party: Whig
Resident KY County: Lincoln
Election Returns:
William Owsley - 59,792 (52.1%);
William O. Butler - 55,089 (48.0%)
Born: 3/24/1782 - Died: 12/9/1862
Occupation(s): Teacher, Deputy Surveyor, Deputy
Sheriff, Lawyer, Judge

Governor John J. Crittenden

Term: 1848-1850
Party: Whig
Resident KY County: Logan
Election Returns:
John J. Crittenden - 64,982 (53.4%);
Lazarus Powell 56.675 (46.6%)
Born: 9/10/1786 - Died: 7/26/1863
Occupation(s): Lawyer

Governor John L. Helm

Term: 1850-1851
Party: Whig
Resident KY County: Hardin
Election Returns: Succeeded Gov.
John J. Crittenden, who resigned
(1850)
Born: 7/4/1802 - Died: 9/8/1867
Occupation(s): Lawyer

Governor Lazarus Powell

Term: 1851-1855
Party: Democrat
Resident KY County: Henderson
Election Returns:
Lazarus Powell - 54.821 (48.8%);
Archibald Dixon 54,023 (48.1%)
Born: 10/6/1812 - Died: 7/3/1867
Occupation(s): Lawyer

Governor Charles Slaughter Morehead

Term: 1855-1859
Party: American ("Know-Nothing")
Resident KY County: Franklin
Election Returns:
Charles Morehead 69,8- 70 (51.6%); Beverley Clark 65,570 (48.4%)
Born: 7/7/1802 - Died: 12/21/1868
Occupation(s): Lawyer

Governor Beriah Magoffin

Term: 1859-1862
Party: Democrat
Resident KY County: Mercer
Election Returns:
Beriah Magoffin - 76,631 (53.2%); Joshua Bell - 67,504 (46.8%)
Born: 4/18/1815 - Died: 2/28/1885
Occupation(s): Lawyer

Governor James F. Robinson

Term: 1862-1863
Party: Democrat
Resident KY County: Scott
Election Returns: Succeeded Gov. Beriah Magoffin, who resigned (1862)
Born: 10/4/1800 - Died: 10/31/1882
Occupation(s): Farmer, Lawyer

Governor Thomas E. Bramlette

Term: 1863-1867
Party: Democrat
Resident KY County: Jefferson
Election Returns:
Thomas Bramlette - 68,422 (79.6%); Charles Wickliffe - 17,503 (20.4%)
Born: 1/3/1817 - Died: 1/12/1875
Occupation(s): Lawyer, Soldier, Judge

Governor John L. Helm

Term: 1867
Party: Democrat
Resident KY County: Hardin
Election Returns:
John Helm - 90,216 (65.7%); Sidney Barnes - 33,939 (24.7%); William Kinkead - 13,167 (9.6%)
Born: 7/4/1802 - Died: 9/8/1867
Occupation(s): Lawyer

Governor John W. Stevenson

Term: 1867-1871
Party: Democrat
Resident KY County: Kenton
Election Returns: Succeeded Gov. John Helm, who died while in office (1867)
Born: 5/4/1812 - Died: 8/10/1886
Occupation(s): Lawyer

Governor Preston H. Leslie

Term: 1871-1875
Party: Democrat
Resident KY County: Barren
Election Returns:
Succeeded Gov. John Stevenson, who resigned (1871), then elected to office in 1871 election.
Preston Leslie - 126,455 (58.6%); John Harlan - 89,083 (41.4%)
Born: 3/8/1819 - Died: 2/7/1907
Occupation(s): Deputy Clerk, Farmer, Lawyer

Governor James B. McCreary

Term: 1875-1879
Party: Democrat
Resident KY County: Madison
Election Returns:
James McCreary - 126,976 (58.3%); John Harlan - 90,795 (41.7%)
Born: 7/8/1838 - Died: 10/8/1918
Occupation(s): Soldier, Lawyer

Governor Luke Blackburn

Term: 1879-1883
Party: Democrat
Resident KY County: Jefferson
Election Returns:
Luke Blackburn 125,399 (55.4%); Walter Evans 81,881 (36.2%); C.W. Cook 18,954 (8.4%)
Born: 7/16/1816 - Died: 9/14/1887
Occupation(s): Doctor

Governor James Proctor Knott

Term: 1883-1887
Party: Democrat
Resident KY County: Marion
Election Returns:
James Knott 133,615 (60.0%); Thomas Morrow 89,181 (40.0%)
Born: 8/29/1830 - Died: 6/18/1911
Occupation(s): Lawyer

Governor Simon Bolivar Buckner

Term: 1887-1891
Party: Democrat
Resident KY County: Hart
Election Returns:
Simon Buckner - 143,466 (50.7%); William Bradley - 126,754 (44.8%)
Born: 4/1/1823 - Died: 1/8/1914
Occupation(s): Soldier, Businessman, Newspaperman

Governor John Young Brown

Term: 1891-1895
Party: Democrat
Resident KY County: Henderson
Election Returns:
John Young Brown - 144,168 (49.9%); Andrew Wood - 116,087 (40.1%); S.B. Erwin - 25,631 (8.9%)
Born: 6/28/1835 - Died: 1/11/1904
Occupation(s): Lawyer

Governor William O. Bradley

Term: 1895-1899
Party: Republican
Resident KY County: Garrard
Election Returns:
William Bradley - 172,436 (48.3%); Parker Hardin - 163,524 (45.8%)
Born: 3/18/1847 - Died: 5/23/1914
Occupation(s): Lawyer

Governor William S. Taylor

Term: 1899-1900
Party: Republican
Resident KY County: Butler
Election Returns:
William Taylor - 193,727 (48.1%); William Goebel - 191,331 (47.5%)
Born: 10/10/1853 - Died: 8/2/1928
Occupation(s): Teacher, County Clerk, Lawyer, Farmer

Governor William Goebel

Term: 1900
Party: Democrat
Resident KY County: Kenton
Election Returns: Appointed by the General Assembly after Gov. William Taylor's election was declared unconstitutional
Born: 1/4/1856 - Died: 2/3/1900
Occupation(s): Lawyer
Note: First Kentucky Governor assasinated while holding office

Governor John Crepps Wickliffe (J.C.W.) Beckham

Term: 1900-1907
Party: Democrat
Resident KY County: Nelson
Election Returns: By special election, succeeded Gov. William Goebel, who was assasinated while holding office.
Special Election
John Beckham - 233,197 (49.9%); John Yerkes - 229,468 (49.1%)
1903 Regular Election
John Beckham - 229,014 (52.1%); M.B. Belknap - 202,862 (46.2%)
Born: 8/5/1869 - Died: 1/9/1940
Occupation(s): Principal of Public Schools, Lawyer

Governor Augustus E. Willson

Term: 1907-1911
Party: Republican
Resident KY County: Jefferson
Election Returns:
Augustus Willson - 214,478 (51.2%); Hager - 196,428 (46.9%)
Born: 10/13/1846 - Died: 8/24/1931
Occupation(s): Lawyer

Governor James B. McCreary

Term: 1911-1915
Party: Democrat
Resident KY County: Madison
Election Returns:
James McCreary - 226,549 (53.7%); E.C. Orear - 195,672 (46.3%)
Born: 7/8/1838 - Died: 10/8/1918
Occupation(s): Soldier, Lawyer

Governor Augustus Owsley Stanley

Term: 1915-1919
Party: Democrat
Resident KY County: Henderson
Election Returns:
Augustus Stanley - 219,991 (49.1%); Edwin Morrow - 219,520 (49.0%)
Born: 5/21/1867 - Died: 8/12/1958
Occupation(s): Teacher, Lawyer

Governor James Dixon Black

Term: 1919
Party: Democrat
Resident KY County: Knox
Election Returns: Succeeded Gov. Augustus Stanley, who resigned
Born: 9/24/1849 - Died: 8/5/1938
Occupation(s): Teacher, President of Union College, Lawyer

Governor Edwin P. Morrow

Term: 1919-1923
Party: Republican
Resident KY County: Pulaski
Election Returns:
Edwin Morrow - 254,472 (53.8%);
James Black - 214,134 (45.3%)
Born: 11/28/1877 - Died: 6/15/1935
Occupation(s): Lawyer

Governor William J. Fields

Term: 1923-1927
Party: Democrat
Resident KY County: Carter
Election Returns:
William Fields - 356,045 (53.3%);
Charles Dawson - 306,277 (45.8%)
Born: 12/29/1874 - Died: 10/21/1954
Occupation(s): Farmer, Businessman, Lawyer

Governor Flem D. Sampson

Term: 1927-1931
Party: Republican
Resident KY County: Knox
Election Returns:
Flem Sampson - 399,698 (52.1%);
John Beckham - 367,698 (47.9%)
Born: 1/25/1875 - Died: 5/25/1967
Occupation(s): Bank President, Teacher, Judge, Lawyer

Governor Ruby Laffoon

Term: 1931-1935
Party: Democrat
Resident KY County: Hopkins
Election Returns:
Ruby Laffoon - 438,513 (54.3%);
William Harrison - 366,982 (45.4%)
Born: 1/15/1869 - Died: 3/1/1941
Occupation(s): Lawyer

Governor A.B. ("Happy") Chandler

Term: 1935-1939
Party: Democrat
Resident KY County: Woodford
Election Returns:
A.B. Chandler - 556,262 (54.5%); King Swope - 461,104 (45.1%)
Born: 7/14/1898 - Died: 6/15/1991
Occupation(s): Coach, Lawyer, Baseball Commissioner

Governor Keen Johnson

Term: 1939-1943
Party: Democrat
Resident KY County: Madison
Election Returns: Succeeded Gov.
A.B. Chandler, who resigned (1939)
1939 Election; Keen Johnson - 460,834 (56.5%);
King Swope - 354,704 (43.5%)
Born: 1/12/1896 - Died: 2/7/1970
Occupation(s): Soldier, Journalist, Businessman

Governor Simeon S. Willis

Term: 1943-1947
Party: Republican
Resident KY County: Boyd
Election Returns:
Simeon Willis - 279.144 (50.5%); J.
Lyter Donaldson - 270,525 (48.9%)
Born: 12/1/1879 - Died: 4/2/1965
Occupation(s): Teacher, Lawyer, Judge

Governor Earle C. Clements

Term: 1947-1950
Party: Democrat
Resident KY County: Union
Election Returns:
Earle Clements - 387,795 (57.2%);
Eldon Dummit - 287,756 (42.5%)
Born: 10/22/1896 - Died: 3/12/1985
Occupation(s): Coach, Teacher, Soldier, Deputy, Sheriff, Public Servant

Governor Lawrence W. Wetherby

Term: 1950-1955
Party: Democrat
Resident KY County: Jefferson
Election Returns: Succeeded Gov.
Earle Clements, who resigned (1950)
1951 Election; Lawrence Wetherby - 346,345
(54.6%); Eugene Stiler - 288,014 (45.4%)
Born: 1/2/1908 - Died: 3/27/1994
Occupation(s): Lawyer, Judge

Governor A.B. ("Happy") Chandler

Term: 1955-1959
Party: Democrat
Resident KY County: Woodford
Election Returns:
A.B. Chandler - 451,647 (58.0%); Edwin Denney - 322,671 (41.5%)
Born: 7/14/1898 - Died: 6/15/1991
Occupation(s): Coach, Lawyer, Baseball Commissioner

Governor Bert T. Combs

Term: 1959-1963
Party: Democrat
Resident KY County: Floyd
Election Returns:
Bert Combs - 516,549 (60.6%); John
M. Robsion - 336,456 (39.4%)
Born: 8/13/1911 - Died: 12/4/1991
Occupation(s): Lawyer

Governor Edward ("Ned") Breathitt

Term: 1963-1967
Party: Democrat
Resident KY County: Christian
Election Returns: Edward Breathitt
- 449,551 (50.7%); Louie B. Nunn - 436,496 (49.3%)
Born: 11/26/1924 - Died: 10/14/03
Occupation(s): Lawyer

Governor Louie B. Nunn

Term: 1967-1971
Party: Republican
Resident KY County: Barren
Election Returns:
Louie B. Nunn - 454,123 (51.2%);
Henry Ward - 425,674 (48.0%)
Born: 3/8/1924 - Died: 1/29/04
Occupation(s): Soldier, Lawyer

Governor Wendell Ford

Term: 1971-1974
Party: Democrat
Resident KY County: Daviess
Election Returns:
Wendell Ford - 470,720 (50.6%);
Tom Emberton - 412,653 (44.3%)
Born: 9/8/1924
Occupation(s): Soldier, Businessman

Governor Julian Carroll

Term: 1974-1979
Party: Democrat
Resident KY County: McCracken
Election Returns: Succeeded Gov.
Wendell Ford, who resigned (1974)
1975 Election; Julian Carroll - 470,159 (62.8%);
Robert Gable - 277,998 (37.2%)
Born: 4/16/1931
Occupation(s): Lawyer

Governor John Y. Brown, Jr.

Term: 1979-1983
Party: Democrat
Resident KY County: Fayette
Election Returns:
John Y. Brown - 558,088 (59.4%);
Louie B. Nunn - 381,278 (40.6%)
Born: 12/28/1933

Governor Martha Layne (Hall) Collins

Term: 1983-1987
Party: Democrat
Resident KY County: Woodford
Election Returns:
Martha Layne Collins - 561,674 (54.6%);
Jim Bunning - 454,650 (44.2%)
Born: 12/7/1936
Occupation(s): Teacher

Governor Wallace Wilkinson

Term: 1987-1991
Party: Democrat
Resident KY County: Fayette
Election Returns:
Wallace Wilkinson - 504,367 (64.9%);
John Harper - 273,035 (35.1%)
Born: 12/12/1941 - Died: 7/5/2002
Occupation(s): Farmer, Businessman

Governor Brereton C. Jones

Term: 1991-1995
Party: Democrat
Resident KY County: Woodford
Election Returns:
Brereton Jones - 540,468 (64.7%); Larry
Hopkins - 294,452 (35.3%)
Born: 6/27/1939
Occupation(s): Businessman

Governor Paul E. Patton

Term: 1995-2003
Party: Democrat
Resident KY County: Pike
Election Returns:
1995 Election; Paul Patton - 500,787
(51.1%)Larry Forgy - 479,227 (48.9%)
1999 Election; Paul Patton - 352,099 (60.6%);
Martin & Cornelius - 128,788 (22.2%); Galbraith &
Lyons - 88,930 (15.3%); Others 6,934 (1.2%)
Born: 5/26/1937
Occupation(s): Engineer, Businessman

Governor Ernie Fletcher

Term: 2003-
Party: Republican
Resident KY County: Fayette
Election Returns:
Ernie Fletcher 593, 058; Ben Chandler
484,804
Born: 11/12/1952
Occupation(s): U.S. Congressman, physician, CEO
Medical Foundation, pastor of a Baptist church
Source: www.kdla.ky.gov & Kentucky Historical Society

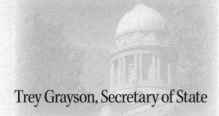

Trey Grayson, Secretary of State

Historical
Elections

Kentucky's rich history reveals a tradition of strong political leaders, dominated by the governor's leading role. From the election of Isaac Shelby as the first governor of the Commonwealth, Kentucky governors have wielded clout and power.

In its early history influential Kentucky governors such as John Breathitt (1832) and James Clark (1836) mapped the state's political history by using their terms in office to set the stage for their party's eventual rise in power, such as Breathitt's Demo-

✕✕✕✕✕ ✕✕✕✕✕✕✕✕✕✕

In 1883 perhaps one of the

most influential and efficient

administrations came into power

through the leadership of

J. Proctor Knott, who completely

reformed Kentucky's antiquated

tax code, thereby stabilizing its

economy during a most

difficult time.

✕✕✕✕✕ ✕✕✕✕✕✕✕✕✕✕

cratic Party, or for their party's domination, as was the case with Clark's Whig Party. In fact Kentucky did not see evidence of a strong two-party political system until the election of William O'Connell Bradley in 1895 as the first Republican governor. Such a two-party system would also be absent for much of the 20th century.

As a border state in the Civil War, Kentucky's gubernatorial leadership became critical to its place in history. If Beriah Magoffin's (1859) influence were greater, he might have taken the state

out of the Union. His resignation in 1862 due to disagreements with the legislature over Kentucky's role in the war assured the Commonwealth would stay in the Union. Just a few years later Thomas Bramlette (1863) would heal Kentucky's Civil War wounds by pardoning most ex-Confederate soldiers and restoring some civil rights to former slaves. He also worked to create the public univer-

Isaac Shelby

sity that would eventually become the University of Kentucky.

In 1883 perhaps one of the most influential and efficient administrations came into power through the leadership of J. Proctor Knott, who completely reformed Kentucky's antiquated tax code, thereby stabilizing its economy during a most difficult time.

While some elections helped to stabilize Kentucky, others sent it into disarray. In 1899 Republican William S. Taylor was elected governor only to have the election deemed unconstitutional by the Democratic legislature. The legislature, in turn, elected Democrat William Goebel (1890) as governor. Shortly thereafter Goebel was the first Kentucky governor to be assassinated while holding office. These events nearly brought Kentucky

Gov. A. B. "Happy" Chandler
Source: Happy Chandler Foundation

Gov. Louie B. Nunn
Source: Governor Louie B. Nunn Foundation

to its own civil war.

In 1934 one of Kentucky's most popular governors, A.B. "Happy" Chandler (1935 and 1955), used his time as acting governor to call a special session of the General Assembly to change the gubernatorial election process. (At that time, when governors left the Commonwealth, the lieutenant governor assumed acting governor status.) The following year, Chandler used this change, the addition of a run-off election in the primary, to win the Democratic nomination and eventually the governorship.

Later in the century the civil rights movement swept across the country, and two Kentucky governors, Bert T. Combs (1959) and Ned Breathitt (1963), took steps to push the state toward equality for all of its citizens. Combs established the state's first human rights commission and desegregated all public accommodations; his successor passed the equal employment opportunity bill, which further removed barriers against minorities.

The latter half of the 20th century saw a partial

Gov. Martha Layne Collins
Source: Kentucky Department for Libraries & Archives

**Governors Ned Breathitt, Bert Combs, Wendell Ford,
Lawrence Wetherby and Happy Chandler**
Source: Happy Chandler Foundation

return to one-party rule, but elections such as Simeon Wills (1943), Louie Nunn (1967) and Ernie Fletcher (2003) indicated a growing competitive spirit among parties and their candidates. In 1984 a competitive two-party system was solidified through the election of Mitch McConnell to the U.S. Senate. This election served as a catalyst to the resurgence of the Republican Party in Kentucky. The increased competition from two parties, along with more affluent candidates, gave rise to the multimillion-dollar campaigns that first became evident in the election of John Y. Brown, Jr. (1979).

Some of Brown's successors set other records for the Commonwealth. In 1983 Martha Layne Collins became the first woman to be elected governor. In 1999 Paul Patton became the first governor to be elected to two consecutive terms since the 19th century.

Beyond the governor's race, however, there were a number of elections that made a significant impact on the Commonwealth. In 1896 Emma Guy Cromwell became the first woman elected to a statewide office as the state librarian. She later became the first woman in the country to be elected as a state secretary of state. In 1935 Charles W. Anderson was the first African American elected to the Kentucky House of Representatives since Reconstruction. Later he sponsored bills to fund out-of-state tuition for black students denied higher education in Kentucky. In 1967 Georgia Powers made history by becoming the first African American woman elected to the Kentucky Senate.

These leaders shared a vision of a brighter Kentucky and a commitment to public service. Through their civic engagement we reap great benefits. Today the challenge is to follow in their pioneering footsteps and sow the seeds for tomorrow's change. Each election reaffirms a commitment to democracy and to the unbridled spirit of those who paved the way.

STATE GOVERNMENT & POLITICS

Inaugural History   Chris Kellogg

Preparation, parades, military flyovers, swearing-in ceremonies, balls – inaugurals reverberate with historical significance. Kentucky has seen 57 inaugurations throughout its more than two centuries of statehood. Most have preserved traditional activities to mark the beginning of a new administration. However, traditions have adapted

Louis B. Nunn
Source: Governor Louie B. Nunn Foundation

over time, often because of circumstance and the press of current events.

The very first inauguration in Kentucky included a colorful parade and the traditional swearing-in ceremony, just like we see today. Isaac Shelby began his term in Lexington, which then served as Kentucky's capital. It was his successor, James Garrard, who began the succession of state leaders to be sworn in at Frankfort.

Dates of inaugural ceremonies have changed through the years too. Initially held in June, then September, the first Tuesday in December was established by the 1890-1891 Constitutional Convention as the date for new leaders to take the helm in Frankfort.

In the 19th century the ceremonies took place at the Old Capitol under the "governor's elm tree," preceded by colorful parades that emphasized the state's military might and patriotism.

Sometimes less than ideal conditions that face the inaugurals of today were more daunting for times gone by. One article in the Dec. 7, 1859, "State Journal" says: "Regardless of the mud and the unpaved streets of the city, and of the hogs wandering through the stores and of the bad boys who threw rocks at the railroad engineers taking their trains along Broadway, the inauguration was sure to be a social and political success." During the 1911 inauguration of James McCreary, the first held in the New State Capitol, the organizers worried about feeding the hordes of visitors and arranged for burgoo and bread to be sold in two locations.

In time the parades began to embrace various civic organizations and school marching bands. Today each county is invited to send a marching band.

Today the parade serves as the precursor to the swearing-in ceremony. While little is known about the early ceremonies, it is likely they share the same basic program as modern-day events: welcoming remarks, brief remarks by the new lieutenant governor, an inaugural address by the new governor, then the oath of office administered by the chief justice to the lieutenant governor and then to the governor. One tradition that has faded through the past quarter century is farewell remarks delivered by the outgoing governor.

One tradition has been maintained for more than a century. Beginning in 1796 as a housewarming gesture from the outgoing first lady to the new matron of the house, now a delegation of Frankfort residents call on their new neighbors bringing beaten biscuits, country ham and white cake as a welcoming gift from the host community.

The day itself is a test of stamina for the new governor and first lady. Beginning with the official midnight private swearing-in at the executive residence and ending in the wee hours of the following day after visiting various balls around Frankfort, work begins early on December 8 for the first day of a new administration.

STATE GOVERNMENT & POLITICS
State Capitol

Chris Kellogg

Approaching her century mark, Kentucky's majestic state capitol sits on a bluff above the Kentucky River valley, its recently restored lantern and dome lighted at night, visible from points throughout Franklin County. Referred to as the New State Capitol, this is the fourth state house since Kentucky became a commonwealth in 1792. Construction began in 1904 and was completed in 1910 in time for the General Assembly to meet. The following June dedication ceremonies were held amid great pomp and circumstance on Capitol Avenue. The building opened to the public in 1909. It has been on the National Register of Historic Places since the early 1970s.

Irreplaceable by today's standards, the building was designed by the distinguished architect Frank Mills Andrews for a total cost of $1.8 million (by comparison the 1998-1999 restoration of the dome cost $2 million). Its beaux arts style includes elements of classical architecture and is a combination of

Source: Department of Tourism

Greek architecture with the highly ornate elegance of French styling. The first floor was largely used as public space where day-to-day business was conducted. The governor's office was on the second floor where the state reception room is located now.

Today there are more than 350 offices carved out of the three-story building and in the attic and basement, which were intended for storage. The first or executive floor includes the offices of the governor, lieutenant governor, secretary of state and the attorney general. The dome, which towers seven stories over the rotunda, is modeled after the one above Napoleon's tomb in Paris, France. A statue of Abraham Lincoln in the center of the rotunda stands above other famous Kentuckians: Henry Clay, Alben Barkley, Ephraim McDowell and Jefferson Davis. Elsewhere on the first floor are likenesses of Thelma Stovall, Happy Chandler and Colonel Sanders.

Massive marble stairways modeled after the Paris Grand Opera House lead to the second floor, or the judicial floor, where the Supreme Court, the state law library and the state reception room are located. The state reception room, restored in 1994, was designed in the Louis XIV period and includes a handwoven Austrian carpet designed for the room when the capitol was built. French-style furniture, elegant murals and intricate faux finishes adorn the room. Portraits of state Supreme Court justices line the grand halls, which afford expansive views of other areas of the building. The court chamber was the most expensive room when the capitol was constructed at a cost $25,000. It has solid Honduras mahogany paneling and an elegant coffered ceiling covered in "Old Dutch" metal leafing.

The Kentucky House of Representatives and Senate chambers are located on opposite ends of the third floor. Entrances are highlighted by decorative lunettes of frontier scenes with Daniel Boone painted in oil by T. Gilbert White. Both chambers continue the classical styles of the building and are furnished with mahogany desks and leather-upholstered chairs. Offices of the leadership are also here.

STATE GOVERNMENT & POLITICS

Governor's Executive Mansion

Chris Kellogg

WHERE KENTUCKY GOVERNORS HAVE CALLED HOME

If the walls of the Executive Mansion, which has served as the residence for Kentucky's governors since 1914, could talk, they would tell of weddings, galas, visits by royalty and world leaders, midnight swearing-in ceremonies and innumerable other

tects C.C. and E.A. Weber, although there is some question as to how much of the work they completed and whether a Cincinnati firm assisted with the designs. The exterior of the building was modeled after the Petit Trianon, Queen Marie Antoinette's villa near the Palace of Versailles in France. This opulent design was executed despite Gov. Augustus E. Willson's advice that the new mansion,

Source: Sid Webb

events that could provide a rich view of the Commonwealth's varied history.

Since the doors opened to the current and fourth domicile of the head of state, 23 governors and their families have lived at 704 Capitol Avenue, which sits just to the east of the New State Capitol on a bluff overlooking the Kentucky River in Frankfort. The mansion was designed by Fort Thomas archi-

to be set away from the existing residence on High and Clinton Streets, would best be constructed in a manner consistent with the lifestyles of the men who were generally elected to serve the office.

Despite the "sticker shock" throughout the legislature that resulted from the cost overrun of the capitol construction, the General Assembly approved funds to purchase land and pay for construction of the governor's mansion in early 1912. The splendid design might owe its origin to Gov. McCreary, who, according to the book "Kentucky's Governors, 1792-1975," was said to be a man of "aristocratic bearings and notions" and was quite the socialite. Problems and changes became the order of the day, but by January 1914 the man-

Source: Sid Webb

sion was completed to the point of allowing Gov. McCreary to move in. The cost overrun was more than $19,000 – a significant sum for the time – but that did not include furnishings. The grand opening kicked off on January 20, 1914, with an elegant event, the likes of which have rarely been seen at the mansion since and which was followed the next evening by a 10-course dinner and grand ball.

The development of a formal garden on the grounds was delayed due to lack of funds. A straight walkway through the front yard and a driveway between the mansion and the capitol would serve until the administration of John Y. Brown Jr. (1979-1983), when the original garden plans were finally

implemented during a major restoration of the home.

A stone balustrade and terrace adorned with a front portico with four pairs of Ionic columns provide the entrance to the mansion. Most lighting fixtures and other decorative features remain original to the building, which is referred to frequently by the occupants as the "People's House." Indeed the mansion sits at the head of a residential neighborhood that was incorporated as South Frankfort at the time of the building's construction.

The first official governor's residence was constructed in 1796 – four years after statehood – because the commissioners of public buildings determined it would be more cost effective to build a residence than rent one. Completed in 1798, the Old Governor's Mansion has recently been restored to resemble its original interior after surviving fires and years of neglect. Referred to early in its history as the "palace," Maria Crittenden, wife of Gov. John J. Crittenden, dispensed with that moniker in favor of the "governor's house" when they moved from the other side of downtown Frankfort in 1849.

After years of fragmented redecorating, the house, which served as the residence for Kentucky's lieutenant governors for years, has a newly restored interior that reflects the style at the time of its construction.

The Executive Mansion underwent a major restoration in the early 1980s to correct wiring hazards and to return it to its adapted beaux arts style. This renovation project was privately funded at a cost of $3.5 million by a "Save the Mansion" foundation and included the construction of the formal garden and furnishings. Nevertheless, the mansion is once again showing signs of wear and tear. According to its current occupants, Gov. and Glenna Fletcher, paint is chipping and peeling from walls and doors, floors are cracked and the patio to the rear of the building is sinking. Again, the heating and ventilation systems are wreaking havoc on the interior. Mrs. Fletcher announced that many areas of the mansion need serious attention, so she has launched the first major renovation since the Brown administration. She has consulted with a historic preservation expert and an architect and kicked off a $5 million private fundraising drive to support the renovation.

STATE GOVERNMENT

State Legislature

Bob Babbage

KENTUCKY'S GENERAL ASSEMBLY: THE GROWING TRANSITION TO INFLUENCE

Worthy of a novel, given the complexity and fabric of its critical decisions, Kentucky's General Assembly has become an equal, at times dominating, branch of state government in the modern generation.

༺༻༺༻༺༻༺༻༺༻༺༻

In addition to the partisan cast
that shades Kentucky's – and most of
America's – public decision making,
only 17 women serve in the
General Assembly, making
Kentucky's one of the least balanced
legislative bodies as to gender.

༺༻༺༻༺༻༺༻༺༻༺༻

With its highly visible personalities and widely varying priorities, the 100 representatives and 38 senators have become a focus of power as well as home to epic confrontations of will and direction. Structural changes eventually brought the legislature into its own — free of domination by the executive branch. As recently as the 1970s Kentucky's governors hand-picked legislative leaders and gave direct orders for expected floor votes. But things changed. The Kenton Amendment to the state constitution, championed by late-House Speaker William G. Kenton in 1978, re-sequenced legislative races out from under the election for governor.

When Governor John Y. Brown, Jr. became chief executive in 1979, he had no interest in traditional legislative control, and freed the General Assembly to choose its own leaders. All the while an influential subset of legislators, dubbed the "Black Sheep

Squadron," prodded lawmakers toward an active agenda for the people's branch of government. Then, too, Kentucky Educational Television network played a key role in summarizing the daily events in Frankfort during meetings of the General Assembly.

A more recent constitutional amendment ushered a sea change when voters approved annual meetings in 2001, a question rejected by the electorate in three prior votes. A combination of advocates, led by House Speaker Jody Richards, a Bowling Green Democrat, and Senate President David Williams, a Burkesville Republican, spearheaded media support matched with a grassroots understanding for consistent deliberation.

While these advances in process have created a more visible, bully pulpit for leaders, the political world changed dramatically when a coalition of Senate Republicans joined disaffected Democrats to take control of the state Senate in 1997. As the conservative national wave took hold, Kentucky Republicans won – and kept – the upper chamber.

As Democrats continue to hold the House 57-43, including election gains in 2004 for Republicans, giving them their largest House contingent in decades. The Senate edge for Republicans is 22-15 with one Independent. The House and Senate failed to give Gov. Paul Patton, a two-term Democrat, his last executive budget on time, raising unique questions about executive power to expend unbudgeted funds. Likewise, Governor Ernie Fletcher, the first Republican to hold the top seat in 32 years, could not get legislative approval for his first budget in 2004.

In addition to the partisan cast that shades Kentucky's – and most of America's – public decision making, only 17 women serve in the General Assembly, making Kentucky's one of the least balanced legislative bodies as to gender. As Senate president pro tem, Republican Katie Kratz Stine is the highest ranking female on the Capitol's third floor. Only five African Americans serve in the House joined by a single member in the Senate.

KY SENATE

PERSON (Party-District)	ADDRESS1	ADDRESS2	CITY	ZIP	PHONE	CAPITOL PHONE	EMAIL	FAX
Walter Blevins Jr (D-27)	777 Broadway		West Liberty	41472	(606) 743-1212	(502) 564-8100	http://lrc.ky.gov/mailform/s027.htm	(606) 743-1214
Charlie Borders (R-18)	700 Capitol Ave	Rm 203 Annex	Frankfort	40601	(606) 475-0237	(502) 564-2450	http://lrc.ky.gov/mailform/s018.htm	
David E Boswell Sr (D-8)	5591 Panther Creek Rd		Owensboro	42301	(270) 926-8000	(502) 564-8100	david.boswell@lrc.ky.gov	(270) 926-9047
Tom Buford (R-22)	105 Crosswoods Pl		Nicholasville	40356	(859) 885-0606	(502) 564-8100	http://lrc.ky.gov/mailform/s022.htm	(502) 564-0456
Julian M Carroll (D-7)		PO Box 1491	Frankfort	40601	(502) 223-8806	(502) 564-8100	jmc75farm@aol.com	(502) 227-4849
Julie Denton (R-36)	1708 Golden Leaf Way		Louisville	40245	(502) 489-9058	(502) 564-8100	http://lrc.ky.gov/mailform/s036.htm	(502) 564-6543
Carroll Gibson (R-5)		PO Box 506	Leitchfield	42755	(270) 230-5866	(502) 564-8100		
Brett Guthrie (R-32)	1005 Wrenwood Dr		Bowling Green	42103	(270) 781-0049	(502) 564-8100	http://lrc.ky.gov/mailform/s032.htm	
Denise Harper Angel (D-35)	2521 Ransdall Ave		Louisville	40204	(502) 452-9130	(502) 564-8100	dhangel@bellsouth.net	(502) 452-9130
Ernie Harris (R-26)		PO Box 1073	Crestwood	40014	(502) 241-8307	(502) 564-8100	http://lrc.ky.gov/mailform/s026.htm	
Tom Jensen (R-21)	303 S Main St		London	40741		(502) 564-8100	http://lrc.ky.gov/mailform/s021.htm	
Ray S Jones II (D-31)		PO Drawer 3850	Pikeville	41502	(606) 432-5777	(502) 564-8100	http://lrc.ky.gov/mailform/s031.htm	(606) 432-5154
Dan Kelly (R-14)	324 W Main		Springfield	40069	(859) 336-7723	(502) 564-2450	dan.kelly@lrc.ky.gov	
Alice Forgy Kerr (R-12)	3274 Gondola Dr		Lexington	40513	(859) 223-3274	(502) 564-8100	alice.kerr@lrc.ky.gov	
Robert J Leeper (I-2)	229 S Friendship Rd		Paducah	42003	(270) 554-9637	(502) 564-8100	bob.leeper@lrc.ky.gov	(270) 554-5337
Vernie D McGaha (R-15)	4787 W Hwy 76		Russell Springs	42642	(270) 866-3068	(502) 564-8100	http://lrc.ky.gov/mailform/s015.htm	
Daniel Mongiardo (D-30)	200 Medical Ctr Dr		Hazard	41701	(606) 439-4466	(502) 564-8100	daniel.mongiardo@lrc.ky.gov	(606) 439-1941
Gerald A Neal (D-33)	One Riverfront Plz	401 W Main St	Louisville	40202	(502) 584-8500	(502) 564-8100	http://lrc.ky.gov/mailform/s033.htm	(502) 584-1119
R J Palmer II (D-28)	1391 McClure Rd		Winchester	40391	(859) 745-7604	(502) 564-8100	rj.palmer@lrc.ky.gov	(859) 737-2348
Joey Pendleton (D-3)	905 Hurst Dr		Hopkinsville	42240	(270) 885-1639	(502) 564-2470	joey.pendleton@lrc.ky.gov	(502) 564-5508
Jerry P Rhoads (D-6)	9 E Center St	PO Box 2002	Madisonville	42431	(270) 825-1490	(502) 564-8100	jerry.rhoads@lrc.ky.gov	(270) 821-8512
Dorsey Ridley (D-4)	4030 Hidden Creek Dr		Henderson	42420	(270) 869-8400	(502) 564-8100	dorsey.ridley@lrc.ky.gov	
Richard L Roeding (R-11)	2534 Kearney Ct		Lakeside Park	41017	(859) 331-1684	(502) 564-3120	http://lrc.ky.gov/mailform/s011.htm	(606) 331-1238
Richie Sanders Jr (R-9)	901 Maple Leaf Dr		Franklin	42134	(270) 586-5473	(502) 564-2450	richie.sanders@lrc.ky.gov	
Ernesto Scorsone (D-13)	511 W Short St		Lexington	40507	(859) 254-5766	(502) 564-8100	ernesto.scorsone@lrc.ky.gov	(859) 255-5508
Dan (Malano) Seum (R-38)	1107 Holly Ave		Fairdale	40118	(502) 749-2859	(502) 564-2450	dan.seum@lrc.ky.gov	(502) 749-2859
Dana Seum-Stephenson (R-37)*	7628 Manslick Rd		Louisville	40204	(502) 564-2470	(502) 367-1020	http://lrc.ky.gov/mailform/s037.htm	
Tim Shaughnessy (D-19)	250 E Liberty Ste 103		Louisville	40202	(502) 584-1920	(502) 564-8100	http://lrc.ky.gov/mailform/s019.htm	
Katie Kratz Stine (R-24)	15 Cliffview Ave		Ft Thomas	41075	(859) 781-5311	(502) 564-3120	http://lrc.ky.gov/mailform/s024.htm	
Robert Stivers (R-25)	207 Main St		Manchester	40962	(606) 598-2322	(502) 564-8100	robert.stivers@lrc.ky.gov	(606) 598-2357
Gary Tapp (R-20)	2154 Buzzard Roost Rd		Waddy	40076	(502) 829-9220	(502) 564-8100	gary.tapp@lrc.ky.gov	
Damon Thayer (R-17)	102 Grayson Way		Georgetown	40324	(502) 867-3046	(502) 564-8100	http://lrc.ky.gov/mailform/s017.htm	(502) 868-6086
Elizabeth J Tori (R-10)	2851 S Wilson Rd		Radcliff	40160	(270) 351-1829	(502) 564-2450	elizabeth.tori@lrc.ky.gov	(270) 351-1829
Johnny R Turner (D-29)		PO Box 5	Drift	41619	(606) 377-6962	(502) 564-6136	johnny.turner@lrc.ky.gov	
John (Jack) Westwood (R-23)	2072 Lakelyn Ct		Crescent Springs	41017	(859) 344-6154	(502) 564-8100	jack.westwood@lrc.ky.gov	(859) 344-1878
David L Williams (R-16)		PO Box 666	Burkesville	42717	(270) 864-5636	(502) 564-3120	http://lrc.ky.gov/mailform/s016.htm	
Kenneth W Winters (R-1)	1500 Glendale Rd		Murray	42071	(270) 759-5751	(502) 564-8100		(270) 759-5751
Ed Worley (D-34)		PO Box 659	Richmond	40475	(859) 623-6524	(502) 564-2470	http://lrc.ky.gov/mailform/s034.htm	(859) 623-6557

Status being contested in court
Source: *The Kentucky Directory Gold Book 2005*

KY HOUSE OF REPRESENTATIVES

PERSON (Party-District)	ADDRESS1	ADDRESS2	CITY	ZIP	PHONE	CAPITOL PHONE	FAX	EMAIL
Royce W Adams (D-61)	580 Bannister Rd		Dry Ridge	41035	(859) 824-3387	(502) 564-8100	(859) 824-7589	royce.adams@lrc.ky.gov
Rocky Adkins (D-99)		PO Box 688	Sandy Hook	41171	(606) 928-3433	(502) 564-5565	(606) 929-5913	rocky.adkins@lrc.ky.gov
Adrian K Arnold (D-74)	3589 Aarons Run Rd		Mt Sterling	40353	(859) 498-3034	(502) 564-8100		http://lrc.ky.gov/mailform/h074.htm
John A Arnold Jr (D-7)	1301 N Lee St	PO Box 124	Sturgis	42459	(270) 333-4641	(502) 564-8100		john.arnold@lrc.ky.gov
Eddie Ballard (D-10)		PO Box 1736	Madisonville	42431	(270) 821-4767	(502) 564-8100		eddie.ballard@lrc.ky.gov
Joe Barrows (D-56)	152 Stout Ave		Versailles	40383	(859) 873-9768	(502) 564-7756		http://lrc.ky.gov/mailform/h056.htm
Sheldon E Baugh (R-16)	252 W Valley Dr		Russellville	42276	(270) 726-7616	(502) 564-8100	(270) 726-7618	sheldon.baugh@lrc.ky.gov
Carolyn Belcher (D-72)	51 Blevins Valley Rd		Owingsville	40360	(606) 674-2417	(502) 564-8100		carolyn.belcher@lrc.ky.gov
Joe Bowen (R-13)	2031 Fieldcrest Dr		Owensboro	42301	(270) 683-0236	(502) 564-8100	(270) 685-0840	jr_bowen@msn.com
Kevin D Bratcher (R-29)	10215 Landwood Dr		Louisville	40291	(502) 231-3311	(502) 564-8100		kevin.bratcher@lrc.ky.gov
Scott W Brinkman (R-32)	6001 Two Springs Ln		Louisville	40207	(502) 560-4244	(502) 564-8100	(502) 627-8744	http://lrc.ky.gov/mailform/h032.htm
James E Bruce (D-9)	6750 Ft Campbell Blvd		Hopkinsville	42240	(270) 886-2422	(502) 564-8100		http://lrc.ky.gov/mailform/h009.htm
Thomas J Burch (D-30)	4012 Lambert Ave		Louisville	40218	(502) 454-4002	(502) 564-8100	(502) 564-5640	tom.burch@lrc.ky.gov
Denver Butler (D-38)	6712 Morocco Dr		Louisville	40214	(502) 366-7195	(502) 564-8100		repbutler@aol.com
Dwight D Butler (R-18)		PO Box 9	Harned	40144	(270) 756-5931	(502) 564-8100		butlerdd@bbtel.com
James R Carr (D-8)	1300 Liberty St		Hopkinsville	42240	(270) 887-0912	(502) 564-8100		http://lrc.ky.gov/mailform/h008/.htm
Michael E Cherry (D-4)	803 S Jefferson St		Princeton	42445	(270) 365-7801	(502) 564-8100	(270) 365-7801	mike.cherry@lrc.ky.gov
Perry B Clark (D-46)	5716 New Cut Rd		Louisville	40214	(502) 366-1247	(502) 564-8100		perry.clark@lrc.ky.gov
Larry Clark (D-37)	5913 Whispering Hills		Louisville	40219	(502) 968-3546	(502) 564-7520		larry.clark@lrc.ky.gov
Hubert Collins (D-97)	72 Collins Dr		Whitinsville	41274	(606) 297-3361	(502) 564-8100	(606) 297-3361	http://lrc.ky.gov/mailform/h097.htm
James R Comer (R-53)	407 4th St Blvd		Tompkinsville	42167	(270) 487-5585	(502) 564-8100		jcomer@scrtc.com
Howard Cornett (R-94)	20 El Paso Dr		Whitesburg	41858	(606) 832-4827	(502) 564-8100		http://lrc.ky.gov/mailform/h094.htm
Tim Couch (R-90)		PO Box 710	Hyden	41749	(606) 672-8998	(502) 564-8100	(606) 672-8998	http://lrc.ky.gov/mailform/h090.htm
Jesse Crenshaw (D-77)	121 Constitution		Lexington	40507	(859) 259-1402	(502) 564-8100	(859) 259-1441	http://lrc.ky.gov/mailform/h077.htm
Ronald E Crimm (R-33)		PO Box 43244	Louisville	40253	(502) 245-2118	(502) 564-8100	(502) 245-3811	ron.crimm@lrc.ky.gov
Robert R Damron (D-39)	231 Fairway W		Nicholasville	40356	(859) 229-4219	(502) 564-2217	(502) 564-1544	robert.damron@lrc.ky.gov
David Osborne (R-59)		PO Box 8	Prospect	40059	(502) 228-3201	(502) 564-8100		david.osborne@lrc.ky.gov
Jim DeCesare (R-21)	136 Cedar Trail Ave		Bowling Green	42101	(270) 792-5779	(502) 564-8100		dj951@insightbb.com
Milward Dedman (D-55)		PO Box 610	Harrodsburg	40330	(859) 734-2880	(502) 564-8100	(859) 734-4946	mdedman@bellsouth.net
Mitchel (Mike) Denham (D-70)	306 Old Hill City Rd		Maysville	41056	(606) 759-5167	(502) 564-8100		http://lrc.ky.gov/mailform/h070.htm
Bob M DeWeese (R-48)	6206 Glen Hill Rd		Louisville	40222	(502) 426-5565	(502) 564-4334		bob.deweese@lrc.ky.gov
Jon E Draud (R-63)	3081 Lyndale Ct		Edgewood	41017	(859) 572-5757	(502) 564-8100	(859) 341-3887	jon.draud@lrc.ky.gov or jbdraud@fule.net
Ted (Teddy) Edmonds (D-91)	1257 Beattyville Rd		Jackson	41339	(606) 666-4823	(502) 564-8100		http://lrc.ky.gov/mailform/h091.htm
C B Embry Jr (R-17)		PO Box 1215	Morgantown	42261	(270) 526-6237	(502) 564-8100		http://lrc.ky.gov/mailform/h017.htm

KY HOUSE OF REPRESENTATIVES

PERSON (Party-District)	ADD1	ADD2	CITY	ZIP	PHONE	CAPITOL PHONE	FAX	EMAIL
Bill Farmer (R-88)	3361 Squire Oak Dr		Lexington	40515	(859) 272-1425	(502) 564-8100	(859) 272-1579	http://lrc.ky.gov/mailform_temp/farmer.htm
Joseph M Fischer (R-68)	126 Dixie Pl		Ft Thomas	41075	(513) 794-6442	(502) 564-8100		joe.fischer@lrc.ky.gov
David W Floyd (R-50)	102 Maywood Ave		Bardstown	40004	(502) 349-6214	(502) 564-8100	(502) 349-0116	david.floyd@lrc.ky.gov
Danny R Ford (R-80)		PO Box 1245	Mt Vernon	40456	(606) 679-2212	(502) 564-8100		danny.ford@lrc.ky.gov
Jim Gooch Jr (D-12)	125C E Main St		Providence	42450	(270) 667-9900	(502) 564-8100	(270) 667-9909	jim.gooch@lrc.ky.gov
Derrick W Graham (D-57)	Capitol Annex Rm 451B		Frankfort	40601	(502) 875-8655	(502) 564-8100	(502) 564-6834	http://lrc.ky.gov/mailform/h057.htm
J R Gray (D-6)	3188 Mayfield Hwy		Benton	42025	(270) 527-8376	(502) 564-8100	(502) 564-6543	jr.gray@lrc.ky.gov
W Keith Hall (D-93)	155 McCoy Caney Rd		Phelps	41553	(606) 835-4666	(502) 564-8100	(606) 835-4999	http://lrc.ky.gov/mailform/h093.htm
Mike Harmon (R-54)		PO Box 458	Junction City	40440	(859) 238-9717	(502) 564-8100	(781) 846-1098	mikeharmon@yahoo.com
Mary C Harper (R-49)	5550 N Preston		Shepherdsville	40165	(502) 957-4467	(502) 564-8100		http://lrc.ky.gov/mailform/h049.htm
Melvin B Henley (R-5)	1305 S 16th St		Murray	42071	(270) 753-3855	(502) 564-8100		henlem02@charter.net
Jimmy Higdon (R-24)	507 W Main		Lebanon	40033	(270) 692-3881	(502) 564-8100	(270) 692-1111	jimmyhigdon@alltel.net
Charlie Hoffman (D-62)	406 Bourbon St		Georgetown	40324	(502) 863-4807	(502) 564-8100		charlie.hoffman@lrc.ky.gov
Jeffrey Hoover (R-83)		PO Box 985	Jamestown	42629	(270) 343-5588	(502) 564-5413	(270) 343-5590	jeff.hoover@lrc.ky.gov
Dennis Horlander (D-40)	1806 Farnsley Rd		Shively	40216	(502) 447-2498	(502) 564-8100		dennis.horlander@lrc.ky.gov
Joni Jenkins (D-44)	2010 O'Brien Ct		Shively	40216	(502) 447-4324	(502) 564-8100		jonijenkins@aol.com
Dennis Keene (D-67)	1040 Johns Hill Rd		Wilder	41076	(859) 912-2096	(502) 564-8100		http://lrc.ky.gov/mailform_temp/h067.htm
Thomas Robert Kerr (R-64)	5415 Old Taylor Mill Rd		Taylor Mill	41015	(859) 431-2222	(502) 564-8100	(859) 428-1864	thomas.kerr@lrc.ky.gov
Jimmie Lee (D-25)	901 Dogwood Dr		Elizabethtown	42701	(270) 765-6222	(502) 564-8100	(859) 259-2927	jimmie.lee@lrc.ky.gov or jolu25@msn.com
Stan Lee (R-45)		PO Box 2090	Lexington	40588	(859) 252-2202	(502) 564-8100		stan.lee@lrc.ky.gov
Gross C Lindsay (D-11)		PO Box 19	Henderson	42419	(270) 827-9824	(502) 564-8100		http://lrc.ky.gov/mailform/h011.htm
Gerry Lynn (R-27)	46 Lakeshore Pkwy		Brandenburg	40108	(270) 422-4343	(502) 564-8100	(270) 422-1622	http://lrc.ky.gov/mailform_temp/h027.htm
Paul H Marcotte (R-60)	10674 Palestine Dr		Union	41091	(859) 384-1097	(502) 564-8100		http://lrc.ky.gov/mailform/h060.htm
Mary Lou Marzian (D-34)	2007 Tyler Ln		Louisville	40205	(502) 451-5032	(502) 564-8100		marylou.marzian@lrc.ky.gov
Thomas M McKee (D-78)	1053 Cook Rd		Cynthiana	41031	(859) 234-5879	(502) 564-8100	(859) 234-3332	tom.mckee@lrc.ky.gov
Charles (Chuck) Meade (D-95)		PO Box 283	McDowell	41617	(606) 285-0196	(502) 564-8100	(606) 874-9102	http://lrc.ky.gov/mailform/h095.htm
Reginald K Meeks (D-42)		PO Box 757	Louisville	40201	(502) 852-3042	(502) 564-8100		srmeeks42@aol.com
Charles Miller (D-28)	3608 Gateview Cir		Louisville	40272	(502) 937-7788	(502) 564-8100	(502) 749-7815	charles.miller@lrc.ky.gov
Harry Moberly Jr (D-81)		PO Box 721	Richmond	40475	(859) 622-1501	(502) 564-8100		harry.moberly@lrc.ky.gov
Russ Mobley (R-51)	900 Holly St		Campbellsville	42718	(270) 789-5266	(502) 564-8100		russ.mobley@lrc.ky.gov
Brad Montell (R-58)	543 Main St	PO Box 1016	Shelbyville	40066	(502) 633-7017	(502) 564-8100		brad.montell@lrc.ky.gov
Lonnie Napier (R-36)	302 Danville St		Lancaster	40444	(859) 792-2535	(502) 564-8100		lonnie.napier@lrc.ky.gov
Rick G Nelson (D-87)	Rt 3 Box 686		Middlesboro	40965	(606) 337-0957	(502) 564-8100	(606) 248-8828	rick.nelson@lrc.ky.gov
Fred Nesler (D-2)	400 St Rt 440		Mayfield	42066	(270) 623-6184	(502) 564-8100		fred.nesler@lrc.ky.gov

KY HOUSE OF REPRESENTATIVES

PERSON (Party-District)	ADD1	ADD2	CITY	ZIP	PHONE	CAPITOL PHONE	FAX	EMAIL
Stephen R Nunn (R-23)	136 Fairway Pl		Glasgow	42141	(270) 651-4865	(502) 564-8100	(270) 651-5552	snunnstaterep@glasgow-ky.com
Darryl T Owens (D-43)	1300 W Broadway		Louisville	40203	(502) 584-6341	(502) 564-8100	(502) 584-6342	owenscommish@aol.com
Ruth Ann Palumbo (D-76)	10 Deepwood Dr		Lexington	40505	(859) 299-2597	(502) 564-8100		ruthann.palumbo@lrc.ky.gov
Don Pasley (D-73)	5805 Ecton Rd		Winchester	40391	(859) 749-2976	(502) 564-8100		http://lrc.ky.gov/mailform/h073.htm
Tanya Pullin (D-98)	1026 Johnson Ln		South Shore	41175	(606) 932-2505	(502) 564-8100	(502) 564-5640	http://lrc.ky.gov/mailform/h098.htm
Marie L Rader (R-89)		PO Box 323	McKee	40447	(606) 287-3300	(502) 564-8100	(606) 287-3300	marie.rader@lrc.ky.gov
Rick Rand (D-47)		PO Box 273	Bedford	40006	(502) 225-3286	(502) 564-8100	(502) 255-9911	http://lrc.ky.gov/mailform/h047.htm
Frank Rasche (D-3)	2929 Jefferson St		Paducah	42001	(270) 443-6206	(502) 564-8100	(270) 442-6565	http://lrc.ky.gov/mailform/h003.htm
Jon David Reinhardt (R-69)	323 Poplar Thicket Rd		Alexandria	41001	(859) 635-3455	(502) 564-8100		jondavid.reinhardt@lrc.ky.gov
Jody Richards (D-20)	817 Culpeper St		Bowling Green	42103	(270) 781-9946	(502) 564-2363	(270) 781-9963	jody.richards@lrc.ky.gov
Steven Riggs (D-31)	8108 Thornwood Rd		Louisville	40220	(502) 499-6050	(502) 564-8100	(502) 564-6543	http://lrc.ky.gov/mailform/h031.htm
Tom Riner (D-41)	1143 E Broadway		Louisville	40204	(502) 584-3639	(502) 564-8100		tom.riner@lrc.ky.gov
Steven J Rudy (R-1)	221 Mt Pleasant Rd		LaCenter	42056	(270) 462-3156	(502) 564-8100	(270) 462-3158	steven@rudysfarmcenter.com
Terry Shelton (R-19)	7725 N Jackson Hwy		Magnolia	42757	(270) 528-5654	(502) 564-8100	(270) 528-5654	http://lrc.ky.gov/mailform_temp/h019.htm
Charles L Siler (R-82)	3570 Tackett Creek Rd		Williamsburg	40769	(606) 549-0900	(502) 564-8100		charles.siler@lrc.ky.gov
Arnold Simpson (D-65)	112 W 11th St		Covington	41011	(859) 261-6577	(502) 564-8100		arsimp@yahoo.com
Ancel Smith (D-92)	1812 Wiley Fork Rd		Leburn	41831	(606) 785-3844	(502) 564-8100		http://lrc.ky.gov/mailform/h092.htm
Brandon Smith (R-84)	350 Kentucky Blvd		Hazard	41701	(606) 436-4526	(502) 564-8100	(606) 436-2398	http://lrc.ky.gov/mailform/h084.htm
John Will Stacy (D-71)		PO Box 135	West Liberty	41472	(606) 743-1516	(502) 564-8100	(606) 743-1516	
Kathy W Stein (D-75)	183 N Upper St		Lexington	40507	(859) 225-4269	(502) 564-8100	(859) 254-0491	kathy.stein@lrc.ky.gov
Jim Stewart (R-86)	141 KY 223		Flat Lick	40935	(606) 542-5210	(502) 564-8100		jim.stewart@lrc.ky.gov
Tommy Thompson (D-14)		PO Box 458	Owensboro	42302	(270) 926-1740	(502) 564-8100	(270) 685-3242	tommy.thompson@lrc.ky.gov
Tommy Turner (R-85)	175 Clifty Grove Church		Somerset	42501	(606) 274-5175	(502) 564-8100		tommy.turner@lrc.ky.gov
Kenneth H Upchurch (R-52)		PO Box 991	Monticello	42633	(606) 340-6490	(502) 564-4334		ken.upchurch@lrc.ky.gov
John Vincent (R-100)		PO Box 2528	Ashland	41105	(606) 329-8338	(502) 564-8100	(606) 325-8199	john.vincent@lrc.ky.gov
Jim Wayne (D-35)	1280 Royal Ave		Louisville	40204	(502) 456-4856	(502) 564-8100		http://lrc.ky.gov/mailform/h035.htm
John (Mike) Weaver (D-26)	131 Mayer Ln		Elizabethtown	42701	(270) 351-0958	(502) 564-8100		http://lrc.ky.gov/mailform/h026.htm
Robin L Webb (D-96)	404 W Main St		Grayson	41143	(606) 474-5380	(502) 564-8100		robin.webb@lrc.ky.gov
Susan Westrom (D-79)		PO Box 22778	Lexington	40522	(859) 266-7581	(502) 564-8100		susan.westrom@lrc.ky.gov
Rob Wilkey (D-22)	220 N Homestead Ct		Scottsville	42164	(800) 952-3454	(502) 564-8100	(270) 843-8607	robwilkey@aol.com
Addia Kathryn Wuchner (R-66)		PO Box 911	Burlington	41005	(859) 525-6698	(502) 564-8100	(859) 525-6698	http://lrc.ky.gov/mailform_temp/h066.htm
Brent Yonts (D-15)	232 Norman Cir		Greenville	42345	(270) 338-0816	(502) 564-8100	(270) 338-1639	brent.yonts@lrc.ky.gov

Source: The Kentucky Directory Gold Book 2005-2006

STATE GOVERNMENT & POLITICS
Judiciary

Robert F. Stephens (1927 - 2002)

In a speech to the Circuit Clerk's Association on Nov. 15, 1985, the late Robert F. Stephens, then serving as Chief Justice of the Kentucky Supreme Court, compared the famed Judicial Article Amendment to a camel. "As with most political documents, the amendment is a compromise of many views. It is frequently said that a camel with one hump is a horse designed by one committee, and a camel

Chief Justice Robert F. Stephens
Source: Kentucky Department
for Libraries & Archives

with two humps is a horse designed by two committees. One can temper this simile by recalling that the camel – with either one or two humps – is a durable and efficient beast of burden, capable of carrying heavy weights for long distances with little sustenance." An apt analogy for the Amendment that has created one of the best judicial systems in the world, according to Stephens. His speech was meant to remind those involved with the legal system the many battles that had been fought to bring about an effective system of justice in Ken-

tucky. Yes, problems still existed, but Stephens was quick to remember the struggle and continue to have hope for the future. Voters in the state passed the Judicial Article Amendment to the Kentucky Constitution on Nov. 4, 1975, after years of rejecting drafted bills and even a new Constitution. The Amendment gave the state its present Court of Justice, with four tiers and a central administration. It also stipulated the election of judges with law background, who are popularly elected by ballot and must adhere to a code of discipline lest they be suspended, removed or impeached. According to Stephens, where once "1,000 city and county courts were staffed with lay judges without any central administration, with disgraceful courtroom facilities, no secretarial or administrative help and yet constituting the only system of justice seen by 99 out of 100 citizens," the acceptance of the Judicial Article Amendment brought efficiency, timeliness and a greater sense of integrity and fair dealing. Efforts to allay the backlogs, disorganization and confusion had begun in the 1960s when the General Assembly drafted a new Constitution for the state that was rejected in November of 1966. Speakers' bureaus, seminars, polls and public relations campaigns were tools to educate and gauge support in the state for a new Amendment. But, it was all in vain as voters rejected two Constitutional Amendments during the 1973 general election. Back to the drawing board, lawmakers continued to convene, gather feedback from citizens and mold a new Amendment to meet the needs of Kentuckians. Lawyers were chosen from each county to educate its constituents. The summer fairs provided venues to reach voters. According to Stephens, the months from March of 1974 to November 1975 were spent educating as many people as possible and spreading the word about the new Amendment guaranteed to help ease the burden of Kentucky's court system. By a vote of 54.2 percent, the Amendment passed on Nov. 4, 1975. The result still stands today as a testament to hard work and a vision for the citizens of Kentucky.

Kentucky Supreme Court

Front row from left to right: Donald C Wintersheimer, Joseph E Lambert (Chief Justice), J William GravesBack row from left to right: William S Cooper, Martin E Johnstone, James Keller (retired), Will T Scott.
(Governor Fletcher appointed John Roach on June 10, 2005 to replace Justice James Keller)

1st District
Justice John William (Bill) Graves
Capitol Bldg Rm 216   222 Kentucky Ave
700 Capital Ave   PO Box 993
Frankfort 40601   Paducah 42003
(502) 564-4163   (270) 575-7039
FAX (502) 564-2665

2nd District
Justice William S Cooper
Capitol Bldg Rm 223   Hardin Co Justice Ctr
700 Capital Ave   120 E Dixie Ave
Frankfort 40601   Elizabethtown 42701
(502) 564-4159   (270) 766-5179
FAX (502) 564-2665

3rd District
Chief Justice Joseph E Lambert
Capitol Bldg Rm 231   101 Rockcastle Judicial Ctr
700 Capital Ave   PO Box 989
Frankfort 40601   Mt Vernon 40456
(502) 564-4161   (606) 256-9030
FAX (502) 564-1933

4th District
Justice Martin E Johnstone
Capitol Bldg Rm 201   700 W Jefferson St
700 Capital Ave   Ste 1000
Frankfort 40601   Louisville 40202
(502) 564-4157   (502) 595-3199
FAX (502) 564-2665

5th District
Justice John Roach
Capitol Bldg Rm 245   155 E Main St Ste 200
700 Capitol Ave   Lexington 40507
Frankfort 40601   (859) 246-2220
(502) 564-6753
FAX (502) 564-2665

6th District
Justice Donald C Wintersheimer
Capitol Bldg Rm 239   PO Box 387
700 Capital Ave   Covington 41012
Frankfort 40601   (859) 292-6300
(502) 564-4165
FAX (502) 564-2665

7th District
Justice Will T Scott
Capitol Bldg Rm 226   PO Box 1316
700 Capital Ave   Pikeville 41502
Frankfort 40601   (606) 432-2030
(502) 564-4168
FAX (502) 564-2665

Clerk of the Court
Susan Stokley Clary
Capitol Bldg Rm 235
700 Capital Ave
Frankfort 40601
(502) 564-5444
FAX (502) 564-2665
susanclary@kycourts.net

Kentucky Court of Appeals

1st Appellate District
Judge David C Buckingham
312 S 8th St
Murray KY 42071
(270) 753-4324
Judge Rick A Johnson
2380 St Rt 45 N
Mayfield KY 42066
(270) 247-1052
2nd Appellate District
Judge John D Minton Jr
Warren Co Justice Ctr
1001 Center St 2nd Fl Rm 204
Bowling Green KY 42101
(270) 746-7867
Judge Jeff S Taylor
Corporate Centre No A102, 401 Frederica St
Owensboro KY 42303
(270) 687-7116
3rd Appellate District
Judge Robert W Dyche III
National City Bank Bldg 4th Fl
400 S Main St, PO Box 5190
London KY 40745
(606) 864-7661
Judge Michael Henry
KY Court of Appeals
205 W Columbia St
Somerset KY 42501
(606) 677-4226
4th Appellate District
Judge William L Knopf
700 W Jefferson St Ste 1020
Louisville KY 40202
(502) 595-3440

Judge William E McAnulty Jr
700 W Jefferson St Ste 1010
Louisville KY 40202
(502) 595-3430
5th Appellate District
Judge Julia K Tackett
Tate Bldg Ste 140, 125 Lisle Industrial Ave
Lexington KY 40511
(859) 246-2734
Judge Laurance B VanMeter
1999 Richmond Rd Ste 5
Lexington KY 40502
(859) 246-2053
6th Appellate District
Judge Daniel T Guidugli
1 Moock Rd Ste 4
Newport KY 41071
(859) 291-9966
Judge Wilfrid A Schroder
2734 Chancellor Dr Ste 109
Covington KY 41017
(859) 292-6574
7th Appellate District
Chief Judge Sara W Combs, Chief Judge
323 E College Ave, PO Box 709
Stanton KY 40380
(606) 663-0651
Judge David Barber
2980 KY Rt 321
Prestonsburg KY 41653
(606) 886-0795
Clerk of the Court
George M Geoghegan III
360 Democrat Dr
Frankfort KY 40601 (502) 573-7920

Did you Know?

The Kentucky Supreme Court is the court of last resort and the final interpreter
of state law. It consists of seven justices that hear appeals of decisions from the
lower courts and issue decisions or "opinions" on cases. The Court of Appeals is
exactly what its title implies. Nearly all cases come to it on appeal from a lower
court. If a case is tried in District or Circuit court, and the losing parties involved
are not satisfied with the outcome, they may ask for a higher court
to review the correctness of the trial court's decision.

Source: Kentucky Court of Justice, www.kycourts.net

Circuit Judges

COUNTY	CIRCUIT	DIVISION	JUDGE	TITLE	PHONE
Adair	29th	1st Div	James G Weddle	Circuit Judge	(606) 787-6991
Allen	49th	1st Div	William R Harris	Circuit Judge	(270) 586-8058
Anderson	53rd	1st Div	Charles Hickman	Circuit Judge	(502) 633-3412
Ballard	1st	1st Div	William L Shadoan	Circuit Judge	(270) 335-5189
Barren	43rd	1st Div	Phillip Patton	Circuit Judge	(270) 651-2744
Barren	43rd	2nd Div	William Mitchell Nance	Family Court Judge	(270) 651-9923
Bath	21st	1st Div	William B Mains	Circuit Judge	(606) 784-5190
Bath	21st	2nd Div	Beth Lewis Maze	Circuit Judge	(859) 498-0488
Bell	44th	1st Div	James L Bowling Jr	Circuit Judge	(606) 337-5949
Boone	54th	1st Div	Anthony W Frohlich	Circuit Judge	(859) 586-6565
Boone	54th	2nd Div	Linda Rae Bramlage	Family Court Judge	(859) 334-3520
Bourbon	14th	1st Div	Robert G Johnson	Circuit Judge	(859) 873-3109
Bourbon	14th	2nd Div	Paul F Isaacs	Circuit Judge	(502) 863-4781
Boyd	32nd	1st Div	Marc I Rosen	Circuit Judge	(606) 739-5844
Boyd	32nd	2nd Div	C David Hagerman	Circuit Judge	(606) 739-6122
Boyle	50th	1st Div	Darren W Peckler	Circuit Judge	(859) 239-7009
Boyle	50th	2nd Div	Douglas Bruce Petrie	Family Court Judge	(859) 239-7090
Bracken	19th	1st Div	John W McNeill	Circuit Judge	(606) 735-3328
Breathitt	39th	1st Div	William Larry Miller	Circuit Judge	(606) 668-7590
Breckinridge	46th	1st Div	Sam H Monarch	Circuit Judge	(270) 756-6278
Breckinridge	46th	2nd Div	Robert A Miller	Circuit Judge	(270) 422-7800
Bullitt	55th	1st Div	Thomas L Waller	Circuit Judge	(502) 543-4776
Butler	38th	1st Div	Ronnie C Dortch	Circuit Judge	(270) 298-7250
Caldwell	56th	1st Div	Bill Cunningham	Circuit Judge	(270) 388-5182
Calloway	42nd	1st Div	Dennis R Foust	Circuit Judge	(270) 527-1480
Campbell	17th	1st Div	Julie Reinhardt Ward	Circuit Judge	(859) 292-6301
Campbell	17th	2nd Div	Fred A Stine V	Circuit Judge	(859) 292-6303
Campbell	17th	3rd Div	Michael D Foellger	Family Court Judge	(859) 292-6717
Carlisle	1st	1st Div	William L Shadoan	Circuit Judge	(270) 335-5189
Carroll	15th	1st Div	Stephen L Bates	Circuit Judge	(859) 824-7516
Carter	37th	1st Div	Samuel C Long	Circuit Judge	(606) 743-4075
Carter	37th	2nd Div	Kristi Hogg-Gossett	Family Court Judge	(606) 475-1801
Casey	29th	1st Div	James G Weddle	Circuit Judge	(606) 787-6991
Christian	3rd	1st Div	Edwin M White	Circuit Judge	(270) 889-6536
Christian	3rd	2nd Div	John L Atkins	Circuit Judge	(270) 889-6537
Christian	3rd	3rd Div	Judy A Hall	Family Court Judge	(270) 889-6038
Clark	25th	1st Div	Julia H Adams	Circuit Judge	(859) 737-7263
Clark	25th	2nd Div	William T Jennings	Circuit Judge	(859) 624-4750
Clark	25th	3rd Div	Jean Chenault Logue	Family Court Judge	(859) 737-7021
Clark	25th	4th Div	Jeffrey M Walson	Family Court Judge	(859) 737-7491
Clay	41st		Gene Clark	Family Court Judge	(606) 599-0948
Clay	41st	1st Div	R Cletus Maricle	Circuit Judge	(606) 598-5251
Clinton	40th	1st Div	Eddie C Lovelace	Circuit Judge	(606) 387-5986
Crittenden	5th		William E Mitchell	Family Court Judge	(270) 639-5094
Crittenden	5th	1st Div	C Rene' Williams	Circuit Judge	(270) 639-5506
Cumberland	40th	1st Div	Eddie C Lovelace	Circuit Judge	(606) 387-5986
Daviess	6th	1st Div	Henry M Griffin III	Circuit Judge	(270) 687-7226
Daviess	6th	2nd Div	Thomas O Castlen	Circuit Judge	(270) 687-7228
Edmonson	38th	1st Div	Ronnie C Dortch	Circuit Judge	(270) 298-7250
Elliott	37th	1st Div	Samuel C Long	Circuit Judge	(606) 743-4075
Elliott	37th	2nd Div	Kristi Hogg-Gossett	Family Court Judge	(606) 475-1801
Estill	23rd	1st Div	William W Trude Jr	Circuit Judge	(606) 723-3320
Fayette	22nd	1st Div	Timothy N Philpot	Family Circuit Judge	(859) 246-2703
Fayette	22nd	2nd Div	Gary D Payne	Circuit Judge	(859) 246-2214
Fayette	22nd	3rd Div	James Ishmel Jr	Circuit Judge	(859) 246-2218
Fayette	22nd	4th Div	Pamela R Goodwine	Circuit Judge	(859) 246-2216
Fayette	22nd	5th Div	Mary C Noble	Circuit Judge	(859) 246-2212
Fayette	22nd	6th Div	Jo Ann Wise	Family Court Judge	(859) 246-2786
Fayette	22nd	7th Div	Sheila R Isaac, Chief Judge	Circuit Judge	(859) 246-2531
Fayette	22nd	8th Div	Thomas L Clark	Circuit Judge	(859) 246-2533
Fayette	22nd	9th Div	Kimberly Nell Bunnell	Family Court Judge	(859) 246-2210
Fleming	19th	1st Div	John McNeil III	Circuit Judge	(606) 564-9736
Floyd	31st	1st Div	Danny P Caudill	Circuit Judge	(606) 889-1653
Floyd	31st	2nd Div	John David Caudill	Circuit Judge	(606) 889-1900
Floyd	31st	3rd Div	Julie Paxton	Family Court Judge	(606) 889-1676
Franklin	48th	1st Div	Roger L Crittenden	Circuit Judge	(502) 564-8383
Franklin	48th	2nd Div	William R Graham	Circuit Judge	(502) 564-8382
Franklin	48th	3rd Div	Orville Reed Rhorer	Family Court Judge	(502) 564-2278
Fulton	1st	1st Div	William L Shadoan	Circuit Judge	(270) 335-5189
Gallatin	54th	1st Div	Anthony Frohlich	Circuit Judge	(859) 334-3270
Garrard	13th	1st Div	Hunter Daugherty	Circuit Judge	(859) 885-6722
Grant	15th	1st Div	Stephen L Bates	Circuit Judge	(859) 824-7516
Graves	52nd	1st Div	Tim Stark	Circuit Judge	(270) 247-8726
Grayson	46th	1st Div	Sam H Monarch	Circuit Judge	(270) 756-6278
Grayson	46th	2nd Div	Robert A Miller	Circuit Judge	(270) 422-7800
Green	11th	1st Div	Douglas M George	Circuit Judge	(606) 336-3903
Greenup	20th	1st Div	Lewis Dunn Nicholls	Circuit Judge	(606) 473-7165
Hancock	38th	1st Div	Ronnie C Dortch	Circuit Judge	(270) 298-7250

Source: Kentucky Directory Gold Book 2005-2006

CIRCUIT JUDGES, CONTINUED

COUNTY	CIRCUIT	DIVISION	JUDGE	TITLE	PHONE
Hardin	9th	1st Div	Pamela Addington	Circuit Family Court Judge	(270) 766-5293
Hardin	9th	1st Div	Thomas Steven Bland	Circuit Family Court Judge	(270) 766-5003
Hardin	9th	2nd Div	Janet P Coleman	Circuit Judge	(270) 766-5039
Hardin	9th	3rd Div	Kelly Mark Easton	Circuit Judge	(270) 766-5259
Harlan	26th	1st Div	Ron (Ronnie) Johnson	Circuit Judge	(606) 573-3242
Harrison	18th	1st Div	Robert W McGinnis	Circuit Judge	(859) 234-3431
Harrison	18th	3rd Div	David Melcher	Family Court Judge	(859) 234-0190
Hart	10th	1st Div	Charles C Simms III	Circuit Judge	(270) 524-5135
Henderson	51st	1st Div	Stephen A Hayden	Circuit Judge	(270) 827-1295
Henderson	51st	2nd Div	Sheila Nunley-Farris	Family Court Judge	(270) 869-0460
Henry	12th	1st Div	Karen Conrad	Circuit Judge	(502) 222-2112
Henry	12th	2nd Div	Timothy Edward Feeley	Family Court Judge	(502) 222-2112
Hickman	1st	1st Div	William L Shadoan	Circuit Judge	(270) 335-5189
Hopkins	4th	1st Div	Charles W Boteler Jr	Circuit Judge	(270) 824-7422
Jackson	41st		Gene Clark	Family Court Judge	(606) 599-0948
Jackson	41st	1st Div	R Cletus Maricle	Circuit Judge	(606) 598-5251
Jefferson	30th	10th Div	Kathleen V Montano	Circuit Judge	(502) 595-4363
Jefferson	30th	11th Div	Geoffrey (Geoff) Morris	Circuit Judge	(502) 595-4400
Jefferson	30th	12th Div	Kenneth Conliffe	Circuit Judge	(502) 595-3012
Jefferson	30th	13th Div	Ann O'Malley Shake	Circuit Judge	(502) 595-3011
Jefferson	30th	17th Div	Jerry J Bowles	Family Court Judge	(502) 595-4502
Jefferson	30th	18th Div	Paula Sherlock	Family Court Judge	(502) 595-4699
Jefferson	30th	19th Div	Stephen M George	Family Court Judge	(502) 595-4998
Jefferson	30th	1st Div	Barry Willett	Circuit Judge	(502) 595-4054
Jefferson	30th	1st Div	Joan L Byer	Family Court Judge	(502) 595-4656
Jefferson	30th	20th Div	Eleanore M Garber	Family Court Judge	(502) 595-4988
Jefferson	30th	21st Div	Hugh Smith Haynie Jr	Family Court Judge	(502) 595-4996
Jefferson	30th	22nd Div	Kevin L Garvey, Chief Judge	Family Court Judge	(502) 595-4043
Jefferson	30th	23rd Div	Joseph W O'Reilly	Family Court Judge	(502) 595-4993
Jefferson	30th	2nd Div	James M Shake, Chief Judge	Circuit Judge	(502) 595-4062
Jefferson	30th	3rd Div	Lisabeth H Abramson	Circuit Judge	(502) 595-4919
Jefferson	30th	3rd Div	Patricia FitzGerald Walker	Family Court Judge	(502) 595-4326
Jefferson	30th	4th Div	Denise M Clayton	Circuit Judge	(502) 595-4604
Jefferson	30th	4th Div	Patricia W Fitzgerald	Family Court Judge	(502) 595-4392
Jefferson	30th	5th Div	Joan L Byer	Family Court Judge	(502) 595-4988
Jefferson	30th	5th Div	Stephen P Ryan	Circuit Judge	(502) 595-4799
Jefferson	30th	6th Div	Martin F McDonald	Circuit Judge	(502) 595-4311
Jefferson	30th	7th Div	Stephen K Mershon	Circuit Judge	(502) 595-4103
Jefferson	30th	8th Div	Thomas B Wine	Circuit Judge	(502) 595-4294
Jefferson	30th	9th Div	Dolly Berry	Family Court Judge	(502) 595-4998
Jefferson	30th	9th Div	Dolly W Berry	Circuit Judge	(502) 595-4969
Jefferson	30th	9th Div	Judith McDonald-Burkman	Circuit Judge	(502) 595-4356
Jessamine	13th	1st Div	Hunter Daugherty	Circuit Judge	(859) 885-6722
Johnson	24th		John David Preston	Family Court Judge	(606) 788-7154
Johnson	24th	1st Div	Daniel R (Dan) Sparks	Circuit Judge	(606) 788-7157
Kenton	16th	1st Div	Steven R Jaeger	Circuit Judge	(859) 292-6538
Kenton	16th	2nd Div	Douglas M Stephens	Circuit Judge	(859) 292-6533
Kenton	16th	3rd Div	Gregory M Bartlett	Circuit Judge	(859) 292-6530
Kenton	16th	4th Div	Patricia M Summe	Circuit Judge	(859) 292-6531
Knott	36th	1st Div	Kim Cornett Childers	Circuit Judge	(606)785-3842
Knott	36th	3rd Div	Julie Paxton	Family Court Judge	(606) 886-9901
Knox	27th	1st Div	Gregory A Lay	Circuit Judge	(859) 625-0601
Knox	27th	2nd Div	Roderick Messer	Circuit Judge	(606) 878-8111
Larue	10th	1st Div	Charles C Simms III	Circuit Judge	(270) 358-4633
Laurel	27th	1st Div	Gregory A Lay	Circuit Judge	(859) 625-0601
Laurel	27th	2nd Div	Roderick Messer	Circuit Judge	(606) 878-8111
Lawrence	24th	1st Div	John David Preston	Family Court Judge	(606) 789-6701
Lawrence	24th	2nd Div	Daniel R (Dan) Sparks	Circuit Judge	(606) 789-6861
Lee	23rd	1st Div	William W Trude Jr	Circuit Judge	(606) 723-3320
Leslie	41st	1st Div	R Cletus Maricle	Circuit Judge	(606) 598-5251
Leslie	41st	2nd Div	Gene Clark	Family Court Judge	(606) 599-0948
Letcher	47th	1st Div	Samuel T Wright III	Circuit Judge	(606) 633-2259
Lewis	20th	1st Div	Lewis Dunn Nicholls	Circuit Judge	(606) 473-7165
Lincoln	28th	1st Div	David A Tapp	Circuit Judge	(606) 677-4091
Lincoln	28th	2nd Div	Jeffrey T Burdette	Circuit Judge	(606) 677-4098
Lincoln	28th	3rd Div	Debra Hembree Lambert	Family Court Judge	(606) 677-4186
Livingston	56th	1st Div	Bill Cunningham	Circuit Judge	(270) 388-5182
Logan	7th	1st Div	Tyler Gill	Circuit Judge	(270) 726-2242
Lyon	56th	1st Div	Bill Cunningham	Circuit Judge	(270) 388-5182
Madison	25th	1st Div	Julia H Adams	Circuit Judge	(859) 737-7263
Madison	25th	2nd Div	William T Jennings	Circuit Judge	(859) 624-4750
Madison	25th	3rd Div	Jean Chenault Logue	Family Court Judge	(859) 625-0601
Madison	25th	4th Div	Jeffrey M Walson	Family Court Judge	(859) 737-7491
Magoffin	36th	1st Div	Kim Cornett Childers	Circuit Judge	(606) 785-9273
Magoffin	36th	3rd Div	Julie M Paxton	Family Court Judge	(606) 886-9901
Marion	11th	1st Div	Doughlas M George	Circuit Judge	(859) 336-3903
Marshall	42nd	1st Div	Dennis R Foust	Circuit Judge	(270) 527-1480
Martin	24th	1st Div	John David Preston	Family Court Judge	(606) 789-6701

CIRCUIT JUDGES, CONTINUED

COUNTY	CIRCUIT	DIVISION	JUDGE	TITLE	PHONE
Martin	24th	2nd Div	Daniel R (Dan) Sparks	Circuit Judge	(606) 789-6861
Mason	19th	1st Div	John McNeil	Circuit Judge	(606) 564-9736
McCracken	2nd	1st Div	R Jeffrey Hines	Circuit Judge	(270) 575-7292
McCracken	2nd	2nd Div	Craig Z Clymer	Circuit Judge	(270) 575-7400
McCracken	2nd	3rd Div	Cynthia Sanderson	Family Court Judge	(270) 575-7133
McCreary	34th	1st Div	Jerry D Winchester	Circuit Judge	(606) 528-3013
McCreary	34th	2nd Div	Paul E Braden	Circuit Judge	(606) 528-3013
McLean	45th	1st Div	David H Jernigan	Circuit Judge	(270) 338-5930
Meade	46th	1st Div	Sam H Monarch	Circuit Judge	(270) 756-6278
Meade	46th	2nd Div	Robert A Miller	Circuit Judge	(270) 422-7800
Menifee	21st	1st Div	William B Mains	Circuit Judge	(606) 784-5190
Menifee	21st	2nd Div	Beth Lewis Maze	Circuit Judge	(859) 498-0488
Mercer	50th	1st Div	Darren W Peckler	Circuit Judge	(859) 239-7009
Mercer	50th	2nd Div	Bruce Petrie	Family Court Judge	(859) 239-7291
Metcalfe	43rd	1st Div	Phillip Patton	Circuit Judge	(270) 651-2744
Metcalfe	43rd	2nd Div	William Mitchell Nance	Family Court Judge	(270) 651-9923
Monroe	40th	1st Div	Eddie C Lovelace	Circuit Judge	(606) 387-5986
Montgomery	21st	1st Div	William B Mains	Circuit Judge	(606) 784-5190
Montgomery	21st	2nd Div	Beth Lewis Maze	Circuit Judge	(859) 498-0488
Morgan	37th		Kristi Hogg-Gossett	Family Court Judge	(606) 475-1801
Morgan	37th	1st Div	Samuel C Long	Circuit Judge	(606) 743-4075
Muhlenberg	45th	1st Div	David H Jernigan	Circuit Judge	(270) 338-5930
Nelson	10th	1st Div	Charles C Simms III	Circuit Judge	(502) 348-7313
Nicholas	18th	1st Div	Robert W McGinnis	Circuit Judge	(859) 234-3431
Nicholas	18th	3rd Div	David Melcher	Family Court Judge	(859) 234-0190
Ohio	38th	1st Div	Ronnie C Dortch	Circuit Judge	(270) 298-7250
Oldham	12th	1st Div	Karen A Conrad	Family Court Judge	(502) 222-2112
Oldham	12th	1st Div	Karen Conrad	Circuit Judge	(502) 222-2026
Oldham	12th	2nd Div	Timothy Edward Feeley	Family Court Judge	(502) 222-2112
Owen	15th	1st Div	Stephen L Bates	Circuit Judge	(859) 824-7516
Owsley	23rd	1st Div	William W Trude Jr	Circuit Judge	(606) 723-3320
Pendleton	18th	1st Div	Robert W McGinnis	Circuit Judge	(859) 234-3431
Pendleton	18th	3rd Div	David Melcher	Family Court Judge	(859) 234-1918
Perry	33rd	1st Div	William (Bill) Engle III	Circuit Judge	(606) 435-6004
Pike	35th	1st Div	Eddy Coleman	Circuit Judge	(606) 433-7554
Pike	35th	2nd Div	Steven D Combs	Circuit Judge	(606) 433-7551
Pike	35th	3rd Div	Larry Thompson	Family Court Judge	(606) 433-7061
Powell	39th	1st Div	William Larry Miller	Circuit Judge	(606) 668-7590
Pulaski	28th	1st Div	David A Tapp	Circuit Judge	(606) 677-4091
Pulaski	28th	2nd Div	Jeffrey T Burdette	Circuit Judge	(606) 677-4098
Pulaski	28th	3rd Div	Debra Lambert	Family Court Judge	(606) 677-4186
Robertson	18th	1st Div	Robert W McGinnis	Circuit Judge	(859) 234-3431
Robertson	18th	3rd Div	David Melcher	Family Court Judge	(859) 234-1918
Rockcastle	28th	1st Div	David A Tapp	Circuit Judge	(606) 677-4091
Rockcastle	28th	2nd Div	Jeffrey T Burdette	Circuit Judge	(606) 677-4098
Rockcastle	28th	3rd Div	Debra Hembree Lambert	Family Court Judge	(606) 677-4186
Rowan	21st	1st Div	William B Mains	Circuit Judge	(606) 784-5190
Rowan	21st	2nd Div	Beth Lewis Maze	Circuit Judge	(859) 498-0488
Russell	57th	1st Div	Vernon Miniard Jr	Circuit Judge	(270) 343-2131
Scott	14th	1st Div	Robert G Johnson	Circuit Judge	(859) 873-3109
Scott	14th	2nd Div	Paul F Isaacs	Circuit Judge	(502) 863-4781
Shelby	53rd	1st Div	Charles R Hickman	Circuit Judge	(502) 633-3412
Simpson	49th	1st Div	William R Harris	Circuit Judge	(270) 586-8058
Spencer	53rd	1st Div	Charles R Hickman	Circuit Judge	(502) 633-3412
Taylor	11th	1st Div	Douglas M George	Circuit Judge	(859) 336-3903
Taylor	11th	2nd Div	Allen Ray Bertram	Circuit Judge	(270) 465-6603
Todd	7th	1st Div	Tyler Gill	Circuit Judge	(270) 726-2242
Trigg	56th	1st Div	Bill Cunningham	Circuit Judge	(270) 388-5182
Trimble	12th	1st Div	Karen Conrad	Circuit Judge	(502) 222-1692
Trimble	12th	1st Div	Karen Conrad	Family Court Judge	(502) 222-1692
Trimble	12th	2nd Div	Timothy Edward Feeley	Family Court Judge	(502) 222-2490
Union	5th	1st Div	C Rene' Williams	Circuit Judge	(270) 667-9318
Union	5th	2nd Div	William E Mitchell	Family Court Judge	(270) 639-5094
Warren	8th	1st Div	Steve Wilson	Circuit Judge	(270) 746-7412
Warren	8th	2nd Div	John Grise	Circuit Judge	(270) 746-7408
Warren	8th	3rd Div	Margaret R Huddleston	Family Court Judge	(270) 746-7144
Washington	11th	1st Div	Douglas M George	Circuit Judge	(859) 336-3903
Wayne	57th	1st Div	Vernon Miniard Jr	Circuit Judge	(270) 343-2131
Webster	5th	1st Div	C Rene' Williams	Circuit Judge	(270) 667-9318
Webster	5th	2nd Div	William E Mitchell	Family Court Judge	(270) 639-5094
Whitley	34th	1st Div	Jerry D Winchester	Circuit Judge	(606) 528-3013
Whitley	34th	2nd Div	Paul E Braden	Circuit Judge	(606) 528-8996
Wolfe	39th	1st Div	William Larry Miller	Circuit Judge	(606) 668-7590
Woodford	14th	1st Div	Robert G Johnson	Circuit Judge	(859) 873-3109
Woodford	14th	2nd Div	Paul F Isaacs	Circuit Judge	(502) 863-4781

Source: Kentucky Directory Gold Book 2005-2006

District Judges

COUNTY	DISTRICT	DIVISION	DISTRICT JUDGE	PHONE
Adair	29th	1st Div	Roger P Elliott	(606) 787-6761
Allen	49th	1st Div	Frank H Wakefield II	(270) 586-8717
Anderson	53rd	1st Div	Linda S Armstrong	(502) 633-4130
Anderson	53rd	2nd Div	Michael Harrod	(502) 633-6313
Ballard	59th	1st Div	Louis Keith Myers	(270) 335-5138
Barren	43rd	1st Div	Barlow Ropp	(270) 651-9839
Bath	21st	2nd Div	John R Cox	(606) 784-6888
Bath	21st	1st Div	William (Bill) E Lane	(859) 498-6622
Bell	44th	1st Div	Robert Vincent Costanzo	(606) 337-1149
Boone	54th	2nd Div	Charles T Moore	(859) 334-2230
Boone	54th	1st Div	Michael P Collins	(859) 334-2230
Bourbon	14th	1st Div	Mary Jane Wilhoit Phelps	(859) 879-9871
Bourbon	14th	2nd Div	Vanessa Dickson	(859) 987-5562
Boyd	32nd	1st Div	George W Davis III	(606) 739-5444
Boyd	32nd	2nd Div	Gerald Brock Reams Jr	(606) 739-5525
Boyle	50th	2nd Div	Jeff L Dotson	(859) 734-6343
Bracken	19th	1st Div	William (Todd) Walton	(606) 845-1037
Breathitt	39th	1st Div	Kenny Profitt	(606) 663-4123
Breckinridge	46th	2nd Div	Shan Embry	(270) 259-5890
Breckinridge	46th	1st Div	Tom Lively	(270) 259-6785
Bullitt	55th	2nd Div	A Bailey Taylor	(502) 543-2243
Bullitt	55th	1st Div	Rebecca S Ward	(502) 543-2243
Butler	38th	2nd Div	John M McCarty	(270) 298-3223
Butler	38th	1st Div	Renona Carol Browning	(270) 298-3223
Caldwell	56th	2nd Div	Jill Clark	(270) 522-7979
Caldwell	56th	1st Div	William G McCaslin	(270) 365-6656
Calloway	42nd	1st Div	Jeanne Carroll	(270) 753-0059
Campbell	17th	1st Div	Gregory T Popovich	(859) 292-6322
Campbell	17th	3rd Div	Karen A Thomas	(859) 292-6322
Carlisle	59th	1st Div	Louis K Myers	(270) 335-5138
Carroll	15th	1st Div	James L Purcell	(502) 732-5880
Carroll	15th	2nd Div	Thomas M Funk	(859) 824-7516
Carter	37th	1st Div	Kimberly I Gevedon	(606) 473-3866
Casey	29th	1st Div	Roger P Elliott	(606) 787-6761
Christian	3rd	2nd Div	Arnold B Lynch	(270) 889-6544
Christian	3rd	1st Div	James G Adams Jr	(270) 889-6544
Clark	25th	3rd Div	Bill Clouse	(859) 624-4719
Clark	25th	2nd Div	Brandy Oliver Brown	(859) 624-4719
Clay	41st	2nd Div	Oscar Gayle House	(606) 598-6170
Clay	41st	1st Div	Renee H Muncy	(606) 672-3350
Clinton	40th	2nd Div	James (Mike) Lawson	(606) 387-8181
Clinton	40th	1st Div	Robyn Williams	(606) 387-7008
Crittenden	5th	1st Div	Tommy Simpson	(270) 639-5506
Cumberland	60th	2nd Div	Steve D Hurt	(270) 864-5600
Daviess	6th	2nd Div	David C Payne	(270) 687-7214
Daviess	6th	3rd Div	Joseph (Joe) Castlen III	(270) 687-7217
Daviess	6th	1st Div	Lisa Jones	(270) 687-7216
Edmonson	38th	2nd Div	John M McCarty	(270) 927-8800
Edmonson	38th	1st Div	Ranona Carol Browning	(270) 298-3223
Elliott	37th	1st Div	Kimberly I Gevedon	(606) 473-3866
Estill	23rd	1st Div	Ralph E McClanahan II	(606) 723-2000
Fayette	22nd	4th Div	David F Hayse	(859) 246-2247
Fayette	22nd	1st Div	Joseph Bouvier	(859) 246-2247
Fayette	22nd	3rd Div	Maria Ransdell	(859) 246-2247
Fayette	22nd	6th Div	Megan Lake Thornton	(859) 246-2247
Fayette	22nd	2nd Div	Thomas Bruce Bell	(859) 246-2247
Fleming	19th	1st Div	William (Todd) Walton	(606) 845-1037
Floyd	31st	2nd Div	Eric D Hall	(606) 889-1661
Floyd	31st	1st Div	James R Allen	(606) 889-1816
Franklin	48th	1st Div	Thomas D Wingate	(502) 564-7073
Franklin	48th	2nd Div	William (Guy) Hart Jr	(502) 564-7073
Fulton	1st	1st Div	Hunter B Whitesell II	(270) 236-2839
Gallatin	54th	2nd Div	Charles T Moore	(859) 334-2230
Gallatin	54th	1st Div	Michael Collins	(859) 334-2230
Garrard	13th	1st Div	Bill Oliver	(859) 885-5615
Garrard	13th	2nd Div	Janet Carroll Booth	(859) 885-5615
Grant	15th	1st Div	James L Purcell	(859) 824-0189
Grant	15th	2nd Div	Thomas M Funk	(859) 824-0189
Graves	52nd	1st Div	Deborah Hawkins Crooks	(270) 247-0580
Grayson	46th	2nd Div	Shan Embry	(270) 259-5890
Grayson	46th	1st Div	Tom Lively	(270) 259-6785
Green	11th	2nd Div	Connie Phillips	(270) 465-8424
Green	11th	1st Div	James L Avritt Jr	(270) 699-9951
Greenup	20th	1st Div	Robert B Conley	(606) 473-6339
Hancock	38th	2nd Div	John M McCarty	(270) 298-3223
Hancock	38th	1st Div	Renona C Browning	(270) 298-3223
Hardin	9th	1st Div	John David Simcoe	(270) 766-5004
Hardin	9th	2nd Div	Kimberly Winkenhofer Shumate	(270) 766-5005

DISTRICT JUDGES, CONTINUED

COUNTY	DISTRICT	DIVISION	DISTRICT JUDGE	PHONE
Harlan	26th	1st Div	Phillip A Hamm	(606) 573-7209
Harrison	18th	2nd Div	William D Probus	(859) 234-1918
Hart	10th	1st Div	Clyde Derek Reed	(270) 358-9501
Henderson	51st	2nd Div	Kenton J Watson	(270) 826-4755
Henderson	51st	1st Div	Robert K Wiederstein	(270) 826-4755
Henry	12th	1st Div	Jerry D Crosby	(502) 222-7447
Henry	12th	2nd Div	Jerry D Crosby	(502) 222-7447
Hickman	1st	1st Div	Hunter B Whitesell II	(270) 236-2839
Hopkins	4th	2nd Div	Robert F Soder	(270) 824-7512
Hopkins	4th	1st Div	W Logan Calvert	(270) 824-7513
Jackson	41st	2nd Div	Oscar Gayle House	(606) 598-6170
Jackson	41st	1st Div	Renee H Muncy	(606) 672-3350
Jefferson	30th	12th Div	Angela Bisig	(502) 595-3013
Jefferson	30th	15th Div	Anne Haynie	(502) 595-4997
Jefferson	30th	16th Div	Audra J Eckerle	(502) 595-4990
Jefferson	30th	3rd Div	Claude Prather	(502) 595-4610
Jefferson	30th	8th Div	Deborah Deweese	(502) 595-4696
Jefferson	30th	5th Div	Donald E Armstrong Jr	(502) 595-4632
Jefferson	30th	17th Div	Eleanore M Garber	(502) 595-4988
Jefferson	30th	18th Div	Hugh Smith Haynie Jr	(502) 595-4996
Jefferson	30th	22nd Div	Jacquelyn Poole Eckert	(502) 595-4983
Jefferson	30th	19th Div	Janice P Martin	(502) 595-4999
Jefferson	30th	13th Div	Joan (Toni) A Stringer	(502) 595-4960
Jefferson	30th	21st Div	Joseph W O'Reilly	(502) 595-4993
Jefferson	30th	23rd Div	Judith Bartholomew	(502) 595-4162
Jefferson	30th	9th Div	Kathleen Voor Montano	(502) 595-4699
Jefferson	30th	20th Div	Kevin L Garvey	(502) 595-4043
Jefferson	30th	2nd Div	Kevin W Delahanty	(502) 595-4957
Jefferson	30th	11th Div	Matthew K Eckert	(502) 595-4992
Jefferson	30th	4th Div	Michele Stengel	(502) 595-4989
Jefferson	30th	1st Div	Paula Fitzgerald	(502) 595-4994
Jefferson	30th	6th Div	Sean R Delahanty	(502) 595-4991
Jefferson	30th	10th Div	Sheila Anne Collins	(502) 595-4995
Jefferson	30th	14th Div	Stephen M George	(502) 595-4998
Jefferson	30th	7th Div	William (Bill) Ryan	(502) 595-4611
Jessamine	13th	1st Div	Bill Oliver	(859) 885-5615
Jessamine	13th	2nd Div	Janet Carroll Booth	(859) 885-5615
Johnson	24th	2nd Div	John Kevin Holbrook	(606) 788-7163
Johnson	24th	1st Div	Susan M Johnson	(606) 788-7163
Kenton	16th	1st Div	Ann Ruttle	(859) 292-6576
Kenton	16th	3rd Div	Douglas J Grothaus	(859) 292 -6576
Kenton	16th	2nd Div	Frank Trusty II	(859) 292-6561
Kenton	16th	4th Div	Martin J Sheehan	(859) 292-6561
Knott	36th	1st Div	Dennis B Prater	(606) 785-3078
Knox	27th	1st Div	John Knox Mills	(606) 864-7241
Knox	27th	2nd Div	Michael Caperton	(606) 864-7241
Larue	10th	1st Div	Clyde Derek Reed	(270) 358-9501
Laurel	27th	1st Div	John Knox Mills	(606) 864-7241
Laurel	27th	2nd Div	Michael Caperton	(606) 864-7241
Lawrence	24th	2nd Div	John Kevin Holbrook	(606) 789-8636
Lawrence	24th	1st Div	Susan M Johnson	(606) 789-8636
Lee	23rd	1st Div	Ralph E McClanahan II	(606) 723-2000
Leslie	41st	2nd Div	Oscar Gayle House	(606) 598-6170
Leslie	41st	1st Div	Renee H Muncy	(606) 672-3350
Letcher	47th	1st Div	James (Jim) T Wood Jr	(606) 633-4222
Lewis	20th	1st Div	Robert B Conley	(606) 473-6339
Lincoln	13th	1st Div	Bill Oliver	(606) 885-5615
Lincoln	13th	2nd Div	Janet Carroll Booth	(859) 885-5615
Livingston	56th	2nd Div	Jill Clark	(270) 522-7979
Livingston	56th	1st Div	William G McCaslin	(270) 365-6656
Logan	7th	1st Div	Sue Carol Browning	(270) 726-8080
Lyon	56th	2nd Div	Jill Clark	(270) 522-7979
Lyon	56th	1st Div	William G McCaslin	(270) 365-6656
Madison	25th	3rd Div	Bill Clouse	(859) 624-4719
Madison	25th	2nd Div	Brandy Oliver Brown	(859) 624-4719
Magoffin	36th	1st Div	Dennis B Prater	(606) 785-3078
Marion	11th	2nd Div	Connie Phillips	(270) 465-8424
Marion	11th	1st Div	James L Avritt Jr	(270) 699-9951
Marshall	58th	1st Div	Jack M Telle	(270) 527-3390
Martin	24th	2nd Div	John Kevin Holbrook	(606) 789-8636
Martin	24th	1st Div	Susan M Johnson	(606) 789-8636
Mason	19th	1st Div	William (Todd) Walton	(606) 564-8178
McCracken	2nd	2nd Div	Bard Kevin Brian	(270) 575-7261
McCracken	2nd	1st Div	Donna L Dixon	(270) 575-7261
McCreary	34th	1st Div	Cathy E Prewitt	(606) 528-4430
McCreary	34th	2nd Div	Daniel Ballou	(606) 549-5669
McLean	45th	1st Div	Brian W Wiggins	(270) 273-3966
Meade	46th	2nd Div	Shan Embry	(270) 259-5890

DISTRICT JUDGES, CONTINUED

COUNTY	DISTRICT	DIVISION	DISTRICT JUDGE	PHONE
Meade	46th	1st Div	Tom Lively	(270) 259-6785
Menifee	21st	2nd Div	John R Cox	(606) 784-6888
Menifee	21st	1st Div	William (Bill) E Lane	(859) 498-6622
Mercer	50th	1st Div	Jeff Dotson	(859) 734-6343
Metcalfe	43rd	1st Div	Barlow Ropp	(270) 651-9839
Monroe	60th	2nd Div	Steve D Hurt	(270) 864-5600
Montgomery	21st	2nd Div	John R Cox	(859) 784-6888
Montgomery	21st	1st Div	William (Bill) E Lane	(859) 498-6622
Morgan	37th	1st Div	Kimberly I Gevedon	(606) 473-3866
Muhlenberg	45th	1st Div	Brian Wiggins	(270) 338-0997
Nelson	57th	1st Div	Robert W Heaton	(502) 348-2012
Nicholas	18th	2nd Div	William D Probus	(859) 234-1918
Ohio	38th	2nd Div	John M McCarty	(270) 298-3223
Ohio	38th	1st Div	Ranona Carol Browning	(270) 298-3223
Oldham	12th	1st Div	Diana Wheeler	(502) 222-7447
Oldham	12th	2nd Div	Jerry D Crosby	(502) 222-7447
Owen	15th	1st Div	James L Purcell	(859) 824-0189
Owen	15th	2nd Div	Thomas M Funk	(859) 824-0189
Owsley	23rd	1st Div	Ralph E McClanahan II	(606) 723-2000
Pendleton	18th	2nd Div	William D Probus	(859) 234-1918
Perry	33rd	1st Div	Leigh Anne Stephens	(606) 435-6007
Pike	35th	1st Div	Darrel Mullins	(606) 433-7562
Pike	35th	2nd Div	Kelsey E Friend	(606) 433-7561
Powell	39th	1st Div	Kenny Profitt	(606) 663-4123
Pulaski	28th	2nd Div	David A Tapp	(606) 677-4112
Pulaski	28th	1st Div	Jeffery S Lawless	(606) 677-4112
Robertson	18th	2nd Div	William D Probus	(859) 234-1918
Rockcastle	28th	2nd Div	David A Tapp	(606) 677-4112
Rockcastle	28th	1st Div	Jeffery S Lawless	(606) 677-4112
Rowan	21st	2nd Div	John R Cox	(606) 784-6888
Rowan	21st	1st Div	William (Bill) E Lane	(859) 498-6622
Russell	40th	2nd Div	James (Mike) Lawson	(270) 343-2131
Russell	40th	1st Div	Robyn Williams	(606) 387-7008
Scott	14th	1st Div	Mary Jane Wilhoit Phelps	(859) 879-9871
Scott	14th	2nd Div	Vanessa M Dickson	(859) 987-5562
Shelby	53rd	1st Div	Linda S Armstrong	(502) 633-4130
Shelby	53rd	2nd Div	Michael Harrod	(502) 633-0486
Simpson	49th	1st Div	Frank Wakefield	(270) 586-8717
Spencer	53rd	1st Div	Linda S Armstrong	(502) 633-4130
Spencer	53rd	2nd Div	Michael Harrod	(502) 633-0486
Taylor	11th	2nd Div	Connie Phillips	(270) 465-8424
Taylor	11th	1st Div	James L Avritt Jr	(270) 699-9951
Todd	7th	1st Div	Sue Carol Browning	(270) 726-8080
Trigg	56th	2nd Div	Jill Clark	(270) 522-7979
Trigg	56th	1st Div	William G McCaslin	(270) 365-6656
Trimble	12th	1st Div	Diana Wheeler	(502) 222-7447
Trimble	12th	2nd Div	Jerry D Crosby	(502) 222-7447
Union	5th	1st Div	Tommy Simpson	(270) 639-5506
Warren	8th	2nd Div	Brent J Potter	(270) 746-7060
Warren	8th	1st Div	Catherine Rice Holderfield	(270) 746-7405
Warren	8th	3rd Div	Sam C Potter Jr	(270) 746-7028
Washington	11th	2nd Div	Connie Phillips	(270) 465-8424
Washington	11th	1st Div	James L Avritt Jr	(270) 699-9951
Wayne	40th	2nd Div	James (Mike) Lawson	(270) 343-2131
Wayne	40th	1st Div	Robyn Williams	(606) 387-7008
Webster	5th	1st Div	Tommy Simpson	(270) 639-5506
Whitley	34th	1st Div	Cathy E Prewitt	(606) 528-4430
Whitley	34th	2nd Div	Daniel Ballou	(606) 549-5669
Wolfe	39th	1st Div	Kenny Profitt	(606) 663-4123
Woodford	14th	1st Div	Mary Jane Wilhoit Phelps	(859) 879-9871
Woodford	14th	2nd Div	Vanessa Dickson	(859) 987-5562

Source: Kentucky Directory Gold Book 2005-2006

Well, What about that?

FAMILY COURT — Kentucky voters gave Family Court a resounding victory in November 2002 when the constitutional amendment passed in all 120 counties with more than 75 percent of the vote. Family Court judges handle all family law matters, like dissolution of marriage, child custody, support and visitation, paternity, adoption, domestic violence, dependency, neglect and abuse. ...

Source: Kentucky Court of Justice, www.kycourts.net

State Government & Politics
Kentucky Politics

Commentary by Al Cross

The moonlight falls the softest
　　in Kentucky;
The summer days come oftest
　　in Kentucky;
Friendship is the strongest,
Love's light glows the longest,
Yet wrong is always wrongest
　　in Kentucky.

. . . Orators are the grandest
　　in Kentucky.
Officials are the blandest
　　in Kentucky.
Boys are all the fliest.
Danger ever nighest,
Taxes are the highest
　　in Kentucky.

. . . Song birds are the sweetest
　　in Kentucky.
The thoroughbreds are fleetest
　　in Kentucky.
Mountains tower proudest,
Thunder peals the loudest,
The landscape is the grandest
And politics – the damndest,
　　in Kentucky.

First, middle and last stanzas of
In Kentucky, 1902,
by James Henry Mulligan

When Lexington's Judge Mulligan
wrote those words, Kentucky
politics certainly were
the damndest. Two years
before, Kentucky had
become the only state in
which a governor was the
victim of an assassin.
It is still the only such
state and still often
seems to be struggling
to relieve itself of other
dubious distinctions.
In 1902, Kentucky
still lacked the
"efficient"
system of
public

Statue of Gov. William Goebel, assassinated in 1900
Source: Sid Webb

education promised by the 1890 amendments to the state's constitution. Kentucky leaders couldn't figure out what to do with gambling, which was keeping its horse industry going as automobiles replaced equine transport. As a gambling ban was debated, so was Prohibition, which was to drive the state's other big "sin" industry underground a few years later.

Today, the constitution is much amended but still largely in effect, and it appears there is no longer momentum behind the 1990 education reforms that stemmed from the courts' interpretation of the efficiency clause. Some estimate gambling in adjoining states is draining a billion dollars a year from Kentucky, as political leaders dither about it. The "sin business" that kept rural Kentucky going for most of the 20th century, tobacco, is largely a spent force, with the end of federal quotas and price supports, and we have seen little impact from the cigarette-company money that was supposed to build a new farm economy.

Yet, if Kentucky's political system continues to fail its people, why? Perhaps because those in the system have become more concerned with staying in the system. Instead of the next election being about the sort of government we will have, our government is too often about what sort of election we will have.

Gov. Wendell H. Ford
Source: Kentucky Department of Tourism

Partisan competition and gridlock are ingrained in Kentucky. After the state elected its first Republican governor in 1895, the legislature deadlocked for 103 ballots and failed to elect a U.S. senator. But partisanship has become incessant in the modern era, in which legislators serve longer, party control of the General Assembly is divided, governors can succeed themselves, success comes most often to candidates well-funded by lobbying interests, and even legislative elections are big-money affairs driven by broadcast advertising.

Partisan competition took a back seat to competition between Democratic factions and gubernatorial campaigns in the 60 years from 1943 to 2003, when Kentucky elected only one Republican governor. That was Louie B. Nunn, who undercut his party and his own political career by pushing a 1968 sales-tax increase. The increase continued the pro-

gressive policies of Gov. Edward Breathitt (who had defeated him in 1963) and Gov. Bert Combs (who had succeeded former Gov. and Sen. Earle Clements as head of the progressive Democratic faction that opposed the faction headed by A.B. "Happy" Chandler, who was governor twice, U.S. senator and commissioner of baseball).

The bifactional system died with the 1979 primary. Millionaire John Y. Brown Jr. won it as an anti-politician with his new wife, former Miss America Phyllis George, defeating candidates from various elements of the party. Since then, Democratic primary candidates for governor have always had more than one opponent.

But while Democrats ruled Frankfort, Kentuckians voted Republican in 10 of the state's 14 elections for president and senator from 1952 to 1972. That reflected the essential conservatism of the state's voters, which Republicans capitalized upon after economic concerns were trumped by social issues – beginning with the 1973 U.S. Supreme Court decision legalizing abortion.

Kentucky is one of the most religious states – and Republicans gained further when national Democrats supported gay rights and a Democratic president and Democratic governor admitted infidelity in 1998 and 2002, respectively. Gun control was important, too, and was key in historically Democratic West Kentucky's election of its first Republican congressman, Ed Whitfield, in 1994. Republicans won on "God, gays and guns" and finally on tobacco, after Bill Clinton tried to regulate nicotine as a drug.

Clinton narrowly carried Kentucky twice, following a pattern that had begun in 1952, in which the state voted Republican for president unless a Southerner headed the Democratic ticket. That trend stopped cold in 2000, when Republican George W. Bush of Texas carried the state by 15 percentage points over Al Gore, who was nominally from Tennessee but to most Kentuckians seemed less like a neighbor than Clinton's vice president. The race in Kentucky would have been closer if Gore's campaign had not virtually abandoned the state.

In 2004, John Kerry lost the state by 20 points after making only minimal effort here, other than a successful fundraiser in Louisville (the only Kentucky place of any size he won).

THE MCCONNELL ERA

The architect of Republican success in Kentucky was Mitch McConnell, who narrowly won re-election as Jefferson County judge-executive in 1981 but used smart strategy and Ronald Reagan's national success in 1984 to oust a Democratic U.S. senator.

After McConnell won re-election in 1990, he guided Republicans to victories in federal races, beginning with the 1994 special election of Ron Lewis in the 2nd Congressional District, the forerunner of that fall's national GOP landslide. In regular elections since 1996, Republicans have won five of the state's six House seats, and in 1998 GOP Rep. Jim Bunning won the Senate seat of retiring Democrat and former governor, Wendell Ford.

The night McConnell escaped defeat in 1981, Ford smelled trouble. He told pollster Harrison Hickman, "We'll rue the day we didn't beat this guy." Three years later, McConnell narrowly ousted Walter "Dee" Huddleston, who had managed Ford's 1971 campaign for governor and had defeated Nunn for the Senate in 1972.

**Sen. Mitch McConnell and his wife,
U.S. Secretary of Labor
Elaine L. Chao**
Source: U.S. Senator Mitch McConnell

The hallmark of McConnell's campaign were ads in which bloodhounds searched for Huddleston, putting a humorous, memorable point on McConnell's argument that Huddleston had missed votes to make speeches. The ads were produced by Roger Ailes, who now runs Fox News. Their underlying argument, that Huddleston hadn't done much in the Senate, capitalized on the Democrat's relatively low profile and vote for the treaty that gave up the Panama Canal.

McConnell and Ford were opposites who never got along in their 14 years together in the Senate. Ford disliked McConnell's cold, technical and impersonal approach to politics, while the newcomer dismissed Ford as an old-fashioned hack who was never really happy in the Senate and longed to be governor again. In their final face-off, over competing tobacco bills in 1998, McConnell narrowly prevailed.

Ford was the whip, or assistant leader, of his party caucus in the Senate. McConnell now holds that post for the Republicans, and is in line to become Senate majority leader after the 2006 elections, when Sen. Bill Frist of Tennessee is expected to forgo a re-election bid in order to run for president. McConnell would break Ford's 24-year record service by a Kentucky senator if he is re-elected in 2008.

CURRENT STATE POLITICS

Even as Gov. Paul Patton was coasting to re-election in 1999 (the first governor in 200 years to serve two terms in succession, thanks to a 1992 constitutional amendment), his Democratic Party's control of Frankfort was broken when two state senators became Republicans. The GOP-controlled Senate, led by strong President David Williams of Burkesville, stymied Patton's agenda and killed a centerpiece Democratic program – public subsidies for gubernatorial slates that observed a campaign spending limit. McConnell, a leading national foe of such systems, had said it made a Republican victory in the 1999 race impossible, and openly told Republicans not to run.

Patton could not seek a third term in 2003, but hoped to oust Bunning in 2004. However, Patton's political career crashed when he first denied, and then tearfully admitted, infidelity with a political appointee whose nursing home later came under state investigation. Those were the underlying facts of the campaign theme of Republican Ernie Fletcher, who vowed to "clean up the mess in Frankfort."

Fletcher, a congressman from Lexington, ran with McConnell's encouragement and a McConnell running mate – top senatorial aide Hunter Bates, who pulled out after a judge ruled he had resided too much in Washington and not enough in Kentucky. Bates was replaced by U.S. Attorney Steve Pence, a McConnell appointee who won fame by prosecuting legislators and lobbyists in a big federal sting a decade earlier.

Fletcher won the primary over former Jefferson County Judge-Executive Rebecca Jackson, state Rep. Steve Nunn of Glasgow (Louie's son) and state Sen.

Virgil Moore of Leitchfield. He won a 10.1-percent-age-point victory over Attorney General Ben Chandler of Versailles, Happy's grandson, who had been adverse to Patton but found that it was not a good time to be a Democrat.

Chandler had also been hurt by the final flurry in the Democratic primary. About three and a half days before the polls opened, record-spending multimillionaire Bruce Lunsford ceased his campaign and threw his support to state House Speaker Jody Richards of Bowling Green, creating an anti-Chandler wave that nearly propelled Richards to a huge upset. Chandler looked weak, and a post-election poll showed him trailing Fletcher. He never caught up.

Gov. Ernie Fletcher, State of the Commonwealth Address 2004
Source: Kentucky Commerce Cabinet, Creative Services

In 2004, Chandler won a special election to fill Fletcher's congressional vacancy, defeating state Sen. Alice Forgy Kerr of Lexington.

FACTS AND FIGURES, THE PAST AND THE FUTURE

Kentucky's Republican trend has been reflected not just in elections, but in voter-registration statistics and polls of party preference, which are better long-term measurements than individual elections.

In 1983, Kentucky had nearly five registered Democrats for every two Republicans. Today, that ratio of 2.5-to-1 has declined to less than 1.6-to-1. Polls that ask voters to which party they feel closer, regardless of registration, no longer show a clear Democratic advantage.

The trend is not just the result of social issues and McConnell strategy, but the gradual passing of voters who came of age and formed their political beliefs during the Democratic presidencies of Franklin Roosevelt in 1933-1945 and Harry Truman, who succeeded Roosevelt and was elected in his own right in 1948, with Sen. Alben Barkley of Kentucky as vice president. Roosevelt's legacies, which included the federal tobacco program, rural electrification, the Tennessee Valley Authority, Corps of Engineers lakes and Social Security, were strong in Kentucky.

The impacts of those legacies and the Roosevelt generation were last felt in a big way in 1995, when Patton narrowly defeated Larry Forgy. The difference was a larger-than-expected turnout, driven by a well-funded and smartly run Democratic Party campaign that operated outside the spending limit and federalized the election.

Democrats' turnout and broadcast messages focused on supposed Republican threats to Roosevelt-era programs and featured Kentucky versions of the "Dole-Gingrich" ads that Clinton used to great effect, beginning a few weeks earlier. Clinton and Patton had the same media consultant, the late Bob Squier. The message was so important to Patton that on a final-week swing through southern Kentucky, where Democrats could not afford to buy spots on Nashville television, he preceded his speeches by playing his party's commercials on a TV set sitting in the bed of a pickup truck.

Forgy blamed his loss on Democratic chicanery – later, Patton's campaign manager (who had become his chief of staff) and his labor liaison were indicted on charges of getting unions to pay the labor aide to run a parallel campaign aimed at union members. Courts upheld the indictment, despite arguments – including one from McConnell – that the 1992 campaign law violated First Amendment freedoms. But Patton, already mired in a sex scandal, pardoned his allies, ending the criminal case.

In early 2005, Attorney General Greg Stumbo launched an investigation into the Merit System hiring practices of the Fletcher administration and indicted nine Fletcher appointees on misdemeanor charges of politicizing employment in the Merit System, the state's version of civil service.

In August 2005, Fletcher pardoned several of his indicted appointees. It appears that the probe by Stumbo, a Democrat, has lowered Fletcher's ratings, even among some Republicans. Some suggest Fletcher lacks a strong political base because he was elected in a way unlike almost any American governor – on the combination of a scandal in the other party and the organization and money provided by the rest of the state's congressional delegation.

Once again, you can say Kentucky's politics are the damndest.

Al Cross, veteran political writer, is the Executive Director of the Institute for Rural Journalism and Community Issues at the University of Kentucky.

STATE GOVERNMENT & POLITICS
Two Regional Perspectives

Eastern Kentucky
Ewell Balltrip

EAST KENTUCKIANS — FORGING A NEW REALITY IN THE REGION

East Kentuckians are forging a new reality in their sector of the commonwealth that's quite dif-

Congressman Hal Rogers at the Mountain Laurel Festival in Pine Mountain State Park, Pineville
Source: Kentucky Department of Tourism

ferent from the reputation long identified with the region. Driven by the goal of preserving the place they call "home," its culture and its heritage and propelling the region's economy into the global commercial arena, they're putting into action solutions to challenges that have restricted East Kentucky's advancement. As a result, today's East Kentucky is not the region portrayed by stereotypical images that have traditionally defined the area.

Development in East Kentucky (generally, those Appalachian foothill and mountain counties along and east of I-75 and along and south of I-64) was guided across the course of two centuries by diverse influences. Geographic barriers, disconnections from markets, inadequate transportation networks, the lack of industrial diversification, absentee ownership of the region's natural resources, inadequate infrastructure and uneven economic advancement all affected the way the region and perceptions about it evolved. Now, new influences are guiding the region and laying a foundation for future prosperity.

U.S. Rep. Harold "Hal" Rogers, whose Fifth District includes many of the East Kentucky counties, has organized and led a number of efforts that address regional issues that affect development. For example, East Kentucky PRIDE (Personal Responsibility in a Desirable Environment) is focused on uniting volunteers with the resources of federal, state and local governments in order to clean the region's waterways, end illegal trash dumps and promote environmental awareness and education. PRIDE is part of a strategy to, first, clean up the region and keep it clean, then capitalize on its tourism potential. Supporting the second leg of this strategy is the Southern and Eastern Kentucky Tourism Development Association. The organization's charge is to promote, expand, develop and market the existing and potential tourism industry as a means to economic and cultural growth.

The newest regional organizations are Operation UNITE and The National Institute For Hometown Security. Operation UNITE targets drug abuse and drug trafficking, organizes regional drug task forces for interdiction, confiscation and undercover operations; it also supports drug treatment programs. The National Institute For Hometown Security harnesses the academic capacity of the state's colleges and universities to research and develop homeland security solutions in cooperation with the U.S. Department of Homeland Security.

Building the region's infrastructure is a significant part of the strategy to position East Kentucky for sustained economic advancement. The construction of I-66 will improve the surface transportation network. This major thoroughfare will ultimately complement other highway reconstruction projects undertaken as part of the Appalachian Development Highway System — these projects are eliminating the physical barriers between East Kentucky, the rest of the state and the nation.

Twenty-First Century infrastructure includes more than roads and sewage facilities. It also includes electronic infrastructure that moves information around the corner or the world. The Center for Rural Development at Somerset first reached into East Kentucky to make video conferencing services readily available. That system has now been expanded and upgraded to keep pace with evolving information technology developments.

Additionally, Gov. Ernie Fletcher has launched an initiative to make broadband service available to all Kentuckians by 2007.

On another front, expanded postsecondary education services are providing new opportunities for East Kentuckians to invest in their abilities. Universities provide satellite classes in some East Kentucky towns and community colleges have established branches to make their offerings more accessible at less cost to more people.

Regional heritage and culture are important in East Kentucky. Several initiatives preserve and amplify this rich heritage. The Kentucky School of Craft at Hindman teaches students to be entrepreneurial craftsmen. At Benham and Lynch in Harlan County, the Kentucky Coal Mining Museum and exhibits highlight the coal heritage of the region. U.S. 23, stretching through East Kentucky from Virginia to Ohio, has become known as The County Music Highway as the eight-county area served by the road is the birthplace of many famous country music stars (such as Loretta Lynn, Crystal Gayle, Ricky Skaggs, Patty Loveless and Dwight Yoakam).

While East Kentucky's economic and demographic profiles still trail those of the state as a whole, these efforts combined with many other initiatives are charting the course for the future and wearing away the stereotypical images that have traditionally defined the region.

Northern Kentucky
Paul A. Tenkotte, Ph.D.

NORTHERN KENTUCKY—A UNIQUE REGION

Northern Kentucky encompasses eleven counties with a combined population of over 430,000—Boone, Bracken, Campbell, Carroll, Gallatin, Grant, Kenton, Mason, Owen, Pendleton and Robertson. Sharing historic, commercial and transportation ties, the counties of Northern Kentucky form the northern point of Kentucky's "Golden Triangle." The Golden Triangle—with its three points at Northern Kentucky, Lexington and Louisville—is an economically prosperous area with high employment, investment and job creation rates. The Cincinnati/Northern Kentucky International Airport, located in Boone County, is an important economic engine. With more than 680 daily departures to 140 cities worldwide, the airport generates $4.5 billion annually to the economy of the metropolitan area.

The nucleus of Northern Kentucky is comprised of the heavily-urbanized counties of Kenton, Campbell, and Boone, and is anchored by the historic Ohio River cities of Covington (Kenton) and

Frank Duveneck home in Covington
Source: Kentucky Department for Libraries & Archives, WPA Collection

Newport (Campbell). Newport (incorporated in 1795) is situated at the eastern corner of the confluence of the Licking and Ohio Rivers. Jacob Fowler is credited with building the first cabin there. Covington (incorporated in 1815) lies at the western corner of the confluence of the Ohio and Licking Rivers. Colonel William Peachy, a Revolutionary War veteran from Virginia, obtained 10,000 acres of land in the immediate area. By 1850, Covington was the second-largest city in Kentucky and the 52nd largest in the nation, and, by 1860, Newport placed third in the state.

**Toyota Motor Manufacturing Kentucky
North America - Corporate Headquarters**

Northern Kentucky's prosperity attracted many German and Irish immigrants, who built beautiful Catholic churches like Mother of God Church and the Cathedral Basilica of the Assumption, both in Covington. The Germans in Northern Kentucky became known for their artists, especially, Johann Schmitt (1825-1898), Frank Duveneck (1848-1919), Thomas P. Anshutz (1851-1912) and Leon Lippert (1863-1947).

The Irish gravitated to new jobs opening up in mid-nineteenth century cities like Covington and Newport, for example, as firemen and policemen, positions that required a familiarity with the English language. They also became important in politics and law.

By the 1850s, the continued existence of slavery in Kentucky created a wedge between Northern Kentucky and its Ohio neighbors. This was most clearly demonstrated when the Ohio General Assembly amended the charter of the Covington and Cincinnati Suspension Bridge Company, prohibiting it from building its ramps onto any Cincinnati street. Northern Kentucky, especially Maysville, became an important conduit on the Underground Railroad.

The Civil War divided the loyalties of Northern Kentuckians. Many Germans supported the Union cause, some crossing the Ohio River to join German-speaking Ohio regiments. In September 1862, the Union army's successful construction of a line of defensive fortifications in Northern Kentucky saved Cincinnati from an impending attack.

Boss rule availed itself of immigrants' votes in Covington in the late-nineteenth century, and William Goebel, of German heritage, rose to prominence in the Democratic party. Goebel advocated workingmen's rights. In a highly-contested 1900 election that nearly led to civil unrest, Goebel was shot, pronounced governor, and died of his wounds; to this day the only governor in U.S. history to die of assassination while in office.

The early twentieth century brought challenges to Northern Kentucky. During World War I in Kenton County, the Citizens' Patriotic League harassed law-abiding German-American residents, and committed acts of violence against them in what was called "The Reign of Terror." Libraries destroyed German books, public schools ended the teaching of the German language, cities changed German street names, and ordinary German-American citizens anglicized their surnames.

Today, Northern Kentucky is a vibrant and prosperous area, anchored by an international airport, and headquarters to corporations like Toyota North America, Omnicare, and Ashland. In addition, large health care facilities like St. Elizabeth Medical Center and St. Luke Hospital improve its quality of life, as do institutions of higher learning like Northern Kentucky University, Thomas More College, Gateway Community and Technical College, and Maysville Community and Technical College. In 2005, the U.S. Census Bureau reported an impressive statistic — that the three counties of Boone, Kenton, and Campbell had together created nearly one-third of Kentucky's new jobs during the period 1998-2003. From its historic Ohio River roots, symbolized by the still-used John Roebling Suspension Bridge, Northern Kentucky has retained a sense of its past, while courting a prosperous present, and envisioning a hopeful future.

VOTER REGISTRATION - PARTY AFFILIATION - DATE: 8/15/05

COUNTY NAME	NO.PRECINCTS	DEMOCRAT	REPUBLICAN	OTHER	MALE	FEMALE	TOT REG.
ADAIR	16	3,678	7,794	421	5,785	6,105	11,893
ALLEN	13	4,288	6,665	530	5,551	5,932	11,483
ANDERSON	14	9,451	3,861	534	6,636	7,210	13,846
BALLARD	13	4,948	734	147	2,812	3,017	5,829
BARREN	24	15,610	8,433	1,274	11,839	13,476	25,317
BATH	12	7,110	885	220	4,045	4,170	8,215
BELL	34	10,132	9,398	645	9,406	10,769	20,175
BOONE	58	24,528	34,260	7,661	31,684	34,763	66,449
BOURBON	18	9,330	2,726	610	5,966	6,700	12,666
BOYD	47	20,432	11,277	1,967	15,662	18,013	33,676
BOYLE	25	11,340	5,463	1,044	8,261	9,585	17,847
BRACKEN	8	4,445	979	206	2,748	2,882	5,630
BREATHITT	21	10,058	744	247	5,441	5,607	11,049
BRECKINRIDGE	15	7,159	5,585	634	6,591	6,784	13,378
BULLITT	42	25,865	15,101	3,375	21,494	22,853	44,350
BUTLER	12	1,814	6,200	217	3,976	4,255	8,231
CALDWELL	13	6,943	1,854	276	4,330	4,743	9,073
CALLOWAY	28	15,651	5,312	1,657	10,685	11,935	22,620
CAMPBELL	65	26,114	24,456	5,861	26,262	30,156	56,431
CARLISLE	7	3,364	461	68	1,868	2,025	3,893
CARROLL	11	5,605	809	265	3,225	3,454	6,679
CARTER	23	10,615	6,372	793	8,729	9,051	17,780
CASEY	15	2,029	8,044	236	5,032	5,277	10,309
CHRISTIAN	46	22,656	9,875	2,391	15,642	19,280	34,922
CLARK	25	14,790	6,552	1,163	10,657	11,848	22,505
CLAY	20	1,864	12,536	200	7,202	7,398	14,600
CLINTON	13	1,799	5,270	117	3,423	3,763	7,186
CRITTENDEN	12	3,211	2,643	266	2,930	3,190	6,120
CUMBERLAND	9	1,006	4,036	131	2,499	2,674	5,173
DAVIESS	85	39,056	17,726	3,726	28,058	32,450	60,508
EDMONSON	10	2,569	5,698	208	4,269	4,206	8,475
ELLIOTT	7	4,833	164	62	2,511	2,548	5,059
ESTILL	15	4,147	5,250	352	4,803	4,946	9,749
FAYETTE	251	85,484	59,917	15,493	73,968	86,926	160,894
FLEMING	18	6,828	2,340	291	4,626	4,833	9,459
FLOYD	42	26,876	2,736	507	14,752	15,367	30,119
FRANKLIN	44	24,537	5,656	1,445	14,391	17,202	31,638
FULTON	13	4,024	678	239	2,129	2,811	4,941
GALLATIN	8	3,684	1,227	227	2,570	2,568	5,138
GARRARD	13	3,912	5,969	568	5,056	5,393	10,449
GRANT	23	8,660	4,636	1,283	7,051	7,528	14,579
GRAVES	30	18,468	3,691	720	10,714	12,162	22,879

VOTER REGISTRATION - PARTY AFFILIATION - DATE: 8/15/05

COUNTY NAME	NO PRECINCTS	DEMOCRAT	REPUBLICAN	OTHER	MALE	FEMALE	TOT REG
GRAYSON	23	5,642	10,000	765	7,957	8,450	16,407
GREEN	10	3,232	4,659	191	3,931	4,151	8,082
GREENUP	32	16,444	8,401	1,443	12,600	13,677	26,288
HANCOCK	10	3,728	1,916	215	2,898	2,960	5,859
HARDIN	55	31,828	21,073	4,906	27,110	30,694	57,807
HARLAN	35	14,872	4,462	357	9,441	10,250	19,691
HARRISON	17	8,757	2,441	442	5,557	6,083	11,640
HART	19	7,820	3,562	371	5,647	6,106	11,753
HENDERSON	38	21,104	5,239	1,374	12,895	14,818	27,717
HENRY	19	7,159	2,410	459	4,824	5,204	10,028
HICKMAN	6	2,960	468	116	1,679	1,865	3,544
HOPKINS	40	21,755	6,733	1,264	13,821	15,930	29,752
JACKSON	14	1,092	7,832	174	4,487	4,611	9,098
JEFFERSON	510	264,308	151,022	41,744	206,712	250,360	457,074
JESSAMINE	33	14,377	11,442	1,991	13,191	14,618	27,810
JOHNSON	31	6,753	9,202	403	7,977	8,381	16,358
KENTON	107	43,088	42,305	11,948	45,716	51,623	97,341
KNOTT	30	11,777	438	175	6,066	6,323	12,390
KNOX	30	6,780	13,831	460	10,064	11,006	21,071
LARUE	12	6,420	2,519	370	4,496	4,813	9,309
LAUREL	45	8,732	27,032	1,240	17,875	19,128	37,004
LAWRENCE	18	6,174	4,415	434	5,371	5,650	11,023
LEE	10	2,059	2,917	96	2,495	2,577	5,072
LESLIE	17	1,063	7,929	149	4,502	4,639	9,141
LETCHER	32	12,301	3,380	246	7,695	8,232	15,927
LEWIS	14	2,190	6,726	260	4,587	4,586	9,176
LINCOLN	17	8,669	6,615	559	7,615	8,226	15,843
LIVINGSTON	10	5,695	1,055	205	3,397	3,558	6,955
LOGAN	20	11,735	3,377	819	7,409	8,522	15,931
LYON	6	4,455	940	202	2,741	2,856	5,597
MCCRACKEN	54	29,594	11,553	2,614	19,963	23,798	43,761
MCCREARY	18	3,001	7,426	417	5,283	5,561	10,844
MCLEAN	8	4,803	1,468	278	3,183	3,366	6,549
MADISON	56	24,713	16,851	3,615	21,191	23,985	45,179
MAGOFFIN	14	6,771	2,922	103	4,845	4,951	9,796
MARION	17	9,946	1,499	313	5,617	6,141	11,758
MARSHALL	25	16,198	4,607	711	10,401	11,115	21,516
MARTIN	14	2,121	6,479	147	4,327	4,417	8,747
MASON	20	7,231	2,930	707	5,084	5,783	10,868
MEADE	18	10,895	4,701	1,067	8,103	8,559	16,663
MENIFEE	6	3,833	679	174	2,338	2,348	4,686
MERCER	17	10,606	3,900	767	7,218	8,055	15,273

VOTER REGISTRATION - PARTY AFFILIATION - DATE: 8/15/05

COUNTY NAME	NO.PRECINCTS	DEMOCRAT	REPUBLICAN	OTHER	MALE	FEMALE	TOT REG.
METCALFE	12	4,198	2,443	289	3,368	3,559	6,930
MONROE	12	1,287	7,072	156	4,126	4,389	8,515
MONTGOMERY	17	12,420	3,352	555	7,809	8,518	16,327
MORGAN	12	7,838	658	74	4,221	4,349	8,570
MUHLENBERG	27	16,088	4,319	884	10,135	11,157	21,292
NELSON	27	17,578	6,407	2,256	12,507	13,734	26,241
NICHOLAS	5	4,410	569	165	2,463	2,680	5,144
OHIO	25	7,341	7,453	725	7,472	8,047	15,519
OLDHAM	34	14,249	17,849	3,433	17,215	18,314	35,531
OWEN	13	5,591	1,416	268	3,602	3,673	7,275
OWSLEY	8	890	2,837	40	1,889	1,877	3,767
PENDLETON	12	6,211	2,714	496	4,612	4,809	9,421
PERRY	37	16,104	4,242	366	10,048	10,663	20,712
PIKE	57	32,991	9,254	1,082	21,061	22,264	43,327
POWELL	11	6,719	1,990	303	4,428	4,584	9,012
PULASKI	57	10,886	26,904	2,116	19,143	20,758	39,906
ROBERTSON	5	1,392	211	33	817	819	1,636
ROCKCASTLE	14	2,090	8,495	379	5,374	5,590	10,964
ROWAN	18	8,737	3,328	721	6,112	6,674	12,786
RUSSELL	16	3,106	8,802	277	5,891	6,294	12,185
SCOTT	35	14,601	8,441	1,374	11,664	12,752	24,416
SHELBY	31	13,859	7,719	1,422	10,888	12,110	23,000
SIMPSON	13	7,601	2,272	785	4,945	5,712	10,658
SPENCER	9	6,110	3,291	500	4,878	5,023	9,901
TAYLOR	20	7,576	7,358	599	7,251	8,280	15,533
TODD	13	6,186	1,143	227	3,596	3,960	7,556
TRIGG	14	6,553	2,286	411	4,483	4,767	9,250
TRIMBLE	12	4,706	1,050	253	2,993	3,016	6,009
UNION	16	8,119	1,145	311	4,562	5,013	9,575
WARREN	61	32,780	19,742	3,896	26,333	30,081	56,418
WASHINGTON	14	5,304	2,150	223	3,680	3,996	7,677
WAYNE	19	5,204	7,595	371	6,413	6,757	13,170
WEBSTER	14	7,494	1,190	261	4,259	4,686	8,945
WHITLEY	36	6,034	17,220	900	11,705	12,448	24,154
WOLFE	8	4,763	493	88	2,670	2,674	5,344
WOODFORD	16	10,081	5,172	1,081	7,640	8,693	16,334
STATE TOTALS	3495	1,538,691	971,960	169,888	1,263,841	1,416,551	2,680,540

Source: Secretary of State - http://elect.ky.gov/stats/regstat.htm

Clark's Kentucky Almanac 2006

GENERAL FUND SUMMARY
2004-2006 EXECUTIVE BUDGET

RESOURCES	Recommended FY2005	Recommended FY2006
Beginning Balance	249,475,100	192,531,100
Consensus Revenue Forecast	7,433,000,000	7,665,000,000
Tobacco Settlement- Phase 1	108,800,000	108,600,000
Continuation of Revenue Measures		18,000,000
Other Resources	16,855,500	21,846,700
Fund Transfers	127,004,600	181,219,700
Total Resources	**7,935,135,200**	**8,187,197,500**
Continued Appropriations Reserve		
Budget Reserve Trust Fund	50,764,800	50,764,800
Tobacco Settlement-Phase 1	42,947,500	5,252,400
Executive Branch	5,882,500	7,126,300
Legislative Branch	11,598,100	6,251,800
Judicial Branch	9,004,600	
Total Continued Appropriations Reserve	**120,197,500**	**69,395,300**
TOTAL RESOURCES	**8,055,332,700**	**8,256,592,800**
APPROPRIATIONS		
Executive Branch		
Regular Operating	7,378,308,800	7,804,037,400
Tobacco Settlement-Phase 1	108,800,000	108,600,000
Budgeted Lapse	(15,074,800)	(5,000,000)
Capital Projects	9,375,000	6,140,700
Total Executive Branch	**7,481,409,000**	**7,913,778,100**
Judicial Branch	**220,255,700**	**232,048,900**
Legislative Branch	**40,939,400**	**41,370,500**
TOTAL APPROPRIATIONS	**7,742,604,100**	**8,187,197,500**
BALANCE	**312,728,600**	**69,395,300**
Continued Appropriations Reserve		
Budget Reserve Trust Fund	50,764,800	50,764,800
Tobacco Settlement-Phase 1	42,947,500	5,252,400
Executive Branch	5,882,500	7,126,300
Legislative Branch	11,598,100	6,251,800
Judicial Branch	9,004,600	
Total Continued Appropriations Reserve	**120,197,500**	**69,395,300**
ENDING BALANCE	**192,531,100**	**0**

ROAD FUND SUMMARY
2004-2006 EXECUTIVE BUDGET

	Recommended FY 2005	Recommended FY2006
RESOURCES		
Beginning Balance		
Revenue Estimate: January 19, 2005	1,119,702,900	1,127,126,500
FY 2004 Surplus	23,011,700	
Road Fund Revenue Initiative		53,250,000
TOTAL RESOURCES	**1,142,714,600**	**1,180,376,500**
APPROPRIATIONS		
Transportation Cabinet		
Revenue Sharing	236,928,500	243,540,600
Highways	637,266,800	634,583,700
Vehicle Regulation	15,834,000	15,898,000
Debt Service	116,113,500	157,528,900
General Administration and Support	64,956,100	66,530,000
Capital Construction	13,794,000	4,248,000
Subtotal	**1,084,892,900**	**1,122,329,200**
Justice & Public Safety Cabinet	52,465,700	53,116,300
Finance and Administration Cabinet	4,756,000	4,331,000
Treasury	250,000	250,000
Homeland Security	350,000	350,000
TOTAL APPROPRIATIONS	**1,142,714,600**	**1,180,376,500**
ENDING BALANCE	**0**	**0**

Source: Office of State Budget Director, http://www.osbd.ky.gov.

CAPITAL CONSTRUCTION SUMMARY
2004-2006 EXECUTIVE BUDGET

	Recommended FY 2005	Recommended FY 2006	New Authorization
SOURCE OF FUNDS			
Executive Branch			
General Fund	9,375,000	6,140,700	15,515,700
Restricted Funds	1,534,473,701	102,192,000	1,636,665,701
Federal Funds	83,825,000	14,703,000	98,528,000
Bond Fund	260,501,000		260,501,000
Road Fund	13,794,000	4,248,000	18,042,000
Agency Bond Fund	12,020,000		12,020,000
Capital Construction Surplus	1,892,400	63,000	1,955,400
Investment Income	29,394,000	19,895,000	49,289,000
Tobacco Settlement-Phase 1	660,000		660,000
Other Funds	21,800,000	4,300,000	26,100,000
TOTAL SOURCE OF FUNDS	**1,967,735,101**	**151,541,700**	**2,119,276,801**
EXPENDITURES BY CABINET			
Executive Branch			
General Branch	76,116,100	6,113,700	82,229,800
Commerce	15,092,000	14,612,000	29,704,000
Economic Development	28,825,000	10,985,000	39,810,000
Department of Education	4,514,000	675,000	5,189,000
Education Cabinet	70,550,000	2,560,000	73,110,000
Environmental and Public Protection	34,550,000	7,950,000	42,500,000
Finance and Administration	118,658,400	17,599,000	136,257,400
Health and Family Services	28,684,000	17,500,000	46,164,000
Justice and Public Safety	8,422,000	2,600,000	11,022,000
Personnel	26,250,000		26,250,000
Postsecondary Education	1,542,299,601	66,699,000	1,608,998,601
Transportation	13,794,000	4,248,000	18,042,000
TOTAL EXPENDITURES	**1,967,735,101**	**151,541,700**	**2,119,276,801**

TOBACCO SETTLEMENT-PHASE I SUMMARY
2004-2006 EXECUTIVE BUDGET

	Recommended FY 2005	Recommended FY2006
Revenue Cabinet*	175,000	175,000
Rural Development- (50%)		
Governor's Office of Agriculture Policy	39,195,900	39,099,300
Finance and Administrative Cabinet Debt Service	6,116,600	6,113,200
Environmental and Public Protection Cabinet		
Natural Resources	9,000,000	9,000,000
Subtotal	**54,312,500**	**54,212,500**
Health Improvement- (25%)		
Justice & Public Safety Cabinet Office of Drug Policy	2,226,800	2,222,700
Health and Family Service Cabinet Public Health	2,715,600	2,710,600
Council on Postsecondary Education		
Lung Cancer Research Program	5,431,300	5,421,300
Environmental and Public Protection Cabinet		
Insurance (Kentucky Access)	16,782,600	16,751,700
Subtotal	**27,156,300**	**27,106,300**
Early Childhood Development- (25%)		
Department of Education-LARS		
Division of Early Childhood Development Services	1,888,400	1,888,400
Health and Family Services Cabinet		
Community Based Services	8,300,400	8,300,400
Public Health	14,712,400	14,662,400
Mental Health/Mental Retardation	900,000	900,000
Children with Special Health Care Needs	455,000	455,000
Postsecondary Education		
Kentucky Higher Education Assistance Authority	900,000	900,000
Subtotal	**27,156,200**	**27,106,200**
TOTAL TOBACCO SETTLEMENT-PHASE 1	**108,800,000**	**108,600,000**

* House Bill 390, as enacted by the 2003 General Assembly, appropriated $175,000 of Phase I Tobacco Funds to carry out the provisions of KRS 131. This amount is deducted before the allocations to Rural Development, Health Improvement, and Early Childhood are made.

KENTUCKY STATE GOVERNMENT EMPLOYMENT AND PAYROLL DATA: MARCH 2004

FUNCTION	FULL-TIME EMPLOYEES	FULL-TIME PAYROLL	PART-TIME EMPLOYEES	PART-TIME PAYROLL	PART-TIME HOURS	EQUIVALENT EMPLOYMENT	MARCH PAYROLL
Financial administration	2,820	9,061,802	230	263,486	26,926	2,981	9,325,288
Other government administration	1,017	4,646,664	498	1,183,164	49,344	1,314	5,829,828
Judicial and Legal	4,271	14,682,362	852	1,428,740	114,714	4,962	16,111,102
Persons with power of arrest	967	3,738,714	2	4,892	266	969	3,743,606
Police - Other	1,207	3,834,374	17	27,368	1,802	1,218	3,861,742
Correction	3,712	9,771,694	138	119,492	3,052	3,731	9,891,186
Highways	5,011	16,210,226	162	293,052	14,284	5,097	16,503,278
Public Welfare	6,818	19,884,164	60	113,444	6,676	6,859	19,997,608
Health	2,071	6,778,290	109	88,615	5,726	2,105	6,866,905
Hospitals	5,359	17,393,170	364	1,019,112	47,422	5,631	18,412,282
Social insurance administration	1,082	3,310,834	69	108,690	6,312	1,120	3,419,524
Parks and recreation	1,478	3,311,540	158	154,416	20,574	1,602	3,465,956
Natural resources	3,287	10,258,539	929	987,388	91,403	3,819	11,245,927
Higher Ed Instructional	8,033	45,152,503	7,262	9,705,543	537,580	11,199	54,858,046
Higher Ed - Other	15,944	45,775,057	13,425	6,272,274	667,334	19,890	52,047,331
Other education	2,816	10,395,764	231	264,714	13,220	2,895	10,660,478
All other and unallocable	4,024	13,576,427	206	202,403	11,010	4,089	13,778,830
Total	69,917	237,782,124	24,712	22,236,793	1,617,645	79,481	260,018,917

STATE GOVERNMENT EMPLOYMENT AND PAYROLL DATA: MARCH 2004 (US, Kentucky, and surrounding states)

STATE NAME	POPULATION	FULL-TIME EMPLOYEES	FULL-TIME PAYROLL	PART-TIME EMPLOYEES	PART-TIME PAYROLL	PART-TIME HOURS	EQUIVALENT EMPLOYMENT	MARCH PAYROLL
United States	281,421,906	3,635,273	13,976,250,802	1,405,870	1,501,270,606	96,075,761	4,187,648	15,477,521,408
Illinois	12,419,293	112,831	461,826,137	47,577	42,820,898	3,466,912	133,672	504,647,035
Indiana	6,080,485	75,965	254,893,211	34,263	31,217,585	2,517,362	90,404	286,110,796
Kentucky	4,041,769	69,917	237,782,124	24,712	22,236,793	1,617,645	79,481	260,018,917
Missouri	5,595,211	81,473	240,712,083	25,077	19,076,877	1,626,888	90,730	259,788,960
Ohio	11,353,140	111,052	432,011,644	66,144	63,355,128	4,396,460	136,041	495,366,772
Tennessee	5,689,283	72,330	224,646,682	25,088	21,349,129	1,619,216	81,905	245,995,811
Virginia	7,078,515	101,954	358,372,929	46,811	46,508,413	3,051,561	119,317	404,881,342
West Virginia	1,808,344	34,751	103,998,345	9,288	7,414,143	468,134	37,583	111,412,488

Source: http://www.census.gov/govs/www/apesst04dl.html

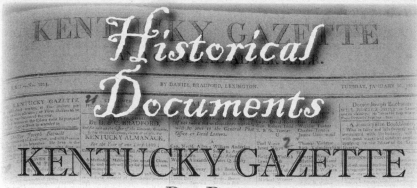

KENTUCKY GAZETTE

Ron Bryant

On August 11, 1787, John Bradford (1749-1830) published the first issue of the *Kentucke Gazette*. As the first newspaper west of the Allegheny Mountains, the *Gazette* provided not only a source for news, but also a printing establishment for the western frontier. Although the paper did not report a great deal of local news, it did serve as a means to advertise local goods and services, and reprint articles of national and international importance.

The need for a printer on the Kentucky frontier became apparent during the second statehood convention in 1785. Delegates to the convention wanted a forum to publish their work and to help unify public opinion. A newspaper would serve their purpose to report to the citizens of Kentucky their efforts to achieve separation from Virginia and to form a new state. Delegates to the statehood convention appointed a committee made up of John

John Bradford

Kentucky Gazette
Source: Lexington Public Library

Coburn, Christopher Greenup and James Wilkinson to persuade a printer to come Kentucky. They endeavored to convince John Dunlap of Philadelphia and Miles Hunter of Richmond to settle on the frontier. Both refused the committee's offer due to concerns that ranged from unhealthful conditions on the frontier to fear of Indians.

When word of the committee's failure reached Kentucky, John Bradford, originally of Fauquier County, Virginia, applied for the position. Bradford had moved to Kentucky in 1779 and became a surveyor. He fought the Indians in the campaigns against the Shawnee at Chillicothe and Piqua. Although he knew nothing about printing, he and his brother Fielding set up the first printing press and newspaper on the frontier. Fielding went to Pittsburgh to learn the printing trade from John Scull, editor of the *Pittsburgh Gazette*.

The Bradford's had the printing press and

type brought from Philadelphia and down the Ohio River to Limestone (now Maysville). Packhorses then carried the printing materials over land to Lexington. With the assistance of Thomas Parvin, an immigrant schoolteacher who had some printing experience, Bradford published the first issue of the *Kentucke Gazette*. The first issue had an apology from Bradford regarding the delay in publication and one advertisement. These two contributions were the only local items in the paper.

Printing on an 18th century press was a laboriously slow process. The sheets of paper measured 8 by 10 inches and were inked with "dog skin" balls (animal skins). The press could only produce 50 to

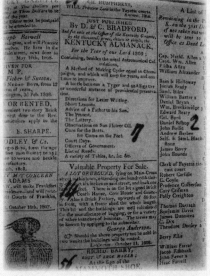

Kentucky Gazette
Source: Lexington Library

60 sheets per hour. The pages of the *Gazette* then had to be dried or else they would smear.

For the first few issues of his paper, Bradford dealt mostly with advertisements and copies of other news articles reporting on national affairs and international affairs. Scarcity of paper may have contributed to the lack of local news, or it may have been easier to reprint articles from other newspapers. The *Gazette* did publish letters from citizens on various issues of the day. It also published congressional debates and the proceedings of the Kentucky General Assembly. The *Gazette* print shop published numerous books, broadsides and pamphlets. One of Bradford's most enduring contributions to the printed word was a series of 66 articles on Kentucky history known as Bradford's

"Notes on Kentucky." Published between August 1825 and January 1829, these invaluable recollections of Kentucky's past are still used by historians and enjoyed by new generations of readers.

In the March 7, 1789, issue of the paper, Bradford changed the spelling on the masthead from *Kentucke* to *Kentucky Gazette*. As times became more settled, the *Gazette* began to publish more local news. From 1792 to 1798 (excepting 1796) Bradford served as public printer for the commonwealth. Until 1795 the *Gazette* was the only newspaper published within 500 miles of Lexington. The paper became a weekly, then a biweekly and at last a triweekly publication. It was originally delivered to subscribers by post rider and then by mail.

Bradford published more than just the *Gazette*. As public printer he printed state documents, including some of the first volumes of the *Acts of the Kentucky General Assembly*. In time he became an excellent printer and more of a journalist. In 1788 he began publication of the *Kentucky Alma-*

The Kentucke Gazette published letters from citizens on various issues of the day as well as congressional debates and proceedings of the Kentucky General Assembly.

nac (1788-1807). This annual publication contained information on the weather as well as astronomy and materials of general interest.

He remained the editor and owner of the *Gazette* until 1802, when he gave ownership of the paper to his son Daniel. In 1809 Daniel sold the paper to Thomas Smith, and in 1814 Smith sold the *Gazette* to Fielding Bradford Jr. In 1825 John Bradford again became editor of the *Gazette*, holding the position until 1827 when Albert G. Merriwether succeeded him.

The *Kentucky Gazette* continued publication from August 11, 1787, until December 29, 1848. No copy of the first issue of the paper has ever been found. The second issue of August 18, 1787, is known to be a near copy of the first edition. Another Lexington newspaper used the name from 1866 to 1910. In 1995, the *Kentucky Gazette* was revived and edited by Lowell Reese as a Frankfort-based political newspaper.

HISTORICAL DOCUMENTS

Constitution of Kentucky

CONSTITUTION OF KENTUCKY
(as amended to 1980)

PREAMBLE

We, the people of the Commonwealth of Kentucky, grateful to Almighty God for the civil, political and religious liberties we enjoy, and invoking the continuance of these blessings, do ordain and establish this Constitution.

BILL OF RIGHTS

That the great and essential principles of liberty and free government may be recognized and established, we declare that:

Sec. 1. Rights of life, liberty, worship, pursuit of safety and happiness, free speech, acquiring and protecting property, peaceable assembly, redress of grievances, bearing arms. All men are, by nature, free and equal, and have certain inherent and inalienable rights, among which may be reckoned:

First: The right of enjoying and defending their lives and liberties.

Second: The right of worshipping Almighty God according to the dictates of their conscience.

Third: The right of seeking and pursuing their safety and happiness.

Fourth: The right of freely communicating their thoughts and opinions.

Fifth: The right of acquiring and protecting property.

Sixth: The right of assembling together in a peaceable manner for their common good, and of applying to those invested with power of government for redress of grievances or other proper purposes, by petition, address or remonstrance.

Seventh: The right to bear arms in defense of themselves and of the State, subject to the power of the General Assembly to enact laws to prevent persons from carrying concealed weapons.

Sec. 2. Absolute and arbitrary power denied. Absolute and arbitrary power over the lives, liberty and property of freemen exists nowhere in a republic, not even in the largest majority.

Sec. 3. Men are equal; no exclusive grant except for public services; property not to be exempted from taxation; grants revocable. All men, when they form a social compact, are equal; and no grant of exclusive, separate public emoluments or privileges shall be made to any man or set of men, except in consideration of public services; but no property shall be exempt from taxation except as provided in this Constitution, and every grant of a franchise, privilege or exemption, shall remain subject to revocation, alteration or amendment.

Sec. 4. Power inherent in the people; right to alter, reform or abolish government. All power is inherent in the people, and all free governments are founded on their authority and instituted for their peace, safety, happiness and the protection of property. For the advancement of these ends, they have at all times an inalienable and indefeasible right to alter, reform or abolish their government in such manner as they may deem proper.

Sec. 5.　Right of religious freedom. No preference shall ever be given by law to any religious sect, society or denomination; nor to any particular creed, mode of worship or system of ecclesiastical polity; nor shall any person be compelled to attend any place of worship, to contribute to the erection or maintenance of any such place, or to the salary or support of any minister or religion; nor shall any man be compelled to send his child to any school to which he may be conscientiously opposed; and the civil rights, privileges or capacities of no person shall be taken away, or in any wise diminished or enlarged, on account of his belief or disbelief of any religious tenet, dogma or teaching. No human authority shall, in any case whatever, control or interfere with the rights of conscience.

Sec. 6.　Elections to be free and equal. All elections shall be free and equal.

Sec. 7.　Right of trial by jury. The ancient mode of trial by jury shall be held sacred, and the right thereof remain inviolate, subject to such modifications as may be authorized by this Constitution.

Sec. 8.　Freedom of speech and of the press. Printing presses shall be free to every person who undertakes to examine the proceedings of the General Assembly or any branch of government, and no shall ever be made to restrain the right there of. Every person may freely and fully speak, write and print on any subject, being responsible for the abuse of that liberty.

Sec. 9.　Truth may be given in evidence in prosecution for publishing matters proper for public information; jury to try law and facts in libel prosecutions. In prosecutions for the publication of papers investigating the official conduct of officers or men in public capacity, or where the matter published is proper for public information, the truth there of may be given in evidence; and in all indictments for libel the jury shall have the right to determine the law and the facts, under the direction of the court, as in other cases.

Sec. 10.　Security from search and seizure; conditions of issuance of warrants. The people shall be secure in their persons, houses, papers and possessions, from unreasonable searches and seizure; and no warrant shall issue to search any place, or seize any person or thing, without describing them as nearly as may be, nor without probable cause supported by oath or affirmation.

Sec. 11.　Rights of accused in criminal prosecution; change of venue. In all criminal prosecutions the accused has the right to be heard by himself and counsel; to demand the nature and cause of the accusation against him; to meet the witnesses face to face, and to have compulsory process for obtaining witnesses in his favor. He cannot be compelled to give evidence against himself, nor can he be deprived of his life, liberty or property, unless by the judgment of his peers or the law of the land; and in prosecutions by indictments or information, he shall have a speedy public trial by an impartial jury of the vicinage; but the General Assembly may provide by a general law for a change of venue in such prosecutions for both the defendant and the Commonwealth, the change to be made to the most convenient county in which a fair trial can be obtained.

Sec. 12.　Indictable offense not to be prosecuted by information; exceptions. No person, for an indictable offense, shall be proceeded against criminally by information, except in cases arising in the land or naval forces, or in the militia, when in actual service, in time of war or public danger, or by leave of court for oppression or misdemeanor in office.

Sec. 13.　Double jeopardy; property not to be taken for public use without just compensation. No person shall, for the same offense, be twice put in jeopardy of his life or limb, nor shall any man's property be taken or applied to public use without just compensation being previously made to him.

Sec. 14.　Right of judicial remedy for injury; speedy trial. All courts shall be open, and every person for an injury done him in his lands, goods, person or reputation, shall have remedy by due course of law, and right and justice administered without sale, denial or delay.

Sec. 15. Laws to be suspended only by General Assembly. No power to suspend laws shall be exercised unless by the General Assembly or its authority.

Sec. 16. Right to bail; habeas corpus. All prisoners shall be bailable by sufficient securities, unless for capital offenses when the proof is evident or the presumption great: and the privilege of the writ of habeas corpus shall not be suspended unless when, in case of rebellion or invasion, the public safety may require it.

Sec. 17. Excessive bail or fine, or cruel punishment, prohibited. Excessive bail shall not be required, nor excessive fines imposed, nor cruel punishment inflicted.

Sec. 18. Imprisonment for debt restricted. The person of a debtor, where there is not strong presumption of fraud, shall not be continued in prison after delivering up his estate for the benefit of his creditors in such manner as shall be prescribed by law.

Sec. 19. Ex post facto law or law impairing the obligation of contract forbidden. No ex post facto law, nor any law impairing the obligation of contracts, shall be enacted.

Sec. 20. Attainder, operation of restricted. No person shall be attainted of treason or felony by the General Assembly, and no attainder shall work corruption of blood, nor, except during the life of the offender, forfeiture of estate to the Commonwealth.

Sec. 21. Descent in case of suicide or casualty. The estate of such persons as shall destroy their own lives shall descend or vest as in cases of natural death; and if any person shall be killed by casualty, there shall be no forfeiture by reason thereof.

Sec. 22. Standing armies restricted; military subordinate to civil; quartering soldiers restricted. No standing army shall, in time of peace, be maintained without the consent of the General Assembly; and the military shall, in all cases and at all times, be in strict subordination to the civil power; nor shall any soldier, in time of peace, be quartered in any house without the consent of the owner, nor in time of war, except in a manner prescribed by law.

Sec. 23. No office of nobility or hereditary distinction, or for longer than a term of years. The General Assembly shall not grant any title of nobility or hereditary distinction, nor create any office the appointment of which shall be for a longer time than a term of years.

Sec. 24. Emigration to be free. Emigration from the state shall not be prohibited.

Sec. 25. Slavery and involuntary servitude forbidden. Slavery and in-voluntary servitude in this State are forbidden, except as punishment for crime, whereof the party shall have been duly convicted.

Sec. 26. General powers subordinate to Bill of Rights; laws contrary there to are void. To guard against transgression of the high powers which we have delegated, We Declare that everything in this Bill of Rights is excepted out of the general powers of government, and shall forever remain inviolate; and all laws contrary thereto, or contrary to this Constitution, shall be void.

For a complete copy of the Kentucky Constitution visit www.lrc.ky.gov/legresou/constitu/intro.htm

It's a Kentucky Thing!
Sec. 4 of the Kentucky Bill of Rights.

"All power is inherent in the people, and all free governments are founded on their peace, safety, happiness and the protection of property."

The Trail of Tears

THE TRAIL OF TEARS POW WOW

Suddenly the throb of drumbeats and the high pitch of singers' voices pierce the late summer morning. Soft breezes flutter the flags carried by the honor guard as they appear from the East. The

Apache, Oklahoma, prepares for Men's Traditional dance competition at 1999 Pow Wow
Source: Library of Congress, photo by Midge Durbin, for "Trail of Tears Powwow," a Kentucky Local Legacies project

eyes catch the brilliant whirl of hundreds of feathers put into motion by the fancy footwork of the dancer. In contrast, he is accompanied into the circle by a woman, garbed in a beautifully beaded buckskin dress. Both keep perfect time with the drumbeats. Following the Head Man and Head Lady Dancers are many other dancers, including children from tiny tots to teenagers. The Trail of Tears Intertribal Pow Wow has begun.

Every year on the first full weekend of September, this event is held at the Trail of Tears Commemorative Park in Hopkinsville. This historic park is one of the few documented sites of actual trail and campsites used during the forced removal of the Cherokee people from their ancestral homes in the southeast, across Mississippi to "Indian Territory," which is now Oklahoma. This tragic, cruel relocation has become known as the "Trail of Tears" and by Native Americans as "The Trail Where They Cried." The forced removal affected Hopkinsville, which was along the trail, and served as a major stopping point for the Cherokees during the harsh winters of 1838 and 1839. Kentucky is particularly relevant to Cherokees, since the state land was once a part of Cherokee ancestral homeland. This park is the burial site for two Cherokee Chiefs who died during the removal, Chief Fly Smith and Whitepath (statues of Chief Whitepath and Fly Smith were crafted by local artist Steve Shields).

The president and founder of the Trail of Tears Commission, Beverly Baker, began work in late 1985 to gain support for the idea for a commemorative park, and to encourage interest in acknowledging this tragic event in local history. City and county governments, and a church donated $1,000 in seed money to the volunteer group. With tremendous enthusiasm, a letter writing campaign to the U.S. Congress was undertaken by community members, schools and government officials. In December 1987, President Ronald Reagan signed a bill creating the Trail of Tears as a National Historic Trail.

A proclamation set 1988 as the Year of the Trail of Tears. With the 150th anniversary approaching, a "competition" Pow Wow was planned to encourage attendance by Native Americans to a "non-Indian" land.

One of the focal points of the Trail of Tears Commemorative Park is a log cabin, which serves as the Heritage Center for the Park. This cabin dates to the Trail of Tears itself. Near the burial area in the park, the Trail of Tears Commission has planted Red Cherokee Chief dogwoods in honor of the seven clans of the Cherokee: Bird, Paint, Deer, Blue, Wolf, Long Hair and Wild Potato.

For the visitor to the Pow Wow, it is an experience not often afforded; for the participants, it is an opportunity to celebrate the great heritage of the American Indian — the original inhabitants and caretakers of this great land.
Source: http://www.trailoftears.org/, and visit http://www.thebearbyte.com/

FEDERAL GOVERNMENT

Kentuckians in Congress

SENATOR MITCH MCCONNELL (R)

In 2004 Senator Mitch McConnell was unanimously re-elected Majority Whip by his Republican colleagues. As Majority Whip, McConnell is the second ranking Republican in the US Senate. First elected to the Senate in 1984, McConnell was the only Republican challenger in the country to defeat a Democrat incumbent, and the first Republican to win a statewide race in Kentucky since 1968. McConnell's landslide victory in 2002 is also one for the record books — he won a fourth term with 65 percent of the vote, the largest margin of victory for a Republican in Kentucky history.

Born on February 20, 1942, and reared in south Louisville, McConnell graduated in 1964 with honors from the University of Louisville. A graduate from the University of Kentucky College of Law, he worked on Capitol Hill as an intern for Senator John Sherman Cooper; as chief legislative assistant to Senator Marlow Cook; and as deputy assistant attorney general under President Gerald R. Ford. Before being elected to the U.S. Senate, McConnell served as County Judge-Executive in Jefferson County from 1978 - 1985.

Senator McConnell is married to U.S. Secretary of Labor, Elaine Chao. He is the father of three daughters.

Mitch McConnell (R)
US Senator, Senate Majority Whip
361A Russell Senate Ofc Bldg
Washington DC 20510
(202) 224-2541
FAX (202) 224-2499
http://mcconnell.senate.gov/index.cfmc

SENATOR JIM BUNNING (R)

Elected to serve a second term as U.S. Senator in 1984, Senator Jim Bunning was first elected to the U.S. Senate in 1998. He had won by a mere 6,766 votes. In 2004 he won by a margin almost 3 ½ times larger than his victory in 1998; he also won 73 of Kentucky's 120 counties and secured 873,507 votes — the most votes ever for a U.S. Senate candidate from Kentucky.

Reared in Northern Kentucky and a graduate of Xavier University, Bunning had a successful 17-year career as a Major League Baseball player. Pitching primarily for the Detroit Tigers and Philadelphia Phillies, Bunning's record won him a seat in the Baseball Hall of Fame in 1996. He was the second pitcher in history (Cy Young was the first) to record 1,000 strikeouts and 100 wins in both the American and National leagues. Retiring in 1971, Bunning was second on the all-time strikeout list—second only to Walter Johnson.

Bunning's political career began in 1977 when he served on the Fort Thomas City Council. In 1979, he was elected to the Kentucky State Senate and then, in 1986, Bunning was elected to the U.S. House of Representatives where he served for 12 years.

Bunning and his wife, Mary, have nine children and 35 grandchildren; they make their home in Southgate.

Jim Bunning (R)
US Senator
SH-316 Hart Senate Ofc Bldg
Washington DC 20510
(202) 224-4343
FAX (202) 228-1373
http://bunning.senate.gov/index.cfm

REPRESENTATIVE ED WHITFIELD
(R-FIRST DISTRICT)

First elected to Congress in 1984, Congressman Ed Whitfield is serving his sixth term as U.S. Representative for the 34 counties of Kentucky's First Congressional District.

A native of Hopkinsville, Whitfield earned a bachelor's degree and a law degree from the University of Kentucky. He served as a 1st Lieutenant in the 100th Division of the U.S. Army Reserves. A practicing attorney in Hopkinsville, Whitfield also operated an oil distributorship in the west Kentucky coalfields. He served in the Kentucky House of Representatives from 1974-75.

In 1979, he became counsel to the president of Seaboard System Railroad in Washington, D.C. Four years later, he was named vice president of State Relations for CSX Corp; and then vice president for Federal Railroad Affairs. Whitfield served as Legal Counsel to the Chairman of the Interstate Commerce Commission (ICC) from 1991 to 1993.

Married to the former Connie Harriman, Whitfield has a daughter, two grandchildren and a Scottish terrier.

Ed Whitfield (R)
US Representative - First District
301 Cannon House Ofc Bldg
Washington DC 20515
(202) 225-3115 • FAX (202) 225-3547
ed.whitfield@mail.house.gov
http://whitfield.house.gov/

REPRESENTATIVE RON LEWIS
(R-SECOND DISTRICT)

Ron Lewis has represented Kentucky's Second District since 1994. The Second District is home to Fort Knox, Mammoth Cave National Park, the birthplace of Abraham Lincoln, and over 50,000 people who depend on agriculture for a living.

The son of a tobacco farmer, Lewis was born Sept. 14, 1946, in Greenup County. He has a bachelor's degree in history and political science; and a master's degree in higher education. Lewis also attended the Southern Baptist Seminary prior to being ordained a minister.

Lewis married the former Kayi Gambill in 1966. They have two children, Ronald Brent and Allison Faye, and live in Cecilia.

Ron Lewis (R)
US Representative - Second District
2418 Rayburn House Ofc Bldg
Washington DC 20515
(202) 225-3501 • FAX (202) 226-2019
ron.lewis@mail.house.gov
http://www.house.gov/ronlewis/

REPRESENTATIVE ANNE M. NORTHUP
(R-THIRD DISTRICT)

Anne M. Northup was elected to represent the Third Congressional District of Kentucky in 1996. She returned to Congress in 1998, 2000, 2002, and 2004. Before her election to Congress, she represented the 32nd Legislative District in the Kentucky House of Representatives for nine years, where she served five consecutive terms from 1987-1996. Congresswoman Northup is a member of the Congressional Coalition on Adoption and traveled to China to work on eliminating growing bureaucratic obstacles that threatened to reduce the number of Chinese orphans available to American families for adoption.

Congresswoman Northup graduated from Saint Mary's College in 1970 with a bachelor of arts degree in economics and business. She has years of service on community boards, is a recipient of numerous civic awards and is an active community volunteer. She has been married to Woody Northup, a small business owner, for over 35 years, and together the Northups have six children.

Anne Northup (R)
US Representative -Third District
2459 Rayburn House Ofc Bldg
Washington DC 20515
(202) 225-5401 • FAX (202) 225-5776
rep.northup@mail.house.gov
http://northup.house.gov/index.asp

REPRESENTATIVE GEOFF DAVIS
(R-FOURTH DISTRICT)

Elected in 2004, Congressman Geoff Davis represents Kentucky's Fourth District, which is the northern part of the state bordering West Virginia, Ohio and Indiana.

Upon graduation from high school, Davis enlisted in the U.S. Army and received an appointment to the U.S. Military Academy at West Point. He served as a helicopter flight commander in the 82nd Airborne Division, and later ran U.S. Army Aviation Operations for Peace Enforcement between Israel and Egypt. Davis is a former Army Ranger and senior parachutist.

In 1992, Davis started a consulting firm specializing in lean manufacturing and high technology systems integration. He and his wife Pat live in Hebron with their six children.

Geoff Davis (R) - US Representative
Fourth District
1541 Longworth House Ofc Bldg
Washington DC 20515
(202) 225-3465 • FAX (202) 225-0003
http://geoffdavis.house.gov/

REPRESENTATIVE HAROLD "HAL" ROGERS
(R-FIFTH DISTRICT)

In his 25th year on Capitol Hill, Congressman Harold "Hal" Rogers was elected to Congress in 1980 and is currently serving his 13th term representing Kentucky's Fifth Congressional District. Rogers has a reputation as a skillful insider with significant influence over federal budget policy in a wide range of areas.

Rogers' congressional district consists of 29 counties in southern and eastern Kentucky. Born in rural Kentucky, Rogers earned his bachelor's and law degrees from the University of Kentucky. An attorney by profession, he stepped into the public arena during the 1960s by promoting industrial development in Somerset. In 1969, he was elected as Commonwealth Attorney for two Kentucky counties and served in that position for 11 years.

Rogers was married to Shirley McDowell Rogers for 37 years until her death in 1995. Together, they reared three grown children, Anthony, Allison and John. Rogers remarried Cynthia Doyle Rogers in 1999, they make their home in Somerset.

Harold Rogers (R)
US Representative - Fifth District
2406 Rayburn House Ofc Bldg
Washington DC 20515
(202) 225-4601 • (202) 225-0940
talk2hal@mail.house.gov
http://www.house.gov/rogers/

REPRESENTATIVE BEN CHANDLER
(D-SIXTH DISTRICT)

Ben Chandler was first elected in a special election in February 2004 to represent Kentucky's Sixth District in the U.S. House of Representatives. He won a full 2-year term in 2004 with 59 percent of the vote.

Before his election to Congress, Chandler served two terms as Kentucky's Attorney General. In 1995, he became the youngest Attorney General in the nation and was reelected in 1999 without opposition to a second term. He previously served a four-year term as Kentucky State Auditor.

Chandler graduated from the University of Kentucky with a bachelor's in history and holds a law degree from the University of Kentucky College of Law.

Born on September 12, 1959, Chandler lives in Woodford County with his wife Jennifer and their three children, Lucie, Albert IV and Branham.

Ben Chandler (D)
US Representative
Sixth District
1504 Longworth House Ofc Bldg
Washington DC 20515
(202) 225-4706 9 • FAX (202) 225-2122
http://chandler.house.gov/

FEDERAL COURTS

COURT	JUDGES/OFFICERS	ADD1	ADD2	CITY	ST	ZIP	PHONE
Supreme Court of the US (The)	John G Roberts Jr, Chief Justice (Nominee)	US Supreme Court Bldg	1 1st St NE	Washington	DC	20543	(202) 479-3211
Supreme Court of the US (The)	Stephen G Breyer, Associate Justice	US Supreme Court Bldg	1 1st St NE	Washington	DC	20543	(202) 479-3211
Supreme Court of the US (The)	Ruth Bader Ginsburg, Associate Justice	US Supreme Court Bldg	1 1st St NE	Washington	DC	20543	(202) 479-3211
Supreme Court of the US (The)	Anthony M Kennedy, Associate Justice	US Supreme Court Bldg	1 1st St NE	Washington	DC	20543	(202) 479-3211
Supreme Court of the US (The)	Sandra Day O'Connor, Associate Justice (Retiring)	US Supreme Court Bldg	1 1st St NE	Washington	DC	20543	(202) 479-3211
Supreme Court of the US (The)	Antonin Scalia, Associate Justice	US Supreme Court Bldg	1 1st St NE	Washington	DC	20543	(202) 479-3211
Supreme Court of the US (The)	David H Souter, Associate Justice	US Supreme Court Bldg	1 1st St NE	Washington	DC	20543	(202) 479-3211
Supreme Court of the US (The)	John Paul Stevens, Associate Justice	US Supreme Court Bldg	1 1st St NE	Washington	DC	20543	(202) 479-3211
Supreme Court of the US (The)	Clarence Thomas, Associate Justice	US Supreme Court Bldg	1 1st St NE	Washington	DC	20543	(202) 479-3211
Supreme Court of the US (The)	William K Suter, Clerk of the Court	1 1st St NE		Washington	DC	20543	(202) 479-3211
Supreme Court of the US (The)	Frank D Wagner, Reporter of Decisions	1 1st St NE		Washington	DC	20543	(202) 479-3211
Supreme Court of the US (The)	Judith A Gaskell, Librarian	1 1st St NE		Washington	DC	20543	(202) 479-3211
Supreme Court of the US (The)	Pamela Talkin, Marshal	1 1st St NE		Washington	DC	20543	(202) 479-3211
Supreme Court of the US (The)	Kathleen L Arberg, Public Information Officer	US Supreme Court Bldg	1 1st St NE	Washington	DC	20543	(202) 479-3211
US Court of Appeals, Sixth Circuit	Danny J Boggs, Chief Judge	220 US Cthse	601 W Broadway	Louisville	KY	40202	(502) 625-3900
US Court of Appeals, Sixth Circuit	Ralph B Guy Jr, Senior Judge	532 Potter Stewart US Cthse	100 E 5th St	Cincinnati	OH	45202	(513) 564-7000
US Court of Appeals, Sixth Circuit	Damon J Keith, Senior Judge	532 Potter Stewart US Cthse	100 E 5th St	Cincinnati	OH	45202	(513) 564-7000
US Court of Appeals, Sixth Circuit	Cornelia G Kennedy, Senior Judge	532 Potter Stewart US Cthse	100 E 5th St	Cincinnati	OH	45202	(513) 564-7000
US Court of Appeals, Sixth Circuit	Gilbert S Merritt, Senior Judge	532 Potter Stewart US Cthse	100 E 5th St	Cincinnati	OH	45202	(513) 564-7000
US Court of Appeals, Sixth Circuit	David A Nelson, Senior Judge	532 Potter Stewart US Cthse	100 E 5th St	Cincinnati	OH	45202	(513) 564-7000
US Court of Appeals, Sixth Circuit	Alan E Norris, Senior Judge	532 Potter Stewart US Cthse	100 E 5th St	Cincinnati	OH	45202	(513) 564-7000
US Court of Appeals, Sixth Circuit	James L Ryan, Senior Judge	310 S Main St Ste 333		London	KY	40741	(606) 877-7930
US Court of Appeals, Sixth Circuit	Eugene E Siler Jr, Senior Judge	532 Potter Stewart US Cthse	100 E 5th St	Cincinnati	OH	45202	(513) 564-7000
US Court of Appeals, Sixth Circuit	Richard F Suhrheinrich, Senior Judge	532 Potter Stewart US Cthse	100 E 5th St	Cincinnati	OH	45202	(513) 564-7000
US Court of Appeals, Sixth Circuit	Deborah L Cook, Judge	532 Potter Stewart US Cthse	100 E 5th St	Cincinnati	OH	45202	(513) 564-7000
US Court of Appeals, Sixth Circuit	Alice M Batchelder, Judge	532 Potter Stewart US Cthse	100 E 5th St	Cincinnati	OH	45202	(513) 564-7000
US Court of Appeals, Sixth Circuit	Eric L Clay, Judge	532 Potter Stewart US Cthse	100 E 5th St	Cincinnati	OH	45202	(513) 564-7000
US Court of Appeals, Sixth Circuit	R Guy Cole Jr, Judge	532 Potter Stewart US Cthse	100 E 5th St	Cincinnati	OH	45202	(513) 564-7000
US Court of Appeals, Sixth Circuit	Martha Craig Daughtrey, Judge	532 Potter Stewart US Cthse	100 E 5th St	Cincinnati	OH	45202	(513) 564-7000
US Court of Appeals, Sixth Circuit	Julia Smith Gibbons, Judge	532 Potter Stewart US Cthse	100 E 5th St	Cincinnati	OH	45202	(513) 564-7000
US Court of Appeals, Sixth Circuit	Ronald Lee Gilman, Judge	209 US Cthse	601 W Broadway	Louisville	KY	40202	(502) 625-3800
US Court of Appeals, Sixth Circuit	Boyce F Martin Jr, Judge	532 Potter Stewart US Cthse	100 E 5th St	Cincinnati	OH	45202	(513) 564-7000
US Court of Appeals, Sixth Circuit	Karen Nelson Moore, Judge	532 Potter Stewart US Cthse	100 E 5th St	Cincinnati	OH	45202	(513) 564-7000
US Court of Appeals, Sixth Circuit	John M Rogers, Judge	532 Potter Stewart US Cthse	100 E 5th St	Cincinnati	OH	45202	(513) 564-7000
US Court of Appeals, Sixth Circuit	Jeffrey S Sutton, Judge	532 Potter Stewart US Cthse	100 E 5th St	Cincinnati	OH	45202	(513) 564-7200
US Court of Appeals, Sixth Circuit	James Higgins, Circuit Executive	532 Potter Stewart US Cthse	100 E 5th St	Cincinnati	OH	45202	(513) 564-7000
Administrative Offices of the US Courts	Leonard Green, Clerk US Court of Appeals 6th Circuit	Office of Public Affairs		Washington	DC	20544	(202) 502-2600
US Sentencing Commission	Leonidas Ralph Mecham, Director	1 Columbus Cir NE		Washington	DC	20002	(202) 502-4500
US District Court Clerk, Eastern District	Judge Ricardo H Hinojosa, Chair	101 Barr St Rm 206	PO Box 3074	Lexington	KY	40588	(859) 233-2503
US District Court Clerk, Eastern District	Leslie G Whitmer, Clerk of the Court	101 Barr St Rm 206	PO Box 3074	Lexington	KY	40588	(859) 233-2503
US District Court Clerk, Eastern District	Mark Armstrong, Chief Deputy	336 Carl Perkins Federal Bldg	1405 Greenup Ave	Ashland	KY	41101	(606) 329-8652
US District Court Clerk, Eastern District	Christina Riley, Deputy in Charge	35 W 5th St		Covington	KY	41012	(859) 392-7925
US District Court Clerk, Eastern District	Lynn Battaglia, Deputy in Charge	313 John C Watts Federal Bldg	330 W Broadway	Frankfort	KY	40601	(502) 223-5225
US District Court Clerk, Eastern District	Shirley Middleton, Deputy in Charge	300 S Main St	PO Box 5121	London	KY	40745	(606) 877-7910
US District Court, Eastern District	Shirley W Allen, Deputy in Charge	110 Main St Ste 203		Pikeville	KY	41501	(606) 437-6160
US District Court, Eastern District	Malinda Bevins, Deputy in Charge	101 Barr St Ste 219	PO Box 2165	Lexington	KY	40588	(859) 233-2625
US District Court, Eastern District	Karl S Forester, Chief Judge (Senior Judge)						

FEDERAL COURTS

COURT	JUDGES/OFFICERS	ADD1	ADD2	CITY	ST	ZIP	PHONE
US District Court, Eastern District	William O Bertelsman, Senior Judge	35 W 5th St Rm 505	PO Box 1012	Covington	KY	41012	(859) 392-7900
US District Court, Eastern District	G Wix Unthank, Senior Judge	320 Federal Bldg	PO Box 5112	London	KY	40741	(606) 878-2731
US District Court, Eastern District	Henry R Wilhoit Jr, Senior Judge	35 W 5th St Rm 410	1405 Greenup Ave	Ashland	KY	41101	(606) 329-2592
US District Court, Eastern District	David L Bunning, Judge	35 W 5th St Rm 410	PO Box 232	Covington	KY	41011	(859) 392-7907
US District Court, Eastern District	Karen K Caldwell, Judge	US District Cthse	310 S Main St Ste 434	London	KY	40741	(606) 877-7950
US District Court, Eastern District	Jennifer B Coffman, Judge	101 Barr St Ste 305	PO Box 2228	Lexington	KY	40588	(859) 233-2453
US District Court, Eastern District	Joseph M Hood, Judge	101 Barr St Ste 135	PO Box 2227	Lexington	KY	40588	(859) 233-2415
US District Court, Eastern District	Danny C Reeves, Judge	US District Cthse	310 S Main St Ste 444	London	KY	40741	(606) 877-7960
US District Court, Eastern District	J B Johnson Jr, Magistrate Judge	US District Cthse	310 S Main St	London	KY	40741	(606) 877-7940
US District Court, Eastern District	Peggy E Patterson, Magistrate Judge	210 Perkins Federal Bldg	1405 Greenup Ave	Ashland	KY	41101	(606) 329-2952
US District Court, Eastern District	James B Todd, Magistrate Judge	101 Barr St Ste 417	PO Box 2058	Lexington	KY	40588	(859) 233-2697
US District Court, Eastern District	J Gregory Wehrman, Magistrate Judge	35 W 5th St Rm 375	PO Box 1229	Covington	KY	41012	(859) 392-7909
US Bankruptcy Court Clerk, Eastern District	Jerry D Truitt, Clerk of the Court	Community Trust Bank Bldg	100 E Vine St Ste 200	Lexington	KY	40507	(859) 233-2608
US Bankruptcy Court, Eastern District	Joe Scott, Chief Judge	100 E Vine St Ste 600	PO Box 1111	Lexington	KY	40588	(859) 233-2608
US Bankruptcy Court, Eastern District	William S Howard, Judge		PO Box 576	Lexington	KY	40588	(859) 233-2465
US Bankruptcy Court, Eastern District	Joe Lee, Judge		PO Box 1111	Lexington	KY	40588	(859) 233-2814
US Probation Office, Eastern District	Rozel L Hollingsworth, Chief Probation Officer	100 E Vine St Ste 600	PO Box 1760	Lexington	KY	40588	(859) 233-2646
US District Court Clerk, Western District	Jeffery A Apperson, Clerk of Court	601 W Broadway Ste 106		Louisville	KY	40202	(502) 625-3500
US District Court Clerk, Western District	William W Clark, Chief Deputy	601 W Broadway		Louisville	KY	40202	(502) 625-3526
US District Court Clerk, Western District	Celia Furlong, Deputy in Charge/Case Administrator	241 E Main St Ste 120		Bowling Green	KY	42101	(270) 393-2508
US District Court Clerk, Western District	Patti May, Deputy in Charge	126 Federal Bldg	423 Frederica St	Owensboro	KY	42301	(270) 689-4400
US District Court Clerk, Western District	Joan Moore, Deputy in Charge	501 Broadway St Ste 127		Paducah	KY	42001	(270) 415-6405
US District Court, Western District	John G Heyburn II, Chief Judge	Gene Snyder Cthse Rm 239	601 W Broadway	Louisville	KY	40202	(502) 625-3620
US District Court, Western District	Edward H Johnstone, Senior Judge	Gene Snyder Cthse Rm 262	601 W Broadway	Louisville	KY	40588	(502) 625-3660
US District Court, Western District	Judge Johnstone's Paducah Office	Federal Bldg Rm 217	501 Broadway St	Paducah	KY	42001	(270) 415-6450
US District Court, Western District	Jennifer B Coffman, Judge	Gene Snyder Cthse Rm 252	601 W Boadway	Louisville	KY	40202	(502) 625-3680
US District Court, Western District	Judge Coffman's Lexington Office	101 Barr St Rm 306	PO Box 2228	Lexington	KY	40588	(859) 233-2453
US District Court, Western District	Joseph H McKinley Jr, Judge	US Cthse Rm 206	423 Frederica St	Owensboro	KY	42301	(270) 689-4430
US District Court, Western District	Thomas B Russell, Judge	Gen Snyder Cthse Rm 202	601 W Broadway	Louisville	KY	40202	(502) 625-3640
US District Court, Western District	Judge Russell's Paducah Office	501 Broadway St Rm 121		Paducah	KY	42001	(270) 415-6430
US District Court, Western District	Charles R Simpson III, Judge	601 W Broadway Ste 247		Louisville	KY	40202	(502) 625-3600
US District Court, Western District	Dave Whalin, Magistrate Judge	Gene Snyder Cthse Rm 200	601 W Broadway	Louisville	KY	40202	(502) 625-3830
US District Court, Western District	E Robert Goebel, Magistrate Judge	US Cthse Rm 117	423 Frederica St	Owensboro	KY	42301	(270) 689-4450
US District Court, Western District	Judge Goebel's Bowling Green Office	241 E Main St Rm 207		Bowling Green	KY	42101	(270) 393-2440
US District Court, Western District	W David King, Magistrate Judge	501 Broadway St Rm 330	601 W Broadway	Paducah	KY	42001	(270) 415-6470
US District Court, Western District	James D Moyer, Magistrate Judge	Gene Snyder Cthse Rm 208		Louisville	KY	40202	(502) 625-3930
US Bankruptcy Court Clerk, Western District	Diane S Robl, Clerk of Court	601 W Broadway Ste 450		Louisville	KY	40202	(502) 627-5800
US Bankruptcy Court, Western District	David T Stosberg, Chief Judge	601 W Broadway		Louisville	KY	40202	(502) 627-5575
US Bankruptcy Court, Western District	Joan L Cooper, Judge	601 W Broadway Ste 541		Louisville	KY	40202	(502) 627-5525
US Bankruptcy Court, Western District	Thomas H Fulton, Judge	601 W Broadway Ste 533		Louisville	KY	40202	(502) 627-5550
US Probation Office, Western District	Patrick Craig, Chief Probate Officer	601 W Broadway Ste 400		Louisville	KY	40202	(502) 681-1000
US Probation Office, Western District	Patrick Craig, Chief Probate Officer	2530 Scottsville Rd Ste 22	PO Box 51607	Bowling Green	KY	42102	(270) 842-6109
US Probation Office, Western District	Jeffery T Litchfield, Supervising Officer	607 Hammond Plz	Ft Campbell Blvd	Hopkinsville	KY	42240	(270) 885-4853
US Probation Office, Western District	Jeffery T Litchfield, Supervising Officer	309 Federal Bldg	423 Frederica St	Owensboro	KY	42301	(270) 684-2351
US Probation Office, Western District	Ronnie E Golden, Supervising Officer	2625 Wayne Sullivan Dr		Paducah	KY	42003	(270) 442-7824

Source: The Kentucky Directory Gold Book 2005-2006

FEDERAL GOVERNMENT
Major Military Installations

Jerry Cecil

Kentucky's role in national security is apparent in its two prominent military installations, Fort Knox and Fort Campbell. However, long before these bases were established, the Commonwealth was playing a significant role in national defense.

HISTORY OF MILITARY INSTALLATIONS

Prior to statehood Kentucky had cemented its geographical importance to the fledgling nation. Early soldiers and frontiersmen such as Gen. George Rogers Clark and Daniel Boone reported on and defended against foreign designs to claim the territory west of the Appalachians. After the American Revolution, European nations threatened the Ohio River valley with attempts to reclaim lost territory. Kentuckians responded willingly and rallied behind Gen. Andrew Jackson in the War of 1812.

Although Kentucky technically remained neutral during the American Civil War, it was a key component to the strategies of both the Union and the Confederacy. As a border state Kentucky displayed the conflicting emotions that arose when families and neighbors split over the conflict, but the state was at the forefront of providing supplies, troops and military posts to support the goals of restoring the Union. Ironically, both wartime presidents, Abraham Lincoln and Jefferson Davis, were Kentucky natives by birth. During the war, Camp Breckinridge, Camp Nelson and Camp Donelson were familiar military bases or posts.

Kentucky's unflinching commitment to providing for national defense continued during the Spanish-American War (1898) through to the Vietnam War (1961-1975). Camp Zachary Taylor, near Louisville, served as a recruiting and training base for hundreds of soldiers during World War I (1917-1918), including medical personnel for the famed Base Hospital #40 or Barrow Unit. Camp Knox, near Radcliffe, was founded during World War I. It later became Fort Knox. World War II triggered another military buildup, hence Fort Campbell, near Hopkinsville, was created to provide training areas and housing for the Army. The importance of Fort Knox and Fort Campbell continued to grow in the early 1960s as America entered the Vietnam War.

After the Vietnam War, the clamor to reduce military spending resurfaced, despite perceived threats from the Cold War (1945-1989). A new era of technology, satellites, bombers and nuclear submarines gave the illusion that military bases would no longer be important, but in fact they are as critical as ever to our nation's security, especially in this time of global terrorism. Once again the two premier federal military installations, Fort Knox and Fort Campbell, demonstrate

Fort Knox
Source: Kentucky Department of Libraries & Archives

their geographical and strategic importance to the Army component of the national strategy.

OTHER IMPORTANT INSTALLATIONS

While Fort Knox and Fort Campbell are the largest and most visible federal military installations in the Commonwealth, there are many other related defense activities in Kentucky that reflect the same level of economic importance. Blue Grass Army Depot, near Richmond, was established to store and repair equipment for World War II. It currently supplies soldiers with ammunition and personal protection equipment. BGAD is also a storage facility for World War II chemical munitions, which are scheduled for destruction this decade. New technologies are being designed to render the toxic material inert.

BGAD's companion depot, Lexington Army Depot, near Avon, was closed in the 1980s by Congressional act. However, new uses for the facility were created in a state and federal partnership that capitalized on its valuable capabilities and location. It is now called Bluegrass Station and is operated by the Commonwealth.

The Naval Ordnance Depot, near Louisville, was closed in the late 1980s and has been leased as a technology park. At its peak the depot provided surface naval gun support, repair and fabrication to the entire fleet. Those functions are now provided by a civilian contractor.

STATE AND FEDERAL MILITARY INSTALLATIONS

The Army and Air National Guard maintain a network of military installations that are funded by state and federal monies. The Kentucky National Guard is headquartered in Frankfort at Boone Center. The Air Guard is stationed near Standiford Field in Louisville. Both of these components are commanded by the adjutant general, who is appointed by the governor. As a state resource, the governor is the commander-in-chief of the Guard. When the Guard is called to federal service, they answer to the president of the United States through the Department of Defense.

The National Guard maintains a network of local armories throughout Kentucky which benefit the local economies. The Guard also has several training and maintenance sites, the largest of which is the recently built Wendell Ford Regional Training Center near Central City in western Kentucky. The Guard uses the training and base facilities at Fort Knox and Fort Campbell as well as other federal sites outside the state.

RESERVE FORCES

The Reserves form an important pillar for national security. Each service – Army, Navy, Air Force, Marines, Coast Guard – maintains Reserve centers in Kentucky. Historically Reservists met and trained less frequently than active or Guard soldiers, but that is no longer the case, as the value of skilled Reservists has shown in recent years.

ARMY CORPS OF ENGINEERS

The Army Corps of Engineers is a special case, both economically and militarily. In wartime the Army Corps of Engineers provides direct and indirect support to the Army in the field with construction (bridge building and water crossings) and destruction projects (mine fields, enemy fortifications). It serves as the project manager on construction projects on federal military installations such as barracks, airfields and training ranges. But it also has an everyday mission directed by Congress, the economic importance of which is often overlooked and underappreciated. The Army Corps of Engineers is responsible for the U.S. waterways to provide for flood control, river commerce, recreation and for the construction of major civil engineering projects such as lakes and dams.

The Army Corps of Engineers is organized into departments and divisions. The Kentucky element is headquartered in Louisville and is commanded by an Army colonel. The chief of engineers at the Pentagon is in charge of the worldwide organization. Because of its unique missions and economic value, the Army Corps of Engineers works closely with the federal Congressional delegation.

COAST GUARD

The Coast Guard is an integral part of the military fabric in Kentucky. Originally it was part of the U.S. Transportation Department, but is now a vital part of the new Transportation Security Agency and performs missions on lakes and rivers, providing search and rescue, boat inspections and interdictions of contraband.

VETERANS FACILITIES

The federal government maintains two Veterans Affairs Medical Centers in Louisville and Lexington. Both facilities are close to medical research universities that provide cutting-edge technology to the care of injured soldiers. In addition to the VAMCs there are a series of clinics throughout the state that seek to place referral and care as close to the patient as possible.

Within the last decade the Commonwealth's Dept. of Veterans Affairs has taken the lead in creating a network of state veteran nursing homes and cemeteries to bring these facilities within reach of more veterans. There are three state veteran nursing homes – in Wilmore, Hazard and near Hopkinsville – with three more planned depending on funding. The new Western Kentucky Veterans Cemetery, near Hopkinsville, opened recently. A second cemetery is under construction near Fort Knox, and a third is being planned near Williamstown.

Useful websites:
- Fort Knox (www.kknox.army.mil)
- Fort Campbell (www.campbell.army.mil)
- Kentucky Historical Society (http://history.ky.gov)
- Kentucky Army National Guard (www.ky.gov/agencies/military/army.htm)
- Army Corps of Engineers (www.usace.army.mil)
- United States Dept. of Veteran Affairs (www.va.gov)
- Kentucky Depart of Veteran Affairs (www.kdva.net)
- State of Kentucky (kentucky.gov)
- Kentucky Commission on Military Affairs (ky.gov/agencies/kcma)
- Kentucky Air National Guard (www.kyang.ang.af.mil)

FEDERAL EXPENDITURES BY COUNTY, 2003

COUNTY	RETIREMENT/ DISABILITY	OTHER DIRECT PAYMENTS (INDIVIDUALS)	DIRECT PAYMENTS (NOT INDIVIDUALS)	GRANTS	PROCUREMENT CONTRACTS	SALARIES & WAGES	TOTAL DIRECT EXPENDITURES OR OBLIGATIONS	TOTAL EXPENDITURES (DEFENSE)	TOTAL EXPENDITURES (NON DEFENSE)	DIRECT LOANS	GUARANTEED/ INSURED LOANS	INSURANCE
Adair	41,173,470	26,826,938	2,500,858	37,307,704	491,235	2,511,971	110,812,176	940,000	109,872,176	3,728,056	2,315,304	582,269
Allen	40,331,733	18,646,615	808,984	31,359,807	562,000	2,141,015	93,850,134	1,044,000	92,806,134	822,611	2,851,713	
Anderson	40,233,901	12,263,078	394,726	10,603,534	545,471	2,409,662	66,450,372	1,894,000	64,556,372	851,961	14,261,259	4,401,123
Ballard	26,798,393	14,860,158	2,112,915	8,761,259	3,051,995	1,995,895	57,580,615	3,291,113	54,289,502	1,036,884	4,046,869	5,538,032
Barren	90,667,754	35,928,041	3,483,042	42,751,667	9,614,878	7,517,299	189,962,681	5,366,261	184,596,420	1,319,344	32,042,810	2,418,304
Bath	26,783,451	10,236,997	660,781	28,435,745	715,176	1,648,686	68,480,836	582,000	67,898,836	4,076,229	1,282,509	4,362,761
Bell	99,969,485	48,669,553	910,009	71,332,278	-158,745,283	12,167,003	74,303,045	5,985,980	68,317,065	-253,012	1,482,439	28,758,961
Boone	164,177,452	48,890,669	595,536	40,259,031	63,929,808	78,608,354	396,460,850	66,884,590	329,576,260	229,996	101,663,978	6,880,416
Bourbon	48,101,960	20,588,710	3,430,951	23,583,431	37,548,699	2,174,015	135,427,766	23,023,924	112,403,842	3,397,469	8,215,061	15,438,015
Boyd	167,667,122	79,052,792	1,175,922	71,082,457	14,536,348	34,054,507	367,569,048	9,335,317	358,233,731	375,288	10,852,238	20,967,364
Boyle	71,374,997	28,690,380	521,898	26,332,603	1,826,119	5,021,732	133,767,729	3,851,199	129,916,530	226,683	10,852,238	3,223,658
Bracken	20,162,231	9,739,892	547,498	11,670,564	413,235	1,570,746	44,104,166	495,000	43,609,166	725,519	2,086,146	9,931,135
Breathitt	49,964,640	20,946,529	224,830	54,849,082	2,130,892	3,831,863	131,947,836	2,741,072	129,206,764	416,742	370,714	6,579,263
Breckinridge	50,055,709	20,289,231	2,199,172	24,106,978	1,387,346	3,753,284	101,791,720	3,450,581	98,341,139	1,338,592	5,875,469	5,310,434
Bullitt	101,194,273	34,604,406	283,125	22,828,853	186,166,776	3,963,964	349,041,375	174,726,128	174,315,247	688,645	71,640,739	50,542,924
Butler	26,995,489	15,388,240	1,394,715	18,399,408	462,823	2,008,836	64,649,511	624,000	64,025,511	1,443,113	959,415	3,804,455
Caldwell	38,630,734	16,680,450	2,719,377	15,302,913	977,784	2,743,925	77,055,173	1,347,000	75,708,173	1,087,570	614,666	6,259,418
Calloway	81,176,857	45,799,116	2,938,078	26,379,833	2,412,767	5,933,269	164,639,920	4,959,531	159,680,389	1,573,245	7,103,242	18,529,150
Campbell	195,991,354	101,128,535	1,496,109	63,478,768	11,562,849	18,264,582	391,922,197	13,584,368	378,337,829	138,227	37,275,443	35,070,840
Carlisle	15,259,038	8,089,076	2,026,468	6,090,108	315,122	1,071,447	32,851,259	353,181	32,498,078	56,986	3,441,039	16,944,171
Carroll	23,954,936	11,456,492	404,978	20,514,137	3,630,440	2,015,776	61,976,759	3,947,675	58,029,084	765,102	2,556,910	6,984,219
Carter	70,408,868	32,961,318	1,522,648	90,739,754	21,926,641	4,876,612	222,437,841	23,332,215	199,105,626	1,864,850	1,556,520	16,944,171
Casey	36,329,905	16,648,893	804,596	27,043,151	564,472	1,755,806	83,146,823	920,000	82,226,823	379,684	813,953	2,998,868
Christian	144,462,794	59,219,433	8,721,542	91,693,011	300,704,552	1,012,421,614	1,617,222,946	1,315,642,146	301,580,800	1,877,177	43,520,177	70,205,495
Clark	86,687,002	28,208,671	1,239,960	40,114,639	1,836,079	7,861,901	165,948,252	3,214,110	162,734,142	1,237,740	492,600,991	15,591,569
Clay	66,458,984	29,812,411	147,738	70,254,231	1,473,292	22,310,224	190,456,880	719,612	189,737,068	1,296,638	1,129,330	5,073,461
Clinton	25,019,689	20,548,808	205,139	38,965,977	1,781,326	2,270,597	88,791,536	806,738	87,984,798	789,200	1,677,764	89,481
Crittenden	26,152,763	14,146,202	2,069,851	10,541,972	396,679	3,170,631	56,478,098	2,340,973	54,137,125	237,706	334,022	2,398,871
Cumberland	19,464,468	13,348,534	299,543	17,064,684	606,974	921,388	51,705,591	1,014,092	50,691,499	75,029	1,003,995	270,054
Daviess	224,935,534	102,362,349	5,154,215	188,190,553	7,467,278	18,943,456	467,053,385	11,902,466	455,150,919	3,098,063	33,999,290	135,292,714
Edmonson	24,727,051	11,088,406	483,090	13,213,461	2,362,303	8,646,476	60,520,787	1,343,520	59,177,267	744,795	1,077,348	578,072
Elliott	12,910,884	5,753,979	140,339	13,570,185	115,705	436,209	32,927,301	77,000	32,850,301	48,660,633	157,400	814,885
Estill	48,785,896	24,099,208	358,117	30,409,188	865,897	2,401,686	106,919,992	1,744,060	105,175,932	793,860	1,262,357	1,410,890
Fayette	498,256,867	281,626,442	5,041,504	372,285,838	259,774,788	207,722,627	1,624,708,066	225,365,591	1,399,342,155	87,362,076	186,984,104	66,209,762
Fleming	32,666,524	13,809,718	2,745,977	23,510,376	654,297	2,578,045	75,964,937	601,768	75,363,169	1,153,306	2,342,545	4,488,599
Floyd	147,838,382	65,246,976	6,185,569	71,865,711	7,998,167	11,247,549	310,380,354	3,492,878	306,887,476	4,498,055	1,579,693	98,640,577
Franklin	263,543,696	61,875,264	27,278,245	977,443,842	2,852,448	31,667,135	1,364,660,630	51,025,063	1,313,635,567	20,714,344	26,143,194	41,503,013
Fulton	25,501,126	14,714,581	2,971,895	17,755,212	1,949,403	2,776,482	65,668,699	2,245,404	63,423,295	777,528	6,578,513	13,961,595
Gallatin	14,258,776	6,574,972	101,235	8,448,322	886,729	1,360,447	31,650,481	1,331,788	30,298,693	115,398	2,739,774	6,502,436
Garrard	35,594,673	12,315,064	533,652	15,735,513	512,412	1,891,925	66,583,239	1,070,000	65,513,239	497,264	8,647,976	2,890,916
Grant	47,282,923	18,387,137	342,035	34,534,908	1,775,781	3,174,314	101,317,098	1,998,487	99,318,611	541,295	17,029,778	570,524
Graves	103,407,709	51,540,583	7,174,995	34,532,321	3,019,429	10,322,568	209,997,605	3,155,142	206,842,463	1,613,919	8,541,628	31,434,131

FEDERAL EXPENDITURES BY COUNTY, 2003

COUNTY	RETIREMENT/ DISABILITY	OTHER DIRECT PAYMENTS (INDIVIDUALS)	DIRECT PAYMENTS (NOT INDIVIDUALS)	GRANTS	PROCUREMENT CONTRACTS	SALARIES & WAGES	TOTAL DIRECT EXPENDITURES OR OBLIGATIONS	TOTAL EXPENDITURES (DEFENSE)	TOTAL EXPENDITURES (NON DEFENSE)	DIRECT LOANS	GUARANTEED/ INSURED LOANS	INSURANCE
Grayson	64,788,217	29,418,997	1,838,109	41,808,879	1,068,124	3,892,642	142,814,968	2,803,588	140,011,380	1,692,535	5,488,546	2,034,440
Green	28,094,200	15,509,671	959,374	14,719,227	330,588	1,386,597	60,999,857	425,000	60,574,657	824,401	509,255	250,239
Greenup	114,531,715	44,914,725	571,104	30,351,939	2,041,772	3,891,552	196,302,807	3,757,066	192,545,741	1,878,331	6,366,533	33,372,318
Hancock	18,074,374	6,432,301	461,188	7,469,987	330,588	1,288,597	34,057,035	746,000	33,311,035	126,335	932,517	8,207,72
Hardin	312,775,661	71,759,463	2,798,457	53,881,931	14,266,478	476,641,986	932,123,976	535,035,831	397,088,145	2,188,602	46,039,472	28,208,124
Harlan	218,678,104	48,068,857	516,222	63,336,808	52,135,763	10,496,230	393,231,984	6,368,968	386,863,016	89,362	1,101,876	35,911,829
Harrison	41,015,988	16,155,874	1,079,624	18,608,126	915,440	3,919,015	81,694,067	2,365,827	79,328,240	1,707,449	4,823,286	15,597,484
Hart	41,012,298	18,378,191	1,323,830	39,801,060	554,352	2,182,015	103,251,746	1,030,000	102,221,746	5,671,287	3,469,060	1,446,099
Henderson	107,572,426	53,980,301	3,278,443	38,166,536	14,813,842	6,694,746	224,506,294	16,646,941	207,859,353	1,603,008	31,334,073	34,371,542
Henry	30,095,535	17,309,800	773,443	15,238,001	1,295,393	3,017,284	67,729,496	1,247,628	66,481,868	1,224,916	4,917,707	2,447,183
Hickman	10,964,612	7,062,497	2,971,421	7,218,058	198,353	1,117,358	29,532,299	198,000	29,334,299	705,159	3,553,667	14,491,273
Hopkins	138,028,422	52,660,871	3,803,263	47,473,797	90,881,459	9,941,687	342,789,499	5,869,363	336,920,196	2,634,018	4,557,694	11,543,450
Jackson	32,839,461	16,765,005	404,299	35,970,783	21,090,657	2,092,836	109,163,041	21,078,834	88,084,207	915,842	4,111,427	3,410,679
Jefferson	1,637,445,459	875,816,936	28,393,508	856,237,932	200,989,469	411,170,110	6,107,353,414	2,348,518,822	3,758,834,592	23,314,261	571,365,523	560,133,772
Jessamine	76,308,223	24,113,376	534,707	32,128,691	20,013,392	5,096,471	158,194,860	3,012,127	155,182,733	2,796,543	115,560,376	38,838,072
Johnson	71,719,774	31,886,264	452,628	49,833,791	2,421,894	3,391,467	159,685,818	2,275,753	157,410,065	667,040	1,635,893	35,473,237
Kenton	309,557,019	150,626,524	4,455,934	150,351,412	29,577,774	196,223,311	840,791,974	18,952,049	821,839,925	726,524	115,560,376	4,262,021
Knott	45,650,406	22,977,001	353,366	44,978,761	1,104,439	2,809,895	117,873,868	786,254	117,127,614	585,450	203,598	4,262,021
Knox	69,305,239	38,682,820	252,828	75,070,728	788,431	13,304,164	197,404,210	5,623,000	191,781,210	802,182	14,708,184	9,532,251
Larue	34,256,259	16,344,438	1,360,583	25,920,362	922,651	2,492,866	81,297,159	1,704,000	79,593,159	1,808,636	3,069,746	3,153,278
Laurel	127,609,223	43,799,483	585,147	70,167,831	5,503,869	19,387,055	267,052,608	5,913,664	261,138,944	813,628	11,534,324	653,773
Lawrence	46,434,898	19,176,319	208,903	30,257,435	732,619	2,431,955	99,242,129	1,299,262	97,942,867	335,016	975,311	3,871,597
Lee	23,407,904	11,314,214	138,695	21,907,986	413,383	1,143,507	58,325,689	396,351	57,929,338	1,378,337	175,015	4,476,605
Leslie	41,501,211	19,602,551	129,486	34,576,751	993,766	1,902,925	98,706,690	189,000	98,517,690	159,518	185,587	2,173,684
Letcher	86,746,424	36,929,762	182,751	48,008,243	1,512,626	4,528,552	177,908,358	748,500	177,159,858	745,791	176,918	3,345,492
Lewis	33,877,968	15,257,391	769,996	25,693,530	314,059	1,205,567	77,118,511	647,000	76,471,511	1,911,116	1,039,178	9,337,317
Lincoln	57,813,270	25,084,024	1,517,274	40,468,885	807,606	8,424,373	134,115,432	6,783,000	127,332,432	461,837	1,356,581	2,707,632
Livingston	29,474,290	14,157,075	2,245,342	10,416,923	32,543,630	4,557,866	93,395,045	19,160,277	74,234,768	309,291	814,251	3,006,052
Logan	64,487,349	35,860,069	6,126,601	34,320,104	977,979	3,814,552	145,586,654	2,620,663	142,965,991	3,237,986	6,961,600	27,692,876
Lyon	24,926,038	9,096,050	944,165	5,873,471	320,079	1,715,537	42,875,460	1,511,550	41,363,910	365,619	246,260	1,945,902
McCracken	183,790,010	87,660,560	3,265,919	66,969,994	1,188,675,268	47,260,066	1,577,621,817	6,833,843	1,570,787,974	1,955,677	21,854,402	23,272,921
McCreary	49,510,873	24,792,607	108,729	34,498,976	29,241,870	5,378,627	143,531,682	29,172,996	114,358,686	972,609	618,170	14,032,506
McLean	26,095,801	13,034,598	3,409,999	9,066,914	429,765	1,854,776	53,891,853	967,000	52,924,853	1,149,984	1,474,269	14,032,506
Madison	145,591,172	75,667,804	1,322,865	95,571,274	28,297,713	31,606,796	378,057,624	56,129,655	321,927,969	1,144,464	37,942,878	8,699,720
Magoffin	35,203,657	18,208,083	689,074	42,545,970	849,059	1,168,567	98,664,410	732,000	97,932,410	168,825	289,163	6,606,270
Marion	41,264,638	18,526,803	2,132,978	28,036,604	760,353	3,092,373	93,813,749	778,000	93,035,749	1,659,352	3,521,300	2,268,731
Marshall	89,857,460	36,735,444	2,218,357	16,425,907	2,852,464	6,205,881	154,295,513	5,052,925	149,242,588	320,682	5,229,729	8,700,988
Martin	39,614,525	14,748,117	381,602	30,519,620	3,125,607	6,640,507	95,029,978	1,340,880	93,689,098	1,376,890	310,212	24,974,279
Mason	37,594,583	19,686,891	2,000,579	26,905,520	709,379	3,854,164	90,751,116	1,437,435	89,313,681	1,249,657	6,035,479	5,552,664
Meade	59,837,454	15,793,546	1,193,090	12,738,711	642,538	2,349,134	92,554,473	6,477,420	86,077,053	286,513	26,629,380	3,481,320
Menifee	16,746,140	6,004,484	120,790	10,249,415	3,250,230	8,976,179	45,347,238	8,938,782	36,408,456	403,618	716,825	321,880
Mercer	51,713,208	17,957,487	846,739	18,266,910	761,751	3,130,164	92,678,259	2,130,185	90,548,074	3,585,471	5,889,502	4,964,208

FEDERAL EXPENDITURES BY COUNTY, 2003

COUNTY	RETIREMENT/ DISABILITY	OTHER DIRECT PAYMENTS (INDIVIDUALS)	DIRECT PAYMENTS (NOT INDIVIDUALS)	GRANTS	PROCUREMENT CONTRACTS	SALARIES & WAGES	TOTAL DIRECT EXPENDITURES OR OBLIGATIONS	TOTAL EXPENDITURES (DEFENSE)	TOTAL EXPENDITURES (NON DEFENSE)	DIRECT LOANS	GUARANTEED/ INSURED LOANS	INSURANCE
Metcalf	24,933,750	12,002,256	1,174,900	16,699,679	488,732	1,765,836	57,065,153	544,909	56,520,244	239,425	179,081	341,236
Monroe	31,947,926	20,423,562	1,138,612	30,382,231	528,941	2,977,955	87,399,227	1,182,000	86,217,227	449,176	6,284,479	498,823
Montgomery	55,544,276	22,366,207	872,574	31,831,021	1,429,811	4,248,198	116,292,087	1,309,148	114,982,939	2,934,465	5,889,628	3,994,088
Morgan	32,126,321	14,091,125	180,135	30,931,784	421,320	1,943,746	79,694,431	414,285	79,280,146	1,167,271	435,751	3,312,128
Muhlenburg	96,438,104	40,599,704	1,990,745	28,835,450	97,939,006	39,945,473	305,748,482	5,016,169	300,732,313	822,624	4,815,037	4,057,698
Nelson	75,259,719	31,620,042	2,111,054	27,708,916	4,469,662	16,230,329	157,399,722	17,403,546	139,996,176	1,639,997	28,416,984	9,183,229
Nicholas	17,622,753	8,758,098	1,375,960	11,042,537	231,411	1,456,418	40,487,177	945,000	39,542,177	379,054	1,197,320	5,323,002
Ohio	59,545,021	26,782,581	1,739,795	20,876,199	1,073,999	4,939,761	114,957,356	1,343,570	113,613,786	948,298	3,133,842	5,291,219
Oldham	50,826,672	19,909,285	527,312	10,878,294	1,360,305	4,921,794	88,423,662	4,982,599	83,441,063	966,805	32,378,803	45,148,425
Owen	18,900,599	9,652,703	223,874	10,527,043	330,588	1,293,597	40,928,404	210,000	40,718,404	635,813	24,376,552	2,676,136
Owsley	14,829,023	9,167,899	40,373	21,668,747	231,411	854,418	46,791,871	190,000	46,601,871	676,796	24,723	290,018
Pendleton	28,172,531	12,474,141	389,426	15,030,596	694,539	1,708,836	58,470,069	802,716	57,667,353	1,238,944	5,313,867	30,511,382
Perry	106,672,271	42,559,893	922,233	60,851,745	11,812,089	9,723,508	232,541,739	2,481,178	230,060,561	1,538,276	939,929	30,179,412
Pike	242,627,204	88,102,016	1,193,970	140,082,490	11,067,135	16,692,975	499,765,790	4,255,493	495,510,297	3,135,673	2,096,225	147,028,080
Powell	27,584,788	8,964,023	175,637	18,463,590	421,204	1,949,657	57,558,899	511,000	57,047,899	617,668	1,823,261	5,572,586
Pulaski	177,153,717	55,836,795	1,534,772	160,692,208	3,208,321	14,197,192	412,623,005	9,670,204	402,952,801	944,240	13,317,648	4,492,707
Robertson	5,219,291	3,373,018	322,002	3,001,161	66,117	293,119	12,274,708	258,000	12,016,708	105,308	656,890	1,207,367
Rockcastle	39,618,008	17,833,645	279,040	49,063,583	853,554	1,729,806	109,377,636	982,260	108,395,376	360,401	2,127,844	1,735,889
Rowan	45,344,951	30,560,113	461,497	37,737,363	1,122,087	5,715,164	120,941,175	2,867,507	118,073,668	46,512,625	3,673,889	14,729,132
Russell	47,797,178	20,361,807	997,306	45,822,661	1,705,965	2,879,895	119,564,812	3,273,974	116,290,838	486,838	1,288,687	391,298
Scott	57,143,118	23,500,036	1,269,859	22,387,919	1,000,769	3,732,702	109,034,403	2,405,460	106,628,943	1,143,766	36,761,154	13,591,706
Shelby	58,997,802	22,507,240	1,943,204	29,042,191	1,817,002	5,689,998	119,997,437	2,417,000	117,580,437	2,626,199	19,311,734	5,942,091
Simpson	34,016,930	19,046,438	2,415,218	15,981,189	666,012	2,139,015	74,264,802	816,012	73,448,790	862,843	4,927,313	9,370,986
Spencer	20,993,711	7,720,198	583,336	6,447,331	428,898	1,606,716	37,780,190	970,192	36,809,998	642,407	9,717,543	4,565,599
Taylor	65,911,514	31,410,970	1,509,017	24,734,801	7,783,582	5,398,403	136,748,287	9,640,649	127,107,638	665,258	3,041,180	790,834
Todd	24,999,875	14,533,129	3,761,207	15,945,583	473,645	2,145,806	61,859,245	1,265,351	60,593,894	1,262,381	4,597,325	14,536,028
Trigg	43,173,416	15,601,967	1,681,134	12,157,061	6,589,764	4,845,716	84,049,058	3,680,794	80,368,264	1,080,005	3,341,036	7,634,316
Trimble	17,656,031	7,874,634	151,474	4,956,979	297,529	1,207,537	32,144,184	288,000	31,856,184	856,587	1,843,240	2,112,994
Union	39,150,034	18,423,941	3,728,148	12,502,798	203,217,244	3,066,194	280,088,359	1,178,060	278,910,299	1,349,719	2,672,415	8,828,747
Warren	192,698,484	105,081,727	5,070,867	120,529,989	13,938,356	41,331,914	478,651,337	14,500,297	464,151,040	5,630,269	43,918,971	17,378,826
Washington	24,208,977	13,049,610	1,337,574	15,810,625	443,397	2,147,716	56,997,899	663,000	56,334,899	920,972	2,644,704	3,789,201
Wayne	48,354,297	25,644,410	466,672	46,878,388	1,927,091	2,466,806	125,737,664	3,137,797	122,599,867	747,559	5,946,888	903,952
Webster	38,655,391	15,920,268	3,382,823	13,633,941	6,026,755	2,472,134	80,091,312	805,000	79,286,312	1,689,716	478,637	6,343,662
Whitley	142,561,434	61,359,228	821,860	60,538,750	73,717,298	7,826,747	346,825,317	67,208,363	279,616,954	2,356,586	2,317,533	6,939,176
Wolfe	22,226,382	8,837,490	109,071	27,283,055	529,972	1,996,895	60,982,865	244,090	60,738,775	705,313	132,250	275,291
Woodford	47,400,459	14,200,289	1,948,107	10,278,441	935,799	3,028,781	77,791,876	2,096,960	75,694,916	2,282,239	12,035,487	19,550,808

Source: http://harvester.census.gov/cffr/asp/Geography.asp

FEDERAL GOVERNMENT OFFICES IN KENTUCKY

Agriculture, US Dept of (USDA) Marketing & Regulatory

ProgramsAgriculture Marketing Service (Tobacco)
www.ams.usda.gov/tob

Ronnie Marrs, Regional Dir.
225 Walton Ave No 100
Lexington KY 40502
(859) 254-7248 • FAX (859) 259-3329

Farm Services Agency (FSA)
FSA-KY State Office
Jeffery S Hall, State Executive Dir.
771 Corporate Dr Ste 100
Lexington KY 40503
(859) 224-7601 • FAX (859) 224-7691
kyfsaso@ky.usda.gov

Forest Service
Daniel Boone National Forest
www.fs.fed.us/r8/boone
Benjamin Worthington, Forest Supv.
1700 Bypass Rd
Winchester KY 40391
(859) 745-3100 • FAX (859) 737-3867
mailroom_r8_daniel_boone@fs.fed.us

Procurement Service
www.fs.fed.us/r8/boone
Sharon Martin, Contract Specialist
1700 Bypass Rd
Winchester KY 40391
(859) 745-3131 • FAX (859) 745-4710

London Ranger District
John Strojan, District Ranger
761 S Laurel Rd
London KY 40744
(606) 864-4163 • FAX (606) 878-0811

Morehead Ranger District
Dave Manner, District Ranger
2375 KY 801 S
Morehead KY 40351
(606) 784-6428 • FAX (606) 784-6435

Redbird Ranger District
Mitch Gandy, District Ranger
91 Peabody Rd
Big Creek KY 40914
(606) 598-2192 • FAX (606) 598-3648

Somerset Ranger District
Jerry Stephens, District Ranger
135 Realty Ln
Somerset KY 42501
(606) 679-2010 • FAX (606) 679-5869

Stanton Ranger District
Joy Malone, District Ranger
705 W College Ave
Stanton KY 40380
(606) 663-2852 • FAX (606) 663-9097

Stearns Ranger District
Fred Noack, District Ranger
3320 N Hwy 27
Whitley City KY 42653
(606) 376-5323 • FAX (606) 376-3734

Frenchburg Job Corps Center
Valerie Scott, Center Dir.
6969 Tarr Ridge Rd
Frenchburg KY 40322
(606) 768-2111 • FAX (606) 768-3080

Pine Knot Job Corps Center
Teresa Dunn-Frank, Center Dir.
Hwy 27 S
PO Box 1990
Pine Knot KY 42635
(606) 354-2176 • FAX (606) 354-2170
1king@fs.fed.us

Natural Resources Conservation Service (NRCS)

NRCS-KY State Office
David G Sawyer, State
Conservationist
771 Corporate Dr Ste 210
Lexington KY 40503
(859) 224-7350 • FAX (859) 224-7399
david.sawyer@ky.usda.gov

NRCS-Area 1 Office
William E Giesecke Jr, AC
Joyce Lynn Kinser, Administrative
Coordinator
1830 Lantaff Blvd
Madisonville KY 42431
(270) 825-2414 • FAX (270) 825-2428
william.giesecke@ky.usda.gov

NRCS-Area 2 Office
J David Stipes, AC
Patricia D Ross, Administrative
Coordinator
103 Lakeview Ct
Frankfort KY 40601
(502) 695-5203 • FAX (502) 695-7996
david.stipes@ky.usda.gov

NRCS-Area 3 Office
Robert L Bradley, AC
Lela Ison, Administrative
Coordinator
509 Willin Way
Mt Sterling KY 40353
(859) 498-8907 • FAX (859) 497-9677
bobby.bradley@ky.usda.gov

Research Education & Economics
Agriculture Research Service (Forage Animal Production Research)
James R Strickland, Supv. Animal
Scientist
USDA, ARA, University of KY
Agricultural Science Bldg N Rm S107
Lexington KY 40506
(859) 257-1647

Agricultural Statistics Service
www.usda.gov/nass/ky
Leland E Brown, State Statistician
William Brannen, Deputy State
Statistician
PO Box 1120
Louisville KY 40201
(800) 928-5277, (502) 582-5293 • FAX
(502) 582-5114
nass-ky@nass.usda.gov

Rural Development (RD)
RD-KY State Office
www.rurdev.usda.gov/ky
Kenneth Slone, State Dir.
771 Corporate Dr Ste 200
Lexington KY 40503
(859) 224-7300 • FAX (859) 224-7340

RD-District I
Kenneth Heath, Area Dir.
320B Traylor St
Princeton KY 42445
(270) 365-6530 • FAX (270) 365-7842
ken.heath@ky.usda.gov

RD-District II
Charles J Blankenship, Area Dir.
957 Campbellsville Rd
Columbia KY 42728
(270) 384-6431 • FAX (270) 384-6351
charles.blankenship@ky.usda.gov

RD-District III
W Gene Floyd, Area Dir.
90 Howard Dr Ste 3
Shelbyville KY 40065
(502) 633-3294 • FAX (502) 633-0552
gene.floyd@ky.usda.gov

RD-District IV
Christine Brewer, Area Dir.
220 W 1st St
Morehead KY 40351
(606) 784-6447 • FAX (606) 784-2076
christine.brewer@ky.usda.gov

RD-District V
Doug Moore, Area Dir.
95 S Laurel Rd Ste A
London KY 40744
(606) 864-2172 • FAX (606) 878-7717
douglas.moore@ky.usda.gov

Commerce, US Dept of (DOC)

Economic Development Administration (EDA)
www.doc.gov/eda/
Bob Hunter, Economic
Development Representative
771 Corporate Dr Ste 200
Lexington KY 40503
(859) 224-7426 • FAX (859) 224-7427

International Trade Administration (ITA)
www.ita.doc.gov
John D Autin, Dir.
601 W Broadway Ste 634B
Louisville KY 40202
(502) 582-5066 • FAX (502) 582-6573

Defense, US Dept of (DOD)

Dept of the Army (DOA)
Army Corps of Engineers, US (USACE)
Steve Furlong, Area Operations Mgr.
2110 Nolin Dam Rd, PO Box 289
Bee Spring KY 42207
(270) 286-4521 • FAX (270) 286-4688
steven.e.furlong@lrl02.usace.army.mil
Terry Peabody, Lockmaster
Lock & Dam No 2
695 W 1st St
Calhoun KY 42327
(270) 273-3152 • FAX (270) 273-3107
C Wayne Rigor, Mgr.
Grayson Reservoir Project
50 Launch Ramp Rd
Grayson KY 41143
(606) 474-5815 • FAX (606) 474-2089

John M East, Superintendent
Barkley Power Plant
8139 US Hwy 62 W
Kuttawa KY 42055
(270) 362-8159 • FAX (270) 362-7403
Robert Rowlette, District Engineer
PO Box 59
Louisville KY 40201
(502) 315-6106 • FAX (502) 315-6109
Mark Barnum, Park Mgr.
Anthony Orr, Park Ranger
Cave Run Lake, 150 KY Hwy 826
Morehead KY 40351
(606) 784-9709 • FAX (606) 784-2400
J C McDaniels, Area Engineer
US Hwy 119, PO Box 247
Pineville KY 40977
(606) 337-6162 • FAX (606) 337-2646
jerry.c.mcdaniels@lrn02.usace.army.mil
Teddy C Music, Resource Mgr.
Dewey Lake, HC 70 Box 540
Van Lear KY 41265
(606) 886-6709 • FAX (606) 886-3483

**Army Corps of Engineers
District Contracting Division**
PO Box 59
Louisville KY 40201
Property & Fiscal Office for KY
Col Micheal Jones, Dir.
120 Minuteman Pkwy
Boone National Guard Ctr
Frankfort KY 40601
(502) 607-1426 • FAX (502) 607-1436

Dept of the Navy (USN)
**Naval Surface Warfare Center,
Port Hueneme Detachment**
Russell Bentley Jr, Site Dir.
160 Rochester Dr
Louisville KY 40214
(502) 364-5052 • FAX (502) 364-5361

**Health & Human Services,
US Dept of (HHS)**
Food & Drug Administration (FDA)
www.fda.gov/
Kathleen Kulver, Consumer Safety
Officer
9600 Brownsboro Rd Ste 302
Louisville KY 40241
(502) 425-0069 • FAX (502) 425-0450

US Coast Guard Marine Safety Center
www.uscg.mil/hq/msc
Terry D Gilbreath, Commander
600 Martin Luther King Jr Pl Ste 360
Louisville KY 40202
(502) 582-5195 • FAX (502) 582-6825
201 Coast Guard Ln
Owensboro KY 42303
225 Tully St
Paducah KY 42003
(270) 442-1621 • FAX (270) 442-1633
US Secret Service
www.secretservice.gov
Paul Sims, Resident Agent
3141 Beaumont Centre Cir Ste 201
PO Box 910570
Lexington KY 40591
(859) 223-2358 • FAX (859) 223-1819

Norman S Jarvis Jr, Special Agent in
Charge
600 Martin Luther King Jr Pl Ste 377
Louisville KY 40202
(502) 582-5171 • FAX (502) 582-6329
**US Customs & Border Protection
(CBP)**
www.cbp.gov
Paul Chambers, Resident Agent in
Charge
207 Grandview Dr Ste 200
Ft Mitchell KY 41017
(859) 578-4600 • FAX (859) 578-4606
Frank Dupre, Resident Agent in
Charge
650 Administration Dr
Louisville KY 40209
(502) 582-5183 • FAX (502) 625-7224
**US Citizenship & Immigration
Services (USCIS)**
www.uscis.gov
Jerry Phillips, Officer in Charge
Gene Snyder Cthse Bldg Rm 390
601 W Broadway
Louisville KY 40202
(502) 582-6953 • FAX (502) 582-6373

**Housing & Urban Development,
US Dept of (HUD)**
KY State Office
www.hud.gov
Ben A Cook, Field Office Dir.
601 W Broadway
Louisville KY 40202
(502) 582-5251 • FAX (502) 582-6074
KY Housing Corp
F Lynn Luallen, CEO
1231 Louisville Rd
Frankfort KY 40601
(502) 564-9946 • FAX (502) 564-9964
lluallen@kyhousing.org
Mike Powers, Dir. of Multi-Family
Housing Program
1231 Louisville Rd
Frankfort KY 40601
(800) 633-8896 • FAX (502) 564-9964
333 Guthrie St Ste 404
Louisville KY 40202
(502) 585-5451
Minnie Le May, Section 8 Program
Coordinator (Acting)
1231 Louisville Rd
Frankfort KY 40601
(502) 564-7630 • FAX (502) 564-9964
mlemay@kyhousing.org
Interior, US Dept of (DOI)
Fish & Wildlife Service (FWS)
PO Box 200
Benton KY 42025
(270) 527-5770 • FAX (270) 527-5330
National Parks Service (NPS)
www.nps.gov/maca/index.htm
Abraham Lincoln Birthplace National
Historic Site
2995 Lincoln Farm Rd
Hodgenville KY 42748
(270) 358-3137 • FAX (270) 358-3874

Ronald R Switzer, Park Mgr.
Mammoth Cave National Park
PO Box 7
Mammoth Cave KY 42259
(270) 758-2254 • FAX (270) 758-2349
ron_switzer@nps.gov
**Surface Mining Reclamation,
Office of**
William J Kovacic, Field Office Dir.
Lexington Field Office
2675 Regency Rd
Lexington KY 40503
(859) 260-8402 • FAX (859) 260-8410
bkovacic@osmre.gov
Appalachia Team
1405 Greenup Ave Box 5
Ashland KY 41101
(606) 324-2828 • FAX (606) 324-2846
jsefton@osmre.gov
Patrick N Angel, Team Leader
London Area Ofc
PO Box 1048
London KY 40743
(606) 878-6440 • FAX (606) 878-6049
pangel@osmre.gov
Michael E Vaughn, Team Leader
Madisonville Area Ofc
100 YMCA Dr
Madisonville KY 42431
(270) 825-4500 • FAX (270) 821-1232
mvaughn@osmre.gov
Patrick N Angel, Team Leader
164 Main St Ste 409
Pikeville KY 41501
(606) 432-8145 • FAX (606) 432-5041
**Geological Survey, Water
Resources Division**
http://water.usgs.gov/
Mark A Ayers, District Chief
9818 Bluegrass Pkwy
Louisville KY 40299
(502) 493-1900 • FAX (502) 493-1909
mayers@usgs.gov

Justice, US Dept of (DOJ)
US Attorney, Eastern District
www.usdoj.gov/usao/offices
Gregory F Van Tatenhove
Vacant, Secretary to US Attorney
110 W Vine St Ste 400
Lexington KY 40507
(859) 233-2661 • FAX (859) 233-2666
US Attorney, Western District
David L Huber
Trent J Sandifur
BB&T Bldg
510 W Broadway 10th Fl
Louisville KY 40202
(502) 582-5911 • FAX (502) 582-5097
**US Marshals Service, Eastern
District**
John Schickel, US Marshal
Federal Bldg Rm 162
PO Box 30
Lexington KY 40588
(859) 233-2513 • FAX (859) 233-2517
Lonnie Lynch, Deputy in Charge
1402 Greenup St
Ashland KY 41101
(606) 329-2587 • FAX (606) 329-2559

Robin Maley, Deputy in Charge
35 W 5th St
Covington KY 41012
(859) 392-7918 • FAX (859) 392-7924
John C Watts Federal Bldg
330 W Broadway Rm 326
Frankfort KY 40602
(502) 223-5608 • FAX (502) 223-2745
David Hines, Deputy in Charge
Federal Bldg 3rd & Main St, Box 5036
London KY 40741
(606) 864-6993 • FAX (606) 878-4310
Rick Newsome, Deputy in Charge
105 Federal Bldg., PO Box 262
Pikeville KY 41502
(606) 437-6524 • FAX (606) 432-8457

US Marshals Service, Western District

Ronald McCubbin, US Marshal
Richard W Knighten, Chief Deputy
601 W Broadway Ste 114
Louisville KY 40202
(502) 588-8000 • FAX (502) 588-8005
Mike De Villez, Deputy US Marshall
US Cthse Rm 110
241 E Main St
Bowling Green KY 42101
(270) 901-2100 • FAX (270) 901-2110
Dwayne DeWitt, Deputy US Marshal
423 Frederica St Rm 216
Owensboro KY 42301
(270) 852-2640 • FAX (270) 852-2650
Isaac F Comte, Deputy US Marshall
501 Broadway St Ste 231
Paducah KY 42001
(270) 415-1700 • FAX (270) 415-1710

Drug Enforcement Administration (DEA)

www.dea.gov
Harvey Goehring, Resident Agent
1500 Leestown Rd Ste 308
Lexington KY 40511
(859) 233-2479 • FAX (859) 233-2590
Tony King, Resident Agent
600 Martin Luther King Jr Pl Ste 1006
Louisville KY 40202
(502) 582-5908 • FAX (502) 582-5535
t.h.king@usdoj.gov

Federal Police Services

Charles E Riley, Special Agent
in Charge
600 Martin Luther King Jr Pl Ste 500
Louisville KY 40202
(502) 582-5455 • FAX (502) 569-3869

Alcohol Tobacco Firearms & Explosives, Bureau of (ATF)

www.atf.gov
Marion Creech, Supv.
976 Bloomfield Rd
Bardstown KY 40004
(502) 348-3829
Kevin Kelm, Resident Agent
PO Box 20046
Bowling Green KY 42102
(270) 781-7090
Alan B Graham, Area Supv.
1040 Monarch St Ste 250
Lexington KY 40518
FAX (502) 223-2720

Carl Vasilko, Resident Agent in
Charge
1040 Monarch St Ste 200
Lexington KY 40513
(859) 219-4500 • FAX (859) 219-4514
Karl Stankovic, Special Agent
in Charge
Agent in Charge
600 Martin Luther King Jr Pl Ste 322
Louisville KY 40202
(502) 753-3400 • FAX (502) 753-3340
Gerald Powers, Inspector
1100 Walnut St Box 45
Owensboro KY 42301
(270) 684-5995

ATF Appeals Office

Mary Alice Gruden, Associate Chief
322 Broadway St Ste 1010
Louisville KY 40202
(502) 582-5445 • FAX (502) 582-6555

Federal Bureau of Investigation (FBI)

www.fbi.gov
Gary J Danzer, Supv. Resident Agent
New Federal Bldg Cthse
1405 Greenup Ave
Ashland KY 41101
(606) 329-8516 • FAX (606) 324-7740
David P Gelios, Senior Supv.
Resident Agent
996 Wilkinson Tr Ste C3
Bowling Green KY 42103
(270) 781-4734 • FAX (270) 842-9710
William O'Leary, SSRA
2220 Grandview Dr Ste 280
Ft Mitchell KY 41017
(859) 341-3901 • FAX (859) 426-3359
Dennis J Dvorjak, Resident Agent
800 Cardinal Dr Ste 101
Elizabethtown KY 42702
(270) 765-7213 • FAX (270) 766-1408
John C Watts, Resident Agent
300 W Broadway
Frankfort KY 40602
(502) 223-3644 • FAX (502) 223-1188
Seldon D Sledd, Resident Agent
607 Hammond Plz Ste 3
Hopkinsville KY 42241
(270) 885-8272 • FAX (270) 887-9772
Clay Mason, Resident Agent
Tate Bldg Ste 120
125 Lisle Industrial Ave
Lexington KY 40511
(859) 254-4038 • FAX (859) 254-9652
Jerry Garner, Resident Agent
201 County Extension Rd
London KY 40741
(606) 878-8922 • FAX (606) 862-2119
Charles D Elder, Special Agent
in Charge
600 Martin Luther King Jr Pl Ste 500
Louisville KY 40202
(502) 583-3941 • FAX (502) 569-3869
www.louisville.fbi.gov
Gary B Coffey, Resident Agent
319 W 10th St Rm 5
Owensboro KY 42302
(270) 926-3441 • FAX (270) 686-8290

Philip Lewzader, Resident Agent
555 Jefferson
Paducah KY 42002
(270) 442-8050 • FAX (270) 442-2962
Vacant, Resident Agent
164 Main St Rm 407
PO Box 938
Pikeville KY 41502
(606) 432-1226 • FAX (606) 432-1846

Labor, US Dept of (DOL)

Federal Contract Compliance Programs, Office of

www.dol.gov/esa/ofccp_org.htm
Carmen Rendon, Assistant
District Dir.
601 W Broadway Ste 15
Louisville KY 40202
(502) 582-6275 • FAX (502) 582-6182

Coal Mine Workers Compensation, Black Lung

Harry Skidmore, District Dir.
164 Main St Ste 508
Pikeville KY 41501
(800) 366-4599 • FAX (606) 432-3574

Coal Mine Workers, Division of

Harry Skidmore, District Dir.
402 Campbell Way
Mt Sterling KY 40353
(859) 498-9700 • FAX (859) 498-5787

Wage & Hour Division

www.dol.gov/esa/whd
Federal Bldg Rm B19
241 E Main St
Bowling Green KY 42101
Wright Executive Bldg Rm 340
1885 Dixie Hwy
Ft Wright KY 41011
3141 Beaumont Centre Cir Ste 202
Lexington KY 40513
Jim P Rogers, District Dir.
Gene Snyder Cthse &
Customhouse Bldg Rm 31
601 W Broadway
Louisville KY 40202
(866) 4US-WAGE • FAX (866) 487-9243
www.wagehour.dol.gov
Federal Bldg Rm B16
423 Frederica St
Owensboro KY 42301
(270) 683-2043
100 Fountain Ave Rm 203
Paducah KY 42001

Apprenticeship & Training, Bureau of

John Delgado, State Dir. (Acting)
600 Martin Luther King Jr Pl Ste 168
Louisville KY 40202
(502) 582-5223 • FAX (502) 625-7081

MSHA (Coal)-Barbourville

William R Johnson, Supv.s
Jim W Langley, Supv.s
3837 S US Hwy 25E
Barbourville KY 40906
(606) 546-5123 • FAX (606) 546-3060
Joseph W Pavlovich, District Mgr.
3837 S US Hwy 25 E
Barbourville KY 40906
(606) 546-5123 • FAX (606) 546-5245
pavlovich_joseph@msha.gov

MSHA-Beaver Dam
Robert A Simms, Supv.
PO Box 81
Beaver Dam KY 42320
(270) 274-9628 • FAX (270) 274-9629

MSHA (Coal)-Belcher
James Hager, Supv.
15169 Ferrells Creek Rd
Belcher KY 41513
(606) 754-4187 • FAX (606) 754-9491

MSHA (Coal)-Harlan
Robert W Rhea, Supv.
Daniel L Johnson, Supv.
133 Readi Mix Rd
Harlan KY 40831
(606) 573-3400 • FAX (606) 573-1774

MSHA (Coal)-Hazard
James D Fields, Supv.
305 Morton Blvd
Hazard KY 41701
(606) 439-2396 • FAX (606) 439-1851

MSHA (Coal)-Hindman
Dave M Jones, Supv.
11 Kentucky Dr
Hindman KY 41822
(606) 785-4191 • FAX (606) 785-0997

MSHA (Coal)-Madisonville
Troy Davis, Supv.s
James H Hackney III, Supv.s
100 YMCA Dr
Madisonville KY 42431
(270) 821-4180 • FAX (270) 825-0949

MSHA (Coal)-Martin
Scott Whitaker, Supv.
1102 Left Beaver
Martin KY 41649
(606) 285-3281 • FAX (606) 285-0255

MSHA (Coal)-Morganfield
Robert Jaco, Supv.
112 E Main St
PO Box 509
Morganfield KY 42437
(270) 389-3134 • FAX (270) 389-9814

MSHA (Coal)-Phelps
Benny Freeman, Supv.
39789 St Hwy 194 E
Phelps KY 41553
(606) 456-3438 • FAX (606) 456-4167

MSHA (Coal)-Pikeville
Franklin Struck, District Mgr.
Thomas Meredith & Robert
Hardman,
Enforcement Assistant District Mgr.
100 Faye Ramsey Ln
Pikeville KY 41501
(606) 432-0944 • FAX (606) 437-9988

MSHA (Coal)-Whitesburg
Larry Little, Supv.
704 Hwy 2034
Whitesburg KY 41858
(606) 633-4882 • FAX (606) 633-9277

MSHA (Metal & Non-Metal)
Dana Haynes, Supv.
152 W Zandale Dr
Lexington KY 40503
(859) 276-1384

Occupational Safety & Health Administration (OSHA)
www.osha.gov
Ron McGill, Area Dir.
330 W Broadway St Ste 108
Frankfort KY 40601
(502) 227-7024 • FAX (502) 227-2348

Employee Benefits Security Administration
www.dol/gov/ebsa
Joseph Menez, Regional Dir.
1885 Dixie Hwy Ste 210
Ft Wright KY 41011
(859) 578-4680 • FAX (859) 578-4688

Veterans Employment & Training Service (VETS)
www.dol.gov/vets/
Rick Netherton, Dir.
Dept for Employment Services
275 E Main St
Frankfort KY 40621
(502) 564-7062 • FAX (502) 564-1476

State, US Dept of
KY Consular Center
www.state.gov
John Coe, Dir.
3505 N Hwy 25W
Williamsburg KY 40769
(606) 526-7401 • FAX (606) 526-7684

Transportation, US Dept of (DOT)
Federal Aviation Administration (FAA)
www.faa.gov
Duff Ortman, Mgr. (Acting)
4051 Terminal Dr
Lexington KY 40510
(859) 233-2509 • FAX (859) 233-2774
Gary R Scannevin, Mgr.
1930 Bishop Ln 11th Fl
Louisville KY 40218
(502) 753-4200 • FAX (502) 582-6735
2200 Airport Rd Ste 30
Owensboro KY 42301
(502) 375-7360
2901 Fisher Rd
Paducah KY 42002
(270) 744-6622 • FAX (270) 744-8044
445 Miller Hunt Rd
Winchester KY 40391

Airport Traffic Control Tower
Robert Head, Mgr.
2710 Moran Ave
Louisville KY 40205
(502) 753-3680 • FAX (502) 753-3690

Sector Field (FAA)
Steve Stoker, Mgr.
755 Grade Ln
Louisville KY 40213
(502) 375-7360

Federal Highway Administration (FHWA)
www.fhwa.dot.gov
Jose M Sepulveda, Division Administrator
330 W Broadway St Ste 264
Frankfort KY 40601
(502) 223-6720 • FAX (502) 223-6735
hdaky@ky.khwa.dot.gov

Federal Railroad Administration (FRA)
www.fra.dot.gov
Barbara Hall, Administrative Officer
629 S 4th St Ste 302
Louisville KY 40202
(502) 549-7454 • FAX (502) 582-6635

Treasury, US Dept of
Comptroller of the Currency
www.occ.treas.gov/
Curtis D Schuman, Field Mgr.
9200 Shelbyville Rd Ste 505
Louisville KY 40222
(502) 429-3422 • FAX (502) 429-0339

Internal Revenue Service (IRS)
www.irs.gov
Processing Center
PO Box 12267
Covington KY 41012
FAX (606) 292-5387

Treasury Inspector General for Tax Administration Office (TIGTA)
www.treas.gov/tigtal
Jim Cupp, Special Agent
601 W Broadway Ste 607, Box 218
Louisville KY 40201
(502) 582-5298 • FAX (502) 625-7501

Criminal Investigation Division
Charles A Jenkins, Special Agent
in Charge
PO Box 2378
Louisville KY 40201
(502) 572-2140 • FAX (502) 572-2142

Associate Area Council
Jillena Warner, Associate Area
Council
332 W Broadway Ste 1100
Louisville KY 40202
(502) 582-5471 • FAX (502) 582-6579

IRS Collection
600 Martin Luther King Jr Pl Rm 351
Louisville KY 40202
(502) 582-6700

IRS Appeals
600 Martin Luther King Jr Pl
Louisville KY 40202

IRS Examination
Walter Jernigan, Chief Examiner
601 W Broadway
Louisville KY 40202
FAX (502) 582-5307

IRS District Council
332 W Broadway Ste 1100
Louisville KY 40202

Taxpayer Advocate Service
Lois Burns, Local Taxpayer Advocate
600 Martin Luther King Jr Pl Ste 325
Louisville KY 40202
(502) 582-6030 • FAX (502) 582-6463
lois.burns@irs.gov

Veterans Affairs, US Dept of (VA)
Regional Office
545 S 3rd St
Louisville KY 40202
(800) 827-1000
Wayne L Peffer, Dir. (Acting)
2250 Leestown Rd
Lexington KY 40511

Vet Center
Phil Godeau, Team Leader
1347 3rd St
Louisville KY 40208
(502) 634-1916 • FAX (502) 636-4002
VA Medical Center
Timothy Shea, Dir.
800 Zorn Ave
Louisville KY 40206
(502) 895-3401
VA Medical Center
Forrest Farley, Dir.
1101 Veteran's Dr
Lexington KY 40502
(859) 233-4511

INDEPENDENT AGENCIES

KY Representative to ARC
www.state.ky.us/patmsg.htm
Gov Ernie Fletcher
700 Capitol Ave Ste 100
Frankfort KY 40601
(502) 564-2611 • FAX (502) 564-2517
Corp for National & Community Service (CNS)
Learn & Serve, KY State Office
www.learnandserve.org
Betsy Irvin Wells, State Dir.
600 Martin Luther King Jr Pl Ste 372D
Louisville KY 40202
(502) 582-6384 • FAX (502) 582-6386
Equal Employment Opportunity Commission (EEOC)
www.eeoc.gov
Marcia Hall-Craig, Dir.
600 Martin Luther King Jr Pl Ste 268
Louisville KY 40202
(502) 582-6082
General Services Administration (GSA)
GSA, SE Sunbelt Region 4
241 Main St
Bowling Green KY 42101
(270) 782-6928
Federal Protective Service Division, Physical Security & Law Enforcement
Michael Wilcox, Security Specialist
600 Martin Luther King Jr Pl Ste 273
267B Federal Ofc Bldg
Louisville KY 40202
(502) 582-5455 • FAX (502) 582-6868
KY Property Management Center
Cindy Jameson, Dir.
600 Martin Luther King Jr Pl Ste 273
Louisville KY 40202
(502) 582-6436 • FAX (502) 582-6868
Public Buildings Service (PBS)
Cindy Jameson, Field Office Mgr.
600 Martin Luther King Jr Pl Ste 273
Louisville KY 40202
(502) 582-6436 • FAX (502) 582-6868
Kenneth King
Federal Cthse, O Box 465
Owensboro KY 42302
(270) 684-2939
Federal Bldg Cthse
501 Broadway St
Paducah KY 42001

Occupational Safety & Health Review Commission (OSHRC)
www.oshrc.gov
Barbara Jessup, Assistant Dir.
4 Mill Creek Pk
Frankfort KY 40601
(502) 573-6892 • FAX (502) 573-4619
Railroad Retirement Board (RRB)
District Office
Gene Guihan, District Mgr.
629 S 4th St Ste 301, PO Box 3705
Louisville KY 40201
(502) 582-5208 • FAX (502) 582-5518
louisville@rrb.gov
Small Business Administration (SBA)
KY District Office
www.sba.gov/ky
Philip D Mahoney, District Dir.
(Acting)
Romano Mazzoli Federal Bldg Rm 188
600 Martin Luther King Jr Pl
Louisville KY 40202
(502) 582-5971 • FAX (502) 582-5009
philip.mahoney@sba.gov
Small Business Development Centers (SBDC)
Central Office
Becky Naugle, State Dir.
UK Ctr for Entrepreneurship
225 CM Gatton Business & Economics Bldg
Lexington KY 40506
(888) 475-SBDC • FAX (859) 323-1907
lrnaug0@pop.uky.edu
KY SBDC's
www.ksbdc.org
Richard S Horn, Dir. Candace Fox, Training Consultant
Bowling Green SBDC
Western KY University
2355 Nashville Rd
Bowling Green KY 42101
(270) 745-1905 • FAX (270) 745-1931
rick.horn@wku.edu
Patricia Krausman, Dir.
University of KY SBDC
1105 Julianna Ct Ste 6
Elizabethtown KY 42701
(270) 765-6737 • FAX (270) 769-5095
pksbdc@kvnet.org
Sutton Landry, Dir./Management Consultant
Sam Asmah, Assistant Dir.
Northern KY University SBDC
BEP Ctr 463
Highland Heights KY 41099
(859) 572-6524 • FAX (859) 572-6177
landrys@nku.edu
DeeDee Harbut, Dir.
Lexington Area SBDC Central Library
140 E Main St Fl 4
Lexington KY 40507
(888) 475-7232• FAX (859) 257-1751

Michael Ashcraft, Dir./Management Consultant
Greater Louisville SBDC
123 E Main St
Louisville KY 40202
(502) 574-4770 • FAX (502) 574-4771
mashcraft@greaterlouisville.com
John D Moore, Dir./Management Consultant
Southeast SBDC
Southeast Community College-Bell Co Campus
Middlesboro KY 40965
(888) 225-7232 • FAX (606) 242-4514
john.moore@kctcs.net
South Central SBDC
Eastern KY Univ
Richmond KY 40475
(877) EKU-SBDC, (606) 622-1384 •
FAX (606) 622-1413
Kathy Moats, Dir./Management Consultant
807 Monticello St
Somerset KY 42501
(877) 358-7232, • FAX (606) 677-6122
sbdc@centertech.com
East KY District
Jason Boggs, Dir./Management Consultant
Morehead SBDC
Morehead State Univ 203 Combs Bldg
Morehead KY 40351
(606) 783-2895 • FAX (606) 783-5020
j.boggs@morehead-st.edu
Kimberly Jenkins, Dir./Management Consultant
1400 College Dr No L282
Ashland KY 41101
(606) 329-8011 • FAX (606) 324-4570
jenkin@morehead-st.edu
Michael Morley, District Dir./Management Consultant
3455 N Mayo Trl No 4
Pikeville KY 41501
(606) 432-5848 • FAX (606) 432-8924
m.morley@morehead-st.edu
Kelli Hall, Management Consultant
MSU/Paintsville SBDC
340 Main St Ste 200
Paintsville KY 41240
(606) 788-7331 • FAX (606) 788-7332
k.hall@morehead-st.edu
West KY District
Vacant, Dir./Management Consultant
403A W 9th St
Hopkinsville KY 42240
(270) 886-8666 • FAX (270) 886-3211
Rosemary Miller, Dir./Management Consultant
MSU Business Bldg Rm 253
Murray KY 42071
(270) 762-2856 • FAX (270) 762-3049
rosemary.miller@murraystate.edu
sara.dixon@murraystate.edu

Mickey Johnson, District Dir./
  Management Consultant
MSU/Owensboro SBDC
3860 US Hwy 60 W
Owensboro KY 42301
(270) 926-8085 • FAX (270) 684-0714
mickeyjohnson@gradd.com
Loretta Daniel, Dir./Management
  Consultant
Paducah SBDC MSU
3000 Irvin Cobb
Paducah KY 42001
(270) 442-3897 • FAX (270) 762-5473
loretta.daniel@murraystate.edu

**KY Business Environmental
Assistance Program**
www.kbeap.org
Gregory C Copley, Dir.
University of KY
227 Gatton College of
  Business & Economics
Lexington KY 40506
(800) 562-2327 • FAX (859) 323-1907
kbeap@uky.edu

SCORE

Bowling Green SCORE
www.score.org
812 State St
Bowling Green KY 4101
(270) 781-3200

Danville SCORE
www.score.org
21B Charleston Dr
Danville KY 40422
(859) 236-3080

Elizabethtown SCORE/BITAC
www.score.org
600 College Street Rd
Elizabethtown KY 42701
(270) 737-0324

Hopkinsville SCORE
www.score.org
101 S Main St
Hopkinsville KY 42240
(270) 885-9016

Lexington SCORE
www.score.org
William Mason, Chapter Chair
389 Waller Ave Ste 130
Lexington KY 40504
(859) 231-9902 • FAX (859) 253-3190
scorelex@pdgweb.com

London SCORE
www.score.org
240 Bennett Cir
London KY 40741
(606) 877-2673 • FAX (606) 877-1964
allegra@kih.net

Louisville SCORE
www.score-louisville.org
Bill Huff, Chair
Mazzoll Federal Bldg Rm 188
600 Martin Luther King Jr Pl
Louisville KY 40202
(502) 582-5976 • FAX (502) 582-5819
louiscore75@aol.com

Louisville SCORE, NIA Center
Louisville Office
2900 W Broadway
Louisville KY 40211
(502) 574-1147

Social Security
Administration (SSA)

KY Offices
www.socialsecurity.gov
1405 Greenup Ave Rm 132
Ashland KY 41101
(800) 772-1213, (606) 324-0516
David K Smith, District Mgr.
1310 Campbell Ln
Bowling Green KY 42104
(800) 772-1213, (270) 842-5691 • FAX
(270) 842-5789
101 Hiestand Farm Rd
Campbellsville KY 42718
(800) 772-1213, (270) 465-4164
159 Future Dr
Corbin KY 40701
(800) 772-1213, (606) 528-1806
1615 Holiday Plz
Danville KY 40422
(800) 772-1213, (859) 236-3935
617 N Mulberry St
Elizabethtown KY 42701
(800) 772-1213, (270) 769-2410
7 Youell St
Florence KY 41042
(800) 772-1213, TDD (800) 325-0778
330 W Broadway 2nd Fl
Frankfort KY 40601
(800) 772-1213, (502) 875-2232
157 Belkway Dr
Harlan KY 40831
(800) 772-1213, (606) 573-6101
310 Roy Campbell Dr
Hazard KY 41701
(800) 772-1213, (606) 439-1351
2000 N Elm Bldg 3
Henderson KY 42420
(800) 772-1213, (270) 826-4451 TTY
(270) 826-4343
2100 Ft Campbell Blvd
Hopkinsville KY 42240
(270) 886-3855
12 Howell Ln
Jackson KY 41339
(800) 772-1213, (606) 666-2462
Joellen Jones, District Mgr.
2260 Executive Dr
Lexington KY 40505
(800) 772-1213 • FAX (859) 294-7592
neatra.adams@ssa.gov
Cthse Custom House Rm 101
601 W Broadway
Louisville KY 40202
(800) 772-1213, (502) 582-6690
2500 W Broadway Ste 500
Louisville KY
(800) 772-1213
10503 Timberwood Cir Ste 50
Louisville KY 40223
(800) 772-1213, (502) 224-0593

4431 Hanson Rd
Madisonville KY 42431
(270) 825-9125
318 S 7th St
Mayfield KY 42066
(270) 247-8095
509 Marketplace Dr
Maysville KY 41056
(800) 772-1213, (606) 564-9987
117 W Lothbury Ave
Middlesboro KY 40965
(800) 772-1213, (606) 248-1527
1100 Walnut St Ste E207
Owensboro KY 42301
(270) 685-3931
125 Brett Chase
Paducah KY 42003
(800) 772-1213, (270) 443-7506
333 Hambley Blvd
Pikeville KY 41501
(800) 772-1213, (606) 432-2177
US 23 N 5322 Auxier Rd
Prestonsburg KY 41653
(800) 772-1213, (606) 886-8525
1060 Gibson Bay Dr
Richmond KY 40475
(800) 772-1213, (859) 624-5714
94 Southport Dr
Somerset KY 42501
(800) 772-1213, (606) 678-0825

Hearings & Appeals, Office of
Gary A Flenner, Hearing Office Chief
  Administrative Law Judge
405 S 7th St
Paducah KY 42003
(270) 443-0440 • FAX (270) 441-7911
Richard C Bentley, Hearing Office
  Chief Administrative Law Judge
Tate Bldg Ste 200
125 Lisle Industrial Ave
Lexington KY 40511
(859) 233-2653 • FAX (859) 233-2402
Lawrence E Shearer, Hearing Office
  Chief Administrative Law Judge
Gene Snyder Cthse Ste 300
601 W Broadway
Louisville KY 40202
(502) 582-6446 • FAX (502) 582-6819
Donald Rising, Hearing Office
  Chief Administrative Law Judge
3504 W Cumberland Ave
Middlesboro KY 40965
(606) 248-5320 • FAX (606) 248-6866

Inspector General, Office of
Pamela J Murphy, Inspector General
c/o Cabinet for Health Services &
  Family Services
275 E Main St 5th Fl
Frankfort KY 40601
(502) 564-2888 • FAX (502) 564-6546
pamelaj.murphy@mail.state.ky.us

Tennessee Valley Authority (TVA)
Shawnee Fossil Plant
7900 Metropolis Lake Rd
West Paducah KY 42086

FEDERAL GOVERNMENT

National Cemeteries

THE NATIONAL CEMETERY SYSTEM

In the U.S., development of national cemeteries began as the Civil War was waged, which tried and tested the very existence of a young nation. During the early years of the war, the dead were buried in fields and churchyards, or close to the hospitals and camps where they died. The number of dead soon exceeded that of any previous conflict of the North American continent.

In 1862, Pres. Lincoln signed legislation authorizing the creation of national cemeteries, "...for the soldiers who shall die in the service of the country." These cemeteries were the beginning of what is now known as the National Cemetery System.

At the end of the Civil War, search and recovery teams visited hundreds of battlefields, churchyards and other locations where hasty combat interments had been made. More than a quarter of a million remains were disinterred. The reinterment process took five years to complete and by 1870, 73 national cemeteries were under the jurisdiction of the federal government.

Today there are a total of 130 national cemeteries — they stand as enduring testimonials to the appreciation of a grateful nation.

Camp Nelson National Cemetery
Source: Sid Webb

KENTUCKY NATIONAL CEMETERIES

Camp Nelson National Cemetery
6980 Danville Rd
Nicholasville, KY 40356
Phone: (859) 885-5727
http://www.cem.va.gov/nchp/campnelson.htm
No. of interments thru FY 2004: 11,666

Cave Hill National Cemetery
701 Baxter Ave
Louisville, KY 40204
Phone: (502) 893-3852
http://www.cem.va.gov/nchp/cavehill.htm
No. of interments thru FY 2004: 5,961

Danville National Cemetery
277 North First St
Danville, KY 40442
(This cemetery is within Bellevue Cemetery)
Phone: (859) 885-5727
http://www.cem.va.gov/nchp/danvilleky.htm
No. of interments thru FY 2004: 393

Lebanon National Cemetery
20 Highway 208
Lebanon, KY 40033
Phone: 859 885 5727, (270) 692-3390
http://www.cem.va.gov/nchp/lebanon.htm
No. of interments thru FY 2004: 4,506

Lexington National Cemetery
833 West Main St
Lexington, KY 40508
(859) 885-5727
http://www.cem.va.gov/nchp/lexington.htm
No. of interments thru FY 2004: 1,390

Mill Springs National Cemetery
9044 West Highway 80
Nancy, KY 42544
(859) 885-5727
http://www.cem.va.gov/nchp/millsprings.htm
No. of interments thru FY 2004: 2,943

Zachary Taylor National Cemetery
4701 Brownsboro Rd
Louisville, KY 40207
Phone: (502) 893-3852
http://www.cem.va.gov/nchp/zacharytaylor.htm
No. of interments thru FY 2004: 13,321

OFFICERS OF THE GOVERNMENT OF THE UNITED STATES.

JOHN ADAMS, Prefident, and Commander in Chief of the Armies and Navy of the United States, Salary 25,000 Dollars.

THOMAS JEFFERSON, Vice-Prefident of the United States and Prefident of the Senate, Salary 5,000 Dolls.

JOHN MARSHALL, Secretary of State, Salary 3,500.

- - - - - - - -, Secretary of the Treafury, Salary 3,500 Dolls.

John Steele, Comptroller, Salary 2,650 Dolls.

Richard Harrison, Auditor, Salary 2,400 Dolls.

- - - - - - - -, Commiffioner of Revenue, Salary 2,400 Dolls.

Joseph Nourse, Regifter, Salary 1,750 Dolls.

Samuel Meredith, Treafurer, Salary 2,400.

Samuel Dexter, Secretary at War, Salary, 3,000 Dolls.

Benjamin Rush, Director of the Mint, Salary 2,000 Dolls.

Joseph Habersham, Poftmafter General, Salary 2,000 Dolls.

Benjamin Stoddard, Secretary of the Navy, Salary *not known.*

Kentucky Counties

Copyright 2005, The Clark Group

● County Seat

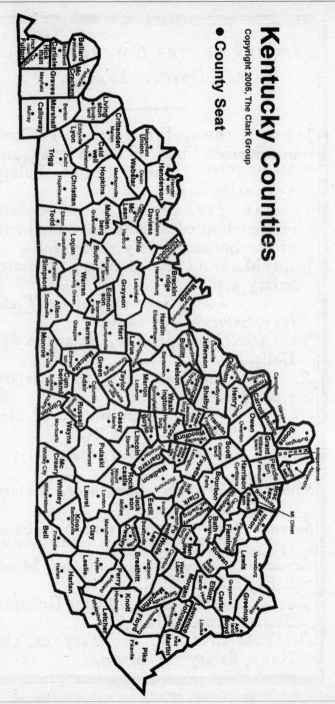

Bob Arnold

COUNTY GOVERNMENTS:
THE CENTER OF OUR COMMUNITIES

Counties are the largest administrative division of most states in the U.S., including the Commonwealth of Kentucky. Counties are the grassroots level of government, where response is local and where neighbors serve their neighbors. Today's counties are the most diverse — varying impressively in size, population, geography, and governmental structure. In their politics and policies, they express the slogan, *"Think globally, act locally."*

Kentucky itself was once a separate county of Virginia. In the early days, Kentucky was known as Fincastle County; it later became Kentucky County in 1776. However, as the number of settlers who came to the rich land through the Cumberland Gap or down the Ohio River grew, so did the needs of these families. There was the need for protection from Indian raids, for laws that applied within each distinctive community, and those needs were difficult to address with the government so far away in Richmond, Va. Finally, Kentucky was admitted to the union as the 15th state on June 1, 1792. Today, from one county Kentucky has grown to 120 counties, each with its own unique history and populace.

As the new state grew, communities were carved into the territory, each of a different size and most named in honor of prestigious political leaders. Counties began to function both as local governments and as arms of the state, but with their own specific roles and powers. County residents elected their own local leaders – judge/ executives, county commissioners, magistrates, county attorneys, county clerks, sheriffs, circuit clerks, jailers, coroners, property valuation administrators, constables and surveyors. Each office has its own history and specific duties.

The election process begins and ends at the county level. County governments are empowered by state law to handle all local, state and national elections. County governments engage in a multitude of tasks to enpower their citizens to vote: register new voters, institute primary elections, publicize election day procedures, mail election information to voters, select voting devices, establish polling sites and certify voting accuracy.

In addition, counties and county officials are responsible for a wide array of other duties. For example, they oversee county roads; provide local law enforcement; operate county jails; provide garbage service; provide emergency and disaster relief services; promote economic development; provide water and sewer services; provide hospitals, ambulances and other health facilities and services; perform marriage ceremonies and operate parks and other recreational facilities for the benefit of county residents.

The evolution of county government reflects the trends of our nation's society as regions that grew dramatically in population fought for equally expanded powers of governance.

County government today is often the mechanism by which geographically or socially pervasive challenges are met with strategies that are locally initiated and accountable.

Adair County

The 44th county in Kentucky was created out of Green County by the General Assembly on Dec. 11, 1801. Adair was so named in honor of Gen. John Adair.

Adair County is located in the Eastern Pennyrile region and Western Appalachian areas. It has 406 square miles of land with a population of 17,244 according to the 2000 U.S. census. The county seat is Columbia and was formed on June 28, 1802. The main waterways are Green River and its tributary, Russell Creek. A few of the earliest settlers in the county were Col. William Casey, Col. James Knox, William Caldwell, William Montgomery and Daniel Trabue.

Adair's first courthouse was completed in 1806. It is one of a select few in Kentucky that was never damaged by fire or raiders from the Civil War. In 1847 renovations were started with a new Greek Revival style. A cupola was added for a bell. Then in 1884, the courthouse was taken completely down and a new courthouse was erected in the Victorian style on its location. In 1974 additions to the courthouse were made and the bell renovated to be operated by electricity instead of hand rung. Also in 1974, the Adair County Courthouse was placed on the National Register of Historic Places.

Adair County has had many notable residents. Henry and Janice Holt Giles moved to Adair County in 1949. The bulk of Janice's literary work was completed while she lived in Adair County.

Col. William Casey came to Adair County in 1789 to help settle the area. He was a state senator for

this district, who died in 1816 at the age of 60. Due to advanced rheumatism, he was buried in his rocking chair in a sitting position.

Col. Frank L. Wolford was born in 1817 in Columbia. He was a colonel in the 1st Kentucky Cavalry in the Union Army. Col. Wolford led his men at the Battle of Mill Springs in January 1862. He was a teacher, lawyer, politician and congressman.

Ed Diddle was born in Adair County in 1895 and went on to become a well known coach of football and basketball. He is best known as the coach of the Western Kentucky Hilltoppers.

Paul Hughes was born in Adair County. Mr. Hughes worked on the Times newspaper for the Courier-Journal. He was instrumental in helping create the Kentucky bookmobile program.

Adair County is rich in education and industry and home to Lindsey Wilson College,

Courthouse in Adair County
Source: Sid Webb

a four-year accredited institution. In 2006, plans will be completed for a new Adair County Elementary School for the county students.

There are a number of historic landmarks, including the home of Mark Twain's great-grandparents, His mother, Jane Clemens, was born in Adair County in 1803; she married John Marshall Clemens in Columbia in 1823. A year later, they moved to Tennessee and later, Missouri where Twain, their sixth child, was born in 1835. Adair County Courthouse, the Trabue-Russell House, the John Field House, Eubank Spring House and the Columbia Presbyterian Church.

Contributed by Lila Ford

Allen County

On Jan. 11, 1815, the Kentucky Legislature created a new county from parts of Warren and Barren Counties. Kentucky's 57th county was named Allen in honor of Lt. Col. John Allen, who lost his life in the War of 1812 at the Battle of the River Raisin, near Detroit. On the extreme southern part Kentucky, the land is somewhat hilly. The first settlements in the area were established around 1797, north and east of the county seat by pioneers from Virginia. On April 10, 1815, four miles northwest of what is currently Scottsville, Gov. Isaac Shelby commissioned seven men as justices of the peace. A site for the county seat was selected near a spring situated on the old Cumberland Settlement Trace. One hundred acres on Bay's Fork were purchased for $2 per acre. The

The county seat was named Scottville in honor of Gov. Charles Scott, the fourth governor of Kentucky. Later the name was changed to Scott(s)ville.

Agriculture and natural resources have been important aspects of Allen County. Mineral springs as well as oil exploration have attracted many to the county.

In wartime, Allen County has provided its best, always supporting and aiding in a justified cause. Many of Allen County's sons and daughters have brought honor to their birthplace. The first woman elected to a political office in Kentucky was Mrs. William (Emma Guy) Cromwell of Allen County.

Allen County is the home of the Dollar General Company. In 1939 J. L. Turner and his son Cal became wholesalers of basic dry goods. By 1955, they owned and operated 35 dry goods stores with annual sales reaching $2 million. Today the Turners' "dollar store" concept has resulted in one of the largest retail companies in the U.S.

Paved roadways throughout the county link the agricultural and scenic landscape to the major cit-

ies. The Jackson Highway (Route 31-E) and Route 231, modern limited-access roadways, create economic development as well as ease in travel, allowing tourists to enjoy the serene environment.

Public Spring, Scottsville
Source: Allen County Historical Society

Religion has always played an important part of family life in Allen County. Revivals and annual homecomings draw large audiences. Today Allen County is the permanent home of the Kentucky State Gospel Singing Convention. Every October this gathering draws hundreds of singers as well as those who enjoy the music. Allen County has two Old Order Mennonite communities, which remind one of the early farming practices and the quiet family life of yesteryear.

Allen County is located in south central Kentucky and is comprised of 364 square miles, bordered on the north by the Barren River Lake, a 10,000 acre wildlife and managed recreational lake. It is capable of 20,150 acres at maximal flood control with 36 miles of Allen County shoreline. The county shares its southern border with Tennessee. Neighboring Barren, Monroe, Simpson, and Warren Counties all share in Allen County's great wealth of resources and unbridled spirit.

Contributed by H.D. Overhold

Anderson County

Anderson County, the eighty-second county in order of formation, is located in the Bluegrass region of central Kentucky. The county is bounded by Spencer, Shelby, Franklin, Woodford, Nelson, Mercer, and Washington counties and covers 204 square miles of rolling hills, grasslands and the meandering water of the Kentucky and Salt Rivers. Lawrenceburg, incorporated in 1820 as Lawrence, is the county seat. The county was established on January 16, 1827, from parts of Franklin, Washington, and Mercer counties. It was named for Richard Clough Anderson, Jr., a Kentucky legislator, U.S. congressman, and minister to Colombia. Anderson was born on August 4, 1788 in Louisville, at which time was then the district of Kentucky.

On July 18, 1773, the first white men set foot on what is now Anderson County. Many early settlers spent time at James Harrod's Fort (now Harrodsburg) and came north to take up land claims. Among them were Richard Benson, Nathan Hammond, William Brayer, and Thomas Baker. Jacob Kaufman, a German immigrant, established Kaufman's Station around 1780. He owned 1,400 acres on the future site of Lawrenceburg. Another early settlement was John Arnold's Station, built around 1783 on the Kentucky River just above the mouth of the Little Benson Creek. In 1798 the Salt River Baptist Church was built two miles south of Lawrenceburg. Its first pastor was John Penney, great-grandfather of J.C. Penney, who founded the chain of retail stores.

Anderson County is home to Four Roses Bourbon Distillery and Wild Turkey Bourbon Distillery, two of only eight working bourbon distilleries in

Anderson County Courthouse
Source: Sid Webb

Kentucky. Complementing the bourbon industry, Anderson County is also home to the commonwealth's largest winery in acreage. Lover's Leap Vineyard and Winery is known for its nationally awarded wines.

In addition to a history of producing bourbon and wine, Anderson County has much more to offer. With many historically preserved homes and recreational opportunities, there is plenty to see and do in Anderson County.

Contributed by Ann Garrison

Ballard County

"Ballard County, the 93rd in order of formation, was organized in 1842, out of parts of McCracken and Hickman counties, and named in honor of Capt. Bland Ballard. It is situated in the extreme western part of the state, opposite Cairo, Illinois; contains 393 square miles; and is bounded on the north by the Ohio river, west by the Mississippi river, south by Hickman County, and east by Graves and McCracken counties. Mayfield creek runs westerly through the entire county, dividing it into north and south Ballard—north Ballard being a beautiful high, level, and comparatively open country, producing more than average in the state, of corn, wheat, rye, oats, potatoes, sorghum, and the finest tobacco in the world (which has sold in several instances, as high as $410 per hundred pounds); south Ballard is more broken, more heavily timbered, and has more depth of soil. The soil of the river-bottoms, a mixture of black loam and sand, is very productive ...

In the first settlement of it, and for many years after, the northern part of the county was an elevated prairie, open, covered with tall grass, five or six feet high, and without timber except along the creeks. Under the timber grew a species of wild rye, with long beards, very troublesome to the eyes of cattle. Wild bees and honey were plentiful, that a man could climb many of the trees and drink metheglin out of the first knot-hole he encountered. Now, the grass and wild rye are gone, and the whole country, except where cultivated, grown up in timber...

Capt. Bland W. Ballard, for whom this county was named, was born near Fredericksburg, Va., Oct. 16, 1761, and died in Shelby co., Ky., Sept. 5, 1853 — aged 92 years. His remains are interred in the State Cemetery at Frankfort. [An elegant portrait, from a sketch taken in life, and finished in Aug. 1873 was presented by the artist, Col. Reuben H. Buckley, to the Public Library at Louisville.] ...

He came to Kentucky, in 1779, when he was 18 years old; joined the militia; served in Col. Bowman's expedition, May 1779; in Gen. Clark's expedition against the Piqua towns, July 1780, where he was dangerously wounded in the hip, and suffered from it until his death; in Gen. Clark's expedition, Nov. 1782, against the same towns; in 1786, was a spy for Gen. Clark, in the Wabash expedition, rendered abortive by mutiny of the soldiers; in 1791, was a guide under Gens. Scott and Wilkinson; and Aug. 20, 1794, was with Gen. Wayne at the battle of the 'Fallen Timbers.'"

An excerpt from pages 38-39 of the entry for "Ballard County," Collins' Historical Sketches of Kentucky, History of Kentucky (Southern Historical Press, 1874).

It's a Kentucky thing...

A state historic site, Wickliffe Mounds, is the archaeological site of a prehistoric Native American village of the Mississippian mound builders. On a bluff overlooking the Mississippi river, the village was occupied from about AD 1100 to 1350. The Mississippians built a complex settlement with permanent houses and earthen mounds situated around a central plaza. (270) 335-3681, http://parks.ky.gov

Barren County

Barren County was formed on Dec. 20, 1798, from parts of Warren and Green counties. It was named not for a governor or soldier as most counties, but for part of the county which was considered barren land. That barren land was devoid of deep timbers, but contained instead lush grasses – a grazing land for the buffalo and a hunting ground for the Indians. The other part of the county was hilly, covered with giant trees and pea vines up to a horse's belly.

Wigwam Villiage
Source: John Perkins

and Louie Nunn; Luska Twyman, the first African American to serve as mayor in the South; Billy Vaughn, the late musician who began his career playing in Glasgow bands; and Gen. Joseph Horace Lewis, the heroic leader of the Orphan Brigade during the Civil War. Haiden Trigg, a Glasgow banker, was the developer and breeder of the noted Trigg Foxhounds. Four-star Gen. Robert Dougherty was the commanding general of the Strategic Air Command. Julian Goodman, Chairman of the Board of NBC, called Barren County home. Stephen Landrum was a African American who owned many houses in Glasgow and was trusted by all for his intellect and honesty. Dr. C. C. Howard was a physician whose fame spread throughout the state. The establishment of the T. B. Hospital in Glasgow was but one of his contributions which also included being known as the father of the Rural Medical Scholarship program in Kentucky. Diane Sawyer of ABC and Johnny Depp have Barren County ties.

There are many small communities, each with their own warmth and charm. Cave City, with its proximity to Mammoth Cave, has grown over the years. Bell's Tavern in Park City was a stagecoach stop carrying visitors to the cave and entertained Jenny Lind and many famous people of the past. Fort Williams, a Union fort, was built during the Civil War. The creation of Barren River Reservoir and Barren River Lodge encouraged further visitor growth.

Despite being devastated in 1854 from a cholera epidemic that killed half the population of Glasgow, the town and county continues to thrive and grow with descendants of the early pioneers still represented and new citizens from many areas and cultures who have come to call Barren County home.

Many of Barren County's earliest settlers came from Virginia, such as soldiers and officers of the Revolutionary War who had been granted land south of the Green River in payment for their services. Soldier John Gorin donated 150 acres of land in July 1799 for the purpose of establishing the town of Glasgow, the county seat.

From this humble beginning, Glasgow and Barren County became a trading, social and cultural center for a wide area. When the War of 1812 raged, Barren County provided many soldiers from among their young men and many of the Revolutionary War soldiers volunteered yet again. During the Civil War, families lost sons to both the Blue and the Gray.

The county has provided many distinguished individuals, including governors Preston Leslie

For more information, contact the South Central Kentucky Historical and Genealogical Society, Post Office Box 157, Glasgow, KY 42142-0157.
Contributed by Sandi Gorin

Bath County

Located on the northeastern edge of the Bluegrass region of Kentucky, the forests and rolling farmland of Bath County gently flow into the foothills of the Appalachian Mountains. The county's rich history precedes that first recorded by hunters, surveyors and colonists like Daniel Boone.

Before modern Native American tribes appeared on the scene, the ancient Mound Builders left evidence of their time here with their famous mounds and the remains of an ancient fort, much of which has been destroyed by time and cultivation.

Two of the earliest businesses in the state, the Bourbon Iron Furnace and the Olympian Springs Hotel, both of which date in the late 1700s, made the area a center for commerce and hospitality that attracted such notables as Henry Clay and the French King Louis Phillippe.

The remains of the furnace, which made household and farm implements as well as cannon balls used during the War of 1812, are now part of a roadside park on state Route 36 south of Owingsville.

Owingsville, the county seat, is famed for its architecture, featuring everything from historic log cabins under new facades to historic Greek Revival mansions. Court House Square includes the Bath County Courthouse; the three-story Owings House, a mansion said to have been designed between 1811 and 1814 by renowned architect Benjamin Latrobe; and the Victorian commercial district surrounding the square. All are on the National Register of Historic Places.

The main part of the present courthouse was built between 1864 and 1867 to replace the one that burned during the Civil War when Union troops making a fast exit accidentally knocked over a stove. The extended front and clock tower were added in 1903.

Sharpsburg, Sherburne, Salt Lick, and Wyoming were all once-thriving communities whose successes fluctuated with the fortunes of their various businesses, including iron, river trade, and timber.

The county has produced and been home to many notable people including Revolutionary War hero Capt. Jack Jouette, who is buried here; Confederate Gen. John Bell Hood; two governors, Alvin Hawkins of Tennessee and Claude Matthews of Indiana; writers William Lightfoot Visscher and Col. John A. Joyce; soldier/diplomat Maj. Gen. Henry Tureman Allen; and artist Joel T. Hart.

Bath County is rich in history, horses, family farming, and opportunities for outdoor activities, including hunting, hiking, biking, fishing, trail riding, camping, photography, water sports, and peace and tranquility. Cave Run Lake is nationally known for

THE OWINGS HOUSE
BUILT BETWEEN 1811 AND 1814
BY IRON MASTER THOMAS DEYE OWINGS
Source: Carol Rison

its muskie and bass fishing; and the Daniel Boone National Forest, which surrounds it, offers endless opportunities for nature lovers. The Owingsville Lions Club Horse Show, a highlight of every Fourth of July weekend for over 60 years and one of the top shows on the circuit, features pleasure riders and high-class show horses.

Bath County, with its unbridled spirit of the land and its history, offers something for everyone.
Contributed by Brenda Vance

Bell County

Bell County is located in the southeastern corner of Kentucky where the state meets Tennessee and Virginia at the famed Cumberland Gap. Its 361 acres are dominated by two mountain ridges, Pine Mountain and Cumberland Mountain. Much of its rugged terrain is thickly forested with picturesque streams cutting through deep valleys. Kentucky's first state park, Pine Mountain State Resort Park, and the country's largest national historical park, Cumberland Gap National

Bell County courthouse
Source: Sid Webb

Historical Park, showcase the county's natural beauty. Kentucky's late Historian Laureate, Dr. Thomas Clark, maintained that Bell County contained the third most important geological feature in American history.

Bell County also contains another unique geological feature: the impact crater of a huge meteorite. The town of Middlesboro is built entirely within this 10.9 square mile crater. It is the only city in the northern hemisphere known to be built within a meteorite crater.

Daniel Boone and his men blazed the way through the Cumberland Gap in 1775 for well over 100,000 frontiersmen and pioneers to travel the Wilderness Road, as it was then called, into the rich interior of Kentucky. Few of these early pioneers settled in what was to become Bell County, and throughout the first

half of the 19th century it was sparsely populated by subsistence farmers and loggers.

Bell County was formed from parts of Harlan and Knox County in 1867. It was named for a Kentucky politician who was the great-grandson of Dr. Thomas Walker. The little settlement at the Cumberland Ford near the Narrows became the county seat. It took the name Pineville.

In the late 1880s, there was a huge developmental boom fueled by foreign investment and the recognition of the wealth of untapped mineral and forest resources in the county. Railroads raced to connect the county with the outside world. Investors plowed millions into a planned city now called Middlesboro. Multiple industries announced plans for large factories, and from 1889-1891 the city boomed. Then several factors, topped off by the Panic of 1893, caused a bust.

In the years that followed, the county gradually rebounded, primarily by exploiting its vast coal resources. For the next 50 years or more, King Coal reigned and county fortunes waxed and waned with the coal's cycle of good and bad times. By 1950, the county population was 44,000. Then coal went into a sustained downward plunge and there was a huge outmigration to the industrial centers of the north.

At the time of the 2000 census, population stood at 30,060. Coal continues to be an important industry, but machinery has greatly reduced the number of miners needed to mine it. Efforts to diversify economically have brought mixed results. Several industrial parks have been developed and have attracted a number of small industries. A tunnel through Cumberland Mountain has greatly improved the transportation system. Bell County now has a community college with a large enrollment. Tourism is becoming an ever larger part of the economy, and the county looks ahead with great optimism.

Contributed by the Bell County Historical Society,
P. O. Box 1344, Middlesboro, KY 40965, 606-242-5622
e-mail: bellhistsociety@hotmail.com
web address: www.geocities.com/bellhistorical.

Boone County

Longe before Kentucky was state, there were three major river navigational landmarks on the Ohio. Two of these are in present-day Boone County: Split Rock, a rare free-standing glacial conglomerate formation, and Big Bone Lick, the most famous depository of Pleistocene vertebrate megafauna fossil remains in North America. Big Bone Lick is designated the Home of Vertebrate Paleontology.

The first documented European visit was in 1739 by Charles Le Moyne, the second Baron de Longueuil, who was the commander of a French Canadian military expedition out of Canada. Boone County was established on Dec. 13, 1798. Named in honor of Daniel Boone, it became the 30th of Kentucky's 120 counties. The total population in the county was just 1500 souls.

The first permanent settlement in Boone County was Tanner's Station, located on a high terrace of the Ohio River, founded in 1789 by John Tanner, a Baptist preacher from North Carolina. Later to be renamed Petersburg in 1814, the settlement was established right on top of two separate prehistoric village sites. The natives and the settlers chose wisely. Unlike many other Boone County river communities, Petersburg has never flooded, not even in the calamitous 1937 record-maker. Other early Boone County settlers include German-heritage pioneers. The current unincorporated town of Burlington was chosen to be the county seat.

The Ohio River played a major role in the settlement patterns and commercial trade of Boone County. Other early pioneer settlers also arrived via the Cumberland Gap, following the Wilderness Road. Boone County has remained predominantly agricultural and rural for most of its history, and since before the Civil War, tobacco has been the main sustaining cash crop for Boone Countians.

All county histories must include their Civil War affiliations and involvement. Being the most northern county in a border state, Boone County proudly claimed military leaders and enlistees in each army. John Hunt Morgan's route through Boone County during his escape from a federal penitentiary in Ohio has always remained a very proud topic

Rabbit Hash General Store
Source: Kentucky Department of Tourism

among residents, which is a good indicator as toward which cause the loyalties predominately leaned.

It wasn't until the second third of the 20th century that things in Boone County really began to change in earnest and shift from an agricultural focus to one of a manufacturing, industrial and service-oriented complexion. The real metamorphosis began in the 1940s with the Greater Cincinnati Airport's growth, along with the building of the major interstate highway systems beginning in the early 1960s. Florence is now is the leading commercial retail epicenter in this mid-west population corridor.

Today, only a handful of family farms are operating and the tobacco settlement is threatening the existence of the part-time farmers. The only lucrative return on their land now is to sell it to developers. That is why Boone County's claim to fame now is the fact that it is the fastest developing county in the Commonwealth.

Contributed by Don Clare

Bourbon County

Bourbon County was the fifth county created from Fayette County in 1786. Bourbon was one of the original nine counties shaped while Kentucky was still a part of Virginia. At one time Bourbon County covered one-fifth of the Commonwealth. The county is located centrally in the part of the state known as the Bluegrass region.

Our first county seat was named Hopewell after Lawrence Protzman's hometown in New Jersey. It was Protzman who bought and divided 250 acres for the new county seat in Bourbon. The name Hopewell was changed to Paris in 1790. The courthouse now standing in Paris is the fourth courthouse built for Bourbon County in 1905. It has been stated by many that it is the finest looking courthouse in the state, modeled after the U.S. Capitol. Millersburg, North Middletown, Little Rock, Centerville and Clintonville are other small communities located in the county.

Bourbon County is known for many fine-looking and historical buildings. Cane Ridge Shrine was the location of the famous Reverend Barton Stone's revival in 1801. This revival is said to have been the peak for early frontier religion drawing as many as 30,000 people.

Another well-known attraction in Bourbon County is Duncan Tavern. Major Joseph Duncan built this three-story tavern in 1788. It is now the headquarters of the Kentucky Society of the Daughters of the American Revolution and home of the John Fox, Jr. Library, one of the best genealogical libraries in our state.

Bourbon County is actually listed in "Ripley's Believe It or Not" as the home of the world's tallest three-story building. The Millersburg Military Academy, the last military school still in operation in the state, has been in continuous operation since 1893. Paris native and African-American inventor Garrett Morgan invented the tri-color traffic light.

Bourbon County is also renowned for the horse Secretariat, which bred, stood and died at Claiborne horse farm in Bourbon County. This Triple Crown winner was the only Kentucky Derby winner to finish in less than two minutes.

Bourbon County is also known for its prime farmland and scenic beauty. This county is known worldwide for its Bourbon whiskey, burley tobacco, purebred livestock and other agricultural products. This county is the center of the horse industry, including thoroughbred, standard bred, walking horses and pleasure horses. The well-drained and fertile soil in Bourbon County produces other crops such as corn, alfalfa hay and clover hay. Farming is in the genes of most people in Bourbon County from generation to generation whether they were landowners or farm employees. The unbeatable combination of prime farmland and history give the people of Bourbon a county to be proud of for a long time.

Contributed by Kellie West

Building a dry stone fence along scenic Paris Pike
Source: Sid Webb

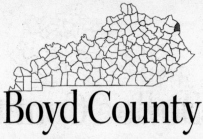

Boyd County

At 160 square miles, Boyd is the third smallest county in Kentucky with a population of 49,752 in 2000. The county was named for Linn Boyd, who had served as Speaker of the House of Representatives in Washington, D.C. He was elected lieutenant governor in 1859, but died before his term was to begin.

The county was created in 1860 from parts of Greenup, Carter, and Lawrence counties and lies at a point where Ohio, West Virginia, and Kentucky meet. Linked to Ohio by two bridges over the Ohio River and with two more to West Virginia (across the Big Sandy River), the county serves as a marketing area for some 420,805 people who live within 60 miles of Ashland (pop. 21,981 in 2000) the largest city, and the county seat of Catlettsburg (pop. 1,960), which stands at the confluence of the Ohio and Big Sandy Rivers.

Paramount Theater
Source: Kentucky Department of Tourism

Coal and iron dominated the area's economy for many years, with abandoned stone-block iron furnaces still dotting the area. Both coal and iron ore were mined extensively in the nineteenth and twentieth centuries, but neither is being produced in Boyd County today.

There has also been a steep decline in the industrial base in recent years. AK Steel (formerly Armco Steel) is still a leading employer with about 1,151 workers, but far fewer than in its heyday in the 1950s with approximately 4,500. Ashland Oil, begun in 1924 and formerly a major employer, moved its headquarters to Covington, Kentucky, in 1999 while retaining its refinery near Catlettsburg (now a part of Marathon Oil).

In spite of this industrial decline, Boyd County has managed quite well with a huge expansion at Kings' Daughter's Medical Center (founded 1898), which employs about 3,000 people. With dozens of other medical offices clustered about the area, Boyd County has become a regional center for the medical arts.

Recreational and cultural opportunities abound, with nearby state parks and man-made lakes, and downtown Ashland's 33-acre Central Park that offers ball fields, tennis courts, play grounds, and mature trees. A publicly owned Tennis Center with 12 outdoor and four indoor courts, and first-class high school athletic facilities add to the recreational mix. Downtown Ashland features the Highlands Museum and Discovery Center, the new Pendleton Artist Center (2005), the Paramount Performing Arts Center (recently restored and enlarged), the Ashland Art Gallery, and the Jesse Stuart Foundation.

Annual celebrations include Poage Landing Days in September, Summer Motion in July, the Catlettsburg Memorial Day Parade, and Central Park's Winter Wonderland of Lights at Christmas. The county has four high schools including Boyd County and Ashland Paul Blazer, where state athletic championships are not a rarity, and two smaller schools, Fairview and Rose Hill Christian. In addition, Ashland Community and Technical College (begun in 1937 as Ashland Junior College) enrolled about 3,200 students in the fall semester of 2005.

Contributed by Ernest M. Tucker.

Boyle County

Although Boyle County is a relatively young county, formed in 1842 from Mercer County, the county seat town of Danville has a rich history. The Wilderness Road, built by Daniel Boone to bring settlers into Kentucky, came through the area. Danville was the first capital of Kentucky, when it was known as the Kentucky District of Virginia. It was in Danville in September 1792 that Kentucky was formed at the present location of Constitution Square State Historic Site after a series of Constitutional Conventions held at the meeting house on the grounds. Boyle County was named for Judge John Boyle, who served as Judge of the Kentucky Court of Appeals from 1809-1826 and Judge of the U.S. District Court for Kentucky from 1827-1834.

Known as the City of Firsts, Danville was the location of the first college in the west, first supreme courthouse, first law school, first meeting house and the first state-supported school for the deaf in the nation. It also is home to Pioneer Playhouse, the oldest outdoor dinner theatre in Kentucky. On Christmas Day, 1809, the first successful abdominal surgery in the world was performed by Dr. Ephraim McDowell at his home on South Second Street. The patient was Jane Todd Crawford from Green County, who rode 60 miles by horseback to have a 22-pound tumor removed without the aid of anesthetic. The home and the adjoining apothecary shop are both open to the public.

Ten miles west of Danville is the community of Perryville, where in October 1862 the bloodiest battle of the Civil War in Kentucky was fought on nearby farmland. The battlefield is now the Perryville Battlefield Historic Site with nearly 600 acres of land preserved much as it was left after the battle. More than 7,600 men were wounded or killed in the battle, and many of the homes, churches and schools still standing in the town of Perryville were used as hospitals and morgues after the battle. Merchants' Row in Perryville, located along the banks of the Chaplin River, contains old commercial buildings and homes that are just like they were in the 1840s with restoration and preservation in progress.

Perryville horse silhouette
Source: Clay Jackson

McDowell House
Source: Danville-Boyle County Convention & Visitors Bureau

One of three rivers that have their headwaters in Boyle County is the Rolling Fork. Along its banks is the beautiful Forkland Valley where many pioneers settled after coming to Kentucky with James Harrod and Daniel Boone. The descendants of these families still live in the valley and its surrounding knoblands. Every October these people celebrate their heritage during the Forkland Heritage Festival and Revue. When their school at Forkland was closed because of consolidation, the people of Forkland bought the school building and turned it into a community center. The public is invited to enjoy the festival with hayrides, Indian artifact displays, craft booths, working sorghum mill, old farm machinery, live drama and a bean supper.
Contributed by Carolyn Crabtree

Bracken County

Bracken County was founded in 1789 by Simon Kenton. Many family records state that George and Laurence Washington were surveying in this area before 1789 when George Washington became President. George Rogers Clark, a man of military genius, became a great benefit to the settlers of Kentucky. In 1778, with his troops, Clark came down the Ohio River on flat boats, bringing with him 20 families, 10 of which located in Bracken County.

The county was named for an early pioneer, William Bracken, whose name well described the lush growth of ferns found nestling in the coves and creek-mouths of the area. The bracken, or large coarse ferns, still grow along many of our inland streams.

Source: SouthEast Telephone

Starting in 1781, Philip Buckner, a captain in the Continental Army of Virginia during the Revolutionary War, came into possession of a number of land grants encompassing thousands of acres in what is now Bracken County. Shortly after having secured these grants he came to visit the area and see for himself the wealth he had gained. In 1796 he returned, bringing with him 40 families from Virginia. Twenty of these families came into Bracken County with Buckner, settled and started many of the present day villages. Their descendants are still to be found in the area. Emigrants from Pennsylvania, Virginia, Ohio and other areas came creating more hamlets and settlements. Civilization finally outgrew the wilderness and progress was on its way. In 1798 Bracken County lost territory to Pendleton County and again in 1867 when Robertson County was formed.

Augusta, Bracken County's largest city, was founded on the Ohio River in 1797 on land given by Philip Buckner. The first session of the court for Bracken County was held in Augusta on Monday, June 12, 1797 and held there regularly until the seat of justice was moved to Woodward's Cross Roads in 1839. At this time the decision was made to rename Woodward's Cross Roads to Brooksville, the current county seat of Bracken County.

With its complete northern border bounded by the Ohio River and its view of freedom only one-fourth mile away, Bracken County became a major route on the Underground Railroad. Many sites in Bracken County have been documented as stops along this journey. In one of the darkest and most challenging eras of our history, many local people were instrumental in helping slaves escape and go north to gain their freedom.

Bracken County is noted for its gently rolling hills, scenic vistas, family farms and places of historic interest. It was one of the largest tobacco producing areas in the state, but with the demise of tobacco production, has diversified with agritourism and value added farm operations. For further information, contact the Bracken County Historical Society at 606-735-3337 or Phil Weber at Bracken County Tourism, City of Augusta Clerk's office, at 606-756-2183.

Sources: A History of Bracken County, Recollections: Yesterday, Today for Tomorrow-1969 and History of Bracken County, Bicentennial Edition Second printing-2002.

Reprinted with the permission of the Bracken County Historical Society.

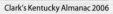

Breathitt County

Breathitt County, located in the foothills of the Appalachian Mountain in the Eastern Coal Field region, was created on April 1, 1839 by an act of the Legislature and named in honor for Gov. John Breathitt (1832-34). The eighty-ninth county in order of creation, Breathitt County covers an area of 494 square miles and is bordered by Lee, Wolfe, Magoffin, Knott, Perry and Owsley counties.

The county seat is located at Jackson, which sits near the geographic center of the county on the North Fork of the Kentucky River. Other major waterways include the Middle Fork of the Kentucky River, Quicksand, Troublesome, Lost and Frozen creeks.

Stone and human artifacts uncovered in the county indicate that generations of prehistoric animals and people inhabited the place leaving behind a rich cultural heritage. Settlers from Virginia and North Carolina first .explored the area in the 1770s but the first permanent settlement was not made until the late 1790s by the Miller, Noble, Neace, Watts, Haddix, Strong, Turner, Back, and Taulbee families.

Most of Breathitt's long history was dominated by periods of quiet subsistence by its inhabitants, with brief periods of economic development involving the early fir and trapping trade, salt making trade, the logging industry and only later by the coal interests.

The violence of the Civil War deeply divided Breathitt County, which was nearly divided equally between the Unionists and Confederates. Shootings, thefts and other actions during the fighting re-ignited many long running feuds and economic disagreements.

Known widely as "Bloody Breathitt," the county garnered national attention through a series of the bloodiest feuds in American history as post Civil War fights ignited in feuds known as the Little-Strong feuds, Hargis-Marcum-Cockrell feud and numerous others. On three separate occasions between 1873 and 1910 the Kentucky State Militia was deployed in Breathitt County to quell fighting and maintain the integrity of the court system.

On July 15, 1891 the Lexington and Eastern Railroad entered the county making Jackson the southern terminus. Business boomed and Breathitt grew and prospered. Seeking the rich cannel coal deposits along Frozen Creek and in neighboring counties, the O & K railroad was built and continued operating until 1935.

The prosperity brought by the railroads brought people to Jackson, and Breathitt's population ballooned from 8,705 in 1890 to 17,540 in 1910. Huge timber tracts brought speculation and investment from lumbermen from across the nation. The largest saw mill in the world operated at Quicksand from the 1890s until 1925 under the Mowbray and Robinson Company brand. E. O. Robinson, owner of the saw mill, later donated fifteen thousand acres of property at Quicksand to the University of Kentucky as the Robinson Agricultural Experiment Substation and Robinson Forest.

Breathitt County is today an important part of the Eastern Kentucky economy with timber and coal as the primary resources transported across a network of roadways including Highways 15, 30 and 1110 to all parts of the nation.

Contributed by, Stephen D. Bowling, Director, Breathitt County Library and Heritage Center

Source: SouthEast Telephone

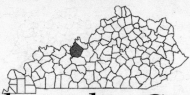

Breckinridge County

Breckinridge County was created in an act passed by the state legislature on December 9, 1799. The 39th county in Kentucky, it was formed from a portion of neighboring Hardin County. Breckinridge County is the sixth largest of the state's 120 counties and contains 565 square miles. Located in western Kentucky on the Ohio River, it is bordered by Hancock, Hardin, Grayson, Meade, and Ohio counties. Part of Meade County was created from a portion of Breckinridge County in 1824, as was Hancock County in 1829.

Breckinridge County was named in honor John Breckinridge, an attorney and statesman, who served as state attorney general from 1793 to 1797 and as a state representative from 1797 to 1801. He was a U.S. senator and became the U.S. attorney general in 1805 during the administration of President Thomas Jefferson.

The county seat of Breckinridge County is Hardinsburg, named for Captain William "Big Bill" Hardin. In 1780 Hardin and three men floated down the Ohio River in a small boat. They reached the mouth of what is today Sinking Creek, traveled upstream to Hardin Creek, and eventually reached a site that became Fort Hardin.

In 1782, lots and streets were laid out for a new town, Hardinsburg. In 1801, the community became the seat of government for the county. Today a county industrial park is located just west of town.

In 1798, a settlement called Joesville was established on the banks of the Ohio River as a trading post. It eventually became the important river port of Cloverport. This community developed into an industrial center for the county. A button factory was built to manufacture buttons from mussel shells taken from the Ohio River. Other industries included railroad shops, a tile plant, a coal oil manufacturing center, and a shipping point for livestock and tobacco.

In 1888 the community of Irvington, was laid out

by civil engineers working for the railroad. By 1927, a federal highway, U.S. Route 60, was established across the county. It was paved by 1931. In 1889 a railroad was built across the county in an east-west direction between Irvington and Cloverport with a branch line built in a southwest direction in order to serve the county seat.

In 1960, Rough River Reservoir

Aerial photo of Hardinsburg,
the county seat
Source: David Hayes

was built on the border with Grayson County and a state resort park was established. A countywide Chamber of Commerce was established in 2001 to help promote business and industrial grown in the county. It also serves as a source of tourism information. The Breckinridge County Historical Society maintains a museum in Hardinsburg, and a community museum is located in a restored train depot in Cloverport.

For more information, interested parties may contact the Greater Breckinridge County Chamber of Commerce at 224 S. Main Street, P.O. Box 725, Hardinsburg, KY 40143. They may phone (270)756-0268 or e-mail the Chamber at chamber@breckinridgeco.com.

Contributed by David Hayes

Bullitt County

Bullitt County is located immediately south of Kentucky's largest city, Louisville. Named for Kentucky's first lieutenant governor, Bullitt was created from Jefferson and Nelson counties on Dec. 13, 1796. Famous frontiersmen Daniel and his brother Squire Boone were among many who forged trails through thick forested hills and valleys following buffalo and deer herds to salt licks.

Bullitt's Lick was the site of the first commercial industry in Kentucky – salt production. The town of Shepherdsville developed near the licks and became the county seat. The Wilderness Trail made a meandering turn here in Bullitt County to the Salt Licks, becoming the first inland intermodal distribution system for commerce in the western frontier. The salt was shipped by flatboats on the Ohio River for distribution from Pittsburgh and New Orleans.

Iron production was another pioneer industry in Bullitt County. During the first half of the 19th century, 30-foot tall stone furnaces, heated by huge quantities of wood and charcoal, smelted iron out of the native rock ore 24 hours a day. Significant remains of two of these old iron furnaces still exist. A massive iron works, powered by a waterwheel on the Salt River, made everything from nails to iron stoves used at Shaker Village at Harrodsburg and, it is said, the first railroad rails west of the Alleghenies.

Bullitt's natural resources, especially timber, suffered greatly at the hands of Kentucky's earliest industrial history. After a century of this early industrial development, both the salt and iron industries faded. In 1929 a successful businessman and visionary formed the Bernheim Foundation, purchased over 14,000 acres of land, and

lovingly guided the return to natural forest. Today Bernheim Arboretum and Research Forest is internationally recognized for its work with native-habitat rehabilitation and its unmatched collections of native-species plants and trees.

About the end of the 18th century, another industry was emerging, and it wasn't long before another Kentucky product was being shipped to the world. The Beam family discovered the smoothness in the limestone water in the Clermont area and began making Jim Beam bourbon. Today, after more than 200 years of continuous operation, the Jim Beam Distillery produces among the finest and most popular bourbons in the world.

From 1826 to 1870, Paroquet Springs, near Shepherdsville, was one of the most noted health and pleasure resorts in the South. The modern-day Paroquet Springs has been reborn as a fresh and attractive new conference center.

Today, rolling knobs, lakes, rivers and forests offer plenty

Bullitt County Courthouse
Source: Bullitt County History Museum

of opportunity to get back to nature, all within close range of Interstate 65. Rapid residential and clean industrial growth is tempered with a growing reawakening to the history and ecology of the area. A first-ever Bullitt County History Museum was opened in October 2004 in the vintage 1900 county courthouse building located in Shepherdsville.

Article submitted by David Strange, Executive Director, Bullitt County History Museum. Learn more about Bullitt County by visiting that museum and its genealogical archives. E-Mail bullittcountyhistory@alltel.net. Or visit on the Internet, www.travelbullitt.org.

Butler County

Butler County was formed on January 18, 1810, from portions of Logan and Ohio counties. It was named for Gen. Richard Butler, a Revolutionary War soldier. The county was 53rd in order of formation and lies in the Western Coal Field region of Kentucky. It contains 444 square miles of land.

Descriptions from early settlers reveal a wild, untouched virgin forest with a cover of numerous species of trees, many being 100 feet high and five and six feet in diameter. Game was abundant. Wild turkeys, deer, elk, bears, and the bellowing of buffalo resounded through the woods like distant thunder. But no resource was more dominant than the Green River, which runs through Butler County. It proved to be a major factor in the growth of the county.

On June 11, 1810 a body of 11 justices of the peace, duly commissioned by Charles Scott, Governor of Kentucky, met to select officers for the newly formed Butler County. One of their first acts was to appoint a commission, which selected as the county seat two acres of land belonging to Christopher Funkhouser. The spot was first called Funkhouser Hill and would later be changed to Morgantown.

In 1833 the Commonwealth of Kentucky inaugurated a navigation system for the Green and Barren rivers. This system was completed in 1842. In the following 20-year period, Butler County's population doubled and two more towns were incorporated along the river — Rochester, located at Lock and Dam No. 3, and Woodbury, located at Lock and Dam No. 4.

With the introduction of the locks and dams, a whole different mode of transportation was launched. This brought a large number of diverse types of people to the county including merchants, miners, loggers, river workers, engineers, carpenters and many more.

After this period of relatively fast growth, the Civil War began and slowed development of the county. Butler County witnessed a few minor incidents during the war, including a skirmish at Big Hill, near Morgantown on Oct. 29,1861, as well as a skirmish the following day at Woodbury where Confederate soldiers had set up camp.

After the war, former soldiers from both sides joined together to raise funds for a Civil War Mon-

> **Descriptions from early settlers reveal a wild, untouched virgin forest with a cover of numerous species of trees, many being 100 feet high and five and six feet in diameter.**

ument that was erected in the courthouse yard and dedicated in May 1907. The monument lists Butler Countians who fought on both sides and is believed to be one of the only two existing memorials which honors both Confederate and Union soldiers.

Butler County is most recently noted for its annual Green River Catfish Festival. Each year numerous tagged catfish are released into the river. Anglers from far and wide attempt to snag one of these tagged catfish for cash prizes, the top prize being $50,000. Once again the river is renowned for bringing people together.

Butler County and her people have a rich and proud heritage and are always ready to seek new paths to secure a bright future.

Contributed by Nancy Cardwell

Caldwell County

"Caldwell county, the 51st erected in the state, was formed in 1809, out of part of Livingston county, and named in honor of Gen. John Caldwell; is situated on the waters of the Cumberland and Tradewater rivers; bounded N. by Crittenden and Hopkins, E. by Hopkins and Christian, S. by Trigg and Lyon, and W. by Lyon and Crittenden counties. The land is generally undulating.

Towns. —*Princeton*, the county seat, on the Elizabethtown and Paducah railroad, 13 miles N.E. of Eddyville, on the Cumberland river, has a handsome brick court house, and 14 lawyers, 5 physicians, 8 churches, Princeton College (an elegant building), and Princeton Female Academy (each with about 100 students), 1 banking house, 3 hotels, 10 dry goods stores, 3 drug stores, 3 furniture stores, 6 groceries, 2 wagon and plough shops, 13 other mechanics' shops, 2 steam flouring mills, and 1 woolen factory; population in 1870, 1,012. *Fredonia*, 12 miles N.W. of Princeton, has 1 church, 2 hotels, 5 stores, 3 doctors, 3 mechanics' shops, and 1 flouring mill.

Gen. John Caldwell, in honor of whom this county received its name, was a native of Prince Edward county, Virginia. He removed to Kentucky in 1781, and settled near where Danville now stands. He took an active part in the conflicts with the Indians, and rose by regular steps from the rank of a common soldier to that of a major general in the militia. He served as a subaltern in the campaign against the Indians in 1786, under Gen. George Rogers Clark. He was a prominent man of his day—esteemed in private and political, as he was in military life. He was a member, from Nelson county, of the conventions held in Danville in 1787 and 1788. In 1792, he was elected from the same county a senatorial elector, under the first constitution; and in the college of electors, he was chosen the senator from Nelson. He took his seat at the session of 1792-93. He was elected lieutenant governor of the state in 1804, and during his term of service removed to the lower part of the State. He died at Frankfort in the year 1804 Nov.19, while the legislature was in session."

An excerpt from pages 108 of the entry for "Caldwell County," Collins' Historical Sketches of Kentucky, History of Kentucky, Volume II (Southern Historical Press, 1874).

y'know what?

The Pennington Folk Music Festival, held in Princeton in June each year, features thumbpicking, bluegrass and lots of other folk music. While in Princeton, visit the historic Adsmore Museum located at 304 North Jefferson Street. A visit to Adsmore, a living home museum, is truly a step back in time. A visitor entering the home will relive an era of top hats and fans, graphophones, lavender scented sheets, elegant china and crystal, and button shoes. Adsmore, meticulously restored, reflects the lifestyle of the prominent Smith-Garrett family at the close of the "Golden Age."

Calloway County

Formed in 1822 from a part of Hickman County, Calloway County is rich in history. Although the two spellings are different, the county is named in honor of Colonel Richard Callaway, a noted lawgiver, defender of the frontier, and friend of Daniel Boone.

Calloway County is part of the Jackson Purchase region and is bordered by Marshall County, Graves County, the Tennessee River and the Tennessee state line. Its primary crops are corn, soybeans, tobacco and wheat.

The first permanent settlement in Calloway County was Wadesboro, established in 1820. Wadesboro served as the county seat until 1842 when Murray became the seat of government for the county.

During the Civil War, the Confederate army built Fort Heiman, one of a trilogy of forts that controlled the Cumberland and Tennessee Rivers and which had a significant impact on the Civil War. Located in extreme southwest Calloway County, Fort Heiman is part of Fort Donelson National Park.

Today the county seat of Calloway County is Murray, named for John L. Murray, a member of Congress in the 19th Century. Murray is the home of Murray State University.

Persons wishing to delve into the history of Calloway County will find several opportunities in Murray. The Wrather West Kentucky Museum is located in the first permanent building constructed on the Murray State campus and is on the National Register of Historic Places. Wrather Museum, featuring both permanent and changing exhibits, provides an understanding of the social, cultural and economic development of West Kentucky and the Jackson Purchase.

Pogue Library
Source: Murray Tourism Commission, Murray

Forrest C. Pogue Special Collections Library also on the Murray State campus, was built in the Renaissance Revival style and features bronze doors on the east and west entrances. On the National Register of Historic Places, Pogue Library contains materials concerning the history and culture of Western Kentucky, including those relating to the Tennessee Valley Authority, the Civil War and local history.

The town of Murray features cosmopolitan amenities complemented by an old-fashioned, small-town friendliness. In an article about Murray, *Southern Living* magazine described the town as "as picturesque as a scene in a Norman Rockwell painting."

Visitors may relax and enjoy stunning scenery, comfortable accommodations, concerts, theater productions, live music, unique shopping, a wide variety of restaurants, sporting events, and a variety of year-round activities.

Murray and Calloway County are known for their access to outstanding outdoor recreation. Kenlake State Resort Park is a popular tourist attraction; and Kentucky Lake, the largest man-made lake in the country, offers excellent opportunities for fishing, swimming, boating, camping, hunting and hiking.

Near the center of the U.S. population, Murray is located within a day's drive from most of the eastern, southern and mid-western United States, with easy and convenient access to both regional and international airports, rail service, and the highway and interstate system. Calloway Countians enjoy all four seasons with a moderate year-round climate.
Contributed by Murray Tourism Commission and the Murray-Calloway County Chamber of Commerce.

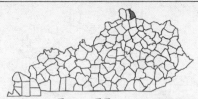

Campbell County

English colonials were exploring the area that would become Campbell County as early as 1750, when Christopher Gist arrived. In the 1770s numerous other explorers and settlers moved into Northern Kentucky. Among them were Simon Kenton, Daniel Boone, Hancock Taylor, George Rogers Clark.

The fist permanent settlement in present day Campbell County was Leitch's Station about six miles upstream from the mouth of the Licking River. It was built in 1789 by Maj. David Leitch, a Revolutionary War officer. The best known of the earliest settlers is James Taylor, whose brother, Hubbard, visited the mouth of the Licking River in 1791 and laid out lots. He named the spot Newport for Christopher Newport, who captained the ship bringing the first permanent English colonists to Jamestown, Virginia, in 1607. In 1793, James Taylor landed at Newport with his wife, two slaves, an English friend, two horses, and a boatload of equipment. Across the Ohio was Fort Washington, a military post protecting the newly settled Cincinnati (1788).

James Taylor was a leader in petitioning the newly recognized state of Kentucky to create a separate county for the Northern Kentucky settlements. In 1794, Campbell County was carved from Scott, Harrison and Mason counties and named for Col. John Campbell, a Revolutionary War officer. Newport was designated the county seat in 1796. In 1840 Alexandria was chosen as a central location for Campbell's courthouse. The greater amount of business in the northern urban portion of the county determined the decision to accept two county seats--Alexandria and Newport.

James Taylor also was instrumental in causing

Newport Aquarium
Source: SouthEast Telephone

the federal government to establish Newport Barracks, a primary military post in the West. In the 1880's, following successive river flooding, Newport Barracks was moved to higher ground and renamed Fort Thomas, a name taken by Campbell County's second largest city and one of Cincinnati's most choice suburban communities.

By the mid 1800s major Irish and German immigration to America, along with the Industrial Revolution, contributed to the growth of Newport and Campbell County.

Although accepting slavery, the majority of Campbell Countians were pro-union when the Civil War began in 1861, with 800 for the Union to 200 for the Confederacy. No significant fighting occurred in Campbell County

Bridges and common carriers connecting Northern Kentucky to Cincinnati led to the evolution in Campbell County of attractive residential suburbs for the Ohio metropolis. Industrially, Campbell County at one time boasted the largest brewery and one of the major steel mills in the South. In the 1880s and the 1890s a second migration of German settlers, many skilled artisans, participated in the development of small factories and businesses.

Prohibition gave rise to syndicated crime in Covington and Newport. The latter was a major headquarters for big-time gambling, Eventually a reform movement was successful in the 1960s.

In the 1970's Campbell County began a period of great growth and prosperity, due in large part to the founding and expansion of Northern Kentucky University and its merger with Chase College of Law.
Contributed by W. Frank Steely.

Carlisle County

Carlisle County, the 119th in order of formation, lies in the Jackson Purchase region of far western Kentucky. Bounded by Ballard, Graves, and Hickman counties, and by the Mississippi River, it has an area of 191 square miles. The area, originally Chickasaw tribal lands acquired by Isaac Shelby and Andrew Jackson in 1818, was part of Hickman County from 1821 to 1842, when it was included in the creation of Ballard County. Carlisle County was created on May 3, 1886. The county was named for John G. Carlisle, a statesman who served at many levels of government.

The mostly flat county has an abundance of fresh water in the many creeks and streams draining into the Mississippi River. In the late 1700s many islands lay offshore in the river, but erosion and the earthquake of 1811-12 along the New Madrid Fault destroyed most of the islands. Most of the area is farmland, growing mainly burley and dark-fired tobacco and livestock.

Among those who settled in the region after the Jackson Purchase was William Milburn of Maryland, who arrived in about 1822 and with a neighbor. William Reddick, established the town of Milburn. Another early landowner was George Reeves, who at about that time owned the site of the present village of Cunningham in the northeastern part of the county. Although fighting took place in the Jackson Purchase during the Civil War... Carlisle County was not greatly affected by the conflict. One hundred and sixty-eight Carlisle County residents joined the Confederate army; only forty-four joined the Union cause.

After the war, the coming of two railroad lines linked the area with Chicago to the north and the Gulf Coast region to the south. The Illinois Central Railroad was completed in 1874 through Arlington, Bardwell, and Winford Junction. The Gulf, Mobile & Ohio Railroad was completed in 1880 in the extreme western part of the county...

Arlington grew as a business and banking center By the mid-1880s the town numbered among its businesses the Arlington Leader newspaper; numerous stores; saw and gristmills; the Flegle Rolling Mill; and several hotels, including William E. Hall's combination hotel and coffin sup-

> The area, originally Chickasaw tribal lands acquired by Isaac Shelby and Andrew Jackson in 1818, was part of Hickman County from 1821 to 1842.

plier. Berkley likewise grew to be a prosperous trading center on the railroad, while Milburn, site of a Methodist seminary, grew in spite of its location away from the rail line. By 1900 a flour mill, livery stable, plow factory, churches, hotel, and drugstore were operating. In 1925 work began on U.S. 51 through the county, and in 1928 U.S. 62, then a gravel road, connected Bardwell with Paducah.

Between 1940 and 1960 the population of the county declined from 7,600 to 5,600. Many residents were engaged in farming, but from 1954 to 1969 the number of farms fell while the average acreage grew, reflecting a statewide trend.

Summary excerpt reprinted with permission of The University Press of Kentucky, The Kentucky Encyclopedia, John Kleber Ed.,. University Press of Kentucky (Lexington 1992).

Carroll County

"Carroll County was formed, the 87th in order, out of part of Gallatin, in the year 1838, and named in honor of Charles Carroll, of Carrollton. It is bounded on the north by the Ohio River, east by Gallatin, south by Owen and Henry, and west by Trimble County. The Ohio River bottom is moderately rolling, with a rich sandy alluvial soil. The soil along the valley of the Kentucky River, which extends through the county is of two classes: the rich alluvial bottoms subject to overflow, and the level uplands, once covered with a yel-

after the residence of Charles Carroll.

This county received its name in honor of Charles Carroll, of Carrollton, one of the signers of the Declaration of Independence, and the last of that immortal band of patriots who descended to the tomb. Mr. Carroll was born at Annapolis, Md., on Sept. 8, 1737. He received his literary education in France, and studied law in England. In 1764 he returned to Maryland, a finished scholar and accomplished gentleman...

Source: John Perkins

An anecdote is told of Carroll, illustrative of the fearlessness and firmness of the man. Immediately after he placed his name to the declaration of Independence, one of his friends jocularly remarked that if the British got hold of him, they would not know whether it were he or the Charles Carroll of Massachusetts, who had signed the declaration; consequently, they would be at a loss which to hang as the rebel. 'In order,' says he, 'that there may be no mistake about that, I will save them the trouble of hanging two of us,' and instantly affixed his residence to his name, and by which he was ever afterwords known as 'Charles Carroll of Carrollton.'"

lowish soil two to four inches deep, over a stratum of bluish clay. The remainder of the county is hilly, and the soil a fertile loam over a stratum of limestone...

Carrollton, the county seat, is on the Ohio River, immediately at and above the mouth of the Kentucky River. Population by the census of 1870 was 1,098 and in 1860 was 1,511. Carrollton was incorporated in 1794 by the name of Port William, but more than 30 years ago changed to "Carrollton,"

An excerpt from pages 118-119 of the entry for "Carroll County," Collins' Historical Sketches of Kentucky, History of Kentucky, Volume II (Southern Historical Press, 1874).

Carter County

Carter County was formed April 10, 1838, from parts of Greenup and Lawrence Counties and named for senator William Grayson Carter. Lands which became Carter County were parts of large Revolutionary War land grants. The town of Grayson, incorporated in 1844, is the county seat. The eastern boundary originally ran to the Big Sandy River, but that segment went to form part of Boyd County in 1860. Another piece was cut off as part of Elliott County in 1869, leaving 397 square miles. An attempt was made in 1904 to form Beckham County with Olive Hill as county seat, but Beckham lasted only 80 days. Other Carter County communities include Hitchins, Denton, Willard, Carter, Soldier, Lawton, and Grahn.

Pioneers began drawing salt from wells along the Little Sandy River in the late 1780s and the industry lasted through 1850. Saltpeter was mined from local caves during the War of 1812. Five large stone furnaces using charcoal to make iron were built in the east end of the county. They were named Pactolus (1824), Mount Savage (1848), Star (1848), Boone (1856) and Iron Hills or Charlotte Furnace (1873). Mount Savage was the last furnace to close in 1882.

Commercial coal mining began in 1850, with cyclical production. After 1960, surface mining had a profound impact on the land and the county's economy. Limestone mining continues near Olive Hill, but a former underground quarry at Lawton no longer operates. It was used in the 1970s as a mushroom farm. Natural deposits of clay brought to Carter County's five brickyards specializing in the kind of brick used in lining metal furnaces and

Carter County native Tom T. Hall
Source: Eddie Pennington

steam locomotives. Two such brickyards remain in operation today.

Tobacco became an important crop in 1883 when entrepreneur William Malone enticed experienced growers from the Owen-Grant county area to come to Carter County. Warehousing and processing of chewing tobacco operated between 1890 and 1925. Current buy-out programs are likely to change agricultural focus to some other crop.

Main highways through the county are U.S Route 60, state Route 1, state Route 2, state Route 7, Interstate 64 and the southern prong of the A-A Highway between Ashland and Alexandria. On the easternmost edge of the county lies a cooperative with Greenup and Boyd counties called EastPark, a wide area of open land suited for industrial, commercial and residential development.

Extractive industries continue, but by 1984 most local jobs were in service or in government. Grayson has become a major retail center, while Olive Hill has reached out to natives to return and live there in their retirement. Many residents drive to work in adjoining counties, especially Boyd and Rowan. Tourists enjoy visiting Carter Caves State Resort Park and Grayson Lake State Park. The community is a jumping-off point for attractions in adjoining counties.

Noted natives include singer-songwriter Tom T. Hall, operatic singer Carol Malone, aviation pioneer Matthew Bacon Seller and King Benjamin Purnell, a religious cult leader and founder of the colorful House of David.

Contributed by George Wollford.

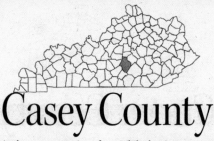

Casey County

Casey County is located in the eastern section of the Pennyrile region of Kentucky and contains 435 square miles. Topography varies from dissected uplands to broad valleys with flat-topped ridges. The headwaters of the Green River and the Rolling Fork of the Salt River are the main water sources. Named in honor of Revolutionary War hero Col. William Casey, it was created on Nov. 14, 1806, the 46th county in order of formation. Revolutionary War veterans who received land grants for their military service selected the town seat's name, Liberty, out of patriotic sentiment.

In 1870 the county produced 95,750 pounds of tobacco and 332,779 bushels of corn. In 1989, 71 percent of the land area was in farms and half of those were in cultivation.

One of the families who settled in the county around 1781 was that of Capt. Abraham Lincoln, the president's grandfather. The Lincolns lived for 2 ½ years on 800 acres on the Green River. Mordecai Lincoln, Capt. Lincoln's heir, sold the land in 1803 to Christopher Riffe for 400 pounds sterling. Another landowner, Enoch Burdett, accumulated 13,000 acres of timberland, and upon his death in 1875, his holdings were sold to Eugene Zimmerman, a Cincinnati businessman who built a wooden train track from King's Mountain to Staffordsville, and in 1884 he organized the Cincinnati & Green River Railway Company.

While there are no records of Civil War skirmishes in the county, Casey is credited with producing one-third of the 1st Kentucky Cavalry, recruited by Col. Frank Wolford and Col. Silas Adams. The 1st Cavalry of the Union Army was active in the Battles of Mill Springs, Perryville, and Lebanon, Tenn. Adams served as state representative and later in the 53rd U.S. Congress (1893-95). The present courthouse was the third one built, completed in 1889. The "Doughboy" statue there was dedicated in 1935 to commemorate the deaths of 32 Casey natives in World War I. On June 1, 1929, Liberty first received continuous electrical service. Known as "the Gate Capital of the World", farm gate production is one of Casey's main businesses, along with lumber firms, clothing manufacturers, and various smaller businesses. Tourism is the bright spot of Casey County's future with a continued emphasis on the growth of rural crafts, the annual Casey County Apple Festival featuring the "World's Largest Pie," the county's new Agriculture/Expo Center, the building of a commemorative Veteran's Park with a marble wall memorializing Casey County veterans, downtown Liberty Renaissance beautification projects and the development of the county's Amish and Mennonite communities and businesses.

Contributed by Jan Banks

Rousey Log Cabin
Source: Casey County Public Library

Christian County

Hopkinsville is an area rich in the history and heritage of the Native Americans. The heritage of Hopkinsville dates back to early settlers of the Cherokee Territory. Established in 1797 on the peaceful banks of the Little River, Hopkinsville's historical significance to Western Kentucky has been the result of its pioneering spirit and the events of the times. The Civil War and its divided loyalties, the Cherokee Trail of Tears and the Night Riders of the Tobacco War of 1904-1909, have all played a part in the creation of the city.

The Cherokee Trail of Tears took place over the harsh winter of 1838-1839. Hopkinsville was the major camp stop in Kentucky for 13,000 Cherokees that moved overland on this infamous trail traversing some 1,200 miles from North Carolina to Oklahoma. Buried along the banks of the Little River that runs through the campsite are Cherokee chiefs Whitepath and Fly Smith. The camp location is off US 41 at the Trail of Tears Commemorative Park.

Hopkinsville, one of the largest cities in Western Kentucky, is the headquarters for shopping in the southeast quadrant of the lakes area. Its large and busy mall, specialty shops, antique stores, and discount stores supply travelers and locals with a variety of shopping opportunities. Restaurants are abundant in Hopkinsville from fine dining and fast food to our famous Western Kentucky Bar-be-cue!

Fort Campbell Memorial Park dedicated to the soldiers of the 1985 Gander, Newfoundland tragedy is located at 41-A and the Pennyrile Parkway. A larger than life sculpture of a member of the Multi-National Peacekeeping Force (MFO) in the Sinai Desert is the focal point.

Several historic cemeteries dot the countryside throughout Christian County. One of these includes the Riverside Cemetery, which serves as the final resting-place for both Union and Confederate soldiers of the Civil War, as well as clairvoyant Edgar Cayce.

Hopkinsville proudly sponsors a variety of festivals and special events throughout the year including the Pennyrile Quilt Show held in April, the Western Kentucky State Fair in August, an Native American Intertribal Pow Wow the weekend after Labor Day and Hopkinsville Salutes Fort Campbell the second week in September. Little River Days Festival held in May is famous throughout the region.

The pride of Christian County is the beautiful Pennyrile Forest State Resort Park, located in the

> **Restaurants are abundant in Hopkinsville from fine dining and fast food to our famous Western Kentucky Bar-be-cue!**

northwest portion of the county. This breathtaking state park is made up of 863 acres including a 55-acre lake. A favorite among visitors to the area, facilities include a lodge, cabins, an 18-hole golf course and walking trails.

Christian County is also home to Fort Campbell's 101st Airborne Division, located 15 miles south of Hopkinsville. Located on the base is the Don F. Pratt Museum with colorful memorabilia and exhibits dealing with the history of the "Screaming Eagles."

For more information on Christian County contact the Hopkinsville-Christian County Convention and Visitor's Bureau, 2800 Ft. Campbell Boulevard, Hopkinsville, KY 42241; (270) 885-9096 or 1-800-842-9959. Visit our website at www.visithopkinsville.com.

Clark County

"Clark County, established in 1792 out of parts of Fayette and Bourbon counties and named after Kentucky's great military chieftain, Gen. George Rogers Clark, was the 14th county formed in the state. It is in the middle section of the state, upon the waters of the Red, Kentucky and Licking rivers; and is bounded on the north by Bourbon, east by Montgomery, southeast by Powell, south by Estill and Madison counties, and west by Fayette. The Kentucky River is the boundary line between Clark and Madison counties, the Red River between Clark and Estill, Boone's Creek between Clark and Fayette, and Lulbegrud Creek between Clark and Powell counties. The remaining streams of the county are Stoner, Strode's, Howard's Upper, Howard's Lower, Four Mile, and Two Mile creeks. The west end, about one-third, of the county is the genuine "Bluegrass Region," exceedingly fertile and highly improved; the middle and northeast portions are more broken yet good farming lands; the east and southeast portions are hilly and poor oak lands. The exports are principally cattle, horses, mules and hogs...

The first child born in Clark County was James Spahr, in 1779; he died about 1862

The first brick building in Clark County was

erected about 1784, near the center of "Bush's Settlement," by Capt. Wm. Bush himself, who came to Boonesborough in Sept. 1775, with Daniel Boone, when he brought out his family.

The "Indian Old Fields," were some ancient cornfields discovered when the country was first settled, about 12 miles east of where Winchester now is. These fields had been cultivated by the Indians, many years before the first visit of the whites.

Winchester was made the county seat of Clark County in 1792, over Strode's and Hood's stations, by one vote...

Gen. George Rogers Clark, whose name is deservedly celebrated in the early history of Kentucky, and conspicuously prominent in the conquest and settlement of the whole west, was born in the county of Albemarle, in the state of Virginia, on the 19th of November, 1752...

In the spring of 1775, he came to Kentucky, drawn hither by that love of adventure which distinguished him through life. He remained in Kentucky during the spring and summer of that year, familiarizing himself with the character of the people and the resources of the country, until the fall, when he returned to Virginia. During this visit, he was temporarily placed in command of the irregular militia of the settlements."

An excerpt from pages 129-133 of the entry for "Clark County," Collins' Historical Sketches of Kentucky, History of Kentucky, Volume II (Southern Historical Press, 1874).

Source: Sid Webb

Clay County

"Clay County, the 47th formed in the state, was carved out of Madison, Knox, and Floyd counties, and named in honor of Gen. Green Clay, in 1806. Since then, parts of its territory have been taken in forming each of the counties of Perry in 1820, Laurel in 1825, Breathitt in 1839, Owsley in 1843, and Jackson in 1858. It lies on the south fork of the Kentucky River, whose tributaries spread through the county, Goose Creek, Red Bird Fork, Collins' Fork, Sexton's, Little Goose, Otter, Bullskin, Big, and Jack's creeks; the Middle fork of the Kentucky River is the east boundary line. The county is bounded north by Owsley and Breathitt, east by Breathitt and Perry, south by Harlan and Knox, and west by Jackson and Laurel. The face of the country is generally hilly and mountainous; the principal products, corn, wheat, and grass, the latter growing spontaneously on the mountains and in the valleys. Coal, iron ore, and fine timber abound. Salt is the leading article of export...

Salt, of the best quality, has been made much more extensively in Clay County, since 1800, than elsewhere in the state. In 1846, 15 furnaces produced 200,000 bushels per annum. So great is the supply and so fine the quality of the salt water that,

with improved facilities, the manufacture could be increased to any extent...

Collins' fork took its name from the first settler; Red Bird fork and Jack's creek, from two friendly Indians bearing those names, to whom was granted the privilege of hunting there; they were both murdered for the furs they had accumulated, and their bodies thrown into the water...

General Green Clay, in honor of whom this county was named, was born in Powhattan County, Virginia on the 14th of August, 1757. He was the son of Charles Clay, and descended from John Clay, a British grenadier, who came to Virginia during Bacon's rebellion, and declined returning when the king's troops were sent back. Green Clay came to Kentucky when but a youth. His education was exceedingly limited. The first few years after his arrival in Kentucky, were spent in examining the country, and aiding to expel the savages. He then entered the office of James Thompson, a commissioned surveyor, where he more thoroughly studied the principles and acquired the art of surveying."

An excerpt from pages 140-142 of the entry for "Clay County," Collins' Historical Sketches of Kentucky, History of Kentucky, Volume II (Southern Historical Press, 1874).

It's a Kentucky thing...

Salt, of the best quality, has been made much more extensively in Clay county, since 1800, than elsewhere in the state. In 1846, 15 furnaces produced 200,000 bushels per annum. So great is the supply and so fine the quality of salt water that, with improved facilities, the manufacture coud be increased to any extent.

Centenarians. — Nothing proves the exceeding healthfulness of Clay county more pointedly than the great age to which many of the citizens attain. Solomon Burchart lived to be 125 years old, John Gilbert 115, and as late as June 22, 1872, David Robinson died, age 102.

(Collins' Historical Sketches of Kentucky, Vol. II, page 141, 1874).

Clinton County

"Clinton County was erected in 1835, out of parts of Wayne and Cumberland counties, the 85th in the order of formation, and named in honor of Gov. DeWitt Clinton, of New York. It lies entirely south of the Cumberland River, on the Tennessee state line, which forms its southern boundary, and is bounded north by Russell, east by Wayne, and west by Cumberland. The surface generally is hilly, much of it adapted to grazing; but the valleys are rich, producing fine crops of corn and wheat...

Albany, the county seat, about 126 miles from Frankfort, was incorporated in 1838. During the war of the Rebellion, the courthouse and many other buildings were burnt....

DeWitt Clinton, whose name this county bears, was a native of New York, and one of the most distinguished men in the United States. He was born at Little Britain, in Orange County, on the 2nd of March, 1769. He was educated at Columbia College, and studied law with the Hon. Samuel Jones. He early imbibed a predilection for political life, and the first office he held was that of private secretary to his uncle George Clinton, then governor of New York. In 1797, Mr. Clinton was elected a member of the New York legislature, where he espoused the political sentiments of the republican or democratic party. Two years after, he was elected to the State senate. In 1801, he received the appointment of United States' senator, to fill a vacancy, where he served for two sessions. After that period, he was chosen mayor of New York, and remained in this position, with an intermission of but two years, until 1815. In 1817, he was elected, almost unanimously, governor of his native State, the two great parties having combined for the purpose of raising him to that dignity. He was re-elected in 1820, but declined a candidacy in 1822. In 1824, he was again nominated and elected to the office of the governor, and in 1826 was re-elected by a large majority. He died suddenly, while sitting in his library, on the 11th of February, 1828, before completing his last term of office. Mr. Clinton was the projector and the active and untiring friend of the canal system on New York, which has been instrumental in adding so largely to the wealth and population of that great State."

An excerpt from pages 143-145 of the entry for "Clinton County," Collins' Historical Sketches of Kentucky, History of Kentucky, Volume II (Southern Historical Press, 1874).

Now, listen here...

On a clear morning the fog seems to rise on the water courses in the distance, and stand just above the trees, when the eye can trace the beautiful Cumberland river in its windings for at least one hundred miles, and may distinctly mark the junction of its tributaries, in a direct line, for thirty miles...

The elevation of the mountain, and the consequent purity of the atmosthere — the beauty and magnificence of the scenery and prospect daily presented to the eye of the visitor, combined with the medicinal virtues of the water, a good host, and intelligent and refined association, would make these springs a most desirable point for a summer excursion.

(Collins' Historical Sketches of Kentucky, Vol. II, page 145.)

Crittenden County

Located in the Pennyrile region of Western Kentucky, Crittenden County covers a land area of 365 square miles and has a population of approximately 9,000. The Tradewater River flows along the northeastern border, while the northwestern boundary is formed by the Ohio River.

By an act of the General Assembly of the Commonwealth on the 26th day of January 1842, a portion of land lying in Livingston County was set apart as Crittenden County and was organized with a court of its own. The new county, the 91st to be formed in Kentucky, was named in honor of John J. Crittenden, then governor of Kentucky and later U.S. senator and attorney general.

Marion, the county seat of Crittenden County was named in honor of Gen. Francis Marion, a Revolutionary War partisan leader of South Carolina, as were several other towns in differing states.

Crittenden County was once one of the nation's largest producers of fluorspar. The famous Saline Trace cuts through the northwestern section of Crittenden County. It was once known both by Flynn's Ferry Road and the Chickasaw Trail, but has now become known as simply the Trace. In 1790, this road was the site of a major battle between the Kaskaskias and Chickasaw tribes. Beginning at a dry creek bed near Piney Fork Church, it continues on to the historic site of Weston on the Ohio River.

Crittenden County's greatest natural resource is its people. Nine thousand men, women and children make Crittenden their home. More than half of these live on small farms or in small towns scat-

Gov. John C. Crittenden
Source: Library of Congress

tered throughout the countryside. The remaining population resides in Marion, the county seat and the area's only metropolis.
Contributed by Brenda Underdown

Cumberland County

"Cumberland County, the 32nd in order of formation, was cut off from Green County in 1798, and so named after Cumberland River, which runs through the county in a northeast and southwest direction. It is one of the tier of counties bordering on the Tennessee state line; is bounded north by Adair, east by Russell and Clinton, south by Mon-

roe County and the Tennessee line, and west by Monroe and Metcalfe Counties. Part of the original territory of Cumberland County was appropriated in the formation of each of five counties, Wayne in 1800, Monroe in 1820, Russell in 1825, Clinton in 1835, and Metcalfe in 1860. The surface of the county is hilly and broken; the soil in the valleys is of more than the average fertility...

Burksville, the county seat, so named in honor of one of the original proprietors, was incorporated in 1810; is situated on the north bank of the Cumberland River, 28 miles from Columbia, 67 miles from Lebenon, 40 miles from Cave City, and about 120 miles from Frankfort...

The American Oil well is situated three miles above Burksville, on the bank of the Cumberland River. About the year 1830, while some men were engaged in boring for salt-water, and after penetrating about 175 feet through a solid rock, they struck a vein of oil, which suddenly spouted up to the height of 50 feet above the surface. The stream was so abundant and of such force, as to continue to throw up the oil to the same height for several days. The oil thus thrown out, ran into the Cumberland River, covering the surface of the water for several miles. It was readily supposed to be inflammable, and upon its being ignited, it presented the novel and magnificent spectacle of a "river on fire," the flames literally covering the whole surface for miles, reaching to the top of the tallest trees on the banks of the river, and continued burning until the supply of oil was exhausted. The salt borers were greatly disappointed, and the well was neglected for several years, until it was discovered that the oil possessed valuable medicinal qualities. It has since been bottled up in large quantities, and is extensively sold in nearly all the states of the Union."

An excerpt from pages 150-151 of the entry for "Cumberland County," Collins' Historical Sketches of Kentucky, History of Kentucky, Volume II (Southern Historical Press, 1874).

Big South Fork of the Cumberland River
Source: Kentucky Department of Tourism

Daviess County

"Daviess county, formed in 1815, out of part of Ohio county, was the 58th erected in the state. It was named in honor of the brilliant and brave Joseph Hamilton Daveiss, although by some oversight not spelled as he spelled his name; just as the orthography of several other counties was changed, apparently without design—Green county being named after Gen. Greene, Muhlenburg after Rev. and Gen Muhlenberg, Calloway after Col. Callaway, and Menifee after Hon. Richard H. Menefee. It is bounded N. by the Ohio river, E. by Hancock and Ohio, S. by Ohio and McLean, and W. by Henderson county; contains 420 square miles, and is the 7th county in the state in population. The soil is a strong clay and rich loam, peculiarly adapted to tobacco, making Daviess, next to Christian, the most extensive tobacco-growing county in the state. It is well watered by the Ohio river, which forms its northern boundary, by the Green river its western boundary (navigable all the year, by locks and dams), and by their tributaries, Panther, North and South, Blackford, Puppy, Rhodes Nos. 1 and 2, Yellow, Two-Mile, Knob Lick, Green and Delaware creeks. It is traversed, from north to south, by the Owensboro and Russellville railroad.

Towns. —Owensboro, the county seat, named in memory of Col. Abraham Owen, who fell at Tippecanoe—originally called Rossborough, and incorporated Feb.3, 1817—is handsomely situated on the bank of the Ohio river, 150 miles below Louisville, upon an extensive and level plateau, surrounded by a rich country, and is the center of a large and growing trade; population in 1870, 3,437, and on Jan. 1, 1873, about 5,500—noted for intelligence, industry, and hospitality…

Generosity—In 1784 or '85, among a party which embarked at the Falls of the Ohio to descend the river, was Andrew Rowan. While the boat stopped at the Yellow banks, on the Indian side, Mr. Rowan borrowed a loaded gun, but no ammunition, and started off in pursuit of amusement rather than game. When he returned, the boat had gone; the party having seen signs of Indians approaching, and not daring to wait for Mr. Rowan, hastened off down stream. Mr. R. started towards the nearest white settlement—Vincennes, 100 miles distant—but soon lost his way, wandered about for three days, and, exhausted, laid down to die. Roused by the

Cooking team preparing mutton International Bar-BQ Festival, Owensboro
Source: Kentucky Department of Tourism

report of a gun, he rose and walked in the direction of the sound. An Indian, seeing him, raised his gun to fire; Rowan turned the butt of his gun, and the Indian, with French politeness, turned the butt of his also. Taking pity upon Rowan's helpless condition, the Indian led him to his wigwam, and treated him with great hospitality until his strength was regained; then took him to Vincennes. Wishing to reward his generosity, Mr. Rowan arranged with a merchant to pay him $300; but the Indian persistently refused to receive a farthing. He, finally, to please Mr. Rowan, accepted a new blanket; and wrapping it around him said, with some feeling, "When I wrap myself in it, I will think of you!"

An excerpt from pages 151-153- of the entry for "Daviess County," Collins' Historical Sketches of Kentucky, History of Kentucky, Volume II (Southern Historical Press, 1874).

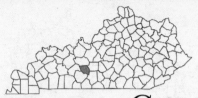

Edmonson County

"Edmonson County, the 79th in the order of erection, was formed in 1825, out of parts of Warren, Hart, and Grayson, and named in honor of Capt. John Edmonson. It lies on both sides of g River; and is bounded north by Grayson, east by Hart and

place has nature exhibited her varied powers on a more imposing scale of grandeur and magnificence. From a letter written in July, 1841, and from other sources, we condense the following information...

The cave is most accessible to visitors from two points, being seven miles from Glasgow Junction, and nine miles from Cave City, stations on the Louisville and Nashville railroad, respectively 91 and 85 miles from Louisville, and 94 and 100 miles from Nashville. Green River is distant from the cave only half a mile...

Capt. John Edmonson, from whom this county derived its

Green River ferry
Source:: Kentucky Department of Tourism

Green River
Source: U.S. Geological Survey

Barren, south by Warren, and west by Warren and Butler counties. The land is generally undulating, and in some places quite hilly. There are several sulphur springs in the county, with ores of various kinds, and an inexhaustible supply of coal...

Brownsville, the county seat, 130 miles from Frankfort, was established in 1828, and named in honor of Gen. Jacob Brown; it contains the usual county buildings; population about 200...

The celebrated Mammoth Cave, the largest in the world, and perhaps the greatest natural wonder, is situated in Edmonson County. In no other

name, was a native of Washington County, Virginia; set- tled in Fayette County in 1790; raised a company of volunteer riflemen, and joined Col. John Allen's regiment in 1812, and fell in the disastrous Battle of the River Raisin, Jan. 22, 1813."

An excerpt from pages 156-165 of the entry for "Edmonson County," Collins' Historical Sketches of Kentucky, History of Kentucky, Volume II (Southern Historical

Elliott County

"Elliott County, the 114th in order, was formed in 1869, out of parts of Morgan, Carter, and Lawrence, and named in honor of Judge John M. Elliott. It is situated in the north-eastern part of the state, and bounded north by Carter, east by Lawrence, south by Lawrence and Morgan, and west by Rowan County. It is surrounded by high hills on three sides, the waters from which shed outwardly into Big Sandy and Licking rivers, but inwardly to Little Sandy River, forming along its tributaries a succession of moderately rich and very pretty valleys...

Martinsburg, formerly Sandy Hook, the county seat, is 21 miles from Grayson, a railroad point, and 30 miles from Louisa, the head of regular steamboat navigation on the Big Sandy; population in 1870, 62...

Elliott county, in eight years of its formation, had no resident Senator. Its first representative was Wm. Kitchen.

Elliott County, it is generally understood, was named in honor of Judge John M. Elliott, now (December, 1873) a resident of Owingsville, Bath County, and circuit judge of the 13th judicial district. Judge E. is a native of Scott County, Virginia; was born May 16, 1820; studied law and was admitted to the bar in 1843; practiced with fine success, at Prestonsburg, Floyd co.; was a representative from Floyd, Pike, and Johnson counties, in the Kentucky legislature, in 1847; a representative in the U.S. congress from six years, 1853-1859; again elected representative in the legislature, from Floyd and Johnson counties, 1861-1863; but an indictment for treason having been found against him, with 31 others, Nov. 6, 1861, in the U.S. district court at Frankfort, and he (although present from Sept. 2 to Oct. 4) not having occupied his seat during the December adjourned session of the legislature, the house, [on] Dec. 21, 1861, expelled him for being 'directly or indirectly connected with, and giving aid and comfort to, the Confederate army, repudiating and acting against the government of the United States and the commonwealth of Kentucky.' He had thus actively united his for-

tunes with the cause of the South; was a member of each successive Regular Congress of the Confederate States, representing the 12th Ky. district, up to the time of the downfall of the Confederacy, over three years in all. In 1868, several years after his return to Kentucky, he was elected, for six years, or until September, 1874, circuit judge of the district embracing Bath, Montgomery, Powell, Estill, Owsley, Lee, Wolfe, Morgan, Elliott, and Menifee (10) counties; and, in 1876, a judge of the court of appeals for 8 years."

An excerpt from pages 165-166 of the entry for "Elliott County," Collins' Historical Sketches of Kentucky, History of Kentucky, Volume II (Southern Historical Press, 1874).

It is surrounded by high hills on three sides, the waters from which shed outwardly into Big Sandy and Licking rivers, but inwardly to Little Sandy River, forming along its tributaries a succession of moderately rich and very pretty valleys...

Estill County

"Estill County, the 50th erected in the state, was formed in 1808, out of parts of Madison and Clark, and named in honor of Capt. Jas. Estill. Parts of its original territory have been taken to help form the counties of Breathitt in 1839, Owsley in 1843, Powell in 1852, Jackson in 1858, and Lee in 1870...

Irvine, the county seat,

Source: John Perkins

was established in 1812 and named in honor of Col. William Irvine...

Population in 1870, 224, and on Jan. 1, 1873, about 300...

The 'Red River Iron District' is mainly confined to Estill County. The iron ores of the region produce iron of unsurpassed excellence. The first iron works in the county were located on Red River, about 1810, and embraced a blast furnace, knobling fire and forge. About 1830, the Estill steam furnace was built on the mountain which divides the waters of Red River from those of the Kentucky, and smelting discontinued at the furnace on Red River; at the same time, the works at the Forge were greatly improved for the manufacture of bar iron, blooms nails, and castings. The Red River iron works soon became celebrated for the good quality of metal produced.

Capt. James Estill, in honor of whom this county received its name, was a native of Augusta County, Virginia. He removed to Kentucky at an early period, and settled on Muddy creek, in the present county of Madison, where he built a station which received the name of Estill's station. In 1781 in a skirmish with the Indians, he received a rifle-shot in one of his arms, by which it was broken. In March, 1782, with a small body of men, believed to be about 25, he pursued a similar number of Wyandotts across the Kentucky River, and into Montgomery County, where he fought one of the severest and most bloody battles on record, when the number of men on both sides is taken into account. Capt. Estill and his gallant Lieutenant, South, were both killed in the retreat which succeeded. Thus fell (says Mr. Morehead in his Boonsborough address), in the ripeness of his manhood, Capt. James Estill, one of Kentucky's bravest and most beloved defenders. It may be said of him with truth, that if he did not achieve the victory, he did more, he deserved it. Disappointed of success, vanquished, slain, in a desperate conflict with an enemy of superior strength and equal valor, he had nevertheless left behind him a name of which his descendants may well be proud. A name which will live in the annals of Kentucky, so long as there shall be found men to appreciate the patriotism and self-devotion of a martyr to the cause of humanity and civilization.

An excerpt from pages 166-168 of the entry for "Estill County," Collins' Historical Sketches of Kentucky, History of Kentucky, Volume II (Southern Historical Press, 1874).

Fayette County

Visitors and newcomers arriving at Lexington's Blue Grass Airport immediately experience one of Lexington's signature features, its gently rolling countryside lined by white wooden fences, home to some of the world's most famous thoroughbred horses. The city, billed as "The Horse Capital of the World," boasts the likes of Keeneland Race Course, The Red Mile and numerous horse farms. It is also known for a diverse economy, a strong work force, a quality education system, great health care, a wide range of higher education options and, of course, big-time college basketball.

The true charm of Fayette County lies in the fact that it has all the amenities. Lexington, with the feel of a big city, still maintains that special small-town feel. In minutes, motorists can drive past horse farms, through downtown and back into rolling countryside.

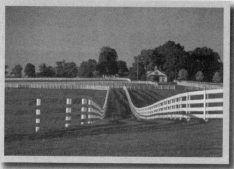

Calumet horse farm
Source: Sid Webb

Fayette Countians are extremely proud of their city's businesses, sports teams, schools and colleges, all of which ensure an exceptional quality of life. Studies have shown that people living in and around Lexington enjoy access to a wide range of religious opportunities, safe neighborhoods, parks, great schools, and a plethora of museums, art galleries, musical performances and historic distilleries.

The Bluegrass Region has gained national prominence in areas such as education, business, health care, agriculture, research and manufacturing.

Part of the economic success of the region is a result of Kentucky's commitment to educational excellence. Lexington is consistently near the top in the nation for the percentage of its population having completed 16 or more years of school.

Meanwhile, unemployment levels in the region continue to be among the lowest in the state and lower than national figures.

It's central location within Kentucky gives Fayette Countians access to other areas via I-75 and 64. Lexington has been called one of the "Best Places for Business" by "FORBES" magazine in 2004; "Best Places to Locate a Company" in "Expansion Management" magazine in 2003; and an "Entrepreneurial Hot Spot" by "Inc." magazine in 2001.

Fayette County is rich in tradition and history. In 1775 Daniel Boone established nearby Boonesboro, paving the way for others to settle an area known as McConnell Springs, Lexington's birthplace. Lexington is named for the site of the opening battle of the Revolutionary War at Lexington, Mass. Fayette County was named in honor of Marquis de Lafayette, France's greatest supporter of the American Revolution.

In 1812, Henry Clay, known as The Great Compromiser, built Ashland, a 400-acre estate, in Lexington. The city opened its first school in 1834. In the 1890s, tobacco replaced hemp as the major cash crop in the Bluegrass. By the early 1900s, Lexington became the world's largest burley tobacco market.

In 1924, Calumet Farm, home of eight Kentucky Derby champion thoroughbreds was launched. Legendary Keeneland Race Course opened to huge crowds in 1936, while planes began taking off from nearby Blue Grass Airport in 1942.

Note: Lexington & Fayette County merged governments January 1, 1974.
Contributed by the Commerce Lexington Inc.

Fleming County

Fleming County was formed in 1798 from part of Mason County. It was the 26th county in order of formation and is located in the northeastern middle part of the state on the Licking River. Flemingsburg, the county seat and principal town with a present population of about 3,500, was founded by Maj. George Stockton and named in honor of his half-brother, Col. John Fleming. These two men built the first settlements in Fleming County—Stockton Station in 1787 and Fleming Station in 1790. It was following

Ringo Mills Covered Bridge
Source: Fleming County Historical Society

the buffalo trails from northeastern Kentucky to Blue Licks that brought George Stockton, John Fleming and Samuel Strode, another explorer, into Fleming County.

The third settlement in Fleming County was Cassidy's Station which was settled in 1791 by Michael Cassidy. He was well regarded and served in the state Legislature but was best known for his bravery in Indian fights.

Another prominent citizen in the early days of Fleming County was John Finley, an associate of Daniel Boone. Finley settled along the banks of the Licking River in 1796 and is buried not far from where he first settled.

Although there are signs of change and growth, Fleming County remains rural and cherishes and preserves its history, especially its covered bridges. Fleming County is fortunate to have three covered bridges

and in 1998, the Kentucky Legislature named Fleming County the "Covered Bridge Capital of Kentucky." To celebrate and recognize the importance of these structures, Fleming County has hosted the "Covered Bridge Festival" for several years on the fourth Saturday of August. The Goddard Covered Bridge, possibly the most photographed bridge in Kentucky, is presently being repaired and restored. The Ringo Mills and Grange City covered bridges are also scheduled to be restored in the near future.

Between 1826 and 1830 a brick courthouse with a clock-tower was built by James Eckles and Samuel Stockwell, using skilled slave labor. Many people still bemoan the loss of this picturesque building which was razed in 1951 and replaced with the present courthouse on the same site. Eckles and Stockwell also built many of the fine homes and other buildings in Fleming County. Many of these are still standing and efforts to preserve them are on going.

Fleming County had some Civil War action. In 1862, Gen. John Hunt Morgan's raiders retreated through Fleming County from their last raid on central Kentucky towns. James J. Andrews lived at the Fleming Hotel in Flemingsburg from 1859-1862. He later led a group of Union soldiers into Georgia and captured the "General," a confederate steam locomotive. The mission failed, the men were captured and Andrews was hanged.

In World War II, a Fleming County native was one of the heroes memorialized in Joe Rosenthal's flag-raising picture. Franklin R. Sousley, who helped to raise the flag on Mt. Suribachi, was later killed in battle and buried at Elizaville, a small community in Fleming County. Years later, a monument was erected in his honor.

Much of Fleming County is located in the Bluegrass region of the state (with the eastern part of the county being located in the Knobs). Although, the county has some industry, it has remained largely agricultural. Until recently, tobacco was the main agricultural product. Corn, soybeans, beef cattle and dairy cattle are also important. Fleming County is considered to be the third largest dairy producing county in the state.
Contributed by Mary Jane Scaggs

Floyd County

On Dec. 13, 1799 the Kentucky General Assembly enacted a bill creating Floyd County from Fleming, Montgomery, and Mason counties. The division became effective June 1, 1800. Floyd County was the 40th county to enter the Commonwealth, and was named for John Floyd, a surveyor and famous pioneer explorer. The county seat was named "Prestons's Station" which would evolve into what is known today as Prestonsburg.

Archaeological evidence shows the Big Sandy Valley was originally occupied by the Adena Indians (Mountain Builders). In fact, the word Kentucky is derived from the Indian word KAIN-TUC-KEE, which means "the dark and bloody hunting ground." The phrase still rings true today, as the hills of Floyd County remain generous to the sport of hunting.

As in many areas of the south, the Civil War reportedly divided the neighbors of Floyd County. Prestonsburg was a Confederate stronghold, but Union victory was claimed in two Floyd County battles. The most popular of these was the Battle of Middle Creek, which took place on Jan. 10, 1862, and is still reenacted today.

The story of the Battle of Middle Creek involved Union Col. James A. Garfield who would later become president of the United States. In addition to a future president, the Civil War brought a twist of fate to Floyd County. Engineers from the north recognized the vast amounts of bituminous coal seams in the area. This occurrence would later contribute to locals selling their land

and mineral resources to northern coal barons for mere pennies, and in some cases they would barter or trade acres of land for chickens.

Floyd County remains today a coal-mining area. However, through economic development by community leaders, the future of Floyd County might prove to be an ideal tourist getaway. Some tourist attractions include the Jenny

Jenny Wiley Festival at the park
Source: SouthEast Telephone

Wiley State Resort Park and beautiful Dewey Lake, with boating, swimming, camp grounds, hiking trails, cottages, convention center, and amphitheater. Thunder Ridge Racetrack offers harness racing with a combination of stock car racing. The Mountain Arts Center, a state of the art performance theater, is home to the Kentucky Opry. The East Kentucky Science Center, on the campus of Big Sandy Community and Technical College, is home to a 40-foot domed planetarium. Stone Crest Golf Course is Kentucky's highest elevated public championship golf course. The Course was recently the site of the 2005 Kentucky Golf Association State Amateur Championship.
Contributed by the Floyd County Chamber of Commerce.

Franklin County

In 1795 Franklin County became the 18th county formed. The county was named for Benjamin Franklin, early American patriot, inventor, diplomat, and signer of the Declaration of Independence. Land was taken from Shelby, Mercer, and Woodford counties to form Franklin County. Frankfort, Kentucky's capital city, has always been the county seat.

Franklin County's countryside has rich, deep soil. Tobacco, corn, hay and vegetables are important crops. Major streams include the Kentucky River, Elkhorn Creek and its branches, and the Big and Little Benson and Flat creeks.

Archaeological excavations have revealed evidence of American Indian villages in Franklin County, and a major Indian trail passed through the area. Originally a trace formed by herds of animals crossed the Kentucky River near Leestown.

Christopher Gist was one of the first explorers to reach Franklin County, arriving in 1751; and Hancock Lee established the county's first settlement at Leestown in 1775 about a mile from modern-day downtown Frankfort. Originally known as Frank's Ford, Frankfort was named for Stephen Frank, a settler killed by Indians near the Kentucky River.

The early 19th century was a time of growth and prosperity in Franklin County. The Marquis de Lafayette visited in May, 1825. Steamboats conducted trade on the Kentucky River. County products found markets at ports on the Ohio and Mississippi rivers. Manufacturers made candles, stovepipes, paper goods, and coaches by the 1830s. A horse drawn railroad began to operate in Franklin County in 1831, and a steam powered line connected Frankfort and Lexington in 1835.

The Civil War saw both armies operating in Franklin County. Between Sept. 3 and Oct. 7, 1862,

Rotunda in the new Capitol building
Source: Kentucky Historical Society

Confederate forces occupied Frankfort — the only pro-Union state capital captured by the Confederates during the war. In June 1864, a detachment of Gen. John Hunt Morgan's cavalrymen attacked Frankfort., but Union troops successfully defended the town. In the postwar years Ku Klux Klan violence was directed at a small African-American community at Bald Knob.

Franklin County's economy recovered slowly from Civil War era disruptions. Emancipation of the slaves left the area with a shortage of farm labor. By 1880 tobacco had replaced hemp as the main cash crop. The livestock industry prospered, and distilleries provided markets for corn.

Early in the 20th century, some Franklin County rural communities lost population as their residents moved to Frankfort or elsewhere in search of factory jobs. Distilling, the county's leading industry at the time, was effectively shut down by prohibition in 1919. The growth of state government helped to reverse the drop in the county's population.

After the repeal of prohibition in 1935, distilleries prospered in Franklin County. In the decades after World War II several industries opened factories in Franklin County. Continued state government expansion and other development in the postwar era led to urbanization of many county areas and the loss of farm land. However, farms still made up nearly three-quarters of the county's area in 1990. The 1990 population of Franklin County was 43,781.
Reprinted with the permission of the Capital City Museum, 325 Ann Street-Frankfort KY

Fulton County

"Fulton County was formed, the 99th in order in the state, in 1845, out of the south-western part of Hickman County, and named in honor of Robert Fulton. It is bound west on north by the Mississippi River, northeast and east by Hickman County, and south by the Tennessee state line. It contains 184 square miles, is the last county west, and is literally cut in two by the Mississippi River, so that in going from the main or eastern part of the county to the western (familiarly known as 'Madrid Bend,") it is necessary to pass over about eight miles of Tennessee territory. The county is divided between Mississippi bottoms, subject for 25 miles to inundation, and uplands; lies well, has no mountains, and but a small portion of hill country; soil generally good, a part very productive; timer good, the finest oak, walnut, poplar, and cypress; principal productions, corn, tobacco, wheat, stock-raising and lumber; the streams, Little Obion River, Bayou du Chien, Mud, Rush, and Dixon creeks...

Hickman, the county seat, was established by act of the legislature in 1834, then called Mills' Point, in honor of Mr. Mills, the first settler there, in 1819, and changed to its present name in 1837, after the maiden name of the wife of G. W. L. Marr, who at one time owned the entire town and several thousand acres around it. It is located on the east bank of the Mississippi, 45 miles below the mouth of the Ohio river...

No Indian Wars, but worse. Fulton County was a sort of dividing line between the combatants during the civil war, and suffered severely, being plundered heavily by both parties...

The Earthquake of 1811. The most alarming and extensive, and the most serious in its effects, that ever occurred within the United States east of the Rocky Mountains, spent its greatest force in Kentucky, in Fulton County, and in the extreme southwest portion of the county and state...

Fulton County received its name in honor of Robert Fulton, the celebrated engineer. He was born in Little Britain, in the State of Pennsylvania, in 1765. In May, 1794, he obtained from the British government a patent for a double inclined plane, to be used for transportation; and in the same year he submitted to the British society for the promotion of arts and commerce, an improvement of his invention on mills for sawing marble."

An excerpt from pages 281-285 of the entry for "Fulton County," Collins' Historical Sketches of Kentucky, History of Kentucky, Volume II (Southern Historical Press, 1874).

Reelfoot Lake was created by the earthquake of 1811

Source: Sid Webb

Gallatin County

Nestled on the fertile banks of the Ohio River in Northern Kentucky, Gallatin County is a pearl amid the Kentucky, Ohio, and Indiana tri-state area. Located in Kentucky's Golden Triangle — the area between interstate highways connecting Cincinnati, Louisville, and Lexington — this rural gem boasts scenic rivers, picturesque country roads, quaint communities, and friendly people.

Gallatin, the 33rd county established, dates from 1798, and was derived from parts of Franklin and Shelby Counties. At that time, Gallatin was a rather large county whose county seat was Port William, now known as Carrollton. Later, parts of Gallatin were pared off to create

Albert Gallatin, pictured on $500 dollar bill, 1863.
Source: Darrell Maines

three additional counties: Owen, Trimble and Carroll. Today, Gallatin County is less than one tenth of its original size, making it the smallest county in Kentucky with just under 100 square miles of territory.

The county was named for Albert Gallatin, a Swiss native who became a financier, a prominent American statesman, and Secretary of the Treasury to President Jefferson.

Warsaw, the county seat of Gallatin County, began as a landing on the Ohio River in 1798. It soon became a busy shipping port and was called Great Landing.

In 1814, Col. Johnson and Henry Yates purchased 200 acres there to establish a river town to be named Fredericksburg after Johnson's hometown in Virginia. In 1831, the town was renamed Warsaw after it was found that there was already a Fredericksburg. In 1837, the Gallatin County seat moved from Port William to Warsaw.

The town of Sparta began as a village named Brock's Station around 1802, on either side of Eagle Creek. Many grist mills, the largest named Sparta, were located along the banks of the creek. A covered bridge once connected the two sides of town. Later, bridges were built upon its pillars. The first public building on what is the Gallatin County side of the creek was the train depot, built when the railroad came through Sparta. This started a time of growth resulting in its incorporation as a town in 1852.

By 1940, Sparta had four general stores, a lumberyard, a stockyard and two tree nurseries, among other businesses. Today, the railroad still runs through Sparta along Eagle Creek, and an Interstate 71 interchange is just a mile away.

Glencoe, on the southeast edge of Gallatin County, is located at the site of a natural mill race on Eagle Creek, which was probably what attracted the first known property owners there by 1790. However, the coming of the railroad in the mid 1800s caused its greatest prosperity.

Glencoe was incorporated in 1876 and reached its highest growth in 1940 when an egg hatchery and canning factory were located there.

Gallatin County's rural roots have helped shape its land and people. While not as agrarian as a century ago, Gallatin County still has many farms and hardworking farmers who serve as stewards of their land.

Contributed by David Hull

Garrard County

"Garrard County, the 25th in order of formation, was formed in 1796, out of parts of Madison, Lincoln, and Mercer, and named in honor of the then governor of the state, James Garrard. It is situated in the middle section of the state, on the east side of Dick's River; and is bounded north by Jessamine County, from which it is separated by the Kentucky River, east by Madison, south by Lincoln, and west by Boyle and Mercer. The face of the country is hilly or gently undulating, but all productive for grains or grasses...

Lancaster, the county seat, is situated two and one-half miles from Dick's River, at the head of Sugar Creek, a branch of the Kentucky River, and on the Richmond branch railroad, 112 1/2 miles from Louisville, 26 from Richmond and 9 from Stanford...

James Garrard, in honor of whom this county received its name, was born on the 14the of January, 1749, in the county of Stafford, in the (then) colony of Virginia. At a very early period in the revolutionary struggle, he engaged in the public service, and in the capacity of a militia officer, shared in the dangers and honors of that memorable war. While in service, he was called by the voice of his fellow citizens to a seat in the Virginia legislature, where he contributed, by his zeal and prudence, as much, or perhaps more than any other individual, to the passage of the famous act securing universal religious liberty...

He was an early emigrant to Kentucky, and was exposed to all the perils and dangers incident to the settlement and occupation of the country. He was repeatedly

Public meeting in Lancaster in the 1st Southern National Bank Meeting room on the town square
Source: John Perkins

called by the voice of his fellow citizens to represent their interests in the legislature of the state; and finally, by two successive elections, was elected to the chief magistracy of the commonwealth, a trust which, for eight years, he discharged with wisdom, prudence and vigor...

As a man, Governor Garrard had few equals; and in the various scenes and different stations of life, he acted with firmness, prudence, and decision. He died on the 19th January, 1822, at is residence, Mount Lebanon, in Bourbon County, in the 74th year of his age."

An excerpt from pages 288-289 of the entry for "Garrard County," Collins' Historical Sketches of Kentucky, History of Kentucky, Volume II (Southern Historical Press, 1874).

Grant County

"Grant County, erected in 1820 out of the western part of Pendleton County, was the 67th formed in the state. In shape it is a parallelogram, nearly a square, 22 ½ miles from the north to south, and 20

> **Mr. John McGill, who published a small gazetteer of Kentucky in 1832, states that this county was named in honor of Col. John Grant, who was born and raised near the Shallow ford of the Yadkin River, North Carolina**

miles from east to west. It is situated in the northern part of the state, and is bounded north by Boone and Kenton counties, east by Pendleton, southeast by Harrison, south by Scott and Owen, and west by Owen and Gallatin counties. The streams are: Eagle Creek, which flows northward through the western part of the county, and finally empties into the Kentucky River, and its tributaries, Clark's, Arnold's, and Ten Mile creeks; and on the eastern side of the county, Crooked, Fork Lick, and Grassy creeks, tributaries of the Licking river. The face of the country is undulating, seldom hilly...

Williamstown, the county seat, so named after William Arnold, probably the first settler, but previously called Philadelphia, was established in 1825; population in 1870 was 281; is situated in the turnpike, 37 miles from Covington, 47 miles from Lexington, and 56 miles from Frankfort...

Mr. John McGill, who published a small gazetteer of Kentucky in 1832, states that this county was named in honor of Col. John Grant, who was born and raised near the Shallow ford of the Yadkin River, North Carolina. He came to Kentucky in the year 1779, and settled a station within five miles of Bryan's Station, in the direction where Paris now stands. When the Indians captured Martin's and Ruddle's stations, he moved back to North Carolina, and thence to Virginia. In the year 1784, he again moved to Kentucky, and settled at his old station. He erected salt works on Licking River, but moved from that place to the United States' saline, in Illinois. He afterwards returned to his residence on the Licking, where he remained until he died. He served his country faithfully and ably in the field and council...

On the other hand, J. Worthing McCann, Esquire, a very intelligent citizen of Grant, and a resident at the time the county was organized, states that Grant was named after Samuel Grant, who was killed by the Indians near the Ohio River in the present State of Indiana, in the year 1794. This gentleman, Mr. M'Cann, further states, that Samuel Grant was a brother of Gen. Squire and Col. John Grant. Maj. William K. Wall, of Harrison, who has been a practitioner at the Grant bar ever since the formation of the county, concurs in the opinion of Mr. McCann, that the county was named in honor of Samuel Grant, and not Col. John Grant, his brother, as stated by Mr. McGill. "

An excerpt from pages 290-292 of the entry for "Grant County," Collins' Historical Sketches of Kentucky, History of Kentucky, Volume II (Southern Historical Press, 1874).

Graves County

In the early 1800s, President Andrew Jackson authorized the negotiation of a land purchase from the Chickasaw Indians; and in Graves County his name is used daily, since the county seat of Mayfield is located in the middle of the Jackson Purchase. This fertile land attracted early settlers from Virginia, North and South Carolina and Tennessee, who brought with them a degree of education and culture and a fierce determination to succeed on the land. Remarkable in their achievements as craftsmen and farmers, they put down roots to blend a political, economic, and social environment unique, perhaps only to Graves County.

The hometown of novelist Bobbie Ann Mason, Mayfield also claims bragging rights in agriculture, history, politics and arts. As one of Kentucky's largest counties boasting 557 square miles, Graves' history of legends and leaders includes a U.S. Vice President, four U.S. Congressmen, famous and infamous heroes, singers and songwriters, noted writers and a legacy of historic sites.

A trip from Paducah and Interstate 24 takes travelers down beautiful four lane Route 45, lined with a mixture of commerce and industry and lush farmland, into Mayfield and is a fitting introduction to Graves County. Downtown Mayfield features a historic district with antique era light fixtures and renovated sidewalks with brick inserts. Mayfield is an all-American town where Glory Days are still celebrated on the main thoroughfare on the Fourth of July.

Regional artisans' work is on display in the local Ice House Art Gallery in the "Arts in the Community" art show every August. Nothing less than the humble gourd is celebrated every fall with the gourd art in the October show of "All About Gourds." The Western Kentucky Museum features artifacts of the historic dark-fired tobacco industry and woolen mills.

Edana Locus House
Source: Mayfield Tourism Commission

Visitors can explore any of the thirteen historical markers commemorating such events as the 1861 convention held in Mayfield to secede from the Union; Alben Barkley's birthplace in Wheel; and the Bayou de Chine Church, oldest congregational church organized in 1826 and used as a hospital during the Civil War. They may wish to search through Camp Beauregard and see the Civil War monument and cemetery, as well as the renowned Wooldridge Monuments in Maplewood Cemetery.

The Fancy Farm Picnic is the premier political event of the region. Every year local sponsors serve up thousands of pounds of delicious barbecued chicken and pork, a variety of lively music and scores of fun filled-games and events. Rumor has it that any Kentucky politician who doesn't speak at the Fancy Farm picnic doesn't have a prayer come election time. This annual event began in 1834 as a family picnic under the limbs of the Lying Oak. Suspended during the Civil War, the event resumed in 1880 as a prime chance for politicians to stump before election day. Politics are BIG in Graves County - part of leaders, legends and lore!

Contributed by Wendy Hunter

Grayson County

"Grayson County was organized in 1810, out of parts of Ohio and Hardin counties, the 54th formed in the state, and named in honor of Col. William Grayson. It is situated in the west middle part of the state, and bounded north by Breckinridge and Hardin counties, east by Hart, south by Edmonson, and west by Ohio and Butler. The face of the country is generally level, and the land about second rate. The county abounds and summer resort, situated two and one-half miles from the railroad and five miles from Leitchfield. The number of white sulphur springs here is remarkable, about 100 of them on a singe quarter-acre of land, said to be more strongly impregnated with sulphur than any in the United States; they very in temperature, some very cold and others very warm, and are valuable for the medicinal properties, their use having effected many wonderful cures. Great improvements in the hotel accommodations have recently been made...

Col. William Grayson, for whom this county was named, was a native of Virginia. He was first elected a member of Congress in 1784. He was a member of the Virginia convention which was called to ratify the constitution of the United States. In this illustrious assembly his talents rendered him conspicuous. He opposed the adoption of the constitution. After the adoption of the constitution he was elected in conjunction with Richard H. Lee to represent his native state in the senate of the United States. He died March 12th, 1790, while on his way to Congress."

Ten Commandments about 5 miles west of Leitchfield
Source: John Perkins

with fine timber, and in portions of it has stone coal and iron ore. Wheat, corn, oats, grass and tobacco are the leading productions. The principal water courses are: Nolin, Rough, Rick, Big Clifty, Little Clifty, Short, Bear, Canoloway, and Caney creeks...

Leitchfield, the county seat, named after Maj. David Leitch (of Leitch's Station, Campbell County, Ky.), who was the patentee of the land on which it stands, and donated the site of the town..."

Grayson Springs is a celebrated watering place

An excerpt from pages 293-294 of the entry for "Grayson County," Collins' Historical Sketches of Kentucky, History of Kentucky, Volume II (Southern Historical Press, 1874).

Green County

Green County was the 16th county created. It was formed out of parts of Lincoln and Nelson counties in 1792. It was named in honor of Gen. Nathaniel Greene, of Revolutionary War fame. Since its creation the following counties have been taken entirely from Green County: Cumberland in 1798, Adair in 1801 and Taylor in 1848. The following counties were taken in part from Green County: Pulaski and Barren in 1796, Hart in 1819 and Metcalfe in 1860. At one time Green County was one of the largest counties in the state. Now it is one of the smallest.

The county seat of Greensburg was established in 1794, and in 1804 a county courthouse was completed. In 1879, on the 75th anniversary of the old courthouse building, a cast iron bell was installed. The bell was rung to celebrate special events, holidays and emergencies. At the end of World War II, the bell tolled the entire day. It is uncertain when the bell was removed from the courthouse. At the present time it remains in storage.

In 1927, an attempt was made to demolish the stone courthouse and replace it with it with a new modern structure. This attempt was met with bitter opposition and became one of the hottest court battles in Green County's history. The old courthouse still sits in the public square as a shrine available for tourists to see and is one of Green County's greatest treasures. It has many uses and served as a place for court when the present courthouse was undergoing renovation.

Early settlements in Green County were: Pitman's Station on Green River near the mouth of Pitman Creek, established about 1779 or 1780; Glover's Station, on the site where Greensburg now stands, established in 1780; Skagg's Station established in 1781; and Gray's Station, about eight miles south of Greensburg, established in 1790.

Green County has been home to many famous people. Among them are Union Generals E. H. Hobson and William T. Ward; the Rev. David Rice, pioneer Presbyterian minister; Mentor Graham, who earned his place in history for being Abraham Lincoln's teacher; Mary Owens, Lincoln's sweet-

heart; William H. Herndon, Lincoln's law partner; and Rueben Creel, U.S. Consul to Mexico.

Green County residents believed in education. Early institutions of learning were the Greensburg Academy, The New Athens Seminary and the Brush

Maj. Nathaniel Greene
Source: Independence National Historical Park Collection

Creek Academy. Many different churches were established as well, including Baptist, Methodist and Presbyterian. The earliest Baptist churches are Mt. Gilead and Brush Creek.

A major contribution to medicine involved Jane Todd Crawford of Green County. On Christmas Day in 1809, Crawford rode 65 miles on horseback to Danville where Dr. Ephraim McDowell, operating without anesthesia, successfully removed from her a life-threatening ovarian tumor. The surgery was the first of its kind. Twenty-five days later Crawford returned home to Green County.

Reprinted with permission of Ray Perkins; Carolyn Scott, Vice President, Green County Historical Society, contributor.

Greenup County

Standing proudly on the banks of the mighty Ohio River, Greenup County, the gateway to the Country Music Highway, is the birthplace of a page in American history. Formed in 1803, out of part of Mason County, Greenup County was named in honor of Christopher Greenup, a Revolutionary War hero from Virginia. After Greenup settled in Kentucky, in 1783, he was sworn in as an attorney at law in the old court for the district of Kentucky.

Boasting unique river communities with a strong sense of heritage rooted deep in their wooded hills, Greenup County is truly Kentucky's natural beauty at its best. Greenup Countians take great pride in our people such as Jesse Stuart

Bennets Mill Bridge
Source: Greenup County Tourism Commission

who was born in W-Hollow here in Greenup. Stuart made Greenup County the setting of his works and masterfully addressed universal themes through the small Appalachia setting. Award winning Billy Ray Cyrus is also a native of Greenup County. Cyrus is known not only for his illustrious singing career, but also for his acting and charitable work through the Billy Ray Cyrus Foundation. He is an exceptional man who has never forgotten his roots in Greenup County.

The Southern roots of Greenup County can be seen in its Georgian architecture style homes and beautiful churches. Nature and beauty surround you at Greenbo Lake State Resort Park and Jesse Stuart Nature Preserve. Two standing covered bridges still grace the county, as well as Native American burial mounds and several iron furnaces. A trip to Greenup County would not be complete without a visit to the McConnell House built in 1834, beautifully restored by Greenup County Historic Society.

Greenup County extends faithful tribute the lonely graves of unknown Civil War soldiers who lost their lives. There are other tributes to the county's war heroes, including a tank and a helicopter, both of which have seen active duty, and a memorial wall dedicated to the memory of the fallen soldiers who made the supreme sacrifice. Jesse Boone's cabin and the grave of Lucy Virgin Downs, the first white child born west of the Allegheny Mountains, are part of the historic sites visitors may see.

A stop at Bryson General Store reveals dry goods for sale, like an iron skillet or miscellaneous hard-to-find hardware items. Family-owned and operated since 1910, it is the oldest continuous operation of its kind in Greenup County. The 1950s era building was once home to the former Walsh and Letitia post offices. Across the road is a field of dreams where the Schultz Creek Bearcats have played baseball on Sunday afternoons since 1967.

A visit to the memorial of Mary Magdalene Pitts will also be a moving experience. The life of Mary Magdalene Pitts, the subject of much controversy in the early part of the 20th Century, is soon to be made into a motion picture, and is sure to touch the heart.

Greenup County is home to many unique festivals and events. Greenup's Old-Fashioned Days, South Shore Quilt Festival and Greenup County Fair are just a few experiences, embracing the cultural heritage and featuring local crafters and musicians.

Remember to visit the Greenup County Tourism Commission, located in the top floor of the Historic McConnell House, and let the staff make the trip to Greenup County a memory that will last a lifetime.
Contributed by Kelly Nelson

Hancock County

1829 was the year Hancock County was formed to become Kentucky's 85th county. It was created by taking parts from Breckinridge, Daviess and Ohio counties. The area was named after John Hancock, the Boston patriot who was president of the Continental Congress and the first signer of the Declaration of Independence.

Hancock County is located geographically in the region known as Western Coal Fields. It was the first county to mine and ship coal. Although the area does not contain large deposits, the quality ranks very high. Miners were active as early as the 1830s, taking coal from the southern part of the county near Victoria. The coal was hauled to Cloverport for shipment on the Ohio River. The Breckinridge Cannel Coal from those mines was once the most famous and highly priced coal in Kentucky.

Hawesville, the county seat was named for Virginian, Richard Hawes. He came to Kentucky in the early 1800s and eventually took residence in the vicinity of Lewisport (then Daviess County). Hawes acquired a large tract of land around present day Hawesville and donated the town site.

For years, a 24-hour ferry connected Hawesville with Cannelton, Indiana. The Bob Cummings-Lincoln Trail Bridge now spans the Ohio River at that point. Many say it was at this place in 1816 that Abe Lincoln crossed from Kentucky into Indiana with his family. In 1827, he returned to Hancock County to face charges of operating a ferry across the Ohio River without a license. The short trial, held at the Pate House that still stands as a museum and was named after the presiding justice of the peace, Squire Pate, ended with the warrant dismissed as the future president won his first law case.

Though it is small in area, Hancock County has become a very progressive industrial center. The County's Industrial Foundation was created in 1985, and in the first ten years it was instrumental in multiple expansions and the site selection of World Source, Roll Coater, Crescent Paper and Tube and the first Alcoa Plant. Since 1995, the Foundation has been successful in attracting in excess of $752 million in new development and more than 650 new jobs to the community. In 2002, local government, industry and the school system founded The Hancock County Industrial Training Consortium to ensure the education and retention of skilled workers.

Hancock County is also considered the Sorghum Capital of the World, with more than half a million gallons of sorghum syrup packaged and shipped from the area each year. One of the annual highlights is the fall Sorghum Festival, where all aspects of production are on display.

Attractions include the Hancock County Museum, located in the restored Railroad Depot built in 1902. It contains a collection of artifacts representing all facets of the history of the county including the influence of farming, river traffic, railroads, schools, art and family life. The museum is open each Sunday from 2 p.m. to 4 a.m., April through October.

Contributed by the Hancock Chamber of Commerce with the permission of Patsy R. Young.

John Hancock
Source: Library of Congress

Hardin County

Hardin County, Kentucky's 15th county, created in November 1792, was named for Col. John Hardin, the notable pioneer of Nelson County. In 1797, the county seat was located on land donated by Col. Andrew Hynes and named Elizabeth Town in honor of Hynes' wife.

The first recorded exploration of this region was in 1766 by Col. John Smith. Ten years later a group of Virginians reconnoitered briefly and left after several Indian attacks. Daniel Boone's brother Squire explored the area repeatedly in the late 1770s, but no permanent settlements were established until 1780, when Col. Andrew Hynes, Capt. Thomas Helm and Samuel Haycraft each built a fort near present-day Elizabethtown.

Hardin County's growth and prosperity is likely due to the fact that it has always been served by good roads and railroads. The Louisville and Nashville Turnpike, a hard-surfaced road, was finished in the late 1830s. Today the county is crisscrossed by highways, including Interstate 65, the Bluegrass and Western Kentucky Parkways, U.S. 31-W, and U.S. 62. Commerce across the county began with these railroads: the Louisville & Nashville, completed in 1859, the Elizabethtown & Paducah (early 1870s) and the Hodgenville & Elizabethtown (1888).

Prior to World War II, the county was primarily agricultural. Farmers raised a variety of crops, including corn, oats, wheat, hay and livestock primarily for their own needs. Later, hemp, fruit, and mules were raised for profit. For many years, tobacco was the money crop of choice. Today, specialization in farming prevails.

In 1917, Camp Knox, now Fort Knox, was created. It grew during World War II and later became the home of the U. S. Bullion Depository and the Patton Museum of Armor and Cavalry.

Following World War II, the town of Radcliff grew at the southern edge of Fort Knox. Today it has absorbed the communities of Rogersville, Red Hill, Long View and New Stithton.

Abraham Lincoln was born on February 12, 1809, in what was then part of Hardin County. His family left Kentucky in the fall of 1816.

In 1813, James Buchanan practiced

The Hardin County History Museum is located in the former Elizabethtown Post Office built in 1931

Source: Kenny Tabb

law for a few months in Hardin County before returning to Pennsylvania.

In 1964 the Elizabethtown Community College, part of the University of Kentucky, opened. In 2003 the community college was separated from the University of Kentucky and joined with the local vocational school to form the Elizabethtown Community and Technical College.

In 1954 Hardin Memorial Hospital opened. Today it boasts 300 beds, the latest medical equipment and a staff of more than 200 physicians.

Industrial development, begun in 1955, has continued to increase. In addition to industrial parks in Elizabethtown and Radcliff, several acres near Glendale have been acquired for future development.

Contributed by Mary Josephine Jones

Harlan County

"Harlan County, the 60th formed in the state, was erected in 1819 out of parts of Floyd and Knox counties, and named in honor of Maj. Silas Harlan. From that date, for a period of 48 years, it was the extreme southeastern county, until Josh Bell County was formed in 1867 out of its southern and southeastern part; this took off about 200 voters. It is bounded north by Perry and Letcher counties, east and south by the Virginia state line, and west by Josh Bell County. It is a high, rugged, and mountainous county, with fertile soil, and heavily timbered with good timber of all kinds. On the southern border lies the great Stone or Cumberland Mountain, surmounted by a stupendous rock one mile long and 600 feet high; on the northern border the Pine Mountain, ranging nearly east and west, and separating this from Letcher and Perry counties; and in the eastern part of the Black Mountain, probably an arm of the Cumberland. The products are corn, wheat, oats, rye, and tobacco; stock raising is carried on to some extent...

Mount Pleasant is the county seat and only town; is 168 miles from Frankfort, 34 miles from Cumberland Ford or Pineville, in Josh Bell County, and 49 miles from Whitesburgh, in Letcher County...

During the Civil War, Harlan County suffered greatly in the loss of some of her best citizens, among them the clerk of the county court. The courthouse and many valuable papers and documents in the clerks' offices, the jail, and a number of other houses in Mount Pleasant and elsewhere

Harlan County Court House, Harlan, Ky.

Harlan County Courthouse
Source: SouthEast Telephone

were burned either by soldiers or guerrillas...

Maj. Silas Harlan, in honor of whom this county received its name, was born in Berkley County, Virginia, near the town of Martinsburg. He came to Kentucky in 1774, and took a very active part in the battles and skirmishes with the Indians. He commanded a company of spies under Gen. George Rogers Clark, in the Illinois campaigns in1779, and proved himself a most active, energetic and efficient officer. Gen. Clark said of him, that 'he was one of the bravest and most accomplished soldiers that ever fought by his side.' About the year 1778, he built a stockade fort on Salt River, seven miles above Harrodsburg, which was called Harlan's Station. He was a major at the battle of the Blue Licks, and fell in that memorable contest at the head of the detachment commanded by him. He was never married. He was universally regarded at a brave, generous and active man."

An excerpt from pages 319-320 of the entry for "Harlan County," Collins' Historical Sketches of Kentucky, History of Kentucky, Volume II (Southern Historical Press, 1874).

Harrison County

"Harrison County, the 17th county in order, and the eighth formed after Kentucky became a state, was made in 1793 out of parts of Bourbon and Scott counties, and named after Col. Benjamin Harrison, who was at the time a representative from Bourbon County in the Kentucky legislature. Main Licking River runs through a small portion of the county in the northeast. About one-half of the county is gently, undulating, rich, and very productive; the other portion, hilly and also quite productive; the whole well adapted to grazing; the soil based on red clay, with limestone foundation...

Cynthiana, the county seat and chief town, named after Cynthia and Anna, two daughters of the original proprietor, Robert Harris, established Dec. 10, 1793, incorporated as a town in 1802 and as a city in 1860, is situated on the right bank of South Licking, or the South fork of Licking, 37 miles from Frankfort and 66 from Cincinnati, being connected with both cities by railroad.

First Battle of Cynthiana. On July 17, 1862, the Confederate general, John H. Morgan, with a force 816 strong when he started, nine days before, upon this first Kentucky raid, attacked the Federal forces at Cynthiana, nearly 500 strong (mainly home guards), under Col. John J. Landram, who after a brave resistance were overpowered and defeated, and the town captured. The Federal pickets were surprised, and captured or driven in; and before the commander had time to dispose his force, the Confederates commenced shelling the town, producing a wild consternation among the inhabitants. Capt. William H. Glass, of the Federal artillery, occupied the public square, from which point he could command most of the roads. Another force took position on the Magee Hill road, south of the town, along which the Confederates were approaching. A third detachment was instructed to hold the bridge on the west side of town, towards which Morgan's main force was pouring. Capt. Glass opened on Morgan's battery, which was planted on an eminence a quarter of a mile distant, between the Leesburg and Fair Ground Turnpikes. The Confederates were now approaching by every road and street, and deployed as skirmishes through every field, completely encircling the Federals. Their battery on the hill having ceased its fire, Capt. Glass with grape and canister swept Pike street from one end to the other. By this time the contestants were engaged at every point. A portion of the Federals made a stand at the railroad depot. A charge upon the Confederate battery at the Licking Bridge, was repulsed and the Confederates, charged upon the force at the depot, while another detachment was pouring deadly fire from the rear, about 125 yards distant."

An excerpt from pages 321-323 of the entry for "Harrison County," Collins' Historical Sketches of Kentucky, History of Kentucky, Volume II (Southern Historical Press, 1874).

I'll tell ya what...

Judge John Trimble, one of the most eminent citizens of Harrison County, was among the earliest natives of Kentucky — born Dec. 4 1783, 8 1/2 years before it became one of the United States. His oldest brother Robert — distinguished as a judge of the court of appeals at 31, appointed chief justice of Kentucky at 33 but declined, judge of the U.S. district court for Kentucky at 39, and on the bench of the U.S. Supreme Court at 49 — was born in Virginia, in 1777... and in 1780, their father, Wm. Trimble, emigrated to Kentucky, and settled in Clark co., not far from Boonesborough, where John and another brother, James, were born. The younger boys were liberally educated by an uncle, who came to live with their father's family.

From Collin's Historical Sketches of Kentucky, Vol. II, page 331.

Hart County

Located in south central Kentucky, Hart County contains miles of scenic country ranging from sultry river bottoms to gently rolling hillsides to steep knobs and hidden hollows. Nolin River and Lake form the western boundary of the county, while beautiful Green River winds through the center, east to west in a series of loops and bends offering delight for the angler and the canoeist alike.

In the late 1700s settlers began arriving. Many were veterans coming to claim land grants awarded for Revolutionary War service. The need for a more accessible government led to

Rolling field in Hart County
Source: John Perkins

the call for a new county. In 1819 Hart County was formed from portions of Hardin and Barren counties. The county was named for Captain Nathaniel Gray Smith Hart, slain in the War of 1812.

Hart County has three incorporated cities: Munfordville, the county seat; Horse Cave and Bonnieville. The county attracted national attention in the 1850s with the construction of an iron railroad bridge over Green River. Hailed as an engineering marvel, three Civil War battles were fought over the control of this vital supply link. The significance of the "Battle for the Bridge" is celebrated each September during the Hart County Civil War Days.

Horse Cave also honors its rich heritage during the month of September with an award-winning festival noted for its diversity of musical entertainment.

Horse Cave is also home to Hidden River Cave and Kentucky Caverns. The enormous entrance to Hidden River Cave can be seen from the city sidewalks, while the tour begins at the American Cave Museum where history and science exhibits intro-

duce visitors to the fascinating world of caves. It is the only museum of its kind in the nation dedicated to caves and their protection. At Kentucky Caverns, experienced guides introduce visitors to some of nature's greatest handiwork including massive columns, delicate coral, and flowing drapery.

Interesting attractions exist above ground, too, including Kentucky Repertory Theatre, designated in 2005 as the State Repertory Theatre. The theatre offers professional performances of classics, comedy and drama. Nearby is Kentucky Down Under, an Australian animal park that offers hands-on opportunities and family fun through its many exhibits and programs. Hart County is also well known for its arts and crafts industry, including white oak baskets that have been a tradition of this area for over 200 years.

Agriculture continues strong in Hart County. Hart ranked 11th in the state for burley tobacco production in 2004. Some of the best dairy and beef herds in Kentucky are located on Hart County farms. The county ranked fifth in the state for alfalfa production in 2004 and is becoming a statewide leader in fruit and vegetable production.

The county continues to preserve its rich heritage and traditional values, but is also ideally positioned for additional economic growth. Dart Container Corp., Louisville Bedding Co., T. Marzetti, Ken-Dec, and Akebono are the county's major industries.

Contributed by Virginia Davis.

For more information about Hart County, contact the Hart County Chamber of Commerce at (270) 524-2892 or visit www.hartcountyky.org.

Henderson County

Richard Henderson, for whom the town and county are named, has been called the political father of Kentucky and one of the greatest of American land speculators and commonwealth builders. He was born in Hanover County, Va., but moved early in life to North Carolina where he studied law and ultimately became associate jus-

that made Hendersonians wealthy. Within 75 years after the town was established it became the largest strip-tobacco market in the world. Fortunes ran into the millions. Henderson at one time was reputed to have more millionaires per capita than any city in the country.

Among the many honored citizens of Henderson are Elizabeth Blackwell, the first woman doctor of medicine in America; Nancy Morgan Hart, Revolutionary War heroine; John James Audubon, artist and ornithologist; Mary Towles Sasseen, founder and originator of Mother's Day; Samuel Hopkins, Henderson's cartographer; Lazarus Whitehead Powell, governor of Kentucky from

Source: Kentucky Department of Tourism

tice of the western district of North Carolina.

Henderson's vision can be traced to 1764 when Daniel Boone returned to Hillsborough, N.C., with a provocative account of the rich trans-Allegheny land. Henderson was convinced that permanent settlement could be made only on land purchased from the Cherokees with a written treaty. Early in 1774 Daniel Boone informed Henderson that the Cherokees were ready to negotiate. In March 1775, three chiefs made their mark on the treaty and eight white men signed as witnesses. The Transylvania Company waited more than 25 years before founding its third city.

Generous grants of land and fertile soil bore rich crops and pasture for flocks. But it was tobacco

1851-1855; Adam Rankin Johnson, Confederate partisan ranger; John Young Brown, governor 1891-95; Augustus Owsley Stanley, governor from 1915-1919; Albert Benjamin Chandler, governor from 1936-39; William Christopher Handy, father of the blues; and Adm. Husband Kimmel, commander of the Pacific Fleet at Pearl Harbor.

The Henderson County Historical and Genealogical Society was founded on April 22, 1922, by Susan Starling Towles. Information about the Society can be found at: http://www.rootsweb.com/~kyhchgs/ The Society also hosts a history website that can be found at: http://www.rootsweb.com/~kyhende2/

Contributed by Netta Mullin

Henry County

The 16,000 people who live in the 289 square miles of Henry County enjoy the simple lifestyle of rural fields, quaint towns, and spectacular scenery. Henry County is a place where people unravel today's complicated world. Deceptively, just 30 minutes down the road is the lure of the big city; but, like Wendell Berry, noted author and environmentalist (and a native Henry countian), people are always happy to come back to the more relaxed style of home in the country.

Founded in 1798, Henry County has an historic courthouse, many restored buildings, and five incorporated towns from which to chose a residence. Eminence, the largest, is home to a number of industries and businesses, but the streetscape has been updated, as it is a silver Renaissance city. A new attraction, the Kentucky Renaissance Faire, is due to open in June 2006.

Historic New Castle, the county seat and home to many of the descendants of the pioneers who settled the region, is also a silver Renaissance city. Its tree-lined streets shade some of the most beautiful and historic homes in the area.

Pleasureville recently was the setting for a movie, and tiny Smithfield is home to Our Best Restaurant, a real tourism destination. The old flour mill and gift shops make Smithfield the place to visit. Flattened by a tornado in the seventies, Campbellsburg, just off Interstate 71, anticipates tremendous growth in the next few years.

Both of the county's school systems, Henry County Public Schools and Eminence Independent Schools, are excellent and offer inno-

vative programs that promote ongoing learning.

The Henry County Historical Society has renovated the Caplinger home as a center for genealogical research for those who enjoy searching for family histories. They also have a museum with changing displays of Henry County history.

The Little Kentucky River Watershed Conservancy operates Lake Jericho, a 137-acre lake, featuring fishing, camping, shelters and outdoor picnic areas. The lake is a wonderful place for family gatherings, company picnics and church outings.

Henry County's most famous place is Bethlehem, where thousands of Christmas cards are stamped with the wise men following the star. Each year in a living nativity scene, live animals and church members portray the First Christmas.

Patrick Henry, who gave his name to Henry County, would be proud of his namesake, where people have always been noted for their independence, spirit and perseverance. Fires and nature destroyed much of the county in the past, and even today, changes in the tobacco program have changed the livelihood of many farmers who make up this rural area. Yet the people continue to go forward. A prime example of farm diversification is the Smith-Berry Winery. After turning the dairy barn into a winery and a buggy shed into a tasting room, the Smiths hold concerts, dinners and weddings. They and others like them prove that the country can offer a rewarding life with good neighbors, good businesses, and a good place to live.
Contributed by Pat Wallace.

Patrick Henry

Hickman County

Hickman County, formed in 1821 out of Caldwell and Livingston Counties (Chickasaw Territory), was the 71st county in Kentucky. It was named in honor of a Revolutionary War hero, Capt. Paschal Hickman who died following the Battle of the River Raisin (near Detroit) in the War of 1812. Capt. Hickman, a native of Virginia, moved to Kentucky when he was very young with his father, Rev. William Hickman, to Franklin County.

Between 1822 and 1886 Hickman County was divided into eight counties that now are Fulton, Hickman, Carlisle, Ballard, McCracken, Graves, Marshall and Calloway. It is bordered by Fulton County to the south, Carlisle to the north, Graves to the east and the Mississippi River to the west. Wolf Island is in fact now connected to Missouri as the river changed courses in the mid 1800s and the river channel shifted from the Missouri side to the Kentucky side.

The county consists of 244.44 square miles with a population of around 5,300. It is made up of a number of unique communities, of which Clinton is the county seat. The original county seat was Columbus, the site of the Columbus — Belmont Battlefield State Park. Located on the Mississippi River, the site was considered a strategic location for control of the Mississippi River during the Civil War — the struggle to control the river led to the Battle of Belmont on November 7, 1861.

Confederate General Leonidas Polk established camps on both the Kentucky and Missouri sides of the river and the more heavily fortified Columbus, which was known as the "Gibraltar of the West."

Anchor and chain at Columbus, Belmont Park
Source: Kentucky Department of Libraries & Archives

But a Union General destined for the White House, Ulysses S. Grant, outflanked the "Gibraltar" and forced evacuation of the Confederates in 1862. From the 1800s until the depression in the 1930s, Hickman County was a very enterprising county with lots of jobs.

During the depression Hickman County lost many of its citizens to larger communities offering more and better job opportunities, a challenging situation for even today's leaders.

Contributed by Wanda Moon

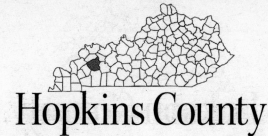

Hopkins County

In 1806, an act was drafted by Senator Daniel Ashby (representing Muhlenberg, Livingston and Henderson Counties) to divide Henderson County and create a new county. Senator Ashby named the new county in honor of his friend and colleague in the Kentucky House of Representatives, General Samuel Hopkins. On May 25, 1807, Hopkins County was established.

Farming was the mainstay of Hopkins County for most of the 1800s. Tobacco was the leading crop, followed by corn. Coal was known to exist but it was not until 1837 that John Wolfolk, a blacksmith from Hall's Store (now Earlington) gathered a sack of coal from an outcrop on Hunting Branch, and

[Tobacco Leaf image]

Tobacco Leaf
Source: Sid Webb

used it to fire his forge. In 1869 the St. Bernard Coal Company opened the No. 11 Mine. Mining coal then became the county's major industry. In 1899 Hopkins County became the first Kentucky county to produce over 1 million tons of coal per year. Hopkins County mines produced 1,265,707 tons of coal that year.

The Evansville, Henderson and Nashville (L & N) Railroad was completed through the county in 1871 and the Elizabethtown, Paducah and St Louis (Illinois Central) Railroad was completed in 1873. The county then had transportation north-south and east-west by rail. The railroads provided transportation for the coal to be shipped nationwide.

Hopkins County was divided by the Civil War. Union supporters joined a regiment recruited by James Shackleford. Al Fowler recruited troops for the Confederacy. The first shots of the Civil War were fired at Burnt Mill Church in Webster County (in Hopkins County before the creation of Webster County in 1860). The courthouse at Madisonville was burned by Gen. Hyland B. Lyon on December 17, 1864, during his courthouse burning march through western Kentucky.

Many communities grew quickly as whistle stops on the railroads, including Hanson, Morton's Gap, Nortonville and White Plains. Dawson Springs, in the southwestern part of the county, began to thrive in the 1880s as a popular health resort, but its popularity had faded by the time of the Great Depression.

In 1970 Hopkins County was the third largest coal producer in the commonwealth, following Muhlenberg and Pike. In 1971 the county also ranked fifth in oil production in Kentucky. Development of resources was aided by the construction of the north-south Pennyrile Parkway (now Edward Breathitt Parkway) and the east-west Western Kentucky Parkway (now Wendell H. Ford Parkway) through the county in the 1970s.

In 1987 farms occupied 41 percent of the land area, with 72 percent of farmland under cultivation. The county has a area of 552 square miles, 353,280 acres.

The population of the county in 1810 was 2,964 and in 1990 it was 46,126.

See "History of Hopkins County" by Maurice K. Gordon; Hopkins County by Ann B. Brown (Kentucky Encyclopedia).

Contributed by J. Harold Utley.

Jackson County

Jackson County was formed out of the present surrounding counties of Madison, Estill, Laurel, Rockcastle, Clay, and Owsley on April 25, 1858. Most of the first families to settle in Jackson County were from the Virginias and Carolinas.

Jackson County is situated on the headwaters of the Kentucky River and the Rockcastle or Cumberland River. The land is hilly and very rough in parts while the southeastern portion is rolling. In the northern area are many small limestone caves, once used by early settlers to store canned food and perishables such as butter and milk. In this same region, settlers found an abundance of water from limestone springs. Sometimes settlers piped the water to their houses. Jackson County was traditionally an agrarian community. The first settlers knew the meaning of hard work, of making do with what they had and sometimes doing without. Today, these same values are evident in the citizens of Jackson County. Many residents are quilters, weavers, farmers, doll makers, basket makers and potters. As they continue to teach their skills to the future generation, they help preserve and honor the heritage of Jackson County.

Jackson County is covered by over 56,000 acres of the Daniel Boone National Forest. The forest encompasses much of the natural and rugged beauty of Jackson County. The U.S. Forest service operates two campgrounds and picnic areas in the county, S-Tree and Turkey Foot. The Sheltowee Trace also runs the length of Jackson County and spills over into other counties. A marker on the courthouse lawn states that the following brave explorers used this trail in explorations across the state before 1779: Dr. Thomas Walker, Christopher Gist, Daniel Boone and John Finley. The Old Boone Trail crosses the southwestern edge of the county. The main county road from Big Hill to Maulden, cut out by oxen and used for hauling goods from Richmond and Lexington, was replaced by a new highway built at the turn of the 21st century.

COUNTY NAMED, 1858

For Andrew Jackson, the 7th US President, 1829-37, first to be elected from west of Appalachians. First Representative in Congress from Tenn., 1796-97. In US Senate twice, 1797 and 1823. Victorious commander at New Orleans, 1815. County formed from small parts of Madison, Estill, Owsley, Clay, Laurel and Rockcastle, every adjoining county, except Lee.

Source: SouthEast Telephone

Today, a spirit of exploration can still be found in the citizens of Jackson County. The county is home to a new state vocational education building and a new adult education facility. New industries are beginning to operate in two of the established industrial parks. In the spring of 2005, construction began on a new public library building. As in the past, there is an urgency to teach the children to honor and preserve their heritage. Future generations may need to tap into that reservoir of past strength, faith, and determination.

This article was contributed by the staff of the Jackson County Public Library.

Jefferson County

Jefferson County was created by the Virginia General Assembly in 1780. Originally a vast territory of 7,800 square miles, its present size is 386 square miles. It is bounded by the Ohio River on the north and by Bullitt, Spencer, Shelby and Oldham Counties.

Jefferson County was named for Thomas Jefferson, governor of Virginia and president of the United States. Louisville, the county seat, was named to honor the French King Louis XVI for his help in the Revolutionary War.

Navigation along the 1,000-mile Ohio River was historically impassable at one place—the Falls of the Ohio at Louisville. In 1773, Virginia surveyors arrived at the falls to map the area, and in 1778 Gen. George Rogers Clark came to the falls with militiamen and a small group of settlers. In 1779, Louisville was platted and the settlers made their home on Corn Island opposite Louisville at the falls. The pioneers built a series of small forts east of Louisville as protection against the Natives. The Chenoweth Massacre (1789) marked the last conflict between settlers and Native Americans.

Pioneers came from eastern states throughout the late 1700s. Many settlers were of German, Irish, Scottish, English and Dutch ancestries. Slaves constituted a portion of the new arrivals.

The first towns outside Louisville were Newtown (1794), Middletown (1797) and Jeffersontown (1797). A network of roads was constructed throughout the first half of the 19th century. Railroads arrived in the mid-19th century, leading to the growth of Lyndon, Anchorage, Valley Station and Pleasure Ridge Park. Soon interurban electric rail lines led to the suburbs of Buechel, Okolona and Valley Station. Today Jefferson County has access to a sophisticated interstate highway system, as well as a mass transit bus system.

Early industries were salt production, distilleries, lumber, brickyards, clothing, tanneries, tobacco production, steamboat building and breweries. Major industries like Ford, General Electric Corporation, International Harvester, Dupont and B.F. Goodrich moved into Jefferson County in the 20th century. Kentucky Fried Chicken (YUM Brands) and Papa John's Pizza are headquartered in Louisville, as is Hillerich and Bradsby.

In addition to some smaller universities, Bellarmine University and the University of Louisville provide outstanding undergraduate and post graduate opportunities. Jefferson County is home to the Southern Baptist Theological Seminary, the Louisville Presbyterian Theological Seminary and the headquarters of the Presbyterian Church – USA. Known for pioneering achievements including the Abiocor artificial heart and the world's first hand transplant, Louisville has a thriving health sciences sector including several world-class hospitals and a downtown research and commercialization park.

Designed by Frederick Olmsted, the metropolitan park system, with more than 14,000 acres, is one of the nation's finest. Louisville's Churchill Downs is home of the world famous Kentucky Derby. Metropolitan Louisville is known internationally for the Louisville Orchestra, the Kentucky Arts Center, the Louisville Ballet, Actor's Theatre, the Speed Art Museum and other fine arts galleries. The Louisville Free Public Library contains nearly a million volumes and circulating collections of art and music.

As America entered the 21st Century, Jefferson County voted to governmentally merge the city with the county. In 2003, Metropolitan Louisville became the 16th largest city in America.

Contributed by Judge Todd Hollenbach

Water Tower
Source: SouthEast Telephone

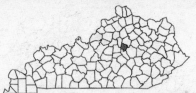

Jessamine County

Jessamine, the only one of the Kentucky's 120 counties with a feminine name, is located near the center of the state in the inner Bluegrass Region. It was named by Col. John Price, state legislator, for the jessamine (jasmine) flower, grown widely in the area, especially along the region's spring fed creeks that flow into the Kentucky River. Popular legend that the county was named for the daughter of a Scottish surveyor, John Douglas, is without foundation. Jessamine Douglas

The first and only fort in Jessamine was established near Keene by Levi Todd in 1779, one year before Lexington was built. At this time the Indians, provided arms by the English, harassed settlers around this part of the state. It was then for the personal safety of those at the fort that Todd felt compelled to abandon the fort and seek protection in other forts around the Lexington area.

The first white man to enter the region was John Finley, a woodsman and hunter from North Carolina. Other hunters, with land grants issued by the British king for service in the French and Indian War, soon followed. On Finley's second trip, he was accompanied by Daniel Boone. The first permanent settlers in Jessamine were John, Jacob and Samuel Hunter, who came here in the spring of 1779 as chain carriers employed by the surveyor, Elias Hite. They settled along the Hickman Creek area, and here was born the first white child in the county, Joseph Hunter.

Bluegrass Festival
Source: SouthEast Telephone

was supposedly tomahawked by an Indian, but historical records proved this to be merely a myth.

Jessamine County was formed from part of Fayette County in 1798, which was a banner year for creation of counties. It was the 36th county in the state. It contains 158 square miles and is one of the smallest in Kentucky, having only 110,080 acres. It is bounded on the east, south, and the southwest by the Kentucky River. Its neighboring counties are Fayette, Madison, Garrard, Mercer and Woodford. Although it became a county in 1798, it had no post office until 1801 and no railroad until 1857. [Camp Nelson, U.S. military cemetery was established in 1863].

Other settlers followed, finding it a beautiful area of rich farmland, rolling hills, valleys, river bottoms, unique palisades and flowing spring waters. At the first census taken (1800) the county had 5,461 residents, and they are still coming. The 1990 census recorded 30,508 citizens.

"Jessamine County Kentucky 1798-1993" reprinted with permission of Howard C. Teater, President, Jessamine County Genealogical and Historical Society.

Johnson County

Johnson County is positioned in the Big Sandy Valley of the Cumberland Plateau in eastern Kentucky. The county's 264 square miles are distinguished by a rolling and hilly terrain combined with many broad and level creek bottoms. The county's sandy soil with clay subsoil is said to be the best in eastern Kentucky. The most important waterway is the Levisa Fork of the Big Sandy River. According to tradition, Dr. Thomas Walker, who is credited with discovering the Cumberland Gap, originally named this river the Louisa River in 1750, but the name has evolved to Levisa.

Matthias Tice Harmon and Samuel Auxier were the first white men to erect a permanent structure in the area which is now Johnson County. In 1787 Harmon led approximately 20 people to start a settlement near the site of his original cabin. In a conflict with a Indian scouting party, Harmon killed a well-known brave. The Indians retaliated.

They killed four settlers and captured Jenny Wiley. Months later she escaped and found her way back to Harmon's settlement. Jenny Wiley's abduction and return has become a local legend.

Paintsville, the county seat of Johnson County, was originally called Paint Lick Station. It was founded in 1790 by Col. John Preston, a Virginia land speculator and fur trader, who established a thriving trading post. By 1834 Paint Lick Station was incorporated as the town of Paintsville.

Paintsville grew rapidly. In 1844 Johnson County was created with Paintsville as its county seat. The county was named for Col. Richard M. Johnson, a Kentuckian who had become a national hero in 1813 by killing Chief Tecumseh at the Battle of the Thames. Johnson was elected to the U.S. Senate in 1819 and became vice president of the United States in 1837.

In 1837 steamboat traffic on the Big Sandy River began an era of economic, social and cultural contact with the rest of the nation. Manufactured goods could be delivered, while raw materials such as fur, hides and timber were sent down the river. During the Civil War Johnson County officially took a neutral stand. Nevertheless, some skirmishes did occur.

By 1880 Johnson County still had no banks, no railroad, no telephones, no electricity and no paved roads. In 1890, John C. C. Mayo began buying, leasing, promoting, and selling coal. A new era of economic progress came to Johnson County and eastern Kentucky. In 1917 a boom in oil and gas production and resulting employment swelled the county's population.

Later, as the coal industry waned, new industry was sought. The most successful and most enduring is American Standard, manufacturer of plumbing fixtures.

Begun in 1962 as an event to celebrate the apple-growing industry, the county's week-long Apple Festival annually attracts enormous crowds during the first week in October.

The establishment of Mayo State Technical College in 1938 led to employment opportunities for thousands of young people from Johnson and surrounding counties. In 2005 the college became part of the statewide Kentucky Community and Technical College System.

Contributed by the Johnson County Public Library staff.

> "The county's 264 square miles are distinguished by a rolling and hilly terrain combined with many broad and level creek bottoms. The county's sandy soil with clay subsoil is said to be the best in eastern Kentucky."

Kenton County

Nineteenth in order of formation with 161.97 square miles, the legislature created Kenton County out of Campbell County in 1840 with the Ohio River, Licking River and Dry Creek at its western edge being natural borders. Kenton has had two courthouse centers with most county business always transpiring at Covington, the largest city in Northern Kentucky. However, the county seat of Independence is now a rapidly growing city of new suburbs. In 2000 the Federal census counted 151,464 people in Kenton County.

In the late 18th century Indian fighters congregated at "The Point," a popular rest area for travelers at the confluence of the Ohio and Licking rivers. The Point was in the 200-acre tract purchased from Pennsylvania by Thomas Kennedy who established a prosperous farm, Ohio River ferry and a tavern. In 1814, Kennedy sold 150 acres to developers of Covington. The legislature established the town of Covington in 1815 and the city in 1834. The early town enjoyed a rolling mill, cotton mill, a flourmill, a nearby a hemp factory on the Ohio, a major slaughterhouse and later, another rolling mill on the Licking River. After the Covington and Lexington Railroad opened in 1854 the focus of commercial activity moved from the river.

Fortifications erected from Ludlow to Campbell County around Covington shielded Cincinnati against the Confederate invasion of Kentucky in 1862. Kenton County was predominantly pro-northern with slaves and some free blacks, but also significant Confederate sympathizers.

Financial collapse in 1857 and the Civil War delayed completion of the Roebling Suspension Bridge to 1867. In the 1890s, electric streetcars replaced horse drawn streetcars and linked Covington neighborhoods (and also its Latonia Race Track, 1883-1939) to surrounding cities, suburbs and Cincinnati.

At the turn of the century the

Catholic dioceses built St Mary's Cathedral, a major architectural landmark. Covington saw major infrastructure construction and annexations south and west. After prolonged heavy Irish and German immigration, and Appalachian northern migration for factory jobs, Covington's population in 1930 reached 65,252.

The state legislature and Campbell County Court first developed the Banklick Road south to the Georgetown Road. County leaders developed the new county seat of Independence on this route. At Walton in Boone County, Gaines' old Stagecoach Inn still stands to commemorate this era.

Very early the legislature also ordered a macadamized road in the direction of present-day Florence in Boone County that became the Covington-Lexington Turnpike. Construction of the Cincinnati Southern Railway in the 1870s encouraged the development of Crescent Springs and Erlanger. In 1913 Kenton County began its segment of Dixie Highway with concrete. Restaurants and service stations developed along this corridor through Park Hill, Fort Mitchell, Erlanger and Florence.

After World War II the "new" Latonia Racetrack opened in Boone County as did the Florence Mall and the Northern Kentucky Industrial Park. Some well-known manufacturing and retail businesses relocated out of Covington. Residents moved to new subdivisions built on the county's dwindling number of family farms. This counterbalanced the decline of historical neighborhoods to keep the population growing. The new suburb of Villa Hills overlooking the Ohio River west of Covington, Ludlow and Bromley exemplified the 1960s accelerated suburban lifestyle. Interstate I-75 replaced the Dixie Highway for interstate travel. It is said that the Cincinnati-Northern Kentucky International Airport dating back to World War II primarily has spearheaded Northern Kentucky "growth."

Contributed by John H Boh

Main Strasse Village in Covington
Source: SouthEast Telephone

Knott County

Located in the mountains of eastern Kentucky, Knott County, with its county seat of Hindman, became the 118th Kentucky county in 1884.

Though Knott County was one of the last counties formed in the state, its history reaches far back to the times of the Long Hunters and American Indians with the early settlers moving into the area in the late 1700s.

No serious attempt to write Knott County's history was made in a comprehensive manner until the formation of the Knott County Historical Society in 1994. An attempt to record oral history was made in the 1970s. Unfortunately, since many of those interviewed were not knowledgeable in the areas about which they were questioned, they could only provide a very focused viewpoint mainly about the history of their particular hollows.

History is second nature to the mountaineer, especially in regard to genealogical knowledge. Regrettably, many of the mini-histories published of Knott have been much embellished by outsiders who have used the plight of some of Knott residents primarily for monetary gains. Contrary to these published stereotypical images, Knott Countians descend from a variety of prestigious families. Their ancestors include the earliest Long Hunters who ventured into Kentucky, including Daniel Boone; early American colonists; several presidential lines, including Abraham Lincoln, Zachary Taylor, James Madison; the Washingtons; and even European royal lineages.

Knott County forefathers have fought in every war since the Revolution, and have been termed "true Jeffersonians." Their love of family, politics, religion and marketing kept them from being isolated in the mountains. They traveled back to the original colonies to visit their families who were unable to migrate with them to Kentucky. Their participation in the various wars kept them in touch with the rest of the world; and their love for farming and husbandry encouraged their frequent travels to Lexington, Louisville, Frankfort, Cincinnati, as well as to cities in the deep South.

Early subscriptions to newspapers, the frequency of the mail, and the advent of the telephone in 1895 brought Knott into the world of communications. Residents kept their Elizabethan speech, folklore, and ballads long into the middle of the 20th century, until mass media impacted the region.

Prior to the Civil War the people of Knott County were very industrious and prosperous, but the results of this war still show its effects to this date. The reconstruction of churches, homes and schools (some of which have been in existence since 1828) has been a slow process. Today the best known educational institutions in Knott County are the Hindman Settlement School and Alice Lloyd College.

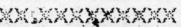

"Though much has been written about the feuds of Eastern Kentucky, a great deal of which has been exaggerated for the sake of yellow journalism, these feuding families were in the minority."

Though much has been written about the feuds of Eastern Kentucky, a great deal of which has been exaggerated for the sake of yellow journalism, these feuding families were in the minority. Most God-fearing mountain people minded their own business and left those men to their own devices. The Knott County Historical Society was created to collect, verify, and preserve the true history of the county's people.

Contributed by David R Smith

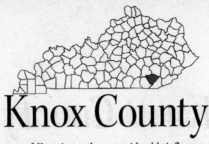

Knox County

Barbourville, the county seat of Knox in southeastern Kentucky, is located in the center of the county on the banks of the Cumberland River and bordered by Richland Creek. Positioned 33 miles north of Cumberland Gap and 15 miles southeast of Corbin, the city is the point where US 25E and KY 11 intersect. After years of suffering from disastrous floods, the city is now protected by a massive floodwall.

In 1750 Dr. Thomas Walker selected a site about six miles southeast of the present location of Barbourville to build the first European settler's house in Kentucky, a requirement by the state of Virginia for staking a claim to the territory.

Dr. Thomas Walker cabin
near Barbourville
Source: Sid Webb

Because Dr. Walker's journal is the first written eyewitness description of the state, it might be argued that documented Kentucky history begins in Knox and its neighboring counties.

Barbourville was created as the county seat of Knox in 1800. The town's basic street design follows closely the initial layout planned in 1801. Barbourville has always enjoyed the advantage of having in its midst elders willing and eager to tell the story of their frontier history and the area's heroic beginnings. This wide appreciation of pioneer Kentucky manifests itself annually in autumn as Barbourville's Daniel Boone Festival.

During the 19th century, Barbourville was the largest and most progressive city south of Richmond, and it was a major stop for settlers and travelers who crossed the Cumberland Gap on an expedition up the Wilderness Road. In the late 1830s and throughout the 1840s the town exercised considerable influence on early state government. One of the nicknames for Barbourville is "Home of Governors," because of the numerous Knox Countians who served as other states' commanders in chief, in addition to two governors of Kentucky, James D. Black and Flem D. Sampson.

In the opening months of the Civil War, Barbourville was the site of the first armed skirmish between Confederate and Union forces in the state and recorded the state's first deaths on either side. At different points in the war, the town was occupied by both military forces, becoming temporary headquarters for Confederate General Kirby Smith in 1862 and hosting Union General U.S. Grant in 1864.

Barbourville experienced boom times in the 1880s and 1890s when railroad expansion opened the hills to coal and timber businesses. Good fields of natural gas and smaller oil deposits furnished incentive for growth in the early 20th century. The founding of Union College, the first college in the mountains, in 1879 continued the town's educational and cultural centrality into the next century.

The Minton Stables, a division of the Minton Hickory Mill, drew worldwide attention to Knox County during the 1920s, as its championship saddlebred horses performed in horse shows across the nation and in Europe. The Hickory Mill was one of the major manufacturers of golf clubs in the 1910s and 1920s, and drew professional golf players, such as Bobby Jones, to visit the company and give public demonstrations.

Contributed by Charles Reed Mitchell

Larue County

"Larue county, the 98th in order of formation, was formed in 1843, out of the southeastern part of Hardin county, and named in honor of John Larue. It is bounded N. by Hardin and Nelson counties, the Rolling fork of Salt river being the dividing line, E. by Marion and Taylor, S. by Hart and Green, and W. by Hardin county, Middle creek forming the dividing line on the N.W. Along the Rolling fork the surface is hilly, being the celebrated Muldrow's Hill; the eastern portion of the county is undulating, and the western is more level; the soil of the latter is red clay, with limestone beneath, while the rolling land is a mulatto clay. The principal products are corn, tobacco, and hogs. Besides the Rolling fork, Nolin (which empties into Green river), its North and South forks, and Otter creek, are the principal streams...

About one mile above Hodgenville on the south side of Nolin creek, there is a *knoll* which may be appropriately termed a natural curiosity. It is about thirty feet above the level of the creek, and contains about two acres of ground, the top of which is level, and a comfortable house has been erected upon it. Benjamin Lynn and others, early pioneers of the county, encamped on this knoll. In a hunting excursion, shortly after they made their encampment, Lynn got lost. The remainder of the company returned to camp, and not finding their companion, some one remarked, "Here is the *Nole* (knoll) but *No Lynn*, from which circumstance the creek which runs hear the knoll took its name—*Nolin*. They immediately started in search of Lynn, and traveled a south course back fifteen miles, and found where he had encamped on a creek, from which circumstance they called the creek *Lynn-camp* creek.

John Larue, for whom the county was named,

emigrated with a considerable company, from Virginia, and settled in Phillips' fort. When they left the fort, Larue bought and settled the land which includes the *knoll*. Robert Hodgen, his brother-in-

Pres. Abraham Lincoln & Son
Source: May 6, 1865 Edition of Harper's Weekly

law, bought and settled the land on which Hodgenville has been erected. They were both noted for their uprightness and sterling moral worth—both of them members of the Baptist church, and beloved for their unobtrusive and devoted piety. Benjamin Lynn was a minister of the same church.

The late president Abraham Lincoln was born in what is now Larue county, two miles S. of Hodgenville, when Larue was a part of Hardin."

An excerpt from pages 456-458 of the entry for "Larue County," Collins' Historical Sketches of Kentucky, History of Kentucky, Vol. II (Southern Historical Press, 1874).

Laurel County

Laurel County was established by an act of the Kentucky General Assembly on December 1, 1825 with its first government taking office early in 1826. It was formed from the surrounding counties of Clay, Rockcastle, Whitley and Knox. It takes its name from the abundant growth of laurel bushes along its creeks and rivers.

the sole transportation route in Kentucky from the south. Blockhouses at various places along the road offered some protection for travelers on the Trace. Wood's Blockhouse, home of John Wood, stood where Boone Trace and Skaggs Trace divided, at a spot called the Hazel Patch, and is said to be the first permanent building in what later became Laurel County.

The Wilderness Road ran through the center of Laurel County, and became the basis for what is now Main Street, London.

John Jackson and his son, Jarvis, donated 25 acres of their own land for the county seat, London, and were active in Laurel County government all their lives. They helped set up the first government and built the first jail and courthouse.

Courthouse
Source: SouthEast Telephone

Laurel County has a land area of 434 square miles, ranking 24th among Kentucky counties. Two historic roads figure prominently in Laurel County's past. The Boone Trace was a well-known packhorse trail from 1775 when Daniel Boone and his company blazed it from Cumberland Gap to Boonesboro and was used until the Wilderness Road was built in 1796. These two routes – often confused as one and the same – were the arteries over which commerce and settlers from Virginia, Pennsylvania, Tennessee and the Carolinas passed through the Cumberland Gap.

Boone Trace was never anything more than a single file path for horses, but for 20 years it was

World Chicken Festival
Source: SouthEast Telephone

Other prominent families in those early days were the Pitmans and the Freemans. It is said that when the time came to name the new seat of government, Pitman, who was Scottish, proposed Edinburgh; Freeman, of Irish descent, wanted Dublin; and Jackson, the Englishman, suggested London. Jackson won, it seems.

To learn more about Laurel County, please visit the Laurel County Historical Society's web site at www.laurelcountyhistoricalsociety.org.
Contributed by Jan Sparkman.

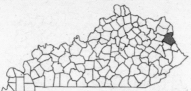

Lawrence County

"Lawrence County, the 69th county formed in Kentucky, dates from 1821. Its territory, comprised of 272,000 acres, was taken from Greenup and Floyd counties. It lies in the extreme eastern part of the state along the Kentucky-West Virginia boundary.

Charles Vancouver of London, England, was issued a patent for a 2,000 acre tract of land by Brit-

munity began to take shape.

Lawrence County was named for James Lawrence, a distinguished American naval officer of the Tripolitan War.

Louisa was established in 1822. It was named for the Louisa (Levisa) Fork of the Big Sandy River, which had been named by Dr. Thomas Walker in honor of the wife of the Duke of Cumberland.

Lawrence County Courthouse
Source: SouthEast Telephone

Paul Patton, 59th governor of Kentucky, was born in Louisa, Ricky Skaggs, popular country music entertainer, is a native of Cordell, in Lawrence County. Ricky's career rises from traditional bluegrass and country roots and has reached around the globe. Ricky is a member of the Grand Ole' Opry and still has family and friends in the area.

Lawrence County's population in 1850 was 6,281. Gradually increasing, it reached 20,067 in 1910. In the years since, the population steadily decreased with the exception of 1940 when it was 17,275. The population started to grow again in the 1970s and 1980s and is now about 15,895 [as of 2005].

ish government in 1772, which contained the present site of Louisa, the county seat. The survey of this grant was made by George Washington during the late 1760s.

Vancouver came to the newly formed United States and settled at the Forks of the Big Sandy in 1789. He erected a fort, built a few cabins and did some farming. However, he abandoned the area because Indians of several tribes used this area as their hunting grounds — until forced out by settlers.

Frederic Moore migrated west to Lawrence County in 1815 and established a trading center at Louisa. Soon after that, the framework for a com-

Yatesville Lake, opened in 1992, has a surface impoundment of 2,242 acres, with 40 miles of shoreline. The lake starts 21 miles upstream from Yatesville Dam and runs along the main stem of Blaine Creek. The Yatesville Lake now offers camping facilities along with a marina that can handle up to 140 boats. And there is a championship golf course now under construction next to the lake. Tourism from the lake helps boost the local economy.

The September Festival, a festival held annually, draws many natives back to enjoy good food, music, crafts and old friends."

Reprinted with the permission of Ruby Arrington.

Lee County

"Lee county, the 115th in order of formation, was established in 1870, out of parts of Breathitt, Estill, Owsley, and Wolfe, and named in honor of the Virginia patriot, Gen. Robert E. Lee. Its territory is among the smallest, and its population, with two exceptions, the smallest of the counties of the state—reaching only 2,924 by the census of 1870. It

Lee County was named in honor of Gen. Robert E. Lee

is bounded N. by Powell and Wolfe counties, E. by Breathitt and Owsley, S. by Owsley, and W. by Estill. It is located on both sides of the main Kentucky river, and includes a large part of the valleys of its South and Middle forks, and their tributaries. The face of the country is hilly and mountainous, while the valleys are rich and in high state of cultivation. Corn, wheat, oats, cattle, and hogs are largely produced, and find a market at home among those engaged in the coal and lumber business…

The Earliest Visitor to any part of what is now Lee county was Dr. Thos. Walker, with his company, in 1750. …The next visitors were the McAfee company, on their return homeward in 1773.
…

Gen Robert E. Lee, in honor of whom Lee county was named, was born in Westmoreland co, Va., Jan. 19, 1807, and died in Lexington, Va., Oct. 12, 1870—aged nearly 64. He was the son of Gen. Henry Lee, better known as "Light Horse Harry Lee," of Revolutionary fame; at 11 years of age he was fatherless; at 18, entered West Point as a cadet and graduated in 1829, without a demerit, second in rank in a class of 46. …

In *Blackwood's* (English) *Magazine* for March 1872, in an article of great power on "General Lee and his Campaign," a contributor maintains that—excepting only Wellington and Marlborough—Lee was the greatest captain who ever spoke with English language. His greatest military error, he maintains, was his failure to attack Gen. Burnside's army on the night of Dec. 13, 1862—after it had been terribly routed in the day. Gen. J.E.B. Steward advised it—inasmuch as Burnside's host, huddled together in and about the little city of Fredericksburg, and with a broad and deep river, spanned only by three pontoon bridges, in its rear, would offer but little resistance. But Lee thought that Burnside was not too much exhausted, and would renew the attack; and so the golden opportunity passed. …"

An excerpt from pages 461-463 of the entry for "Lee County," Collins' Historical Sketches of Kentucky, History of Kentucky, Vol. II (Southern Historical Press, 1874).

Leslie County

Leslie County was created in 1878 from Clay, Harlan, and Perry Counties, as the state's 117th county. It is located in the Eastern Coal Field Region of the state, and was named for Preston Leslie who was governor of Kentucky from 1871-1875.

Hyden, the county seat, is home to the Frontier Nursing Service, a health service organization founded by Mary Breckinridge in 1925. Also located in the county are the Frontier School of Midwifery and Family Nursing and the Leslie County branch of the Hazard Community and Technical College.

Well-known Leslie Countians include: Willie Sandlin, winner of the Medal of Honor in World War I; Mary Breckinridge, health care pioneer; the Osborne Brothers, trailblazers in bluegrass music; and Tim Couch, a former All-American quarterback at the University of Kentucky.

Leslie County's school system is one of the most modern in the state, with computers in every classroom and Internet access in every school.

Most of Leslie County is comprised of the Daniel Boone National Forest. The collaborative efforts of the Rocky Mountain Elk Foundation, Kentucky Dept. of Fish and Wildlife, and the University of Kentucky Department of Forestry led to the "re-introduction" of elk between 1997 and 2001 at two primary locations in Eastern Kentucky, one of which was Leslie County near the Red Bird Wildlife Management Area. In that mostly hilly, wooded setting — with its steep to gentle slopes, bottomlands and ridge tops, ample food, cover and water — the elk have flourished and become the largest herd east of the Mississippi River. Due to the increased local, regional and national interest, efforts are underway to create additional tourism opportunities for wildlife enthusiasts.

Studies are also underway to construct a trail system for motorized off-road vehicles, an increasingly popular pastime and source of revenue for the county. Future plans include the construction of several hundred miles of trails.

Two sites in the county are on the National Historic Register — one is the Big House, home of Mary Breckinridge. It is currently operated as a bed and breakfast. The other is the School of Midwifery and Family Nursing, the oldest and largest school of its kind in the U.S.

Annual events include Wildlife Day, the first Sat-

Fall day on Coon Creek
Source: SouthEast Telephone
Rick Pennington

urday in July; the Osborne Brothers Festival, the first weekend in August; the Mary Breckinridge Festival, the first weekend in October; and the Parade of Lights, the first Friday in December.

Leslie County is also working to fund several new initiatives, including the creation of a Veterans Memorial Cemetery. A recent survey by the Kentucky Department of Veterans Affairs has concluded that Leslie County has one of the best locations for a veterans' cemetery, because it is centrally located between Hazard, London, Middlesboro, and Richmond. The region, known as Southeast Kentucky, boasts one of the largest per capita of veterans in the United States.
Contributed by Mary Ethel Wooten.

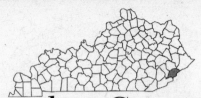

Letcher County

Letcher County was formed in 1842 and was named for Robert P. Letcher, who was the governor of Kentucky at that time. The county seat of Whitesburg is named for U.S. Rep. Daugherty White. Today the area of Letcher County is 339 square miles. In the 2000 census, the population of Letcher County was 25,277.

Letcher County's first schools were called "blab schools" because students recited their lessons aloud. They were held in one-room log buildings with packed earth for floors and stone fireplaces for heat. The two public school systems in the county today are Letcher County and Jenkins Independent Schools. Southeast Community and Technical College is located in Whitesburg, as well.

A number of interesting museums tell the history of Letcher County. They are the David A. Zegeer Coal Railroad Museum in Jenkins, a Coal Miners' Memorial in Jackhorn, a War Memorial Museum in McRoberts and a Veterans Museum in Whitesburg. Other points of interest in the county are the C.B. Caudill Store and History Center in Blackey and the Seco Company Store Bed and Breakfast, home of the Highland Winery in Seco.

There are two local newspapers--"The Mountain Eagle" and "The News Press." The county has four public libraries.

Health care in Letcher County is provided by two community health systems — the Mountain Comprehensive Health Corporation, a primary Health Care Clinic, and the Appalachian Regional Hospital. Both are in Whitesburg.

Recreation opportunities in Letcher County

include Fishpond Lake at Little Laurel Park and Raven Rock Golf Course at Jenkins. The county has a race track and a go-cart track, as well.

During September, Letcher County hosts its Mountain Heritage Festival. Every June Appalshop, Inc. sponsors the "Seedtime on the Cumberlands" festival, famous for music, crafts, theater and films.

The Lillie Cornett Woods is a 554-acre stand of virgin-growth forest, Pound Gap Road Cut is a geological wonder, and Bad Branch Falls State Nature Preserve comprises 2,600 acres on the Cumberland side of Pine Mountain.

Letcher County's Pine Mountain boasts several points of interest. High Rock, atop Pine Moutain, is one of the highest points in the state. Ned's Old Rock House, also at the top of Pine Mountain, was used as a hideout during the Civil War. The Bull Hole is a "bottomless" hole associated with local legends. Rainbow Rock is a natural bridge with a 25-foot arch. Bad Branch Falls plunges for a distance of 165 feet. At Seven Springs near Bad Branch Falls, water bubbles up from clear mountain springs. On top of Pine Mountain is Raven Rock,the point from which Daniel Boone looked down upon the gorgeous hill country of Letcher County. Civil War soldiers used Raven Rock as a lookout post.

John Fox, Jr. was inspired by the land and people of Letcher County to write "Trail of the Lonesome Pine" in 1908 and "The Little Shepherd of Kingdom Come" in 1903. The Little Shepherd Trail runs through the Pine Mountain Wildlife Management Area.

Contributed by Merlene Davis

Woodworker at Seedtime Festival
Source: SouthEast Telephone

Lewis County

In 1794 the first salt wells were dug in Salt Lick Creek near Vanceburg by John Vance, Moses Baird and John Heath. In 1797, Vanceburg was founded and named for John Vance. The land was bought and divided into lots and sold. John Vance and Moses Baird later moved to Ohio where John Vance's son later became governor.

The General Assembly of the Commonwealth passed on Dec. 2, 1806, an act for the division of Mason County, establishing a new county called Lewis.

The first county seat was at Poplar Flat and its first court was held at the house of Oke Hendrickson by the following magistrates: Landen Clavert, George Fearis, Aaron Stratton, John G. McDowell, George Brown, Hugh Hannah, John Doyle and John Stephenson. The first sheriff was Plummer Thomas; the first county clerk, Walker Reid; first county attorney, John G. Heath; and first coroner, Samuel Cox.

In 1809 Rowland T. Parker built a new jail at Clarksburg and gave land for the town of Clarksburg, which became the county seat until December 1863. In January 1864 the county offices were moved to Vanceburg, and the archives of the county were placed in the old city hall on Main Street. Then came the rush of attorneys, court attaches, fortune hunters and adventurers, and Vanceburg rapidly rose from an old meadow, surrounded by swamps, to an incorporated city.

On Jan. 30, 1864, an act was passed by the legislature empowering the county to issue bonds and levy taxes for the purpose of building a new courthouse. The cost of the new courthouse was $25,000, and it was finished in 1865.

In 1939, the old courthouse was torn down and a new courthouse built in the same place. In 2000 it was decided to build a new justice building beside the courthouse. All of the court system was moved to the new building. The courthouse has been renovated with the clerk's office expanding and taking in the sheriff's old office.

In 1795 the Ebenezer Church, also called Cabin Creek Church, was begun in the part of Lewis County now known as Wilson Bottoms on the Ohio River. In the year 1833 or 1834 a new house of worship was built and was moved to a more centralized location. The present edifice was built in 1876. An old cemetery is there by the church. The Ebenezer Cemetery is still receiving bodies today.

East Fork Church was founded in 1802; a rude log cabin was built two miles east of the East Fork Creek, a tributary of Little Cabin Creek. The church doubled as a school and was the focal point of social activities. In 1858 a better log structure was built. In 1933 the members felt a need for a more modern building. The present Church at East Fork was dedicated in 1939 when the indebtedness was cleared. There is a large cemetery around the church where people have been burying since its beginning. It is still receiving bodies today.

The Lewis County Historical Society is open each Friday and Saturday from 11:00 a.m. to 3:00 p.m. It is located in Vanceburg, Kentucky at 318 Lexington Ave. The mailing address is Lewis County Historical Society, PO Box 275, Garrison, Kentucky 41141.

Contributed by Joan Godfrey

Meriwether Lewis

Lincoln County

Lincoln County is one of the original counties formed from Kentucky County, Virginia in 1780 by the Virginia legislature. The county was named for American Revolutionary War General Benjamin Lincoln. The second oldest permanent settle-

William Whitley House
Source: Sid Webb

ment was established in 1775 by Benjamin Logan, founder of Lincoln County, and this settlement would later become Stanford, the county seat. Earliest slaves known in Lincoln County were Molly Logan and her three sons: Matt, Dave and Isaac. They came into Kentucky with Logan and helped build Logan's Fort.

William Whitley, Indian fighter and horseman, was an original inhabitant of Logan's Fort. Legends tell that it was Whitley that killed the infamous Tecumseh at the Battle of the Thames in the War of 1812. Dislike for the British moved him to build a racecourse out of clay in 1788 and raced the horses counterclockwise, opposite of all English racetracks until 1861.

The first two sessions of the Lincoln County court were held at Harrodsburg but were moved to St. Asaph in 1781. In February 1781 Benjamin Logan offered 10 acres of land including the Buffalo Spring for the building of a courthouse, which is now located in the old section of the Buffalo Springs Cemetery. This courthouse was later moved to Stanford and placed on lands conveyed by Benjamin Logan.

Lincoln County played a major role in Kentucky's statehood. All constitutional conventions were held in Danville, located in Lincoln County [now Boyle County], from 1785 through 1792 when the first constitution of Kentucky would be framed. Isaac Shelby would become the first governor of Kentucky. Today his home site, Traveler's Rest, and the cemetery are located on Knob Lock Pike in Lincoln County. This is one of the first turnpikes developed in Kentucky by Isaac Shelby.

In 1800 the population of the county was 8,621, a 2,000 increase over 10 years. Lincoln County would be known for its agricultural production: horses, mules, milk cows, oxen, tobacco, wool, hemp, butter and cheese. Manufacturing was not extensive. The first steam-powered mill was Buffalo Mill, built in 1848 on Hustonville Road near the old Cave Spring just west of Stanford. The structure was four stories high and the millstones were imported from France.

Crab Orchard Springs was a world renowned spa in 1827. Located at the tavern called the Sign of the Golden Bell in the village of Crab Orchard, it was common to have 400 to 500 guests present during the tourist season. In the summer of 1858 John Hunt Morgan and his Lexington Rifles visited Crab Orchard and the group drilled and gave military reviews to the delighted guests. By 1930 the resort was forced to close from the lack of patrons.

Caswell Saufley contributed to the American history of aviation. His accomplishments in the U.S. Navy as a skillful navigator and aviator made a mark in history for this young man from Lincoln County. Today, Saufley Field near Pensacola, Florida, is named in his honor for bringing the U.S. Navy into the modern era of aviation.

Contributed by the Lincoln County Historical Society.

Livingston County

Livingston County, created by the legislature in May, 1798, was formed from Christian County.

The first description included what is now all counties of the Jackson Purchase area: Livingston, Crittenden and portions of Caldwell and Lyon counties. Livingston County, the 29th county formed, was named for Robert R. Livingston of New York, a distinguished statesman. The first county seat of Livingston was in Eddyville where court was held at the home of Daniel Walker. It was later moved to Centerville, on land now in Caldwell County.

In April 1809 the records were sent to Salem, and Salem was the county seat until 1842.

Smithland has been the county seat since 1842.

Record books and papers dated from 1799, lodged in the courthouse, reveal many interesting facts of Livingston county and its people. The courthouse, built in 1842, still stands as one of the most historic land marks in Smithland and Livingston county. There are still several old homes in Smithland. The Gower House still stands. It was built in the early 1800s as a luxury inn on the Ohio and Cumberland rivers, enjoyed by visitors and celebrities alike.

Livingston County is surrounded by rivers. Hamlets on the Ohio were Bayou, Berry's Ferry, Birdsville and the larger town of Carrsville. On the Cumberland, current and former hamlets include Luka, Vicksburg, Tiline and Pickenyville. Ledbetter is near the Tennessee River. Other places are Salem, Grand Rivers, Lola, Joy, Burna and Hampton. Grand Rivers is the gateway to Between the Rivers,

which is a plot of land between the Tennessee and Cumberland rivers.

As travelers pass through the historic town of Smithland and the hamlet of Birdsville, few are aware that they are within a short distance of the grave of the younger sister of one of our greatest Americans and presidents, Thomas Jefferson. She was Lucy Jefferson Lewis, wife of Dr. Charles L. Lewis, brother of Meriwether Lewis. In 1811, Lucy

Kentucky Lake dam
Source: U.S. Army Corps of Engineers

J. Lewis was buried near her home in Livingston County. A few months afterwards, her two sons, Lilburn and Isham, were involved in a tragedy. The brothers murdered an African American servant and then dismembered his body. Both Lilburn and Isham were arrested for the crime, but neither was brought to trial. Lilburn later died from a gunshot wound and Isham disappeared.

Two limestone rock quarries, one being the largest in the world, are in operation near Burna and Grand Rivers. Long past are the flourspar mines that were in operation for many years.

Livingston County has had many historical and fascinating events.

Contributed by Mary Lou Smith

Logan County

In 1780 Logan County was the 13th county formed in Kentucky . It was named after Gen. Benjamin Logan, among the earliest pioneers into the "howling wilderness' of Kentucky. Born of Irish parents in Virginia, Gen. Logan was a distinguised officer of the Revolutionary War. The county seat of Logan County is Russellville.

This fertile land in the Pennyroyal region of western Kentucky attracted early settlers from Vir-

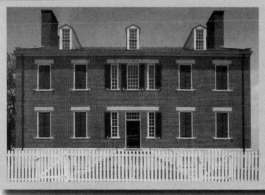

Centre family dwelling, Shaker Village and Museum at South Union
Source: Kentucky Department of Tourism

ginia, North Carolina and the East, who brought with them a high degree of education and culture. Remarkable in their achievements as artists and craftsmen, they put down roots to blend a political, economic, and social environment unique, perhaps, only to Logan County.

As one of Kentucky's oldest counties, Logan's long and colorful history included four Kentucky governors, famous and infamous heroes and a legacy of historic sites and events. The Great Revival of 1800 began at the Red River Meeting House in Logan County. Andrew Jackson fought a duel in Logan County and Jesse James robbed the Southern Deposit Bank in downtown Russellville.

Twelve miles east of Russellville is Shakertown

at South Union, where members of the United Society of Believers on Christ's Second Appearing (Shakers) lived from 1807 to 1922.

During the Civil War when Logan Countians' loyalties were divided between the North and the South, the Confederate Government of Kentucky was organized in Logan County.

Today Logan County offers visitors a variety of pleasant experiences. Those interested in history can seek out the Red River Meeting House, site of the Great Revival of 1800, or tour the Bibb House, an excellent example of antebellum life. Other interesting sites to tour are the Auburn Museum for a journey through the 19th century, the Shaker Museum at South Union, the Saddle Factory Museum, the Schochoh Rosenwald One Room School Museum and the Old Jail and Genealogical Archives.

Others may prefer to stroll through antique and gift shops, tour a winery or take a historic walking tour.

Those who favor the outdoors might choose to fish or boat on beautiful Lake Malone, canoe down the Red River or hike through prairie grass in Logan County's Glade State Nature Preserve.

Overnight accommodations in Logan County include two nationally affiliated motels and several bed and breakfasts. One bed and breakfast provides a Victorian atmosphere while another is a log house. For a leisurely meal, diners may choose to eat overlooking the lake or pick up some of Logan County's famous barbecue.

Many special events and festivals take place annually. Russellville is within 30 minutes of Bowling Green and Clarksville and approximately one hour from Nashville.
Contributed by the Logan County Chamber of Commerce.

Lyon County

Located in the Pennyrile region of Kentucky, Lyon County was formed in 1854. The county is named in honor of Col. Matthew Lyon, born in Wickliffe, Ireland in 1746. The county seat is Eddyville.

Kentucky Dam was constructed on the Tennessee River by the TVA during the early 1940s at the same time as WWII. In the late 1950s and early 1960s, Lyon County was forever changed when the

ing communities in western Kentucky. Amenities will include resorts, campgrounds, marinas, restaurants, golfing, a water park, a fun park (complete with go-carts and laser-tag), riding stables, and many more attractions for people of all ages.

Other attractions include the Lyon County Museum located in the Cobb House, a federal home built in 1832 that is listed on the National

BRANCH PENITENTIARY, Eddyville, Ky.

Source: Kentucky Historical Society

U.S. Army Corps of Engineers started buying property below the 378-foot sea level for the building of Barkley Dam to create Lake Barkley. The Dam measures 157 feet high and 10,180 feet wide, and allows boats and barges to move through its 1,200-foot locks. The project required the relocation of Eddyville and Kuttawa. Eddyville was moved 5-1/2 miles from the old town, and Kuttawa was moved approximately one mile.

At 134 miles long with 1,004 miles of shore line, Lake Barkley was fully impounded in 1966. It has since become a popular tourist destination for boating, swimming, fishing and camping. Many new roads, subdivisions and businesses are being built, making Lyon County one of the fastest grow-

Register of Historic Places. Also, the Kentucky State Penitentiary is a local landmark, known to natives as "The Castle on the Cumberland." The hulking stone building is more than 100 years old and attracts visitors and photographers year round.

The Lyon County School System has one of the highest attendance rates in the state, and the high school ranks in the top 20 in all content areas in state school testing.

Eddyville is home to Seapac Inc., a manufacturer of plastics and chemicals, and Kuttawa Plastics. Tourism is Lyon County's number one industry.
Contributed by Lyon County Chamber of Commerce & Lyon County Joint Tourism Commission.

Madison County

It has been said that in the east there is Eden and in the west there is Kentucky, and deeply embedded in Kentucky is Madison County. Named after the illustrious Virginia statesman James Madison, the county is a study in geographical and cultural contrasts. At one side it touches the rolling Appalachian

Madison County Courthouse
Source: Sid Webb

mountains, and on the other the lush Bluegrass.

The pages of Madison County's history are filled with colorful personalities and exciting events. Not far from Interstate 75 is the old frontier Wilderness Trail on which legendary Daniel Boone and other pioneers traveled to establish Fort Boonesborough in 1775.

Perhaps no other leader dominated the country's early history more than Green Clay, the classic

example of a self-made entrepreneur, who served as a model for aspiring farmers and businessmen. As a member of the county court for nearly forty years, Clay used his political power to develop a vast economic empire which included large estates, ferries, taverns and toll roads.

During the antebellum period the region was primarily pro-slavery in its sentiment; however, it saw the establishment of an antislavery colony at Berea in the violent and turbulent 1850s by the radical abolitionist missionary John G. Gee and the emancipationist Cassius M. Clay. The county also witnessed major battles during both the American Revolution and the Civil War, including the Battle of Richmond in 1862.

Madison County was the birthplace of Cassius M. Clay; Kit Carson; African American man-of-letters, Henry Allen Laine; associate justice of the U.S. Supreme Court, Samuel Freeman Miller; women's rights leaders, Laura Clay and Belle H. Bennett; and five governors.

Cassius Clay
*Source: The New York Public Library,
Astor, Lenox and Tilden Foundations.*

In the 21st century Madison County continues to be known for its institutions of higher education such as Berea College and Eastern Kentucky University, its stable agricultural economy, light industrial development, tourism, and the production of handmade arts and crafts.

Madison County Historical Society brochure; reprinted with permission by Charles Hays, Pres. Madison County Historical Society.

Magoffin County

"Magoffin county, established in 1860 out of parts of Morgan, Johnson and Floyd counties, was named in honor of Beriah Magoffin, then governor. It was the 108th formed in the state. It is situated on the head waters of Licking river, and extends over on to the waters of Big Sandy; the Licking for 60 miles dividing it nearly centrally from S.E. to N.W. It is bounded N. by Morgan and Johnson counties, E. by Johnson and Floyd, S. by Breathitt, and W. by Breathitt and Morgan. The valleys or bottom-lands are rich and quite productive; the face of the country generally is broken and hilly; its minerals are iron ore and coal of a fine quality. The principal streams are Johnson's, Lick, Stateroad, Middle, and Burning Spring forks, and Oakley creek. ...

Magoffin County was first settled about 1800, by emigrants originally from South Carolina — John Williams, Archibald Prather, Clayton Cook, Ebenezer Hanna, and a few others. Some of them had previously attempted a settlement in 1794, but were driven back by Indians. ...

During the late Civil War, on the morning of Nov. 30, 1863, Capt. Peter Everett, with about 200 Confederates, surprised a company of Federals, stationed at Salyersville and on Licking Station hill — killing 1 lieutenant, wounding 4 or 5 privates, and capturing 25 prisoners and 40 horses.

Ex-Gov. Beriah Magoffin, after whom this county was named, was born in Harrodsburg, Mercer co., Ky., April 18, 1815, and is therefore (1873) 58 years old. He still lives on the farm inherited from his father, of the same name, who was from County Down, Ireland. His mother was a granddaughter of Samuel McAfee, one of the original McAfee company who visited Kentucky in 1773 and who settled permanently in 1775. He graduated at Centre College, Danville, 1835; at the Lexington law school, 1938; began the practice of law at Jackson, Mississippi, where he made money rapidly; was reading clerk of the senate of Mississippi, 1838-39; returned in bad health in summer of 1839, and settled at Harrodsburg, in partnership with his brother-in-law, Chas. M. Cunningham, whose death soon after

left him with a heavy and lucrative practice; married Anna N. Shelby, daughter of Isaac Shelby, and granddaughter of Gov. Isaac Shelby, April, 1840; although a Democrat, was appointed police judge of Harrodsburg, by Gov. Robert P. Letcher, (Whig),

Beriah Magoffin, after whom this county was named, was born in Harrodsburg, Mercer co., Ky., April 18, 1815, and is therefore (1873) 58 years old. He still lives on the farm inherited from his father, of the same name, who was from County Down, Ireland.

1840-42; was elected to the senate of Kentucky, without opposition, 1850; offered the nomination for congress, 1851, but declined; Democratic candidate for lieutenant governor in 1855 against the Know Nothings, but defeated by 3,674 votes — but was elected governor in 1859, for 4 years, by 1,804 votes over Joshua F. Bell. ..."

An excerpt from pages 536-537 of the entry for "Magoffin County," Collins' Historical Sketches of Kentucky, History of Kentucky, Vol. II (Southern Historical Press, 1874).

Marion County

Marion County, created in 1834 from the southern part of Washington County, is in the geographical center of Kentucky. It contains approximately 343 square miles. Marion was the 84th county in the state and named for Gen. Francis Marion of Revolutionary fame.

Incorporated towns include Lebanon, Loretto, Bradfordsville and Raywick. Other communities include Calvary, Gravel Switch, Holy Cross, St. Mary, St. Joe, Phillipsburg, Jessetown and New Market. The settlers came largely from Virginia and Maryland.

In 1776 James Sandusky built a station on Pleasant Run six miles northeast of Lebanon. In 1778, Samuel Cartwright erected a station 3.5 miles north of Lebanon on the creek that bears his name. Peter Bradford settled what is now Bradfordsville.

In 1785, 60 Catholic families from Maryland, mostly residents of St. Mary's County, each pledged to immigrate to Kentucky. About 25 families, led by Basil Hayden, settled on Pottinger's Creek in 1785 in what is now Holy Cross. He donated land on which the first Catholic church west of the Allegheny Mountains was built in 1792.

Farming was for nearly 200 years the main occupation. Mills were founded on various streams. Blacksmith shops and distilleries sprung up all over the county. Grain, liquor and other products were floated down the Rolling Fork to Salt River and on to New Orleans. Hunting, trapping and fishing not only provided food, but also fur for trading. Raising horses and mules was a profitable business before, during and after the Civil War.

In Marion County, records show that there are now about 1,500 farms averaging 140 acres. Marion County has only in the past 30 years become a thriving industrialized county, now with 31 factories. Maker's Mark Distillery is the oldest continuously-operated distiller in America. It is a national historic landmark and the county's greatest tourist attraction.

Marion County has a private school at St. Augustine in Lebanon, serving kindergarten through eighth grade. St. Mary's College opened in 1821 and closed in 1976. Many influential people received their education there.

Marion County Courthouse
Source: SouthEast Telephone

The Loretto Sisters, a religious order, was founded by Father Charles Nerinckx in 1812, near St. Charles Church in St. Mary. In 1824 they moved to their present Motherhouse near Loretto. They operated a boarding school for girls in Loretto and an academy at Calvary from 1816-1900.

J. Proctor Knott was born near Cherry Run in Raywick in 1830. He served as governor from 1883-1887. Martin John Spalding was born in Calvary in 1810; he was named bishop of Louisville in 1848 and archbishop of Baltimore in 1864. Edwin Carlille Litsey was named poet laureate of Kentucky in 1954. Wallace Kelly, a noted artist and writer, received the Knopp Fellowship Award in fiction in 1941 for his novel "Days are as Grass." Michael Lanham was named a Rhodes Scholar in 1999.
Contributed by Veronica Hill.

Marshall County

"Marshall county, the 92nd formed in the state, was organized June 7, 1842, out of the northern part of Calloway county, and named in honor of Chief Justice John Marshall, then recently deceased. It is situated in the extreme S.W., and is part of the Jackson purchase; is bounded N. by Livingston and Lyon counties, E. by Lyon and Trigg, S. by Calloway, and W. by Graves and McCracken. Its N. and E. boundary line is the Tennessee river; the East fork of Clark's river passes centrally through it, from N.W. to S.E.; other streams are the West fork of Clark's river, and Jonathan, Cypress, Bear, and Sugar creeks. It contains 328 square miles of land, or 209,920 acres, generally level; the soil in good, of the quarternary formation, and the timber of every variety, and excellent; the river bottoms are about two miles wide, and quite fertile. The principal productions are corn, oats, wheat, and tobacco...

John Marshall, chief justice of the United States, was born in Virginia, on Sept. 24, 1755; and as early as the summer of 1775, received a commission as lieutenant of a company of minute-men, and was shortly afterwards engaged in the battle of Great Bridge, when the British troops under Lord Dunmore were repulsed with great gallantry. He was subsequently engaged in the memorable battles of Brandywine, Germantown, and Monmouth, and in 1780 obtained a license to practice law. He returned to the army shortly after, and continued in the service until the termination of Arnold's invasion.

In the spring of 1782, he was elected a member of the state legislature, and in the autumn of the same year a member of the executive council. He married in 1783. In 1788 he was elected to represent the city of Richmond in the legislature, and continued to occupy that station during the years 1789, 1790, 1791, and upon the recall of Mr. Monroe as minister to France, Pres. Washington solicited Mr. Marshall to accept the appointment as his succes-

John Marshall, Chief Justice of the United States (1801)

sor, but he respectfully declined. In 1799 he was elected and took his seat in congress, and in 1800 was appointed secretary of war.

On the 31st of January, 1801, he became chief justice of the supreme court of the United States, which distinguished station he continued to fill with unsullied dignity and pre-eminent ability until the close of his mortal career. He died at Philadelphia on the 6th of July, 1835."

An excerpt from pages 542-544 of the entry for "Marshall County," Collins' Historical Sketches of Kentucky, History of Kentucky, Vol. II (Southern Historical Press, 1874).

Martin County

Martin County Kentucky is located in the far eastern part of Kentucky. It was carved from four other counties, Pike, Floyd, Johnson and Lawrence Counties on Sept. 1, 1870, becoming the 116th county of Kentucky. The county was named in honor of Senator John Martin. It lies at the foot of the Appalachian Mountains and consists of 231 miles of rugged mountain terrain that elevates to 1,500 feet above sea level.

The Tug River flows down the eastern part and

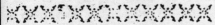

> ### Recreation in the area revolves around the county's scenic landscape — hiking, horseback riding and biking are just a few available options.

separates the county from West Virginia. Martin County's resources are mainly mineral, timber, coal and farming. The county has consolidated its schools to one high school, two middle schools, two elementary schools and a Kentucky Tech School.

In 1766 George Washington surveyed the area along the Tug River and wrote in his journal about the rich resources. By the late 1700s and early 1800s, settlers were drawn to the area by the virgin wilderness that could supply all their material needs. Pioneer James Ward, who had traveled and encountered adventures with "Walker and Boone," returned in 1810 with his family in the area of what is now Inez.

In 1870, Warfield, being the only township, became the county seat. The citizens rallied for a more central location, which happened to be a large fertile cornfield called "Arminta's Bottom" owned by Ward's daughter-in-law. The new town was christened Eden, due to its natural beauty, and was built on the cornfield. The name was later changed to Inez, because Kentucky already had a post office named Eden. In 1873 the county seat was moved there.

There are many villages in historic Martin County. Himlerville, now Beauty, was noted for its Hungarian miners and the vast amount of coal production during the 1920s. Pigeon Roost and Turkey Creek are named for the many pigeons and turkeys in the area. Indians named Rockhouse for the cave-like rocks under which they took shelter.

Several mining companies are large employers in the area and their use of safe and modern equipment has allowed the land to be reclaimed and reused. The Big Sandy Airport and the Big Sandy Penitentiary are built on reclaimed land and serve as examples of these technological advancements.

Recreation in the area revolves around the county's scenic landscapes — hiking, horseback riding and biking are just a few available options. The Milo Lake offers a variety of water activities. Also, Col. Barrett's mansion, in Warfield, and Himler's mansion in Beauty are open to the public for tours. And, the vast resources of deer, elk and turkey make the county a destination for hunters.

In addition to Route 40, a number of other scenic routes lead visitors into Kentucky's westward interior. These roads are carved through mountain rock that are a wonder to imagine and beautiful to see. A four-lane highway to West Virginia is being built.

The county has a community center that boasts four theaters, a gym, inside walking track and three levels of other activities. There are many cafes, restaurants and motels in the county.

Looking for something different to do? Be sure to visit Martin County, Ky., for an unforgettable adventure.

Contributed by Evelynn Cassady, President, Martin County Historical Society

Mason County

Mason County, Kentucky's eighth county, currently spans 241 square miles and is located along the Ohio River 60 miles northeast of Lexington. It was established by the Virginia Legislature on May 1, 1789. The county was named for a Virginian, George Mason, author of the 1776 Virginia Declaration of Rights, which was the foundation for the U.S. Bill of Rights.

The exploration and settlement of Mason County began with French and English fur traders. Christopher Gist and John Filson kept records of their trips to the area. Mary Ingles was the first white woman in the county as she fled from American Indian captors along the Ohio River. Simon Kenton and Daniel Boone surveyed the land and later resided in the county.

Mason County was the northern counterpart of the Cumberland Gap as a point of entry into Kentucky and the west. Limestone Creek provided an excellent landing place for settlers' flatboats; the North Fork of the Licking River provided water for farming. A buffalo trace provided relatively easy access to interior parts of the state. The rich cane land drew many settlers from the East.

Simon Kenton raised the first corn crop there in 1775. Hemp — and later tobacco — became major crops. Maysville was the second largest burley market in the world. Cattle and swine were also important commodities. Steamboats were a boon for Mason County, bringing in trade goods from New Orleans and settlers from Europe.

Originally called Limestone, Maysville was named in 1790 in memory of John May, a casualty of an Indian conflict. Washington, established in 1786, is said to be the first town named for George Washington. Washington was the county seat of Mason until 1848 when that designation was moved to Maysville.

The county historical association received its charter in 1878, making it the oldest historical organization in continuous existence in the state. Education was important from the earliest times and the first school opened in 1790.

The Washington Opera House, built in 1884, is being restored as a live theater. The Rosemary Clooney Music Festival is an annual event and proceeds are used to restore the Russell Theater (a grand 1930s movie theater) to its original glory.

U.S. Supreme Court Justice Stanley F. Reed, renowned singer Rosemary Clooney, and Heather French Henry, Miss America 2000, are from Mason County.

Mason County Courthouse
Source: SouthEast Telephone

The county is a shopping hub for surrounding counties in southern Ohio and Ky., with easy access provided by a good highway system and a local airport. Students attend the Mason County Schools, St. Patrick School, Highland Christian School, the Downing Performing Arts Academy and the Maysville Community and Technical College.

As agricultural diversification has expanded, tobacco has diminished as a cash crop. Browning-Emerson EPT, a power transmission company, is a major employer. Other industries include Temple-Inland Corporation, East-Kentucky Power Cooperative, Stober Drives, and Mitsubishi. Cultural and agritourism are thriving parts of the local economy. Murals of historic events painted on the floodwall are part of the attraction.

Contributed by Sue Ellen Grannis

McCracken County

"McCracken county—in the extreme W. part of the state, one of the earliest counties of the territory known as Jackson's Purchase (see Volume I. of Collins' Historical Sketches)—was established out of part of Hickman county in 1824, and named in honor of Capt. Virgil McCracken. It was the 78th formed in the state, was organized Jan. 17, 1825, and contains 237 square miles. It is bounded N. by the Ohio river, N.E. by the Tennessee river, which separates it from Livingston

Postcard from Paducah
Source: SouthEast Telephone

county, S.E. by Marshall for 8 miles, S. by Graves for 18 miles, and W. by Ballard county. Besides the rivers named, it is watered by Clark's river and Island creek, tributaries of the Tennessee, Mayfield creek, of the Mississippi, and Massac, Willow, Newton's, and Perkins' creeks, and Spring Bayou, which empty into the Ohio. The country is level, and with but little of any thing like stone; the soil of medium quality, except the river bottoms which are very productive. Tobacco is the great staple.

Towns—Paducah, the county seat, is the 5th

city in the state in population and importance; is situated on the Ohio, immediately below the mouth of the Tennessee river . . . was laid out in 1827 by Gen. Clark, of St. Louis and named after the celebrated Indian chief, Paducah, who was buried on the bank of the Tennessee river now in the city; incorporated as a town Jan. 11, 1830, and as a city March 10, 1856. . . .

Capt. Virgil McCracken, in honor of whom this county was named, was a native of Woodford co., Ky. His father, Cyrus McCracken, one of the first adventurers to that region, in conjunction with Hancock Lee, raised cabins one mile below Frankfort, on the east side of the Kentucky river, and named the place Leestown; and lost his life, Nov. 4, 1782, in Gen. George Rogers Clark's expedition against the Piqua towns, to avenge the terrible battle of the Blue Licks. Capt. McCracken was an intelligent, patriotic, and fearless young man. In 1812, he raised a company of riflemen, for the regiment of the brilliant Col. John Allen; and fell at the head of his company, in the battle of the river Raisin, Jan. 22, 1813, while bravely maintaining the honor of his native state on that fatal field."

An excerpt from pages 593-595 of the entry for "McCracken County," Collins' Historical Sketches of Kentucky, Vol. II (Southern Historical Press, 1874).

McCreary County

McCreary County, the 120th and last county in order of formation, is located in south-central Kentucky between the Big South Fork and the main body of the Cumberland River. It was created in 1912 from parts of Pulaski, Wayne, and Whitley counties and is bordered by those counties, by Laurel County, and by the Tennessee state line. The county contains 427 square miles. Although intensely loyal to the Union in the Civil War and overwhelmingly Republican, the county was named for a Confederate army veteran and two-time Democratic governor, James B. McCreary (1875-79, 1911-15).

For the most part, the county is less than 1,500 feet above sea level. Sandstone, which underlies the surface, has led to a terrain of narrow ridges and deep ravines, numerous waterfalls and sandstone arches. Coal production began early in the nineteenth century, and the area led the state in the production of coal from 1836 until 1865.

In 1902 a new group of entrepreneurs arrived, headed by Justus S. Stearns. Well educated and well financed, they built within thirteen months of their arrival a new town named Stearns, an electrical generating plant, America's first all-electric saw-mill, five miles of railroad through rugged terrain, and the first of many mines.

The industrial activity in an area inaccessible to county seats led to the creation of McCreary County, under a resolution by state Sen. William B. Creekmore of Pine Knot. After two elections bitterly contested between the northern and southern parts of the new county, Whitley City was chosen as the county seat.

The first mention of the area in a newspaper probably occurred in 1819 when the Frankfort Argus of Western America reported the discovery of oil on the Big South Fork of the Cumberland River by congressman Martin Beatty. The oil well was Kentucky's first and according to the late newspaper writer Joe Creason, America's oldest commercial well.

The mining and lumber industries grew rapidly after the turn of the century, and the county was quite prosperous until after World War II. The purchase by the federal government of over seventy

> In 1902 America's first all-electric saw-mill opened in Stearns. The oil well on the Big South Fork of the Cumberland River (1819) was Kentucky's first and according to the late newspaper writer Joe Creason, America's oldest commercial well.

percent of the land area of McCreary to form part of the Daniel Boone National Forest and the Big South Fork River and Recreation Area slowed lumber production in a county that once boasted the state's largest lumberyard. With the demise of the coal and timber industries, McCreary's unemployment figures have been among the worst in Kentucky.

Big South Fork River and Recreation Area [was created] in 1974. The restoration of the Blue Heron Mining Community and the Big South Scenic Railway have brought many visitors to the county. The business section of old Stearns has been placed on the National Registry of Historic Places, and the offices of the Stearns Coal & Lumber Company (1907) is now occupied by the Stearns Museum.

FRANK C. THOMAS

Summary excerpt reprinted with permission of The University Press of Kentucky, The Kentucky Encyclopedia, John Kleber, Ed., The University Press of Kentucky (Lexington 1992).

McLean County

McLean County, Kentucky's 103rd county, was formed January 28, 1854, from parts of Daviess, Muhlenberg and Ohio Counties. It was named for Alney McLean, a surveyor, Representative and Circuit Court Judge. Four towns within the county have mayors and boards: Calhoun, the county seat, Livermore, Sacramento and Island, each with an interesting history. The Green River

McLean County Courthouse
Source: Sid Webb

bisects the county and is used for recreation and barge transportation. Bridges are located at Highway 81 through Calhoun and Highway 431 at Livermore.

Three businesses have the distinction of being more than one hundred years old: Muster Funeral Home in Calhoun and Livermore, Sacramento Deposit Bank, and the McLean County News in Calhoun. Other employers in the county include the Board of Education, Twin Rivers Inc. for wooden industrial furniture, and Tyson, with an established chicken hatchery. A listing of existing county businesses is published by the McLean County News, the weekly paper, and is available at the Chamber of Commerce office. An active Industrial Foundation is always searching for ways to bring jobs into the county. McLean benefits from industrial parks in neighboring counties, realizing

tax dollars as well as sharing in the employment opportunities.

Tourism is becoming an attraction, notably the Civil War Battle of Sacramento re-enactment in May, Thunder on the Green Boat Races in August at Livermore, and the Island Wooden Bridge Festival in September. The annual county fair in July acts as a homecoming for native McLean County people living elsewhere.

The McLean County History and Genealogy Museum was established in 2001 and is located at 540 Main Street, Calhoun. The Prentice Smith Home was donated by the Smith Family and is being renovated as funds become available. The house is one of the oldest in Calhoun, dating back to the early 1850s. It is open Monday afternoons from 1 p.m. to 3 p.m., except holidays.

Some of the county's active service clubs and organizations include: Lions Clubs, Chamber of Commerce, Industrial Foundation, VFW, American Legion, Red Cross, Boy Scouts and Girl Scouts, Main Street Renaissance, Audubon Area Community Service, Help Office, 4-H Clubs, Kentucky State Extension Offices, senior citizens groups, McLean County Fair Board and a church sponsored food and clothing pantry. Churches of several faiths serve residents.

The educational system consists of the McLean County High School, County Middle School and elementary schools in Calhoun, Livermore and Sacramento. Parent participation and academics are emphasized and sports are an integral part of the schools, with playgrounds operating during summer months.

Real estate for housing, good schools and country living appeals to many people, making McLean County an attractive place to live and rear a family. Most of the county is now served by city water lines and electric rates are reasonable. Natural gas service is available in some of the towns.

When taking a drive, get off the beaten path and visit this scenic, rural county.
Contributed by Helen Anderson.

Meade County

"Meade county, the 76th in order of formation, was established in 1823, out of parts of Hardin and Breckinridge counties, and named in honor of Capt. James Meade. It is situated in the N. W. middle part of the state; is bounded N. and N.W. for 58 miles, by a great bend of the Ohio river, E. by Hardin, S. by Hardin and Breckinridge, and W. by Breckinridge county. The other streams are—Otter, Doe, Wolf, and Spring creeks. About two-thirds of the county is 'barrens;' the balance, off of the level river bottoms rolling. The soil —based upon clay, with a limestone foundation—is gently rich and fertile. Tobacco and corn are the two leading crops; the other cereals, and live stock, are largely raised. ...

Enoch Boone, son of Squire Boone (and nephew of Daniel Boone), was born 'in a canebrake,' at Boonesborough, Madison co., Ky., Nov. 16,1777. He was among the earlier white children native of Kentucky (probably there were not more than eight born at a prior date), and many of his friends still cherish the pleasant but mistaken thought that he was *the first*. ... Inured to the dangers and hardships of a frontier life, he was a soldier before he was 17, in Wayne's campaign against the Indians, 1794; in 1808, and for 8 years, he lived in Grassy Valley, Harrison co., Indiana (then Indiana territory), and held a captain's commission from Gen. Wm. H. Harrison, then its governor; afterwards removed to Meade co., Ky. He was married in Shelby co., Ky., Feb. 8, 1798, to Lucy Galman, with whom he lived happily for 62 years. He died on his wedding anniversary, Feb. 8, 1862, at the residence of his son-in-law, Judge Collins Fitch, on the Ohio river, near Garnettsville, Meade co., Ky., aged 84 years. ...

This county received its name in honor of Captain James Meade, a native of Woodford county, Kentucky. Captain Meade, when quite a youth, volunteered his services under the lamented Colonel Joseph H. Daveiss, in the Wabash expedition, and fought side by side with that gallant officer in the battle of Tippecanoe. For his bravery on this occasion, combined with his intelligence and military

qualifications, he was promoted to the rank of captain in the regular service.

In 1813, at the battle of the river Raisin, where so many of the gallant young men of Kentucky found a bloody grave, the company of Captain Meade

Captain Meade, when quite a youth, volunteered his services under the lamented Colonel Joseph H. Daveiss, in the Wabash expedition, and fought side by side with that gallant officer in the battle of Tippecanoe.

composed a part of the regular force. He occupied a very exposed position, and fell at the head of his company, while gallantly leading them on, early in the action."

An excerpt from pages 598-600 of the entry for "Meade County," Collins' Historical Sketches of Kentucky, History of Kentucky, Vol. II (Southern Historical Press, 1874).

Menifee County

Menifee County was formed from parts of Bath, Montgomery and Powell Counties in 1869 and was named for Richard H. Menefee, a well-regarded statesman and successful lawyer. The misspelling of the county name occurred in the legislature when the county was chartered.

Menefee, one of Kentucky's great orators, who died at age 32, was the youngest person to have a county named for him in Kentucky. The city of Frenchburg was named for Judge Richard French, who was defeated by Menefee in a race for Congress in 1837.

Menifee County is located in the Daniel Boone National Forest between Cave Run Lake and the Red River Gorge. It has much to offer in outdoor recreation and sightseeing. Spring and summer find wildflowers carpeting the hills, valleys and meadows. Fall offers a breathtaking show of colors. Winter provides a Christmas card type of scenery that is hard to beat. Environments ranging from high cliff areas to wetlands provide habitats for birds and wildlife.

Cave Run Lake, impounded in 1974 with 8,270 surface acres, has a wide variety of recreational opportunities. The lake is known for producing trophy-size musky. There is easy access to the lake at Leatherwood Boat Ramp on Forest Service Road 129 and Longbow Marina on Kentucky 1274.

The Red River Gorge Geological Area and Wild and Scenic River is a 25,500-acre natural scenic wonder of sandstone cliffs, rock formations and magnificent wilderness. There are many hiking trails and campsites. The river is popular for canoeing. The Gorge has the Gladie Cultural and Environmental Learning Center that provides an opportunity for visitors to learn about the rich cultural legacy and environmental uniqueness of the Red River Gorge. The site has a restored historical cabin and displays of farm implements from bygone years.

Also located in Menifee County is the Red River Gorge National Scenic Byway, Frenchburg Job Corps Center, Sheltowee Trace National Recreational Trail, Pioneer Weapons Wildlife Management Area, Beaver Creek Wetlands and Broke Leg Falls.

Although Menifee County is a rural county, a large percentage of its 6,566 residents have city water and sewer. Emergency medical, fire and law enforcement agencies can be reached through the county's 911 system.

Many are employed in farming and logging. Tobacco is a major cash crop and corn, hay and soybeans are grown for livestock feed. Menifee County sorghum has long been a source of pride for

Cabin near Gladie
Source: SouthEast Telephone

Menifee Countians. Cane mills can still be found in operation in Menifee County in the fall.

Woodland cabins provide homes for many retirees and weekend retreats for nonresidents.

An industrial park at Means and a tri-county industrial park at Farmers in Rowan County have sites available for economic development. Many residents find employment here and in surrounding counties.

Contributed by Lola Thomas

Mercer County

"Mercer county—one of the 9 counties erected by the legislature of Virginia before Kentucky was separated and admitted into the Union, the 1st formed out of Lincoln county, and the 6th in numerical order in the state — was established in 1785, and named in honor of Gen. Hugh Mercer. It is situated very near to—if, indeed, it does not embrace within its limits — the exact geographic center of the state; on the waters of both the Kentucky and Salt rivers; and is bounded N. by Anderson and Woodford, E. by Woodford,

lies, who are generally in independent circumstances, well educated, and intelligent. ...

Gen. Hugh Mercer, of Virginia, from whom this county received its name, was native of Scotland, and graduated at an early age in the science of medicine. At the memorable battle of Culloden, he acted as assistant surgeon, and with many of the vanquished sought a refuge in America. In the Indian war of 1755, he served as a captain, under Washington. For his gallantry and military skill in this war, the corporation of Philadel-

Tableau commemorating the first permanent settlement in Kentucky and Fort Harrod, Harrodsburg
Source: Sid Webb

Jessamine, and Garrard, S. by Boyle, and W. by Washington and Anderson counties. Dick's and Kentucky rivers form the entire E. boundary line; Salt river runs centrally through the county, from S. to N.; other streams in Mercer county are—Chapline's, Jennings', Rocky, McCoun's, Lyon's, and Thompson's creeks, and Shawnee run. The surface is undulating, and the land generally of a good quality, some of it very rich; and the whole is finely watered.

This county being settled at the very earliest period of the history of Kentucky, has been finely improved; and the population consists to a large extent of the descendants of pioneer fami-

phia presented him with an appropriate medal. In 1775, he was in command of three regiments of minute-men; and 1776, he was made colonel in the army of Virginia. Having joined the continental army, he was promoted to the rank of brigadier general, and served in that capacity with efficiency and distinction, until the period of his death, which occurred in the battle of Princeton, where he fell mortally wounded, while leading the vanguard of the American forces. He survived nine days, and then died of his wounds."

An excerpt from pages 602-622 of the entry for "Mercer County," Collins' Historical Sketches of Kentucky, History of Kentucky, Vol. II (Southern Historical Press, 1874).

Metcalfe County

Metcalfe, the 106th county established in Kentucky, was named in honor of Kentucky's 10th governor, Thomas Metcalfe. Metcalfe County, located in the south-central portion of the state in the eastern Pennyrile Region, is bounded on the north by Green and Hart counties, on the west by Barren, on the south and southeast by Monroe and Cumberland and on the east by Adair County.

> **It was not until citizens of Glasgow wanted to tax the people of Barren County to pay for a 10-mile section of railroad track from Glasgow Junction to Glasgow that the parent county consented to its [Metcalfe County] formation.**

Metcalfe County contains a land area of 296 square miles. The Little Barren River and its tributaries, including the South and East Fork, drain the northern and central part of the county. Southeastern Metcalfe is drained by the headwaters of Marrowbone Creek.

According to an act of the Kentucky General Assembly, Metcalfe officially became a recognized county on May 1, 1860. It was formed primarily from the county of Barren, with small sections coming from Hart, Green, Adair, Cumberland and Monroe. During the 1855 and 1857 legislatures, proposals were introduced for the formation of a new county from eastern Barren County, but Barren County representatives blocked the issue. It was not until citizens of Glasgow wanted to tax the people of Barren County to pay for a 10-mile section of railroad track that the parent county consented to its formation.

The town of Edmonton was named as its county seat. When the county was surveyed, it was determined that the geographic center of the county was only about one-half mile from the Edmonton public square. Edmonton, which became Metcalfe's largest town, was named for Edmund Rogers who owned the land and laid out the town in 1818.

Shortly after Metcalfe County was established, the county courthouse was built. On March 15, 1865, a band of guerrillas looted the town and burned the courthouse. After rebuilding, it was again burned on July 26, 1868. The present courthouse was begun on Sept. 19, 1868, and was completed before Oct. 15, 1869.

Metcalfe has no large cities or towns; instead there are small villages and rural communities.

Two sites in the county are associated with Metcalfe County's early history. John Filson located Big Blue Spring on his 1784 map of Kentucky as being between the Little and Big Barren rivers in northwestern Metcalfe County. The Great Warriors Path that extended from the Cherokee settlements near Chattanooga to the Falls of the Ohio River intersected a trail that reached from the Lexington-Dick River area to the Indian villages near Nashville.

A second location mentioned in early records was McKinney's Station. Stephen McKinney was granted a military warrant on the South Fork of the Little Barren where he built a station and was killed by Indians in 1792.

Contributed by Jerry Sampson

Monroe County

"Monroe county, formed in 1820 out of parts of Barren and Cumberland counties, and named in honor of James Monroe (who had just been re-elected president of the United States, receiving every vote in the electoral college but one), was the 65th in order of formation. It is situated on the southern border of the state, and lies on the head waters of Big Barren river, while the Cumberland river passes through its S.E. corner; its other streams are McFarland's, Long Fork, East Fork, Line, Sulphur Lick, and Indian creeks; it is bounded N. by Barren, Metcalfe, and Cumberland counties, E. by Cumberland, S. by the Tennessee state line, and W. by Allen and Barren counties. The face of the country is quite diversified—level, undulating, and hilly; the principal growth on the wild lands, poplar, walnut, oak, and beech; for a few years past, a number of citizens have been extensively engaged in transporting poplar and walnut logs to Nashville, Tennessee. Tobacco, corn, wheat and oats are the principal products; hogs are exported in considerable numbers. ...

The Trees have kept, for 96 years, the silent record of the first known visit to what is now Monroe county. A quarter of a mile W. of Tompkinsville, a stately beech bears the name of '*D. Bone, 1777*' and is an object of curious interest and of frequent visits. Other trees, in other neighborhoods, bear the same date, but without a name—indicating that several hunters were here in that year on an excursion. Dr. Thomas Walker and Daniel Smith, the Virginia

commissioners to run the boundary line between Virginia and North Carolina — of which states Kentucky and Tennessee then formed the western parts—marked their names and Feb. 25, 1780, on two beech trees, on the west bank of the Cumberland river, at the point where the state line crosses, in this county.

President James Monroe (1817-1825)

During the War of the Rebellion, Monroe county was nearly devastated. Roving bands of marauders — some professing allegiance to the cause of the Union, some of that of the South, and some to neither cause — overran the county, and rendered life and property precarious and insecure.

Col. S.S. Stanton, of Tennessee led the first Confederate troops into the county, late in the autumn of 1861. He burned Camp Anderson (in the W. portion of the county), which had recently been evacuated by the Federals; and returned, through Tompkinsville, to Tennessee. The celebrated Gen. Pat. Cleburne, with several regiments, passed through the county, during the same autumn; and Gen. Bragg's entire army in 1862. In the winter of 1862, Col. John H. Morgan's Confederate rangers encountered Maj. Jordan, who was encamped half a mine E. of Tompkinsville. After a sharp conflict, the Federals retreated, leaving their tents and most of their baggage. Several were killed and wounded on each side."

An excerpt from pages 629-631 of the entry for "Monroe County," Collins' Historical Sketches of Kentucky, History of Kentucky, Vol. II (Southern Historical Press, 1874).

Montgomery County

Montgomery County was created on Dec. 14, 1796. It is in the outer Bluegrass region, and is bounded by Clark, Bourbon, Bath, Menifee and Powell Counties. The county was named for General Richard Montgomery, who was killed at the Revolutionary War Battle of Quebec. Montgomery County once stretched to the Virginia

Montgomery County Courthouse
Source: SouthEast Telephone

border, but with the formation of Floyd, Bath, Powell and Menifee Counties, it assumed its present size in 1869.

The major town in the county is Mt. Sterling, the county seat, which was founded in 1792. The town originally was called "Little Mountain" for a large Indian mound that was located near the creek where the Queen and Locust Street intersection is today. The 25-foot-tall, 150-foot-diameter mound was excavated in the 1840s, and produced many Indian artifacts and bodies. Another large Indian mound attributed to the Adena people, 800 B.C. to A.D. 700, is the Gaitskill Mound near the bypass just north of town. It is listed on the National Register of Historic Places and has been the origin of some of the best Adena artifacts ever recovered.

Mt. Sterling has a rich and colorful Civil War history. It was primarily a Union garrison town, but fell several times to Confederate forces commanded by Colonel John Hunt Morgan.

Carmago and Jeffersonville have become economic centers of the southern portion of the county. Both towns are enjoying much growth in the 21st century, the population of each now being in excess of 1,000. The population of Montgomery County in 1980 was 20,046, in 2000 it was 22,554, and in 2005, 23,620.

Two important additions to Montgomery County in the past decade have been the Clay Community Center, which opened in 2003, and Easy Walker Park, which opened in 1992.

The Clay Community Center has been the site of meetings and conferences, banquets, proms, weddings and retirement dinners. The Center also serves as the Morehead State University satellite campus, where enrollment continues to increase each year.

The Easy Walker Park on Osborne Road comprises 65 acres and provides hiking paths, soccer, baseball and softball fields, tennis courts, horseshoe pits, picnic areas and a fishing pond and playground suitable for family gatherings.

A broad spectrum of industries exist in the county. Some of the largest employers are Cooper Tire and Rubber Co., Hoffman Engineering, Nestle's, Quality Cabinets and The Walker Company. Other companies manufacture everything from chimney pipes, molded plastics, hermetic motors, candles, equine wraps and bindings and fuel system valves and filters.

Court Day, on the third Monday in October and proceeding weekend, has been an important part of Mt. Sterling history since its early days – the one event the town is most noted for. Originally, this was an occasion for swapping and selling cattle, horses, mules and dogs, as well as guns. The animals are gone now, replaced by an array of vendors from all over the country selling to more than 100,000 people.

With excellent schools, modern medical facilities, and a vibrant economy, the Montgomery County community is truly "THE GATEWAY TO THE MOUNTAINS."

Contributed by George Stone

Morgan County

Morgan County was established in 1822 from parts of Floyd and Bath Counties. Prior to and after the Civil War, four more counties were created from Elk Fork and Caney Creeks, as well as the Licking River Valley.

In the spring the county's hills are a mass of red and white colors, produced by redbud and dogwood trees in full bloom. In the fall, the hills display brilliant colors of red, orange and browns from the maples, sumac, gum, oak and hickory trees.

Source: SouthEast Telephone

The county is largely composed of conservative Scottish and Irish descendants who take pride in their county. The residents of Morgan County, influenced by their churches and schools, have affection for God and country, as well as education.

The annual Morgan County Sorghum Festival in West Liberty attracts thousands of visitors every year as residents celebrate their heritage with food, entertainment, arts and crafts.

a portion of Morgan County.

Morgan County was named for Gen. Daniel Morgan, a hero in the Revolutionary War. Wells Mill was the first settlement in the county and was named for Edmund Wells, who began operating a water mill on the Licking River in 1816. In 1823 the county seat of West Liberty was established.

Morgan County is located in east-central Kentucky in the foothills of the Cumberland Mountain Range. The elevation in the county ranges from 690 to 1400 feet above sea level. The land is characterized by beautiful rolling hills and wide valleys along the Grassy, Blackwater,

Source: SouthEast Telephone

Morgan County has contributed many prominent citizens to various parts of the United States, including a Medal of Honor recipient during the Korean War.

The people are deeply interested in their heritage as evidenced by monuments on the courthouse lawn honoring their founding fathers, World War II veterans and veterans of all wars.

Morgan County is truly the jewel of eastern Kentucky.

Contributed by Linda Bradley

Muhlenberg County

"Muhlenberg County — the 34th in order of formation — was established in 1798, out of parts of Logan and Christian, and named in honor of General Peter Muhlenberg. Its original territory is still intact, except the small northern portion taken in 1854 to help form McLean county. It is situated in

> Gen. Peter Muhlenberg was a native of Pennsylvania. At the breaking out of the Revolution, he was a young man, and pastor of a Lutheran church at Woodstock. In 1776, he received the commission of colonel, and was requested to raise his regiment among the Germans of the valley.

the south-western middle portion of the state, and is bounded N. and N.E. by McLean and Ohio counties, from which it is separated by Green river; E. by Butler county, Big Muddy river being the dividing line; S.E. by Logan; S. by Todd and Christian; and W. by Hopkins county, the dividing line being Pond river. The surface of the county is generally rolling, part of it broken; the northern portion is good farming land, and all the county is fine grass land, and well timbered. The principal products are tobacco, corn, hay and wool. Cattle and hogs are sold in large numbers to drovers. But the great wealth of the county is coal and iron. ...

Antiquities — On a rock bank of Pond creek, four miles from Greenville, tracks of mules and horses are plainly to be seen in the solid sandstone. Some have been removed, and taken, it is said, to the St. Louis museum. On Muddy river is a sandstone rock with flat surface, 30 or 40 feet square, on which are carved hieroglyphics as yet undeciphered; the full form of an Indian, surrounded by different animals; the sun, moon, stars, and other symbolic signs. ...

Gen. Peter Muhlenberg was a native of Pennsylvania. At the breaking out of the Revolution, he was a young man, and pastor of a Lutheran church at Woodstock. In 1776, he received the commission of colonel, and was requested to raise his regiment among the Germans of the valley. Having in his pulpit inculcated the principles of liberty, he found no difficulty in enlisting a regiment. He entered the pulpit with his sword and cockade, preached his farewell sermon, and the next day marched at the head of his regiment to join the army. His regiment was the 8th Virginia, or, as it was commonly called, the German regiment. This corps behaved with honor throughout the war; was at Brandywine, Monmouth, and Germantown, and in the southern campaigns. In 1777, Mr. Muhlenberg was promoted to the rank of brigadier general. After the war, he returned to Pennsylvania — was for many years treasurer of that state, and served three terms in congress. In person, he was tall and well proportioned, and, in his address remarkably courteous. He was a fine disciplinarian, an excellent officer, and esteemed and beloved by both officers and soldiers."

An excerpt from pages 639-643 of the entry for "Muhlenberg County," Collins' Historical Sketches of Kentucky, History of Kentucky, Vol. II (Southern Historical Press, 1874).

Nelson County

"Nelson county was formed in 1784 by the general assembly of Virginia, the 4th county erected in the district (now state) of Kentucky, and named in honor of ex-Gov. Thomas Nelson, of Va. It then embraced all the territory lying between Salt and Green rivers, as far E. as the E. line of Washington county. Out of that original territory have been formed the following counties: Washington, Har-

John Fitch, first inventor of steamboats

din, and part of Green in 1792, part of Bullitt in 1796, Ohio in 1798, Breckinridge in 1799, Grayson and part of Butler in 1810, Daviess in 1815, part of Hart in 1819, Meade in 1823, part of Spencer in 1824, part of Edmonson in 1825, part of Anderson in 1827, Hancock in 1829, Marion in 1834, Larue in 1843, Taylor of 1848, and part of McLean in 1854. In its present limits, it is situated in the northern middle portion of the state, and is bounded N. by Bullitt and Spencer counties, E. by Anderson, Washington, and Marion, S. by Washington, Mar-

ion, and Larue, and W. by Larue, Hardin and Bullitt. Chapline's and Beech forks of Salt river form most of its E. and S.E. boundary line, and the Rolling fork of Salt river its S.W. line. The surface of the county is undulating. The soil generally is excellent, but in the southern portion, off the creek bottoms, is rather thin. Corn and hogs are the largest exports, but cattle, horses, mules, hay, hemp, tobacco, flour, whiskey, and apples are also exported. ...

John Fitch, the first inventor of steamboats, was at two different periods an inhabitant of Nelson county, and at his death a citizen. He was born in Windsor, Conn., Jan. 21, 1743, and died in June or July, 1798, in Bardstown, Ky., aged 55 years. ...

Gov. Thomas Nelson, one of the signers of the Declaration of Independence, for whom this county received its name, was a native of Virginia. He was educated in England; and entered the Virginia house of burgesses, in 1774. In the military organization of Virginia, at the breaking out of the war, he was appointed to the command of a regiment. In 1775, he was sent to the general congress at Philadelphia, and was a member of that body at the time of the Declaration of Independence. About this time he was appointed, by the state of Virginia, a brigadier general, and invested with the chief command of the military state. In 1779, he was again, for a short time, a member of congress, but was forced by ill health to resign his seat. In 1781, he succeeded Mr. Jefferson as governor of Virginia; and continued to unite in himself the two offices of governor and commander of the military forces, until the surrender of Lord Cornwallis. He died in 1789, aged fifty years."

An excerpt from pages 643-650 of the entry for "Nelson County," Collins' Historical Sketches of Kentucky, History of Kentucky, Vol. II (Southern Historical Press, 1874).

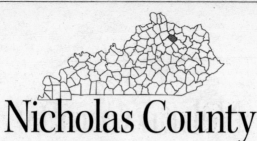

Nicholas County

"Nicholas County — the 42nd in order of formation, and the last before 1800 — was formed in 1799, out of parts of Bourbon and Mason, and named in honor of Col. Geo. Nicholas. A portion of its territory was taken to form Robertson county in 1867. It is situated in the N.E. middle part of the state, and is bounded N. by Robertson

XXXXXXXXXXXXXXX

> If he [Col. George Nicholas] was not a transcendent orator according to the Demosthenian process of resolving eloquence into action alone, his powers of argumentation were of the highest order, and his knowledge of the laws and institutions of his country placed him in the first rank of the distinguished men by whose wisdom and patriotism they were established.
>
> *Governor Morehead - 1792*

XXXXXXXXXXXXXXX

and Fleming counties, E. by Fleming and Bath, S. by Bath and Bourbon, and W. by Bourbon and Harrison. The Licking river flows through the county in a N.W. direction, and forms part of the N.E. boundary line; the other more important streams are Hinkson creek, which forms its southern boundary, Somerset, Cassidy, Beaver, Brushy Fork, and Flat creeks. That portion of the county which borders upon Bourbon and Bath counties is gently undulating, and very rich and productive; the remainder of the county, with the exception of the valleys of the Licking and its

tributaries, is broken oak lands. The soil is based on limestone, with red clay foundation. The staple articles of production and commerce are corn, wheat, rye, oats, tobacco, whiskey, cattle, hogs, and mules. ...

Col. George Nicholas — in honor of whom Nicholas county was named on Dec. 18, 1799, five months after his death — was born about 1743, in Williamsburg, Va.; where is father, Robert Carter Nicholas, was a distinguished lawyer, a member of the house of burgesses, a member of the colonial council, and treasurer of the colony of Virginia. The son was a captain in the war of the Revolution, in the Virginia state line; and after the war, practiced law at Charlottesville, Albemarle county, was elected to the legislature from that county, and was a prominent and influential member of the Virginia convention called to consider the new Federal Constitution, the adoption of which he advocated very ably and zealously. In 1788, he removed to what was then Mercer County, Ky., near Danville. In 1791, he was chosen from that county a member of the convention which framed the first constitution of Kentucky, adopted April 19, 1792. Of that convention, Gov. Morehead said, 'it abounded in talent, integrity, and patriotism.' George Nicholas was its brightest luminary. If he was not a transcendent orator according to the Demosthenian process of resolving eloquence into action alone, his powers of argumentation were of the highest order, and his knowledge of the laws and institutions of his country placed him in the first rank of the distinguished men by whose wisdom and patriotism they were established. A member of the convention that ratified the constitution of the United States, he was the associate of Madison, of Randolph, and of Patrick Henry; and he came to Kentucky in the fullness of his fame and in the maturity of his intellectual strength."

An excerpt from pages 650-664 of the entry for "Nicholas County," Collins' Historical Sketches of Kentucky, History of Kentucky, Vol. II (Southern Historical Press, 1874).

Ohio County

"Ohio County was formed in 1798, out of part of Hardin county, the 35th in order of formation, and named after the beautiful river that forms the northern boundary of the state. From its territory has since been taken the entire county of Daviess in 1815, and parts of Butler and Grayson in 1810, Hancock in 1829, and McLean in 1854. It is situated in the west middle portion of the state, on the waters of Green river; is bounded N. by Daviess and Hancock counties, E. by Breckinridge and Grayson, S.E. by Butler, S.W. by Muhlenberg, W. by McLean, and N.W. by Daviess. Besides Green river, the streams are Rough, East fork of Panther, Muddy, White's Fork, Walton's, Barnett's, and Caney creeks. The soil is considered equal to that of the Green river lands generally—producing excellent crops of corn, tobacco, oats, potatoes, clover and other grasses, but supposed not to contain sufficient lime for the profitable growing of wheat. The timber is heavy and of a superior quality. Iron ore abounds, and coal is inexhaustible. In 1842-48, the morus multicaulis was tried extensively and flourished, showing that the culture of silk might be carried onto any extent. Some specimens of manufactured silk were produced, equal to the best Italian. ...

A Giant.—Early in 1872, in prospecting for coal in Ohio county, about a mile from Rockport, the complete skeleton of a human body of gigantic size was found, 6 feet below the surface. The lower jaw-bone, when fitted over the lower portion of a man's face in the party of explorers, completely covered it; the thigh-bone, from the hip-bone to the knee, was 42 inches long, and the fore-arm bone from wrist to elbow measured 22 inches. This would indicate a giant over 10 feet high."

An excerpt from pages 665-667 of the entry for "Ohio County," Collins' Historical Sketches of Kentucky, History of Kentucky, Vol. II (Southern Historical Press, 1874).

It's a Kentucky thing...

"A Giant — Early in 1872, in prospecting for coal in Ohio county, about a mile from Rockport, the complete skeleton of a human body of gigantic size was found, 6 feet below the surface. The lower jaw-bone, when fitted over the lower portion of a man's face in the party of explorers, completely covered it; the thigh bone, from the hip-bone to the knee, was 42 inches long, and the fore-arm bone from wrist to elbow measured 22 inches. This would indicate a giant over 10 feet high.

Source: Collins' Historical Sketches of Kentucky, page 666, Southern Historical Press, 1874.

Oldham County

"Oldham County, the 74th in order of formation, was established in 1823, out of parts of Jefferson, Shelby, and Henry counties, and named in honor of Col. Wm. Oldham. Part of its territory was taken in 1836, to aid in forming the county of Trimble. It is situated in the north middle part of the state, and lies for 18 miles along the Ohio river; is bounded N. by the Ohio river and Trimble county, E. by Henry, S. by Shelby and Jefferson counties, and W. and N.W. by the Ohio river; and embraces about 170 square miles. The face of the country along the Ohio river and Eighteen Mile Creek, and in the upper part of the county adjoining Trimble, is hilly and broken; the remainder of the country is gently undulating, and generally good, arable land, based on limestone. The principal products and exports are wheat, hemp, tobacco, hogs and cattle. The principal streams of the county are Harrod's creek and Curry's fork of Floyd's fork, both having their source in Henry county. The Louisville, Cincinnati, and Lexington railroad runs through the southern part of the county, in a N.E. direction.

From the records of Jefferson county we have obtained the autograph of Col. William Oldham, in honor of whom this county received its name. He was a native of Berkeley co., Virginia; entered the Revolutionary war as an ensign, in 1775; became a captain, and continued in active service, until the spring of 1779, when he resigned and emigrated to the Falls of the Ohio, now Louisville; commanded a regiment of Kentucky militia in the memorable battle of St. Clair's defeat, Nov. 4, 1791, where he was killed by the Indians. He was a chivalrous and enterprising man, a brave and experienced officer, and very efficient in defending the country against incursions of the Indians. He was one of the first magistrates of Jefferson county, an active, useful, and public-spirited citizen.

Towns. —Lagrange (originally and correctly written La Grange, like Gen. La Fayette's residence in France, after which it was named) is the county seat, at or near the junction of the old main line of the Louisville and Lexington railroad with its Cincinnati or "Short Line" branch; contains a brick court house, 5 churches Baptist, Methodist, and Reformed or Christian, and 2 for colored people), 3 lawyers, 3 physicians, 1 seminary building (formerly known as Masonic College and for a time a flourishing institution), 3 hotels, 3 dry good stores, 3 groceries, drug store and several mechanics' shops, 1 small woolen mill; incorporated in 1840; population in 1870, 612." *An excerpt from page 667 of the entry for "Oldham County," Collins' Historical Sketches of Kentucky, History of Kentucky (Southern Historical Press, 1874).*

Well, I never...

Credited as being one of the greatest film producers of all time, D.W. Griffith was born in 1875 in Oldham County. His most famous production was a story about the Civil War entitled BIRTH OF A NATION (1915).

His movie presented the violence and excitement of war spectacularly. However brilliantly filmed, the movie was a sad testament to the deep prejudice of that era. Audiences were outraged by the racist distortion of history — and, viewed as a contributor to the rise of the Ku Klux Klan, the film prompted riots in a number of black communities. Griffith's other films include Intolerance (1916), Broken Blossoms (1919) and Way Down East (1920).

Owen County

"Owen County, the 67th in order of formation, was erected in 1819, out of parts of Scott, Franklin, and Gallatin counties, and named in honor of Col. Abraham Owen. It is situated in the north middle part of the state. The Kentucky river is its western boundary line for 28 miles; and Eagle creek rises in Scott, flows through the southern part of Owen into Grant in a northern direction-then, making a sudden bend, runs nearly parallel with the Ohio river into the Kentucky river in Carroll county, skirting the northern boundary of Owen in its progress. The county is bounded N. by Carroll, Gallatin, and Grant counties, E. by Grant and Scott, S. by Scott and Franklin, S.W. by Henry, and N.W. by Carroll. The face of the country is undulating, part of it hilly, and the soil generally good-producing fine tobacco, corn, oats, buckwheat, and barley; cattle, sheep, and hogs are raised in large quantities, and stock-growing is rapidly increasing. The county being well adapted to grazing and one of the best watered in the state. Besides the Kentucky river and Big Eagle creek, are Big Twin, Little Twin, Cedar, Big Indian, Caney, Clay Lick, and Severn creeks. The Cincinnati branch of the L., C. & L. railroad (the "Short Line") runs near the northern boundary of Owen County, giving it, in conjunction with the Kentucky river, remarkable access to the best markets.

Colonel Abraham Owen, in honor of whom this county received its name, was born in Prince Edward County, Virginia, in the year 1769, and emigrated to Shelby county, Kentucky, in 1785. His first appearance on the public theatre and in the service of the country, was upon Wilkinson's campaign, in the summer of 1791, in the White and Wabash rivers. He was in the expedition led by Colonel Hardin to White river, and participated in the action which routed Indians in their hunting camps. It is not known that he was in Wayne's campaign; but in 1796, he was surveyor of Shelby county, and afterwards a magistrate. He commanded the first militia company raised in the county, and the late venerable Singleton Wilson, of Shelbyville, brother of the late Dr. Wilson of Cincinnati, was the lieutenant. They had been associates in Wilkinson's campaign, and the humane efforts of Colonel Owen to provide for the wants and promote the comforts of his companion, were illustrative of his general good character. Owen was soon promoted to be a major, and then colonel of the regiment. Lieutenant Wilson was promoted to the rank of captain, having served with distinction as a spy in the campaign led by General Wayne."

An excerpt from pages 669-672 of the entry for "Owen County," Collins' Historical Sketches of Kentucky, History of Kentucky, Volume II (Collins & Co., 1882.)

I didn't know that...

The people of Owen county were almost unanimous in favor of the South; and Confederate soldiers were nearly always in the county, for concealment, for recruiting purposes, or for a dash upon their enemies. Many persecuted Southern Sympathisers and Southern soldiers escaping from norther prisons or cut off form their commands, found a temporary hiding-place in the thick undergrowth in several portions of the county. Mose Webster's most daring operations were, some of them, planned and carried out from or in Owen county. Few, if any, counties in the state furnished so many soldiers to the Confederate army, in proportion to population."

From Collins' Historical Sketches, Vol. II, page 671.

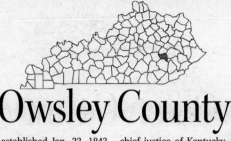

Owsley County

"Owsley county was established Jan. 23, 1843 — the 96th in the state — and named in honor of Judge Wm. Owsley, afterwards governor of Kentucky. It is situated in the eastern middle portion, on the waters of the Kentucky river; is bounded N. by Lee county, E. by Breathitt, S. by Clay, W. by Jackson, and N.W. by Estill. The South Fork of Kentucky river runs quite centrally through the county from S. to N., the main Kentucky forms part of the N. boundary line; and its Middle Fork crosses the N.E. part. The soil along the river valleys is rich and productive; but the face of the country generally is broken and the soil not sufficiently strong for profitable cultivation. Corn is the staple production; rye, wheat, and oats, cattle and hogs are raised. ...

Owsley county is included in the eastern coal field—except the lower portion of the valley of Sturgeon creek, and the valley of the Kentucky river from the mouth of Sturgeon creek to the Estill county line. The coal measures in the vicinity of Proctor and Beattyville—which were in Owsley county when examined by the state geological survey, in 1859, but are now in Lee county—contain four, if not five, veins of coal. The "main coal," which has received most attention from the miners, measures from 42 to 50 inches; and had then been opened and mined at some 9 banks, on the Kentucky river, the South fork, the Duck fork, Sturgeon, Upper and Lower Stufflebean Creeks, and Mike's branch. ...

William Owsley, the 14th governor of Kentucky, was born in 1782 in Virginia. His father, Wm. Owsley, emigrated, the next year, to the county of Lincoln in the then "district of Kentucky," settling on the waters of Drake's creek, near the present town of Crab Orchard. The son, William, succeeded in getting a better education than was common for boys at that day, taught school awhile, became deputy surveyor, and afterwards deputy sheriff, hi father being high sheriff of the county.

It was whilst William Owsley was engaged in his early official pursuits as deputy sheriff, & co., that he attracted the attention of John Boyle, afterwards chief justice of Kentucky. Judge Boyle, perceiving the promise that was in young Owsley, offered him the use of his library, and the advantage of his instructions in the study of law. The offer was accepted, and by perseverance and close application, Owsley soon obtained license and com-

> **William Owsley,**
>
> **the 14ᵗʰ governor of Kentucky,**
>
> **was born in 1782 in Virginia.**
>
> **His father, Wm. Owsley,**
>
> **emigrated, the next year, to**
>
> **the county of Lincoln in the**
>
> **then "district of Kentucky."**

menced the practice of law in Garrard county. His success was immediate. He ranked high at the bar, and became the intimate and firm friend of Judge Boyle. He afterwards represented Garrard county several years in the legislature and lawyer, that, in 1812, when he was only thirty-one years of age, and had been but few years at the bar, Governor Scott appointed him to the supreme bench of the State, as the colleague of Judge Boyle, who had been honored by a seat on the appellate bench three years previously. Judge Owsley resigned this office in a short time, in consequence of the passage of a law reducing the number of judges of the court to three. But a vacancy occurring in 1813, he was immediately re-appointed by Governor Shelby."

An excerpt from pages 673-674 of the entry for "Owsley County," Collins' Historical Sketches of Kentucky, History of Kentucky, Volume II (Southern Historical Press, 1874).

Pendleton County

On Dec. 13, 1798, the General Assembly approved an act to create a Pendleton County out of Campbell and Bracken counties. The county embraces about 300 square miles and was named for Judge Edmund Pendleton, of Carolina County, Va. It was the 28th county in the state of Kentucky.

Falmouth, laying in the center of the county, is the county seat. Some of the first settlements in the county were Falmouth, Grassy Creek, Flour Creek, Unity or Jagg, Gardnersville, Fork Lick, Blanket Creek, Snake Creek, Main Licking, Boston Station, Lock Number 4 (now Butler) and South Licking Grove.

The first roads were: from Falmouth to the Harrison County line; and from John Sanders ferry across the Licking River to intersect with Grassy Creek, now Highway 17.

Source: John Perkins

Toll roads often were present in the county. Travelers passed through the gates with the toll collector's house on one side of the road and another part on the opposite side of the road.

Before 1824 candidates were elected to office largely upon their personal popularity.

After the election of 1824, the two political parties were the Democrats and the Whigs. The Democrats favored a more democratic control of the government, this feeling being strong in the newer parts of the county. They favored a vigorous executive leadership, strict construction of the constitution and states rights. Later, as the slavery question became more acute, the party opposed restrictions upon slavery.

The opposition party, merging with other minor parties became known as the Whigs and were supported by the financial and business classes. They favored liberal construction of the constitution,

a protective tariff and construction of internal improvements. They opposed executive dominance and favored Congressional control of the government.

In the end, the Whigs were strongest in the northeast of the county, but failed as a result of an attempt to compromise on the slavery question.

The land rose quite rapidly in value after the completion of the Kentucky Central Railroad in 1852 from Covington to Lexington. Prior to that, this was considered backwoods country. The only roads were wagon roads through the forest. The principle road in the county led from Falmouth to Foster Landing on the Ohio River. Stagecoaches ran between these points and people went there to take boats to Cincinnati and Louisville and other points.

Until the railroad was built, supplies were brought on barges down the Ohio River to Foster Landing, then hauled by carts and wagons pulled by oxen over mud roads to their respective places. It was known as the Dinkey.

Contributed by Mildred Belew

Perry County

The settlement of Perry County, a hilly and mountainous land, began in 1795 when Elijah Combs set out on foot, accompanied by one slave, to explore Kentucky and find a new place to live. The two traveled by way of the old Wilderness Road, crossing the Clinch River into the Powell Valley, and continuing up to the Big Stone Gap and Pound Gap. In the valley below they found the head of the North Fork of the Kentucky River. Happening upon a salt lick, Combs decided to end his journey. He built two houses

Source: SouthEast Telephone

where Hazard now stands. His seven brothers and their families followed him and settled all along the river.

In 1819 the citizens of Clay County petitioned the state for the creation of a new county, to reduce the distance of their trips to a county seat. The request was granted, and in November 1821, the new county was established. Perry County lies at the headwaters of the North Fork of the Kentucky River in southeastern Kentucky. It is drained by the Middle Fork and the North Fork of the Kentucky River.

Perry County was named in honor of Oliver Hazard Perry, a distinguished officer in the U.S. Navy, from Newport, Rhode Island. A national hero of the War of 1812, at defeat of the British in the Battle of Lake Erie. Hazard was designated the county seat. By the 1820s the county's population growth slowed due to the rugged terrain, which made travel difficult, dooming the mountain people to lives of isolation and solitude.

During the Civil War the region was of no strategic significance to either the Union or the Confederacy. As a result, bands of bushwhackers roamed freely. Many of the guerrillas were locals and their actions spread seeds of hatred that later led to vicious mountain feuds. In 1884, the year Hazard was incorporated, its population was only about 100. Around this time a feud grew out of land grabbing by outside interest. This precipitated the French and Eversole Feud, resulting once again in a deeply anguished community.

Lumber companies sent agents into the mountains and they were stunned by the thousands of acres of untold wealth. By 1890 a number of small local mines were in operation and the timber business was flourishing. Roads remained very poor and in bad weather were impassable. Travel on the river provided the only access. Logs floated down the Kentucky River in huge quantities. Coal was shipped in barges. By 1912, the Lexington and Eastern Railroad extended into Perry County and the coalfields were open to the outside world.

During the 1960s improvement of Route 15 connected eastern Kentucky with the Mountain Parkway. Perry County became a commercial center of Eastern Kentucky with the construction of several malls. The East Kentucky Regional Airport, was opened in 1983, and named in honor of U.S. Sen. Wendell H. Ford. Buckhorn Lake State Resort Park and Carr Creek State Park are great tourist destinations for outdoor enthusiasts, for boating and fishing, and those in need of a relaxing vacation.

Contributed by Martha Quigley, Bobby Davis Museum and Park

Pike County

"Pike county was established in the year 1821, out of part of Floyd; was the 70th in order of formation, and named in honor of Gen. Zebulon M. Pike. A small portion of its territory was taken in 1870, towards forming the county of Martin. It is the easternmost county in the state; and bounded N. by Martin, N.E., E., S.E., and S. by Virginia, S.W. by Letcher, and W. by Floyd county. It is drained by the waters of the Big Sandy river; its Tug Fork forming the N. E. boundary line, and the Levisa (or Louisa) and West Forks running through the county, almost from the E. to W. The surface presents quite a variegated appearance; along the water courses, the lands are of excellent quality and very productive; while the uplands are broken and mountainous, and the soil comparatively poor. Corn, cattle, and hogs are the staple products, but oats, wheat, rye, buckwheat, and some tobacco are raised.

The Court House of Pike county was erected, in 1823, upon a public square in the town of Pikeville, which together with a large portion of the town itself, was in such a disputed situation, that the legislature was appealed to for a remedy; and by law vested the title to the town in trustees, directing to sell the lots, and return the proceeds of sale in secured bonds to the circuit clerk's office, for the benefit of those whom the court should decree to be the rightful owners full pay for their property.

This county was named in honor of General Zebulon M. Pike, born in New Jersey, Jan. 5, 1779. He entered the army while yet a boy, and served as a cadet in his father's company, afterwards as ensign and lieutenant. In 1805 he was sent by the government to explore the Mississippi river to its sources. After his return, he was sent by Gen. Wilkinson on an excursion into the interior of Louisiana, to fix the boundary line between New Mexico and the United States. Upon his return he was appointed a captain, subsequently a major, and in 1810 a colonel. In 1812 he was stationed on the northern frontier, and in 1813 appointed a brigadier general. He was selected to command the land forces in an expedition against York, the capital of Upper Canada, and April 25th sailed from Sackett's Harbor in the squadron commanded by Commodore Chauncey. On the 27th he arrived at York with seventeen hundred chosen men. A landing having been effected under a heavy fire from the enemy, in the course of the attack, large stones were thrown in every direction, one of which struck Pike, inflicting a mortal wound."

An excerpt from pages 679-680 of the entry for "Pike County," Collins' Historical Sketches of Kentucky, History of Kentucky, Volume II (Southern Historical Press, 1874).

Well, what about that?

It seems that Dwight Yoakum has never forgotten he was born in Kentucky...his song "Readin', Writin' and Route 23" pays tribute to his childhood move to Ohio from Kentucky. Born in Pikeville, Dwight grew up in Columbus, Ohio with his mom and step-dad. Legend has it that "Readin', Writin' and Route 23" described a local expression about the highway route many Kentuckians took when they left home to find a job up north. Yes, a drive on Route 23 takes a traveler directly north from Kentucky, through Columbus and Toledo, Ohio, and on to Michigan, to its automotive manufacturing centers and the plentiful jobs that attracted so many Kentuckians. Dwight himself had a white collar job, working in the automotive industry until his country music debut in 1986, with "Guitars, Cadillacs, Etc., Etc." Remember, "Crazy Little Thing Called Love" and the one Elvis Presley made famous first, "Suspicious Minds?"

Powell County

Although Powell County, named in honor of Gov. Lazarus W. Powell, was the 101st county formed in Kentucky when it was officially established on May 10, 1852, its history began much earlier than that.

On June 7, 1769, Daniel Boone viewed the Bluegrass from Pilot Knob, the highest point in Powell County. By 1805, what became the Red River Iron Works was in operation; and, under that name, the first post office in what was to be Powell County was established in 1824. In 1805, the operation was known as Clark and Smith's Iron Works.

When the county was created, Beaver Pond was designated as the county seat.

Natural Bridge
Source: Kentucky Department of Tourism

Later it was renamed Stanton, in honor of U.S. Rep. Richard H. Stanton of Maysville. The courthouse and records were burned by Civil War guerrillas in 1863.

Logging became an important industry in the 1800s; and, in 1917, an oil boom period began. In 1911, while lumber mills and logging were still in their heyday, the Nada Tunnel was built, connecting by rail timber tracts of the Red River Gorge with a trunk line to the south of it. On June 1, 1884, the first run of a Kentucky Union Railway train into Powell County took place. The tracks were taken up in 1942 to aid the war effort.

The county's first newspaper, the "Powell County Journal," was started in March, 1886, but it lasted only six months. Ten years later, the "Spout Spring Times" was begun in Estill County by J.E. Burgher. Moved to Powell County, it continues today as "The Clay City Times," having been given that name in 1901.

The Clay City National Bank was erected in 1889. The building stands today as the Red River Museum. In 1925, Natural Bridge, a huge natural stone arch, was deeded by the railway company to the Commonwealth of Kentucky. Today it is the highlight of the Natural Bridge State Resort Park. The Bert T. Combs Mountain Parkway, so named by Gov. Louie B. Nunn in 1971, was opened to traffic in 1963. Powell County has been visited by two first ladies of the U.S., Eleanor Roosevelt in 1937 and Lady Bird Johnson in 1967.

A long-lasting impact on Powell County was made by the Stanton Academy, a United Presbyterian school, which operated from 1908 until 1931. Author Harriette Simpson Arnow, who wrote "The Dollmaker," attended it during her freshman year of high school. Numerous other persons born in, living in, or having lived in Powell County are well known outside the county. These include: Joe Bowen, cyclist and stilt-walker; the late Gov. Bert T. Combs; Sara Walters Combs, chief judge of the Kentucky Court of Appeals; Lily May Ledford, musician; Larry Meadows, historian and museum curator; Nellie K. Meadows, artist; David Eugene Rule, minister and historian; and Woody Stephens, horse trainer.

Powell County is a growing region. From only 2,257 people in 1860, the county's population increased to 13,237 in 2000.

Contributed by David Eugene Rule

Pulaski County

Pulaski County, located in the south-central part of the state, was the 27th county formed in Kentucky. It was created by an act of the General Assembly on Dec. 10, 1798, out of territory belonging to Lincoln and Green counties.

Being off the beaten path of the first people coming into this land, Pulaski County was not among the most favored Kentucky counties, but it is rich in natural resources and scenic beauty. The valley is very fertile, with gorges cut by swift flowing streams filled with redbud and dogwood during the spring; in the autumn the trees turn many shades of golden hues. It is a historic fact that all of Kentucky was a hunting ground for deer, and it remains a popular sport to this day.

Statue of Sen. John Sherman Cooper in the Somerset town square
Source: Sid Webb

A duel was fought to determine where the county seat would be located — in its present location or south of the Cumberland on Allen's Branch. They compromised on the name Somerset after Somerset, England. The name of the county was the result of the War of Independence: Pulaski County was named after Count Casmir Pulaski, a Polish patriot and Revolutionary war hero, who was considered the "father of the American Cavalry."

A couple of well known people from Pulaski County are author Harriet Simpson Arnow and Edith Pearl Fitzgerald, who was a Broadway actress and screenwriter for MGM.

Contributed by Louann Hardy

**Short Creek,
"The shortest creek in the world"
near Stab, was once the site of a mill**
Source: Sid Webb

Robertson County

"Robertson county, established in 1867, out of fractions of four counties, Nicholas, Harrison, Bracken, and Mason, was named after ex-chief Justice George Robertson, and was the 111th formed in the state. It is situated in the N. E. middle section, and is bounded N. by Bracken and Mason counties, E. by Mason and Fleming, S. by Nicholas, and W. by Harrison. The principal streams are the Licking river, which is the boundary line from the Lower Blue Lick Springs to the Brooksville and Claysville turnpike, opposite the town of Claysville; North fork of Licking river, which is part of its N. boundary; and Shannon, Johnson's fork, Clay's, Cedar, West, Helm's Painter, and Fire Lick creeks, and Drift run. The surface of the county is hilly, but the land can be cultivated. The soil is tolerably good, some of it excellent and admirable adapted to raising tobacco. The timber is mostly oak, but with poplar, sugar tree, beech, hickory, and walnut intermingled. The productions and exports are tobacco, corn, oats, wheat, rye and live stock.

Ex-Chief Justice George Robertson, in honor of whom this county was named, was born Nov. 18, 1790, in Mercer county, Ky. His father, Alexander Robertson, who was born in Augusta county, Va., about a mile from Staunton, Nov. 22, 1748, was the son of James Robertson–who with his own father of the same name, emigrated about 1737 to America from the neighborhood of Coleraine, in the north of Ireland.

George Robertson, after attaining a good elementary education in the English branches, was sent, Aug., 1804, to Joshua Fry (then teaching on his farm five miles west of Danville, once owned and occupied by Col. George Nicholas) to learn Latin, French, and mathematics. From this he entered Transylvania, remaining until 1806; then spent four months in Rev. Samuel Finley's classical school at Lancaster, Ky., for six months more being his assistant in teaching. In the spring of 1808 he went to Frankfort to study law under Gen. Martin D. Hardin, but was disappointed; returned to Lancaster, and, under the direction of his brother-in-law, Samuel McKee, then a member of congress, studied law until Sept., 1809, when Judges Boyle and Wallace granted him license to practice.

In Nov., 1809, when only a few days over 19 years

> In Nov., 1809,
> when only a few days
> over 19 years of age,
> he [George Robertson]
> married Eleanor Bainbridge,
> who was less than 16,
> a daughter of
> Dr. Bainbridge, of Lancaster.
> The young couple set up for
> themselves in a
> small buckeye house
> with only two rooms

of age, he married Eleanor Bainbridge, who was less than 16, a daughter of Dr. Bainbridge, of Lancaster. The young couple set up for themselves in a small buckeye house with only two rooms. A remarkable coincidence of successive events is related with pride. Also setting up housekeeping at the same house and elected to congress were: Judge John Boyle (1803-09); Samuel McKee (1809-17); George Robertson (1817-21); Robert P. Letcher (1823-33)."

An excerpt from pages 686-687 of the entry for "Robertson County," Collins' Historical Sketches of Kentucky, History of Kentucky, Volume II (Southern Historical Press, 1874).

Rockcastle County

"Rockcastle county, the 52nd established in the state, was formed in 1810, out of parts of Lincoln, Pulaski, Madison, and Knox counties, and named after Rockcastle river, which forms its S.E. border. It is situated in the S. E. middle section; is bounded N. by Madison and Garrard counties, E. by Jackson, S. E. by Laurel, S. and S. W. by Pulaski, and W. by Lincoln. The N. E. and S. E. parts of the county are broken and hilly, but interspersed with numerous streams (Brush, Roundstone, Rentfro's, Skaggs', Copper creeks, Dick's and Rockcastle rivers). In the W. part of the county, the surface is level or gently undulating, and the soil quite productive. The timber consists of white, chestnut, black and spotted oak, of hickory, poplar, lynn, walnut, dogwood, and sycamore; in some locations there are orchards of sugar trees creating a large quantity of maple sugar. The staple products are corn, oats, hay, wheat, rye and live stock.

Rockcastle River – "Nearly the whole of the base of the hills on Rockcastle river, in the vicinity of the "*Narrows*" (near the mouth), is composed for upwards of 200 feet of soft shaly materials—on which reposes 150 feet of massive sandstone and conglomerate, forming, the conspicuous escarpment known as the "Bee Cliff," whose summit is 355 feet above the river or about 1,100 feet above tide-water without reckoning the slope above, which is 25 or 50 feet more. In consequence of the crumbling away of the shaly beds supporting these enormous weight of sandstone and conglomerate, the cliffs are rapidly undermined-while immense masses become disjointed, and are precipitated down the abrupt slope into the bed of the river. The stream has thus become blocked up with rocks—that in many places even a canoe can not pass. The river is full of excellent fish. Hence it is a favorite hunting and fishing ground. Rockcastle river is about 75 miles long, and about 200 to 250 feet wide.

Saltpeter Caves. – Among the Rockcastle hills are numerous saltpeter caves, at which large quantities of saltpeter were manufactured during the war

of 1812. One of these, called the "Big Cave" or the "Great Saltpeter Cave," extends through a spur of the mountain or "Big Hill," over half a mile. The saltpeter manufactured here…gave employment to 60 or 70 laborers. There is fine, bold running

> The stream has thus become blocked up with rocks—that in many places even a canoe can not pass. The river is full of excellent fish. Hence it is a favorite hunting and fishing ground.

stream of water in the cave, and works were constructed inside, for the manufacture of saltpeter by torchlight. Carts and wagons passed through, from one side of the mountain to the other, without difficulty. The way is so level and straight, that oxen were soon taught to pass through in perfect darkness, without a driver."

An excerpt from pages 690-691 of the entry for "Rockcastle County," Collins' Historical Sketches of Kentucky, History of Kentucky, Volume II (Southern Historical Press, 1874).

Rowan County

Rowan County is nestled amid the foothills of the Appalachian Mountains on the edge of the Daniel Boone National Forest. It is believed the first Europeans entered this section of Kentucky in 1772 and later settled in the Licking River Valley.

Rowan was established on May 1, 1856, and named for distinguished jurist, attorney John Rowan, the owner of Federal Hill (My Old Kentucky Home) in Bardstown.

Triplett, a tiny community near the geographical

Source: SouthEast Telephone

center of the county was selected as the site of the county seat. Its name was changed to Morehead in honor of Kentucky's Gov. Charles Morehead (1855-1859).

During the Civil War, some of the county's citizens fought on both sides. Morehead's courthouse was burned March 21, 1864, sowing seeds of the Tolliver-Marin Feud or Rowan County War (1884-1887). Rowan became a lawless community and 22 people were killed over a three-year period.

In April, 1887, a "Louisville Courier Journal" headline read, "Rowan, a county without schools, without churches, without judges: missionaries urgently needed." The Morehead Normal School opened on October 3, 1887. Out of that humble beginning came Morehead State University in 1966. In 2005 Morehead State University had

almost 10,000 students and employed over 1,000 people.

In 1911, Moonlight Schools were opened at night to overcome illiteracy throughout the county. This movement was perceived internationally as a model for adult education.

The railroad came through Rowan County in 1881, opening up the market for the region's vast supply of virgin timber, stone and clay.

Shortly after midnight on July 4, 1939, a flash flood roared through Morehead, washing away houses and drowning 25 people. It caused $5,000,000 in property damage. As a result of the devastation, a flood wall was built to prevent a repeat of the tragedy.

On July 1, 1963, the Sisters of Notre Dame opened the St. Claire Hospital, a 41-bed general acute care hospital. By 2005, it was a modern 159-bed regional hospital providing the latest in health care.

In 1973, the U.S. Corps of Engineers completed the Cave Run Dam across the Licking River. The dam created a beautiful 8270-acre lake, providing flood control, water supply to the region, and a popular recreational area.

On July 4, 2002, Freedom Park was dedicated on the grounds of the old courthouse in downtown Morehead to honor all Rowan Countians who served in the military in war and peace. By 2005, there were almost 3,000 names on the wall. Names are added as men and women are discharged from the military.

A regional park for economic development has opened in Rowan County. In 2005 the city and county began building a new convention center in downtown Morehead, and the old courthouse was converted into a Rowan County Arts Center. A regional armory and airport were built, as well. The city, Rowan, Bath, Morgan and Menifee counties cooperated in building a regional development center to benefit the entire region.

Contributed by Jack D. Ellis.

Russell County

"Russell County, the 81st formed in Kentucky, was established in 1825, out of parts of Adair, Wayne, and Cumberland, and named after Col. Wm. Russell. It is a small county, situated in the south middle section of the state, and lies on both sides of Cumberland River; is bounded N. and N.E. by Casey, E. by Pulaski, S.E. by Wayne, S. by Clinton, and W. and N.W. by Cumberland and Adair counties. The beautiful level bottom lands on the Cumberland are very fertile; but the surface of the county generally is hilly and broken, and the soil not well adapted for profitable agriculture. Good streams of water abound, and the water power of the county is remarkably fine; one cotton and two woolen factories were established before 1847, and many other factories might be advantageously established.

The Towns are all small. — Jamestown, the county seat, is 23 miles S.E. of Columbia, 18 N.W. of Monticello, 43 S.E. of Lebanon, and about 96 S. of Frankfort; population in 1870, 138; incorporated Dec. 23, 1827. ...

Columbia
Source: SouthEast Telephone

Col. William Russell in honor of whom this county was named was born in Culpepper co., Va., in 1758, and died in Fayette co., Ky., July 3, 1825—aged 67 years. While yet a boy his father removed into the extreme southwestern part of the province of Virginia. In 1774, the son, when only 15, joined an expedition under Daniel Boone against the Indians, and was in similar excursions repeatedly until 1780. In that year he visited Kentucky and Middle Tennessee, spending the summer near Nashville, and returning to Virginia in the fall. As a lieutenant in the mounted regiment, or as aid to Col. Wm. Campbell, he engaged in the famous battles of the Revolution, at King's Mountain, Whitsell's Mills, and Guilford Court House, and in an expedition against the Cherokee Indians.

Soon after the close of the war of Independence, Capt. Russell emigrated to Fayette county, Ky. In the several expeditions under Gen. Chas. Scott, Col. James Wilkinson, and Gen. Anthony Wayne, against the Indians, in 1791 and 1794, Col. Russell acted a gallant and distinguished part, exhibiting military capacity of a high order. In 1808, President Madison appointed him to the command of a regiment in the regular army. In 1811, after the battle of Tippecanoe, where his courage and skill were again prominent, Gen. Harrison was transferred to the command of the northwestern army, and Col. Russell succeeded him in the important command of the frontiers of Indiana, Illinois, and Missouri. After Hopkins' campaign, Col. Russell in conjunction with Gov. Ninian Edwards, of Illinois planned the expedition against the Peoria Indians, which was crowned with complete success. When peace was restored, Col. Russell retired to his farm.

No man thus distinguished in arms has ever, in Kentucky, been allowed to remain entirely out of civil life. Col. Russell was almost continuously honored with the confidence of the people."

An excerpt from pages 694-696 of the entry for "Russell County," Collins' Historical Sketches of Kentucky, History of Kentucky, Volume II (Southern Historical Press, 1874).

Scott County

As one of the six counties in and around Lexington referred to as the "Horse Capital of the World," Scott County is home to farms devoted to producing the finest American Saddlebred trotters and pacers anywhere. Scott County boasts three Kentucky Derby Winners: Kingman, Venetian Way and Winning Colors.

Because of area soil content, tobacco was historically one of the county's major crops. Scott County farmers, however, were among the state's first to begin diversifying crops. Fields once planted with tobacco are transitioning to producing beef, vegetables and flowers.

Rooted in industrial ingenuity, Georgetown was founded by Elijah Craig, a Baptist minister and accomplished businessman. Craig built a fulling mill for making fabrics and the first sawmill and gristmill. He is also reputed to be the creator of Kentucky bourbon.

Scott County prospered greatly in the early 1900s, and stately mansions and other edifices were built along Georgetown's main streets. Today, over 300 of them are listed on the National Register of Historic Places.

The 1960s brought a major change with the construction of Interstate 75 and Interstate 64. The interstates crossed near Georgetown, and the interchange drew commerce, causing the town's commercial shift.

With one of the lowest overall business costs in the nation, Kentucky caught the eye of Toyota Motor Corporation. In 1986 Toyota located a major manufacturing facility in Georgetown, where they now employ over 7,000 people. As a result other manufacturers have located in the area to support and supply Toyota, expanding even more the county's sound economic base.

From the halls of historic mansions to the assembly lines of Toyota, from Thoroughbred horse farms and the banks of Elkhorn Creek to the sidelines of pro football and the koi pond at Yuken, Georgetown and Scott County form a community where its heritage reflects the future. One might agree with residents and tourists alike: it's one of the best places on earth to live or to visit.

Once considered as a possible site for Kentucky's state capital, Scott County's elegant Ward Hall represents architectural innovation and the development of the state's lifestyle throughout history. Situated on 40 acres, the house was originally constructed in Greek Revival splendor in 1856 for the Junis Ward family. In its nearly 150-year existence, numerous families have called Ward Hall home and it once served, on a limited basis, as a house museum. It has attracted many admirers over the years and was noted by architectural historian, Rexford Newcomb, as "the most fabulous home in Central Kentucky."

Scott County Courthouse in Georgetown
Source: Sid Webb

Reprinted with permission Georgetown/Scott Co. Chamber of Commerce Magazine and Lanham Media Service.

Shelby County

Formed from a part of Jefferson County, Shelby County was the third county established after Kentucky became a state in 1792. It was named in honor of Isaac Shelby (1750-1826), Kentucky's first governor (1792-96) who was re-elected (1812-1816). Shelby served in the Revolutionary War, the Indian campaigns, and the War of 1812. He came to Kentucky in 1783, and was a member of the Statehood and Constitutional Conventions of 1784-1792.

Pioneer settlers, including Squire Boone, William Shannon, Bland Williams Ballard, Benjamin Logan, Brackett Owen, Acquilla Whitaker and Nicholas Meriwether made significant contributions to early Shelby County and Kentucky.

Shelby County is noted for many outstanding citizens, including natives Martha Layne Collins, the first woman governor of Kentucky (1984-87); famed author Alice Hegan Rice ("Mrs. Wiggs of the Cabbage Patch"); the first black graduate of the University of Louisville Law School, Willie Fleming; Robert F. Matthews Jr., the only Shelby Countian to serve as Kentucky's attorney general; Mark J. Scearce, who made Wakefield-Scearce a nationally recognized purveyor of quality antiques; noted sculptor Barney Bright; A.O. Stanley, elected governor of Kentucky in 1915 and to the U.S. Senate in 1917; Whitney M. Young, prominent African American educator who headed Lincoln Institute in Shelby County from 1936 to 1964; and his son, Whitney M. Young, Jr. who emerged in the 1960s as a national civil rights leader and headed up the National Urban League.

Other Shelby County residents who, while not native to the county, have enjoyed state or national prominence, include Col. Harland D. Sanders of fried chicken fame; Charles Stewart Todd, lawyer and soldier who was appointed by Pres. John Tyler in 1841 to serve as Envoy Extraordinaire and Minister Plenipotentiary to the Court of Russia; Marnel Moorman, who in 1992 became the first African American to be elected president of the Kentucky Education Association.; and Hall of Fame Saddle-bred owner, trainer and rider Helen Crabtree.

Shelby County has close ties to Pres. Harry S. Truman because his great-grandparents on both sides were married and lived in Shelby County.

Former Gov. Martha Layne Collins, in her foreword to "The New History of Shelby County" wrote,

Shelby County Courthouse
Source: SouthEast Telephone

"Shelby County is a special place. From the days when Indians roamed the forests, savannas, and waterways of what is now Kentucky to the present day, Shelby County has grown, developed and changed. Throughout these many years, history has been made which has created the character of this place, influencing its landscape, its people, its economy, its education, and the quality of life. Several years ago, the Shelby County Chamber of Commerce adopted a slogan, 'Good People, Good Land, Good Living.' The history of Shelby County is woven tightly into all three of these components."

Helping contribute to this good living is a strong mix of industry and agriculture. In 2005 Shelby County was named the fifth fastest growing county in Kentucky. Additionally, the state legislature has named Shelby County as the Saddlebred capital of the world.

Contributed by William E Matthews

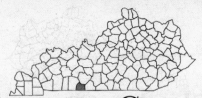

Simpson County

Simpson County came into existence on January 28, 1819, when the General Assembly passed an act using land from Logan, Warren and Allen counties to make a new and separate county. The story told is that it was too far to ride a horse to and from the area to any of the other county seats in one day. The county was named

tells us that land owned by William Hudspeth was viewed most favorably, but since an adequate water supply at this location was uncertain, Hudspeth agreed to dig a well. After several days of unsuccessful digging, commissioners gave him only one more day. In desperation Hudspeth hauled water all night from Drakes Creek and filled the well. When the commissioners checked the full well, they chose his property. The water from the creek primed the well and started a stream of water, which supplied Franklin, named for Benjamin Franklin, with water until about the time of the Civil War at which time it was declared unfit for use.

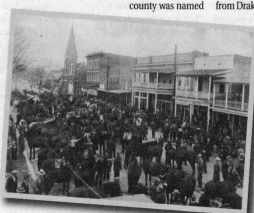

Mule Days
Source: Simpson County archive file

From 1939 until 1942, Simpson County boasted the second largest mule market in the world. At one time, people journeyed here to bathe in and drink the mineral waters.

Simpson County has thrived partially because of its excellent combination of agriculture and industry. Antique shops grace the downtown Franklin area and attract many visitors. A new technical school is being constructed and a plan to create a recreational vehicle mecca beginning in 2005 could make the county the number one tourist attraction in the state.

Simpson   in honor of Capt. John Simpson, one of Kentucky's Indian fighters and heroes in the War of 1812.

Simpson County is unique in that the southern boundary line of Kentucky takes an almost triangular entrance south, adding extra land into the state. The jag is a mystery with many rumors abounding, but the best known concerns Sanford Duncan, who lived about a mile north of the state line. In order to keep a certain portion of his land in Kentucky, it is said he entertained the surveyors with Kentucky hospitality, food and drink. The next day, his land was in Kentucky. A small amount of additional land was added from Allen County in 1822 and more from Logan County in 1869. However, Simpson County remains one of the smallest counties in area in the state.

The act, which created the county also provided for the selection of a permanent seat of justice. Legend

A few of the better known Simpson Countians include Jim Bowie, an Alamo hero with a well-known knife; Alexander Majors, founder of the Pony Express; T. O. Chisholm, music composer; Annie Potts, television and movie actress; Kenny Perry, PGA golfer; and Olivia Mayes Hall, worldwide author with the pen name Laurie Paige.

Information provided by the Simpson County Historical Society, Inc., 206 North College Street, Franklin, KY 42134, phone (270) 586-4228, FAX (270) 586-4429, e-mail: oldjail@comcats.net, web site: www.simpsoncountykyarchives.com. Compiled by Dr. James Henry Snider, President, with assistance from Nancy Thomas, Secretary, and Sara Jo Cardwell, Consultant and past president.

Spencer County

Spencer County, the 77th in order of formation, is located in western central Kentucky. It is bordered by Bullitt, Jefferson, Nelson, Shelby and Anderson counties and contains 193 square miles. As with most of the country, Spencer County was first settled by American Indians.

The county was named after Capt. Spear Spencer, a captain in the Cornstalk Militia in the early 1800s, a militia which used corn stalks for drills because of a shortage of rifles.

Born in Pennsylvania, Spencer and his family moved to Kentucky in 1792. Spencer formed the Yellow Jackets rifle company in 1809 and joined William Henry Harrison's command in the Tippecanoe campaign where he was killed on November 7, 1811.

The county seat is Taylorsville, incorporated in 1829, which sits in a lovely valley of about 160 acres. Taylorsville was named for Richard Taylor who owned the tract of land on which the town was laid out.

Taylorsville Park
Source: Kentucky Department of Tourism

The topography is rolling and hilly with Salt River cutting valleys 200 to 250 feet deep. Primarily an agricultural county from the arrival of the first settlers in 1776, Spencer had a slave-based economy. The county had sufficient labor to produce corn, raise livestock and hay, along with wheat and barley. Tobacco was for many years the major cash crop, but with government price support ending, many farmers are turning to raising soybeans.

A large number of Spencer Countians are employed outside the county, many in Louisville and in Shelby County.

Tourism expenditures are beginning to boost the county's economy.

Although Spencer County was not the scene of any major battles during the Civil War, it experienced much guerrilla activity. The threats of injury and theft of personal property by these and other guerrilla troops made life difficult for Spencer Countians during those times. Most notorious of the guerrillas was William Clark Quantrill who had gone through an apprenticeship in Bleeding Kansas before the war and continued his nefarious career during it. Seriously wounded, Quantrill died in a Louisville military prison on June 6 before he could be hanged.

Before the construction of the dam on Salt River and the creation of Taylorsville Lake in 1982, the town of Taylorsville was subject to periodic flooding.

Not only has the formation of the lake controlled flooding, but its 3,050 acres provide fishing and boating activities. Over 10,000 acres surrounding the lake are devoted to wild life preservation and recreation.

The Army Corps of Engineers operates a visitor's center at the dam, along with boat ramps and a marina. There are also two beautiful restored historic building — Ashes Creek Schoolhouse, probably built in the early 1800s and the Yates Log Cabin, which may be even older.

Since the impounding of Taylorsville Lake in 1982, and with the state park continuing to develop, Spencer County has experienced much growth. Now Spencer County is the fastest growing county in Kentucky. According to the Kentucky Data Center, as of July 1, 2004, the population of Spencer County was 14,822.

Contributed by Hilda Snider

Taylor County

"Taylor County, the 100th in the order of formation, was erected in 1848, out of the N.E. half of Green county, and named in honor of the then most popular soldier in the Union, Gen. Zachary Taylor. It is situated in the west middle portion of the state; is bounded N. by Larue and Madison counties, E. by Casey, S.E. and S. by Adair, and S.W. and W. by Green; and has an area of about 218 miles. It is well timbered; and finely watered by Green river (which forms part of its southern boundary), and by Robinson's, Wilson, Stoner, Blockhouse, Black Lick, Long Branch, Meadow, Big and Little Brush, and south, Middle and North Pitman creeks. The surface is generally undulating, in some places broken and hilly. Muldrow's Hills and the Knobs are in the eastern portion. The staple products are tobacco, corn, wheat, and oats. Brush Creek is of a very fine fiber; fruits of all kinds are grown in abundance. The soil of a portion of the county are quite thin. About 150 families of thrifty Pennsylvania farmers settled in the county in 1869-70 and are making their mark by substantial improvements in farming. ...

During the Civil War, Camps Hodson and Andy Johnson were both established in Taylor county. In Dec., 1864, guerrillas attacked some Federal soldiers stationed at Campbellsville; and at another time made a charge on the town, killing 2 Federal soldiers before resistance was effectual. On July 4, 1863, near the Green river bridge on the Lebanon and Columbia turnpike, in the southern corner of Taylor county, occurred one of the bravest assaults but bloodiest repulses of the war—the Confederate forces being driven off, with terrible slaughter, in only half an hour. (For details see Collins' Annals, Vol. 1, page 125).

The following is an excerpt from 'Jefferson County' describing the life of Pres. Zachary Taylor, Vol. 1, pages 380, 387, of Collins' Historical Sketches of Kentucky, History of Kentucky: "Among the distinguished men, whom Jefferson county enrolls with her worthies, a prominent place belongs to Major General Zachary Taylor, of the United States' army. Although not a Kentuckian by birth, he was brought by his parents to this State when only nine months old, and received his first impressions of the world amid the hardy hunters, the tall forests and romantic scenery of the dark and bloody ground. ...

He [Zachary] was brought and educated in the neighborhood, and grew up to manhood with the yell of the savage and the crack of the rifle almost constantly ringing in his ears. General Zachary Taylor may be literally said to have been cradled in war, nor have the deeds of his subsequent life done discredit to his early training."

Zachary Taylor

Note: President Taylor became the 12th president on March 5, 1849. He fell ill after the 4th of July celebrations and died July 9, 1850. [www.whitehouse.gov/history/presidents/].

An excerpt from pages 725-726 of the entry for "Taylor County," Collins' Historical Sketches of Kentucky, History of Kentucky, Vol. II (Southern Historical Press, 1874).

Todd County

"Todd County, named in honor of Col. John Todd, and established in 1819 out of parts of Logan and Christian, was the 64th of the counties of Kentucky in order of formation. It is situated in the southern part of the state, on the Tennessee line; is one of the most easterly of the S.W. counties; is bounded N. by Muhlenburg, E. by Logan, S. by the state line of Tennessee (or by the county of Montgomery in that state), and W. by Christian. The county is finely watered by Elk, West and East forks of Pond River, Whippoorwill, and Big, Little, and West Clifty creeks—tributaries of Red river in the south, and of Muddy and Pond rivers in the north. But for a small portion in the N.W. end of the county, the territory would form an oblong square; it comprises about 330 square miles. The S. and a portion of the N. part of the county is level or gently undulating—the soil based upon limestone, and very productive; the remainder is rolling and hilly—the soil of inferior quality, but producing fine grass. The principle products are corn, wheat, oats, and tobacco; and exports—horses, mules, cattle, sheep, and hogs...

Col. John Todd, for whom this county was named, was the eldest of three brothers, and a native of Pennsylvania. He was educated in Virginia, at his uncle's—the Rev. John Todd,—and, at maturity, entered upon the study of the law, and finally obtained a license to practice. He left his uncle's residence, and settled in the town of Fincastle in Virginia, where he practiced law for several years;

but Daniel Boone and others having discovered Kentucky, Col. Todd, lured with the descriptions given him of the fertility of the country, about the year 1775, came first to Kentucky, where he found Col. Henderson and others at Boonsborough. He joined Henderson's party, obtained a pre-emption right, and located sundry tracts of land in the now county of Madison, in Col. Henderson's office. He afterwards returned to Virginia; and, in the year 1786, again set out from Virginia with his friend, John May, and one or two other, for Kentucky. The proceeded some distance together on the journey, when, for some cause, Mr. May left his servant with Col. Todd, to proceed on to Kentucky, and returning to Richmond, Virginia. Col. Todd proceeded on to the place where Lexington now stands, and, in its immediate vicinity, improved two places,—the one in his own name, and the other in that if his friend, John May,—for both of which he obtained certificates for settlement and pre-emption of fourteen hundred acres. These pre-emptions adjoin, and lie in the immediate vicinity of the now city of Lexington. It appears from depositions, taken since his death, that he accompanied Col. Clark, since Gen. Clark, in his expedition against Kaskaskia and Vincennes, and was at the capture of those places."

An excerpt from pages 727-729 of the entry for "Todd County," Collins' Historical Sketches of Kentucky, History of Kentucky, Volume II (Southern Historical Press, 1874).

Well, I never...

Col. Todd's widow told this story after his death: "That, during the winter succeeding their marriage [in 1780], the provisions of the fort at Lexington became exhausted to such an extent, that, on her husband's return home with George [his aid] one night, almost famished with hunger, she had been able to save for him a small piece of bread, about two inches square, and about a gill of milk, which she presented to him; on which he asked, if there was nothing for George? She answered, 'not a mouthful.' He called George, and handed him the bread and the milk, without taking any of it for himself."

Collins' Historical Sketches of Kentucky, Vol. II, page 730.

Trigg County

Trigg County, the 66th county in order of formation, is located on the southwestern edge of the Pennyroyal region. It is bounded by Tennessee to the south and by Kentucky Lake to the west. Containing 421 square miles, Trigg County is sur-

✘✘✘✘✘✘✘✘✘✘✘✘✘

The first census of 1820 listed Trigg County's population at 3,874 inhabitants. The first government was organized on May 15, 1820.

✘✘✘✘✘✘✘✘✘✘✘✘✘

rounded by Calloway, Marshall, Lyon, Caldwell and Christian counties. It was created on January 27, 1820, and was formed principally from Christian County and a small portion of Caldwell. The county was named for Col. Stephen Trigg, a native of Virginia, and a soldier of great renown, who came to Kentucky in the fall of 1779 as a land commissioner. Col. Trigg was fatally wounded on August 19, 1782, in the disastrous Battle of Blue Licks. The first census of 1820 listed Trigg County's population at 3,874 inhabitants. The first government was organized on May 15, 1820, in a log structure at Warrington, occupied as a residence by Samuel Orr.

Cadiz, the county seat of Trigg County, is located just 30 miles west of Fort Campbell. The fort's west military boundary joins the southeastern tip of Trigg County. This unique city nestles in rolling countryside at an elevation of 540 feet above sea level and enjoys a favorable and moderate climate. Cadiz has interesting legends behind its name. One version is that a group of Spaniards encamped on Little River attended all town meetings. The towns' people were so impressed with the visitors the town was named "Cadiz," for the Spaniard's hometown of Cadiz, Spain.

A history of the first settlement of Cadiz district would not be complete without a short statement about four men who began life almost with the beginning of Trigg County. Major Matthew Mayes, Collins D. Bradley, and T. W. Hammond, where three young lawyers who came to Cadiz in 1820, even before there was a court house, and began to practice law. The fourth man, Linn Boyd, probably attained more prominence than any other citizen. He was born November 22, 1800, and like most others of his day, received a very scant education. At 21, he was appointed paymaster of the Kentucky Militia; in 1823, he was appointed a deputy sheriff of Trigg County; he then represented Trigg County in the legislature in 1831; was elected to U.S. Congress for 18 years; and in 1859 became Lieutenant Governor of Kentucky. However, he never took office due to poor health and died in Paducah later that year.

With more than 340 miles of shoreline (comprising up to one-third of the Land Between The Lakes 170,000 acres), favorite pastimes, such as fishing, boating, swimming, the beach and loafing, are within easy reach for Trigg County, especially around Barkley Lake State Park Resort. Precipitation is well distributed throughout the year. In the fall of the year, colorful trees and mild, sunny days make recreational and family oriented activities abound. Well known for its festivals, recreation and location, the city is surrounded by many of nature's wonders that add to the many charms of Trigg County and the surrounding area.

Source: Cadiz-Trigg County Chamber of Commerce; www.barkleylake.com/trigg_county.html

Trimble County

"Trimble County, the 86th formed in the state, was established in 1836, out of parts of Gallatin, Henry, and Oldham counties, and named in honor of Judge Robert Trimble. It is situated in the northern part of the state, immediately on the Ohio River; is bounded W. and N. by the Ohio River for 21 miles, N.E. by Carroll, and S.E. and S. by Henry and Oldham counties; and contains about 145 square miles, being one of the smallest counties (there are but six smaller). Little Kentucky river flows northward entirely across or through the E. part of the county, and empties into the Ohio, in Carroll county, one mile below the mouth of Kentucky River; among the other streams are Spring, Corn, Barebone, Middle, and Patton creeks. The valleys on the Ohio River are unsurpassed in fertility; and the uplands, through hilly and broken, are quite productive. The principle productions and exports are tobacco, blackberries, corn, wheat, oats, hogs, and cattle. ...

The Hon. Robert Trimble, in honor of whom this county received its name, was born in Berkeley County, Virginia, and when three years old, his father immigrated to Kentucky. His parents were not affluent, but occupied a respectable position in the agricultural population of the country. He received but the imperfect rudiments of an education — such only as could be had in a new settlement, so distant from the seats of learning in the older States. He, however, improved himself, by teaching for a few years, and reading carefully the scanty libraries afforded by his neighborhood. After so imperfect a probation, he commenced the study of law, under George Nicholas. That eminent man dying before he had completed his studies, he continued them under James Brown; and, in 1803, was licensed by the court of appeals to practice his profession. He commenced his career in Paris, and in the same year was elected a member of the legislature from the county of Bourbon. But the stormy life of a politician not being congenial to his disposition or taste, he ever afterwards refused to be a candidate for political office — even

to be nominated, on two occasions, for the United States' senate, when his assent only was necessary to secure his election. He devoted himself exclusively to his profession, and rapidly rose to the first class of jurist. In 1808, he was commissioned sec-

...but the stormy life of a politician not being congenial to his disposition or taste, he (Judge Robert Trimble) ever afterwards refused to be a candidate for political office...

ond judge of the court of appeals. He retained this place but a short time, but long enough to greatly distinguish himself in it by his rectitude, learning and ability. He was appointed chief justice of Kentucky in 1810, but, in consequence of his limited circumstances, declined the first judicial station in the commonwealth. After retiring from the bench, he resumed, with great assiduity, the practice of his profession; and, in 1813, was appointed a district attorney for the State. He continued at the bar, with eminent and profitable success, until 1816, when he was appointed by President Madison judge of the Kentucky district. He filled this office until 1826, when he was prompted by John Quincy Adams to the Supreme Court of the United States. He died the 25th day of August, 1828, in the fifty-second year of his age, and in the full vigor of his power."

An excerpt from pages 732,734 of the entry for "Trimble County," Collins' Historical Sketches of Kentucky, History of Kentucky, Volume II (Southern Historical Press, 1874).

Union County

"Union County, the 55th formed in the state, was taken entirely from the W. part of Henderson county, in 1811, and thus described: Beginning at the upper point of the Eighteen-mile island (formerly called Elk island, and in 1840 known to boatmen as Slim island), on the Ohio River; people assented to the proposed division of the old county. Thus, it is bounded N., N.W., and W. by the Ohio River, for 41 miles; N.E. by Henderson county; S.E. by Webster; and S.W. by Crittenden county; and embraces about 316 square miles of territory. Shawneetown, Illinois, and

Camp Breckinridge Museum & Arts Center, Morganfield
Source: Kentucky Department of Tourism

thence a straight line to Highland creek, one mile above Higgins' mill (measured along the meanders of the creek); thence up the said creek to the White-lick fork thereof; thence a direct and straight line, by "Harpes Head," to the line of Hopkins county; thence with that line, to Tradewater river; thence down the same to the Ohio River, and up the Ohio to the beginning.

The origin of the name is in doubt; but the generally received opinion is that it was so named because of the hearty unanimity with which the the mouths of the Wabash and Saline rivers, are all opposite this county. The face of the country is level, undulating, and in some parts hilly. The soil is good. Corn and tobacco are the staple products, but all other crops usual in the state are cultivated, and horses, mules, cattle, sheep and hogs exported."

An excerpt from pages 735-736 of the entry for "Union County," Collins' Historical Sketches of Kentucky, History of Kentucky, Volume II (Southern Historical Press, 1874).

Warren County

"Warren County, the 24th formed in the state, was established in 1796 out of part of Logan, and named in honor of Gen. Jos. Warren, the hero of Bunker Hill. It embraces about 560 square miles; and is bounded N. by Butler and Edmonson counties, E. by Barren, S. by Allen and Simpson, and W. by Logan and Butler. Big Barren river, which heads near the Cumberland river, runs through this county; its tributaries in the county are Bay's fork, Drake's and Jennings' creeks, and Gaspar river. There are several mineral springs in the county, one of which, 3 miles from Bowling Green, in the character of its water is much like the Lower Blue Lick, in Nicholas county. The face of the country is gently undulating; the soil fertile and productive based mostly on red clay and limestone foundation. The principle articles of export are tobacco, wheat, corn, and pork. ...

The First Railroad in Kentucky ran from where the new court house in Bowling Green stands, along Plain street, to the Double Springs on Green river. It was over a mile long, and built about 1832, by James R. Skiles and Jacob Vanmeter. Some of the wooden cross-ties were still visible in 1872. The cars were drawn by horse.

Warren County, in 1851, subscribed $300,000 stock in the Louisville and Nashville railroad, issuing bonds in payment. A tax, to meet interest, was collected for some year—since which the dividends from the road have paid the interest and part of the principle of the debt, each year. In 1872, the sinking fund treasurer recommended the sale of stock enough to pay the outstanding bonds; there would remain $175,000 stock, yielding over $11,000 yearly. The population of the county in 1840 was 15,446, fell off to 15,123 in 1850, but increased to 21,742 in 1870 — and increase, from 1850 to 1870, of 43 ¾ per cent. The taxable property in 1851 was $5,028,141 and in 1872, $8,029,631 — an advance in 21 years of 59 2/3 per cent, and from being the 16th county in wealth in the state to the 7th. ...

Maj. Gen. Joseph Warren, M.D., in honor of whom this county was named, was one of the most dis-

tinguished patriots of the American Revolutionary war; was born at Roxbury, near Boston, in 1741— the son of a farmer; entered Harvard University, at

> ## Maj. Gen Joseph Warren, M.D., in honor of whom this county was named, was one of the most distinguished patriots of the American Revolutionary war...

14, and was there remarkable for his talents, fine address, and bold and independent spirit; studied medicine, and had rapid and high success in the practice; on two occasions, delivered eloquent orations on March 5th, the anniversary of the Boston massacre, and became prominent in politics, as a public speaker and writer; was president of the provincial congress of Massachusetts, in 1775; participated in the battle of Lexington, April 19, 1775; June 14,1775, was appointed major general of the military force of Massachusetts province; and at the battle of Bunker Hill, in Boston, on June 17,1775, when the American troops — after three times repelling the British troops — exhausted their ammunition and were compelled to retire, he was killed by a random shot, among the last to abandon the entrenchments. Congress passes a resolution to erect a monument to his memory, which long occupied the site of the present Bunker Hill monument."

An excerpt from pages 736,737,747 of the entry for "Warren County," Collins' Historical Sketches of Kentucky, History of Kentucky, Volume II (Southern Historical Press, 1874)

Washington County

Before the Revolution, pioneers discovered Washington County. Settlers followed the Wilderness Trace to Sandusky's and Cartwright's stations and the lands along the Beech Fork. Rich woodlands and farmlands attracted the settlers to Washington County and several communities had sprung into being by the time Kentucky was admitted to statehood. Today's traveler is still drawn to the colors and beauty of the landscapes, the fine structures built by early hands and one of the few remaining covered bridges in the state.

Washington County is centrally located within the state, and lies within a day's drive of two-thirds of the population of the U.S. Foremost among Washington County's attractions is Lincoln Homestead State Park, land once owned by members of the Lincoln family. The house in which Abraham Lincoln's parents were married is there, as are other historic buildings tied to our 16th president. The Washington County Courthouse, completed in 1816, is the oldest courthouse in the state west of the Alleghenies still in daily use. Among the records dating from 1792 is the marriage certificate of Pres. Abraham Lincoln's parents, Thomas and Nancy Hanks Lincoln. Other attractions include:

- Mt. Zion Covered Bridge – the longest covered bridge in Kentucky
- Eleanores, the Elizabeth Madox Roberts Home – where the famed author lived and wrote
- The John Pope House – Pope was governor of the Arkansas Territory
- St. Catharine Motherhouse – home of the Dominican Sisters founded in 1822
- Kalarama Farm – home of the fine Kalarama strain of Saddlebred horses
- The Arnold Home – built in 1843, served as a hospital for soldiers wounded during the Civil War

- The Jesse Head Homesite – Methodist minister who married Thomas Lincoln and Nancy Hanks
- House of History – oldest house still standing in Springfield, built of logs circa 1800
- Elmwood – built in 1851, used as headquarters by Civil War General Don Carlos Buell
- Maple Hill Manor – stately mansion circa 1851 and named Kentucky's most historic B&B for the past two years
- St. Rose Priory – founded in 1806, the first Catholic educational institution west of the Alleghenies and attended by Confederate President Jefferson Davis in 1815-1816

Washington County residents view their spirituality as an important part of life. In May 2005 many members of local churches took turns reading the entire Bible on the courthouse steps. Washington County is considered part of the Catholic Church's "American Holy Land." In addition to the Catholic churches in the county, there are nearly 20 Baptist churches, as well as Presbyterian, Methodist, Church of Christ, Church of God of Prophecy, Christian, AME Zion, Pentecostal and nondenominational churches.

Source: SouthEast Telephone

One of Washington County's biggest assets is its agriculture industry. In the past, this centered around tobacco and livestock. As tobacco production has fallen off, more emphasis is being placed on beef cattle and agritourism, with the latter holding great promise for the future. As local farmers learn more about modern agriculture and technology, they ensure that one of Washington County's historically important industries is adapting to the changes coming in the 21st century.
Contributed by the Springfield-Washington County Chamber of Commerce.

Wayne County

The known history of Wayne County and its county seat, Monticello, began with the Paleo-Indian people who lived in south central Kentucky 9,000 to 12,000 years ago. The following centuries were characterized by the development of the civilizations of the American Indian. Next came the European explorers and the Long Hunters like Benjamin Price, Nathaniel Buckhannon, and Jerry Pearce, are believed to have established the first permanent settlement in Wayne County.

After the Revolutionary War, as many as 15,000 of that war's brave American soldiers settled in Kentucky. At least 46 of them settled in Wayne County. The bodies of these courageous pioneers lie buried in the hallowed soil of Wayne County; their legacy of freedom lives on in the lives of the thousands of their descendants.

Soon after Kentucky became the 15th state in the union in 1792, the state legislature passed an act that led to the formation of Wayne County. In 1800 Monticello with its population of 27 people became the county seat of Wayne County.

These humble, yet noble, beginnings have served as the foundation stones upon which all Wayne County's modern history rests.

The proud determination of those pioneer fathers and their intense work ethic caused them to carve out of the wilderness a home for their families. Their wisdom and intelligence helped to develop industry and a business community that thrives to this day. Their love of country has sent many of them into battle to defend the principles of freedom and democracy. A devotion to God caused them to establish churches that created an environment for the growth of character and integrity. Schools were built to nurture the quest for knowledge.

The pioneer spirit is still present in the heart of those men and women who, almost daily, start a new business venture. The patriotic spirit is proudly expressed in the presence of veterans groups and an active National Guard made up of citizens who stand ready to respond to the call of a free people to go to the ends of the earth to protect and preserve this country's freedoms. The community spirit is expressed in the scores of volunteer and civic organizations whose members provide a helping hand to those in need. The religious spirit is to be witnessed in the number of houses of worship that open their doors to those who look for an expression of man's higher calling.

A progressive spirit exists in Monticello and Wayne County that makes it attractive to vacationers, seniors looking for retirement homes, corporations seeking a work force for their business ventures, and for migrant workers looking for a place to start a new life.

Two hundred years of hard work and determination, commitment and vision, pride and glory, make Monticello and Wayne County one of the most desirable places for people of all ages, all backgrounds, and all dreams to make their homes.

Wayne Countians are a proud people, who treasure their heritage, enjoy their prosperity, and are building their future on their vision.

Contributed by Harlan Ogle, Executive Director and Curator, William Crenshaw Kennedy, Jr. Memorial Museum.

Webster County

Webster County is situated in the western part of Kentucky. It was established in 1860 out of parts of Henderson, Hopkins and Union counties, and was the 109th county in order of formation. It was named in honor of Daniel Webster, one of the greatest American orators, statesmen and lawyers. It contains 292 square miles.

The central portion of the county is moderately broken, but the greater part of the northern and southern portion is comparatively level. Green River bounds the northern portion for a distance of 12 miles and is a navigable stream. Once it provided considerable business through shipping produce and rafting logs. The Tradewater River forms the southwestern boundary for 12 miles.

The soil in general is very fertile and adapted to corn, wheat and tobacco. Webster County has been rated as one of the most important counties in western Kentucky and the eighth largest in the state for growing tobacco.

William Jenkins from Virginia is believed to have been the first settler in Webster County. He received a land warrant for his services in the Revolutionary War.

Dixon was incorporated as the county seat of Webster County on Feb. 6, 1861. Dixon is pleasantly situated on a moderately elevated plateau in the central portion of the county. It was named for Archibald Dixon, lieutenant governor of Kentucky from 1844-1848 and member of the U.S. Senate from 1852-1855. The town was laid out on land owned by Ambrose Mooney, who gave the land where the court-

Daniel Webster

house now stands.

Originally, vast quantities of excellent timber consisting of white oak, black oak, poplar, sweet gum, hickory and dogwood grew in Webster County. A portion of the timber was rafted in form of saw-logs to Evansville, In., and other points

In 1905 there was a large quantity of building stone in the county, but the principle mineral deposit was coal. Webster County is situated in the Western Coalfield of Kentucky; and, as the outcrop of the coalfield runs through the southern portion of the county, the coal was easily mined and was of excellent quality. At one time more than 40 mines operated in the county.

Because of the coal industry and the building of the Henderson railroad bridge, the Louisville and Nashville Railroad was built in Providence in 1882.

At one time there were only dirt roads and each man in the county gave so many days work each year on them. Later the poll tax of $1.50 for every man 21 years or older was passed and this money used for maintaining the roads. Today Webster County has some form of hard surface roads over most of the county, as well as four-lane roads, super highways and toll roads paid for by those who travel them.

In addition to the county seat, there are several other towns in Webster County. Providence, the largest, was incorporated Feb. 18, 1840. Others include Sebree, Clay, Slaughters, Vanderburg, Onton, Poole, Tilden, and Wannamaker.

Contributed by Lowell Childress

Whitley County

"Whitley county, formed in 1818 out of the W. part of Knox, and named in honor of the great Indian fighter, Col. Wm. Whitley, was the 59th in order of formation. Part of its territory was taken, in 1825, to help form Laurel county. It is situated on the southern border, in the S.E. section of the state; and is bounded N. by Laurel, E. by Knox and Josh Bell, S. by the Tennessee state line (and Scott and Campbell counties, Tenn.), and W. by Wayne and Pulaski counties. It is about the 10th largest county in the state, and embraces over 450 square miles. It is drained by the Cumberland and its tributaries—that river winding through it for 45 miles, in a general western course, and quite centrally, except that it enters on the N.E. and flows out on the N.W. border; Laurel river, with 4 miles of the Cumberland, forms the N. boundary line. The face of the country, except the river valleys, is hilly and broken; two spurs of the Cumberland mountain penetrating the S.E. corner, to within a short distance of Williamsburg, on the Cumberland river. Corn is the staple product, and cattle and hogs to principle exports of the county.

Towns.—*Whitley Court House*, formerly and still generally called *Williamsburg*, on the right bank of the Cumberland river, about 100 miles nearly S.E. of Frankfort, 30 S. of London, and 47 ½ S.E. of Somerset, is a small village; incorporated in 18—; population in 1870, 139—an increase of 14 in ten years. The other villages or post offices of the county are—*Boston, Lot, Marsh Creek, Meadow Creek, Young's Creek, and Rockhold's.*

The Falls of the Cumberland River, in Whitley county, about 14 miles below Williamsburg, are among the most remarkable objects in the state. The river here is precipitated over a perpendicular fall of 62 feet; the fall and rapid is 70 feet. On a clear morning, the roar of the waters may be heard for a distance of 10 or 12 miles above and below the falls. Immediately behind the falling sheet of water, there is a cave in the surface of the rock; and a person can go almost across the river by this passage — through an arch formed on one side by the rock, and on the other by the flashing waters. Just below the falls, large fish are to be caught in great numbers. The country, for 6 or 8 miles above and below the falls, is very irregular, and presents to the eye of the traveler a succession of scenery as romantic

> Immediately behind the falling
> sheet of water, there is a cave
> in the surface of the rock; and a
> person can go almost across the
> river by this passage—through
> an arch formed on one side by
> the rock, and on the other by the
> flashing waters.

and picturesque as any in the state. The hills and mountains rise upon one another like clouds upon the horizon. ...

William Whitley, from whom this county received its name, was one of the most distinguished of those early pioneers, whose adventurous exploits have shed a coloring of romance over the early history of Kentucky. He was born on the 14th of August, 1749, in that part of Virginia then called Augusta, and which afterwards furnished territory of Rockbridge county. Unknown to early fame, he grew to manhood in the laborious occupation of tilling his native soil, in which his corporal powers were fully developed, with but little mental cultivation. He possessed, however, the spirit of enterprise, and the love of independence."

An excerpt from pages 757-760 of the entry for "Whitley County," Collins' Historical Sketches of Kentucky, History of Kentucky, Volume II (Southern Historical Press, 1874).

Wolfe County

"Wolfe county, the 110th formed in the state, was established in 1860, out of parts of Morgan, Breathitt, Owsley, and Powell counties, and named in honor of Nathaniel Wolfe, then a state senator from the city of Louisville. It is situated in the central eastern portion of the state, on the waters of Red river, which runs from E. to W. through the county, while the North fork of the Kentucky river forms its southern boundary; is bounded on the N. and E. by Morgan, S.E. by Breathitt, S. by Lee, and W. by Lee and Powell counties; and contains an area of about 170 square miles. Besides the above, the streams are Gilmore's, Stillwater, Swift, Parched Corn, Wolf Pen, Gilladie, Upper Devil and Lower Devil creeks. The surface of the county generally is hilly and broken, with some rich level land along the river and creek bottoms. Corn is the principle product; but wheat, oats, hay, and some tobacco are raised, and cattle, hogs, horses, and mules to a very limited extent.

Swift's Silver Mine...is too beautiful and fanciful to be confined to those counties [Carter & Bell], but must needs have a local habitation also in Wolfe county—on Lower Devil creek, 6 miles in an air-line from Compton, the county seat (which is 30 miles from Mountsterling). Swift's name is carved on both rocks and trees—by whom, is not known.

In Feb., 1871, three Cherokee Indians (two men and a squaw), came from the Indian Territory to Irvine, Estill co., Ky.; thence about 15 miles E. to the farm of Jacob Crabtree. One of the men, who claimed to be a young chief, was educated, talked English, and was well informed about minerals. The object of their journey was quite mysterious — except that it seemed to have connection with the time-out-of-mind tradition about Swift's silver mine; indeed, the Indians said they were within half a days' journey of that mine. Leaving the squaw at Crabtrees's, the Indians followed up Little Sinking creek to its source, crossed over on to Big Sinking creek, and after riding some miles, hitched their horses; then—warning the whites who out of curiosity were following at a little distance, that they would turn back if followed further — disappeared

in the thick undergrowth. Late in the evening they returned to Crabtree's, bearing upon their horses two buckskin sacks or bags heavily laden. By these sacks one of the Indians kept watch, all night, with a revolver in his hand; and in the morning the three departed, on the return road toward Irvine. The whites went immediately to the neighborhood, visited by the Indians, but did not succeed in finding any mineral but iron ore.

Two caves, known as the Ashy and the Bone (or Pot) caves, are about a mile apart, on Lower Devil's creek. In the latter, on a visit in 1871, were found 27 pots or crucibles, about 1 ½ feet across and same depth, in three rows of 9 each, and each pot of about half a barrel capacity. The road to it, although unused for many years, was plainly perceptible — being worn down 4 or 5 feet deep, and with trees, apparently 100 to 125 years old, growing in it. A large deposit of sulphur, in ore or rocks, and deposits of iron and of bismuth are found near, but with no road leading to them."

An excerpt from pages 761-763 entry for "Wolfe County," Collins' Historical Sketches of Kentucky, History of Kentucky, Volume II (Southern Historical Press, 1874).

y'know what?

Many legends surrounding John Swift's lost silver mine place it in the Red River Gorge area of present-day Wolfe and Menifee Counties. Wolfe County today boasts many reminders of the lost treasure — places with names like Silvermine Branch, Silvermine Arch, Swift Camp Creek, and the town of Campton (originally "Camp Town," so named because it was widely believed to be the site of Swift's main camp). Many strange markings on the trees and rocks of Wolfe County recall similar markings described in Swift's journals.

Source: John Swift's Lost Silver Mine Historic Campground, www.swiftcampground.com

Woodford County

Woodford County was created by an act of the Virginia Legislature on November 12, 1788, in response to a petition signed by residents of Fayette County, from which Woodford was formed. Woodford County was the ninth, and last county created while what would become the Commonwealth of Kentucky was still part of Virginia. The Woodford County government was formed at the first meeting of the County Court on May 5, 1789. It was on this date that the first official county records were recorded, so the 1789 date is most often given as the date the county was formed. Woodford County was named for General William Woodford, a Revolutionary War officer who died while a prisoner of war of the British.

Woodford County Courthouse
Source: Sid Webb

Settlers began moving into the area in the 1770s and often clashed with Native Americans who wanted to preserve the area as their hunting ground. Although Native Americans were not living in Woodford County in the late 18th century, the Adena tribe and perhaps others, had lived here in prehistoric times. Their burial mounds and earthworks have been identified by archaeologists at Lovedale, about two miles northwest of Versailles. One of the earliest churches in the county was Pisgah Presbyterian Church, founded in 1784. A school started by the church, Kentucky Academy, became part of Transylvania University in 1799. Half a century later, in 1849, Dr. Lewis Pendleton and James Parrish established the Kentucky Female Orphan School in Midway, which later became Midway College, the only women's college in Kentucky.

Agriculture, distilling, cattle and horses have been important industries for the county since its earliest settlement. Historic horse farms such as Woodburn, Nantura and Bosque Bonita gained legendary status in the mid to late 1800s by producing some of the finest thoroughbreds in the world. Horse farms are still a dominant force in Woodford County's economy and the international horse industry. Woodford Reserve Distillery, Castle Hill Farm and Equus Run Vineyard wineries carry on a tradition of manufacturing that can be traced back almost two centuries in Woodford County.

The Woodford County Historical Society has been collecting and preserving historical artifacts and documents since 1966. The former Big Spring Church on Rose Hill in Versailles, built circa. 1819, houses the Society's library and museum. The Society is open 10 a.m. to 4 p.m., Tuesday through Saturday, and is free and open to the public.

Other historical organizations in the county include the Jack Jouett House, the Bluegrass Railroad Museum, and the Midway Museum. Woodford County contains 192 square miles and is bordered by Anderson, Fayette, Franklin, Jessamine, Mercer and Scott counties. Versailles, established in June 1792, is the county seat. Midway, the county's only other incorporated town, was established in 1835.

There are also several small communities in the county, including Clifton, Davistown, Duckers, Elm Corner, Faywood, Firmantown, Germany, Huntertown, McKee's Crossroads, Millville, Milner, Mortonsville, Mundy's Landing, Nonesuch, Nugent Crossroads, Pinckard, Pisgah, Spring Station, Troy, Wallace, and Warwick.

Woodford County Historical Society 121 Rose Hill Rd., Versailles, KY 40383, Free admission, (859) 873-6786 , www.woodfordkyhistory.org
Contributed by Danna Estridge

COUNTIES AND JUDGE/EXECUTIVES

COUNTY	JUDGE/EXECUTIVE	ADDRESS1	ADDRESS2	CITY	ZIP	PHONE	FAX
Adair	Jerry Vaughan	Adair Co Cthse Annex	424 Public Sq Ste 1	Columbia	42728	(270) 384-4703	(270) 384-9754
Allen	Johnny Hobdy	City-Co Bldg	PO Box 115	Scottsville	42164	(270) 237-3631	(270) 237-9155
Anderson	Anthony D Stratton	137 S Main St		Lawrenceburg	40342	(502) 839-3131	(502) 839-8151
Ballard	Bob Buchanan	437 Ohio St	PO Box 276	Wickliffe	42087	(270) 335-5176	(270) 335-3010
Barren	Davie Greer	117 N Public Sq Ste 3A		Glasgow	42141	(270) 651-3338	(270) 651-2844
Bath	Walter Shrout	Cthse Annex	PO Box 39	Owingsville	40360	(606) 674-6346	(606) 674-6658
Bell	William (Bill) Kelley	Cthse Sq	PO Box 339	Pineville	40977	(606) 337-3076	(606) 337-9807
Boone	Gary W Moore	2950 Burlington Pk	PO Box 900	Burlington	41005	(859) 334-2242	(859) 334-3105
Bourbon	Donnie R Foley	Bourbon Co Cthse	301 Main St Rm 203	Paris	40361	(859) 987-2135	(859) 987-2136
Boyd	Bill F Scott	Boyd Co Cthse	PO Box 423	Catlettsburg	41129	(606) 739-4134	(606) 739-5446
Boyle	Tony Wilder	Boyle Co Cthse	321 W Main St Ste 111	Danville	40422	(859) 238-1100	(859) 238-1108
Bracken	Leslie Newman	Bracken Co Cthse	PO Box 264	Brooksville	41004	(606) 735-2300	(606) 735-2615
Breathitt	Lewis H Warrix	Breathitt Co Cthse	1137 Main St	Jackson	41339	(606) 666-3800	(606) 666-3813
Breckinridge	George Monarch	Co Cthse Annex	PO Box 227	Hardinsburg	40143	(270) 756-2269	(270) 756-2364
Bullitt	Kenneth J Rigdon	Bullitt Co Cthse 300 S Buckman St	PO Box 768	Shepherdsville	40165	(800) 672-5058	(502) 543-1577
Butler	Hugh C Evans	Butler Co Cthse	PO Box 626	Morgantown	42261	(270) 526-3433	(270) 526-2658
Caldwell	Van Knight	100 E Market St Rm 27		Princeton	42445	(270) 365-6660	(270) 365-6637
Calloway	Larry Elkins	Calloway Co Cthse	101 S 5th St	Murray	42071	(270) 753-2920	(270) 753-3911
Campbell	Steven Pendery	Campbell Co Fiscal Court	24 W 4th St	Newport	41071	(859) 292-3822	(859) 292-3888
Carlisle	John G Roberts III	77 E Court St	PO Box 279	Bardwell	42023	(270) 628-5451	(270) 628-0190
Carroll	Harold (Shorty) Tomlinson	Carroll Co Cthse 2nd Fl	440 Main St	Carrollton	41008	(502) 732-7000	(502) 732-7023
Carter	Charles Wallace	Carter Co Cthse Rm 227	300 W Main St	Grayson	41143	(606) 474-5616	(606) 474-6991
Casey	Ronald D Wright	625 Campbellsville St	PO Box 306	Liberty	42539	(606) 787-6154	(606) 787-6154
Christian	Steve Tribble	515 Weber St		Hopkinsville	42240	(270) 887-4100	(270) 885-7501
Clark	John Myers	Clark Co Cthse Rm 103 3rd Fl	34 S Main St	Winchester	40391	(859) 745-0200	(859) 737-5678
Clay	James G Garrison	102 Richmond Rd Ste 201		Manchester	40962	(606) 598-2071	(606) 598-7849
Clinton	Donnie McWhorter	100 S Cross St		Albany	42602	(606) 387-5234	(606) 387-7651
Crittenden	Fred Brown	Crittenden Co Cthse	107 S Main St	Marion	42064	(270) 965-5251	(270) 965-5252
Cumberland	Tim Hicks	Cumberland Co Cthse	PO Box 826	Burkesville	42717	(270) 864-3444	(270) 864-1757
Daviess	Louis Reid Haire	Daviess Co Cthse	212 St Ann St	Owensboro	42303	(270) 685-8424	(270) 685-8469
Edmonson	N E Reed	Edmonson Co Cthse	PO Box 353	Brownsville	42210	(270) 597-2819	(270) 597-2494
Elliott	Charles R Pennington	Elliott Co Cthse Main St	PO Box 710	Sandy Hook	41171-	(606) 738-5821	(606) 738-4509
Estill	Wallace Taylor	Estill Co Cthse Rm 101		Irvine	40336	(606) 723-7524	(606) 723-5471
Fayette	Sandra Varellas	167 W Main St Ste 1310		Lexington	40507	(859) 255-1790	(859) 252-4476
Fleming	Larry Foxworthy	Fleming Co Cthse		Flemingsburg	41041	(859) 845-8801	(606) 845-1312
Floyd	Paul M Thompson	Floyd Co Cthse		Prestonsburg	41653	(606) 886-9193	(606) 886-1083
Franklin	Robert Roach	315 W Main St Ste 302	149 S Central Ave	Frankfort	40601	(502) 875-8751	(502) 875-8755
Fulton	Harold M Garrison	2004 S 7th St		Hickman	42050	(270) 236-2594	(270) 236-7904
Gallatin	George W Zubaty	Gallatin Co Cthse Annex II	PO Box 144	Warsaw	41095	(859) 567-5691	(859) 567-4764
Garrard	E J Hasty	Garrard Co Cthse	15 Public Sq	Lancaster	40444	(859) 792-3531	(859) 792-2010
Grant	Darrell L Link	Grant Co Cthse	101 N Main St	Williamstown	41097	(859) 823-7561	(859) 428-4567
Graves	Anthony Doyle (Tony) Smith	Graves Co Cthse	101 E South St Ste 1	Mayfield	42066	(270) 247-3626	(270) 247-1274
Grayson	Gary L Logsdon	10 Public Sq		Leitchfield	42754	(270) 259-3159	(270) 259-0512
Green	Mary Ann Blaydes Baron	Green Co Cthse	203 W Court St	Greensburg	42743	(270) 932-4024	(270) 932-3635
Greenup	Robert W Carpenter	Greenup Co Cthse Rm 102		Greenup	41144	(606) 473-6440	(606) 473-9878
Hancock	Jack B McCaslin	Hancock Co Admin Bldg	PO Box 580	Hawesville	42348	(270) 927-8137	(270) 927-8138
Hardin	Harry Berry	Hardin County Cthse 3rd Fl	PO Box 568	Elizabethtown	42701	(270) 765-2350	(270) 737-5590
Harlan	Joseph A Grieshop	210 E Central St Ste 111	PO Box 956	Harlan	40831	(606) 573-2600	(606) 573-3522
Harrison	Dean Peak	Harrison Co Cthse	111 S Main St	Cynthiana	41031	(859) 234-7136	(859) 234-6647
Hart	Terry L Martin	Hart Co Cthse	PO Box 490	Munfordville	42765	(270) 524-5219	(270) 524-9732
Henderson	Sandy Lee Watkins	Henderson Co Cthse		Henderson	42420	(270) 826-3971	(270) 827-6002
Henry	John Brent	Henry Co Cthse Annex	PO Box 202	New Castle	40050	(502) 845-5707	(502) 845-4916
Hickman	Gregory D Pruitt	Hickman Co Cthse	110 E Clay St	Clinton	42031	(270) 653-4369	(270) 653-4360
Hopkins	Patricia Hawkins	Hopkins Co Govt Bldg	PO Box 523	Madisonville	42431	(270) 821-8294	(270) 821-8295

COUNTIES AND JUDGE/EXECUTIVES

COUNTY	JUDGE/EXECUTIVE	ADDRESS1	ADDRESS2	CITY	ZIP	PHONE	FAX
Jackson	Tommy Slone		PO Box 339	McKee	40447	(606) 287-8562	(606) 287-7190
Jefferson	Ken Herndon	1442 Christy Ave		Louisville	40204	(502) 583-0794	(502) 583-1677
Jessamine	William Neal Cassity	Jessamine Co Cthse	101 N Main St	Nicholasville	40356	(859) 885-4500	(859) 885-2545
Johnson	Roger T Daniel	338 2nd St	PO Box 868	Paintsville	41240	(606) 789-2550	(606) 789-2555
Kenton	Ralph Drees	Kenton Co Bldg	PO Box 792	Covington	41012	(859) 392-1400	(859) 392-1412
Knott	Donnie Newsome	Knott Co Cthse	PO Box 505	Hindman	41822	(606) 785-5592	(606) 785-0966
Knox	Raymond Smith	Knox Co Cthse	PO Box 173	Barbourville	40906	(606) 546-6192	(606) 546-6196
LaRue	Tommy Turner	Larue Co Cthse Ste 4	209 W High St	Hodgenville	42748	(270) 358-4400	(270) 358-4528
Laurel	Lawrence Kuhl	Laurel Co Cthse Rm 204	101 S Main St	London	40741	(606) 864-4640	(606) 864-3867
Lawrence	Phillip Carter	Lawrence Co Cthse	122 S Main Cross St	Louisa	41230	(606) 638-4102	(606) 638-0618
Lee	LC (Bub) Reese	Lee Co Cthse	PO Box G	Beattyville	41311	(606) 464-4100	(606) 464-4107
Leslie	Kenneth Witt	Leslie Co Cthse	PO Box 619	Hyden	41749	(606) 672-3200	(606) 672-7373
Letcher	Carroll A Smith	Letcher Co Cthse	156 Main St Ste 107	Whitesburg	41858	(606) 633-2129	(606) 633-7105
Lewis	Steven Applegate	Lewis Co Cthse	514 2nd St	Vanceburg	41179	(606) 796-2722	(606) 796-0822
Lincoln	R W (Buckwheat) Gilbert	Lincoln Co Cthse	102 E Main St	Stanford	40484	(606) 365-2534	(606) 365-4514
Livingston	Christopher Lasher	Livingston Co Cthse	PO Box 70	Smithland	42081	(270) 928-2106	(270) 928-3262
Logan	John H Guion III	Logan Co Cthse	PO Box 365	Russellville	42276	(270) 726-3116	(270) 726-3117
Lyon	Sara Jean Boyd	Lyon Co Cthse	PO Box 598	Eddyville	42038	(270) 388-7311	(270) 388-0715
Madison	Kent Clark	Madison Co Cthse	101 W Main St	Richmond	40475	(859) 624-4700	(859) 624-9140
Magoffin	Bill May	Magoffin Co Cthse	PO Box 430	Salyersville	41465	(606) 349-2313	(606) 349-2109
Marion	David R Hourigan	102 W Main St		Lebanon	40033	(270) 692-3451	(270) 692-9487
Marshall	Mike Miller	Marshall Co Cthse	1101 Main St	Benton	42025	(270) 527-4750	(270) 527-4795
Martin	Kelly E Callaham		PO Box 309	Inez	41224	(606) 298-2800	(606) 298-4404
Mason	James L (Buddy) Gallenstein	221 Court St		Maysville	41056	(606) 564-6706	(606) 564-7315
McCracken	Danny Orazine	McCracken Co Cthse	301 S 6th St	Paducah	42003	(270) 444-4707	(270) 444-4731
McCreary	Blaine Phillips	McCreary Co Cthse	PO Box 579	Whitley City	42653	(606) 376-2413	(606) 376-9499
McLean	Larry B Whitaker	McLean Co Cthse	PO Box 127	Calhoun	42327	(270) 273-3213	(270) 273-9965
Meade	William Haynes	Meade Co Cthse	516 Fairway Dr	Brandenburg	40108	(270) 422-3967	(270) 422-3262
Menifee	James Trimble		PO Box 105	Frenchburg	40322	(606) 768-3482	(606) 768-2144
Mercer	John D Trisler	Fiscal Court Bldg	134 S Main St	Harrodsburg	40330	(859) 734-6300	(859) 734-6345
Metcalfe	Donald M Butler II	Metcalfe Co Cthse	PO Box 149	Edmonton	42129	(270) 432-3181	(270) 432-3726
Monroe	Wilbur Graves	Monroe Co Cthse	200 N Main St Ste C	Tompkinsville	42167	(270) 487-5505	(270) 487-0591
Montgomery	B D Wilson Jr	44 W Main St		Mt Sterling	40353	(859) 498-8707	(859) 498-1040
Morgan	Timothy Conley	Morgan Co Ofc Bldg	450 Prestonsburg St	West Liberty	41472	(606) 743-3896	(606) 743-3895
Muhlenberg	Rodney Keith Kirtley	Muhlenberg Co Cthse	PO Box 137	Greenville	42345	(270) 338-2520	(270) 338-6116
Nelson	Dean Watts	Old Cthse	PO Box 578	Bardstown	40004	(502) 348-1801	(502) 348-1873
Nicholas	Larry D Tincher	Nicholas Co Cthse	PO Box 167	Carlisle	40311	(859) 289-3725	(859) 289-3705
Ohio	Wayne Husaker	Ohio Co Cthse	PO Box 146	Hartford	42347	(270) 298-4400	(270) 298-4408
Oldham	Mary Ellen Kinser	Oldham Co Fiscal Court Bldg	100 W Jefferson St	LaGrange	40031	(502) 222-9357	(502) 222-3210
Owen	William P O'Banion	Owen Co Cthse	100 N Thomas	Owenton	40359	(502) 484-3405	(502) 484-1004
Owsley	Cale Turner	Owsley Co Cthse	PO Box 749	Booneville	41314	(606) 593-6202	(606) 593-6381
Pendleton	Henry W Bertram	233 Main St Rm 4		Falmouth	41040	(859) 654-4321	(859) 654-5047
Perry	Denny Ray Noble	Perry Co Cthse	PO Box 210	Hazard	41702	(606) 439-1816	(606) 439-1686
Pike	William M Deskins	Pike Co Cthse	146 Main St	Pikeville	41501	(606) 432-6247	(606) 432-6242
Powell	Robert Ray (Bobby) Drake	Powell Co Cthse	PO Box 506	Stanton	40380	(606) 663-2834	(606) 663-2905
Pulaski	Darrell Beshears	Pulaski Co Cthse	PO Box 712	Somerset	42502	(606) 678-4853	(606) 679-8642
Robertson	Bradley Gifford	Court St	PO Box 76	Mt Olivet	41064	(606) 724-5615	(606) 724-5022
Rockcastle	Buzz Carloftis	Rockcastle Co Cthse	PO Box 755	Mt Vernon	40456	(606) 256-2856	(606) 256-8104
Rowan	Clyde A Thomas	Rowan Co Cthse	627 E Main St	Morehead	40351	(606) 784-5151	(606) 784-3535
Russell	Ronnie McFall	Russell Co Cthse	PO Box 397	Jamestown	42629	(270) 343-2112	(270) 343-2134
Scott	George H Lusby	101 E Main St	PO Box 973	Georgetown	40324	(502) 863-7850	(502) 863-7852
Shelby	Rob Rothenburger	Shelby Co Cthse	501 Main St Ste 13	Shelbyville	40065	(502) 633-1220	(502) 633-7623
Simpson	Jim Henderson	Main St	PO Box 242	Franklin	42135	(270) 586-7184	(270) 586-9505
Spencer	David Jenkins	12 W Main St	PO Box 397	Taylorsville	40071	(502) 477-3205	(502) 477-3206

Clark's Kentucky Almanac 2006

COUNTIES AND JUDGE/EXECUTIVES

COUNTY	JUDGE/EXECUTIVE	ADDRESS1	ADDRESS2	CITY	ZIP	PHONE	FAX
Taylor	Paul Patton	Taylor Co Cthse	203 N Court St Ste 4	Campbellsville	42718	(270) 465-7729	(270) 789-3675
Todd	Carl Knight	Todd Co Cthse	PO Box 355	Elkton	42220	(270) 265-2451	(270) 265-3277
Trigg	Berlin S Moore Jr	38 Main St	PO Box 672	Cadiz	42211	(270) 522-8459	(270) 522-7786
Trimble	Randy Stevens	123 Church St	PO Box 251	Bedford	40006	(502) 255-7196	(502) 255-4618
Union	Frank J Eiter	Union Co Cthse	PO Box 60	Morganfield	42437	(270) 389-1081	(270) 389-0406
Warren	Michael O Buchanon	Warren Co Cthse	429 E 10th St	Bowling Green	42101	(270) 843-4146	(270) 731-2777
Washington	John A Settles	Washington Co Cthse	PO Box 126	Springfield	40069	(859) 336-5410	(859) 336-5407
Wayne	Bruce Ramsey	Wayne Co Cthse	PO Box 439	Monticello	42633	(606) 348-4241	(606) 348-6647
Webster	James R (Jim) Townsend	Webster Co Cthse	PO Box 155	Dixon	42409	(270) 639-5042	(270) 639-7009
Whitley	Michael Patrick	Whitley Co Cthse	PO Box 237	Williamsburg	40769	(606) 549-6000	(606) 549-6095
Wolfe	Raymond Hurst	Wolfe Co Cthse	PO Box 429	Campton	41301	(606) 668-3040	(606) 668-3367
Woodford	Joe D Gormley	Woodford Co Cthse Rm 200	103 S Main St	Versailles	40383	(859) 873-4139	(859) 873-0196

Source: The Kentucky Directory Gold Book 2005

Autumn in Kentucky
Source: Kentucky Department of Tourism

Autumn Comes to Kentucky
Charlie Hughes

Drawn to nakedness and held

in the bare arms of ash and locust,

I am most alive in summer's death, awakened

each autumn by the chainsaw's scream, blood

stirred by great vees of geese.

I become as sharp and crisp as the taste

of woodsmoke on October's cool, clear wind.

I begin to speak in metaphor,

have the midnight eloquence

of the condemned

awaiting the morning's hangman.

A strange paradox, to be so alive, while

all around me life ending.

…

Tonight the sky will once again rise

in the east with wonder not seen in summer.

The trees will reach toward the heavens

where stars burn holes in the darkness.

Barns will cast dark shapes in the fescue

and the tin of their roofs will mirror

the brilliant moon, and I, in amazement,

will walk in this light and shadow

one last time before the snow.

Reprinted with permission of Wind Publications, Autumn Comes to Kentucky from "Shifting for Myself," Charlie Hughes, Wind Publications, pages 74-75 (Nicholasville: 2002).

LEXINGTON.

Lexington, the seat of justice of Fayette county, is situated 38 deg. 6 min. north latitude, and 10 deg. 8 min. north longitude from Philadelphia. It is 64 miles from the Ohio river. The Kentucky river runs round it in the form of a semi-circle, being 18 miles distant at Boonsborough, and 22 at Frankfort the seat of the Government of the State; by water the difference between there place is upwards of 180 miles.

The business of the country dependant upon this river, is done principally in Lexington, as well as a great part of the whole commercial business of the State. The town contains   houses and about 3,500 inhabitants; but it is progressing with unexampled rapidity; and there can be little question that many years will not roll away before it will become the largest inland town in the United States. It is situated in the centre of the largest body of rich soil which is perhaps to be found in the world. The inhabitants are devoting themselves to the manufacturing system. There are established seven rope walks, and five factories of coarse linen; in which upwards of 500 workmen are employed. There are three establishments for cotton spinning, one of which is on an extensive plan. A steam engine is recently erected, which promises to be of considerable importance. Perhaps no manufactory which is to be met with in other towns in the United States, which is not known here. The market is well supplied with provisions; some of the streets are already paved, and this part of the improvements of the town is progressing in every part. A theatre has been recently erected—As to churches, there are two Presbyterian, one Baptist, one Methodist and one Episcopalian. There is an incorporated Circulating Library in a prosperous situation. The Kentucky Academy is fixed here. It is the seat of the Trannsylvania University, an Institution endowed with ample funds, has a handsome library and philosophical apparatus, and professorships in the various departments of law, medicine, philosophy and literature.

** In this town there is established an Insurance Company with banking priviliges—and a Branch of the Bank of Kentucky, both of which give considerable assistance to the commerce and manufactures of the place.

Source: Johnson & Warner's Kentucky Almanac 1810, published by
Johnson & Warner, Lexington, Ky.

PERSONAL INCOME, RACE, BIRTHS, DEATHS AND UNEMPLOYMENT FOR KENTUCKY COUNTIES

AREA NAME	TOTAL POPULATION	WHITE	BLACK OR AFRICAN-AMERICAN	OTHER RACES	*HISPANIC OR LATINO	BIRTHS	DEATHS	PERSONAL INCOME ($000)	PER CAPITA PERSONAL INCOME ($)	UNEMPLOYMENT PERCENT**	POVERTY LEVEL
Kentucky	4,041,769	3,640,889	295,994	104,886	59,939	53,805	40,120	104,263,983	25,494	6.6%	12.7%
Adair	17,244	16,555	440	249	132	233	182	333,517	19,192	5.5%	18.2%
Allen	17,800	17,376	191	233	147	215	193	389,357	21,498	6.6%	13.2%
Anderson	19,111	18,448	449	214	153	217	176	484,252	24,766	4.8%	4.8%
Ballard	8,286	7,898	238	150	52	113	115	214,923	26,426	7.3%	10.7%
Barren	38,033	35,864	1,556	613	355	424	422	871,810	22,491	4.7%	11.8%
Bath	11,085	10,738	205	142	89	154	120	217,978	19,131	8.4%	16.4%
Bell	30,060	28,864	720	476	194	348	375	525,478	17,521	7.0%	26.7%
Boone	85,991	81,822	1,306	2,863	1,702	1,388	583	2,780,666	29,703	4.7%	4.4%
Bourbon	19,360	17,497	1,343	520	503	204	198	547,079	28,045	5.0%	0.1%
Boyd	49,752	47,747	1,267	738	558	603	601	1,280,980	25,795	6.0%	11.5%
Boyle	27,697	24,311	2,680	706	398	297	305	701,445	25,327	6.2%	9.1%
Bracken	8,279	8,153	51	75	39	108	78	176,492	20,887	8.6%	7.6%
Breathitt	16,100	15,889	63	148	106	177	201	279,501	17,559	7.4%	28.1%
Breckinridge	18,648	17,872	534	242	134	233	222	384,342	20,317	7.7%	11.8%
Bullitt	61,236	60,052	233	951	383	750	384	1,524,370	23,927	5.4%	6.2%
Butler	13,010	12,734	68	208	135	164	136	246,472	18,737	7.1%	13.1%
Caldwell	13,060	12,262	628	170	80	153	169	289,184	22,578	5.9%	12.2%
Calloway	34,177	31,950	1,218	1,009	473	355	339	822,506	23,927	5.1%	9.8%
Campbell	88,616	85,636	1,394	1,586	765	1,112	878	2,479,433	28,049	5.4%	7.3%
Carlisle	5,351	5,232	51	68	44	46	50	116,600	21,733	8.3%	15.0%
Carroll	10,155	9,663	197	295	330	140	102	236,769	23,036	5.9%	10.4%
Carter	26,889	26,625	35	229	158	373	281	481,942	17,798	9.3%	19.2%
Casey	15,447	15,184	51	212	198	203	183	289,067	18,276	5.6%	20.7%
Christian	72,265	50,529	17,148	4,588	3,494	1,547	553	1,666,017	23,444	6.0%	12.1%
Clark	33,144	31,023	1,582	539	393	404	362	905,655	26,944	5.5%	8.4%
Clay	24,556	23,063	1,178	315	333	285	249	361,297	14,798	7.6%	35.4%
Clinton	9,634	9,546	10	78	118	119	118	183,305	19,031	6.3%	20.2%
Crittenden	9,384	9,219	61	104	48	83	118	183,711	20,040	6.1%	14.7%
Cumberland	7,147	6,810	244	93	43	97	95	130,773	18,328	8.2%	0.2%
Daviess	91,545	85,772	3,982	1,791	845	1,245	888	2,325,761	25,310	5.7%	9.4%
Edmonson	11,644	11,457	67	120	65	129	114	197,760	16,728	7.4%	14.2%
Elliott	6,748	6,683	2	63	40	63	68	99,111	14,601	11.6%	20.8%
Estill	15,307	15,165	17	125	81	215	185	272,148	17,747	7.9%	22.5%
Fayette	260,512	211,120	35,116	14,276	8,561	3,618	2,047	8,681,237	32,932	3.9%	8.2%
Fleming	13,792	13,424	195	173	103	183	146	263,310	18,606	6.2%	14.8%
Floyd	42,441	41,478	546	417	260	542	490	828,370	19,568	7.1%	26.9%
Franklin	47,687	41,953	4,463	1,271	531	570	495	1,370,821	28,481	4.4%	6.9%
Fulton	7,752	5,823	1,798	131	56	92	121	169,217	22,398	7.5%	20.1%
Gallatin	7,870	7,612	125	133	82	115	98	162,705	20,828	7.3%	11.6%
Garrard	14,792	14,163	453	176	195	162	121	320,535	20,513	5.8%	11.6%
Grant	22,384	22,006	57	321	232	362	183	498,350	21,195	5.7%	9.0%
Graves	37,028	34,335	1,645	1,048	888	488	427	818,459	22,070	9.7%	13.1%

PERSONAL INCOME, RACE, BIRTHS, DEATHS AND UNEMPLOYMENT FOR KENTUCKY COUNTIES

AREA NAME	TOTAL POPULATION	WHITE	BLACK OR AFRICAN-AMERICAN	OTHER RACES	*HISPANIC OR LATINO	BIRTHS	DEATHS	PERSONAL INCOME ($000)	PER CAPITA PERSONAL INCOME ($)	UNEMPLOYMENT PERCENT **	POVERTY LEVEL
Grayson	24,053	23,634	120	299	186	278	257	462,078	19,038	8.1%	13.9%
Green	11,518	11,079	301	138	109	144	151	210,960	18,091	5.9%	15.2%
Greenup	36,891	36,179	212	500	204	399	422	839,441	22,795	6.4%	11.6%
Hancock	8,392	8,222	71	99	64	106	78	170,526	20,219	6.7%	11.4%
Hardin	94,174	77,217	11,178	5,779	3,159	1,529	704	2,439,028	25,468	5.4%	8.2%
Harlan	33,202	31,728	869	605	216	404	408	564,389	17,354	7.1%	29.1%
Harrison	17,983	17,200	454	329	207	210	211	405,268	22,423	5.6%	9.4%
Hart	17,445	16,150	1,081	214	150	253	192	302,339	17,110	6.4%	18.6%
Henderson	44,829	40,866	3,181	782	433	592	415	1,140,611	25,356	5.2%	9.7%
Henry	15,060	14,152	497	411	339	195	168	355,919	23,222	6.4%	10.4%
Hickman	5,262	4,649	521	92	54	63	69	169,337	32,359	8.4%	14.2%
Hopkins	46,519	42,808	2,887	824	423	530	586	1,070,212	23,039	5.5%	13.6%
Jackson	13,495	13,383	7	105	72	163	155	198,954	14,588	7.1%	25.8%
Jefferson	693,604	536,721	130,928	25,955	12,370	9,710	7,173	23,300,262	33,466	5.4%	9.5%
Jessamine	39,041	36,871	1,222	948	512	541	314	1,036,492	25,429	4.2%	8.4%
Johnson	23,445	23,126	59	260	143	304	260	473,002	20,159	6.5%	21.7%
Kenton	151,464	142,357	5,810	3,297	1,669	2,175	1,340	4,600,382	30,382	5.1%	7.1%
Knott	17,649	17,344	129	176	112	178	162	302,466	17,047	6.5%	26.2%
Knox	31,795	31,108	262	425	180	428	362	574,617	18,139	6.3%	29.6%
Larue	13,373	12,657	473	243	140	158	154	326,908	24,295	6.4%	12.6%
Laurel	52,715	51,484	331	900	291	751	523	1,114,855	20,468	5.2%	17.8%
Lawrence	15,569	15,403	15	151	64	183	176	267,742	16,853	7.9%	25.3%
Lee	7,916	7,528	300	88	29	75	107	129,870	16,433	7.5%	25.2%
Leslie	12,401	12,296	9	96	77	137	132	215,272	17,513	7.8%	30.2%
Letcher	25,277	24,952	129	196	110	283	310	481,485	19,337	6.8%	23.7%
Lewis	14,092	13,940	29	123	62	129	166	208,424	15,057	10.4%	23.5%
Lincoln	23,361	22,454	592	315	208	324	258	445,770	18,458	6.7%	16.4%
Livingston	9,804	9,656	14	134	74	94	119	222,318	22,623	6.7%	7.6%
Logan	26,573	24,101	2,025	447	288	329	256	574,143	21,476	6.1%	10.8%
Lyon	8,080	7,422	543	115	59	66	90	163,653	20,095	8.2%	10.2%
McCracken	65,514	56,841	7,128	1,545	694	821	747	1,898,114	29,313	4.5%	11.4%
McCreary	17,080	16,737	108	235	106	201	155	255,317	14,912	12.7%	26.1%
McLean	9,938	9,797	36	105	83	138	107	262,270	26,351	5.4%	13.7%
Madison	70,872	65,918	3,150	1,804	685	934	600	1,527,134	20,808	6.8%	12.0%
Magoffin	13,332	13,238	20	74	56	170	115	231,129	17,389	7.7%	31.2%
Marion	18,212	16,240	1,661	311	144	269	168	390,066	21,105	6.4%	15.8%
Marshall	30,125	29,694	37	394	229	318	377	749,109	24,792	5.5%	6.6%
Martin	12,578	12,484	4	90	78	164	123	215,133	17,152	9.0%	33.3%
Mason	16,800	15,268	1,203	329	160	216	205	390,234	23,126	7.6%	12.9%
Meade	26,349	24,339	1,088	922	567	303	159	594,657	21,687	7.1%	9.3%
Menifee	6,556	6,401	90	65	73	82	58	102,838	15,356	9.4%	23.4%
Mercer	20,817	19,568	769	480	265	259	215	483,495	22,911	5.8%	10.0%
Metcalfe	10,037	9,762	165	110	53	127	150	177,505	17,761	4.8%	18.8%

Clark's Kentucky Almanac 2006

PERSONAL INCOME, RACE, BIRTHS, DEATHS AND UNEMPLOYMENT FOR KENTUCKY COUNTIES

AREA NAME	TOTAL POPULATION	WHITE	BLACK OR AFRICAN-AMERICAN	OTHER RACES	*HISPANIC OR LATINO	BIRTHS	DEATHS	PERSONAL INCOME ($000)	PER CAPITA PERSONAL INCOME ($)	UNEMPLOYMENT PERCENT**	POVERTY LEVEL
Monroe	11,756	11,235	324	197	170	127	142	224,023	19,098	5.2%	20.0%
Montgomery	22,554	21,442	784	328	259	336	236	496,967	21,398	7.7%	12.5%
Morgan	13,948	13,193	611	144	85	154	133	215,797	15,153	10.7%	23.5%
Muhlenberg	31,839	29,989	1,480	370	232	372	389	654,185	20,632	8.3%	15.5%
Nelson	37,477	34,792	2,064	621	395	523	311	1,000,785	25,732	6.6%	10.0%
Nicholas	6,813	6,698	57	58	37	101	93	145,341	21,052	9.6%	9.7%
Ohio	22,916	22,391	171	354	231	292	264	450,354	19,435	6.9%	13.9%
Oldham	46,178	43,230	1,943	1,005	602	522	263	1,580,063	32,120	4.1%	2.9%
Owen	10,547	10,234	119	194	105	132	97	198,508	18,053	5.8%	12.1%
Owsley	4,858	4,820	5	33	35	53	76	83,966	17,644	7.1%	41.7%
Pendleton	14,390	14,159	71	160	97	187	102	303,138	20,445	6.3%	9.8%
Perry	29,390	28,609	482	299	154	444	353	615,460	20,926	7.4%	26.1%
Pike	68,736	67,599	312	825	450	743	799	1,435,298	21,172	6.3%	20.6%
Powell	13,237	13,046	82	109	88	212	121	243,793	18,341	8.6%	18.9%
Pulaski	56,217	54,798	604	815	454	736	642	1,259,175	21,986	5.6%	14.8%
Robertson	2,266	2,235	1	30	21	25	24	39,657	17,227	7.6%	17.5%
Rockcastle	16,582	16,385	23	174	102	238	182	277,128	16,615	7.0%	19.1%
Rowan	22,094	21,205	345	544	235	255	178	430,716	19,309	5.5%	15.9%
Russell	16,315	16,044	95	176	140	207	190	315,432	19,139	7.2%	20.4%
Scott	33,061	30,397	1,769	895	531	559	228	993,257	28,022	4.6%	7.3%
Shelby	33,337	28,874	2,942	1,521	1,505	497	274	982,079	28,034	4.5%	6.5%
Simpson	16,405	14,410	1,676	319	150	213	179	383,939	23,107	4.8%	8.5%
Spencer	11,766	11,472	133	161	132	187	76	287,405	21,150	5.1%	7.7%
Taylor	22,927	21,465	1,159	303	189	298	247	473,473	20,391	5.2%	14.2%
Todd	11,971	10,692	1,048	231	199	151	132	242,358	20,121	5.0%	14.7%
Trigg	12,597	11,128	1,233	236	113	114	155	324,402	25,419	6.4%	8.8%
Trimble	8,125	7,954	24	147	111	102	56	147,889	17,109	6.5%	10.0%
Union	15,637	13,297	2,015	325	244	198	173	359,036	22,934	4.9%	9.3%
Warren	92,522	80,474	7,934	4,114	2,466	1,286	790	2,376,512	25,183	4.3%	10.8%
Washington	10,916	9,892	820	204	175	144	108	231,200	20,732	5.0%	10.3%
Wayne	19,923	19,321	297	305	291	240	200	346,422	17,231	5.0%	24.6%
Webster	14,120	13,220	660	240	268	201	156	358,051	25,417	5.1%	12.6%
Whitley	35,865	35,280	123	462	249	471	378	713,644	19,388	5.6%	21.6%
Wolfe	7,065	7,011	17	37	36	122	105	114,326	16,407	10.6%	29.9%
Woodford	23,208	21,371	1,256	581	695	301	200	803,775	34,135	3.5%	5.2%

Source: Regional Economic Information System, U.S. Bureau of Economic Analysis. (CA05N).

* based on survey results and are included in the Other Races Column

** 2002 Income, Race, Births, Deaths and Unemployment for Kentucky Counties

Vital Staistics from: http://ksdc.louisville.edu/sdc/vitalstats/vs1960_2002.xls

http://www.workforcekentucky.ky.gov/cgi/dataanalysis/AreaSelection.asp?tableName=Labforce, Jan 2005 Data

COUNTIES WITH YEAR FORMED, COUNTY SEAT, AREA, POPULATION, & DENSITY

COUNTY	FORMED	COUNTY SEAT(S)	AREA	POP.	DENSITY	NO OF HOUSEHOLDS	POP. PER HOUSEHOLD
Adair	1802	Columbia	406.8	17,244	42.3	6,747	2.44
Allen	1815	Scottsville	346.1	17,800	51.4	6,910	2.55
Anderson	1827	Lawrenceburg	202.6	19,111	94.2	7,320	2.59
Ballard	1842	Wickliffe	251.1	8,286	32.9	3,395	2.39
Barren	1799	Glasgow	490.9	38,033	77.4	15,346	2.44
Bath	1811	Owingsville	279.4	11,085	39.6	4,445	2.47
Bell	1867	Pineville	360.7	30,060	83.3	12,004	2.44
Boone	1799	Burlington	246.2	85,991	349.1	31,258	2.73
Bourbon	1786	Paris	291.4	19,360	66.4	7,681	2.49
Boyd	1860	Catlettsburg	160.1	49,752	310.6	20,010	2.38
Boyle	1842	Danville	181.9	27,697	152.2	10,574	2.38
Bracken	1797	Brooksville	203.2	8,279	40.7	3,228	2.55
Breathitt	1839	Jackson	495.1	16,100	32.5	6,170	2.54
Breckinridge	1800	Hardinsburg	572.4	18,648	32.5	7,324	2.51
Bullitt	1797	Shepherdsville	299	61,236	204.7	22,171	2.75
Butler	1810	Morgantown	428	13,010	30.3	5,059	2.52
Caldwell	1809	Princeton	346.9	13,060	37.6	5,431	2.36
Calloway	1823	Murray	386.2	34,177	88.4	13,862	2.25
Campbell	1795	Alexandria, Newport	151.5	88,616	584.7	34,742	2.49
Carlisle	1886	Bardwell	192.4	5,351	27.7	2,208	2.4
Carroll	1838	Carrollton	130	10,155	78	3,940	2.51
Carter	1838	Grayson	410.6	26,889	65.4	10,342	2.54
Casey	1807	Liberty	445.6	15,447	34.64	6,260	2.44
Christian	1797	Hopkinsville	721.3	72,265	100.1	24,857	2.66
Clark	1793	Winchester	254.3	33,144	130.3	13,015	2.51
Clay	1807	Manchester	471	24,556	52.1	8,556	2.62
Clinton	1836	Albany	197.4	9,634	48.7	4,086	2.34
Crittenden	1842	Marion	362.1	9,384	25.9	3,829	2.42
Cumberland	1799	Burkesville	305.8	7,147	23.3	2,976	2.37
Daviess	1815	Owensboro	462.3	91,545	197.9	36,033	2.47
Edmonson	1826	Brownsville	302.6	11,644	38.4	4,648	2.47
Elliott	1869	Sandy Hook	233.9	6,748	28.8	2,638	2.54
Estill	1808	Irvine	253.9	15,307	60.2	6,108	2.48
Fayette	1780	Lexington	284.5	260,512	915.6	108,288	2.29
Fleming	1798	Flemingsburg	350.8	13,792	39.3	5,367	2.55
Floyd	1800	Prestonsburg	394.2	42,441	107.6	16,881	2.45
Franklin	1795	Frankfort	210.4	47,687	226.5	19,907	2.3
Fulton	1845	Hickman	208.9	7,752	37	3,237	2.32
Gallatin	1799	Warsaw	98.8	7,870	79.6	2,902	2.68
Garrard	1797	Lancaster	231.2	14,792	63.9	5,741	2.56
Grant	1820	Williamstown	259.9	22,384	86.1	8,175	2.72
Graves	1824	Mayfield	555.5	37,028	66.6	14,841	2.44
Grayson	1810	Leitchfield	503.6	24,053	47.7	9,596	2.47
Green	1793	Greensburg	288.6	11,518	39.9	4,706	2.41
Greenup	1804	Greenup	346.1	36,891	106.5	14,536	2.51
Hancock	1829	Hawesville	188.8	8,392	44.4	3,215	2.59
Hardin	1793	Elizabethtown	627.9	94,174	149.9	34,497	2.62
Harlan	1819	Harlan	467.2	33,202	71	13,291	2.47
Harrison	1794	Cynthiana	309.6	17,983	58	7,012	2.53
Hart	1819	Munfordville	415.9	17,445	41.9	6,769	2.54
Henderson	1799	Henderson	440.1	44,829	101.8	18,095	2.43
Henry	1799	New Castle	289.3	15,060	52	5,844	2.57
Hickman	1822	Clinton	244.4	5,262	21.5	2,188	2.34
Hopkins	1807	Madisonville	550.5	46,519	84.4	18,820	2.43
Jackson	1858	McKee	346.3	13,495	38.9	5,307	2.52
Jefferson	1780	Louisville	385	693,604	1801.1	287,012	2.37
Jessamine	1799	Nicholasville	173.1	39,041	225.5	13,867	2.69
Johnson	1843	Paintsville	261.5	23,445	89.6	9,103	2.52
Kenton	1840	Covington, Independence	161.9	151,464	935.1	59,444	2.52
Knott	1884	Hindman	352.1	17,649	50.1	6,717	2.54

COUNTY	FORMED	COUNTY SEAT(S)	AREA	POP.	DENSITY	NO OF HOUSEHOLDS	POP. PER HOUSEHOLD
Knox	1800	Barbourville	387.6	31,795	82	12,416	2.51
Larue	1843	Hodgenville	263.2	13,373	50.8	5,275	2.49
Laurel	1826	London	435.6	52,715	120.9	20,353	2.56
Lawrence	1822	Louisa	418.7	15,569	37.1	5,954	2.59
Lee	1870	Beattyville	209.8	7,916	37.7	2,985	2.41
Leslie	1878	Hyden	404	12,401	30.6	4,885	2.52
Letcher	1842	Whitesburg	339	25,277	74.5	10,085	2.48
Lewis	1807	Vanceburg	484.4	14,092	29	5,422	2.56
Lincoln	1780	Stanford	336.2	23,361	69.4	9,206	2.51
Livingston	1799	Smithland	316	9,804	31	3,996	2.42
Logan	1792	Russellville	555.6	26,573	47.8	10,506	2.5
Lyon	1854	Eddyville	215.7	8,080	37.4	2,898	2.26
McCracken	1825	Paducah	251	65,514	260.9	27,736	2.31
McCreary	1912	Whitley City	427.7	17,080	39.9	6,520	2.55
McLean	1854	Calhoun	254.3	9,938	39	3,984	2.47
Madison	1786	Richmond	440.6	70,872	160.8	27,152	2.42
Magoffin	1860	Salyersville	309.4	13,332	43	5,024	2.62
Marion	1834	Lebanon	346.3	18,212	52.5	6,613	2.58
Marshall	1842	Benton	304.8	30,125	98.8	12,412	2.38
Martin	1870	Inez	230.7	12,578	54.5	4,776	2.62
Mason	1789	Maysville	241.1	16,800	69.6	6,847	2.41
Meade	1824	Brandenburg	308.5	26,349	85.4	9,470	2.77
Menifee	1869	Frenchburg	203.9	6,556	32.1	2,537	2.49
Mercer	1786	Harrodsburg	250.9	20,817	82.9	8,423	2.45
Metcalfe	1860	Edmonton	290.9	10,037	34.5	4,016	2.47
Monroe	1820	Tompkinsville	330.8	11,756	35.5	4,741	2.45
Montgomery	1797	Mount Sterling	198.5	22,554	113.5	8,902	2.49
Morgan	1823	West Liberty	381.2	13,948	36.5	4,752	2.55
Muhlenberg	1799	Greenville	474.7	31,839	67	12,357	2.45
Nelson	1785	Bardstown	422.6	37,477	88.6	13,953	2.64
Nicholas	1800	Carlisle	196.6	6,813	34.6	2,710	2.48
Ohio	1799	Hartford	593.7	22,916	38.5	8,899	2.54
Oldham	1824	La Grange	189.1	46,178	244	14,856	2.85
Owen	1819	Owenton	352.1	10,547	29.9	4,086	2.55
Owsley	1843	Booneville	198	4,858	24.5	1,894	2.51
Pendleton	1799	Falmouth	280.5	14,390	51.2	5,170	2.75
Perry	1821	Hazard	342.1	29,390	85.8	11,460	2.53
Pike	1822	Pikeville	787.6	68,736	87.2	27,612	2.46
Powell	1852	Stanton	180.1	13,237	73.4	5,044	2.6
Pulaski	1799	Somerset	661.6	56,217	84.9	22,719	2.42
Robertson	1867	Mount Olivet	100	2,266	22.6	866	2.54
Rockcastle	1810	Mount Vernon	317.5	16,582	52.2	6,544	2.49
Rowan	1856	Morehead	280.8	22,094	78.6	7,927	2.39
Russell	1826	Jamestown	253.5	16,315	64.3	6,941	2.33
Scott	1792	Georgetown	284.7	33,061	116.1	12,110	2.61
Shelby	1792	Shelbyville	384.1	33,337	86.7	12,104	2.63
Simpson	1819	Franklin	236.1	16,405	69.4	6,415	2.52
Spencer	1824	Taylorsville	185.9	11,766	63.2	4,251	2.74
Taylor	1848	Campbellsville	269.8	22,927	84.9	9,233	2.41
Todd	1820	Elkton	376.3	11,971	31.8	4,569	2.59
Trigg	1820	Cadiz	443.1	12,597	28.4	5,215	2.39
Trimble	1837	Bedford	148.8	8,125	54.5	3,137	2.57
Union	1811	Morganfield	345.1	15,637	45.3	5,710	2.5
Warren	1797	Bowling Green	545.2	92,522	169.6	35,365	2.46
Washington	1792	Springfield	300.5	10,916	36.3	4,121	2.57
Wayne	1800	Monticello	459.4	19,923	43.3	7,913	2.49
Webster	1860	Dixon	334.7	14,120	42.1	5,560	2.49
Whitley	1818	Williamsburg	440.1	35,865	81.4	13,780	2.52
Wolfe	1860	Campton	222.7	7,065	31.7	2,816	2.45
Woodford	1789	Versailles	190.6	23,208	121.7	8,893	2.57
TOTALS			**39728.1**	**4,041,769**	**101.7**	**1,590,647**	**2.5025**

Sources: www.uky.edu/KentuckyAtlas/kentucky-counties.html and ksdc.louisville.edu

Clark's Kentucky Almanac 2006

COUNTIES
Wet-Dry Counties

It's a Kentucky Thing

It isn't that easy knowing where one can legally purchase a bottle of bourbon or a mug of Kentucky Ale. Out of Kentucky's 120 counties, the Office of Alcoholic Beverage Control lists 54 counties as dry (absolutely no legal liquor sales); 30 "wet" counties; 16 "moist" (wet cities within a dry county); 19 cities or counties with "limited" alcohol sales (sales of alcohol by the drink only in restaurants with at least 100 seating and 70 percent food sales); 13 wet for alcohol by the "drink only" at golf courses; and 13 small and farm wineries in a dry territory.

COUNTY	STATUS	COUNTY	STATUS
ADAIR	DRY	KNOX	LTD
ALLEN	DRY	LARUE	DRY
ANDERSON	WET	LAUREL	LTD
BALLARD	DRY	LAWRENCE	DRY
BARREN	DRY	LEE	DRY
BATH	DRY	LESLIE	DRY
BELL	LTD	LETCHER	WI
BOONE	WET	LEWIS	M
BOURBON	WET	LINCOLN	DRY
BOYD	M	LIVINGSTON	DRY
BOYLE	LTD & WI & G	LOGAN	M
BRACKEN	WET	LYON	LTD
BREATHITT	DRY	McCRACKEN	WET
BRECKINRIDGE	DRY	McCREARY	DRY
BULLITT	WET	McLEAN	DRY
BUTLER	DRY	MADISON	M & G & WI
CALDWELL	WI	MAGOFFIN	WET
CALLOWAY	LTD & G	MARION	WET
CAMPBELL	WET	MARSHALL	LTD
CARLISLE	DRY	MARTIN	DRY
CARROLL	WET	MASON	WET
CARTER	DRY	MEADE	WET
CASEY	DRY	MENIFEE	DRY
CHRISTIAN	WET	MERCER	LTD
CLARK	WET	METCALFE	DRY
CLAY	DRY	MONROE	DRY
CLINTON	DRY	MONTGOMERY	M
CRITTENDEN	DRY	MORGAN	DRY
CUMBERLAND	DRY	MUHLENBERG	M
DAVIESS	WET	NELSON	WET
EDMONSON	DRY	NICHOLAS	WET
ELLIOTT	DRY	OHIO	DRY
ESTILL	DRY	OLDHAM	LTD & G
FAYETTE	WET	OWEN	WI
FLEMING	DRY	OWSLEY	DRY
FLOYD	WET	PENDLETON	M
FRANKLIN	WET	PERRY	WET
FULTON	WET	PIKE	M
GALLATIN	WET	POWELL	DRY
GARRARD	DRY	PULASKI	WI & LTD
GRANT	LTD	ROBERTSON	DRY
GRAVES	LTD & G	ROCKCASTLE	DRY
GRAYSON	DRY	ROWAN	M
GREEN	DRY	RUSSELL	DRY
GREENUP	DRY	SCOTT	LTD & WI & G
HANCOCK	DRY	SHELBY	M & LTD & G
HARDIN	LTD & G	SIMPSON	LTD
HARLAN	M	SPENCER	DRY
HARRISON	WET	TAYLOR	DRY
HART	DRY	TODD	LTD
HENDERSON	WET	TRIGG	DRY
HENRY	M & WI	TRIMBLE	DRY
HICKMAN	DRY	UNION	WET & G
HOPKINS	M	WARREN	WET
JACKSON	DRY	WASHINGTON	M & WI
JEFFERSON	WET	WAYNE	DRY
JESSAMINE	M & G & WI	WEBSTER	DRY
JOHNSON	DRY	WHITLEY	LTD
KENTON	WET	WOLFE	WET
KNOTT	DRY	WOODFORD	WET

LTD = Limited, M = Moist, G = Golf, WI = Winery
Source: Kentucky Alcoholic Beverage Control Board

First Things in Kentucky

"LIKE ALL THINGS, KENTUCKY HAD HER BEGINNING — her day of First Things. These first things were generally types of better things to come — forerunners of something to come after, indicating social and civil life, progress, power. From the day of her first settlement by white Americans on Thursday, June 16, 1774, at Harrodsburg, to the present, 1874, just one hundred years have elapsed! The adventurers of that day found it a desert land and a waste howling wilderness. For their descendants, even for the children of the pioneer, the wilderness and the solitary place have been made glad, and the desert has rejoiced and blossomed as the rose.

The First Village in Kentucky was on the bank of the Ohio river, in Greenup county, opposite now Portsmouth, Ohio-built after 1756 (except one cabin), by the Shawnee Indians and some French traders, when driven from their own Shawnee town opposite, by probably the highest flood ever known in the Ohio. It only existed some twenty years — having, in 1773, 19 or 20 log cabins, with clapboard roofs, doors, windows, chimneys, and some cleared ground; but disappeared in a few years after.

The First Settlement of Kentucky was on Thursday, June 16, 1774, at Harrodsburg.

The First Families who settled in Kentucky were those of Daniel Boone at Boonesborough, and of Hugh McGary, Thomas Denton, and Richard Hogan, at Harrodsburg, each on September 8, 1775. They came from Virginia, in company, through Cumberland Gap.

The First Census of any part of Kentucky was taken on May 7, 1777, and another on September 2, 1777, of the population of the station at Harrodsburg, which latter gave 65 children under 10 years, 24 women, and 198 in all. Boonesborough was then nearly as large and there were families at McClelland's (Georgetown), Logan's (near Stanford), and several other stations.

The First Public Printer—John Bradford; succeeded by James H. Stewart in 1796, John Bradford in 1797, Hunter & Beaumont in 1798, Wm.

Hunter in 1799 to 1808, Gerard & Bledsoe in 1809, Wm. Gerard in 1810-11, Gerard & Berry, 1812-15.

The First Fine House (frame) was built by Alexander Robertson, father of ex-chief justice George Robertson, about 1780, at Harlan's spring, the head of Cane Run, in Garrard County.

The First Jail was built at Danville, in 1783

The First Lunatic Asylum in the West, and the second state lunatic asylum in the United States, was that at Lexington, founded in 1816.

The First Advertisement of legal notice in a newspaper, by law, was in the Kentucky Gazette, in 1789; and the first posted up at the courthouse door, in 1780.

The First Nightwatchman on duty in a town was in Lexington, in the spring of 1811. He cried "in a shrill, unearthly tone, the time of night and the weather."

The First Division of Town Lots by drawing (lottery, they called it) was set for Saturday evening, April 22, 1775, at Boonesborough. There were 54 lots, and no blanks; but dissatisfaction arising, the drawing was postponed until next day. Next morning, Sunday, April 23, Col. Henderson's journal says they 'drew lots'. ...

The First Almanac printed in the west, was at Lexington, in 1788.

The First Marriage was in the fort at Boonesborough, August 7, 1776—Samuel Henderson, one of the three lovers just referred to, to the oldest of the three girls, Elizabeth (or Betsy) Callaway. The ceremony was performed—most probably without any legal license first obtained, because of the distance to the county seat of Fincastle county (of which all Kentucky was then the western portion)—by Squire Boone (a younger brother of Daniel), who was an occasional preacher in the Calvinistic Baptist church.

Source: Collins' Historical Sketches of Kentucky, selections from "A Chapter of First Things in Kentucky," Vol. I, pages 508 - 520 (Southern Historical Press:1874).

Cities

Sylvia Lovely

"Thus …
we will transmit this city
greater and more beautiful
than it was transmitted to us."

That excerpt from the ancient Athenian Oath of citizenship says it best. The heart and soul of citizenship and thus the highest order of human responsibility to one another is inexplicably bound to the idea of "city." In fact the Greek word civitas, meaning citizenship, is the word from which city is derived.

So what is this thing called city and why devote a chapter of this Almanac to it? I dare say that when the first almanac was written in 1792, a chapter on cities probably didn't exist. The American republic was founded as a reaction against the overly rigid rules and laws of the British monarchy.

Those who relocated across the pond did so in an act of defiance against the tyranny of rules and regulations and in favor of wide open spaces and small informal gatherings. As a result, city was not a favorable concept because it suggested rigid rules and government oppression, as chronicled in early writings about Kentucky and doubtless other states as well.

Yet cities have survived. They continue to evolve and have flourished throughout the history of humankind for reasons that have never changed since the beginning of time. Cities began as gathering places for worshiping gods and revering the dead – where stability of place was a requirement.

Downtown Lexington Fountain
Source: Sid Webb

For the same reasons, they were where children were reared, crops were raised and cultural and religious symbols were erected.

The critical mass of workers could come together in cities to synergize their work leading to the stunning inventions that have paralleled the evolution of civil society. Even in the heady frontier American west where individualism was prized, cowhands gathered in saloons to share tales of lonely nights and high noon adventure on the plains.

Here in Kentucky, from Paducah to Ashland and from the more rural Williamsburg to the urban Covington, we identify with each of our 400-plus cities. The truth is that as people we are born alone but spend the remainder of our time on earth searching for warmth and comfort and a higher level of civilization – through togetherness.

Today, there are 18,000 cities and towns across the U.S., and they are at yet another crossroads. More people live in urban Kentucky and urban America than in the wide open spaces. Our world has changed and so have cities and their role in our lives. America's heartland continues to empty out and the coasts fill up and become congested and compromised in the quality of life that they offer.

The events of 9/11 along with the proliferation of information and televised images of unrest throughout the world have instilled an unprecedented fear of the loss of connection with one another. For that reason, our cities – where togetherness equates with civilized society - are threatened.

Our work as citizens of the 21st century is cut out for us. Experts tell us that the paradox of the 21st "global" century will be that local is where we begin. As we view the flickering images on our TV screens, we are more than aware of the fragility of our world and our own local places. We must with deliberate intent, a base of knowledge and newfound leadership, redefine city in the 21st Century. It remains as it has been throughout history as the very heart, soul and repository of our collective spirit.

In the year 2050, it is forecast that people will have gravitated to just eight "super cities" throughout the nation. Those super cities would know no boundaries – state or local. They must sort out the issues raised by the sheer numbers of people who gravitate to them, and manage the ills that come with fast and unplanned growth. And while Kentucky is not considered a site for one of those super cities, it is a place of unprecedented opportunity.

We have the opportunity to meet the yearning for city life that is planned and promoted to meet the needs of people. It will involve connecting people with one another and the outside world, embracing what is new and different and building economic prosperity with the idea that people are the greatest natural resources in a world where they can live and work anywhere.

We would do well to memorize the Athenian Oath and remember our ultimate responsibility: to leave our cities more beautiful and thriving for future generations.

Ashland

The Scot-Irish Poage family settled Ashland after coming from the Shenandoah Valley in Virginia. They were attracted to the area because of its location on the Ohio River and its abundance of natural resources. The Poages settled in 1786 and established a homestead known as Poage's Landing. For a long while, the community was made up only of extended family.

In 1854, a group of Ohio industrialists approached the Poage family and asked them to become partners in forming a development community. They searched for stockholders and chartered the Kentucky Iron, Coal and Manufacturing Co. and soon named the city when Levi Hampton, a stockholder, suggested calling it Ashland after the name of Henry Clay's Lexington estate.

The city became a regional hub for industrialization. In the early part of the 1900s, Ashland became a destination for timber that was shipped down the Big Sandy River and to the Ohio River. Railroads carried coal and timber. There were plenty of jobs available and lots of opportunities for growth. Ashland Oil became a major part of the city's economy, bringing in revenue and jobs. So did Armco, the steelmaker that was a major employer.

Ashland's major growth came in the 1920s when the population doubled to 30,000. The population hit its peak in the 1960s at around 34,000.

A regional center for business, industry, health care and education, Ashland offers families urban advantages within a small community atmosphere. The downtown area supports a diverse group of service and retail businesses, an art and entertainment district and a medical facility in King's Daughters Hospital. Special events and attractions include the Ashland Brass Band Festival in June, and the Kentucky Music Trail in July and August.

Native sons and daughters include former UK basketball player and TV basketball color announcer Larry Conley;

Downtown Ashland
Source: SouthEast Telephone

Dr. Thomas B. Zerfoss Sr., who founded Vanderbilt University's student health center in 1926 and served as its director until 1967; Ellis Johnson, who led an unbeaten Ashland basketball team to the National High School Basketball Tournament Championship in 1928 and later became Adolph Rupp's first All-American player while also lettering in football, baseball and track at the University of Kentucky; TV game show host Chuck Woolery; George Reeves, the original Superman of the TV series; country music singers Billy Ray Cyrus, Naomi and Wynonna Judd, and actress Ashley Judd, who was born in Los Angeles, but was named after the city where she spent much of her youth and graduated from Ashland's Paul Blazer High School. *Contributed by NewCities Foundation Staff*

Berea

The town of Berea was named by Rev. John G. Fee after a Greek town mentioned in Acts 17:11 where people were receptive to the preaching of Paul. In 1853, Fee himself had been invited by Cassius M. Clay, a wealthy Madison County politician and landowner, to preach at the Christian church located in the southern Madison County area known as the Glade, then only a community of scattered farms with a racetrack and residents sympathetic to emancipation. He later returned to establish a church and school which became Berea College.

In 1859, Fee and his followers were forced out of Berea by armed vigilantes from the slave owner sec-

an education for all races, charges no tuition and requires each student to work 10 hours a week to earn money for books, room and board.

The railroad came to Berea in 1883, and the town incorporated in 1890 with a population exceeding 500. In 1909, Berea elected its first mayor, John Gay, who served continuously for 48 years.

Berea is recognized nationally for its arts and crafts and has hosted artisan fairs since 1896. Twenty-five working-artisan studios and retail galleries exhibit fine crafts ranging from woodwork to jewelry; glass creations to fiber arts. Berea is designated the Folk Arts and Crafts Capital of Kentucky,

Boone Tavern - Berea
Source: SouthEast Telephone

tion of Madison County. Undaunted, he returned after the Civil War and invited black army veterans from Camp Nelson to settle in Berea. The school and church he founded worked to achieve interracial brotherhood until the Day Law, which prohibited interracial education, was passed in 1904 and sustained by the United States Supreme Court in 1908. Today, Berea College continues to provide

was chosen as the site of the Kentucky Artisan Center, and is home to many celebrated artists, writers and musicians, including music pioneer, Red Foley. With 12 manufacturing plants, Berea is also an important part of central Kentucky's economy. The unbridled spirit of Kentucky is on display daily in Berea.

Contributed by Mayor Steve Connelly

Bowling Green

In 1775, a ragtag band of explorers called "long hunters" reached the banks of a meandering river where they carved their names on beech trees to mark their passage through this vast wilderness. Their explorations led them to a fertile land nourished by numerous rivers and streams, blanketed with thick forests, and composed both of gently rolling hills and rugged, rocky terrain. Within a few years, hardy pioneers followed in an attempt to establish more permanent settlements. The first, McFadden's Station, was located on the north side of the newly named Barren River. Robert Moore paused for a few days at the rough-hewn station in the early 1790s before continuing to his own homestead — a cabin alongside a spring at what later became Bowling Green.

By 1792, the Kentucky territory had become the 15th state. Within four years, land grants were offered to Virginia's Revolutionary War veterans. At the behest of the new residents, Warren County was established in 1797 and named to honor Dr. Joseph Warren, a hero of the Battle of Bunker Hill.

Two brothers, Robert and George Moore, donated land on which to build a log county courthouse and jail. Later, they offered more acreage for the creation of a town. At the first county commissioners meeting in early 1798, the pioneers decided the new town would be "known by the name of Bolin Green," after Bowling Green Square in New York City, where patriots pulled down a statue of King George III and used the lead to make bullets during the American Revolution.

Within only a few decades, Bowling Green was established as a commercial and transportation center for the south central Kentucky area. Bowling Green gained the official designation of county seat in 1809.

Ambitious business leaders, such as James Rumsey Skiles, were instrumental in ensuring Bowling Green's success as a commercial center in the region. During the 1830s, their stock companies funded the clearing of Barren River to improve its navigability and the construction of the Portage Railroad to connect the docks to the center of town.

Agriculture provided the town's economic base, with the main trade products being tobacco, hay and livestock. Paddle

Historic Capitol Movie Theater
SouthEast Telephone

wheelers and steamboats began to traverse the Barren River with increasing frequency. Completion of the Louisville and Nashville Turnpike in 1838 further strengthened Bowling Green's ties to the rest of the region.

By the 1840s, Bowling Green was no longer a lonely settlement in the midst of a vast wilderness. By the late 1850s, Bowling Green boasted several manufacturing facilities, including an iron foundry, woolen factory, candle factory and several flour mills. A strong industrial base continues to grow and thrive.

Home to the Corvette Plant and Museum (where all Corvettes are made), Bowling Green is only 20 miles away from the longest cave system in the world, Mammoth Cave, and home to Lost River Cave. Western Kentucky University is located in Bowling Green and the downtown area continues to grow and thrive.

Contributed by Mayor Elaine Walker.

Corbin

Corbin, situated in the Daniel Boone National Forest, has made its mark on the nation due to its location. Viewed as a convenient gateway between north and south, the Louisville & Nashville Railroad opened its rail station in Corbin in the late 1800s. Later, US Hwy 25 led an enterprising colonel (with a flair for frying chicken) to capitalize upon the many folks driving

Col. Sanders Kentucky Fried Chicken Museum
Source: Kentucky Department of Tourism

by on their travels between north and south. Eventually, as the nation's interstate highway system emerged, I-75 served as a major transportation route for vehicles traveling from northern Michigan to south Florida. It is estimated that over 40,000 people pass Corbin on this still important route.

Corbin's forefathers paved the way for another landmark when they built the Corbin-Cumberland Falls Road. Created by the Kiwanis Club of Corbin, the road enabled the first round trip by auto through the wilderness from Corbin to the falls. Dedicated in 1931, the road opened Cumberland Falls to the public. The mist of the "Little Niagara" of Cumberland Falls creates the only moonbow in the Western Hemisphere.

Corbin, as noted earlier, is the birthplace of the original Colonel Sanders Cafe and Museum. Listed in the National Register of Historic Places, the museum and dining room still serve the traditional (and still secret recipe) fried chicken. The Laurel River Lake provides another great place to visit, especially for fishing, boating and swimming.

The Corbin area offers great opportunity for business to thrive — it has an abundance of clean water and a plentiful supply of electricity and natural gas. With the cost of operating a business at only 80 percent of the national average, Corbin has a wide range of businesses that provide job opportunities. In addition to numerous small businesses, Corbin has a number of manufacturers. The highly respected Baptist Regional Medical Center has nearly 1,000 highly skilled medical professionals.

Corbin ranks in the top 10 percent of the high schools and middle schools in Kentucky. The Corbin middle school has won the State Science Olympiad two out of the past four years. The area schools have achieved success in education and in the 2004-2005 school year, Corbin athletic teams led Kentucky with regional championship teams.

Although Colonel Harland Sanders is the most famous person in modern times, Corbin produced a number of renowned athletes. As coach for Eastern Kentucky University, Roy Kidd became the seventh college coach in NCAA history to win over 300 games and was inducted in College Football's Hall of Fame. The Bird brothers (Jerry, Calvin, Rodger and Billy) were high school All Americans and went on to stardom at the University of Kentucky and in professional sports. The Selvy brothers are another great sports family from Corbin. Other notable Corbin citizens include Karl Bays, who was posthumously inducted in the Medical Industry Hall of Fame, and K. Norman Berry, inducted in the Architectural Industry Hall of Fame.

Corbin welcomes all to this wonderful place to live, work, raise a family or just stop in for a visit. *Contributed by Bob Terrell.*

Covington

"Covington, the largest city in northern Kentucky, is located in northwestern Kenton County at the confluence of the Licking and Ohio rivers. The city is built principally on a flat plain that is bordered on the south and west by hills. Covington lies across the Ohio River from Cincinnati and is connected to it by four bridges.

In the eighteenth century the area at the confluence of the Licking and Ohio rivers was known as the Point, a popular rendezvous place for explorers and pioneers. Christopher Gist, an agent for the Ohio Company, visited the area in 1751. On February 14, 1780, the site was presented as a two-hundred-acre military warrant to George Muse in recognition of his service during the French and Indian War. Thomas Kennedy acquired it in 1791 and established a prosperous farm, a ferryboat service, and a tavern.

Roebling Suspension Bridge
Source: Sid Webb

On February 8, 1815, the Kentucky legislature approved an act creating the town of Covington. The community was named in honor of Gen. Leonard Wales Covington, of Maryland, who had been mortally wounded at the Battle of Chrysler's Field in the War of 1812. Covington's growth was negligible during the years of the national depression following 1819, but by 1830 the town had a population of 715, a log church, several inns, and a schoolhouse where the town trustees met.

Large numbers of Irish and German immigrants helped make Covington the state's second-largest city by 1850 and a recognized power in state politics by the time of the Civil War. Despite a highly vocal minority of Confederate sympathizers, the community remained overwhelmingly Unionist throughout the war. During the Confederate invasion of Kentucky in the late summer of 1862, southern troops commanded by Gen. Edmund Kirby Smith threatened northern Kentucky, and martial law was declared in Covington by Union Gen. Lew Wallace.

A pontoon bridge was laid over coal barges in the Ohio River to rush Cincinnati militia troops over to Covington to build and occupy earthen fortifications south of the city. In 1867 the suspension bridge designed by John Roebling was opened.

In the early 1900s Covington expanded its boundaries. To the south it annexed the city of Central Covington (also known as Peaselburg) in 1906 and Latonia in 1909. To the west it annexed the city of West Covington in 1909, but failed in attempts to annex Ludlow. The annexations boosted Covington's population to more than 53,000 by 1910. That year, the Roman Catholic Cathedral Basilica of the Assumption was completed, patterned after Notre Dame Cathedral in France.

In 1930 the population of Covington peaked at 65,252 as many eastern Kentuckians flocked to the city in search of jobs during the Great Depression. In the decades that followed, the population of Covington declined as suburban cities began to grow in Kenton and surrounding counties."

Summary excerpt reprinted with permission from the University Press of Kentucky, The Kentucky Encyclopedia, John E. Kleber, Ed., page 236 (Lexington, 1992).

Danville

"Danville, the county seat of Boyle County, is located at the junction of U.S. 150 and U.S. 127. The community began as Crow's Station, founded in 1782 by John Crow, a settler in the area. Danville was founded in 1783-84 by Walker Daniel, the first district attorney of Kentucky, and was named in his honor. The Virginia leg-

Source: Bell South

islature granted a charter for the town in 1787, and Danville was incorporated on March 1, 1836. In 1783 the legislature of Virginia created a supreme court for the District of Kentucky; the court met first in Harrodsburg but soon moved to Danville to hold its deliberations in a log courthouse built in the town square. Danville's convenient location, plus the presence of three hospitable taverns nearby, brought ten conventions to the log courthouse where the delegates discussed the future of Kentucky. The first convention met in December 1784 and the last in April 1792, producing an eighteen-page document that became the first constitution of the Commonwealth of Kentucky. Danville was the home of Dr. Ephraim McDowell, who performed the first successful ovariotomy in December 1809.

During the antebellum period, Danville was a prosperous and growing community in spite of two major disasters. In 1819 a tornado devastated a portion of the city and on February 22, 1860, a fire destroyed sixty-four businesses, churches, and homes and caused over $300,000 in damages. Among the structures destroyed was the 1844 courthouse. Its replacement, an Italianate-style brick structure, was completed in 1862 and used as a military hospital following the Battle of Perryville on October 8, 1862. During the Civil War, the town was occupied by both Confederate and Union soldiers, and in October 1863 a large force of guerrillas passed through, causing damage.

With the coming of the Cincinnati, New Orleans & Texas Pacific Railroad (now Norfolk Southern) to Danville in the 1870s, the city prospered as a transportation and commercial hub as well as an educational center. The railroad built a large yard, a locomotive roundhouse, and repair shops there; Danville became an important division point on the north-south line. Industrial development proceeded steadily throughout the nineteenth and twentieth centuries. An out-of-the ordinary business in the 1870s distilled lubricating oil from hog fat. In 1891 an electrical clock company was built in Danville, along with three carriage factories, a hemp works, brick manufacturer, shoe factory, and a glassware plant.

In 1942 the state of Kentucky dedicated the John G. Weisiger Memorial Park in the center of Danville. Later known as Constitution Square State Shrine, the park celebrates the city's role in Kentucky statehood and contains log reproductions of an early courthouse, church, and jail, as well as an original log structure that is reputed have been the first post office west of Alleghenies."

RICHARD C. BROWN Summary excerpt reprinted with permission from the University Press of Kentucky, The Kentucky Encyclopedia, John E. Kleber, Ed., page 252 (Lexington, 1992).

Elizabethtown

Located 35 miles south of Louisville, Elizabethtown is strategically positioned in the center of Kentucky's crossroads – Interstate 65, the Bluegrass Parkway and the Western Kentucky Parkway. Elizabethtown encompasses 25 square miles and has a population of approximately 23,239. The county seat of Hardin County, Elizabethtown is

City Hall, Elizabethtown
Source: SouthEast Telephone

surrounded by some of the state's richest historic landmarks, breathtaking lakes, forests and natural wonders.

In 1779, three early settlers, Capt. Thomas Helm, Col. Andrew Hynes, and Col. Samuel Haycraft built forts with block houses to use as stockades for defense against the American Indians. The forts, being one mile apart, formed a triangle. At the time, there were no other settlements between the Ohio River and the Green River. Soon, however, other people came and settled around these forts.

In 1793, Colonel Hynes had thirty acres of land surveyed and laid off into lots and streets to establish Elizabethtown. Named in honor of the wife of Andrew Hynes, Elizabethtown was legally established on July 4, 1797.

Elizabethtown has a rich history. Thomas Lincoln practiced carpentry in the area while raising a future president. John James Audubon, an early

merchant of Elizabethtown, later became distinguished as a great ornithologist and illustrator. Gen. George Armstrong Custer and his wife took summer walks along tree-lined streets of Elizabethtown.

Elizabethtown features Freeman Lake Park with a beautiful lake, picnic facilities, fishing, paddleboat and canoe rentals, and a wonderful view. Nature lovers may also enjoy hiking one of the many maintained trails that surround the lake.

Other points of interest in Elizabethtown include the Schmidt's Museum of Coca-Cola Memorabilia, Swope's Cars of Yesteryear Museum, the Hardin County History Museum, the Brown-Pusey House, the Lincoln Heritage House, the Sarah Bush Johnston Lincoln Memorial Cabin, and a restored one-room schoolhouse.

Elizabethtown is centrally located to many of the State's attractions including the historic town of Glendale with its antique shops and uniquely Kentucky dining. Not far away in Hodgenville is the Abraham Lincoln Birthplace National Historic Site with the Lincoln Museum and Lincoln's Boyhood Home. Another nearby destination of interest is historic Bardstown, the setting of My Old Kentucky Home State Park and the famous production of "Stephen Foster--The Musical." Other interesting attractions in the vicinity of Elizabethtown include Loretto, where visitors may tour the Maker's Mark Distillery; New Haven with the Kentucky Railway Museum; and world famous Mammoth Cave National Park. About 30 miles from Elizabethtown in Louisville is the Kentucky Derby Museum and Churchill Downs, home of the Kentucky Derby.

Today, Elizabethtown is still a growing community with an ever-increasing industrial and commercial economy. There are also many cultural and recreational opportunities in the area. The city seal, with the inscription "Elizabethtown, Strong and Growing Since 1779," still rings true today.

Visit the city of Elizabethtown's website at www.elizabethtownky.org .

Contributed by Mary Chaudoin

Erlanger

Erlanger, also know as the "Friendship City," was incorporated Jan. 25, 1897. It is a suburban city located in the northern part of Kenton County on the Dry Ridge Plateau which extends from the Ohio River down into Central Kentucky. The 2000 census lists the population of Erlanger at 16,676.

Various modes of transportation have contributed tremendously towards the growth and development of Erlanger. In the 18th century it was the

> Feb. 12, 1874, was one of the most important days in Erlanger history as the trustees of the Cincinnati Southern Railroad announced that they would build a bridge over the Ohio River into Ludlow and that the railroad would follow the Lexington Pike.

buffalo trails along the Dry Ridge Plateau leading to the salt deposits. A legislative act in 1793 provided for the clearing of a wagon trail extending from Frankfort to Cincinnati. The road was called George Town Road, then Lexington Pike and later Dixie Highway. Stagecoaches ran year round along the old George Town Road and farmers used the road to drive livestock to market. As early as 1839, half of the pork packed in Cincinnati and Covington came from central Kentucky. About 70,000 hogs in addition to 10,000 cows traveled the George Town Road through Erlanger.

The Cincinnati, New Orleans & Texas Pacific Railway Co.-Queen & Crescent Route also played an important role. Feb. 12, 1874, was one of the most important days in Erlanger history as the trustees of the Cincinnati Southern Railroad announced that they would build a bridge over the Ohio River into Ludlow and that the railroad would follow the Lexington Pike. Passenger service on the Cincinnati Southern was initiated on July 23, 1877, with a train running daily in each direction with one of its stops being Erlanger Station. Baron d'Erlanger's railroads ran from Cincinnati to New Orleans and became known as the Queen & Crescent route.

The impact of the railroad on the community cannot be overestimated. This railroad station is a museum and home of the Erlanger Historical Society. It is the last remaining southern station between Cincinnati and Chattanooga. The small community that grew up around a tollgate on the buffalo trails along the Dry Ridge was originally known as Timberlake in honor of a local physician, William Timberlake. However, in 1882 the Erlanger post office was established and the name of the city was changed from Timberlake to Erlanger, honoring Baron Frederic Emile d'Erlanger.

The town grew quickly after the Dixie Highway was paved in 1921. In 1946, the Greater Cincinnati Northern Kentucky International Airport was dedicated. When Interstate 75 was constructed in the early 1960s, subdivisions and industrial areas built up along the interstate, and Erlanger led the Cincinnati metropolitan area in new construction for several years.

Erlanger has a reputation for steady growth, a stable government and active volunteers. A mayor and 12 council persons govern Erlanger. Over 600 businesses, large and small, call Erlanger home.
Contributed by Patricia A. Hahn and John A. Scheben, Erlanger Historical Society.

Florence

As you look at Florence today, it may be difficult to envision this area as it appeared when Boone County was organized in 1798. At that time, families of primarily German descent began to purchase land on the divide between Dry Run and Gunpowder creeks, along what was known as the George Town Road. This village, originally called Crossroads, in 1830 was named Florence and incorporated with a population of 63.

Among the earliest town businesses were a post office, tavern, blacksmith shop and later a wool carding mill. Shortly after Florence was established, the George Town Road was chartered as the Covington-Lexington Turnpike. In the early 1840s, one could ride the stage from Cincinnati to Lexington, a daylight ride that ran from 5 a.m. to 9 p.m. Florence was the first stop to change horses.

These stagecoaches, and the increasingly heavy turnpike traffic, were instrumental in the growth of Florence, which could boast two churches, two stores, two taverns, two schools, three doctors, four mechanic shops and a population of 200 by the late 1840s. The Covington-Lexington Turnpike was the primary route for transporting farm goods from southern Kentucky to the markets of Cincinnati and points north.

Following the Civil War, Florence and Boone County quietly prospered. In 1869, the Odd Fellows built a three-story lodge building at the corner of Main and Youell. By the 1870s, Florence was the second largest town in Boone County (Petersburg was the largest) with a population of 374.

In the early 1900s, the automobile made its debut, with a speed limit of 6mph hour. The Covington- Lexington Pike became known as Dixie Highway, or Route 25. Blacksmith shops began supplying auto repair services, and hitching posts and water troughs were removed to provide space for parking. Electric lights replaced coal oil lamps, eliminating the need for the village lamplighter to light the street lamps each evening. By 1910, the school had grown to four rooms, and in 1915 the first Florence High School class, with four graduates, received their diplomas.

In the late 1950s, the Northern Kentucky Industrial Foundation developed the Florence Industrial Park. Soon, Interstate 75 would run through Florence, bringing volumes of automobile traffic never before seen. Construction on the Florence Mall began in November 1974. Originally billed as the largest shopping

Old Florence
Source: Lloyd Library

center in the southwest, the mall offered over 130 shops. Whether you're visiting or just passing through, it's hard not to notice the city's most recognized landmark: The Florence Y'all water tower.

Growth in Florence has been steady since 1830, with major increases in retail shopping and residential development. Once only the third largest city in Boone County, Florence is now the second largest city in northern Kentucky. The little city that began with only 63 residents is now home to over 23,000 and features such attractions as Turfway Park Race Track, Florence Family Aquatic Center, Florence-Boone County Skate Park, a minor league baseball team known as the Florence Freedom, Boone County Veterans Memorial and the Florence Government Center.

Contributed by William Conrad and Joe Christofield

Frankfort

"Frankfort, Kentucky's capital and the Franklin County seat, is located astride a double curve in the Kentucky River about sixty miles upstream from the Ohio, at U.S. 60 and U.S. 127.

The first English explorer to visit the area was Ohio Company surveyor Christopher Gist, who followed an ancient buffalo trace to its junction with the Kentucky River and arrived on March 19, 1751. The event that probably gave Frankfort its name occurred in 1780 when Indians attacked a salt-boiling party from Bryan's Station at a ford on the Kentucky River, killing a

Floral Clock on the Capitol Grounds
Source: Kentucky Department of Tourism

pioneer named Stephen Frank. The crossing soon became known as Frank's Ford.

In August 1786, Gen. James Wilkinson, a former Continental army officer, bought a 260-acre tract on the north side of the Kentucky River from Humphrey Marshall. Two months later, the Virginia legislature designated one hundred acres of Wilkinson's land as the town of Frankfort. When Kentucky became a state…[in 1792] the legislature appointed a commission to select a capital. The commissioners were instructed to choose the town that pledged the largest contribution toward construction of a statehouse. Several towns, including Lexington, made serious proposals. But Holmes's offer of several town lots, rents from a tobacco warehouse, and assorted building materials, in addition to an offer of $3,000 in specie by eight local citizens, overwhelmed all other bids. On December 5, 1792, the commissioners recommended Frankfort as the capital.

As a border state capital, Frankfort felt deeply the

sectional tensions that led to the Civil War. Numerous families were divided, notably that of U.S. Sen. John J. Crittenden, whose sons, George B. Crittenden and Thomas L. Crittenden, served as generals in the Confederate and Union armies, respectively.

During the Confederate invasion in September 1862, Frankfort was captured and occupied until after the Battle of Perryville on October 8. The governor, the legislature, and other state officials fled to Louisville.

The postwar years were punctuated with incidents of racial and political violence, which culminated in the fatal shooting of William Goebel, the Democratic candidate in the challenged 1899 gubernatorial election, on January 30, 1900. Nevertheless, Frankfort saw considerable growth during this period.

Frankfort grew dramatically during the twentieth century, largely because of the expansion of state government. An impressive indicator of governmental expansion was the proliferation of government buildings. After nearly two decades of agitation, an imposing new capitol was constructed in south Frankfort. Designed in the French renaissance style by Frank Mills Andrews, it was dedicated in June 1910.

State government remains Frankfort's primary business, but the city has experienced substantial economic diversification since World War II."
CARL E. KRAMER
Excerpt reprinted with permission from the University Press of Kentucky, The Kentucky Encyclopedia, John E. Kleber, Ed., pages 353-354 (Lexington 1992).

Glasgow

The city of Glasgow, established in 1799, was named by John Matthews, one of the early pioneers in the county. Matthews, a native of Glasgow, Scotland, was active in the early history of the town, being employed by the court to clear the square and holding almost every office in the county at one time or another. In September 1853 the city was struck by its greatest disaster, Asiatic cholera, which threatened to wipe out the populace. A traveling circus brought the disease to town and the big spring, the main water source for the city, soon became polluted, infecting members of almost every family in town. Some fled, but many stayed to nurse the sick and bury the dead until the disease had run its course.

Today Glasgow is a great place to live and work. It is home to many unique attractions including the historic Plaza Theatre, the South Central Cultural Center and Fort Williams, which is within a few miles of Barren River State Park and Mammoth Cave National Park. Each year Glasgow hosts a number of events including the Glasgow Highland Games, the Beaver Creek Music Festival, Global Fest and wide array of outdoor music and downtown festivals.

In recent years Glasgow has been named the most wired small town in America. Far ahead of other communities, Glasgow's city-owned utility initiated fiber optics in 1988 and today sells electricity, competitive cable television, telephone service and wireless technology, creating a state-of-the-art network of networks at rates lower than anyone in the area. These goals have been accomplished through the construction of 120 miles of

Glasgow Highland Games
Source: Glasgow Renaissance Main Street

bidirectional broadband plant which touches each home and business within the city. As a result, residents enjoy information age services today that the rest of the country is only beginning to anticipate.

The community offers an excellent educational system with award winning schools in Glasgow and Barren County. We are home to the Glasgow Post-Secondary Regional Center and the Glasgow campus of Western Kentucky University. The WKU campus offers four-year and two-year degrees for both traditional and non-traditional students.

Glasgow, with our three industrial parks, serves as a business, service and industrial hub for communities to the north, east and south with easy access to Interstate 65 and the Cumberland Parkway (future Interstate 66). Glasgow has an active Chamber of Commerce and Industrial Development Economic Authority assisting with business and industrial development. The Glasgow Regional Landfill accepts over 70,000 tons of waste annually serving the disposal need of 14 counties in south-central Kentucky.

Local recreational facilities include a private golf and country club, four public golf courses, three swimming pools, walking trails, bowling, an eight-screen cinema complex, soccer and softball complexes and five municipal parks.

With our active downtown revitalization program, new outer loop and growing economy, Glasgow has a lot to offer and we invite visitors to the community to experience our unique community spirit that takes pride in our past and plans for the future.

Contributed by Rhonda Riherd Trautman,
Director, Glasgow Renaissance Main Street

Harrodsburg

An excellent way to begin a getaway in Kentucky would be to visit the state's oldest town and discover that Harrodsburg is blessed with a distinct character all its own. Once a frontier territory, Harrodstown was founded in 1774 as the first permanent English settlement west of the Allegheny Mountains. It is possible to lose oneself for awhile in this small town that is bursting with historic charm. Harrodsburg is a place where the pioneer past has a strong presence, and southern hospitality is the backdrop for an appealing mix of history, architecture and culture.

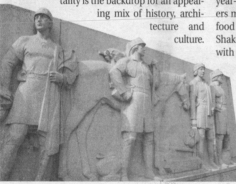

Monument at Fort Harrod
Source: Sid Webb

Located in the heart of Kentucky's famous Bluegrass Region near Lexington, Mercer County is nestled among breathtaking palisades and gently rolling countryside scattered with hand-laid stone fences and some the state's most pristine horse farms. A well-beaten path leads to a place rich in heritage, warm hospitality and simple pleasures.

The townspeople of Harrodsburg invite travelers to experience the relaxing atmosphere of their historic area. A tour of the area might begin with nearby Shaker Village of Pleasant Hill, one of the finest examples of historic restoration in the country. From there, visitors can marvel at the Kentucky River's natural surroundings aboard the Dixie Belle riverboat, which charts a course that runs through some of America's most beautiful scenery. Oth-

ers may choose to explore frontier life at Old Fort Harrod State Park, where Harrodsburg's history is showcased. A self-guided walking/driving tour of Harrodsburg highlights the town's architectural treasures. Shoppers may stroll through the downtown's historic district and shop for quality antiques and handmade crafts.

Visitors who are hungry can savor a taste of history at the Beaumont Inn, where diners feast on yellow-legged fried chicken, corn pudding or two year-old sugar cured Kentucky country ham. Others may choose to sample delicious country-style food in the famous Trustees' Office Dining Room at Shaker Village, where meals are served family style with plenty of hot breads, country-cooked vegetables, delicious entrees and special desserts.

A variety of amenities make this community as contemporary as any in the Bluegrass area. Golfers can indulge their passion at Bright Leaf Golf Resort, which offers a challenging championship course. Fans of fishing may cast their lines or enjoy recreational boating at Herrington Lake or at the Kentucky River. Horseback riders can gallop over more than a thousand acres of lush bluegrass farmland at Big Red Stables.

Every year Harrodsburg hosts the Fort Harrod Heritage Festival, a lively two-day event commemorating the heritage of the town. Another popular annual event is the Mercer County Fair and Horse Show, believed to be the oldest continually run event of its type in North America. The Christmas season is ushered in with the annual Historic Holiday Homes Tour, which is the highlight of the Come Home to Christmas Celebration.

Harrodsburg's tourism advocates like to say, "Come anytime. We've been preparing for your visit since 1774."

Reprinted with permission of Harrodsburg/Mercer County Tourist Commission, PO Box 283 Harrodsburg, KY 40330. For vacation planning ideas, phone (800) 355-9192 or visit www.harrodsburgky.com

Hazard

Elijah Combs was the founder of the town first officially called Perry Court House when it was established as the county seat of Perry County in 1821. However, in early court records it was referred to as Hazard. The name came from the hero of the War of 1812 Commodore Oliver Hazard Perry. He had recently succumbed to malaria in Venezuela. The name of the town was changed to Hazard by the state in 1854 and the town was incorporated in 1884.

Hazard grew very slowly in the years following its founding. By the outbreak of the Civil War there were only about a dozen families in the town. The Civil War brought Hazard an era of suffering and misery that was to last over a generation. During the Civil War the town was subject to guerrilla raids by small bands of outlaws. A mountain feud that followed the war in the late 1880s also was a reason for many inhabitants to flee.

After the train entered Hazard in 1912, coal mining surpassed logging. In the 1920s Hazard became the major mining center in the southeastern coalfields. By 1947 there were a total of 259 truck mines in Perry County. A steadily progressive coal industry continues today with operations by a very few large coal corporations.

Each year in September Hazard's coal heritage is celebrated with the Black Gold Festival in downtown Hazard.

Hazard Community College opened in 1968 with 166 students housed in a few rooms on the upper floor of the "Lower Broadway" school building. Today, and three college presidents later, it is called the Hazard Community and Technical College with campuses in five locations and an enrollment

of 3,802 in 2004 just on the main campus. The Challenger Center on the main campus gives elementary students and teachers from subscribing school systems outstanding experiences in space travel and education.

Hazard ARH Regional Medical Center follows a tradition of more

Hazard City Hall
Source: Charlie Hammonds

than 50 years of providing quality healthcare to Eastern Kentucky. Along with the Center for Rural Health, that has a building on the same campus as the hospital, healthcare professionals and students offer superior treatment and attention for the whole range of patients in eastern Kentucky.

Civic organizations which provide funding and support to the whole community are Hazard-Perry County Community Ministries, Inc., Rotary, Lions, Kiwanis, Chamber of Commerce, Hazard Women's Club, and sororities. Fraternal organizations active in Hazard are VFW, Masons, and Daughters of American Revolution. Many of these organizations provide scholarships, and fundraising to make the community a better place in which to live. Churches of all faiths are active in Hazard.

Contributed by Martha Quigley.

Henderson

"Henderson, the seat of Henderson County, is located on the Ohio River at the junction of U.S. 60 and 41. The town site was part of the 200,000 acres granted to Col. Richard Henderson's Transylvania Company by the Virginia Assembly in 1778. In the 1790s, the company's heirs established the town at an existing settlement known as Red Bank. When Henderson County was formed in 1798, Henderson was named the county seat. A log schoolhouse

> **Ironically, it was the Great Flood of 1937 that started economic recovery. Henderson was the only city between Pittsburgh and Cairo that was not inundated in the deluge, and new industry was attracted to the location.**

was used for county government until a permanent structure, a two-story brick building, was completed in 1814. A third courthouse, of Greek Revival style, was completed in 1843 and went through several renovations and additions before it was torn down in 1963.

Henderson's location on the Ohio River just below the confluence with the Green River made it an important river port; yet because the city was built on a bluff, it did not suffer flood damage as did many other of Kentucky's Ohio River towns. The rich agricultural region made it a tobacco market, and its proximity to western Kentucky coal mines attracted industry.

In 1810 Henderson was incorporated as a city.

Among the 160 town residents at the time was ornithologist John J. Audubon, who operated a general store there. In 1811 the first steamboat on the Ohio River arrived at the city, and by 1814 a tobacco warehouse had been built

The city was divided by the Civil War. A Federal recruiting station was established there in October 1861, while some of those who inclined toward the Confederacy were recruited by Col. Adam R. Johnson, a native of Henderson. Johnson's Confederates captured the town on July 17, 1862, and took away guns and military stores. Federal troops occupied the city for a time in 1863 and used the courthouse as a prison and a garrison in 1864.

Substantial growth took place in the city after the war. In March 1869, the Evansville, Henderson & Nashville Railroad (now part of CSX Transportation) was completed to Madisonville. By 1871 trains were running between Henderson and Nashville, and in 1885 a railroad bridge connected Henderson with Evansville, Indiana. In 1889 a second railroad, the Louisville, St. Louis & Texas (now CSX) reached Henderson from the east.

The railroads increased Henderson's status as a market city. By the early 1890s, eighteen tobacco factories were located there along with several distilleries and a brewery. The Henderson Wagon Works, the Henderson Cotton Mills, and the Henderson Woolen Mills, which made the well-known Kentucky jeans, were all important industries in the late nineteenth and early twentieth centuries.

From 1916 until 1937, prohibition of alcohol and overseas tobacco tariffs hit the Henderson economy hard, and the wagon works lost out to the rising automobile industry. Ironically, it was the Great Flood of 1937 that started economic recovery. Henderson was the only city between Pittsburgh and Cairo that was not inundated in the deluge, and new industry was attracted to the location."

BOYNTON MERRILL, JR.

Excerpt reprinted with permission from the University Press of Kentucky, The Kentucky Encyclopedia, John E. Kleber, Ed., pages 423-424 (Lexington 1992).

Hopkinsville

"Hopkinsville, the county seat of Christian County, is located at U.S. 41 and U.S. 68 in the Pennyroyal Region. The site was settled in 1796 by Bartholomew and Martha Ann Wood, a couple from Jonesborough, Tennessee. The Wood family established a permanent settlement in the vicinity of present-day West Seventh and Bethel Streets, near what would become known as the Old Rock Spring.

Wood donated five acres of land and a half interest in his spring for the county seat. The following year a log courthouse, jail, and "stray pen" were built on the public square facing Main Street. The plat for the town, first called Christian Court House, was surveyed by John Campbell and Samuel Means in 1799. In honor of Wood's eldest daughter, the town was renamed Elizabeth that same year. However, a town in Hardin County had the same name, and in April 1804, the General Assembly renamed the settlement Hopkinsville, in honor of Gen. Samuel Hopkins of Henderson County. A colonel in the Revolutionary War, Hopkins had settled in Kentucky in 1797 and was promoted to the rank of general during the War of 1812.

Although Kentucky was tardy in the establishment of a public school system, Hopkinsville was fortunate to have several quality private schools. The first of these was in operation by 1812, preceding the establishment of public schools in the city by almost thirty years. South Kentucky College, established in 1849, and Bethel Female College, organized five years later, provided formal higher education for young women. Circuit riders established a Methodist church in Hopkinsville about 1800, and in 1804 Little River Baptist Church was constituted. Other religious denominations organized in Hopkinsville included: Presbyterian, 1813; Cumberland Presbyterian, 1825; Episcopal, 1831; and Christian Church, 1832.

From the first issue of the Western Eagle on Jan.1, 1813, through 123 years of the Kentucky New Era, 45 newspapers have been printed in Hopkinsville and Christian County. Thirty-eight were weekly publications, one was tri-weekly, five were semi-weekly, and four were daily papers. Two papers were morning editions and three were monthly.

Railroad construction and operation in the late 1860s opened markets for agricultural and industrial products. Railroad service was inaugurated in Hopkinsville on April 8, 1868, by the Evansville,

On December 7, 1907, some 250 masked night riders captured police and sheriff posts and cut off the town from outside contact. They then pursued city officials and tobacco executives who were buying cheap tobacco from farmers not members of the Dark Tobacco District Planters' Protective Association.

Henderson, & Nashville Railroad.

On Dec. 7, 1907, 250 masked night riders captured police and sheriff posts and cut off the town from outside contact. They then pursued city officials and tobacco executives who were buying cheap tobacco from farmers not members of the Dark Tobacco District Planters' Protective Association. Three warehouses were burned during a night of lawlessness.

The building of the Pennyrile Parkway in 1969 and the city's proximity to I-24, the Land Between the Lakes region, and to Fort Campbell Military Reservation have been important factors in the Hopkinsville's growth."

WILLIAM T. TURNER

Excerpt reprinted with permission from the University Press of Kentucky, The Kentucky Encyclopedia, John E. Kleber, Ed., pages 440-441 (Lexington 1992).

Lexington

Founded in 1775 and named for the first battle site of the American Revolution, Lexington is Kentucky's second largest city. Early settlers started the town near the McConnell Springs branch of South

Lexington Financial Center
Source: Sid Webb

Elkhorn Creek. The city's growth followed the creek southward, with an early fort and cemetery being established near the city's Triangle Park area prior to 1800. Lexington was officially established by an act of the Virginia Assembly in 1782, a decade before Kentucky statehood.

An early center of learning, Lexington is home to Transylvania University, founded in 1780 and the oldest institution of higher learning west of the Alleghenies. Established in Lexington in 1865, the University of Kentucky is the state's flagship public university. The University of Kentucky currently has the distinction of being the city's largest employer.

Lexington is regarded as the center of the Bluegrass region and capital of the thoroughbred industry. Horse breeding and racing are economically important to the region. The Kentucky Horse Park, located just north of the city, is one of the few such facilities in the world celebrating man's relationship with the horse. The Keeneland Association holds world-renowned horse sales and race meets at its track just west of Lexington. Likewise, the Red Mile, one of the standardbred horse industry's most distinguished tracks, is located near downtown.

Lexington and Fayette County have shared a merged government since 1974, making it Kentucky's first such combined government. The Lexington-Fayette Urban County Government's structure consists of a mayor as head of its executive branch, and a 15-member council as its legislative branch. Twelve of the council members represent districts throughout Fayette County, and are elected to two-year terms. The remaining three members are elected at-large, with the candidate who acquires the most votes becoming the government's vice mayor.

According to the Kentucky Cabinet for Economic Development, more than $97 million has been invested in new and expanded businesses in Fayette County since 2002. The U.S. Census Bureau estimates that more than 266,000 people were living in Lexington-Fayette County at the beginning of 2005. In the latest U.S. Department of Commerce figures, the estimated average household income in Lexington-Fayette County is just under $40,000. The unemployment rate for Fayette County, according to the U.S. Department of Labor Statistics, is 3.2 percent. Major employers in Lexington include the University of Kentucky, LexMark International, Trane Co., Amazon.com and Valvoline.
Contributed by Claude Hammond

Louisville

You could say Louisville's story is a Tale of Two Cities. Not the 19th century novel by Charles Dickens, but a 21st century saga about my hometown.

The first city of Louisville was born in 1828 – a river town at the falls of the Ohio River with 7,063 residents. By 2000, the 61 square miles were home to 256,000 – and a reputation for lively and historic neighborhoods, visual and performing arts, baseball bats and basketball, the Kentucky Derby and Muhammad Ali.

The second city is the new city of Louisville – born Jan. 6, 2003, created through the merger of our city and county governments. It's now home to some 695,000 residents, covers 386 square miles and stretches from downtown to the county line with 83 incorporated suburban cities. Louisville zoomed from being the 64th largest city in the United States to 16th – overnight.

The new Louisville is the economic heart of a region that includes 16 Kentucky counties and seven in southern Indiana with a total population of about 1.4 million. One of every four Louisville workers lives in a nearby county.

The 21st century Louisville has a diverse economy. From health-care giant Humana to Papa John's . . . from Ford to General Electric... from Brown-Forman to YUM!, several world-class companies have headquarters or strategic operations located here. Our new UPS WorldPort global air hub employs more than 20,000 people and makes Louisville International Airport one of the busiest cargo airports in the world.

As Louisville has stretched in new ways, it has also kept in touch with our roots.

Louisville's very first settlers were pioneers. Our new Louisville has pioneered, too -- in different terrain. It is a health-sciences center where the first hand transplants in the United States were performed. It is a city of vibrant historic neighborhoods – with a renaissance of new housing downtown. It is a city of parks, building on our system of historic parks designed by Frederick Law Olmsted and the 5,500-acre Jefferson Memorial Forest.

Today, our new, award-winning Waterfront Park attracts 1.5 million visitors to the edge of the Ohio River each year. And we will add 3,000 additional acres of parkland in the coming decade – including a 100-mile loop encircling the city for the benefit of walkers and bicyclists to enjoy.

The first Louisville got its name from the King of France who aided American colonies in the Revolutionary War. The new Louisville has received national attention since our voters made the revolutionary decision to say "yes" to one merged local government. We are the first city our size to merge in 30 years.

Just as Louisville's early years were shaped by waves of immigrant arrivals from Ireland, Italy and Germany, its recent years have seen increasing numbers of international residents. In fact, half the population growth in the last Census came from residents with roots in Africa and Asia, South and Central America and Eastern Europe.

Louisville Slugger Museum

Source: Kentucky Commerce Cabinet, Division of Creative Services

Charles Dickens wrote another novel that could be the title of the next chapter of Louisville's life: "Great Expectations."

We're committed to making our hometown even greater for our children and our grandchildren.
Contributed by Mayor Jerry E. Abramson.
Louisville Metro Mayor Jerry E. Abramson took office in 2003. He served three terms as Mayor of the old city of Louisville from 1986-1998, the maximum allowed by state law.

Mayfield

"Mayfield, the county seat of Graves County in the Jackson Purchase region, is located at the junction of U.S. 45 and KY 80, just south of the Purchase Parkway in the center of the county.

Mayfield presumably was settled in 1819 by John and Nancy (Davenport) Anderson, who migrated to far western Kentucky from South Carolina. Anderson evidently started a post office at May-

> ...the same year [1823] the legislature created Graves County and established Mayfield as its county seat. The town was named for nearby Mayfield Creek, which possibly was named for George Mayfield, who had been kidnapped and murdered along the creek.

field in 1823, the same year the legislature created Graves County and established Mayfield as its county seat.

The town was named for nearby Mayfield Creek, which possibly was named for George Mayfield, who had been kidnapped and murdered along the creek.

In 1854, the New Orleans & Ohio Railroad (now part of the Paducah & Louisville) entered May-

field, boosting the town's growth. In 1830, Mayfield numbered forty-four inhabitants; its population was 556 in 1860.

During the Civil War, Mayfield, like the rest of the Jackson Purchase, was strongly pro-Confederate. In 1861, at a meeting in Mayfield attended by politicians and other leaders from the region, the secession of western Kentucky and the forming of a Confederate state with western Tennessee were discussed. Although nothing came of the plan, Confederate volunteers from Mayfield far outnumbered Union recruits from the city. In 1864, a small Union force occupied the town and ordered citizens to help build an earthen fort around the courthouse. Confederate sympathizers accused the Union commander, Gen. E.A. Paine, of a reign of terror; it was said that he executed more than sixty-one people in the region.

After the war, Mayfield's population grew steadily; by 1870, it was 779. It also was the center of one of the largest tobacco-producing areas in the state; Graves County grew more than 4.6 million pounds in 1870. In the 1990s the city is a tobacco marketing town with large sale barns.

In the early twentieth century, Mayfield became synonymous with clothing that was made and shipped nationwide. The town's minor league baseball team was the Clothiers. In 1990, Mayfield's and the region's largest employer was the General Tire and Rubber Co. plant, with a payroll of more than 2,000 union and management employees. Other local industries produce clothing, air compressors, and processed poultry.

In 1988, much of the Warner Brothers movie *In Country* was filmed in Mayfield. Starring Bruce Willis and Emily Lloyd, the Norman Jewison-directed film was based on a novel by Mayfield native Bobbie Ann Mason about a Vietnam veteran and his niece."

BERRY CRAIG

Excerpt reprinted with permission from the University Press of Kentucky, The Kentucky Encyclopedia, John E. Kleber, Ed., pages 619-620 (Lexington 1992).

Maysville

Virtually every Kentucky city has its own interesting history and unique features, and Maysville is no exception.

Despite having a population of only 8,993, Maysville is anything but a sleepy little town. The city has its own dedicated bus service, two newspapers and enough industry to attract a regional workforce that more than doubles the city's actual resident population each day throughout the work week.

Located on the banks of the Ohio River, Maysville has been home to an impressive array of noteworthy figures, including Supreme Court Justices Stanley Forman Reed and John McLean, and entertainers Rosemary and Nick Clooney, along with his son, actor George Clooney. Heather French Henry, Miss America 2000, also lived in Maysville.

The Clooneys still have a presence in Maysville—highlighted by the Rosemary Clooney Festival, which annually draws huge crowds to see entertainers such as Linda Ronstadt.

The town also has a sizable tourist industry, with a number of historic buildings. Daniel Boone was one of the town's trustees and his first cousin, Jacob, once owned a tavern here.

In addition, Maysville and the nearby town of Washington (which merged with Maysville in 1991) were key destination end points to freedom for many slaves who escaped to the south via the Underground Railroad. The Harriet Beecher Stowe Slavery to Freedom Museum is located in "Old Washington," which has a number of historic buildings dating as far back as the 1700s.

In 1775, Simon Kenton built a station three miles inland near present day Washington. Maysville, located 51 miles southeast of Cincinnati and 135 miles northeast of Louisville, was founded in 1784 as Limestone. It was the port through which many settlers traveling west on the Ohio River entered the Bluegrass State.

Maysville's port attracted the likes of French Gen. Lafayette, whose signature adorns the register of one of the local inns, and Henry Clay, who often used it as a departure point via boat after making the 60-mile journey north from Lexington.

Maysville was once the largest hemp market outside of the Bluegrass as well as the world's second largest burley tobacco market, producing about $70 million for the local economy. It remains a strong agri–industrial community.

Maysville has a full-service local government and its two newspapers include a daily, The Ledger Independent, and a weekly, the Mason County Beat.

An excellent quality of life, a low unemployment rate and certified retirement community amenities give the city overall appeal.

Like many other Kentucky cities, Maysville has a small town personality with big city aspirations and services. Maysville has succeeded in retaining the best of its past while also adapting to the rapid changes of 21st century life.

Contributed by Mayor David Cartmell

Downtown Maysville
Source: Sid Webb

Middlesborough

"MIDDLESBOROUGH (MIDDLESBORO)

Middlesborough, the largest city in Bell County in southeastern Kentucky, is located in the southeastern part of the county just northwest of the Cumberland Gap at the junction of U.S. 25E and KY 74. The city is situated in the valley of Yellow Creek, a large bowl-like depression. A popular but unlikely theory holds that the cause of the depression was the impact of a colliding meteorite 30 million to 300 million years ago.

Located at the base of the Cumberland Gap, Middlesborough witnessed Indians on the Warriors' Path, explorations of early pioneers, and the movement of thousands of settlers...via the Wilderness Road. At or near the city site, the pioneer Yellow Creek settlement was made around 1810 by John Turner of Virginia.

A few industrious farmers mined coal from the creek banks as early as the 1850s... Surface and mineral rights were sold to wealthy businessmen in the East beginning around 1870, but large-scale mining and logging operations did not go into full swing until the 1890s. Alexander Alan Arthur of Scotland, who arrived on Yellow Creek in the 1880s, had been involved in iron, coal, and steel enterprises in Great Britain...and saw great economic potential in the mineral and natural resources of the Yellow Creek Valley. He convinced European backers of easily obtainable wealth in the Kentucky hills and formed the American Association Limited. The company purchased 100,000 acres in Kentucky and nearby Tennessee and Virginia, and in 1889 Arthur began planning for a new city to be named after the industrial and manufacturing center of Middlesborough, England. A tunnel through

The World War II P-38 "Glacier Girl" was recovered from under 268 feet of ice from a Greenland ice-cap and restored to flying condition

Source: Kentucky Department for Libraries & Archives

Cumberland Mountain connected the Louisville & Nashville Railroad with Pineville...

Middlesborough was incorporated in 1890 and was a town of 5,000 with long, wide avenues, an iron furnace, tannery, city hall, opera house, hospital, two schools, four banks, five churches, sixteen hotels, and numerous homes and businesses of English-style architecture. By the end of the year, a number of the English backers went bankrupt and Arthur's grandiose plans were scaled down. When it was discovered that local iron deposits were not as rich as originally thought, new investment in the town virtually ceased. The financial panic of 1893 almost completely dried up American and British investment capital and much of Middlesborough went bankrupt. ...[c]oal mining was the backbone of the local economy for most of the twentieth century. The economy boomed during World War I, suffered during the postwar recession of 1920-22, rose during the latter part of the 1920s, and fell again with the Great Depression that began in 1929. A flood the same year did half a million dollars damage to the town.

During the 1930s, the federal government decided to proceed with plans to create the Cumberland Gap National Historical Park in the depressed area...which was not dedicated until July 4, 1959.

Although the name is commonly spelled Middlesboro, the city was incorporated as Middlesborough, which continues to be the official spelling."

DAVID F. WITHERS

Excerpt reprinted with permission from the University Press of Kentucky, The Kentucky Encyclopedia, John E. Kleber, Ed., pages 634-635 (Lexington 1992).

Murray

Murray, the county seat of Calloway County, is located on U.S. 641 and KY 94. A post office and trading center was established in the 1820s and named Williston, for James Willis, an early settler. Later, the community was called Pooltown, in honor of Robert Pool, a local merchant. The name was again changed to Pleasant Hill. Murray was incorporated Jan. 17, 1844, and named for John L. Murray, who represented the area in the U.S. Congress (1837-39).

The first courthouse was constructed in Wadesboro in 1823, and was a one-room log structure. The second Wadesboro courthouse, a two-story brick structure, was completed in 1831. The first courthouse in Murray was a two- story brick building constructed in 1843. The present courthouse, a three- story brick edifice in the Beaux Arts style, was built in 1913. Portions of the business district were burned in the Civil War by Union soldiers. By the 1870s, the town had recovered and was a prosperous community that had several mills and factories. Murray Seminary was established in 1858, the Murray Male and Female Institute in 1871, and Murray Normal School in 1922, which later became Murray State University. The proximity of Murray to Kentucky Lake and the Land Between the Lakes has aided the economic growth of the town. It is the home of the national Boy Scouts Museum.

Perhaps the best-known resident of Murray was Nathan B. Stubblefield, who, in 1888, created a wireless telephone, and, in 1892, made a wireless voice transmission. The population of the third-class city was 13,537 in 1970; 14,248 in 1980; and 14,439 in 1990. In 1987, Rand McNally's Retirement Places chose Murray as the top ranked retirement spot in the nation for quality of life. The Murray community is extremely proud of this honor and feels that this represents the spirit of this cosmopolitan and diverse community of 35,000. Murray is just minutes away from Kentucky Lake and Lake Barkley, two of the largest man-made lakes in the country, and the recreation area, Land Between the Lakes. This uncommercialized outdoor oasis attracts more than 2 million visitors to the area each year, with Murray being the closest city for shopping, dining and lodging. Golf, swimming, camping, hiking, boating, fishing and tennis are among the many popular activities of our residents and visitors.

> The first courthouse was constructed in Wadesboro in 1823, and was a one-room log structure. The second Wadesboro courthouse, a two-story brick structure, was completed in 1831.

Murray is also the home of Murray State University. With record enrollment of more than 10,000 students, MSU is consistently ranked as one of the nation's best educational values by U.S. News & World Report. It is also among the top three state institutions of higher learning in number of nationally accredited degree programs. The city is also a regional medical center with facilities that include a 216-bed hospital and a medical staff of more than 50 physicians representing 25 different medical specialties.

The Murray/Calloway County Chamber of Commerce and Ambassadors can be reached at 1-800-900-5171.

See E.A. Johnston, HISTORY OF CALLOWAY COUNTY, KENTUCKY (Murray, KY, 1931). RON D. BRYANT

Reprinted with permission from the University Press of Kentucky, The Kentucky Encyclopedia, John E. Kleber, Ed., pages 663-664 (1992).

Newport

"Newport is one of the two county seats of Campbell County, the other being Alexandria. Newport is located in the northwestern part of the county, across the Licking River from Covington to the west, and across the Ohio River from Cincinnati to the north. The city is the oldest river settlement on the south shore of the Ohio River in the Cincinnati area. It was laid out in the early 1790s by Hubbard Taylor, a young Virginia Revolutionary War veteran, who named it for Christopher Newport, commander of the first ship to reach Jamestown, Virginia, in 1607. James Taylor, Jr., a cousin of James Madison, brought the first settlers to Newport and was influential in having Kentucky create Campbell County in 1794. He also convinced Madison, who had become President Thomas Jefferson's secretary of state, to establish a military barracks in Newport, which had been incorporated as a village in 1795. The

Source: Bell South

Newport barracks was the mustering center for U.S. troops in the west when they marched on Canada in the War of 1812.

In 1830, Newport had only 715 inhabitants, but was elevated to the status of a city by 1835. The first large influx of population came in the 1840s with Irish and German immigrants. By the 1850 census, Newport boasted almost 6,000 people. There were no bridges across the Ohio River before the Civil War, and the Licking River was not bridged until 1854. The initial structure collapsed in two weeks but was quickly rebuilt, reopening travel to Covington. Lack of bridges led to more autonomous growth of the river-separated communities in their early decades. William Shreve Bailey, a self-styled "poor mechanic," edited an abolitionist newspaper, the Free South in Newport in the 1850s. The large German immigration in the 1880s and 1890s, and the completion of bridges from northern Kentucky to

Cincinnati, promoted the development of Newport as a residential suburb of the Ohio metropolis. One of the largest steel mills in the South and the largest brewery in the United States south of the Ohio River, Wiedemann, were industrial bases for Newport's development in the early twentieth century.

In the 1920s, national prohibition gave birth to organized syndicate crime, which was a dominant force in Newport and throughout northern Kentucky until the early 1960s. In the 1930s, 1940s, and 1950s, the city was a major headquarters for big-time gambling, especially layoff betting, in which one bookmaker, inundated with a large sum of money bet on a single horse, would move a portion of the bets to another bookmaker; if the horse won, the payoff was split. State government in Kentucky did not undertake to stamp out this illicit activity until the local Protestant Ministerial Association, and later the Committee of 500 (led by local businessmen), gave support to a reform movement. Assistance from the U.S. attorney general's office helped to banish syndicate criminals to other points in the early 1960s.

The Northern Kentucky Chamber of Commerce and Northern Kentucky University were factors in the growth of Newport in the early 1970s. The university, located in suburban Highland Heights, helped to raise the percentage of local high school graduates who attended college and went on to become leaders of Newport and the other northern Kentucky communities. The population of the second-class city was 25,998 in 1970; 21,587 in 1980; and 18,871 in 1990. "

WILL FRANK STEELY
Reprinted with permission from the University Press of Kentucky, The Kentucky Encyclopedia, John E. Kleber, Ed., page 680 (1992).

Nicholasville

"James Douglas, a surveyor from Virginia, came into the Bluegrass in 1774. He found a stream and called it Jessamine, after his daughter. The area later became Jessamine County, the only county in Kentucky with a feminine name. The city of Nicholasville, laid out in 1798, was named for Col. George Nicholas, a professor of law at Transylvania University during that time.

Entered into the National Register of Historic Places in 1984, the Nicholasville Historic District is the historic core of the city. The district consists of a concentrated group of nineteenth and early twentieth century commercial, governmental, residential and religious structures.

Camp Nelson is just a few miles from downtown Nicholasville. The site includes the Camp Nelson National Cemetery, where 4,000 Civil War dead are buried, and the Camp Nelson Heritage Park, which served as a Union Army supply depot, enlistment and training post and a refugee camp for the families of the enlisted African American soldiers.

J.D. Crowe, Bluegrass Festival
Source: SouthEast Telephone

Nicholasville is the birthplace of Dr. Lena Madesin Phillips, the founder of the Business and Professional Women's Clubs in America and the Business and Professional Women's Clubs International. Nicholasville is also the birthplace of Morgan and Marvin Smith, twins famous in the field of photography, particularly for their artistic rendering of Harlem.

Nicholasville and Jessamine County have a rich music history. Some of the area's famous citizens include country music recording performers, writers and bluegrass music legends, including John Michael Montgomery, Eddie Montgomery, J.D. Crowe and composer James Curnow. Jessamine County hosts an interesting variety of festivals and events. The J.D. Crowe Bluegrass Music Festival is held in August. Each spring 20,000 young people flock to Jessamine County for the Ichthus Christian Music Festival, the oldest of its kind in America.

Jessamine County has a rich agriculture history that includes hemp and tobacco. Although many other crops are grown in the county, one that is of importance historically is grapes. Jessamine County was the site of the first U.S. commercial wine grape vineyard, established in 1798. Today the county has 12 vineyards. Chrisman Mill Vineyards and Winery produces over 3,000 gallons of wine per year. Jessamine County has 74 horse farms, including Taylor Made Farms, Ramsey Farm, and Almahurst Stud.

Memorial Sports Complex in Nicholasville is a new facility and is the site of the AAA and Majors 18 and Under World Series. It is one of the few youth sports facilities in the country that will be completely wired for TV production. The National Softball Association Hall of Fame Museum is also located in Jessamine County. Each year the area hosts golf tournaments including the Kentucky Pro Football Hall of Fame Weekend.

The Kentucky River and Sugar Creek Resort offer venues for outdoor recreation. Valley View Ferry is the oldest continuously operating business in Kentucky. At High Bridge Park, you can picnic while viewing trains cross the first cantilever bridge in North America, designated an engineering marvel."
Reprinted with the permission of Nicholasville Now! Kentucky Renaissance/Main Street Program.

Owensboro

Owensboro, Kentucky's third largest city with a population of more than 54,000, is located on the south bank of the Ohio River in Daviess County. The city operates under a city manager form of government. The mayor and four city commissioners appoint a city manager.

The community has exceptional school systems, with schools consistently ranking among the top in the state in standardized testing and have received awards and recognition at both the state and national levels. There are four individual institutions of higher learning: Brescia University, Kentucky Wesleyan College, the Owensboro Community and Technical College and Western Kentucky University's Owensboro campus, which offers extensive undergraduate and graduate programs.

Owensboro has excellent public recreation

Mississippi Queen docked during International Bar BQ Festival, Owensboro
Source: Kentucky Department of Tourism

facilities, including numerous parks, playgrounds and spraygrounds, swimming pools, an ice arena, skatepark, golf course, tennis courts, softball and baseball diamonds, basketball courts and a greenbelt park that surrounds the city limits for easy access to walking and biking. The Jack C. Fisher Park Softball Complex and the Thompson-Berry Park Soccer Complex, which serve as host to several national softball and soccer tournaments during the summer, as well as the Waymond Morris Park Football Complex, are among the reasons Owensboro was selected by Sports Illustrated magazine as Sports-town Kentucky.

Well-known for its commitment to the arts, Owensboro boasts a premium symphony orchestra, as well as art, history, science and bluegrass museums. RiverPark Center, one of the finest performing arts centers in the country, brings some of the nation's most popular shows to its stage. RiverPark Center is becoming known as Broadway West to New York stage productions since it began providing Broadway shows with a venue where they may come to rehearse and perfect their shows before going on the road.

On the second weekend of each May, the Owensboro riverfront, from the Executive Inn Rivermont Hotel to the RiverPark Center, is bustling with thousands of locals and visitors who come to celebrate the International Bar-B-Q Festival. While the Bar-B-Q Festival is Owensboro's largest event, there are many others throughout the year in what has become known as Festival City. One of the most popular events is the Friday After Five free concert series that runs throughout the summer. Owensboro's long-range riverfront development plan included the expansion of the RiverPark Patio and the creation of Mitch McConnell Plaza. These beautiful additions allowed more space for the public to come downtown, relax and enjoy concerts and outdoor movies.

About five years ago, Owensboro began to organize its 12 neighborhood boards to give citizens more input in city government. The program has been so successful that the National League of Cities has added the Owensboro Neighborhood Alliance Program to its database of proven city solutions. Another popular program is the Citizen's Academy that was created to educate citizens on how city government works, to gain new ideas for improving operations from the participants and to produce future community and government leaders.

Contributed by Mayor Tom Watson

Paducah

"Paducah, the county seat of McCracken County and the largest city in the Jackson Purchase region, is located on the Ohio River at U.S. 60 and U.S. 45. The city may have been named for a legendary Chickasaw leader, Chief Paduke. The site was selected by George Rogers Clark during the Revolutionary War. His brother William, of Lewis and Clark fame, established the settlement and selected the name.

Paducah was the last town to be developed in Kentucky west of the Tennessee River, yet it quickly became the largest community. Its location at the junction of the Ohio and Tennessee rivers made trade and commerce prosper. As a break-in-bulk point on the inland waterway, Paducah became a center of wholesale trade for southern Illinois and western Kentucky. In 1831, the county seat was moved from Wilmington to Paducah. After the Civil War, Paducah became the midpoint in a railroad system linking Louisville and Memphis. Other lines connected Paducah to Nashville and to points north. A railroad bridge over the Ohio River opened in 1917, and the next year was used by the Illinois Central. In 1927, the Illinois Central built one of the largest locomotive repair and maintenance shops of that time in Paducah. In 1942-43, large steam locomotives were manufactured in Paducah. In 1990, VMV Enterprises operated the shops, and the Paducah & Louisville Railroad operated the former Illinois Central tracks in the city. Being a commercial center, Paducah was more cosmopolitan than the rest of the county or the surrounding region. German immigrants arriving in Paducah in the 1840s soon acquired leadership positions, including the third mayor of the city,

Vice President Alben Barkley
Source: Kentucky Department for Libraries & Archives

John G. Fisher, and Meyer Weil, a German Jew, who served as mayor during the economic Depression of 1873 and helped the city through financial crisis. In fact, a large Jewish influx occurred and the city's Temple Israel is one of the oldest Reform congregations in the United States.

Paducah was flooded in 1884, 1913, and 1937, when thousands of refugees fled the city, and many went as far as Nashville to find shelter. A floodwall was completed in 1946. Dams on the Cumberland, Tennessee, and Ohio helped alleviate the threat of floods.

The construction of the U.S. Atomic Energy Commission's gaseous diffusion plant, the Tennessee Valley Authority's Shawnee steam plant, and the power plant of Electric Energy Inc. at Joppa, Illinois, caused an influx of more than 20,000 people into the Paducah area in 1951. Educational opportunities include the Paducah Community College, a pioneer in the use of cable television to serve community needs.

Annual events include the Dogwood Festival, the Paducah Summer Festival, and the National Quilt Show.

Paducah's most well-known citizens include Alben Barkley, vice-president under President Harry Truman; Irvin S. Cobb, a noted correspondent, writer, humorist, and actor; Linn Boyd, twice Speaker of the U.S. House of Representatives; and Gov. Julian Carroll (1974-79). The population of the second-class city was 31,627 in 1970; 29,315 in 1980; and 27,256 in 1990."

See John E.L. Robertson, PADUCAH, 1830-1980: A SESQUICENTENNIAL HISTORY (Paducah, Ky., 1980). JOHN E.L. ROBERTSON
Reprinted with permission from the University Press of Kentucky, The Kentucky Encyclopedia, John E. Kleber, Ed., pages 705-706 (1992).

Paris

"Paris, the seat of Bourbon County, is located in the center of the county approximately fifteen miles northeast of Lexington. Pioneers lived in the area as early as 1776. In 1786, Lawrence Protzman bought land near the present site of Paris and offered 250 acres of it for the establishment of the county seat. In 1789, the Virginia legislature officially established the town, naming it Hopewell after Protzman's New Jersey hometown. A year later the town was

Duncan Tavern
Source: SouthEast Telephone

renamed Paris, to correspond with the naming of the county after the French royal house.

The post office was established in 1795 and was referred to as Bourbontown; contrary to a widely held belief, however, there is no evidence that the town itself ever went by that name. The first courthouse was completed in 1787; fire destroyed the second and third courthouses in 1872 and 1901, respectively. Paris's fourth and present courthouse was constructed during the period 1902-5 and was listed on the National Register of Historic Places in 1974.

The Bourbon Academy was established in Paris in 1798 by the Kentucky legislature on 6,000 acres of land and opened for classes in 1800. Lyle's Female Academy opened in 1806. William H. McGuffey, the author of the famous "McGuffey Reader," taught in Paris from 1823 to 1826, between his periods of attendance at Washington College.

Paris was an agricultural center boasting market houses, warehouses, taverns, and hotels as well as mills, carding factories, distilleries, stockyards, and groceries. The Lexington & Covington Railroad was completed as far as Paris in 1853. This railroad, which later became the Kentucky Central, helped make Paris the urban and commercial center of Bourbon County. Paris boomed during Reconstruction as freedmen and railroad workers tripled the population to 5,000 by 1875.

At the close of the century, Paris converted from gas to electric lights and enjoyed telephones, streetcars, city sewers, a fire fighting company, and public mail service. New public schools and a Paris High Alumni Association (1892) supported the expanding community consciousness. The Commercial Club (1908) underlined Paris's economic development in the early 1900s. Many new city services were established, including a sewer system, a water company, a lighting plant, hospitals, a YMCA Center, and a power plant. Parisians built magnificent churches and converted hundreds in well-known religious revivals.

Today Paris is a major tobacco market and the site of industrial interests as well. John Fox, Jr., is buried in the Paris Cemetery. Paris is also the location of the Duncan Tavern, built by Maj. Joseph Duncan in 1788.   The population of Paris was 7,823 in 1970; 7,935 in 1980; and 8,730 in 1990."

See G.R. Keller and J.M. McCann, SKETCHES OF PARIS (Paris, Ky., 1876). H.E. EVERMAN
Reprinted with permission from the University Press of Kentucky, The Kentucky Encyclopedia, John E. Kleber, Ed., pages 709-710 (1992).

Pikeville

"Pikeville, the county seat of Pike County in eastern Kentucky, is located on U.S. 23/ 460 and U.S. 119 on the Levisa Fork of the Big Sandy River. It is the county's largest city and has become the major trade and service center for the upper Big Sandy Valley. In 1990 it was served by the Chesapeake & Ohio Railroad (CSX Transportation), three banks (making it the state's third largest financial center), a regional hospital, a tri-weekly newspaper, an independent school district, and a four-year college. It was also the headquarters for several major coal companies.

The first proposed location of the new Pike County seat – the present Garden Village – was rejected because of public opposition. On Dec. 24, 1823, a commission selected a site owned by Elijah Adkins on Peach Orchard Bottom, on the west side of the Levisa Fork across from the mouth of Lower Chloe Creek. From the outset the town was called Pikeville in honor of the western explorer and U.S. Army officer, Zebulon Montgomery Pike, for whom the county and Pikeville's northeast suburb of Zebulon were also named. The site was surveyed and a town was laid out by James Honaker in the spring of 1824. The county court first convened there in May 1824. No court buildings were erected at the first proposed site, originally called Liberty, so court proceedings were held instead at the home of Spencer Adkins, near the mouth of Russell Fork. When the post office was established on Aug. 5, 1825, with William Smith as the first postmaster, it was called simply Pike. In 1829 the post office was renamed Piketon, the name given to the town incorporated in 1848. The town became Pikeville in 1850, but this name was not adopted by the post office until 1881. Pikeville was officially chartered as a city in 1893.

In October 1987, Pikeville completed one of the most ambitious engineering efforts east of the Mississippi River: a $77.6 million federally funded cut-through project designed to eliminate frequent flooding, relieve traffic congestion, and alleviate the critical shortage of level land in the downtown

Hillbilly Days
Source: Kentucky Department of Tourism

area. The Levisa Fork was diverted from its looping course through the city into a half-mile-long cut through Peach Orchard Mountain. Railroad tracks and streets were rerouted from the area and bridges were removed. The former river channel was filled in with dirt and rock from the cut-through, the end result giving the city nearly four hundred acres of new level land for commercial and institutional development.

Pikeville College, established in 1889 by the Presbyterian Church (USA) as a preparatory school for mountain youth, is a four-year liberal arts college with an enrollment of more than 900 students. The population of the third-class city was 4,576 in 1970; 5,583 in 1980; and 6,324 in 1990."

ROBERT M. RENNICK

Reprinted with permission from the University Press of Kentucky, The Kentucky Encyclopedia, John E. Kleber, Ed., pages 722-723 (1992).

Radcliff

Radcliff is a city in northern Hardin County located on U.S. 31W six miles northwest of Elizabethtown and adjacent to the western boundary of Fort Knox Military Reservation. The city was founded in 1919 when Col. Horace McCullum, one of Kentucky's well-known auctioneers, purchased land on Dixie Highway and sold building lots to

> One of the top destinations in Kentucky is the General George S. Patton Museum of Cavalry and Armor, located on Fort Knox. The museum contains personal artifacts of General George S. Patton, as well as one of the most extensive collections of tanks and armored vehicles in the world.

military personnel stationed at nearby Fort Knox. McCullum named his town Radcliff as a token of his friendship with a Major Radcliff, one of the U.S. Army Corps of Engineers supervisors in charge of building the federal military establishment, then known as Camp Henry Knox, in 1918 and 1919. Radcliff was incorporated as a sixth-class city on March 6, 1956. At that time its population was estimated to number 2,000. In 1962 it became a fifth-

class city. Radcliff's first mayor was Elmer Hargan. The next significant step in Radcliff's history happened during the 1930s when Fort Knox expanded and dislocated the towns of Stithton and New Stithton, causing various residents and businesses of those communities to move to Radcliff. During World War II, thousands of soldiers trained at Fort Knox and spend their leisure hours at the USO in Radcliff.

Fort Knox is home to the U.S. Bullion Depository, which stores 100 billion dollars worth of gold bullion. One of the top destinations in Kentucky is the General George S. Patton Museum of Cavalry and Armor, located on Fort Knox. The museum contains personal artifacts of General George S. Patton, as well as one of the most extensive collections of tanks and armored vehicles in the world.

Economically, Radcliff is dependent on Fort Knox. Many residents are employed on the base and many retired military personnel have chosen to live in Radcliff after leaving the service. Radcliff regards Fort Knox as its largest industry, with a payroll of millions of dollars. The city recognizes the importance of the military base to the city's economy by holding an annual weeklong Golden Armor Festival on the military base. For entertainment, local talent is on display at the Hardin County Playhouse and the Hardin County Schools Performing Arts Center, both in Radcliff. And, recreational activities such as hiking, biking and walking abound at the Saunders Spring Nature Preserve. Radcliff participates in the Sister City Program, and is paired with Munster, Germany, a partnership that has spanned more than 20 years.

During the 1970s and 1980s Radcliff was one of the fastest growing cities in the state. Its population was 7,881 in 1970; 14,656 in 1980; and 19,772 in 1990.

Sources: Reprinted with permission from the University Press of Kentucky, The Kentucky Encyclopedia, John E. Kleber, Ed., page 752 (1992) and Radcliff-Ft. Knox Tourism Convention Commission, www.radclifftourism.org.

Richmond

"Richmond, the county seat of Madison County, is located near the center of the county at the junction of U.S. 25/421 and KY 52, just east of I-75. The area was settled in 1785 by Col. John Miller, a Virginia-born Revolutionary War veteran. He donated fifty acres on Town Fork of Dreaming Creek for the transfer of the county seat from Milford, located four and a half miles to the southwest. Richmond was created by legislative act on July 4, 1798, and became the county seat that year. It was named for Miller's birthplace in Virginia.

In 1799, a courthouse was erected, which served the county until a Greek Revival-style structure was built between 1849 and 1852. In 1809, Richmond was incorporated. In 1810, the town had 110 citizens, which made it the fifteenth largest town in the state. By 1812 a hotel had been constructed, and in 1817 a bank opened.

Although a private school had been established in 1799 by Israel Donaldson, it was not until 1821 that Madison Seminary, a city-sponsored school, was opened. In 1858, the Madison Female Institute began enrollment and provided a classical preparatory education for young women until 1919. Following the Civil War Battle of Richmond on Aug. 30, 1862, it was used as a hospital for several months, with teachers and students caring for the wounded.

After the Civil War, Richmond grew both in population and in size as it expanded the city limits four times between 1866 and 1890. Numerous industries and institutions grew in Richmond after 1865. A baseball club was organized in 1868, and a cheese factory was started in 1869. As a city, Richmond secured modern public utilities relatively early. Gas lamps illuminated streets in 1874, and in 1879 the town had the only telephone system in the state outside of Louisville. A water plant opened in 1891, and public electricity was produced in 1899.

Curtis Field Burnam, a staunch Republican and friend of Abraham Lincoln, dominated politics between 1850 and 1900 and acted as a strong advocate for locating Central University, a predecessor of Eastern Kentucky University (EKU), to Richmond. The university was formally founded in 1906 as Eastern Kentucky State Normal School. During World War II, the Blue Grass Ordinance Depot was constructed just south of Richmond and provided a major boost in the area's employment. In 1948, the Westinghouse Electric Corporation opened a large light bulb manufacturing plant

Downtown Richmond
Source: Bell South

in Richmond, but in the early 1980s the plant was sold to the North American Phillips Company.

In 1963, I-75 was completed from Richmond to Athens in Fayette County. The interstate highway helped to spur commercial and residential development in the county. Richmond's largest employers are EKU and college-related service businesses, and many residents of the city and county commute into Lexington for work. The population of the second-class city was 16,861 in 1970; 21,705 in 1980; and 21,155 in 1990."

FRED ALLEN ENGLE

Reprinted with permission from the University Press of Kentucky, The Kentucky Encyclopedia, John E. Kleber, Ed., pages 771-772 (1992).

Somerset

On Feb. 24, 1801, the county court named Somerset as the county seat of Pulaski County. According to tradition, the first courthouse was located in the center of the public square in 1808. The town was incorporated in 1810, and on March 13, 1888,

governor, Edwin P. Morrow elected in 1918.

The first raw silk in Kentucky was produced in Somerset in 1842.

The first church in Somerset, organized on June 8, 1799 was originally called Sinking Creek and is now known as First Baptist Church. During the Civil War, the church

Downtown Somerset
Source: Sid Webb

Farmers market in Somerset
Source: Sid Webb

was used as a hospital for the sick and wounded. The church cemetery, now known as Town Springs Cemetery, is where some of our Revolutionary soldiers were buried.

The first hospital was started in 1893 by Dr. George Reddish. The William Fox House, built in 1818 and 1819, was used as military hospital during the Civil War to care for the wounded of both sides. It was where Confederate General Felix Zollicoffer, slain in battle of Mill Springs lay in state for three days.

it was incorporated as a city. The first mayor chosen was Abe Wolfe.

The public square has a statue of one of the prominent citizens, state Senator John Sherman Cooper. The county courthouse faces the square. The clock, built in 1874, used to be on top of the old courthouse, but is now on the northeast corner of the square.

Somerset was the birthplace of one Kentucky

A street car was operated in Somerset from 1907 until 1926. The first railroad came to Somerset in 1877. The first post office was established shortly before Jan. 1, 1803. Somerset Academy was established in 1802, then the Masonic College, and in 1886 the Somerset Graded School was approved. The first newspapers were published between 1850 and 1860. The first bank was established in 1818.

Contributed by Judith Burdine

Winchester

The City of Winchester was created in 1793 from 66 acres of land donated by a frontiersman, John Baker. It was a wilderness — a 330 acre farm of cane-covered hills and its one advantage was a spring large enough to provide water for over 500 people. Baker divided the land into lots, laid out streets and provided free land to the county for a courthouse, a school, a jail and a stray animal pen. The town was named in honor of Baker's home, Winchester, Virginia. By 1797 Winchester consisted of 11 homes connected by a series of paths, through the cane. The streets were laid out, but not cleared and there were stumps in the middle of Main Street well into 1800. By 1800 there were 20 stores, six taverns, 10 churches, six lawyers and perhaps one doctor. In 1812, Winchester was listed as the seventh largest town in Kentucky. It was a thriving town of 412 people when boardwalks were built to permit crossing muddy streets. There was little organized education in the early years, but in 1810 a school was built at the corner of Hickman and Highland and continued on this site until 1974. Winchester Downtown Commercial District was placed on the National Register of Historic Places in 1982. The courthouse, completed in 1853, stands rigidly in the center and is a symbol of a history rich in tradition and legend.

Winchester's Main Street is known as the "White Way" because of the five-globed lampposts that were originally gas-burning lights. The name comes from a poem written by eastern Kentucky renowned Kentucky poet and author, Jesse Stuart. In his poem, "Up Silver Stairs," Jesse Stuart expresses his reaction to seeing the lights while flying over Winchester one night. The lamps remained in place for many years until they were removed in the mid-1950s in favor of brighter lights. In 1983, 10,000 people gathered in Winchester to celebrate the re-lighting and rebirth of the White Way, with two of the original fixtures and many replicas.

Winchester has one of few elevated sidewalks in Kentucky giving this downtown area the name, "High On Main." Main Street was a dirt pathway until 1910 when the city council accepted the plea to cover it with bricks. During the 19th Century, an

Downtown Winchester
Source: SouthEast Telephone

electric streetcar traveled Main Street to Moundale Avenue. At that point, the car was pushed around manually to make its return journey. At the end of the day, the driver would go into a store, call the electric company and have them turn off the electricity to the streetcar.

Winchester is centrally located, with breathtaking scenery, great history nettled in rich traditions, and friendly smiles waiting. Visitors are welcome to come visit the past, but will be pleased and surprised to discover that Winchester not only has great history but a bright future. The founders of Winchester left a great foundation upon which its citizens continue to build.

Contributed by the Winchester Chamber of Commerce

CITIES AND MAYORS—1st - 6th Class Cities

CITY	CLASS	POP	COUNTY	MAYOR	ADDRESS	CITY	ZIP	PHONE	FAX
Adairville	5	917	Logan	James Wilkerson	PO Box 185	Adairville	42202	(270) 539-6731	(270) 539-5503
Albany	4	2,255	Clinton	John N (Nicky) Smith	204 Cross St	Albany	42602	(606) 387-6011	(606) 387-6105
Alexandria	4	8,206	Campbell	Daniel M McGinley	8330 W Main St	Alexandria	41001	(859) 635-4125	(859) 635-4127
Allen	6	150	Floyd	Sharon S Woods	PO Box 510	Allen	41601	(606) 874-2953	
Anchorage	4	2,457	Jefferson	W Thomas Hewitt	1306 Evergreen Rd	Anchorage	40223	(502) 245-4654	(502) 245-5651
Arlington	6	395	Carlisle	Charles Burton	PO Box 399	Arlington	42021	(270) 655-6811	(270) 655-2261
Ashland	2	21,491	Boyd	Stephen Gilmore	1700 Greenup Ave	Ashland	41105	(606) 327-2001	(606) 327-2055
Auburn	5	1,468	Logan	Dewey Roche	103 E Main	Auburn	42206	(270) 542-4149	(270) 542-4143
Audubon Park	5	1,533	Jefferson	Michael Scalise	3340 Robin Rd	Louisville	40213	(502) 637-5066	(502) 637-1574
Augusta	4	1,222	Bracken	John Laycock	219 Main St	Augusta	41002	(606) 756-2183	(606) 756-2185
Bancroft	5	545	Jefferson	Kimberly Reinhardt	7608 Wesleyan Pl	Louisville	40242	(502) 425-8369	(502) 429-6141
Barbourmeade	5	1,280	Jefferson	Albert A Tomassetti	3516 Breeland Ave	Louisville	40241	(502) 429-6141	
Barbourville	4	3,493	Knox	W Patrick Hauser	196 Daniel Boone Dr	Barbourville	40906	(606) 546-3914	(606) 546-4543
Bardstown	4	10,458	Nelson	Dixie Hibbs	220 N 5th St	Bardstown	40004	(877) 348-5947	(502) 348-2433
Bardwell	5	796	Carlisle	Joe C Ross	265 Front St	Bardwell	42023	(270) 628-5415	(270) 628-3246
Barlow	5	705	Ballard	Ruth Negley	PO Box 309	Barlow	42024	(270) 334-3500	(270) 334-3564
Beattyville	5	1,178	Lee	Charles Beach III	309 W 2nd	Beattyville	41311	(606) 464-3631	(606) 464-2123
Beaver Dam	4	3,054	Ohio	Mary Pate	PO Box 127	Beaver Dam	42320	(270) 274-7106	(270) 274-5640
Bedford	6	719	Trimble	Russell Dale Clifton	147 Victory Ave	Bedford	40006	(502) 255-3684	(502) 255-3222
Beechwood Village	5	1,186	Jefferson	Joyce Louden	220 Sage Rd	Louisville	40207	(502) 893-5087	
Bellefonte	6	830	Greenup	Thomas R (Tom) Bradley	422 Bellefonte Princess Rd	Ashland	41101	(304) 529-5375	
Bellemeade	4	882	Jefferson	Arthur (Wes) Amos	108 Tristan Rd	Louisville	40222	(502) 425-0485	
Bellevue	4	6,138	Campbell	John Jack Meyer	616 Poplar St	Bellevue	41073	(859) 431-8866	(859) 261-8387
Bellewood	6	302	Jefferson	Bruce Gale	3907 Brookfield Ave	Louisville	40207	(502) 893-0237	
Benham	5	560	Harlan	Betty Joy Howard	463 Cumberland Ave	Benham	40807	(606) 848-5506	(606) 848-5506
Benton	4	4,165	Marshall	Larry Spears	1009 Main St	Benton	42025	(270) 527-8677	(270) 527-2251
Berea	4	11,259	Madison	Steven Connelly	212 Chestnut St	Berea	40403	(859) 986-8528	(859) 986-7657
Berry	6	300	Harrison	Don Adams	PO Box 96	Berry	41003	(859) 234-1268	(859) 234-3185
Blackey	6	147	Letcher	Cathy Back	265 Main St Loop	Blackey	41804	(606) 633-4111	(606) 633-4111
Blaine	6	249	Lawrence	Ella V Seals	PO Box 66	Blaine	41124	(606) 652-9175	
Bloomfield	5	856	Nelson	Ronnie Bobblett	141 Depot St	Bloomfield	40008	(502) 252-8222	(502) 252-9013
Blue Ridge Manor	5	630	Jefferson	Albert M Hardesty	120 Blue Ridge Rd	Louisville	40223	(502) 245-5139	(502) 245-5106
Bonnieville	6	357	Hart	Rose Bostic	347 Campground Rd	Bonnieville	42713	(270) 531-5693	
Booneville	6	109	Owsley	Charles Long	1 Mulberry St	Booneville	41314	(606) 593-6800	(775) 414-9363
Bowling Green	2	50,063	Warren	Elaine Walker	PO Box 430	Bowling Green	42102	(270) 793-9055	(270) 393-3698
Bradfordsville	6	314	Marion	David Edelen	Main St	Bradfordsville	40009	(270) 337-3796	(270) 337-2085
Brandenburg	6	2,158	Meade	Ronnie C Joyner	737 High St	Brandenburg	40108	(270) 422-4981	(270) 422-4983
Bremen	6	365	Muhlenberg	Roy A Shaver	PO Box 334	Bremen	42325	(270) 525-3493	
Briarwood	6	559	Jefferson	William H Vaughan	2006 Japonica Way	Louisville	40242	(502) 425-2515	
Brodhead	5	1,185	Rockcastle	Walter Lee Cash	7 W Main St	Brodhead	40409	(606) 758-8635	(606) 758-8635
Broeck Pointe	5	298	Jefferson	Leonard P Wiseman	PO Box 22205	Louisville	40222	(502) 426-4471	(502) 426-4471
Bromley	5	800	Kenton	James G Miller	211 Rohman Ave	Bromley	41016	(859) 261-2498	(859) 261-6791
Brooksville	6	601	Bracken	John H Corlis	320 Frankfort St	Brooksville	41004	(606) 735-2501	
Brownsboro Farm	6	686	Jefferson	Eric Cerro	8455 Brownsboro Rd	Louisville	40241	(502) 426-1113	
Brownsboro Village	6	320	Jefferson	Robert L Desensi Jr	310 Lotis Way	Louisville	40207	(502) 895-0708	
Brownsville	5	933	Edmonson	Timothy M Houchin	PO Box 238	Brownsville	42210	(270) 597-3814	(270) 597-3274
Buckhorn	6	144	Perry	Veda Wooton	191 Buckhorn Ln	Buckhorn	41721	(606) 398-7381	(606) 398-7912
Burgin	5	880	Mercer	John D Brown	117 Maple St	Burgin	40310	(859) 748-5220	(859) 748-9900
Burkesville	5	1,765	Cumberland	Mike Irby	214 Upper River St	Burkesville	42717	(270) 864-5391	(270) 864-1795
Burnside	5	659	Pulaski	Dean Lovins	7968 S Hwy 27	Burnside	42519	(606) 561-4113	
Butler	5	626	Pendleton	Delbert Reid	102 Front St	Butler	41006	(859) 472-5015	(859) 472-5173
Cadiz	5	2,443	Trigg	Lyn Bailey	63 Main St	Cadiz	42211	(270) 522-8244	(270) 522-0025
Calhoun	5	812	McLean	Thomas Fulkerson	325 W 2nd St	Calhoun	42327	(270) 273-3092	(270) 273-9717
California	6	83	Campbell	Franklin D Smith	45 Madison St	California	41007	(859) 635-1808	

CITIES AND MAYORS — 1st - 6th Class Cities

CITY	CLASS	POP	COUNTY	MAYOR	ADDRESS	CITY	ZIP	PHONE	FAX
Calvert City	4	2,723	Marshall	Lynn B Jones	1315 5th Ave	Calvert City	42029	(270) 395-7138	(270) 395-5554
Camargo	5	952	Montgomery	Greg Beam	4406B Camargo Rd	Mt Sterling	40353	(859) 498-9075	
Cambridge	6	194	Jefferson	Camille Mills	2907 Cambridge Rd	Louisville	40220	(502) 473-8043	(502) 584-3091
Campbellsburg	5	706	Henry	Carl Rucker	8142 Main St	Campbellsburg	40011	(502) 532-6050	(502) 532-0039
Campbellsville	3	10,689	Taylor	Brenda Allen	100 Terri St	Campbellsville	42718	(270) 465-7001	(270) 789-0251
Campton	6	405	Wolfe	Gay Campbell	Main St	Campton	41301	(606) 668-3574	(606) 668-7426
Caneyville	6	637	Grayson	James P Embry	PO Box 222	Caneyville	42721	(270) 879-8711	(270) 879-3333
Carlisle	4	2,002	Nicholas	Eugene Kelley	107 E Chestnut St	Carlisle	40311	(859) 289-3700	(859) 289-7704
Carrollton	4	3,802	Carroll	Ann C Deatherage	750 Clay St	Carrollton	41008	(502) 732-7051	(502) 732-6738
Carrsville	6	62	Livingston	Deana Jo Gerding	1810 Fleet St	Carrsville	42081	(606) 988-3632	
Catlettsburg	4	1,908	Boyd	Roger M Hensley	PO Box 533	Catlettsburg	41129	(606) 739-0104	(606) 739-5754
Cave City	4	1,920	Barren	Bob Y Hunt	103 Duke St	Cave City	42127	(270) 773-2188	(270) 773-4522
Centertown	6	413	Ohio	Jeanene Reeneer	816 Main St	Centertown	42328	(270) 232-5067	(270) 232-5969
Central City	4	5,787	Muhlenberg	Hugh W Sweatt Jr	214 N 1st St	Central City	42330	(270) 754-5097	(270) 754-5745
Clarkson	6	808	Grayson	Bonnie Henderson	510 Millerstown St	Clarkson	42726	(270) 242-6997	(270) 242-2841
Clay	5	1,166	Webster	Rick Householder	9100 St Rt 132 W	Clay	42404	(270) 664-2444	(270) 664-9185
Clay City	5	1,314	Powell	Jimmy Caudill	4651 Main St	Clay City	40312	(606) 663-2224	(606) 663-0672
Clinton	5	1,387	Hickman	Tommy Kimbro	City Hall	Clinton	42031	(270) 653-6419	(270) 653-6422
Cloverport	6	1,248	Breckinridge	Tom Wheatley	212 W Main St	Cloverport	40111	(270) 788-6632	(270) 788-3751
Coal Run Village	6	565	Pike	Phyllis S Muncy	3515 N Mayo Trl	Pikeville	41501	(606) 437-6032	
Cold Spring	5	4,772	Campbell	Mark Stoeber	5694 E Alexandria Pk	Cold Spring	41076	(859) 441-9604	(859) 441-4640
Coldstream	4	970	Jefferson	Winfred McBroom	9462 Brownsboro Rd No 140	Louisville	40241	(502) 243-7002	
Columbia	4	4,152	Adair	Pat Bell	116 Campbellsville St	Columbia	42728	(270) 384-6183	(270) 384-3799
Columbus	5	221	Hickman	Lynn Bencini	PO Box 121	Columbus	42032	(270) 677-2701	
Concord	6	26	Lewis	Lovell Polley	Rt 2 Box 510	Vanceburg	41179	(606) 798-6922	
Corbin	3	7,932	Whitley/Knox	Eddie Amos Miller	PO Drawer 1343	Corbin	40702	(606) 523-6520	(606) 523-6500
Corinth	6	184	Grant	William H Hill	215 Thomas Ln	Corinth	41010	(859) 824-5922	(859) 824-5922
Corydon	6	753	Henderson	Larry Thurby	531 7th St	Corydon	42406	(270) 533-6576	(270) 533-6721
Covington	2	42,687	Kenton	Irvin T Callery	City Bldg	Covington	41011	(859) 292-2127	(859) 292-2137
Crab Orchard	6	860	Lincoln	Michael Ramey	723 Meadowlark Dr	Crab Orchard	40419	(606) 355-2394	
Creekside	6	341	Jefferson	Michael B Watson	PO Box 221076	Louisville	40241	(502) 426-1633	(502) 327-0080
Crescent Springs	4	3,964	Kenton	Claire F Moriconi	739 Buttermilk Pk	Crescent Springs	41017	(859) 341-3017	(859) 341-3518
Crestview	6	471	Campbell	Janet Krebs	14 Circle Dr	Crestview	41076	(859) 441-5898	(859) 441-5898
Crestview Hills	5	3,232	Kenton	Paul W Meier	50 Crestview Hills Mall Rd	Crestview Hills	41017	(859) 341-7373	(859) 341-6993
Crestwood	5	2,095	Oldham	Dennis L Deibel	PO Box 186	Crestwood	40014	(502) 241-7088	(502) 241-3159
Crittenden	5	2,506	Grant	James Livingood	104 N Main St	Crittenden	41030	(859) 428-2597	(859) 428-2419
Crofton	6	794	Christian	Michael Croft	PO Box 42	Crofton	42217	(270) 424-5111	(270) 424-9332
Crossgate	5	254	Jefferson	Peggy W Swain	1804 Crossgate Ln	Louisville	40206	(502) 426-3086	(502) 426-3086
Cumberland	4	2,380	Harlan	Carl Hatfield	402 W Main St	Cumberland	40823	(606) 589-2107	(606) 589-2107
Cynthiana	4	6,260	Harrison	Virgie Florence Wells	PO Box 67	Cynthiana	41031	(859) 234-7153	(859) 234-0035
Danville	3	15,294	Boyle	John W D Bowling	445 W Main St	Danville	40423	(859) 238-1200	(859) 238-1236
Dawson Springs	4	2,978	Hopkins	Stacia Peyton	200 W Arcadia Ave	Dawson Springs	42408	(270) 797-2781	(270) 797-2221
Dayton	4	5,677	Campbell	Kenneth Rankle	1203 Dayton Ave	Dayton	41074	(859) 491-1600	(859) 491-3538
Dixon	6	604	Webster	Colin E Todd	10 N Main St	Dixon	42409	(270) 639-5088	(270) 639-5864
Douglass Hills	4	5,648	Jefferson	Sheri Fetter	11013 Finchley Rd	Louisville	40243	(502) 245-3600	(502) 245-3648
Dover	6	317	Mason	Ed Sidell	PO Box 161	Dover	41034	(606) 882-2306	
Drakesboro	5	622	Muhlenberg	Jesse Gibson	Main St	Drakesboro	42337	(270) 476-8986	(270) 476-7714
Druid Hills	5	320	Jefferson	Ben Franklin	4006 Druid Hills Rd	Louisville	40207	(502) 637-0631	(502) 637-0148
Dry Ridge	5	2,068	Grant	William W Cull	PO Box 145	Dry Ridge	41035	(859) 824-3335	(859) 824-3598
Earlington	4	1,599	Hopkins	Steve Everly	305 E Clark St	Earlington	42410	(270) 821-4897	(270) 383-2041
Eddyville	5	2,353	Lyon	Judith Stone	PO Box 744	Eddyville	42038	(270) 388-2017	(270) 388-5683
Edgewood	4	9,188	Kenton	John D Link	385 Dudley Rd	Edgewood	41017	(859) 331-5910	(859) 331-5912
Edmonton	5	1,578	Metcalfe	Howard D Garrett	207 East St	Edmonton	42129	(270) 432-2811	(270) 432-3949
Ekron	6	176	Meade	Gwynne Ison	307 4th St	Ekron	40117	(270) 828-3801	

CITIES AND MAYORS —1st - 6th Class Cities

CITY	CLASS	POP	COUNTY	MAYOR	ADDRESS	CITY	ZIP	PHONE	FAX
Elizabethtown	4	23,239	Hardin	David Willmoth Jr	200 W Dixie Ave	Elizabethtown	42702	(270) 765-6121	(270) 737-5362
Elkhorn City	4	1,038	Pike	Richard Vaughn Salyer	395 Patty Loveless Dr	Elkhorn City	41522	(606) 754-5080	(606) 754-8588
Elkton	4	1,964	Todd	John E Walton	71 Public Sq	Elkton	42220	(270) 265-9877	(270) 265-5816
Elsmere	4	8,059	Kenton	Billy Bradford	910 Garvey Ave	Elsmere	41018	(859) 342-7911	(859) 342-7910
Eminence	4	2,242	Henry	Douglas Bates	PO Box 163	Eminence	40019	(502) 845-4159	(502) 845-8066
Erlanger	3	16,826	Kenton	Marc T Otto Sr	505 Commonwealth Ave	Erlanger	41018	(859) 727-2525	(859) 727-7944
Eubank	6	364	Pulaski	Frey Todd	10 Depot St	Eubank	42567	(606) 379-2703	(606) 379-2023
Evarts	5	1,068	Harlan	Burl Fee	101 Harlan St	Evarts	40828	(606) 837-2477	(606) 837-2093
Ewing	6	285	Fleming	Nellie Ellison	PO Box 63	Ewing	41039	(606) 267-4010	(606) 564-2257
Fairfield	6	133	Nelson	Mary Ellen Marquess	PO Box 42	Fairfield	40020	(502) 252-5171	(502) 348-3475
Fairview	6	150	Kenton	Harold Parks	8394 Decoursey Pk	Fairview	41015	(859) 291-7885	(859) 291-4697
Falmouth	4	2,103	Pendleton	Gene Flaugher	230 Main St	Falmouth	41040	(859) 654-4730	(859) 654-3603
Ferguson	5	894	Pulaski	James Muse	414 Murphy Ave	Ferguson	42533	(606) 679-6800	(606) 678-9638
Fincastle	6	837	Jefferson	Raymond H Elms	4411 Amelia Ct	Fincastle	40241	(502) 429-6629	(502) 429-6629
Flatwoods	4	7,593	Greenup	Bobby F Crager	2513 Reed St	Flatwoods	41139	(606) 836-9661	(606) 836-4222
Fleming-Neon	5	818	Letcher	Susan Polis	Main St	Fleming-Neon	41840	(606) 855-7900	(606) 855-7995
Flemingsburg	5	3,097	Fleming	Larry H Foxworthy	201 Court Sq	Flemingsburg	41041	(606) 845-8801	(859) 647-5411
Florence	3	24,689	Boone	Diane Ewing Whalen	8100 Ewing Blvd	Florence	41042	(859) 371-5491	
Fordsville	6	535	Ohio	Wilda G Hardesty	66 Ratliff St	Fordsville	42343	(270) 276-5268	(270) 276-5268
Forest Hills	6	508	Jefferson	Kenneth W Griffin	2401 Merriwood Dr	Jeffersontown	40269	(502) 261-0348	(502) 491-5567
Fountain Run	6	234	Monroe	Eldon Veach	202 Main St	Fountain Run	42133	(270) 434-3544	(270) 434-2211
Fox Chase	6	484	Bullitt	Joe Laswell	4814 Fox Chase Dr	Shepherdsville	40165	(502) 957-2471	
Frankfort	2	27,408	Franklin	William I May Jr	315 W 2nd St	Frankfort	40602	(502) 875-8500	(502) 875-8502
Franklin	3	8,009	Simpson	Jim Brown	PO Box 2805	Franklin	42135	(270) 586-4497	(270) 586-9419
Fredonia	6	411	Caldwell	Mike Board	Rt 36	Fredonia	42411	(270) 545-3925	(270) 545-3925
Frenchburg	5	554	Menifee	Dwain E Benson	PO Box 58	Frenchburg	40322	(606) 768-3457	(606) 768-6277
Ft Mitchell	4	7,822	Kenton	Thomas E Holocher	PO Box 17157	Ft Mitchell	41017	(859) 331-1212	(859) 331-6102
Ft Thomas	4	16,019	Campbell	Mary H Brown	140 Highland Ave	Ft Thomas	41075	(859) 441-2964	(859) 441-3519
Ft Wright	4	5,580	Kenton	Gene Weaver	409 Kyles Ln	Ft Wright	41011	(859) 331-1700	(859) 331-0454
Fulton	4	2,636	Fulton	Edward Crittendon	PO Box 1350	Fulton	42041	(270) 472-1320	(270) 472-6526
Gamaliel	6	435	Monroe	Roger Geralds	298 Lil Taylor Rd	Gamaliel	42140	(270) 457-4561	
Georgetown	4	19,448	Scott	Everette L Varney	100 Court St	Georgetown	40324	(502) 863-9800	(502) 863-9810
Germantown	6	192	Bracken	James Campbell	PO Box 57	Germantown	41044	(606) 728-2403	(606) 728-2225
Ghent	6	381	Carroll	Robert Sundermeyer	501 Main St	Ghent	41045	(502) 347-0161	
Glasgow	3	13,614	Barren	Darrell Pickett	126 E Public Sq	Glasgow	42142	(270) 651-1777	(270) 659-2114
Glencoe	6	250	Gallatin	Michael Murphy	112 N Main St	Glencoe	41046	(859) 643-2211	(859) 643-2211
Glenview	6	610	Jefferson	Gar Davis	2211 Brownsboro Rd	Louisville	40206	(502) 893-3333	
Glenview Hills	6	342	Jefferson	Fred R Simon	2908 Lightheart Rd	Louisville	40222	(502) 426-9863	(502) 897-6093
Glenview Manor	6	195	Jefferson	Michael Patterson	6 Glenwood Rd	Louisville	40222	(502) 429-6988	
Goose Creek	6	276	Jefferson	Don Zitnik	8709 Banbridge Rd	Louisville	40242	(502) 426-2480	
Goshen	5	935	Oldham	Todd Hall	1111 Crestview	Goshen	40026	(502) 228-2377	(502) 228-4277
Grand Rivers	5	338	Livingston	Tom Moodie	122 W Cumberland Ave	Grand Rivers	42045	(270) 362-8272	(270) 362-2572
Gratz	6	92	Owen	Charles Redmon	583 Crittenden St	Gratz	40359	(502) 484-2053	
Graymoor-Devondale	4	2,957	Jefferson	John Vaughan	1508 Valley Brook Rd	Louisville	40222	(502) 426-9561	(502) 425-5721
Grayson	4	3,980	Carter	Leda Dean	302 E Main St	Grayson	41143	(606) 474-6651	(606) 474-6653
Green Spring	6	774	Jefferson	William M Huff	7103 Green Spring Dr	Louisville	40241	(502) 228-3951	
Greensburg	5	2,443	Green	George Cheatham	105 W Hodgenville Ave	Greensburg	42743	(270) 932-4298	(270) 932-7778
Greenup	5	1,173	Greenup	Charles Veach	1005 Walnut St	Greenup	41144	(606) 473-7331	(606) 473-7831
Greenville	5	4,315	Muhlenberg	Billie Ruth Lewis	PO Box 289	Greenville	42345	(270) 338-3966	(270) 338-3007
Guthrie	5	1,449	Todd	Albert Scott Marshall	110 Kendall St	Guthrie	42234	(270) 483-2511	(270) 483-9062
Hanson	6	622	Hopkins	Charles Young	7580 Hanson Rd	Hanson	42413	(270) 322-8760	(270) 322-8575
Hardin	6	567	Marshall	Randal Scott	PO Box 377	Hardin	42048	(270) 437-4910	(270) 437-4934
Hardinsburg	5	2,393	Breckinridge	Wayne Macy	220 S Main St	Hardinsburg	40143	(270) 756-2213	(270) 756-2029
Harlan	4	1,945	Harlan	Daniel E Howard	PO Box 783	Harlan	40831	(606) 573-2912	(606) 573-9947

CITIES AND MAYORS — 1st – 6th Class Cities

CITY	CLASS	POP	COUNTY	MAYOR	ADDRESS	CITY	ZIP	PHONE	FAX
Harrodsburg	4	8,085	Mercer	Lonnie Campbell	208 S Main St	Harrodsburg	40330	(859) 734-7705	(859) 734-6231
Hartford	5	2,603	Ohio	Earl Russell	116 E Washington St	Hartford	42347	(270) 298-3612	(270) 298-3220
Hawesville	5	961	Hancock	Charles M King	395 Main St	Hawesville	42348	(270) 927-8707	(270) 927-8184
Hazard	3	4,745	Perry	William D Gorman	700 Main St	Hazard	41702	(606) 436-3171	(606) 436-3252
Hazel	6	439	Calloway	Harold Pittman	PO Box 184	Hazel	42049	(270) 492-6464	(270) 492-8862
Hebron Estates	5	1,120	Bullitt	Jerry Clark	3407 Burkland Blvd	Shepherdsville	40165	(502) 955-8973	
Henderson	2	27,468	Henderson	Henry Lackey	PO Box 716	Henderson	42419	(270) 831-1206	(270) 831-1206
Hickman	4	2,442	Fulton	Richard H White	PO Box 199	Hickman	42050	(270) 236-2535	(270) 236-2537
Hickory Hill	6	146	Jefferson	Patricia J Rayburn	3001 Creekside Dr	Louisville	40241	(502) 423-9302	
Highland Heights	4	6,472	Campbell	Charles W Roetiger	175 Johns Hill Rd	Highland Heights	41076	(859) 441-8575	(859) 441-8293
Hills and Dales	6	157	Jefferson	Ralph Johanson	3209 Mt Rainier Dr	Louisville	42024	(502) 426-7948	
Hillview	4	7,179	Bullitt	James Eadens	298 Prairie Dr	Louisville	40229	(502) 957-5280	
Hindman	5	771	Knott	Janice Jarrell	Main St	Hindman	41822	(606) 785-5544	(606) 785-0799
Hiseville	6	224	Barren	Bill Phillips	PO Box 149	Hiseville	42152	(270) 453-2605	(270) 453-2941
Hodgenville	4	2,787	Larue	Roger Truitt	PO Box 189	Hodgenville	42748	(270) 358-3832	(270) 358-9757
Hollow Creek	5	826	Jefferson	Robert A Wagner Jr	6410 Watch Hill Rd	Louisville	40228	(502) 231-0856	
Hollyvilla	6	494	Jefferson	Charles David Clemons Sr	10721 Charlene Dr	Fairdale	40118	(502) 363-4939	
Hopkinsville	2	28,678	Christian	Richard G Liebe	101 N Main St	Hopkinsville	42240	(270) 887-4000	
Horse Cave	4	2,272	Hart	JoAnne Smith	PO Box 326	Horse Cave	42749	(270) 786-2680	(270) 786-2688
Houston Acres	6	497	Jefferson	Charles G Bartman	4302 Martha Ave	Louisville	40220	(502) 454-3355	(502) 957-4205
Hunters Hollow	6	376	Bullitt	Linda S Parker	11300 Angelina Rd	Louisville	40229	(502) 957-4205	(502) 426-4889
Hurstbourne	4	3,959	Jefferson	Furman Wallace	304 Whittington Pkwy Ste 100	Louisville	40222	(502) 426-4808	
Hurstbourne Acres	5	1,517	Jefferson	Sean P Fore	1808 Addington Ave	Louisville	40220	(502) 491-5419	
Hustonville	6	351	Lincoln	Larry Doss	PO Box 172	Hustonville	40437	(606) 346-2501	(606) 346-4312
Hyden	6	200	Leslie	Eugene Stewart	22035 Main St	Hyden	41749	(606) 672-2300	(606) 672-5810
Independence	3	17,070	Kenton	Chris Moriconi	5409 Madison Pk	Independence	41051	(859) 356-5302	(859) 356-6843
Indian Hills	4	2,967	Jefferson	Thomas O Eifler	PO Box 6289	Louisville	40206	(502) 895-0005	(502) 893-0330
Inez	6	456	Martin	Dick Young	PO Box 427	Inez	41224	(606) 298-7051	
Irvine	4	2,748	Estill	W T (Tom) Williams	142 Broadway	Irvine	40336	(606) 723-2554	(606) 723-2558
Irvington	5	1,292	Breckinridge	Ricky Lucas	806 Michelle Way	Irvington	40146	(270) 547-6623	
Island	6	431	McLean	Charles R Strole	145 N Washington St	Island	42350	(270) 486-3992	(270) 486-9303
Jackson	4	2,407	Breathitt	Michael D Miller	333 Broadway St	Jackson	41339	(606) 666-7069	(606) 666-7046
Jamestown	5	1,666	Russell	June McGaha	202 Monument Sq	Jamestown	42629	(270) 343-4594	(270) 343-4929
Jeffersontown	3	26,331	Jefferson	Clay S Foreman	10416 Watterson Trl	Jeffersontown	40299	(502) 267-8333	(502) 267-6338
Jeffersonville	5	1,867	Montgomery	Richard Henderson	PO Box 127	Jeffersonville	40337	(859) 498-5808	(859) 497-6267
Jenkins	4	2,321	Letcher	Robert Pud Shubert	8531 Lakeside Dr	Jenkins	41537	(606) 832-2142	(606) 832-2362
Junction City	5	2,163	Boyle	Glen Harmon	794 Shelby St	Junction City	40440	(859) 854-3900	(859) 854-3900
Kentonvale	6	149	Kenton	Michael Pendery	464 Kuhrs Ln	Kentonvale	41015	(502) 331-7977	
Kevil	6	565	Ballard	Charles Burnley	PO Box 83	Kevil	42053	(270) 462-3151	(270) 462-3104
Kingsley	6	426	Jefferson	Phyllis A Breuer	PO Box 5515	Louisville	40205	(502) 452-2515	(502) 452-2515
Kuttawa	5	613	Lyon	Lee McCollum	82 Cedar St	Kuttawa	42055	(270) 388-7151	(270) 388-7695
LaCenter	5	1,026	Ballard	Lewis Hicks	PO Box 420	LaCenter	42056	(270) 665-5162	(270) 665-9113
LaFayette	6	183	Christian	Nancy A Reece	PO Box 240	Lafayette	42254	(270) 271-2185	(270) 271-2859
LaGrange	4	5,865	Oldham	Elsie Carter	410 W Jefferson St	LaGrange	40031	(502) 222-1433	(502) 222-5875
Lakeside Park	5	2,791	Kenton	Karen Gamel	258 N Ashbrook Cir	Lakeside Park	41017	(859) 331-8707	(859) 331-8707
Lakeview Heights	6	248	Rowan	David Bolt	385 Circle Dr	Morehead	40351	(606) 780-7613	(606) 780-7613
Lancaster	4	4,014	Garrard	Billy Carter Moss	101 Stanford St	Lancaster	40444	(859) 792-2241	(859) 792-3341
Langdon Place	4	986	Jefferson	Carolyn S Weitlauf	PO Box 22294	Louisville	40252	(502) 426-3701	(502) 426-3701
Latonia Lakes	6	313	Kenton	William Dorgan Jr	6132 Clubhouse Dr	Latonia Lakes	41015	(859) 356-0417	(859) 356-9111
Lawrenceburg	4	9,246	Anderson	Bobby Sparrow	205 E Woodford St	Lawrenceburg	40342	(502) 839-5372	(502) 839-5106
Lebanon	4	5,821	Marion	Gary D Crenshaw	PO Box 840	Lebanon	40033	(270) 692-6272	(270) 692-4638
Lebanon Junction	5	1,854	Bullitt	George Haik	271 Main St	Lebanon Junction	40150	(502) 833-4311	(502) 833-4688
Leitchfield	4	6,263	Grayson	William H (Turkey) Thomason	314 W White Oak St	Leitchfield	42755	(270) 259-4034	(270) 259-5858
Lewisburg	5	911	Logan	Kenneth Whitson	204 S Main St	Lewisburg	42256	(270) 755-2516	(270) 755-4829

CITIES AND MAYORS — 1st - 6th Class Cities

CITY	CLASS	POP	COUNTY	MAYOR	ADDRESS	CITY	ZIP	PHONE	FAX
Lewisport	5	1,628	Hancock	Chad Gregory	1010 Market St	Lewisport	42351	(270) 295-6665	(859) 258-3194
Lexington	2	266,798	Fayette	Teresa Isaac	200 E Main St	Lexington	40507	(859) 258-3100	(606) 787-7992
Liberty	5	1,871	Casey	Steve Sweeney	PO Box 127	Liberty	42539	(606) 787-9973	(270) 787-9092
Lincolnshire	6	156	Jefferson	Lewis Hudson		Louisville	40220		(502) 895-6552
Livermore	5	1,467	McLean	Eldon Easton	105 W 3rd St	Livermore	42352	(270) 278-2113	
Livingston	6	225	Rockcastle	J Griffin	PO Box 39	Livingston	40445	(606) 453-2205	
London	4	7,653	Laurel	Ken Smith	501 S Main St	London	40741	(606) 864-6995	(606) 864-5184
Lone Oak	6	445	McCracken	Frank M Galliher	254 S Friendship Rd	Paducah	42003	(270) 554-5929	(270) 534-8477
Loretto	6	635	Marion	Robert G Miles	9215 Loretto Rd	Loretto	40037	(270) 865-4174	(270) 865-4422
Louisa	5	2,007	Lawrence	Teddy Preston	215 N Main Cross St	Louisa	41230	(606) 638-4038	(606) 638-3414
Louisville	1	248,762	Jefferson	Jerry Abramson	Louisville Metro Hall	Louisville	40202	(502) 574-2003	(502) 574-5354
Loyall	6	731	Harlan	Charles Wattenberger	306 Carter St	Loyall	40854	(606) 573-6396	(606) 573-2283
Ludlow	4	4,283	Kenton	Ed F Schroeder	306 Stokesay St	Ludlow	41016	(859) 291-1243	(859) 491-2966
Lynch	4	843	Harlan	Thomas E Vicini	6 E Main St	Lynch	40855	(606) 848-2873	(606) 848-2147
Lyndon	4	10,293	Jefferson	Susan M Barto	515 Wood Rd	Lyndon	40222	(502) 423-0932	(502) 339-9722
Lynnview	6	974	Jefferson	Lawrence Shaughnessy	1241 Gilmore Ln	Louisville	40213	(502) 966-4086	(502) 966-5507
Mackville	6	211	Washington	Carl Gabhart	151 N Church St	Mackville	40040	(859) 262-5175	
Madisonville	4	19,321	Hopkins	Karen L Cunningham	37 E Center St	Madisonville	42431	(270) 824-2100	(270) 821-6161
Manchester	4	1,668	Clay	Daugh K White	239 Memorial Dr	Manchester	40962	(606) 598-3456	(606) 599-1763
Manor Creek	6	224	Jefferson	Paul Veatch	PO Box 22133	Louisville	40252	(502) 425-3000	(502) 425-2007
Marion	6	3,087	Crittenden	Michael D Alexander	108 E Bellville St	Marion	42064	(270) 965-2266	(270) 965-5235
Martin	4	636	Floyd	Thomasine Robinson	11729 Main St	Martin	41649	(606) 285-9335	(606) 285-3309
Maryhill Estates	6	178	Jefferson	Linda Jedlicki	4116 Ormond Rd	Louisville	40207	(502) 895-3158	
Mayfield	4	10,228	Graves	Arthur Byrn	211 E Broadway	Mayfield	42066	(270) 247-1981	(270) 247-2485
Maysville	3	8,941	Mason	David Cartmell	216 Bridge St	Maysville	41056	(606) 564-4811	(606) 564-9416
McHenry	6	426	Ohio	Dennis Chinn	59 Hillard Moseley Rd	McHenry	42354	(270) 274-4831	
McKee	5	856	Jackson	Dwight K Bishop	US 421 Main St	McKee	40447	(606) 287-8305	(606) 287-7179
Meadow Vale	5	776	Jefferson	Roy Fey	9818 Boxford Way	Louisville	40242	(502) 425-8329	
Meadowbrook Farm	6	148	Jefferson	Timothy (Tim) Roe	2114 Terriwood Ct	Louisville	40223	(502) 429-8356	
Meadowview Estates	6	425	Jefferson	Henry Glass	2912 Meadowview Cir	Louisville	40250	(502) 574-3579	
Melbourne	6	451	Campbell	Helen P Lutz	7 Raintree Dr	Melbourne	41059	(859) 781-6664	(859) 781-9444
Mentor	6	177	Campbell	David Gearding	PO Box 3	Mentor	41007	(859) 635-9365	
Middlesboro	3	10,266	Bell	Ben Hickman	PO Box 756	Middlesboro	40965	(606) 248-5670	(606) 248-1202
Middletown	4	6,005	Jefferson	J Byron Chapman	PO Box 43048	Middletown	40253	(502) 245-2762	(502) 245-6047
Midway	5	1,591	Woodford	Becky Moore	101 E Main St	Midway	40347	(859) 846-4237	(859) 846-4411
Millersburg	5	833	Bourbon	Samuel (Sam) Chanslor	5th St	Millersburg	40348	(859) 484-3899	(859) 484-3901
Milton	6	575	Trimble	Donald Oakley	206 Peck Pk	Milton	40045	(502) 268-5224	
Minor Lane Heights	5	1,508	Jefferson	Fred D Williams Sr	11642 Reality Trl	Louisville	40229	(502) 290-5413	(502) 290-0224
Mockingbird Valley	6	196	Jefferson	John Hanley	606 Club Ln	Louisville	40207	(502) 893-3767	(502) 290-5423
Monterey	6	170	Owen	Dennis Atha	10335 Hwy 127S	Monterey	40359	(502) 484-0672	
Monticello	4	6,053	Wayne	Thurston Frye	PO Box 550	Monticello	42633	(606) 348-5719	(606) 348-0267
Moorland	6	469	Jefferson	William L Daniel II	1802 Ashmoor Ln	Louisville	40223	(502) 245-7150	
Morehead	4	7,627	Rowan	Bradley H Collins	105 E Main St	Morehead	40351	(606) 784-8505	(606) 784-2216
Morganfield	4	3,481	Union	Jerry R Freer	130 E Main St	Morganfield	42437	(270) 389-2525	(270) 389-2157
Morgantown	5	2,545	Butler	Charles T Black	117 N Main St	Morgantown	42261	(502) 526-3557	(270) 526-6295
Mortons Gap	5	954	Hopkins	Frank D Stafford	102 S Main St	Mortons Gap	42440	(270) 258-5362	(270) 258-9353
Mt Olivet	6	294	Robertson	Phillip Insko	PO Box 166	Mt Olivet	41064	(606) 724-5816	(606) 724-5816
Mt Sterling	4	6,033	Montgomery	Gary Williamson	33 N Maysville St	Mt Sterling	40353	(859) 498-8725	(859) 498-8727
Mt Vernon	5	2,589	Rockcastle	Clarice R Kirby	125 Richmond St	Mt Vernon	40456	(606) 256-3437	(606) 256-3443
Mt Washington	4	8,605	Bullitt	Frank Sullivan	PO Box 285	Mt Washington	40047	(502) 538-4216	(502) 538-4064
Muldraugh	4	1,346	Meade	Danny J Tate	120 S Main St	Muldraugh	40155	(502) 942-2824	(502) 942-2892
Munfordville	3	1,581	Hart	John Johnson	PO Box 85	Munfordville	42765	(270) 524-2635	(270) 524-3021
Murray	3	15,311	Calloway	Tom Rushing	104 N 5th St	Murray	42071	(270) 762-0350	(270) 762-0306
Murray Hill	6	621	Jefferson	Eric Higdon	PO Box 22302	Louisville	40252	(502) 454-3083	

CITIES AND MAYORS — 1st - 6th Class Cities

CITY	CLASS	POP	COUNTY	MAYOR	ADDRESS	CITY	ZIP	PHONE	FAX
Nebo	6	223	Hopkins	Wayne Kelley	8695 Nebo Rd	Nebo	42441	(270) 249-3116	
New Castle	5	919	Henry	James Brammell	37 E Cross Main St	New Castle	40050	(502) 845-5750	(502) 845-5702
New Haven	6	854	Nelson	Tessie R Cecil	379 Center St	New Haven	40051	(502) 549-3569	
Newport	3	16,243	Campbell	Thomas Guidugli	998 Monmouth St	Newport	41071	(859) 292-3666	(859) 292-3669
Nicholasville	3	22,251	Jessamine	John P Martin	517 N Main St	Nicholasville	40356	(859) 885-1121	(859) 881-0750
Norbourne Estates	6	461	Jefferson	Timothy (Tim) Kraus	4020 Norbourne Blvd	Louisville	40207	(502) 895-7731	
North Middletown	6	558	Bourbon	Buddy Mers	213 Liberty St	North Middletown	40357	(859) 362-7776	(859) 362-7052
Northfield	5	987	Jefferson	Jack Kaiser	6401 Lime Ridge Ct	Northfield	40222	(502) 425-3997	
Nortonville	5	1,259	Hopkins	James L Noel	199 S Main St	Nortonville	42442	(270) 676-3384	(270) 676-7067
Norwood	6	399	Jefferson	Kenneth Schueler	405 Hidden Oak Way	Louisville	40252	(502) 426-2818	
Oak Grove	4	7,564	Christian	Colleen Ochs	PO Box 250	Oak Grove	42262	(270) 439-6552	(270) 439-1201
Oakland	6	255	Warren	William P Mansfield Jr	701 N Vine St Box 145	Oakland	42159	(270) 663-4033	
Old Brownsboro Place	5	390	Jefferson	Maurice H (Mick) Wagner	7247 Heatherly Sq	Louisville	40242	(502) 426-8447	
Olive Hill	4	1,794	Carter	Danny Sparks	415 Oak St	Olive Hill	41164	(606) 286-5220	(606) 286-8538
Orchard Grass Hills	5	1,361	Oldham	Jim Burke	PO Box 25	Crestwood	40014	(502) 241-7963	(502) 243-0028
Owensboro	2	54,312	Daviess	Tom Watson	PO Box 10003	Owensboro	42302	(270) 687-8550	(270) 687-8585
Owenton	5	1,453	Owen	David M Woller	220 S Main St	Owenton	40359	(502) 484-2322	(502) 484-5156
Owingsville	4	1,515	Bath	Don Kincaid	19 Goodpaster Ave	Owingsville	40360	(606) 674-6361	(606) 674-3068
Paducah	2	25,565	McCracken	William F Paxton	300 S 5th St	Paducah	42002	(270) 444-8530	(270) 443-5058
Paintsville	4	4,031	Johnson	Douglas Pugh	101 Euclid Ave	Paintsville	41240	(606) 789-2600	(606) 789-2602
Paris	3	9,271	Bourbon	Donald Kiser	525 High St	Paris	40361	(859) 987-2110	(859) 987-4640
Park City	5	527	Barren	David Lyons	388 Riherd Estate Rd	Park City	42160	(270) 749-5700	
Park Hills	4	2,880	Kenton	Michael J Hellmann	1106 Amsterdam Rd	Park Hills	41011	(859) 431-6252	(859) 431-6410
Park Lake	6	553	Oldham	James Kramer	PO Box 310	Crestwood	40014	(502) 243-0467	
Parkway Village	6	707	Jefferson	Betty Shelton	850 Parkway Dr	Louisville	40217	(502) 636-2726	
Pembroke	6	754	Christian	Freddy Shelton	PO Box 308	Pembroke	42266	(270) 475-9171	(270) 475-9766
Perryville	5	749	Boyle	Bruce Richardson	206 S Buell St	Perryville	40468	(859) 332-8361	(859) 332-7682
Pewee Valley	5	1,490	Oldham	Clayton Stoess	109 LaGrange Rd	Pewee Valley	40056	(502) 241-1964	(502) 241-0006
Pikeville	3	6,286	Pike	Frank Justice	118 College St	Pikeville	41501	(606) 437-5108	(606) 437-5100
Pineville	4	2,060	Bell	Bruce Hendrickson	PO Box 688	Pineville	40977	(606) 337-2207	(606) 337-7111
Pioneer Village	6	2,569	Bullitt	Gary W Hatcher	3300 Cardinal Dr	Louisville	40229	(502) 957-3800	(502) 975-4580
Pippa Passes	6	294	Knott	Richard Kennedy	100 Purpose Rd	Pippa Passes	41844	(606) 368-6082	(606) 368-6217
Plantation	5	914	Jefferson	Becky Peak	PO Box 22698	Louisville	40242	(502) 425-4449	(502) 425-4747
Pleasureville	6	873	Henry	William Rodney Young	111 Roberts St	Pleasureville	40057	(502) 878-4273	(502) 878-9952
Plum Springs	6	452	Warren	Thomas Clayton	124 Owl Dr	Bowling Green	42101	(270) 843-1593	
Poplar Hills	6	398	Jefferson	W Grayson Flood Jr	201 Huntington Park Dr	Louisville	40213	(502) 962-9090	(502) 966-8666
Powderly	5	851	Muhlenberg	Donald C Hancock	PO Box 106	Powderly	42367	(270) 338-5123	(270) 338-4990
Prestonsburg	4	3,677	Floyd	Jerry S Fannin	200 N Lake Dr	Prestonsburg	41653	(606) 886-2335	(606) 886-0563
Prestonville	6	169	Carroll	Tommy Couch	PO Box 306	Carrollton	41008	(502) 732-4576	
Princeton	4	6,394	Caldwell	Vickie Hughes	206 N Jefferson St	Princeton	42445	(270) 365-9575	(270) 365-4661
Prospect	4	4,824	Jefferson	Lawrence C (Lonnie) Falk	PO Box 1	Prospect	40059	(502) 228-1121	(502) 228-9542
Providence	4	3,544	Webster	Eddie Gooch	220 N Willow St	Providence	42450	(270) 667-5463	
Raceland	5	2,388	Greenup	Bill Selvage	50 Bellifonte Rd	Raceland	41169	(606) 836-5151	
Radcliff	2	21,894	Hardin	Sheila C Enyart	411 W Lincoln Trail Blvd	Radcliff	40159	(270) 351-4714	(270) 351-7329
Ravenna	5	672	Estill	Charles Crowe	609 Elm St	Ravenna	40472	(606) 723-3332	(606) 723-3332
Raywick	6	144	Marion	Marilyn Mullins	5720 Raywick Rd	Raywick	40060	(270) 692-2216	
Richlawn	6	459	Jefferson	Sandra Banta	202 Heady Ave	Louisville	40207	(502) 893-9461	
Richmond	2	29,080	Madison	Connie Lawson	239 W Main St	Richmond	40476	(859) 623-1000	(859) 623-7618
River Bluff	6	416	Oldham	Bryan Dillon	PO Box 792	Prospect	40059	(502) 426-1542	
Riverwood	6	479	Jefferson	Joseph Helm	2004 Round Ridge Rd	Louisville	40207	(502) 896-1892	
Robards	6	572	Henderson	Ron Iler	8933 N Easy St Loop	Robards	42452	(270) 521-7621	
Rochester	6	185	Butler	Horace B Hammers	PO Box 125	Rochester	42273	(270) 934-3851	
Rockport	6	337	Ohio	Kermit Geary	PO Box 184	Rockport	42369	(270) 274-9763	
Rolling Fields	6	659	Jefferson	Bill Conway	425 Club Ln	Rolling Fields	40207	(502) 895-5004	(502) 895-5661

CITIES AND MAYORS — 1st - 6th Class Cities

CITY	CLASS	POP	COUNTY	MAYOR	ADDRESS	CITY	ZIP	PHONE	FAX
Rolling Hills	5	916	Jefferson	Leslie Faust	9405 Aylesbury Dr	Louisville	40242	(502) 426-7895	(606) 836-3795
Russell	4	3,574	Greenup	Bill Hopkins	410 Ferry St	Russell	41169	(606) 836-9666	(270) 866-3860
Russell Springs	5	2,464	Russell	Brian Walters	72 High St	Russell Springs	42642	(270) 866-3981	(270) 726-5043
Russellville	4	7,202	Logan	Shirlee Yassney	16 .S Main St	Russellville	42276	(270) 726-5001	
Ryland Heights	6	802	Kenton	Bob Miller	9985 Decoursey Pk	Ryland Heights	41015	(859) 356-5662	
Sacramento	6	510	McLean	Pam Jennings	PO Box 245	Sacramento	42372	(270) 736-5114	(270) 736-5042
Sadieville	6	281	Scott	Robbie Wagoner	PO Box 129	Sadieville	40370	(502) 857-4576	(502) 859-4555
Saint Charles	6	314	Hopkins	Louise Foe	PO Box 164	St Charles	42453	(270) 669-9432	
Saint Matthews	4	17,441	Jefferson	Arthur K Draut	4306 Churchill Rd	St Matthews	40207	(502) 893-2751	(502) 895-0510
Saint Regis Park	6	1,541	Jefferson	William Bohnert	4607 Stormon Ct	St Regis Park	40250	(502) 451-3776	
Salem	6	753	Livingston	Andrew Fox	111 Court St	Salem	42078	(270) 988-2600	(270) 988-4662
Salt Lick	6	346	Bath	Brad Frizzell	200 Caney Ave	Salt Lick	40371	(606) 683-5041	
Salyersville	4	1,587	Magoffin	Stanley Howard	PO Box 954	Salyersville	41465	(606) 349-7990	(606) 349-2449
Sanders	6	247	Carroll	Jackie Ogden	14373 Hwy 36 E	Sanderson	41083	(502) 347-9809	
Sandy Hook	5	690	Elliott	James (Robby) Adkins	PO Box 274	Sandy Hook	41171	(606) 738-6489	(606) 738-5192
Sardis	6	148	Mason	Bonnie Tuel	PO Box 14	Sardis	41056	(606) 763-6693	(606) 763-6693
Science Hill	6	641	Pulaski	MacDonald M Phelps	PO Box 14	Science Hill	42553	(606) 423-4109	(606) 423-2384
Scottsville	4	4,413	Allen	Rob Cline	City County Bldg	Scottsville	42164	(270) 237-3238	(270) 237-4922
Sebree	5	1,566	Webster	Jerry L Hobgood	36 S Spring St	Sebree	42455	(270) 835-7501	(270) 835-9807
Seneca Gardens	6	694	Jefferson	James F (Jim) MacDonald	2501 Denham Rd	Seneca Gardens	40205	(502) 451-8221	
Sharpsburg	6	299	Bath	Roberta Shrout	PO Box 176	Sharpsburg	40374	(606) 247-2931	
Shelbyville	4	10,390	Shelby	Tom Hardesty	315 Washington St	Shelbyville	40066	(502) 633-0011	(502) 633-4292
Shepherdsville	4	8,600	Bullitt	Joseph G Sohm	170 Frank E Simon Ave	Shepherdsville	40165	(502) 543-2923	(502) 543-6201
Shively	4	15,343	Jefferson	Sherry Sinegra Conner	PO Box 16007	Shively	40216	(502) 449-5000	(502) 449-5004
Silver Grove	5	1,181	Campbell	Carl John Schwarber	308 Oak St	Silver Grove	41085	(859) 441-6390	(859) 441-4363
Simpsonville	5	1,329	Shelby	Steve Eden	503 Garden Ct	Simpsonville	40067	(502) 722-5711	(502) 722-0060
Slaughters	6	237	Webster	Donald W Winstead	51 W 2nd St	Slaughters	42456	(270) 884-7000	(270) 884-7009
Smithfield	6	102	Henry	Les Bryant	PO Box 22	Smithfield	40068	(502) 845-6300	
Smithland	6	392	Livingston	Thomas N (Tom) Cothron	PO Box 262	Smithland	42081	(270) 928-4287	(270) 928-2446
Smiths Grove	5	762	Warren	James Gilley	146 S Main St	Smiths Grove	42171	(270) 563-4014	
Somerset	3	11,786	Pulaski	J P Wiles	400 E Mt Vernon St	Somerset	42502	(606) 679-6366	(606) 679-2481
Sonora	6	342	Hardin	Larry D Copelin	330 E Western Ave	Sonora	42776		
South Carrollton	6	183	Muhlenberg	David Anderson	PO Box 44	South Carrollton	42374	(270) 754-9820	
South Park View	6	201	Jefferson	Glenn Byerly	9108 Aria Dr	Louisville	40219	(502) 969-2069	
South Shore	5	1,225	Greenup	Kenneth M Ratliff	PO Box 89	South Shore	41175	(606) 932-6910	
Southgate	4	3,444	Campbell	Charles (Chuck) Melville	122 Electric Ave	Southgate	41071	(859) 441-0075	(859) 441-0244
Sparta	6	232	Owen/Gallatin	Brenda Henry	Rt 1 Box 133A Boone Rd	Sparta	41086	(859) 643-4471	(859) 643-3500
Spring Mill	6	384	Jefferson	Robert Schmitt	6902 Peppermill Ln	Louisville	40228	(502) 231-0040	
Spring Valley	6	680	Jefferson	Patrick Long	7400 Lanfair Dr	Louisville	40241	(502) 339-7237	
Springfield	4	2,739	Washington	Mike Haydon	127 W Main St	Springfield	40069	(859) 336-5440	(859) 336-5455
Stamping Ground	6	612	Scott	Jared Hollon	3206 Main St	Stamping Ground	40379	(502) 535-6114	(502) 535-6523
Stanford	4	3,423	Lincoln	Eddie Carter	305 E Main St	Stanford	40484	(606) 365-4509	(606) 365-1023
Stanton	4	3,026	Powell	Virginia Wills	PO Box 370	Stanton	40380	(606) 663-4459	(606) 663-4433
Strathmoor Manor	6	327	Jefferson	Dennis Boyd	2018 Lowell Ave	Louisville	40205	(502) 452-9104	
Strathmoor Village	6	621	Jefferson	Dewey Cornell Jr	2303 Emerson Ave	Louisville	40205	(502) 456-1620	
Sturgis	4	2,027	Union	Mike Cowan	23 N Main St	Sturgis	42459	(270) 333-2166	(270) 333-2724
Sycamore	6	160	Jefferson	Cleveland A Parkins	123 Sycamore Dr	Anchorage	40223	(502) 245-3766	
Taylor Mill	4	6,866	Kenton	Mark Kreimborg	5225 Taylor Mill Rd	Taylor Mill	41015	(859) 581-3234	(859) 581-0015
Taylorsville	6	1,107	Spencer	Walter E Hahn Sr	106 Maple St	Taylorsville	40071	(502) 477-3235	(502) 477-1310
Ten Broeck	6	140	Jefferson	Robert Roos	3704 Ten Broeck Way	Louisville	40241	(502) 425-7687	
Thornhill	6	177	Jefferson	Patricia Lay	2309 Thornhill Rd	Louisville	40222	(502) 429-8467	
Tompkinsville	5	2,654	Monroe	Windell Carter	207 Carrier St	Tompkinsville	42167	(270) 487-6862	(270) 487-6940
Trenton	6	419	Todd	Craig Hines	PO Box 72	Trenton	42286	(270) 466-3332	
Union	5	3,135	Boone	Don Kirby	984 Lakepointe Ct	Union	41091	(859) 384-4467	(859) 384-7760

CITIES AND MAYORS — 1st - 6th Class Cities

CITY	CLASS	POP	COUNTY	MAYOR	ADDRESS	CITY	ZIP	PHONE	FAX
Uniontown	5	1,079	Union	Kevin Ferguson	3rd & Main Sts	Uniontown	42461	(270) 822-4277	(270) 822-4773
Upton	6	638	Hardin/Larue	Debra Riggs	438 N Walnut St	Upton	42784		
Vanceburg	4	1,680	Lewis	William T Cooper	PO Box 336	Vanceburg	41179	(606) 796-3044	(606) 796-6096
Versailles	4	7,487	Woodford	Fred Siegelman	PO Box 625	Versailles	40383	(859) 873-4581	(859) 873-5969
Vicco	6	315	Knott/Perry	Harry Ward	PO Box 153	Vicco	41773	(606) 476-2418	(606) 476-2676
Villa Hills	4	7,919	Kenton	Michael Sadouskas	719 Rogers Rd	Villa Hills	41017	(859) 341-1515	(859) 341-0012
Vine Grove	4	4,066	Hardin	Gary Minter	300 W Main St	Vine Grove	40175	(270) 877-2422	(270) 877-2875
Wallins Creek	6	242	Harlan	Freddy Burke	PO Box 483	Wallins Creek	40873	(606) 664-3093	
Walton	4	2,598	Boone/Kenton	Phillip W Trzop	40 N Main St	Walton	41094	(859) 485-4383	(859) 485-9710
Warfield	6	279	Martin	Clayborne Tom Hayes	PO Box 502	Warfield	41267	(606) 395-6423	(606) 395-6423
Warsaw	5	1,808	Gallatin	Travis Simpson	101 W Market St	Warsaw	41095	(859) 567-5900	(859) 567-5931
Water Valley	6	320	Graves	Murrel Stephens	Box 63	Water Valley	42085	(270) 355-2294	
Watterson Park	5	1,039	Jefferson	Norman R Liebert	4264 Regina Ln	Watterson Park	40213	(502) 458-7613	(502) 458-7613
Waverly	6	295	Union	David Wolfe	100 S Maple St	Waverly	42462	(270) 389-4270	
Wayland	6	290	Floyd	Tom Murphy	PO Box 181	Wayland	41666	(606) 432-2993	
Wellington	6	562	Jefferson	Tim McNally	3111 Lowell Ave	Wellington	40205	(502) 452-2458	
West Buechel	5	1,332	Jefferson	Richard Richards	3713 Marvin Ave	West Buechel	40218	(502) 456-2822	(502) 456-0727
West Liberty	4	3,344	Morgan	Robert W Nickell	City Hall	West Liberty	41472	(606) 743-3330	(606) 743-2202
West Point	5	1,062	Hardin	Eric Duvall	1501 Elm St	West Point	40177	(502) 922-4775	(502) 922-0126
Westwood	6	172	Jefferson	Robert M Groemling	9003 Trentham Ln	Westwood	40242	(502) 426-1395	
Wheatcroft	6		Webster	Patsy J Clark	PO Box 7	Wheatcroft	42463	(270) 664-2802	
Wheelwright	5	1,025	Floyd	David Marlee Sammons	Box 175	Wheelwright	41669	(606) 452-4202	(606) 452-4203
White Plains	5	817	Hopkins	Ronald D (Ronnie) Lewis	161 Greenville Rd	White Plains	42464	(270) 676-8164	(270) 676-8622
Whitesburg	5	1,542	Letcher	Nathan Baker	72 Bentley Ave	Whitesburg	41858	(606) 633-8827	(606) 633-3712
Whitesville	6	599	Daviess	John Boarman	10184 Hwy 54	Whitesville	42378	(270) 233-4103	
Wickliffe	5	781	Ballard	Sylvio L Mayolo	321 Court St	Wickliffe	42087	(270) 335-3557	(270) 335-3557
Wilder	5	2,766	Campbell	Stanley Turner	520 Licking Pk	Wilder	41071	(859) 581-8884	(859) 581-0823
Wildwood	6	251	Jefferson	Dwight Riggle	PO Box 24036	Wildwood	40224	(502) 326-9146	
Williamsburg	4	5,033	Whitley	Roger (Roddy) Harrison	PO Box 119	Williamsburg	40769		
Williamstown	5	3,362	Grant	Glenn V Caldwell	400 N Main St	Williamstown	41097	(859) 824-6351	(859) 824-6320
Willisburg	6	313	Washington	Bruce Welch	2952 Lawrenceburg Rd	Willisburg	40078	(859) 375-9215	
Wilmore	4	5,818	Jessamine	Harold L Rainwater	335 E Main St	Wilmore	40390	(859) 858-4411	(859) 858-3595
Winchester	3	16,378	Clark	Dodd D Dixon	PO Box 40	Winchester	40392	(859) 744-9815	(859) 744-8822
Windy Hills	5	2,520	Jefferson	Louis A Phillips	5614 Coach Gate Wynde	Windy Hills	40207	(502) 899-9971	(502) 899-7645
Wingo	5	582	Graves	Charles W Shelby	95 St Rt 45 S	Wingo	42088	(270) 376-5580	(270) 376-2286
Woodburn	6	327	Warren	Chip Jenkins	9555 Three Springs Rd	Woodburn	42104	(270) 529-9719	(270) 846-4663
Woodbury	6	86	Butler	Vickie House	117 Orchard St	Woodbury	42288	(270) 526-4638	
Woodland Hills	6	667	Jefferson	Robert Robinson	PO Box 43032	Woodland Hills	40243	(502) 245-9997	
Woodlawn	6	257	Campbell	Ronald (Ron) Barth	14 W Crescent Ave	Woodlawn	41071	(859) 781-7146	
Woodlawn Park	5	1,046	Jefferson	Tim Robertson	4254 Westport Ter	Woodlawn Park	40207	(502) 896-6499	(502) 895-6620
Worthington	5	1,657	Greenup	Jerry Epling	512 Ferry St	Worthington	41183	(606) 836-6821	(606) 833-2593
Worthington Hills	6	1,612	Jefferson	Beth Kreakie	PO Box 22586	Worthington Hills	40252	(502) 732-5937	(502) 243-8416
Worthville	6	212	Carroll	Melanie Stewart	PO Box 123	Worthville	41098		
Wurtland	6	1,043	Greenup	Donna K Hayes	500 Wurtland Ave	Wurtland	41144	(606) 836-9166	(606) 836-5544

Source: The Kentucky Directory Gold Book 2005

POPULATION, HOUSING UNITS, AREA, AND DENSITY FOR 1-4 CLASS CITIES

CITY	CLASS	COUNTY	POPULATION	HOUSING UNITS	AREA IN SQ MILES			DENSITY PER SQ MILE OF LAND AREA	
					TOTAL AREA	WATER AREA	LAND AREA	POPULATION	HOUSING UNITS
KENTUCKY			4,041,769	1,750,927	40,409	681	39,728	102	44
Albany	4	Clinton	2,220	1,165	3	0	3	653	343
Alexandria	4	Campbell	8,286	2,989	5	0	5	1,539	555
Anchorage	4	Jefferson	2,264	750	3	0	3	744	247
Ashland	2	Boyd	21,981	10,763	12	1	11	1,984	972
Augusta	4	Bracken	1,204	605	2	0	1	991	498
Barbourville	4	Knox	3,589	1,646	3	0	3	1,027	471
Bardstown	4	Nelson	10,374	4,488	7	0	7	1,445	625
Beaver Dam	4	Ohio	3,033	1,411	3	0	3	1,201	559
Bellevue	4	Campbell	6,480	2,936	0	0	0	6,904	3,128
Benton	4	Marshall	4,197	1,922	4	0	4	1,065	488
Berea	4	Madison	9,851	4,115	9	0	9	1,055	441
Calvert City	4	Marshall	2,701	1,203	14	0	14	195	87
Campbellsville	3	Taylor	10,498	4,876	6	0	6	1,761	818
Carlisle	4	Nicholas	1,917	982	1	0	1	1,500	768
Carrollton	4	Carroll	3,846	1,709	2	0	2	1,715	762
Catlettsburg	4	Boyd	1,960	959	2	0	1	1,529	748
Cave City	4	Barren	1,880	914	4	0	4	435	212
Central City	4	Muhlenberg	5,893	2,313	5	0	5	1,126	442
Columbia	4	Adair	4,014	1,789	3	0	3	1,168	521
Corbin	3	Knox/Whitley	7,742	3,704	7	0	7	1,046	500
Corbin (part)	3	Knox	1,865	907	2	0	2	800	389
Corbin (part)	3	Whitley	5,877	2,797	5	0	5	1,159	551
Covington	2	Kenton	43,370	20,448	14	0	13	3,301	1,557
Crescent Springs	4	Kenton	3,931	1,760	1	0	1	2,741	1,227
Cumberland	4	Harlan	2,611	1,288	5	0	5	571	281
Cynthiana	4	Harrison	6,258	2,909	3	0	3	1,874	871
Danville	2	Boyle	15,477	6,734	16	0	16	980	427
Dawson Springs	4	Caldwell/Hopkins	2,980	1,353	4	0	4	756	343
Dawson Springs (part)	4	Caldwell	0	0	0	0	0	0	0
Dawson Springs (part)	4	Hopkins	2,980	1,353	4	0	4	760	345
Dayton	4	Campbell	5,966	2,401	2	0	1	4,495	1,809
Douglass Hills	4	Jefferson	5,718	2,553	1	0	1	4,286	1,914
Earlington	4	Hopkins	1,649	798	4	0	3	493	239
Edgewood	4	Kenton	9,400	3,149	4	0	4	2,251	754
Elizabethtown	4	Hardin	22,542	10,043	24	0	24	937	417

POPULATION, HOUSING UNITS, AREA, AND DENSITY FOR 1-4 CLASS CITIES

CITY	CLASS	COUNTY	POPULATION	HOUSING UNITS	AREA IN SQ MILES			DENSITY PER SQ MILE OF LAND AREA	
					TOTAL AREA	WATER AREA	LAND AREA	POPULATION	HOUSING UNITS
Elkhorn City	4	Pike	1,060	506	2	0	2	526	251
Elkton	4	Todd	1,984	928	2	0	2	959	449
Elsmere	4	Kenton	8,139	3,126	3	0	3	3,256	1,251
Eminence	4	Henry	2,231	998	2	0	2	1,039	465
Erlanger	3	Kenton	16,676	6,865	8	0	8	2,002	824
Falmouth	4	Pendleton	2,058	988	1	0	1	1,599	768
Flatwoods	3	Greenup	7,605	3,338	4	0	4	1,692	743
Flemingsburg	4	Fleming	3,010	1,434	3	0	3	1,178	561
Florence	3	Boone	23,551	10,322	10	0	10	2,386	1,046
Fort Mitchell	4	Kenton	8,089	3,744	3	0	3	2,582	1,195
Fort Thomas	4	Campbell	16,495	7,028	6	0	6	2,910	1,240
Fort Wright	4	Kenton	5,681	2,573	3	0	3	1,642	744
Frankfort	2	Franklin	27,741	13,422	15	0	15	1,883	911
Franklin	4	Simpson	7,996	3,609	7	0	7	1,075	485
Fulton	4	Fulton	2,775	1,388	3	0	3	983	492
Georgetown	4	Scott	18,080	7,209	14	0	14	1,318	525
Glasgow	3	Barren	13,019	6,153	15	0	15	883	417
Graymoor-Devondale	4	Jefferson	2,925	1,157	0	0	0	4,003	1,583
Grayson	4	Carter	3,877	1,538	3	0	3	1,549	615
Greenville	4	Muhlenberg	4,398	2,047	5	0	5	922	429
Harlan	4	Harlan	2,081	1,060	2	0	2	1,187	605
Harrodsburg	4	Mercer	8,014	3,709	5	0	5	1,511	699
Hazard	3	Perry	4,806	2,291	7	0	7	685	326
Henderson	2	Henderson	27,373	12,652	17	2	15	1,829	845
Hickman	4	Fulton	2,560	1,177	4	0	4	718	330
Highland Heights	4	Campbell	6,554	2,787	2	0	2	2,882	1,226
Hillview	4	Bullitt	7,037	2,460	4	0	4	1,690	591
Hodgenville	4	Larue	2,874	1,349	2	0	2	1,668	783
Hopkinsville	2	Christian	30,089	13,260	24	0	24	1,252	552
Horse Cave	4	Hart	2,252	1,091	3	0	3	758	367
Hurstbourne	4	Jefferson	3,884	1,887	2	0	2	2,077	1,009
Independence	3	Kenton	14,982	5,391	17	0	17	893	321
Indian Hills	4	Jefferson	2,882	1,162	2	0	2	1,460	589
Irvine	4	Estill	2,843	1,409	2	0	2	1,872	928
Jackson	4	Breathitt	2,490	1,111	3	0	3	935	417
Jeffersontown	2	Jefferson	26,633	11,220	10	0	10	2,676	1,127

POPULATION, HOUSING UNITS, AREA, AND DENSITY FOR 1-4 CLASS CITIES

CITY	CLASS	COUNTY	POPULATION	HOUSING UNITS	AREA IN SQ MILES			DENSITY PER SQ MILE OF LAND AREA	
					TOTAL AREA	WATER AREA	LAND AREA	POPULATION	HOUSING UNITS
Jenkins	4	Letcher	2,401	1,122	9	0	9	281	131
La Grange	4	Oldham	5,676	2,330	4	0	4	1,515	622
Lawrenceburg	4	Anderson	9,014	3,733	4	0	4	2,427	1,005
Lebanon	4	Marion	5,718	2,555	4	0	4	1,297	579
Leitchfield	4	Grayson	6,139	2,797	9	0	9	700	319
Lexington-Fayette	2	Fayette	260,512	116,167	286	1	285	916	408
London	4	Laurel	5,692	2,676	8	0	8	738	347
Louisville	1	Jefferson	256,231	121,275	67	5	62	4,125	1,952
Ludlow	4	Kenton	4,409	1,888	1	0	0	5,142	2,202
Lyndon	4	Jefferson	9,369	4,934	3	0	3	2,719	1,432
Madisonville	4	Hopkins	19,307	8,889	19	0	18	1,085	500
Manchester	4	Clay	1,738	844	2	0	2	1,148	558
Marion	4	Crittenden	3,196	1,595	3	0	3	972	485
Martin	4	Floyd	633	339	0	0	0	1,358	727
Mayfield	3	Graves	10,349	4,907	7	0	7	1,550	735
Maysville	3	Mason	8,993	4,416	22	2	20	452	222
Middlesborough	3	Bell	10,384	4,955	8	0	8	1,359	649
Middletown	4	Jefferson	5,744	2,543	5	0	5	1,181	523
Monticello	4	Wayne	5,981	2,730	6	0	6	984	449
Morehead	4	Rowan	5,914	2,347	9	0	9	641	254
Morganfield	4	Union	3,494	1,581	2	0	2	1,672	756
Mount Sterling	4	Montgomery	5,876	2,768	3	0	3	1,709	805
Mount Washington	4	Bullitt	8,485	3,294	5	0	5	1,589	617
Murray	3	Calloway	14,950	6,622	10	0	10	1,542	683
Newport	2	Campbell	17,048	7,828	3	0	3	6,268	2,878
Nicholasville	3	Jessamine	19,680	7,783	9	0	8	2,320	917
Oak Grove	4	Christian	7,064	2,912	10	0	10	685	283
Olive Hill	4	Carter	1,813	886	2	0	2	904	442
Owensboro	2	Daviess	54,067	24,302	19	1	17	3,103	1,395
Owingsville	4	Bath	1,488	720	2	0	2	684	331
Paducah	2	McCracken	26,307	13,221	20	0	19	1,350	679
Paintsville	4	Johnson	4,132	1,901	5	0	5	786	362
Paris	3	Bourbon	9,183	4,222	7	0	7	1,351	621
Park Hills	4	Kenton	2,977	1,523	0	0	0	3,840	1,965
Pikeville	3	Pike	6,295	2,981	15	0	15	408	193
Pineville	4	Bell	2,093	961	1	0	1	1,452	667

POPULATION, HOUSING UNITS, AREA, AND DENSITY FOR 1-4 CLASS CITIES

CITY	CLASS	COUNTY	POPULATION	HOUSING UNITS	AREA IN SQ MILES			DENSITY PER SQ MILE OF LAND AREA	
					TOTAL AREA	WATER AREA	LAND AREA	POPULATION	HOUSING UNITS
Pioneer Village	4	Bullitt	2,555	900	1	0	1	2,187	770
Prestonsburg	4	Floyd	3,612	1,683	11	0	11	332	155
Princeton	4	Caldwell	6,536	3,150	9	0	9	716	345
Prospect	4	Jefferson/Oldham	4,657	1,847	4	0	4	1,158	459
Prospect (part)	4	Jefferson	4,564	1,819	4	0	4	1,183	472
Prospect (part)	4	Oldham	93	28	0	0	0	573	173
Providence	4	Webster	3,611	1,754	6	0	6	587	285
Radcliff	2	Hardin	21,961	9,487	11	0	11	1,914	827
Richmond	2	Madison	27,152	11,857	19	0	19	1,420	620
Russell	4	Greenup	3,645	1,584	4	0	4	911	396
Russellville	4	Logan	7,149	3,458	11	0	11	672	325
St. Matthews	4	Jefferson	15,852	8,537	4	0	4	3,938	2,121
St. Regis Park	4	Jefferson	1,520	595	0	0	0	4,252	1,664
Salyersville	4	Magoffin	1,604	710	2	0	2	758	336
Scottsville	4	Allen	4,327	2,059	6	0	6	750	357
Shelbyville	4	Shelby	10,085	4,117	8	0	8	1,334	544
Shepherdsville	4	Bullitt	8,334	3,402	11	0	11	791	323
Shively	3	Jefferson	15,157	6,929	5	0	5	3,271	1,495
Somerset	3	Pulaski	11,352	5,428	11	0	11	1,007	482
Southgate	4	Campbell	3,472	1,665	1	0	1	2,439	1,170
Springfield	4	Washington	2,634	1,239	3	0	3	1,049	493
Stanford	4	Lincoln	3,430	1,522	3	0	3	1,115	495
Stanton	4	Powell	3,029	1,340	2	0	2	1,538	680
Sturgis	4	Union	2,030	973	2	0	2	1,343	644
Taylor Mill	4	Kenton	6,913	2,604	6	0	6	1,105	416
Vanceburg	4	Lewis	1,731	752	1	0	1	1,502	653
Versailles	4	Woodford	7,511	3,330	3	0	3	2,669	1,183
Villa Hills	4	Kenton	7,948	2,855	4	0	4	2,144	770
Vine Grove	4	Hardin	4,169	1,779	6	0	6	708	302
West Liberty	4	Morgan	3,277	758	4	0	4	739	171
Williamsburg	4	Whitley	5,143	2,118	5	0	5	1,103	454
Wilmore	4	Jessamine	5,905	1,740	3	0	3	2,239	660
Winchester	3	Clark	16,724	7,400	8	0	8	2,188	968

Source: U.S. Census Bureau, Census 2000 Summary File 1 and The Kentucky Directory Gold Book 2005-2006

this industry which never left him till his death. So hasten to your vines and see that the bugs do not take them.

—JUNE—

Plant more Cucumbers, Weed your garden. Weed your flax, and throw off bad habits. Water tender plants, and cultivate virtues.

Attend to your cattle see that they do not faint for want of a little salt Cut your clover. Plough your fallows. Do not let your bees take French leave of you. Do not be in a rage to be done haying ; 'tis a boyish notion. Set cabbages for winter. Repine not at the good of thy neighbours ; nor rejoice at the misfortune of any one. Drink little cold water.

When it rains pottage, hold out your dish.

—JULY—

Ladies, for mercy's sake, see about the bed bugs. Perhaps you will think that this business does not exactly fall into the agricultural department ; nevertheless 'tis of such consequence to farmers that one nights lodging among those poisonous vermin will render a man unfit for business all the succeeding day.

Steady is the word with good farmers. You may begin to hoe your corn for the last time ; but 'tis said that Captain Bluster in the heat of his passion to finish haying before any other in town, has forgotten to hoe his corn but once ! The proverb says, *he who fixeth his soul on show, loseth reality.* Keep your earliest cucumbers for seed. Take care that you do not kill yourself with cold water. Keep the boys from running to the ponds and rivers to bathe. Gather herbs in their bloom. This month keeps the haymakers and reapers attentively employed ; the females we hope will not be neglectful of their care. Doily, my dear, you will be kind enough to send out the drink and the puncheon. Take heed, lest the weeds overtop the other growth of your garden. Attend to your flax—Burn new lands.

—AUGUST—

All things must give way to necessity ; yet what need is there for a woman to leave her domestic concerns, go in the field and like an Amazon wield the pitchfork and the rake ? 'Tis abominable ! Is this the duty of a wife ? Is such the tenderness of a husband. *Remember she is the mistress of thy house ; treat her therefore with respect that thy*

Source: Johnson & Warner's Kentucky Almanac 1810, Lexington, Ky.

Geology

Dr. Gary O'Dell

Kentucky displays a wide variety of physical landscapes, from the scenic mountain vistas of eastern Kentucky, to the gently rolling pastures of the central Bluegrass, to the fertile Mississippi River floodplains of extreme western Kentucky. These landscapes are the result of tectonic, erosional and depositional processes that have taken place over a very long span of time and are still modifying the landscape today. Kentucky's terrain is still very much a work in progress. If the geological record tells us anything, it is that landscapes are not static and unchanging, but are dynamic and subject to dramatic alterations from a variety of geologic processes. Given enough time, great mountains are reduced to fragments by the inexorable erosion of wind and water; the debris transported to the sea-bottoms and other low places of the earth where, through long accumulation, they are compressed into solid rock and ocean

Chimney Rock near Danville
Source: Kentucky Department of Libraries & Archives

floors are uplifted by the ponderous but irresistible movements of colliding crustal plates. Thus it has continued throughout the history of our planet, a continuous cycle of conflict between the processes that build land and those that wear it away. Mountains become dust and the dust becomes the stuff of new mountains.

The shaping of Kentucky's landscape is a story written in the rocks for those who can interpret the geological text. Each layer is a page in the ancient history of the land. The rocks of the surface speak of more recent events; beneath these are tales more deeply buried in place and in time, miles beneath the surface and representing a span of years greater than our comprehension. To understand the forces and processes that produced modern-day Kentucky we must peel away the layers of time and bedrock to recreate landscapes of hundreds of millions of years ago, when the world was a very different place. Kentucky's geologic history is part of a drama played out on a grand scale, a story of continents slowly colliding to form giant supercontinents and of those same giant land masses rupturing and splitting apart, even as great oceans were created and destroyed.

Centered around Hudson Bay in Canada is a region of ancient granitic igneous rock, the nucleus or craton, of the original continent of North America known as the Canadian Shield. Some of the rocks of the Shield have been dated to more than four billion years in age. The North American continent grew around the Canadian Shield by the gradual process of accretion as other, and usually smaller, land masses were carried into contact with the craton by the movement of crustal plates and often became permanent additions to the continent. Around the margin of the core area, more extensive to the south and west, is the relatively stable region known as the platform, which, while submerged, accumulated massive sediment deposits eroded from the craton. Kentucky is positioned on the platform of the southeastern margin of the Canadian Shield.

From approximately 1.3 to 1.0 billion years ago, during Precambrian time, this core region was located along the equator and the eastern edge was in the process of colliding with a continental block. The collision, which took place over several hundred million years, led to the formation of a supercontinent called Rodinia (homeland) by geologists and a massive mountain-building event known as the Grenville Orogeny. The western edge of the collision zone, the Grenville Front, traverses central Kentucky, but is today buried beneath thousands of feet of sedimentary rock. Rodinia remained stable for a long period of time, and the Himalaya-scale mountain ranges generated during the orogeny were leveled by erosion near sea level. About 700 million years ago, Rodinia began to split ("rift") apart in the vicinity of the previous suture zone, and a new ocean, the Iapetus, separated the parts of the former supercontinent.

At the beginning of the Paleozoic Era, more than a half billion years before the present, the crustal plates containing the continents of North America, Europe, and Africa were again on a collision course. The Iapetus Ocean, the predecessor of the modern Atlantic, was shrinking as the floor of the ocean plunged beneath the eastern coastal margin of North America in a process known as subduction. Along the subduction boundary, as the subducting plate melted and magma rose to the surface, lines of volcanic islands were produced.

Red River Gorge
Source: Sid Webb

As the continental masses converged, these island arcs and wedges of crustal material were compressed between them in several major episodes of mountain-building. During the later Paleozoic, beginning in the Pennsylvanian Period about 310 million years ago, a full contact collision began to occur that lasted for nearly 60 million years and created the supercontinent of Pangea. This supercontinent persisted for about 100 million years and then began to split apart during the Triassic Period of the Mesozoic Era. The rift that developed to separate the continents was the origin of the present-day Atlantic Ocean, which is still widening today as the crustal plates move farther apart.

Each of the major mountain-building episodes of the Paleozoic produced major deformations and disruptions of the crust. These earlier mountain ranges, uplifted by plate collisions, and ancestral to the modern Appalachian Mountains, no longer exist, having been long-since leveled by erosion. The by-products of their disintegration were deposited as broad sheets of sediment in adjacent ocean areas.

During most of the Paleozoic Era, which spanned nearly 300 million years, the region that is now Kentucky was covered by a shallow sea and only intermittently exposed. Much of the bedrock that is today at or near the land surface was deposited as sediments in this marine environment and was compressed and transformed to solid rock by the accumulating weight of overlying material. Because of their origin as marine deposits, the sedimentary bedrocks of Kentucky occur in layers that are more-or-less horizontal, except where they have been disturbed. Features associated with Precambrian tectonic events, such as the Grenville Front, lie deeply buried beneath thousands of feet of sedimentary rocks. Reactivation of several of these lines of structural weakness in later eras resulted in fracturing of the sedimentary cover to produce fault zones, some of which are active today.

Rocks such as sandstone and shale originated as particulate (clastic) sediments received from eroding highland areas eastward. The extensive limestone strata of Kentucky were also deposited during the Paleozoic, not as transported sediments, but as a calcium-rich ooze consisting largely of the remains of organisms who extracted calcium from seawater to make their hard body parts. The type of sedimentary rock being deposited at any given time largely depended upon the nature of the rock being eroded from adjacent highlands, prevailing environmental conditions and the configuration

of land and sea. Deposition of clastic sediments dominated some eras and carbonates (limestone, dolomite) during others.

This has produced a stratigraphic sequence for Kentucky in which the lowermost Precambrian and early Paleozoic sedimentary rocks are of clastic origin, then a period of carbonate deposition fol-

Natural Bridge State Park
Source: Sid Webb

lowed by more sandstones and shales, then a thick sequence of carbonates in the middle to late Paleozoic, and, closing the era, a thick layer of sandstones and other clastics. Embedded within the late Paleozoic rocks are seams of bituminous coal, derived from massive accumulations of organic matter in vast lowland swamps that represented the explosion of plant and animal life on land at this time.

The proto-Appalachian ranges that were uplifted by continental collisions during the Paleozoic were reduced to a flat, eroded plain in North America by the end of the Mesozoic. Regional uplift during the Cenozoic Era brought the Paleozoic marine sedimentary rocks of the interior to the surface, exposing them to weathering and erosion. The uplift rejuvenated regional streams and rivers, which began to cut deeply into the plateau surface formed by sedimentary rock. Differential rates of weathering, according to the nature of the bedrock, developed a new mountainous topography influenced by ancient mountain roots, preserving the geologic structures of rocks folded and overthrust during previous orogenies. These are our present-day Appalachian Mountains of North America.

Although we might like to think of our Appalachian Mountains as uniquely American, in the geologic sense they are quite international. With the breakup of the Pangean supercontinent, the ancestral Appalachians were divided among three continents, so that the largest remnant is today in North America, another section comprises the Atlas Mountains of Africa, and a third piece forms the Pyrenees that separate France and Spain.

In eastern Kentucky, the Appalachian Mountains tend to be more erosional than tectonic in origin, because the platform area was the marine dumping ground for Paleozoic sediments which accumulated in horizontal layers. Unlike the overthrust and folded mountains farther east, the Kentucky mountains are erosional remnants left by the carving of deep valleys into these horizontal rock strata rather than the product of an orogeny.

During the post-Grenville episodes of slow-motion tectonic violence, Kentucky's location on the cratonic platform was far enough to the west of the collision zone that the sedimentary rocks of the region were generally spared major distortions and faulting, except in the extreme southeast corner. Instead, the tectonic events that built mountains in the east produced a series of gradually diminishing accordian pleats or waves in the bedrock of the continent westward away from the collision zone.

In Kentucky, this flexing of the bedrock produced a slight structural upwarp, known as the Cincinnati Arch, flanked by downwarps to the east and west, known as the Appalachian Basin and the Illinois Basin, respectively. The axis of the Arch runs diagonally through the state from Ohio through Tennessee, and is one of the defining features of Kentucky's overall geology. The concept involved may be somewhat confusing to the non-geologist. The upward flex of the Arch is

primarily expressed in the bedrock rather than the topography. Millions of years of erosion concurrent with and subsequent to the uplifts have leveled the surface, cutting across the rock layers and planing away the convexity. The structure of the Arch is revealed at the surface

Pine Mountain Thrust Fault in the Pound Gap road cut near Jenkins, Letcher County
Source: Steve Greb, KY Geological Survey

only by a very subtle upward bulge in the center as a consequence of exposed strata that have been more resistant to erosion than layers higher in the sequence.

The Arch has two major domes: one centered nearly under Lexington called the Jessamine Dome, and another near Nashville. Because of the upward bulge of the rock structure and subsequent erosion, the oldest rocks in the state are exposed in the center of the Jessamine Dome (in the gorge of the Kentucky River) and become progressively younger as one travels outward in any direction. The surface geology of Kentucky resembles a vast bull's eye target comprised of concentric rings of bedrock of similar age. Driving across Kentucky is like traveling through time, with tens of millions of years of bedrock time passing for every hour on the road.

The oldest rocks at the center of the planed-down dome are limestones, formed in shallow tropical seas that dominated the region 500 million years ago during the Ordovician Period. Surrounding this Ordovician core are younger rock belts of Silurian and Devonian age. During this geologic time period, less carbonate and a greater amount of silt and mud was deposited from eroding mountains to the east, so that shales and siltstones are dominant. Moving still further out from the central region, the traveler again enters a zone representing carbonate deposition; limestones deposited during the Mississippian Period, and, at last, Pennsylvanian sandstones with their seams of coal.

The basins to either side of the Arch served as reservoirs for sediment accumulation, and the tremendous weight of these sediments augmented the tectonic downwarp to depress these areas still farther into the crust. The Ordovician strata that are exposed at the center of the Cincinnati Arch lie buried beneath more than 3,000 feet of sedimentary rock in the Appalachian Basin to the east and more than 4,000 feet of rock in the Illinois Basin to the west. Both sides of the Illinois Basin are present in Kentucky, so that the pattern of bedrock at the surface forms a series of roughly concentric circles similar to the pattern exhibited by the Jessamine Dome. On the Dome, however, the rocks become older toward the center, whereas on the Basin the youngest rocks are toward the center. Only the western side of the Appalachian Basin is present in Kentucky, so that rock strata in the state continue dipping downward toward the east. During the later Paleozoic Era, the eastern coastline of the Appalachian Basin was dominated by numerous river deltas and wetlands, formed of riverborne sediments eroded from the ancestral Appalachians in the east. These were the coal swamps of the Pennsylvanian and Permian periods, in which organic matter accumulated and was eventually transformed to bituminous coal.

Because of the Cenozoic uplift, the region was no longer underwater and accumulation of marine sediments ceased across most of the area that is now Kentucky. Deposition was replaced by erosion, and much of the uppermost Paleozoic bedrock was worn away to form the present day surface landscape. In far western Kentucky, however, beginning in the late Mesozoic, gradual subsidence along an ancient rift zone combined with higher sea levels than at present allowed the ocean to invade the land mass along a broad corridor. Known as the Mississippi Embayment, this longitudinal dent in the southern margin of the continent stretches from southern Louisiana to Illinois. Since the Cretaceous Period, thousands of feet of marine sediments eroded from the adjacent land areas accumulated in this depositional trough. As sea levels subsequently dropped and the ocean retreated from the embayment, particularly during the last 2 million years as a consequence of

Quaternary glaciation, the Mississippi River became established in this location.

The multiple episodes of recent Ice Age continental glaciation of the Quaternary Period had other significant effects in Kentucky, although the landscape was directly impacted by ice sheets only in northern Kentucky. The direct effects of glaciation exist as a thin strip of till, outwash, and lacustrine (glacial lake) deposits along the Ohio River from Kenton County to Oldham County. These deposits reach a thickness of several hundred feet. Glacial outwash deposits mixed with alluvium are found further westward along the river to the embayment area, which served as an outlet for a tremendous outpouring of meltwaters during periods of glacial retreat. Deposits of wind-blown silt and fine sand (loess) as much as 70 feet thick occur mixed with glacial deposits in some locations, and as a thin layer in much of western Kentucky. The presence of massive ice sheets covering the lands bordering Kentucky to the north blocked existing rivers and caused a reorganization of regional drainage. The major rivers of Kentucky, including the Kentucky, Licking and Green, were forced to find shorter pathways to the sea. The reduction in the overall length of these rivers increased the gradient, or steepness of the flow path, so that the streams began downcutting their channels. Consequently, rivers in Kentucky were entrenched, and the residual alluvium of former flood plains exists in numerous locations as high-level terrace deposits above the present-day river courses.

In summary, during virtually the entire 300 million year span of the Paleozoic, the region that includes present-day Kentucky was under water – a depositional environment. Sediments eroded from land areas to the east, north, and west accumulated in this low area and were compacted and cemented to form thick layers of sedimentary rock. These initially flat-lying rock strata were several times disturbed by tectonic events to the east, producing an alternating series of upwarps and downwarps that are today visible in the rock structure. The region was uplifted during the Cenozoic and has remained dry land to the present day, so that no further accumulation of marine sediments occurred except in the area of the Mississippi Embayment to the extreme west. As a result, Kentucky was transformed from a region of deposition to an erosional environment, and about 2,000 feet of accumulated sedimentary rock were subsequently worn away to produce the modern landscape.

Fault Lines & Earthquakes
Dr. Gary O'Dell

An earthquake is generated as the result of a sudden movement along a fault. Stress builds up along a fracture in the earth's crust until slippage occurs, releasing energy in the form of seismic waves. These waves radiate outward through the earth from the point of origin, or focus; the location on the surface directly above the focus is known as the epicenter. Generally, the longer movement along the fault is hindered, allowing stress to build, the greater will be the displacement along the fault and the associated severity of the quake. There are hundreds of earthquakes around the globe every day, most of which are so slight that the vibrations cannot be detected except by sensitive instruments.

Most earthquakes take place near the boundaries of tectonic plates, but approximately one in ten is an intraplate quake, located far from an active plate margin. The New Madrid Seismic Zone (NMSZ), is such a region, and is situated above a failed rift zone. This zone trends approximately SW-NE from northeast Arkansas, through southeast Missouri, western Tennessee, and western Kentucky to southern Illinois, but is deeply buried beneath thousands of feet of Mississippi River alluvial deposits. About 750 million years ago, when the supercontinent Rodinia began to break apart, the rupture that began in the location now occupied by the NMSZ ceased before a split could take place. The rifting process produced a zone of weakness here that has persisted to the present day and is known as the Reelfoot Rift, located in the most northerly part of the Mississippi Embayment. Most of the fault systems in Kentucky appear to be related to failed rift zones that developed in the late Precambrian, associated with the breakup of the Rodinia supercontinent.

During the Mesozoic breakup of Pangaea, stretching of the crust reactivated the long-dormant faults of the Reelfoot Rift, which were subsequently covered by many thousands of feet of sediments as a consequence of the downwarping of the Mississippi Embayment later in the Mesozoic. Some geologists have lately come to believe that the most recent episodes of continental glaciation – the "Ice Ages" – have also played a role in stimulating seismic activity along the NMSZ. The tremendous weight of the ice sheets, thousands of feet in thickness, that periodically covered much of the North American continent during the last two million years actually depressed the earth's crust. After the glaciers melted, most recently about 10,000 years ago, the crust slowly rebounded upward toward its original position and is still recovering today.

There are several other fault systems located within Kentucky or nearby that appear to be related to the New Madrid Seismic Zone, although these are far less active. Although the NMSZ lies buried in the Mississippi River floodplain and is detected

y'know what...?

ACTIVE FAULT ZONES POTENTIALLY AFFECTING KENTUCKY:

- New Madrid Fault System
- Wabash Valley Fault System
- Eastern Tennessee Fault System
- Unmapped fault system responsible for 1980 Sharpsburg quake

through seismic activity, other faults can often be traced along surface exposures. The fault complex known as the Fluorspar District emerges from the covering sediments of the Mississippi Embayment in western Kentucky. These faults are aligned with the NMSZ but have exhibited very little recent seismicity. The District was once of economic significance to Kentucky as a source of certain vein minerals of hydrothermal origin, including fluorite and galena, which were deposited along the fault pathways

East of the Fluorspar District is the Rough Creek Graben, which appears to be an extension of the Reelfoot Rift. The graben is a section of the crust that has been displaced gradually downward between two east-west trending faults, the Rough Creek Fault System to the north and the Pennyrile

Fault System southward. The Rough Creek system traverses the central part of the Western Kentucky Coal Field, and the Pennyrile system is located near the southern edge of the Coal Field. These fault systems are relatively inactive, although the monitoring system established in the vicinity of the NMSZ has recorded a number of minor earthquakes here, too small to be detected by human senses.

The Wabash Valley Fault System, located in southeastern Illinois and southwestern Indiana, has experienced at least five earthquakes from magnitude 5.0 to 5.8 during the last 100 years, and geologic evidence indicates an event of at least magnitude 7.0 took place here within the last 5,000 years. Although the seismic zone associated with this fault system lies mainly outside Kentucky,

System. This system, inactive today, is a zone of ancient faulting that traverses the Bluegrass region of central Kentucky from southwest to northeast, passing through eastern Lexington, and is aligned with the much older Grenville Front zone of structural weakness. Tectonic events during the Paleozoic that developed the Cincinnati Arch upwarp produced faulting associated with the line of the Grenville Front. The Lexington Fault system parallels the Arch along the eastern flank.

Several fault zones which are roughly parallel with the Eastern Tennessee Fault System extend eastward from the Lexington Fault System. The major structural feature associated with these faults is the Rome Trough, bounded to the north by

STRONGEST EARTHQUAKES IN THE CONTIGUOUS UNITED STATES (EXCLUDES ALASKA)

Location	Date	Time UTC	Magnitude
1. New Madrid, Missouri	1811 Dec 16	08:15	8.1
2. New Madrid, Missouri	1812 Feb 07	09:45	˜8
3. Fort Tejon, California	1857 Jan 09	16:24	7.9
4. New Madrid, Missouri	1812 Jan 23	15:00	7.8
5. Imperial Valley, California	1892 Feb 24	07:20	7.8
6. San Francisco, California	1906 Apr 18	13:12	7.8
7. Owens Valley, California	1872 Mar 26	10:30	7.6
8. N Cascades, Washington	1872 Dec 15	05:40	7.3
9. California - Oregon Coast	1873 Nov 23	05:00	7.3
10. Charleston, South Carolina	1886 Sep 01	02:51	7.3
11. West of Eureka, California	1922 Jan 31	13:17	7.3
12. Kern County, California	1952 Jul 21	11:52	7.3
13. Hebgen Lake, Montana	1959 Aug 18	06:37	7.3
14. Landers, California	1992 Jun 28	11:57	7.3

Source: US Geological Survey

earthquakes generated here have been felt in Kentucky and have sometimes caused minor damage. The Wabash system of faults overlies what appears to be a failed rift zone that is probably associated with the same tectonic stresses that produced the Reelfoot Rift, although faulting is not directly continuous across the Rough Creek Graben from the NMSZ to the Wabash Valley Fault System.

Midway between the New Madrid and the Eastern Tennessee fault systems is the Lexington Fault

the Kentucky River Fault System and to the south by the Rockcastle River- Warfield Fault System, with the Irvine-Paint Creek Fault System running parallel between these. The Irvine-Paint Creek faulting can be traced at the surface through much of central and eastern Kentucky, but much of the Kentucky River Fault System and all of the Rockcastle River-Warfield fault zone lies buried. The Rome Trough may be associated with a Precambrian failed rift, although most of the subsidence occurred during the Cambrian Period. There also appears to be something of an association with the Rough Creek Graben. The Rough Creek Graben and the Rome Trough (a graben-like structure) are approximately aligned west-to-east. The Rome Trough extends eastward through West Virginia into Pennsylvania, but has not been traced west of the Lexington Fault System. Displacement within the Rough Creek Graben is downward to the north, opposite from the Rome Trough which exhibits downward to the south displacement. The fault systems associated with the Rome Trough have been reactivated numerous times since the Cambrian, although none have been active during historic times.

The most dramatic fault zone in Kentucky is the Pine Mountain Thrust Fault in the southeastern part of the state, and differs considerably from the types of faults noted previously. Displacement along a thrust fault (also called an overthrust fault) is primarily horizontal, rather than vertical, as is the case for faults such as those associated with the Rough Creek Graben or Rome Trough, where one side of a fault block drops down relative to the other. Thrust faults are the result of compressional forces so extreme as to cause one section of the rock strata, thousands of feet in thickness, to be pushed up and over another. The Pine Mountain fault originated about 275 million years ago during the late Paleozoic as one of a series of overlapping fault blocks generated by the collision of land masses that formed the Pangaea supercontinent. The total horizontal displacement along the fault, which extends through Virginia into Tennessee, ranges from 4 to 11 miles, and created a ridge more than 100 miles long known as Pine Mountain. A number of small earthquakes have occurred along this fault during historic times, including a January 19, 1976, event that registered magnitude 4.0 and was felt in five states.

A previously unknown and therefore unmapped fault system was responsible for the strongest earthquake ever to originate within Kentucky during historic times, which occurred on July 27, 1980. The 5.2 magnitude quake, centered near Sharps-

Breaks Interstate Park
Source: Sid Webb

burg in Bath County, was felt in 15 states and in Ontario, Canada. Property damage amounted to more than $3 million. The most severely affected community was Maysville, located on the Ohio River about 30 miles north of the epicenter, where 37 commercial structures and 269 homes were damaged. This quake may possibly have been associated with the Kentucky River Fault System, which is not too very far from the apparent epicenter.

There is an additional category of rather exotic small-scale, very localized fracture systems which do not represent an earthquake hazard. In years past, before their origin and nature was well understood, these were referred to as "cryptovolcanic" or "cryptoexplosive" structures. These terms are still found on topographic maps and in older geological publications, but they may be more properly referred to as "astroblemes." Recent theorization holds that these are not of tectonic origin but from the impact of extraterrestrial objects such as large meteors or cometary fragments. Traveling at speeds measured in miles per second, such bodies shatter the rock strata upon impact in a roughly circular pattern and may bring up rocks from deep underground that rebound into a central uplift structure within the crater. At such sites, rocks are often found that have been metamorphosed, transformed and partially melted by the tremendous heat and pressure of an impact.

Three such possible astrobleme structures are known in Kentucky: Jeptha Knob in Shelby County, a site in Woodford County near Versailles, and the Middlesboro Impact Structure in southeastern Kentucky near the Virginia border, within which the city of Middlesboro is situated. The Middlesboro structure, the largest, is about 4 miles in diameter and was produced by a body estimated to be about 1,600 feet in diameter. As all of these impacts occurred long ago, time and weather have eroded the former craters so that only the core of the central uplift area remains. The Jeptha Knob is the most easily viewed of these structures, a low hill clearly visible from Interstate 64 between Frankfort and Shelbyville, to the north of the highway.

ENVIRONMENT & NATURAL RESOURCES

Caves & Karst

Dr. Gary O'Dell

In his 1784 book, "Discovery, Settlement and Present State of Kentucke," John Filson wrote: "Caves are found in this country amazingly large; in some of which you may travel several miles under a fine limestone rock, supported by curious arches and pillars: in most of them runs a stream of water." The size and splendor of Kentucky's caves are today still a source of amazement to visitors. Kentucky is home to Mammoth Cave, which, with more than 360 miles of mapped passageways, is the world's longest cave. Although Mammoth is certainly the most significant cave in the state, the geology of Kentucky has promoted the formation of many thousands of other caves contained within a distinctive landscape type known as "karst." Karst landscapes are characterized by subsurface drainage and landscape features such as sinkholes, sinking streams, caves and springs. In karst, the typical patterns of drainage by surface streams found elsewhere are absent or interrupted, since flow takes place underground through a network of conduits. This network develops as bedrock fractures are enlarged by the circulation of naturally acidic groundwater that slowly dissolves limestone, dolomite and other carbonate sedimentary rocks. Approximately half of Kentucky's land area displays such features and is considered karst terrain. Precipitation falling to the earth is naturally slightly acidic, the result of carbon dioxide and water vapor combining in the atmosphere to form carbonic acid. This acidity is increased as water filters through the soil and absorbs more carbon dioxide from organic matter. The relatively weak solution of carbonic acid in groundwater is capable of dissolving rocks such as limestone. Acidic water percolates downward through the soil cover and into the bedrock, following the network of joints and bedding planes. Vertical bedrock fractures, or joints, are largely the result of past tectonic

Decorations in a Breckinridge County cave
Source: Chris Anderson, Darklight Imagery

stresses that have cracked the rock layers, providing pathways for downward penetration of groundwater. Bedrock structure is thus an important control upon the conduit pathways that develops as acidic groundwater dissolves the rock. As vertical fractures just beneath the soil cover are enlarged by removal of the rock, eventually the soil slumps downward to form an enclosed depression known as a sinkhole.

This "blue hole" or artesian spring in Allen County is one of the largest in Kentucky
Source: Gary O'Dell

Water enters a karst conduit system through direct inlet points such as sinkholes and sinking streams, and by a more diffuse and widespread recharge that takes place beneath the soil. The enlargement of bedrock fractures creates an extensive plumbing system of tubes and conduits that carry groundwater to lower elevations, where it is discharged as springs. As the channel of a surface stream becomes wider and deeper downstream as tributaries join, the conduits in an underground system increase in diameter in a downstream direction.

There are four distinct cave regions in Kentucky: the Pine Mountain Karst Region, Inner Bluegrass Karst Region, Eastern Pennyroyal Karst Region and the Western Pennyroyal Karst Region. These four regions are differentiated primarily by the age of the carbonate rocks in which the cave and conduit systems are developed and their geography.

The Pine Mountain Karst Region is a long narrow strip at the extreme southeastern corner of the state, representing a band of limestone of Mississippian age exposed at the northwestern edge of the Pine Mountain thrust fault.

The Inner Bluegrass Karst Region is very nearly centered on Lexington, a roughly circular area of limestones and dolomites of Ordovician age exposed by the weathering of the upward bulge of the Jessamine Dome. The rock strata are nearly horizontal, with a very slight dip away from the center in all directions except to the southeast where the Lexington Fault System comprises the boundary of the karst area. The rocks in the region tend to be rather thinly bedded, and often interbedded with shales, which tends to limit development of extensive cave networks. Although several hundred caves are known in the region, with few exceptions, most of these are short, low and wet.

The Eastern and Western Pennyroyal Karst Regions are both developed on carbonate sedimentary rocks of Mississippian age. These carbonate rocks are relatively pure, thickly bedded, and often of considerable vertical extent, allowing the development of multi-level cave systems and large passages. Carter Caves State Resort Park is located in the northern part of the Eastern Pennyroyal, and many large cave systems are found in the southeastern section. The most famous cave system in the world, Mammoth Cave, is found in the Western Pennyroyal Karst Region. The karst area stretches in an arc around the hilly, non-karst Western Coal Field region. The edge of the coalfield region is a dissected landscape of ridges and valleys in which cavernous limestones are capped by non-soluble sandstones and shales. The Mammoth Cave system is located in this area. The area around Mammoth Cave is probably the best-known and most intensively studied karst region in the world, and has been designated a World Heritage Region by the U.N. Educational, Scientific, and Cultural Organization.

The first explorers and settlers of Kentucky, as Filson noted, were greatly impressed by the many caves and abundant springs of clear water in this land. Spring water was then, as today, perceived as being the highest quality water supply, and the location of springs had a strong influence upon the early settlement pattern. As the land was surveyed, claimed and settled, first priority was given to tracts containing a significant spring. Individual settlements or stations were often situated in close proximity to a significant spring. In the Inner Bluegrass Karst Region, for example, communities originally sited to take advantage of a particular spring include Lancaster, Georgetown, Versailles, Paris and Lexington. Early deeds recorded in Kentucky courthouses exhibit a well-developed terminology describing karst features such as springs, "sinking springs," and "blue holes." Urban growth and land development upon a karst landscape also imposes certain problems not evident in other terrain types. Groundwater contamination by chemical pollutants and pathogenic organisms is a particular hazard. Karst aquifers exist at relatively shallow depths and are easily contaminated by a variety of causes, ranging from runoff of agricultural chemicals to leaking sewer lines. Since water flows swiftly through karst conduits and thus spends relatively little time underground there is only a slight reduction in potential pathogens, nor is there any filtration of the water flow as occurs in sand and gravel aquifers. Too often sinkholes are regarded by a property owner simply as a convenient place to dispose of trash or waste, unaware that what is dumped into a sinkhole today may show up in his neighbor's drinking water spring tomorrow.

"300 Springs" in Hart County
Source: Gary O'Dell

ENVIRONMENT & NATURAL RESOURCES

Physical Regions

Dr. Gary O'Dell

The present-day physical landscape of Kentucky, as we have seen, is a result of both ancient and recent geological processes. The accumulation of transported sediments during the Paleozoic, when this region was a shallow marine environment, produced a veneer of sedimentary strata thousands of feet in thickness over the much older basement rocks. Tectonic processes, involving the movement of crustal plates, fractured, warped and folded the rock layers to impose structural features within the bedrock mass. Because these structural features vary across the length and width of the Commonwealth, and because different types of sedimentary rocks vary in their resistance to weathering and erosion, there is

Lexington reservoir
Source: Sid Webb

a distinct pattern of variation of the surface landscape. Kentucky's 40,409 square miles of land and water can thus be divided into discrete physiographic regions according to characteristics of the topography. As one travels across the state, moving from one region to another, the natural scenery often changes rather dramatically.

The five main physical regions of Kentucky, from east to west, are: the Eastern Kentucky Coal Field, the Bluegrass, the Mississippian Plateau, the Western Kentucky Coal Field, and the Mississippi Embayment. The labels used for these regions are not completely standardized, so that books about Kentucky may refer to a region by different names. For example, the Mississippian Plateau is sometimes known as the Penny-royal (or Pennyrile) Plateau, named for a plant of the mint family found in the region, and the Mississippi Embayment has historically been referred to as the Purchase or Jackson Purchase region, since it was added to the state in 1818 during the administration of Andrew Jackson. Multiple designations also apply to some of the major features within the regions; the western edge of the Eastern Kentucky Coal Field is sometimes known as the Pottsville Escarpment and sometimes as the Cumberland Escarpment.

Adding to the potential confusion, the physical regions of Kentucky are included within the larger geomorphic provinces of the United States. The Eastern Kentucky Coal Field is part of the Appalachian Plateaus that stretch from New York to Georgia; the Bluegrass, Mississippian Plateau and the Western Kentucky Coal Field are contained within the Interior Low Plateaus that include parts of southern Illinois, Indiana and Ohio; and the Mississippi Embayment is a section of the much larger Gulf Coastal Plain.

Broadly speaking, the landscape of Kentucky consists of dissected highland plateaus, east and west, separated by escarpments from gently rolling plains in central and southern Kentucky. The plateau areas; the two coal field regions, are capped by sandstones and conglomerate rocks, which have eroded less rapidly than the limestones and shales of the Bluegrass and Mississippian plateau. The Eastern Kentucky Coal Field can be described as mountainous (part of the Appalachians), and the Western Kentucky Coal Field as hilly. The Bluegrass and the Mississippian Plateau are characterized by karst topography; a landscape of sinkholes, sinking streams, springs and caves resulting from the dissolution of carbonate bedrock by the percolation of acidic groundwater. The Mississippi Embayment is a low-lying dissected plain situated on thick deposits of Mesozoic and Cenozoic sand and gravel. Elevations range from more than 4,000 feet above sea level in the eastern mountains, between 800 to 1,000 feet in the Bluegrass, to less than 300 feet in the embayment.

EASTERN KENTUCKY COAL FIELD
(Cumberland Plateau, Eastern Kentucky)

The Eastern Coal Field region, an area of about 10,500 square miles, is part of the Central Appalachian Mountains and has very mature and rugged terrain. The long-standing economic significance of numerous seams of bituminous coal is reflected in the name given to the region. The heavily forested topography consists of steep and narrow ridges separated by v-shaped valleys, with the mountain elevations increasing toward the southeast. Black Mountain in Harlan County is the highest point in the state, with an elevation of 4,145 feet.

Cumberland Mountain, a narrow linear ridge, marks part of the southeastern boundary with Virginia, and is paralleled within Kentucky by the very similar Pine Mountain that continues the boundary with Virginia to the northeast. These mountain ridges were formed by folding and faulting during the late Paleozoic Allegheny Orogeny associated with the assembly of Pangea. The steep northwestern face of Pine Mountain is the leading edge of an overthrust fault block shoved, in places, nearly a dozen miles past underlying strata. These ridges, which were significant barriers to the pioneer settlement of the state, are cut by gaps in only a few locations, notably Cumberland Gap in the Cumberland Mountain and the Pineville Gap in Pine Mountain. The Pine Mountain ridge reaches a height of 3,200 feet in Letcher County.

Northwest of Pine Mountain, the much larger area of mountainous terrain in Eastern Kentucky is of lesser height and is often referred to as the Cumberland Mountains (as distinct from the Cumberland Mountain of the Virginia border). These mountains are not of tectonic origin and are thus unlike the Pine and Cumberland ridges, and the folded and fault block mountains farther east. The mountains of the Eastern Coal Field, except in the southeast corner, are the result of a deep and intricate dissection by stream erosion of a plateau of relatively flat-lying rock strata, alternating layers of sandstone, shale, coal, and limestone.

The western boundary of the Eastern Coal Field is defined by the Pottsville (Cumberland) Escarpment, which trends in a southwestern direction from Lewis County, on the Ohio River, toward the Tennessee border. The escarpment rises 200 to 300 feet from the adjacent terrain and is capped by sandstone and conglomerate rocks that are highly resistant to erosion. The edge of the escarpment is thoroughly dissected, and is bordered by conical hills known as "Knobs" that are erosional remnants left by the retreat of the escarpment. The escarpment area is very scenic, with many attractive stream-carved gorges, waterfalls, and natural arches produced by the narrowing of ridges. More than 450,000 acres of the Daniel Boone National Forest are located along the escarpment area, as are the Red River Gorge Geological Area and the nearby Natural Bridge State Park. The escarpment also contains numerous caves developed in limestone exposed by the erosion of the landscape.

Most of the region is drained by four streams and their tributaries, all of which flow northward to the Ohio River: the Big Sandy River, which forms the boundary between Kentucky and West Virginia; the Licking River; the Cumberland River, which flows southward into Tennessee but returns to Kentucky in the western part of the state; and the Kentucky River, which is divided into three separate branches. Because of the very steep and rugged terrain, most communities in the region are located in floodplains. As a consequence, flooding is a serious hazard for these towns.

BLUEGRASS

Adjacent to the Eastern Coal Field and sharing the Escarpment as a border is the Bluegrass region, which contains about 8,000 square miles and is subdivided into the Inner and Outer Bluegrass sub-regions, separated by the Eden Shale belt. The fertile lands of the Bluegrass were the first to be settled by the pioneers, and in this region today resides most of the population of the state. Frankfort, the state capital, is located here, as are the two largest cities: Louisville and Lexington, and the metropolitan areas of Newport and Covington, across the Ohio River from Cincinnati. The region is named for a grass, *Poa pratensis*, that was introduced by the early settlers of the area, probably by accident. The Bluegrass is bordered to the north by the Ohio River and separated from the rest of the state by the Knobs, which extend completely around the region in a belt 10 to 15 miles wide from Lewis County in the east to Jefferson County in the west. The Knobs range from about 50 feet to nearly 1,000 feet in height, with the highest toward eastern Kentucky. The terrain is gently rolling, with a belt of low hills that separates the Inner from the Outer Bluegrass.

The topography is developed upon the upwarped rock strata of the Cincinnati Arch. The Bluegrass region is centered upon the Jessamine Dome, the highest point of the Arch, so that the older rocks in the middle are surrounded by irregular concentric bands of younger strata, wider to the north and west. The changing nature of the bedrock, nearly all of Ordovician age, accounts for the changing nature of the terrain. The Inner Bluegrass is a karst landscape of about 2,000 square miles situated upon limestone, and characterized by numerous sinkholes and natural springs. Many sinkholes contain small ponds. This is one of the most fertile agricultural regions in Kentucky. Surrounding the Inner Bluegrass is the Eden Shale belt, sometimes referred to as the Hills of the Bluegrass because the topography is more rugged and contains little level land, with many low hills and narrow valleys. Because shale is the dominant bedrock, soils in this region are generally thin and infertile. The Outer Bluegrass encircles the region outside the shale belt, and, as a gently rolling karst plain, is very similar to that of the Inner Bluegrass.

The Bluegrass region is drained by the Kentucky River and its tributaries, which, as they flow through the Bluegrass, are entrenched in sinuous meanders 200 to 300 feet below the adjacent uplands.

MISSISSIPPIAN PLATEAU
(Pennyroyal Plateau, Pennyrile Plateau)

The Mississippian Plateau, with 12,000 square miles, is the largest region of Kentucky and shares borders with all of the other regions. From the Pottsville Escarpment, which forms the eastern boundary, the region extends west to the Mississippi Embayment and northward to the Knobs of the Bluegrass and nearly encircles the Western Coal Field region. Except for the southern boundary with Tennessee, which is political, the geographic bounds of the region are derived from the underlying geologic structure. The upwarp of the Cincinnati Arch extends from Ohio to Tennessee, and contains two structural highs, the Jessamine Dome, centered nearly on Lexington, and the similar Nashville Dome, centered near Nashville, Tenn. The rock strata dip away from the two domes, so that each dome is surrounded by belts of younger rock, but between the Jessamine and Nashville domes is a slight structural low known as the Cumberland Saddle in which the surface bedrock is all of Mississippian age. The region is separated from the Western Coal Field by an escarpment similar to the Pottsville Escarpment along the boundary with the Eastern Kentucky Coal Field, but of lesser relief.

Two women on a rock in the Big Sandy River
Source: Kentucky Department of Libraries & Archives

The topography of the region, and associated land use, is related to the surface bedrock. Where the bedrock is limestone, the terrain generally consists of gently rolling hills that are good farmland. Where resistant sandstone caprock still exists to protect the limestone from erosion, the terrain tends to be more rugged, cut up into steep hills and valleys. Since the rocks of the Mississippian Plateau are mainly limestones, a large proportion of the region is considered karst and much of the regional drainage is subsurface. Mammoth Cave and many others are located in the stream-dissected Chester Upland near the southeastern border of the Western Coal Field, developed in the limestones underlying a band of sandstone caprock known as the

Big Clifty that encircles the Coal Field.

The outer edge of the Chester Upland is the Dripping Springs Escarpment, which rises 150 to 300 feet above the surrounding landscape. Southeast from the escarpment is an area of complex sinkhole patterns known as the Sinkhole Plain, in which surface streams are almost entirely absent since the local drainage is underground. The early settlers referred to this area as the "Barrens," a term used for a grassland prairie. Northward from the Sinkhole Plain, the Mississippian Plateau is separated from the Bluegrass region by the Muldraugh's Hill limestone escarpment, at the base of which is the most extensive area of Knobs in the state.

Much of the landscape of the eastern and central Mississippian Plateau is also karst. The eastern section of the Mississippian Plateau tends to have a more rugged topography, particularly near the border with the Eastern Coal Field and in the vicinity of the deeply entrenched Cumberland River, Lake Cumberland, and Dale Hollow Lake. North and west from the lakes, the terrain is more suitable for agriculture. Most of the Mississippian Plateau region is drained by the Green River and its tributaries, and to a lesser extent by the Cumberland River in the eastern and western parts of the region. The Mississippian Plateau topography extends southward into Middle Tennessee, where it is known as the Highland Rim.

WESTERN KENTUCKY COAL FIELD

The 4,680 square-mile Western Kentucky Coal Field, like its eastern counterpart, owes its name to the long-standing economic significance of coal mining in the region. The Ohio River forms the northern border, and elsewhere the Coal Field is surrounded by the Mississippian Plateau region on all sides. The topography of the region is derived from the underlying structural downwarp feature: the Illinois Basin. The basin originated during the early Paleozoic, slowly subsiding as it accumulated a great thickness of marine sediments. Most of the 60,000 square-mile basin lies in Illinois and Indiana; only the southern tip extends into Kentucky. Since this is a basin, the oldest strata are on the perimeter, unlike the structure of the Jessamine Dome in the Bluegrass where the oldest rocks are in the center.

The margin of the Western Coal Field is a narrow belt of rough, hilly land whose outer edge forms an escarpment, very similar to the Pottsville Escarpment bordering the Eastern Kentucky Coal Field but not as high. Within the rim of hills is a lower interior of rolling hills. The region is drained by the Green, Tradewater and Ohio rivers. The Green and Tradewater rivers, and their tributaries, flow through wide valleys which contain an alluvial fill nearly 200 feet thick in places, deposited as floodplain and lake sediments during periods of glaciation when glacial outwash dammed the mouths of the rivers. Radical alterations of the topography have been made across broad areas by the surface mining of coal carried on extensively in the region.

MISSISSIPPI EMBAYMENT

(Jackson Purchase, Purchase)

The Embayment region is completely unlike any other part of Kentucky in its geology and topography. The landscape is geologically the youngest and lowest terrain of the state, and, historically, the most recent territory incorporated into the Commonwealth. This region has traditionally been called The Jackson Purchase because it was acquired in 1818 from the Chickasaw Indians during the administration of Andrew Jackson. The 2,396 square-mile region is bounded by the Tennessee River and the impoundment of Kentucky Lake to the east, by the Ohio River to the north, and by the Mississippi River to the west. The Tennessee state line forms the southern boundary. There are some boundary anomalies along the Mississippi River border with Missouri. This boundary was originally established as a line down the center of the Mississippi river, but shifts over time in the course of the river have stranded small sections of Kentucky on what is now the opposite side of the river. An error made in the 1780 Walker survey created the Kentucky Bend enclave, the state's most western territory. This tract of about 5 square miles is isolated within a hairpin bend of the Mississippi, completely separated from the rest of the state and accessible only from Tennessee.

The region is located at the head of the Mississippi Embayment, a depositional trough that formed during the late Mesozoic and accumulated thick deposits of marine sediments overlain by more recent deposits of alluvium and loess. Low hills and rolling plains of deeply weathered gravel in the eastern part slope gradually to low, flat plains of sand, gravel, silt and clay in the west. The landscape is poorly drained in the southern part, dissected by a network of low-gradient creeks and small rivers often bordered by wetland areas, but well-drained farmland is found to the north. In the west, the uplands end in a line of bluffs along the Mississippi River, 100 to180 feet high, overlooking the floodplain of the great river. The flows of the Ohio and Mississippi join just above Wickliffe in Ballard County, and the floodplains of these rivers exhibit many meander scars and oxbow lakes.

ILLUSTRATED PHYSIOGRAPHIC DIAGRAM OF KENTUCKY

KGS KENTUCKY GEOLOGICAL SURVEY
James C. Cobb, State Geologist and Director
UNIVERSITY OF KENTUCKY, LEXINGTON

View the KGS World
Wide Web site at
www.uky.edu/kgs

Note: Numbers on map indicate
where the photographs were
taken.

For information on obtaining copies
of this map and other Kentucky
Geological Survey maps and
publications call:
Publication Sales
(859) 257-3896

MAP AND CHART 24
Series XII, 2001

modified from A.K. Lobeck

ENVIRONMENT & NATURAL RESOURCES

Water Resources   Dr. Gary O'Dell

Kentucky is an exceptionally well-watered state. Nearly 90,000 miles of rivers and streams give the Commonwealth more flowing water than any other state except Alaska. Each year more than 100 million tons of commodities, mainly coal and grain, are shipped to and from Kentucky by way of more than 1,000 miles of navigable rivers. Seven hundred miles of streams in the state have been designated as "outstanding resource waters"

Echo River in Mammoth Cave
Source: Kentucky Department of Libraries & Archives

for their high water quality, and 114 miles in eight streams are protected as "wild rivers" under the provisions of the 1972 Kentucky Wild Rivers Act. The state contains more than 2,700 surface water impoundments, both natural and artificial, although nearly all of the larger lakes are of human construction. Approximately one-third of the impoundments are greater than 10 acres in size. As elsewhere in the nation, much of Kentucky's

wetland area has been reduced by development, from an estimated 1.5 million acres at the time of settlement to less than 640,000 acres today. Groundwater in bedrock and granular aquifers is an important water supply resource for communities and individual households.

RIVERS

All streams within the state are contained within the Ohio River basin, which in turn is part of the Mississippi River system. Excepting only the headwaters of the Cumberland River, which initially flow southward to Tennessee, all of the major rivers in Kentucky flow to the north. The primary drainage basins in Kentucky are those of the Green River, Kentucky River, Cumberland River (upper and lower segments), Licking River, Salt River, Big and Little Sandy rivers, Tradewater River, Tennessee River and Tygarts Creek. In addition, substantial areas parallel to the courses of the Ohio and Mississippi drain directly to those rivers. The basins of the Kentucky, Licking, Salt, Tradewater, Little Sandy and Tygarts are entirely contained within the state, as is all but a fraction of the Green River drainage.

The Green River, the longest river in the state (370 miles), has the largest drainage area (9,430 square miles) and the greatest number of miles navigable to commercial shipping (108.5). Originating in Lincoln County at the eastern edge of the Mississippian Plateau, the river flows west, passing through Mammoth Cave National Park, and then turns northwest, flowing through the Western Coal Field to join the Ohio River across from Evansville. A series of locks and dams were built on the river, beginning in 1842, which once allowed river navigation as far as Bowling Green. The lowermost two locks and dams remain in service and facilitate a substantial amount of shipping, mainly coal and aluminum ore.

Although most of the Cumberland River flows through Tennessee, the beginning and end sections are located within the Commonwealth and are known as the Upper and Lower Cumberland River basins. The headwaters of the Cumberland River originate in the mountains of southeastern Kentucky. The Cumberland flows south and west for over 300 miles across the Eastern Coal Field region, crossing the Tennessee border in Monroe County, Kentucky, and returns to Kentucky in south-central Trigg County. The Upper Cumberland and its tributaries are exceptionally scenic: six of the state's eight wild rivers are found here, including 10.2 miles of the Big South Fork in Whitley County, one of the nation's finest stretches of whitewater. Cumberland Falls, sometimes called the "Niagara of the South," is located on the river at the border of McCreary and Whitley counties. The falls are 68 feet high and span about 125 feet.

The Licking River rises in southeastern Magoffin County in the Eastern Coal Field Region and follows a meandering course northwestward through the Bluegrass for 310 miles, joining the Ohio River in northern Kentucky opposite Cincinnati, where it separates the cities of Covington and Newport. The river was named for the many mineral springs near the river that attracted animals to salt licks. The river was an important transportation route for native Americans and during the settlement of Kentucky and a trade route during the 19th century.

The headwaters of the Kentucky River arise in the mountainous terrain of the Eastern Coal Field. The North Fork, Middle Fork and South Fork of the Kentucky flow northward from the vicinity of Pine Mountain, roughly parallel to each other, and join near Beattyville. From this confluence, the river flows northwestward for 255 miles through the Bluegrass Region to join the Ohio River at Carrollton in

northern Kentucky. The nearly 7,000-square-mile area of the Kentucky River basin is second largest in the state. Other major tributary streams include the Red River, Dix River, Elkhorn Creek and Eagle Creek. The Palisades, a 100-mile stretch of scenic limestone gorge, lies between Clays Ferry in Madison County and Frankfort. The river once provided access to the mineral and timber resources of the Coal Field, aided by a series of 14 locks and dams constructed on the river beginning in the early 19th century, but is today navigable only as far as Frankfort, a distance of 65 river miles from the mouth. The Kentucky is an important regional resource for 63 municipal water systems that withdraw from the river, supplying over 700,000 residents with water.

The Salt River rises in Boyle County, west of Danville, flows northward and then west to the Ohio River at West Point. The river was named for the saline licks and springs along the lower reaches of the stream. Early settlers established a salt works at Bullitt's Lick near in 1779 and in several other locations.

The Big Sandy was named for the presence of many sand bars in the river channel. The main stem of the Big Sandy is a relatively short stretch of river, only 27 miles long, formed by the confluence of the Levisa Fork and Tug Fork at Louisa. The Big Sandy is navigable due to lock and dam construction, as are the lower parts of the Levisa and Tug Forks, and carries commercial shipping, primarily coal.

In northeastern Kentucky, Tygarts Creek and the Little Sandy River are the smallest of the Kentucky drainage systems of significance that flow to the Ohio River; both are less than 100 miles in length.

The Tennessee River is the largest tributary of the Ohio River, but only about 10 percent of its 620-mile length is within the Commonwealth, and most of that is impounded as Kentucky Lake.

The Tennessee flows into the Ohio River at Paducah. The Kentucky Dam is located about 22 miles from the river mouth, creating the largest impoundment in the eastern U.S., 184-mile-long Kentucky Lake. This lake is linked by a navigation canal to Lake Barkley, an almost equally large and parallel impoundment of the Cumberland River. The area is known as "Land Between the Lakes" National Recreation Area.

The Mississippi River forms a short section of Kentucky's far western boundary, flowing 49 miles from its confluence with the Ohio River at Wickliffe to the Tennessee state line. In addition, the Mississippi comprises another 15.5 miles of boundary for the Kentucky Bend enclave, a small area within a hairpin bend of the river not directly connected to another part of the state.

**Wolf Creek Dam
on the Cumberland River**
Source: Sid Webb

The Ohio River is one of the most important tributaries of the Mississippi, flowing 981 miles from the confluence of the Allegheny and Monongahela rivers in downtown Pittsburgh to join with the Mississippi near Wickliffe in far western Kentucky. The Ohio forms the boundary between West Virginia and Ohio and, for a distance of 665 miles, the northern boundary of Kentucky that separates it from Indiana and Illinois. Unlike most boundary rivers, the boundaries between states along the Ohio were established along the centerline of the river. This situation derives from the January 2, 1781, resolution of the General Assembly of Virginia that the Commonwealth of Virginia would cede to the U.S. all those lands granted to it under the Virginia Charter "northwest of the river Ohio." This was interpreted to mean that Virginia owned the Ohio River to the far shore, a right of possession that was extended to Kentucky and West Virginia when those states were formed. In the years since the original boundary was established, many locks and dams have been built on the river to improve navigation.

During the settlement of Kentucky and the western territory, the Ohio River was a primary transportation route and remains today an important artery for commerce. The only significant navigation obstacle on the river is the Falls of the Ohio, a series of cascading rapids over limestone ledges that drops 26 feet in a 2-1/2 mile stretch of the river. The river barrier created a natural stopping point for travelers, and the city of Louisville was founded on the south side of the rapids. The first canal and locks around the Falls was completed in 1830 by a private stock company charted by the Commonwealth. In 1874 the canal and locks were appropriated by the U.S. government. The U.S. Army Corps of Engineers has widened and improved the original canal and locks and constructed an additional route to bypass the falls. About 20 barge tows pass through the canals and locks every day.

LAKES

Since most of Kentucky lies south of the farthest glacial advance, there are few natural lakes of significant size within the state. Swan Lake in Ballard County is the largest natural lake wholly contained within Kentucky and is of about 300 acres extent. The lake is situated in the bottom land of the Ohio River, surrounded by cypress swamps and part of the 2,200 acre Swan Lake Wildlife Management Area. The far larger Reelfoot Lake, 15,500 acres at normal pool, is almost entirely within Tennessee, except for a tiny section that extends north into Fulton County, Kentucky. This is a very shallow lake, surrounded by cypress swamps and marshes and a habitat for bald eagles and is included within the Reelfoot National Wildlife Refuge.

Nearly all of Kentucky's larger lakes are artificial impoundments formed by the damming of a stream or river. With the exception of Kentucky Lake, managed by the Tennessee Valley Authority, these lakes are under the jurisdiction of the U.S. Army Corps of Engineers and the Kentucky Dept. of Fish and Wildlife Resources. Most of these lakes were built during the 1960s and early 1970s for flood control, recreation and hydroelectric power generation. Lake Herrington, built in the 1920s, was the first major impoundment in the state, and supplied hydroelectric power for many years. The most recent large impoundment was Cedar Creek Lake, a reservoir of 762 acres that finished filling in 2002. Kentucky Lake is one of the largest artificial lakes in the eastern U.S., although only a little more than a third of its 160,000 acres are contained within the Commonwealth. The largest lake entirely within Kentucky is Lake Cumberland in the southeastern section of the state, which contains over 50,000 acres at normal pool and more than 1,000 miles of shoreline. Five lakes in the state produce hydroelectric power – Kentucky, Cumberland, Barkley, Dale Hollow and Laurel lakes – with a total capacity of nearly 2.9 billion annual kilowatt-hours.

WETLANDS

Kentucky's wetlands are an important natural resource that is often unappreciated by the general public. Wetlands are areas that may be flooded on a permanent, seasonal or occasional basis, or are saturated by groundwater seepage, and are characterized by specialized plants (hydrophytic) that are adapted to wet environments and soils (hydric) that are sufficiently wet during the growing season to develop anaerobic conditions in the upper part. Freshwater wetlands include marshes, swamps, bogs and fens. Wetlands were once perceived as undesirable wastelands, breeding grounds for mosquitoes and flies and sources of diseases and unpleasant odors. Because of this viewpoint, more than half of America's original wetlands have been destroyed, drained or filled for agriculture or development. More recently, we have come to understand that wetlands provide important benefits to people and the environment. Wetlands help to control water levels within watersheds, improve water quality, reduce flood damages, provide fish and wildlife habitat and support recreational activities.

About 2.5 percent of Kentucky is wetlands. At the time of settlement the state contained an estimated 1,566,000 acres of wetlands; today only about 637,000 acres remain – a 60 percent loss. Most of the wetland loss has occurred in the western part of the state as a result of conversion to cropland and pasture-land. The Kentucky Division of Water estimates that about 3,600 acres of existing wetland are lost annually, being drained or filled. Most of the wetlands of the state are privately owned. The 2005 General Assembly authorized the Environmental and Public Protection Cabinet to investigate the possibility of administrating the federal wetlands program at the state level, and the state has received a grant from the EPA to help fund development of a proposed program.

GROUNDWATER

Nearly one-fifth of the earth's fresh water is contained underground, more than three times as much as can be found in all the rivers, streams and lakes combined. Groundwater is an important water-supply resource for the planet, and in Kentucky, more than 1.6 million citizens depend upon groundwater from wells and springs for drinking water and other household needs. Groundwater sources also supply commercial, agricultural and industrial uses in the state. The normal flow and dry-weather flow of Kentucky's rivers and streams is maintained by groundwater seepage. The use of groundwater in the state is increasing, although contamination from urban, industrial and agricultural sources poses an increasing threat to quality.

Just over half of Kentucky's public water supplies (226 of 435) depend upon groundwater sources, supplying a combined population of over 1.2 million persons. This represents about 30 percent of the total population. An estimated 400,000 persons are self-supplied, of which about 90 percent rely on groundwater from private wells and springs. Over 35,000 private water wells for domestic use have been drilled in Kentucky since 1985.

The Kentucky Division of Water has monitored groundwater quality across the state since 1995. Overall water quality is considered good, though impacts from human activity, primarily related to agriculture, occur in the karst regions where shallow conduit aquifers are particularly vulnerable to contamination. Pesticides are routinely detected in groundwater samples only in the karst regions. Local groundwater contamination from causes such as landfills, leaking underground storage tanks, Superfund and hazardous waste sites is of concern in Kentucky as elsewhere, but does not represent a widespread disruption of groundwater use.

MAJOR RIVERS

RIVER BASIN	TOTAL DRAINAGE AREA (mi)	DRAINAGE AREA IN KENTUCKY (sq. mi.)	TRIBUTARY STREAMS	LENGTH IN KENTUCKY (mi)*	DRAINAGE AREA IN KENTUCKY (sq. mi.)
Mississippi River	> 1.2 million	40,424 total; 39,124 by Ohio River and tributaries; 1,300 by main stem and minor tributaries	Main stem and minor tributaries	49 (main stem)	329
			Mayfield Creek	60	436
			Obion Creek		320
			Bayou du Chien	33	215
Ohio River	204,000	39,124	Major tributaries	see below	34,974
			Main stem and minor tributaries	665 (main stem)	4,150
Green River	9,233	8,810	Main stem and minor tributaries	366 (main stem)	3,319
			Rough River	147	1,077
			Pond River	133	798
			Nolin River	71	726
			Panther Creek	92	375
			Mud River	31	389
			Russell Creek	50	
Kentucky River	6,972	6,975	Main stem and minor tributaries	249 (main stem)	2,335
			North Fork	134	1,335
			South Fork	78	750
			Middle Fork	95	560
			Eagle Creek	100	519
			Elkhorn Creek	78	492
			Red River	78	497
			Dix River	99	442
Cumberland River	17,913	5,180 Upper Cumberland	Main stem and minor tributaries	288 (main stem)	3,056
			Rockcastle River	57	764
			Big South Fork	50	405
			Buck Creek	63	294
			Laurel River	41	489
			Poor Fork	52	118
			Clover Fork	33	105
		2,040 Lower Cumberland	Main stem and minor tributaries	70 (main stem)	1,439
			Little River	58	601
Licking River	3,712	3,710	Main stem and minor tributaries	267 (main stem)	2,244
			South Fork	62	908
			North Fork		308
			Stoner Creek		230
Salt River	2,920	2,920	Main stem and minor tributaries	130 (main stem)	924
			Rolling Fork	109	1,284
			Floyds Fork	62	262
			Brashear Creek	37	
Big Sandy River	4,288	2,290	Main stem and minor tributaries	27 (main stem)	1,475
			Levisa Fork	94	478
			Tug Fork	46	265
			Blaine Creek		
Tennessee River	40,879	1,040	Main stem and minor tributaries	63 (main stem)	362
			Clarks River		678
Tradewater River	943	943	Main stem and minor tributaries	65 (main stem)	943
Little Sandy River	726	726	Main stem and minor tributaries	86 (main stem)	572
			East Fork		154
Tygarts Creek	340	340	Main stem and minor tributaries	88 (main stem)	340

* "Length" is length of stream section bearing that name. For example, the given length of Elkhorn Creek is for that section downstream from the junction of North Elkhorn Creek and South Elkhorn Creek, which merge to form Elkhorn Creek.

Primary sources: Carey, Daniel I. Catalog of hydrologic units in Kentucky. Kentucky Geological survey 2003. Online at: http://kgsweb.uky.edu/download/rivers/CATHUCS.pdf ;
U.S. Geological Survey. Hydrology of Kentucky. Online at: http://kygeonet.ky.gov/kyhydro/viewer.htm;
U.S. Geological Survey. High Resolution National Hydrography Dataset (by Basin) Coverage Area: Kentucky. Online at: http://www.uky.edu/KGS/gis/kyhuc8pic.htm;
Dr. Steven Parkansky, Morehead State University; and
Erik Siegel, Kentucky Environmental Quality Commission

MAJOR LAKES & DAMS

LAKE	COUNTY LOCATION	STREAM IMPOUNDED	AREA (Acres)*	SHORELINE (Miles)*	DAM	DAM HEIGHT & WIDTH (Feet)	WHEN CONSTRUCTED	GENERATING CAP (kwh/year)
Kentucky Lake	Calloway, Lyon, Marshall, Trigg	Tennessee River	160,300 total 51,000 Kentucky	2,064 total	Kentucky Dam	206 by 8,422	1938 - 1944	1.3 billion
Lake Cumberland	Clinton, Laurel, Pulaski, Russell, Wayne	Cumberland River	50,250	1,085	Wolf Creek Dam	258 by 5,736	1941 - 1943; 1946 - 1950	800 million
Lake Barkley	Caldwell, Livingston, Trigg	Cumberland River	57,920 45,600 Kentucky	1,004 total	Barkley Dam	157 by 10,180	1959 - 1964	582 million
Barren River Lake	Allen, Barren, Monroe	Barren River	10,000	300	Barren River Lake Dam	146 by 1,272	1961 - 1964	
Cave Run Lake	Bath, Menifee, Morgan, Rowan	Licking River	8,270	166	Cave Run Lake Dam	148 by 2,700	1969 - 1974	
Green River Lake	Adair, Casey, Taylor	Green River	8,210	250	Green River Dam	141 by 2,350	1964 - 1969	
Nolin River Lake	Edmonson, Grayson, Hart	Nolin River	5,795	172	Nolin Dam	166 by 980	1959 - 1963	
Laurel Lake	Laurel, Whitley	Laurel River	5,600	192	Laurel Dam	282 by 1,420	1964 - 1974	67 million
Rough River Lake	Breckinridge, Grayson, Hardin	Rough River	5,100	220	Rough River Dam	132 by 1,590	1955 - 1958	
Dale Hollow	Clinton, Cumberland	Obey River	27,700 total 4,933 Kentucky	620 total 112 Kentucky	Dale Hollow Dam	200 by 1,717	1942 - 1943	127 million
Taylorsville Lake	Anderson, Nelson, Spencer	Salt River	3,050	75	Taylorsville Lake Dam	163 by 1,280	1982 - 1983	
Lake Herrington	Boyle, Mercer, Garrard	Dix River	2,335	325	Dix Dam	287 by 1,080	1923 - 1925	
Yatesville Lake	Lawrence	Blaine Creek	2,242	93	Yatesville Dam	109 by 760	1984 - 1991	
Grayson Lake	Carter, Eliot	Little Sandy River	1,512	74	Grayson Dam	120 by 1,460	1965 - 1968	
Buckhorn Lake	Leslie, Perry	Middle Fork, Kentucky River	1,230	65	Buckhorn Lake Dam	162 by 1,020	1956 - 1961	
Fishtrap Lake	Pike	Russell Fork	1,131	43	Fishtrap Lake Dam	195 by 1,000	1962 - 1968	
Dewey Lake	Floyd	John's Creek	1,100	52	Dewey Dam	118 by 920	1946 - 1949	
Paintsville Lake	Johnson, Morgan	Paint Creek	1,139	57	Paintsville Dam	160 by 1,660	1976 - 1980	
Lake Malone	Logan, Muhlenberg, Todd	Rocky Creek	826	30	Mud River MP5 No. 51	56 by 610	1959 - 1961	
Cedar Creek Lake	Lincoln	Cedar Creek	762	23	Cedar Creek Dam	86 by 2110	2000 - 2002	
Lake Beshear	Caldwell, Christian	trib. Tradewater R	760	24	Beshear Lake Dam	38 by 550	Completed 1962	
Carr Creek Lake	Knott	Carr Creek	710	24	Carr Creek Dam	130 by 720	1966 - 1976	
Wood Creek Lake	Laurel	Wood Creek	672	33.6	Wood Crk Lake Dam	163 by 800	Completed 1968	
Martins Fork Lake	Harlan	Martins Fork	340	10	Martins Fork Dam	97 by 504	1973 - 1978	
Guist Creek Lake	Shelby	Guist Creek	325	27	Guist Crk Lake Dam	60 by 1010	Completed 1961	
Williamstown Lake	Grant	Grassy Creek	300	13.5	Williamstown Lake Dam	55 by 680	Completed 1956	
Lake Linville	Rockcastle	Renfro Creek	273	8.2	Renfro Lake Dam	72 by 1100	Completed 1978	
Cannon Creek Lake	Bell	Cannon Creek	243	7.7	Cannon Crk Lake Dam	125 by 900	Completed 1972	
Cranks Creek Lake (Herb Smith Lake)	Harlan	Cranks Creek	219	9	Cranks Crk Lake Dam	120 by 635	Completed 1963	
Kincaid Lake	Pendleton	Kincaid Creek	183	12.5	Kincaid Lake Dam	61 by 480	Completed 1961	
Greenbo Lake	Greenup	Claylick Creek	181	7.6	Greenbo Lake Dam	70 by 570	1954 - 1955	

*Acreage and shoreline vary according to pool elevation of lakes. Figures represent summer pool.

Compiled by Gary A. O'Dell
Primary sources: U.S. Army Corps of Engineers, Kentucky Division of Water,
Kentucky Department of Fish and Wildlife Resources, Kentucky Department of Parks

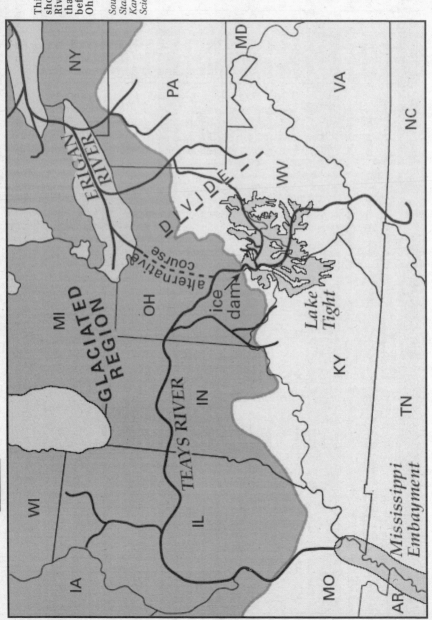

This image shows the Teays River drainage that existed before the Ohio River.

Source: Emporia State University, Kansas, Earth Science Dept.

ENVIRONMENT & NATURAL RESOURCES
Minerals

Royal Berglee

Metallic, Non-metallic and Vein Minerals
MINERAL MINING

Numerous metallic and non metallic mineral resources have been mined in Kentucky, including iron, titanium, phosphates, and vein minerals such as fluorite, barite, sphalerite, galena, gypsum and calcite. Vein mineral deposits occur in 20 counties in the central, western and southern Kentucky mineral districts. Iron ore has been used for steel products. Titanium is used as a high-strength alloy in aircraft and ship building. Phosphates are used as fertilizer. Vein minerals such as fluorite and barite are used in the steel and oil-field industries, respectively. Sphalerite and galena are metallic minerals used in automobiles, electronics and radiation protection. Gypsum has a very low thermal conductivity (hence its use in *drywall* as insulating filler).

Kentucky was a major center for mining iron, phosphates, barite and fluorite during the early 1900s. Occasionally, small operators still mine some of these mineral deposits, but currently no large commercial mines are operating in Kentucky. Principal mining companies have, however conducted exploration activity. The geology of Kentucky is not favorable for the natural occurrence of large quantities of precious metals such as gold or silver, though they both have been found in the state. The same can be said for gemstones such as diamonds, which are not common in Kentucky's geological formations. A number of additional minerals can be found in the state but not in large enough quantities to be economically feasible to extract. For example, naturally occurring potassium nitrate (saltpeter) was once mined in various caves and similar locations in Kentucky to produce gunpowder.

LIMESTONE AND DOLOSTONE

Limestone and dolostone, both carbonate rocks, can be found at the surface of 25 percent of Kentucky, mainly in the central and western regions. Kentucky has attained the position of one of the nation's major producers of limestone. Since the year 2000, Kentucky has been rated as

Coal miners underground entrance
Source: Kentucky Department of Libraries & Archives

Strip mine in Western Kentucky
Source: (WPA) Kentucky Department of Libraries & Archives

high as the fifth-largest stone producer in the United States. Kentucky produced 58.8 million short tons of limestone and dolostone in 1992, which had a value of $251.1 million, averaging $4.25 per ton. Stone is being produced at 72 open-pit quarries and 17 underground mines in 62 of the state's 120 counties. In recent years, the Reed Quarry in western Kentucky has been listed as the largest producer of crushed limestone in the U.S. The Reed Quarry has produced over 10 million short tons of crushed stone annually. Fine-grained dolomitic limestone of the Oregon Formation, which has been labeled Kentucky River marble, was once used as building stone for central Kentucky residences and commercial and public buildings.

Industrial and miscellaneous applications of limestone and dolostone include chemically pure stone for the manufacture of lime and cement; filter stone; sorbent stone for removing sulfur dioxide emissions from coal-burning plants; rock dust for explosion abatement in

residential, commercial and government construction; riprap and jetty stone; and railroad ballast. Sand and gravel are obtained from the valley

Coal mine
Source: (WPA) Kentucky Department of Libraries & Archives

Coal miner
Source: (WPA) Kentucky Department of Libraries & Archives

of the Ohio River from land-based pits in fluvioglacial and alluvial deposits and from the channels of the Ohio and Mississippi Rivers, by floating operations from bars, islands and other channel and bedload deposits in the streams themselves. Combined, these sources constitute more than three-fourths of the sand and gravel produced in Kentucky. Floating dredge operations provide the greatest amount. Sands and gravels are also found in numerous stream channels within the state.

underground coal mines; and acid-water treatment. Agricultural uses include limestone applied to soils to adjust their pH, poultry grit, and mineral feed. The second and third largest lime plants in the U.S. are in Kentucky, along the Ohio River in Mason and Pendleton counties.

SAND AND GRAVEL

Sand and gravel deposits can mainly be found along the Ohio River Valley and in the western-most region of the state. The largest market for sand, gravel and crushed stone produced in Kentucky is the construction industry, which includes aggregate for road construction and maintenance;

CLAY

Current clay and shale supplies are being extracted primarily from deposits in the western coal fields and the Ohio River Valley. Of historical importance is the formerly large firebrick industry that developed around clay deposits found in the northeastern portion of the state; an example is the Olive Hill clay bed. Also, clay from the Irvine Formation (high-level fluvial deposits) in east-central Kentucky has been the source of raw material for a small but well-known pottery in Madison County for many years.

SHALE

Commonly used locally for fill and for a base course for road construction, shales have also been used for the manufacture of face brick, drain tile and quarry or roofing tile. Shales on both the east and west sides of the Cincinnati arch are located near potential markets but appear to offer little possibility for structural clay products. Shales in northern Lewis County near the Ohio River appear to be relatively free of deleterious materials and offer potential for further exploitation. The carbon-rich Chattanooga-New Albany-Ohio shales constitute a present and potential energy resource. When oil shales are heated to 900 F, they can give off a gas similar to natural gas and a type of oil not much different from conventional crude oil.

SANDSTONE

Often resistant to erosion, sandstone can be seen in places like rock outcroppings, ridges and cliff faces. Comprised of mineral grains and cemented together by silica, iron oxide or calcium carbonate, sandstone is porous and easily crushed into sand. Silica sands of high quality and purity are used in the glass industry for windows, light bulbs and containers. Glass sands have been extracted from deposits in Calloway County. Certain types of dense sandstone have been used for building stone throughout the state.

Kentucky Coal Resources

Kentucky has two distinct coalfields: one in western Kentucky and one in eastern Kentucky. Each contains numerous deposits of bituminous coal of varied characteristics, and mines of every type and size. Original resource estimates for western and eastern Kentucky were 41 and 64 billion tons respectively. The resources currently remaining after 200 years of mining are estimated to be 35.8 billion tons in western Kentucky and 52.3 billion tons in eastern Kentucky. Of Kentucky's 130.7 million tons of 2000 coal production, 80.2 million tons were produced by underground mining methods and 50.5 million tons were produced by surface mining methods.

Electricity: Average electricity costs in Kentucky were 4.1 cents per kilowatt-hour in 2001, the lowest in the U.S. Coal provides 51.8 percent of the electricity in the U.S. and 97 percent in Kentucky.

Production: Kentucky produced 131 million tons of coal in 2000, compared to the record production of 179 million tons set in 1990. Kentucky has been one of the top three coal producers in the U.S. for the last 50 years.

Employment: The Kentucky coal industry paid $678.4 million in direct wages in 2000, directly employing 14,812 persons and indirectly providing three additional jobs for every miner employed.

Types of coal mining in Kentucky

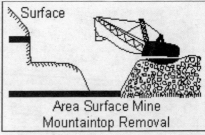

Area Surface Mine
Mountaintop Removal

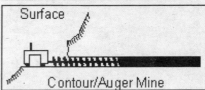

Contour/Auger Mine

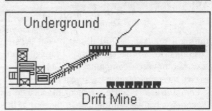

Drift Mine

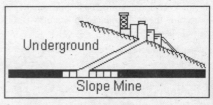

Slope Mine

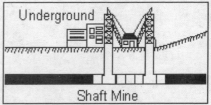

Shaft Mine

Graphic Source: U.S. Department of Energy

The average weekly wage for coal miners in Kentucky was $880 during 2000. The Kentucky coal mining industry has a current work force of approximately 17,042 people directly employed in coal mining jobs. The western Kentucky coalfield directly employs approximately 2,524 persons, while the eastern Kentucky coal field provides 14,518 direct mining jobs.

Economy: The Kentucky coal industry brought over $2.5 billion into Kentucky

Coal haul sled in the middle fork of the Kentucky River
Source: Kentucky Department of Libraries & Archives

during fiscal year 2000-01, through coal sales to customers in 27 other states and 11 foreign countries. Kentucky coal companies paid $141.2 million in coal severance taxes in fiscal year 2000-01.

Coal Markets: Electric power plants located in 27 states accounted for almost 79 percent of the Kentucky coal sold during 2000. Approximately 80 percent of the coal produced in Kentucky is sold out-of-state each year.

Coal Prices: There are as many coal price averages as there are coal qualities.

Average Value of Kentucky Coal FOB Mine in 2002 was $27.77 dollars per ton.

Eastern Coal Average = $29.04 -- **Underground** = $29.77 -- **Surface** = $28.11

Western Coal Average = $22.23 -- **Underground** = $22.37 -- **Surface** = $21.81

Kentucky Oil and Gas Production

Oil production in Kentucky is most prominent in the western coalfield and south-central region. The eastern coalfield produces mostly natural gas. Kentucky has an estimated 18,000 producing oil wells and over 19,000 producing gas wells. The majority of those producing wells are in the "stripper" category, having daily production rates of 10 barrels of oil or 60,000 cubic feet of gas or less. Many wells are reported with initial daily production rates in excess of 100 barrels of oil or 580,000 cubic feet of gas. Daily production per well averages much lower, at around 0.5 barrels for oil and 19,000 cubic feet for gas. Since the year 2000, annual production has averaged 2.8 million barrels of oil and 85 billion cubic feet of natural gas with a total annual value of $457 million. On an annual basis Kentucky only produces about 10 percent of the oil and natural gas consumed in the state.

It's a Kentucky thing...

Most of the major coal beds were formed as widespread peat swamps during the Pennsylvanian Period. During that period the area that is now Kentucky was near the equator and had a climate much like that of Indonesia. Tropical climates allowed lush vegetation to accumulate into widespread peats. Plant and animal remains, buried by the sediments, were preserved and became fossils.

Source: Kentucky Geological Survey, http://www.uky.edu/KGS/coal/coalbear.htm

EASTERN KENTUCKY COAL RESOURCES, 2002

COUNTY	ORIGINAL	MINED	REMAINING
Bell	3,194.70	299.09	2,596.52
Boyd	630.68	19.93	590.82
Breathitt	4,112.20	206.09	3,700.02
Carter	501.96	18.61	464.74
Clay	1,536.11	61.42	1,413.27
Elliott	316.32	9.85	296.62
Floyd	4,168.08	453.55	3,260.98
Greenup	204.87	10.42	184.03
Harlan	7,881.12	894.43	6,092.26
Jackson	375.87	11.23	353.41
Johnson	1,419.44	95.78	1,227.88
Knott	4,385.10	304.83	3,775.44
Knox	1,381.93	74.34	1,233.25
Laurel	408.04	35.81	336.42
Lawrence	2,024.68	24.58	1,975.52
Lee	363.98	8.45	347.08
Leslie	3,554.65	249.43	3,055.79
Letcher	3,692.80	542.10	2,608.60
McCreary	444.97	55.34	334.29
Magoffin	1,969.10	54.85	1,859.40
Martin	3,319.97	376.01	2,567.95
Morgan	849.40	15.19	819.02
Owsley	574.14	9.83	554.48
Perry	3,596.70	569.59	2,457.52
Pike	11,391.70	1,363.38	8,664.94
Whitley	987.44	91.12	805.20
Wolfe	443.92	7.16	429.60
Other***	334.89	33.18	268.53
EKY Total	64,064.76	5,895.59	52,273.58

WESTERN KENTUCKY COAL RESOURCES, 2002

COUNTY	ORIGINAL	MINED	REMAINING
Butler	413.69	30.20	353.29
Daviess	1,330.32	62.26	1,205.80
Henderson	6,852.78	70.32	6,712.14
Hopkins	8,814.80	761.98	7,290.84
McLean	3,576.41	19.73	3,536.95
Muhlenberg	4,723.84	741.03	3,241.78
Ohio	1,824.55	264.13	1,296.29
Union	6,506.98	325.10	5,856.78
Webster	6,322.95	314.71	5,693.53
Other*	623.08	25.44	572.20
WKY Total	40,989.40	2,614.90	35,759.60

2000 MINING TYPE ESTIMATES

MINE TYPE	NO. OF MINES	PRODUCTION (million tons)
Surface	**162**	**50.5**
Surface Only*	--	12.6
Surface & Auger*	--	36.3
Auger Mining*	--	1.6
Underground	**246**	**80.2**
Continuous**	--	68.3
Conventional**	--	1.7
Longwall**	--	10
Other**	--	0.2
State Totals	408	130.7

ENVIRONMENT & NATURAL RESOURCES

Soils

Dr. Gary O'Dell

Much of Kentucky's agricultural prosperity can be attributed to the fertile and productive soils that are found in many regions of the state. Soil is far more than simply dirt. The late Dr. William G. Survant, much-beloved instructor of soil science at the University of Kentucky, always took pains to emphasize the difference. "Soil," he said, "is a complex substance that supports the growth of plants; dirt is what you sweep up off the floor."

To say that soils are complex is no exaggeration: the soil of a region is the result of many factors that interact over time and contribute to the specific characteristics of that soil. Nor should an existing soil be considered as an end product of these processes, because soils continue to develop and evolve. Soils are made up of both inorganic and organic components: mineral particles, decaying organic matter, living organisms, liquid solutions and various gases.

The inorganic substrate can be either residual; derived in place by the decomposition of bedrock through weathering, or transported from elsewhere by wind, water or ice. In Kentucky, most soils are residual, the product of weathered sedimentary rocks such as sandstone, shale, and limestone. Bottomlands along streams contain alluvial deposits

Source: Sid Webb

of sediments transported by water, and much of the western part of the state is blanketed with a layer of wind-blown dust – loess – that thins out toward the east.

The upper part of this mineral matter is transformed into soil by biological activity at the surface, through which organic matter is incorporated. The mineral component is classed according to particle size as gravel, sand, silt, and clay. The best soils are comprised of 10-20 percent clay with equal proportions of silt and sand, which provides a soil texture that allows both good drainage and nutrient availability. Soils with high clay content are poorly drained, and those with a high sand content tend to be relatively infertile.

The soils of Kentucky are mainly of three broad groups, inceptisols, ultisols, and alfisols. Inceptisols are immature gray-brown soils associated with young geomorphic surfaces, steep slopes, and resistant parent rock, and occur mainly in the Eastern Coal Field, the Outer Bluegrass and the Western Coal Field.

Ultisols are mature soils, with little humus and a subsurface accumulation of clay. These soils, which occur in the Eastern Coal Field and eastern Mississippian Plateau regions, have a high content of iron and aluminum, which causes their acidic nature and yellow to reddish color. Ultisols tend to be deep, and are generally of low fertility, although they can be quite productive with the addition of lime and fertilizers.

Alfisols are mature, well-developed soils with a subsurface clay horizon, and occur in the Bluegrass, western section of the Mississippian Plateau, and Mississippian Embayment regions. The alfisols are among the most productive in Kentucky, and tend to a more basic pH since they are derived from limestone. These soils are light in color and fertile, with a well-balanced and generous availability of nutrients. The high calcium and phosphate content of the soils of the Inner Bluegrass is one important reason that the thoroughbred industry has flourished in this area, for these nutrients tend to develop strong-boned horses.

ENVIRONMENT & NATURAL RESOURCES

Forests & Plant Life

Zachary J. Bortolot

Forests are very important to Kentucky. Kentucky has 12.7 million acres of forested land, which covers 50 percent of the state's land area. Although 92 percent of the forested land is privately owned, there is also an extensive amount of publicly owned forest land, including 628,000 acres of National Forest land. In addition to the wildlife and recreational benefits of the forest, Kentucky's forest-related industries employ 30,000 Kentuckians and generate $2 billion of revenue each year.

FOREST HISTORY

During the height of the last ice age 18,000 years ago, the forests of Kentucky were much different than they are now. In place of Kentucky's primarily broadleaf forests was a coniferous boreal forest similar to the forests found in northern Canada today. This forest was well adapted to the brutally cold climate that existed at that time. The boreal forest lasted until about 11,500 years ago, at which point the climate began to warm up and forests similar to Kentucky's modern forests began to appear. This transition was complete by about 10,000 years ago. Between 10,000 years ago and the arrival of large numbers of settlers of European descent, the region was occupied by several groups of Native Americans. The level of impact these groups had on Kentucky's forests varied quite a bit from one Native American group to another. Groups with a hunting and gathering-based culture had a minimal impact on the forests, whereas groups with extensive settlements and agricultural production had much more of an impact. Examples of these impacts include a reduction in forest land as a result of harvesting for fuel and construction and agriculture-related burning.

Large numbers of settlers of European descent arrived in Kentucky about 200 years ago. With this new settlement came the widespread clearing of land for raising crops and livestock, building factories and mining. By 1900, the amount of forested land in Kentucky had been reduced from 23.1 million acres before settlement began to 10.0 million acres. Since 1900 there has been a slow increase in the amount of forested land, and currently there are 12.7 million acres of forest land. This increase is primarily due to the abandonment of poor quality farmland. Researchers predict that in the future, urban development will again reduce the amount of forested land in Kentucky. They predict that by 2020, 1.3 percent of the forested land will have been converted to other uses and by 2040, 3.4 percent will have been converted. Most of the forests found in Kentucky today are secondary growth forests of relatively recent origin.

Besides clearing the land, European settlers also changed the forests through the introduction of disease. One of the most important was the chestnut blight which affects the American chestnut tree. Prior to the introduction of the blight, American chestnut was one of the most common trees in Kentucky. The American chestnut tree was prized for its excellent timber and delicious nuts and was an important species for wildlife due to its reliable production of large quantities of food. The chestnut blight was accidentally brought to North America from Asia in 1904 by the Bronx Zoo in New York City. The disease spread to Kentucky in the 1930s and killed nearly all mature chestnut trees. Luckily other tree species have filled in the gaps left vacant by the disappearance of the American chestnut, but these trees are often not as valuable commercially or to wildlife.

FOREST REGIONS

There are a number of ways in which the forests of Kentucky can be divided. One of the most popular is the system developed by Bailey for the U.S. Forest Service. Bailey divides Kentucky's forests into four ecosystem provinces: the Central Appalachian Broadleaf Forest - Coniferous Forest - Meadow Province (CABF), the Eastern Broadleaf (Oceanic) Province (EBOP), the Eastern Broadleaf (Continental) Province (EBCP), and the Lower Mississippi Riverine Forest Province (LMRF). The boundaries of these ecosystem provinces are shown in the map.

The CABF is found in southeastern Kentucky, a region that contains the hilliest terrain in the state. These forests are greatly affected by the variability in elevation, and if you were to walk from a valley to the top of a hill, you would see large changes in the forest species present. In the bottom of the valley you would likely find a forest consisting of oaks and pines. As you walk up the mountain, the pines would gradually become less common, and you would find mostly oaks. This oak forest would then give way to a maple, beech and birch forest, and finally near the top of the hill, you would find spruce and fir.

As you move towards the north and west, the terrain becomes increasingly flat, and the climate becomes drier. This change in topography and precipitation results in gradual changes in species composition as one moves west to the EBOP and then the EBCP. As you move west, oaks and hickories become less dominant, and there are fewer maple, beech, and birch forests. Many of the trees found in the western part of the state are species that thrive in dry conditions. At the same time, pines become more common, and you start seeing more elm, ash and cottonwood.

In the low lying areas near the Mississippi, one encounters the LMRF. Although this forest has been greatly affected by human activity, this province still contains a much different mixture of trees that those found in the rest of the state. Oaks are much less prevalent in the LMRF than in areas to the east, and in their place are large numbers of elm, ash and cottonwoods. Maple, beech and birch are also much more common here than in the rest of the state, and there are large numbers of vines in the forest.

Non-Forest Vegetation
Christine E. McMichael

OVERVIEW

In addition to forests, which comprise the major vegetation community type in Kentucky, there are a number of other important plant communities that deserve mention – namely wetland and grass-dominated communities. Unfortunately, these communities occupy an ever-shrinking portion of Kentucky's landscape as our population grows and our urban areas continue to expand into natural areas.

WETLAND COMMUNITIES
Forested Wetlands

There are two major types of forested wetlands in Kentucky; swamp forests and floodplain forests. Swamp forests generally occupy areas that are either permanently or frequently covered with standing water; they are also associated with high water tables, sinkholes and depressions. These forested wetlands are found throughout Kentucky, but are most common in the western part of the state where bald cypress and water tupelo thrive in areas with deep standing water. Oak, sycamore, black gum and red maple species dominate swamp forests in central and eastern Kentucky where sinkholes provide suitable watery habitat. Localized depressions occurring within the eastern part of the state may contain swamp forest dominated by red maple, black gum, tulip tree and white oak. Floodplain forests are found along the banks of major waterways throughout the state, as well as in the adjacent floodplain areas, particularly in western and central Kentucky. Hardy trees such as black willow and sycamore are common canopy species in stream-bank communities, while a variety of vines and herbs thrive in the understory. Typically, there is a greater diversity of tree species associated with forested wetland communities in floodplain areas. In addition to containing species having statewide distributions such as American elm, red maple, black gum and green ash, floodplain forests also include species with more localized distributions – e.g., American beech in the Appalachians.

NON FORESTED WETLANDS

Nonforested wetland communities can be found across the state, but are most common in central and western lowland areas that are fairly flat, generally (but not always) submerged in water and dominated by herbaceous and shrub vegetation. There are a number of nonforested wetland community types including those associated with standing water (ponds, lakes, reservoirs) or running water (streams and rivers), as well as those dominated by emergent vegetation (marshes and wet meadows) or shrubs. Some of the plants commonly found in standing water communities include the mosquito fern, bladderwort, water lily and alligator weed; rushes and sedges typify running water communities. Cattails, irises and cardinal-flowers may be found in emergent wetland communities, while buttonbush, pawpaw, willow, false indigo and highbush blueberry are common in shrub dominated wetlands.

Despite the range of important "services" they provide (e.g., flood control, water supply, fisheries and wildlife habitat), most wetland communities in Kentucky have been destroyed by, or are currently threatened by, ongoing human activities including agriculture and urban expansion.

GRASS-DOMINATED COMMUNITIES

It is thought that prairie grasses began extending their range into Kentucky 4,000 years ago, but it is unclear whether their current distribution throughout the state is a relic of the last glacial retreat or a more recent result of the agricultural-related burning practices of Native American peoples. Today, grass-dominated communities are most common in the western and central areas of the state. The two major grassland regions in Kentucky include the Big Barrens in west central Kentucky and the hill prairies of central Kentucky. The Big Barrens region occupies flat to steep hilly terrain in the Shawnee Hills and is dominated by perennial grasses and herbs, with occasional shrubs and small trees. The rolling hill prairies of the Knobs and Bluegrass regions are thought to be remnants of tallgrass prairie communities. While little bluestem grass dominates these communities, other grasses are commonly found throughout these areas including big bluestem grass, gama grass and prairie cord grass. Flowering plants found here include hairy sunflower, blazing stars, coneflowers and lobelia; common shrubs and small trees include red maple, sassafras, persimmon and mockernut hickory. Altogether, these grass-dominated communities cover a fairly small area within Kentucky, however they contain some of the state's rarest plants including Short's goldenrod, Eggert's sunflower, blue wild indigo, buffalo clover and Carolina larkspur.

y'know what?

The U.S. Forest Service estimates that there are 6.7 billion trees in Kentucky. That's 1,700 trees for each person in Kentucky.

The most common tree in Kentucky is the red maple. There are 803 million of them.

Cumberland County has the most trees per person: 13,330. Fayette County has the fewest, "only" seven trees per person.

Kentucky's state tree is the yellow poplar, also known as the tulip poplar or tulip tree.

The largest tree in Kentucky is a 168-foot tall yellow poplar in McCreary County.

KENTUCKY'S FEDERAL THREATENED & ENDANGERED SPECIES

COMMON NAME	SCIENTIFIC NAME	FEDERAL STATUS
Crustaceans		
Mammoth Cave Shrimp	Palaemonias ganteri	Endangered
Mussels		
Catspaw	Epioblasma obliquata obliquata	Endangered
Clubshell	Pleurobema clava	Endangered
Cumberland Bean Mussel	Villosa trabalis	Endangered
Cumberland Elktoe *	Alasmidonta Atropurpurea	Endangered
Cumberlandian Combshell *	Epioblasma Brevidens	Endangered
Fanshell	Cyprogenia stegaria	Endangered
Fat Pocketbook	Potamilus capax	Endangered
Little-wing Pearlymussel	Pegias fabula	Endangered
Northern Riffleshell	Epioblasma tarulosa rangiana	Endangered
Orange-foot Pimpleback	Plethobasus cooperianus	Endangered
Oyster Mussel *	Epioblasma Capsaeformis	Endangered
Pink Mucket	Lampsilis abrupta	Endangered
Ring Pink	Obovaria retusa	Endangered
Rough Pigtoe	Pleurobema plenum	Endangered
Fish		
Blackside Dace	Phoxinus cumberlandensis	Threatened
Duskytail Darter *	Etheostoma Percnurum	Endangered
Palezone Shiner	Notropis sp.	Endangered
Pallid Sturgeon	Scaphirhynchus albus	Endangered
Relict Darter *	Etheostoma Chienense	Endangered
Birds		
Bald Eagle	Haliaeetus leucocephalus	Endangered
Interior Least Tern	Sterna antillarum athalassos	Endangered
Paregrine Falcon *	Falco Peregrinus	Endangered
Red-cockaded Woodpecker	Picoides borealis	Endangered
Mammals		
Gray Myotis (bat)	Myotis grisescens	Endangered
Indiana Myotis (bat)	Myotis sodalis	Endangered
Virginia Big-eared Bat	Plecotus townsendii virginianus	Endangered
Insects		
American Burying Beetle	Nicrophorus americanus	Endangered
Plants		
Chaffseed	Schwalbea americana	Endangered
Cumberland Rosemary	Conradina verticillata	Threatened
Cumberland Sandwort	Minvartia cumberlandensis	Endangered
Price's Potato-bean	Apios priceana	Threatened
Running Buffalo Clover	Trifolium stoloniferum	Endangered
Short's Goldenrod	Solidago shortii	Endangered
Virginia Spiraea	Spiraea virginiana	Threatened
White-haired Goldenrod	Solidago albopilosa	Threatened

* Included in some Federal listings
Source: Kentucky State Nature Preserves Commission

ENVIRONMENT & NATURAL RESOURCES
Wildlife Refuges

CLARKS RIVER NATIONAL WILDLIFE REFUGE

Clarks River National Wildlife Refuge is a beautiful bottomland hardwood forest lying along the East Fork of the Clarks River and is a seasonal home to over 250 different species of migratory birds. The refuge is located in the western Kentucky counties of Marshall, McCracken and Graves, between Paducah and Benton. The bottomlands are dominated with overcup oaks, bald cypress, and tupelo gum, and the slightly higher, better drained areas, are covered with willow oak, swamp chestnut oak, red oak, sweet gum, sycamore, ash and elm.

Clarks River National Wildlife Refuge is the only National Wildlife Refuge located solely within the State of Kentucky. It is located in close proximity to the National Recreational Area Land Between the Lakes and a number of state Wildlife Management Areas offering a multitude of outdoor activities.

The most significant resource values of this area are the wetland habitat complexes formed by the river, creeks, beaver ponds, and natural ponding.

This natural wetland ecosystem is relatively intact and has high wildlife habitat values, particularly for migratory birds and other species representative of bottomland hardwood systems. The hardwood dominated forests are used as breeding, wintering and migration habitat by many species of neotropical migratory birds.

The refuge provides habitat for a natural diversity of wildlife associated with the Clarks River floodplain and includes: wintering habitat for migratory waterfowl, habitat for nongame migratory birds and opportunities for wildlife dependent recreation.

The refuge offers the public opportunities for hunting and fishing (special regulations do apply), wildlife observation and photography and hiking.

For more information, call (270) 527-5770 or http:// southeast.fws.gov/clarksriver.

THE CENTRAL KENTUCKY WILDLIFE REFUGE

The Central Kentucky Wildlife Refuge is a 500-acre preserve, located 13 miles from Danville in the Parksville (Boyle County) knob land and bordering a stretch of the beautiful North Rolling Fork. The refuge is open to all as a protected area for the enjoyment and study of nature in its many fascinating forms. It is set aside as a permanent sanctuary for plant and animal forms native to Central Kentucky, to be enjoyed by future generations. The refuge depends upon donations and volunteer labor to operate; there is no paid staff.

The bird blind near the caretaker's home provides close-up views of feeding birds for study and photography. Birds include Purple Finches and House Finches, Evening Grosbeaks, Car-

Source: Kentucky Department of Fish & Wildlife

dinals, Towhees, Carolina Chickadees, Flickers and Nuthatches, just to name a few.

Hundreds of wildflowers grow and many animals such as Deer, Foxes, Grey and Fox Squirrels, Flying Squirrels and more. The refuge has five main trails rated easy to strenuous.

For information, call 800-755-0076.

WOLF RUN WILDLIFE REFUGE & EDUCATIONAL FACILITY

Wolf Run is a non-profit wildlife refuge in Central Kentucky. State and federally licensed, this refuge houses, heals and cares for abused, abandoned and injured wild and exotic animals. A 501(c)(3) non-profit organization, there is no paid staff and all profit is used 100 percent in the care of the animals. The refuge houses everything from opossums to lions, and all in between. The refuge, located in Jessamine Co., is near Camp Nelson National Cemetery.

For more information, call (859) 887-2256.

ENVIRONMENT & NATURAL RESOURCES
Wildlife Management Areas

Most of the public wildlife areas listed in this guide are owned by various agencies of the state and federal government. Many areas were purchased with dollars from hunting and fishing license sales. Funding from the same sources pay for wildlife management programs on more than 70 percent of these areas. Kentucky's public-use lands total 1,602,978 acres, or 6.3 percent of the state.

Wildlife management practices on these areas provide food, cover and water for a wide variety of species. Since wild creatures are more active at dawn and dusk, these are the best times to watch wildlife. The widest variety of species can be seen during spring and fall migrations.

PURCHASE REGION

Reelfoot Lake National Wildlife Refuge (2,500 acres): Fulton Co. (731) 538-2481

Obion Creek WMA (3,521 acres): Hickman, Fulton, Carlisle Cos. (270) 753-6913

Meadwestvaco WMA (3,600 acres): Hickman, Carlisle Cos. (270) 753-6913

Winford WMA (237 acres): Carlisle Co.

Boatwright WMA (6,975 acres): 9 units in Ballard, Carlisle Cos., Peal Unit (1,724 acres) (270) 224-2244

Ballard Hunting Unit (400 acres): Ballard Co., 4 mi. S. of Oscar off KY 1105 on Salle Crice Rd. Area is not part of Ballard WMA. No roads or trails within area. (270) 224-2244

Big South Fork National River and Recreation Area

Ballard WMA (8,473 acres): Ballard Co. (270) 224-2244

West Kentucky WMA (6,463 acres): McCracken Co. (270) 488-3233

Ohio River Islands WMA (1,375 acres): Livingston Co. (270) 753-6913

Kaler Bottoms WMA (1,930 acres): Graves Co.

Clarks River National Wildlife Refuge (5,000 acres): Marshall Co. (270) 527-5770

Kentucky Lake WMA (3,500 acres): Calloway, Marshall, Lyon Cos.

Beechy Creek WMA (122 acres): Calloway Co.

Land Between the Lakes National Recreational Area (107,000 acres): Trigg, Lyon Cos., between Kentucky and Barkley lakes. (270) 924-2065

Lake Barkley WMA (5,429 acres): Trigg, Lyon, Livingston Cos.

Fort Campbell Military Reservation (85,000 acres): Christian, Trigg Cos. (270) 798-2175

Pennyrile State Forest (17,000 acres): Christian Co.

Tradewater WMA (724 acres): Hopkins-Christian County line, shares boundary with Pennyrile Forest

Jones-Keeney WMA (2,250 acres): Caldwell Co.

GREEN RIVER REGION

White City WMA (5,472 acres): Hopkins Co. (270) 273-3569 or 3568

Lee K. Nelson WMA (70 acres): Webster Co. Gift to Ky. Dept. Fish and Wildlife Resources from former wildlife biologist Lee K. Nelson

Higginson-Henry WMA (5,424 acres): Union Co. (270) 389-3580

Sloughs WMA (10,481 acres): 6 units in Henderson, Union Cos. (270) 827-2673

Daviess Demonstration Area (72 acres): Daviess Co., (270) 273-3569 or 3568

L. B. Davison WMA (150 acres): Ohio Co.

Peabody WMA (60,000 acres): Ohio, Muhlenberg Cos.

Yellowbank WMA (6,000 acres in 4 tracts): Breckinridge Co. (270) 547-6856

Rough River Lake WMA (3,425 land acres at summer pool): Portions of lake shoreline, Breckinridge, Grayson Cos. (270) 746-7130

Nolin River Lake WMA (5,210 land acres at summer pool): Portion of lake shoreline, Grayson, Edmonson, Hart Cos. (270) 746-7130

Barren River Lake WMA (10,100 land acres at summer pool): Barren, Allen Cos. (270) 646-5167

BLUEGRASS REGION

Fort Knox Military Reservation (109,068 acres): Hardin, Bullitt, Meade Cos. (502) 624-2712

John C. Williams WMA (384 acres): Nelson Co. (502) 477-9024

Taylorsville Lake WMA (10,571 acres): Spencer, Anderson, Nelson Cos. (502) 477-9024

Central Kentucky WMA (1,847 acres): Madison Co. (859) 986-4130

Breaks Interstate National Park
Source: Sid Webb

Blue Grass Army Depot (14,596 acres): Madison Co. (859) 625-6420

Dr. James C. Salato Wildlife Education Center (132 acres): Franklin Co. (800) 858-1549, M-F, 7:30 a.m.-5:30 p.m. Eastern Time

T. N. Sullivan WMA (155 acres): Franklin Co. (502) 535-6335

John A. Kleber WMA (2,605 acres): Owen, Franklin Cos. (502) 535-6335

Dr. James R. Rich WMA (1,567 acres): Owen Co. (502) 535-6335

Kentucky River WMA (1,604 acres): Henry, Owen Cos., (502) 535-6335

Twin Eagle WMA (166 acres): Owen Co. (502) 535-6335

Curtis Gates Lloyd WMA (1,179 acres): Grant Co. (859) 428-2262

Mullins WMA (266 acres): Kenton Co. (859) 428-2262

Dr. Norman And Martha Adair WMA (631 acres): Boone Co. (859) 428-2262

NORTHEAST REGION

Claude Cummins Property (100 acres): Mason Co. (606) 564-6706

Ohio River Islands National Wildlife Refuge (1,450 acres in 12 islands, 2 islands in Ky.) (304) 422-0752

Chain Rock at Pine Mountain Park
Source: Kentucky Department of Tourism

Lewis County WMA (1,161 acres): Lewis Co. (606) 686-3312.

Daniel Boone National Forest (670,000 acres; 141,457 acres in the Northeast Region including Pioneer Weapons WMA).

Fleming WMA (2,070 acres): Fleming Co. (859) 289-2564.

Clay WMA (5,790 acres): Nicholas and Fleming Cos. (859) 289-2564

Pioneer Weapons WMA (7,610 acres): Bath, Menifee Cos. (606) 745-3100

Tygarts State Forest (800 acres): Carter Co.

Grayson Lake WMA (10,598 acres in land at summer pool): Carter, Elliott Cos. (606) 474-6856.

Yatesville Lake WMA (17,370 acres in land at summer pool): Lawrence Co. (606) 686-3312)

Paintsville Lake WMA (12,103 acres in land at summer pool): Johnson, Morgan Cos. (606) 297-6312

Dewey Lake WMA (9,870 acres in land at summer pool): Floyd Co. (606) 789-4521

Fishtrap Lake WMA (10,691 acres in lake at summer pool): Pike Co.

George Washington-Jefferson National Forest (961 acres; 116 acres are in Pike Co. The rest lies in the Southeast Region)

SOUTHEAST REGION

George Washington-Jefferson National Forest (961 acres): Pike Co. 845 acres and Letcher Co. 116 acres

Hensley-Pine Mountain WMA (6,000 acres): Letcher Co.

Carr Creek Lake WMA (2,849 acres): Knott Co. (606) 642-3308

Addington Enterprises WMA (16,000 acres): Breathitt, Knott, Perry Cos. (606) 378-3474

Buckhorn Lake WMA (3,480 acres): Lake shoreline in Perry Co. (606) 398-7154

Redbird WMA (25,529 acres): Leslie and Clay Cos.

Beech Creek WMA (1,260 acres): Clay Co.

Kentenia State Forest (3,624 acres): Harlan Co.

Cranks Creek WMA (2,167 acres): Harlan Co.

Martins Fork Lake WMA (1,394 acres): Harlan Co.

Begley WMA (20,000 acres): Bell, Harlan and Leslie Cos.

Shillalah Creek WMA (2,640 acres): Bell and Harlan Cos.

Kentucky Ridge Forest WMA (3,600 acres): Bell Co.

Kentucky Ridge State Forest (11,363 acres): Bell Co.

Mill Creek WMA (13,558 acres): Jackson Co.

Daniel Boone National Forest (670,000 acres): From Tenn. line in McCreary Co. N. to Fleming and Lewis Cos.

Cane Creek WMA (6,672 acres): Laurel Co.

Beaver Creek WMA (17, 347 acres): McCreary and Pulaski Cos.

Big South Fork National River and Recreation Area (55,000 acres): McCreary Co. Visitor Center, (606) 376-5073

Lake Cumberland WMA (39,484 acres in land at summer pool): Lake shoreline in Pulaski, Russell, Wayne, Clinton Cos. (606) 376-8083

Dale Hollow Lake WMA (3,130 acres): Lake shoreline in Cumberland, Clinton Cos. and Dale Hollow State Resort Park

Mud Camp Creek WMA (600 acres): Cumberland Co.

R. F. Tarter WMA (1,300 acres): Adair, Russell Cos.

Dennis-Gray WMA (70 acres): Adair Co.

Green River Lake WMA (20,500 acres): Taylor, Adair Cos. (270) 465-5039

Source: Kentucky Department of Fish and Wildlife Resources, (800) 858-1549

Climate & Seasons

Dr. Stuart Foster

Location plays a vital role in determining the distinct seasonal variations in Kentucky's climate. Its inland location on the North American continent contributes to seasonal swings in average temperature, while its position relative to the Gulf of Mexico contributes to ample precipitation that is well distributed throughout the year. Upper-level westerly winds, which steer storm systems across North America, also contribute to the variability of Kentucky's weather.

Average temperature has varied over the past century. While concerns about the quality of temperature observations over time raise questions about the assessment of temperature trends, nearly all of Kentucky's high temperature records were achieved in the early 1900s. The recent rise in average temperature since the late 1980s is more evident in the average winter temperatures than in the average summer temperatures, which remain unremarkable in comparison with historical observations. Currently, the mean annual temperature in Kentucky ranges from 53 F in the northeast to 59 F in the southwest.

Precipitation is generally abundant across Kentucky. Average annual precipitation increases from 42 inches in the north to 52 inches in the south. A strong precipitation gradient during the winter season is less evident over the summer months. After a relatively dry period through the mid-1900s, the average annual precipitation across Kentucky has increased by an average of nearly three inches over the past three decades.

SPRING

Spring is an active weather season in Kentucky. While the warm, sunny days of spring are always welcome, springtime weather can be very changeable. Temperatures reaching above 80 F in early spring can be followed by temperatures dipping to near 20 F. The clash between cold, dry air masses from the north and warm, moist air masses from the south brings the risk of severe weather in the form of thunderstorms producing damaging winds, hail and tornadoes.

Average temperatures rise significantly throughout spring. Mid-spring daily high temperatures

No Trespassing
Source: Sid Webb

average in the low to mid 70s across Kentucky with higher values to the south and west. In extreme cases, high temperatures above 90 F have been recorded as early as March, while subfreezing temperatures have been recorded up until the first of June. The average date of the last spring freeze ranges from early April in the southwest to early

May in the northeast.

While precipitation is distributed rather evenly throughout the year, Kentucky's wettest months on average occur during spring. May averaged more than 5 inches of rain across the state, with slightly higher amounts in the south and central portions of Kentucky. Though early spring snowstorms are not common, they can bring significant accumulations of heavy, wet snow.

SUMMER

Summer days in Kentucky are typically quite warm. Weather prognosticators often bring out the three H's, forecasting "hazy, hot and humid, with the chance of an isolated, afternoon thunderstorm." As the upper level winds weaken and migrate further north during the summer months, the passage of frontal systems becomes less frequent. Kentucky's summer weather is thus less changeable than during other seasons, and weather patterns often persist for several days or even weeks. When summertime frontal systems do move through Kentucky, cool and dry air from Canada brings pleasant conditions that may persist for a few days.

The average daily high temperature for July increases from about 86 F in the east to 90 F in the west. High temperatures exceed 90 F for an average of 20 days per year in the north and east and 40 or more days in the south and west. Temperatures occasionally exceed 100 F. Nighttime low temperatures average near 63 F in the east to 68 F in the west, but during a heat wave they may not dip below the 70s.

Summertime precipitation is produced largely from thunderstorms, though severe weather is less frequent than during spring. Moist, tropical air from the Gulf of Mexico helps to fuel thunderstorms and normally contributes sufficient rains to support crops and pastureland. Still it is not uncommon for a location to go for a period of two weeks without measurable precipitation at some point during the summer.

FALL

Fall, like spring, is a transitional season. Weather is influenced by a reduced flow of moist air from the south and by the more frequent passage of weak frontal systems bringing cool, dry air from the north. Together, these contribute to an increased frequency of warm, sunny days and cool, clear nights. While severe weather is possible during the fall, it is much less common than during spring. Instead, fair weather and colorful fall foliage make this a favorite time of year for many people.

Average temperatures decline steadily throughout fall. High temperatures drop from the mid to upper 70s in early fall to the mid to upper 40s by the time winter arrives. As during spring, weather patterns can be quite variable. Freezing temperatures have been recorded as early as September, while temperatures well into the 90s have been observed even in October. The average date of the first fall freeze ranges from early October in the northeast to late October in the southwest, resulting in an average growing season of 165 to 200 days.

Kentucky's driest season is fall. Thunderstorms are much less frequent than during summer, and the passage of frontal systems rarely brings heavy rain during early fall. October is normally the driest month of the year, averaging about 3.5 inches of rain in the west and less than 3 inches in the east. The remnants of occasional tropical storms add significantly to Kentucky's precipitation total during the fall. Average precipitation increases through November and into December, often providing relief from any dry spells that may have persisted through early fall.

WINTER

Winters in Kentucky are typically mild. The polar jet stream is strong and plays a vital role in Kentucky's winter weather, bringing an increased frequency of cloudy days. When it moves north of Kentucky, the jet stream can bring spring-like temperatures in the midst of winter. When it dips to the south, it can usher in arctic air that sends the mercury plummeting. Further, it can steer storm systems bringing cold, steady rains or heavy snows across Kentucky.

The average daily high temperature for January ranges from 38 F in extreme northern Kentucky to 44 F along the Kentucky-Tennessee border. Daily low temperatures average near 20 F in the north and 25 F in the south and southwest. When polar air masses visit Kentucky, their stay is usually short. Subzero temperatures occur an average of five days in the north and only two days in the south. During many winters, temperatures never drop below zero.

Most winter precipitation is in the form of rain. Seasonal snowfall totals average from less than 10 inches in the south to more than 20 inches in the north. But totals can vary greatly from year to year. Some winters, particularly in the south, may pass without any significant accumulation. Meanwhile, seasonal accumulations of more than 2 or 3 feet occur periodically, typically reflecting a small number of heavy snow events. Snow seldom covers the ground for more than a week at a time in the south or more than two weeks in the north.

CLIMATE & SEASONS

Weather Highlights
2003-2005

Dr. Stuart Foster

Jan 2003—28.7 F / 1.84 inches (average statewide temperature / precipitation)

January was cold and dry, but most precipitation was in the form of snow. The 16th brought 3 to 4 inches of snow over areas of the west, and a storm on the 16th and 17th left 4 to 8 inches in the southeast. Light snow from the west to the north central regions on the 22th was followed by sub-zero temperatures in some areas. Snow accumulated up to 3 inches in the southwest on the 26th.

Feb 2003—33.7 F / 6.73 inches (9th wettest)

February was cold and wet with several stormy periods. Two accumulating snows occurred in the west during the first 10 days. A winter storm on the 15th and 16th left 1 to 2 inches of sleet and ice in a band from the central to the northeastern regions. The cities of Frankfort and Lexington received extensive damage. Heavy rains bringing 4 to 6 inches to some areas resulted in widespread flooding across much of the state during the second half of the month. A rare February tornado touched down in Breathitt County on the 22nd, resulting in two deaths.

Mar 2003—49.0 F / 2.05 inches

March was warm and dry with relatively little active weather. Thunderstorms producing hail were widespread across the central and eastern regions on the 19th. A late season snowstorm brought 4 inches to parts of Harlan County.

Apr 2003—57.9 F / 5.47 inches

April was warm and wet. Severe thunderstorms

Source: Kentucky Department of Libraries

moved across the central and eastern regions on the 4th and 5th. Heavy rains in the southeast contributed to flooding on the Cumberland River between the 9th and 14th. Severe thunderstorms on the 20th dropped nearly 4 inches of hail in Hart County, and a weak tornado touched down in Christian and Muhlenberg counties. Another weak tornado touched down in Marshall County on the 25th. Thunderstorms on the 29th led to minor flooding in the west.

May 2003—64.3 F / 6.40 inches

May was wet with near normal temperatures. It was an active weather month. Severe storms with damaging winds, hail and tornadoes were reported on several days over the first half of May. Tornadoes in the west on the 4th and again on the 6th caused widespread but minor damage. A tornado touched down in Pulaski County on the 5th. A tornado moved through Mason and Lewis Counties on the 10th. Tornadoes touched down in several counties on the 11th, with the greatest damage in Mercer and Hardin counties. One death was reported in Mercer County. Flash flooding was also widespread during this period, though damage was not extensive.

Jun 2003—69.0 F / 6.04 inches

June was cool and wet. A period of active weather between the 11th and 18th produced widespread thunderstorms, heavy rain, hail and flash flooding. A weak tornado touched down in Marshall County on the 11th and another in Bell County on the 18th. Flash flooding on the 16th and 17th was widespread in the east with the greatest damage reported in southern Pike County and Floyd County.

Jul 2003—75.4 F / 4.65 inches

July was near normal in both temperature and precipitation. Thunderstorms were widespread between the 9th and 13th, from the 21st to the 23rd and restricted to the west on the 28th. Some damage from wind, hail and lightning were reported. Only minor flash flooding occurred

Aug 2003—76.0 F / 4.94 inches

August was slightly warmer and wetter than normal. Severe thunderstorms were widespread on the 4th causing damage at Barren River Lake. Intense lightning caused power outages in Somerset on the 11th, and storms led to minor flash flooding in the east. Thunderstorms developed over a wider area on the 22nd, and a flash flood claimed two lives and damaged numerous homes in Franklin County.

Sep 2003—66.3 F / 5.66 inches (7th wettest)

Heavy rains from the end of August continued into the first week of September, resulting in minor flooding and flash flooding in parts of the central and eastern regions. The most extensive damage occurred in Breathitt County.

Oct 2003—56.7 F / 2.49 inches

October brought near normal temperatures and slightly below normal precipitation. Weather-wise, it was a quiet month. An early season frost occurred in the northeast on the morning of the 3rd.

Nov 2003—50.5 F / 5.60 inches (8th warmest)

November was warm and wet. Precipitation was distributed throughout the month. Thunderstorms brought high winds, heavy rains and localized flash flooding to the central and eastern regions on the 12th. High winds were reported on the 24th in the east. The first heavy snow of the season accumulated 5 inches on Black Mountain on the 29th.

Dec 2003—37.5 F / 3.30 inches

December temperatures were near normal, and precipitation was below normal. No severe weather was reported. Light snow covered the west beginning on the evening of the 13th. Snow accumulated up to 4 inches at higher elvations in the east between the 18th and 20th.

Jan 2004—33.2 F / 3.91 inches

January temperatures and precipitation were near normal. Minor flooding and flash flooding occurred across the central and eastern regions on the 2nd through the 4th, followed by minor river flooding in the southwest through midmonth. Heavy snow, with up to 7 inches in upland areas, occurred on the 9th in the east. Following an intrusion of arctic air, widespread freezing rain on the 25th caused power outages and traffic accidents. On the 26th, lightning strikes, including one at the Kentucky State Penitentiary at Eddyville, damaged buildings.

Feb 2004—36.9 F / 2.82 inches

February temperatures were near normal, and precipitation was slightly below normal. Thunder-snow was reported on the 5th in the west, where 1 to 3 inches of wet snow fell. Flash flooding occurred in the east on the 5th and 6th. Minor flooding along rivers in the central and western regions was reported during mid month. Dry weather in the west during the final three weeks led to widespread grass and brush fires by month's end.

Mar 2004—49.5 F / 4.28 inches

March was warm with near normal precipitation. Flash flooding was widespread in the east from the 5th through the 7th, resulting in two deaths. A 6-inch snowfall was reported in Bell County on the 9th. Thunderstorm winds on the 20th caused damage at locations in the central and eastern regions. Dry, windy weather contributed to a wildfire in the Land-Between-the-Lakes area on the 28th.

Apr 2004—55.9 F / 4.69 inches

April temperatures were near normal and precipitation was slightly above normal. A late season snow on the 13th brought 2 to 4 inches over areas from the Mayfield to Hopkinsville and north to Owensboro, causing limited power outages and numerous traffic accidents that resulted in four fatalities. Minor flash flooding was reported in the east on the 13th and 14th. Severe thunderstorms on the 30th caused minor wind damage and flash flooding in the west.

May 2004—69.2 F (6th warmest) / 8.31 inches (5th wettest)

May was very warm and very wet. Severe weather at month's end caused widespread damage. Tornadoes in Fayette and Henry counties on the 27th caused considerable damage, while weaker tornadoes touched down in Henderson and Pulaski counties. Severe weather was also widespread on the 30th. Tornadoes were reported on the 29th and 30th in the west and on the 31st in the east. Overall damage was minor. Thunderstorms dumped heavy rain causing widespread flooding and flash flooding in the east, resulting in millions of dollars in damage.

Jun 2004—72.3 F / 4.00 inches

June temperatures and precipitation were near normal. Severe weather continued into the first days of the month. Minor flooding along the Ohio River continued from late May through the first third of June. On the 12th, thunderstorms contributed to flash flooding in the northern and eastern regions. Damage was greatest in Fleming and Letcher counties.

Jul 2004—74.4 F / 5.67 inches

July temperatures were below normal, while precipitation was above normal. The dominant weather for the month came in the form of severe thunderstorms. On the 5th and 6th, storms brought very strong winds, causing extensive power outages, fallen trees, and damage to structures. One week later, on the 13th, another line of strong thunderstorms with damaging winds moved southeastward across the state. Damage and power outages were widespread over the central portion of the state.

Aug 2004—71.2 F (6th coolest) / 4.10 inches

August was cool with near normal precipitation. Severe thunderstorms with damaging winds and hail were widespread on the 4th. Otherwise, there were no widespread outbreaks of severe weather.

Sep 2004—68.8 F / 3.86 inches (1st wettest in east, 2nd driest in west)

September brought near normal temperatures, but it was a month of precipitation extremes. Many locations in central and western areas received barely a drop of rain the entire month. Meanwhile, the east was inundated by heavy rains brought by the remnants of Hurricane Frances, bringing 3 to 6 inches of rain on the 7th and 8th, and Hurricane Ivan, bringing similar totals on the 16th and 17th. These storms, during a normally dry time of year, caused minor flooding that was widespread in the eastern half of the state, and led to one death.

Oct 2004—59.9 F / 4.83 inches (8th wettest)

October was warm and wet. A weak tornado was reported on the 15th in Caldwell County. Thunderstorms bringing strong winds and heavy rain moved through on the 18th causing minor damage.

Nov 2004—50.4 F (9th warmest) / 5.83 inches

November was warm and wet. Still, there was very little active weather. Ashland reported some urban flooding at the result of heavy rains on the 4th.

Dec 2004—36.4 F / 4.60 inches

December was near average in temperature and precipitation. However, it will be marked for the historic winter storm on the 22nd and 23rd. A combination of snow, sleet and freezing rain moved northeastward across the western half of the state. Snow accumulated to record depths with 14 inches at Paducah to as much as 19 inches in Hancock County. Louisville received 9 inches, but Lexington received only a thin coating of ice. Farther south, ice and sleet accumulated more than 1 inch. Following the storm, low temperatures dropped below zero in many snow-covered areas.

Jan 2005—39.1 F / 4.68 inches

January was warm with slightly above normal precipitation. The first part of the month was very warm, and some areas remained above freezing from December 29th through January 13th. Heavy rains in early January, combined with runoff from melting snow, caused flooding on the Ohio River and tributaries. Floodwaters were the highest since 1997, but damage was minor. A winter storm on the 20th dropped up to 5 inches of snow in northern Kentucky near the Ohio River. Another storm on the 22nd left 3 to 6 inches in the east.

Feb 2005—40.6 F / 2.59 inches

February was warm with below normal precipitation. Two snowstorms in the east left significant accumulations. The first storm on the 10th left 6 inches on Black Mountain. The second storm on the 28th left 14 inches on Black Mountain.

Mar 2005—42.9 F / 3.95 inches

March was cool with slightly below normal precipitation. A weak tornado touched down in Spencer County on the 19th. Severe weather on the 27th caused wind damage near Kentucky Lake, and hail accumulated to 4 inches in Calloway County. Minor flooding was reported in the western and central regions near the end of the month.

WEATHER & CLIMATE

Temperature & Precipitation Records

Dr. Stuart Foster

KENTUCKY RECORD MAXIMUM DAILY TEMPERATURES

TEMPERATURE	YEAR	MONTH	DAY	LOCATION
83 F	1907	Jan	20	Loretto
86 F	1890	Feb	11	Princeton
94 F	1929	Mar	24	Hopkinsville
98 F	1925	Apr	24	Farmers
106 F	1896	May	10	Ashland
110 F	1936	Jun	29	St. John's Academy
114 F	1930	Jul	28	Greensburg
113 F	1930	Aug	5	St. John's Academy
110 F	1925	Sep	6	Beaver Dam
98 F	1953	Oct	1	Frankfort & Hopkinsville
90 F	1902	Nov	14	Pikeville
87 F	1982	Dec	3	Pikeville

KENTUCKY RECORD MINIMUM DAILY TEMPERATURES

TEMPERATURE	YEAR	MONTH	DAY	LOCATION
-37 F	1994	Jan	19	Shelbyville
-32 F	1951	Feb	2	Princeton
-14 F	1960	Mar	6	Bonnieville
10 F	1857	Apr	2	Millersburg
20 F	1966	May	10	Falmouth
29 F	1966	Jun	1	Cumberland
34 F	1988	Jul	1	Ashland
36 F	1946	Aug	31	Clermont
24 F	1928	Sep	26	Farmers
10 F	1962	Oct	27	Dewey Dam
-9 F	1929	Nov	30	Shelbyville
-24 F	1989	Dec	24	Farmers

KENTUCKY RECORD GREATEST DAILY PRECIPITATION

PRECIPITATION	YEAR	MONTH	DAY	LOCATION
8.52"	1966	Jan	2	Mayfield
6.20"	1949	Feb	14	Turkey Creek School
10.25"	1997	Mar	2	Madisonville
9.05"	1911	Apr	30	Edmonton
6.00"	1983	May	19	Elkton
10.40"	1960	Jun	28	Dunmor
8.44"	1965	Jul	24	Middlesboro
8.20"	1982	Aug	31	Gilbertsville Dam
8.20"	1982	Sep	2	Jamestown
5.60"	1910	Oct	6	Earlington
6.66"	1957	Nov	18	Mammoth Cave
6.16"	1917	Dec	7	Bowling Green

"Well, what about that?"

In January of 1937, rains began to fall throughout the Ohio River Valley, triggering what is known today as the "Great Flood of 1937." Total damage for Kentucky was $250 million, an incredible sum in 1937.

Kentucky State Climatology Center, http://kyclim.wku.edu

CLIMATE & SEASONS
Destructive Weather

Dr. Stuart Foster

Floods

Kentucky, with nearly 90,000 miles of waterways ranging from small mountain streams to the broad Ohio and Mississippi rivers, is quite prone to flooding. A distinction can be drawn between river floods that inundate broad flood plains and flash floods that sweep through narrow stream valleys with little or no advance warning. River flooding results from an extended period of heavy precipitation over a large region and it is most common during the winter and early spring when weather systems become stalled or recurring storm systems move over Kentucky one after another. The best-known flood affecting Kentucky dates to January of 1937. Flash flooding can be highly localized and is particularly troublesome in upland watersheds in the Appalachians of eastern Kentucky. It is more likely to be associated with intense and sometimes persistent thunderstorms that bring copious amounts of rain in a short period of time.

The list below is not comprehensive, but it highlights some of the most destructive and deadly floods in Kentucky history.

Accounts of Selected Kentucky Floods

1937 – January of 1937 brought hardship across Kentucky. Storm systems, one after another, trained along the nearly stationary boundary between air masses that stretched through the Ohio River Valley. More than 20 inches of rain fell

The Ashland flood of 1884
Source: Carl & Nellie Griffith

in areas of central Kentucky during the month, and totals of at least 15 inches were common throughout Kentucky and portions of neighboring states. The heaviest rains occurred from Jan. 17 to Jan. 23 and sent the Ohio River and its tributaries to levels that had never been seen. A final day of heavy rain on Jan. 24 sent floodwaters even higher. At the crest on Jan. 27, waters were 30 feet above flood stage in Louisville, and the river and its backwaters were as much as 20 to 25 miles wide. Towns all along the Ohio River were inundated. In Louisville alone, 175,000 people were evacuated to towns across Kentucky. Paducah was nearly deserted, as residents were forced to leave the city where floodwaters nearly 10 feet deep engulfed the downtown business district. Cities all along the Ohio River were left without drinking water, electricity and communication, and explosions started numerous fires. The flood exceeded previous devastating floods of 1883, 1884 and 1913, and no flood since has approached the magnitude of the 1937 event. Hundreds of people died in Kentucky as a result of the flood, and damage was estimated at $250 million.

1939 – On the night of July 4th and early morning of July 5th, intense, localized thunderstorms dropped torrents of rain in the hills of Rowan and Breathitt counties. A storm lasting three hours began at 9:30 p.m. in Rowan County and dumped anywhere from 4 to 10 inches of rain, according to unofficial gages. The storm left 25 people dead and destroyed 10,800 acres of crops, 5,000 chickens, 200 farm animals, 50 homes and 300 other farm buildings. Later that evening, a storm produced an even more deadly flash flood along Troublesome, Frozen, and Quicksand creeks in Breathitt County. The worst flooding was concentrated along Frozen Creek, where houses with unsuspecting families sleeping inside were swept into the floodwaters. Only the remnants of communities remained. A total of 51 people were found dead as the floodwaters receded.

1957 – Late January of 1957 saw heavy rains spread across eastern Kentucky and parts of Tennessee, Virginia, and West Virginia causing widespread flooding. From 4.5 to 9 inches of rain fell on already saturated soils in the headwaters of the Big Sandy, Kentucky and Cumberland rivers. Rapidly rising floodwaters forced thousands to leave their homes without time to collect belongings. Hazard was one of 13 towns and many smaller communities to suffer heavy damage. Aid was rushed to the area as food and drinking water were in short supply, and electric power was out. Washed out roads and bridges forced supplies to be brought in by helicopter. Damage in the town of Pineville was limited by a floodwall. But in numerous other eastern Kentucky towns, homes were washed away and business districts were under water. The flood claimed five lives, left nearly 8,000 homeless and caused $50 million damage. The magnitude of the flood exceeded previous floods in 1927 and 1937, and it was compared to the flood of 1862.

1977 – A storm system moving slowly northeastward brought 3 to 6 inches across southeastern Kentucky, with locally higher amounts reported up to 15 inches. Floodwaters swept through the Appalachian valleys from April 4 through April 7. Communities along the Upper Cumberland and Big Sandy rivers were hardest hit. The flood on the Upper Cumberland broke historical records. The floodwall and levee at Pineville was topped by floodwaters. Officials in Williamsburg, recognizing that their efforts would not save the town, moved documents from the courthouse as floodwaters threatened the building. Roads were blocked preventing people from trying to enter Harlan, Barbourville and Pineville. Communities along tributaries of the Big Sandy River, including Pikeville, Elkhorn City, Prestonsburg, South Williamson, Martin and Inez, also suffered extensive damage. In Pikeville, the hospital was surrounded by floodwaters, and patients had to be ferried by boat. Flooding was less extensive on the Kentucky and Licking rivers. Five deaths were reported, thousands were left homeless, and damage estimates reached as high as $175 million.

1997 – March ushered in heavy rains across Kentucky. Upper level winds brought a steady flow of moisture-laden air into the Ohio River Valley. Rain that began falling on the last day of February intensified as March arrived, bringing more than 7 inches of rain to Louisville and over 5 inches to Lexington in one day. By March 3, rainfall totals had reached from 6 to 12 inches over much of central and northern Kentucky. The Licking River, a stream that normally runs 4 feet deep through the town of Falmouth, rose to 52 feet, some 24 feet above flood stage, nearly destroying the town, as residents fled in disbelief. The death toll in Kentucky reached 21, and damage was estimated as high as $500 million.

Tornadoes

Severe thunderstorms producing dangerous lightning, damaging winds, large hail and tornadoes are most frequent during spring. These storms frequently form in warm, moist air in advance of an approaching cold front. They are more common in the afternoon and early evening hours but can occur at any time of day. The air-mass thunderstorms prevalent in midsummer are less likely to produce severe weather. But there are no certainties when it comes to severe weather. Thunderstorms producing hail and tornadoes have been reported in every month of the year in Kentucky, with an average of about 10 tornadoes per year.

Improved weather radar systems, better knowledge of the atmospheric conditions that lead to severe weather and the adoption of modern communication systems provide advance warning that helps to save lives. Many Kentuckians, however, will vividly recall the tornado outbreak of April 3, 1974, that brought devastation to communities scattered across the state with little or no warning of what was to come.

SIGNIFICANT TORNADOES

March 27, 1890

The myth that Louisville was protected from tornadoes was dispelled on the evening of March 27, 1890. Following a day when snow flurries swirled in the air, evening thunderstorms bore down on the city. Around 8 p.m., in the midst of vivid lightning display, a tornado touched down and ripped through residential and commercial districts before crossing the Ohio River into Indiana. The death toll in Louisville and environs reached 76, and 200 people were injured. Damage was estimated at more than $2 million, including tobacco warehouses, hotels and churches. On the same day, eight other tornadoes were also reported in western and southern Kentucky, killing another 44 people.

May 27, 1917

An outbreak of tornadoes stretched from Alabama to Kentucky and westward into Arkansas. Heavy thunderstorms blew through western Kentucky in the late afternoon bringing destruction. A tornado crossed from Tennessee into Kentucky killing 68 people. The greatest loss of life was in Fulton County, where 42 people were killed, but Hickman, Carlisle and Graves counties also suffered losses from the storm.

March 18, 1925

On the same day that the deadliest tornado in U.S. history cut a path through Missouri, Illinois and Indiana, four tornadoes struck Kentucky. The most deadly of these crossed from Tennessee into southeastern Allen County at about 5 p.m. and continued to move through Barren, Monroe and Metcalfe counties. Four deaths were reported near Scottsville in Allen County and six at Beaumont in Metcalfe County. Tornadoes in Jefferson and Oldham counties killed seven and injured 100. Near 6:30 p.m., another tornado passed through Marion, Washington, Mercer, Jessamine, Fayette and Bourbon counties, leaving two people dead and injuring 40.

May 9, 1933

On an evening when severe thunderstorms brought damaging winds and hail across Kentucky, a midnight tornado left a path of destruction through Monroe, Adair, Cumberland and Russell counties in southern Kentucky. The tornado destroyed about 60 houses in Tompkinsville and left 17 people dead. Significant damage was also reported near Russell Springs, but most of the damage was in rural areas, where an estimated 100 barns were destroyed. A total of 36 deaths were reported in Kentucky, with additional fatalities in Tennessee.

March 16, 1942

Tornadoes raked through the South and Midwest. In Kentucky, a tornado touched down in Muhlenberg County around 5:30 p.m. without warning, killing 11 people. The storm carved a path northeastward through Grayson, Hardin and Nelson counties, moving through Bardstown before dissipating. Fortunately, much of the path was through sparsely populated areas. A total of 24 deaths were reported, and 60 people were injured.

April 3, 1974

Kentucky was one of 13 states in the South and Midwest that were hit by a massive outbreak of 148 tornadoes. At least 26 tornadoes struck Kentucky alone, killing 77 people and injuring another 1,377. Damage estimates exceeded $110 million. The most devastating tornado packed winds estimated at 260 miles per hour and tore a path 500 yards wide through the small town of Brandenburg in Meade County shortly after 4 p.m., leaving 31 people dead. Louisville was also hit, leaving a path of damage that included the Kentucky State Fair Grounds, Cherokee Park and suburban residential areas. Tornadoes, many with little or no advance warning, carved through southern and central Kentucky, leaving behind death and destruction in Boyle, Clinton, Franklin, Hardin, Madison, Nelson, Simpson and Warren counties. Pulaski County was hit by three tornadoes that evening before the storm system moved out of Kentucky.

Droughts

Drought is commonly referred to as a "creeping" hazard. The onset of drought is difficult to identify, but when lawns have turned brown and crops withered in the field, the presence of a drought is easier recognized.

Definitions of drought abound. From a meteorological perspective, drought is defined as an extended period with deficit precipitation. Other definitions are based on observed impacts of drought. An agricultural drought reflects dry soil conditions that stunt the growth of crops and pasture. If the dry spell persists long enough, hydrological drought may become evident as water levels drop in reservoirs and streams and freshwater springs and groundwater wells cease to produce. In the case of severe droughts, water supplies of entire cities may be threatened.

Make no mistake: Drought is a recurrent feature of Kentucky's climate. Agricultural droughts can develop quickly during the spring and summer and can be localized in extent.

Kentucky's most intense and widespread drought of record occurred through the summer of 1930. If drought is thought of in terms of its impacts on water availability, then one may conclude that Kentucky's growing population and growing demand for water make the state more vulnerable to drought than in the past.

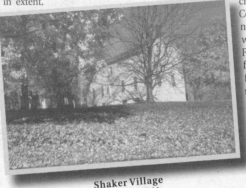

Shaker Village
Source: Sid Webb

about the change of temperature during the summer long, yet we have had nothing but suffocating hot and dry temperatures. Of course, if we got a tornado from the south and a blizzard from the north, all at the same time, the temperature might condescend to drop a few points, but at the present we will be skeptical about any chance until we really see it."

Precipitation remained below normal each month for the remainder of the year. The tobacco crop was worthless. Corn failed to pollinate, and cornstalks were cut for silage. Farmers, lacking feed and water, were forced to sell livestock for any price. Small streams were dry, and large ones had only pools of water in places. By winter, when water supplies are normally recharged, the shortage forced some municipalities to seek other sources of drinking water. Exceptionally dry weather through January left dirt roads dusty in some areas. It was not until late March that a return of more normal precipitation brought flow back to streams.

SELECTED KENTUCKY DROUGHTS

1930

In contrast to many droughts whose beginnings can be traced to a dry spell that emerges through the late fall and winter months, the onset of the drought in 1930 was sudden and harsh. Dry weather in March of 1930 was followed by hot, dry weather in April. Temperatures reached above 90 F before midmonth, and the ground became too dry for farmers to work. Many areas received less than 1 inch of rain during the month. Drought quickly became evident in the north and lower Green River region. The shortage of stock water became severe in upland areas. Then came the worst. July and August brought record heat, including an all-time high of 114 F on the 28th of July at Greensburg. Meanwhile, Bowling Green experienced 22 days with temperatures over 100 F from early July through early August, as day after day passed without significant precipitation. A newspaper writer from the Russellville News-Democrat summarized the mood:

"Various reports are received, some predicting thundershowers for today, tomorrow, or the next day. However, there have been so many reports

1952-1954

The early 1950s was an extended period of generally dry weather. The onset of drought was evident in western Kentucky with each passing day of June 1952, which proved the warmest on record. The town of Hicksville in Graves County did not record a drop of precipitation the entire month. Hot, dry weather dominated the weather pattern. The temperature reached 110 F at both Murray and Princeton in July, and precipitation averaged half of the normal monthly total. Drought conditions spread into the central portion of Kentucky. Temperatures above 100 F became a frequent occurrence. Pasture and hay crops wilted in the hot, dry fields, and the fire danger was high. Farmers were forced to buy feed for their livestock, and many chose to reduce their herds. The dry weather continued through the fall and winter seasons with few exceptions and set the stage for persistent drought in 1953. Hot, dry weather returned in the summer of 1953, but farmers were more prepared for drought this time. Many had built silos and increased their allocation of pasture. But crops faired no better than the previous year. Temperatures that reached above 100 F in September remained in the 90s for several days in October. Louisville went 36 days in a row without rain beginning on Sept. 20. Water was increasingly in short supply, as below normal precipitation continued through December. A wet January helped to improve soil moisture into the spring of 1954, but a return of hot, dry weather by July quickly depleted the moisture available to crops and pasture. Drought was worse in the western areas. But the late summer and fall of 1954 brought a return to more normal precipitation, and heavy precipitation during January and February of 1955 marked the clear end to a prolonged drought.

1999-2000

Following a wet spring in 1998, a pattern of dry weather settled over Kentucky during the summer and fall of 1998. Though it received little attention, it helped set the stage for severe drought in the coming year. While January of 1999 brought above normal precipitation, the weather pattern again turned dry. By the end of June, a water shortage watch was issued for counties in the eastern and bluegrass regions, as drought moved westward into Kentucky. Precipitation during July averaged less than one-half of normal, while temperatures soared. Temperatures from the 90s to the 100s held over the second half of July. The maximum reading was 107 F at Rough River Lake. Conditions deteriorated rapidly, as the period of July through September was the driest on record statewide with an average of only 5.3 inches of rain. By the end of September, 96 of Kentucky's 120 counties had been placed under a water shortage warning, and the remaining counties were under a water shortage watch. Mandatory curtailments of water usage for some residential and commercial activities were implemented in some areas. The drought reduced crop yields, particularly for late season crops. Poor pasture and a shortage of water for livestock led many farmers to sell cattle and hogs. Precipitation returned to normal seasonal amounts throughout much of the state by the summer of 2000, but the dry pattern persisted in parts of southern and central Kentucky, and concerns about the availability of municipal water supplies continued in some areas through the end of the year.

Ice & Snow

Kentucky normally enjoys mild winters but is vulnerable to a wide variety of hazardous winter weather, including snow, ice and arctic cold waves. Low-pressure systems that bring winter storms to Kentucky often track eastward across the southern United States before turning toward the northeast. Those that track along the western margin of the Appalachian Mountains are most likely to bring heavy precipitation. With cold air in place over Kentucky, the precipitation is often in the form of heavy snow, but it can also be freezing rain and sleet, resulting in destructive ice storms. Occasionally, a strong cold front will move into the region and send temperatures plunging below zero. Gusty winds often magnify the impact and create dangerous wind chills.

Many Kentuckians will recall the winter of 1977-1978, while a few still recall the winter of 1917-1918, as long cold winters willed plenty of snow. Those winters, along with a recollection of the win-

Heavy snow hits Lexington
Source: Sid Webb

ter storm of January 1994, are highlighted below.

Winter of 1917-1918

December ushered in a cold, snowy winter season. An early snowstorm on the 7th and 8th dumped a foot or more of snow across parts of Kentucky. The blizzard was followed by a period of extreme cold with temperatures dropping to near or below zero for several days. Farmers were snowbound and unable to bring poultry to market for the Christmas season. The average temperature of 26.5 F for December was some 11 F below normal. Snow returned before the end of the month, and December's totals ranged from 9 inches in southeastern Kentucky to 28 inches in the Louisville area, with an average of 17.3 inches across the state. Harsh winter conditions persisted through January. Temperatures as low as minus 20 F combined with winds of 30 miles per hour on Jan. 12 to produce the most severe weather conditions recalled since New Year's Day of 1864. Heavy snow returned. Average snowfall across the state in January was 23.3 inches, while more than 30 inches fell in western and southern counties. The average temperature of 20.6 F for January was nearly 15 F below normal. Many stations reported temperatures of zero or below on 10 days during the month. The cold snap finally broke on Feb. 6, and snow that had covered the ground in some areas since early December began to melt.

Winter of 1977-1978

A brief, early December cold snap brought light snow and subzero temperatures to parts of northern and central Kentucky on the 6th and 7th. But warm temperatures quickly returned as the mercury touched 60 F again before Christmas, and early January remained seasonably warm. The weather changed for the worse however, on January 16th and 17th, when a major winter storm dumped at least 10 inches of snow from western Kentucky through the north central portion of the state. Some of the heavier totals included 12 inches at Paducah, 16 inches at both Henderson and Louisville and 11 inches at Lexington and Covington. At La Grange in Oldham County, where 18 inches fell, accumulation from January storms reached a record depth of 31 inches on Jan. 20. Blizzard conditions returned on the 25th and 26th and roads were declared closed in all but the southeast counties. All told, snow fell somewhere in Kentucky on 19 days in January, 12 days in February, and even seven days more in March. With a heavy snow cover from mid-January and persistent snows in the following weeks, snow remained on the ground well into March at some northern locations. Owenton measured snow 15 inches deep on March 8, and La Grange still had 3 inches of snow cover as late as the 12th. Over the course of the winter, snowfall totals ranged from 31 inches at Scottsville, near the Kentucky-Tennessee border and 84 inches at La Grange. While there were no record-setting cold waves during the winter, the continued influx of polar air resulted in a long, cold winter. Cities ran short of road salt, and disruptions of river traffic due to icing at locations on the Ohio River delayed shipments. School children, particularly in rural areas, missed week upon week of classes. When spring finally arrived, it was a welcome sight indeed.

January 1994

January of 1994 started out as a typical winter month in Kentucky. Light snow in the first week of the month was followed by warmer weather with temperatures reaching well into the 40s. The uneventful weather took a sudden and unexpected change beginning on the 16th. Heavy snow, accumulating up to 3 inches per hour, blanketed the northern half of the state, covering Paducah with 15 inches, Louisville with 16 inches, Shelbyville with 19 inches, Lexington with 10 inches and Jackson with 15 inches. Unofficial totals in the northern counties reached 20 inches or more. To the south, accumulations of 4 to 8 inches fell on top of a thick coating of ice, as freezing rain and sleet preceded the snowfall. In Louisville, it was an all-time record snowfall.

Ice and snow was followed by frigid arctic air that rushed in over Kentucky. Temperatures plummeted, and Shelbyville broke the all-time record low temperature for Kentucky with a reading of minus 37 F on the morning of the 19th. Temperatures dropping to at least minus 30 F were also recorded at Cynthiana (minus 33 F), Falmouth (minus 30 F), Gray Hawk (minus 35 F), Manchester (minus 30 F), Somerset (minus 32 F) and West Liberty (minus 30 F).

The record-shattering burst of winter weather brought Kentucky to a near standstill. A state of emergency was declared. All interstate highways were ordered closed to all but emergency vehicles on the 17th, and they remained closed until the 20th. Emergency personnel struggled across the state to reach people in need. Schools and businesses were closed. Thousands were without power, many for several days. The danger of fire increased as people resorted to fireplaces and kerosene heaters to keep warm. Manufacturers depending upon just-in-time delivery of inventory were shut down, as the transportation industry struggled to deliver shipments.

"Well, go figure..."

The Kentucky Climate Center was created in 1978 by agreement among Western Kentucky University, the National Weather Service and the National Climatic Data Center.

State Climatologist, Stuart Foster (2000 to present)
State Climatologist Emeritus, Glen Conner 1978-2000

CLIMATE & SEASONS
Weather Records

Dr. Stuart Foster

10 WARMEST YEARS

Year	Avg Temp(°F)
1921	59.2
1998	58.3
1931	57.9
1938	57.7
1922	57.7
1991	57.6
1933	57.5
1953	57.5
1990	57.5
1946	57.4

10 WARMEST SUMMERS**

Year	Avg Temp(°F)
1936	78.8
1952	77.9
1921	77.7
1934	77.5
1943	77.2
1914	77.1
1913	77.1
1901	77.0
2002	76.9
1900	76.9

10 WARMEST WINTERS*

Year	Avg Temp(°F)
1931-32	44.7
1948-49	41.7
1949-50	41.5
1956-57	40.3
1951-52	40.2
1997-98	40.0
1952-53	40.0
1998-99	39.9
1936-37	39.8
2001-02	39.8

10 COLDEST YEARS

Year	Avg Temp(°F)
1917	52.6
1958	53.7
1976	53.8
1912	52.8
1978	53.9
1940	54.0
1963	54.0
1979	54.0
1966	54.2
1924	54.2

10 COLDEST SUMMERS**

Year	Avg Temp(°F)
1967	71.4
1992	71.8
1927	71.9
1976	72.1
1950	72.1
1915	72.3
1974	72.4
2004	72.6
1946	72.7
1961	72.7

10 COLDEST WINTERS*

Year	Avg Temp(°F)
1977-78	27.1
1917-18	27.4
1976-77	28.2
1935-36	29.4
1962-63	29.4
1904-05	29.6
1901-02	30.3
1898-99	30.6
1939-40	30.8
1978-79	30.9

* (December, January, February)
** (June, July, August)
Photo Source: Kentucky Historical Society

CLIMATE & SEASONS

Folklore Weather

Glen Conner

Humans have long had a desire to foretell the weather based on what we can see and feel. There are many sayings about the weather that have been passed down through the generations. Some have a basis in fact but others don't: "If you wash your car, it is likely to rain." Such sayings are proof that faith in them persisted but not necessarily proof that they are true.

Red skies at night, sailor's delight; red skies at dawning, sailor take warning. The red clouds seen before sunset are reflecting the reds from sunlight. It must be clear to the west if the sunlight is making it through to them. Good weather must be coming because most weather systems move from the west.

Count the fogs in August and that is the number of snows for the coming winter. If that were true, then there could never be more than 31 snows in a winter. There is no predictive capability in this saying. However, the average number of fogs in August and the average number of days with an inch of snow or more on the ground are roughly similar. In weather, unlike mathematics, things equal to the same thing aren't necessarily equal to each other.

Rainbow in the morning is the shepherd's warning. A rainbow is only visible when the sun is behind you and the rain is in front of you. Because most rain events approach from the southwest, when you see a rainbow in the morning, it is from a rain shower that is approaching from the west. Conversely, when you see a rainbow in the eve-

Barren River area
Source: Betty Hall

ning, it is from a rain shower that has passed and is going away from you.

Damp salt is a sign of coming rain. Salt does absorb moisture from the air and high humidity is a major ingredient in conditions that precede rain.

When leaves show their undersides, be sure that rain betides. The topsides of leaves are green but the undersides of leaves are a lighter color (poplar, sycamore, silver maple, etc.). An approaching thunderstorm is preceded by instability and rapidly changing wind direction, which can flip the leaves upside down.

When the dew is on the grass, rain will not come to pass. Dew forms during a cloudless night, which permits the Earth's surface to cool rapidly by radiation of heat, causing condensation to form on the grass. The presence of clear skies during the night is a good indicator of a rainless day to follow.

Curls that kink are signs of rain. Human hair is sensitive to changes in humidity. Rising relative humidity is associated with approaching rain events and people with curls may be the first to know.

All signs fail in a drought. This saying about sayings is true of most weather lore as well. Nevertheless, a remarkable number of them have some truth. Reduction of the activity of our enormously complicated weather patterns to a short saying seems unlikely. But, we love to try.

CLIMATE & SEASONS

Glen Conner   *Climate Folklore*

Folklore has given us the names of hot spells and cool spells that are recurring periods of unseasonable weather. Some of those names are generally recognized across Kentucky. Recognition of their arrival is subjective rather than quantitative. People just know them when they see them!

Indian Summer. The term Indian Summer may be the oldest of the climate lore seasons. The dictionary defines it as a period of warm temperature in early winter that is characterized by a cloudless sky that appears smoky or hazy. In Kentucky, a warm spell that follows some winter weather in November would be recognized as Indian Summer. The origin of the name is uncertain and debatable. One origin suggestion was that, in areas like Kentucky, Indian hunting parties were absent during winter but would return during the warm spell in November. Thus, the Indian Summer.

January Thaw. A warm spell in late January that is sufficient in warmth and duration to thaw the ground after a period of it being frozen would be recognized as the January Thaw. In modern times, a warm spell in late January provides a welcomed temporary relief to winter. In earlier times, before paved roads, the January Thaw was not welcomed because the roads turned into mud and became impassable.

Dogwood Winter. The dictionary defines Dogwood Winter as a brief spell of wintry weather in spring. In Kentucky, the climate lore refers to the very cold spell that comes while the dogwoods are in bloom. In the parts of Kentucky that do not

have dogwoods, the same cold spell may be called Locust Winter because it occurs while the locust trees are in bloom.

Blackberry Winter. When the prickly brambles of the Blackberry are in bloom, they are seen as large mounds of white blossoms. Once, those mounds of white were a common sight in the springtime countryside. The decline of home canning and the inclination toward mowed pastures have made blackberry patches a less common sight. Climate lore says that Blackberry Winter arrives while the blackberries are in bloom. They bloom sometime in early May after spring has fully arrived and cool periods have become more infrequent and shorter in duration. Kentuckians would see a cool spell during the blackberry bloom period as Blackberry Winter

Dog Days. The name Dog Days comes from a Mediterranean reference to Sirius (the Dog Star) that rose and set with the sun for this period. The name and its summer period were adapted in climate lore to represent a long uninterrupted period of hot, sultry and muggy days in mid summer. Dog Days occur when the annual march of temperature reaches highest during the last two weeks of July. Rather than reaching a peak, it is more likely to plateau. Add an area of high pressure that remains over Kentucky for several consecutive days, builds up pollutants in its stable, stagnating air, and accumulates heat day after breezeless day. The result would be known as Dog Days.

Contributed by: Glen Conner, Kentucky State Climatologist Emeritus

Source: Sid Webb

Culture
& the Arts
Lindy Casebier

Rosemary Clooney

Jean Ritchie

KY Artisan Center, Berea, KY

Loretta Lynn

David Wright - Whitley Chamber...

The Judds

Louisville Ballet

Boots Randolph

John Lair

Sources: Kentucky Artisan Center
Kentucky Music Hall of Fame
Kentucky Department of Tourism

Clark's Kentucky Almanac 2006

Kentucky is blessed with a rich artistic and cultural heritage. Through the years Kentuckians have led the way in sharing their extensive talents: Jesse Stuart, Robert Penn Warren, Wendell Berry, Joel Tanner Hart, Lionel Hampton, Rosemary Clooney, Bill Monroe, Loretta Lynn, the Everly Brothers, Ed Hamilton, Ricky Skaggs, John Michael Montgomery, Naomi, Wynonna & Ashley Judd, Diane Sawyer and Johnny Depp –to name a few. These Kentuckians have received national and international acclaim for their contributions. Every day many other talented Kentuckians make their artistic contribution to the commonwealth and the nation by sharing their gifts.

Kentucky's arts offerings are as diverse as our people, and can be found in every corner of the state. Bluegrass or blues, opera or opry, craft fairs or art museums—wherever your tastes may lead you, we've got it in the Bluegrass state.

In Kentucky, crafts are revered and the traditions live on in the pieces that grew out of necessity from early frontier days, like quilts and coverlets, baskets, furniture, pottery, brooms and dulcimers. That strong foundation in craft has also made way for contemporary expressions in sculpture, ceramics, jewelry, glass, metal and fiber arts. With the newly inaugurated Kentucky Artisan Center at Berea and the Berea College and the Kentucky Guild of Artist and Craftsmen's craft fairs, Berea earns its title as the Folk Arts and Crafts Capital of Kentucky. Centrally located in the state, this enclave of tradition is the gateway into a world of wonderful crafts that can be found from the hills and hollers of eastern Kentucky all the way west to the Mississippi River, including our urban centers.

When it comes to theatre and the performing arts, Kentucky has something for everyone including professional theatre, community theatre, summer stock, outdoor drama, touring companies and student

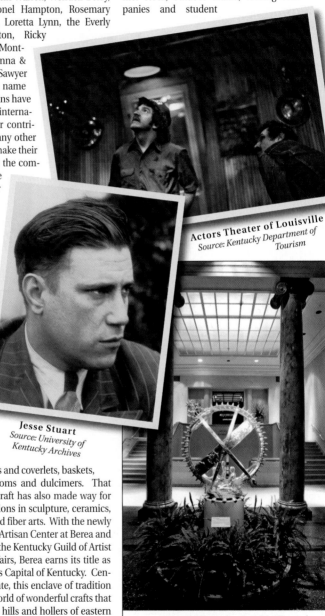

Actors Theater of Louisville
Source: Kentucky Department of Tourism

Jesse Stuart
Source: University of Kentucky Archives

Speed Museum, Louisville
Source: Kentucky Department of Tourism

productions.

The Music Theatre Louisville, performing at the Iroquois Amphitheater is a must see for family fun, along with The Jenny Wiley Theatre in Prestonsburg, the Ragged Edge Community Theatre in Harrodsburg, or the Walden Theatre with youth performers in Louisville. The Kentucky Repertory Theatre at Horse Cave is nationally acclaimed for artistic excellence with a unique program to develop Kentucky playwrights. The Actors Guild of Lexington can always be depended upon for high-quality, thought-provoking productions.

Speed Museum, Louisville
Source: Kentucky Department of Tourism

Actors Theatre of Louisville has incredible theatrical productions and is home to the Humana Festival of New American Plays. This internationally celebrated showcase of groundbreaking stage premieres features up-to-the-minute modern comedies and dramas written by America's best playwrights.

Great theatre can also be found in Paducah at the Market House Theatre, and Bowling Green's Public Theatre of Kentucky. Owensboro boasts the Owensboro Theatre Workshop, and there's also the Unicorn Players of Union County and the Kincaid Regional Theatre in Falmouth. The Artist Collaborative Theatre in Elkhorn City annually performs the "Kentucky Cycles."

Berea Crafts
Source: Kentucky Artisan Center

The state strongly supports the performing arts, with the Kentucky Center (www.kentuckycenter.org) in Louisville as the cultural heart of the city, region, and state. It is a showcase for Kentucky performance and visual arts as well as for national and international performances in orchestra, theatre, dance,

opera, jazz, and contemporary music.

Other venues include The Mountain Arts Center (www.macarts.com) in Prestonsburg, which serves as home to the Kentucky Opry. The Paramount Arts Center in Ashland offers performances by artists from the Country Music Highway such as Ricky Skaggs, Loretta Lynn and Wynonna Judd, as does Renfro Valley Entertainment Center in Renfro Valley. Appalshop in Whitesburg offers an authentic view of Appalachian culture through performance, visual and media arts.

In Lexington, the University of Kentucky's Singletary Center for the Arts serves the greater Lexington community, and the Norton Center at Centre College's provides nationally acclaimed performances. Owensboro is home to the International Thumbpickers Hall of Fame, which honors a distinctive style of guitar playing that originated in the western coalfields.

With world-renown works on display, the Speed Art Museum, in Louisville, is Kentucky's oldest and largest art museum with over 12,000 pieces in its permanent collection. Its extensive collection spans 6,000 years, ranging from ancient Egyptian to contemporary art, and also includes a strong Kentucky collection of paintings, sculpture and decorative arts.

The Owensboro Museum of Fine Art features a permanent collection of 19th-and 20th-century paintings and sculptures, decorative arts dating back as far as the 16th century, and the spectacular Stained Glass Gallery.

If quilts are your fancy, visit the Museum of the American Quilters Society in Paducah, which

BLUEGRASS STATE

Kentucky
UNBRIDLED SPIRIT™

0000

Capture the Spirit of the Arts

The mission of the Commerce Cabinet is to spread the message that the Arts are vital to our lives, our communities and our economy. The Arts can help move Kentucky forward and become more competitive nationally and globally. We have a wonderful message to share with others. To that end the Cabinet has unveiled a new license plate inviting Kentuckians to "Capture the Spirit of the Arts."

houses the largest collection of art quilts in the world. Lexington's Headley-Whitney Museum tops the list for small treasures. Dedicated to the decorative arts, the museum's signature collection is comprised of intricately jeweled sculptures known as bibelots.

The Carnegie Center for Visual and Performing Arts in Covington has five art galleries showcasing local, regional and national artists. A wonderful blend of regional natural history, cultural history and art can be found at Covington's Behringer-Crawford Museum. The Janice Mason Art Museum in Cadiz features local and regional collections. In Paducah, the Yeiser Art Center's permanent collection of American, European, African and Asian art is highlighted each year by the prestigious 'Fantastic Fibers" exhibition with a national call to fiber artists.

Lexington's oldest and largest visual arts organization, the Lexington Art League, offers regular exhibitions at the MetroLex Gallery of the National City Bank Building and their home base at the Loudon House.

Kentucky's cultural landscape is as varied as the high winding eastern mountain roads, the rolling hills of central Kentucky and the vast farms and lakes of the west. The Kentucky Arts Council can provide current contact information for any of the listed arts organizations or cultural attractions. Call 888-833-ARTS or kyarts@ky.gov.

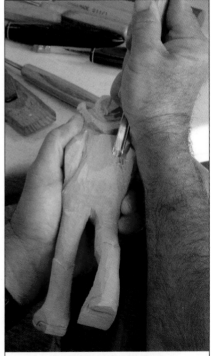

Larry Smith carving
Source: Kentucky Artisan Center

KET

facilitating **Lifelong Learning**

sharing **Kentucky's Stories**

fostering **Civic Dialogue**

CULTURE & THE ARTS

Governor's Awards in the Arts

KENTUCKY GOVERNOR'S AWARDS RECIPIENTS

Milner Award: Governor Julian Carroll, Moritz Bomhard, Jon Jory, James Still, Wendell Cherry, Harriet Simpson-Arnow, Jean Ritchie, Anna L. Huddleston, Barry Bingham, Sr., Wendell Berry, Robert Penn Warren, Jesse Stuart, Harlowe Dean, Rude Osolnik, Lucille Little, Sherry Jelsma, Homer Ledford, Marilyn Moosnick, Alun Jones, Robert Bruce French, Roy P. Peterson, Crit Luallen, Donna S. Hall, Bill and Josephine D'Amato Richardson, David A. Jones.

National Award: George Wolfe, Marsha Norman, Marvin and Morgan Smith, Rosemary Clooney, Christine Johnson Smith, Joe Downing, Sam Gilliam, Barbara Kingsolver, John Henry, The Judd Family (Naomi, Wynonna and Ashley), Ricky Skaggs.

Artist Award: Harlan Hubbard, Robert S. Whitney, Alma Lesch, Helen Starr, Barney Bright, Adale O'Brien, Ray Fry, Paul Owen, John Tuska, Warren Hammack, Ed Hamilton, Minnie Adkins, David Livingston, George Zack, Lee Sexton, Lee Luvisi, Melvin Dickinson, Moses Goldberg, Arturo Alonzo Sandoval, Elizabeth Hartwell.

Business Award: Brown-Forman Corporation, South Central Bell, Ashland Oil Inc., Philip Morris USA, Humana Inc., Martin Coal Company, Texas Gas Transmission, Liberty National Bank, Toyota Motor Manufacturing, Trans Financial Inc., Charlie Johnson (Active Transportation), Commercial Bank of Grayson, William and Meredith Schroeder, Bank of Louisville, Peoples Bank of Madison County, J.W. Kinzer Drilling Co., Fifth Third Bank, Community Trust Bank, Julius Friedman.

Community Arts Award: Elmer Lucille Allen, Wayne Smith, Mary Yeiser, Bowling Green-Warren County Arts Commission, G. Caliman Coxe, Emily Wolfson, Ft. Knox Alumni Performing Arts Center, Donna Bradley-Morton, Elizabeth Paxton, Rowan County Arts Council, Fohs Hall Community Arts Foundation, Dorothy Brockman, John Edmonds, Tom Sternal, Appalshop, Jenny Wiley Theatre, Ashland Area Art Gallery, Princeton Art Guild, Cumberland County Arts Council, Living Arts and Science Center, Billie Jean Osborne, Roots and Heritage Festival, Kenneth H. Clay, Paramount Arts Center, Saundra Kilijian, Master Musicians Festival, Covington Community Center, Jarrett Boyd, Louisville Central Community Centers, Montgomery County Council for the Arts, Nana Yaa Awantewaa, Singeltary Center for the Arts.

Education Award: Henrietta Roush Scott, Water Tower Art Association, Hindman Settlement School, Lila Davis Bellando, Kentucky Educational Television, Norma E. Brown, Christian County Schools, Mildred Berkey, Hancock County Schools, Westport Middle School, Jean Green, Bige Towery, Jr., Ballard High School, Judy Sizemore, Very Special Arts Kentucky, Daviess County Public Schools, Diane Roketenetz/James E. Biggs Early Childhood Education Center, Nancy Carpenter, Collaborative for Teaching and Learning, Diane Downs, Deborah M. Shannon, Vernell Bennett, Kentucky Shakespeare Festival, Carnegie Visual and Performing Arts Center.

Folk Heritage Award: Eddie Pennington, J.D. Crowe, Lynwood Montell, Lestel Childress, John Harrod.

Government Award: Senator David Karem, Mayor Scotty Baesler, Representative Jody Richards, Congressman Ron Mazzoli, Representative Harry Moberly, Sue Larison, Louisville Regional Airport Authority, Senator Wendell Ford, Mammoth Cave National Park, Mayor Pam Miller, Secretary Ann R. Latta, Center for Economic Development Entrepreneurship and Technology, City of Paducah Artist Relocation Project, City of Berea, Hindman/Knott County Community Development Initiative.

Media Award: Barry Bernson, Cass Irvin, William Mootz, Jane S. Blake, WYMT-TV (Hazard), WKMS Radio (Murray), WEKU/WEKH Radio (Richmond), Lexington Herald Leader, Kentucky Educational Television, Public Radio Service of Western Kentucky University, WHAS-TV (Louisville), Byron Crawford, Nick Lawrence, Arts Across Kentucky Magazine, The Lane Report, Business First of Louisville, WTCR Radio.

Pioneer Award: Eben Henson, Arthur Harvey, Phyllis George, Fund for the Arts.

Special Recognition: Harry Caudill.

CULTURE & THE ARTS
Poets, Writers, Novelists & Playwrights

Kentucky's Poets Laureate

Kentucky has an illustrious literary tradition. As Richard Taylor (Poet Laureate, 1999) has said, "Kentucky is increasingly recognized as a state that has produced important national voices in fiction, drama, and poetry. . . a state that values its rich literary heritage." Since 1926 the state of Kentucky has appointed 21 persons as Poets Laureate, thus honoring worthy poets among its citizens, while paying tribute to the art of poetry. This recognition of the importance of poetry in Kentucky occurred well before 1986, when Kentuckian Robert Penn Warren — one of America's most distinguished scholars and writers —was the first to be appointed U.S. Poet Laureate.

Robert Penn Warren, born in Guthrie, Kentucky in 1905, is the only person to have been awarded the Pulitzer Prize in both fiction and poetry, and having won twice in poetry, is the only three-time Pulitzer Prize winner. Over the years the post of Kentucky Poet Laureate has evolved from a chiefly honorary title to a position with the appointees assuming responsibility for promoting the literary arts across the state during their two-year tenure. Kentucky's laureates have come from diverse backgrounds and occupations, and have included farmers, lawyers, educators, homemakers, bankers, legislators, writers, and businessmen. Each of these persons has, in their own unique way, contributed to the outstanding literary tradition and heritage of Kentucky.

In 1990 legislation provided for appointment of the Kentucky Poet Laureate by the governor. Prior to 1991 poets were appointed to lifetime terms and several poets held the position simultaneously. The nomination and selection process is coordinated by the Kentucky Arts Council.

1926 J.T. Cotton Noe
1928 Edward G. Hill
1945 Louise Scott Phillips
1954 Edwin Carlisle Litsey
1954 Jesse Hilton Stuart
1956 Lowell Allen Williams
1974 Lillie D. Chaffin
1976 Tom Mobley
1978 Agnes O'Rear
1984 Clarence 'Soc"Clay
1984 Lee Pennington
1984 Paul Salyers
1986 Dale Faughn
1986 Jim Wayne Miller
1986 Henry E. Pilkenton
1990 James H. Patton
1995 James Still
1997 Joy Bale Boone
1999 Richard Taylor
2001 James Baker Hall
2003 Joe Survant
2005 Sena Jeter Naslund

Reprinted with permission from Wind Publications, Poets Laureate of Kentucky, Betty J. Sparks (2004) and special thanks to the Kentucky Arts Council, http://www.kyarts.org/.

JESSE HILTON STUART (b. 1907 – d. 1984) - **Poet Laureate, 1954**
Jesse Stuart, author, poet and teacher, was born in 1907 to tenant farmers in Greenup County. Stuart published 200 articles, approximately 2000 poems, 60 books and he wrote 460 short stories.

"Kentucky is neither southern, northern, eastern, western, It is the core of America. If these United States can be called a body Kentucky is its heart." – *Jesse Stuart*
Reprinted with permission from Wind Publications, Poets Laureate of Kentucky, Betty J. Sparks (Nicholasville:2004)

Notable Kentucky Authors

James Lane Allen
Harriette Arnow
Garry Barker
Wendell Berry
Harry Brown
Charles Neville Buck
Billy C. Clark
Thomas D. Clark
Irvin S. Cobb
Richard H. Collins
Joseph S. Cotter
Alfred Leland Crabb
Olive Tilford Dargan
David Dick
Lalie Dick
Michael Dorris
Leon V. Driskell
John Fox, Jr.
Janice Holt Giles
Caroline Gordon
Sue Grafton
A. B. Guthrie
Tom T. Hall
Wade Hall
Elizabeth Hardwick
Silas House
Fenton Johnson

Barbara Kingsolver
Lisa Koger
Jim and Freda Klotter
Sylvia Lovely
George Ella Lyon
Bobbie Ann Mason
Taylor McCafferty
Ed McClanahan
Jim Wayne Miller
Sena Jeter Nasland
Gurney Norman
Marshal Norman
Chris Offutt
Lee Pennington
Joe A. Porter
Betty Layman Receveur
Elizabeth Madox Roberts
James Still
Jesse Stuart
Hollis Summers
Walter Tevis
Tom Wallace
Robert Penn Warren
Crystal Wilkinson

Source: Eastern Kentucky University, Dept. of English, www.english.eku.edu/services/kylit/default.htm

---

MAN WITH A BULL-TONGED PLOW
from
Kentucky is My Land by Jesse Stuart

I didn't have any choice
as to where I was born,
But if I had had my choice,
I would have chosen Kentucky.
And if could have chosen
wind to breathe, I would
have chosen a Kentucky wind
with the scent of cedar,
pinetree needles,
green tobacco leaves, pawpaw,
persimmon and sassafras.
I would have chosen too,
Wind from the sawbriar and
greenbriar blossoms.

Reprinted with permission from Wind Publications, Poets Laureate of Kentucky, Betty J. Sparks (Nicholasville: 2004).

Louise Scott Phillips (b.1911 — d.1983)
Sesquicentennial Poet Laureate, 1945
An excerpt from
MEMORIES FROM CHILDHOOD
— from *Deep End*

...In my memories I linger
Near the mound of greening earth,
Where my father long has rested
By the one who gave me birth.
'Tis so sweet in early evening,
In the sunset's last golden glow,
To recall the scenes of childhood,
And the days of long ago!

Reprinted with permission from Wind Publications, Poets Laureate of Kentucky, Betty J. Sparks (Nicholasville: 2004).

CULTURE & THE ARTS

Film & Television

Robert S. Boles

Kentucky has a very rich heritage when it comes to the Film Industry. Successful films such as **The Kentuckian, Seabiscuit, How the West was Won, Coal Miner's Daughter, Eight Men Out,** and **Stripes** are but a few of the films that were filmed on location in the state.

Whether Hollywood film makers are looking the town with the largest concentration of horse farms in the world, but the film industry learned long ago that Lexington has a lot more than just horses to offer. Scattered throughout the Lexing-

Director Cameron Crowe during a break of filming in the Versailles, Ky. part of the movie, "Elizabethtown"
Source: Lexington Herald-Leader

for period towns, scenic outdoor areas or bluegrass horse farms, Kentucky has a wide variety of extraordinary locations to choose from.

Kentucky is known throughout the world for its thoroughbred industry, and that's especially true in Hollywood. Our horse farms, the 1,032-acre Kentucky Horse Park and our beautiful tracks, including Keeneland, Turfway Park and Churchill Downs, have been featured in a wide variety of commercials, television shows and feature films. Horse related feature films that were shot totally or partially in the Commonwealth include **Seabiscuit, The Thoroughbreds, Black Beauty, The Champions, Bluegrass, A Horse for Danny, Simpatico, Dreamer** and many others.

Lexington, "The Horse Capital of the World," is located in the heart of central Kentucky and home to many world-famous farms. Lexington may be

Jay King preparing special effects for the movie "Seabiscuit"
Source: Lexington Herald-Leader

ton area are period neighborhoods, antebellum mansions, two universities and one of the largest basketball venues in the nation, Rupp Arena, and these are only a few of the city's assets that film makers have used over the years. In 1978, the feature film **Steel** was filmed on location at a downtown Lexington construction site. Other films that have been shot in central Kentucky include **Seabiscuit** and **Dreamer.**

Kentucky's largest river city is Louisville, home

of the Kentucky Derby, the Belle of Louisville and Tony-award winning Actors Theatre. Modern office towers contrast with historic neighborhoods, including blocks of Victorian homes such as Farmington, built in 1810 using a design by Thomas Jefferson. These venues have been used by film producers for decades. The recently released movie, *Elizabethtown,* was filmed in Oldham County and in Jefferson County.

Inflatable people were used as the crowd in the stands for filming of "Seabiscuit" at Keeneland
Source: Lexington Herald-Leader

Many of the communities in northern Kentucky reflect the ethnic backgrounds of Irish and German heritage. These period neighborhoods manifest the character and variety of an age not so long ago. These areas have also attracted Hollywood film companies. Films shot in this region include *Little Man Tate*, *City of Hope* and *A Rage in Harlem* to name a few. The blockbuster film, **Rain Man,** was also filmed at locations throughout this area of Kentucky, and even required the closing of a nearby interstate for one scene.

Kentucky also has many small towns scattered throughout the state that evoke the charm of main street America. River towns along the Ohio River have welcomed *Lost in Yonkers*, a PBS American Playhouse version of Huckleberry Finn, and the television mini-series *Centennial.*

Many of Kentucky's small towns are well-preserved, intact period towns that frequently attract film producers. The Kentucky Main Street Program manages the revitalization of downtown areas statewide, providing towns with period appearances ranging from 1880-1920. Part of *A League of Their Own* was filmed in the Main Street community of Henderson, featuring the Soaper Hotel and a private home as a boarding house. Kentucky has many historic sites, including a wide variety of private homes and public buildings. The Southern

charm of Spindletop Hall welcomed the television mini-series **Bluegrass**. White Hall, a unique blend of Gothic, Georgian Revival and Italianate architectural styles, has been featured in the opening credits of the television series **Sister Kate** and in the mini-series **Centennial.**

Although Kentucky has more miles of navigable water than any other state except Alaska, Kentucky's waterlands aren't all rivers. In Western Kentucky, there are huge lakes that surround Land Between the Lakes National Recreation Area. Farther west, swamplands were featured in Norman Jewison's **In Country** as Vietnam.

Military bases have also been proven to be popular film loca-

Film crews shoot a scene from the movie "Elizabethtown," staring Orlando Bloom and Kirsten Dunst in Versailles, Kentucky
Source: Lexington Herald-Leader

tions through the years. *Stripes* was filmed at Fort Knox with the cooperation of the U.S. Army. The army base also worked with a major Hollywood studio to make the set realistic for the James Bond feature film *Goldfinger.*

FILM STARS FROM KENTUCKY

Ned Beatty was born in Louisville and has appeared in over 100 films. His most recognized roles include Lex Luthor's henchman Otis in *Superman*, and as rape victim Bobby Trippe in *Deliverance*, his debut role. Beatty was nominated for the Academy Award for Best Supporting Actor in the movie *Network*.

Rebecca Gayheart was born in Hazard and is a coal miner's daughter. She left Kentucky at age 15 to start acting. Gayheart appeared in a series of commercials for *Noxzema* and then joined the cast of the soap opera *Loving*. Gayheart also had a role in the series *Beverly Hills, 90210* and other TV shows. Gayheart has several film appearances.

Grandpa Jones was a banjo player and country and gospel music singer. Jones was born in Niagra and left Kentucky as a teenager and sang songs on the radio. His career led to Boston, MA where he met musician/songwriter Bradley Kincaid who gave him the nickname "Grandpa". He moved to Nashville, TN, and played the banjo and sang and joined the *Grand Ole Opry*. He was best known for his role on the popular TV show *Hee Haw*. Grandpa Jones was inducted into the Country Music Hall of Fame.

Lily Tomlin was born in Michigan but her mother moved them to Paducah during the Depression. She is an actress and comedian and became very well-known for her character on the TV show *Laugh-In*. Her most notable character was the wisecrack-ing and snorting telephone opera-tor Ernestine and her other famous character was a five-year-old brat Edith Ann, which she performed from an oversized rock-ing chair. Tomlin did stand-up comedy in nightclubs after college and had her first TV appearance

Ashley Judd
Source: Lexington Herald-Leader

on *The Merv Griffin Show*. She was a versatile actor and played the role of the secretary Violet Newstead in *Nine to Five*. More recently she has played a role on the popular TV series *The West Wing*. Recently, she was awarded the Mark Twain Prize for American Humor.

Lee Majors was born in Michigan and is an actor best known for playing the part of Steve Austin with bionic limbs in the television series *The Six Million Dollar Man*. Majors was adopted by his uncle and aunt after his mother was killed in an automo-bile accident. His new family moved to Middles-boro, where he graduated from Middlesboro High School and earned a degree from Eastern Ken-tucky University in Richmond. Majors had a role on the 1960s television show *The Big Valley* and years later starred in another popular series, *The Fall Guy*. Married several times his most famous marriage was to actress Farrah Fawcett.

James Best was born in Powderly and played the role of Sheriff Rosco P. Coltrane in the television series *The Dukes of Hazzard.*

William Conrad was born in Louisville and had a marvelous baritone voice. His large size, deep, resonant voice led to a number of noteworthy roles

in radio drama, most prominently his originating the role of Marshal Matt Dillon on *Gunsmoke*.

Foster Brooks was born in Louisville. Brooks was an actor and comedian and was most famous for his ongoing portrayal of a drunken man in Las Vegas

Nick and George Clooney
Source: Lexington Herald-Leader

nightclub performances and television programs. He regularly appeared on *The Dean Martin Show.*

George Timothy Clooney is an actor born in Lexington and known for his for-mer role in the long-running television drama *ER*. He started his acting career in a similarly named sitcom, *E/R,* and played a handyman on the series *The Facts of Life.* He had starring roles in *Batman & Robin, The Perfect Storm, O Brother, Where Art Thou?, Ocean's Eleven and Ocean's Twelve.*

Nick Clooney was born in Maysville and is a for-mer television news anchorman and politician from the state of Kentucky. He is the brother of singer Rosemary Clooney and the father of noted actor George Clooney. He writes a column for *The Cincinnati Post.*

Billy Ray Cyrus was born in Flatwoods and is a country singer, best known for the hit single "*Achy Breaky Heart*". In 2001, Cyrus began playing the lead role on the PAX Network comedy-drama *Doc*. In 2004, Blender magazine selected *Achy Breaky Heart* as the magazine's choice for second worst song ever.

Ashley Judd was born in California and is an actress. Her mother Naomi Judd and sister Wynonna Judd are country singers. She graduated with honors in 1990 from the University of Ken-tucky and is often seen at UK Basketball games.

She earned early acclaim in **Smoke** and publicity in **Heat**. By the end of the 1990s, she managed to achieve significant fame and success as an actress in movies like **Double Jeopardy** and **Someone Like You.**

Victor Mature was a film actor born in Louisville and considered a handsome leading man. His best known role was Samson in **Samson and Delilah**. He played opposite stars like Betty Grable and Rita Hayworth. He served in World War II and played the role of Doc Holliday with Henry Fonda as Wyatt Earp.

Annie Potts was born in Nashville, TN, but grew up in Franklin and is a television and film actress.

She is probably best known for her roles in the television sitcom **Designing Women** and in the movie **Ghostbusters**. She is currently a visiting professor of Drama at Stephens College in Missouri.

Diane Sawyer was born and raised in Glasgow and is a television journalist for **ABC News** and co-anchor of **ABC's Good Morning America**. She served as a reporter for WLKY-TV in Louisville, Kentucky. In 1970 she was hired by Ron Ziehler, White House press secretary for President Richard Nixon. In 1978, she became a political correspondent for CBS, becoming a co-anchor of the **CBS Morning News** in 1981. In 1984, she became a correspondent for **60 Minutes**, where she stayed for five years. In 1989, she moved to ABC to co-anchor **Primetime Live** with Sam Donaldson.

Rosemary Clooney was a very popular singer and actress. She was born in Maysville. Rosemary's sister

Many television and feature films have been shot at Kentucky Race tracks including Turfway Park
Source: Kentucky Department of Tourism

Kentucky Educational Television Control Room
Source: Sid Webb

Betty and brother Nick (his son is George Clooney) all became entertainers. In 1945, the Clooney sisters won a spot on Cincinnati's radio station WLW as singers. Rosemary's first recordings were in May of 1946 for Columbia Records. In 1951 her record of "*Come On-a My House*" became her first of many hits. In 1954 she teamed up with Bing Crosby, Danny Kaye, and Vera-Ellen in the movie *White Christmas*. She was a close friend of Robert F. Kennedy and was present at his assassination. One of her five children includes actor Miguel Ferrer.

Tom Cruise was born in Syracuse, NY, but he grew up in Louisville. He was known then as Tom Mapother. Cruise is an actor and producer who has starred in a number of top-grossing movies including his first leading role in a blockbuster movie *Risky Business*. He received Academy Award nominations for *Born on the Fourth of July* and *Jerry Maguire*, both as Best Actor; and for *Magnolia*, as Best Supporting Actor. In 1996, he became the first actor in history to star in five consec-

utive films that grossed $100 million in domestic release. The films were *A Few Good Men, The Firm, Interview with the Vampire, Mission: Impossible,* and *Jerry Maguire.*

Kassie DePaiva was born Katherine Virginia Wesley in Morganfield and is an actress on the soap opera *One Life to Live.* She started her soap opera career on *Guiding Light.* DePaiva is also a singer, and has released two albums: Naked and No Regrets.

John Christopher Depp II or Johnny Depp was born in Owensboro and is a well-known film actor. He dropped out of school to become a rock musician. Depp's film debut was in Wes Craven's **A *Nightmare on Elm Street*** as teenager Glen Lantz, who dies

Stripes was filmed at Fort Knox with the cooperation of the U.S. Army
Source: Kentucky Historical Society

White Hall, a unique blend of Gothic, Georgian Revival and Italianate architectural styles, has been featured in the opening credits of the television series Sister Kate and in the mini-series Centennial
Source: Kentucky Historical Society

after being swallowed by a bed. In the late '80s, he starred in the TV police drama *21 Jump Street*, and later he distinguished himself as an acclaimed lead actor in unique roles beginning with *Edward Scissorhands* in 1990. Other movies include *The Curse of the Black Pearl*, *Donnie Brasco* and *The Brave*.

Lynn Ryan was born in Germany and is an actress known for playing the shapely Borg Seven of Nine on *Star Trek: Voyager*. Her father served in the military and raised the family on military bases all over the country until they finally settled in Paducah, when Ryan was 11. Early in her career she was on TV

The 1,032 acre Kentucky Horse Park has been featured in a variety of television and feature films.
Source: Kentucky Department of Tourism

shows like *Melrose Place* and *Matlock*, and had a role in David E. Kelley's *Boston Public*. She gained national attention when details of her divorce proceedings with Jack Ryan, a candidate for the U.S. Senate, were unsealed by a California judge.

Roger Davis is an actor who is best known for his role in the early 1970s television series, *Alias Smith and Jones*. Davis was born in Bowling Green, KY, and first appeared on television in 1959. He first gained attention playing multiple characters on the daytime gothic soap TV series *Dark Shadows*.

Charles Napier was born in Scottsville and is an actor usually known to play tough guys and military types. He made his film debut in *Russ Meyer's Cherry, Harry & Raque.!* Napier had roles in *Silence of the Lambs*, *Rambo: First Blood Part II* and in *The Blues Brothers*. Napier served in the military before becoming an actor.

A.J. Bakunas was a stunt man who died while filming the movie *Steel*. He was killed when his landing pad malfunctioned.

David Llewelyn Wark (D.W.) Griffith was born in Crestwood and became a famous film director and was best known for his film *The Birth of a Nation*. His father was a Confederate Army colonel and Civil War hero Jacob "Roaring Jake" Griffith. Griffith contributed or mastered techniques in the film industry. In addition, he worked on many of his best films with the legendary silent star Lillian Gish. *The Birth of a Nation* was very controversial and helped revive the Ku Klux Klan. Griffin founded United Artists along with Charlie Chaplin, Mary Pickford, and Douglas Fairbanks.

Josh Hopkins is an actor born in Lexington and is the son of former U.S. Congressman Larry Hopkins. His film and television credits include *Ally McBeal*, *Cold Case* and the movie *The Perfect Storm*.

Irene Dunne was born in Louisville and was a film actress and a major star through the 1930s. Later in her career she best known for her role in *The Awful Truth* and the original film of *Anna and the King of Siam*. In 1995, she was appointed one of five alternate U.S. delegates to the United Nations by President Dwight Eisenhower.

Kelly Rutherford starred on the TV series *Melrose Place* and was born in Elizabethtown. She became famous in Turkey for a role in the TV series *Generations*. She has had numerous TV roles and guest appearances

Charles Albert Browning with the nickname "Tod" was born in Louisville and attended Louisville Boys High School. He left home around 1900 to join a circus and became a clown and contortionist. He later became an actor for director D.W. Griffith. Browning played a crook in Griffith's movie *Intolerance* and served as an assistant director in the movie.

James Albert Varney Jr. was an actor born in Lexington and is best known for his character Ernest P. Worrell, which was used in numerous television commercials. His character became so popular that it became a TV series called *Hey Vern, its Ernest.*

Patsy Neal was born in Packard, KY, and grew up in Tennessee. She appeared on Broadway and won a Tony Award for *Voice of the Turtle* and later appeared in her first film opposite Ronald Reagan in *John Loves Mary*. She had an affair with actor Gary Cooper that became public. Neal won the

Academy Award for Best Actress for her role in the movie *Hud.* Neal did television work late in her career and appeared in a TV movie which became the pilot TV series *The Waltons.*

FILMS SHOT IN KENTUCKY

1955 – The Kentuckian
1957 – April Love; Raintree County
1958 – Some Came Running
1962 – How the West Was Won
1964 – Goldfinger
1965 – The Great Race
1967 – The Film-Flam Man
1975 – Escape to Witch Mountain
1976 – The Treasure of Matecumbe; The Thoroughbreds; The Greatest
1977 – A Child of Glass; Black Beauty; Lawman Without a Gun
1978 – Centennial; Steel
1979 – Coal Miner's Daughter
1980 – Stripes
1981 – Rare Breed
1982 – The Act; And They're Off; Kentucky Woman
1983 – The Champions; The River Rat; Carnauba
1984 – Sylvester
1985 – Huckleberry Finn
1987 – Big Business; Bluegrass; Eight Men Out
1988 – Fresh Horses; Rain Man; In Country; Next of Kin
1990 – A Rage in Harlem; Little Man Tate; City of Hope
1991 – The Pickle
1992 – Lost in Yonkers
1993 – Airborne
1995 – A Horse for Danny; Jimmy Crack Corn; Pharaoh's Army
1996 – Fire Down Below; Lawn Dogs
1997 – The Mighty; U S Marshals
1998 – The Insider; Nice Guys Sleep Alone; Simpatico
1999 – Madison
2000 – Traffic; Greatest Adventure of My Life
2002 – Zombie Planet; Paper Cut; Peoples; Fake ID; End of the Party; Finish Line; Coming Down the Mountain; Seabiscuit
2003 – Dance With a Vampire; Keep Your Distance; The Gray; Andy's Logic; Zombie Planet II; Breaking & Entering; Trade Paperback; Forever In Blackhills; Uncle Smiley's Comin' Home;
2004 – Stray; Sweet William; The Death Tunnel; Shadow's Light; Elizabethtown; Dreamer; Jimmy & Judy; A Second More; 12 Steps NOWHERE; The Perfect Stranger; The Deer Path
2005 – Saint Joseph College; The Humane Game; Wrong Number; Halloween; Life Without Harriett

Kentucky Film Office
2200 Capital Plaza Tower
500 Mero Street
Frankfort, Kentucky 40601
Ph: 800-345-5691 (800-FILM KY 1)

KENTUCKY FILM PROFILE
MONEY SPENT IN KENTUCKY BY PRODUCTIONS COMPANIES

PROFILE	2005 (Jan-July)	2004	2003
Feature Films	$118,000	$7,195,000	$9,939,000
Television Series	$36,000	$185,000	$95,000
Documentary	$3,000	$26,000	$87,000
Commercial	$300,000	$285,000	$258,000
Industrial	$35,000	$49,800	$71,000
Music Video	$0	$77,000	$150,000
Still Photo	$52,000	$112,000	$8,000
TOTAL	$544,000	$7,929,800	10,608,000

Based on data reported to the Kentucky Film Commission.

CULTURE & THE ARTS

Music

Robert Lawson

No one can question the fact that Kentucky is rich in music and musicians. From the early days of European settlers bringing their folk music traditions to the area as well as African American gospel and working songs, these are the building blocks of our rich musical heritage today.

The Kentucky Music Hall of Fame & Museum in Renfro Valley, KY, honors the state's performers, songwriters, publishers, promoters, managers, broadcasters, comedians and other music professionals who have made significant contributions to the music industry in Kentucky and around the world.

What follows is a list of artists, past and present, that have influenced and inspired our current musical environment.

Akemon, David 'Stringbean" (1915-1973)

Place of Birth –Annville

Born ito a musical family, young David was taught to play banjo by his father. His moniker 'Stringbean" came from his tall and thin stature. In the 1940's Akemon became the banjo player with Bill Monroe using a two-finger style. In 1969 he became a founding member of the television show 'Hee Haw."

Asher & Little Jimmy (Sizemore)

Sizemore, Asher (1906 - 1975)
Place of Birth: Manchester

Sizemore, 'Little" Jimmie (b. 1928)

Place of Birth: Paintsville

Asher Sizemore and his son Little Jimmie were very popular radio personalities in the Depression years. Father and son duo were regulars on WSM's Grand Ole Opry broadcasts from 1933 to around 1943. Little Jimmie became a favorite of children and adults

Sam Bush
Source: Kentucky Music Hall of Fame

alike with songs like 'Chawin' Gum and the show's sign off song 'As I Lay Me Down To Sleep."

Kenny Baker (b. 1926)

Place of Birth: Jenkins

Kenny was born and grew up in the east Kentucky coal mining town of Jenkins. Both his father and grandfather were fiddlers. Baker made his recording debut with the Blue Grass Boys in 1957. Baker has made many solo recordings through the years and is considered one of the most influential fiddle players of modern times.

Frank 'Hylo"Brown (1922 –2003)

Place of Birth: Johnson County

A Bluegrass and country singer, Frank Brown earned the nickname 'Hylo" because of his considerable vocal range.

Brown joined Flatt and Scruggs becoming a featured vocalist. Due to their increasing popularity, Flatt and Scruggs formed a second group called the Timberliners with Brown as the frontman.

Bush, Sam (b. 1952)

Place of Birth: Bowling Green

Sam Bush expanded the known capabilities of the mandolin and the fiddle in a blend of bluegrass, soul, rock, jazz, and reggae. The founder, leader and member of the New Grass Revival and Strength in Numbers where he expanded the traditions even further. Bush was an integral member of Emmylou Harris' backup band the Nash Ramblers.

Carlisle, Bill (1908 –2003)

Place of Birth: Wakefield

Bill Carlisle, in a duo with his brother Cliff, was a singer, comedian, guitarist, songwriter, and a showman. In the early 1920s he and his brother Cliff were performing in their family's band on WLAP in Lexington. While working in Knoxville he expanded his craft with his comic alter ego Hot Shot Elmer and had audiences laughing for years.

Carson, Martha (b. 1921)

Place of Birth: Neon

Born Irene Amburgey, "The First Lady of Gospel Music," Martha began as a guitar player with her sisters Jean and Berthey ("Mattie and Minnie") as "The Sunshine Sisters"in 1936. At the Renfro Valley Barn Dance, she and her sisters performed with Lily Mae Ledford in 1939 as the Coon Creek Girls (replacing some original members), and by themselves in 1940 as the Hoot Owl Holler Girls. Her single, "Satisfied,"sold more than one-million copies. On the strength of "Satisfied," Martha was invited to join the Grand Ole Opry in 1952.

Martha toured with Elvis Presley, Ferlin Huskey, Del Reeves, Little Jimmy Dickens, and Patsy Cline. Elvis also recorded "Satisfied" and borrowed Martha's dramatic set-ending stance of dropping to one knee and holding the mic stand at an angle. Martha appeared on a number of early television programs including those hosted by Arthur Godfrey, Ray Bolger, Ralph Emery, Tennessee Ernie Ford, Steve Allen, and Ed Sullivan. In 1996, a highway near Neon, Kentucky was named the "Martha Carson Highway"in her honor.

Chapman, Steven Curtis (b. 1962)

Place of Birth: Paducah

Steven has been one of the biggest stars of contemporary Christian music since the late 1980s.

Chesnut, Jerry (b. 1931)

Place of Birth: Harlen County

A guitarist and prolific song writer, Chesnut became a regular on Hee Haw in the 1970s. Some of his most famous songs are: "Another Place Another Time" written for Jerry Lee Lewis; "Good Year for

the Roses"by George Jones; "The Wonders You Perform" by Tammy Wynette and "They Don't Make 'Em Like My Daddy Anymore"by Loretta Lynn. Elvis regarded Chesnut as his favorite songwriter recording 12 of his songs. In 1996, he was inducted into the Nashville Songwriters Foundation Hall of Fame, and in 1999 the International Songwriters Association Hall of Fame. He was a member of the 2006 induction class into the Kentucky Music Hall of Fame & Museum.

Rosemary Clooney
Source: Kentucky Music Hall of Fame

Clooney, Rosemary (1928-2002)

Place of Birth: Maysville

Rosemary Clooney was a renowned pop, jazz, and blues singer on film and radio. She became a band vocalist and rose to instant fame with her recording of "Come-On-A-My-House." She starred in a number of films, most notably "White Christmas," co-starring with Bing Crosby. In the National Broadcaster's Hall of Fame, she won the "Pied Piper Award," describing her as "an American Musical Treasure." She was a member of the 2002 class inducted into the Kentucky Music Hall of Fame.

Conlee, John B. (b. 1946)

Place of Birth: Versailles

John Conlee is one of the most respected vocalists to emerge during the urban cowboy era. John Conlee was known for his superb taste in material and his distinctively melancholy voice. Conlee was born on a tobacco farm in Versailles, and took up the guitar as a child, performing on local radio at age ten. Conlee's hits made the Top Ten 19 times through 1987.

John Conlee
Source: Kentucky Music Hall of Fame

Coon Creek Girls

Ledford, Lily May (1917 – 1985)
Place of Birth: Pilot
Ledford, Rosie (1923-1987)
Place of Birth: Pilot

In 1917, Lily May Ledford (banjo) was born in the Red River Gorge area of Powell County, Kentucky. When the Renfro Valley Barn Dance was born, so was the world's first all girl string band, "The Coon Creek Girls"featuring Lily May Ledford, her sister

Rosie, Esther Koehler, and Evelyn Lange. In 1939, they performed at the White House for President and First Lady, Franklin and Eleanor Roosevelt and King George IV and Queen Elizabeth of England. In 2002, they were inducted into the Kentucky Music Hall of Fame.

Cousin Emmy (1903-1980)
Place of Birth: Lamb

Born Cynthia May Carver, Cousin Emmy became known as 'the first hillbilly to own a Cadillac."She began recording for Decca in the late '40s, her album winding up a cherished item among folk music revivalists of the '60s. Showmanship was always a big deal with her, and she once played almost two dozen different instruments during her show.

Crowe , J.D. (b. 1936)
Place of Birth: Lexington

One of bluegrass music's most talented and influential artist, James Dee Crowe, was born in Lexington in 1937. In the 1950s he played banjo with Jimmy Martin and Mac Wiseman. Jn the 1960s, he formed his own band, the Kentucky Mountain Boys. In 1971 he formed The New South and in 1975 released one of the most influential bluegrass records of all time. Crowe with The New South won a Grammy for their instrumental 'Fireball"in 1983.

Cyrus, Billy Ray (b. 1961)
Place of Birth: Flatwoods

Cyrus is a country singer, best known for the hit single 'Achy Breaky Heart"in 1992, which helped renew the popularity of line dancing and made Cyrus a star. In 2001, Cyrus began playing the lead role on the PAX Network comedy-drama 'Doc." Cyrus continued to chalked up a string of top 40 singles, including 'It Could Have Been Me"and 'When I'm Gone."

Davis, Skeeter (1931-2004)
Place of Birth: Dry Ridge

Mary Frances Penick was born in a two-room cabin near Dry Ridge, KY, in 1931. Her grandfather, impressed by her energy, nicknamed her 'Skeeter."

Davis was a pioneering female vocalist in country music blazing the trail for female singers to follow. She and Betty Jack Davis began the Davis Sisters. Signed by RCA Victor they had their first hit with 'I Forgot More Than You'll Ever Know."

DeShannon, Jackie (b. 1944)
Place of Birth: Hazel

Jackie DeShannon (Sharon Myers) began singing country tunes at age six; by age 11, she hosted her own radio program. Considered the first female singer songwriter of the rock 'n' roll period, DeShannon wrote the soundtrack for Splendor in the Grass (1961); 'Don't Doubt Yourself Babe"for The Byrds debut album; and in 1965, she recorded Bacharach and David's 'What the World Needs Now Is Love." These hits were followed by 'Put a Little Love in Your Heart" and 'Bette Davis Eyes" (a worldwide Number 1 single for Kim Carnes in 1981 and a 1982 Grammy Award for Song of the Year for DeShannon).

Todd Duncan
Source: Kentucky Music Hall of Fame

Duncan, Todd (1903-1998)
Place of Birth: Danville

Duncan was the first Black vocalist to join the New York City Opera. Duncan, considered one of the groundbreaking figures in American artsong, sang the original Porgy in George Gershwin's Porgy and Bess. In 1934 Duncan started his opera career with a production of Mascagni's Cavalleria Rusticana with the Aeollian Opera, and sang with various black opera companies, when the opera stage was still segregated. Duncan was a 2006 inductee into the Kentucky Music Hall of Fame.

Everly Brothers
Everly, Don (b. 1937)
Everly, Phil (b.1939)
Place of Birth: Central City

The Everly Brothers hit the Top 10 singles chart 15 times and sold more than 35 million records in the first five years of their career. Their first hit 'Bye-Bye Love,"reached number one on the country charts in less than a month and remained in the Top 10 for six months to become their first Gold record. 'Bye-Bye Love" and 'All I Have To Do Is

Dream"are identified by the Rock and Roll Hall of Fame as two of '500 songs that shaped Rock and

The Everly Brothers
Source: Kentucky Music Hall of Fame

Roll." They were among the first inductees into the Rock and Roll Hall of Fame 1986, and in 2002, were inducted into the Kentucky Music Hall of Fame.

Foley, Red (1910-1968)
Place of Birth: Blue Lick

Clyde Julian, better known as 'Red" Foley, was a native of Blue Lick, close to Berea. Foley was a country, gospel and pop artist. A member of the Grand Ole Opry (1946) & the Country Music Hall of Fame (1967), his song, 'Peace in the Valley"was the first gospel record to sell a million copies. He was the first Kentuckian to be elected to the Country Music Hall of Fame (1967). He was a member of the 2002 induction class into the Kentucky Music Hall of Fame.

Gayle, Crystal: (b. 1951)
Place of Birth: Paintsville

One of the most popular and widely recognized female country singers of her era, Crystal Gayle, supported her trademark of nearly floor-length hair with a supple voice, a flair for ballads, and a crossover-friendly country-pop style that netted her the occasional mainstream hit. Gayle was born Brenda Gail Webb in Paintsville, KY, in 1951. Her older sister was future superstar Loretta Lynn, though Lynn had already left home by the time Brenda was born. Inspired in part by Lynn's success, Brenda learned guitar and started performing folk songs in high school, also singing backing

vocals in her brother's band. Lynn encouraged her younger sister, and started bringing her out on tour for a few weeks each summer. Lynn's label, Decca, signed the young singer as soon as she was done with high school, but suggested a name change so as to avoid confusion with labelmate Brenda Lee. Lynn suggested the name Crystal, inspired by the Krystal hamburger chain, and Brenda adopted her middle name to come up with Crystal Gayle.

Gillespie, Haven (1888–1975)
Place of Birth: Covington

Haven Gillespie, one of the great Tin Pan Alley writers, is the composer and lyricist of the timeless classics 'You Go To My Head," 'Honey," 'By the Sycamore Tree"and 'Santa Claus is Coming to Town." For the past 60 years, Gillespie's songs have been recorded by the greatest singers of their time, including Dean Martin, Frank Sinatra, Michael Jackson, Louis Armstrong, Sarah Vaughn, Margaret Whiting, Bruce Springsteen, and George Straight.

'Wandering Soul" (Rebel)(1980) 'At Their Best" (Old Homestead)(1981) 'Sweet Sunny South"(Old Homestead)(1985).

Hall , Tom T. (b. 1936)
Place of Birth: Olive Hill

Tom T. Hall was a country and bluegrass singer, songwriter, storyteller and author. He began playing at age 10; his early musical work was on WMOR

Tom T. Hall
Source: Kentucky Music Hall of Fame

in Morehead. Hall's first two singles, 'I Washed My Face in the Morning Dew"and 'A Week in the County Jail" were Top 10 hits. His song, 'Harper Valley P.T.A.," sung by Jeannie C. Riley went to number one on the U. S. Pop Charts. He was a member of the 2002 class inducted into the Kentucky Music Hall of Fame.

Hampton, Lionel (1909–2002)
Place of Birth: Louisville

Hampton was the first jazz vibraphonist and was one of the jazz giants beginning in

Lionel Hampton
Source: Kentucky Music Hall of Fame

the mid-'30s. His big band in the early 1940s enjoyed hit records such as: "Sunny Side of the Street," "Central Avenue Breakdown," "Flying Home," and "Hamp's Boogie-Woogie."

Hampton, Pete (1871-1916)
Place of Birth: Kentucky

Pete Hampton was the first African American to be recorded playing a harmonica. A banjo soloist and singer, his recordings were made in Britain and Germany between 1903-1911. Hampton lived and toured in Europe, returning to the U.S. in 1913. It is believed that Hampton recorded more than any other contemporary African American.

Hill, Mildred (1859-1916)
Hill, Patty (1868-1946)
Place of Birth: Louisville

These sisters both taught nursery school or kindergarten. In 1893, Mildred wrote a melody, Patty added the lyrics and "Good Morning to All" was created. The original lyrics were Good morning to you, Good morning to you, Good morning, dear children, Good morning to all.

Later, the lyrics became "Happy Birthday To You," appearing in a songbook in 1924. Numerous movies and radio shows started using the song

as a birthday greeting. After a court contest, the Hill sisters were granted the copyright to "Happy Birthday To You" in 1934.

Jones, Grandpa (1913-1998)
Place of Birth: Niagra

Born Louis Marshall in Niagra, Grandpa Jones was given his "old" nickname at the age of 22, because he sounded like a "grumpy old man." A country music singer who excelled on his primary instrument, the banjo, he was equally known for his open comedy routines. He was one of the original cast members of the popular television show,

Grandpa Jones
Source: Kentucky Music Hall of Fame

"Hee Haw." Jones was elected to the Country Music Hall of Fame in 1978. He was a 2002 inductee into the Kentucky Music Hall of Fame.

Judds, The
Judd, Naomi (b. 1946)
Place of Birth: Ashland
Judd, Wynonna (b. 1964)
Place of Birth: Ashland

Both Naomi Judd and her daughter, Wynonna, (born Christina Ciminella) are natives of Ashland. The mother and daughter duo were the most commercially successful duo in country music history, until the fame of Brooks & Dunn. Acclaimed as one of the most popular country music acts in the 1980s, the Judds sustained a run of 14 number-one singles from 1984 to 1989. Their debut single, "Had a Dream (For the Heart)," reached the country Top 20; the Judds' second single, "Mama He's Crazy," was a knockout hit that went all the way to number one and later won a Grammy for Best Country Vocal by a Duo or Group. The Judds were inducted into the Kentucky Music Hall of Fame in 2006.

John Lair
Source: Kentucky Music Hall of Fame

Lair, John (1894 –1985)

Place of Birth: Livingston

Radio Pioneer, Folklorist, Writer, Entrepreneur and Founder Renfro Valley Barn Dance. Lair was instrumental in discovering and developing the talents of many country music performers such as Lulubelle, Karl & Harty, "Red" Foley, Doc Hopkins, Linda Parker, "Whitney" Ford, Lily Mae & the Coon Creek Girls, Merle Travis, Homer & Jethro, "Slim" Miller, and Old Joe Clark, among others.

On Nov. 4, 1939 John Lee Lair stepped to the microphone on the stage of the big barn and said: "This is the Renfro Valley Barn Dance, coming to you direct from a real barn in Renfro Valley, Kentucky--the first and only barn dance on the air presented by the actual residents of an actual community.".

Loveless, Patty (b. 1957)

Place of Birth: Pikeville

One of the most popular female country singers of the 1990s, Patty Loveless rose to stardom thanks to her mix of honky tonk and emotive country ballads. She is a distant cousin of sisters Loretta Lynn and Crystal Gayle. Perhaps her crowning achievement was her album, "When Fallen Angels Fly." It won the Country Music Association's Album of the Year award and gave her four Top 10 singles.

Lynn, Loretta (b. 1935)

Place of Birth: Butcher Hollow

Born in Butcher Hollow, Loretta Lynn is one of country music's most well-known personalities and performers. Her biography, "Coal Miner's Daughter," made her famous worldwide. In 1972, Lynn was the first woman to become the Country Music Association's Entertainer of the Year, and she shared the Vocal Duo of the Year award with Conway Twitty. Making the cover of Newsweek in 1973, Lynn was the first woman in country music to become a millionaire. She was inducted into the Kentucky Music Hall of Fame in 2002.

Loretta Lynn
Source: Kentucky Music Hall of Fame

Montgomery Gentry
Montgomery, Gerald Edward (Eddie) (b.1963)

Place of Birth: Danville

Gentry, Troy (b. 1967)

Place of Birth: Lexington

Montgomery Gentry's first musical effort was in a band named Young Country. After several years with the band, Gentry left to try a solo career. In 1994, he was the opener for Patty Loveless, Tracy Byrd and John Michael Montgomery (Eddie's younger brother). He won the Jim Beam National Talent Contest. Later, Gentry forged a duo with Montgomery, building on their rowdy fan base in Kentucky clubs. They won the CMA vocal duo award in 2000.

Montgomery, John Michael (b. 1965)

Place of Birth: Danville

John Michael Montgomery arrived on the country music scene in 1993 with a debut album, "Life's a Dance," that became the only million-seller on the country charts by a new artist that year. Its title was a No. 4 hit single and was followed by his first country chart-topper, "I Love the Way You Love Me." The follow-up album hit the top spot on both the country and adult contemporary charts and produced four more successful singles. At this point, Montgomery was one of the hottest artists in country music, appealing to lovers of both Garth Brooks and Lynyrd Skynyrd.

Monroe, Bill (1911-1996)
Place of Birth: Rosine

Bill Monroe is rightly known as the 'Father of Bluegrass." As a singer, songwriter and mandolin player, he is credited with developing and perfect-

Bill Monroe
Source: Kentucky Music Hall of Fame

ing the Bluegrass music form and teaching it to many great artists. Monroe formed his first band, the Kentuckians, and then the Bluegrass Boys in the 40s. His song 'Blue Moon of Kentucky" is an icon in the Bluegrass music world.

Niles, John Jacob (1892-1980)
Place of Birth: Louisville

He began collecting folk songs at a young age and composed his first song by 1907. Although he specialized in folk music, he was trained at the Cincinnati Conservatory, sang with the Lyric Opera of Chicago, and studied in France. Among his better known folk compositions are 'I Wonder As I Wander" and 'Black is the Color of My True Love's Hair." He was inducted into the Kentucky Music Hall of Fame in 2006.

Molly O'Day (1923 –1987)
Place of Birth: Pike County

Born Lois LaVerne Williamson, Molly O'Day pioneered the position of solo female Country vocalist. She recorded 36 solo and duet numbers for Columbia (each considered a classic) . O'Day started out in a string band playing guitar and singing, with her brothers 'Skeets" on fiddle and 'Duke" on ban-

jo and later recorded songs by Alabama songwriter Hank Williams for Columbia Records. Beginning in 1973, she and her husband had a daily Gospel record program at WMMN-FM Huntington.

Osborne, The Brothers
Osborne, Bobby (b. 1932)
Osborne, Sonny (b. 1937)
Place of Birth: Hyden

The Osborne Brothers Invented the 'High Lead Trio" style of Bluegrass music. In 1963, they joined

Osborne Brothers
Source: Kentucky Music Hall of Fame

the Grand Ole Opry and had several country chart successes including 'Rocky Top," which has the distinction of being the state song in Tennessee. The first to play Bluegrass at the White House, they are the only band to win both the Country Music Association award and Bluegrass Vocal Group of the Year award in the same year. They were inducted into the Kentucky Music Hall of Fame in 2002.

Osborne, Joan (b. 1963)
Place of Birth: Anchorage

Joan's early desire was filmmaking, which led her to New York City where she was a film student at New York University's prestigious film school. Faced with the daunting task of financing her own education, circumstances resulted in a lapse in enrollment. It was during this break that Joan found herself in a little blues bar singing Billie Holiday's 'God Bless The Child" after a friend's late night dare. The realization of a great talent was, thus, born. What followed next was Joan's full blown induction into New York City's thriving blues and roots music scene. In 1992 she formed her own label, Womanly Hips, releasing the live-recorded Soul Show. Her album, 'Relish," earned eight Grammy Award nominations, including one for Album of the Year.

Price, Kenny (1931 –1987)
Place of Birth: Florence

A man of many musical talents, singer and songwriter Kenny Price played drums, guitar, banjo, stand-up bass. Price learned to play on a Sears Roebuck catalog guitar at age five. Drafted into the Army in 1952, Price was stationed in Korea where he played with the USO Show. After his discharge from the Army, he attended the Cincinnati Conservatory of Music. His biggest hits were 'Sea Of Heartbreak" (1972) and "Turn On Your Light" (1973). Price joined the cast of Hee Haw in 1973, singing in the Hee Haw Gospel Quartet with Roy Clark, Grandpa Jones and Buck Owens.

Rambo, Dottie (b. 1934)

Place of Birth: Madisonville

Rambo is considered by many to be the queen of gospel music and a recording artist of international fame. Rambo started writing songs sitting

Dottie Rambo
Source: Kentucky Music Hall of Fame

on a creek bank near her Morganfield home when she was only eight years old. 'Stand By The River," a duet with Dolly Parton, has received wide acclaim by The Christian Country Music Association. Named the Songwriter of The Century (1994), the CCMA presented her with the Living Legend award (2002). Rambo was a member of the 2006 class inducted into the Kentucky Music Hall of Fame.

Ritchie, Jean (b. 1922)

Place of Birth: Viper

Mountain Dulcimer Performer, Folk Singer, Songwriter. Jean Ritchie was the youngest of 14 children from a well-known family of traditional singers. Jean's father taught her to play the Mountain Dulcimer and she was first recorded in 1948. In 2002, she was inducted into the Kentucky Music Hall of Fame.

Roberts, Fiddling Doc (1897 –1978)

Place of Birth: Madison County

One of the best old-time fiddlers from coun-

Jean Ritchie
Source: Kentucky Music Hall of Fame

try music's first commercial decade, Phil ('Doc') Roberts, spent most of his adult life as a farmer in Madison County, Kentucky. Two or three times a year Roberts would journey to the recording studios and make discs for such companies as Gennett, Paramount and the ARC group, logging a total of more than 80 tunes.

Shultz, Arnold (1886-1931)

Place of Birth: Racine

Arnold Shultz was a blues guitarist and fiddler. He is credited as a major influence on white guitarists in western Kentucky and more noteably, on a young Bill Monroe. Shultz is buried in Morgantown Colored Cemetery.

Skaggs, Ricky (b. 1954)

Place of Birth: Eastern Kentucky, reared in Cordell

An accomplished singer and mandolin player, Scaggs was a master by the age of 21. He began his professional career playing bluegrass in 1971, when he and friend, late country singer, Keith Whitley, were invited by Ralph Stanley to join his band. He performed with J.D. Rowe and the New South on their 1975 debut album, which has become one of the most influential bluegrass albums ever released.

As a member of Emmylou Harris' Hot Band in the late 70's, Ricky began exploring the country scene. He reached the top of the country charts in 1981 with the release of his own album, 'Waitin' for the Sun to Shine,"and in 1982 became the youngest member included in the Grand Ole Opry at that time. Ricky was awarded many honors throughout the 80's including the 1985 CMA entertainer of the year, four Grammy awards and dozens of other awards. At a time when the Nashville sound was becoming more and more popish, Ricky carried the torch for returning country to its traditional elements. He was a member of the 2006 class inducted into the Kentucky Music Hall of Fame.

Lonzo & Oscar
John Y. Sullivan 'Lonzo,"
(1919- 1967)
Rollin Sullivan 'Oscar"(b. 1917)

Place of Birth: Edmonton

Ranked as the Grand Ole Opry's premier musical comedy team for more than 25 years. There were really three "Lonzos," brother John being the first and most significant; then, Lloyd George (known as Ken Marvin) and was David Hooten. Lonzo & Oscar hit the Country singles chart with "I'm My Own Grandpa" in 1948.

Mary Travers
Source: Kentucky Music Hall of Fame

Travers, Mary (b. 1937)

Place of Birth: Louisville

Mary Travers was a major influence on the folk music scene during the 1960s and 1970s. Travers, a founding member of Peter, Paul And Mary, became one of the most commercially successful folk performers. She became an inspirational political spokesperson and performed at civil rights rallies with Dr. Martin Luther King and at numerous anti-Vietnam War demonstrations. She was a member of the 2006 class inducted into the Kentucky Music Hall of Fame.

Travis, Merle (1917-1983)

Place of Birth: Rosewood

Travis was a guitar stylist, singer, and songwriter. The son of a tobacco farmer and coal miner, he and

Merle Travis
Source: Kentucky Music Hall of Fame

Grandpa Jones did many radio shows together and recorded as the Shepard Brothers. Travis's "Walkin' The Strings" is a highly regarded album of acoustic guitar solos. In 1948, he developed the solid-body guitar. He was elected to the Country Music Hall of Fame in 1977, and inducted into the Kentucky Music Hall of Fame in 2002.

Vaughn, Billy (1919-1991)

Place of Birth: Glasgow

Born Richard Smith Vaughn, Billy Vaughn is credited with being one of the top most popular orchestra leaders and pop music arrangers of the 1950s and early 60s. Though the Vaughn's were a musical family, Billy was encouraged by his father to seek a career path that was more stable. He began writing songs in his spare time as a barber, and later a factory worker in Glasgow. In 1952, he organized the musical group, "the Hilltoppers" with Jimmy Sacca, Don McGuire and Seymour Spiegelman. Their song, "Trying" became a hit record, and the group enjoyed almost a decade of success. Billy formed an orchestra in Gallatin, TN, and became Dot Records' top moneymaker with hits like "Melody of Love" and "Sail Along Silvery Moon," which sold over 3 million copies, and which also featured what would be his trademark "twin sax" sound. Billy Vaughn became the first American artist to be awarded a gold record in Europe and the first musician to receive a platinum record for achieving sales well over 3 million. He was a member of the 2006 class inducted into the Kentucky Music Hall of Fame.

Billy Vaughn
Source: Kentucky Music Hall of Fame

Whitley, Keith (1955-1989)

Place of Birth: Sandy Hook

A talented new country singer and songwriter, Whitley was just beginning to emerge as a superstar at the time of his death in 1989. The first three singles from his hit album, "Don't Close Your Eyes" -- "Don't Close Your Eyes," "When You Say Nothing At All," and "I'm No Stranger to the Rain"–all reached number one.

Yoakam, Dwight (b. 1956)

Place of Birth: Pikeville; reared in Columbus, Ohio.

When he began his career, Nashville was oriented towards pop Urban Cowboy music, and Yoakam's brand of Bakersfield honky tonk was not considered marketable. His debut LP was 1986's Guitars, Cadillacs, Etc., Etc. and it instantly launched his career. "Honky Tonk Man" and "Guitars, Cadillacs" were hit singles. Yoakam's song Readin', Writin', and Route 23 pays tribute to his childhood move from Kentucky, and is titled after a local expression describing the route that rural Kentuckians need to take to find a job.

CULTURE & THE ARTS

Orchestras & Symphonies

Bowling Green Chamber Orchestra
(270) 846-2426

The Bowling Green Chamber Orchestra changes lives through music education and exciting concerts featuring a wide variety of music.

Bowling Green Western Symphony Orchestra
(270) 745-7681

A cooperative venture between Western Kentucky University's Department of Music and the Bowling Green Western Symphony Orchestra Association, BGWSO is composed of Western students and faculty members as well as musicians from the surrounding region.

Central Kentucky Youth Orchestra
(859) 254-0796

The Central Kentucky Youth Orchestras is one of the oldest, independently chartered, youth orchestras dating back to 1947.

Centre College
(859) 238-5424

Centre's Music Program offers a wide variety of performance and academic opportunities. Any student may take private lessons, participate in ensembles, and take courses ranging from music theory and history to world music.

Eastern Kentucky University
(859) 622-3266

The Eastern Kentucky University Symphony Orchestra is open to all string performers and to selected woodwind, brass and percussion performers by auditions.

Lexington Philharmonic
(859) 233-4226; Toll Free: (888) 494-4226

LPO has a long and vibrant tradition that enhances thousands of lives each year through the beauty of timeless symphonic music.

Louisville Orchestra
(502) 587-8681

Founded in 1937 by conductor Robert Whitney and Charles Farnsley, Mayor of Louisville, the Louisville Orchestra has been called the cornerstone of the Louisville arts scene.

Louisville Youth Orchestra
(502) 896-1851

The Louisville Youth Orchestra (LYO), founded in 1958, provides an extraordinary musical experience for young people from grade school through age 21.

Morehead State University
(606) 783-2473

The MSUO is composed of Morehead State University students and faculty members, as well as musicians from the surrounding region.

Murray State University
(270) 762.6456

The Symphony Orchestra meets on Monday from 6:30 to 8:20, and on Thursday from 2:30 to 3:50 in the Fine Arts Building.

Northern Kentucky Symphony Orchestra
(859) 431-6216

The Kentucky Symphony Orchestra offers the Northern Kentucky and Greater Cincinnati area unique, affordable symphonic experience in a relaxed setting.

Owensboro Symphony
(270) 684-0661

The Owensboro Symphony Orchestra is a premier producer of live classical and pops music.

Paducah Symphony Orchestra
(270) 444-0065

Founded in 1979, the Paducah Symphony Orchestra performs classical, pops and children's concerts featuring internationally recognized guest artists. A regional orchestra, it has played in Kentucky, southern Illinois, southwest Tennessee and southeast Missouri. The Orchestra also has a Children's Chorus and Symphony Chorus.

University of Kentucky
(859) 257-4900

The school has achieved awards and national recognition for high-caliber education in opera, choral and instrumental music performance, as well as for music education, composition, theory and music history.

CULTURE & THE ARTS

Legend of the White Buffalo

Momfeather Erickson

**WHITE BUFFALO CALF WOMAN
(LAKOTA STORY)**

One summer nobody knows how long, the **Oceti**-*Shakowin,* the seven sacred council fires of the *Lakota Oyate,* the nation, came together and camped. The sun shone all the time, but there was no game and the people were starving. Every day they sent scouts to look for game, but the scouts found nothing.

Early one morning the chief sent two of his young men to hunt for game. They went on foot, because at that time the Sioux didn't have horses. They searched everywhere but could find nothing. Seeing a high hill, they decided to climb it in order to look over the whole country. Halfway up, they saw something coming toward them from far off, but the figure was floating instead of walking. From this they knew that the person was *wakan,* holy.

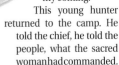

**Rare White Buffalo - born July 2005
at Buffalo Crossing, Shelbyville, KY**
Source: Betty Hall

At first they could make out only a small moving speck and had to squint to see that it was a human form. But as it came nearer, they realized that it was a beautiful young woman, more beautiful than any they had ever seen, with two round, red dots of face paint on her cheeks. She wore a wonderful white buckskin outfit, tanned until it shone a long way in the sun. It was embroidered with sacred and marvelous designs of porcupine quill, in radiant colors no ordinary woman could have made. This wakan stranger was *Ptesan-Wi,* White Buffalo Woman. In her hands she carried a large bundle and a fan of sage leaves. She wore her blue-black hair loose except for a strand at the left side, which was tied up with buffalo fur. Her eyes shone dark and sparkling, with great power in them.

The two young men looked at her open-mouthed. One was overwhelmed, but the other desired her body and stretched his hand out to touch her. This woman was very sacred, and could not be treated with disrespect. Lightning instantly struck the brash young man and burned him up.

To the other scout who had behaved in a good way, the White Buffalo Woman said: 'Good things I am bringing, something holy to your nation. A message I carry for your people from the buffalo nation. Go back to the camp and tell the people to prepare for my arrival. Tell your chief to put up a medicine lodge with twenty-four poles. Let it be made holy for my coming.'

This young hunter returned to the camp. He told the chief, he told the people, what the sacred woman had commanded. The chief told the *eyapaha,* the crier, and the crier went through the camp circle calling: 'Someone sacred is coming. A holy woman approaches.' So the people put up the big medicine tipi and waited. After four days they saw the White Buffalo Woman approaching, carrying her bundle before her. Her wonderful white buckskin dress shone from afar. The chief invited her to enter the medicine lodge. She went in and circled the interior sunwise. The chief addressed her respectfully, saying: 'Sister, we are glad you have come to instruct us.'

She told him what she wanted done. Halting before the chief, she now opened the bundle. The holy thing it contained was the *chanunpa,* the sacred pipe. She held it out to the people and let them look at it. She was grasping the stem with her right hand and the bowl with her left, and thus the pipe has been held ever since.

Again the chief spoke, saying: 'Sister, we are glad. We have had no meat for some time. All we can give you is water.' They dropped some wacanga, sweet grass, into a skin bag of water and gave it to her, and to this day the people dip sweet grass or an eagle wing in water and sprinkle it on a person to be purified.

The White Buffalo Woman showed the people how to use the pipe. She told them that the smoke rising from the bowl was *Tunkashila's* breath, the living breath of the great Grandfather Mystery.

The White Buffalo Woman showed the people the right way to pray, the right words and the right gestures. She taught them how to sing the pipe-filling song and how to lift the pipe up to the sky, toward Grandfather, and down toward Grandmother Earth, to Unci, and then to the four directions of the universe.

'Look at this bowl,' said the White Buffalo Woman. 'Its stone represents the buffalo, but also the flesh and blood of the red man. The buffalo represents the universe and the four directions, because he stands on four legs, for the four ages of man.

The White Buffalo Woman had many things for her Lakota sisters in her sacred womb bag: corn, *wasna* (pemmican) and wild turnip. She taught them how to make the hearth fire. She filled a buffalo paunch with cold water and dropped a red-hot stone into it. 'This way you shall cook the corn and the meat,' she told them.

The White Buffalo Woman also talked to the children, because they have an understanding beyond their years. She told them: 'You are the coming generation, that's why you are the most important and precious ones. Some day you will hold this pipe and smoke it. Some day you will pray with it.'

She spoke once more to all the people: 'The pipe is alive; it is a red being showing you are a red life and a red road. She told the Lakota that they were the purest among the tribes, and for that reason Tunkashila had bestowed upon them the holy cha-nunpa. They had been chosen to take care of it for all the Indian people on this turtle continent.

She spoke one last time to Standing Hollow Horn, the chief, saying: 'Remember: this pipe is very sacred. Respect it and it will take you to the end of the road. The four ages of creation are in me; I am the four ages. I will come to see you in every generation cycle. I shall come back to you.'

The sacred woman then took leave of the people, saying: '*Toksha ake wacinyanktin ktelo,* I shall see you again.'

The people saw her walking off in the same direction from which she had come, outlined against the red ball of the setting sun. As she went, she stopped and rolled over four times. The first time, she turned into a black buffalo; the second into a brown one; the third into a red one; and finally, the fourth time she rolled over, she turned into a white female buffalo calf. A white buffalo is the most sacred living thing you could ever encounter.

The White Buffalo Woman disappeared over the horizon. Sometime she might come back. As soon as she had vanished, buffalo in great herds appeared, allowing themselves to be killed so that the people might survive. And from that day on, our relations, the buffalo, furnished the people with everything they needed, meat for their food, skins for their clothes and tipis, bones for their many tools.

Two very old tribal pipes are kept by the Looking Horse family at Eagle Butte in South Dakota. One of them is the Sacred Pipe brought to the people by White Buffalo Woman.

On July 9, 2005, a white buffalo calf was born in Shelby County and named by Steve McCullough a Lakota Elder. The new calf was named 'Medicine Spirit.'

Story submitted by Momfeather Erickson.

"MEDICINE SPIRIT — A MOST SACRED LIVING THING"

As she went, she stopped and rolled over four times.

The first time, she turned into a black buffalo;

the second into a brown one; the third into a red one; and finally,

the fourth time she rolled over, she turned into a white female buffalo calf.

A white buffalo is the most sacred living thing you could ever encounter.

CULTURE & THE ARTS

Craft & Folk Art

Glass, steel, iron, fabric, fiber, clay, wood, sticks, beads, even coal from time immemorial humans have found many ways to express their creativity, their dreams, their very souls. Out of the celebration of Kentucky's folklife naturally comes an interest in the crafts and folk art created by its people.

We humbly pay hom-

Folk artist Minnie Adkins
at home, Isonsville
Source: Sid Webb

age to all folk art-
ists and whatever means they select to share their visions with us and thank them for their generosity in permitting a glimpse into their genius.

The Kentucky Artisan Center at Berea offers an outstanding opportunity to explore Kentucky artisan works and their stories –it offers Kentucky crafted items, recordings by Kentucky musicians, books by Kentucky authors, and specialty foods grown or produced in Kentucky. Berea is officially the 'Crafts Capital" of Kentucky, recognition earned from a long-time tradition as a center of craftsmanship. At the heart of Berea and its crafts tradition is Berea College, where students do not pay tuition, but work ten to 15 hours per week in

one of the college's industries. As part of the Berea College Crafts Program, students create fine furniture, woven items, ceramics, brooms and wrought iron pieces.

In 1980, former First Lady of Kentucky, Phyllis George, helped propel into the spotlight the amazing

Creations of folk artist Minnie Adkins
Source: Sid Webb

skills and talents of the state's artisans.

The effort began when Kentucky crafts were featured in 'Oh, Kentucky" shops at Bloomingdales department store in New York City. In 1981 the Kentucky Museum of Art and Craft, in Louisville, was organized as a non-profit organization to promote the rich art and craft heritage of Kentucky through three main areas of programming: exhibition, education, and support of artists through the retail Gallery Shop.

The Museum of Art and Craft has supported more than 400 artists and provided educational programs to more than 500,000 school children. The Museum is supported in part by the Fund for the Arts and Kentucky Arts Council, a state agency of the Commerce Cabinet. The Gallery Shop features the work of over 200 artists at any one time, offering work in all media from folk art to furniture.

In Morehead, the Kentucky Folk Art Center offers visitors one of the most unique and important cultural experiences to be found anywhere in Appalachia. From the fun and quirky to the fantastical, the folk art exhibited and conserved by the Folk Art Center is an engaging and vital piece of the region's history and contemporary culture.

With a growing permanent collection of nearly 1,000 works by regional folk artists, the Folk Art Center strives to preserve and promote a broader understanding of traditional and contemporary folk art through exhibitions that range in content from folk art works, such as textiles to contextually related subject matter, including photography and food traditions.

Events around the state celebrating the gifts from Kentucky hands include the biannual Arts and Crafts Fairs at the Folk Art Center, which creates a market for regional crafts people. "A Day in the Country" folk art show, formerly held on Minnie Adkin's farm in Elliott County, brings more than 50 folk artists to Morehead on the first Saturday of June each year. More than 100 artists and craft persons from Kentucky and surrounding states reveal their creations at each of the two annual Appalachian Arts and Crafts Fair on the first Saturday of December and the last Saturday of June in the

Louisville Stoneware
Source: Sid Webb

Traditional Kentucky pattern on woven coverlet
Source: Sid Webb

Laughlin Health Building on the campus of Morehead State University, Morehead.

Another extremely popular event is Kentucky Crafted: The Market, held annually at the Kentucky Fair and Exposition Center in Louisville. Now in its 24th year, the show is an extension of the Kentucky Craft Marketing Program (also established under George's leadership in 1981). The program's mission is, among other things, to develop the state's craft industry, support and empower Kentucky artisans and craftspeople, and create an economically viable environment for craft entrepreneurs.

Kentucky Crafted: The Market was selected as one of the Top 25 Art Fairs and Festivals in the country by "American Style Magazine," and, for the tenth time, the Southeast Tourism Society has named it one of the Top Twenty Events in the Southeast. More than 300 exhibitors participate offering fine traditional, folk and contemporary crafts, two-dimensional visual art, musical recordings, books and food products. The Market is a collaborative effort among several state agencies and cabinets, and generates $2-$3 million dollars in direct sales.

The craft industry in Kentucky contributes $252 million dollars to the state's economy and has an impact of additional $147 million dollars from out-of-state sales. Kentucky is recognized as a model for its craft programs and its role in the $14 billion national craft industry.

Sources: The Kentucky Artisan Center, www.kentuckyartisancenter.ky.gov; The Kentucky Museum of Art and Craft, www.kentuckyarts.org/index.cfm; Kentucky Crafted: the Market, http://kycraft.ky.gov/; The Kentucky Folk Art Center at Morehead, www.morehead-st.edu/units/folkart.

Paintings • Drawings • Giclée

Visit the online gallery

www.sidwebb.com

859-226-9943

Food & Traditional Recipes

MINT JULEP

3 cups sugar
3 cups water
Sprigs of fresh mint
Crushed ice
Bourbon (not whisky)
Silver Julep Cups

Make a simple syrup by boiling sugar and water together for about five minutes. Cool and place in a covered container with eight - ten sprigs of fresh mint, and refrigerate overnight. Make one julep (only one) at a time by filling a julep cup with crushed ice, adding one tablespoon syrup and two ounces of Bourbon. Stir briskly with a spoon in order to frost the outside of the julep cup. Garnish with a sprig or two of fresh mint. Enjoy.

SHAKER LEMON PIE

2 large lemons
4 eggs, well beaten
2 C sugar

Slice lemons as thin as paper, rind and all. Combine with sugar and mix well; Let stand 2 hours, or preferably overnight, blending occasionally. Add beaten eggs to lemon mixture and mix well. Turn into nine-inch pie shell, arranging lemon slices evenly. Cover with top crust. Cut several slits near center. Bake at 450 degrees for 15 minutes, reduce heat to 375 degrees and bake for about 20 minutes or until silver knife inserted near edge of pie comes out clean. Cool before service.

NOTE: In the 1800's lemons had a much thinner layer of rind than are found today. For this reason, look for a variety of lemons with a very thin rind.

(From the Trustees House Daily Fare, Pleasant Hill, Kentucky. Compliments of Shaker Village at Pleasant Hill, http://www.shakervillageky.org)

SIMPLE SHAKER COOKIES

½ C butter
¾ C granulated sugar
1 egg
1 tsp vanilla
1-1/2 C flour
1 tsp baking powder
¼ tsp salt

Cream butter and sugar until well blended. Beat in egg and vanilla, mixing well. Sift dry ingredients together. Add to creamed mixture. Chill for at least two hours, then roll and cut on floured surface. (This dough can be rolled in a wax paper cylinder and sliced and baked after chilling. For cookie presses omit the chilling. Place on greased cookie sheet. Bake at 400 degrees until firm but not brown. This recipe has many uses. It's basic for fancy-shaped holiday cookies, plain icebox cookies or drop cookies.

(Also from the Trustees House Daily Fare, Pleasant Hill, Kentucky.)

WOODFORD PUDDING

1 C flour
½ C butter
1 tsp soda
1 tsp cinnamon
1 C sugar
1 C blackberry jam
½ C sour milk
3 eggs

Mix all together well. Bake in pudding dish at 375 for 40 minutes or until lightly firm.

(Also from the Trustees House Daily Fare, Pleasant Hill, Kentucky.)

ANGEL BISCUITS

5 C all purpose flour (not sifted)
3 Tbsp sugar
3/4 C vegetable shortening
1 pkg. yeast, dissolved in ½ c. lukewarm water
1 tsp baking soda
1 tsp salt
2 C buttermilk
3 tsp baking powder

Sift dry ingredients together. Cut in shortening until mixed thoroughly. Add buttermilk and dissolved yeast. Stir with a large wooden spoon until all flour is moistened. Put in large bowl in refrigerator until ready to use.

When ready to use, take out as much as needed and let rest 5 minutes on floured board. Roll to ½ inch thickness and cut. Melted margarine may be brushed on biscuit before or after baking.

Biscuits are best if they have been refrigerated at least overnight. The longer they are refrigerated, the more the yeast flavor comes through. (They will refrigerate for several weeks.)

Baking Temperature: 400 degrees. Baking time: 12 minutes. Yield or number of servings: 6 dozen.

(From "A Book of Favorite Recipes," compiled by the Washington County Homemakers, 1979, compliments of Mrs. Elizabeth Breeding, Springfield, Ky.)

CARAMEL ICING FOR JAM CAKE

4 C light brown sugar
2 tsp vanilla
1 C butter or margarine
2 Tbsp bourbon (your favorite)
1 C cream

Stir the sugar, butter or margarine, and cream over medium heat until dissolved. Then boil the mixture to the soft ball stage (238 degrees.) Remove mixture from heat and beat with electric mixer until it is cool. Then add vanilla and bourbon. If icing needs to be thicker, add sifted powdered sugar gradually until it is the right consistency.

Yield or number of servings: generously frosts a 3 layer cake. Beware: if the icing "cracks" when the cake is cut, it's been cooked too long. Adjust next time.

(Also from "A Book of Favorite Recipes,")

STELLA HALL'S JAM CAKE

"If you just follow the directions, it'll come out good."

2 ½ C white sugar
6 egg yolks, well beaten
1 C of butter or margarine
1 tsp soda dissolved in 1 cup of buttermilk
1 C of jam or jelly
1 C of raisins
1 C of strawberry preserves
1 C of pear preserves, finely minced
1 C nut meats {pecans} broken
1 tsp ground cloves
1 tsp allspice
1 tsp cinnamon
31/2 C sifted flour
6 egg whites, stiffly beaten

Sift flour with spices. Cream butter or margarine with sugar until very light. Add egg yolks and beat thoroughly. Add buttermilk and soda alternately with dry ingredients.

Mix the jam or jelly, raisins, strawberry preserves, pear preserves, and nuts together. Add this to the creamed mixture. Best served with hot coffee after a very large dinner with family and friends.

(Also from "A Book of Favorite Recipes,")

CHESS PIE

2 C sugar
5 egg yolks
2 Tbsp flour
½ C butter
2 Tbsp corn meal
1 C whole milk

Bake at 400 degrees for 15 minutes. Then back at 350 degrees until the filling is set. Yield or number of servings: 6

(Also from "A Book of Favorite Recipes,")

RECIPE FOR A HAPPY HOME

4 C of love
3 C of forgiveness
2 C of loyalty
3 C of forgiveness
2 C of loyalty
1 C of friendship
5 Tbsp of hope
2 Tbsp of tenderness
4 Qt of faith
1 Barrel of laughter

Take love and loyalty, mix thoroughly with faith. Blend it with tenderness, kindness and understanding. Add friendship and hope, sprinkle abundantly with laughter. Bake it with sunshine. Serve daily with generous helpings.

A Few Kitchen Ideas

* For quick and handy seasoning while cooking, keep on hand a large shaker containing six parts of salt and one of pepper.
* It is important when and how salt is added in cooking. To blend with soups and sauces, put it in early, but add it to meats just before taking from stove.
* In cake ingredients, salt can be mixed with eggs.
* When cooking vegetables always salt the water in which they are cooked.
* Put salt in the pan when frying fish.
* It is easy to remove the white membrane from oranges-for fancy desserts or salads by soaking them in boiling water for five minutes before peeling.

Words

The six most important words in the English language:
I admit I made a mistake.
The five most important words: *You did a good job.*
The four most important words: *What is your opinion?*
The three most important words: *If you please.*
The two most important words: *Thank you.*
The one most important word: *We.*
The one least important word: *I.*

(Also from "A Book of Favorite Recipes.")

CULTURE & THE ARTS

Preservation

Since 1966, the Kentucky Heritage Council / State Historic Preservation Office has been assisting individuals, communities and local governments with making historic preservation an important component of comprehensive community planning and economic development. Kentucky has a rich heritage expressed in its historic buildings, sites and cultural landscapes. Making a concerted effort to preserve this heritage and the built environment is integral to building successful, thriving communi-

ties. At its heart, fostering a preservation ethic in Kentucky is essential to community revitalization and quality of life.

As set forth by federal and state legislation, the Kentucky Heritage Council is charged with identifying, preserving and protecting the historic resources of Kentucky, and seeking to build a greater awareness of Kentucky's past while ensuring it for the future. To this end, the Heritage Council has successfully encouraged the adaptive reuse of historic buildings in all contexts and advocated that historic preservation should be a key public policy initiative to encourage economic development, provide affordable housing, revitalize downtowns and neighborhoods, provide life-long learning opportunities and enhance Kentucky's quality of life. As an agency of the Kentucky Commerce Cabinet, the Heritage Council has consistently and successfully partnered with other agencies, local governments, preservation and community organizations and individuals to achieve this mission.

Kentucky Heritage Council programs include surveying historic structures and archaeological sites, nominating properties to the National Register of Historic Places, rebuilding and revitalizing Ken-

tucky Main Streets, and administering and overseeing federal rehabilitation tax incentives, Certified Local Governments, historic preservation grants, environmental review, archaeology programs, and public education and outreach.

Through the years, several special emphasis programs (including Civil War, Rural Preservation, Heritage Tourism, the African American Heritage Commission, the Native American Heritage Commission, Military Sites, Underground Railroad, and the Kentucky Archaeological Survey) have been developed and proven highly successful in reaching diverse audiences and expanding preservation efforts to encompass important new partners. Along with the strength of core programs, these additional initiatives have made Kentucky a leader in the national historic preservation movement. For more information, see www.heritage.ky.gov.

The National Historic Preservation Act of 1966 authorized the National Park Service to create and maintain the National Register of Historic Places, the official federal listing of properties deemed to be of historic, cultural and architectural significance. Because of the Kentucky Heritage Council's early emphasis on surveying, identifying and evaluating our state's historic resources, the agency has consistently been successful in nominating properties to the National Register.

National Register listing can be applied to buildings, objects, structures, districts and archaeological resources. Properties proposed for listing must be significant in architecture, engineering, American history or culture, or possess a special role in the development of our country. National Register status does not affect property ownership rights. Owners of National Register properties, however, may qualify for federal or state tax credits for certified rehabilitation of these properties or for making charitable contribution of preservation easements.

Kentucky ranks fourth in the nation in the number of properties listed in the National Register with more than 3,100 listings of districts, sites and structures totaling more than 41,000 historic features. For more information about the National Register in Kentucky, see www.heritage.ky.gov/national_register.htm

Introduced in 2003, *Preserve America* is a White House initiative that encourages and supports community efforts in historic preservation. Led by honorary chair First Lady Laura Bush, the program was developed in cooperation with the federal Advisory Council on Historic Preservation, the U.S. Department of the Interior, and the U.S. Department of Commerce to focus attention on President and Mrs. Bush's commitment to preserving our national heritage.

Preserve America goals include a greater shared knowledge about the nation's past, strengthened regional identities and local pride, increased local participation in preserving the country's cultural and natural heritage assets and support for the economic vitality of communities.

Taking advantage of this important opportunity, the Kentucky Heritage Council initiated an early push to get Kentucky Main Street communities designated in the *Preserve America* program. Today, Kentucky has the largest and most unique group of community designations among all states – a total of 60. For more information about Preserve America, see www.preserveamerica.gov.

Created and administered by the Kentucky Heritage Council, the Kentucky Main Street Program is the oldest statewide downtown revitalization program in the nation, celebrating its 26th anniversary in 2005. Kentucky Main Street Program strategy is based on a four-point approach developed by the National Main Street Center of the National Trust for Historic Preservation, which emphasizes organization, promotion, design and economic restructuring within the context of historic preservation as principles for successful downtown revitalization.

Downtowns throughout Kentucky feature substantial historic resources embodied in their buildings and structures. Fortunately, the Kentucky Main Street Program's emphasis on historic preservation as a sound economic development strategy not only helps promote development along Main Street, but also creates a halo effect to encourage neighborhood investment and redevelopment. Fostering strong partnerships between the public and private sector to achieve downtown revitalization has been the key to this success.

Today more than 100 communities – a record number – participate in the Kentucky Main Street Program and reap the economic benefits of preserving the business core of their communities. For more information, see www.heritage.ky.gov/kyheritage_mainstreet.htm

National Historic Landmarks are nationally significant historic places designated by the Secretary of the Interior because they possess exceptional value or quality in illustrating or interpreting the heritage of the United States. Today, fewer than 2,500 historic places bear this national distinction. Working with citizens throughout the nation, the National Historic Landmarks Program draws upon the expertise of National Park Service staff, who nominate new landmarks and provide assistance to existing landmarks.

KENTUCKY'S 30
NATIONAL HISTORIC LANDMARKS

Daniel C. Beard Boyhood Home, Covington
Belle of Louisville (Steamboat), Louisville
Burks' Distillery, Loretto
Churchill Downs, Louisville
Ashland, the Henry Clay Home, Lexington
Covington and Cincinnati Suspension Bridge
Fort Boonesborough Site, Richmond
Green River Shell Middens Archaeological District
Indian Knoll, McHenry
Jacobs Hall, Kentucky School for the Deaf, Danville
Keeneland Race Course, Lexington
Labrot and Graham's Old Oscar Pepper Distillery, Versailles
Liberty Hall, Frankfort
Lincoln Hall, Berea College, Berea
Locust Grove, Louisville
Louisville Water Company Pumping Station, Louisville
Mayor Andrew Broaddus Lifesaving Station, Louisville
Dr. Ephraim McDowell House, Danville
Middle Creek Battlefield, Prestonsburg
Mill Springs Battlefield
Old Bank of Louisville (Actors Theatre), Louisville
Old Morrison, Transylvania College, Lexington
Old State House, Frankfort
Perryville Battlefield, Perryville
Pine Mountain Settlement School, Bledsoe
Shaker Village of Pleasant Hill and vicinity
Zachary Taylor House, Louisville
United States Marine Hospital, Louisville
Wendover, Hyden
Whitney M. Young Birthplace and Boyhood Home, Simpsonville

Ida Lee Willis was named the first Executive Director of the Kentucky Heritage Council / State Historic Preservation Office (formerly the Kentucky Heritage

Commission) in 1966. The Ida Lee Willis Memorial Foundation was chartered in 1979 to honor Mrs. Willis, widow of former Governor Simeon Willis. Awards are presented annually to individuals and organizations who have demonstrated an understanding of and an appreciation for the value of preserving and reusing Kentucky's historic and prehistoric resources, whether through the restoration of an important structure or community resource or through a lifetime commitment to encouraging and promoting historic preservation. **The Ida Lee Willis Memorial Award** for historic preservation is given annually to the individual who has demonstrated outstanding dedication to the cause of historic preservation in the Commonwealth. The award is the highest honor given by the foundation.

The history of African American life in Kentucky is filled with a host of rich experiences. African American history in Kentucky has roots in the Commonwealth's earliest history, as African Americans accompanied and assisted Daniel Boone upon his arrival to the new frontier in 1769.

As a border state during the Civil War, Kentucky's unique condition did not lessen the cruelty and pain of slavery. These experiences left a lasting legacy of places that Kentucky takes pride in preserving.

The Kentucky Heritage Council / State Historic Preservation Office and the Kentucky African American Heritage Commission are dedicated to preserving buildings and places important to the history of Kentucky African Americans. These efforts include building a statewide network of grassroots preservationists working through the Northern and Western Kentucky African American Task Forces.

Kentucky offers an array of sites that tell the story of slavery, the Underground Railroad, Civil War, education (including an historically black college) and civil rights, as well as a variety of historically significant architecture and museums that promote local history. For more information, see www.kcaah.com.

Native Americans have called Kentucky home for more than 12,000 years. To date, more than 22,000 Native American archaeological sites have been documented in the state. These sites range from small seasonal camps to burial mounds, to rock art, to large villages that were occupied by hundreds of people.

To learn more about the Native Americans who once called Kentucky home, visit exhibits on Kentucky prehistory at the Kentucky History Center in Frankfort, the University of Kentucky William S. Webb Museum of Anthropology in Lexington or the Gladie Creek Cultural and Environmental Learning Center at the Daniel Boone National Forest. The Kentucky Archaeological Survey's web site, at www.heritage.ky.gov/kas.htm is a joint program of the Kentucky Heritage Council / State Historic Preservation Office and the University of Kentucky Department of Anthropology.

A SAMPLER OF HISTORIC PLACES

Pine Mountain Settlement School, Harlan County

This National Historic Landmark campus in the heart of Appalachia is open for tours by appointment and also offers weekend and weeklong programming for those interested in historic preservation and the environment.

Stearns, McCreary County

Visit this coal company town and ride the train to the Big South Fork River and Recreational Area to see the interpreted coal camp of Blue Heron.

Dinsmore House, Boone County / Adsmore, Princeton / Conrad Caldwell House, St. James Court, Louisville / Liberty Hall, Frankfort

These house museums do an exceptional job of telling their stories to visitors.

Highway 31 Corridor / Highway 68 Corridor

Kentucky's historic highways are scenic experiences, and the small towns along the way offer varied opportunities for the visitors.

Covered Bridges, north central Kentucky

A sense of nostalgia is inevitable at the sight of one of Kentucky's surviving covered bridges. Visit the Covered Bridge Museum in Flemingsburg to learn more about these fascinating structures.

Belle of Louisville, Louisville

Take a ride on this steamboat, a National Historic Landmark, and get a sense of the importance of river history to Kentucky's development.

Shaker Village of Pleasant Hill, Harrodsburg / Shakertown at South Union, Auburn

Shaker Village is a premier living history site where costumed interpreters chronicle Shaker life. The Shaker Museum at South Union is filled with scores of original artifacts exemplifying the Shakers' fine craftsmanship.

Stone Walls and Rock Fences

Travel along Kentucky's highways and enjoy the craftsmanship of dry laid stone walls and rock fences that border fields, pastures and roadways. The skills required of this construction method are being revived to continue this traditional building technique.

For more information on how you can help with the preservation and interpretation of historic places, contact the Kentucky Heritage Council / State Historic Preservation Office, 300 Washington Street, Frankfort, KY 40601, 502-564-7005 or see www.heritage.ky.gov.

CULTURE & THE ARTS
Museums
& Related Organizations

ART MUSEUMS

Behringer-Crawford Museum
Covington
(859) 491-4003

Bill Monroe Museum
Rosine
(270) 298-3551

The Crane House
Louisville
(502) 635-2240

Emma Reno Connor's Black History Gallery
Elizabethtown
(270) 769-5204

Headley-Whitney Museum
Lexington
(859) 255-6653

International Museum of the Horse
Kentucky Horse Park
Lexington
(859) 233-4303

Janice Mason Art Museum
Cadiz
(270) 522-9056

John James Audubon Museum & Nature Center
Henderson
(270) 826-2247

Kentucky Derby Museum
Louisville
(502) 637-1111

Kentucky Museum of Arts & Design
Louisville
(502) 589-0202

Magoffin Co. Historical Society Pioneer Village
Salyersville
(606) 349-1607

Mayfield/Graves County Art Guild
Mayfield
(270) 247-6971

Museum of the American Quilter's Society
Paducah
(270) 442-8856

Owensboro Museum of Fine Arts
Owensboro
(270) 685-3181

Portland Museum
Louisville
(502) 776- 7678

The Speed Art Museum
Louisville
(502) 634-2700

UNIVERSITY ART MUSEUMS

Berea College Museum
Berea
(859) 985-3373

Clara M. Eagle Art Gallery
Murray State University
Murray
(270) 762-3052

Fine Arts Center
Henderson Community College
Henderson
(270) 827-1867

Godbey Appalchian Center
Southeast Community College
(606) 589-2145

Kentucky Folk Art Center
Morehead State University
Morehead
(606) 783-2204

The Kentucky Museum
Western Kentucky University
Bowling Green
(270) 745-2592

Museum of Anthropology
Northern Kentucky University
Highland Heights
(859) 572-5259

University of Kentucky Art Museum
University of Kentucky
Lexington
(859) 257-5716

David Wright, Windsor chairmaker
Source: Kentucky Department of Tourism

ART CENTERS

The Gateway Regional Center for the Arts
Mt. Sterling
(859) 498-6264

Kentucky Artisan Center
Berea
(859) 985-5448

Kentucky Center
Louisville
(859) 562-0100

Kentucky Folk Art Center
Morehead
(606) 786-2204

Minds Wide Open Art Center
Lexington
(859) 259-2637

Yeiser Art Center
Paducah
(270) 492-2453

Dawson Springs Museum And Art Center
Dawson Springs
(270) 797-3503

Living Arts and Sciences Center
Lexington
(859) 252-5222

Camp Breckinridge Museum and Arts Center
Moranfield
(270) 289-4420

Richmond Area Arts Center
Richmond
(859) 624-4242

Henderson Fine Arts Center
Henderson
(270) 831-9800

NON-PROFIT ORGANIZATIONS

Arts Kentucky
Louisville
(502) 561-0701

Kentucky Art & Craft Foundation
Louisville
(502) 589-0102

Kentucky Arts Council
Frankfort
(502) 564-3757

Kentucky Citizens for the Arts
Louisville
(502) 589-3116

Kentucky Crafted
Frankfort
(502) 564-3757

Lexington Art League
Lexington
(859) 254-7024

Lexington Arts & Cultural Council
Lexington
(859) 225-2951

Louisville Visual Art Association
Louisville
(502) 896-2146

VSA Arts of Kentucky
Bowling Green
(270) 781-0872

Background Photo Source: Kentucky Department of Tourism

Kentucky Artisan Center
Source: Kentucky Commerce Cabinet

CULTURE & THE ARTS

Kentucky Chautauqua

Kentucky Humanities Council

**KENTUCKY CHAUTAUQUA —
BRINGING HISTORY TO LIFE**

"Kentucky Chautauqua," presented by the Kentucky Humanities Council, are historically accurate impersonations of 16 fascinating characters from Kentucky's past. Intended for audiences of 40 or more, Kentucky Chautauqua performances offer a unique combination of education and entertainment. KHC offers a limited number of reduced-cost ($125) Kentucky Chautauqua performances supported by the generosity of sponsors.

The characters are: Ruth Hanly Booe, Bourbon Ball Belle (1891-1973); George Rogers Clark, Revolutionary War Hero (1752-1818); Anna Mac Clarke, Military Pioneer (1919–1944); Catherine Conner, Political Powerhouse (1900-2002); Henry Clay, Kentucky's Great Statesman (1777–1852); Price Hollowell, Black Patch War Hero (1895–1975); Grandpa Jones, Country musician and Comic (1913–1998); Maxine Lacey, Toby Tent Show Actress (1916–1996); Lily May Ledford, Coon Creek Girl (1917–1985); Rose Will Monroe, Rosie the Riveter (1920–1997); Adolph Rupp, The Coach (1901–1977); Dinnie Thompson, No Ordinary Woman (1857–1939); Dr. Thomas Walker, Pioneer Physician (1715–1794); Simon Kenton, Frontiersman (1755–1836); John C. C. Mayo, Coal Baron (1864–1914); and Sallie Ward, Queen of Society (1827–1896).

Book Kentucky Chautauqua by callng (859) 257-5932 or by going to http://www.kyhumanities.org.

**Ruth Hanly Booe
(Kelly Brengelman)**
*Source: Kentucky
Humanities Council*

**Catherine Connor
(Suzi Schuhmann)**
*Source: Kentucky
Humanities Council*

Ruth Hanly Booe: Borbon Ball Belle (1891-1873): Ruth Booe, inventor of the world-famous bourbon ball, founded the Rebecca Ruth candy company of Frankfort. Her grandson now runs the business. Portrayed by Kelly Brengelman of Midway.

Catherine Conner: Political Powerhouse (1900-2002): Born on a farm in Bullitt County, Kentucky, Conner's political career carried her all the way to the inner councils of Franklin D. Roosevelt's White House. Portrayed by Suzi Schuhmann of Louisville.

Price Hollowell: Black Patch War Hero (1895-1975): Hollowell was just thirteen when the Night Riders attacked his family's farm in western Kentucky (Caldwell County). His testimony in court brought the villains to justice. Portrayed by Ethan Sullivan Smith of Cynthiana.

Rose Will Monroe: Rosie the Riveter (1920-1997): Monroe, a native of Pulaski County, Kentucky, was working in a bomber factory when she was picked to play World War II icon Rosie the Riveter in a film. Portrayed by Angela Bartley of Louisville.

Adolph Rupp: The Coach (1901-1977): The legendary coach's winning teams and genius for public relations made University of Kentucky basketball a statewide phenomenon. Portrayed by Edward B. Smith of Cynthiana.

Dr. Thomas Walker: Pioneer Physician (1715-1794): Walker, a politically well connected doctor and land speculator from Virginia, led the first English expedition into Kentucky in 1750. Portrayed by Danny W. Hinton of Livingston/

**Dr. Thomas Walker
(Danny W. Hinton)**
*Source: Kentucky
Humanities Council*

**Rose Will Monroe
(Angela Bartley)**
*Source: Kentucky
Humanities Council*

**Price Hollowell
(Ethan Sullivan Smith)**
*Source: Kentucky
Humanities Council*

**Adolph Rupp
(Edward B. Smith)**
*Source: Kentucky
Humanities Council*

CULTURE & THE ARTS

Kentucky Department for Libraries & Archives

The Department for Libraries & Archives dates its origins to 1825, when the Kentucky State Library was established by the General Assembly to serve the government in Frankfort. Today, KDLA is one of 10 state agencies in the United States which combine library, archival and public records programs, and is guided by the motto, "Serving Kentucky's Need to Know."

Kentucky's Historian Laureate Dr. Thomas D. Clark played a key role in the passage of the state's public records law in 1958 and in construction of the Department for Libraries and Archives. Clark began lobbying governors and legislators in the 1930s to appropriate funds for a suitable home for the state's permanent public records and pled his case to every governor over a 40 year period. His tenacity was rewarded when Gov. Julian Carroll supported a $10.5 million appropriation for a combined library and archival facility of almost 140,000 square feet. The building, located on 300

Kentucky Department for Libraries & Archives
Source: Kentucky Deaprtment for Libraries & Archives

Coffee Tree Road in Frankfort, was dedicated on October 8, 1982. The structure, which houses the State Archives, the State Library, and the Kentucky Talking Book Library, was named the Clark-Cooper building in honor of Dr. Clark and prominent Hazard banker C. Vernon Cooper, who was also a champion of Kentucky's library system.

Today, KDLA fulfills its mission through services to the public, to libraries and to government agencies.

At KDLA's Archives Research Room, researchers find access to local, state, and judicial records. The Friends of Kentucky Public Archives, Inc., a private, not-for-profit membership organization open to all, supports the department's archival programs through outreach and advocacy, planned giving and fiscal support, and education and professional development.

Additionally, the State Library is a major information and referral center in Kentucky. State Library Services maintains information and resources sharing among all types of libraries and information centers – including state agencies.

Working in cooperation with the Library of Congress, KDLA also provides visually and physically disabled Kentuckians with a large selection of reading materials through the Kentucky Talking Book Library.

Kentuckians have public library services in 118 counties. The abilities of these libraries vary greatly; KDLA works with local library staffs and governing boards to enhance each public library's efforts. Resources available to Kentucky's public libraries include: reference services, interlibrary loan, cataloging assistance, quick access through KDLA's website, and circulation of multimedia and large print book collections. In addition, regional library consultants are located in offices throughout the state, and work directly with public librarians and their boards, providing assistance in a variety of management and planning functions. Statewide consultants provide assistance in bookmobile services, children's services, certification of public librarians, technology and automation, conservation of materials, and library construction and renovation, among others. Direct financial assistance is also provided.

KDLA provides the information government employees need to conduct official business and furnishes other important services to government agencies, including records storage, records and information management, records grants to local governments, disaster assistance, document preservation, and imaging and micrographics.

Additional information about KDLA is available at http://www.kdla.ky.gov.

PUBLIC LIBRARIES

LIBRARY	ADDRESS1	ADDRESS2	CITY, ZIP	PHONE	WEBSITE
Adair County Public Library	307 Greensburg St		Columbia, 42728	270-384-2472	
Allen County Public Library	106 West Main St		Scottsville, 42164	270-237-3861	http://www.allencountylibrary.com/
Anderson County Public Library	114 North Main St		Lawrenceburg, 40342	502-839-6420	http://www.andersonpubliclibrary.org/
Ballard/Carlisle/Livingston Public Library System		P.O. Box 428	Bardwell, 42023	270-335-5059	
Bath County Memorial Library	24 West Main St	P.O. Box 380	Owingsville, 40360	606-674-2531	http://www.youseemore.com/bath/
Boone County Public Library	8899 U.S. 42		Union, 41091	859-384-5550	http://www.bcpl.org/
Bowling Green Public Library	1225 State St		Bowling Green, 42101	270-781-4882	http://www.bgpl.org/
Boyd County Public Library	1740 Central Ave		Ashland, 41101	606-329-0090	http://www.thebookplace.org/
Bracken County Public Library	310 West Miami St	P.O. Box 305	Brooksville, 41004	606-735-3620	http://brackenlibrary.com
Breathitt County Public Library	1024 College Ave		Jackson, 41339	606-666-5541	http://www.breathittcountylibrary.com/
Breckinridge County Public Library	112 South Main St	P.O. Box 248	Hardinsburg, 40143	270-756-2323	
Butler County Public Library	116 West Ohio St	P.O. Box 247	Morgantown, 42261	270-526-4722	
Calloway County Public Library	710 Main St		Murray, 42071	270-753-2288	
Campbell County Public Library	3920 Alexandria Pike		Cold Spring, 41076	859-781-6166	http://www.cc-pl.org/
Carroll County Public Library	136 Court St		Carrollton, 41008	502-732-7020	http://www.carrollcolibrary.org
Casey County Public Library	238 Middleburg St		Liberty, 42539	606-787-9381	http://www.caseylibrary.org/
Clark County Public Library	370 South Burns Ave		Winchester, 40391	859-744-5661	http://www.clarkpublib.org
Clay County Public Library	211 Bridge St		Manchester, 40962	606-598-2617	http://www.claycountypubliclibrary.org
Clinton County Public Library	302 King Dr		Albany, 42602	606-387-5989	
Crittenden County Public Library	204 West Carlisle St		Marion, 42064	270-965-3354	
Cumberland County Public Library	114 Hill St	P.O. Box 440	Burkesville, 42717	270-864-2207	http://www.cumberlandlibrarylcd.com
Cynthiana-Harrison County Public Library	104 North Main St		Cynthiana, 41031	859-234-4881	http://harrisonlibrary.org/
Daviess County Public Library	450 Griffith Ave		Owensboro, 42301	270-684-0211	http://www.dcpl.lib.ky.us/
Duerson-Oldham Co. Public Library	106 East Jefferson St		LaGrange, 40031	502-222-1141	http://www.oldhampl.org/
Edmonson County Public Library	503 Washington St	P.O. Box 219	Brownsville, 42210	270-597-2146	
Estill County Public Library	246 Main St		Irvine, 40336	606-723-3030	http://www.youseemore.com/estill/
Fleming County Public Library	303 South Main Cross		Flemingsburg, 41041	606-845-7851	http://www.youseemore.com/fleming
Floyd County Public Library	161 North Arnold Ave		Prestonburg, 41653	606-886-2981	http://www.fclib.org/
Fulton County Public Library	312 Main St		Fulton, 42041	270-472-3439	http://www.fultonlibrary.com
Gallatin County Public Library	209 West Market St	P.O. Box 848	Warsaw, 41095	859-567-2786	http://www.gallatincountylibrary.org/
Garrard County Public Library	101 Lexington St		Lancaster, 40444	859-792-3424	http://garrardpublib.state.ky.us/
George Coon Public Library	114 South Harrison St	P.O. Box 230	Princeton, 42445	270-365-2884	
Goodnight Memorial Library	203 South Main St		Franklin, 42134	270-586-8397	http://www.goodnightlibrary.org/
Grant County Public Library	201 Barnes Rd		Williamstown, 41097	859-824-2080	http://www.grantcountypubliclibrary.org
Graves County Public Library	601 North 17th St		Mayfield, 42066	270-247-2911	http://www.gcpl.org
Grayson County Public Library	130 East Market St		Leitchfield, 42754	270-259-5455	http://www.graysoncountylibrary.org
Green County Public Library	116 South Main St		Greensburg, 42743	270-932-7081	http://www.gcpl.info
Greenup County Public Library	614 Main St		Greenup, 41144	606-473-6514	http://greenuplib.state.ky.us/
Hancock County Public Library	240 Court Square	P.O. Box 249	Hawesville, 42348	270-927-6760	http://www.hancockcopubliclibrary.ky.gov
Hardin County Public Library	100 Jim Owen Dr		Elizabethtown, 42701	270-769-6337	http://www.hcpl.info/
Harlan County Public Library	107 North Third St		Harlan, 40831	606-573-5220	http://www.harlancountylibraries.org/
Harry M. Caudill Memorial Library	220 East Main St		Whitesburg, 41858	606-633-7547	http://lcld.org
Hart County Public Library	500 East Union St	P.O. Box 337	Munfordville, 42765	270-524-1953	http://www.hartcountypubliclibrary.org
Harvey Helm Memorial Library	301 Third St		Stanford, 40484	606-365-7513	
Helen H. Rayburn Public Library	422 Second St		Vanceburg, 41179	606-796-2532	
Henderson County Public Library	101 South Main St		Henderson, 42420	270-826-3712	http://www.hcpl.org/

PUBLIC LIBRARIES

LIBRARY	ADDRESS1	ADDRESS2	CITY, ZIP	PHONE	WEBSITE
Henry County Public Library	172 Eminence Terrace		Eminence, 40019	502-845-5682	http://www.youseemore.com/henry
Hickman County Memorial Library	209 Mayfield Rd		Clinton, 42031	270-653-2225	
Hopkins County–Madisonville Public Library	31 South Main St		Madisonville, 42431	270-825-2680	http://www.publiclibrary.org/
Hopkinsville-Christian County Library	1101 Bethel St		Hopkinsville, 42240	270-887-4263	http://hccpl.org/
Jackson County Public Library	Second St	P.O. Box 160	McKee, 40447	606-287-8113	
Jessamine County Public Library	600 South Main St		Nicholasville, 40356	859-885-3523	http://www.jesspublib.org/
Johnson County Public Library	444 Main St		Paintsville, 41240	606-789-4355	http://mywebpage.netscape.com/johnsoncolibrary/
Kenton County Public Library System	502 Scott Blvd		Covington, 41011	859-962-4060	http://www.kenton.lib.ky.us/
Knott County Public Library	238 Route 160	P.O. Box 667	Hindman, 41822	606-785-5412	
Knox County Public Library	206 Knox St		Barbourville, 40906	606-546-5339	
LaRue County Public Library	201 South Lincoln Blvd		Hodgenville, 42748	270-358-3851	http://www.laruelibrary.org
Laurel County Public Library	120 College Park Dr		London, 40741	606-864-5759	http://www.laurellibrary.org
Lawrence County Public Library	102 West Main and Jefferson		Louisa, 41230	606-638-4497	http://lawrencecountypubliclibrary.org
Lee County Public Library	123 Center St	P.O. Box 600	Beattyville, 41311	606-464-8014	
Leslie County Public Library	22065 Main St	P.O. Box V	Hyden, 41749	606-672-2460	
Lexington Public Library	140 East Main St	P.O. Box 498	Lexington, 40507	859-231-5504	http://www.lexpublib.org/
Lexington Public Library - Beaumont Branch	3080 Fieldstone Way		Lexington, 40513	859-231-5570	http://www.lexpublib.org/
Lexington Public Library - Eagle Creek Branch	101 North Eagle Creek Dr		Lexington, 40509	859-231-5560	http://www.lexpublib.org/
Lexington Public Library - Northside Branch	1737 Russell Cave Rd		Lexington, 40505	859-231-5590	http://www.lexpublib.org/
Lexington Public Library - Tates Creek Branch	3628 Walden Dr		Lexington, 40517	859-231-5580	http://www.lexpublib.org/
Lexington Public Library - Village Branch	2185 Versailles Rd		Lexington, 40504	859-231-5575	http://www.lexpublib.org/
Logan County Public Library	201 West Sixth St		Russellville, 42276	270-726-6129	http://www.loganlibrary.org/
Louisville Free Public Library	301 York St		Louisville, 40203	502-574-1600	http://www.lfpl.org/
Louisville Free Public Library - Bon Air Regional Branch	2816 Del Rio Place		Louisville, 40220	502-574-1795	http://www.lfpl.org/
Louisville Free Public Library - Crescent Hill Branch	2762 Frankfort Ave		Louisville, 40206	502-574-1793	http://www.lfpl.org/
Louisville Free Public Library - Fairdale Branch	10616 West Manslick Rd		Fairdale, 40118	502-375-2051	http://www.lfpl.org/
Louisville Free Public Library - Fern Creek Branch	6768 Bardstown Rd		Louisville, 40291	502-231-4605	http://www.lfpl.org/
Louisville Free Public Library - Highlands-Shelby Park Branch	1250 Bardstown Rd		Louisville, 40204	502-574-1672	http://www.lfpl.org/
Louisville Free Public Library - Iroquois Branch	601 West Woodlawn Ave		Louisville, 40215	502-574-1720	http://www.lfpl.org/
Louisville Free Public Library - Jeffersontown Branch	10635 Watterson Trail		Louisville, 40299	502-267-5713	http://www.lfpl.org/
Louisville Free Public Library - Middletown Branch	200 North Juneau Dr		Louisville, 40243	502-245-7332	http://www.lfpl.org/
Louisville Free Public Library - Okolona Branch	7709 Preston Hwy		Louisville, 40219	502-964-3515	http://www.lfpl.org/
Louisville Free Public Library - Portland Branch	3305 Northwestern Pkwy		Louisville, 40212	502-574-1744	http://www.lfpl.org/
Louisville Free Public Library - Saint Matthews/Eline Branch	3940 Grandview Ave		Louisville, 40207	502-574-1771	http://www.lfpl.org/
Louisville Free Public Library - Shawnee Branch	3912 West Broadway		Louisville, 40211	502-574-1722	http://www.lfpl.org/
Louisville Free Public Library - Shively/Newman Branch	3920 Dixie Hwy		Louisville, 40216	502-574-1730	http://www.lfpl.org/
Louisville Free Public Library - Southwest Regional Branch	10375 Dixie Hwy		Louisville, 40272	502-933-0029	http://www.lfpl.org/
Louisville Free Public Library - Western Branch	604 South Tenth St		Louisville, 40203	502-574-1779	http://www.lfpl.org/
Louisville Free Public Library - Westport Community Library	Westport Middle School	8100 Westport	Louisville, 40222	502-394-0379	http://www.lfpl.org/
Lyon County Public Library	261 Commerce St	P.O. Box 546	Eddyville, 42038	270-388-7720	
Madison County Public Library	507 West Main St		Richmond, 40475	859-623-6704	http://www.madisonlibrary.org/
Magoffin County Public Library	141 Church St	P.O. Box 435	Salyersville, 41465	606-349-2411	
Marion County Public Library	201 East Main St		Lebanon, 40033	270-692-4698	http://geocities.com/marioncountypubliclibrary/
Marshall County Public Library	1003 Poplar St		Benton, 42025	270-527-9969	http://www.marshalllibrary.org
Martin County Public Library	Main St	P.O. Box 1318	Inez, 41224	606-298-7766	
Mary Wood Weldon Memorial Public Library	107 West College St		Glasgow, 42141	270-651-2824	http://www.weldonpubliclibrary.org

PUBLIC LIBRARIES

LIBRARY	ADDRESS1	ADDRESS2	CITY ZIP	PHONE	WEBSITE
Mason County Public Library	218 East Third St		Maysville, 41056	606-564-3286	http://maysvillelibrary.com/
McCracken County Public Library	555 Washington St		Paducah, 42003	270-442-2510	http://www.mclib.net/
McCreary County Public Library	6 North Main St	P.O. Box 8	Whitley City, 42653	606-376-8738	http://www.mccrearylibrary.org/
Meade County Public Library	400 Library Place		Brandenburg, 40108	270-422-2094	http://www.meadereads.org/
Menifee County Public Library	P.O. Box 49	1585 Main St	Frenchburg, 40322	606-768-2212	
Mercer County Public Library	109 West Lexington St		Harrodsburg, 40330	859-734-3680	http://www.mcplib.info/
Metcalfe County Public Library	200 South Main St	P.O. Box 626	Edmonton, 42129	270-432-4981	http://www.scrtc.com/~metcolib/
Middlesborough-Bell Co. Public Library	126 South 20th St	P.O. Box 1677	Middlesborough, 40965	606-248-4812	http://www.bellcountypubliclibraries.org
Morgan County Public Library	151 University Ave		West Liberty, 41472	606-743-4151	http://www.youseemore.com/mcpl/
Mount Sterling-Montgomery County Public Library	241 West Locust St		Mount Sterling, 40353	859-498-2404	http://www.youseemore.com/mtsterling/
Muhlenberg County - Central City Public Library	108 East Broad St		Central City, 42330	270-754-4630	
Nelson County Public Library	90 Court Square		Bardstown, 40004	502-348-3714	http://www.nelsoncopublib.org/
Nicholas County Memorial Library	223 North Broadway St		Carlisle, 40311	859-289-5595	http://www.nicholascountylibrary.com/
Ohio County Public Library	413 Main St		Hartford, 42347	270-298-3790	
Owen County Public Library	118 North Main St		Owenton, 40359	502-484-3450	http://www.youseemore.com/Owen/
Owsley County Public Library	#2 Action Place	P.O. Box 280	Booneville, 41314	606-593-5700	
Paris-Bourbon County Public Library	701 High St		Paris, 40361	859-987-4419	http://bourbonlibrary.org
Paul Sawyier Public Library	305 Wapping St		Frankfort, 40601	502-223-1658	http://www.pspl.org/
Pendleton County Public Library	228 Main St	P.O. Box 928	Falmouth, 41040	859-654-8535	http://perrycountylibrary.com/
Perry County Public Library	479 High St	P.O. Box 471	Hazard, 41701	606-436-2475	
Pikeville Public Library	119 College St		Pikeville, 41502	606-432-1285	
Powell County Public Library	725 Breckenridge St		Stanton, 40360	606-663-4511	http://www.geocities.com/powellcountylibrary
Pulaski County Public Library	107 North Main St	P.O. Box 36	Somerset, 42502	606-679-8401	http://www.pcplib.org/
Ridgway Memorial Library	127 North Walnut St	P.O. Box 146	Shepherdsville, 40165	502-543-7675	http://www.rcpl.state.ky.us/
Robertson County Public Library	148 North Main St	P.O. Box 282	Mount Olivet, 41064	606-724-5746	http://www.rockcastlelibrary.com/
Rockcastle County Public Library	60 Ford Dr		Mount Vernon, 40456	606-256-2388	
Rocky J. Adkins Public Library	Main St	P.O. Box 750	Sandy Hook, 41171	606-738-5796	
Rowan County Public Library	185 East First St		Morehead, 40351	606-784-7137	http://www.youseemore.com/rowan/
Russell County Public Library	94 North Main St	P.O. Box 970	Jamestown, 42629	270-343-3545	http://www.russellcountylibrary.com/
Scott County Public Library	104 South Bradford Lane		Georgetown, 40324	502-863-3566	http://www.scottpublib.org/
Shelby County Public Library	309 Eighth St		Shelbyville, 40065	502-633-3803	http://www.scpllibrary.net
Spencer County Public Library	168 Taylorsville Rd		Taylorsville, 40071	502-477-8137	http://members.iglou.com/scpl/
Taylor County Public Library	205 North Columbia Ave		Campbellsville, 42718	270-465-2562	http://www.taylorcountypubliclibrary.org/
Todd County Public Library	302 East Main St		Elkton, 42220	270-265-9071	http://www.angelfire.com/ky/toddcopl/
Trigg County - John L. Street Library	244 Main St	P.O. Box 249	Cadiz, 42211	270-522-6301	http://www.tclibrary.org/
Trimble County Public Library	112 Hwy 42 East		Bedford, 40006	502-255-7362	
Union County Public Library	126 South Morgan St		Morganfield, 42437	270-389-1696	
Washington County Public Library	210 East Main St		Springfield, 40069	859-336-7655	http://www.wcpl.ky.gov
Wayne County Public Library	159 South Main St		Monticello, 42633	606-348-8565	http://www.waynepubliclibrary.net
Webster County Public Library	101 State Route 132 East	P.O. Box 50	Dixon, 42409	270-639-9171	
Whitley County Public Library	285 South Third St		Williamsburg, 40769	606-549-0818	http://www.whitleylibrary.org
William B. Harlan Memorial Library	500 West Fourth St		Tompkinsville, 42167	270-487-5301	http://www.wbhmlibrary.org
Wolfe County Public Library	176 Kentucky 15 North	P.O. Box 10	Campton, 41301	606-668-6571	http://www.wolfcountypubliclibrary.org
Woodford County - Logan Helm Woodford Co. Library	115 North Main St		Versailles, 40383	859-873-5191	http://www.woodfordcountylibrary.org

Source: http://www.kdla.ky.gov

Astronomical Calendar 2006

Col. Claude E. Hammond

Introduction to the Kentucky Almanac Calendar for 2006

The second year after Bissextile or Leap Year; as of July 4th, 2006, the 230th of American Independence; the 217th of Federal Government; and as of June 1, 2006, the 214th of this Commonwealth.

ABBREVIATIONS, SYMBOLS & DEFINITIONS

☿ Mercury	♀ Venus	⊕ Earth	♂ Mars	♃ Jupiter
♄ Saturn	♅ Uranus	♆ Neptune	♇ Pluto	☉ Sun
☾ Qtr. Moon	◯ Full Moon	● New Moon		

A calendar is a system of organizing units of time for the purpose of reckoning time over extended periods. There are six principal calendars in current use. These are the Gregorian, Hebrew, Islamic, Indian, Chinese, and Julian Calendars. These calendars replicate astronomical cycles according to fixed rules.

The principal astronomical cycles are the day (based on the rotation of the Earth on its axis), the year (based on the revolution of the Earth around the Sun), and the month (based on the revolution of the Moon around the Earth). The complexity of calendars arises because the year does not comprise an integral number of days or an integral number of lunar months.

All times given are in Eastern Standard Time, so West Kentucky residents living in the Central Time Zone will need to subtract an hour when using information from Clark's Kentucky Almanac. Corrections are made in Almanac times for Daylight Savings Time, saving the reader additional calculating effort.

The times given are calculated, specifically for Frankfort, Kentucky's capital city.

EXPLANATION OF CALENDAR PAGES

The first column shows the day of the Month (with Sunday in bold); the second Remarkable Days & Judgement of Weather, proverbs to live by and certain details of note; the second column shows the Moon's Phase & Astrological events; the third column shows the Moon's Place in the Zodiac; and the fourth through seventh columns indicate the Rising and Setting of the Sun and Moon.

THE
ANATOMY OF MAN'S BODY,
AS GOVERNED BY THE TWELVE CONSTELLATIONS.

♈ Head and Face G

♉ Neck. B
♊ Arms. B
♋ Breast. M
♌ Heart. B
♍ Bowels. M
♎ Reins. G
♏ Secrets. M
♐ Thighs. M
♑ Knees. B
♒ Legs. G

♓ The Feet G

TO KNOW WHERE THE SIGN IS,
First find the day of the month, and against that day you have the sign or place of the moon in the 6th column. Then finding the sign above, it shows the part of the body it governs.

THE TWELVE SIGN OF THE ZODIAC.

♈ Aries, the Ram.	♎ Libra, the Balance.
♉ Taurus, the Bull.	♏ Scorpio, the Scorpion.
♊ Gemini, the Twins.	♐ Sagittarius, a Bowman
♋ Cancer, the Crab.	♑ Capricornus, the Goat.
♌ Leo, the Lion.	♒ Aquarius, a Waterman.
♍ Virgo, the Virgin.	♓ Pisces, the Fishes.

Source: Kentucky Almanac 1818,
published by William Sebree, Georgetown, Ky.

JANUARY—hath 31 days.

	REMARKABLE DAYS, JUDGEMENT OF WEATHER.			MOON PHASE LOCATION	ZODIAC SYMBOL	SUN RISE	SUN SET	MOON RISE	MOON SET
1	New Year's Day	Circumcision	2nd Sunday of Christmas	Minor conj. ☾ ♀	♒	7:56am	5:30pm	9:39am	7:20am
2	New Year's Day observed – Federal holiday.			Minor conj. ☾ ♆	♒	7:56am	5:31pm	10:19am	8:39am
3	Troops of Gen. Hylan Lyons, CSA, burn Cumberland County Courthouse, 1865.			Conj. ☾ ⛢	♓	7:56am	5:32pm	10:52am	9:55pm
4	After trudging through winter mire, stand closer to the fire.		Perihelion		♓	7:56am	5:33pm	11:20am	11:08pm
5	Johnson Newlon Camden, co-founder of Standard Oil, born in Woodford Co., 1855.				♈	7:56am	5:34pm	11:45am	-:-------
6	Epiphany	Old Christmas		FIRST QTR. ☾	♈	7:56am	5:35pm	12:10pm	12:18am
7	Calhoun, Ky. incorporated, 1852.				♈	7:56am	5:35pm	12:36pm	1:27am
8	1st Sunday of Epiphany	Battle of New Orleans: Kentucky troops help whip the British, 1815.		Conj. ☾ ♂	♉	7:56am	5:36pm	1:04pm	2:35am
9	Gen. James Franklin Bell, Spanish-American War hero, born in Shelby County, 1856.				♉	7:56am	5:37pm	1:37pm	3:44am
10	Have garden planned by today and prevent worries in May.				♊	7:56am	5:38pm	2:16pm	4:52am
11	Benton incorporated, 1845.				♊	7:56am	5:39pm	3:01pm	5:56am
12	Construction of Third Kentucky State Capitol authorized, 1827.				♋	7:56am	5:40pm	3:54pm	6:55am
13	Stephen Foster died, 1864: "Weep no more, my lady."			Close passage ♀ ☉	♋	7:55am	5:41pm	4:53pm	7:45am
14	Capt. Harrison Ford enrolls in 39th Ky. Mounted Infantry (U.S.), Peach Orchard, Ky., 1863.			FULL ○	♋	7:55am	5:42pm	5:55pm	8:28am
15	Bath County formed, 1811.		2nd Sunday of Epiphany		♌	7:55am	5:43pm	6:57pm	9:03am
16	Martin Luther King Jr.-Federal holiday John C. Breckinridge born, 1821.				♌	7:54am	5:44pm	7:58pm	9:31am
17	Muhammed Ali born, Louisville, 1942.				♍	7:54am	5:46pm	8:58pm	9:56am
18	Confession of St. Peter		*Kentucky Almanac* first appears by that name (not *Kentucke*) 1803.		♍	7:54am	5:47pm	9:56pm	10:18am
19	Robert E. Lee Day – state holiday				♍	7:53am	5:48pm	10:54pm	10:39am
20	Alben Barkley becomes U.S. Vice President, 1949.				♎	7:53am	5:49pm	11:53pm	10:59am
21	Centre College founded, 1819.				♎	7:52am	5:50pm	-:-------	11:21am
22	Movie pioneer D.W. Griffith born, 1875, Oldham Co.		3rd Sunday of Epiphany	LAST QTR. ☾	♏	7:52am	5:51pm	12:54am	11:44am
23	Anti-Darwinism bill introduced to Ky. House, 1922.			Minor conj. ☾ ♃	♏	7:51am	5:52pm	1:58am	12:12pm
24	Don't let sunny days put you in a daze, there's still ice and haze.				♏	7:50am	5:53pm	3:05am	12:46pm
25	Gov. Ned Breathitt signs Ky. Civil Rights Bill of 1966.				♐	7:50am	5:54pm	4:16am	1:30pm
26	Sharpen your hoe, even if there's snow.				♐	7:49am	5:55pm	5:25am	2:25pm
27	Albany, Ky. incorporated, 1837.				♑	7:48am	5:57pm	6:30am	3:33pm
28	Judge Louis Brandeis, from Louisville, appointed to the U.S. Supreme Court, 1916.				♑	7:48am	5:58pm	7:25am	4:50pm
29	Chinese New Year: Year of the Dog.		4th Sunday of Epiphany	NEW ●	♒	7:47am	5:59pm	8:11am	6:11pm
30	Franklin D Roosevelt Day - state holiday				♒	7:46am	6:00pm	8:48am	7:31pm
31	Col Jack Chinn, Mercer Co's greatest horseman, died, 1920.				♓	7:45am	6:01pm	9:19am	8:48pm

FEBRUARY—hath 28 days.

	REMARKABLE DAYS, JUDGEMENT OF WEATHER.			MOON PHASE LOCATION	ZODIAC SYMBOL	SUN RISE	SUN SET	MOON RISE	MOON SET
1	Thomas Campbell born, 1763: founder of Church of the Disciples of Christ.				♓	7:44am	6:02pm	9:46am	10:02pm
2	Groundhog Day	Presentation			♈	7:43am	6:03pm	10:12am	11:14pm
3	William Lowther Jackson, CSA general & famed Louisvilled jurist, born, 1825	Start tomato seeds today.			♈	7:43am	6:04pm	10:38am	-:-------
4	James Gillespie Birney, abolitionist, born in Danville, 1792.				♉	7:42am	6:06pm	11:06am	12:25am
5	4th Sunday before Lent Cave Hill Cemetery chartered, Louisville, 1848.			FIRST QTR. ☾	♉	7:41am	6:07pm	11:38am	1:36am
6	Ohio River Flood of 1937 began to recede this day.				♊	7:40am	6:08pm	12:15pm	2:44am
7	Gen. John C. Breckinridge made CSA Secretary of War, 1865.				♊	7:39am	6:09pm	12:58pm	3:50am
8	Smith D. Broadbent born in Trigg Co., 1914: Agriculture's Great Innovator.				♊	7:38am	6:10pm	1:49pm	4:51am
9	Beckham County formed from part of Carter Co., 1904.				♋	7:37am	6:11pm	2:46pm	5:43am
10	Barry Bingham Sr. born in Louisville, 1906.				♋	7:35am	6:12pm	3:47pm	6:28am
11	Catlettsburg organized, 1858.				♌	7:34am	6:13pm	4:49pm	7:04am
12	Lincoln's Birthday—state holiday*	3rd Sunday before Lent		FULL ○	♌	7:33am	6:15pm	5:50pm	7:35am
13	George Rogers Clark died in Louisville, 1818.				♌	7:32am	6:16pm	6:50pm	8:00am
14	St. Valentine's Day; Confederate Army evacuates Bowling Green, Ky.'s Confederate capital, 1862.				♍	7:31am	6:17pm	7:49pm	8:23am
15	Ballard Co. founded, 1842				♍	7:30am	6:18pm	8:47pm	8:44am
16	Brooksville becomes seat of Bracken Co., 1839.				♎	7:29am	6:19pm	9:46pm	9:04am
17	Mary Carson Breckinridge, founder of East Ky.'s Frontier Nursing Service, born 1881.				♎	7:27am	6:20pm	10:45pm	9:25am
18	Lexington author James Lane Allen died, 1924.				♎	7:26am	6:21pm	11:47pm	9:47am
19	2nd Sunday before Lent	Eddie Arcaro born, 1916: Winning jockey in five Ky. Derbys.			♏	7:25am	6:22pm	-:-------	10:13am
20	President's Day		Fertilize brambles.		♏	7:24am	6:23pm	12:52am	10:43am
21	The greatest waste of energy is anger.			LAST QTR. ☾	♐	7:22am	6:24pm	1:59am	11:21am
22	Agricultural & Mechanical College of Ky. founded, 1865 (later known as the University of Kentucky).				♐	7:21am	6:25pm	3:07am	12:09pm
23	Calhoun, Ky. named for Judge John Calhoun, 1849.				♑	7:20am	6:26pm	4:12am	1:09pm
24	February gets ready to go, ice storms will replace the snow.				♑	7:18am	6:28pm	5:10am	2:20pm
25	Muhammad Ali KO's Sonny Liston in the 7th round, 1964.				♒	7:17am	6:29pm	6:00am	3:39pm
26	Last Sunday before Lent			Inferior conj. ☾☉	♒	7:16am	6:30pm	6:40am	4:59pm
27	The Marquis Calmes, founder and namer of Versailles, died, 1834.			NEW ●	♓	7:14am	6:31pm	7:14am	6:18pm
28	Madison County novelist Walter Stone Tevis, Jr., born, 1928.				♓	7:13am	6:32pm	7:43am	7:36pm

Artwork source at the top of each month: The Kentucky Almanac 1820, published by John Bradford, Esq., Lexington, Ky.

MARCH—hath 31 days.

	REMARKABLE DAYS, JUDGEMENT OF WEATHER.	MOON PHASE LOCATION	ZODIAC SYMBOL	SUN RISE	SUN SET	MOON RISE	MOON SET
1	Ash Wednesday Robert Bell Anderson, author, born a slave near Greensburg, 1843.		♈	7:11am	6:33pm	8:10am	8:51pm
2	Benjamin Avery, inventor of the Avery plow, died in Louisville, 1884.		♈	7:10am	6:34pm	8:37am	10:05pm
3	Sarah Blanding, from Lexington, Vassar's first female president, died in 1985.		♉	7:09am	6:35pm	9:05am	11:19pm
4	Lucian Anderson, W. Ky.'s pioneering Republican, begins congressional term, 1863.		♉	7:07am	6:36pm	9:36am	-:------
5	1st Sunday of Lent Martin Luther King led Ky.'s largest civil rights march to date, Frankfort, 1964.		♊	7:06am	6:37pm	10:12am	12:31am
6	Col. James Bowie and 13 other Kentuckians are among the 189 who die defending the Alamo, 1836.	FIRST QTR. ☾	♊	7:04am	6:38pm	10:54am	1:41am
7	Wix Howard kills Bob Turner and the Howard-Turner feud begins, Harlan Co., 1882.		♊	7:03am	6:39pm	11:43am	2:44am
8	Richard Callaway and Pemberton Rawlings killed by Wyandots, Callaway Creek, 1780.		♋	7:01am	6:40pm	12:39pm	3:40am
9	The fastest horse can be slowed by a bad shoe.		♋	7:00am	6:41pm	1:39pm	4:27am
10	Humorist Irvin S. Cobb of Paducah died, 1944.		♌	6:58am	6:42pm	2:41pm	5:06am
11	Chattaroi Railway Co. incorporated, Ashland, 1873.		♌	6:57am	6:43pm	3:43pm	5:38am
12	2nd Sunday of Lent "Sue Mundy" (Marcellus Clarke) hanged for murder, Louisville, 1865.		♌	6:55am	6:44pm	4:43pm	6:05am
13	Can spring be that far away?		♎	6:54am	6:45pm	5:42pm	6:28am
14	Purim Casey Jones, engineer, born in Fulton County, 1864. Lunar Eclipse at sundown	FULL ○	♎	6:52am	6:46pm	6:41pm	6:50am
15	IDES (Great Caesar's Ghost!) Rufus B. Atwood, "Mr. Kentucky State," born in Hickman, 1897.		♎	6:51am	6:47pm	7:39pm	7:10am
16	Dig and divide rhubarb plants.		♎	6:49am	6:48pm	8:39pm	7:30am
17	St. Patrick's Day (Erin Go Braugh!)		♎	6:48am	6:48pm	9:40pm	7:52am
18	William O. Bradley, Ky's first Republican Governor, born in Garrard Co., 1847.		♏	6:46am	6:49pm	10:44pm	8:16am
19	3rd Sunday of Lent Gay Brewer, Lexington golfing legend, born 1932.		♏	6:45am	6:50pm	11:50pm	8:45am
20	Vernal Equinox: Spring begins		♐	6:43am	6:51pm	-:-------	9:20am
21	Confederate troops fire on US troops in the Bath Co. Courthouse. It burns down, 1864.		♐	6:42am	6:52pm	12:57am	10:03am
22	Coach Blanton Collier died, 1983.	Conj. ⛢☿ LAST QTR. ☾	♐	6:40am	6:53pm	2:01am	10:57am
23	Prolific poet Madison Cawein born in Louisville, 1865.		♑	6:38am	6:54pm	3:01am	12:02pm
24	A sage is one who follows his own advice.		♑	6:37am	6:55pm	3:51am	1:15pm
25	Jennie Carter Benedict, Louisville chef, inventor of Benedictine cheese, born, 1860.		♒	6:35am	6:56pm	4:34am	2:32pm
26	4th Sunday of Lent Duncan Hines born in Bowling Green, 1880.	Conj. ☾♀	♒	6:34am	6:57pm	5:09am	3:49pm
27	Dr. Tim Lee Carter, former 5th District congressman, died in Glasgow, 1987.		♓	6:32am	6:58pm	5:40am	5:06pm
28	Beattyville incorporated, 1872.		♓	6:31am	6:59pm	6:07am	6:22pm
29	Looking forward to April showers. Adolph Rupp's UK Wildcats defeat Baylor 77-59, 1948	NEW ●	♈	6:29am	7:00pm	6:34am	7:38pm
30	James Graham Brown, Louisville hotelier, died, 1969.		♈	6:28am	7:01pm	7:02am	8:53pm
31	Delaware Indians perpetrate Tick Creek Massacre, 1788.		♉	6:26am	7:02pm	7:32am	10:08pm

APRIL—hath 30 days.

	REMARKABLE DAYS, JUDGEMENT OF WEATHER.		MOON PHASE LOCATION	ZODIAC SYMBOL	SUN RISE	SUN SET	MOON RISE	MOON SET
1	April Fool's Day	Construction of Boonesborough begins, 1775.		♉	6:25am	7:03pm	8:06am	11:22pm
2	5th Sunday of Lent	Daylight Savings Time begins, 2am.		♊	7:23am	8:04pm	9:47am	-:------
3	Deadly tornado strikes Brandenburg: 31 killed, 1974.			♊	7:22am	8:04pm	10:35am	1:31am
4	Fertilize your garden today or tomorrow.			♋	7:20am	8:05pm	11:29am	2:32am
5	If you stop learning, you'll stop living.		FIRST QTR. ☽	♋	7:19am	8:06pm	12:29pm	3:23am
6	Belle Brezing's "house" (59 Megowan St., Lexington) is closed by order of U.S. Army, 1917.			♋	7:17am	8:07pm	1:31pm	4:06am
7	Ky.'s Confederate Governor, George Johnson, mortally wounded at Shiloh, 1862.			♌	7:16am	8:08pm	2:34pm	4:40am
8	Author Barbara Kingsolver born in Carlisle, 1955.			♌	7:14am	8:09pm	3:35pm	5:09am
9	Palm Sunday	Charles Scott born in Va. He became Ky. Governor from 1808-1812.		♍	7:13am	8:10pm	4:34pm	5:33am
10	Carter Co. formed, 1838.			♍	7:11am	8:11pm	5:33pm	5:55am
11	April reigns with ample rains.			♍	7:10am	8:12pm	6:31pm	6:15am
12	Henry Clay born, 1777.			♎	7:08am	8:13pm	7:31pm	6:36am
13	Passover	Alexander Scott Bullitt, pioneer leader, died at Oxmoor, 1813.	FULL ○	♎	7:07am	8:14pm	8:32pm	6:57am
14	Julia Allen, educator and activist, born in Burkesville, 1896.			♏	7:05am	8:15pm	9:35pm	7:21am
15	These are taxing times.			♏	7:04am	8:16pm	10:42pm	7:48am
16	Easter Sunday	Julian Carroll born, McCracken Co., 1931.		♐	7:03am	8:17pm	11:49pm	8:21am
17	Federal income taxes due.	Louisville's Paul Hornung suspended from NFL for gambling, 1963.		♐	7:01am	8:17pm	-:------	9:02am
18	Capt. John Cannon, former master of the steamer Robert E. Lee, died in Frankfort, 1882.			♐	7:00am	8:18pm	1:55am	9:53am
19	Fr. Stephen Theodore Badin, pioneering Ky. priest, died, 1853.			♑	6:58am	8:19pm	1:55am	10:53am
20	Spelunker Floyd Collins born, Edmonson County, 1887		LAST QTR. ☽	♑	6:57am	8:20pm	2:48am	12:02pm
21	David C. Alexander, mystery writer, born in Shelbyville, 1907.			♒	6:56am	8:21pm	3:32am	1:16pm
22	Earth Day	Survey completed of Boonesborough, 1775.		♒	6:54am	8:22pm	4:08am	2:31pm
23	2nd Sunday of Easter / Orthodox Easter	Rosemary Clooney born in Maysville, 1928.		♓	6:53am	8:23pm	4:39am	3:45pm
24	Robert Penn Warren born in Guthrie, 1905.		Minor conj. ☽♀	♓	6:52am	8:24pm	5:07am	4:59pm
25	Fine days without haze precede May.			♈	6:50am	8:25pm	5:33am	6:12pm
26	John James Audubon born in Haiti, 1785.			♈	6:49am	8:26pm	5:59am	7:27pm
27	Richard Patrick Maloney, Democratic power broker, born in Lexington, 1902.		NEW ●	♉	6:48am	8:27pm	6:28am	8:42pm
28	Joseph Allen, hero of the War of 1812, died at Hardinsburg, 1862.			♉	6:47am	8:28pm	7:00am	9:57pm
29	Court of Appeals dissolves Beckham Co., 1904.			♊	6:45am	8:29pm	7:38am	11:10pm
30	3rd Sunday of Easter	Alben Barkley died after making a speech at Washington & Lee University, 1956.		♊	6:44am	8:30pm	8:23am	-:------

MAY—hath 31 days.

	REMARKABLE DAYS, JUDGEMENT OF WEATHER.		MOON PHASE LOCATION	ZODIAC SYMBOL	SUN RISE	SUN SET	MOON RISE	MOON SET
1	Daniel Boone leads hunting party of six into Kentucky, 1769.			♊	6:43am	8:31pm	4:19am	2:18pm
2	Alexander S. Bullitt appointed Louisville trustee, 1786.			♋	6:42am	8:32pm	4:54am	3:32pm
3	Author, Appalachian social critic Harry Caudill born in Letcher County, 1922.			♋	6:41am	8:33pm	5:23am	4:43pm
4	J. Winston Coleman, Kentucky historian, died at his Lexington home, 1983.			♌	6:40am	8:33pm	5:48am	5:51pm
5	Zounds! Pollen abounds!	Secretariat wins the Kentucky Derby, 1973.	FIRST QTR. ☽	♌	6:38am	8:33pm	6:13am	6:59pm
6	The Kentucky Derby			♍	6:37am	8:33pm	6:37am	8:06pm
7	4th Sunday of Easter	Barrier Awareness Day in Ky.		♍	6:36am	8:34pm	7:03am	9:14pm
8	Steamboat "Mechanic" sank near Owensboro with the Marquis de Lafayette aboard, 1825. He was rescued.			♍	6:35am	8:35pm	7:32am	10:21pm
9	Jefferson County buys old steamer "Avalon" this day, 1962. Restored, it's now the "Belle of Louisville."			♎	6:34am	8:36pm	8:06am	11:27pm
10	The young raccoons walk early.			♎	6:33am	8:37pm	8:46am	-:--------
11	Foster Brooks, comedian, born in Louisville, 1912.			♏	6:32am	8:38pm	9:32am	12:29am
12	'Tis Spring: Your fancy may get romancy.			♏	6:31am	8:39pm	10:25am	1:24am
13	Best week of spring fishing should begin this morning.		FULL ○	♏	6:30am	8:40pm	11:23am	2:12am
14	5th Sunday of Easter/Mother's Day	Gen. Simon Bolivar Buckner Jr.'s troops break through enemy lines at Okinawa, 1945.		♐	6:30am	8:41pm	12:23pm	2:52am
15	Lafayette arrives in Fayette County (which was named for him), 1825.			♐	6:29am	8:42pm	1:24pm	3:25am
16	An honest apology works wonders.			♑	6:28am	8:43pm	2:26pm	3:54am
17	John C. Breckinridge, former U.S. Vice President & CSA Secretary of War, died in Lexington, 1875.			♑	6:27am	8:44pm	3:26pm	4:18am
18	May days have warm charms.			♒	6:26am	8:45pm	4:27pm	4:41am
19	James Dixon Black begins 7-month term as Governor, 1919.			♒	6:25am	8:46pm	5:30pm	5:03am
20	Armed Forces Day	Owsley Co. formed, 1820.	LAST QTR. ☽	♓	6:25am	8:47pm	6:35pm	5:26am
21	6th Sunday of Easter			♓	6:24am	8:48pm	7:43pm	5:50am
22	Your garden should be planted by now (except the pumpkins).			♈	6:23am	8:49pm	8:56pm	6:19am
23	Lexington's Gen. John B. Castleman, first president of American Saddlebred Horsemen's Association, died, 1918.			♈	6:23am	8:49pm	10:11pm	6:53am
24	Turtles rise: Prepare your soup pot.		Minor conj. ☽ ♀ ☽	♈	6:22am	8:50pm	11:26pm	7:37am
25	May in Kentucky is cat-like: First it purrs, then it scratches!			♉	6:21am	8:51pm	-:--------	8:31am
26	Hart County's Gen. Simon Bolivar Buckner Sr., CSA, surrenders to U.S. Army, 1865.			♉	6:21am	8:52pm	12:34am	9:37am
27	Select flowers for your loved ones.		NEW ●	♊	6:20am	8:53pm	1:32am	10:51am
28	7th Sunday of Easter			♊	6:20am	8:54pm	2:19am	12:07pm
29	Memorial Day			♋	6:19am	8:55pm	2:56am	1:23pm
30	George Mortimer Bibb becomes Chief Justice of Kentucky's Supreme Court, 1809.			♋	6:19am	8:56pm	3:27am	2:35pm
31	Trout line weather begins.	It's a lovely day for a birthday party.		♌	6:18am	8:56pm	3:53am	3:43pm

JUNE—hath 30 days.

	REMARKABLE DAYS, JUDGEMENT OF WEATHER.			MOON PHASE LOCATION	ZODIAC SYMBOL	SUN RISE	SUN SET	MOON RISE	MOON SET
1	Kentucky Statehood Day				♌	6:18am	8:57pm	4:17am	4:50pm
2	Shavuot	June is joyous and jaunty.			♌	6:18am	8:58pm	3:41am	5:57pm
3	Confederate Memorial Day and Jefferson Davis Day – double state holiday			FIRST QTR. ☾	♍	6:17am	8:58pm	5:06am	7:03pm
4	Pentecost	Plant pumpkins this week.			♍	6:17am	8:59pm	5:34am	8:09pm
5	John Allen commissioned Colonel of 1st Kentucky Rifles, 1812.				♎	6:17am	8:59pm	6:05am	9:15pm
6	Fort Harrod established, 1774.				♎	6:17am	9:00pm	6:42am	10:18pm
7	Morning work prevents afternoon worries.				♎	6:16am	9:01pm	7:26am	11:16pm
8				Superior conj. ☉☿	♏	6:16am	9:01pm	8:16am	-:------
9	George Madison, cousin of James Madison and Ky. Gov. for five weeks in 1816, born this day in Va.				♏	6:16am	9:02pm	9:13am	12:06am
10	This time is fine for hook and line.				♐	6:16am	9:02pm	10:13am	12:49am
11	Trinity Sunday	Confederate Infantry captures Scottsville, 1863.		FULL ○	♐	6:16am	9:03pm	11:14am	1:25am
12	Living only for yourself isn't living at all.				♑	6:16am	9:03pm	12:15pm	1:55am
13	Florence Cantrill born, 1888: first woman to serve in Ky. legislature.				♑	6:16am	9:03pm	1:15pm	2:20am
14	Flag Day	ACC's birthday! Happy Birthday!			♒	6:16am	9:04pm	2:14pm	2:43am
15	A.B. "Happy" Chandler died at home, Versailles, 1991.				♒	6:16am	9:04pm	3:15pm	3:05am
16	Daniel Boone escapes the Shawnee, 1778.				♒	6:16am	9:05pm	4:17pm	3:27am
17	Choose to be happy.				♓	6:16am	9:05pm	5:22pm	3:50am
18	1st Sunday after Trinity	Fathers' Day		LAST QTR. ☾	♓	6:16am	9:05pm	6:32pm	4:16am
19	Juneteenth National Freedom Day				♈	6:16am	9:06pm	7:45pm	4:47am
20	Benjamin Helm Bristow born in Elkton, 1832. He became the 1st U.S. Solicitor General.				♈	6:16am	9:06pm	9:01pm	5:25am
21	Jim Bunning pitches perfect game for the Phillies, beating the Mets 4-0, 1964.	Summer Solstice			♉	6:16am	9:06pm	10:14pm	6:15am
22	Thomas H. Barlow of Nicholas County, inventor of the rifled cannon, died, 1865.				♉	6:17am	9:06pm	11:19pm	7:17am
23	Luke Blackburn, Ky.'s first physician governor, born in Woodford County, 1816.	Moon & Venus very close			♊	6:17am	9:06pm	-:------	8:30am
24	Kentucky National Guard Day	Gen. George Rogers Clark and his men shoot the Falls of the Ohio during a full solar eclipse, 1778.			♊	6:17am	9:06pm	12:12am	9:48am
25	Second Sunday after Trinity			NEW ●	♋	6:18am	9:07pm	12:54am	11:07am
26	First known ad for Bourbon Whiskey appears in Paris "Western Citizen," 1821.				♋	6:18am	9:07pm	1:28am	12:23pm
27	Folks that sleep late usually pay their bills the same way.				♋	6:18am	9:07pm	1:56am	1:34pm
28	A dose of responsibility solves a lot of problems.	Thomas D. Clark, Historian Laureate died at age 101.			♌	6:19am	9:07pm	2:22am	2:43pm
29	Sts. Peter & Paul, Sts of the day				♌	6:19am	9:07pm	2:46am	3:50pm
30	Isaac Caldwell, early U of L President, born in Adair County, 1824.				♍	6:19am	9:07pm	3:10am	4:56pm

JULY—hath 31 days.

	REMARKABLE DAYS, JUDGEMENT OF WEATHER.		MOON PHASE LOCATION	ZODIAC SYMBOL	SUN RISE	SUN SET	MOON RISE	MOON SET
1	Retired Veterans' Day – Ky. holiday			♍	6:20am	9:07pm	12:00pm	-:-------
2	Blanton Collier born in Millersburg, 1904: He became football coach at UK, then for the Cleveland Browns.			♍	6:20am	9:06pm	12:57pm	12:46am
3	John Mason Brown, America's great 20th Century drama critic, born in Louisville, 1900.		FIRST QTR. ☾	♎	6:21am	9:06pm	1:56pm	1:06am
4	Independence Day			♎	6:21am	9:06pm	2:55pm	1:27am
5	Writ of habeas corpus in Kentucky suspended by President Lincoln, 1864.			♏	6:22am	9:06pm	3:58pm	1:50am
6	Ned Beatty, actor, born in St. Matthews, 1937.			♏	6:23am	9:06pm	5:03pm	2:17am
7	Young Ewing Allison, poet, author of "15 Men on a Dead Man's Chest," died in Louisville, 1932.			♐	6:23am	9:05pm	6:11pm	2:49am
8	Lancaster's cholera epidemic subsides, 1833.			♐	6:24am	9:05pm	7:19pm	3:30am
9	James Campbell Cantrill, U.S. & Ky. legislator, born in Georgetown, 1870.			♐	6:24am	9:05pm	8:23pm	4:21am
10	Stable boys and lawyers have similar duties.			♑	6:25am	9:04pm	9:19pm	5:23am
11	Charles A. Browning, inventor of the horror film, born in Louisville, 1881.		FULL ○	♑	6:26am	9:04pm	10:05pm	6:35am
12	Adm. Claude Charles Brock born in Butler County,1878.			♒	6:26am	9:04pm	10:43pm	7:52am
13	Harrodsburg's Matthew H. Jouett made Capt. of 28th U.S. Infantry, 1814. He later became a painter.			♒	6:27am	9:03pm	11:15pm	9:10am
14	Thomas D. Clark, history professor, historian, Kentucky Historian Laureate, born, 1903.			♓	6:28am	9:03pm	11:42pm	10:25am
15	Jackson connects to the Kentucky Union R.R., 1891.			♓	6:28am	9:02pm	-:--------	11:38am
16	Thistles get numerous.			♈	6:29am	9:02pm	12:08am	12:50pm
17	Chenoweth Massacre, Jefferson County, 1789.		LAST QTR. ☾	♈	6:30am	9:01pm	12:34am	2:01pm
18	WHAS, Ky.'s first radio station, goes on the air, Louisville, 1922.			♉	6:31 am	9:00pm	1:01am	3:12pm
19	In a home game, the Louisville Grays beat Nashville: first pro baseball game west of the Alleghenies, 1865.			♉	6:31am	9:00pm	1:31am	4:24pm
20	Detroit Tiger Jim Bunning pitches a no-hitter against the Red Sox, 1958.		Moon Day	♊	6:32am	7:59pm	2:07am	5:34pm
21	Orlando Brown, Whig editor of "The Frankfort Commonwealth," died, 1867.			♊	6:33am	8:58pm	2:50am	6:39pm
22	Cassius Marcellus Clay died during a thunder-storm at White Hall, 1903.			♋	6:34am	8:58pm	3: 41am	7:37pm
23	Parents' Day			♋	6:34am	8:57pm	4:39am	8:26pm
24	Sunny day? Get outside and play.	Congressman Richard Clough Anderson died, 1824	NEW ●	♋	6:35am	8:56pm	5:41am	9:05pm
25	Lawyer & Lincoln scholar William Townsend died in Lexington, 1964.			♌	6:36am	8:55pm	6:46am	9:38pm
26	Get thee to a Farmer's Market!	Pres. Cabinet Secy John J. Crittenden died, 1863.	Minor conj. ☾♄	♌	6:37am	8:55pm	7:49am	10:05pm
27	U.S. Army orders Louisville's Camp Zachary Taylor closed, 1920.			♍	6:38am	8:54pm	8:51am	10:28pm
28	The fishin' hole has become the swimmin' hole by now.			♍	6:39am	8:53pm	9:50am	10:50pm
29	"Freedom" is a poor excuse for being irresponsible.		Close qtrs. ☿♀	♍	6:39am	8:52pm	10:48am	11:10pm
30	Never date a tennis player: To them, love means nothing.			♎	6:40am	8:51pm	11:46am	11:30pm
31	Whitney Young Jr. born in Shelbyville, 1921.			♎	6:41am	8:50pm	12:44pm	11:52pm

AUGUST—hath 31 days.

REMARKABLE DAYS, JUDGEMENT OF WEATHER.		MOON PHASE LOCATION	ZODIAC SYMBOL	SUN RISE	SUN SET	MOON RISE	MOON SET
1	Bell Co. established, 1867.		♏	5:42am	7:49pm	1:45pm	-:--------
2	Disability Day in Ky. Clinton Co. Courthouse burns, 1980.	FIRST QTR. ☽	♏	5:43am	7:48pm	2:48pm	12:16am
3	Sophio Kindrick Alcorn born in Stanford, 1883: pioneer educator of the deaf and blind.		♏	5:44am	7:47pm	3:53pm	12:45am
4	Desha Breckinridge born, 1867: he became publisher of the "Lexington Herald."		♐	5:45 am	7:46pm	5:00pm	1:21am
5	Wendell Berry born in Henry Co., 1934.		♐	5:45am	7:45pm	6:06pm	2:06am
6	"Bloody Monday" anti-Catholic riots in Louisville, 1855.		♑	5:46am	7:44pm	7:05pm	3:03am
7	First sermon in Louisville history preached by Squire Boone, 1776.		♑	5:47am	7:43pm	7:56pm	4:10am
8	Jesse Stuart born in Greenup Co., 1906.		♒	5:48am	7:42pm	8:38pm	5:26am
9	Confederate guerillas capture Calhoun, 1862.	FULL ○	♒	5:49am	7:40pm	9:12pm	6:45am
10	Diane Sawyer of Glasgow becomes reporter for "60 Minutes" in 1984.		♓	5:50am	7:39pm	9:42pm	8:04am
11	First issue of The Kentucky Gazette published, Lexington, 1787.		♓	5:51am	7:38pm	10:09pm	9:20am
12	Author Robert S. Cotterill born in Fleming Co., 1884.		♈	5:52am	7:37pm	10:36pm	10:35am
13	Bert T. Combs born in Clay Co., 1911.		♈	5:52am	7:36pm	11:03pm	11:48am
14	Last public hanging in the U.S., Owensboro, 1936.		♉	5:53am	7:34pm	11:33pm	12:02pm
15	Barry Bingham Sr. died, Louisville, 1988.	LAST QTR. ☾	♉	5:54am	7:33pm	-:--------	2:15pm
16	Attack of Tories and Wyandots repelled at Bryan's Station, 1782.		♊	5:55am	7:32pm	12:07am	3:26pm
17	Problems can't be solved from afar.		♊	5:56am	7:30pm	12:48am	4:33pm
18	James Graham Brown born, 1881: Founder of the Brown Hotel.		♊	5:57am	7:29pm	1:36am	5:33pm
19	Battle of Blue Licks, Robertson County, 1782.		♋	5:58am	7:28pm	2:32am	5:24pm
20	Ohio & Big Sandy R.R. founded: Ashland, 1889.		♋	5:59am	7:26pm	3:33am	7:06pm
21	Complaint and inaction are dreadful partners.	Major conj. ☿♄	♌	5:59am	7:25pm	4:37am	7:40pm
22	Alexander Kimbrough, duelist from Cynthiana, died, 1921.		♌	6:00am	7:24pm	5:40am	8:09pm
23	John Sherman Cooper born in Somerset, 1901.	NEW ●	♌	6:01am	7:23pm	6:42am	8:33pm
24	Katherine Bowersox, educator of women at Berea College, born, 1869.		♍	6:02 am	7:21pm	7:42am	8:55pm
25	"Sue Mundy" (Marcellus Jerome Clark), Civil War bandit, born in Simpson County, 1845.		♍	6:03am	7:19pm	8:40am	9:15pm
26	Discipline solves more problems than money.		♎	6:04am	7:18pm	9:38am	9:35pm
27	Unwilling to work, unhappy in life.	Major conj. ♀♄	♎	6:05am	7:17pm	10:36am	9:56pm
28	William C. Breckinridge born, 1837: Editor, Confederate officer, civil rights advocate.		♎	6:06am	7:15pm	11:35am	10:19pm
29	L&N Railroad line arrives at Madisonville, 1870.		♏	6:06am	7:14pm	12:37am	10:45pm
30	Alexander Arthur, Middlesborough's founder, born, 1846, Glasgow, Scotland.		♏	6:07am	7:12pm	1:40pm	11:18pm
31	Parents are happy-hearted: school has started.		♐	6:08am	7:11pm	2:46pm	11:58pm

SEPTEMBER—hath 30 days

	REMARKABLE DAYS, JUDGEMENT OF WEATHER.		MOON PHASE LOCATION	ZODIAC SYMBOL	SUN RISE	SUN SET	MOON RISE	MOON SET
1	Martin Co. formed, 1870.			♐	6:09am	7:09pm	3:50pm	-:---------
2	Adolph Rupp born, 1901.			♑	6:10am	7:08pm	4:51pm	12:48am
3	Troops commanded by Gen. Leonidas K. Polk, CSA, capture Columbus, Ky., 1861.			♑	6:11am	7:06pm	5:44pm	1:48am
4	Labor Day	Lexington's Gen. John Hunt Morgan died at the Battle of Greenville, Tenn., 1864.		♑	6:12am	7:05pm	6:29pm	2:59am
5	John Griffen Carlisle born in Kenton County, 1835: He became Pres. Cleveland's Secretary of the Treasury.			♒	6:12am	7:03pm	7:07pm	4:16am
6	To rush is to miss.			♒	6:13am	7:02pm	7:39pm	5:34am
7	U of L President George Colvin born in Washington Co., 1875.		FULL MOON ○	♓	6:14am	7:00pm	8:07pm	6:53am
8	Patience is a virtue only when not combined with laziness.			♓	6:15am	6:58pm	8:35pm	8:10am
9	Col. Harland Sanders born, 1890.			♈	6:16am	6:57pm	9:02pm	9:26am
10	Grandparents' Day	Gov. John J. Crittenden born this day, Woodford Co., 1786.		♈	6:17am	6:55pm	9:32pm	10:42am
11	A government is a reflection of its citizens.			♉	6:18am	6:54pm	10:05pm	11:58am
12	Sen. Joseph C.S. Stiles born, Woodford County, 1918.			♉	6:18am	6:52pm	10:45pm	1:13pm
13	Plant radishes, spinach and mustard for fall.			♊	6:19am	6:51pm	11:32pm	1:24pm
14	Gov. Luke Blackburn died, 1887.		LAST QTR. ☾	♊	6:20am	6:49pm	-:---------	3:28pm
15	Muhammed Ali regains heavyweight title from Leon Spinks, 1978.		Superior conj. ☿☌	♋	6:21am	6:48pm	12:26am	4:22pm
16	Gov. Leslie sends militia to stop Breathitt Co. feuding, 1874.			♋	6:22am	6:46pm	1:26am	5:07pm
17	Citizenship Day	UK & NFL football star George Blanda born, 1927.		♌	6:23am	6:44pm	2:29am	5:43pm
18	Confederate troops occupy Bowling Green, 1861.			♌	6:24am	6:43pm	3:33am	6:13pm
19	Ashland Oil founder Paul Blazer born, 1890.			♌	6:25am	6:41pm	4:35am	6:38pm
20	Confederate Gen. Benjamin Hardin Helm, Lincoln's brother-in-law, killed at Chickamauga, 1863.			♍	6:25am	6:40pm	5:35am	7:00pm
21	Gen. William O. Butler, of Jessamine Co., wounded at the Battle of Monterey, 1846.			♍	6:26am	6:38pm	6:34am	7:21pm
22	John Bryan Bowman died, 1891: principle founder of UK.		Autumnal Equinox NEW MOON ●	♎	6:27am	6:36pm	7:32am	7:41pm
23	Rosh Hashanah	KET goes on the air, 1968.		♎	6:28am	6:35pm	8:30am	8:01pm
24	Black Patch War begins, Guthrie, 1904.			♎	6:29am	6:33pm	9:29am	8:24pm
25	Boones and five other families first try to settle in Ky., 1773.			♏	6:30am	6:32pm	10:29am	8:49pm
26	Orlando Brown, prominent early Ky. journalist, born in Frankfort, 1801.			♏	6:31am	6:30pm	11:32am	9:19pm
27	Col. Basil Duke, CSA, and Ky. Cavalry defeat Home Guards and loot Augusta, 1862.			♐	6:32am	6:29pm	12:36pm	9:55pm
28	Apple-picking time in Kentucky.			♐	6:32am	6:27pm	1:40pm	10:40pm
29	U.S. Gen. Jefferson Davis kills Gen. William Nelson in a dispute, Louisville, 1862.			♐	6:33 a.m.	6:26pm	2:41pm	10:36pm
30	"Thrilla in Manila" – Ali defeats Frazier, 1975.		FIRST QTR. ☾	♑	6:34am	6:24pm	3:35pm	-:---------

OCTOBER—hath 31 days.

	REMARKABLE DAYS, JUDGEMENT OF WEATHER.		MOON PHASE LOCATION	ZODIAC SYMBOL	SUN RISE	SUN SET	MOON RISE	MOON SET
1	Sen. Joseph Blackburn born near Versailles, 1838.			♑	7:35am	7:22pm	4:22pm	12:40am
2	Yom Kippur	Muhammad Ali's last fight: he was defeated by Larry Holmes in the 11th round, 1980.		♒	7:36am	7:21pm	5:01pm	1:52am
3	McNitt's Defeat: 20 settlers killed by Cherokees in Laurel Co., 1786.			♒	7:37am	7:19pm	5:35pm	3:07am
4	Richard Hawes installed as Confederate Gov. of Ky., Bowling Green, 1862.			♓	7:38am	7:18pm	6:04pm	4:24am
5	Battle of the Thames: Ky. soldiers save the day, 1813.			♓	7:39am	7:16pm	6:32pm	5:40am
6	Louisville's Charles Browning, pioneer film maker, died, 1962.		FULL ○	♈	7:40am	7:15pm	6:59pm	6:56am
7	Start curing pumpkins for jack-o-lanterns.			♈	7:41am	7:13pm	7:28pm	8:13am
8	Battle of Perryville, 1862.			♉	7:42am	7:12pm	8:00pm	9:31am
9	Columbus Day (Observed)	Gen. Edmund K. Smith, CSA, gets lost on way to reinforce Bragg at Perryville. Rebels retreat.		♉	7:42am	7:10pm	8:38pm	10:49am
10	Pick Indian Corn & Popcorn			♊	7:43am	7:09pm	9:23pm	11:05am
11	Gen. Casimir Pulaski Day - Ky. holiday	Oakland Race Course opens in Louisville, 1832.		♊	7:44am	7:07pm	10:16pm	1:15pm
12	Columbus Day (Traditional)	Lexington founder Robert Patterson and others leave Fort Pitt for Ky., 1775.		♋	7:45am	7:06pm.	11:16 p.m	2:15pm
13	Levisa Fork River cut-through completed, Pikeville, 1987.		LAST QTR. ☾	♋	7:46am	7:05pm	-:-------	3:04pm
14	Start drying gourds for spring use.			♋	7:47am	7:03pm	12:20am	3:44pm
15	U.S. Rep. Carl Perkins born in Hindman, 1912.			♌	7:48am	7:02pm	1:24am	4:16pm
16	Cleanth Brooks, literary critic, born, Murray, 1906.			♌	7:49am	7:00pm	2:27am	4:43pm
17	UK begins WBKY, first university-owned radio station, 1940.			♍	7:50am	6:59pm	3:28am	5:06pm
18	Though Autumn is glorious; the race track can be uproarious.			♍	7:51am	6:58pm	4:27am	5:26pm
19	Cassius Marcellus Clay, emancipationist, Lincoln's ambassador to Russia, born in Madison County, 1810.			♍	7:52am	6:56pm	5:25am	5:47pm
20	Gen. John Hunt Morgan's men burn a U.S. Army wagon train at Coxes Creek, 1862.			♎	7:53am	6:55pm	6:23am	6:07pm
21	Jim Wayne Miller, poet from Berea, born, 1936.			♎	7:54am	6:54pm	7:22am	6:29pm
22	Gov. Earl Clements born in Morganfield, 1896.		NEW ●	♏	7:55am	6:52pm	8:22am	6:53pm
23	Adlai Stevenson, U.S. Vice President, born in Christian Co., 1835.			♏	7:56am	6:51pm	9:24am	7:22pm
24	United Nations Day	Dann Byck, Louisville clothier, born, 1899.		♏	7:57am	6:50pm	10:29am	7:56pm
25	9th Mich. Infantry moves on Louisville	1861	Super. conj. ♀♂	♐	7:58am	6:48pm	11:33am	8:39pm
26	In Kentucky, there are almost as many October brides as June brides.			♐	7:59am	6:47pm	12:34pm	9:30pm
27	Barbourville selected as seat of Knox Co., 1800.			♑	8:00am	6:46pm	1:30pm	10:31pm
28	Get out the pumpkin pie recipes!			♑	8:01am	6:45pm	2:19pm	11:39pm
29	Centre 6, Harvard 0	Daylight Savings Time ends	FIRST QTR. ☾	♒	7:02am	5:44pm	1:59pm	11:51pm
30	David Barrow, Mt. Sterling abolitionist, born in Va., 1753.			♒	7:03am	5:42pm	2:33pm	-:-------
31	Halloween	Otis A. Singletary, former UK president, born, 1921.		♓	7:04am	5:41pm	3:03pm	1:04am

NOVEMBER—hath 30 days.

	REMARKABLE DAYS, JUDGEMENT OF WEATHER.		MOON PHASE LOCATION	ZODIAC SYMBOL	SUN RISE	SUN SET	MOON RISE	MOON SET
1	All Saints	Mann Butler, early Ky. historian, died, 1855.		♓	7:05am	5:40pm	3:30pm	2:17am
2	Daniel Boone born in Penn., 1734.			♓	7:07am	5:39pm	3:57pm	3:31am
3	First state capitol building occupied, 1794.			♈	7:08am	5:38pm	4:24pm	4:45am
4	Second state capitol building burns, 1824.			♈	7:09am	5:37pm	4:54pm	6:02am
5	J. Winston Coleman, writer & historian, born near Lexington, 1898.		FULL ○	♉	7:10am	5:36pm	5:29pm	7:20am
6	John Beckham elected governor, 1900.			♉	7:11am	5:35pm	6:11pm	8:38am
7	Election Day	Battle of Belmont, 1861.		♊	7:12am	5:34pm	7:02pm	9:53am
8	John Adair begins term in U.S. Senate, 1805.			♊	7:13am	5:33pm	8:00pm	10:59am
9	Martin V.B. Bates, "The Kentucky Giant" born in Letcher Co., 1845. He grew to 7'11".			♋	7:14am	5:32pm	9:05pm	11:55am
10	Veterans' Day (Observed)			♋	7:15am	5:31pm	10:11pm	12:40pm
11	Veterans' Day (Traditional) / Alben Barkley announces gubernatorial candidacy, 1922.		Close conj. ☿ ♂	♌	7:16am	5:30pm	11:16pm	1:16pm
12	"The old raccoon walks late."		LAST QTR. ☾	♌	7:17am	5:30pm	-:--------	1:45pm
13	Louis Brandeis, great jurist, born in Louisville, 1856.			♍	7:18am	5:29pm	12:19am	2:09pm
14	Surveyor's error creates Black Jack Corner, 1780.			♍	7:19am	5:28pm	1:19am	2:31pm
15	Kentucky Harvest Day	Commercial flights begin, Standiford Field, Louisville, 1947.		♍	7:21am	5:27pm	2:17am	2:51pm
16	Have your hunting dogs ready.		Close conj. ♀ ♃	♎	7:22am	5:26pm	3:14am	3:11pm
17	Be thankful during the rest of the year, too.			♎	7:23am	5:26pm	4:13am	3:33pm
18	Ky.'s Confederate state government formed, Russellville, 1861.			♏	7:24am	5:25pm	5:12am	3:56pm
19	George Rogers Clark born, 1752.			♏	7:25am	5:25pm	6:14am	4:23pm
20	Be thankful today and every day.	George B. Hodge, Fleming Co., made a CSA General.	NEW ●	♏	7:26am	5:24pm	7:19am	4:56pm
21	Campbell-Rice religious debates rage in Lexington, 1843.			♐	7:27am	5:23pm	8:24am	5:37pm
22	Sarah Blanding, Vassar's first woman president, born in Lexington, 1898.			♐	7:28am	5:23pm	9:27am	6:25pm
23	THANKSGIVING	Make sure that your turkey or ham comes from Kentucky, not Alabama!		♑	7:29am	5:22pm	10:26am	7:25pm
24	"Have Leftovers For Dinner Day"			♑	7:30am	5:22pm	11:17am	8:32pm
25	First Kentucky state capitol building burns, 1813.			♑	7:31am	5:21pm	11:59am	9:42pm
26	Christ the King (Advent approaches)	Gov. Ned Breathitt born, 1924.		♒	7:32am	5:21pm	12:35pm	10:34pm
27	John Hunt Morgan escapes from Ohio State Penitentiary, 1863.			♒	7:33am	5:21pm	1:05pm	-:-------
28	James Buckner Brown, owner of old "Louisville Herald-Post," born, 1872.		FIRST QTR. ☽	♓	7:34am	5:20pm	1:32pm	12:05am
29	Harry M. Caudill died, Letcher Co., 1990.			♓	7:35am	5:20pm	1:58pm	1:16am
30	Get rid of turkey leftovers (make catfish bait).			♈	7:36am	5:20pm	2:23pm	2:27am

DECEMBER—hath 31 days.

	REMARKABLE DAYS, JUDGEMENT OF WEATHER.		MOON PHASE LOCATION	ZODIAC SYMBOL	SUN RISE	SUN SET	MOON RISE	MOON SET
1	Kentucky Christian College founded, Grayson, 1919.			♈	7:37am	5:20pm	2:51pm	3:40am
2	The year's last month can the best month.			♉	7:38am	5:19pm	3:23pm	4:55am
3	Advent Sunday	Louisville's Benjamin Avery, inventor of the Avery Plow, born, 1801.		♉	7:39am	5:19pm	4:01pm	6:11am
4	Former Gov. Bert T. Combs drowns in a Powell County flash flood, 1991.		FULL ○	♊	7:40am	5:19pm	4:47pm	7:27am
5	U.S. Army's Camp Breckinridge (near Morganfield) closed, 1962.			♊	7:41am	5:19pm	5:42pm	8:38am
6	St. Nicholas Day	A jolly day in many ways.		♋	7:42am	5:19pm	6:45pm	9:40am
7	Martha Layne Collins born, Shelby County, 1936.			♋	7:43am	5:19pm	7:53pm	10:31am
8	Frankfort chosen as state capital city, 1792.			♌	7:43am	5:19pm	9:00pm	11:11am
9	James Black ends 7-month term as governor, 1919.			♌	7:44am	5:19pm	10:05pm	11:43am
10	Ky. admitted into Confederacy without secession, 1861: George Johnson declared governor.		☿ Conj. & ♂♃	♌	7:45am	5:19pm	11:07pm	12:10pm
11	Gov. Isaac Shelby born, 1750.		Conj. ♂♃	♍	7:46am	5:19pm	-:-------	12:33pm
12	William Goebel made governor, 1899: he'd be assassinated in six weeks.		LAST QTR. ☾	♍	7:47am	5:20pm	12:06a. m.	12:54pm
13	Boone Co. founded, 1798.			♎	7:47am	5:20pm	1:04am	1:14pm
14	Lawrence Co. formed, 1821.			♎	7:48am	5:20pm	2:02am	1:35pm
15	Bill of Rights Day	Shuck beans and cornbread weather!		♎	7:49am	5:20pm	3:01am	1:58pm
16	Hanukkah			♏	7:49am	5:21pm	4:01am	2:23pm
17	Campbell County formed, 1794	No better time for a festival of lights, than these dark winter nights.		♏	7:50am	5:21pm	5:05am	2:54pm
18	Ky. General Assembly considers public education, 1821.			♐	7:51am	5:21pm	6:10am	3:32pm
19	Cut your Christmas tree before tomorrow afternoon.			♐	7:51am	5:22pm	7:15am	4:18pm
20	Lincoln countermands Gen. Grant's order expelling Jews from Ky., 1862.		NEW ●	♐	7:52am	5:22pm	8:16am	5:15pm
21	Author James Lane Allen born in Fayette Co., 1849.	Winter Solstice		♑	7:52am	5:23pm	9:11am	6:21pm
22	St. Nick came to Kentucky, then said, "I'll trade my reindeer for just one Thoroughbred!'			♑	7:53am	5:23pm	9:57am	7:32pm
23	Armed mob forcibly closes Berea College for its abolitionist views, 1859.			♒	7:53am	5:24pm	10:36am	8:45pm
24	Kit Carson born, Madison Co., 1809.			♒	7:54am	5:24pm	11:08am	9:57pm
25	Christmas Day	Gen Hylan Lyon, CSA, orders Taylor Co. courthouse burned, 1864.		♓	7:54am	5:25pm	11:36am	11:08pm
26	The sooner you take down the Christmas tree, the better.	Kwanzaa starts (ends Jan. 1)		♓	7:55am	5:26pm	12:01pm	-:-------
27	"Fish and visitors stink after three days." – Benjamin Franklin.		FIRST QTR. ☾	♈	7:55am	5:26pm	12:27pm	12:18am
28	John Y. Brown Jr. born in Lexington, 1933.			♈	7:55am	5:27pm	12:53pm	1:29am
29	John Hunt Morgan's cavalry encamps at Bardstown, 1862.			♉	7:55am	5:28pm	1:22pm	2:41am
30	Col. John Allen born, 1771 (Allen Co. was named for him).			♉	7:56am	5:28pm	1:56pm	3:54am
31	Start the New Year out great: Go to bed early, don't stay out late!			♊	7:56am	5:29pm	2:38pm	5:08am

Curious Animal

IN February laſt, a detachment of mounted infantry, commanded by Captain John Baird, penetrated fifteen miles into the Cumberland mountain :. On Cove creek, enſign M'Donald and another man, in advance of the party as ſpies, they diſcovered a creature about three ſteps from them, it had only two legs, and ſtood almoſt upright, covered with ſcales of a black, brown, and light yellow colour, in ſpots like rings, a white tuft or crown on the top of its head, about four feet high, with a head as big as a two pound ſtone & large eyes of a firey red. It ſtood about three minutes in a daring poſture, (orders being given not to fire a gun, except at Indians) Mr. M'Donald advanced and ſtruck at it with his ſword, when it jumped up, at leaſt eight feet, and lit on the ſame ſpot of ground, ſending forth a red kind of matter out of its mouth reſembling blood, and then retreated into a Laurel thicket, turning round often, as if it intended to fight. The tracks of it reſembled that of a gooſe, but larger. The Indians report, that a creature inhabits that part of the mountain, of the above deſcription, which, by its breath, will kill a man, if he does not inſtantly immerſe himſelf in water.

Note — until the late 1780s, American publishers practiced the English method of typesetting the letter "s" as an "f." Source: The Kentucky Almanac 1795, published by John Bradford, Lexington, Ky.

Notable Kentuckians

NOTE — *Any attempt to list remarkable, distinguished or "notable" individuals carries with it an inherent risk that someone will be omitted. The people named here are a brief cross-section of individuals who have achieved noteworthy accomplishments, some obscure and others with international fame. Be assured, many more will be featured in future editions of the Kentucky Almanac and at www.kyalmanac.com.*

(1715-1794) **Dr. Thomas Walker**, physician & surveyor, led an exploratory party to Ky. in 1750

(1734-1820) **Daniel Boone**, hunter, woodsmen & early explorer, settled Boonesborough in 1775

(1738-1813) **Rebecca Boone**, early settler, Boonesborough

(1743-1798) **John Fitch**, invented the first American steam boat (1786), Nelson Co.

(1743-1808) **Elijah Craig**, early Kentucky preacher & entrepreneur thought to have invented the distillery of bourbon whiskey, Scott County

(1745-1808) **Benjamin Harrison**, soldier & pioneer, Cynthiana

(1752-1818) **George Rogers Clark**, Revolutionary War General & early Kentucky surveyor

(1753-1788) **John Filson**, Kentucky surveyor & historian, Louisville

(1760-1831) **Virginia "Jenny" Wiley**, heroic pioneer mother, buried in Johnson Co.

(1771-1830) **Dr. Ephraim McDowell**, pioneer surgeon, Danville

(1810-1903) **Cassius Marcellus Clay**, emancipationist & ambassador to Russia, Madison Co.

(1777-1852) **Henry Clay**, American statesman & farmer, Lexington

(1785-1851) **John James Audubon**, artist, "Birds of America," Henderson

(1789-1865) **Thomas Harris Barlow**, inventor, Nicholas Co.

(1789-1883) **Josiah Henson**, alleged to be Uncle Tom in "Uncle Tom's Cabinet," by Harriet Beecher Stowe, Owensboro

(1793-1858) **Mother Catherine Spalding**, missionary, founder of Spalding University, Louisville

(1802-1888) **Gideon Shryock**, architect, designed the Old State Capitol (Greek Revival style), Lexington

(1808-1889) **Jefferson Davis**, president of the Southern Confederacy, Fairview

(1809-1865) **Abraham Lincoln**, U.S. president, Hodgenville

(1809-1868) **Christopher Kit Carson**, scout & pioneer of the West, Madison Co.

(1810-1877) **Joel Tanner Hart**, sculptor, Clark Co.

(1816-1901) **Rev. John G. Fee**, noted abolitionist, founder of Berea College, Berea

(1820-1867) **Theodore O'Hara**, author, "Bivouac of the Dead," Louisville

(1829-1915) **James Morrison Heady**, invented the "talking glove," Spencer Co.

(1833-1911) **John Marshall Harlan**, U.S. Supreme Court Justice, Boyle Co.

(1842-1922) **Lucy Dupey Montz**, Kentucky's first woman dentist, Warsaw

(1844-1912) **James Breckinridge Speed**, capitalist & philanthropist, established The Speed Art Museum, Louisville

(1846-1911) **Carry A. Nation**, temperance crusader known as "the lady with a hatchet," Garrard Co.

(1848-1919) **Frank Duveneck**, painter & etcher, Covington

(1849-1925) **James Lane Allen**, author, Lexington

(1849-1941) **Laura Clay**, early feminist, Madison Co.

(1856-1929) **John E. Madden**, horseman, founder of Hamburg Place & breeder of six Kentucky Derby Winners, Fayette Co.

(1856-1941) **Louis D. Brandeis**, U.S. Supreme Court justice, Louisville

(1860-1940) **Belle Brezing** (Mary Belle Cox), served as the prototype for Belle Watling in Margaret Mitchell's "Gone With the Wind," Lexington

(1860-1940) **John T. Thompson**, inventor of the Tommygun machine gun, Newport

(1861-1896) **Isaac Murphy**, first jockey to win three Kentucky Derbies, Fayette Co.

(1862-1919) **John Fox Jr.**, novelist, "Little Shepherd of Kingdom Come," Bourbon Co.

(1864-1900) **Casey Jones** (John Luther Jones), heroic locomotive engineer, Fulton Co.

(1866-1945) **Thomas Hunt Morgan**, Nobel Prize winner 1933 in Physiology or Medicine, Lexington

(1866-1946) **John A. "Bud" Hillerich**, inventor (Louisville Slugger baseball bat), Louisville

(1867-1933) **Mary Elliott Flanery**, first woman to serve in a southern state legislature, Carter Co.

(1872-1967) **Isaac S. Hathaway**, first African American to design a U.S. coin, Lexington

(1876-1944) **Irvin S. Cobb**, humorist & author, Paducah

(1876-1962) **Alice Lloyd**, social reformer, helped establish what is now Alice Lloyd College, Knott Co.

(1877-1956) **Alben W. Barkley**, U.S. vice president, Graves Co.

(1877-1963) **Garrett Morgan**, African-American, invented gas masks used in WWI, Paris

(1881-1941) **Elizabeth Madox Roberts**, novelist & poet, Perryville

(1881-1965) **Mary Carson Breckinridge**, founded the Frontier Nursing Services, Southeastern Ky.

(1883-1967) **Sophia Kindrick Alcorn**, invented methods to teach deaf-blind children, Stanford

(1884-1980) **Stanley Reed**, justice of the U.S. Supreme Court, Maysville

(1886-1974) **Arthur Krock**, Pulitzer Prize winning journalist & author, Glasgow

(1887-1925) **Floyd Collins**, explorer whose entrapment & death in Sand Cave became a widely reported story, Barren Co.

(1890-1953) **Frederick M. Vinson**, chief justice of the U.S. Supreme Court (1946-1953), Louisa

(1890-1980) **Col. Harland Sanders**, restaurateur & founder of Kentucky Fried Chicken, Corbin

(1892-1971) **Margaret Ingels**, first U.S. woman to obtain a mechanical engineering degree, Bourbon Co.

(1892-1980) **John Jacob Niles**, author, composer & balladeer, Louisville

(1894-1949) **Wiley B. Rutledge**, U.S. Supreme Court justice, Cloverport

(1895-1970) **Edgar A Diddle**, legendary basketball coach, Western Kentucky University

(1898-1983) **J. Winston Coleman**, Jr., historian & non-fiction writer, Lexington

(1898-1990) **Irene Dunne**, actor, Louisville

(1898-1991) **Albert B. "Happy" Chandler**, two-time Governor of Kentucky, Corydon

(1899-1976) **Earle Bryan Combs**, professional baseball player, Owsley Co.

(1899-1979) **John Orley Allen Tate**, poet & critic, Winchester

(1900-1976) **Annie L. Sandusky**, pioneer in social work, Louisville

(1900-1991) **George Speri Sperti**, scientist & inventor (radiation lamp for rheumatism), Covington

(1901-1977) **Adolph Rupp**, UK basketball coach, won 875 games in 41 years of coaching, won four NCAA championships, Lexington

(1901-1991) **A.B. Guthrie**, journalist & novelist, Lexington

(1901-1991) **John Sherman Cooper**, U.S. Senator & diplomat, Somerset

(1903-2005) **Thomas D. Clark**, author & Historian Laureate of Kentucky, Lexington

(1904-1995) **Mary Bingham**, patron of the arts, civic leader & philanthropist, Louisville

(1905-1989) **Robert Penn Warren**, poet & writer, Guthrie

(1906-1988) **George Barry Bingham, Sr**, president of the Louisville Courier-Journal & the Louisville Times, Louisville

(1906-1997) **Lyman T. Johnson**, school teacher, led non-violent picketing against racial discrimination, Louisville

(1906-2001) **James Still**, author, Wolfpen Creek

(1907-1982) **Thruston Ballard Morton**, U.S. congressman & Assist. Secretary of State, Louisville

(1907-1984) **Jesse Stuart**, teacher & writer, Greenup Co.

(1907-1990) **Charles P. Farnsley**, former state & U.S. Congressman, mayor of Louisville, 1948-1953

(1908-1986) **Harriette Arnow**, author, Wayne Co.

(1908-2002) **Lionel Hampton**, jazz musician, composer, Louisville

(1909-1999) **May Street Kidd**, businesswoman & Kentucky state representative, Louisville

(1910-1972) **Wade Hall**, author, Louisville

(1911-1996) **Bill Monroe**, legendary Bluegrass musician & songwriter, Rosine

(1912-1984) **Carl Perkins**, U.S. congressman & teacher, Hindman

(1912-2001) **Foster Brooks**, comic & actor, Louisville

(1914-1941) **Marion Miley**, internationally-known woman golfer, Lexington

(1915-1968) **Thomas Merton**, Trappist monk & writer, Nelson Co.

(1915-1984) **Ed Prichard**, chairman, Prichard Committee for Academic Excellence, Maysville

(1915-1999) **Victor Mature**, actor & producer, Louisville

(1916-1998) **Elvis Jacob Stahr, Jr.**, secy. of U.S. Army & pres. of the National Audubon Society, Hickman

(1917-) **Marvin Finn**, internationally-known urban folk artist, Louisville

(1918-2004) **William T. Young**, businessman, horseman, community leader & philanthropist

(1919-1944) **Anna Mac Clarke**, first female black officer to command a white unit, Anderson County

(1919-1989) **Lois Morris**, founder of National Black Women for Political Action, Louisville

(1919-1994) **Thelma Stovall**, elected as Kentucky's first female lieutenant governor (1975), Munfordville

(1920-2002) **Anita Y. Boswell**, first national director for Project Head Start, Shelby Co.

(1921-1971) **Whitney M. Young, Jr.**, executive director of the National Urban League, Shelby Co.

(1922-1990) **Harry M. Caudill**, historian & non-fiction writer, Whitesburg

(1923-) **Georgia Davis Powers**, first female African-American state senator in Ky. (1968), Springfield

(1924-2003) **Edward T. "Ned" Breathitt, Jr.**, governor (1963-1967), signed the Ky. Civil Rights Act into law (1966), Hopkinsville

(1924-2004) **Louie Broady Nunn**, attorney & statesman, governor of Kentucky (1967-1971), Barren County

(1926-) **Patricia Neal**, Oscar-winning actress, Whitley Co.

(1926-1996) **Clarence "Cave" Wilson, Sr.**, basketball player for Harlem Globetrotters, Horse Cave

(1926-2001) **Carl "Kingfish" Helm**, played guard for the Harlem Globetrotters, Horse Cave

(1926-2001) **Caywood Ledford**, Hall of Fame sportscaster, "voice" of the UK Wildcats, Harlan Co.

(1928-) **Joe B. Hall**, head UK basketball coach 1972-1985, Cynthiana

(1928-) **Gene Snyder**, state court judge 1957-61, U.S. Representative, Louisville

(1928-1982) **Warren Oates**, actor, Louisville

(1928-2002) **Rosemary Clooney**, actor & premier jazz & pop singer, Maysville

(1930-) **Davey L. Whitney**, ranked among the top six active coaches, Midway

(1931-) **Roy Kidd**, head football coach, Eastern Kentucky University, Corbin

(1931-2004) **Skeeter Davis**, 60s pop & country singer, Dry Ridge

(1935-) **Paul "Golden Boy" Hornung**, football player, Louisville

(1935-) **Loretta Lynn**, country songwriter & singer, Butcher Hollow

(1936-) **Martha Layne Collins**, first woman governor, Shelby Co.

(1937-) **Ned Beatty**, motion picture, television & stage actor, St. Matthews

(1937-) **Denzel "Denny" Edwin Crum**, college basketball coach, University of Louisville

(1937-) **Donald Isaac Everly &** (1939 -) **Phil Everly**, pop singers, Brownie

(1937-) **Sallie Bingham**, philanthropist & writer, Louisville

(1937-2005) **Hunter S. Thompson**, "Gonzo" journalist & writer, Louisville

(1939-) **Lily Tomlin**, actress & comedienne, Paducah

(1939-) **William Stamps Farish, III**, business magnate & horseman, Woodford Co.

(1940-) **Sue Grafton**, author of the Kinsey Milhone mystery series, Louisville

(1940-) **Bobbie Ann Mason**, author, Mayfield

(1942-) **Muhammad Ali**, three-time heavyweight champion of the world, Louisville

(1942-) **Betty Lou Evans**, golfer & coach, inducted in National Golf Coaches Hall of Fame , Lexington

(1943-) **Wendell Berry**, writer & activist, Lexington

(1943-) **Arthur B. Hancock III**, musician & breeder of three Kentucky Derby Winners, Bourbon Co.

(1944-) **Bernie Bickerstaff**, head coach of the University of San Diego at 25, youngest college coach in the U.S., Benham

(1945-) **Diane Sawyer**, broadcast journalist, Glasgow

(1945-1996) **Ralph Gabbard**, visionary television newsman & former president of WKYT-TV

(1946-) **Wes Unseld**, played 13 years with the Baltimore Bullets, NBA's seventh all-time leading rebounder, Louisville

(1946-) **Naomi Judd** (Diane Ellen Judd), singer & actor, Ashland

(1949-) **Phyllis George**, former Miss America, former First Lady (married to Gov. John Y. Brown, Jr.), Lexington

(1950-) **Tom Payne**, first African American player to sign with UK, Louisville

(1950-) **Danny Sullivan**, race car driver, Louisville

(1951-) **Richard Thomas**, actor, Paintsville

(1951-) **Tubby Smith**, first African American basketball coach at UK, Lexington

(1952-) **Annie Potts**, actress, Franklin

(1954-) **George C. Wolfe**, African-American writer, Broadway producer & director, Frankfort

(1956-) **Jack "Goose" Givens**, first African American All-American in Kentucky, Lexington

(1956-) **Dwight Yoakam**, country singer, Pikeville

(1958-) **Bernadette Locke**, first woman & first African American assistant coach in Division I Men's NCAA basketball, Lexington

(1958-) **Donna L. Murphy**, first Miss Kentucky Basketball, inducted into the Kentucky Athletic Hall of Fame, Newport

(1960-) **Steve Cauthen**, youngest jockey to win the Triple Crown on Affirmed in 1978, Covington

(1961-) **George Clooney**, film & television actor, Augusta

(1963-) **John "Johnny" Christopher Depp III**, actor, Owensboro

(1963-) **Joan Osborne**, singer, Anchorage

(1963-) **Tori Murden-McClure**, first woman & first American to row solo across the Atlantic and first woman & first American to ski to the South Pole, Louisville

(1964-) **Wynonna Judd** (Christina Ciminella), singer & actor, Ashland

(1964-) **Mary T. Meagher**, winner of three gold medals at 1984 Olympic Games, Louisville

(1968-) **Ashley Judd**, actor & UK graduate, enthusiastic UK basketball fan

(1970-) **Diane Crump**, first female jockey to ride in a Kentucky Derby (1970)

(1970-) **Kevin Richardson**, singer & member of Back Street Boys, Irvine

(1975-) **Brian Littrell**, singer & member of Back Street Boys, Lexington

(1975-) **Heather French Henry**, Miss America 2000, Maysville

"Words may show a man's wit but actions his meaning."
— Benjamin Franklin

KENTUCKY GROSS STATE PRODUCT (GSP), BY COMPONENT: 1995, 2000, and 2001 (In Millions of Dollars)

CODE	INDUSTRY	GSP: CURRENT DOLLARS			% CHG	REAL GSP: CHAINED			% CHG
		1995	2000	2001		1995	2000	2001	
5000	**Total Gross State Product**	91,472	117,233	120,266	0.315	92,794	109,537	110,074	0.186
	Private industries	78,522	101,566	103,632	0.320	79,452	95,601	95,771	0.205
10000	Agriculture, forestry, & fishing	1,874	2,681	2,498	0.333	2,126	3,569	3,093	0.455
10010	Farms	1,413	1,983	1,775	0.256	1,650	3,070	2,518	0.526
30000	Mining	2,426	1,986	2,235	-0.079	2,323	2,424	2,786	0.199
30120	Coal mining	2,135	1,598	1,820	-0.148	2,006	2,062	2,417	0.205
40000	Construction	3,588	5,500	5,635	0.571	3,703	4,506	4,366	0.179
50000	Manufacturing	25,848	30,891	30,297	0.172	26,103	28,733	27,946	0.071
51000	Durable goods	14,024	18,871	18,986	0.354	13,966	20,341	20,764	0.487
51330	Primary metal industries	1,801	1,362	1,402	-0.222	1,686	1,523	1,662	-0.014
51340	Fabricated metal products	1,404	2,130	1,891	0.347	1,482	1,996	1,732	0.185
51350	Industrial machinery & equipment	1,952	1,816	2,274	0.165	1,833	2,614	3,415	0.863
51360	Electronic & other elec. equipment	1,495	1,075	912	-0.390	1,310	2,069	2,137	0.631
51371	Motor vehicles & equipment	5,420	10,209	10,255	0.892	5,692	9,946	9,985	0.754
52000	Nondurable goods	11,825	12,019	11,311	-0.043	12,144	9,152	8,231	-0.322
52200	Food & kindred products	2,551	2,728	2,718	0.065	2,807	2,388	2,342	-0.166
52210	Tobacco products	1,767	1,622	1,359	-0.231	1,835	472	320	-0.826
52270	Printing & publishing	1,383	1,689	1,675	0.211	1,526	1,430	1,351	-0.115
52280	Chemicals & allied products	2,549	2,182	1,964	-0.230	2,502	2,103	1,896	-0.242
60000	Transportation & public utilities	7,574	9,433	9,905	0.308	7,433	8,954	9,214	0.240
62000	Transportation	3,393	5,170	5,415	0.596	3,251	4,651	4,846	0.491
62420	Trucking & warehousing	1,300	1,891	1,944	0.495	1,265	1,586	1,533	0.212
62450	Transportation by air	1,207	2,187	2,351	0.848	1,123	2,018	2,294	1.043
64000	Communications	1,557	1,797	1,939	0.245	1,557	1,846	2,142	0.376
66000	Electric, gas, & sanitary services	2,624	2,466	2,551	-0.028	2,629	2,436	2,233	-0.151
70000	Wholesale trade	5,332	7,502	7,461	0.399	5,145	8,078	8,206	0.595
80000	Retail trade	8,300	10,947	11,369	0.370	8,231	11,218	11,607	0.410
90000	Finance, insurance, & real estate	9,979	13,731	14,162	0.418	10,372	12,070	12,210	0.177
90600	Depository institutions	2,516	3,417	3,398	0.350	2,863	2,719	2,741	0.022
90650	Real estate	5,596	7,258	7,506	0.341	5,731	6,566	6,647	0.142
100000	Services	13,599	18,895	20,081	0.477	14,023	16,388	16,684	0.190
100730	Business services	2,130	3,436	3,599	0.690	2,215	2,958	3,039	0.372
100800	Health services	5,849	7,456	8,064	0.379	6,000	6,633	6,853	0.142
100840	Other services	1,060	1,775	1,916	0.808	1,090	1,559	1,596	0.464
110000	Government	12,950	15,667	16,633	0.284	13,346	13,983	14,313	0.072
110100	Federal, civilian	2,881	3,098	3,193	0.108	2,984	2,789	2,780	-0.082
112000	Federal military	1,904	2,395	2,646	0.337	2,020	2,161	2,226	0.102
113000	State & local	8,165	10,175	10,895	0.334	8,362	9,013	9,306	0.113
51999	Electronic equip. & instr.	1,633	1,232	1,190	-0.271	1,482	2,147	2,407	0.646
90999	Depository & nondepository institutions	2,749	3,824	3,891	0.415	2,909	3,149	3,209	0.103
100999	Business serv. & other serv.	3,191	5,211	5,515	0.728	3,305	4,518	4,635	0.402

Note: Sub-categories with less than $1 billion were not included in this chart.

Source: U.S. Department of Commerce, Bureau of Economic Analysis. See: http://www.bea.gov/bea/regional/gsp/

For GSP glossary, see http://www.bea.gov/bea/glossary/glossaryIndex.htm

Business & Economy

Charles Thompson

From the beginning, Kentucky was all about business. Dr. Thomas Walker, a Virginia physician, led the first organized English expedition into Kentucky in 1750. Dr. Walker didn't come here for his health. He was also a businessman — a land speculator — and he was looking for territory suitable for settlement.

Mill at Mill Springs
Source: Sid Webb

After months of searching, Walker went home disappointed. He and his party had never gotten beyond the heavily forested hills of eastern Kentucky — good for hunting, Walker noted in his journal, but not for farming.

A more famous businessman arrived by way of North Carolina in 1769. Daniel Boone hunted for deerskins and furs he could sell for a profit back home. He soon learned that business is risky no matter where you are. Kentucky's Native Americans, who had their own centuries-long tradition of doing business with their neighbors, didn't appreciate trespassers. The Shawnee relieved Boone of a small fortune in pelts that he had spent months collecting, and warned him not to come back.

Brenda Adams, owner of A.D. Campbell Dress Shop, which has been in business more than a hundred years
Source: Sid Webb

Boone and many others ignored that warning. As settlers streamed into Kentucky, entrepreneurs founded businesses to serve them; from banks and general stores to well digging services, taverns, ferries, and even a saltpeter business run by a former slave called Free Frank.

A remarkable number of old Kentucky businesses have survived to the twenty-first century. While there are hardly any from the early pioneer days, there are quite a few from the first half of the nineteenth century, and hundreds that date from 1850 to 1900. About three hundred of these survivors have registered with the Kentucky Historical Society's Centennial Business Program. Most are small businesses which, as historian James C. Klotter has written, "are little known but affect so many people every day. They are the human side of economic history."

How does a business survive for a century, or even two centuries? "Bend over backward and bite your tongue 20 times to satisfy a customer," said Elmore Tonini, third generation president of Tonini Church Supply in Louisville, founded in 1886. Tonini's explanation of his company's longevity is, in so many words, the same one nearly every owner of a century-old business ultimately falls back on. Service, to customers and communities, is truly the bottom line. It can take many forms, from the local bank that uses its financial power to nurture a community's well being to the pharmacist who's on call to fill a prescription any time, night or day.

"I think the reason we're here today is because we continue to do the same things we were doing a hundred years ago, and that is personal customer service," said Willie D. Patton of Grayson, owner of Horton Bros. and Brown Pharmacy (founded 1889). "We know or soon become acquainted with everyone that comes in our store. I think the people of Grayson have rewarded us for that."

Banks are the biggest category of century-old businesses in Kentucky. Retail establishments and newspapers are close behind. Then come service providers – funeral homes and monument companies are big. Kentucky companies make everything from salsa to shoelaces to hair straighteners.

All these businesses have played a vital role in the commonwealth's history, both as providers of indispensable services and products and as beacons of continuity in an ever changing commercial and cultural landscape. As Thomas D. Clark, the late historian laureate of Kentucky, wrote: "These

Roger Kephart of Fall & Fall Ins. in Fulton, a 100-plus year old business
Source: Sid Webb

survivors have established rock-solid assets of integrity, personal service, patron loyalties, and a dedication to the sense of community. Collectively, the centennial businesses have reached far beyond the doorways of their stores and shops to knit a rich Kentucky heritage into a meaningful tradition and history of time and place."

***A list of century-old Kentucky businesses can be found at kyhumanities.org.**

BUSINESS & ECONOMY

Pioneer Industries

Thomas J. Kiffmeyer
Dr. Gary O'Dell

Kentucky's earliest industries were home-based production of tools and clothing for self-sufficient family farms. Other important early industries included salt mining, iron mining and smelting, hemp and rope production, and niter mining and gunpowder production.

Because it served as a preservative, long hunters and settlers highly valued salt and the production of this mineral represented one the state's first industries. Existing under the state's sandstone formations, salt was deposited in the soils as natural springs leached it from the rock. These deposits, known as "licks" because wild game licked the salt from the ground—became the sites of Kentucky salt works. After pioneer-producers excavated a salt spring, they dug a long trench, the longest was about three miles, which served as a "furnace." Salt makers placed large kettles, some of which held over twenty gallons, over a fire built in the furnace to evaporate the water and leave the salt.

Many salt producers obtained their kettles from yet another of Kentucky's pioneer industries—iron. In 1791 Jacob Myers constructed what probably was Kentucky's first iron furnace near what is now Owingsville, in Bath County. Iron makers constructed stone furnaces forty feet high in which they smelted limestone and ore with charcoal to produce iron. While some furnaces cast finished items including pots and stoves, others simply produced wrought iron for local blacksmiths.

Due to the number of interdependent operations, from woodcutters and miners to highly skilled furnace masters, the larger operations, such as the Aetna Furnace, built in 1816 in Hart County, utilized the labor of hundreds of people, both slave and free. These iron plantations, which included company houses, stores, and schools represented an interesting juxtaposition of antebellum labor systems with the company town system most commonly associated with the modern coal mining industry. The height of Kentucky's

iron industry was in the 1830s and 1840s, when the state ranked third in production behind Pennsylvania and New York. Kentucky's iron industry fell to seventh in the nation in 1870 and all but ceased by 1910.

Evidence indicates that niter mining at Saltpeter

Fort Boonesborough
Source: Photo by Sid Webb

Cave in Carter County became a full-time operation during the War of 1812.

At Great Saltpeter Cave in Rockcastle County and at Mammoth Cave, the works essentially became large saltpeter factories that employed hundreds of laborers, free and slave, and utilized more advanced processing technology. These mines ran twenty-fours hours a day all year at the height of their operations. Moreover, saltpeter mining intensified in the Red River Gorge rock-shelters during the war. This increase in niter production gave rise to what was the last, though not least of Kentucky's pioneer industries, gunpowder manufacturing.

Gunpowder, a combination of saltpeter, charcoal and sulfur, production began in Lexington as early as 1793, when Richard Foley advertised gunpowder for sale at his South Elkhorn mill. During the War of 1812 powder mills such as those owned by the Trotter family of Lexington became big business.

Products manufactured in Kentucky (1810)

ITEM	MEASURE[2]	US RANK[3]	% US TOTAL[3]
Hemp[1]	5,755 tons	1	99.9
Hemp bagging	453,750 yards	1	98.0
Saltpeter[1]	201,937 lbs	1	47.0
Salt	324,870 bushels	2	26.2
Maple sugar[1]	2,471,647 lbs	2	25.6
Blended & unnamed cloths	4,685,385 yards	1	21.2
Hemp rope	1,991.5 tons	2	18.4
Distilleries	2,000 establishments	3	14.0
Gunpowder	115,716 lbs	6	8.3
Looms for cotton or wool	23,559 looms	4	7.2
Tanneries	267 establishments	5	6.2
Cotton manufacturing	15 establishments	6	5.6
Iron furnaces	4 furnaces	9	2.6
Paper	6,200 reams	8	1.5
Spindles	1,656 spindles	12	1.3
Nails	196,000 lbs	11	1.2
Carding machines	75,100 lbs carded	11	1.0
Fulling mills	53,058 yards fulled	8	1.0
Flaxseed oil	4,605 gallons	11	< 1.0
Bar iron	52.5 tons	12	< 1.0

[1] *The census noted that these products might not be considered as manufactured and listed them separately from the other products. Notable product groupings NOT shown as manufactured in Kentucky were most metals and metal products, finished wood products (wagons, barrels, furniture, etc.), ceramics and glassware, and chemical products such as paints and dyes.*

[2] *Measures chosen for this table are those for which data was most complete or best represented production. For these reasons value of production was not used as an indicator for individual products. Value of total US manufacturing production reported as $153,545,397, of which Kentucky's share was $5,153,863 or 3.4 percent.*

[3] *US ranking and percent of total national production based on data reported for 26 states and territories. Leading manufacturing states, in order according to value of production, were Pennsylvania, New York, Massachusetts, and Virginia.*

Source: Coxe, Tench. 1814. A statement of the arts & manufactures of the United States for the year 1810. Philadelphia. Available online at http://www2.census.gov/prod2/decennial/documents/1810v2-01.pdf. The 1810 manufacturers census, the first such, was quite controversial at the time; representatives of several states claimed that production had been greatly underreported. The marshal for Kentucky noted, in particular, that iron production in the state was far greater than reported. This census should therefore be taken as indicative rather than definitive of manufacturing production.

Economic Development

Marvin E. Strong, Jr.

Imagine you're shopping for a new house. You find one that's appealing, you attend a showing, and you and your agent start speaking with the

Toyota assembly line, Georgetown
Source: Kentucky Historical Society

might go ahead with the negotiations, or the sudden change might unnerve you enough to make you walk away from the deal.

This instability existed in the state's economic development efforts prior to 1992, and this did not always result in the best outcome for Kentucky's economy. The art of economic development lies in building relationships. A corporate CEO doesn't wake up one morning and decide, "Hey, I think I'll build my new facility in Kentucky." These things take time, a great deal of study, and a carefully cultivated sense of trust.

Recognizing the value of continuity, the Kentucky General Assembly passed HB 89 in 1992, creating the Kentucky Economic Development Partnership Board.

The 13-member Board, chaired by the governor, is a true public-private partnership. In addition to the governor, voting members include the secretaries of the state's Finance and Administration Cabinet and Environmental and Public Protection Cabinet, plus eight private-sector members serving staggered terms and representing a variety of business sectors from across Kentucky. The secretaries of the Commerce and Economic Development cabinets serve as non-voting members. This dual structure allows the board to stay mindful of its duties to the commonwealth while maintaining a business-like approach in its dealings with existing and prospective Kentucky companies.

The board serves as the governing body of the Cabinet for Economic Development. Not only does it have the authority to hire and fire the Cabinet secretary, it also oversees such functions as strategic planning, finance, business assistance, marketing and promotion, community development, workforce development and innovation, all of which are designed to make it easier for business to prosper here.

seller and his or her agent. Negotiations begin, it's all running smoothly, and just as you write up your offer, you notice that the agent and the seller have both walked away, to be replaced by two other people you've never met.

You'd get an uneasy feeling, wouldn't you? You

And business is indeed prospering in Kentucky. For the period from July 1, 1992, to July 31, 2005, investment announcements in Kentucky's manufacturing and supportive-service sectors totaled more than $31.7 billion. During that period, companies in those sectors made 7,705

Between 1998 and 2004, exports grew 63.4 percent to $13 billion. That figure puts Kentucky ninth in per capita exports.

To further the goal of growing Kentucky's economy to an even stronger level, a new strategic plan was recently unveiled by Gov. Ernie Fletcher and Department of Commercialization and Innovation Commissioner Deborah Clayton of the Cabinet for Economic Development calling for Kentucky to become a world leader in the research, development and marketing of life science and

announcements of either new locations or expansions of operations in Kentucky, creating 265,627 jobs at full employment.

From 1992-2004, Kentucky's average unemployment rate fell in line with the

Buffalo Trace Distillery, Frankfort
Source: Department of Tourism

national average to 5.5 percent, significantly improving from the state's 8.3 percent average unemployment rate from 1979-1991. Additionally, Kentucky's rank among the 50 states jumped from 41st in 1991 to 34th in 2003 in average annual wage.

For more than 20 years now, foreign investment has grown increasingly vital to Kentucky's economy. This trend began in a big way in the mid-1980s when Toyota decided to open its manufacturing plant in Georgetown. That was the company's largest plant outside Japan and it continues today. In all, foreign companies made 915 announcements of new locations or expansions from July 1, 1992, to July 31, 2005. These announcements represented investments of more than $8.5 billion and 43,565 new employees.

While foreign direct investment continues to play a crucial role in the state's economy, Kentucky has also become one of the nation's most aggressive exporters. Over the past decade, Kentucky has ranked sixth in export growth quite a feat for a state that is not on a coast or an international border.

bioscience innovations.

The growth potential in areas such as pharmaceuticals, nutraceuticals, biotechnology, medical services, bio and health informatics, as well as services related to these industries, is enormous. Kentucky has already started to realize some of this potential. A recent article in "The Chronicle of Higher Education" referenced the impressive gains made by the University of Kentucky and the University of Louisville in attracting federal research funding and potentially patentable inventions. And biotech and other science-based companies around the state—both startups and relocations from elsewhere—are on the rise. By building on these strengths, Kentucky will hasten its ascent within the life-sciences industry.

Combined with the continuity and stability provided by the Economic Development Partnership Board, this climb means Kentucky will assure its place in an evermore sophisticated and demanding global economy.

BUSINESS & ECONOMY
International Trade

Gov. Martha Layne Collins

Increasingly, Kentucky companies are competing at the international level and reaping the benefits of an expanded marketplace.

If we consider that almost $13 billion worth of sales (2004) makes up the state export business, and new markets such as China and India represent over 2 billion of the world's population, how can we not fully consider the advantages of taking our business international? Every week, Kentucky-based businesses ship computer products to France, hospital and medical supplies to Malaysia and India, building equipment to Uzbekistan and software technology to Brazil.

Kentucky is the 11th largest exporter per capita in the United States, and this trend shows signs of continuing over the next decade. As the internationalization push has intensified, Kentucky now ranks sixth in export growth among all states. The direct benefit of selling on the global market means more money to the local economy, more jobs created and ultimately an increased standard of living in our state.

Companies that once never dreamed of entering other markets are now considering such far-flung destinations such as South Africa, Ghana, Indonesia or Russia. These countries all represent an opportunity for growth and demand for what we have to offer. Individuals who have never traveled outside the state are now traveling abroad and signing deals with their counterparts in every corner of the world.

Of course, everyone knows what Kentucky is famous for: Kentucky Fried Chicken, the Kentucky Derby and good old-fashioned Kentucky bourbon. But other products such as steel, plastics and lumber are the traditional focus of local exports. Now products as diverse as food flavoring and colorants, wine, Kentucky-made crafts, financial services, technical expertise, textiles and even chocolate are being exported outside our borders.

Hand-made Basket
Source: Kentucky Crafted

We are all interconnected and the global village concept is not too far off. As they say, the world is getting smaller every day and our neighbors are now those living in Africa, South America and Asia. We can communicate just as easily with someone across the world as with someone across the street. Why not take advantage of the benefits of an expanded market and "Go Global?" The benefits far outweigh the obstacles.

TOTAL U.S. EXPORTS (Origin of Movement) VIA KENTUCKY
TOP 25 COMMODITIES BASED ON DOLLAR VALUE
(In Millions of Dollars)

RANK	HS CODE	COMMODITY	VALUE 2001	VALUE 2002	VALUE 2003	VALUE 2004	%SHARE 2001	%SHARE 2002	%SHARE 2003	%SHARE 2004	% CHANGE 2004/2003
		Total All Commodities via Kentucky and % Share of U.S. Total	9,048	10,607	10,734	12,992	1	2	2	2	21
		Total Top 25 Commodities and % of Kentucky Total	4,112	5,432	4,968	6,784	45	51	46	52	37
1	841191	Turbojet And Turboproller Parts	1,166	1,622	1,545	2,204	13	15	14	17	43
2	870323	Passenger Vehicles Spark-Ignition Engine >1500 < 3M Cc	194	234	141	406	2	2	1	3	188
3	870421	Trucks, Diesel and Semi-Diesel Engine, Gvw 5 Metric Tons	0	350	256	375	0	3	2	3	46
4	847330	Parts For Automatic Data Processing Machines & Units	750	440	288	316	8	4	3	2	10
5	300210	Antisera And Other Blood Fractions	220	354	348	288	2	3	3	2	-17
6	284420	Uranium Enriched In U235 Plutonium	100	208	105	265	1	2	0	2	154
7	870899	Parts And Accessories Of Motor Vehicles	278	320	280	244	3	3	3	2	-13
8	870324	Passenger-Vehicle Spark-Ignition Engine > 3000 Cc	100	271	133	242	1	3	1	2	82
9	870422	Motor Vehicle Transport of Goods Spark Ignition, Gvw> 5 < 20 Mtn	0	41	40	231	0	0	0	2	474
10	870431	Motor Vehicle Transport of Goods Spark Ignition, Gvw< 5 Mtn	53	208	115	225	0	2	1	2	96
11	940190	Parts Of Seats (Excluding Medical, Barber, Dental)	84	91	117	200	0	0	1	2	71
12	700319	Cast Or Rolled Glass In Nonwired Sheets	104	137	191	181	1	1	2	1	-5
13	391000	Silicones, In Primary Forms	20	47	134	167	1	1	1	1	24
14	010190	Live Horses, Asses, Mules And Hinnies	0	24	77	157	0	0	0	1	103
15	847990	Parts Of Machines/Mechanical Appliances With Individual Function	25	79	76	153	0	0	0	1	100
16	220830	Whiskies	118	111	124	149	1	1	1	1	20
17	847160	Automatic Data Processing Input Or Output Units, Storage Or Not	90	104	103	137	0	0	0	0	33
18	870829	Parts & Accessories Of Bodies Of Motor Vehicles	41	65	69	127	0	0	0	0	85
19	390690	Acrylic Polymers, In Primary Forms	92	113	97	127	1	1	0	0	30
20	290321	Vinyl Chloride (Chloroethylene)	65	57	101	124	0	0	0	0	23
21	880330	Parts Of Airplanes Or Helicopters	310	195	258	106	3	2	2	0	-59
22	870839	Brakes And Servo-Brakes & Parts For Motor Vehicles	89	111	98	99	0	1	0	0	1
23	852439	Discs For Laser Reading Systems	56	74	78	94	0	0	0	0	20
24	840790	Spark-Ignition Reciprocating/Rotary Internal Combustion Engine	62	83	91	88	0	0	0	0	-4
25	760612	Aluminum Alloy Rectangular Plates, Over .2 Mm Thick	96	92	104	81	1	0	0	0	-21

Source: U.S. Census Bureau, Foreign Trade Division

BUSINESS & ECONOMY

Robert G. Clark

Small Businesses

Small businesses in the Commonwealth make a significant contribution to Kentucky's economy. More than half of Kentucky's non-farm private output and employment is generated by small firms with 500 or fewer employees. Small business owners, including women, minorities and home-based individuals, continue to be leaders in the state's economy.

The estimated total number of small businesses in Kentucky in 2003 was 309,000. Of the 81,407 employer firms in 2003, 96.9 percent, or an estimated 78,900, were small firms. The most recent data available show that non-employer businesses numbered 230,083 in 2001.

KENTUCKY MINORITY-OWNED BUSINESSES

In 1997 there were 12,664 minority-owned firms in Kentucky with $2.46 billion in sales and receipts and 24,572 employees. Minority-owned firms accounted for 4.5 percent of the firms and just over one percent of the sales and receipts in Kentucky's economy. In the U.S. 14.6 percent of the firms were minority-owned, and 3.2 percent of sales and receipts were from minority-owned businesses.

For Kentucky and the United States, the number of minority-owned businesses is low relative to the number of minorities in the population. According to the 2000 Census, approximately 10 percent of Kentucky's population are non-white and 1.5 percent Hispanic. In the U.S., around 25 percent of the population are non-white and 12.5 percent Hispanic. The percentage of minority-owned, African American-owned, and Hispanic-owned firms in Kentucky is much less than the percentage of minorities, African Americans, and Hispanics in Kentucky's population. The relative number of Asians and

Lisa Howlett (L) & Ida Elliott
Auburn Leather Auburn, KY
Source: Sid Webb

Pacific Islander-owned and American Indian and Alaska Native-owned firms is greater than the relative number of Asians and Pacific Islanders and American Indians and Alaska Natives in the population.

In 1997 the Services industry contained around 43 percent of the minority-owned firms with 5,377 firms. Minority-owned businesses in the services industry had over $660 million in sales and receipts and over 9,200 employees. Retail trade was the other significant industry for minority-owned businesses in Kentucky with over $600 million in sales and receipts and 6,700 employees. The category of industries not classified had the second most minority-owned firms with 2,884. Of the minority groups, there were more firms owned by African Americans than any other minority group. There were 5,629 firms owned by African Americans. These firms employed over 7,700 people, and they had over $650 million in sales and receipts. A majority of the firms owned by African Americans were in the Services industry.

American Indians and Alaska Natives owned 3,069 firms, and these firms had $242 million in sales and receipts and 2,257 employees. Firms owned by American Indians and Alaska Natives were predominantly in the Construction and Services industries.

Even though Asian and Pacific Islander-owned firms accounted for only 20 percent of the minority-owned firms in Kentucky, sales receipts from Asian and Pacific Islander-owned firms accounted for over half of all the sales and receipts from minority-owned businesses. Sales and receipts from these firms totaled $1.29 billion, and they employed 11,843 people. Most of the firms owned by Asian and Pacific Islanders were in the Services industry.

KENTUCKY WOMEN-OWNED BUSINESSES

With a total of 65,965 firms, women-owned businesses accounted for 23.4 percent of Kentucky firms in 1997. U.S. women-owned firms accounted for 26 percent of total firms. Kentucky businesses owned by women generated $9.87 billion in sales, four percent of the state's total sales and receipts. Revenues from U.S. women-owned firms comprised 4.4 percent of total business sales and receipts.

Demosthenes Hunn cuts Eugene Thompson's hair in Hunn's Lexington, KY barbershop
Source: Sid Webb

Businesses that were equally male-female-owned in 1997 numbered 51,032, 18 percent of all Kentucky firms. Sales receipts from these firms was over $11 billion. Almost 52 percent of Kentucky's women-owned firms were in the Service sector. Retail trade comprised the second highest number of firms with approximately 21 percent of firms. Following retail trade in order of number of firms were: finance, insurance, and real estate; construction; transportation, communication, and utilities; agriculture services, forestry, fishing, and mining; wholesale trade; and manufacturing. Nationwide, women-owned firms were also concentrated in the service area with almost 43 percent of total women-owned firms, followed by retail trade and construction.

Kentucky women-owned firms with paid employees accounted for 16 percent of the total women-owned firms. These firms employed 95,453 employees, almost 7 percent of the people employed in Kentucky businesses. The largest numbers of these people were employed in the service sector – almost 40 percent of employees in women-owned businesses. The retail trade sector accounted for 24 percent of employees, followed by manufacturing with 15.6 percent. Following manufacturing in order of employment size were: construction; wholesale trade; and finance, insurance, and real estate.

Thirty-nine percent of the sales and receipts generated by Kentucky's women-owned firms were concentrated in the retail and wholesale trade sectors. Manufacturing accounted for almost 27 percent of sales and receipts; services accounted for 16 percent.

Average sales and receipts per firm for all Kentucky women-owned firms was $149,725 in 1997 compared to $873,007 for all Kentucky firms. Women-owned firms with paid employees averaged $827,485 in sales and receipts compared to an average of $3,492,018 for all Kentucky firms with paid employees.

The estimated number of new employer businesses was 8,155 in 2003.

Employment. Small businesses with fewer than 500 employees numbered 69,651 in 2001 and employed 752,830 people or 50.3 percent of the state's non-farm private workforce. Total net employment loss in the state amounted to 15,781 between 2000 and 2001. Of that number, 10,419 are attributable to MSAs (metropolitan statistical areas). During the same time period, firms with fewer than 20 employees gained 7,742 jobs.

Small Business Income. Small business proprietors' income in 2003 increased by 8.4 percent, from $7.4 billion in 2002 to $8 billion in 2003.

Finance. Small firms typically use commercial bank lenders and rely on local bank services. The Small Business Administration Office of Advocacy has identified banks in each state that make the most loans to small businesses. This information is available in its banking studies available at www.sba.gov/advo/stats.

For the complete report on Kentucky's small business profile, go to www.sba.gov/advo/stats/profiles/04ky.pdf.

Resources available to Kentucky small business entrepreneurs:

Kentucky's Small Business Development Centers with 15 service centers statewide have experienced and knowledgeable staff for both existing business owners and potential entrepreneurs. This is a free service co-sponsored by the U.S. Small Business Administration administered by the University of Kentucky and the Gatton College of Business and Economics, in partnership with regional universities, community and private colleges and the private sector. http://www.ksbdc.org/.

The Small and Minority Business Branch in Kentucky's Economic Development Cabinet coordinates Small Business Enterprise, Minority Business Enterprise and Women Business Enterprise activities throughout the state's administrative structure. The branch acts as an advocacy agency for the furtherance and expansion of Kentucky-based small, minority and women-owned businesses through

Scott Berryman owner of Valentine's Ice Cream makes "Mint Julep Ice Cream" with real bourbon
Source: Sid Webb

the utilization of resources available through the state or under the purview of the state. www.thinkkentucky.com/SMBD/

The Kentucky Commission on Small Business Advocacy (KCSBA) has 13 members appointed by the governor. The CSBA promotes a cooperative and constructive relationship between state agencies and the small business community to ensure coordination and implementation of statewide strategies that benefit small business in the commonwealth.The cost to comply with federal regulations by Kentucky small businesses is estimated at more than $9.1 billion and this does not include state and local regulations. Kentucky was the eighth state to pass a Regulatory Flexibility Act that gives small businesses a voice in the development of government regulations.

The Small Business Administration (SBA) provides technical assistance in areas such as entrepreneurial development, SCORE, Small Business Training Network, Womens Business Ownership and International Trade. SBA provides financial assistance through Loan Programs, Investment Division (SBICs), Surety Guarantees and International Trade. SBA also provides contracting assistance through programs like 8a Business Development, HUBZone, Government Contracting, Small Disadvantaged Business and Technology (SBIR/STTR). The SBA Kentucky District Office: The Romano Mazzoli Federal Building, 600 Dr. MLK Jr. PL, Louisville, KY 40202, (502) 582-5971 or www.sba.gov/ky.

One-stop Business Licensing Program

The Secretary of State offers a One-stop Business Licensing Program. There are over 1,800 business types and over 600 business licenses required from various agencies at the state level in Kentucky. This program allows users to instantly receive a complete listing of all licenses that could be required at the state level. In addition to this streamlined process, users can obtain detailed information about the license or permit, such as the contact person in state government, the fees and requirements for the license, and hyperlinks to forms available on the Internet. http://apps.sos.ky.gov/business/onestop/onestop.aspx

Assistance can also be obtained by contacting the state Business Information Clearinghouse at (800) 626-2250.

(Sources: Kentucky Economic Development Cabinet and Small Business Administration)

BUSINESS & ECONOMY
Manufacturing

In 2003, 4,202 manufacturing establishments in Kentucky employed 260,951 people. However since 1998, the manufacturing sector lost 29,714 jobs or a drop of 10.2 percent. The manufacturing sector contributed $88.6 billion or 39.2 percent of total state industry receipts in 2002, which represents a two percent growth since 1997 with $86.63 billion.

Transportation equipment manufacturing (Ford, General Motors and Toyota) lead the way with $30.3 billion or slightly more than a third of total manufacturing receipts.

The chemical manufacturing sector is the second largest manufacturing group, generating receipts of $7.08 billion in 2002, which was down from the 1997 totals of $7.46 billion. The chemical industry employed 13,231 in 2003, down from 14,331 in 1998.

In 1998 textile mills, textile mill products and apparel manufacturing industry sub-sectors employed 25,641, but in 2003 the number dropped 52 percent or to just 12,291 employees due to moving operations out of Kentucky and overseas. Overall value of shipments by these industry sub-sectors dropped in 1997 from $2.93 billion to $1.77 billion in 2002, a nearly 40 percent drop.

The largest employers in Kentucky are in transportation (42,423), fabricated metal products (26,590) and machinery manufacturing (25,459).

The Automobile Industry in Kentucky

Auto manufacturers, along with their suppliers and dealers, provide a major driving force in the U.S. economy, and Kentucky has capitalized on this industry. In Kentucky, approximately 2.98 percent of the state's employment is in either the automobile industry or in a job dependent on the auto industry.

The automobile industry has contributed to Kentucky in a number of ways. For instance, Kentucky's automobile industry represents 5.2 percent of the state's gross state product. Kentucky's automotive industry gross state product for 2002 was over $6.3 billion. Kentucky has the nation's third highest level of auto industry related employment as a percent of total state employment in the United States.

Ford first came to Kentucky in 1913, when Henry Ford began a "factory" at the Summers-Herman dealership in Louisville. In 1925 Henry Ford created what was called "the first modern assembly plant" in Louisville. The plant turned out Model A's and other Ford trucks and cars. During World War II, the plant geared up to produce military equipment.

In 1955 Ford began operations at the Louisville assembly plant, and in 1969, began operations at the eastern Jefferson County truck plant. The Lou-

Vintage Corvettes
Source: Kentucky Department of Tourism

isville assembly plant employs 3,855. In late 1997 Ford announced expansion plans at its Louisville operations, adding 1,000 jobs and 130,000 square feet to the Kentucky truck plant. Total employment at the truck plant now stands at 6,000. The expanded facility, at 4.6 million square feet, is the second-largest Ford assembly plant in North America.

On June 1, 1981, General Motors moved production of the Corvette from St. Louis to Bowling Green, which remains today the exclusive home of Corvette production. The 1,000 employees in 2003 built over 35,000 vehicles at the one million square foot plant. The new Cadillac XLR has been produced in Bowling Green since the end of 2002.

Georgetown, which began production in 1988, is Toyota's largest production plant in North America. With two vehicle production lines and a powertrain engine and axle facility, more than 7,600 team members build about 500,000 vehicles and nearly 400,000 engines each year. In addition, Toyota's North American headquarters is located in Erlanger, employing 800. Toyota's North American Parts Logistics Division, located in Hebron, employs 400.

Motor Vehicle Production & Facilities

In 2003, 1,164,967 cars and light trucks were assembled in Kentucky. In addition to the Corvettes and Cadillac XLRs produced in Bowling Green, Kentucky plants produce a number of other models: Ford's Louisville plant produces the Ford Explorer and Mercury Mountaineer SUV models and the Sport Trac. The Ford Kentucky truck plant manufactures Ford Super Duty F Series trucks and Excursion SUV models. Toyota's plant in Georgetown manufactures the Toyota Camry, Avalon and Solara.

Ford truck plant, Louisville
Source: Kentucky Department of Tourism

19,500 in the motor vehicle manufacturing industry. In Kentucky, employment in the motor vehicle manufacturing industry has grown by more than 35 percent between 1995 and 2000, compared to 14 percent for all industries and 2.5 percent for manufacturing. Kentucky's employment growth in the motor vehicle manufacturing industry between 1995 and 2000 ranks second among the top ten automobile producing states.

The Gross State Product (GSP) for the motor vehicles industry in 2002 was $6.354 billion, and it experienced growth rates of 225 percent and 71 percent for the periods 1991-2001 and 1996-2001, respectively. The growth rate of 71 percent from 1996-2001 ranks first among the top automobile producing states. The Annual Survey of Manufacturers, January 2003 issue, lists the value of shipments for the auto manufacturing industry in Kentucky at over $30 bil-

AUTO MANUFACTURING IMPACT ON THE KENTUCKY ECONOMY

The automobile manufacturing industry's strong presence in Kentucky has grown significantly over the last several years. In 2004, the automobile industry employed over 90,000 in Kentucky, with

Impact of Automobile Manufacturing Industry on Kentucky

	Industry	Manufacturing	Auto Manufacturing
Employees (2000)	1,816,900	307,200	53,451
Employment Growth (1995 2000)	11.1%	2.5%	37.7%
Total Annual Wages	$52,136,852,000	$11,138,577,000	$2,624,724,235
GSP (2002 Current Dollars)	$122,282,000,000	$25,471,000,000	$6,354,000,000
Real GSP Growth (1991-2001)	41.38%	45.95%	225.14%
GSP per Capita (2002)	$29,899	$6,228	$1,554

lion, which ranks third among the top automobile producing states. The value of shipments grew by a rate of 26 percent between 1995 and 1999.

The automobile manufacturing industry has affected the economy and people of the Commonwealth in a very positive manner. It provides thousands of well-paying jobs to the people of Kentucky. In 2001, the average weekly wage for this industry was $1,333 compared to $732 for manufacturing industries and $576 for all industries. Employers in the auto industry paid over $2.6 billion in wages to employees in 2002, and wages paid totaled over $1.4 billion in the motor vehicle manufacturing segment of the industry. The motor vehicles industry component accounted for 5.2 percent of Kentucky's total GSP in 2002.

Sources: The Alliance of Automobile Manufacturers; The Automobile Industry in Kentucky, Division of Research, Kentucky Cabinet for Economic Development, December 2004; The 1997 and 2002 Economic Census; 2003 and 1998 County Business Patterns.

Associated Industries of Kentucky

The manufacturing industry has long been promoted and represented by the Associated Industries of Kentucky, which was established in 1911. The Association's mission is to enhance the competitiveness of manufacturers by shaping a legislative and regulatory environment conducive to economic growth and to increase understanding among policy makers, the media and the general public about the importance of manufacturing to America's economic strength.

The board consists of top executives at these and other major Kentucky companies: Kentucky Power; Air Products & Chemicals, Inc.; MeadWestvaco Corporation (new name); Sumitomo Electric Wiring Systems; Toyotetsu America, Inc.; Brown-Forman Distillery; United Parcel Service; Altria Corporate Services; DuPont Fluoroproducts; LG&E Energy Corp.; Kentucky Farm Bureau Mutual Insurance; RJ Reynolds Tobacco Co.; The Valvoline Co., a Division of Ashland Inc.; Delta Air Lines, Inc.; Toyota Motor Manufacturing, KY; Columbia Gas of Kentucky, Inc.; Anthem; and Alcoa.

The organization's original name was the Kentucky Manufacturers and Shippers Association but was changed to Kentucky Manufacturers Association in December 1917. Phillip Speed Tuley was the first president from 1911-1918 and later in 1935-36. Tuley was president of the Louisville Cotton Mills Com-

Associated Industries of Kentucky's Industry of the Year Awards

pany (Louisville Textiles).

Eight of the charter companies are still in business: Ashland Steel, now called AK Steel; Brinly Hardy Company (est. 1839 in Louisville); Browning Manufacturing (est. 1886 in Maysville, now owned by Emerson Electric); Hirsch Brothers (est. 1886, now known as Paramount Foods); January and Wood Company (est. 1831 in Maysville); Louisville Bedding Company (est. 1889); Standard Corp. (est. 1859 in Louisville, now called American Standard); and Henry Vogt Machine Company (est. 1880 in Louisville, now owned by Babcock Power, Inc.).

Annually, Associated Industries of Kentucky presents the Industry of the Year Awards for large, medium and small industry categories:

2004 Winners - LG&E Energy LLC, Louisville; McCoy & McCoy Laboratories, Inc., Madisonville; and LSI Graphic Solutions Plus, Erlanger.

2003 Winners - Webasto, Lexington; Modine, Harrodsburg; and OnLine Printing, Louisville.

2002 Winners - American Electric Power, Ashland; Boneal, Inc., Means; and Clark Publishing & Communications (now The Clark Group), Lexington.

2001 Winners - Griffin Industries and Shelby Industries were the inaugural winners at the 90th Anniversary celebration.

For more information: www.aik.org.

BUSINESS & ECONOMY

Technology

Dr. Lee Todd

KENTUCKY'S NEW ECONOMIC FRONTIER: A KNOWLEDGE-BASED ECONOMY

The history of technology in Kentucky is not nearly as storied as that of our agricultural, mining or distilling industries. Technology, however, holds the key to the economic future of the Commonwealth.

This state has traditionally lured good-paying manufacturing jobs through a combination of cheap land, cheap labor and tax incentives. Though traditional Kentucky industries have served this state admirably for decades, economic times are changing in the Commonwealth – and across the globe. The days of recruiting companies to Kentucky by providing cheap land and cheap labor are dwindling. As more and more traditional American businesses choose to expand their operations outside the U.S., Kentucky must find a new way to compete in the global marketplace.

The future of this state's economy must be rooted in the commercialization of knowledge. We must develop a new generation of innovators and entrepreneurs. Of course that mission starts in the classroom, as we prepare Kentucky students for global competition. But after preparing a new generation of critical thinkers, we need to provide them with an economy that will allow them to compete and excel in the modern world.

The recipe for growing and sustaining a successful, modern economy is no secret. Take one look at the hot-beds of innovation across the U.S.:

Before there was a Silicon Valley, there was a Stanford University and a University of California-Berkley. Before there was a Research Triangle Park in North Carolina, there was a University of North Carolina, a North Carolina State University and a Duke University. Before Massachusetts had a biotechnology corridor, there was a Harvard University and a Massachusetts Institute of Technology.

All these universities have one thing in common – a strong research infrastructure. If Kentucky is serious about competing globally, we must invest resources into expanding and enhancing our research nerve centers. We must realize that our ability to commercialize knowledge is intrinsically tied to the economic health of the Commonwealth.

Even though the development of knowledge is crucial to the future of the Commonwealth, we can not forget our past. We must conduct the type of research that will assist the corporations and companies that already call Kentucky home. We have to add value to our local organizations.

We must conduct research to help make Kentucky's thoroughbred industry even stronger; we must work alongside aluminum manufacturers to ensure that industry can grow and thrive in the Bluegrass; we must help develop clean coal technologies so Kentucky can be an environmental and energy leader; and we must discover new medical technologies so Kentuckians can live healthier, more productive lives.

The Commonwealth of Kentucky needs technology and innovation to be at the forefront of our economic future. We need to invest in education and research. We need to cultivate our new ideas and commercialize our intellectual property. Once we do all these things, we will then provide our next generation of Kentuckians with the type of economy that will allow them to compete in a changing world.

U.K. Coldstream Research Campus
Source: University of Kentucky

Did you know?

Lee Todd became the 11th president of the University of Kentucky on July 1, 2001, after serving as senior VP of Lotus Development Corp. Since assuming the leadership of the university, Todd has applied his background as a successful, high tech entrepreneur by emphasizing the university's role as an economic engine.

Todd earned his bachelor's degree in electrical engineering from UK and his master's and doctoral degrees in electrical engineering from the Massachusetts Institute of Technology. While at MIT, he received six patents for high-resolution display technology.

After returning to UK as a professor, Todd founded Projectron Inc. to make projection cathode ray tubes for flight simulators. He left UK in 1983 to begin product development at a second company, DataBeam Corp. In 1990, he sold Projectron to Hughes Aircraft Co. He sold DataBeam, the world's leading provider of real-time collaboration and real-time distance learning software and development platforms, to IBM.

Kentucky's New Economy Focus

The Dept. of Commercialization and Innovation was created by the Kentucky Innovation Act of 2000; a state-wide strategic plan for development of a technology-centered economy in the Commonwealth was the outcome. Drawing on area-wide strategic plans covering six regions of Kentucky, a state-wide strategic plan focuses on five Priority Research Focus Areas and seven Special Opportunities identified as areas in which Kentucky already has developed a national or international reputation.

Implementation of the plan is being coordinated by the Dept. of Commercialization and Innovation with assistance from the Kentucky Innovation Commission. It includes participation from the Council on Postsecondary Education, Cabinet for Economic Development, the State Chamber of Commerce and other state-wide partners. Kentucky is also focusing on the great potential the Commonwealth has to build a strong biotechnology industry.

Providing young high-tech firms access to capital is critical to growing firms to fuel economic development in the emerging economy. Product development can be expensive and many young firms find it difficult to raise capital. These firms must turn to alternative forms of financing. Since resources are generally not available in Kentucky, the state decided to act aggressively to improve access to capital for fledgling, high-potential technology firms.

The Postsecondary Education Reform Act of 1997 created the Research Challenge Trust Fund to support nationally recognized research programs at the University of Kentucky and the University of Louisville, and to strengthen key programs at the comprehensive universities. These funds, along with the Endowment Match Program (Bucks for Brains), have been used primarily to recruit exceptional faculty to these research universities.

Kentucky has a limited research and development infrastructure as is evidenced in the state's 47th place ranking in per capita R&D spending. The Commonwealth has no significant corporate research and development presence, nor does it have a federal research laboratory. To address these deficiencies the New Economy strategic plan advances the development of a globally competitive research and development infrastructure at Kentucky's research universities. The Commonwealth's resources are deployed to bolster targeted research areas where Kentucky stands to gain national prominence.

The Dept. of Commercialization and Innovation, after consultation with scholars and scientific experts across the Commonwealth, identified five research priority focus areas for Kentucky: (1) Human Health and Development; (2) Biosciences; (3) Information Technology and Communications; (4) Environmental and Energy Technologies; and (5) Materials Science and Advanced Manufacturing

These are the research areas that will afford Kentucky the best opportunity to build centers of research excellence around which competitive technology-based clusters can grow and thrive. These centers and associated business clusters will have the greatest influence on the creation of the New Economy in Kentucky. *Source: http://www.one-ky.com/*

It's a Kentucky Thing

The McConnell Technology & Training Center projects will allow a cost avoidance for the U.S. Navy of approximately $1,000,000,000 over the next 15 years. The MTTC resolves nagging and costly shipboard problems by inserting into the U.S. Fleet commercially available innovative products and technologies, thus providing the Navy with significant cost savings, manpower savings and important safety improvements.

Historically, when refueling U.S. Navy ships at sea, three sailors on each ship used ropes with a flag every 20 yards to show the distance between ships when refueling in order to stay a safe distance from each other. MTTC proposed the use of laser range finders connected to large LED signs on each ship to more precisely measure the distance between ships, provide an immediate digital readout of the distance, and remove sailors from a potentially hazardous task.

MTTC is located in Louisville and may be reached at (888) 778-8786.

U.S. Navy Replenishment ship
Source: McConnell Technology & Training Center

BUSINESS & ECONOMY
Mining, Oil & Gas

THE KENTUCKY COAL INDUSTRY

In 1750 Dr. Thomas Walker was the first recorded person to discover and use coal in Kentucky. Later in 1820, the first commercial mine, known as the "McLean drift bank," opened in Kentucky near the Green River and Paradise in Muhlenberg County. It produced and sold 328 short tons of coal. Prior to the Civil War, Kentucky produced a record 285,760 tons; however, by 1870 production had decline to 150,582 tons. In 1877 a steam-powered shovel was introduced and coal production jumped to more than one million tons in 1879. In 1890 a steam turbine was built and produced 5,000 kilowatt of electricity. By the beginning of World War I, demand for coal increased substantially and Kentucky produced 20.3 million tons.

In 1932 walking dragline excavators were built and four years later coal production jumped to 47.7 million tons. Just as before, World War II increased demand and caused production to soar to 72.4 million tons. By the early 1960s railroads began using unit coal trains, and the first longwall mining with powered roof supports was first introduced. By 1963 coal production jumped to more than 100 million tons.

In 1983 the U.S. Clean Coal Technology Demonstration Program was established with $2.5 billion in federal matching funds to assist the private sector in developing improved clean coal technologies. In 1988, for the first time, Wyoming displaced Kentucky as the leading coal producing state but just two years later Kentucky reach a record production level of 179.4 million tons.

Source: Ford Collection, University of Louisville

KENTUCKY COAL PRODUCTION

YEAR	SURFACE	UNDERGROUND	TOTAL
1998	58,941,761	97,937,265	156,879,026
1999	55,150,235	89,249,086	144,399,321
2000	50,346,219	81,499,769	131,845,988
2001	53,107,358	85,107,965	138,215,323
2002	50,595,329	80,807,468	131,402,797

Source: http://www.coaleducation.org/

EMPLOYMENT

The Kentucky coal mining industry in 2002 employed 20,956 persons, down 6.5 percent since 1997. The Western Kentucky Coal Fields directly employed approximately 2,524 persons, while the Eastern Kentucky coalfield provided 14,518 direct mining jobs. In 2002, Kentucky produced 124,142 million tons. Eastern Kentucky averaged just over 85 percent of Kentucky's coal mining work force and accounted for about 80 percent of Kentucky's total coal production. Western Kentucky averaged approximately 15 percent of Kentucky's coal mining work force and about 20 percent of Kentucky's total coal production. Direct mining employment declined in Eastern Kentucky, but increased in the Western Kentucky Coal Fields.

THE KENTUCKY COAL INDUSTRY:

- employed 14,812 miners earning over $678.4 million in wages during 2000
- created a total of 56,219 jobs statewide
- paid over $141.23 million in severance taxes during FY 2000-01 and generated total state tax revenues of about $403.2 million
- was a $3.15 billion industry, which brought into Kentucky receipts totaling about $2.5 billion from 27 states and 11 countries in 2000
- created economic activity throughout Kentucky totaling $6.84 billion

*NOTE: Estimated values of coal sold in each state are based upon average per ton gross value of coal produced and processed.

KENTUCKY COAL MINING EMPLOYMENT, 1979-2002

YEAR	WESTERN KENTUCKY			EASTERN KENTUCKY			KENTUCKY
	SURFACE	UNDERGROUND	TOTAL	SURFACE	UNDERGROUND	TOTAL	TOTALS
1998	747	2,763	3,510	5,493	9,924	15,417	18,927
1999	615	2,309	2,924	4,973	9,314	14,287	17,211
2000	450	2,060	2,510	4,162	8,828	12,990	15,500
2001	558	1,864	2,422	5,197	9,915	15,112	17,534
2002	495	2,029	2,524	5,237	9,281	14,518	17,042

Source: U.S. DOE - EIA; Coal Industry Annual, 1993-2002, Coal Production, 1979-1992.

TABLE 1. COAL PRODUCTION AND NUMBER OF MINES BY STATE AND MINE TYPE, 2003-2002 (THOUSAND SHORT TONS)

	2003		2002		Percent Change	
	NO. OF MINES	PRODUCTION	NO. OF MINES	PRODUCTION	NO. OF MINES	PRODUCTION
Kentucky	399	112,680	427	124,142	-6.6	-9.2
Underground	213	69,238	233	75,589	-8.6	-8.4
Surface	186	43,442	194	48,553	-4.1	-10.5
Eastern	374	91,184	399	99,398	-6.3	-8.3
Underground	201	52,078	219	56,413	-8.2	-7.7
Surface	173	39,106	180	42,984	-3.9	-9.0
Western	25	21,496	28	24,744	-10.7	-13.1
Underground	12	17,160	14	19,176	-14.3	-10.5
Surface	13	4,337	14	5,569	-7.1	-22.1

Source: http://www.coaleducation.org/

Oil & Gas Industry

Kentucky's oil and gas industry began in the early 19th century with pioneers searching for salt brines for use in tanning, food preservation and livestock agriculture. In 1818 Martin Beatty was searching for brine in what is now the Big South Fork National River and Recreation Area in southeastern Kentucky. This shallow well initially produced up to 100 barrels per day. Between 1818 and the Civil War few oil wells were drilled, but they were often spectacular. The "Old American Well," drilled near Burkesville, produced more than 50,000 barrels from its discovery in 1829 until about 1860. The end of the Civil War began the era of exploration for oil and gas.

The first commercial gas wells in Kentucky were drilled between 1863 and 1865 in Meade County. The gas was used as fuel to evaporate brines and was later delivered by pipeline to Louisville for lighting and domestic heat. Historic production data are sparse. The record for statewide oil production starts in 1883. Western Kentucky natural gas production data are available from 1933 to 1949. Statewide natural gas data are available beginning 1950. These data indicate Kentucky's total historic oil and gas production exceeds 9.85 quadrillion Btu (765 million barrels of oil and 5.4 trillion cubic feet of natural gas).

Two of Kentucky's potential energy resources have largely been ignored because of a lack of information. Preliminary data indicate natural gas is present in coal beds (coal bed methane) in both of the state's coal regions. A small pilot project is currently producing coal bed methane in eastern Kentucky. Natural asphalt, known as tar sand, was mined early in the 20th century for road paving material. The tar sand was successfully produced in the late 1970s and early 1980s when the price of oil was sufficiently high to make this resource economical.

All of Kentucky's counties have been tested to varying depths for oil and gas resources. In 2004, production was reported from 65 counties. In general, oil production dominates in the Western Coal Field and south-central areas of Kentucky; the Eastern Coal Field produces mostly natural gas. Kentucky has an estimated 18,000 producing oil wells and 13,000 producing gas wells. The majority of those producing wells are in the "stripper" category, having daily production rates of 60 million Btu or less (10 barrels of oil or 60,000 cubic feet of gas). Many wells are reported with initial daily production rates in excess of 580 million Btu (100 barrels of oil or 580,000 cubic feet of gas). Daily production per well averages much lower, however: 2.4 million Btu (0.5 barrels) for oil and 19 million Btu (19,000 cubic feet) for gas in 2004. In 2004, production totaled 109 trillion Btu (2.54 million barrels of oil and 94 billion cubic feet of natural gas) with a total value of $583 million ($26 million severance tax paid). Annually, Kentucky produces only about 12 percent of the 921 trillion Btu of oil and natural gas consumed in the state.

Ashland Oil Refinery, Ashland
Source: University of Kentucky,
John Jacob Niles Collection

Petroleum is produced at various depths from limestone, sandstone and shale of Cambrian through Pennsylvanian age. In some areas of the state oil is still produced from depths of less than 100 feet. Wells producing natural gas from the Cambrian Rome Formation are currently Kentucky's deepest producers, with some zones exceeding 7,500 feet. The overall average total depth of oil and gas wells drilled in the state is less than 1,500 feet. The average depth for wells drilled in 2001 is more than 2,700 feet. This increase represents the exploration for deeper producing zones and the continuing efforts to develop the Devonian shale natural gas resource. Both occur primarily in eastern Kentucky.

As the price of oil and gas has increased, interest in coalbed methane and Devonian shale gas production have grown especially in western Kentucky.

Reprinted with permission from Kentucky Geological Survey, University of Kentucky, www.uky.edu/kgs.

A typical setup of an air rotary rig in south-central Kentucky. The flatbed truck on the right is used in the transport of drill pipe. As the flatbed is nearly empty, this well is nearing total depth. The vertical mast is a draw-works with pulleys and hydraulics used to add or remove sections of pipe. The rig works by rotating the string of pipe at the surface. A bit at the bottom of the string of pipe works like a rotating jackhammer to crush rock. The pressure of the air used to drive the bit also blows the crushed rock out of the hole.

Kentucky Geological Survey, University of Kentucky, www.uky.edu/kgs.

Did you know?

Leading Counties in Oil and Gas Production

In 1997, Union County in western Kentucky produced 425 thousand barrels of oil, mostly from the Mississippian age Chester sandstones and carbonates. Pike County in eastern Kentucky, produced 29.8 billion cubic feet of natural gas, mostly from the Devonian Ohio (black) Shale.

The Deepest Well in Kentucky is in Webster County

The deepest well in Kentucky is the Exxon No. 1 Duncan, Webster County, in the western Kentucky portion of the Illinois Basin, south of the Rough Creek Fault System. Drilled to a total depth of 15,200 feet in the Eau Claire Formation of Cambrian age in 1977, it was plugged and abandoned.

Source: Kentucky Geological Survey, University of Kentucky, www.uky.edu/kgs.

BUSINESS & ECONOMY

Kentucky Industry Profiles

CONSTRUCTION

The Construction Industry Sector is a major employer in Kentucky, employing a total of 83,946 people in 2002. The industry sub-sector for Construction of Buildings employed 19,088; Heavy and Civil Engineering Construction employed 13,814 and the Specialty Trade contractors accounted for the majority of employees in the construction industry with 51,044 people. Employment figures show increased employment of 8.4 percent since 1997. The value of construction industry business in 2002 was $12.64 billion, up from $9.9 billion in 1997.

FINANCE AND INSURANCE

The Finance and Insurance Industry employed 68,764 with an annual payroll of $2.58 billion in 2002. This industry sector includes banks, credit unions securities, insurance carriers and funds and trust organizations. Census data does not have industry wide revenue figures, but credit related businesses generated $2.47 billion in 2002. Insurance agencies and brokers generated sales of $1.07 billion.

REAL ESTATE, RENTAL AND LEISURE

The Real Estate, Rental and Leisure industry sector employed 18,019 people in 2002, up from 16,284 people in 1997. The primary industry sub-sector is Real Estate generated $2.47 billion in sales in 2002, up from $1.96 billion in 1997. Rental and Leasing services contributed $907 million in sales in 2002, while non-financial intangible assets accounted for $139 million.

TRANSPORTATION AND WAREHOUSING

The Transportation and Warehousing Industry

Source: Sid Webb

Source: Sid Webb

is a growing industry in Kentucky with 67,163 employees in 2002, up from 49,545 employees in 1997. This industry is broken into the following sub-sectors: Air, Water, Truck, Transit & Ground Passenger Transportation and Pipeline Transportation. In 1997 the sub-sectors employed: Air Transportation (49,545); Water Transportation (2,548); Truck Transportation (20,222); Transit & Ground Passenger Transportation (1000-2499); Support activities from transportation (3,326); Couriers & Messengers (7,518); Pipeline transportation (1,205); Scenic & Sightseeing transportation (250-499); and Warehousing and Storage (1,706).

Due to the small number of establishments in the Air, Water and Rail transportation sub-sectors, revenue data is not available. Information about revenue is available for 2002 in the following transportation sub-sectors: Trucking ($2.61 billion); Pipeline ($562 million); Support Activities ($732 million); Couriers messengers ($2.82 billion); and Warehousing and Storage ($248 million).

HEALTH CARE AND SOCIAL ASSISTANCE

The Health Care and Social Assistance industry is obviously big business in Kentucky. The industry employed 218,732 people in 2002, up from 194,876 people in 1997. Annual payroll in 2002 was $6.71 billion and total receipts were $16.6 billion.

28,732. Total receipts for each industry sub-sector in 2002 and 1997 respectively in billions: Ambulatory Health Care Services ($6.5/$4.5); Hospitals ($7.6/$5.6); Nursing and Residential Care Facilities ($1.6/$1.3); and Social Assistance ($933 million/$617 million).

ARTS, ENTERTAINMENT AND RECREATION

Based on the 2002 Economic Census, the Arts, Entertainment and Recreation industry directly generated more than $1 billion in sales employing 16,057 people with an annual payroll of $273.4 million. Amusement, Gambling and Recreation Industry sub-sector employed 10,607 people with a payroll $148.8 million, followed by Performing Arts, Spectator Sports and related industries, which employed 4,414 people with an annual payroll of $105.8 million. Museums, Historical Sites and similar institutions employed 1,036 people and generated sales of $1.04 million.

January & Wood Cotton Mills, Maysville
Source: Sid Webb

This industry includes: Ambulatory Healthcare Services; Hospitals; Nursing and Residential Care Facilities; and Social Assistance agencies. Hospitals were the largest employers in 2002 with 82,447 followed by Ambulatory Health Care service with 67,423; Nursing and Residential Care Facilities with 40,130; and Social Assistance agencies with

ACCOMMODATION AND FOOD SERVICES

The Accommodation and Food Services Industries in 2002 employed 136,442 people with an annual payroll of $1.4 billion and sales of $4.91 billion. Food Services and Drinking Places accounted for the majority of sales with $4.1 billion and employed 121,346 people. The size of this industry had very little growth since 1997 when the industry employed 129,442 people and sales of $4.01 billion.

Combined establishments in the **Information Industry Sector** and the **Professional, Scientific and Technical Services Sector** in Kentucky employed 84,987 in 2002 up from 71,089 or a 17.4 percent since 1993. Combined annual payroll was $2,242,574,000 in 2002, which is an increase of 7.5 percent or $2,074,827,000. Total receipts for this industry sector were not available in the 2002 Economic Census but in 1997, sales totaled $5,056,056; the number of business entities in this sector increased by almost 20 percent with 1,261 establishments in 1997 and 1,546 in 2002.

The **Professional, Scientific, and Technical Services** sector comprises establishments that specialize in performing professional, scientific and technical activities for others. These activities require a high degree of expertise and training. The businesses in this sector specialize according to expertise and provide these services to clients in a variety of industries. Activities performed include: legal advice and representation; accounting, bookkeeping, and payroll services; architectural, engineering, and specialized design services; computer services; consulting services; research services; advertising services; photographic services; translation and interpretation services; veterinary services; and other professional, scientific and technical services. This sector excludes establishments primarily engaged in providing a range of day-to-day office administrative services, such as financial planning, billing and recordkeeping, personnel, and physical distribution and logistics.

The **Professional, Scientific and Technical Services Sector** employed 55,537 in 2002 with an annual payroll of almost $2 billion. Total receipts for this industry sector totaled $5,190,416,000 in 2002. The number of business entities in this sector increased by almost 18 percent with 6,189 establishments in 1997 and 7,503 in 2002. The sub-sector with the highest number of employees in 2002 was Legal Services with 11,030 employees. Accounting, Tax Preparation, Bookkeeping and Payroll Services were next with 10,922 people followed by Architectural, Engineering and Related Services with 9,107 people. The next three subsectors are Computer System Design and Related Services (7,536); Other Professional, Scientific and Technical Services (6,187) and Management, Scientific and Technical Consulting Services (5,204).

Employee keeps an eye on bottles at the Ale-8 assembly line in Winchester
Source: Sid Webb

The top four revenue producing sub-sectors in 2002 was Legal Services topping $1 billion with total sales of $1,235,972,000; Architectural, Engineering and Related Services ($930,037,000); Computer System Design and Related Services ($847,387,000) and Accounting, Tax Preparation, Bookkeeping and Payroll Services ($576,989,000). This industry sector grew by 26 percent since 1997 with total receipts of $3,853,289,000 and $5,190,416,000 in 2002.

The Information Industry Sector comprises establishments that produce and distribute information and cultural products, provide the means to transmit or distribute these products (including data or communications) and process data.

The main components of this sector are the publishing industries, including software publishing, motion picture and sound recording industries, broadcasting and telecommunications industries, and the information services and data processing industries.

The expressions "information age" and "global information economy" are used with considerable frequency today. The general idea of an "information economy" includes both the notion of industries primarily producing, processing and distributing information, as well as the idea that every industry is using available information and information technology to reorganize and become more productive.

The Information Industry Sector of Kentucky industries employed 29,450 in 2002 with an annual payroll of $243,717,000. Total receipts for this industry sector were not available in the 2002 Economic Census but in 1997, sales totaled $5,056,056. The number of business entities in this sector increased by almost 20 percent with 1,261 establishments in 1997 and 1,546 in 2002.

In 2002, **Publishing** entities excluding Internet publishers had total sales receipts of $1,669,901, while Broadcasting generated sales of $303,366,000. Internet Service Providers, Web Search Portals and Data Processing Services came close to the Broadcasting sub-sector of $303,034,000 and employed 3,634 people, which was down 28 percent from 5,023 in 1997. The Telecommunications industry sub-sector employed 12,573 people in 2002.

The Wholesale Trade and Retail Trade industries in Kentucky combined employed 285,155 people, in 2002, with a total payroll $6,546,349,000. There were 21,698 establishments that generated sales of $92,134,422,000 in 2002. Total receipts since 1997

for the Wholesale Trade industries increased 38.2 percent and the Retail Trade industries receipts increased by 22 percent.

There were 4,630 wholesale businesses in Kentucky in 2002. The **Wholesale Trade Sector** comprises establishments engaged in wholesaling merchandise, generally without transformation, and rendering services incidental to the sale of merchandise. Wholesalers are organized to sell or arrange the purchase goods for resale, capital or durable non-consumer goods, and raw and intermediate materials and supplies used in production. This sector comprises two main types of wholesalers: those that sell goods on their own account and those that arrange sales and purchases for others for a commission or fee. Establishments that sell goods on their own account are known as wholesale merchants, distributors, jobbers, drop shippers, import/export merchants, and sales branches. Other businesses that arrange for the purchase or sale of goods owned by others or purchasing goods on a commission basis are known as agents and brokers, commission merchants, import/export agents and brokers, auction companies, and manufacturers' representatives. These establishments operate from offices and generally do not own or handle the goods they sell. Wholesaling normally denotes sales in large volume, durable non-consumer goods may be sold in single units. Sales of capital or durable non-consumer goods used in the production of goods and services, such as farm machinery, medium and heavy-duty trucks, and industrial machinery, are always included in wholesale trade. **The Wholesale Trade and Durable Goods** industry sector is divided into two categories: durable goods and nondurable goods.

DURABLE GOODS

The sub-sectors of the wholesale durable goods that employ the most Kentuckians in 2002 included Machinery, Equipment and Supplies (10,567); Professional and Commercial Equipment and Supplies (7,184); Motor Vehicle and Motor Vehicle Parts and Supplies (5,186); Electrical and Electronic Goods (3,245); Miscellaneous Durable Goods (2,748); Metal and Mineral, except petroleum (2,651) Hardware, Plumbing and Heating Equipment and Supplies (2,269); Lumber and Other Construction Materials (2,186); and Furniture and Home Furnishings (1,017).

Based on 2002 total receipts in billions, the Wholesale Trade and Durable Goods industry sub-sectors of Professional and Commercial Equipment and Supplies ($4.816); Electrical and Electronic Goods ($4.318); Machinery, Equipment and Supplies ($3.687); Motor Vehicle, Motor Vehicle Parts and Supplies ($2.988); Metal and Mineral, except petroleum ($1.947); Miscellaneous Durable Goods ($.908). The Furniture and Home Furnishings sub-sector was had the 9th highest number of employees but only generated sales of $.292 billion, while the sub-sector Hardware, Plumbing, Heating Equipment and Supplies totaled $.738 billion.

NON-DURABLE GOODS

The sub-sectors of Wholesale Non-durable Goods employed a total of 29,541 people in 2002. In 2002, the largest industry sub-sector was Grocery and Related Products (8,375) followed by the Miscellaneous Non-Durable Goods (7,799); Petroleum and Petroleum Products (2,845); Wholesale Electronic Markets (2,598); and Chemical and Allied Products (1,630). Total receipts in 2002 for the Wholesale Non-durable Goods sub-sector were $27,189,640. The breakdown for the sub-sectors in this category in billions of dollars: Miscellaneous Non-durable goods ($7.204); Wholesale Electronic Markets ($4.082); Grocery and Related Products ($4.075); Petroleum and Petroleum Products ($3.976); Apparel, Piece Goods and Notions ($1.970) and Farm Product Raw Material ($1.567)

In 2002 there were 16,847 retail businesses in Kentucky with 919,619 employees and total sales of $40,062,561. The **Retail Trade** industry sector comprises establishments engaged in retailing merchandise, generally without transformation, and rendering services incidental to the sale of merchandise. The retailing process is the final step in the distribution of merchandise and retailers sell merchandise in small quantities to the general public. This sector comprises two main types of retailers: store and non-store retailers. Store retailers operate fixed point-of-sale locations, located and designed to attract a high volume of walk-in customers. They typically sell merchandise to the general public for personal or household consumption, but some also serve business and institutional clients. In addition to retailing merchandise, some types of store retailers are also engaged in the provision of after-sales services, such as repair and installation. Non-store retailers reach customers and market merchandise with methods such as the broadcasting of "infomercials," the broadcasting and publishing of direct-response advertising, the publishing of paper and electronic catalogs, door-to-door solicitation, in-home demonstration, selling from

portable stalls, and distribution through vending machines. Establishments engaged in the direct sale (non-store) of products, such as home heating oil dealers and home delivery newspaper routes are included in this category.

General Merchandise with 181,917 employees edged out Motor Vehicle and Parts Dealers with 181,392 employees as the largest retail industry sector employer. Other retail industry sub-sectors that employ large numbers are as follows: Food and Beverage (131,292); Building Material and Garden Equipment and Supplies Dealers (98,316); Health and Personal Care (66,400); Gasoline Stations (63,914); Clothing and Clothing Accessories (46,721); Miscellaneous Stores (39,574) and Non-Store Retailers (36,590).

The Motor Vehicle and Parts Dealers industry sub-sector led the way in total sales in 2002 were $9.55 billions followed by the following sub-sectors in billions of dollars: General Merchandise ($7.60); Food and Beverage ($5.53); Gasoline Stations ($4.59); Building Material and Garden Equipment and Supplies Dealers ($3.64); Health and Personal Care (2.65); Clothing and Clothing Accessories ($1.59); Miscellaneous Stores ($1.41) and Non-Store Retailers ($1.09).

Source: 2002 Economic Census, http://www.census.gov/

BUSINESS & ECONOMY
Utilities

Paul Wesslund

POWER IN THE COUNTRY
THE ELECTRIC CO-OP STORY

Kentucky historian Dr. Thomas Clark, writing about the coming of electricity to rural America in a July 1998 essay in "Kentucky Living" magazine, said, "No other great national enterprise on the globe wrought so quickly so many fundamental modifications in the rural way of life."

Clark added a

Wire swinging in Maysville
Source: Kentucky Utilities

personal note about rural electrification coming to his own house: "My father turned on every light on the place. I suggested he turn off most of them; it was costing him money. He retorted, 'Leave them on. I have been in the dark all my life.'"

The results of that excitement over electricity can still be seen in the network of nearly 1,000 local, consumer-owned electric cooperatives that provide power for some 34 million people in 47 states.

In the 1930s, several trends came together for rural America. One was an activist populism that focused on making natural resources available to everyday people. Many of our national parks and economic development projects like the Tennessee Valley Authority came from this movement.

Another force was the effort to end the Great Depression with government programs that targeted different areas of the economy.

But the most powerful force may have been the longing by American farm families as they looked at the glowing cities, and realized they were cut off from the benefits of modern society. Farmers didn't have access to lights, washing machines, radios, irons or indoor plumbing. Power companies didn't believe they could make a profit stringing lines to remote farmsteads.

But several politicians found support for the farmers, and in 1935 President Roosevelt created the Rural Electrification Administration, which offered loans for utilities to serve rural areas.

Power companies still weren't interested, but loan applications poured in from groups of people organizing themselves into cooperatives. REA staff were split over the advisability of lending to these groups. But within months it became obvious that local, member-owned, not-for-profit co-ops would be the primary providers of electricity in the countryside. Local organizers rode from farm to farm, signing up members for $5.

In the 1950s the rural electric co-ops could no longer grow efficiently by buying power from the city utilities. So many of these distribution co-ops that delivered power to their members got together to form power supply co-ops. These generation and transmission co-ops had the resources to build the relatively expensive power plants and lines the distribution co-ops needed.

Today, much of non-urban Kentucky, representing some 1.5 million people, gets electricity from cooperatives. There are 16 distribution co-ops in the eastern part of the state, and they receive their power from East Kentucky Power Cooperative, the generation and transmission co-op based in Winchester. Three co-ops in the west are served by Big Rivers generation and transmission co-op based in Henderson. Five other Kentucky distribution co-ops in the western part of the state receive power from the Tennessee Valley Authority, which produces power for co-ops and municipal utilities in seven states.

Electric co-ops serve about 11 percent of the people in the U.S., and have been keeping pace with other changes under their overall mission of providing a better quality of life. As user-owned, community-based organizations, co-ops are able to fight for other concerns facing people living outside the city. Promoting economic development to keep jobs from moving away, setting up subsidiaries to provide hard-to-find services in rural areas like cell phones and Internet access, and providing more than $100,000 a year in scholarships are examples of how electric co-ops today keep their members connected to the benefits of the modern world.

Lady sees an electric lamp for the first time
Source: Kentucky Living Magazine

The Kentucky Association of Electric Cooperatives provides services for the 24 local, consumer-owned electric distribution utilities in the state, as well as the two "generation and transmission" cooperatives. KAEC publishes "Kentucky Living" magazine, which is distributed monthly to more than 500,000 Kentuckians.

Utilities in Kentucky

The utility industry in Kentucky is big business and in 2002, employed 7,711 people with an annual payroll of $441,701,000. Employment in the utility industry has dropped by almost 32 percent since 1997 when there were 11,367 employees. Annual receipts in 2002 totaled 5.3 billion down from 8.2 billion or an almost 36 percent drop. Below are some of the major utilities operating in Kentucky:

East Kentucky Power (EKP) is headquartered in Winchester. The member cooperatives set up EKPC as a not-for-profit generation and transmission utility. Its purpose is to generate energy and ship it to co-ops that distribute it to retail customers. EKPC provides wholesale energy and services to 16 distribution cooperatives through power plants, peaking units, hydro power and more than 2,600 miles of transmission lines. Together, EKPC and member cooperatives are known as Kentucky's Touchstone Energy Cooperatives. The distribution cooperatives supply energy to about 500,000 Kentucky homes, farms, businesses and industries across 89 counties. http://www.ekpc.com/

Big Rivers Electric Corporation is based in Henderson Kentucky and serves 22 western Kentucky counties. LG&E entered into a 25-year lease of Big Rivers Electric's generating facilities. Big

Linemen at work
Source: Kentucky Living Magazine

Rivers is an electric generation and transmission cooperative supplying the wholesale power needs of its three member cooperatives and marketing power to non-member utilities and power markets. These members provide retail electric power and energy to in-dustrial, residential and commercial customers in portions of 22 western Kentucky counties. Big Rivers Electric Corporation serves 98,000 customers. See http://www.bigrivers.coop/ For more information on Kentucky's Rural Electric Cooperatives, visit http://www.kaec.org/.

Kentucky Power/ American Electric Power provides service to approximately 175,000 customers in all or part of 20 eastern Kentucky counties. Its distribution operations are based in Ashland with service centers in Pikeville and Hazard and area offices in Paintsville and Whitesburg. Kentucky Power maintains 1,233 miles of transmission lines, has 1,060 megawatts of generating capacity and 1.22 billion in assets. See http://www. kentuckypower. com/.

Louisville Gas & Electric (LG&E) is a diversified energy

Source: University of Kentucky, John Jacob Niles Collection

services company that is a member of a German family of companies. E.ON is the world's largest investor-owned utility company. LG&E is a regulated electric and natural gas utility, based in Louisville, serving Louisville and 16 surrounding counties. Founded in 1838, investors formed Louisville Gas and Water to provide gas-fired street lighting mandated by Louisville's city fathers to deter crime. The company sold gas from its local coal plant to fuel the gaslights. In 1998, LG&E Energy acquired KU Energy, which owned neighboring utility, Kentucky Utilities. LG&E serves 384,139 electric customers, 312,146 natural gas customers and their

service area covers 700 square miles. LG&E's total regulated generation capacity is 3,514 megawatts. http://www.lgeenergy.com/

Union Light, Heat and Power (ULH&P) is owned by Cinergy based in Cleveland, OH. ULH&P serves 129,602 Kentucky customers. ULH&P also serves 87,002 gas customers. Cinergy has 7,055 megawatts of generating capacity serving a total of 1.5 million electric customers and 500,000 gas customers. See http://www.cinergy.com/.

In fiscal year 2004, **Tennessee Valley Authority (TVA)**, sold more than 7.9 billion kilowatt-hours of electricity to 14 municipal and five cooperatively owned power companies serving customers in Kentucky. Distributors of TVA power provided three billion kilowatt-hours of electricity to more than 220,000 households in 28 counties in western and central Kentucky. Distributors of TVA power served more than 47,700 commercial and industrial customers with sales of more than 4.3 billion kilowatt-hours. TVA power revenues in Kentucky totaled more than $733 million. See http://www.tva.gov/.

Columbia Gas of Kentucky, based in Lexington, is a subsidiary of Columbia Gas of Kentucky serving over 145,000 energy customers in 31 Kentucky counties in central and eastern Kentucky. See http://www.columbiagasky.com/.

Atmos Energy serves 3.1 million natural gas utility customers in 12 states. It ranks as the largest pure gas utility in the U.S. Its nonutility operations serve wholesale customers in 22 states. In 1987, Atmos Energy expanded its operations into Kentucky with the acquisition of Western Kentucky Gas Company. See http://www.atmosenergy.com/

1999 SUMMARY STATISTICS

ITEM	VALUE	U.S. RANK
National Energy Regulatory Commission Region(s)		ECAR/SERC
Primary Energy Source		Coal
Net Summer Capability (megawatts)	16,542	20
Utility	14,708	20
Nonutility	1,834	15
Net Generation (megawatthours)	93,107,763	16
Utility	81,658,150	18
Nonutility	11,449,613	12
Emissions (thousand short tons)		
Sulfur Dioxide	796	5
Nitrogen Oxide	369	5
Carbon Dioxide	105,601	6
Sulfur Dioxide/sq. mile	20	6
Nitrogen Oxide/sq. mile	9	6
Carbon Dioxide/sq. mile	2,658	10
Electricity Consumption (MWh) (excludes line losses)	79,696,434	17
Utility Retail Electricity Sales (megawatthours)	79,098,015	16
Nonutility Retail Sales and Direct Use (megawatthours)	598,419	34
Utility Average Retail Price (cents/kWh)	4.17	49

Source: http://www.eia.doe.gov/cneaf/electricity/st_profiles/kentucky/ky.html#t3

Louisville Hydro Electric Company power plant, Ohio River Falls 1929
Source: University of Louisville

APPROPRIATIONS,

For the support of the Civil Government of the United States, for the year 1800.

	D.	C.
For the Prefident & Vice Prefident of the U. States,	30,000	00
For the expences of congrefs,	211,839	40
For the judiciary officers &c.	78,900	00
For the office of &c. of the treafury department,	75,507	94
For the commiffioner of the revenue &c.	7,753	06
For the purveyor of public fupplies &c.	3,716	00
For the fecretary of the finking fund.	250	00
For the officers &c. of the loan office department,	28,556	00
For the officers &c. of the department of ftate,	24,808	6
For officers &c. of the mint,	17,600	00
For the officers &c. of the war department.	29,466	56
For the officers &c. of the navy department,	23,707	84
For the furveyor general &c.	4,000	00
For the officers &c. of the general poft office,	13,381	40
For the governor &c. of the North Weftern territory,	5,500	00
For the governor &c. of the Miffiffippi territory,	5,500	00
Total,	**560,525**	**89**

Note — until the late 1780s, American publishers practiced the English method of typesetting the letter "s" as an "f." Source: The Kentucky Almanac 1800, published by John Bradford, Lexington, Ky.

BUSINESS & ECONOMY

Economic Impact of Tourism

Bob Stewart

An incredible abundance of natural resources, breathtakingly beautiful scenery, and a well-earned reputation for outstanding hospitality offered by its residents are the perfect components for the thriving tourism industry that has evolved in the Commonwealth of Kentucky. These elements, combined with a rich array of significant historic and cultural sites, outstanding state parks, reasonable prices, and the perception of Kentucky as a safe, family-friendly destination have helped to stoke the state's tourism industry to the point where it is undeniably a major economic force.

Visitors come to Kentucky for all sorts of reasons. Visiting family and friends, participating in one of the hundreds of festivals and special events throughout the year, attending the races at one of Kentucky's signature race-tracks, or simply checking into a state resort park to enjoy the wonderful natural amenities that are available all across Kentucky are all top reasons visitors give for coming to spend leisure time in the state. Regardless of the reason, visitors love to come to Kentucky and many return over and over again, year after year.

Bluegrass jam at the Watermelon Festival, Tompkinsville
Source: Sid Webb

These visitors leave behind a significant amount of money. In 2003, the travel and tourism industry contributed $5.6 billion directly to Kentucky's economy. When factoring in the total impact these travel and tourism activities have once these visitors' dollars are pumped throughout the various sectors of Kentucky's economy, the total economic impact of tourism spending in Kentucky for 2003 totaled nearly $9.3 billion.

This spending also generated $144 million in tax revenues to local governments throughout Kentucky and $807.2 million in state tax receipts, for a total tax impact of $951.2 million in 2003. Additionally, this spending generated and supported over 162,000 jobs in Kentucky. These jobs are spread throughout over 3,500 businesses across the state which directly serve visitors: hotels, motels, resorts, bed and breakfasts, restaurants, campgrounds, marinas, museums, historic sites, race tracks, state parks and other attractions. These are the obvious tourism-related businesses. However, visitor spending also helps support many other jobs in other sectors as well that may not be so obvious: food & beverage directors at hotels and convention centers, marketing specialists, airport personnel, transportation specialists, and even farmers who grow the produce that is consumed in state parks and restaurants and sold at farmers' markets to visitors all across the state. Also, various goods and services that support the state's bustling meetings and convention industry are also part of the travel and tourism economy. These vendors include special event planners, sound and lighting providers, audio/visual specialists, florists, printers and caterers to mention only a few.

Competition for the visitor dollar is intense. All 50 states have aggressive marketing campaigns to attract the attention and spending of potential visitors. Traditionally, Kentucky has been outspent by half the states, and in some cases dramatically outspent. To help address this, in 2004, a 1 percent statewide hotel bed tax was passed by the General Assembly that is dedicated specifically to tourism marketing, the first such tax ever approved in Kentucky on a statewide basis.

Tourists at the Kentucky Horse Park get up close after the Parade of Breeds, Lexington
Source: Sid Webb

Although very important, marketing alone is no longer enough to sustain and grow a vibrant tourism economy. Like other more traditional sectors of Kentucky's economy, such as manufacturing, the tourism industry must be carefully nurtured and continually developed in order to remain fresh and appealing to new and repeat visitors. In order for this to happen, strategies and incentives need to be in place to continue the growth and development of this industry.

Recognizing this, the General Assembly in 1996 passed the historic Tourism Development Act, the first such legislation in the nation designed specifically to attract tourism business investment to the commonwealth. Historically, most of Kentucky's economic development incentive programs had been aimed primarily at traditional manufacturing operations. With the establishment of tourism business incentives, Kentucky became very competitive in the area of attracting development that expands and enhances the state's tourism infrastructure. Essentially what this piece of legislation did was to allow a tourism developer to recover 25 percent of the cost of a project through a rebate of the state sales taxes collected from visitors to the attraction. Initially, in order to qualify for this tax incentive, the project had to cost a minimum of $1 million. In its first seven years, the Tourism Development Act attracted over a half billion dollars in new investment. Projects such as the Newport Aquarium, Newport on the Levee, Hofbrauhaus and the Kentucky Speedway became reality, further bolstering the state's ability to draw visitors.

And while the sales tax rebate offered by this program is certainly a valuable incentive to developers looking for locations for new tourism attractions, it is projected that the sales tax revenues generated by the new businesses will far exceed the total rebates recovered by the developers. In the first 10 years of the Tourism Development Act, it is estimated that approved projects will create $140 million more in taxes than they could have received in rebates. Thus, the net impact on Kentucky's economy resulting from these new tourism businesses is a strong and positive one.

A healthy tourism industry also supports a desirable and appealing quality of life throughout Kentucky, which can also play a key role in the state's ability to attract investment and retain businesses.

Source of economic impact statistics: Kentucky Department of Travel's Report on Tourism and Travel Industry Expenditures for 2002-2003, based on analysis using economic models updated to 1996 and described in Benjamin H. Stevens, George I. Treyz, David J. Erhlich and James R. Bower, State Input-Output Models for Transportation Impact Analysis (Hightstown, NJ: Regional Science Research Institute, 1981) Discussion Paper Series No. 128.

Source of Tourism Development Act statistics: News Release, Tourism Development Cabinet, September 23, 2003.

Wigwam Village, Cave City
Source: Sid Webb

BUSINESS & ECONOMY
Equine

The Kentucky Equine Education Project (KEEP) was formed in May 2004 to raise awareness of Kentucky's horse industry and its economic impact throughout the state. To that end, KEEP brought together horse owners, breeders and trainers of all disciplines and breeds on a scale never seen before to create a unified voice and build a grassroots

ing more horses to remain in Kentucky.

At its core, KEEP endeavors to reach those willing to help foster the horse industry's everyday contributions to the state's agricultural and tourism sectors as well as facilitate public discussions relating to land preservation and the environment. While some 30 percent of Kentucky's modern-day econ-

Source: Sid Webb

organization to better inform the public about the equine economy.

Former Kentucky Gov. Brereton Jones (1991-1995) served as the impetus for KEEP's organization and development and was asked to lead the group as its first chairman. Jones and his wife, Libby, own and operate Airdrie Stud farm in Woodford County.

In a little over a year, KEEP has grown its membership ranks to more than 7,000, including members in 114 Kentucky counties representing every breed of horse, not just Thoroughbreds. In addition, KEEP has established a 29-member governing board, added six full-time staff and assigned team leaders in every county in the state. KEEP's maiden lobbying effort during the state legislature's 2005 session yielded legislation that not only established a $15 million breeder incentive fund but also eliminated a tax on out-of-state buyers, encourag-

omy is based on agriculture, including horses, the equine industry has also become a key component of the state's $8 billion tourism trade, the second leading source of revenue and jobs in Kentucky.

KEEP's mission focuses on coalition building among a diverse group of state and local organizations, including chambers of commerce, rotaries, nonprofits, educational foundations, businesses, organized labor and trade associations. KEEP advocates expanding the reach of state-sponsored programs like the Kentucky Thoroughbred and Standardbred development funds — which encourage ownership of Kentucky-bred horses — to include economic incentives and added tax reform to stimulate job growth and spur economic expansion.

Today, roughly 320,000 horses of varied breeds are raised on more than 13,000 farms owned and operated by Kentuckians in every county. Big and small, these farms require feed, fencing, veterinary services, trucks, tractors and manpower to operate, which taken together, create and sustain businesses that contribute more than $4 billion to Kentucky's annual gross domestic product. Incredibly, 100,000 or more jobs are directly or indirectly

Source: Sid Webb

related to the state's horse industry.

It is estimated that more than half the farm equipment sold in Kentucky, for instance, is used on horse farms. Those farms collectively purchase 400,000 tons of hay and 200,000 tons of feed each year, and the average horse farm builds and maintains roughly 22 miles of fence. Rural and suburban automobile dealerships sell an average of three new trucks for every new car, and no other small business increases the property value of nearby

real estate as dramatically as acreage devoted to horses. In short, horse farm operations contribute significantly to the bottom line of businesses across a broad spectrum of industries.

In Kentucky, horses are not just a business — they are a way of life. Owners, breeders and industry officials across the country and around the world covet the concentration of bloodstock, investment and expertise that have kept Kentucky atop the horse industry for so long. Simply put, they want to be where Kentucky is now and are challenging the state's position like never before.

KEEP's entrance into the public discussion in 2004 on how to best preserve and promote the state's signature industry brought about a renewed sense of purpose for many industry leaders. Indeed, it quantified in real terms, through tax and breeder incentive legislation enacted by the state legislature, the effectiveness of KEEP's broad-based grassroots advocacy and its potential to help shape the industry's future.

Contributed by the Kentucky Equine Education Project

"Well, what about that"

From 1932–1982, Calumet Farm (Lexington) recorded 2,401 wins, 508 of which were in stakes races. Of its 148 homebred stakes winners, nine won in excess of $500,000. Calumet was number one on the list of Leading Money-Winning Owners 12 times and in the top three from 1939 to 1954, acquiring total earnings of $26,410,941.

BUSINESS & ECONOMY
Distilleries

Bill Ambrose

Bourbon (bou' r' bon) – 1.) "The Whiskey That Made Kentucky Famous" and 2.) a whiskey distilled primarily from corn and aged in charred oak barrels.

In 1790 Kentucky was still considered the western frontier of the new United States. Even before Kentucky was admitted to the new union in 1792, local farmers were converting their surplus corn crops into a rough form of whiskey. This whiskey was known as "Western Whiskey" to distinguish it from the rye-based whiskies from the east.

Also, according to legend, during this period a Baptist minister named Elijah Craig acquired a number of used oak barrels to store his distilled whiskey. Reverend Craig is said to have burned the insides of these barrels to avoid cleaning the remnants out. The liquor he stored in these barrels turned out to have distinctive characteristics and a rich caramel brown color. Thereafter charred oak barrels were used for shipping bourbon.

In 1833 Oscar Pepper hired Dr. James Christopher Crow as Master Distiller of his family distillery, Glassy Spring Branch of Glenn's Creek in Woodford County. This distillery is still operating today

Source: Bill Ambrose

and is known as the Woodford Reserve Distillery. Dr. Crow was a physician trained in Edinburgh, Scotland. Dr. Crow brought a scientific approach to distilling – using the saccharimeter (alcohol measurer) and thermometer to study fermentation. *Old Crow Bourbon* was named in his honor. He was the first to perfect the sour mash process – where a portion of the "sour" stillage from the prior day was mashed in the next day. This created consistency between batches. Henry Clay, noted Kentucky Senator, would annually ship a barrel of Crow's whiskey to Washington "to lubricate the wheels of government." Other famous customers included Andrew Jackson, John C. Calhoun, Ulysses S. Grant, William Henry Harrison and Daniel Webster.

During the Civil War, the Revenue Act of 1862 authorized the Federal government to impose a temporary excise tax on distilled sprits. This tax was signed into law by President Lincoln to offset the cost of the war. The tax was $2.00 per gallon and due at the time the whiskey was distilled. This temporary tax – for some unknown reason – is still being collected to this day. Excise Taxes accounted for twenty-five to fifty percent of the Federal budget between the Civil War and Prohibition.

The distilling industry expanded rapidly after the Civil War, and because of its quality Kentucky Bourbon Whiskey became known as a "gentleman's drink". Fine Kentucky Bourbon was available in most western saloons – a number of lawmen and outlaws in Dodge City were known to partake.

Maker's Mark Distillery
Source: Sid Webb

The roots of Prohibition can be traced to the 1890s, with the founding by a group of preachers, teachers and businessmen of the Anti-Saloon League. After the United States entered the First World War the temperance movement made major strides towards a national prohibition. The National Prohibition Act, also known as the Volstead Act after its sponsor Andrew Volstead of Minnesota, was approved in October 1918. President Wilson vetoed this legislation, but Congress quickly overrode his veto. After January 17, 1920 it was against the law to manufacture or sell any beverage with more than one-half of one percent alcohol. The first offense was punishable with a fine of up to $1,000 and a prison term of up to six months. The "Great Experiment" had begun.

After 1919, the remaining bourbon inventory was bottled for medicinal sales. Medical doctors could write a prescription for whiskey, which was then filled at drug stores. Prescriptions were limited to one quart at a time, later one pint every ten days. Doctors were limited to one hundred prescriptions annually, but many turned a blind eye and exceeded these limitations.

Prohibition ended in 1934 but only 34 of 157 distilleries reopened. Over the next 30 years, ownership of these remaining distilleries was consolidated into a half dozen major corporations. In 1968 Congress passed a resolution naming Bourbon Whiskey as America's native spirit.

Kentuckians still celebrate their heritage of fine bourbon whiskey. The Kentucky Bourbon Festi-

val is held annually in Bardstown during September. The Kentucky Bourbon Trail was established for tours of Kentucky's operating distilleries. The tour includes Buffalo Trace in Frankfort (*Ancient Age, Buffalo Trace* and *W. L. Weller*); Jim Beam Brands in Clermont (*Booker's, Jim Beam, Knob Creek, Old Crow, Old Grand-Dad, Old Taylor* and *Sunny Brook*); Four Roses Distillery in Lawrenceburg (*Four Roses*); Heaven Hill Distillery in Bardstown (*Elijah Craig, Evan Williams* and *Heaven Hill*) Woodford Reserve in Versailles (*Woodford Reserve*); Maker's Mark Distillery in Loretto (*Maker's Mark*); and Wild Turkey in Lawrenceburg (*Wild Turkey*).

Bourbon whiskey is today one of Kentucky's leading exports with over 400 million dollars in revenue.

It's a Kentucky Thing!

Bourbon whiskey by federal regulation must contain at least 51 percent but not more than 80 percent corn, and no coloring or flavoring agents can be added. It must be distilled at less than 160 proof and racked into barrels at no more than 125 proof and barrels must be made of new charred oak To qualify as Kentucky Bourbon the whiskey must be distilled and stored in the commonwealth for at least one year.

(U.S. Code, Title 27, Part 5, Section 5.22)

TOP 100 MANUFACTURERS AND/OR SUPPORTIVE SERVICE FACILITIES BY FULL-TIME EMPLOYMENT

NO	COMPANY	PRODUCTS	EMPL	COUNTY	YR	ADDRESS	CITY	ZIP
1	UPS	Courier services, admin offices, airline offices	9,942	Jefferson	2004	1400 N Hurstbourne Pkwy	Louisville	40223
2	Toyota Motor Manufacturing Ky	Automobiles–Camry sedan, Avalon sedan, engines (4 cyl & V6), axles, steering components, blocks/cylinder heads/crankshafts	7,400	Scott	2004	1001 Cherry Blossom Way	Georgetown	40324
3	Ford Motor Co	Medium & commercial light truck assembly	6,600	Jefferson	2004	3001 Chamberlain Ln	Louisville	40241
4	GE Consumer and Industrial	Major household appliances; dryers, washers, refrigerators & dishwashers	5,650	Jefferson	2004	AP35-1113	Louisville	40225
5	Delta Connection Comair	Air terminal, maintenance, training, office facility	4,900	Boone	2004	77 Comair Blvd	Erlanger	41018
6	Humana Inc	Corporate office	4,000	Jefferson	2004	500 West Main Street	Louisville	40202
7	Lexmark International Inc	Printers & information processing supplies, headquarters	3,600	Fayette	2004	740 W New Circle Rd	Lexington	40550
8	Ford Motor Co	Automobile assembly (Ford Explorer, Mercury Mountaineer, Ford Explorer Sport-Trac)	3,454	Jefferson	2004	2000 Fern Valley Rd	Louisville	40213
9	Fidelity Investments	Financial services	2,900	Kenton	2005	100 Magellan Way	Covington	41015
10	Citicorp Credit Services	Credit card service center	2,500	Boone	2004	4600 Houston Road	Florence	41042
11	Brown-Forman Corp	Distilled spirits, wooden barrels, headquarters	1,800	Jefferson	2003	850 Dixie Hwy	Louisville	40210
12	Cagle's Keystone Foods Inc	Fresh & frozen poultry	1,530	Clinton	2004	RR 4 Box 439	Albany	42602
13	National Processing Company LLC	Data processing (credit/debit card)	1,350	Jefferson	2004	1231 Durrett Lane	Louisville	40213
14	Tyson Foods Inc	Chicken slaughtering, processing & packaging	1,350	Henderson	2004	14660 US Hwy 41 S	Robards	42452
15	R R Donnelley	Offset printing, computer typesetting, saddle stitch & perfect binding	1,315	Barren	2004	120 Donnelley Dr	Glasgow	42141
16	USEC Paducah Plant	Government & uranium enrichment	1,270	McCracken	2004	5600 Hobbs Rd	Paducah	42001
17	BA Merchant Services	Processor of credit- and debit-card transactions, headquarters	1,253	Jefferson	2004	1231 Durrett Lane	Louisville	40213
18	Citicorp Credit Services Inc USA	Customer service call center and collections	1,200	Jefferson	2004	12501 Lakefront Place	Louisville	40299
19	General Motors Corp	Automobiles – Corvette, Cadillac XLR	1,200	Warren	2004	600 Corvette Dr	Bowling Green	42101
20	CSX/GE Transportation	Repair locomotives and rail cars	1,200	Whitley	2004	1500 Lynn Av	Corbin	40701
21	Briggs & Stratton Corp	Lawn mower engines	1,160	Calloway	2004	110 Main St	Murray	42071
22	Schwan's Food Manufacturing Inc	Frozen pizzas	1,150	Boone	2005	7605 Empire Dr	Florence	41042
23	AMBRAKE Manufacturing LTD	Automotive disc & drum brakes	1,134	Hardin	2004	300 Ring Rd	Elizabethtown	42701
24	Amazon.com	Distribution - Fulfillment Center	1,100	Fayette	2002	1850 Mercer Rd	Lexington	45011
25	Trane Co	Air conditioning, heating & air handling equipment & supplies	1,100	Fayette	2004	1515 Mercer Rd	Lexington	40511
26	Nestle Prepared Foods	Specialty microwavable lunch foods	1,094	Montgomery	2004	150 Oak Grove Dr	Mt. Sterling	40353
27	Dana Corporation	Pick up truck/SUV frames	1,036	Hardin	2004	750 Dana Dr	Elizabethtown	42701
28	Perdue Farms Inc	Chicken slaughtering, processing & packaging	1,025	Ohio	2004	489 Cromwell Rd	Cromwell	42333
29	Swift & Co	Pork processing	1,023	Jefferson	2004	1200 Story Ave	Louisville	40206
30	Panasonic Home Appliances Co of Am	Vacuum cleaners	1,000	Boyle	2004	1355 Lebanon Rd	Danville	40422
31	Kindred Healthcare Operating Inc	National corporate headquarters, computer service center & help desk	1,000	Jefferson	2004	680 South Fourth St	Louisville	40202
32	NACCO Materials Handling Group	Lift trucks	1,000	Madison	2004	2200 Menelaus Rd	Berea	40403
33	Gibbs Die Casting Corp	Aluminum & magnesium die castings, headquarters	1,000	Henderson	2004	369 Community Dr	Henderson	42420
34	Pilgrim's Pride	Poultry processing & packing	960	Graves	2004	2653 State Rt 1241	Hickory	42051
35	North American Stainless	Stainless steel coils, sheets, and long products (bar, wire, and rod)	960	Carroll	2004	6870 Highway 42 E	Ghent	41045
36	Cingular Wireless LLC	Wireless sheet stock	952	Carter	2004	828 East Park Rd	Grayson	41143
37	Logan Aluminum Inc	Aluminum rolled sheet stock	950	Logan	2004	US Highway 431 N	Russellville	42276
38	Tyco Adhesives	Pipeline coatings; industrial, athletic & consumer adhesive tapes & bandages	944	Simpson	2004	2320 Bowling Green Rd	Franklin	42134
39	ThyssenKrupp Budd	Automobile parts stamping	935	Shelby	2004	1000 Old Brunerstown Rd	Shelbyville	40065
40	R R Donnelley & Sons Co	Offset printing, side & saddle stitch binding, patent binding	921	Boyle	2004	3201 Lebanon Rd	Danville	40422
41	SHPS	Corporate Office	900	Jefferson	2004	11405 Bluegrass Pkwy	Louisville	40299
42	AK Steel Corp	Flat rolled carbon steel	900	Boyd	2004	US Hwy 23	Ashland	41101
43	Catlettsburg Refining LLC	Petroleum refining; gas	890	Boyd	2004	11631 US Rt 23	Catlettsburg	41129
44	Courier-Journal	Daily newspaper publishing offset printing and mass distribution	887	Jefferson	2004	525 W Broadway	Louisville	40202
45	Quebecor World	Book publishing & printing; staple saddle stitch & perfect binding	883	Woodford	2002	100 US Bypass 60 E	Versailles	40383
46	Valvoline Co	Administrative offices and lab	858	Fayette	2004	3499 Blazer Pkwy	Lexington	40509
47	Wal-Mart Distribution Center 6066	Distribution	855	Christian	2004	690 Crenshaw Blvd	Hopkinsville	42240
48	Fruit of the Loom	Fabric for underwear & sportswear	850	Russell	2004	Hwy 127	Jamestown	42629
49	Publishers Printing Co	Offset & lithographic printing typesetting, saddle stitch & perfect binding	845	Bullitt	2004	100 Frank E Simon Ave	Shepherdsville	40165
50	Commonwealth Alum Corp Lewisport	Coils, aluminum tubing & flexible conduits	830	Hancock	2004	1372 State Rt 1957	Lewisport	42351
51	Super Service	Freight carrier	821	Pulaski	2004	250 Super Service Dr	Somerset	42501

TOP 100 MANUFACTURERS AND/OR SUPPORTIVE SERVICE FACILITIES BY FULL-TIME EMPLOYMENT

NO	COMPANY	PRODUCTS	EMPL	COUNTY	YR	ADDRESS	CITY	ZIP
52	Huish Detergents Inc	Detergent	808	Warren	2004	385 Southwood Ct	Bowling Green	42101
53	Dart Container Corp	Plastic food containers	805	Hart	2004	975 S Dixie St	Horse Cave	42749
54	Humana Customer Service Center	Call center, customer service	800	Jefferson	2004	101 East Main	Louisville	40202
55	Con Agra Foods	Hams	800	Carter	2004	800 Cw Stevens Blvd	Grayson	41143
56	Tokico (USA) Inc	Automobile shock absorbers, struts, brake systems & air compressors	800	Madison	2004	301 Mayde Rd	Berea	40403
57	L-3 Communications Integrated Sys	Support activities - DOD contract	785	Fayette	2004	5749 Briar Hill Rd	Lexington	40516
58	GE Aircraft Engine Div	Aircraft engines, turbines, blades & vanes	780	Hopkins	2004	3050 Nebo Rd	Madisonville	42431
59	Bank One Kentucky	Check processing and administrative services	761	Jefferson	2004	Grade Lane Operations	Louisville	40213
60	Cox Interior Inc	Hardwood moldings, trim, stair parts, interior doors & mantels	760	Taylor	2004	1751 Old Columbia Rd	Campbellsville	42718
61	Hitachi Automotive Products USA	Automobile electric & electronic components	760	Mercer	2005	955 Warwick Rd	Harrodsburg	40330
62	Publishers Printing Co	Printing publications or magazines	760	Bullitt	2004	13487 S Preston Hwy	Lebanon Jnct	40150
63	Johnson Controls Inc	Automobile & truck seat frames	751	Trigg	2004	Hwy 68 E	Cadiz	42211
64	Emerson Power Transmission	V-belts, drives, sprockets, gears, ball & roller bearing units, sheaves, bushings, couplings, gear boxes and gear reducers, motorized conveyor pulleys	750	Mason	2004	1248 E 2nd St	Maysville	41056
65	Bank One Kentucky	Regional loan servicing center	750	Fayette	2004	201 E. Main St	Lexington	40507
66	Eagle Industries LLC	Oak furniture	750	Warren	2001	610 Hope St	Bowling Green	42101
67	Toyotetsu America LLC	Structural automotive components & stampings	740	Pulaski	2004	100 Pin Oak Dr	Somerset	42503
68	Century Aluminum of Kentucky LLC	Aluminum castings, sows & smelting	739	Hancock	2004	1627 State Rt 271 N	Hawesville	42348
69	American Greetings	Distribution and paper product packaging center	712	Boyle	2004	2601 Lebanon Rd	Danville	40422
70	Dana Corporation	Truck axles & brake components	700	Henderson	2004	1491 Dana Dr	Henderson	42420
71	Mother's Cookie Co	Cookies	700	Jefferson	2003	2287 Ralph Ave	Louisville	40216
72	ASTAR Air Cargo	Airfreight delivery service	700	Boone	2004	236 Wendell H Ford	Erlanger	41018
73	Wal-Mart	Distribution Center	700	Laurel	2004	3701 Russel Dyche Hwy	London	40741
74	McLane Cumberland	Food distribution center	700	Jessamine	2004	1040 Baker Ln	Nicholasville	40356
75	Kroger Limited Partnership I	Distribution center	700	Jefferson	2004	2000 Nelson Miller Pkwy	Louisville	40223
76	Thomson Learning Distribution Ctr	Book distribution center	700	Kenton	2004	10650 Toebben Dr	Independence	41051
77	US Bank Home Mortgage	Loan processing and underwriting service center, loan servicing center	685	Daviess	2004	4801 Frederica St	Owensboro	42301
78	Mid-South Electronics Inc	Injection molded products, printed circuit boards, control panels, ice makers, electromechanical & electronic assemblies	673	Jackson	2004	2500 Highway 30 W	Annville	40402
79	DESA International	Portable gas heaters & generators- distribution	669	Warren	2004	2901 Industrial Dr	Bowling Green	42101
80	Square D Company	Electrical safety switches & distribution panels, load centers	666	Fayette	2003	1601 Mercer Rd	Lexington	40511
81	Montaplast of North America	Plastic injection molding automotive wheel covers, center caps, and intake manifolds	651	Franklin	2004	2011 Hoover Blvd	Frankfort	40601
82	Dollar General Corp	Storage warehouse	650	Allen	2004	427 Beech St	Scottsville	42164
83	Presbyterian Church [USA]	Headquarters	650	Jefferson	2004	100 Witherspoon St	Louisville	40202
84	Alcan Primary Metal Group	Aluminum extrusion billets & ingots	650	Henderson	2004	9404 Hwy 2096	Robards	42452
85	Dana Corporation	Automobile frames	650	Christian	2004	301 Bill Bryan Blvd	Hopkinsville	42240
86	TG Kentucky LLC	Rubber molded & plastic interior automobile parts	650	Marion	2004	633 E Main St	Lebanon	40033
87	Cooper Standard Automotive	Molded & extruded rubber products, reinforced rubber hoses & automotive parts, fuel delivery systems	650	Montgomery	2004	250 Oak Grove Dr	Mt. Sterling	40353
88	Toyota Motor Manufacturing NA Inc	Corporate headquarters	650	Kenton	2005	25 Atlantic Ave	Erlanger	41018
89	Pella Corporation	Windows and doors manufacturer	625	Calloway	2004	307 Pella Way	Murray	42071
90	Papa John's International	Corporate office and make dough	617	Jefferson	2004	2002 Papa John Blvd	Louisville	40299
91	Aisin Automotive Casting LLC	Automotive aluminum die cast components	615	Laurel	2004	4870 E Hwy 552	London	40744
92	Bremner Inc	Cookies & crackers	610	Caldwell	2004	1475 US Hwy 62 W	Princeton	42445
93	AGC Automotive Americas	Automobile glass	603	Hardin	2004	1 Auto Glass Dr	Elizabethtown	42701
94	Flynn Enterprises Inc	Men's, ladies & children's jeans, shorts & skirts	600	Christian	2002	1121 Skyline Dr	Hopkinsville	42240
95	Field Packing Co Inc	Processed meat products	600	Daviess	2004	6 Dublin Ln	Owensboro	42301
96	DESA LLC	Portable gas heaters & generators	600	Warren	2004	2701 Industrial Dr	Bowling Green	42101
97	Topy Corp	Road wheels for passenger cars and light trucks.	600	Franklin	2004	980 Chenault Rd	Frankfort	40601
98	American Greetings Corp	Greeting cards	598	Nelson	2004	800 American Dr	Bardstown	40004
99	Gall's Inc	Corporate office, inbound call center, distribution, shipping	596	Fayette	2003	2680 Palumbo Dr	Lexington	40509
100	Sara Lee US Foods	Sausage & hot dogs, deli meats	594	Campbell	2004	401 Bob Huber Dr	Alexandria	41001

Source: Kentucky Economic Development Cabinet - www.thinkkentucky.com/kyedc/pdfs/top200mf.pdf

BUSINESS & ECONOMY

Economic Indicators

JUNE 2005 INDICATORS
AS OF AUGUST 26, 2005

KY Composite Index of Leading Indicators increased 6.2 percent for June.

- The Leading Index increased for the fourth time this year.
- The Leading Index rose by 1.4 percent over the same month last year.
- Component indicators were mostly positive, 4:1.
- KY Labor Intensity Index decreased 1.7 percent.
- The U.S. Leading Index increased 15.0 percent.
- The Index of KY Initial Unemployment Insurance Claims increased 10.4 percent.
- U.S. Retail Sales increased 22.4 percent.
- Component weights for June are 52.44, 19.81, 15.31, 10.68 and 1.77 respectively.
- KY Composite Index of Coincident Indicators increased 5.7 percent for June.
- The Coincident Index was positive for the fifth consecutive month.
- Same-month-last-year growth is positive for the 23rd consecutive month at 2.7 percent.
- Component indicators were all positive for June.
- KY Total Nonagricultural Employment increased 3.0 percent.
- U.S. Industrial Production Index increased 10.1 percent.
- U.S. Personal Income Less Transfers increased 6.5 percent.

Component weights for June are 32.61, 29.80 and 26.72 respectively. Component weights do not sum to one because the two U.S. components were discounted to allow the Kentucky component more weight.

The Kentucky Leading Index increased substantially in June. The June increase is the third largest single month increase since the recession of 2001. Four of the five components showed solid growth this month. Only the Kentucky Labor Intensity Index declined.

Employment activity was mixed among the five manufacturing sectors of the Labor Intensity Index. Transportation equipment and Rubber and Plastic Products employment showed small declines for June. Fabricated Metals employment remained unchanged. Chemical Products and Lumber and Wood Products rose slightly. The majority of the movement in the Labor Intensity Index was in the average weekly hours side of the equation. Average weekly hours for Fabricated Metals, Chemical Products and Lumber and Wood products fell by moderate to large amounts for June, while Transportation Equipment and Rubber and Plastic Products average weekly hours rose slightly.

The newly designed US Leading Index exhibited its highest growth in over two years. The Kentucky and US Leading Indices have both performed quite differently since the trough of the 2001 recession. The Kentucky Leading Index showed a small second downturn in early 2003, which hindered its recovery.

Meanwhile, the U.S. Leading Index had already surpassed its previous pre-recession peak and was increasing its growth over its 1990s growth trend. It has taken Kentucky nearly two additional years to surpass its 2001 peak and only now has regained its high growth similar to the 1990s growth trend.

Kentucky Nonagricultural Employment continues to do well. Kentucky has gained 31,500 positions since July 2004. That is almost the same amount that was lost in all of Manufacturing during the 2001 recession. Manufacturing Employment continues to struggle. After three consecutive months of moderate growth, 1,000 jobs were lost in June. The loss almost wiped out the combined gains of the previous three months.

For a complete description of the Index of Leading Indicators and methodology, see University of Kentucky Center for Business and Economic Research Kentucky Annual Economic Report, 2000.

Source: Office of State Budget Director, www.osbd.ky.gov

2002 SURVEY OF BUSINESS OWNERS
PRELIMINARY ESTIMATES OF BUSINESS OWNERSHIP BY GENDER, HISPANIC OR LATINO ORIGIN AND RACE

	KY FIRMS (Number)	KY PERCENT	U.S. FIRMS (Number)	U.S. PERCENT	KY SALES & RECEIPTS ($1000)	KY PERCENT	U.S. SALES & RECEIPTS ($,1000)	U.S. PERCENT
TOTALS	300,732		22,977,164		284,127,673		22,634,870,406	
Female	77,232	25.68%	6,492,795	28.26%	9,482,166	3.34%	950,600,079	4.20%
Male	174,984	58.19%	13,185,703	57.39%	84,647,270	29.79%	7,096,465,049	31.35%
Equally male-/female-owned	39,343	13.08%	2,691,722	11.71%	8,237,792	2.90%	731,051,431	3.23%
Hispanic	2,082	0.69%	1,574,159	6.85%	782,891	0.28%	226,468,398	1.00%
Non-Hispanic	289,477	96.26%	20,796,061	90.51%	101,584,338	35.75%	8,551,648,161	37.78%
White	280,029	93.12%	19,894,823	86.59%	99,681,772	35.08%	8,303,716,399	36.69%
Black	7,595	2.53%	1,197,988	5.21%	1,090,724	0.38%	92,681,562	1.12%
American Indian and Alaska Native	1,324	0.44%	206,125	0.90%	79,406	0.03%	26,395,707	0.12%
Asian	3,243	1.08%	1,105,329	4.81%	1,473,543	0.52%	343,321,501	1.52%
Native Hawaiian and Other Pacific Islander	S	na	32,299	0.14%	11,385	0.00%	5,220,795	0.02%
Publicly-held, foreign-owned, and not-for-profit	7,333	2.44%	491,715	2.14%	179,737,815	63.26%	13,790,327,139	60.93%

Note: "S" Estimates are suppressed when publication standards are not met. Suppression occurs when one or more of the following criteria are met: the firm count is less than 3; or the Relative Standard Error is 50 percent or more.

Source: U.S. Census Bureau, Company Statistics Division, Economic Census Branch (http://www.census.gov/csd/sbo/state/st21.HTM, http://www.census.gov/csd/sbo/state/st00.HTM)

INDUSTRY EMPLOYMENT PROJECTIONS 2002 - 2012

CODE	INDUSTRY	EST YR - PROJ YR	CHANGE	PERCENT CHANGE
110000	Agriculture, Forestry, Fishing and Hunting	2002-2012	712	9.5
210000	Mining	2002-2012	-5,025	-25.6
220000	Utilities	2002-2012	-1,912	-28.6
230000	Construction	2002-2012	12,667	15.2
310000	Manufacturing	2002-2012	7,913	2.9
420000	Wholesale Trade	2002-2012	16,976	23.7
440000	Retail Trade	2002-2012	27,621	13
480000	Transportation and Warehousing	2002-2012	17,345	21.5
510000	Information	2002-2012	11,759	36.9
520000	Finance and Insurance	2002-2012	8,397	13.3
530000	Real Estate and Rental and Leasing	2002-2012	4,196	21.2
540000	Professional, Scientific, and Technical Services	2002-2012	14,616	25.8
550000	Management of Companies and Enterprises	2002-2012	2,017	15
560000	Administrative and Support and Waste Management and Remediat	2002-2012	15,139	17.9
610000	Educational Services	2002-2012	38,875	24.8
620000	Health Care and Social Assistance	2002-2012	46,670	23
710000	Arts, Entertainment, and Recreation	2002-2012	4,611	26
720000	Accommodation and Food Services	2002-2012	30,864	22.8
810000	Other Services (Except Government)	2002-2012	10,137	14.8
900000	Government	2002-2012	17,048	12.3
910000	Federal Government	2002-2012	-1,997	-5.3
920000	State Government, Excluding Education and Hospitals	2002-2012	4,318	10.1
930000	Local Government, Excluding Education and Hospitals	2002-2012	14,727	25.1
6010	Self-Employed Workers, Primary Job	2002-2012	36,472	27.9
6010	Total Employment, All Jobs	2002-2012	316,011	16.8

Source: http://www.workforcekentucky.ky.gov/

Of the FEDERAL MONEY.

By an Ordinance of Congress, the money of account of the United States, is to be expressed in Dollars or Units; Dimes* or Tenths; Cents or Hundredths; and Mills or Thousandths.

TABLE I.

Ten Mills make one Cent. Ten Cents one Dime. Ten Dimes one Dollar. Ten Dollars one Eagle.

Source: The Kentucky Almanac 1795, published by John Bradford, Lexington

REAL GROSS STATE PRODUCT (GSP) 1991-2001 (Millions of Chained 1996 Dollars)

STATE	1991	1992	1993	1994	1995	1996	1997	1998	1999	2000	2001	US GSP	1991-2001	2000-2001
US	6,615,685	6,774,505	6,918,388	7,203,002	7,433,965	7,715,901	8,093,396	8,502,663	8,882,613	9,298,227	9,335,399		41.11%	0.40%
Alabama	85,518	88,853	90,225	93,575	96,624	99,286	102,646	106,367	110,426	112,295	112,026	1.20	31.00%	-0.24%
Alaska	25,085	25,130	25,438	25,268	26,535	25,774	26,056	25,064	25,064	24,725	24,490	0.26	-2.37%	-0.96%
Arizona	79,726	85,316	89,911	98,339	105,397	112,882	120,763	130,720	141,368	148,806	153,684	1.65	92.77%	3.17%
Arkansas	46,172	48,652	50,174	52,921	54,689	56,796	58,585	59,967	63,207	64,046	63,701	0.68	37.96%	-0.54%
California	912,709	906,189	898,829	911,249	941,853	973,395	1,029,232	1,096,091	1,169,845	1,258,449	1,260,041	13.50	38.06%	0.13%
Colorado	89,421	94,035	99,789	105,850	111,244	117,118	127,314	135,590	145,524	158,173	159,308	1.71	78.16%	0.71%
Connecticut	114,576	114,830	115,725	117,489	120,792	124,157	132,620	138,159	142,699	151,987	152,985	1.64	33.52%	0.65%
Delaware	25,791	25,639	25,984	26,657	28,236	29,001	30,142	30,594	31,961	33,381	35,745	0.38	38.59%	6.61%
District of Col.	49,943	50,646	51,216	50,657	49,737	48,505	49,265	49,613	51,291	54,080	56,077	0.60	12.28%	3.56%
Florida	305,752	314,129	325,760	339,110	350,565	366,318	382,250	400,891	420,176	438,639	446,482	4.78	46.03%	1.76%
Georgia	167,161	175,614	183,173	195,330	206,415	219,520	231,808	245,966	261,522	274,886	273,876	2.93	63.84%	-0.37%
Hawaii	38,516	39,120	38,809	38,332	37,948	37,490	37,668	37,622	38,047	38,860	38,839	0.42	0.84%	-0.05%
Idaho	20,510	21,783	23,654	25,331	27,395	28,101	29,322	31,015	34,888	37,089	36,832	0.39	79.58%	-0.70%
Illinois	317,857	328,462	334,735	345,882	364,080	375,949	394,497	411,417	424,851	441,904	441,797	4.73	38.99%	-0.02%
Indiana	126,605	133,621	138,501	145,882	150,037	155,096	161,059	171,703	175,395	181,542	178,184	1.91	40.74%	-1.88%
Iowa	63,891	66,147	66,324	71,576	73,111	76,976	81,541	82,332	84,376	87,454	86,968	0.93	36.12%	-0.56%
Kansas	60,507	61,872	62,367	65,016	65,618	68,160	72,113	74,830	77,480	79,919	80,680	0.86	33.34%	0.94%
Kentucky	77,856	81,890	84,543	89,569	92,794	95,536	100,210	104,359	106,590	109,537	110,074	1.18	41.38%	0.49%
Louisiana	107,664	100,696	102,847	100,509	116,496	116,867	120,699	120,783	129,495	125,733	125,295	1.34	16.38%	-0.35%
Maine	27,010	27,046	27,286	27,755	28,256	28,925	29,958	31,121	32,418	33,746	34,020	0.36	25.95%	0.81%
Maryland	134,540	133,947	136,070	140,338	142,140	145,061	151,478	157,610	164,001	170,747	175,256	1.88	30.26%	2.57%
Massachusetts	181,901	182,789	186,680	195,171	200,537	210,127	219,716	233,981	247,354	266,840	265,722	2.85	46.08%	-0.42%
Michigan	219,814	226,548	237,214	255,812	258,329	265,130	275,591	285,449	299,525	306,437	297,475	3.19	35.33%	-3.01%
Minnesota	116,918	122,706	123,146	130,178	133,804	141,540	150,415	158,919	165,644	176,841	175,371	1.88	49.99%	-0.84%
Mississippi	45,946	47,963	49,925	53,020	55,420	56,575	57,794	57,893	61,797	62,295	61,527	0.66	33.91%	-1.25%
Missouri	124,568	127,157	127,578	135,048	141,926	146,537	153,392	158,123	161,395	166,677	167,370	1.79	34.36%	0.41%
Montana	15,852	16,577	17,245	17,679	17,858	18,074	18,614	19,422	19,698	20,461	20,708	0.22	30.63%	1.19%
Nebraska	39,968	41,308	41,376	44,009	45,247	47,772	48,924	50,296	52,047	53,517	53,563	0.57	34.01%	0.09%
Nevada	38,129	40,266	43,019	47,030	50,062	54,564	57,518	60,522	64,375	68,216	69,538	0.74	82.38%	1.90%
New Hampshire	27,528	28,373	28,808	30,122	32,630	35,068	37,131	39,965	42,529	46,082	45,270	0.48	64.45%	-1.79%
New Jersey	257,597	258,156	262,674	268,019	275,002	285,738	294,088	305,186	316,040	332,927	332,897	3.57	31.79%	-0.01%
New Mexico	32,672	34,081	37,795	42,183	42,708	44,114	47,621	49,554	50,305	52,361	54,930	0.59	68.13%	4.68%
New York	562,563	586,798	587,982	600,674	609,090	633,830	651,107	695,186	717,677	756,573	766,526	8.21	33.88%	1.30%
North Carolina	162,742	170,297	176,163	188,574	197,500	204,329	218,108	232,122	242,941	249,784	246,291	2.64	51.34%	-1.42%
North Dakota	13,112	14,016	13,795	14,627	14,988	15,855	15,819	16,884	16,825	17,787	17,757	0.19	35.43%	-0.17%
Ohio	263,160	271,844	276,024	290,068	299,232	306,333	322,050	337,650	344,957	352,654	349,331	3.74	32.74%	-0.95%
Oklahoma	66,588	67,641	69,173	70,081	71,819	74,855	78,111	80,759	82,990	85,092	85,948	0.92	29.07%	1.00%
Oregon	67,556	69,392	73,009	76,642	81,330	91,709	97,097	103,218	111,388	124,781	124,847	1.34	84.81%	0.05%
Pennsylvania	292,974	300,806	306,134	312,197	322,915	329,660	340,924	351,920	362,533	374,012	374,500	4.01	27.83%	0.13%
Rhode Island	24,676	24,884	25,226	25,385	26,182	26,656	28,766	29,541	30,058	33,349	33,451	0.36	35.56%	0.30%
South Carolina	76,509	77,984	80,440	84,567	87,750	89,854	94,252	98,360	102,379	106,108	106,485	1.14	39.18%	0.35%
South Dakota	15,932	16,603	17,429	18,097	18,744	19,372	19,673	20,323	21,456	22,937	23,165	0.25	45.40%	0.98%
Tennessee	114,320	121,959	127,108	134,440	138,632	142,051	149,239	156,836	162,665	166,632	168,412	1.80	47.32%	1.06%
Texas	447,200	461,434	480,045	504,252	527,685	553,180	597,889	631,688	660,534	688,473	698,547	7.48	56.20%	1.44%
Utah	37,752	39,024	40,932	43,952	46,965	51,523	53,999	57,011	59,663	63,565	63,353	0.68	69.35%	0.58%
Vermont	12,972	13,524	13,794	14,115	14,133	14,662	15,304	15,921	16,611	17,387	18,048	0.19	39.13%	3.66%
Virginia	173,420	175,916	181,231	187,578	192,486	199,953	207,892	208,406	224,464	236,945	241,539	2.59	39.28%	1.90%
Washington	139,654	144,389	148,188	152,882	153,987	161,779	172,216	185,474	198,264	202,812	202,470	2.17	44.98%	-0.17%
West Virginia	32,016	33,033	33,813	35,723	36,569	37,220	37,668	37,791	39,111	38,665	39,012	0.42	21.85%	0.89%
Wisconsin	116,704	121,928	126,748	131,788	135,169	141,046	146,903	154,512	160,224	166,019	167,299	1.79	43.35%	0.77%
Wyoming	14,558	14,486	15,264	15,264	15,617	15,879	15,983	16,470	16,852	17,528	18,254	0.20	25.39%	3.98%

Source: U.S. Department of Commerce, Bureau of Economic Analysis. See: http://www.bea.gov/bea/regional/gsp/

When issues that affect the future of agriculture come before Kentucky's governing bodies, who speaks up for farmers? Who promotes growth of agribusiness? Who defends the rural values and lifestyle that are so much the backbone of this great state? Since 1919, that has been a role played by Kentucky Farm Bureau. And it's no different today. With representatives and offices in all 120 counties, Kentucky Farm Bureau sees the big picture and understands the local issues. That's why people on the farm, in small towns, and even in major cities, benefit from the voice of Kentucky Farm Bureau.

Yes, we represent special interests in Frankfort. Yours.

KENTUCKY FARM BUREAU BIG ON COMMITMENT.

AGRICULTURE

John Mark Hack

CULTIVATING PRIDE AND PROSPERITY, PAST AND FUTURE

Agriculture has always occupied a special place in the hearts and minds of Kentuckians. Since well before the Commonwealth was established, these lands have yielded a bounty that has formed our economy, influenced our culture, and fashioned our communities. Kentucky agriculture has cultivated a legacy of hard work, production excellence and innovation that impacts every Kentucky community, from our most rural towns to our largest urban centers.

The economic contributions of this industry are well documented, and have formed the Commonwealth's financial foundation since the frontier days. Crops have been cultivated on Kentucky soils since well before the first European settlers arrived. Native Americans raised tobacco, establishing the roots of the state's deep devotion to the golden leaf. Upon the arrival of the pioneers, agriculture became the primary economic activity, and remained so through the Civil War. These early subsistence farmers first raised corn, a crop used as food for both humans and livestock. Women often tended vegetable gardens in those early days, and a milk cow, hogs, chickens and fruit trees contributed to the diet of early settlers. Sheep, flax and hemp were used for clothing, rope and other fiber needs.

As the state matured, so did its agricultural economy. Production specialties emerged in various regions of the state, linked directly to the diversity of terrain and natural resource assets. Western Kentucky grew into a major grain production area, with its vast flatlands producing crops of corn, wheat and soybeans

Photo Source: Sid Webb

on par with many of the Midwestern "breadbasket" states. Central Kentucky's rolling hills produced the majority of the state's tobacco crop, as well as its beef cattle and horse industries. Eastern Kentucky retained the closest semblance to the small production scale typical of the early days, buoyed in most of the 20th century by the federal tobacco program with its guaranteed markets and prices.

The urban centers of Louisville and Lexington, as well as smaller cities, played critically important roles as major markets, forging a relationship with rural areas that remains today, albeit in a diminished status. Kentucky farms now produce close to $4 billion in cash receipts annually, while annual business activity linked to agriculture is estimated at more than $20 billion. There is probably no other sector within the state that accounts for more economic activity on a per capita basis than agriculture. As the state's urban areas grew with the expansion of the manufacturing sector, agriculture's economic significance lessened somewhat, but farming remains today a defining characteristic of the state and its residents.

Most Kentuckians are no more than a generation or two removed from the farm. This cultural linkage is manifested in many ways, from a strong devotion of many residents to farmers markets, to the state's rich literary heritage. Nationally know writers such as Wendell

Source: Sid Webb

Berry, Barbara Kingsolver and Bobbie Ann Mason have relied on their agrarian upbringings as inspiration for best-selling works, as have dozens of other authors of growing acclaim.

The cultural influence, while defined less clearly in the historic record than economic contributions, is probably far more significant in terms of how Kentuckians have always defined themselves and their sense of place. Virtually every Kentucky community, from small towns to major urban centers, is rooted in the farms that surrounded them. In the early days, non-farm businesses existed largely to serve the needs of farm families. Towns served as meeting places for families coming from various locations throughout a county or region, places of enjoyment and relaxation from the rigors of farm life.

The labor intensiveness of early farm life produced a work ethic that endures today. From the

pioneers' back-breaking work of clearing fields for crops, to the back-straining work of harvesting a tobacco crop, hard work and pride in it have always typified the Kentucky farm family. Today, this ethic is readily visible across the state in all walks of life, as is a commitment to production excellence.

Kentucky leads the nation and the world in many agricultural sectors. Thoroughbred horses have been perfected on the central Kentucky pastures fed by the limestone waters beneath them, and the world recognizes the Bluegrass state as the international center of equine excellence. The state has in years past produced 70% of the nation's burley tobacco crop, and has long been recognized as the global leader in tobacco quality. Kentucky boasts more beef cattle than any state east of the Mississippi River, and ranks eighth nationally.

These accomplishments have not come easy though. Kentucky farmers have always been faced with tribulation, and in most cases have responded with innovation. No-till crop production, a practice that has saved untold amounts of topsoil in the U.S., was invented here as a method of reducing production costs and increasing yields of corn and other cash grain crops. Today, Kentucky corn producers feed a 30-million gallon ethanol production facility in Hopkinsville, while soybean growers are turning the oil from their crop into diesel fuel in Union County. Farmers once almost entirely dependent on tobacco have now turned their attention to a wide variety of other farm enterprises. In the wake of profound changes to the tobacco economy, state government, under the leadership of Governor Paul Patton, decided to invest hundreds of millions of dollars in agricultural diversification so that the state's rich agricultural heritage can continue to play its critical role well into the future.

Agriculture has meant far more than dollars to our Commonwealth. It has come to define who we are as a people, how we interact with one another, and how our state looks. It has shaped our economy, forged our culture, and formed our communities, producing a strong work ethic, a pride in production excellence, and a spirit of innovation. Our past is rooted in our farms, and our future will be shaped by their prosperity.

AGRICULTURE

Heirloom Seeds

Rosemary O. Gordon

Kentucky grower and educator Bill Best knows beans about beans — and tomatoes.

TOMATOES and beans. Lots of people grow them. Not all, however, appreciate the story behind different varieties like Bill Best does. Coming from a farming family with roots in North Carolina, Best has a very colorful history that includes being a professor at a local college.

From growing up in Haywood County, NC, where his mother collected bean seeds, to raising his own heirloom crops in Berea, Kentucky, Best has spent years planting and harvesting numerous bean and tomato varieties and their seeds. In fact, he is growing some heirloom bean varieties from seed his mother collected. While operating Best Farms, however, he also had a career for 40 years as an administrator and professor at Berea College in Berea.

Despite the demands of his career as an educator, Best always had time to farm. And, although he focuses on the heirloom beans and tomatoes, he also grows heirloom okra and pumpkins as well as some field corn.

What has caught the attention of local chefs, though, are his heirloom tomatoes. The chefs are interested in these tomatoes because of their great flavor, he says. In fact, Best is currently growing heirloom tomato plants for a local restaurant. The plan of the restaurant, he says, is to grow its own tomatoes in an adjacent garden this summer. Now, Best says, chefs also are showing an interest in heirloom beans for much of the same reason.

In addition to selling to chefs, he also sells his fresh produce at a farmers market in Lexington, Kentucky. Of the tomato varieties he grows, the best sellers are the pinks of all varieties and German yellow tomatoes, which include Mammoth German Gold, Mr. Stripey, Pineapple, and many others. The German yellows, he says,

are characterized with red streaks and have a very sweet flavor.

Best also grows four unreleased commercial tomato varieties that he received from Randy Gardner, a professor of horticultural sciences at North Carolina State University. "One was a pink

Bill Best of Berea
Source: Sid Webb

plum tomato that is outstanding," he says. "I also tried a yellow pear tomato and it is the best yellow pear tomato I have ever seen." To please customers, Best also grows some hybrid varieties.

The heirloom tomatoes, however, are definitely

worth any extra trouble, he says. Last summer the heirlooms were bringing $3.50 a pound for wholesale and $7 for retail in Atlanta, Georgia.

In terms of the beans, though, he grows strictly the heirloom varieties. About 20 years ago, he gave up on commercial beans because he didn't want the "tough" gene added to the mix.

"The reason I don't grow any commercial beans

Michael Best of Berea sorts tomatoes at Lexington's Farmers Market
Source: Sid Webb

at all is that I don't want them to cross with my heirloom beans, which are known for flavor, texture, and nutrition," explains Best. "Commercial beans were genetically 'toughened' in order to withstand the rigors of machine harvest without breaking. The downside of this toughening process was that by the time a mature bean appeared in the pod, the hull was too tough to eat."

Because heirloom beans can't be harvested mechanically, they are harder to produce than other vegetables, says Best, but they are definitely a worthy cause. "A lot of hand labor is involved, but I think that is made up for in the price they command," he adds. Heirloom beans, especially the greasy varieties, typically bring from $2 to $2.50 per pound.

In the past, Best says heirloom beans were grown

in cornfields using cornstalks for supports and then later they were grown on poles, like a tepee. Now he uses trellises because they are more efficient.

"I can create a trellis in a 200 foot row with four rolls of twine on a dowel rod in about 20 minutes," he says. The tomatoes also are on trellises where Best uses tall stakes to create a "Florida weave."

This "weave," he says, is the most efficient way he's found to grow tomatoes, including the heirlooms. The Florida weave is a way of building a close fence on both sides of a row of tomatoes so the plants remain upright, he explains.

When asked how many acres he farms, Best says he prefers to think in number of plants rather than acres. He currently has about 8000 tomato plants and about 20,000 linear feet of heirloom beans. "I'll be covering about 5 acres with beans but the area isn't going to be thick because I need to accommodate my B7100 Kubota tractor," he says. "I do most of the work myself." The same situation applies with tomatoes. He has about two acres, but he wants to avoid crowding the plants.

Reprinted with permission by American Vegetable Grower magazine, June 2005. Direct comments or questions about this article to rogordon@meistermedia.com.

Well, go figure...

Greasy beans really aren't greasy

Many of the beans Bill Best grows were grown by Native Americans. In fact, he says some of the varieties are more than 500 years old, the evidence coming from campsites and burial areas. For example, he says cut-short beans have been in the area for hundreds of years. Cut-shorts don't have anything to do with the size of the bean but rather the configuration of the bean inside of the hull. These beans, with a high protein content, are squared off within the hull, and, like the name implies, they are "cut short," Best explains.

The term greasy bean, however, does have something to do with how the bean looks. A greasy bean doesn't have the fuzz like other beans and instead is slick in appearance. "The shine of such beans makes them appear greasy, hence the name greasy bean," Best adds.

2002 CENSUS OF AGRICULTURE UNITED STATES: Released June 3, 2004, by the National Agricultural Statistics Service (NASS), Agricultural Statistics Board, U.S. Department of Agriculture

Table 1. Kentucky Summary Highlights: 2002

Farms	number	86,541
Land in farms	acres	13,843,706
Average size of farm	acres	160
Median size of farm	acres	94
Estimated market value of land and buildings:		
Average per farm		$294,056
Average per acre		$1,824
Estimated market value of all machinery and		
Average per farm		$41,458
Farms by size:		
1 to 9 acres		5,342
10 to 49 acres		24,758
50 to 179 acres		36,628
180 to 499 acres		14,950
500 to 999 acres		3,175
1,000 acres or more		1,688
Total cropland	farms	80,927
	acres	8,412,354
Harvested cropland	farms	65,815
	acres	4,978,994
Irrigated land	farms	3,606
	acres	36,751
Market value of agricultural products sold		$3,080,080,000
Average per farm		$35,591
Crops		$1,110,209,000
Livestock, poultry, and their products		$1,969,871,000
Farms by value of sales:		
Less than $2,500		32,918
$2,500 to $4,999		11,778
$5,000 to $9,999		13,561
$10,000 to $24,999		13,154
$25,000 to $49,999		6,525
$50,000 to $99,999		3,486
$100,000 or more		5,119
Government payments	farms	22,825
		$94,053,000
Total income from farm-related sources, gross before taxes and expenses	farms	33,083
		$210,952,000
Total farm production expenses		$2,604,069,000
Average per farm		$30,073
Net cash farm income of operation	farms	86,591
		$847,511,000
Average per farm		$9,788

Table 1. Kentucky Summary Highlights: 2002 (cont'd)

Principal operator by primary occupation:		
Farming	number	46,939
Other	number	39,602
Principal operator by days worked off farm:		
Any	number	49,176
200 days or more	number	36,532
Livestock and poultry:		
Cattle and calves inventory	farms	47,447
	number	2,395,476
Beef cows	farms	40,234
	number	1,125,183
Milk cows	farms	2,939
	number	120,748
Cattle and calves sold	farms	40,429
	number	1,291,026
Hogs and pigs inventory	farms	1,254
	number	385,811
Hogs and pigs sold	farms	1,220
	number	986,704
Sheep and lambs inventory	farms	1,230
	number	27,443
Layers 20 weeks old and older inventory	farms	2,197
	number	4,343,328
Broilers and other meat-type chickens sold	farms	669
	number	271,176,998
Selected crops harvested:		
Corn for grain	farms	7,446
	acres	1,043,990
	bushels	108,721,040
Corn for silage or greenchop	farms	2,307
	acres	82,820
	tons	1,287,831
Wheat for grain, All	farms	2,145
	acres	318,856
	bushels	16,447,721
Winter wheat for grain	farms	2,145
	acres	318,856
	bushels	16,447,721
Spring wheat for grain	farms	-
	acres	-
	bushels	-

Note: Some data based on survey samples.
Source: http://www.nass.usda.gov/census/census02/volume1/us/index2.htm

FARMER'S MARKETS

NAME	COUNTY	CONTACT	PHONE
Adair County Farmers' Market	Adair County	David Herbst	(270) 384-2317
Allen County Farmers' Market	Allen County	Nina Jones	(270) 622-8029
Anderson County Farmers' Market	Anderson County	Dennis Cantrill	(502) 859-4845
Cave City Farmers' Market	Barren County	Patricia Switzer	(270) 786-4991
Bath County Farmers' Market	Bath County	Sandra Ellington	(606) 683-6316
Boone County Farmers' Market	Boone County	Jerry Brown	(859) 586-6101
Bourbon County Farmers' Market	Bourbon County	Pat Wasson	(859) 987-6614
Boyd County Farmers' Market	Boyd County	F. H. Bradley	(606) 324-4047
Boyle County Farmers' Market	Boyle County	Treina Miller	(859) 236-2631
Heart of Danville Farmers' Market	Boyle County	Julie Wagner	(859) 236-1909
Bracken County Farmers' Market	Bracken County	James Fields	(606) 735-3278
Breckinridge County Farmer's Market	Breckinridge County	Carol M Hinton	(270) 756-2182
Caldwell County Farmers' Market	Caldwell County	David Adams	(270) 365-3053
Downtown Saturday Market	Calloway County	Deana Wright	(270) 759-9474
Campbell County Farmers' Market	Campbell County	Vonnie Black	(859) 635-1390
Dayton Farmer's Market	Campbell County	Marvin Knobloch	(859) 491-1600
Riverview Farmers' Market	Carroll County	Jenny Urie	(502) 732-8410
Carter County Farmers' Market	Carter County	John Ruggles	(606) 474-6686
Bradford Square Farmers' Market	Christian County	Samantha Hancock	(270) 886-5434
Winchester - Clark County Farmers' Market	Clark County	Shella McCord	(859) 744-4860
Clay County Community Farmers' Market	Clay County	Jess Casada	(606) 598-2789
Marion Farmers' Market	Crittenden County	Rose Crider	(270) 965-5015
Owensboro Regional Farmers' Market, Inc.	Daviess County	Earl and Peggy Castlen	(270) 264-1681
Edmonson County Farmers' Market	Edmonson County	David Embrey	(270) 597-3628
Elliott County Farmers' Market	Elliott County	Ben Meredith	(606) 738-6440
Estill County Farmers' Market	Estill County	Esther McKinney	(606) 723-4106
Lexington Farmers' Market	Fayette County	John Garey	(859) 576-1063
Fleming County Farmers' Market	Fleming County	Darrell W. Doyle	(606) 784-0855
Franklin County Farmers' Market	Franklin County	Edie Greer	(502) 695-9035
Garrard County Farmers' Market	Garrard County	Kathy Simpson	(859) 792-3828
Dry Ridge Farmers' Market	Grant County	Jeff Nehring	(859) 824-0552
Grant County Farmers' Market	Grant County	Edna Whaley	(859) 428-1769
Greenup County Farmers' Market	Greenup County	Linda S. Hieneman	(606) 473-9881
Hancock County Farmers' Market	Hancock County	Pam McGee	(270) 314-5688
Hardin County Farmers' Market	Hardin County	Brenda Thomas	(270) 862-9509
Harlan County Farmers' Market	Harlan County	Jeremy Williams	(606) 573-4464
Harrison County Farmers' Market	Harrison County	Allyson Arthur	(859) 234-3521
Green River Area Farmers' Market	Henderson County *	George Warren	(270) 826-9531
Henry County Farmers' Market	Henry County	Maryellen Garrison	(502) 845-2811
Dawson Spring Main Street Market	Hopkins County	Emily Barbour	(270) 797-4248
Pennyrile Area Farmers' Market	Hopkins County	Lisa Miller	(270) 821-3435
Jackson County Farmers' Market	Jackson County	Juanitta Welborn	(606) 364-5482
Bardstown Road Farmers' Market	Jefferson County	Patrick Dennedy	(502) 477-8561
Jeffersontown Farmers' Market	Jefferson County	Barbara Carby	(502) 267-1674
Middletown Farmers' Market	Jefferson County	Ed Nelson	(502) 845-2117
Portland Shawnee Farmers' Market	Jefferson County	Cassia Herron	(502) 775-4041
Rowan Street Farmers' Market	Jefferson County	LaDonna Barrick	(502) 252-9305
Smoketown Shelby Farmers Market	Jefferson County	Cassia Herron	(502) 775-4041
The Temple Farmers Market	Jefferson County	Jack Benjamin	(502) 423-1818
Jessamine County Farmers' Market	Jessamine County	Mary E. Stevens	(859) 887-2797
Johnson Co. Farmer's Market	Johnson County	Brian Jeffers	(606) 789-8108
Northern Kentucky Regional Market	Kenton County	Patrick H. Baxter	(859) 431-1500
The Dixie Farmers' Market	Kenton County	Robert Yoder	(859) 342-7912
London/Laurel County Farmers' Market	Laurel County	Fred King	(606) 864-4167
Lawrence County Farmers' Market	Lawrence County	John E. Sparks	(606) 638-9495
Mountain Farmers' Market	Lee County	Neil Hoffman	(606) 593-6584
Lewis County Farmers' Market	Lewis County	Ruley S. Kegley	(606) 796-2987
Lincoln County Farmers' Market	Lincoln County	Andrea Miller	(606) 365-4118
Logan County Farmers' Market	Logan County	Chris Milam	(270) 726-6323
Lake Barkley Farmers' Market at Eddyville	Lyon County	Yolanda Sanderson	(270) 388-7013
Berea Farmers' Market	Madison County	Bill Best	(859) 986-3204
Madison County Farmers' Market	Madison County	Myra E. Isbell	(859) 624-9573
MERJ Clean & Green Farmers Market	Madison County	Jane Post	(859) 228-0062
Marion County Farmers' Market	Marion County	Kathryn A. Alford	(270) 699-9651
Martin County Farmers' Market	Martin County	Roger Mollett	(606) 298-7742
Mason County Farmers' Market	Mason County	Bill Peterson	(606) 564-6808
Paducah Downtown Farmers' Market	McCracken County	Carol Gault	(270) 444-8649
Calhoun Farmer's Market	McLean County	Alden McElwain	(270) 273-3854
Meade County Farmers' Market	Meade County	Kathy Packard	(270) 496-4218
Menifee County Farmers' Market	Menifee County	Charlene Smallwood	(606) 768-3724
Mercer County Farmers' Market	Mercer County	Tony Shirley	(859) 734-4378
Monroe County Farmers' Market	Monroe County	Kevin Lyons	(270) 487-5504
Montgomery County Farmers Market	Montgomery County	Gayle Arnold	(859) 498-1898
Morgan County Farmers' Market	Morgan County	Karen Wright	(606) 522-3756
Muhlenberg County Farmers' Market	Muhlenberg County	Dorothy Walker	(270) 338-5422
Bardstown Farmers' Market	Nelson County	Danielle Ballard	(502) 348-5947
Botland Food Co-op	Nelson County	Beverly Mardis	(502) 348-8976
Nicholas County Farmers' Market	Nicholas County	Kimberly Adams-Leger	(859) 289-2313
Discover Downtown LaGrange Farmers'	Oldham County	Keli Quinn	(502) 269-0126
Owen County Farm & Craft Market	Owen County	Frank Downing	(502) 484-9900
Pendleton County Farmers' Market	Pendleton County	Charley Herron	(859) 654-8670
Powell County Farmers' Market	Powell County	Mike Reed	(606) 663-6405
Pulaski Growers Association	Pulaski County	Twila VanHook	(606) 423-2939
Rockcastle Farmers' Market	Rockcastle County	Noah C. Campbell	(606) 256-4040
Rowan County Farmers' Market	Rowan County	Bob Marsh	(606) 784-5457
Russell County Farmers' Market	Russell County	Darrell Andrew	(270) 343-4475
Scott County Farmers' Market, Inc.	Scott County	Mark Reese	(502) 863-0989
Shelby County Farmers' Market	Shelby County	Wanda Bennett	(502) 829-9375
The Farmers Market Assoc. of Taylor	Taylor County	Cathy Bunnell	(270) 384-5412
Cadiz/Trigg County Farmers' Market	Trigg County	Carole Schafer	(270) 522-3269
Bowling Green Farmers Market	Warren County	Dorothy Richmond	(270) 782-8465
Southern Kentucky Regional Farmers' Market	Warren County	Paul Wiediger	(270) 749-4600
Washington County Farmers' Market	Washington County	Kathy Taylor	(859) 336-3810
Southeastern Ky Regional Farmers' Market	Whitley County	Bonnie Sigmon	(606) 864-4167
Wolfe County Farmers' Market	Wolfe County	Ted Johnson	(606) 668-3712
Woodford County Farmers' Market	Woodford County	John Wilhoit	(859) 873-6861

Photos Source: Sid Webb

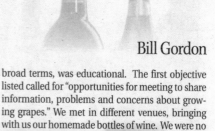

AGRICULTURE
Vineyards and Wineries

Bill Gordon

THE ROMANCE OF THE VINE:
The Beginnings of the Kentucky Vineyard Society

Like many other vintners across the state, I had fallen in love with the romance of the vine. Yet with few exceptions, vintners across the state were unaware of others who were growing grapes and making wine.

That was to change one fall day in 1980. Three people sat around a kitchen table at Colcord Winery in Paris. The owners, Carlton and Ann Colcord, chatted with Robert Miller, who had planted a vineyard in Richmond. During their conversation, Ann pointed out that a Swiss named Jean Jacques Dufour had planted grapes and created the Kentucky Vineyard Society in 1780. She suggested the Vineyard Society be re-established and that a newsletter be published to share and introduce information about grapes and wine.

Bob Miller became the key figure in bringing this idea to the public. The first organizational meeting was in April 1981 at the Colcord Winery. Seventeen grape growers from across the state walked in with great energy and curiosity, and the first official meeting of the Kentucky Vineyard Society occurred in May 1981.

The purpose of the Vineyard Society, in very broad terms, was educational. The first objective listed called for "opportunities for meeting to share information, problems and concerns about growing grapes." We met in different venues, bringing with us our homemade bottles of wine. We were no longer lonely vintners, but bound by friendship in a common endeavor.

The very serious business before us was the study of the survival of different species of grapes, as well as an understanding of the quality of the wine they made. Kentucky has a good climate, many diversified microclimates and many areas of good soil for grapes, but it has one predominant problem - extremes of temperature within a short period of time.

Different aspects of growing grapes were addressed by outside experts and by experienced members. And starting in 1982, Bob Miller and I, as president and vice president, worked hard with the legislature to amend the winery law to improve the situation for wineries to make and sell wine in Kentucky.

From that simple beginning, we have seen an explosion of interest. According to a recent count, Kentucky has 91 vineyards and the society lists 250 members. At present an estimated 40 wineries are producing and selling wine in Kentucky.

One of many fine Kentucky wines
Source: Sid Webb

AGRICULTURE

New Trends

Changes are taking place for tobacco producers because of the social and economic pressures from the markets, regulatory agencies and the health industry. Kentucky farm families, political leadership, agricultural organizations, and many others confront the question of how to best help farm families make the adjustment away from tobacco production in a way that allows them to capture the value of their assets, while adjusting to a sustainable, alternative asset base. Many producers are leading the way by having already made a successful effort to replace lost tobacco income. The Kentucky Department of Agriculture and the Governor's Office of Agricultural Policy are using a wide variety of resources to determine how to help Kentucky farmers build on the models of our agricultural leaders, maximize the value of their assets, and explore new opportunities in production and marketing of agricultural products. Here is a list of what's going on right now: **Kentucky's Near-Term Comprehensive Plan for Agricultural Development:** represents the first step in the planning process for Kentucky's agricultural future. Provides a blueprint for action in the near-term and lays the groundwork for the long-term plan; **Kentucky's Long-term Plan for Agricultural Development:** represents the cumulative efforts of hundreds of Kentuckians across the Commonwealth, including members of county agricultural development councils, many interested citizens and the Agricultural Development Board. The primary aim of this plan is to preserve and enhance the social fabric of rural Kentucky, while building a sustainable economic base rooted in local communities and local ecology. Plus, the Governor's Office of Agricultural Policy administers three advisory boards, each charged with addressing different issues related to the future of agriculture in Kentucky: **Governor's Commission on Family Farms** [advises the Governor on issues directly impacting the farm families of the Commonwealth. The commission is a 24 member board, comprised primarily of farmers.]; **Kentucky Agricultural Finance Corpo-**

ration: provides access to capital programs for agricultural diversification and infrastructure projects. This 12 member board consists of agriculture leaders, financial institution leaders, farmers, and political leaders.]; and **Kentucky Agriculture Resources Development Authority** [advises the governor and

**Cheese maker and dairy farmer,
Ken Mattingly, Jr.**
Source: Sid Webb

other state officials on economic development initiatives that will improve the farm economy in Kentucky. This 27 member board consists of agriculture leaders, commodity and industry representatives, farmers and political leaders.]

Besides aquaculture, here is what else Kentucky farmers are raising to make up for the loss in tobacco income (of course, some farmers have been doing these things for a while already): goats (goat meat, milk, gourmet goat cheese and ice cream); grapes (an acre of vineyard can produce five to six tons of grapes); bees (the state has purchased honey extractors that make honey easier to get to and use)...and there is more, like agritourism (visiting a working farm or any agricultural, horticultural, or agribusiness operation for the purpose of having fun, learning, or being actively involved in farming activities).

For more information, visit http://www.kyagr.com/ or http://agpolicy.ky.gov/contact.shtml

Aquaculture in Kentucky

Dr. James H. Tidwell

Aquaculture is a growing alternative farm enterprise to traditional crop and livestock production in Kentucky. Improved production methods will not only help diversify Kentucky farms but will also address the U.S. trade deficit in seafood, which exceeds $7 billion annually.

Kentucky State University's Aquaculture Program aids and assists farmers by conducting research and providing education and information

Susan Harkins - Bubba Sue's Shrimp - with fresh water shrimp
Source: Sid Webb

regarding fish, shrimp and crayfish production, fish health, water quality, pond management and marketing. Researchers are currently conducting commercial-scale-field-trials on paddlefish polycultured with catfish, hybrid striped bass, largemouth bass, and freshwater prawn. In addition, researchers and extension agents educate and disseminate new research information through many workshops and field days. In 1999 in order to support the growing aquaculture industry further, KSU began to offer a Masters of Science degree in Aquaculture to attract and train qualified personnel in the Commonwealth and the U.S.

In recent years commercial freshwater prawn production has grown dramatically in Kentucky and surrounding states. Since 1999, the number of Kentucky's commercial hatchery and four regional nurseries were operational in 2003. The total sales from freshwater shrimp production is projected to have reached approximately $850,000. Channel catfish production has also increased approximately 50 percent in western Kentucky as a result of the newly established processing plant operated by the Purchase Area Aquaculture Cooperative. Catfish production accounted for over $2 million in 2003. Rainbow trout production, which is limited by available spring water, remains stable and is projected to account for sales of approximately $1 million annually. In addition, largemouth bass are now being commercially produced in Kentucky (three growers), as well as several farmers growing paddlefish and hybrid striped bass as a result of efforts by KSU. Further, in 2002, the first group of Masters students graduated from KSU's Aquaculture Program.

In 1999 the Aquaculture Program was named KSU's Program of Distinction. This significantly increased the program's funding base. For more information, contact Dr. James H. Tidwell, KSU Coordinator of Aquaculture Programs, jtidwell@gwmail.kysu.edu.

y'know what?

Kentucky's goat population ranks sixth in the nation with 70,000 animals, according to a survey released earlier this year by the Kentucky Agricultural Statistics Service, a huge leap from 16,223 goats in 1997.

AGRICULTURE

Hemp

Gatewood Galbreath

Hemp is the name given to the *Cannabis sativa* plant when it is cultivated and used in its industrial and textile capacity. Hemp is as integral a part of Kentucky and its history as racehorses and bourbon. Hemp was Kentucky's first cash crop and was its largest cash crop for over 100 years (almost twice as long as tobacco held that distinction). Indeed, the Commonwealth was the world's largest hemp producer from 1810 until 1911.

The cannabis plant, also known as marijuana when cultivated for its medicinal and

SPREADING HEMP IN KENTUCKY.

intoxicating properties, has been a valuable commodity to mankind for thousands of years. Civilizations have depended on hemp to create sails and rigging for ships and cloth for clothing. During the War of 1812, Napoleon's ill-fated invasion of Russia was prompted by his need to cut off shipments of hemp to England. Without hemp Great Britain's formidable navy would have been rendered useless within three months.

In addition to canvas, ropes, thread and linens, hemp can also be used to make fine paper with a useful life of centuries. Interestingly, the Vatican continues to print its most important documents on hemp paper.

When the colonists landed on the shores of North America, hemp was such an integral part of survival that a law was passed compelling citizens to grow hemp as a crop, and they could pay their taxes with it. The first pioneers passing into Kentucky through the Cumberland Gap brought hemp seeds for planting in order to furnish their day-to-day needs and to barter with.

Hemp cultivation is labor-intensive, and turning it into finished products became a major industry in Kentucky. The seeds were a valuable source of oil for paints, lubricants, inks and medicinal balms. The seedcake remaining after the oil was derived was a valuable food for humans and animals and today it is prized as birdseed.

Kentucky remained the world's largest producer of hemp until 1911, when it lost ground to cheaper imports and synthetic products such as nylon. After a long period of vilification of the cannabis plant, Congress outlawed growing cannabis in the 1937 Marijuana Tax Act. The hemp market was destroyed.

Hemp enjoyed a rebirth in 1941, and Kentucky farmers' income rose when its cultivation was encouraged to produce goods for the war effort including oil for motor lubrication of high altitude aircraft. Farmers in a seven-state area were required to view a 14-minute film produced by the U.S. military entitled "Hemp for Victory". Moreover, hemp farmers were exempt from the draft. However, as the Allies regained access to major oil supplies in 1944, the hemp program was discontinued, and marijuana was maligned again as criminal.

Nevertheless, cannabis is a very useful plant. Hemp can be converted to a biofuel called methanol, which may one day be a viable fuel source, and it is becoming more widely accepted as a medicine, with 11 states now allowing its use by prescription.

Family Trends & Society

Harry Caudill (1922 – 1990), a long-time Whitesburg attorney and state legislator, was one of Kentucky's most beloved and influential writers. The following story is a selection from "Slender Is The Thread, Tales from a Country Law Office."

"It was the season of golden summer and by dint of much effort the physician-to-be had acquired enough money to buy himself a new suit, shirt, and hat from Sears, Roebuck and Company. He was very proud of all his splendor, but was most proud of his new high-top, black patent leather shoes. They were a perfect fit and when he got into his crisp, fresh attire, he felt mighty handsome. The cause of all this effort was a lissome, blond, blue-eyed girl whose father owned broad bottomlands amid his thousand or more hillside acres. Doc was 'struck on' the girl and intended to do something about it. He didn't know what, precisely, but he was strong-willed and inventive. He had met her only once, at a square dance a few weeks before, and being immediately smitten hastily expended all his small hoard on suitable garments. Unfortunately for his incubating schemes, the damsel's father had gotten wind of their chance meeting and the mutual interest they had shown in one another. He sternly forbade his daughter to see young Wright again because he was destitute and his people were notorious feudists. He planned to marry her in due time to someone with far better prospects. This, of course, only increased the young woman's interest in seeing the forbidden youth, and she managed to get a message to him that she would be spending the coming Saturday night at the home of a cousin. They met at the cousin's house, he in his impressive new garments and she so beautiful of face and form that he scarcely noticed what she wore." ...

Reprinted with permission, "Slender Is The Thread, Tales from a Country Law Office," by Harry M. Caudill, pages 90-91, University Press of Kentucky (Lexington: 1987).

Jeff & Elsie Dungan of Science Hill
Source: Sid Webb

FAMILY TRENDS & SOCIETY
Gender, Race and Ethnicity

Steven H. Jones

This essay focuses on the gender, race and ethnicity of the Kentucky population at the beginning of the 21st century. Gender followed by race represents some of the most salient features of cultural diversity of the state's residents. What follows is an overview of the major social and demographic trends for males, females, Caucasians, African Americans and Hispanics.

GENDER

The Kentucky population of 4,041,769 is composed of 51.1 percent females and 48.9 percent males. Males and females have

Family Reunion
Source: Sid Webb

roughly the same amount of education at the high school level: 82.9 percent of females have a high school diploma or higher; the comparable percentage for males is 82.6 percent. However, at the college level 22.8 percent of males have a bachelor's degree or higher, while the equivalent figure for females is only 19.9 percent. Kentucky ranks 49th in the U.S. for the number of women aged 25 and older with four or more years of college.

When the average yearly salary of men and women is compared (holding educational level constant for both groups), women in the Commonwealth earn only about 67 percent of the salary of men. As this suggests, women in the state are more poverty stricken than men – 15.6 percent of women live below the poverty line as compared to 11 percent of men. In 1999, 54.4 percent of women in Kentucky participated in the labor force. The most significant national comparison is that Kentucky ranks 40th in the nation for women's labor force participation, and it ranks 47th for women's overall employment and earnings. Many social scientists maintain that these disparities are primarily caused by institutional discrimination. Women in Kentucky, like their counterparts in the nation at large, do not enjoy the same access to economic and political resources that men enjoy.

Women in American society generally, and in Kentucky specifically, play an important role in preserving and enriching family life. Female-centered families represent an especially sensitive barometer of family and female well-being. An examination of the period between 1980 and 2000 indicates that two-parent families in the state decreased from 84 percent of the total number of families to 73 percent. Female-centered families climbed from 16 percent to 26 percent of the state total – a 63 percent increase. In 1999, 43 percent of female-headed families lived in poverty compared to only 18 percent of all families in the state.

RACE

The major categories based on race are composed of Caucasians and African Americans. In 2003 Caucasians formed 88 percent of the population, and African Americans constituted 8 percent. In order to encourage a general comparison of the Kentucky populace on the basis of gender, race and ethnicity, the socioeconomic categories listed below will generally mirror those presented in the section on gender.

African Americans in Kentucky numbered 305,820 in 2000. In 1990, 61.7 percent of African Americans over the age of 25 had a high school diploma; the comparable figure for Caucasians was 64.7 percent. In 2000, 80.5 percent of African Americans had a high school diploma, and the same figure for Caucasians was 83.3 percent. Differences between blacks and whites in educational attainment are greatest at the college level. In 1990, 25.4 percent of Caucasians over the age of 25 had a bachelor's degree; the comparable figure for African Americans was 14.8 percent. And in 2003, 29.8 percent of whites over age 25 had a bachelor's degree, while only 17.2 percent of blacks had an undergraduate degree.

The median household income for African Americans in 2000 was $22,080 in the Commonwealth, while the median household income for Caucasians was $35,600. The average household size for blacks was 2.44 persons; at the same time the average size of white households was 2.5. When the mean annual income and education level for black females and white females is compared in Kentucky, as income and education increase, the difference in income between the two groups becomes greater. White females earn approximately $2,000 more at the ninth-grade level, and they earn approximately $4,000 more at the doctorate degree level.

Family structure is a key variable in determining African American progress in the nation and the state. A high percentage of female-headed families for a group (especially a gender, racial or ethnic group) usually means elevated levels of poverty. While 22 percent of Caucasian families are headed by females, 63.7 percent of African American families are headed by females in Kentucky. An overwhelming percentage of the mother-centered families live below the poverty line. Thirty-one percent of the black population lives below the poverty level in the state of Kentucky.

African Americans in our state and in the nation face a health care crisis because they suffer from high rates of HIV/AIDS. In 2004 blacks in the U.S. were just under 14 percent of the total population, but they constituted nearly 40 percent of all AIDS

cases. By 2005 blacks represented over 50 percent of all AIDS cases in the country. Even though blacks are only about 8 percent of the population in the Commonwealth, they represent 30 percent of all the AIDS cases. There is a ray of hope – the black AIDS rate decreased from 39 percent of the total cases in the state in 1999 to 30 percent in 2004.

Source: Sid Webb

ETHNICITY

Hispanics numbered approximately 70,910 in 2003, representing 2 percent of the total population in the state. In 1990, 75.6 percent of Hispanics 25 years and older had a high school diploma; in 2000 this number plummeted to 46.5 percent. In 1990, 7.1 percent of Hispanics 25 years and older had a bachelor's degree, but this number had only increased to 7.7 percent by 2000. Thirty-three percent of Hispanics in Kentucky live below the poverty level.

CONCLUSION

As cultural diversity in Kentucky's population continues to evolve, one trend is striking – high rates of poverty afflict select diverse communities suffering from inadequate socioeconomic resources. There are differences of opinion about causes of this conundrum. Critics of the poor and their way of life and those who blame inefficient institutions agree on one issue: education must play a major role in any solution. Bold new education programs must target women and minorities.

FAMILY TRENDS & SOCIETY

Aging & Elder Care

A PERSONAL PERSPECTIVE —
ONE DAUGHTER'S STORY

There comes a time when the child becomes the parent…and the whole world tilts drastically when it happens. I have traveled a great distance, in time and emotion, since the day nine years ago when my mother could no longer stay by herself. She needed someone with skill to care for her 24 hours a day. The horrible reality was she couldn't stay with me

In the garden at Ashland Terrace, Lexington
Source: Ashland Terrace Retirement Home

— and circumstances starkly pointed to the dreaded realization most of us shun for as long as possible. I had to "put" my darling, precious mother in a nursing home.

I spent a lot of time thinking about the way we phrase that responsibility. Dishes are "put" away, books are "put" back on the shelf, the dog is "put" outside. I had to "put" my mother in a nursing home — why do we say it that way?

Avoidance is a wonderful game…and there are a myriad of tricks a child will play before they "put" their elderly loved one in a "facility." I sure pulled every one in the book when my time came.

The strength of my will — actually, my very sanity — was challenged as I tried to stop what had to be done. My friends (my chosen family) stuck with me as they have in every other gargantuan event in my

life. We made it through but it hurt so much.

My sweet mother's life followed a typical path: a productive and loving wife and mother; a widow living alone; a move from her home to a retirement home (lovely, lovely Ashland Terrace)…and then, the nursing home.

I am my mother's advocate and champion. To my deep despair, the nursing home I "put" my mother in was as awful and dismal as one can ever imagine. Not a day went by that I didn't cry — desperate for a way to change what could not be changed. The depth of my anguish was similar to the day my father passed from this earth…a day one has to experience to understand the emptiness that day brings.

Daily visits were essential, sometimes twice a day. It is true — the nursing home staff needs to see family — visiting, caring, talking. But I had to go because my mother was alone there.

The day came that my mother was accepted by another (highly recommended) home and, I cried then too.

We went to a home that was so different it made my head spin. Not that we haven't had our "issues," but as a good daughter I have learned which battles to fight (well…most of the time). A trailblazer in the complex world of Medicaid, Medicare and eligibility determinations, I serve as counselor to my friends. No…don't lose your mind because your mom didn't have on a bra today. No…don't call the police because her house shoes are missing. And (one of my better ones), No…no one has stolen your mom's false teeth.

After nine years I am a seasoned warrior in the world of "skilled nursing care." My parting words of advice: live the Serenity Prayer. And, be glad, no matter what happens, for the little things like brushing your dad's hair, or hanging a cheerful picture, or just sitting and holding your precious mother's hand.

FAMILY TRENDS & SOCIETY

Health Services

The **Kentucky Cabinet for Health and Family Services** and the **Department for Public Health** rely on local health departments to carry out two important functions for the state: core public health activities required by statute or regulation, and preventive services to specific populations mandated by budget appropriations.

The seven core functions are: enforcement of public health regulations; surveillance of public health; communicable disease control; public health education; public health policy development; reduction of risk to families and children; and disaster preparedness. Preventive services for specific populations include family planning, prenatal care, pediatric preventive check-ups, Women, Infants, and Children supplemental nutrition services (WIC), adult preventive services, and chronic disease monitoring and support services. Local health departments may provide additional services depending on the availability of alternative revenue sources. Examples of these services include home health services, physician based ambulatory primary care services, and expanded school health services.

William Hacker, Public Health Commissioner, serves as the **State Health Officer** for the Commonwealth. A role that continues to expand is the creation and management of anti-bioterrorism initiatives and coordination of emergency response capabilities with federal and other state agencies. The Commissioner's Office is responsible for the leadership, management, oversight, and policy direction of the Dept. for Public Health. The Commissioner advises the heads of major agencies in state government on policies, plans, and programs relating to matters of public health including actions necessary to respond to extraordinary events in order to safeguard the health of the citizens of the Commonwealth. The following is a list of primary offices located in the commissioner's office:

The **Chief Nurse for Public Health** provides professional consultation, support, and technical assistance to the commissioner and state and local health departments including approximately 1,000 nurses practicing in local health departments.

The **Epidemiology and Health Planning Program** assesses the occurrence of, and risk factors for, preventable and reportable diseases and injuries in the Commonwealth.

The **Adult and Child Health Improvement Program** promotes and improves the health status of all Kentuckians through early childhood development programs. Although improvements have been made in several areas, the overall health of Kentucky's citizens still ranks near the bottom nationally. focus.

The **Laboratory Services Program** provides essential examinations of clinical and environmental specimens required to support other state programs and local health department programs.

The **Public Health Protection and Safety Program** provides a variety of environmental services, from monitoring exposure to radiation to insuring sanitation of food, milk, and public facilities.

2005-2006 Budget
Health and Family Services Cabinet

GENERAL FUNDS

2005	$ 282,226,100
2006	$ 330,210,800

FEDERAL FUNDS

2005	$ 874,541,700
2006	$ 877,148,600

The Public Safety program conducts lead abatement activities, especially in areas occupied by children. The program investigates unsafe products and provides education on safety issues.

The Certificate of Need process ensures that the citizens of the Commonwealth will have safe, adequate and efficient medical care.

The **Dept. for Human Support Services** is made up of five separate divisions: Women's Physical and Mental Health, Aging Services, Family Resource and Youth Service Centers, Child Abuse and Domestic Violence Services and the Kentucky Commission on Community Volunteerism and Services.

The Kentucky Education Reform Act (KERA) of 1990 created the **Division of Family Resource and Youth Services Centers**. The primary goal of these centers is to enhance student ability to succeed in school by developing and sustaining partnerships that promote early learning and successful transition into school, academic achievement and well-being, and graduation and transition into adult life.

The **Office of Child Abuse and Domestic Violence Services** was established to address the need to increase the efficiency and accountability of state and community systems and other organizations that provide services to victims of child abuse, domestic violence and sexual assault.

Aging Services is responsible for aging issues on behalf of all older persons in Kentucky.

The **Office of Women's Physical and Mental Health** serves as a repository for data and information affecting women's health and mental health; analyzing and communicating trends in women's health issues and mental health; recommending data elements affecting women's health and mental health that should be collected, analyzed and reported; and administering a Women's Health Resource Center to focus on targeted preventive and comprehensive health education.

The Dept. for Disability Determination Services determines medical eligibility for residents who apply for Social Security and Supplemental Security Income disability benefits from the federal government.

The Dept. for Community Based Services is responsible for administering the following programs: Family Support (including Temporary Assistance to Needy Families (TANF), Food Stamps, Medicaid Eligibility,and State Supplementation), Child Support, Energy Assistance, Child Care, and Family and Community Based Services (including Family Based Services, Adult Services and Alternatives for Children). These programs benefit Kentuckians who, because of social, educational, mental, or physical impairments are without sufficient resources to meet their basic needs.

Temporary Assistance for Needy Families: Federal "block grants" are provided to states for Temporary Assistance for Needy Families (TANF). These federal funds support the program's administrative and benefit expenditures that include personnel, operating, and indirect costs; contracts with partnering agencies; cash assistance subsidies; supportive services; child care; and transportation.

The Kentucky Transitional Assistance Program (K-TAP) is the Commonwealth's cash assistance program for families with a dependent child who is deprived of parental support due to the continued absence, unemployment, incapacity, or death of one or both parents.

The Kentucky Works Program assists recipients with their transition into the workforce and attainment of self-sufficiency. Adults receiving K-TAP benefits must participate in this program amd develop a Transitional Assistance Agreement. *Source: For the full document, see 2004-2006 Budget of the Commonwealth, www.osbd.ky.gov.*

Receipt for the Jaundice.

TAKE about a pound of pigeons' dung, boil it in sweet milk, strain it, drink about half a pint of it every two or three hours; and in less than twelve hours it has been known to effect a cure.

For the bite of a Snake.

Tie up the wound with dry salt: it has been found very powerful in extracting the poison. Salt applied as above, is also an excellent remedy for the bite of a mad dog

Source: The Kentucky Almanac 1800, published by John Bradford, Lexington, Ky.

RECIPES.

To cure the Dysentary.

TAKE a large apple, pick out the core, and fill the cavity with honey-comb, (the honey being ſtrained out) cover it in hot aſhes till roaſted ſoft, then mix it together, and eat it all at once. It commonly gives eaſe in about half an hour.

For the Whooping Cough.

TAKE a ſmall handful of garlic, and throw it into a quantity of melted lard, perhaps half a pint, and after boiling it till the ſtrength of the garlick is got out, rub the ſoles of the child's feet every few hours.— The effects have ſometimes been aſtoniſhing.

For the Hydrophobia.

TAKE the leaves of rue, picked from the ſtalks and bruiſed—venice treacle or mithridate, and ſcrapings of pewter, each four ounces—boil all theſe over a ſlow ſire in two quarts of ale, till one pint is conſumed—keep it in a bottle cloſe ſtopped. Give of it nine ſpoonfuls, a little warm, to the perſon bit, ſeven mornings ſucceſſively, and ſix to a dog, to be given for nine days after the bite ; apply alſo ſome of the ingredients to the part bitten.

N. B. This recipe was taken out of Cathrop church, in Lincolnſhire, the whole town almoſt being bitten, and not one perſon that took this medicine but what was cured.

Note — until the late 1780s, American publishers practiced the English method of typesetting the letter "s" as an "f". Source: The Kentucky Almanac 1801, published by John Bradford, Lexington, Ky.

WAIT FOR ME
Chester Powell

If I'm not here when you come,
Wait for me; I won't be gone long…
I'm going into the woods away
to bring you back a present.

Do you remember the mossy bank
where we sat one day looking through
the trees to where the world ended?

Well, when I was there yesterday
I saw a small patch of Lady Slippers,
like children playing under the trees
with streaks of sunlight in their hair.

Oh, there now; I've given away my secret;
but I'm bringing one back just for you,
I'll lift it from the ground in its own
clump of dirt, a way of adding my love.

So, if I'm not here when you come,
wait for me; I won't be gone long…
I'm going into the woods away
to bring you back a present.

*Reprinted with permission
"Thanks for Coming By," Chester Powell,
Plum Lick Publishing (Paris, Ky.: 1997).*

FAMILY TRENDS & SOCIETY

Feuds

"The feuds of Eastern Kentucky have always been the stuff of legend and folklore, in part because there is so little substantial evidence on which the writer can depend. Courthouse fires have destroyed many records relating to the feuds. Much of the feud violence never reached the courts, as the feudists, whether distrusting the courts or dissatisfied with jury verdicts, preferred to settle matters themselves. In many cases all we have is word of mouth, handed down over the years like folk songs, with the facts bent to reflect the loyalties of the speaker. Probably for this reason, every tale, every account, every magazine article or newspaper story concerning a feud is invariably contrary to, in conflict with, or contradicted by another account. This applies as well to the recollections of the few surviving descendents of the feudists.

For that reason, I cannot claim that the accounts in this book are the truth, the whole truth, and nothing but the truth. They are as near to the truth as I can find. Generally speaking, the newspaper accounts of the time are almost always sensational and inaccurate. Magazine articles were worse. Courthouse records, when they are available, tend to be incomplete and confusing. Even some accounts of feuds written by reputable authors contain legend for which I can find no supporting evidence. One Book states that

the Clay County feuds erupted when Dr. Abner Baker called Daniel Bates' dog a cur. The French-Eversole War is said to have begun over a woman. They are good stories; it is always disappointing

Headstone of McCoy clan leader Randolf McCoy in a cemetery in Pikeville. Randolph was a leader in the famous Hatfield-McCoy feud
Source: Sid Webb

to find that they are not true.

In writing about the feuds, there is always a tendency to fall into stereotypes. The image of the bearded, one-gallus, barefoot mountaineer, sucking his corncob pipe, his jug of

Old photo of Hatfield family,
famous for feuding with the McCoy clan
Source: Sid Webb

moonshine on his shoulder and his trusty rifle ready to deal death to his neighbors, has for more than a century made the mountain people objects of ridicule and contempt. The feuds undoubtedly fed this stereotype. But for the most part the feudists were ordinary Americans, surging across the Appalachian Mountains in the aftermath of the Revolutionary War, in which many of them had fought, trying in a harsh, raw land to establish an acceptable society in which to live and rear families.

As in most frontier regions, few Kentucky mountaineers were of aristocratic background. Most Cumberland settlers were of English or Scotch-Irish descent, farmers or lower middle-class workmen, hoping to better themselves in a rich, new land. Inevitably some were, as author Harry Caudill has described them, the sweeping of the streets of London and Liverpool, or poor people who had earned their passage to America as indentured servants, "temporary slaves." As might be expected, such people were flinty, volatile mix. They had escaped the oppression of throne and aristocracy, had found a new way of life in a new land, and did not want anyone, including the law, to infringe upon rights they were willing to defend to the death. This made law enforcement difficult in an area where law was still vaguely defined, precariously established, and haphazardly enforced."

Reprinted with permission, Days of Darkness, The Feuds of Eastern Kentucky, John Ed Pearce, University Press of Kentucky (1994).

Another Story from Days of Darkness

"A rugged, scenic recess in the heart of the Cumberland Mountains of the Appalachian range, Clay County seemed doomed to trouble from its beginning. In the early days the rough terrain made road-building so difficult and costly that settlers could seldom manage more than rocky trails, though every able-bodied man was required to work on the roads or contribute to their construction. This lack of roads helped to isolate them from the mainstream of America as the tide of settlement swept westward, and made it hard to develop trade with the booming towns of Central Kentucky.

And Clay had wealth to trade. The wide, beautiful hills contained some of the finest virgin timber in the eastern United States — beech, oak, poplar, walnut, hickory, chestnut. Under the dark hills lay coal seams whose value had not been guessed. And along the banks of Goose and Sexton Creeks were wells that yielded water rich with salt, that mineral so precious on the frontier.

It was the salt wells that drew the earliest settlers into Clay County... The first settler who made salt there was James Collins, a long hunter who in 1775 tracked some animals to a large salt lick on what is now Collins Fork of Goose Creek, and the following year returned to stake a claim. Word of his discovery spread slowly...and the fledgling state of Kentucky considered the salt so valuable that it built the first road into the county to get the salt out. It was not much of a road, but a road.

Considering the isolation of Clay County and the difficulty of transportation, the salt industry grew fairly rapidly...By 1845 there were fifteen deep wells-some drilled to depths of a thousand feet-whose waters yielded a pound and a quarter of salt per gallon. With the accompanying furnaces, they were producing 250,000 bushels a year, and with salt selling for a dollar and half to tow dollars a bushel at the well, or as much as five dollars a bushel downriver, the producers soon became rich, influential men...

There was also abundant game in the dark, hollowed hills... It was an elk hunt, incidentally, that in 1806 triggered the first burst of bloodshed in the region in what became know as the Cattle Wars. In that year Clay County was formed. Manches-

ter, a rough village of about a hundred people, was chosen county seat, and plans were made to open roads west to London, south to Barbourville, and toward present-day Leslie, Owsley, and Breathitt Counties to the north. ...[h]unting was still a popular way to replenish the family larder, and in the early fall of 1806 a group of men living on the South Fork of the Kentucky River (now Clay County) went over to the Middle Fork (now Leslie and Perry Counties) to hunt elk. They found not only elk but, on an upland meadow above the river, a herd of cattle, apparently abandoned or left to graze by Middle or North Forkers. Adopting the convenient view that finders were keepers, they killed and dressed one cow for food and were driving the rest home when North Forkers appeared and took exception to their casual roundup. A gunfight ensued in which one man on each side was killed, several were wounded, and the South Forkers were obliged to retreat. But bitter resentment had been planted, gunfights between the two settlements continued for years, and until the Civil War, travel through the area was often risky business..."

Reprinted with permission, Days of Darkness, The Feuds of Eastern Kentucky, John Ed Pearce, University Press of Kentucky (Lexington, KY., 1994).

The Kentucky Feudist

James P. Webb - 1947

Ye ask why I'm a-settin' here, a-hidin'
    in the laurel,
A-gazin' with such eager look along this
    rifle barr'l?
Ye air a snoopin' furriner; I wants no
    truck with ye;
I'm settin' here a-sunnin' some, as any
    fool could see;
I'm waitin' fer a man to pass along the
    yander trace--
My rifle-gun's a-yearnin' just to see his
    ugly face.
Ye ask why we's a feudin with the family
    over yander?
As nigh as I kin make hit out, hit started
    'bout a gander.
But that air fifty year gone by, the gander he is dead,
And still the feudin' goes right on, a-pluggin' right ahead.
Why do I lay a-hidin' fer to shoot my
    feller' man?
I'm danged if I know. Stranger--tell me,
    if ye think ye can.

I only know that ary man, a-workin' like
    the malt,
What wouldn't do as I will do ain't wuth
    a pinch o' salt.
My Pap he kilt a man o' their'n, and now
    they've shot my Pap
Whilst he war settin' on a log a-takin'
    him a nap.
'The man Pap filled so full o' lead warn't
    rightly called a man---
He war a stinkin' polecat, like their hull
    bushwhackin' clan.
Thar ain't a one what's wuth his salt
    that I have ever saw,
And now I'm layin' fer the snake
    what up and shot my Paw;
So that's why I'm a-waitin' here, a-hidin'
    in the laurel,
Caressin' of my rifle-gun and sightin'
    down hits barr'l.
I dunno why I'm settin' here, and wants
    no truck with ye:
The reason down beneath hit all is more
    than I kin see.

ON TOLERATION.

DO always what you yourself think right, and let others enjoy the same privilege.— The latter is a duty you owe to your neighbour, the former as well as the latter are duties you owe to your Maker.

Receipt for the Jaundice.

TAKE about a pound of pigeons' dung, boil it in sweet milk, strain it, drink about half a pint of it every two or three hours; and in less than twelve hours it has been known to effect a cure.

DANIEL LAMBERT, *Aged Thirty-six Years.*

The astonishing weight of this man is fifty stone and upwards, being more than seven hundred pounds ; the surprising circumference of his body is three yards four inches : his leg, one yard and an inch ; and his height, five feet eleven inches : and though of this amazing size, entirely free from any corporeal defect.

Note — until the late 1780s, American publishers practiced the English method of typesetting the letter "s" as an "f." Sources: The Kentucky Almanac 1807, published by John Bradford, Lexington, Ky. and Johnson & Warner's Kentucky Almanac 1810, Lexington, Ky.

HEALTH & SCIENCE
Frontier Medicine & Nursing

Lisa Thompson

As early as 1750 a physician journeyed to the territory that was to become the Commonwealth of Kentucky. Thomas Walker, a doctor and land speculator from Albemarle, Va. led the first organized English expedition through Cumberland Gap into Kentucky.

In 1775 Dr. Frances Jane Coomes arrived in Kentucky and first practiced medicine at Harrod's Fort, she then moved to Bardstown, where she died in 1816. Dr. Coomes performed surgery and made medical compounds in addition to providing medical services. She was the first female doctor to practice in Kentucky.

In 1781 the turbulence of the times is evident in a report that a midwife, "the celebrated Mrs. Harper," was sent for, under armed guard, to McConnell's Station.

It was common for physicians to learn the healing arts through a combination of reading and studying with a mentor. However, with the establishment of Transylvania Medical School in 1799, Kentucky became the second state in the country to provide an opportunity for receiving a formal medical education. Many of the faculty at the time had obtained medical training in Europe.

In 1806 Dr. Walter Brashear performed the first successful amputation at the hip joint in the United States. The patient was a 17-year-old slave from Nelson County.

Dr. Ephraim McDowell performed the nation's first successful ovariotomy on a patient in Danville in 1809, long before the use of anesthesia during surgery.

In the 1840s two of the nation's most prominent medical schools were located in Kentucky: Transylvania Medical School, and Louisville Medical School. More medical training institutions would be established in the following decade, making Kentucky a leader in the training of medical practitioners before the Civil War.

In 1851 Dr. William Loftus Sutton instigated the formation of the State Medical Society. This was the beginning of formal collaboration in the medical community in Kentucky.

The following year, at the urging of the State Medical Society and Dr. Sutton in particular, Kentucky became the first state west of the Alleghenies to collect vital statistics about the population. The recording of birth and death rates would provide valuable information and

Dr. Mary Edwards Walker, U.S. Army surgeon, wearing her Medal of Honor
Source: Library of Congress

statistics, aiding in the prevention of disease and a more effective response to epidemics.

Dr. Mary Edwards Walker, the first female surgeon in the U.S. Army and one of two female Medal of Honor recipients, briefly practiced medicine in

Louisville in 1864-65 upon her release from a Confederate prison.

The State Board of Health was organized in 1878, establishing a governmental regulating agency which dealt chiefly with examining and licensing physicians. Among the board's functions was

Staff of Frontier Nursing in Hyden, June 26, 1928
Source: Kentucky Department of Libraries & Archives

determining which colleges and universities provided acceptable medical training. The board was also required to collect information on vital statistics and dispense information on hygiene and disease in an annual report.

The following year a physician, Dr. Luke Pryor Blackburn, was elected governor. Throughout his years of medical practice (which he resumed in 1883 upon leaving the governor's office), Gov. Blackburn was renowned for his role in the medical community's response to yellow fever.

In 1886 Kentucky's first nursing school was organized at Norton Memorial Infirmary in Louisville. Several more nursing educational institutions were established around this time in Kentucky. Over time training would focus on the medical practices of the nurse as a medical practitioner, rather than as an assistant to a physician.

The Louisville National Medical College was cre-

**Mary Breckinridge,
Frontier Nursing**
*Source: University of
Louisville*

ated for the education of blacks in 1888. Instrumental in establishing this institution was Dr. J. Henry Fitzbutler, one of the first African-American physicians to practice medicine in Kentucky.

In 1893 in an effort to eliminate medical quackery, the General Assembly passed an anti-empiricism law, requiring certification of physicians practicing in Kentucky. All practicing physicians were required to obtain a license from the State Board of Health by providing proof of medical training. In the absence of formal education, doctors were to provide proof of having begun practicing medicine prior to 1864.

In 1903 a law was passed by the General Assembly which required newly licensed physicians to pass a State Board exam, administered by the Board of Health.

In 1911 legislation was passed making it mandatory to record births and deaths. The Bureau of Vital Statistics was created at this time to administer the process and to compile statistical reports from the information gathered. Guidelines were created, making for a more consistent set of records, which became invaluable in analyzing medical occurrences.

Dr. Lillian South, a Kentucky physician who served as vice president of the American Medical Association in 1913, was instrumental in organizing a reserve corps of female physicians during World War I. She held the position of state bacteriologist on the State Board of Health for 40 years, which involved, among other duties, administering the public school inoculation program.

Further strides in Kentucky's healthcare came when Mary Carson Breckinridge founded the Frontier Nursing Service in 1925. The goal of this organization, based in Hyden, was to provide infant and maternal care in the mountains of southeastern Kentucky, thereby furthering the concept of professional midwifery.

Health Statistics

POPULATION DISTRIBUTION BY INSURANCE STATUS, STATE DATA 2002-03, U.S. 2003

	KY TOTAL	KY PERCENTAGE	US TOTAL	US PERCENTAGE
Employer	2,168,220	54%	156,270,570	54%
Individual	179,420	4%	13,593,990	5%
Medicaid	580,430	14%	38,352,430	13%
Medicare	563,640	14%	34,190,710	12%
Uninsured	560,970	14%	44,960,710	16%
Total	4,052,680	100%	287,368,410	100%

DISTRIBUTION OF PERSONAL HEALTH CARE EXPENDITURES BY SERVICE (in millions), FY2000

	KY TOTAL	KY PERCENTAGE	US TOTAL	US PERCENTAGE
Hospital Care	6,208	38.7%	413,131	36.4%
Physician & Other Professional Services	4,207	26.2%	328,983	29%
Drugs & Other Medical Nondurables	2,420	15.1%	151,926	13.4%
Nursing Home Care	1,383	8.6%	95,296	8.4%
Dental Services	587	3.7%	60,726	5.3%
Home Health Care	523	3.3%	31,616	2.8%
Medical Durables	184	1.1%	17,750	1.6%
Other Personal Health Care	514	3.2%	36,687	3.2%
Total	16,027	100%	1,136,115	100%

DISTRIBUTION OF MEDICAID SPENDING BY SERVICE, FY2003

	KY TOTAL	KY PERCENTAGE	US TOTAL	US PERCENTAGE
Acute Care	2,523,671,975	66.1%	155,517,818,840	58.3%
Long Term Care	1,126,692,215	29.5%	97,026,007,372	36.4%
Disproportionate Share Hospital Payments	168,464,730	4.4%	14,273,275,198	5.3%
Total	3,818,828,920	100%	266,817,101,410	100%

TOTAL SOCIAL SECURITY DISABILITY INSURANCE(SSDI) BENEFICIARIES AGES Ages 18-64 AS A PERCENT OF POPULATION (18-64), 2003

	KY PERCENTAGE	US PERCENTAGE
Total Beneficiaries	6.4%	3.6%

MEDICAID PAYMENTS PER ENROLLEE BY ENROLLMENT GROUP, FY2001

	KY TOTAL	US TOTAL
Children	1,683	1,315
Adults	2,635	1,736
Elderly	9,487	10,619
Blind and Disabled	7,654	10,642
Total	4,268	4,011

FEDERAL MEDICAID EXPENDITURES PER CAPITA, FY2004

	KY TOTAL	US TOTAL
Total Expenditures	$753	$627

CIGARETTE SMOKING RATE BY GENDER, 2002

	KY PERCENTAGE	US PERCENTAGE
Male	34.7 %	25.1 %
Female	30.3 %	20.0 %

RETAIL PRESCRIPTIONS FILLED PER CAPITA, 2003

	KY TOTAL	US TOTAL
No of Prescriptions	15.5	10.7

DISTRIBUTION OF NONELDERLY UNINSURED BY GENDER STATE DATA 2002-2003, U.S. 2003

	KY TOTAL	KY PERCENTAGE	US TOTAL	US PERCENTAGE
Female	277,690	50 %	21,001,460	47%
Male	282,270	50 %	23,672,840	53 %
Total	559,970	100 %	44,674,300	100 %

NUMBER OF BIRTHS PER 1,000 POPULATION BY RACE/ETHNICITY, 2002

	KY RATE / 1000	US RATE / 1000
White	12.8	11.7
Black	15.8	16.1
Hispanic	23.7	22.6
Asian/Pacific Islander	20.1	16.5
American Indian	9.9	13.8

RATE OF TEEN BIRTHS PER 1,000 POPULATION BY RACE/ETHNICITY, 2002

	KY RATE / 1000	US RATE / 1000
White	48.6	28.5
Black	69.9	68.3
Hispanic	91.8	83.4
Asian/Pacific Islander	26.2	18.3
American Indian	NSD	53.8

NUMBER OF DEATHS PER 100,000 POPULATION BY RACE/ETHNICITY, 2001

	KY RATE / 100,000	US RATE / 100,000
White	981	833.7
Black	1,154.5	1,099.2
Other	330.7	521.9

NUMBER OF DEATHS PER 100,000 POPULATION BY GENDER, 2001

	KY RATE / 100,000	US RATE / 100,000
Male	1,207.9	1,023.9
Female	825.7	719.9

Source: Kaiser Family Foundation , http://www.statehealthfacts.org

Clark's Kentucky Almanac 2006

HOSPITALS

CITY	HOSPITAL	COUNTY	PHONE	NO OF BEDS	OWNER
Albany	Clinton County Hospital	Clinton	(606) 387-6421	42	Clinton County Hospital, Inc.
Ashland	King's Daughters Medical Center	Boyd	(606) 327-4000	366	Ashland Hospital Corporation
Ashland	Our Lady of Bellefonte Hospital	Greenup	(606) 833-3333	194	Bon Secours Health System, Inc.
Barbourville	Knox County Hospital	Knox	(606) 546-4175	42	Knox County Fiscal Court
Bardstown	Flaget Memorial Hospital	Nelson	(502) 350-5000	40	Catholic Health Initiatives
Benton	Marshall County Hospital	Marshall	(270) 527-4800	46	Marshall County Fiscal Court
Berea	Berea Hospital	Madison	(859) 986-3151	48	Catholic Health Initiatives
Bowling Green	Commonwealth Regional Specialty Hospital	Warren	(270) 796-6200	28	Commonwealth Health Corporation
Bowling Green	Greenview Regional Hospital	Warren	(270) 793-1000	211	HCA - The Healthcare Company
Bowling Green	Rivendell Behavioral Health Services	Warren	(270) 843-1199	72	Universal Health Services
Bowling Green	Southern Kentucky Rehabilitation Hospital (SKY)	Warren	(270) 782-6900	60	Highmark Healthcare, LLC
Bowling Green	The Medical Center/Bowling Green	Warren	(270) 745-1000	330	Commonwealth Health Corporation
Burkesville	Cumberland County Hospital	Cumberland	(270) 864-2511	25	Cumberland County Fiscal Court
Cadiz	Trigg County Hospital Inc.	Trigg	(270) 522-3215	25	Trigg County Hospital, Inc.
Campbellsville	Taylor Regional Hospital	Taylor	(270) 465-3561	90	Taylor County Hospital District
Carlisle	Nicholas County Hospital	Nicholas	(859) 289-7181	18	Johnson Mathers Healthcare, Inc.
Carrollton	Carroll County Hospital	Carroll	(502) 732-4321	49	Associated Healthcare Systems Inc.
Columbia	Westlake Regional Hospital	Adair	(270) 384-4753	25	Adair County Hospital District
Corbin	Baptist Regional Medical Center	Whitley	(606) 528-1212	240	Baptist Healthcare System
Corbin	Oak Tree Hospital	Whitley	(606) 523-5150	25	Baptist Healthcare System
Covington	NorthKey Community Care	Kenton	(859) 578-3200	57	Northern Ky Mental Health/Mental Retardation Bd
Covington	St. Elizabeth Medical Center	Kenton	(859) 344-2000	621	Diocese of Covington
Cynthiana	Harrison Memorial Hospital	Harrison	(859) 234-2300	61	Harrison Memorial Hospital, Inc.
Danville	Ephraim McDowell Regional Medical Center	Boyle	(859) 239-1000	177	Ephraim McDowell Health, Inc.
Edgewood	HEALTHSOUTH Rehabilitation Hospital of Northern Kentucky	Kenton	(859) 341-2044	40	HealthSouth Corporation
Edgewood	St. Elizabeth Medical Center South	Kenton	(859) 344-2000	654	Diocese of Covington
Elizabethtown	Hardin Memorial Hospital	Hardin	(270) 737-1212	285	Hardin County Fiscal Court
Elizabethtown	HEALTHSOUTH Rehabilitation Hospital of Central Kentucky	Hardin	(270) 769-3100	40	HealthSouth Corporation
Flemingsburg	Fleming County Hospital	Fleming	(606) 849-5000	52	Fleming County Fiscal Court
Florence	Gateway Rehabilitation Hospital	Boone	(859) 426-2400	40	EPI Corporation
Florence	St. Luke Hospital West	Boone	(859) 962-5200	153	St. Luke Hospital, Inc.
Fort Thomas	St. Luke Hospital East	Campbell	(859) 572-3100	284	St. Luke Hospital, Inc.
Frankfort	Frankfort Regional Medical Center	Franklin	(502) 875-5240	173	HCA - The Healthcare Company
Franklin	The Medical Center at Franklin	Simpson	(270) 598-4800	25	Commonwealth Health Corporation
Fulton	Parkway Regional Hospital	Fulton	(270) 472-2522	70	Community Health Systems, Inc.
Georgetown	Georgetown Community Hospital	Scott	(502) 868-1100	75	LifePoint Hospitals, Inc.
Glasgow	T.J. Samson Community Hospital	Barren	(270) 651-4444	180	T.J. Samson Community Hospital, Inc.
Greensburg	Jane Todd Crawford Memorial Hospital	Green	(270) 932-4211	64	Green County Fiscal Court
Greenville	Muhlenberg Community Hospital	Muhlenberg	(270) 338-8000	90	Muhlenberg Community Hospital, Inc.
Hardinsburg	Breckinridge Memorial Hospital	Breckinridge	(270) 756-7000	27	Breckinridge County Buildings Commission
Harlan	Harlan Appalachian Regional Hospital	Harlan	(606) 573-8100	175	Appalachian Regional Healthcare
Harrodsburg	James B. Haggin Memorial Hospital	Mercer	(859) 734-5441	50	Community

HOSPITALS

CITY	HOSPITAL	COUNTY	PHONE	NO OF BEDS	OWNER
Hartford	Ohio County Hospital	Ohio	(270) 298-7411	68	Ohio County Fiscal Court
Hazard	ARH Regional Medical Center	Perry	(606) 439-6600	308	Appalachian Regional Healthcare
Henderson	Methodist Hospital	Henderson	(270) 827-7700	209	Community United Methodist Hospital
Hopkinsville	FHC Cumberland Hall	Christian	(270) 886-1919	58	First Hospital Corporation
Hopkinsville	Jennie Stuart Medical Center	Christian	(270) 887-0100	194	Jennie Stuart Medical Center, Inc.
Hopkinsville	Western State Hospital	Christian	(270) 886-4431	495	Commonwealth of Kentucky
Horse Cave	Caverna Memorial Hospital Inc.	Hart	(270) 786-2191	25	Caverna Memorial Hospital, Inc.
Hyden	Mary Breckinridge Healthcare, Inc.	Leslie	(606) 672-2901	40	Frontier Nursing Service, Inc.
Irvine	Marcum & Wallace Memorial Hospital	Estill	(606) 723-2115	25	Catholic Healthcare Partners, Cincinnati
Jackson	Kentucky River Medical Center	Breathitt	(606) 666-6000	55	Community Health Systems, Inc.
Jenkins	Jenkins Community Hospital	Letcher	(606) 832-2171	60	Gregory Johnson
LaGrange	Baptist Hospital Northeast	Oldham	(502) 222-5388	90	Baptist Healthcare System
Lebanon	Spring View Hospital	Marion	(270) 692-3161	65	Spring View Hospital, LLC
Leitchfield	Twin Lakes Regional Medical Center	Grayson	(270) 259-9400	75	Grayson County Hospital Foundation
Lexington	Cardinal Hill Rehabilitation Hospital	Fayette	(859) 254-5701	108	The Kentucky Easter Seal Society, Inc.
Lexington	Central Baptist Hospital	Fayette	(859) 260-6100	371	Baptist Healthcare System
Lexington	Eastern State Hospital	Fayette	(859) 246-7000	323	Commonwealth of Kentucky
Lexington	Ridge Behavioral Health System	Fayette	(859) 269-2325	110	Universal Health Services
Lexington	Samaritan Hospital	Fayette	(859) 226-7000	302	Associated Healthcare Systems Inc.
Lexington	Shriners Hospital for Children – Lexington	Fayette	(859) 268-5630	50	Shriners
Lexington	St. Joseph East	Fayette	(859) 967-5000	166	Catholic Health Initiatives
Lexington	St. Joseph Healthcarewww.sjhlex.org	Fayette	(859) 313-1000	468	Catholic Health Initiatives
Lexington	University of Kentucky Hospital	Fayette	(859) 323-5000	473	Commonwealth of Kentucky
Lexington	VA Medical Center – Lexington	Fayette	(859) 233-4511	285	Federal Government
London	Marymount Medical Center	Laurel	(606) 878-6520	76	Catholic Health Initiatives
Louisa	Three Rivers Medical Center	Lawrence	(606) 638-9451	90	Community Health Systems, Inc.
Louisville	Baptist Hospital East	Jefferson	(502) 897-8100	407	Baptist Healthcare System
Louisville	Caritas Medical Center	Jefferson	(502) 361-6000	331	Catholic Health Initiatives
Louisville	Central State Hospital	Jefferson	(502) 253-7060	192	Commonwealth of Kentucky
Louisville	Gateway Rehabilitation Hospital at Norton Healthcare Pavilion	Jefferson	(502) 315-8433	40	EPI Corporation
Louisville	Jewish Hospital	Jefferson	(502) 587-4011	442	Jewish Hospital HealthCare Services
Louisville	Kindred Hospital – Louisville	Jefferson	(502) 587-7001	337	Kindred, Inc.
Louisville	Kosair Children's Hospital	Jefferson	(502) 629-6000	255	Norton Hospitals, Inc.
Louisville	Norton Audubon Hospital	Jefferson	(502) 636-7111	432	Norton Hospitals, Inc.
Louisville	Norton Healthcarewww.nortonhealthcare.com	Jefferson	(502) 629-8000	737	Norton Hospitals, Inc.
Louisville	Norton Hospitalwww.nortonhealthcare.com	Jefferson	(502) 629-8000	972	Norton Hospitals, Inc.
Louisville	Norton Southwest Hospital	Jefferson	(502) 933-8100	127	Norton Hospitals, Inc.
Louisville	Norton Suburban Hospital	Jefferson	(502) 893-1000	343	Norton Hospitals, Inc.
Louisville	Ten Broeck Hospital – DuPont	Jefferson	(502) 896-0495	66	United Medical Corporation
Louisville	Ten Broeck Hospital – KMI	Jefferson	(502) 426-6380	82	United Medical Corporation
Louisville	University of Louisville Hospital	Jefferson	(502) 562-3000	404	Commonwealth of Kentucky
Louisville	VA Medical Center – Louisville	Jefferson	(502) 287-4000	114	Federal Government

HOSPITALS

CITY	HOSPITAL	COUNTY	PHONE	NO OF BEDS	OWNER
Madisonville	Regional Medical Center	Hopkins	(270) 825-5100	390	Trover Foundation
Manchester	Memorial Hospital Inc.	Clay	(606) 598-5104	63	Adventist Health System
Marion	Crittenden Health System	Crittenden	(270) 965-5281	50	Crittenden Health Systems
Martin	Our Lady of the Way Hospital	Floyd	(606) 285-5181	25	Catholic Health Initiatives
Mayfield	Jackson Purchase Medical Center	Graves	(270) 251-4100	107	LifePoint Hospitals, Inc.
Maysville	Meadowview Regional Medical Center	Mason	(606) 759-5311	111	LifePoint Hospitals, Inc.
McDowell	McDowell Appalachian Regional Hospital	Floyd	(606) 377-3400	50	Appalachian Regional Healthcare
Middlesboro	Middlesboro Appalachian Regional Hospital	Bell	(606) 242-1100	96	Appalachian Regional Healthcare
Monticello	Wayne County Hospital, Inc.	Wayne	(606) 348-9343	30	Wayne County Hospital, Inc.
Morehead	St. Claire Regional Medical Center	Rowan	(606) 783-6500	159	Sisters of Notre Dame
Morganfield	Methodist Hospital Union County	Union	(270) 389-5000	41	Community United Methodist Hospital
Mt. Sterling	Gateway Regional Health System	Montgomery	(859) 498-1220	64	Gateway Regional Health System
Mt. Vernon	Rockcastle Hospital Inc.rockcastlehospital.org	Rockcastle	(606) 256-2195	26	Rockcastle Hospital, Inc.
Murray	Murray-Calloway County Hospital	Calloway	(270) 762-1100	176	Murray Callaway Co. Public Hospital Corp.
Owensboro	Owensboro Medical Health System, Inc.	Daviess	(270) 688-2000	447	Owensboro Mercy Health System
Owensboro	River Valley Behavioral Health Hospital	Daviess	(270) 689-6500	80	Green River MH/MR Board
Owenton	New Horizons Health Systems, Inc.	Owen	(502) 484-2771	25	New Horizon Health System
Paducah	Lourdes	McCracken	(270) 444-2444	389	Catholic Healthcare Partners, Cincinnati
Paducah	Western Baptist Hospital	McCracken	(270) 575-2100	367	Baptist Healthcare System
Paintsville	Paul B. Hall Regional Medical Center	Johnson	(606) 789-3511	72	Health Management Association, Inc.
Paris	Bourbon Community Hospital	Bourbon	(859) 987-3600	58	LifePoint Hospitals, Inc.
Pikeville	Pikeville Medical Center	Pike	(606) 437-3500	261	Pikeville Medical Center, Inc.
Pineville	Pineville Community Hospital	Bell	(606) 337-3051	120	Pineville Community Hospital Assn., Inc.
Prestonsburg	Highlands Regional Medical Center	Floyd	(606) 886-8511	184	Consolidated Health Systems, Inc.
Princeton	Caldwell County Hospital	Caldwell	(270) 365-0300	48	Caldwell County Fiscal Court
Radcliff	Lincoln Trail Behavioral Health System	Hardin	(270) 351-9444	77	Southeastern Hospital Corporation
Richmond	Pattie A. Clay Regional Medical Center	Madison	(859) 623-3131	105	Pattie A. Clay Infirmary Association, Inc.
Russell Springs	Russell County Hospital	Russell	(270) 866-4141	45	Alliant Management Services, Inc.
Russellville	Logan Memorial Hospital	Logan	(270) 726-4011	92	LifePoint Hospitals, Inc.
Salem	Livingston Hospital and Healthcare Services	Livingston	(270) 988-2299	26	Livingston Hospital and Healthcare Services Inc.
Scottsville	The Medical Center/Scottsville	Allen	(270) 622-2800	47	Commonwealth Health Corporation
Shelbyville	Jewish Hospital - Shelbyville	Shelby	(502) 647-4000	70	Jewish Hospital HealthCare Services
Somerset	Lake Cumberland Regional Hospital	Pulaski	(606) 679-7441	222	LifePoint Hospitals, Inc.
South Williamson	Williamson Appalachian Regional Hospital	Pike	(606) 237-1700	123	Appalachian Regional Healthcare
Stanford	Fort Logan Hospital	Lincoln	(606) 365-2187	43	Fort Logan Hospital Foundation
Tompkinsville	Monroe County Medical Center	Monroe	(270) 487-9231	49	Monroe Medical Foundation, Inc.
Versailles	Bluegrass Community Hospital	Woodford	(859) 873-3111	25	LifePoint Hospitals, Inc.
West Liberty	Morgan County Appalachian Regional Hospital	Morgan	(606) 743-3186	30	Appalachian Regional Healthcare
Whitesburg	Whitesburg Appalachian Regional Hospital	Letcher	(606) 633-3500	90	Appalachian Regional Healthcare
Williamstown	St. Elizabeth Medical Center of Grant County	Grant	(859) 824-8240	30	Diocese of Covington
Winchester	Clark Regional Medical Center	Clark	(859) 745-3500	100	Clark Regional Medical Center, Inc.

Source: Kentucky Hospital Association, www.kyha.com

Clark's Kentucky Almanac 2006

HEALTH & SCIENCE
Alternative Medicine

Conventional medicine is medicine practiced by medical doctors (M.D.s) or doctors of osteopathy (D.O.s) and by allied health professionals, such as physical therapists, psychologists and registered nurses. Conventional medicine is considered to be practices that are approved by the politically dominant health system of a society in a given historical time period.

There are many terms used to describe approaches to health care that are outside the realm of conventional medicine as practiced in Kentucky and the U.S. Complementary therapies and alternative medicine, commonly referred to as CAM, focuses on maintaining a healthy lifestyle, treating illness and preventing disease. CAM embraces a holistic approach to wellness — addressing physical, emotional and spiritual needs through a variety of therapies and practices, many of which are centuries old. CAM is defined as a group of diverse medical and health care systems, practices and products that are not considered to be part of conventional medicine at present. CAM may lack biomedical explanations but, as they become better researched, some, such as physical therapy, diet and acupuncture, may become widely accepted. Therapies are termed as complementary when used in addition to conventional treatments and as alternative when used instead of conventional treatment.

Alternative therapies include, but are not limited to, the following disciplines: folk medicine, herbal medicine, homeopathy, faith healing, new age healing, chiropractic, acupuncture, naturopathy, massage and music therapy.

According to the Centers for Disease Control and Prevention's 2002 National Health Interview Survey, 36 percent of U.S. adults aged 18 years and over use some form of CAM. When prayer, specifically for health reasons, is included in the definition of CAM, the number of U.S. adults using some form of CAM rises to 62 percent.

It is interesting to note that the practice of CAM extends to animals, including dogs, cats and horses. In this concept, "holistic" veterinary medicine goes beyond addressing the problem the animal is having and considers the whole horse. See also www.iseekhealth.com/animal and www.equestrian.org.

The University of Kentucky, Colleges of Medicine and Health Sciences, Complementary and Alternative Medicine is engaged in a project that seeks to integrate CAM knowledge and interdisciplinary care skills into existing curricula of the University of Kentucky's Department of Family Practice (College of Medicine) and the Department of Clinical Nutrition (College of Health Sciences), including medical and health professionals' education, residency training and continuing education. The project's aim is to enhance the development of critical thinking skills for learners and to develop CAM practitioners to teach and precept. See http://www.mc.uky.edu/com.

Richard and Hilda Rosenthal Center - Alternative Medicine (New York)

The Rosenthal Center research program has a broad spectrum of research methodologies and approaches, including survey research, clinical trials, basic science, ethnobotanical studies and information science research. The work to date has focused on women's health and aging, with an emphasis on botanical remedies from traditional systems of medicine. See http://www.rosenthal.hs.columbia.edu/.

The National Center for Complementary and Alternative Medicine is the federal government's lead agency for scientific research on CAM. It is one of the 27 institutes and centers that make up the National Institutes of Health (NIH). NCCAM is dedicated to exploring complementary and alternative healing practices and disseminating authoritative information to the public and professionals. See http://nccam.nih.gov/.

Kentucky Legislative Task Force on Complementary and Alternative Medicine, Report on Complementary and Alternative Medicine, 2000, See http://www.lrc.state.ky.us/lrcpubs/Rm491.pdf.

HEALTH & SCIENCE
Medical Trends
& Advances

James R. Bean, M.D.

The pace of change in medical care is fast and shows no sign of slowing. Three kinds of advances are driving the trend toward more effective medical care in prevention, diagnosis and treatment.

The first and most important factor is new scientific knowledge and technical innovation in medical treatment. Discoveries in molecular and genetic science, in pharmacology and drug research, and in minimally invasive surgery have all spawned new forms of treatment that render some therapies and procedures obsolete.

The international Human Genome Project, which aimed to map the entire human genome, completed its 13-year initial work in 2003. Current investigations look to correct genetic defects by using chemical carriers to deliver correct genes to cells in people with genetically faulty or absent genes. Conditions under investigation are heart disease, cancer, Parkinson's disease, Huntington's disease and cystic fibrosis.

The pace of drug development has led to the introduction of new forms of therapy for common conditions. For instance, the treatment of hypertension now includes many different classes of drugs, such as diuretics, beta-adrenergic blockers and others. Combinations of these compounds, along with single day dosing, have made treatment of hypertension more complicated but considerably more effective.

Minimally invasive procedures are being introduced in virtually every specialty of medicine. Current advances include stents that contain coatings of drugs to keep the artery from reclosing and brachytherapy, which uses radioactive isotopes to prevent the later buildup of excessive scar tissue in the artery.

The second advance driving profound change in medical care is new information technology. Patients can glean a wealth of information from the Internet on virtually every medical condition, and this has changed the relationship between doctor and patient. Hospitals and medical offices are steadily converting to electronic medical records,

with information now accessible from any PC with an Internet connection. Pharmacy prescribing via Internet is now possible, improving the accuracy of prescriptions, and eliminating lost prescriptions or illegible handwriting. Many radiology studies are recorded as digital images and transmitted by Internet or copied to a CD, eliminating the need for X-ray film.

The third advance in medical care is educational, administrative and political change. Many medical conditions are simply lifestyle choices and are preventable or correctable by changes in daily habits. For instance, heart attack, stroke, diabetes, gallbladder disease and colon cancer can be a direct result of obesity, which has become epidemic in the American and Kentucky populations. However, simple dietary change, weight loss

Source: Cathy Jamieson MSP

and regular exercise can eliminate future medical disease and in some cases may increase lifespan. Similarly, smoking causes emphysema, heart disease, strokes and lung cancer; secondhand smoke is known to have similar effects. Lexington passed the first Kentucky public smoking ban in 2003, Georgetown passed one in 2005 and Louisville is considering a similar ban. Though the regulation is controversial, the long-term effect in preventing smoking-related illness justifies the ban.

HEALTH & SCIENCE
Veteran's Affairs

OUR VETERANS

The Department of Veterans Affairs offers a variety of programs for the nation's 26 million veterans. In Kentucky, the VA spent more than $958 million in 2003 to serve about 366,000 veterans. Last year, 85,971 people received health care and 55,643 veterans and survivors received disability compensation or pension payments from VA in Kentucky. More than 5,930 veterans, reservists or survivors used GI Bill payments for their education, 32,978 owned homes with VA home loans and 643 were interred in Kentucky's seven national cemeteries.

Health Care: In Kentucky, VA operates major medical centers in Lexington and Louisville. The state's facilities offer health care including, primary, extended and specialty care, nuclear medicine, blind rehabilitation, cardiovascular surgery, urology, podiatry, post-traumatic stress disorder, substance abuse and numerous programs for the aging veteran. In fiscal year 2003, the Louisville medical center had 6,144 inpatient admissions and the Lexington medical center had 5,737 inpatient admissions.

Source: Department of Defense

The Lexington and Louisville medical centers use modern advances in pharmacology, surgery and medical technology that continue to shape national health care. VA operates outpatient clinics in Bowling Green, Fort Knox, Paducah, Shively and Somerset. The Lexington VA plans to open community-based clinics in Morehead and Hazard in 2005.

The Louisville VAMC and Ireland Army Community Hospital at Ft. Knox are developing an agreement to staff a mobilization and demobilization clinic that medically processes approximately 20,000 mobilized Reserve and National Guard soldiers returning to Ft. Knox each year. As of June 2004, a total of 174 Operation Enduring Freedom and Operation Iraqi Freedom veterans were treated at Louisville VAMC.

Geriatric Care: Long-term care is a critical issue for America's veterans. Approximately 38.5 percent of living veterans are at least 65 years, compared with 12.4 percent of the general population. In Kentucky, 29,112 veterans aged 65 and older received medical care in 2003. Both Lexington and Louisville medical centers offer a continuum of services, including adult day health care, hospice, home health care, palliative care, rehabilitation and extended care services.

Disabilities and Pensions: VA's Louisville Regional Office serves veterans and their survivors in Kentucky who are seeking VA financial benefits. In fiscal year 2003, the Louisville office processed 13,148 disability compensation claims. The total includes 4,256 veterans applying for the first time for disability compensation.

Homeless: Nearly 23 percent of homeless adults are veterans, and many more veterans who live in poverty are at risk of becoming homeless. VA is the only federal agency that provides substantial hands-on assistance directly to the homeless. Lexington and Louisville medical centers have extensive outreach and treatment programs for homeless veterans in need of mental health, substance abuse treatment and other long-term assistance.

Memorial Affairs: Most men and women who have been in the military, their dependent children and usually their spouses, are eligible for burial in a national cemetery. VA has seven national cemeteries in Kentucky. VA provided 6,617 headstones and markers for the graves of veterans in Kentucky.

Source: U.S. Department of Veterans Affairs, http://www.va.gov/. For additional state summaries see: http://www.va.gov/opa/fact/statesum/index.htm.

HEALTH & SCIENCE
Scientists &
Related Programs

Kentucky has several notable scientists who were born, lived or worked in Kentucky, including William Kelly, inventor of the "air-boiling" process of steel production; David Dale Owen, Kentucky's first state geologist in 1854 and regarded as the premier scientist of the Midwest; Curtis Gates Lloyd, a self-taught botanist of international renown; and John Uri Lloyd, chemist and novelist who promoted the use of plant extracts in treating patients and has been called the father of colloidal chemistry.

Space Shuttle Discovery at the International Space Station
Source: NASA

Robert Shepherd was the first Kentucky scientist elected to the National Academy of Sciences. He was a professor of plant pathology at the University of Kentucky's Tobacco and Health Institute.

George Speri Sperti, a Covington-born scientist and inventor, founded the Basic Science Research Laboratory at the University of Cincinnati, where he concentrated on cancer research. Mary Eugenia Wharton, author, botanist, geologist, educator, and activist was born in Jessamine County and discovered an unnamed species of dewberry in Montgomery County, Ky., which was named in her honor, Rubus Whartoniae.

One of Kentucky's most famous scientists is Story Musgrave (M.D.), a NASA astronaut. He was born Aug. 19, 1935, in Boston, Mass., but considers Lexington to be his hometown. He graduated from

Astronaut Story Musgrave M.D.
Source: NASA

St. Mark's School, Southborough, Mass., in 1953; received a bachelor of science degree in mathematics and statistics from Syracuse University in 1958; a master of business administration degree in operations analysis and computer programming from the University of California at Los Angeles in 1959; a bachelor of arts degree in chemistry from Marietta College in 1960; a doctorate in medicine from Columbia University in 1964; a master of science in physiology and biophysics from the University of Kentucky in 1966; and a master of arts in literature from the University of Houston in 1987.

Musgrave entered the U.S. Marine Corps in 1953, where he served as an aviation electrician, instrument technician, and as an aircraft crew chief while completing duty assignments in Korea, Japan, Hawaii, and aboard the carrier USS WASP in the Far East. He has flown 17,700 hours in 160 different types of civilian and military aircraft, including 7,500 hours in jet aircraft.

He is an accomplished parachutist, who has made more than 500 free falls – including more

clinical and scientific training as a part-time surgeon at the Denver General Hospital and as a part-time professor of physiology and biophysics at the University of Kentucky Medical Center.

Dr. Musgrave was selected as a scientist-astronaut by NASA in August 1967. He completed astronaut academic training and then worked on the design and development of the Skylab Program. He was the backup science-pilot for the first Skylab mission, and was a CAPCOM for the second and third Skylab missions. Dr. Musgrave participated in the design and development of all Space Shuttle extravehicular activity equipment including spacesuits, life support systems, airlocks, and manned maneuvering units. Dr. Musgrave first flew on STS-6, which launched from the Kennedy Space Center, Florida, on April 4, 1983, and landed

International Space Station
Source: NASA

than 100 experimental free-fall descents involved with the study of human aerodynamics. He served a surgical internship at the University of Kentucky Medical Center in Lexington from 1964 to 1965, and continued there as a U. S. Air Force post-doctoral fellow (1965-1966), working in aerospace medicine and physiology, and as a National Heart Institute post-doctoral fellow (1966-1967), teaching and doing research in cardiovascular and exercise physiology. From 1967 to 1989, he continued

at Edwards Air Force Base, California, on April 9, 1983. During this maiden voyage of Space Shuttle *Challenger*, the crew performed the first Shuttle deployment of an IUS/TDRS satellite, and Musgrave and Don Peterson conducted the first Space Shuttle extravehicular activity (EVA) to test the new space suits and construction and repair devices and procedures.

On STS-51F/Spacelab-2, the crew aboard *Challenger* launched from the Kennedy Space Center,

Florida, on July 29, 1985, and landed at Edwards Air Force Base, California, on August 6, 1985. This flight was the first pallet-only Spacelab mission, and the first mission to operate the Spacelab Instrument Pointing System (IPS).

On STS-33, he served aboard the Space Shuttle *Discovery*, which launched at night from the Kennedy Space Center, Florida, on November 22, 1989. This classified mission operated payloads for the Department of Defense. Following 79 orbits, the mission concluded on November 27, 1989.

STS-44 mission on Nov. 24, 1991 was accomplished with the successful deployment of a Defense Support Program (DSP) satellite with an Inertial Upper Stage (IUS) rocket booster. In addition, the crew also conducted two Military Man in Space Experiments, three radiation-monitoring experiments, and numerous medical tests to support longer duration Shuttle flights.

STS-61 was the first Hubble Space Telescope (HST) servicing and repair mission. Launched on Dec. 2, 1993, the *Endeavour* rendezvoused with and captured the HST. During this 11-day flight, the HST was restored to its full capabilities through the work of two pairs of astronauts during a record 5 spacewalks. Dr. Musgrave performed 3 of these spacewalks and traveled 4,433,772 miles in 163 orbits of the Earth.

On STS-80 (November 19 to December 7, 1996), the crew aboard Space Shuttle *Columbia* deployed and retrieved the Wake Shield Facility (WSF) and the Orbiting Retrievable Far and Extreme Ultraviolet Spectrometer (ORFEUS) satellites. The free-flying WSF created a super vacuum in its wake in which to grow thin film wafers for use in semiconductors and the electronics industry.

For more information, access these science related programs in Kentucky:

The Kentucky Science and Technology Corporation, established in 1987, is a nonprofit corporation committed to the advancement of science, technology and innovative economic development founded on Kentucky know-how. KSTC is a fast-paced leader with a reputation for developing and managing creative initiatives in education, economic competitiveness and scientific research. KSTC is an entrepreneurial company dedicated to enhancing the capacity of people, companies and organizations to develop and apply science and technology and compete responsibly in the global marketplace. See http://www.kstc.com/.

The Kentucky Academy of Science was founded at the University of Kentucky in 1914 to improve scholarly communication among scientists in the Commonwealth. See http://kas.wku.edu/kas/.

Kentucky Science Olympiad is part of "The Science Olympiad," an international nonprofit organization with a primary purpose to increase student interest in science and to recognize outstanding achievement in science education for teachers and students. See http://www.jctc.kctcs.net/kso/.

The Kentucky Science Support Network (KSSN) is designed to provide classroom teachers in Kentucky a direct link to "experts" across the Commonwealth. Teachers can select an area of expertise and instantly generate a list of contacts willing to provide content information, consultation on research/projects, and/or suggestions. See http://oapd.kde.state.ky.us/kssn/.

Source: The Kentucky Encyclopedia, University Press of Kentucky (Lexington:1992) and NASA.

Well, what about that?

During his maiden voyage of Space Shuttle *Challenger*,
Dr. Story Musgrave and Astronaut Don Peterson
conducted the first Space Shuttle extravehicular activity
to test the new space suits and construction and
repair devices and procedures.
In 1993, Musgrave performed three space walks to repair
the Hubble Space Telescope. He traveled 4,433,722 miles
in 163 orbits of the Earth.

THE KENTUCKY ALMANACK ADVERTISEMENT PUBLISHED IN THE KENTUCKY GAZETTE JANUARY 10, 1809

Source: The Kentucky Gazette 1809, published by John Bradford, Lexington, Ky. Photo from Lexington Public Library and masthead from the Kentucky Gazette, Frankfort, published by Lowell Reese.

JUST PUBLISHED
By D. & C. BRADFORD,
And for sale at the Office of the Kentucky Gazette,
by the thousand, gross, dozen or single, the
KENTUCKY ALMANACK,
For the Year of our Lord 1809 ;

Containing, besides the usual Astronomical Calculations,

A Method of Making Cyder equal to Champaigne, and which will keep for years, and continue to improve.

A battle between a Tyger and an Alligator or wonderful instance of providential preservation.

Directions for Letter Writing.
Short Lessons.
Advice of a Father to his Son.
The Protest.
The Lottery.
Observations on Sun Flower Oil.
Cure for the Botts.
    for Corns on the Feet.
Court Days.
Officers of Government.
List of Roads.
A variety of Tables, &c. &c. &c.

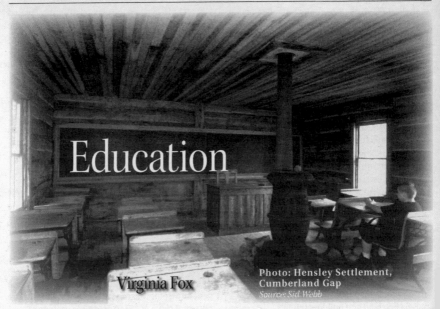

Education

Virginia Fox

Photo: Hensley Settlement,
Cumberland Gap
Source: Sid Webb

*i*t is tempting to look at where Kentucky is in its educational journey and feel as though we have not made much progress compared to other states. But those Kentuckians who were taught in one-room schoolhouses with a class ranging from first through eighth grades just a couple of generations ago can see the dramatic improvements that we have made.

When measured against where we have come from, the growth of our public school system is phenomenal. If the children in those rural counties were fortunate enough to have a one-room schoolhouse nearby, they did not have a yellow school bus to pick them up and transport them on paved roads or a teacher with a college degree or even a book for every student. Many of those things we take for granted now have come about in the last 60 years or so. In fact, the last operating one-room schoolhouse in Kentucky closed in 1989.

Kentucky has been near the bottom of the education ladder relative to other states for most of its history. The first private school in Kentucky was established in the mid-1770s even before the first Kentucky General Assembly was created, but few Kentucky children could attend. In fact, education was so insignificant to most early Kentucky leaders that the state's first two constitutions did not even address the subject.

It was not until 1838 that the first public school system was established in the state. Most Kentucky children could not attend classes regularly because they were poor and were needed at home to help their families, they lived in remote rural areas of the state that did not have a school or teacher, or they were not allowed to attend because of their color. Then, as now, we struggled with financing education, hiring and retaining qualified teachers, compensating teachers, providing adequate instructional materials and textbooks, as well as purchasing land and building schools.

Even more than a lack of funds, the biggest drawback was indifference and even opposition to public education in Kentucky. Many Kentuckians did not see a need for much education when they earned a living doing physical labor, and children were more valuable to their families when they were home planting and harvesting crops. Most people certainly did not want to pay taxes to support public schools or mandate attendance. For women and African-Americans, school was discouraged or forbidden. Education was not seen as practical for most Kentuckians, but fortunately that attitude has changed over the years.

When talk turns to sweeping education change in Kentucky, most people think of the Kentucky Education Reform Act of 1990. But there have been several ground-breaking pieces of legislation that have attempted to move the state forward, and every generation has had education prophets literally crying in the Kentucky wilderness for the state to develop accessible public education for all Kentuckians.

In 1838 the state's first superintendent, Joseph J. Bullock, was appointed and began gathering data on the rate of illiteracy in Kentucky (a problem that still plagues us today). Even though he showed the profound need for basic education, he did not receive the support necessary to develop a statewide public school system. In fact, many people opposed the idea of school as unnecessary and a waste of time.

Even in 1845 when the general assembly created a permanent office of superintendent of public education, a state board of education, and encouraged the creation of common schools in every county, there was no enforcement power on the local or state level to make these changes happen. However, this was a turning point. It was the first time that legislators had adopted an education provision in the Kentucky Constitution.

As early as 1821 there was movement toward establishing government funding of public education by way of a literary fund through a state bank called the Bank of Kentucky, but that venture failed. In 1837 the Kentucky legislature debated using surplus federal money from the sale of public lands to fund common schools, but that idea became embroiled in political bickering. The money that was designated for education was diverted for internal improvement when transportation issues became a priority of the legislature.

The people of Kentucky voted the first state property tax for public education in 1848 after the general assembly agreed to put it on the ballot. The tax was 2 cents per $100 of taxable property. These and other revolutionary school initiatives were lead by strong-willed Supt. Robert J. Breckinridge. Supt. Breckinridge organized The Friends of Public Education for a meeting in 1851 to make recommendations on curriculum, length of school, which was only three months a year at that time, and standard textbooks among other important issues.

Supt. Breckinridge felt the winds of change as the whole state was starting to organize a complete general education system. Many tens of thousands of the sons and daughters of the state have received, in these schools, the first elements of education; great multitudes of whom, but for these schools, would never have received any education at all. And perhaps more important than all, a public sentiment, and what is better and deeper, a public principle, fixed, general, and earnest has been begotten in the mind and settled in the heart of our people, that the work is a good work, that it can be done, and shall be done," he wrote. Finally, Breckinridge could see and feel that Kentuckians across the state were starting to support schools with their funds and truly to value education. Unfortunately, the Civil War destroyed much of the progress that Breckinridge and The Friends of Public Education made during those years.

It wasn't until education legislation was enacted in 1908 that Kentucky made school attendance mandatory in every county and required counties to organize high schools. At this point, there were fewer than 50 high schools with fewer than 5,000 students enrolled in the state. Two years earlier, the general assembly established two normal schools to train teachers, Eastern and Western, creating a systematic approach to properly preparing Kentucky teachers for the classroom.

However, equal funding of schools was not mandatory until a 1949 amendment addressed the inadequate funding of schools in poor counties, and even then equal funding did not materialize.

It was another 40 years before 66 Kentucky school districts, seven boards of trustees and 22 public school students demanded equal support of education for all students by suing the state. The case went all the way to the Kentucky Supreme Court where it ruled in 1989 that the entire system of elementary and secondary public schools was unconstitutional because the Kentucky general assembly was not providing an efficient system of public schools.

The resulting study by the general assembly and reform in 1990 was at least the fourth time that the state's legislature had proposed a detailed proposal for the establishment of significant changes of Kentucky's public education system since 1821.

Over the years, the Kentucky legislature has commissioned many studies on the need for education to move the state forward, but most of the time the reports have been disregarded with little or no action. Yet, even though change has been slow, progress is happening.

Anyone who doesn't believe that attitudes have changed toward education, should talk to the 73-year-old woman who grew up in a "holler" in Rockcastle County with a father who told her women didn't need an education as long as they could cook and change a diaper. She has made the best of an eighth-grade education and worked in physically demanding jobs to give her children the support she lacked as a child. While she did not have the opportunity to go to high school, she and her husband have made sure their children went and even put one daughter through college. In a mere generation, the attitude in this family changed from "Who needs an education?" to "School is a necessity."

Consider the African-American grandfather who can remember in the not-so-distant past when "separate but equal" schooling was the law in the U.S., but education for black children was not equivalent by any measure. It wasn't until the 1954

Freedom School in Freedom
Source: Sid Webb

U.S. Supreme Court decision of Brown vs. Board of Education that all children could be legally educated together. Now, for students of all races learning together is the norm, and it's hard for today's students to believe it was any other way.

There was another segment that had to fight to be educated—people with disabilities.

One Magoffin County native recalls that he was so nearsighted as a child that, even with glasses, he had to stand near the chalkboard to read it. When his mother asked for assistance from the superintendent in his school district, she was told to keep him at home and let him catch butterflies. Fortunately, his mother did not heed that advice and today he is a teacher and an artist. He is only 35 years old. It seems unbelievable that such an attitude toward children with disabilities was around as recently as 30 years ago, but the truth is that it still lingers in some areas today.

A separate school for children who were deaf or hearing impaired, called The Kentucky Asylum for the Tuition of the Deaf and Dumb, was created in 1822, and in 1842 The Kentucky Institute for the Blind was founded. For children with these disabilities, that was a huge leap forward because they would have received little, if any, formal education otherwise. Yet another leap came when all students with disabilities were included in the 1975 Education for All Handicapped Children Act, which effectively integrated children with disabilities into regular classes with other children. The federal law took time to be implemented, but by 1990 the renamed Individuals with Disabilities Education Act (IDEA) was making a difference in classrooms where children with disabilities were being educated, included in activities with their peer group and receiving the help they needed to succeed. Now, whenever possible, the regular classroom is the first option for children with disabilities, not the last.

As of the 2003-2004 school year, Kentucky had 176 school districts with 1,249 schools and more than 40,800 teachers instructing more than 653,000 students. In the school years around 1950, there were actually more school districts with 237 and more schools with 5,424 across the state with about 20,000 teachers. About 60 percent of those schools had only one teacher. The average teacher's salary was $2,350 compared to $40,849 in 2003-2004. The state education budget in 1950 was $49 million compared to $3.15 billion in 2004.

While Kentucky still has a long journey ahead in education, one recent report gave particular cause for hope: The average Kentucky composite score from the ACT college admission test rose to 20.4 compared to 20.9 for the nation in 2005. It followed three years of steady improvement. Maybe even *more* encouraging is that more high school students, about three-fourths of high school graduates, took the ACT this year, which means that they are at least considering higher education.

Recent developments in Kentucky education are geared toward accountability by testing children to accurately measure the progress of every school and student. In the near future, the state plans to track each child by computer from preschool to high school graduation and to use information on his progress to find out where help is needed. Computer technology will help teachers more quickly analyze test scores so they can detect areas where a child needs extra attention. It will help educators find out what teaching methods are successful before children go to the next level.

Kentucky's education history is both rich and complex. Understanding where we've come from can offer very useful insights on our promising educational future.

y'know what...?

"To me the sole hope of human salvation lies in teaching."

- George Bernard Shaw

The Kentucky Education Professional Standards Board was established as part of the 1990 Kentucky Education Reform Act to oversee the education profession. EPSB is the standards and accreditation agency for Kentucky teachers and administrators, and for programs of education at Kentucky colleges and universities. The board is charged with establishing standards of performance both for preparation programs and practitioners.

(Source: Ky. Education Professional Standards Board, www.kyepsb.net/)

EDUCATION

KET

O. Leonard Press

The decade of the 1950s was a period of educational ferment. There was growing acknowledgment of the woeful inequities and inadequacies in American education. State and federal governments undertook major corrective actions. In Kentucky, the Minimum Foundation Program, an attempt to equalize school funding, was passed in 1954. The same year, the U.S. Supreme Court declared the doctrine of "separate but equal" unconstitutional. Two years later, Kentucky's Day Law, compelling segregation in higher education, was declared unconstitutional by Kentucky's highest court.

Around the country, especially in the South where educational deficiencies were greatest and, consequently, the pressure for out-of-the box progress most pressing, the new technology of television was tried and proved promising.

Gov. Bert Combs signs bill authorizing Kentucky Educational Television.

Kentucky Governor Bert T. Combs at desk, Len Press at far right, (L to R) Bill Small, WHAS News Director; Ron Stewart, WBKY Chief Engineer; Harry King Lowman, Speaker of the House; Townes Ray, Majority Leader of the House; Wendell Butler, Superintendent of Public Instruction.

Source: UK Radio Photographic Collection

It was against this backdrop that the plan for a statewide Kentucky educational television network, first drafted at the University of Kentucky's Radio-TV Department in 1958, took shape.

The Kentucky Educational Television Network (KET) grew out of the zeal of thousands of co-founders, citizens at all levels of influence from the schoolhouse to the state house, who promoted the idea with their legislators, with teachers and school administrators, and with a succession of governors. Finally, on September 23, 1968, ten years after conception, a string of TV transmitters from Murray to Ashland went on the air as the largest state educational TV network in the nation.

From the beginning, KET's primary mission was to provide educational enhancement for every child and every adult in the Commonwealth, no matter how rural or remote their schools and homes.

Early on, KET gained national recognition for outstanding production. Its GED series "GED ON TV" has enrolled more than 1.25 million adults throughout the nation since it was released in 1974. More than 120,000 Kentucky adults have so far registered in KET's college courses broadcast in partnership with Kentucky's colleges and universities.

To encourage a more informed citizenry, KET offers every home a front-row seat in the chambers of state government. Further, it provides penetrating insight into current events through analyses, such as "Comment on Kentucky" with Al Smith and "Kentucky Tonight" with Bill Goodman.

A pioneer in the use of new age technology, KET created one of the first systems in the nation for interactive teaching by satellite and the only one that, at once, connected every school building in the state and all its universities and libraries. KET's multi-casting Star Channels serve curriculum needs for students in many other states as well as in Kentucky.

From its inception, KET has been institutionally mindful of a concern best expressed by Kentucky's late historian laureate, Dr. Thomas D. Clark. "It is highly frustrating," Dr. Clark said, "to see Kentuckians fail to live up to the potential of their land and place." With its world-class staff and its advanced technology, KET is an instrument of education and cultural enrichment designed to address that very concern, to help fulfill the historical promise of this, our "land and place."

O. Leonard Press is the founder of KET and was its executive director until his retirement in 1991.

EDUCATION

Home Schooling　　　　Jan Fletcher

Homeschooling is a tutorial method of education in which the parents retain direct responsibility for their children's education. It is the fastest growing educational movement in the U.S., and in Kentucky, too.

According to the National Center for Education, about 1.1 million students were homeschooled in the U.S. in the spring of 2003. The Kentucky Department of Education estimates 12,075 children were homeschooled in Kentucky in the school year 2003-2004.

Source: Sid Webb

Home education is based in the home, but children are also educated in museums, libraries, places of business, art centers, the seashore, the mountains, in backyards, in kitchens and even in cars. Home education allows a student to work at his or her own pace and learning is not limited to six hours a day.

Having a sincere desire to homeschool qualifies a parent to homeschool but homeschooling is a serious responsibility. Parents should be fully informed about both the benefits and responsibilities of homeschooling before making decisions about their child's education.

One of the benefits of homeschooling is better academic performance. According to Brian D. Ray, Ph.D., of the National Home Education Research Institute, in Salem, Ore., "In study after study, the home educated score better, on average, than those in conventional state-run schools."

Homeschooling parents are often asked about socialization. Many families have found that participation in a church, 4-H club, music or dance lessons, or scouts offers plenty of social opportunities for a child. Several homeschooling families can join together to share experiences, such as field trips.

In Kentucky homeschools are considered private schools. Kentucky compulsory attendance laws require that every child between the ages of 6 and 16 be enrolled in school. This requirement may be met by attending public school, private school (including homeschool), parochial school, or church regular day school.

Homeschooling parents must notify the local superintendent of schools by letter within the first two weeks of each school year of their intent to homeschool their children. The letter must include the names, ages and place of residence of each pupil in attendance at the school.

In an effort to clarify the Kentucky statutes for both homeschooling families and educational personnel who enforce compulsory attendance laws, two state homeschooling organizations, Kentucky Home Education Association and Christian Home Educators of Kentucky, met with the Kentucky Directors of Pupil Personnel in August 1997 and created *A Home School Information Packet and Best Practice Document*. This free document is available at www.khea.info, and will answer most questions about Kentucky homeschooling statutes. Home School Legal Defense Association also has information about Kentucky's statutes on the web at www.hslda.org.

Jan Fletcher, and her husband, Charles Fletcher, live in Columbia, Ky. They have homeschooled since 1992 and have five children. Their oldest child, Samuel, who was homeschooled since the second grade, graduated valedictorian from Campbellsville University in 2005. Kentucky Home Education Association is a non-sectarian organization open to all conscientious supporters of home education – without regard to race, color, creed or religion.

Prichard Committee for Academic Excellence

In 1985, 66 property-poor Kentucky school districts filed a lawsuit against the governor, legislature, superintendent of public schools and the state school board, alleging that state school funding was inadequate and inequitable. On June 9, 1989, the Kentucky Supreme Court upheld a ruling by the Franklin Circuit Court known as the Corns Ruling. This decision declared Kentucky's entire system of common schools to be unconstitutional on the basis of the Kentucky Constitution, Section 183. The court directed the Kentucky General Assembly to re-create a "substantially uniform" system of schools that provided each child with an equal opportunity to have an adequate education. On April 11, 1990, the Kentucky Education Reform Act of 1990 was signed into law. Each part of the law was designed to fit with the others in a comprehensive framework.

The Kentucky Education Reform Act of 1990 establishes student performance outcomes for all students and requires schools to help all students successfully meet them. This is the key provision of the legislation, and it is the basis for all other provisions.

Professional development funds have been increased to help teachers prepare for the changes in the law and learn how to better help students learn. To ensure students acquire the desired outcomes, the law holds educators accountable. Significant consequences, including monetary rewards and the possibility of dismissal, are established for educators. Since they face these significant consequences, educators are given the authority in school-based decision-making councils to determine how to help students learn. Parents are included on the school councils, since they also have an important stake in whether schools are successful.

New student performance assessments are used to determine if students are successful. These new assessments are performance-based; that is, they measure students' abilities to actually use the knowledge and skills they have gained rather than their ability to choose one of four possible answers in a paper and pencil test.

EDUCATION
KERA

Several other programs have been established to support the work of educators to help students learn. Preschool programs offer four-year-olds at risk of educational failure and three-year-olds and four-year-olds with disabilities an opportunity. Parents are an important part of this program.

The primary school program replaces grades kindergarten through third to allow students to progress at their own pace without the stigma of failure. Students move into fourth grade when they have mastered the skills they need to be successful in fourth grade.

Edward F. Prichard Jr., architect of education reform in Kentucky
Source: Lexington Herald-Leader

Extended School Services provides extra instructional time for students who need more time to meet specific performance goals. Help may be provided before or after school, on weekends or during summer.

Technology is used to help students learn and connect teachers and students to other resources in order to stimulate and improve learning. It is also used to collect information about school districts across the state.

Family Resource and Youth Services Centers provide students with access to needed services in schools where 20 percent or more students are on the free lunch program. Since students bring their family, social, emotional, economic and childcare needs to school, these centers help meet the non-academic needs of students and allow teachers and principles to focus on instruction.

New laws provided more money to schools in order to help students learn. Support Education Excellence in Kentucky is the new funding formula that ensures students a more equal opportunity for a high quality education no matter where they live.

Education by the numbers (Public Schools)

Number of school districts: 176
(20 female superintendents; 156 male; 1 minority)

Number of public schools: 1,249
(Does not include dependent districts Ft. Campbell and
Ft. Knox, alternative schools or the Kentucky School for
the Deaf and Kentucky School for the Blind)

Number of public schools by grade level:

> **Elementary** - 770
> **Middle** - 218
> **High** - 231
> **Preschool** - 26
> **9th Grade** - 1

Number of public school teachers
(full-time equivalent)...40,833.44

Number of public school students
(actual headcount of enrolled
students on the last day of
the school year) 653,248

Ethnicity of public school students
> **White** - 85.7%
> **African American** - 10.4%
> **Hispanic** - 1.6%
> **Asian** - less than 1%
> **Native American** - less than 1%
> **Other** - 1%

Number of employed certified staff,
minus teachers (full-time equivalent) 7,712.25

Average teacher salary $40,849

Number of classified staff (actual head count) 49,249

Average per-pupil current expense spending
(excludes debt service, facilities and fund transfers)
[2002-03]...$7,022

Total SEEK budget
[2004-05]..$2.027 billion

Total state education budget
[FY 2004]...$3.155 billion

Total federal education revenue
[2002-03]...$499 million

Total local education revenue
[2002-03]..$1.464 billion

Length of school year ....185 days
(includes 4 days of professional development;
4 holidays; 2 planning days)

Number of districts with alternative calendars 32
(Individual schools in Fayette and Jefferson Counties and
Ashland Independent also have alternative calendars.)

Number of local school board seats 882
(5 for each district; Jefferson County has 7 because of its size)

Gender breakdown of local school board members:

> **Male** - 574 (65%)
> **Female** - 278 (32%)
> **Not Reported** - 30 (3%)

Racial breakdown of local school board members:

> **White** - 812 (92%)
> **Non-White** - 34 (4%)
> **Not reported** - 36(4%)

State dropout rate
[2002-03]..3.31%

State retention rate
[2002-03] 3.39%

State attendance rate 94.31%
[2002-03]

State graduation rate...78.99%
[2002-03]

Percentage of high school graduates
attending college, vocational/technical
schools, entering the military, employed
or a combination of the above
[2002-03]..96.02%

Number of exceptional children ages 3-5 20,219
[as of December 2003]

Number of exceptional children ages 6-21
[as of December 2003]..83,564

Percentage of networked schools with Internet access 100%

Percentage of schools using e-mail 100%

Number of family resource/youth services centers 782
(399 family resource; 233 youth services; 150 combined)

Number of students served in extended
school services programs
(includes daytime and summer programs) [2002-03] 259,698

ESS grant monies provided to school districts................$32.9 million
[2002-03]

Number of homeschools 9,130

Number of homeschooled students 12,075

*All numbers are for the 2003-04 school year un-
less otherwise noted.*
*Source: Kentucky Department of Education,
http://www.education.ky.gov/; for national
statistics, visit the National Center for Education
Statistics, http://nces.ed.gov/.*

SCHOOL BOARDS

COUNTY	DISTRICT	SUPERINTENDENT	ADDRESS1	ADDRESS2	CITY	ZIP	PHONE	FAX
Adair	Adair County Schools	Darrell Treece	1204 Greensburg St		Columbia	42728	(270) 384-2476	(270) 384-5841
Allen	Allen County Schools	Larry Williams	238 Bowling Green Rd		Scottsville	42164	(270) 237-3181	(270) 237-3898
Anderson	Anderson County Schools	Kim Shaw	103 N Main St		Lawrenceburg	40342	(502) 839-3406	(502) 839-2501
Ballard	Ballard County Schools	Ed Adami	3465 Paducah Rd		Barlow	42024	(270) 665-8400	(270) 665-9844
Barren	Barren County Schools	Jerry Ralston	202 W Washington St		Glasgow	42141	(270) 651-3787	(270) 651-8636
Barren	Caverna Independent Schools	Samuel Dick		PO Box 240	Cave City	42127	(270) 773-2530	(270) 773-2524
Barren	Glasgow Independent Schools	Fred Carter	1108 Cleveland Ave		Glasgow	42142	(270) 651-6757	(270) 651-9791
Bath	Bath County Schools	Nancy Hutchinson	405 W Main St	PO Box 1239	Owingsville	40360	(606) 674-6314	(606) 674-2647
Bell	Bell County Schools	George W Thompson	211 Virginia Ave	PO Box 340	Pineville	40977	(606) 337-7051	(606) 337-1412
Bell	Middlesboro Independent Schools	Darryl Wilder	220 N 20th St		Middlesboro	40965	(606) 242-8800	(606) 242-8805
Bell	Pineville Independent Schools	Michael White	401 Virginia Ave	PO Box 959	Pineville	40977	(606) 337-5829	(606) 337-9983
Boone	Boone County Schools	Bryan Blavatt	8330 US Hwy 42		Florence	41042	(859) 283-1003	(859) 282-2376
Boone	Walton-Verona Independent Schools	Bill Boyle	16 School Rd		Walton	41094	(859) 485-4181	(859) 485-1810
Boone*	Covington Diocese	Lawrence Bowman	947 Donaldson Rd	PO Box 18548	Erlanger	41018	(859) 283-6230	(859) 283-6237
Bourbon	Bourbon County Schools	Lana Fryman	3343 Lexington Rd	PO Box 3000	Paris	40361	(859) 987-2180	(859) 987-2182
Bourbon	Paris Independent Schools	Janice Cox Blackburn	310 W 7th St		Paris	40361	(859) 987-2160	(859) 987-6749
Boyd	Ashland Independent Schools	Phil Eason	1420 Central Ave		Ashland	41101	(606) 327-2706	(606) 327-2705
Boyd	Boyd County Public Schools	Vacant	1104 Bob McCullough Dr		Ashland	41102	(606) 928-4141	(606) 928-4771
Boyd	Fairview Independent Schools	Bill Musick	2100 Main St		Ashland	41102	(606) 324-3877	(606) 324-2288
Boyle	Boyle County Schools	Steve Burkich	352 N Danville Bypass		Danville	40422	(859) 236-6634	(859) 236-8624
Boyle	Danville Independent Schools	Robert (Bob) E Rowland	152 E Martin Luther King Blvd		Danville	40422	(859) 238-1300	(859) 238-1330
Bracken	Augusta Independent Schools	John Cordle	207 Bracken St		Augusta	41002	(606) 756-2845	(606) 756-2149
Bracken	Bracken County Schools	Anthony Johnson	348 W Miami St		Brooksville	41004	(606) 735-2523	(606) 735-3640
Bracken*	Covington Diocese	Lawrence Bowman	947 Donaldson Rd	PO Box 18548	Erlanger	41018	(859) 283-6230	(859) 283-6237
Breathitt	Breathitt County Schools	Arch Turner	420 Court St		Jackson	41339	(606) 666-2491	(606) 666-2493
Breathitt	Jackson Independent Schools	Timothy Spencer	940 Highland Ave	PO Box 750	Jackson	41339	(606) 666-4979	(606) 666-4350
Breckinridge	Breckinridge County Schools	Evelyn Neely	86 Airport Rd	PO Box 148	Hardinsburg	40143	(270) 756-3000	(270) 756-6888
Breckinridge	Cloverport Independent Schools	James (J B) Skaggs	214 W Main St	PO Box 37	Cloverport	40111	(270) 788-3910	(270) 788-6290
Bullitt	Bullitt County Schools	Michael M Eberbaugh	1040 Hwy 44 E		Shepherdsville	40165	(502) 543-2271	(502) 543-3608
Butler	Butler County Schools	Larry Woods	203 N Tyler St	PO Box 339	Morgantown	42261	(270) 526-5624	(270) 526-5625
Caldwell	Caldwell County Schools	Carrell Boyd		PO Box 229	Princeton	42445	(270) 365-8000	(270) 365-5742
Calloway	Calloway County Schools	Steve Hoskins	2110 College Farm Rd	PO Box 800	Murray	42071	(270) 762-7300	(270) 762-7310
Campbell	Bellevue Independent Schools	Wayne Starnes	219 Center St		Bellevue	41073	(859) 261-2108	(859) 261-1708
Campbell	Campbell County Schools	Anthony Strong	101 Orchard Ln		Alexandria	41001	(859) 635-2173	(859) 448-2428
Campbell*	Covington Diocese	Lawrence Bowman	947 Donaldson Rd	PO Box 18548	Erlanger	41018	(859) 283-6230	(859) 283-6237
Campbell	Dayton Independent Schools	William Gary Rye	200 Clay St		Dayton	41074	(859) 491-6565	(859) 292-3995
Campbell	Fort Thomas Independent Schools	Larry Stinson	28 N Ft Thomas Ave		Ft Thomas	41075	(859) 781-3333	(859) 442-4015
Campbell	Newport Independent Schools	Michael Brandt	301 E 8th St		Newport	41071	(859) 292-3004	(859) 292-3073
Campbell	Silver Grove Independent Schools	Danny Montgomery	101 W 3rd St		Silver Grove	41085	(859) 441-3894	(859) 441-4299
Campbell	Southgate Independent Schools	Curtis Hall	6 William Blatt Ave		Southgate	41071	(859) 441-0743	(859) 441-6735
Carlisle	Carlisle County Schools	Danny Brown	RR 1 Box 237		Bardwell	42023	(270) 628-3800	(270) 628-5477
Carroll	Carroll County Schools	Carroll Yager	813 Hawkins St	PO Box 400	Carrollton	41008	(502) 732-7070	(502) 732-7073
Carter	Carter County Schools	Larry Prichard	228 S Carol Malone Blvd		Grayson	41143	(606) 474-7696	(606) 474-6125
Casey	Casey County Schools	Linda Hatter	1922 N US 127		Liberty	42539	(606) 787-6941	(606) 787-5231
Christian	Christian County Schools	Robert (Bob) Lovingood	200 Glass Ave	PO Box 609	Hopkinsville	42241	(270) 887-1302	(270) 887-1316
Christian	Fort Campbell Dependent Schools	Martha Brown	77 Texas Ave		Ft Campbell	42223	(270) 439-1927	(270) 439-3179
Clark	Clark County Schools	Robert E Lee	1600 W Lexington Ave		Winchester	40391	(859) 744-4545	(859) 745-3935
Clay	Clay County Schools	Douglas Adams	128 Richmond Rd		Manchester	40962	(606) 598-2168	(606) 599-7829
Clinton	Clinton County Schools	Mickey McFall	rt 4 Box 100 Hwy 127		Albany	42602	(606) 387-6480	(606) 387-5437
Crittenden	Crittenden County Schools	John W Belt	601 W Belt	PO Box 420	Marion	42064	(270) 965-3525	(270) 965-9064
Cumberland	Cumberland County Schools	John Hurt	810 N Main St		Burkesville	42717	(270) 864-3377	(270) 864-5803
Daviess	Daviess County Schools	Tom Shelton	1622 Southeastern Pkwy	PO Box 21510	Owensboro	42304	(270) 852-7000	(270) 852-7010
Daviess	Owensboro Diocese	Jim Mattingly	600 Locust St		Owensboro	42301	(270) 683-1545	(270) 683-6883
Daviess	Owensboro Independent Schools	Larry D Vick	1335 W 11th St	PO Box 249	Owensboro	42302	(270) 686-1000	(270) 684-5756

SCHOOL BOARDS

COUNTY	DISTRICT	SUPERINTENDENT	ADDRESS1	ADDRESS2	CITY	ZIP	PHONE	FAX
Edmonson	Edmonson County Schools	Patrick Waddell	100 Wildcat Way	PO Box 129	Brownsville	42210	(270) 597-2101	(270) 597-2103
Elliott	Elliott County Schools	John Williams	Main St Cthse Sq	PO Box 767	Sandy Hook	41171	(606) 738-8002	(606) 738-8050
Estill	Estill County Schools	Vacant	253 Main St	PO Box 930	Irvine	40336	(606) 723-2181	(606) 723-6029
Fayette	Fayette County Schools	Stu Silberman	701 E Main St		Lexington	40502	(859) 381-4104	(859) 381-4303
Fayette	Lexington Diocese	Bernadette McManigal	1310 W Main St		Lexington	40508	(859) 253-1993	(859) 254-6284
Fleming	Fleming County Schools	Kelley F Crain	211 W Water St		Flemingsburg	41041	(606) 845-5851	(606) 849-3158
Floyd	Floyd County Schools	Paul Fanning	106 N Front Ave		Prestonsburg	41653	(606) 886-2354	(606) 886-4532
Franklin	Frankfort Independent Schools	Judith M Lucarelli	309 Shelby St		Frankfort	40601	(502) 875-8661	(502) 875-8663
Franklin	Franklin County Schools	Monte Chance	916 E Main St		Frankfort	40601	(502) 695-6700	(502) 695-6708
Fulton	Fulton County Schools	Charles Holliday	2780 Moscow Ave		Hickman	42050	(270) 236-3923	(270) 236-2184
Fulton	Fulton Independent Schools	Dianne Owen	313 Main St		Fulton	42041	(270) 472-1553	(270) 472-6921
Gallatin	Gallatin County Schools	Dorothy Perkins	600 Main St		Warsaw	41095	(859) 567-2828	(859) 567-4528
Garrard	Garrard County Schools	Raymond Dean Woosley	322 W Maple Ave	PO Box 147	Lancaster	40444	(859) 792-3018	(859) 792-4733
Grant	Grant County Schools	Donald Martin	505 S Main St		Williamstown	41097	(859) 824-3323	(859) 824-3508
Grant	Williamstown Independent Schools	Charles Ed Wilson	300 Helton St		Williamstown	41097	(859) 824-7144	(859) 824-3237
Graves	Graves County Schools	Brady Link	2290 St Rt 121 N		Mayfield	42066	(270) 247-2656	(270) 328-1561
Graves	Mayfield Independent Schools	Lonnie Burgett	709 S 8th St		Mayfield	42066	(270) 247-3868	(270) 247-3854
Grayson	Grayson County Schools	Teddy White	909 Brandenburg Rd		Leitchfield	42755	(270) 259-4011	(270) 259-4756
Green	Green County Schools	Marshall Lowe	206 W Court St	PO Box 4009	Greensburg	42743	(270) 932-5231	(270) 932-3624
Greenup	Greenup County Schools	John Younce	8000 US 23 N		Greenup	41144	(606) 473-5830	(606) 473-5710
Greenup	Raceland-Worthington Independent Schools	John Stephens	600 Ram Blvd	PO Box 369	Raceland	41169	(606) 836-2144	(606) 833-5807
Greenup	Russell Independent Schools	Susan E Compton	409 Belfont St		Russell	41169	(606) 836-9679	(606) 836-2865
Hancock	Hancock County Schools	Mike Gray	83 St Rt 271 N		Hawesville	42348	(270) 927-6914	(270) 927-6916
Hardin	Elizabethtown Independent Schools	Gary French	219 Helm St		Elizabethtown	42701	(270) 765-6146	(270) 765-2158
Hardin	Fort Knox Community Schools	Michael Minutelli	Crittenberger Central Ofc	4553 Fayette Ave	Ft Knox	40121	(502) 624-2345	(502) 624-3969
Hardin	Hardin County Schools	Richard Hughes	65 W A Jenkins Rd		Elizabethtown	42701	(270) 769-8800	(270) 769-8888
Hardin	West Point Independent Schools	Charles Roberts	209 N 13th St	PO Box 367	West Point	40177	(502) 922-4617	(502) 922-9372
Harlan	Harlan County Schools	Timothy Saylor	251 Ball Park Rd		Harlan	40831	(606) 573-4330	(606) 573-8711
Harlan	Harlan Independent Schools	David Johnson	420 E Central St		Harlan	40831	(606) 573-8700	(606) 573-8711
Harrison*	Covington Diocese	Lawrence Bowman	947 Donaldson Rd	PO Box 18548	Erlanger	41018	(859) 283-6230	(859) 283-6237
Harrison	Harrison County Schools	Roy Woodward	324 Webster Ave		Cynthiana	41031	(859) 234-7110	(859) 234-8164
Hart	Hart County Schools	Ricky Line	511 W Union St		Munfordville	42765	(270) 524-2631	(270) 524-2634
Henderson	Henderson County Schools	Thomas Richey	1805 2nd St		Henderson	42420	(270) 831-5000	(270) 831-5009
Henry	Eminence Independent Schools	David Baird	114 S Penn Ave	PO Box 146	Eminence	40019	(502) 845-4788	(502) 845-2339
Henry	Henry County Schools	Tim Abrams	326 S Main St		New Castle	40050	(502) 845-8600	(502) 845-8601
Hickman	Hickman County Schools	Steve Bayko	416 Waterfield Dr		Clinton	42031	(270) 653-2341	(270) 653-6007
Hopkins	Dawson Springs Independent Schools	Alexis Seymore	118 E Arcadia Ave		Dawson Springs	42408	(270) 797-8698	(270) 797-5201
Hopkins	Hopkins County Schools	James L Stevens	320 S Seminary St		Madisonville	42431	(270) 825-6000	(270) 825-6062
Jackson	Jackson County Schools	Ralph Hoskins	Hwy 421	PO Box 217	McKee	40447	(606) 287-7181	(606) 287-4514
Jefferson	Anchorage Independent Schools	Larry R Harrison	11400 Ridge Rd		Anchorage	40223	(502) 245-8927	(502) 245-2124
Jefferson	Jefferson County Schools	Stephen Daeschner	Flaget Ctr	PO Box 34020	Louisville	40232	(502) 485-3251	(502) 485-3991
Jefferson	Louisville Diocese	Leisa Speer	1935 Lewiston Dr		Louisville	40216	(502) 448-8581	(502) 448-5518
Jessamine	Jessamine County Schools	Lu Young	871 Wilmore Rd		Nicholasville	40356	(859) 885-4179	(859) 887-4811
Johnson	Johnson County Schools	Orville L Hamilton	253 N Mayo Trl		Paintsville	41240	(606) 789-2530	(606) 789-2506
Johnson	Paintsville Independent Schools	Coy Samons	305 2nd St		Paintsville	41240	(606) 789-2654	(606) 789-7412
Kenton*	Beechwood Independent Schools	Fred Bassett	50 Beechwood Rd		Ft Mitchell	41017	(859) 331-3250	(859) 331-7528
Kenton*	Covington Diocese	Lawrence Bowman	947 Donaldson Rd	PO Box 18548	Erlanger	41018	(859) 283-6230	(859) 283-6237
Kenton	Covington Independent Schools	Jack Moreland	25 E 7th St		Covington	41011	(859) 392-1000	(859) 292-5916
Kenton	Erlanger-Elsmere Independent Schools	Michael Sander	500 Graves Ave		Erlanger	41018	(859) 727-2009	(859) 727-5653
Kenton	Kenton County Schools	Susan Cook	1055 Eaton Dr		Ft Wright	41017	(859) 344-8888	(859) 344-1531
Kenton	Ludlow Independent Schools	Elizabeth Grause	525 Elm St		Ludlow	41016	(859) 261-8210	(859) 291-6811
Knott	Knott County Schools	Harold Combs	140 School St	PO Box 869	Hindman	41822	(606) 785-3153	(606) 785-0800
Knox	Barbourville Independent Schools	Larry Warren	200 Daniel Boone Dr	PO Box 520	Barbourville	40906	(606) 546-3120	(606) 546-3452
Knox	Knox County Schools	Michael J Jones			Barbourville	40906	(606) 546-3157	(606) 546-2819

SCHOOL BOARDS

COUNTY	DISTRICT	SUPERINTENDENT	ADDRESS1	ADDRESS2	CITY	ZIP	PHONE	FAX
Larue	Larue County Schools	Sam Sanders	296 E Hwy 30	PO Box 39	Hodgenville	42748	(270) 358-4111	(270) 358-3053
Laurel	East Bernstadt Independent Schools	Homer Radford Jr		PO Box 128	East Bernstadt	40729	(606) 843-7373	(606) 843-6249
Laurel	Laurel County Schools	James Francis	275 S Laurel Rd		London	40744	(606) 862-4600	(606) 862-4609
Lawrence	Lawrence County Schools	Jeff May		PO Box 607	Louisa	41230	(606) 638-9671	(606) 638-0128
Lee	Lee County Schools	Frank Kincaid		PO Box 668	Beattyville	41311	(606) 464-5000	(606) 464-5009
Leslie	Leslie County Schools	Thomas Sizemore		PO Box 949	Hyden	41749	(606) 672-2397	(606) 672-4224
Letcher	Jenkins Independent Schools	John Shook	224 Park St	PO Box 74	Jenkins	41537	(606) 832-2183	(606) 832-2181
Letcher	Letcher County Schools	Anna C Craft	520 Plummer Ln	PO Box 768	Whitesburg	41858	(606) 633-4455	(606) 633-4724
Lewis	Lewis County Schools	Maurice Reeder		PO Box 159	Vanceburg	41179	(606) 796-2811	(606) 796-3081
Lincoln	Lincoln County Schools	Teresa T Wallace		PO Box 265	Stanford	40484	(606) 365-2124	(606) 365-1660
Livingston	Livingston County Schools	Jack Monroe		PO Box 219	Smithland	42081	(270) 928-2111	(270) 928-2112
Logan	Logan County Schools	Marshall Kemp	2222 Bowling Green Rd		Russellville	42276	(270) 726-2436	(270) 726-8892
Logan	Russellville Independent Schools	Vacant	355 S Summer St		Russellville	42276	(270) 726-8405	(270) 726-4036
Lyon	Lyon County Schools	Lee Gold	217 Jenkins Rd		Eddyville	42038	(270) 388-9715	(270) 388-4962
Madison	Berea Independent Schools	Gary Conkin	3 Pirate Pkwy		Berea	40403	(859) 986-8446	(859) 986-1839
Madison	Madison County Schools	Michael (Billy) Caudill	755 E Main St	PO Box 768	Richmond	40476	(859) 624-4500	(859) 624-4508
Magoffin	Magoffin County Schools	Donald Cecil	86 High School Rd	PO Box 109	Salyersville	41465	(606) 349-6117	(606) 349-3417
Marion	Marion County Schools	Roger L Marcum			Lebanon	40033	(270) 692-3721	(270) 692-1899
Marshall	Marshall County Schools	Steve Knight		PO Box 366	Benton	42025	(270) 527-8628	(270) 527-0804
Martin	Martin County Schools	Mark Blackburn		PO Box 18548	Inez	41224	(606) 298-3572	(606) 298-4427
Mason*	Covington Diocese	Lawrence Bowman	947 Donaldson Rd		Erlanger	41018	(859) 283-6230	(859) 283-6237
Mason	Mason County Schools	Timothy Moore	435 Berger Rd	PO Box 130	Maysville	41056	(606) 564-5563	(606) 564-5392
McCracken	McCracken County Schools	Randy J Greene	800 Caldwell St		Paducah	42003	(270) 538-4000	(270) 538-4001
McCracken	Paducah Independent Schools	Tim Heller	120 Raider Way	PO Box 2550	Paducah	42002	(270) 444-5600	(270) 444-5645
McCreary	McCreary County Schools	Ray Ball		PO Box 245	Stearns	42647	(606) 376-2591	(606) 376-5584
McLean	McLean County Schools	Earl Melloy		PO Box 337	Calhoun	42327	(270) 273-5257	(270) 273-5259
Meade	Meade County Schools	Mitch Crump		PO Box 110	Brandenburg	40108	(270) 422-7500	(270) 422-5494
Menifee	Menifee County Schools	Charles Mitchell		PO Box B	Frenchburg	40322	(606) 768-8002	(606) 768-8050
Mercer	Burgin Independent Schools	Richard Webb	140 Burgin/Danville Rd		Burgin	40310	(859) 748-4000	(859) 748-4010
Mercer	Harrodsburg Independent Schools	H M Snodgrass	371 E Lexington St		Harrodsburg	40330	(859) 734-8400	(859) 734-8404
Mercer	Mercer County Schools	Bruce Johnson	961 Moberly Rd		Harrodsburg	40330	(859) 734-4364	(859) 734-4852
Metcalfe	Metcalfe County Schools	Patricia Hurt	1007 W Stockton St		Edmonton	42129	(270) 432-3171	(270) 432-3170
Monroe	Monroe County Schools	George Wilson	309 Emberton St	PO Box 10	Tompkinsville	42167	(270) 487-5456	(270) 487-5571
Montgomery	Montgomery County Schools	Daniel Freeman	212 N Maysville Rd		Mt Sterling	40353	(859) 497-8760	(859) 497-8780
Morgan	Morgan County Schools	Joe Gold	460 Prestonsburg St	PO Box 489	West Liberty	41472	(606) 743-8002	(606) 743-8050
Muhlenberg	Muhlenberg County Schools	R Dale Todd	510 W Main St	PO Box 167	Greenville	42345	(270) 338-8800	(270) 338-0529
Nelson	Bardstown Independent Schools	Brent Holsclaw	308 N 5th St		Bardstown	40004	(502) 331-8800	(502) 331-8830
Nelson	Nelson County Schools	Janice Lantz	1200 Cardinal Dr	PO Box 2277	Bardstown	40004	(502) 349-7000	(502) 349-7004
Nicholas	Nicholas County Schools	Gregory Reid	395 W Main St		Carlisle	40311	(859) 289-3770	(859) 289-3777
Ohio	Ohio County Schools	Soretta Ralph	315 E Union St	PO Box 70	Hartford	42347	(270) 298-3249	(270) 298-3886
Oldham	Oldham County Schools	Paul Upchurch	1350 N Hwy 393	PO Box 218	Buckner	40010	(502) 222-8880	(502) 222-8885
Owen	Owen County Schools	Mark Cleveland	1600 Hwy 22 E		Owenton	40359	(502) 484-3934	(502) 484-9095
Owsley	Owsley County Schools	Stephen Jackson	Court & Main	PO Box 340	Booneville	41314	(606) 593-6363	(606) 593-6368
Pendleton	Pendleton County Schools	James Robert Yost	2525 Hwy 27 N		Falmouth	41040	(859) 654-6911	(859) 654-6143
Perry	Perry County Schools	John Amis	315 Park Ave	PO Box 3097	Hazard	41701	(606) 439-5814	(606) 439-2512
Pike	Pike County Schools	Frank Welch	401 N Mayo Trl		Pikeville	41502	(606) 433-9200	(606) 432-3321
Pike	Pikeville Independent Schools	Jerry Green	691 Breckinridge St	PO Box 430	Pikeville	41501	(606) 432-8161	(606) 432-2119
Powell	Powell County Schools	Lonnie Morris		PO Box 1055	Stanton	40380	(606) 663-3300	(606) 663-3303
Pulaski	Pulaski County Schools	Tim Eaton	501 University Dr		Somerset	42501	(606) 679-1123	(606) 679-1438
Pulaski	Science Hill Independent Schools	Rick Walker	6007 N Hwy 27	PO Box 108	Science Hill	42553	(606) 423-3341	(606) 423-3313
Pulaski	Somerset Independent Schools	Wilson Sears Jr	305 College St		Somerset	42501	(606) 679-4451	(606) 678-0864
Robertson	Robertson County Schools	Chuck Brown	110 Deming Hwy		Mt Olivet	41064	(606) 724-5431	(606) 724-5921
Rockcastle	Rockcastle County Schools	Larry Hammond	245 Richmond St		Mt Vernon	40456	(606) 256-2125	(606) 256-2126
Rowan	Rowan County Schools	Marvin Moore	121 E 2nd St		Morehead	40351	(606) 784-8928	(606) 783-1011

SCHOOL BOARDS

COUNTY	DISTRICT	SUPERINTENDENT	ADDRESS1	ADDRESS2	CITY	ZIP	PHONE	FAX
Russell	Russell County Schools	Scott Pierce	404 S Main St	PO Box 440	Jamestown	42629	(270) 343-3191	(270) 343-3072
Scott	Scott County Schools	Dallas Blankenship	2168 Frankfort Pk	PO Box 578	Georgetown	40324	(502) 863-3663	(502) 863-5367
Shelby	Shelby County Schools	Elaine Farris	403 Washington St	PO Box 159	Shelbyville	40066	(502) 633-2375	(502) 633-1988
Simpson	Simpson County Schools	Jim Flynn	430 S College St	PO Box 467	Franklin	42135	(270) 586-8877	(270) 586-2011
Spencer	Spencer County Schools	R Larry Holt	207 W Main St		Taylorsville	40071	(502) 477-3250	(502) 477-3259
Taylor	Campbellsville Independent Schools	Diana W Woods	136 S Columbia Ave		Campbellsville	42718	(270) 465-4162	(270) 465-3918
Taylor	Taylor County Schools	Gary Seaborne	1209 E Broadway St		Campbellsville	42718	(270) 465-5371	(270) 789-3954
Todd	Todd County Schools	David A Eakles	804 S Main St		Elkton	42220	(270) 265-2436	(270) 265-5414
Trigg	Trigg County Schools	Tim McGinnis	202 Main St		Cadiz	42211	(270) 522-6075	(270) 522-7782
Trimble	Trimble County Schools	Marcia Dunaway	68 Wentworth Ave	PO Box 275	Bedford	40006	(502) 255-3201	(502) 255-5105
Union	Union County Schools	Gerald L Novak	510 S Mart St		Morganfield	42437	(270) 389-1694	(270) 389-9806
Warren	Bowling Green Independent Schools	John C Settle	1211 Center St		Bowling Green	42101	(270) 746-2200	(270) 746-2205
Warren	Warren County Schools	E Dale Brown	303 Lover's Ln	PO Box 51810	Bowling Green	42102	(270) 781-5150	(270) 781-2392
Washington	Washington County Schools	Larry Graves	120 Mackville Hill Rd		Springfield	40069	(859) 336-5470	(859) 336-5480

Source: The Kentucky Directory Gold Book 2005-2006

The Covington Dioceses serves Boone, Bracken, Campbell, Harrison, Kenton and Mason counties

INDEPENDENT SCHOOL DISTRICTS

DISTRICT	COUNTY
Anchorage Independent Schools	Jefferson County
Ashland Independent Schools	Boyd County
Augusta Independent Schools	Bracken County
Barbourville Independent Schools	Knox County
Bardstown Independent Schools	Nelson County
Beechwood Independent Schools	Kenton County
Bellevue Independent Schools	Campbell County
Berea Independent Schools	Madison County
Bowling Green Independent Schools	Warren County
Burgin Independent Schools	Mercer County
Campbellsville Independent Schools	Taylor County
Caverna Independent Schools	Barren County
Cloverport Independent Schools	Breckinridge County
Corbin Independent Schools	Whitley County
Covington Independent Schools	Kenton County
Danville Independent Schools	Boyle County
Dawson Springs Independent Schools	Hopkins County
Dayton Independent Schools	Campbell County
East Bernstadt Independent Schools	Laurel County
Elizabethtown Independent Schools	Hardin County
Eminence Independent Schools	Henry County
Erlanger-Elsmere Independent Schools	Kenton County
Fairview Independent Schools	Boyd County
Fort Thomas Independent Schools	Campbell County
Frankfort Independent Schools	Franklin County
Fulton Independent Schools	Fulton County
Glasgow Independent Schools	Barren County
Harlan Independent Schools	Harlan County
Harrodsburg Independent Schools	Mercer County
Hazard Independent Schools	Perry County
Jackson Independent Schools	Breathitt County
Jenkins Independent Schools	Letcher County
Ludlow Independent Schools	Kenton County
Mayfield Independent Schools	Graves County
Middlesboro Independent Schools	Bell County
Monticello Independent Schools	Wayne County
Murray Independent Schools	Calloway County
Newport Independent Schools	Campbell County
Owensboro Independent Schools	Daviess County
Paducah Independent Schools	McCracken County
Paintsville Independent Schools	Johnson County
Paris Independent Schools	Bourbon County
Pikeville Independent Schools	Pike County
Pineville Independent Schools	Bell County
Providence Independent Schools	Webster County
Raceland-Worthington Independent Schools	Greenup County
Russell Independent Schools	Greenup County
Russellville Independent Schools	Logan County
Science Hill Independent Schools	Pulaski County
Silver Grove Independent Schools	Campbell County
Somerset Independent Schools	Pulaski County
Southgate Independent Schools	Campbell County
Walton-Verona Independent Schools	Boone County
West Point Independent Schools	Hardin County
Williamsburg Independent Schools	Whitley County
Williamstown Independent Schools	Grant County

Source: The Kentucky Directory Gold Book 2005-2006

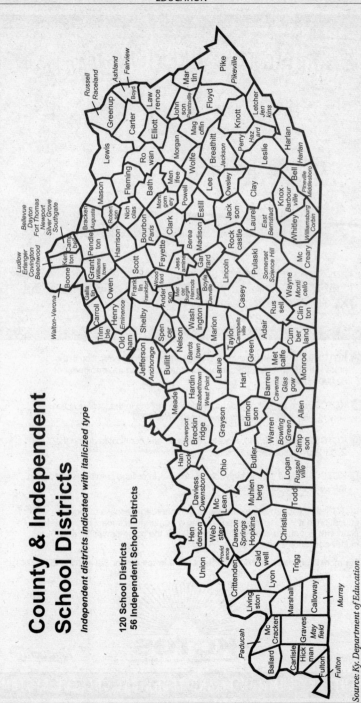

County & Independent School Districts

Independent districts indicated with italicized type

120 School Districts
56 Independent School Districts

Source: Ky. Department of Education

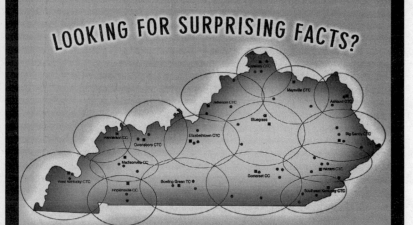

LOOKING FOR SURPRISING FACTS?

Here are just a few of the historical achievements the Kentucky Community and Technical College System (KCTCS) has made in only eight short years:

1 KCTCS is the largest provider of undergraduate college education in the state with 16 colleges, 65 campuses statewide, and an enrollment of 82,000 students.

2 KCTCS is the largest provider of workforce training in the state and has served over 7,700 Kentucky businesses since 2000.

3 KCTCS awarded 12,740 degrees, diplomas and certificates during the 2003-2004 academic year alone.

4 KCTCS enrolled 18,056 high school students in college credit courses during the 2004-2005 school year.

KCTCS' ability to provide Kentuckians with affordable access to a quality education that is close to home is having a tremendous impact on the state's economy. For successful Kentuckians all over the commonwealth, it's where higher education starts.

For more information, visit our website at **www.kctcs.edu** or call at **1-877-528-2748**.

An equal opportunity institution

KCTCS
Kentucky Community & Technical College System

Kentucky UNBRIDLED SPIRIT

KENTUCKY COMMUNITY AND TECHNICAL COLLEGE SYSTEM

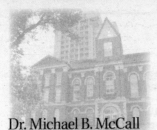

EDUCATION
Colleges & Universities

Dr. Michael B. McCall

THE TRANSFORMATION OF LEARNING AND WORK

Our economy is undergoing a profound transformation, one equivalent in scope and depth to the Industrial Revolution. Technology is revolutionizing every aspect of our lives. Knowledge is at the core of this revolution, and education has become the key to success.

Technology has virtually erased all borders and created a worldwide marketplace where wealth is created by combining science and business to apply innovative ideas and technologies to services, products and manufacturing processes. The New Economy demands that Americans work with their brains, not their hands.

This demand is placing increasing pressure on American workers to embrace a philosophy of lifelong learning. Labor economist Tony Carnevale says, "We've moved from a system in which hard work and showing up for a job, the blue collar economy, was one way to make a living. Now the only way you can get ahead is by going to college and getting some form of postsecondary education or training."

Today's high school graduates face a very different workplace than the one their grandparents faced. This fast-changing economy is exposing vast numbers of workers to global labor competition. Countries like China and India are turning out large numbers of well-educated young people fully qualified to work in our information-based economy.

Fortunately, Kentucky has been blessed with visionary leadership. In 1997 state leaders recognized that the only way Kentucky could succeed in the New Economy was to link postsecondary education to economic development by opening up higher education paths to its citizens. The result was the 1997 Postsecondary Education Improvement Act. The Act overhauled the state's higher education system in order to provide Kentuckians with the knowledge and skills needed to succeed in an information-based economy. It redefined the mission of Kentucky's public colleges and universities, giving each the flexibility to build on its strengths.

For the University of Louisville and the University of Kentucky this meant committing their resources into research—developing knowledge that will open the door for new business and industries. The six regional universities were asked to focus their efforts on their unique educational expertise and concentrate on undergraduate baccalaureate programs. The greatest change in the reform act was combining the state's community colleges and technical schools into one institution, creating the Kentucky Community and Technical Education System (KCTCS). KCTCS has quickly become the largest provider of postsecondary education and workforce training in the state. Its 16 colleges and 65 campuses provide citizens with a quality and affordable education close to home and a seamless path from high school to postsecondary education and on into the workplace.

Old Morrison Hall, Transylvania University, Lexington
Source: Sid Webb

What was once a narrow doorway for a privileged few is now an open gateway for every Kentuckian. We have moved from a K-12 system to a K-16 system. The 1997 Postsecondary Education Improvement Act has given each of us the educational tools for success. It is now in our hands to write a new future for our state, a future that links higher education to economic development and personal success.

Colleges & Universities

ALICE LLOYD

Alice Lloyd is a co-educational, private, four-year institution based on Christian principles and dedicated to leadership training. The college offers a tuition guarantee for qualified students from its 108 county Central Appalachia service area. This is valued at $6,360 per year and is awarded for a total of 10 semesters, provided that reasonable progress is made toward the completion of a degree. This program is guaranteed to all students, regardless of income, from the 108-county service area who qualify to attend Alice Lloyd College.

ASBURY COLLEGE

Asbury College, founded in 1890, is a four-year, multi-denominational institution located 20 minutes southwest of Lexington in Wilmore. U.S. News & World Report has ranked Asbury College among the top comprehensive colleges in the South for the last 13 years. Within the 17 academic departments, 49 majors are available at the college, as well as several masters degrees in education, including alternative certification programs. With a commitment to academic excellence and spiritual vitality, Asbury College encourages 1,300 students to study, worship and serve together.

BELLARMINE UNIVERSITY

Bellarmine University, nestled on 135 acres in Louisville's Highlands neighborhood, is ranked as one of the top universities in the South by U.S. News & World Report. Bellarmine is an independent, Catholic liberal arts based university that also offers undergraduate and graduate professional programs in business, education and health sciences, as well as international programs and study abroad opportunities in 40 countries. Over 700 of 1600 full-time undergraduates live on campus.

BEREA COLLEGE

Founded in 1855, Berea provides a high-quality liberal arts education within the context of a non-sectarian and inclusive Christian tradition. The college limits enrollment to 1,500, charges no tuition and takes 80 percent of its students from the Southern Appalachian area and Kentucky. The college seeks those who have high ability, but limited financial resources. In addition to carrying a full academic load, students work 10-15 hours per week in a college job, which permits them to earn at least a portion of their educational expenses.

BRESCIA UNIVERSITY

Brescia University, a liberal arts college located in Owensboro, offers 31 undergraduate degrees, nine pre-professional programs, a master of science in management, and a master of science in curriculum and instruction. Brescia is a NAIA school with 10 varsity sports competing in the Kentucky Intercollegiate Athletic Conference. Founded in 1950 by the Ursuline Sisters of Mount Saint Joseph, the university is committed to providing academic excellence and value-centered education in the Catholic tradition.

CAMPBELLSVILLE UNIVERSITY

Founded in 1906 and affiliated with the Kentucky Baptist Convention, Campbellsville University is one of the fastest-growing Christian comprehensive universities in the South. The university has experienced an increase of 150 percent in student enrollment during the past decade. Much of this growth can be attributed to the expansion of academic and athletic programs as well as the addition of seven master's degree programs.

CENTRE COLLEGE

Centre College, located in Danville, is known for its outstanding liberal arts academic program and the extraordinary career success of its graduates. Enrollment is around 1,100 and alumni span the range of occupations—from U.S. vice presidents, to Supreme Court Justices (including a chief justice), to the founder of the Hard Rock Café. The Centre record of accomplishment is based on rigorous academic standards and one-to-one teacher/student interaction. Centre College hosted the 2000 Vice Presidential Debate, and the city of Danville was recently featured by Time magazine as one of the nation's outstanding small towns.

EASTERN KENTUCKY UNIVERSITY

Located in Richmond, Madison County, EKU is an accredited four-year institution that offers a variety of undergraduate programs leading to the Associate of Arts and Bachelor's Degrees and several pre-professional programs, as well as masters programs. EKU was founded in 1906 and in 1909, when the first commencement was held, 11 people received degrees. Over the last century, EKU has grown to a full-fledged comprehensive university offering 168 degree programs and serving more than 15,000 students a year.

GEORGETOWN COLLEGE

Chartered in 1829 and affiliated with the Kentucky Baptist Convention, GC is dedicated to teaching the liberal arts in a Christian environment. GC offers bachelor of science, bachelor of arts and bachelor of music education degrees, and students can select a field of study from 37 majors and 28 minors. Georgetown also offers a graduate program in education. Enrollment is 1,361 undergraduate students and 342 graduate students. The school has forged a unique agreement with Oxford University in London, England, to allow its students, faculty and associates to participate in an academic partnership with Regent's Park, the Baptist college at Oxford. The Regent's Park College link enhances GC's reputation as a center for innovative Christian thought and produces widespread benefits to both institutions.

KENTUCKY CHRISTIAN UNIVERSITY

Founded in 1919, Kentucky Christian University's mission is to educate students for Christian leadership and service throughout the world. The university, which is located in Grayson in northeastern Kentucky, offers more than 20 baccalaureate majors and two master's degrees. KCU is regularly recognized as one of the best comprehensive schools in the south by the U.S. News & World Report.

KENTUCKY STATE UNIVERSITY

As an 1890 Land Grant institution, KSU is committed to providing quality reserach and other community outreachinitiatives. KSU's liberal arts programs draw upon the unique diversity of KSU and its African-American heritage. With around 2,300 students, KSU provides students with a public liberal-arts studies and vocational-oriented courses of instruction such as business, computer sciences, medical technology, office administration, and nursing. Pre-professional programs in law, dentistry, medicine, veterinary medicine, optometry, allied health, and engineering are also offered.

KENTUCKY WESLEYAN COLLEGE

High-quality teaching and a commitment to a career-oriented liberal arts education are hallmarks of Kentucky Wesleyan College (KWC). Established in 1858, the mission of Kentucky Wesleyan College is clear and concise: Kentucky Wesleyan College, in partnership with the United Methodist Church, fosters a liberal arts education that nourishes, stimulates, and prepares future leaders intellectually, spiritually and physically to achieve success in life. Kentucky Wesleyan is home to nearly 700 students from 23 states and numerous foreign countries.

LINDSEY WILSON COLLEGE

Founded in 1903 to train teachers for South central Kentucky, Lindsey Wilson College has evolved into a vibrant liberal arts college with 16 baccalaureate majors and a master's degree program. Lindsey Wilson is affiliated with the Kentucky Conference of the United Methodist Church. The campus is located on 45 partially wooded acres in Columbia, Ky., a small town about 20 miles from scenic Lake Cumberland in South central Kentucky.

MIDWAY COLLEGE

Established in 1847, Midway College is Kentucky's only women's college. Midway offers baccalaureate degrees in fourteen disciplines and associate degrees in four disciplines through the traditional day program. The college's School for Career Development meets the needs of working men and women by offering accelerated degree programs in the evening and at extension sites. Midway College's pillar degree programs are equine studies, business and organizational management, nursing, and teacher education.

MOREHEAD STATE UNIVERSITY

Located in the Appalachian foothills, the university's main campus facilities are in the city of Morehead in Rowan County. MSU offers 76 undergraduate degree programs and 12 pre-professional programs of study, as well as masters degrees. Art and music facilities provide cultural programs and activities for the campus and surrounding area. MSU consistently has been recognized as one of the top 25 public universities in the South by U.S. News & World Report.

MURRAY STATE UNIVERSITY

The 232-acre campus located in Murray, Calloway County, is home to more than 9,920 students with a full-time teaching faculty of 390. The university is a comprehensive institution comprised of five colleges and one school. Additionally, the university offers interactive television and web distance learning, extended campus, correspondence and evening classes.

NORTHERN KENTUCKY UNIVERSITY

NKU is located in Highland Heights in Campbell County and meets the needs of the surrounding northern Kentucky region, providing associate, bachelor's, masters and first professional degree programs. Started in 1948 as an extension center of the University of Kentucky, and later as part of the UK's Community College System, NKU became an autonomous senior institution in 1968 by an act of the Kentucky General Assembly.

PIKEVILLE COLLEGE

Pikeville College is a private, four-year, liberal arts and sciences college in the heart of Appalachia. Founded in 1889 by Presbyterian ministers to provide educational opportunity to mountain youth, Pikeville College has played an integral role in the economic, academic, and social development of its area for more than a century. In addition to a range of undergraduate degrees, Pikeville also offers the Doctor of Osteopathic Medicine degree, through the Pikeville College School of Osteopathic Medicine.

SPALDING UNIVERSITY

Spalding University is a Catholic, independent, coeducational, urban university located in downtown Louisville, Ky. Founded by the Sisters of Charity of Nazareth, it remains dedicated to value-oriented education and ethical principles. Spalding is now owned and operated by an independent board of trustees, broadly representative of the community that it serves.

ST. CATHARINE COLLEGE

St. Catharine College is located in south central Kentucky in the town of Springfield. An independent, co-educational college in the Dominican tradition, the college was formally founded in 1931, but dates its educational heritage to the formation of the Dominican sisters in 1822. The college offers certificate, associate and bachelor degrees in a variety of fields including humanities, social sciences, education, mathematics, natural sciences and business topics. Welcoming students of all social and religious backgrounds, the college is committed to the value of the liberal arts, environmental awareness and its Catholic heritage in a supportive learning community.

THOMAS MORE COLLEGE

Thomas More College, named for the English saint, scholar and statesman, is located on 60 acres in Crestview Hills. The suburban campus is eight miles south of Cincinnati, Ohio. Thomas More serves some 1,500 students. Although primarily from Greater Cincinnati and Northern Kentucky, students from 12 states and six countries attend the college.

TRANSYLVANIA UNIVERSITY

Chartered in 1780, Transylvania is the 16th oldest institution of higher learning in the U.S. and the first college west of the Allegheny Mountains. Located in Lexington, the liberal-arts school, with an enrollment of 1,100 students, is consistently recognized by publications such as U.S. News & World Report, Peterson's Top Colleges for Science, and Barron's Best Buys in College Education. The student body consists of bright, highly motivated students who thrive due in part to the university's low student/faculty ratio of 13:1.

UNION COLLEGE

Union College is located in Barbourville, KY, and offers a liberal arts education. The famous Wilderness Road spans the east side of the campus and Cumberland Gap National Historic Park is a mere 30 miles away. This, along with four state parks, miles of lake, river and stream and endless opportunities for outdoor learning, make Union College the place where students can really experience life beyond the classroom.

UNIVERSITY OF THE CUMBERLANDS

University of the Cumberlands (formerly Cumberland College) is in its 117th year of operation. It offers undergraduate degrees in 38 major fields of study, 30 minors and nine pre-professional programs, as well as opportunities such as studying abroad. Cumberland, located in Williamsburg, is affiliated with the Kentucky Baptist Convention and has long been known for its outstanding academic programs and graduates who enter the work force well prepared for success and service.

UNIVERSITY OF KENTUCKY

UK serves as the principal research and graduate-degree granting institution in the Commonwealth serving more than 30,000 students. It is a comprehensive land-grant institution located in Lexington, Fayette County. UK offers baccalaureate, professional, master's, specialist, doctoral, and postdoctoral programs and conducts joint doctoral programs in cooperation with other institutions. UK is ranked among the top 100 research universities in the nation.

UNIVERSITY OF LOUISVILLE

Established in 1798, U of L is a preeminent metropolitan research university that emphasizes undergraduate and graduate-level education, as well as research. With a student population of more than 22,000, U of L offers graduate, professional, baccalaureate, and associate degrees, as well as certificates, in more than 170 fields of study through 12 schools and colleges on three campuses. U of L receives more than $82.3 million (excluding financial aid) in federally-funded research.

WESTERN KENTUCKY UNIVERSITY

WKU, located in Bowling Green in Warren County, offers associate, baccalaureate, and masters degrees, and certificate programs. "The home of the Hilltoppers," Western's campus crowns a hill overlooking the city of Bowling Green and is proclaimed as one of the most beautiful in the nation.

Kentucky Community & Technical Colleges

The Postsecondary Education Improvement Act of 1997 created the Kentucky Community and Technical College System (KCTCS) with a mission "to be the primary provider of two-year transfer and technical programs, workforce training for existing and new businesses and industries, and remedial and continuing education to improve the quality of life and employability of the citizens of the Commonwealth of Kentucky." One of the goals of KCTCS is to develop a "seamless, integrated system of postsecondary education that is strategically planned and adequately funded to enhance economic development and quality of life."

KCTCS is composed of 16 community and technical college districts comprising 28 community and technical colleges plus several branch campuses and distance learning centers strategically located across the Commonwealth. The Kentucky Community and Technical College System's enrollment in credit courses has increased from 45,529 in the fall of 1999 to 72,000 in the fall of 2003. Thirteen community colleges formerly under the jurisdiction of the University of Kentucky are part of KCTCS. All of the postsecondary technical institutions formerly a part of Kentucky Tech in the Workforce Development Cabinet are part of KCTCS. KCTCS has been streamlining and improving service delivery including consolidation of programs and services at many of the colleges. KCTCS is developing state-of-the-art technology infrastructure to improve the quality of instruction, enhance and expand professional development opportunities, increase access through distance learning, and streamline administrative functions.

With more than 65 campuses and other locations open or under construction, the KCTCS College Districts:

Ashland Community and Technical College
  Ashland
Big Sandy Community and Technical College
  Paintsville, Pikeville, Prestonsburg
Bluegrass Community and Technical College District
  Lawrenceburg, Lexington, Danville, Winchester
Bowling Green Technical College
  Bowling Green, Glasgow
Elizabethtown Community and Technical College
  Elizabethtown, Fort Knox
Gateway Community and Technical College
  Covington, Edgewood, Highland Heights
Hazard Community and Technical College
  Hazard, Jackson, Hindman
Henderson Community College
  Henderson
Hopkinsville Community College
  Hopkinsville, Fort Campbell
Jefferson Community and Technical College
  Louisville, Shelbyville, Carrollton
Madisonville Community College
  Madisonville, Central City
Maysville Community and Technical College
  Maysville, Morehead, Cynthiana
Owensboro Community and Technical College
  Owensboro
Somerset Community College
  Somerset, London
Southeast Kentucky Community and Technical College
  Cumberland, Middlesboro, Pineville, Whitesburg, Harlan
West Kentucky Community and Technical College
  Paducah
(Source: KCTCS, www.kctcs.edu)

Medical Schools

Kentucky has two fine institutions training doctors: The University of Louisville School of Medicine and the University of Kentucky College of Medicine.

The Louisville School of Medicine traces its beginnings to 1833, when the Louisville Common Council set up a committee to investigate the possibility of establishing a medical college in the city. With improved river travel made possible by the steamboat, Louisville grew to be one of the largest cities in the South and sought to develop its own cultural institutions. The Louisville Medical Institute began classes in temporary quarters in the fall of 1837. A few weeks later, the 80 students and seven faculty members moved into a splendid Greek Revival structure designed by Kentucky architect Gideon Shryock. The school instituted clinical teaching in the wards of the public hospital, then known as the Louisville City Hospital, as an integral part of the medical curriculum, and founding faculty included several of the most distinguished professors from Lexington's Transylvania University. More than 15,800 medical students have earned the M.D. degree from the University of Louisville School of Medicine.

The institution can boast several milestones throughout its history, including the establishment of one of the country's first surgical laboratories in 1841. Also, in 1911 the facility launched the nation's first trauma care center when it began offering "accident service."

According to the National Institutes of Health (NIH) ranking information, the U of L School of Medicine is now ranked 42nd among public schools for the research funding received from NIH, according to recently released rankings for the 2004 fiscal year. The Dept. of Neurosurgery ranks fourth, the Dept. of Ophthalmology ranks 14th, and the Dept. of Anesthesiology ranks 20th. Anatomical Sciences and Pediatrics also are ranked in the top 30. Major research areas include: Cancer (including breast cancer, head and neck, and tumor immunology), Bioethics, Health Policy and Law, Cardiovascular Disease, Digestive Health, Neurosciences, Opthalmology and Visual Sciences, Pediatrics, and Spinal Cord Injury.

Recent milestones include:

- 1999 – U of L surgeons perform the first human hand transplant in the U.S. at Jewish Hospital's Kleinert, Kutz Hand Care Center
- 2001 – U of L surgeons implant the first fully-implantable artificial heart at Jewish Hospital.
- 2005 – U of L received approval for construction of a third biomedical research building, funded in part by a $39 million appropriation from the Kentucky Legislature and a $10.25 million federal earmark secured with the assistance of U.S. Senator Mitch McConnell.

The University of Kentucky, located in Lexington, enrolled its first medical school class in 1960. Four years later, the College of Medicine graduated its first class of 32 students. Since then, 3,391 medical students have earned the M.D. degree from the University of Kentucky College of Medicine.

The UK College of Medicine is now ranked 31st among public schools for the research funding received from the National Institutes of Health (NIH), according to recently released rankings for the 2004 fiscal year. In 2005, UK dedicated a $74.4 million Biomedical Biological Sciences Research Building, which will house 185,000 square feet of laboratory and workspace for prominent faculty scientists from the UK College of Medicine, College of Pharmacy, and College of Arts and Sciences. Also in 2004, a research breakthrough in the field of DNA mismatch repair by professor Guo-Min Li, Ph.D., of UK's Markey Cancer Center, was the cover story in the September issue of the premier international research science journal, Cell Magazine.

Other NIH rankings based on 2004 fiscal year figures include:

- UK College of Medicine ranks 35th among public medical schools
- The Center on Aging ranks third
- The Department of Physiology ranks eighth
- Molecular and Biomedical Pharmacology ranks 10th among public medical schools

The Departments of Anatomy and Neurobiology; Microbiology, Immunology, and Molecular Genetics; Molecular and Cellular Biochemistry and Surgery also are ranked in the top 20.

Sources: University of Louisville School of Medicine and University of Kentucky College of Medicine.

COLLEGES, UNIVERSITIES, COMMUNITY & TECHNICAL COLLEGES

COLLEGE	ADD1	ADD2	CITY	ZIP	PHONE	WEB PAGE
Alice Lloyd College	100 Purpose Rd		Pippa Passes	41844	(606) 368-2101	www.alc.edu
Asbury College	1 Macklem Dr		Wilmore	40390	(859) 858-3511	www.asbury.edu
Asbury Theological Seminary	204 N Lexington Ave		Wilmore	40390	(800) 2-ASBURY	www.asburyseminary.edu
Ashland Community & Technical College	1400 College Dr		Ashland	41101	(800) 928-4256	www.ashland.kctcs.edu
Bellarmine University	2001 Newburg Rd		Louisville	40205	(800) 274-4723	www.bellarmine.edu
Berea College	CPO 2182		Berea	40404	(859) 985-100	www.berea.edu
Big Sandy Community & Technical College	One Bert T Combs Dr		Prestonsburg	41653	(888) 641-4132	www.bigsandy.kctcs.edu
Bluegrass Community & Technical College	209 Oswald Bldg	Cooper Dr	Lexington	40506	(866) 774-4872	www.bluegrass.kctcs.edu
Bowling Green Technical College	1845 Loop Ave		Bowling Green	42101	(270) 901-1000	www.bowlinggreen.kctcs.edu
Brescia University	717 Frederica St		Owensboro	42301	(270) 685-3131	www.brescia.edu
Campbellsville University	1 University Dr		Campbellsville	42718	(800) 264-6014	www.campbellsville.edu
Centre College of Kentucky	600 W Walnut St		Danville	40422	(859) 238-510	www.centre.edu
Clear Creek Baptist Bible College	300 Clear Creek Rd		Pineville	40977	(606) 337-3196	www.ccbbc.edu
Eastern Kentucky University	521 Lancaster Ave		Richmond	40475	(800) 262-7493	www.eku.edu
Elizabethtown Community & Technical College	600 College Street Rd		Elizabethtown	42701	(877) 246-2322	www.elizabethtowncc.com
Gateway Community & Technical College	300 Buttermilk Pk Ste 334		Fort Mitchell	41017	(859) 441-4500	www.gateway.kctcs.edu
Georgetown College	400 E College St		Georgetown	40324	(502) 863-8000	www.georgetowncollege.edu
Greater Cincinnati Consortium of Colleges & Universities	The Union Institute	440 E McMillan St	Cincinnati	45206		www.gcccu.org
Hazard Community & Technical College	One Community College Dr		Hazard	41701	(800) 246-7521	www.hazcc.kctcs.edu
Henderson Community College	2660 S Green St		Henderson	42420	(800) 696-9958	www.hencc.kctcs.edu
Hopkinsville Community College	720 North Dr	PO Box 2100	Hopkinsville	42241	(270) 886-3921	www.hopkinsville.kctcs.edu
Jefferson Community & Technical College	109 E Broadway		Louisville	40202	(502) 213-5333	www.jefferson.kctcs.edu
Kentuckiana Metroversity	200 W Broadway Ste 700		Louisville	40202		www.metroversity.org
Kentucky Advanced Technology Institute	1127 Morgantown Rd		Bowling Green	42101	(270) 746-7807	
Kentucky Christian College	100 Academic Pkwy		Grayson	41143	(606) 474-100	www.kcc.edu
Kentucky Community & Technical College System	300 N Main St	PO Box 10	Versailles	40383	(859) 256-3100	www.kctcs.edu
Kentucky Mountain Bible College	855 KY Hwy 541		Vancleve	41385	(606) 666-5000	www.kmbc.edu
Kentucky State University	400 E Main St		Frankfort	40601	(502) 597-6000	www.kysu.edu
Kentucky Wesleyan College	3000 Frederica St	PO Box 1039	Owensboro	42302	(270) 926-3111	www.kwc.edu
Lexington Baptist College	183 N Ashland Ave		Lexington	40502	(859) 252-1130	
Lexington Theological Seminary	631 S Limestone		Lexington	40508	(859) 252-0361	www.lextheo.edu
Lindsey Wilson College	210 Lindsey Wilson St		Columbia	42728	(270) 384-2126	www.lindsey.edu
Louisville Bible College	8013 Damascus Rd	PO Box 91046	Louisville	40291	(502) 231-5221	www.louisvillebiblecollege.org

COLLEGES, UNIVERSITIES, COMMUNITY & TECHNICAL COLLEGES

COLLEGE	ADD1	ADD2	CITY	ZIP	PHONE	WEB PAGE
Louisville Presbyterian Theological Seminary	1044 Alta Vista Rd		Louisville	40205	(502) 895-3411	www.lpts.edu
Madisonville Community College	2000 College Dr		Madisonville	42431	(270) 821-2250	www.madcc.kctcs.edu
Maysville Community & Technical College	1755 US Hwy 68		Maysville	41056	(606) 759-7141	www.maycc.kctcs.edu
Metropolitan College	1000 Community College Dr		Louisville	40272		
Mid Continent College	99 E Powell Rd		Mayfield	42066	(859) 846-4421	www.midcontinent.edu
Midway College	512 E Stephens St		Midway	40347		www.midway.edu
Morehead State University	201 Howell-McDowell Admin Bldg	University Blvd	Morehead	40351	(606) 783-2221	www.moreheadstate.edu
Murray State University		PO Box 9	Murray	42071	(800) 272-4678	www.murraystate.edu
Northern Kentucky University		Nunn Dr	Highland Heights	41099	(859) 572-5100	www.nku.edu/
Owensboro Community & Technical College	4800 New Hartford Rd		Owensboro	42303	(866) 755-OCTC	www.octc.kctcs.edu
Pikeville College	147 Sycamore St		Pikeville	41501	(606) 218-5250	www.pc.edu
Portland Christian School of Bible Studies	2500 Portland Ave		Louisville	40212		
Saint Catharine College	2735 Bardstown Rd		St Catharine	40061	(859) 336-5082	www.sccky.edu
Simmons Bible College	1811 Dumesnil St		Louisville	40210	(502) 776-1443	www.sbcollege.edu
Somerset Community College	808 Monticello St		Somerset	42501	(877) 629-9722	www.somerset.kctcs.edu
Southeast Kentucky Community College	700 College Rd		Cumberland	40823	(888) 274-SECC	www.southeast.kctcs.edu
Southern Baptist Theological Seminary	2825 Lexington Rd		Louisville	40280	(800) 626-5525	www.sbts.edu
Spalding University	851 S 4th St		Louisville	40203		www.spalding.edu
Spencerian College, Lexington Campus	2355 Harrodsburg Road		Lexington	40504	(859) 223-9608	www.spencerian.edu/lexington
Spencerian College, Louisville Campus	4627 Dixie Hwy	PO Box 16418	Louisville	40256	(502) 447-1000	www.spencerian.edu
Sullivan College	3101 Bardstown Rd		Louisville	40205	(502) 456-6504	www.sullivan.edu
Sullivan College, Lexington Campus	2355 Harrodsburg Rd		Lexington	40504	(800) 467-6281	www.sullivan.edu
Sullivan University, Ft Knox Campus	63 Quartermaster St	PO Box 998	Ft Knox	40121	(270) 942-8500	www.sullivan.edu
Thomas More College	333 Thomas More Pkwy		Crestview Hills	41017	(800) 548-7044	www.thomasmore.edu
Transylvania University	300 N Broadway		Lexington	40508		www.transy.edu
Union College	310 College St		Barbourville	40906	(606) 546-4151	www.unionky.edu
University of Kentucky	101 Gillis Bldg	Central Admin	Lexington	40506	(859) 257-9000	www.uky.edu
University of Louisville	102 Grawemeyer Hall	Ofc of the President	Louisville	40292	(800) 334-8635	www.louisville.edu
University of the Cumberlands	6191 College Station Dr		Williamsburg	40769	(606) 549-210	www.cumberlandcollege.edu
West Kentucky Community & Technical College	4810 Alben Barkley Dr	PO Box 7380	Paducah	42002	(270) 554-9200	www.westkentucky.kctcs.edu
Western Kentucky University	1 Big Red Way St		Bowling Green	42101	(270) 745-0111	www.wku.edu

Source: The Kentucky Directory Gold Book 2005

EDUCATION
Adult Education and Literacy

For all Kentuckians to prosper, every citizen must be prepared to function well in the workforce, the community and the home. Experts tell us that 80 percent of all jobs to be created over the next two decades will require some postsecondary education. Kentucky is far from ready for this new reality, with about 40 percent of working-age citizens functioning at the two lowest levels of literacy. According to 2004 census data, Kentucky ranks 44th in the nation in the percentage of adults with at least a high school education (81.8 percent).

Without a good education, Kentuckians can't compete for good jobs to make enough money to support their families and their children are less likely to succeed in school and beyond. This means the Commonwealth can't make a compelling case for companies opening or expanding their business in Kentucky.

Recognizing that an undereducated workforce is a hindrance on the state's economy, the 2000 General Assembly passed The Kentucky Adult Education Act. This legislation created a partnership between Kentucky Adult Education (KYAE) and the Council on Postsecondary Education, increased funding and set the stage for dramatic improvements in the educational status of adult Kentuckians who lacked a high

WPA Packhourse Librarians
Source: Kentucky Department of Libraries & Archives

Source: Kentucky Department of Libraries & Archives

school diploma, functioned at low levels of literacy or wanted to learn the English language.

In fiscal year 2004, 120,051 students enrolled in Kentucky Adult Education programs. This was more than double than the number enrolled in

2000.

Kentucky Adult Education places a particular emphasis on family literacy because efforts to improve the educational attainment of children will fail without a strong outreach to their first teachers — their parents. Kentucky is one of only

English-as-a-second language programs help adults become more fluent in English, pass U.S. citizenship tests, work on job-seeking skills and improve their ability to cope with society.

With the help of Kentucky Department of Correction and federal funds, KYAE provides adult education in state prisons and local jails. In addition to adult basic education services, this program provides appropriate life skills courses.

KYAE has funded pilot programs designed to increase the number of GED graduates who move on to post-

Source: Kentucky Department of Libraries & Archives

two states with family literacy programs in every county. KYAE partners with the Kentucky Institute for Family Literacy and the National Center for Family Literacy, which provides professional development and technical assistance to help improve Kentucky's family literacy program.

KYAE funds workforce education to meet the needs of business and industry. Many businesses are using KYAE's SkillMobiles — state-of-the-art mobile computer labs that feature online curriculum.

The first of its kind in the nation, the Kentucky Virtual Adult Education website (www.kyvae.org) allows adults to learn anywhere, anytime, at their convenience.

secondary education. The percentage of GED graduates who went on to college increased from 12 percent in 1998 to 19 percent in 2002. Kentucky's recent reforms have enhanced KYAE collaborations with other programs, agencies, educational systems and services.

Source: Kentucky Adult Education

Well, I declare!

"Children are made readers on the laps of their parents." — Emilie Buchwald

Cora Wilson Stewart (1875-1958) was an outstanding Kentucky educator from the community of Farmers in Rowan County. Her novel idea of the "Moonlight School," which she started in 1911, brought her national fame. Instead of children, the school was opened for uneducated adults and held at night. It was so successful that many such schools were soon opened across the U.S.

General Education Development
Sid Webb

The General Educational Development test was developed over 50 years ago to help returning veterans from WW II pick up their educations where they left off and enable them to continue on to college. A GED certificate is the equivalent of a high school diploma. Kentucky leads the nation in providing an alternative to high school dropouts who discover that good paying jobs are scarce for people who have not attained a high school education.

Nearly 35 years ago, KET, the public television network in Kentucky, developed a comprehensive television series to aid people in studying for the GED test. Since then, KET has remade the series twice, improving on it each time with feedback from both teachers and students.

Contrary to what many think, the GED is not an easy test. Its developers at the American Council on Education (ACE) see to that. Each time they remake the test and update it they ask high school seniors to take it. The pass/fail score for the test is set at a level that would have failed 25 percent of the high school seniors who took it.

While KET was making their first GED series, a small, respected book company in New York formed a partnership with KET to publish and sell the GED videotapes and accompanying workbooks to other states. The partnership proved fruitful for KET. By the end of the decade adult education centers in every state in the union, including the U.S. military, were using the KET/GED series.

In the 70s, the use of videotapes was not common in homes. Videotape machines were bulky and expensive. By the early 80s, however, videotape machines had become small and affordable. More and more people had them in their homes. Now GED students who depended on TV for instruction could tape and replay at their convenience GED programs broadcast on KET and other stations. This widened the potential audience and changed the market dynamics.

KET had always partnered with the Kentucky Department of Education and schools in Kentucky, and during the 70s it had left the promotion and recruitment of GED students to the state department. KET felt it was reaching students in rural communities that were under-served by adult education programs; but when it took a hard look at what other states were accomplishing with its GED program, KET decided it time to take an active role in promoting the series in Kentucky.

About the same time, several things happened that gave new impetus to the GED series for KET. The network dropped its partnership with the book company and started publishing and distributing its own books. Secondly, ACE decided it was time to update and revise the GED test. Thirdly, there was a move on the national level to promote the KET/GED series as an important educational contribution that public television could do well.

KET decided to provide its new KET/GED series at no cost to other public TV stations across the nation to stir new life and enthusiasm into GED. KET also began actively enrolling, tracking and aiding GED-ON-TV students.

Today the KET/GED series is still going strong in Kentucky and attracting new students in the state and around the U.S. KET revised the GED series again in 2002 as part of the broader Workplace Literacy series. Each year about 1,000 people watch the series, take and pass the GED test in Kentucky. In the past three decades KET estimates that as many as a million people in the nation may have gotten their GED certificates by using its series.

EDUCATIONAL ATTAINMENT: YEARS OF SCHOOL COMPLETED, 1970-2000

AREA	TOTAL PERSONS 25 YEARS AND OLDER				8 YEARS OF SCHOOL OR LESS				HIGH SCHOOL				4 OR MORE YEARS OF COLLEGE			
	1970	1980	1990	2000	1970	1980	1990	2000	1970	1980	1990	2000	1970	1980	1990	2000
Kentucky	1,713,298	2,086,692	2,333,833	2,646,397	44.8	31.3	19.0	11.7	38.5	53.1	64.6	74.1	7.2	11.1	13.6	17.1
Adair	7,629	9,291	9,885	11,270	69.4	52.2	36.6	23.6	21.6	34.6	46.3	60.1	3.4	5.3	7.4	10.9
Allen	7,749	8,779	9,463	11,643	66.7	48.7	32.2	18.9	23.8	38.5	51.1	64.5	2.6	5.0	4.6	9.1
Anderson	5,330	7,393	9,421	12,600	47.7	33.5	16.8	8.0	38.2	50.3	66.7	80.4	5.3	7.3	9.9	12.0
Ballard	5,186	5,521	5,328	5,766	41.7	29.6	16.8	9.9	39.3	53.4	64.2	76.3	2.7	7.7	8.7	10.6
Barren	16,676	20,864	22,627	25,751	58.7	43.0	28.8	16.3	29.6	44.0	54.5	69.5	4.9	8.0	8.3	11.1
Bath	5,183	5,908	6,341	7,451	65.1	49.6	36.1	22.8	21.6	35.6	46.3	59.0	3.3	6.4	6.2	10.1
Bell	16,696	19,319	19,644	20,042	61.9	49.7	33.5	25.0	25.2	36.2	46.7	56.6	5.5	6.5	9.3	9.0
Boone	16,536	25,095	35,347	54,166	32.5	17.9	9.3	4.8	47.0	65.3	76.4	85.1	6.7	11.8	15.3	22.8
Bourbon	10,481	11,628	12,332	13,015	40.7	31.1	16.4	9.3	41.8	53.6	64.0	75.4	6.6	9.2	11.8	13.5
Boyd	29,531	33,759	34,809	34,697	34.2	24.3	13.0	8.2	48.3	59.0	68.9	78.0	7.8	9.8	11.9	14.1
Boyle	11,967	14,648	16,693	18,491	37.9	28.6	16.2	9.5	44.3	55.6	65.4	76.6	9.8	12.6	14.4	19.3
Bracken	4,225	4,627	5,016	5,460	53.1	39.7	24.4	14.2	30.1	43.7	56.0	69.6	3.1	5.4	6.5	9.5
Breathitt	6,867	8,776	9,455	10,393	69.5	48.1	34.8	24.2	21.2	37.0	47.8	57.5	6.0	8.9	8.6	10.0
Breckinridge	8,254	9,892	10,615	12,501	60.2	44.1	28.1	15.9	26.4	42.1	56.7	68.9	2.0	5.7	6.3	7.4
Bullitt	12,335	22,177	28,596	39,307	44.7	26.8	15.0	7.8	34.9	53.0	64.7	76.0	3.1	5.8	6.3	9.2
Butler	5,584	6,504	7,252	8,489	68.6	52.6	34.9	20.3	20.3	34.6	46.6	60.7	3.1	3.1	5.1	6.4
Caldwell	8,022	8,625	8,928	9,265	45.4	34.7	19.0	11.3	37.2	49.5	61.9	73.1	4.4	7.6	8.2	10.0
Calloway	14,198	16,883	18,542	21,032	40.4	26.6	15.7	9.9	43.8	59.8	69.1	77.9	11.4	18.1	19.4	24.0
Campbell	47,257	47,773	52,731	57,184	39.7	26.3	12.7	7.1	40.1	55.6	71.0	80.8	5.7	9.8	14.9	20.5
Carlisle	3,399	3,457	3,508	3,690	47.6	33.4	19.2	11.9	34.3	52.5	62.3	73.4	2.1	4.6	6.6	10.6
Carroll	4,781	5,517	5,938	6,690	49.5	33.4	18.9	15.0	32.2	46.5	59.6	68.1	5.6	7.6	10.7	8.3
Carter	10,546	13,753	15,035	17,394	62.1	45.7	29.5	19.2	23.9	38.0	51.3	64.4	4.4	5.4	7.6	8.9
Casey	7,293	8,665	9,152	10,423	71.1	55.2	38.6	24.9	19.4	33.2	43.1	57.4	4.9	5.8	6.5	7.4
Christian	25,507	32,876	38,693	40,344	42.9	25.1	14.2	10.2	41.2	60.5	72.2	77.2	6.2	8.7	10.4	12.5
Clark	13,064	16,521	19,172	22,187	43.6	28.8	17.8	10.4	40.1	55.9	65.1	75.0	6.8	9.6	13.0	15.6
Clay	8,765	11,718	12,818	16,083	75.1	59.9	43.5	31.9	17.2	27.6	38.9	49.4	5.0	7.3	7.4	8.0
Clinton	4,738	5,588	5,987	6,594	74.4	55.3	38.1	29.3	17.5	30.5	44.4	53.5	3.1	4.7	6.6	8.0
Crittenden	5,264	5,776	6,102	6,460	53.6	40.0	24.4	17.6	33.5	45.4	59.6	67.0	3.6	5.9	5.1	7.3
Cumberland	4,106	4,551	4,583	4,972	73.1	61.3	43.6	28.2	18.4	29.0	39.5	56.0	4.3	6.7	6.1	7.1
Daviess	41,289	48,965	55,048	59,745	32.7	22.6	12.6	6.7	48.9	61.3	72.3	80.7	8.7	11.0	14.1	17.0
Edmonson	4,769	5,772	6,570	7,865	65.2	47.8	32.1	20.3	19.7	35.5	48.6	61.7	2.2	5.3	5.4	4.9
Elliott	3,095	3,742	3,912	4,422	74.5	55.0	37.0	27.1	18.8	31.3	44.0	52.6	3.4	7.1	5.6	7.8
Estill	6,964	8,301	9,170	10,189	65.5	50.5	35.5	25.1	23.1	38.4	46.5	58.5	2.9	6.5	5.4	6.9
Fayette	89,217	115,055	142,116	167,235	24.2	15.9	8.3	5.1	60.1	71.6	80.2	85.8	17.2	25.6	30.6	35.6
Fleming	6,583	7,326	7,946	9,154	60.2	48.3	31.1	20.5	27.9	40.2	53.8	66.5	3.3	6.3	8.7	8.8
Floyd	18,863	29,961	26,566	28,370	63.8	45.9	31.3	20.4	24.5	39.9	50.8	61.3	4.2	6.0	7.4	9.7
Franklin	19,347	25,064	28,819	32,388	35.1	22.7	12.0	8.7	51.0	64.0	76.0	78.8	11.9	18.0	21.3	23.8
Fulton	6,067	5,495	5,512	5,111	46.9	33.8	25.0	10.7	37.8	45.2	54.4	69.5	4.9	6.6	10.3	11.5
Gallatin	2,296	2,761	3,349	5,007	51.6	36.9	21.2	11.6	32.1	43.2	59.8	68.0	2.2	5.5	5.0	6.9
Garrard	5,592	6,741	7,776	9,951	51.3	36.8	26.0	13.3	31.9	44.5	54.3	69.4	4.7	7.2	6.3	10.5

EDUCATIONAL ATTAINMENT: YEARS OF SCHOOL COMPLETED, 1970-2000

AREA	TOTAL PERSONS 25 YEARS AND OLDER				8 YEARS OF SCHOOL OR LESS				HIGH SCHOOL				4 OR MORE YEARS OF COLLEGE			
	1970	1980	1990	2000	1970	1980	1990	2000	1970	1980	1990	2000	1970	1980	1990	2000
Grant	5,756	7,630	9,635	13,861	48.1	34.0	19.8	9.3	33.5	49.0	61.6	72.4	3.7	5.6	7.2	9.4
Graves	18,967	21,686	22,682	24,932	43.9	32.2	18.7	10.7	36.3	50.0	62.0	73.4	3.6	7.9	8.8	12.6
Grayson	9,200	12,203	13,615	15,940	66.4	49.1	32.0	20.3	21.7	37.2	48.3	62.8	4.0	5.6	6.1	7.7
Green	6,154	6,918	7,093	7,983	70.6	55.2	38.6	24.7	21.1	35.6	49.0	61.4	3.1	3.9	6.8	9.1
Greenup	17,403	22,402	24,051	25,323	43.4	27.1	18.6	10.5	38.9	57.1	64.7	75.1	4.3	9.1	11.1	11.5
Hancock	3,747	4,253	4,844	5,427	45.8	29.0	17.3	8.8	38.9	57.2	69.3	77.2	3.9	6.3	6.9	8.1
Hardin	28,263	39,986	49,643	58,358	32.7	20.9	12.1	6.7	51.7	66.5	75.3	82.3	7.5	10.9	12.9	15.4
Harlan	19,821	22,992	22,506	22,041	61.2	45.1	31.7	21.9	23.9	38.2	49.5	58.7	4.3	5.7	6.4	8.9
Harrison	8,408	9,271	10,490	12,000	46.1	34.8	19.5	10.7	37.2	46.9	62.4	74.2	6.2	7.3	8.6	10.6
Hart	8,005	9,123	9,659	11,474	63.6	47.8	34.6	21.0	23.0	37.2	45.3	58.2	3.2	6.4	5.2	7.0
Henderson	19,705	23,811	27,643	29,960	37.7	25.2	14.3	8.0	44.2	57.2	68.5	78.3	5.5	10.2	11.1	13.8
Henry	6,492	7,776	8,389	10,032	49.0	34.0	21.4	10.7	36.0	50.9	60.9	73.4	4.6	7.4	8.2	9.8
Hickman	3,741	3,830	3,852	3,734	45.1	30.3	23.0	15.0	34.6	53.2	56.8	64.4	2.6	7.5	7.6	8.8
Hopkins	22,200	27,410	29,896	31,464	47.1	34.3	20.9	12.8	35.5	49.7	62.5	71.3	5.0	7.5	9.6	10.6
Jackson	5,294	6,693	7,324	8,611	76.4	62.5	43.6	27.7	13.6	25.3	38.3	52.9	3.5	4.2	4.9	6.8
Jefferson	370,404	406,868	439,055	464,284	31.9	19.1	9.7	5.4	47.3	63.6	74.1	81.8	9.7	15.3	19.3	24.8
Jessamine	9,594	14,032	18,458	24,182	41.5	26.3	14.2	8.7	41.5	59.7	69.0	79.1	11.8	17.3	19.1	21.5
Johnson	9,923	13,944	14,571	15,735	62.8	44.7	28.1	18.0	25.2	42.8	54.7	63.8	4.5	7.4	9.3	9.3
Kenton	68,985	78,036	88,454	97,727	35.9	22.9	10.7	6.1	42.4	59.0	74.4	82.1	7.1	12.2	17.0	22.9
Knott	7,181	9,283	10,619	11,427	70.4	50.7	35.9	25.0	18.8	36.2	45.1	58.7	4.9	6.1	8.2	10.2
Knox	12,441	16,552	17,934	20,401	66.5	50.9	35.2	27.0	21.9	36.0	46.6	54.1	4.3	7.3	8.0	8.8
Larue	6,042	7,232	7,814	9,017	57.5	40.4	24.3	14.7	29.3	43.9	59.0	71.0	4.6	5.0	8.1	10.9
Laurel	14,566	21,732	27,037	34,431	61.4	43.5	27.6	18.1	26.8	42.5	52.7	63.9	5.3	6.7	8.2	10.6
Lawrence	6,080	7,982	8,677	10,256	64.2	48.9	36.0	23.7	23.2	36.0	46.4	58.2	3.8	5.5	6.2	6.6
Lee	3,562	4,544	4,654	5,381	70.3	49.8	37.7	25.6	16.6	34.6	43.4	50.9	2.8	5.7	5.8	6.3
Leslie	5,313	7,448	8,048	8,214	72.9	55.0	38.0	27.0	16.0	30.6	40.4	52.5	4.5	7.0	6.6	6.3
Letcher	12,154	16,618	16,645	16,930	66.5	46.5	33.6	22.7	19.3	37.9	45.6	58.5	3.1	6.7	6.7	7.7
Lewis	6,336	7,805	8,127	9,256	66.2	54.7	38.8	23.4	22.0	33.0	45.4	57.4	3.5	5.3	6.7	6.4
Lincoln	9,339	11,159	12,759	15,440	58.9	45.5	30.1	18.3	26.1	37.0	50.4	64.6	4.0	4.7	6.2	8.4
Livingston	4,565	5,723	6,200	6,851	56.3	33.0	21.2	10.2	29.8	50.9	63.1	74.3	3.0	5.4	5.4	8.4
Logan	12,653	14,495	15,856	17,471	52.3	38.9	24.9	15.4	31.7	45.1	57.7	68.5	4.7	6.6	8.1	9.6
Lyon	3,720	4,373	4,959	6,185	52.8	30.6	18.7	9.5	33.7	54.1	61.0	68.0	3.3	6.4	9.1	10.1
McCracken	34,129	38,193	42,531	45,038	32.7	22.1	11.7	7.4	47.8	62.9	73.1	80.3	7.4	11.5	14.3	18.1
McCreary	6,194	8,145	9,118	10,668	74.0	56.0	39.4	26.6	14.8	28.8	40.2	52.6	4.1	5.2	4.6	6.7
McLean	5,346	6,149	6,316	6,737	51.9	36.3	23.5	11.0	32.1	47.1	58.6	70.8	2.8	5.6	6.6	8.7
Madison	19,544	26,152	32,274	42,125	44.3	30.4	19.2	11.9	40.6	54.9	64.8	75.2	12.0	17.8	19.1	21.8
Magoffin	5,087	6,841	7,567	8,410	71.4	55.0	40.4	28.5	17.5	30.1	38.2	50.1	2.5	5.5	4.6	6.3
Marion	8,010	9,606	10,339	11,772	54.1	38.7	23.3	15.2	31.1	44.9	58.9	70.5	4.9	6.7	6.4	9.1
Marshall	12,120	16,184	18,824	21,278	42.9	28.5	16.2	8.4	39.5	56.4	67.6	76.9	4.1	8.4	9.6	13.7
Martin	4,389	6,874	7,208	7,835	75.5	50.4	35.3	25.0	13.9	34.5	44.4	54.0	3.8	5.9	6.0	9.0
Mason	9,947	10,708	10,895	11,372	35.2	33.8	19.0	10.1	37.4	49.2	60.7	73.3	4.8	9.7	10.2	14.4

EDUCATIONAL ATTAINMENT: YEARS OF SCHOOL COMPLETED, 1970-2000

AREA	TOTAL PERSONS 25 YEARS AND OLDER				8 YEARS OF SCHOOL OR LESS				HIGH SCHOOL				4 OR MORE YEARS OF COLLEGE			
	1970	1980	1990	2000	1970	1980	1990	2000	1970	1980	1990	2000	1970	1980	1990	2000
Meade	8,481	11,623	13,790	16,131	34.0	22.4	13.7	7.0	51.6	64.2	74.3	77.9	14.0	12.2	11.0	11.3
Menifee	2,075	2,761	3,122	4,213	73.6	54.8	34.8	23.2	15.8	31.8	46.0	57.6	2.9	4.2	4.9	8.4
Mercer	9,361	11,520	12,757	14,158	43.1	30.9	20.5	9.6	39.9	52.3	62.8	75.8	6.3	9.2	8.9	13.5
Metcalfe	2,075	5,370	5,873	6,729	72.8	55.5	39.8	24.7	17.3	33.1	45.2	58.0	3.3	5.2	5.0	6.6
Monroe	6,683	7,454	7,553	7,896	71.3	57.0	38.3	26.4	20.4	32.4	47.1	57.8	4.0	5.2	6.9	8.4
Montgomery	8,241	11,405	12,460	15,033	50.4	37.4	25.7	14.7	34.1	46.8	56.1	70.5	6.5	8.0	9.2	13.4
Morgan	5,454	6,680	7,325	9,321	70.4	55.5	39.1	24.5	20.5	30.5	44.1	56.4	4.8	6.3	6.7	7.7
Muhlenberg	16,062	18,947	20,133	21,676	51.9	37.1	24.9	15.5	30.8	44.8	54.9	65.8	3.2	6.5	6.2	8.1
Nelson	11,095	14,802	18,159	23,785	47.0	29.8	16.9	9.6	37.8	56.0	67.4	79.0	7.1	10.0	9.3	13.4
Nicholas	3,741	4,329	4,420	4,636	54.0	39.1	25.0	16.5	28.7	42.0	55.4	62.9	3.0	6.3	6.0	7.5
Ohio	10,930	12,863	13,562	15,237	55.9	38.3	25.5	15.9	28.3	44.1	53.1	67.0	3.5	5.1	6.2	7.4
Oldham	7,789	15,518	21,049	30,366	38.3	17.1	7.9	4.8	42.4	69.3	80.2	86.5	7.1	16.4	22.9	30.6
Owen	4,596	5,460	5,887	6,999	54.5	40.3	24.8	14.1	31.2	41.6	55.2	67.9	3.5	7.0	7.4	9.1
Owsley	2,680	3,237	3,187	3,242	76.8	59.5	49.1	33.8	12.6	29.3	35.5	49.2	4.4	6.9	9.8	7.7
Pendleton	5,523	6,238	7,336	9,081	49.5	36.1	20.1	10.8	34.1	47.5	60.1	72.8	3.1	6.0	6.8	9.7
Perry	12,941	17,943	18,362	19,596	62.9	47.9	32.5	21.5	24.2	37.3	47.6	58.3	5.1	6.0	6.7	8.9
Pike	31,121	43,648	44,941	46,153	64.0	45.3	31.5	21.3	23.4	38.3	50.2	61.8	4.1	6.2	7.7	9.9
Powell	3,896	5,973	7,012	8,485	66.8	50.8	33.8	23.9	21.9	34.0	50.1	56.1	3.4	5.5	5.3	6.5
Pulaski	20,038	27,175	32,512	38,430	59.3	43.1	28.5	18.1	28.8	44.5	56.2	65.6	5.2	7.1	9.2	10.5
Robertson	1,360	1,424	1,408	1,566	58.6	45.1	29.7	21.3	27.0	40.7	50.8	60.9	3.4	6.6	7.7	8.7
Rockcastle	6,490	8,008	9,249	11,109	69.9	53.1	37.9	24.4	19.7	34.4	44.9	57.7	3.6	6.2	5.9	8.3
Rowan	6,910	9,205	10,476	12,455	52.9	36.6	27.4	16.8	35.0	51.0	57.9	70.9	12.4	16.9	17.3	21.9
Russell	6,162	8,384	9,839	11,437	67.2	48.9	32.7	22.7	22.0	37.4	50.2	61.8	4.7	6.0	6.2	9.6
Scott	9,261	12,203	14,554	20,459	40.7	28.5	13.9	7.6	42.6	55.2	69.1	80.5	8.6	11.6	15.2	20.3
Shelby	10,882	13,909	16,318	22,708	42.7	28.3	14.8	8.0	40.1	55.1	69.9	79.1	6.1	11.3	12.9	18.7
Simpson	7,381	8,586	9,730	10,680	49.6	32.7	21.9	12.5	36.0	49.8	58.9	73.6	5.4	7.6	8.8	11.9
Spencer	2,923	3,455	4,343	7,672	62.2	43.9	25.9	12.1	25.1	39.7	57.5	75.4	3.9	5.4	9.9	11.1
Taylor	9,549	12,533	13,792	15,253	55.1	41.3	27.4	20.1	30.8	44.1	57.4	68.0	5.5	8.2	10.1	12.2
Todd	6,232	7,090	7,028	7,758	55.3	45.4	30.0	20.7	30.6	41.3	50.6	63.5	5.5	5.8	7.1	9.2
Trigg	4,984	5,956	7,223	8,897	56.0	36.9	22.4	10.6	28.6	49.0	58.9	72.1	3.8	9.4	11.4	12.0
Trimble	2,895	3,699	3,931	5,340	46.4	29.8	19.7	11.0	33.4	49.2	61.6	70.7	2.9	5.3	7.3	7.6
Union	7,682	8,864	9,408	9,524	36.9	24.1	12.5	8.1	43.4	56.4	68.1	76.9	5.7	6.7	8.9	10.9
Warren	28,146	38,216	46,161	56,069	40.5	25.4	15.0	7.8	45.6	63.1	70.9	80.3	10.6	16.6	19.2	24.7
Washington	5,725	6,135	6,669	7,144	52.3	38.9	26.2	17.1	34.2	45.9	57.8	68.8	5.0	8.6	8.6	13.3
Wayne	7,818	9,759	11,030	13,153	73.5	58.8	39.4	26.1	18.2	29.6	44.6	57.8	2.6	5.3	5.5	7.2
Webster	8,084	8,902	9,089	9,424	51.5	34.2	19.9	12.5	30.2	47.3	60.7	70.9	3.2	5.2	6.0	7.1
Whitley	13,472	18,554	20,195	22,708	58.7	44.0	28.8	19.0	26.9	40.5	53.0	61.3	5.5	8.7	11.3	13.4
Wolfe	2,994	3,688	4,052	4,571	75.4	57.9	38.8	25.9	16.6	26.8	42.8	53.6	3.3	6.7	7.7	10.6
Woodford	7,749	10,267	12,840	15,546	36.8	24.6	12.2	7.5	46.0	60.8	73.5	82.6	9.6	15.6	19.5	25.9

Produced by the Kentucky State Data Center
Source: 1970, 1980, 1990, and 2000 Census of Population and Housing

Religion
Nancy Jo Kemper

Kentucky religion in 2005 shows all the hallmarks that characterized the religious outlook of the first pioneers. That early environment was characterized by separatism, individualism, local autonomy, biblicism, emotional fervor, and theological diversity. Moreover, the religious culture of Kentucky, over its long history, has played important roles in the nation's religious history and culture.

The majority of pioneers in the first three decades of exploration and settlement, from roughly 1769 to 1800, were either dissenting Baptists or people who were not so much anti-religion as areligious. The long hunters didn't have much time to worry about religion. The Anglican state religion of Virginia had forced many dissenters into North Carolina. Given the wild, sparse and ill-governed nature of the land beyond the mountains, churches had almost no hold on believers. South of Virginia, religion was not organized and churches were weak, due to the lack of trained clergy and because of the wide diversity of religious views.

Squire Boone II is said to have preached the first sermon in the state, and the first worship services were held in Harrod's Town in 1776. Two Roman Catholics, a school teacher and a doctor, came to Harrod's Town in 1776 and were the first of their particular professions. Jews also had a hand in early settlements. A Virginia mercantile business of Cohen

Statue at the Abbey of Gethsemani, Trappist, KY
Source: Sid Webb

and Isaacs secured the services of Daniel Boone to check out possibilities in the new territory for them, and the Gratz family of Philadelphia were among the first settlers of Lexington.

Currently, Baptists remain the largest religious group in the state with 45.4 percent of all religious adherents claiming that they are Baptists. Approximately 18.8 percent of religious adherents claim that they are Roman Catholic. The Jewish community remains strong and vibrant with 11 synagogues or temples around the state, while still amounting to less than 1 percent of all persons who claim some form of religion.

Today, as in the early days, although the state's culture is predominantly Christian and fundamentalist, only 53.4 percent of Kentuckians identify themselves as religious. In the third millennium, moreover, one can see even more religious pluralism in the commonwealth. The state universities have been largely responsible for introducing Asian and middle-eastern immigrants to the population, and these people have brought with them their rich religious heritages as Muslims, Hindus, Jains, Baha'is, and Buddhists. Although small in numbers, these religious traditions add to the cultural and spiritual vitality of the commonwealth.

With the exponential multiplication of population in Kentucky's first three decades, and the establishment in numerous towns in the land beyond the mountains, churches become more numerous. Their diversity, however, and the shortage of clergy, led to the inability of Christians to participate in the Lord's Supper or Holy Communion. With energy trickling down from the Great Revival in New England and new ideas generated by such Enlightenment thinkers as John Locke, coupled with spiritual hunger on the frontier, the ideas generated by these influences began to have consequences.

In Logan County, in 1797, Presbyterian James McGready started a great religious revival. In 1801, a crowd that some estimated at 25,000 gathered at Cane Ridge in Bourbon County, under the leadership of Barton W. Stone, for what would become the Second Great Revival in the history of the fledging country. Here was born a new movement, known as the Christian Church. "We are not the only Christians," they claimed, "but we are Christians only." They created a more vital, simple, and biblical approach to church life that was to become, at one time in the early 20th century, the largest indigenous American denomination, the Christian Church (Disciples of Christ).

As a result of divisive religious convictions, the descendants of the original followers of Barton W. Stone and another Christian Church founder, Alexander Campbell, are now separated into three branches from that original vine. Today those churches are the Christian Church (Disciples of Christ); the Christian Churches and Churches of Christ (often called Independent Christians); and the (non-instrumental) Churches of Christ. Their numbers together equal that of the United Methodists, which after Baptists and Catholics, formed the third largest denomination in Kentucky in 2005. Two congregations of this Stone-Campbell movement that emerged from the great revival at Cane Ridge are among the largest mega-churches in the United States: Southeast Christian in Louisville and Southland Christian in Lexington.

In 1806 and 1807 learning of the great revival and spiritual vitality in the new state west of the mountains, followers of Mother Anne Lee's United Society of Believers in Christ's Second Appearing, came to Kentucky and established communities near Harrodsburg at Pleasant Hill and at South Union, near Bowling Green. With a strong commitment to communal living, celibacy, the virtues of work and excellence in working, and a rigorous moral code, the Shakers, as they were called, contributed much to Kentucky agricultural life, architecture, tool making, and industry.

Catholics also saw the state of Kentucky as a great fertile place for the creation of religious houses and monasteries. In the area around Bardstown, now known as the "Kentucky Holy Land," a new diocese was created in 1808, and under the leadership of Bishop Benedict Joseph Flaget began to build their cathedral. The Basilica of St Joseph Proto-Cathedral was completed in 1823 with lavish gifts of art and other items from many European royal houses as well as from Pope Leo XII. The official seat of the diocese was moved to Louisville in 1841. Catholics, however, suffered from anti-papal sentiments during riots that occurred in Louisville in 1855. In an election day riot a mob of Know-Nothings entered the Louisville Cathedral, and 25 Irish-Americans were killed.

Nelson and Washington Counties are still home to the great Trappist Monastery of Gethsemani, home to the late writer and theologian Thomas Merton, and to the Sisters of Charity of Nazareth, Ky.

In recent years, two major Supreme Court cases dealing with church and state issues, most notably regarding the Ten Commandments, originated in Kentucky. In 1980, in Graham v. Stone, Superintendent of Public Instruction of Kentucky, the U.S. Supreme Court declared unconstitutional a Kentucky statute that required posting a copy of the Ten Commandments, purchased with private contributions, in each public school classroom in the state. With the issue of the Ten Commandments and their role in American history still simmering in people's memories, county courthouses in McCreary County and in Pulaski County decided to display the Ten Commandments. They were sued successfully by the ACLU. They followed this lawsuit by changing the displays to include other historical documents, and were again sued. Again, a Kentucky case about the Ten Commandments went to the U.S. Supreme Court where it was decided in June 2005, that the displays were unconstitutional because the intention of the counties was substantially to promote religion, and therefore were in violation of the First Amendment.

Today, Kentucky's religious environment might be best described as a kind of moralistic individualism. Christians are the clear majority, and much of the population, even those who do not attend church, would identify themselves as Christian. Christian denominations that believe in local church autonomy and individual responsibility before God predominate the religious landscape of the state. For the majority, the Bible has primary authority in structuring church life and in the formation of the believers' lives. Revivalism continues to be a means of bringing some excitement to small communities, and of reaching out to convert new believers.

RELIGION
Seminaries & Church Related Colleges

Nancy Jo Kemper

Kentucky has four theological seminaries, accredited by the Association of Theological Schools in the U.S. and Canada.

Louisville Presbyterian Theological Seminary
Established 1853
1044 Alta Vista Road
Louisville, KY 40205
Ph. (800) 264-1839

Southern Baptist Theological Seminary
Established 1859
2825 Lexington Road
Louisville, KY 40280
Ph. (800) 626-5525

Lexington Theological Seminary
Established 1865
631 S. Limestone
Lexington, KY 40508
Ph. (859) 252-0361

Asbury Theological Seminary
Established 1923
204 North Lexington Avenue
Wilmore, KY 40390
Ph. (800) 2.ASBURY, (859) 858-3581

Kentucky has 17 church-related, accredited colleges, affiliated with the Association of Independent Kentucky Colleges and Universities. They are:

- Asbury College
- Bellarmine University
- Brescia University
- Campbellsville University
- Centre College
- Cumberland College
- Georgetown College
- Kentucky Christian University
- Kentucky Wesleyan College
- Lindsey Wilson College
- Midway College
- Pikeville College
- St. Catharine College
- Spalding University
- Thomas More College
- Transylvania University
- Union College

There are numerous Bible colleges and institutions for preparation for ministry, including: Kentucky Christian University (Grayson); Clear Creek Bible College (Pineville); Kentucky Mountain Bible College (Van Cleve), Louisville Bible College; and Simmons Bible College (Louisville). *For full detail refer to the Education Section.*

Well, what about that?

Thomas Merton, a Trappist monk at Gethsemani (outside Bardstown), was a famous poet, peace activist and public scholar who came to his God through the poetry of William Blake. In "Seven Storey Mountain," Merton wrote, "I became more and more conscious of the necessity of a vital faith... I became conscious of the fact that the only way to live was to live in a world that was charged with the presence and reality of God." (Contributed by Frederick Smock, poet-in-residence at Bellarmine College, Louisville. His newest book, "Poetry & Compassion: Essays on Art & Craft," is forthcoming.

RELIGION

Amish & Shakers

Michelle Edwards

The Amish and Mennonites were part of the early Anabaptist movement in Europe, which took place at the time of the Reformation. The Anabaptists (late baptizers) believed that only adults who had confessed their faith should be baptized and that they should remain separate from the larger society. Both Catholics and Protestants put many early Anabaptists to death as heretics, and many others fled to the mountains of Switzerland and southern Germany. Here began the tradition of self-sufficient farming and home-based worship services. In 1536, a young Catholic priest from Holland named Menno Simons joined the Anabaptist movement. His writings and leadership united many of the Anabaptist groups, who were nicknamed "Mennonites." In 1693, a Swiss bishop named Jacob Amman broke from the Mennonite church. His followers were called the "Amish." Although the two groups have

Shakertown, Pleasant Hill
Source: Sid Webb

split several times, the Amish and Mennonite churches still share the same beliefs concerning baptism, non-resistance, and basic Bible doctrines. They differ in matters of dress, technology, language, form of worship, and interpretation of the Bible. The Amish and Mennonites both settled in Pennsylvania as part of William Penn's "holy experiment" of religious tolerance. The first sizable group of Amish arrived in Lancaster County in the 1720s. In 1824, they declared themselves separate from the home church in Europe.

Today, Amish and Mennonite settlements exist throughout Kentucky; many communities offer handcrafted Amish furniture, dry goods and specialty items are available. The first Amish settlement in Crittenden County was established in 1977. At present the Amish population has grown to almost 400 residents.

Shaker Village of Pleasant Hill

Diana Ratliff

The Shakers, more properly known as the United Society of Believers in Christ's Second Appearing, are one of the most compelling religious and social movements in American life. Originating in the religious ferment of Manchester, England, in the mid-18th century, the "Shaking Quakers" reached fruition after settlement in America in 1774.

"Mother" Ann Lee, the English-born leader of the Shakers, began her public ministry in America in 1780. She lived only until 1784, but her charismatic preaching had sparked a revolutionary new movement which has had enduring impact on

American religion and culture.

After reading of the great religious revivals being held in Kentucky in the early 1800s, three Shaker missionaries journeyed to Kentucky in 1805 to attend the Cane Ridge meetings in Bourbon County. They quickly converted three Kentuckians.

Being a communal society, one of the converts, Elisha Thomas, gave over his 100+ acre farm on the banks of Shawnee Run Creek and began to establish what is known today at Shaker Village of Pleasant Hill in Mercer County.

The Shakers were ardent believers in the millennialist principle of establishing "heaven on earth" through the practice of communitarian social organization, pacifism, celibacy, racial and gender equality, and the public confession of sin. The community at Pleasant Hill reached its peak numbers in the mid 1850s. Pleasant Hill was closed as an operating Shaker village in 1910, and the last Shaker remaining at Pleasant Hill died in 1923.

The restoration began in 1960, opened to the public in 1968 and has served thousands of guests from around the world each year. In "Pleasant Hill and Its Shakers," the late and much beloved Dr. Thomas D. Clark wrote: " 'Shakertown,' or Pleasant Hill, stands not so much as a monument to a narrow religious concept of a celibate society, guided by a willful woman and a prevailing streak of spiritualism, as to the ever-recurring dream in American history that somewhere on this vast continent man could find a hallowed spot to achieve two objectives: first, the redemption of man from his original sin, and, second, the creation of the prefect society in which simplicity, integrity, and quiet love of one's fellowman could prevail free from the machination of a highly materialistic world."

A premier history site, a visitor may talk with costumed interpreters about Shaker life in the 1850s. A National Historic Landmark, it's 34 pristinely restored 19th century buildings are set on 2,900 acres of rolling farmland. Overnight stays, daily programs of Shaker music and dance, skilled artisans demonstrating the 19th century trades of broom making, wood working, coopering, spinning, and weaving are available. Riverboat excursions and horse-drawn wagon rides offer a great way to enjoy the village and surrounding area.

The Shakers in South Union
Michelle Edwards

In 1807 Shakers came to South Union in Logan County and lived there until 1922. The Shakers kept meticulous journals of their activities and from these journals, we catch a glimpse of the history of their daily lives, their belief in work and worship, their inventions and contributions, the birth of the seed industry, textile production and what it was like to live during that period of time. A visit to this wonderful historic site takes one back in time and perhaps gives a better understanding of the challenges facing the Shakers. The Shaker Museum sits upon the historic site of the South Union Shaker Village in the commercial district of South Union. Located in the 40-room 1824 Centre House, the museum houses the nation's largest collection of western Shaker furniture. South Union was one of 24 villages established by the Shakers. During the village's 100-year history, the Shakers acquired and worked 6,000 acres of farmland, constructed over 200 buildings, and maintained industries that developed for them a national reputation.

Built in 1869 the Shaker Tavern was maintained by the Shakers as a thriving business for 40 years, catering to Victorian railroad travelers who stopped at South Union. The Shaker Tavern Bed & Breakfast became a private residence after the Shaker village closed in 1922 and was

1824 Centre House, South Union

reopened in 1992. Set in a beautiful country setting and operated by the Shaker Museum, the features include Victorian style furnishings, a full breakfast and admission to the museum.

See: http://www.shakervillageky.org/; http://www.bbonline.com/ky/shaker; http://www.shakermuseum.com/; http://religiousmovements.lib.virginia.edu/nrms/Shakers.html#profile

RELIGION
Appalachian
Pentecostalism

Patsy Sims

One of the most popular images of religion in Appalachia is that of serpent handlers. The sensationalism that has popularized this tradition since its inception has condescendingly described its followers, at best, as naive and misguided; at worst, as psychologically disturbed cultists. To themselves, they are ordinary people following their religious beliefs. Historically, serpent handlers as a group are considered to be part of the Pentecostal movement in America, but later they formed independent Pentecostal holiness churches.

There has been much debate over exactly where serpent handling originated, but there is much evidence that it spread out of Tennessee during the early years of the 20th century. The necessary elements were present in Tennessee to encourage the ritual of serpent handling. Vital to its growth was the presence of a fervent fundamentalist religious community with a traditional approach to biblical interpretation — with traditional values that would evoke and reinforce the practice.

Another critical factor in the growth of serpent handling was that it was necessary for the right person to take up a serpent first. This person, at least in East Tennessee, was George Hensley. Hensley may not have been the first person in the 20th century to handle a serpent in obedience to bibli-

Serpent handlers are dedicated believers
Source: Lexington Herald-Leader

cal text, but he did lay claim to being the first (Burton, 418). Hensley traveled throughout the South spreading serpent handling throughout the region. He eventually died from a snakebite on July 25, 1955 in Florida at the age of 70.

Serpent handlers are fundamentalists, and to the dedicated believers they are just carrying out the words of Jesus in St. Mark 16:17-18: "And these signs shall follow them that believe: in my name they shall cast out devils; they shall speak with new tongues: they shall take up serpents and if they drink any deadly thing, it shall not hurt them; they shall lay hands on the sick and they shall recover."

Most fundamentalist churches take the healing sign, but very few take the Bible literally on serpent handling. Of those that do handle serpents, they are not testing their faith, nor do they feel that they are testing God, as many Christians have accused

them of doing. They will not handle snakes unless they are "anointed" or that the power of God was sufficient to protect them. Serpent handlers say that they are "anointed" to pick up serpents and that without this divine intervention, they would be bitten. They feel that they are protected because they take the Bible literally. In serpent handling churches, no one is required to handle the snakes, and in most, no one under the age of 18 is allowed to handle snakes. When they do handle snakes, it is in the summer and fall months when the rattlers, cottonmouths and copperheads which are commonly handled can be caught. Church members capture their own snakes.

Source: Lexington Herald-Leader

Reprinted with permission of the publisher, University Press of Kentucky, Patsy Sims, "The Snake-Handlers: With Signs Following, Can Somebody Shout Amen,!" The University Press of Kentucky, (Lexington:1996).

DID YOU KNOW?

The practice of serpent handling is based in the Gospel according to St. Mark, Chapter 16, verses 17 and 18. In this passage, Jesus says, "And these signs shall follow them that believe; In my name shall they cast out devils; they shall speak with new tongues; they shall take up serpents; and if they drink any deadly thing, it shall not hurt them; they shall lay hands on the sick, and they shall recover."

JUSTICE.

The peace of society dependeth on Justice; the happiness of individuals, on the safe enjoyment of all their possessions. Keep the desires of thy heart, therefore, within the bounds of moderation; let the hand of Justice lead them aright. Cast not an evil eye on the goods of thy neighbour, let whatever is his property be sacred from thy touch. Let not temptation allure, nor any provocation excite thee to lift up thy hand to the hazard of his life. Defame him not in his character; bear no false witness against him. Corrupt not his servant to cheat or forsake him; and the wife of his bosom, O, tempt not to sin! It will be a grief to his heart, which thou canst not relieve; an injury to his life, which no reputation can atone. In thy dealings with men, be impartial and just; and do unto them as thou wouldst they should do unto thee. Be faithful to thy trust, and deceive not the man that relieth upon thee; be assured it is less evil in the sight of God to steal than to betray. Oppress not the poor, and defraud not of his hire the labouring man. When thou sellest for gain, hear the whisperings of conscience, and be satisfied with moderation; nor from the ignorance of the buyer make advantage to thyself. Pay the debts which thou owest: for he who gave thee credit relied upon thy honor; and to withhold from him his due, is both mean and unjust. Finally, O son of society! examine thy heart, call remembrance to thy aid; and if in any of those things thou findest thou hast transgressed, take sorrow and shame to thyself, and make speedy reparation to the utmost of thy power.

Note — until the late 1780s, American publishers practiced the English method of typesetting the letter "s" as an "f". Source: The Kentucky Almanac 1818, published by William Sebree, Georgetown, Ky.

Law Enforcement & Crime

Glen Cordner

Kentucky is 46th among the 50 states in the number of state and local police officers per population, with 1.77 police per 1,000 residents. (Louisiana is first with 4.15). In other words, only four states have fewer police officers per population than Kentucky. (They are Minnesota, West Virginia, Vermont, and Washington.) That might seem worrisome, except for another statistic – Kentucky has the sixth lowest reported crime rate in the nation. The big picture, then, is that Kentucky has a low crime rate and few police officers, compared to other states.

Every state has a mixture of four types of police officers: (1) federal, such as FBI agents and customs enforcement officers; (2) state, such as state police or highway patrol troopers; (3) local, such as town police officers and sheriff's deputies; and (4) special, such as campus police and game wardens. Kentucky's 7,144 non-federal police officers are distributed as follows:

State	937 (13.1%)
Local	5,924 (82.9%)
Special	283 (4.0%)

When Kentucky is compared to the other 49 states, it has a typical or average profile in many respects. For example, it is 24th in the number of federal officers, 28th in the number of state and local officers, and 19th in the number of law enforcement agencies (382). It has some other distinctive features.

Kentucky is 4th in the number of sheriff depart-

Luther Risner
Kentucky State Highway Patrol
Source: Risner Family

ments (120).

Kentucky is 30th in the number of sheriffs and sheriff's deputies (1,406).

Kentucky is 36th in the average number of sworn officers per agency (18.7). (Hawaii is #1 at 416.3, California #2 at 142.5.)

Kentucky is ninth in the portion of its total state and local police officers accounted for by the state police (13.1 percent).

These statistics show that Kentucky has many sheriff departments, but they are relatively small. The state also has a large number of town and city police departments, most of which are rather small. The state police in Kentucky represent a larger share of the total law enforcement community than in most other states. In comparative law enforcement terms, Kentucky is a strong state police, weak sheriff state with a heavy preponderance of small town police departments.

SHERIFF DEPARTMENTS

Kentucky's 120 sheriff departments vary widely in size, from small offices with only a sheriff (Robertson County) or a sheriff and one deputy (Elliott, Lee, Nicholas, and Trimble Counties) to the Jefferson County sheriff's office with 240 deputies. Sheriff departments in Kentucky are authorized to perform police and law enforcement duties, but their primary obligations are to collect certain taxes and fees and serve writs for the courts. These are historically common sheriff functions around the U.S. that hark back to English traditions. Kentucky sheriffs have retained these historical functions to a greater extent than sheriffs in many other states, though, probably due to the Commonwealth's numerous small counties that have not seen fit, or been financially able, to appoint other officials to perform such tasks. As a result, because of these fiscal and civil priorities, many Kentucky sheriff departments do not exercise their police and law enforcement authority to the degree that otherwise might be expected in a predominantly rural state.

Sheriffs, of course, are elected. As such they are independent of other political and government officials. However, they typically derive part of their funding from the county fiscal court, and consequently have to negotiate with county judge executives and other elected county officials on budgetary matters. Also, they derive much of their funding in the form of a percentage of the taxes and fees that they collect and through fees for serving writs for the court. Realistically, the primacy of these duties follows from their revenue-producing nature.

The most distinctive characteristic of Kentucky sheriffs is something they do not do. They do not run jails. In other states, running the county jail is one of the sheriff's primary responsibilities and jail duties typically account for half or more of sheriff department employees. In Kentucky, however, each county has a separate constitutional office of elected jailer. This unique bifurcation of the sheriff and jailer positions helps explain the small size of many of Kentucky's sheriff offices and the relatively weak role that sheriffs play in Kentucky law enforcement.

TOWN AND CITY POLICE

Kentucky's largest police agency is the Louisville Metro Police Department with 1,192 sworn officers. This agency was formed in 2003 through the merger of the Louisville Police Department and the Jefferson County Police Department, which prior to the merger were the second and third largest police agencies in the state, respectively (after the state police). The second largest local police agency in Kentucky is now the Lexington Division of Police, with 516 authorized sworn officers. Of course, most of Kentucky's municipal police agencies are much smaller. Nationally, 50 percent of police departments have ten or fewer sworn police officers. In Kentucky, 75 percent have ten or fewer officers.

STATE POLICE

The Kentucky State Police, like state police in other states, were a fairly late addition to the commonwealth's law enforcement system. The Kentucky Highway Patrol was formed in 1936 with 40 officers. It evolved into the Kentucky State Police in 1948.

The Kentucky State Police hired its first black trooper in the 1960s and its first female trooper in the 1970s. The distinctive gray uniform has not changed, but patrol vehicle colors have changed over the years from black to gray to blue and white to white and finally back to gray. The agency was given its nickname The Thin Gray Line in the 1960s by then Director Ted Bassett.

Today the Kentucky State Police have over 1,000 authorized sworn positions. The agency operates in all 120 counties but particularly in rural areas, providing front-line police patrol and investigations as well as important support services such as central criminal records, the state crime lab, and the Law Information Network of Kentucky (LINK) computer system.

EDUCATION AND TRAINING

Police education and training programs in Kentucky primarily date from 1966, when Eastern Kentucky University began offering law enforcement classes and the Kentucky Peace Officer's Standards and Training Council was established within state government. The first college course attracted 49 students and initial police training was only one to three weeks in length. From those modest beginnings, EKU's College of Justice and Safety now boasts 44 full-time faculty, 1,500 students, over $60 million per year in federal and state grants and contracts, and the university's Program of Distinction banner. The Kentucky Law Enforcement Council now oversees mandated police recruit training of 16 weeks duration, as well as the 40 hours of in-service training required every year for every peace officer, including chiefs of police. Much of the training is provided by the Department of Criminal Justice Training, a nationally-accredited state agency that operates out of modern, state-of-the-art facilities on the EKU campus.

Kentucky's police training system is the envy of most other states. Part of the credit is owed to a succession of leaders of the Department of Criminal Justice Training, from Robert Stone through Dr. John Bizzack. Importantly as well, the architects of the system in Kentucky had the foresight to establish a surcharge on property and casualty insurance as the funding mechanism for police training. This surcharge has provided steady revenue year after year that self-adjusts for inflation. Without this funding source, the last 40 years of police training in Kentucky would have been much more susceptible to the vagaries of state finances and certainly would not have resulted in the national leadership position now enjoyed.

LAW ENFORCEMENT OFFICERS KILLED IN THE LINE OF DUTY (1950 - 2004)

Name	Date	Location	Name	Date	Location
CLARENCE L MEENACH	5/11/1950	Russell	JOHN W HUTCHINSON	6/4/1975	KSP
EZRA SUTHERLAND	6/19/1950	Jefferson Co.	BOBBY A MCCOUN JR	9/1/1975	KSP
ROY CONWAY	7/28/1950	Pike Co.	WILLIAM F PICKARD	1/21/1976	KSP
ROBERT R MILLER	2/14/1951	KSP	MICHAEL T SMITH	3/11/1976	Jefferson Co.
OWEN FLACK	6/17/1951	Hopkinsville	WILSON McLAIN	4/17/1976	Harlan Co.
WILLIAM M CARRICO SR	9/15/1951	Carrollton	WILLIAM D COBB	8/20/1976	Hart Co.
CLAUDE STRONG	1/8/1952	Hickman	MARK W HINES	8/29/1976	Jefferson Co.
JAMES B JASPER	7/3/1952	Pulaski Co.	MICHAEL L WILLIAMS	8/29/1976	Salyersville
LAITH WARREN	9/18/1952	Bell Co.	WILLIS D MARTIN	4/26/1977	KSP
JOHN P MINOGUE	10/4/1952	Louisville	GWEN DOWNS	5/16/1977	Louisville
CREED J. JOHNSON	10/31/1952	Lewis Co.	JOE C LYKINS	10/2/1977	Boyle Co.
ALVIN L KEOWN	11/8/1952	Jefferson Co.	JIMMY R TOLSON	6/26/1978	Campton
LEE T HUFFMAN	5/4/1953	KSP	KENNETH R NALLY	11/6/1978	Jefferson Co.
ROBERT HENSLEY	3/27/1954	Owsley Co.	LESTER E REID	1/5/1979	Warren Co.
CLARENCE TAYLOR	3/27/1954	Owsley Co.	CLINTON E CUNNINGHAM	2/11/1979	KSP
HENRY E StCLAIR	4/5/1954	Jefferson Co.	CLAUDE E FLINCHUM	3/4/1979	Wolfe Co.
HUBBARD FERGUSON	6/18/1954	Gallatin Co.	ALBERT B SALLEE JR	5/12/1979	Louisville
WILLIAM D PORTER	2/25/1955	LaGrange	EARL SMITH	5/15/1979	Pike Co.
JACK W RANIER SR	11/21/1955	Henderson	DANIEL L HAY	10/16/1979	Maysville
OWEN DAVENPORT	7/13/1956	Corrections	EDWARD R HARRIS	11/7/1979	KSP
EDWARD R FROEDGE	11/4/1956	Owensboro	CHRISTOPHER M DUNN	4/3/1980	Jefferson Co.
WILLIE LEWIS SR	1/1/1957	Leslie Co.	HIRAM A RITCHIE	6/30/1980	Perry Co.
LUTHER W HAMMOND	2/18/1957	Corrections	HORACE HALL JR	8/14/1980	Bell Co.
NOVEL McREYNOLDS	4/29/1957	Murray	JEROME S CLIFTON	10/1/1980	KSP
ARLIN E. CURNEAL	6/20/1957	Hopkins Co.	RONNIE E SEELYE	1/27/1981	Louisville
EDWARD P NOWAKOWSKI	7/10/1957	Louisville	DARRELL V PHELPS	8/7/1981	KSP
WILLARD C MILSTEAD	10/15/1957	Princeton	RANDALL COOK	4/16/1982	Knott Co.
PAGE W MASON	6/27/1958	Irvine	ALEX EVERSOLE	1/4/1983	Perry Co.
AUSTIN E VANOVER SR	8/13/1958	Henderson	CHARLES D WENTWORTH	4/12/1983	Shelby Co.
WILLIAM L LONG	10/4/1958	Louisville	JACK D CLAYWELL	6/16/1983	Grayson
HERBERT C BUSH	10/11/1958	KSP	RICKY A LAFOLLETTE	8/18/1983	Louisville
STANLEY PITAKOS	10/16/1958	Newport	PATRICIA ROSS	3/1/1984	Corrections
ELVIN PATRICK	1/17/1959	Whitley Co.	DONALD R WILLIAMS	6/16/1984	West Point
ORVILLE C TRINKLE JR	3/29/1960	Louisville	CARNIE F HOPKINS	9/9/1984	Livingston Co.
DELMAR WHITWORTH SR	5/24/1960	Jefferson Co.	ANTHONY E JANSEN	12/30/1984	Newport
WESLEY S. FANNIN	8/1/1961	Floyd Co.	WILLIAM R BURNS	7/5/1985	Radcliff
DOUGLAS F HUTTON	12/2/1961	Pulaski Co.	ROY H MARDIS	8/23/1985	Lexington
SAM L GREEN	1/1/1962	Rowan Co.	MICHAEL R GREEN	1/26/1986	Corrections
JAMES C SMITH	7/20/1962	Barbourville	JOHN R WEISS	2/12/1986	Shively
LEONARD ADAMS SR	12/6/1962	Letcher Co.	ROBERT T WALKER	2/16/1986	Irvine
WILLIAM E TEVIS	5/26/1963	KSP	CHARLES F CASH	5/9/1986	Corrections
COSBY H WHITTED JR	8/23/1963	Louisville	JACK S DEUSER	7/29/1986	Jefferson Co.
ELMER MOBLEY	5/28/1964	KSP	JOHN R HERRON	12/20/1986	Falmouth
CECIL W UZZLE	5/28/1964	KSP	RUSSELL J ESTEP	1/2/1987	Louisa
WARREN C CAMPBELL SR	8/29/1964	Montgomery Co.	ROBERT C BANKER	3/19/1987	Fish & Wildlife
HAROLD L CATRON SR	9/16/1964	Somerset	JAMES M RICHARDSON	2/1/1988	Pulaski Co.
JAMES SANSBURY	2/21/1965	Louisville	ALTON EMBRY JR	5/7/1988	Louisville
DELANO G POWELL	7/8/1965	KSP	THOMAS A NOONAN	9/10/1988	Highland Heights
CALEB DEHART	8/22/1965	Leslie Co.	JOSEPH M ANGELUCCI	11/23/1988	Fayette Co.
GLEN A STEPHENS	9/3/1965	Olive Hill	JOHNNY M EDRINGTON	12/21/1988	KSP
AUTHUR G DOTSON	2/16/1966	Russellville	FRANK W PYSHER JR	1/10/1989	Jefferson Co.
JAMES STRONG JR	5/28/1966	Corydon	CURTIS E LOBB	5/17/1989	Greensburg
MACK E BRADY	11/9/1966	KSP	SHELBY W NEASE	7/18/1989	Hazard
WALTER L MEEK	11/26/1966	Johnson Co.	TERRY L SANDERS	9/15/1989	Mayfield
DANNY L REDMON	1/3/1967	Lexington	DONALD L FERGUSON	4/28/1990	Albany
CLOYD A CHARLTON	2/6/1967	Adairville	ROBERT P PALMER	9/25/1990	Elsmere
WILLIAM F MEYER	9/1/1967	Louisville	EDWARD E FLORA	10/26/1990	Warren Co.
JOHN L THOMAS	11/21/1967	Lexington	GARY E KIDWELL	1/20/1991	Stanford
JOSEPH L PRICE	11/29/1967	Louisville	KENNETH M McCARTY	5/23/1991	Bourbon Co.
DONALD RONNEBAUM	7/26/1968	Covington	STEVE L BENNETT	1/30/1992	Powell Co.
EARL J BERTRAM	8/18/1968	Jefferson Co.	ARTHUR C BRISCOE	1/30/1992	Powell Co.
JAMES RYAN SR	11/4/1968	Danville	CECIL E CYRUS	3/18/1992	Johnson Co.
OSCAR BURKHART	11/7/1968	Harlan Co.	CHARLES K TODD	8/23/1992	Mayfield
DONALD W GASKIN	12/30/1969	Louisville	FLOYD W CHEEKS	10/27/1993	Jefferson Co.
JAMES RATLIFF	12/30/1969	Louisville	JOHN L BECK	1/27/1994	Rowan Co.
JOHN SCHAEFER	5/2/1971	Louisville	MICHAEL R CARRITHERS	8/17/1995	Louisville
WILBUR HAYES	5/2/1971	Louisville	ERIC S STAFFORD	6/26/1996	Edmonson Co.
RAYMOND OYLER JR	5/8/1971	Louisville	GREGORY HANS	3/10/1997	Jefferson Co.
AMOS A FAULKNER JR	7/20/1971	Hopkinsville	COLEMAN BINION	9/5/1997	Carter Co.
JACK BROCK	12/7/1971	Harlan Co.	MICHAEL A PARTIN	1/4/1998	Covington
WILLIAM H BARRETT	12/19/1971	KSP	BRANDON H THACKER	4/16/1998	ABC
JAMES W McNEELY	4/8/1972	KSP	REGINA W NICKLES	10/14/1998	Harrodsburg
LAWRENCE CONLEY	4/12/1972	Floyd Co.	JOEY T VINCENT	6/27/1999	Greenville
BILLY F WOOD	8/8/1972	Williamstown	JASON W CAMMACK	4/23/2000	KVE
WALTER O THURTELL	9/29/1972	KSP	BILLY R. WALLS III	11/13/2001	Jessamine Co.
ORIE HICKS	10/8/1972	Harlan Co.	CHARLES B MORGAN JR	11/28/2001	Jessamine Co.
TOMMY RAY	4/20/1973	Louisville	SAMUEL W CATRON	4/13/2002	Pulaski Co.
JOE WARD JR	4/23/1973	KSP	HOWARD B. CALLIS	12/10/2002	Corrections
WILLIAM C SMITH	4/26/1973	KSP	RAY B. FRANKLIN	12/12/2002	Charitable Gaming
DENVER TABOR	7/20/1973	Fish & Wildlife	EDDIE MUNDO JR	4/16/2003	LaGrange
BRISTOL TAYLOR	11/23/1973	Knott Co.	DOUGLAS W BRYANT	5/19/2003	Fish & Wildlife
JONAH D COX	2/23/1974	Louisville	ROBERT T HANSEL	10/2/2003	Lynch
WILLIAM C FREDERICK	4/24/1974	Paris	STEVEN L HUTCHINSON	6/17/2004	Grayson Co.
ARMAND VANCLEAVE	4/27/1974	Shively			

Source: Kentucky Law Enforcement Memorial Foundation

LAW ENFORCEMENT & CRIME

Crime & Traffic Report

2004 KENTUCKY CRIME FACTS

- 113,635 serious crimes were committed in 2004
- A serious crime was committed every 4 minutes, 38 seconds
- Murder was committed every 40 hours, 33 minutes
- Firearms were used in 65 percent of all murders
- 71 percent of all murder victims were white; 66 percent were male
- Rape was committed every 7 hours, 14 minutes
- Robbery was committed every 2 hours, 34 minutes
- 57.4 percent of violent crimes were solved
- 768 police officers were assaulted
- 19.4 percent of property crimes were solved
- Property crimes outnumbered violent crimes by 9.7 to 1
- 23,444 persons were arrested for DUI
- 40,793 arrests were made for drug violations
- A total of 252,298 arrests were made in 2004

The overall crime rate in Kentucky in 2004 decreased by 0.7 percent compared to 2003. The categories that show an increase are murder, rape, robbery and auto theft. Aggravated assault, burglary, larceny-theft, and arson reflect decreases. The largest percentage of decrease was in arson, showing 188 fewer reported offenses.

The offense of murder, the most serious of all crimes, shows an increase of 19.3 percent

The murder clearance rate is one of the highest at 83.3 percent. Although some murders are difficult to solve, the intensity of police investigations, together with solvability factors, account for the high clearance rate for murder. The circumstances of the 216 murders in Kentucky show that an argument was involved in 72 murders; a felony involved in 26; a lover's quarrel in nine murders; gangland – 0; other – 36; unknown – 73. Sixty-five percent of murder victims were killed with a firearm (handgun: 101; shotgun: 15; rifle: 13; unknown: 11). Sixty-six percent of murder victims were male; 32 percent female; 2 percent unknown sex; 71 percent of murder victims were African American; 26 percent were white.

Kentucky's crime index for 2004 is based on the current estimated population of 4.15 million. The crime rate is tabulated on seven major offenses designated Index Crimes by the Federal Bureau of Investigation's Uniform Crime Reporting program. These seven categories include four violent offenses (murder, rape, robbery and aggravated assault) and

OFFENSES REPORTED, 2003 & 2004

	2004	2003	% CHANGE	% DIST.
1. MURDER	216	181	19.30%	0.20%
2. RAPE	1,251	1,124	11.30%	1.10%
3. ROBBERY	3,372	3,224	4.60%	3.00%
4. AGGRAVATED ASSAULT	5,232	5,703	-8.30%	4.60%
5. BURGLARY	25,784	26,034	-0.80%	22.70%
6. LARCENY THEFT	68,478	69,083	-0.60%	60.30%
7. MOTOR VEHICLE THEFT	8,669	8,253	9.70%	7.60%
8. ARSON	633	821	-22.90%	0.50%
TOTAL	113,635	114,423	-0.70%	100.00%

Source: Kentucky State Police, 2004 Crime Report, www.kentuckystatepolice.org.

three nonviolent crimes (burglary, larceny theft and auto theft).

Consider the following explanation to help clarify the data classification process:

1) Murder is the unlawful killing of a human being with malice aforethought; it does not include suicides, negligent manslaughters, accidental deaths, assaults to murder, traffic fatalities and attempted murders.

2) Rape (37.6 percent clearance rate) reflects the number of offenses for each female victim raped or upon whom an assault to rape or attempt to rape has been made.

3) Robbery (69.0 percent clearance rate) with $16,186,156.97 in property stolen, is a crime committed in the presence of the victim who is directly confronted with the perpetrator and is threatened with force or put in fear that force will be used.

4) In the absence of force or threat of force (as in pocket-picking or purse-snatching), robbery is classified as larceny (22.1 percent clearance rate).

the Anti-Arson Act of 1982, includes only fires determined through investigation to have been willfully or maliciously set.

FAMILY OR DOMESTIC VIOLENCE IN KENTUCKY IN 2004

Domestic violence is a problem that has been of major news focus both nationally and in Kentucky. The number of reported cases and victims assisted in protective shelters is proof that this is a serious public safety issue worthy of priority response. Domestic violence includes any of the following crimes when committed by one family member/partner against another: homicide, kidnapping, sex offenses, stalking, assault, and terroristic threatening.

In FY04, the Administrative Office of the Courts reported that 17,237 petitions were filed by persons seeking Domestic Violence Protective Orders. There were 18,811 disposition case closings. (AOC does not distinguish between cases dismissed and types of orders issued).

DOMESTIC VIOLENCE

Total Kentucky Adult Protection Reports Received by DSS in FY'04 (Adult Abuse, Spouse Abuse, Self Neglect, Caretaker Neglect and Exploitation)	35,319
Total Number of Resulting Allegations	7,694
Domestic Violence Allegations Investigated (Spouse, Ex-Spouse, Paramour)	22,269
Adult Abuse Allegations Investigated	6,097
Caretaker Neglect, Self Neglect and Exploitation Allegations Investigated	7,198
Percent of Total Adult Protection Allegations due to Domestic Violence	63.1 percent
Percent Decrease of Domestic Violence Allegations from FY'03	-26.1 percent

Source: Kentucky State Police, 2004 Crime Report, www.kentuckystatepolice.org.

5) Aggravated assaults (53.7 percent clearance rate) include all assaults by one person upon another with the intent to kill, maim, or inflict severe bodily injury with the use of any dangerous weapon. If a dangerous weapon is used, it is not necessary that injury result from the assault.

6) The offense of burglary (13.3 percent clearance rate) includes all offenses known as burglary (any degree) plus attempts to commit burglary.

7) Motor vehicle theft (16.6 percent clearance rate) also includes attempted theft of a motor vehicle. Of the 8,669 vehicles stolen in Kentucky, 19.7 percent were recovered.

8) The offense of arson (20.7 percent clearance rate), in keeping with the passage of

HATE BIAS CRIMES IN KENTUCKY IN 2004

A "hate crime" is a criminal offense committed against a person or property which is motivated, in whole or in part, by the offender's bias against a race, religion, disability, ethnicity/national origin, or sexual orientation. These criminal offenses fall into the major crimes (murder, rape, robbery, aggravated assault, burglary, larceny-theft, motor vehicle theft and arson), plus lesser crimes of simple assault, intimidation and vandalism. The most common offenses involving hate-bias crimes for 2004 were "intimidation," and "destruction/damage vandalism." In 2004 the most commonly reported bias motivation was racial. The second largest percentage was sexual orientation, followed by religious for third place, ethnicity/national origin for fourth place, and disability for fifth place.

By far, individuals (61 or 80.3 percent) were reported to be the main hate crime target.

The most frequently reported location of bias crimes in 2004 was residence/homes. The second most common location was parking lot/garages. The most common race of suspected offender of hate crimes was white.

DRUG ARRESTS
IN KENTUCKY IN 2004

There were 40,793 individuals arrested for drug violations in Kentucky in 2004: 5,092 for opium or cocaine; 15,911 for marijuana; 2,205 for synthetic narcotics and 17,585 for other dangerous non-narcotic drugs. DUI (driving

Department for Community
Based Services
Adult and Child Abuse
24-hour Toll Free
Reporting Hotline
1-800-752-6200

under the influence) arrests totaled 23,444; adults counted for 22,342 of the arrests; 18,895 males and 4,067 females; 20,149 were white and 2,049 African Americans.

Traffic Facts

2004 COLLISION SUMMARY

TYPE COLLISION REPORTED	2003	2004	% CHANGE
Fatal (Public Roads)	845	854	1.1
Nonfatal injury (Public Roads)	31,075	29,933	-3.7
Property Damage Only (Public Roads)	97,908	102,931	5.1
Total Number Reported (Public Roads)	129,828	133,718	3
Parking Lots/ Private Property	24,247	23,514	2.9
Total All Reported	154,075	157,232	2
Fatal (Total)	860*	866**	0.7
*Includes 15 fatal collisions on parking lots/private property			
**Includes 12 fatal collisions on parking lots/private property			

Approximately one of every 4,900 Kentucky residents died as a result of a fatal traffic collision on a public road. About one in 102 Kentucky residents was injured in a traffic collision.* [*Based on 4,145,922 population estimates.] Approximately one of every 14 drivers licensed in Kentucky was involved in a traffic collision in Kentucky. About one of 2,500 Kentucky drivers was involved in a fatal collision.** [**Based on 2,888,354 licensed drivers (including learner permits)].

There were 133,718 total collisions in Kentucky. Total collisions increased 3.0 percent from 2003 to 2004.

Collisions with moving motor vehicles (89,932 or 65 percent) and collisions with fixed objects (24,661 or 24 percent) account for 89 percent of the fatalities and injuries. Sixty-seven (67) percent of all collisions reported involved collisions between two or more moving vehicles (not in a parking lot). Eighteen (18) percent of all collisions involved collisions with fixed objects. Fourteen (14) percent of all collisions did not involve a col-

lision with either a moving vehicle or a fixed object. About 11 percent were other types of collisions.

Fifty (50) pedestrians were killed and 849 were injured in traffic collisions in 2004. Twenty-five (25) percent of the pedestrians killed or injured were 14 years of age or younger, while 7 percent were age 65 or older.

Forty-two (42) percent of all fatal collisions involved a collision with another moving vehicle. Thirty-nine (39) percent of the fatal collisions reported during 2003 involved collisions with fixed objects. Collisions with pedestrians accounted for 6 percent of the fatal collisions. Fourteen (14) percent of the fatal collisions were other type collisions. Most of these (10 percent) were non-collisions (vehicle overturning or other non-collision). Four of the 20 persons killed in hit-and-run collisions were pedestrians and none were pedalcyclists. One hundred three (103) pedestrians and 40 pedalcyclists were injured.

Most collisions (63 percent) occurred in urban areas. However, the majority of fatal

DEATH AND INJURY SUMMARY

	2003	2004	% CHANGE
Persons Killed – Public Roads	928	964	3.9
Persons Killed – Parking Lots/Private Property	17	14	-17.6
Persons Killed (Total)	945	978	3.5
Perons Injured – Public Roads	46,966	44,986	-4.2
Persons Injured – Parking Lots/ Private Property	1,623	1,226	-24.5
Persons Injured (Total)	48,589	46,212	-4.9

collisions (57 percent) took place in rural areas of Kentucky. Although nonfatal injury collisions were divided between urban and rural areas, nearly twice as many property damage collisions were reported in urban areas; 79 percent of all collisions occurred on straight roads and 21 percent on curved roads. Thirty-nine (39) percent of the fatal collisions during 2004 occurred on curved roads.

Seventy-two (72) percent of all collisions reported occurred during daylight hours. Twenty-three (23) percent of all collisions occurred during dark hours, and 5 percent occurred at dawn or dusk. Fifty-six (56) percent of all fatal collisions occurred during daylight hours, 37 percent occurred during dark hours, and 7 percent at dawn or dusk.

Twenty-three (23) percent of all collisions and 32 percent of fatal collisions occurred on weekends (Saturday and Sunday combined). November ranked highest for total number of collisions and February showed the lowest number of total collisions. August reported the highest number of fatal collisions; January showed the lowest.

The total number of persons killed in holiday periods in 2004 was 65 as compared to 44 in 2003. The Labor Day holiday period registered the highest number of fatalities. The lowest number of holiday fatalities occurred over the Christmas holiday.

There were 10,015 collisions in which a truck was involved. This resulted in 137 fatalities

and 2,806 injuries. Twenty-three (23) percent of the truck collisions occurred on county or city streets, 20 percent on interstates, and 47 percent on U.S. and state-numbered routes. Twenty (20) percent of the hazardous cargo collisions occurred on interstates and 54 percent on U.S. and state-numbered routes.

Fifty-seven (57) percent of the drivers who were involved in collisions during 2004 (where sex was listed) were male; 43 percent were female. In fatal collisions, 71 percent of the drivers were male and 29 percent were female; there were 640 males versus 324 females killed. Twenty-six (26) percent of all persons killed in traffic collisions were in the 15- to 24-year old age group; there were 154 fatalities in collisions involving a teenage driver (76 of these fatalities were the teenage driver). There were 24 fatalities in alcohol-related collisions involving teenage drivers (10 of these fatalities were the teenage driver).

ASSAULTS ON LAW ENFORCEMENT OFFICERS IN 2004

In 2004, no Kentucky law enforcement officer was required to pay the supreme sacrifice of giving their life in the line of duty for the citizens of this great Commonwealth. However, 768 police officers were assaulted. Of the officers assaulted, 299 officers received personal injury (38.9 percent of the total number of officers assaulted); and 92.1 percent of police assaults were cleared.

Source: Kentucky State Police, 2004 Crime Report, www.kentuckystatepolice.org.

TOTAL DEATH RATES
(deaths per 100 million miles traveled*)

YEAR	KILLED	KY	RATE** U.S.
1989	776	2.4	2.3
1990	851	2.5	2.2
1991	828	2.4	2
1992	819	2.2	1.8
1993	875	2.2	1.8
1994	791	2	1.8
1995	856	2.1	1.8
1996	846	2	1.8
1997	865	1.9	1.7
1998	869	1.9	1.6
1999	819	1.7	1.5
2000	823	1.8	1.5
2001	843	1.8	1.5
2002	915	2	1.6
2003	928	2	1.5
2004	964	2.1	1.5

*miles raveled in Kentucky in 2004=47.2 billion
**Includes Public Roads

Did you know?

In 2004, in Kentucky, there were 5,645 alcohol-related crashes in which 199 people were killed. This number represents a 12 percent increase in alcohol-related fatalities from the previous year.

LAW ENFORCEMENT & CRIME
Federal & State Prisons

Federal Prisons

Federal Bureau of Prisons
www.bop.gov
Harley G Lappin, Director
Home Owners Loan Corp Bldg Rm 654
320 1st St NW
Washington DC 20534
(202) 307-3250

FMC Lexington
Joe W Booker Jr, Warden
3301 Leestown Rd
Lexington KY 40511
(859) 255-6812
An administrative facility for male inmates. It has a population of approximately 1933.

FCI Ashland
Linda Sanders, Warden
St Rt 716
PO Box 888
Ashland KY 41105
(606) 928-6414
A low security institution housing 1218 male inmates.

FCI Manchester
Jose Barron Jr, Warden
PO Box 3000
Manchester KY 40962
(606) 598-1900
A medium security facility with a male population of 1124.

USP Big Sandy
US Penitentiary
1197 Airport Road
Inez KY 41224
(606) 433-2400
A high security satellite prison camp housing approximately 1541 male inmates.

USP McCreary
US Penitentiary
330 Federal Way
Pine Knot, KY 42635
(606) 354-7000
A high security facility that houses 1567 male offenders.

State Prisons

ADULT INSTITUTIONS

Blackburn Correctional Complex - Lexington
Steve Haney, Warden
3111 Spurr Rd
Lexington 40511
(859) 246-2366
Largest adult male minimum security institution (594) providing care, housing, custody, control and governmental services jobs to inmates.

Eastern KY Correctional Complex - West Liberty
John Motley, Warden
US 460 Index Hill
PO Box 636
West Liberty 41472
(606) 743-2800
A medium security institution with a current population of 1689.

Frankfort Career Development Ctr - Frankfort

Cookie Crews, Warden
PO Box 538
Frankfort 40601
(502) 564-2120

A 205-capacity minimum security facility. The majority of inmates are assigned to the Governmental Services Program Work Detail.

Green River Correctional Complex

Patti Webb, Warden
1200 River Rd
PO Box 9300
Central City 42330
(270) 754-5415

A medium/minimum security adult male correctional facility housing 982 inmates.

KY Correctional Institution for Women - Pewee Valley

Doris Deuth, Warden
Box 337 Ash Ave
Pewee Valley 40056
(502) 241-8454

Houses 726 women. The only adult female institution in the Commonwealth for the purpose of housing felons from all 120 counties.

KY State Penitentiary – Eddyville

Thomas L. Simpson, Warden
Rt 2 Box 128
Eddyville 42038
(270) 388-2211

The oldest and only maximum-security facility. This facility houses Kentucky's 36 Death-Row inmates. Total population is 856 inmates.

KY State Reformatory - LaGrange

Larry Chandler, Warden
3001 W Hwy 146
LaGrange 40032
(502) 222-9441

A medium security facility and the state's second largest institution in term of inmate population with a 1908-bed capacity.

Luther Luckett Correctional Complex –LaGrange

Ralph Dailey, Warden
Dawkins Rd Box 6
LaGrange 40031
(502) 222-0363

A medium/minimum security prison. The population is currently at 1073.

Northpoint Training Center - Burgin

Jim Morgan, Warden
Hwy 33 Box 479
Burgin 40310
(859) 239-7012

A medium-security institution with a current bed capacity of 1,256 inmates. Currently consists of 1,108 general population medium-security beds, 60 special management beds, and 40 minimum-security beds.

Roederer Correctional Complex

James Sweatt, Warden
3001 W Hwy 146
LaGrange 40031
(502) 222-0170

A medium/minimum security with 997 inmates.

Western KY Correctional Complex

Becky Pancake, Warden
374 New Bethel Rd
Fredonia 42411
(270) 388-9781

PRIVATE PRISONS

Lee Adjustment Center - Beattyville

Randall Stovall, Warden
Fairground Ridge
PO Box 900
Beattyville 41311
(606) 464-2866

Can house up to 390 medium security inmates.

Marion Adjustment Center - St Mary

Caroline Mudd, Warden
95 Raywick Rd
PO Box 10 Hwy 94
St Mary 40063
(270) 692-9622

The first private minimum-security prison in the country has 826- beds.

OCCC—Otter Creek Correctional Complex

Joyce Arnold, Warden
Hwy 306 Box 500
Wheelwright 41669
(606) 452-9700

Kentucky Travel Map

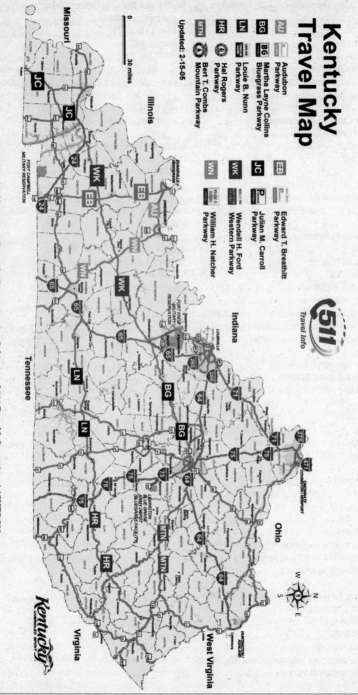

Updated: 2-15-05

AU	Audubon Parkway
BG	Martha Layne Collins Bluegrass Parkway
LN	Louie B. Nunn Parkway
HR	Hal Rogers Parkway
MTN	Bert T. Combs Mountain Parkway
EB	Edward T. Breathitt Parkway
JC	Julian M. Carroll Parkway
WK	Wendell H. Ford Western Parkway
WN	William H. Natcher Parkway

Source: Original base map, Kentucky Transportation Cabinet and 511 Travel Information, AASHTO 511.

Recreation & Travel

Herb Sparrow

entucky has a long history of attracting tourists. It could be argued that Daniel Boone was the first tourist, as he gazed at the verdant Bluegrass Region from atop Pilot Knob. Although Boone's interest in the state was economic — an untouched area to hunt, trap and settle — he was also enticed by the state's scenic wonders and beauty.

By the early 1800s, just a few years after it became a state, Kentucky was drawing tourists. Curious visitors came to see the saltpeter works at Mammoth Cave shortly after the War of 1812, and by the 1830s "tourists," including notables such as Ralph Waldo Emerson and Swedish soprano Jenny Lind, were traveling rough

Photo Source: Scott Risner

roads and staying in a "modernized" log cabin to view the underground wonders of the cave, where black guide Stephen Bishop became a legend during more than 20 years of leading tours by torch light.

Kentucky continued to exert a magnetic allure over the years. In his 1947 bestseller, Inside USA, author John Gunther said Kentucky was the state

Hiking Eastern Kentucky
Source: Sid Webb

that the most people wanted to see. Today, tourism is a major industry in the state. Numerous factors help the Bluegrass State draw millions of visitors each year from throughout the United States and many foreign countries.

Kentucky is home to bourbon and bluegrass music; quilts and Louisville Slugger baseball bats; Corvettes and Camrys; Fort Knox's gold and the Run for the Roses; the Niagara Falls of the South and the Grand Canyon of the East; historic mansions and pioneer forts; horse farms and stone fences; black bear and elk; hot browns and barbecue; Shakers and Civil War battlefields; award-winning professional theaters and outdoor dramas; folk art and fine art; horse racing and basketball; small towns and cosmopolitan cities; rolling bluegrass fields and tree-covered mountains.

Kentucky is the state of Abraham Lincoln and Mary Todd Lincoln, Henry Clay and Jefferson Davis,

Robert Penn Warren and Alben Barkley, Muhammad Ali and Colonel Sanders, Lionel Hampton and Loretta Lynn and sites associated with them. As Americans finally breached the Appalachian Mountains through the Cumberland Gap in the late 18th century and began their relentless push westward, their first stop was Kentucky, bequeathing the state a rich history and heritage. Heritage tourism is one of the top travel trends in the United States, and Kentucky visitors can trace the state's fascinating history at numerous museums and historic sites throughout the state.

Kentucky was a leader in developing state parks. Its system of parks, which includes 17 resort parks with lodges and a range of activities, showcase the state's scenery and history. Many of the parks are located on water, and with Kentucky having more miles of navigable water than any state other than Alaska, water recreation is a major component of the state's tourism scene. Outdoor enthusiasts take to rivers and large manmade lakes throughout Kentucky to fish, swim, water ski, jet boat, sail or just relax aboard houseboats with all the comforts of home. Kentucky's varied scenic wonders also include Cumberland Falls and its unusual moonbow; the 1,000-foot-deep gorge at Breaks Interstate Park; fascinating rock formations of the Big South Fork National River and Recreation Area and the natural arches of the Red River Gorge.

Kentucky's heritage and scenic beauty come together in the Bluegrass Region's horse country, where miles of white and black fence, rock walls, imposing barns and grazing thoroughbreds stamp an indelible image of the state. Other integral parts of Kentucky's appeal are its strong sense of place, its easily accessible location and the warm welcome that visitors receive.

Author Jesse Stuart summed up the universal attraction of his native state:

"Kentucky is neither southern, northern, eastern, western.

It is the core of America.

If these United States can be called a body,

Kentucky is its heart."

White water rafting on the Cumberland River
Source: Kentucky Department of Tourism

RECREATION & TRAVEL

Horses

The Kentucky Horse Park
Bill Cooke

The Kentucky Horse Park is a working horse farm with 1,200 acres surrounded by 30 miles of white plank fencing. The park is like none other in the world. Dedicated to man's relationship with the horse, the park features two outstanding museums, twin theaters

Three Day Event at Kentucky Horse Park
Source: Kentucky Department of Tourism

and nearly 50 different breeds of horses. All of these elements combine to make a visit to the park an enjoyable learning experience for everyone - from those unfamiliar with the horse to the horse expert.

The Kentucky Horse Park officially opened to the public on November 30, 1978. The final project cost $35,000,000. Fourteen original structures were renovated along with the construction of 23 new buildings, an interstate exit ramp, three bridges, a seven-acre lake, a resort campground, nine miles of paved roads, a one-mile steeplechase course, plus a cross-country course and dressage and stadium jumping areas.

Throughout the years the rolling hills and white plank fences of the Kentucky Horse Park have become the quintessential image of Kentucky and the horse industry. By 2005, the Park welcomes nearly one million visitors and hosts over 60 world-class equestrian events annually. The Kentucky Horse Park has introduced thousands of people from around the world to the fascinating and exciting world of the horse and will continue to entertain and educate the public for years to come.

For decades, central Kentucky horse farms had provided an anchor for tourism in the Bluegrass. During the late 1960s, however, many horse farms had to close their doors to the public as a result of vandalism and increased labor costs. In response to this, Lexington horseman, John R. Gaines and Department of Parks' Commissioner, Jim Host, suggested to Governor Louie Nunn and members of the Kentucky Legislature that the Commonwealth of Kentucky should open a theme park dedicated to the horse and the horse industry, as a way to gain back tourism revenue. Their idea was to create a public attraction where visitors could experience a Kentucky horse farm to maintain the identity of Lexington as the "Horse Capital of the World."

In April 1972, Mary Edwards Jenney sold her Walnut Hall Stud property to the Commonwealth of Kentucky for $2,700,000 to become the Kentucky Horse Park. Ground was officially broken by then Governor Wendell Ford in 1974 which also marked the first horse-related special event to be held on the grounds, when the High Hope Steeplechase moved its annual one- day meet to the Park's newly constructed course.

In 1975, the Park was chosen as the site of the 1978 World Three-Day Event Championship, the first equestrian world championship to ever take place in North America. On June 23, 1977, Man o' War and African-American jockey, Isaac Bums Murphy, were reinterred at the Park and in April 1978, the campground became the first element of the new Park to open to the public.

Museums, Carriage Rides, Riding Stables, Camps and Trails, & Racetracks

MUSEUMS

American Saddlebred Museum is located in Lexington and is dedicated to Kentucky's oldest native breed of horse, the American Saddlebred (859) 259-2746; The **Carriage Museum in** Maysville showcases transportation before the automobile (606) 759-7305; The Kentucky Horse Park's **International Museum of the Horse** is the largest and most comprehensive equestrian museum in the world. It is dedicated to describing the relationship between man and horse (800) 678-8813;

(606) 876-5591; **Double J Stables & Horsemans Camp** is located in Mammoth Cave National Park with guided trail rides through Mammoth Cave National Park. Primitive camping is also available (270) 286-8167;

Happy Trails Riding Stables in Eddyville (270) 871-4370; **Jesse James Riding Stables** (800) 798-0560; **Keith Stables** in Monticello (606)561-6458;

Churchill Downs
Source: John Perkins

Studying the Daily Racing Form
Source: Sid Webb

Kentucky Derby Museum. The new 10,000 square foot expansion has created a whole new environment full of the sounds, images and artifacts that bring the pageantry and excitement of the Kentucky Derby to life for all visitors. The new exhibits include high-tech computerized hands-on displays and video graphics (502) 637-1111.

CARRIAGE RIDES

Carriage rides are available at **Annie's Horse-drawn Carriage Rides** in Paducah (270) 210-6095; **Around the Town Carriage** Bardstown (502) 348-0331; **Buena Vista Carriage** in Louisville (502) 417-7109 and **Louisville Horse Trams** (502) 581-0100; and **Lexington Livery Horse Drawn Carriage Tours in Lexington** (859) 259-0000

RIDING STABLES, CAMPS & TRAILS

A Little Bit of Heaven Riding Stables in Frankfort (502) 223-8925**; Big Red Stables** in Harrodsburg (859) 734-3118; **Deer Run Stables L.L.C.** in Richmond (859) 527-6339; **DH Resorts, Inc.** in Flemingsburg 1200-acre "Dude Ranch" featuring the Mountain Lake Manor & Western Villages

Kinlee Stables in East Bernstadt (606) 843-2645; **Sugar Creek Resort** (859) 885-9359; **Sugar Creek Resort** in Nicholasville (859) 885-9359; **Whispering Woods Riding Stables** in Georgetown (502) 570-9663; and **Wranglers Riding Stables** in Cadiz (270) 752-8266.

RACETRACKS

Churchill Downs, Louisville - (502) 636-4400; **Ellis Park Race Course Inc.,** Henderson - (270) 826-0608; **Keeneland Race Course,** Lexington (859) 254-3412; **Kentucky Downs Race Course,** Franklin, (270) 586-7778; **Players Bluegrass Downs,** Paducah - (270) 444-7117; **Red Mile Harness Track,** Lexington - (859) 255-0752; **Thunder Ridge Racing & Entertainment Complex,** Prestonsburg - (606) 886-7223; **Turfway Park Race Course,** Florence - (859) 371-0200.

Source: Kentucky Deparment of Tourism (www.kentuckytourism.com).

This information, and more, can be found at the Kentucky Department of Travel's website www.KentuckyTourism.com.

RECREATION & TRAVEL

Hunting, Fishing & Wildlife

Jon Gassett

The quality, quantity and variety of hunting, fishing, and wildlife observation available to Kentucky's residents and visitors are, perhaps, unsurpassed within the continental United States. Hunters enjoy large and healthy populations of deer, wild tur-

and other wildlife. The locations for observation include state parks, wildlife refuges, national forests and nature sanctuaries and preserves.

Since the beginning of our country, fishing and hunting have been significant activities within our culture. Whether for pleasure or necessity, people have always wanted to pursue and take fish and game. Deer, rabbit, squirrel, quail, grouse, elk, bear and hundreds of other species have graced this country, and this wildlife has been taken for granted.

The Bluegrass State was, and is, one of the most abundant and popular places any-

Deer and Elk exhibit, Salato Center
Source: KY Dept. of Fish & Wildlife

key, rabbit, squirrel, quail, grouse, dove and waterfowl. With the recent reintroduction of elk to the Commonwealth, hunters have, on a limited basis, the opportunity to pursue one of the largest members of the deer family.

Kentucky's fishing opportunities are also plentiful. The Commonwealth has more miles of navigable waterways than any other state in the continental 48. There are also thousands of smaller streams and ponds for fisherman to enjoy.

The wildlife that may be observed in Kentucky is surprising to many. In addition to the game animals listed above, there are numerous bald eagles, hawks, bobcats, coyotes, beaver, otters, black bears

Bobcat (Felis Rufus), Salato
Source: Source: KY Dept. of Fish & Wildlife

where to enjoy the outdoors. People from all over fish our lakes, hunt our lands and just enjoy our splendid wildlife. But to truly understand what we have and where we are going, we must first look at the past.

Daniel Boone came through the Cumberland

Gap to the prosperous land the Indians called Kentucke. This land was filled with more animals, trees and open land than anyone had ever seen. There were even some species of game that were too plentiful. The new land fell under Virginia law and one of those laws required all male citizens to kill

White Tail Deer
Source: KY Dept. of Fish & Wildlife

the overabundant squirrels.

By this time, settlers were calling Kentucky home. But still conservation was an unpracticed word, almost unheard. The population of humans were killing off the game and fish at an alarming rate.

The new occupants could not believe the number of species and animals that occupied the new land. In early Europe, only royalty or the upper class could use wildlife in any way. In England, the king owned everything, even the fish, game and birds, until 1215. Here it was all open and free. There was nobody to say what, when or where to hunt and fish. It was an abundance that was new and exciting, but it wouldn't last.

Over the next 20 years, people started to notice that the game wasn't as plentiful as it once was. They had to go as far as 30 miles to find food. People had been able to hunt and take any and as much game as necessary. The huge fish and game populations began thinning out.

What was the reason for all of the destruction of game, fish and birds? One reason is still a problem today: a lack of education. A number of people still have no idea how important conservation and preservation are to nature.

Settlers at Fort Boonesborough decided to do something about the dwindling populations. Daniel Boone was put in charge of the settlement's

game committee, making him the state's first game warden.

In 1792, Kentucky became a state, but not until 1861 was a law established to close seasons on certain game birds and deer. It had taken over 100 years since the first people came through Cumberland Gap to establish some type of law to protect our natural resources.

In 1874, the first fish hatchery was built in Louisville and the Division of Game and Fish was installed with the Department of Agriculture. Two years later a law passed prohibiting destruction of fish by trap, dipnet or seining. After these early decisions by government, things really got moving for the betterment of wildlife.

In February of 1894, one of the biggest steps in the Commonwealth's brief history was made. Kentucky's legislature enacted the first game and fish laws. This provided protection for certain types of fish, wild birds and game, but left the enforcement of the laws to local officials. This was a major feather in the cap of the conservation movement and set the tone for further growth in the 1900s.

The turn of the century saw the beginnings of major change in Kentucky. The Lacey Act of 1900 made it unlawful to transport illegally taken wildlife, and non-resident hunting licenses were first seen around this time. People were really starting to take notice of the problems facing the future of wildlife.

Kentucky was not the only state that got involved in the protection of wildlife. Conservation and control of nature was becoming a nationwide topic of discussion. With the election of Theodore Roosevelt in 1901 came an all-new look at conservation in our country. Roosevelt's idea of "conservation through wise use" was used all across the United States. Reproduction of renewable resources before over-harvest was the main idea behind this theory.

The Doctrine of Conservation recognized the importance of a holistic approach to the management of natural resources. The doctrine also made a statement that is true today. Conservation is a responsibility of the public. Conservation isn't something that should be practiced or watched over by sportsmen. It is something for which everyone on the planet should be concerned.

During Roosevelt's "period of conservation," he made sure the Lacey Act was strictly enforced and made numerous other strides to improve wildlife in America. Three other major steps made during his term set a precedent that others tried to follow. The creation of the first federal bird refuge was created at Pelican Island, Florida, the new Division of Forestry was expanded by over 140 million acres of national forest and national parks were greatly improved and expanded.

1904 saw the creation of county "game wardens" in Kentucky, the forefathers of today's Conservation Officers. Their only duty was to enforce fish and wildlife laws and regulations. These men didn't do it for the money; they did it for the love and protection of our natural resources.

One problem with which the early game wardens dealt was landowner rights. There has been an ongoing battle between landowners and sportsmen for many, many years. The main cause of this feud: posted land. In 1878, the Kentucky legislature passed a law making it "unlawful to enter the closed lands of another to hunt, shoot or fish without the consent of the owner after the property has been posted." This was an important law, but it has not kept the illegal hunter off private property. Only the hunter or angler can keep himself or herself off posted land.

Private land covers almost 95 percent of Kentucky. Why is so much of the land posted? Poachers and inconsiderate sportsmen can take most of the credit. Private landowners don't need the hassle and worry of people leaving gates open or destroying crops. So it is up to the honest sportsmen to improve relations with landowners. Help out the farmers with chores, share the game and fish that you remove from the land and just be considerate.

Female Canada Goose nesting in Dragonfly marsh at Salato Center
Source: KY Dept. of Fish & Wildlife

The first 120 years in Kentucky were slow and inconsistent on the conservation front. Most of the moves by government were late coming and could have been much better, but they were making strides. Improvements on the state and national scene were being seen and felt. The "age of conservation expansion" would take place over the next 40 years in Kentucky, but had it not been for a few visionaries in the past two centuries we would have had much less to conserve.

The work and caring of just a few people got the ball rolling in the 1700s; now it is our turn to take over and make sure our state is a better place to live. Using private land is a privilege. Conserving our wildlife resources is a responsibility.

Hunting
Jon Gassett

Two of the favorite game animals for hunters in Kentucky are whitetail deer and wild turkey. The Kentucky Department of Fish and Wildlife Resources has done an excellent job of managing deer and turkey populations.

Whitetail males can attain a height of 3 ½ feet and a weight of 250 pounds. Females usually weigh much less. The size and health of the deer herd has grown remarkably in recent decades. Sixty years ago Kentucky's deer population was less than 1,000. It is estimated that in 2005 the herd numbers 900,000. The herd has grown to the point that in some areas the population of deer is too high. The department continues to manage the herd by increasing the length of the hunting seasons as well as the number of deer each hunter may harvest. A hunter may take one antlered (male) deer per season but may take up to four deer total in three of the four hunting zones. In the fourth zone a hunter may take an unlimited number of antlerless (presumed female) deer with bonus antlerless-only permits. Hunters can choose one or more of several hunting seasons. There are seasons for modern firearms, archery and black powder or muskets. The deer harvest in 2004 in Kentucky was estimated to be 125,000. A healthy deer herd such as Kentucky's can be reduced by up to 40 percent without negatively affecting its future population. Hunting rarely depletes a herd more than 15 percent.

Source: KY Dept. of Fish & Wildlife

The wild turkey flock has also shown rapid growth through the restoration and restocking efforts of the department. In 1958 the population was approximately 1,500 birds, but has grown to an estimated 230,000, with the 2005 harvest estimated to be 25,000.

It is once again possible to hunt elk (also known as wapiti) in the Commonwealth, for the first time since the 1850s. Kentucky began its modern-day elk restoration program in December 1997 with the release of seven elk from Kansas. Continuing releases and reproduction have increased the herd to over 5,300, the largest population east of the Mississippi River. The target population is 7,500.

Bull elk can reach a height of five feet at the shoulder and a mature weight of 700 pounds, making it one of the largest members of the deer family. The first modern-day elk hunt in Kentucky was in 2001, and was limited to 10 hunters that won a lottery entered by 9,235 hopeful hunters. All 10 hunters successfully harvested an elk. The number of permits issued has increased to 100 and will be increased further as the herd increases in number.

The Department of Fish and Wildlife Resources has also led successful restoration projects for quail and grouse. Squirrel and rabbit seasons are also very popular in Kentucky.

To inquire about hunting licenses or regulations contact, the Kentucky Department of Fish and Wildlife Resources at (800) 858-1549.

Fishing
Jon Gassett

Many of the most popular fishing destinations for Kentucky residents and visitors are the lakes located in Kentucky's magnificent state resort park system. The following is a summary of some of those lakes.

BARREN RIVER LAKE STATE RESORT PARK

Barren River Lake State Resort Park is in the center of some of the best fishing in Kentucky for largemouth bass, black and white crappie and hybrid striped bass. Anglers can also have good success catching spotted (Kentucky) and smallmouth bass. White bass, bluegill, channel catfish and flathead catfish also offer good fishing. Excellent fishing also occurs

Jim Mattingly of Somerset with the state record rainbow trout caught Sept. 10, 1972 from the Cumberland tailwater. The 14-pound, 6-ounce fish measured 32 ½ inches long and had a girth of 18 ½ inches.
Source: KY Dept. of Fish & Wildlife

occurs in the tailwaters below Barren River Lake Dam, particularly during the spring and early summer, for crappie, hybrid striped bass and channel catfish. Bluegill, white bass and flathead catfish can also be caught in the tailwaters. You can fish for rainbow trout at Peter Creek, which is less than 10 miles from the state park. This stream is stocked each month from April through September.

BUCKHORN LAKE STATE RESORT PARK

Buckhorn Lake State Resort Park overlooks Buckhorn Lake, which is one of the best fishing lakes in eastern Kentucky. Anglers can fish for largemouth bass, white crappie, bluegill, channel catfish or muskie at this lake. Buckhorn Lake is one of three lakes in Kentucky that are stocked with muskie by the Kentucky Department of Fish and Wildlife Resources. Muskie used to naturally range in Middle Fork Kentucky River where the lake now stands. Middle Fork Kentucky River below Buckhorn Lake Dam attracts anglers interested in catching white crappie, bluegill, channel catfish, muskie and rainbow trout. The Kentucky Department of Fish and Wildlife Resources stocks a total of 5,600 rainbow trout below the dam each year during April through November. Float fishing access is available at a ramp just below the dam. Boaters can float 5 miles downstream to the ford at Johnson Branch. Three sections of Middle Fork Kentucky River above Buckhorn Lake can be floated by anglers from Route 1850 Bridge downstream 7.5 miles to Asher, from this bridge downstream 5 miles to Hoskinston, and from Hoskinston downstream 9.6 miles to the Route 2431 Bridge just above Hyden. Floating during the summer may be difficult due to low flow, except after a heavy rain. Anglers can catch smallmouth bass, spotted (Kentucky) bass and rock bass in this stretch of river. Watch for obstructions such as log jams and deadfall trees that may require portaging.

CARTER CAVES STATE RESORT PARK

Carter Caves State Resort Park offers a variety of fishing opportunities, including fishing at 36 acre Smoky Valley Lake for largemouth bass, bluegill and channel catfish. Fishing is allowed only during daylight hours on this lake. No internal combustion engine may be operated on the lake. Anglers can also fish for smallmouth bass, spotted (Kentucky) bass, muskie and panfish in Tygart's Creek that borders the park. A 12-mile float-fishing trip is possible on Tygart's Creek in the spring and after heavy rains in the summer, from Olive Hill downstream through a scenic gorge to the Highway 182 Bridge at the park entrance. Another 10-mile section is floatable from the Highway 182 Bridge

downstream to Iron Hill. The first 5 miles of this section goes through the lower end of the gorge.

CUMBERLAND FALLS STATE RESORT PARK

Cumberland Falls State Resort Park is known for having one of the South's greatest natural wonders in Cumberland Falls, but there are also several places to fish within and near the park. Bank fishing is popular just below Cumberland Falls in the park. The Kentucky Wild River section of Cumberland River can be float fished from Forest Road 536 downstream 7.5 miles to the park's picnic area just above Highway 90 Bridge. Anglers can also float from the lower end of Jellico Creek at Highway 478 Bridge downstream 0.75 mile to Cumberland River, and then float 13 miles down to the picnic area. You will be only 0.25 mile from the Cumberland Falls when approaching the Highway 90 Bridge, so stay far to the right in order to reach the picnic area on the right-hand bank and avoid the falls. The Wild River section of Cumberland River offers fishing for smallmouth bass, spotted (Kentucky) bass, rock bass, redbreast sunfish, bluegill, walleye and channel catfish. Bark Camp Creek is a 13-mile drive from Cumberland Falls State Resort Park to Forest Road 193 Bridge, where both rainbow and brown trout can be caught. The Kentucky Department of Fish and Wildlife Resources stocks a total of 3,600 rainbow trout into this stream during March through June and October. Another 500 brown trout are stocked in late winter. During October 1 through March 31, a catch and release season is in effect, during which all anglers must fish with artificial baits and immediately release all trout back into the stream. Trout may be kept after March 31. Marsh Creek can be float fished from Highway 478 Bridge downstream 6 miles to Laurel Creek Road Bridge during the spring and after heavy rains in the summer. Anglers can catch smallmouth bass, spotted (Kentucky) bass, rock bass and redbreast sunfish on this float trip. You may experience logjams and deadfall trees that require portaging.

DALE HOLLOW LAKE STATE RESORT PARK

A fishing trip to Dale Hollow Lake State Resort Park will place you at one of the best smallmouth and spotted (Kentucky) bass lakes in the Southeast. Good fishing is also the norm for largemouth bass, crappie, bluegill and walleye at Dale Hollow Lake. A boat ramp and marina are at the park to accommodate boat anglers. The Wolf River arm of the lake in Tennessee is also open to fishing with a Kentucky fishing license above the reciprocal zone boundary as shown on the map. Fish for trout at the Cumberland River in the Burkesville area, which is less than a 15-mile drive from Dale Hollow Lake State Resort Park. A fishing walkway and boat ramp is located above Highway 90 Bridge in Burkesville. A second boat ramp is 4 miles downstream, just below the Highway 61 Bridge. Lake Cumberland Dam is only 20 miles from the park. There is a boat ramp below the dam and bank access is available along the river and at the hatchery creek below Wolf Creek National Fish Hatchery. This stream is stocked with trout each week from February through December. Dale Hollow Lake State Resort Park is the second largest state park in Kentucky. Most of the 3,398 acres in the park are forested and surrounded on three sides by the lake. Anglers can plan an overnight stay at Mary Ray Oaken Lodge that overlooks the lake or the park's campground.

JENNY WILEY STATE RESORT PARK
AT DEWEY LAKE

Jenny Wiley State Resort Park borders almost one entire side of Dewey Lake, where anglers can fish for largemouth bass, white crappie, bluegill and channel catfish. Dewey Lake has three boat ramps within the park. The headwaters of Dewey Lake can be float fished on Johns Creek from near the Pike County border at a ford near Thomas off Highway 194 downstream 4.8 miles to the German Bridge boat ramp. Largemouth bass, white bass, bluegill and channel catfish can be caught in this section of Johns Creek. Anglers can also fish Johns Creek at the picnic area below Dewey Lake Dam. The Kentucky Department of Fish and Wildlife Resources stocks a total of 2,200 rainbow trout in this area during April, May, October and November. Johns Creek also offers fishing for largemouth bass, smallmouth bass, spotted (Kentucky) bass, white crappie, bluegill and channel catfish. A 3.8 mile float trip is possible on Johns Creek from the picnic area below the dam downstream to a pulloff on 2381. Look for obstructions such as log jams and deadfall trees that may require portaging. Levisa Fork is another stream suitable for float fishing, from the Kentucky Department of Fish and Wildlife Resources ramp at Prestonsburg downstream 6.6 miles to Auxier. The same species of fish can be caught in Levisa Fork as in Johns Creek, except for trout and white crappie.

GREENBO LAKE STATE RESORT PARK

Greenbo Lake State Resort Park offers some of the best trout fishing in Kentucky in Greenbo Lake (181 acres). The Kentucky Department of Fish and Wildlife Resources stocks a total of 15,000 rainbow trout in this lake during January and October each year. Anglers have the best success at catching trout from mid-May through early September at night from dusk until 1 a.m. Fish at depths of 12 to 20 feet from a boat with a floating light over the deepest area of the lake. Motorboats must be operated at idle speed on Greenbo Lake. Anglers can also experience good fishing for largemouth bass, bluegill and channel catfish. A fishing pier is located in the upper lake area near the boat ramp and a fishing walkway parallels the face of the dam. Because this lake is so deep and clear, fishing is best during early morning, late afternoon or at night.

KINCAID LAKE STATE PARK

Kincaid Lake State Park overlooks Kincaid Lake, where one of the best populations of largemouth bass in Kentucky resides. Kincaid Lake is also known for bluegill, crappie and channel catfish. Nearby, the South Fork of the Licking River can be float fished from Cynthiana downstream to Falmouth for smallmouth bass, rock bass, largemouth bass and spotted (Kentucky) bass. This stream is one of the best smallmouth streams in Kentucky. There are several canoe entry and takeout sites along this stretch of South Fork. The South Fork of the Licking River is floatable during the spring and after heavy rains in the summer. Keep a watch for log jams and deadfall trees that may require portaging. Another float fishing venture can be taken on the Licking River from McKinneysburg downstream 13.6 miles to the Kentucky Department of Fish and Wildlife Resources boat ramp at Falmouth. Smallmouth bass, spotted (Kentucky) bass, flathead catfish, channel catfish, panfish species and freshwater drum can be caught in this section of river.

LAKE CUMBERLAND STATE RESORT PARK

Lake Cumberland State Resort Park, one of Kentucky's largest state parks, is surrounded on three sides by Lake Cumberland. Anglers can fish for largemouth bass, smallmouth bass, spotted (Kentucky) bass, crappie, walleye, striped bass, bluegill and channel catfish. Lake Cumberland is known for having good fishing particularly for smallmouth bass, striped bass and walleye. The striped bass fishery is one of the best in the U.S. Several boat ramps are available in and around the park. The 75 miles of Cumberland River from Lake Cumberland Dam downstream to the Tennessee border is known as one of the premier trout fisheries in the Southeast for rainbow and brown trout. Striped bass and walleye are also present. The upper 16 miles of river has fishing access for bank and wade anglers just below the dam, near Long Bottom, Helm's Landing, Rockhouse and

Winfrey's Ferry. Boat anglers can launch at ramps just below the dam, Helms landing and Winfrey's Ferry. Trout fishing is good throughout the 75 miles of river. Other boat ramps are at Burkesville (mile 34 below the dam), Highway 61 (mile 38), Cloyd's Landing (mile 51), and McMillan's Ferry (mile 67). Wolf Creek National Fish Hatchery is located below Lake Cumberland Dam. This hatchery raises nearly 800,000 trout each year to stock Kentucky's waters. The creek just below the hatchery is stocked with rainbow trout each week during February through December.

NEW TROUT FISHERY AT NATURAL BRIDGE STATE RESORT PARK

Middle Fork Red River will be stocked with 1,000 rainbow trout in early October throughout the 2.2 mile section that flows through Natural Bridge State Resort Park to provide a catch and release trout fishery from October 1 through March 31 each year. During this period, all anglers must fish with artificial baits only and immediately release all trout back into the stream. Trout will be available for harvest after March 31 each year. Middle Fork Red River will also continue to receive 1,000 rainbow trout in the park each month in March, April and May. Beginning in 2005, the March stocking will provide additional trout to catch and release until April 1, when trout can then be harvested. No fishing is allowed on Hoedown Island Lake. The lower end of Middle Fork in the park offers smallmouth bass fishing in the spring. Rainbow trout can also be caught in the 41-acre Mill Creek Lake located in Natural Bridge State Resort Park. A total of 5,500 rainbow trout are released into the lake in January, April, May and October. A good night-fishery for trout occurs during mid-May through early September. Anglers need to fish over the deepest area of the lake at depths of 12 to 20 feet. Best success is from dark until 1 a.m. Largemouth bass, bluegill and channel catfish are also available to anglers at this lake. No internal combustion engines may be operated on Mill Creek Lake.

ROUGH RIVER DAM STATE RESORT PARK

Rough River Dam State Resort Park sits along the banks of Rough River Lake, where anglers can catch largemouth bass, spotted (Kentucky) bass, white crappie, bluegill, hybrid striped bass and chan-

nel catfish. Boat anglers may access Rough River Lake at one of seven boat ramps, including a ramp at the park. Rough River below Rough River Lake Dam provides both bank and float fishing opportunities for the same fish species listed for the lake. A 6.6 mile section of the river may be floated from near the campground below the dam downstream to just above the Falls of Rough. The Kentucky Department of Fish and Wildlife Resources from April through September stocks a total of 6,300 rainbow trout

London resident Dale Wilson holds the state record largemouth bass, caught in Wood Creek Lake on April 14, 1984. The 13-pound, 10-ounce bass measured 25 1/4 inches long and 21 1/2 inches around.
Source: KY Dept. of Fish & Wildlife

in Rough River at Hihgway 54 Bridge near Hites falls. Another 2,000 rainbow trout are stocked just below Rough River Lake Dam in June.

OTHER LAKES, STREAMS AND PONDS

Excellent fishing is also found at a number of other lakes such as Lake Barkley and Kentucky Lake in Western Kentucky, McNeely Lake in Jefferson County, Pan Bowl Lake in Breathitt County, Beshear Lake in Caldwell and Christian counties, and Taylorsville Lake in Spencer County.

There are abundant trout stream fishing opportunities available, with a total of 321.4 miles of trout fisheries in 71 streams. Kentucky's farm ponds offer the best early spring fishing in the state because the water warms earlier in smaller bodies of water. Farm ponds produce numerous trophy sized fish. It is important to ask permission before fishing in private ponds.

Fishing licenses can be purchased at most bait stores.

Wildlife
Jon Gassett

Eagles, bobcats and bears - these are three of the most difficult and most exciting animals to be seen in the wild in Kentucky.

American bald eagles can be observed on a regular basis in the Land Between the Lakes region in Western Kentucky, and occasionally in other portions of the state. These birds, which can have a wingspan of eight feet, have been upgraded from the endangered species list to the threatened species list. They can fly level at 60 miles per hour and dive at 100 miles per hour. Their eyesight is so keen that they can see a rabbit two miles away.

There are approximately 10,000 bobcats (also known as wildcats) in Kentucky. They are difficult to observe due to their nocturnal and solitary habits. Their diet includes mostly small animals such as rabbits, rodents, fish and birds. A large bobcat (they can weigh as much as 30 pounds) can catch a small deer.

Starfire Elk
Source: KY Dept. of Fish & Wildlife

In the early 1900s black bears disappeared from Kentucky due to unregulated hunting and a loss of habitat, but they are making a comeback. Bears have been sighted in Eastern Kentucky over the last two decades. Sightings have increased dramatically as roaming bears from surrounding states of Tennessee, Virginia and West Virginia make forays into the state. Bears, which can attain weights in excess of 450 pounds, have been reported in more than two dozen counties in the Cumberland Plateau Region, with the greatest concentrations in Harlan, Bell and Pike counties.

There is a great variety of other wildlife to be seen in Kentucky. The game animals that may be observed include whitetail deer, elk, wild turkey, squirrel and rabbit. Herons, Canada geese and other waterfowl are common throughout the state. Beaver and otters are making a comeback. Peregrine falcons have been reintroduced to the Commonwealth, and coyotes have found their own way in, with an expanding population that may be causing a reduction in fox numbers. Birdwatchers enjoy observing songbirds, hawks and other birds.

One of the best places to see wildlife (although not in the wild) is at the Dr. James C. Salato Wildlife Education Center in Frankfort. There are outdoor live exhibits that include bald eagles, black bear, elk, bobcat, whitetail deer, wild turkey and bison. Indoor exhibits include venomous snakes, frogs and toads, alligator snapping turtle, a bee hive and warm and cold water aquariums. Resident Canada geese and mallard ducks freely roam the grounds. The center has a backyard-style wildlife viewing area, mini wetland, two fishing lakes and a shaded picnic area.

Kentucky has an excellent state park system with abundant wildlife viewing opportunities. The Daniel Boone National Forest, which includes the Red River Gorge and the Big South Fork National Recreation Area are popular wildlife observation destinations. In addition to numerous nature preserves and nature sanctuaries, there are 82 wildlife management areas in Kentucky.

The Kentucky Department of Fish and Wildlife Resources offers a Kentucky Wildlife Viewing Guide. This guide contains information including 66 viewing sites, descriptions, and special viewing tips. For more information, call (800) 858-1549.

Article compiled by Mark Reinhardt

RECREATION & TRAVEL
Boating
& Marinas

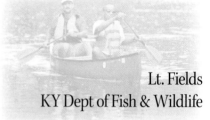

Lt. Fields
KY Dept of Fish & Wildlife

Boating, America's number one family sport, is enjoyed by thousands of new enthusiasts each year. For mid-Americans, Kentucky is the place to come to enjoy cruising, sail-

For canoe and kayak enthusiasts, Kentucky offers waters ranging from tranquil to raging – both found on the Elkhorn Creek in central Kentucky, the Cumberland River near the Cumberland Falls, and on many other waterways that offer the ultimate paddling experience.

Family recreation is endless on the many major impoundments in Kentucky. Since the 1960s, many lakes have been created, such as Barkley, Malone, Barren, Green, Laurel, Cave Run, Fishtrap, Dewey and numerous other state and federal impoundments. During this period, motorboat registration has climbed to over

Sailboats docked at Land Between the Lakes
Source: Kentucky Department of Tourism

ing, skiing, fishing and floating in its broad waterway system of lakes, rivers, and streams.

Kentucky offers endless opportunities to boaters of every kind. Whether you enjoy the quietness of floating down a lazy stream in a canoe or kayak, taking a raft through challenging class 4 rapids, pulling the family behind the boat on a tube or on skis, slowly making your way down the lake on a luxury houseboat filled with friends and relatives, taking a month long trip from one end of the state to the other, or simply trying to catch the "big one," Kentucky has exactly what you are looking for.

170,000. In addition to these registered boats, there are thousands of non-registered vessels such as canoes, rowboats and sailboats, as well as large houseboats and cruisers that are registered by the Federal Government. And thousands of tourists from neighboring states bring their boats to Kentucky. Although Kentucky's waterways are not yet crowded, it is obvious that boating is growing rapidly.

Learn more about recreational opportunities on Kentucky's beautiful waterways by contacting the Kentucky Department of Fish and Wildlife Resources at 1-800-858-1549 or visit fw.ky.gov.

MARINAS

CITY	REGION	NAME	PHONE
ALBANY	So Lakes	Grider Hill Dock & Indian Creek Lodge	(606) 387-5501
ALBANY	So Lakes	Wisdom Dock	(800) 840-8523
ALBANY	So Lakes	Wolf River Resort	(606) 387-5841
AUGUSTA	No Ky	Augusta River Park Marina	(606) 756-2183
BELLEVUE	No Ky	Riverside 4 Marina	(859) 261-8114
BENTON	W Lakes	Bee Spring Lodge and Marina	(800) 732-0088
BENTON	W Lakes	Big Bear Resort and Marina	(800) 922-2327
BENTON	W Lakes	Cedar Knob Resort and Marina	(800) 428-7986
BENTON	W Lakes	Hester's Spot in the Sun	(800) 455-7481
BENTON	W Lakes	Hickory Hill 5 Star Resort	(800) 280-4455
BENTON	W Lakes	King Creek Resort and Marina	(800) 733-6710
BENTON	W Lakes	Lakeside Campground & Marina Inc.	(270) 354-8157
BENTON	W Lakes	Lakewood Camping Resort	(270) 354-9122
BENTON	W Lakes	Malcolm Creek Resort	(800) 733-6713
BENTON	W Lakes	Shawnee Bay Resort	(270) 354-8360
BENTON	W Lakes	Sportsman's Anchor Marina	(800) 326-3625
BENTON	W Lakes	Whispering Oaks Resort	(800) 788-1061
BUCKHORN	Boone	Buckhorn Lake State Resort Park	(800) 325-0058
BURGIN	Bluegrass	Chimney Rock Marina	(859) 748-9065
BURKESVILLE	So Lakes	Dale Hollow Lake State Resort Park	(800) 325-2282
BURKESVILLE	So Lakes	Hendricks Creek Resort	(800) 321-4000
BURKESVILLE	So Lakes	Sulphur Creek Resort	(270) 433-7272
BURNSIDE	So Lakes	Burnside Marina	(800) 844-8862
CADIZ	W Lakes	Boat Haven Resort & Marina	(888) 557-7638
CADIZ	W Lakes	Lake Barkley State Resort Park	(800) 325-1708
CADIZ	W Lakes	Prizer Point Marina & Resort	(800) 548-2048
CAMPBELLSVILLE	So Lakes	Emerald Isle Resort and Marina	(888) 815-2000
CAMPBELLSVILLE	So Lakes	Green River Lake State Park	(270) 465-8255
CAMPBELLSVILLE	So Lakes	Green River Marina & Resort	(800) 488-2512
CAWOOD	Boone	Stone Mountain Boat Dock	(606) 573-7352
CLARKSON	Derby	Ponderosa Boat Dock	(270) 242-7215
CLARKSON	Derby	Wax Marina	(888) 624-9951
COLUMBIA	So Lakes	Holmes Bend Marina-Resort	(800) 801-8154
CORBIN	Boone	Grove Marina	(606) 523-2323
CRITTENDEN	No Ky	Eve's Boatdock	(859) 428-1644
DANVILLE	Bluegrass	Gwinn Island Resort & Marina Inc.	(859) 236-4286
DAWSON SPRINGS	W Lakes	Pennyrile Forest State Resort Park	(800) 325-1711
DAYTON	No Ky	RiverCity Marina	(859) 292-8688

CITY	REGION	NAME	PHONE
DAYTON	No Ky	Watertown Yacht Club	(859) 261-8800
DRY RIDGE	No Ky	Ruby's Boat Dock	(859) 824-9967
DUNMOR	Audobon	Lake Malone State Park	(270) 657-2111
EDDYVILLE	W Lakes	Eddy Creek Marina Resort	(800) 626-2300
EDDYVILLE	W Lakes	Holiday Hills Resort	(800) 337-8550
FALLS OF ROUGH	Derby	Rough River Dam State Resort Park	(800) 325-1713
FALMOUTH	No Ky	Kincaid Lake State Park	(859) 654-3531
FRANKFORT	Bluegrass	Frankfort Boat Dock	(502) 227-9481
FRENCHBURG	Ky Appalachians	Long Bow Marina	(606) 768-2929
GILBERTSVILLE	W Lakes	Kentucky Dam Marina	(800) 648-2628
GILBERTSVILLE	W Lakes	Kentucky Dam Village State Resort Park	(800) 325-0146
GILBERTSVILLE	W Lakes	Moors Resort and Marina	(800) 626-5472
GLASGOW	Caves	Narrows Marina	(270) 646-5253
GLASGOW	Caves	Sawyers Landing Marina	(800) 470-2223
GRAND RIVERS	W Lakes	Green Turtle Bay Houseboat Rentals	(800) 844-8862
GRAND RIVERS	W Lakes	Green Turtle Bay Resort	(800) 498-0428
GRAND RIVERS	W Lakes	Lighthouse Landing	(800) 491-7245
GREENUP	Ky Appalachians	Greenbo Lake State Resort Park	(606) 473-7324
HARDIN	W Lakes	Kenlake State Resort Park	(800) 325-0143
HARRODSBURG	Bluegrass	Cane Run Fishing Marina	(859) 748-5487
HARRODSBURG	Bluegrass	Cummins Ferry Campground & Marina	(859) 865-2003
HARRODSBURG	Bluegrass	Pandora Marina	(859) 748-9121
HARRODSBURG	Bluegrass	Royalty's Fishing Camp	(859) 748-5459
HARRODSBURG	Bluegrass	Walker's Mid-Lake Marina	(859) 748-5520
JAMESTOWN	So Lakes	Jamestown Resort and Marina	(800) 830-5131
JAMESTOWN	So Lakes	State Dock	(888) 782-8336
KUTTAWA	W Lakes	Buzzard Rock Resort & Marina	(800) 826-6238
KUTTAWA	W Lakes	Kuttawa Harbor Marina	(270) 388-9563
LANCASTER	Bluegrass	Herrington Marina	(859) 548-2282
LANCASTER	Bluegrass	Kamp Kennedy Marina	(859) 548-2101
LANCASTER	Bluegrass	Kings Mill Marina	(859) 548-2091
LANCASTER	Bluegrass	Sunset Marina	(859) 548-3591
LAWRENCEBURG	Bluegrass	Fair Winds At Beaver Lake Inc	(502) 839-4402
LEITCHFIELD	Derby	Bill's Marina and Service Center	(270) 259-4859
LEITCHFIELD	Derby	Moutardier Marina	(270) 286-4069
LEWISBURG	Caves	Shady Cliff Resort & Marina	(270) 657-9580
LONDON	Boone	Holly Bay Marina	(606) 864-6542
LONDON	Boone	London Dock and Rockcastle Campground	(606) 864-5225
LONDON	Boone	Wood Creek Boat Dock	(606) 878-5420
LOUISA	Ky Appalachians	Yatesville Lake State Park	(606) 673-1492
LUCAS	Caves	Barren River Lake State Resort Park	(800) 699-Boat
MAYSVILLE	No Ky	Maysville River Park Marina	(606) 564-2520
MONTICELLO	So Lakes	Beaver Creek Resort	(800) 844-8862
MONTICELLO	So Lakes	Conley Bottom Resort, Inc.	(606) 348-6351
MOREHEAD	Ky Appalachians	Scott's Creek Marina	(606) 784-9666
MORGANTOWN	Caves	Steamboat Landing Marina	(270) 662-0019
MOUNT VERNON	Boone	Lake Linville Marina and Campgrounds	(606) 256-9696
MURRAY	W Lakes	America's Paradise Resort	(800) 340-2767
MURRAY	W Lakes	Irvin Cobb Resort	(800) 225-2415
MURRAY	W Lakes	Kentucky Beach Resort and Marina	(888) 244-2277
MURRAY	W Lakes	Water's Edge RV Park & Marina	(888) 651-3084
MURRAY	W Lakes	Wildcat Creek Recreation Area	(270) 436-5628
NANCY	So Lakes	Lee's Ford Resort Marina	(877) LEES-FORD
NEW CONCORD	W Lakes	Cypress Springs Resort	(270) 436-5496
NEW CONCORD	W Lakes	Lakeview Cottages & Marina	(877) 895-5876
NEW CONCORD	W Lakes	Missing Hills Resort	(270) 436-5519
OWENSBORO	Audobon	Executive Marina of Owensboro	(270) 683-2405
RICHMOND	Bluegrass	Wilgreen Lake Marina & Bait & Tackle Shop	(859) 623-1881
RUSSELL SPRINGS	So Lakes	Indian Hills Resort Alligator II Marina & KOA	(877) 363-9911
RUSSELL SPRINGS	So Lakes	Popplewell's Alligator #1	(270) 866-3634
SASSAFRAS	Boone	Carr Creek State Park	(606) 642-4050
SCOTTSVILLE	Caves	Browns Ford Boat Ramp	(270) 434-2329
SCOTTSVILLE	Caves	Walnut Creek Marina	(270) 622-5858
SHELBYVILLE	Derby	Guist Creek Marina and Campground	(502) 647-5359
SOMERSET	So Lakes	Buck Creek Boat Dock	(606) 382-5542
STAFFORDSVILLE	Ky Appalachians	Paintsville Lake State Park	(606) 297-5253
TAYLORSVILLE	Derby	Taylorsville Lake Dock	(502) 477-8766
TAYLORSVILLE	Derby	Taylorsville Lake State Park	(502) 477-8766
UNION	No Ky	Big Bone Landing Marina & Campground	(859) 384-1713
UNION	No Ky	Farmlands Marina	(606) 384-3140
WARSAW	No Ky	Dan's Marina and Motel	(888) 326-7386
WARSAW	No Ky	Pier 99 Marina	(859) 567-8811
WILLISBURG	Derby	Captain Bobs Boat Dock	(859) 375-0093
WINCHESTER	Bluegrass	Stan's Restaurant and Boat Dock	(859) 527-3146

Source: Kentucky Dept. of Fish & Wildlife

SIMPLY SPECTACULAR.

Breathtaking scenery. Fabulous food. All kinds of recreation. Unmatched hospitality. At Kentucky State Parks, you'll find everything you need to make your next getaway a thing of beauty. With 52 different locations to choose from, including 17 resorts with lodging, you'll find the perfect setting for just relaxing or having an unforgettable adventure. Discover how easy it is to unleash your unbridled spirit at a Kentucky State Park. Call or visit our Web site – now with online reservations – today, and reserve your next unbridled adventure.

KENTUCKY STATE PARKS

Kentucky
UNBRIDLED SPIRIT

1-800-255-PARK
www.parks.ky.gov

RECREATION & TRAVEL

Introduction to State Parks

Jim Carroll

The Kentucky State Park system can be described with superlatives. It has more resort park lodges than any other state. It has three golf courses named among the best in the country by Golf Digest magazine. It preserves some of Kentucky's most valued historic treasures. And Kentucky parks offer easy access to some of the best boating and fishing anywhere.

Kentucky's extensive park system had humble beginnings. In 1924 that the Kentucky General Assembly passed a law that established a Kentucky State Parks Commission and allocated the princely sum of $1,100 to help the new board find likely sites for Kentucky state parks. The panel's first director was the state geologist, Dr. Willard R. Jillson.

Within two years, the commission located four properties for park development and moved to acquire them. Three of the sites – encompassing Pine Mountain State Resort Park, Natural Bridge State Resort Park and Old Fort Harrod State Park — remain in the park system today.

The focal point for Kentucky State Parks is 17 resort parks scattered throughout the state. All feature comfortable lodges with modern conveniences, but each has its own atmosphere. In western Kentucky, Kentucky Dam Village and Lake Barkley are large, busy parks. Yet a third park just down the road – Kenlake – has a quiet, inn-like atmosphere. Not far away is another rural gem, Pennyrile Forest State Resort Park.

Some resort parks are known for their natural features – such as Cumberland Falls, Carter Caves, Pine Mountain and Natural Bridge. For others, the big selling point is access to lake activities, including Lake Cumberland, Jenny Wiley, Rough River Dam, Dale Hollow Lake, Buckhorn Lake, Greenbo Lake and Barren River Lake.

Kentucky's unique history is preserved at two resort parks. General Butler in Carrollton maintains the home of a famous military family, while Blue Licks Battlefield marks the site of the last Revolutionary War battle in Kentucky.

Golf is hot in Kentucky state parks. The park sys-

tem maintains six championship courses dubbed the Signature Series of outstanding courses. Four of the courses are new, having opened in 2003. They are Mineral Mound in western Kentucky, Dale Hollow Lake in south-central Kentucky, and two courses in northeastern Kentucky – Grayson Lake and Yatesville Lake. Pine Mountain's course opened for play in 2001, while the sixth is the popular course at Kentucky Dam Village.

Besides resort parks, the park system maintains 35 other state parks and historic sites. Two of them are urban parks with extensive recreational facilities – E.P. "Tom" Sawyer in Louisville and Ben Hawes State Park in Owensboro. Others interpret Kentucky's history. John James Audubon State Park in Henderson honors the noted 19th century artist and naturalist, while My Old Kentucky Home in Bardstown is the antebellum mansion that tradition holds inspired Stephen Foster to write his famous song.

Reconstructed pioneer forts can be found at Fort Boonesborough and Old Fort Harrod. Columbus-Belmont and Perryville Battlefield, mark the sites of important Civil War battles. White Hall near Richmond was the home of emancipationist Cassius M. Clay. The latest addition to the park system, Wickliffe Mounds at Wickliffe in western Kentucky, preserves and interprets a Native American community dating from 1100 A.D.

2004 was an eventful year for the park system, reports Parks Commissioner George Ward. Guest rooms were improved with new bedding, hair dryers, and irons and ironing boards. The park system began offering online reservations in the summer of 2004. In August state resort parks began enhancing their dining room menus by buying local produce directly from Kentucky farmers, which makes for excellent fare after a long day of recreation.

Each year, Kentucky parks draw 7 million visitors and contribute $317 million to the economy. For more information on Kentucky parks, visit http://www.parks.ky.gov

RECREATION & TRAVEL

State Parks, Resort Parks & Historic Sites

Western Region

Western Lakes Region

COLUMBUS-BELMONT STATE PARK

A visit to Columbus-Belmont, high above the Mississippi River, recalls the November 7, 1861 Battle of Belmont and the fight to control this waterway. Confederate General Leonidas Polk established camps on both the Kentucky and Missouri sides of the river and named the more heavily fortified Columbus the "Gibraltar of the West." But a Union General destined for the White House, Ulysses S. Grant, outflanked the "Gibraltar" and forced evacuation of the Confederates in 1862. Today, you can still see the massive chain and anchor used by the South to block passage of the Union gunboats and the earthen trenches dug to protect 19,000 Confederate troops. The farmhouse that served as the Civil War hospital is now a museum that interprets many historic events at this site. At one time, national leaders wanted to move the Capital of the United States from Washington to Columbus. The park has a beautiful campground with a spectacular view of the Mississippi River and Activity Center. The park is 36 miles southwest of Paducah on KY 80.

Columbus- Belmont State Park
PO Box 9, 350 Park Road
Columbus KY 42032-0009
270-677-2327
http://parks.ky.gov/stateparks/cb/

JEFFERSON DAVIS STATE HISTORIC SITE

Jefferson Davis was elected President of the Confederate States of America on February 18, 1861, less than a month before the inauguration of Abraham Lincoln as President of the Union, and two months before the outbreak of the Civil War, on April 12, 1861. Ironically, these two destined adversaries were born in Kentucky in log cabins within one year and 100 miles apart. The 351-foot obelisk marks the birthplace of Jefferson Davis, born on

**Jefferson Davis
birthplace monument and marker.**
Source: Sid Webb

June 3, 1808. Outstanding views of the countryside are available from the top of the monument accessible by elevator. A visitor's center has exhibits and a gift shop. The site is 10 miles east of Hopkinsville on US 68.

Jefferson Davis State Historic Site
PO Box 157, 258 Pembroke-Fairview Road
Fairview KY 42221
270-886-1765
http://parks.ky.gov/statehistoricsites/jd/

KENLAKE STATE RESORT PARK

Located on the western shore of Kentucky Lake, Kenlake offers a choice of quiet relaxation or active recreation. Take to the net at the tennis center, a seasonal facility with temperature-controlled courts, racquet rentals and a pro shop. Nature lovers can explore 200 miles of trails at Land Between the Lakes. The resort is 40 miles southeast of Paducah. From Paducah, take I-24 to the Purchase Parkway, then US 68E. From I-24 north, exit US 68/KY 80W.

Kenlake State Resort Park
(Mail Address)
542 Kenlake Road, Hardin KY 42048
(Resort Location)
Aurora KY
Lodge: 270-474 - 2211
Reservations: 800-325-0143
Marina: 270-474-2245
http://parks.ky.gov/resortparks/kl/

KENTUCKY DAM VILLAGE STATE RESORT PARK

Kentucky Dam Village is one of three state resorts near Land Between the Lakes National Recreation Area, a 170,000 acre wooded peninsula bound by Kentucky Lake and Lake Barkley. The abundance of water offers uncrowded cruising, water-skiing and fishing.With its wide choice of accommodations, excellent marina and fine dining, Kentucky Dam Village is one of Kentucky's most popular resorts. During the winter, take tours to see American bald eagles. Relax in one of the cottages or in the main lodge with private balconies or patios overlooking Kentucky Lake. If golf is your game, stay at the Village Green Inn, next to the 18-hole golf course. The course is part of the Signature Series of premiere golf courses. Kentucky Dam Village is 21 miles southeast of Paducah. From Paducah, take I-24 east to US 62 to US 641 East.

Kentucky Dam Village State Resort Park

PO Box 69, 113 Administration Drive
Gilbertsville KY 42044
270-362-4271 Reservations: 800-325- 0146
Marina: 270-362-8386
Golf Pro Shop: 800-295-1877
http://parks.ky.gov/resortparks/kd/

LAKE BARKLEY STATE RESORT PARK

The world-class, Lake Barkley lodge, designed by Edward Durrell Stone, is indigenous with the wooded shoreline that surrounds it. The grand scale, post-and-beam wood construction features 3 1/2 acres of glass offering outstanding views of Lake Barkley. In addition to the outdoor pool overlooking the lake, the resort has a heated, indoor pool. The Fitness Center offers executive treatment with Nautilus equipment, fitness cycles, a weight room, racquet ball court, tanning beds, sauna, whirlpool and fitness trainers. In addition to accommodations in the main lodge, the resort has the secluded Little River Lodge and several cottage styles to choose from. The 18-hole Boots Randolph golf course, par 72, 6,751 yards, is a challenge for the most avid of golfers. Resort guests can also enjoy a spacious campground, full-service marina, a lighted airstrip and trails for hiking and mountain biking. The resort is 29 miles west of Hopkinsville. Take US 68W to KY 1489.

Eagle
Source: Kentucky Department of Fish & Wildlife

Lake Barkley State Resort Park
PO Box 790, 3500 State Park Road
Cadiz KY 42211
Lodge: 270-924-1131
Reservations: 800-325-1708
Marina: 270-924-9954
Golf Pro Shop: 800-295-1878
http://parks.ky.gov/resortparks/lb/

MINERAL MOUND STATE PARK

This peaceful setting on the shores of Lake Barkley is historically linked to the author F. Scott Fitzgerald. The property was once the farm of Willis B. Machen, grandfather of Zelda Sayre Fitzgerald. It's not hard to imagine the serene, Gatsby-style era from this park, with idyllic days of playing golf and cruising the lake. The park has a challenging Signature Series 18-hole golf course. The front 9 holes are situated in a wooded area and many of the back 9 holes are flanked by lake views. A pro shop offers rental carts, clubs and golf merchandise. The park also has a picnic area, a fishing pier and a boat ramp. Mineral Mound is 1 mile south of Eddyville on KY 93, off US 62/641. The park entrance is north of the I-24 exit.

Mineral Mound State Park
PO Box 489, 48 Finch Lane, Eddyville KY 42038
270-388-3673
Golf Pro Shop toll-free 866-904-7888 (PUTT)
http://parks.ky.gov/stateparks/mm/

PENNYRILE FOREST STATE RESORT PARK

Named for the tiny Pennyroyal plant found in the woodlands surrounding this resort, Pennyrile Forest is the perfect back-to-nature hideaway. Relax in the rustic wood and stone lodge or in one of the charming cottages near the lodge or beside the lake. In either case, the only sounds to wake you may be the gentle splash of a beaver or the melodic song of the wood thrush. The resort offers a newly expanded 18-hole golf course, par 72, 6,793 yards, set in an oak-pine forest. Other recreational pursuits include tennis, hiking, canoeing, fishing and swimming at

the pool or beach. Enjoy mountain biking on trails in the adjoining Pennyrile State Forest. The resort is 20 miles northwest of Hopkinsville on KY 109.

Pennyrile Forest State Resort Park
20781 Pennyrile Lodge Road
Dawson Springs KY 42408
Lodge: 270-797-3421
Reservations: 800-325- 1711
Golf Pro Shop: toll-free 866-427-7888 (PUTT)
http://parks.ky.gov/resortparks/pf/

WICKLIFFE MOUNDS STATE HISTORIC SITE

Wickliffe Mounds preserves a village inhabited by prehistoric Native Americans known as Mississippian Mound Builders. This culture built large ceremonial earthen mounds and farmed along the great river valleys of the Eastern United States from AD 800 until AD 1500.Wickliffe Mounds preserves the site and exhibits the historic artifacts.

Wickliffe Mounds State Historic Site
94 Green Street, PO Box 155,Wickliffe KY 42087
270-335-3681
http://www.kystateparks.com/statehistoricsites/wm/

Bluegrass, Blues and Barbeque

BEN HAWES STATE PARK

Golf is the name of the game at Ben Hawes in Owensboro. Choose from the 18 hole course or a 9-hole, par-3 course. Pros and duffers will find everything they need from a pro shop. The park also has 4 miles of trails for hiking and mountain biking. The park is 4 miles west of Owensboro off US 60.

Ben Hawes State Park
400 Boothfield Road, Owensboro KY 42301
270-684-9808 Pro Shop: 270-685-2011
http://parks.ky.gov/stateparks/bh/

John James Audubon
Source: Kentucky Department of Libraries & Archives

JOHN JAMES AUDUBON STATE PARK

Relax in a cottage in the woods where the famed naturalist studied the subjects of his paintings during the years he lived in Henderson, from 1810-1819. The world-renowned museum interprets Audubon's life through his art and personal memorabilia,

framed within a timeline of world events. The nature center features a wildlife observatory. A giant bird's nest is the centerpiece of the Discovery Center, with hands-on exhibits and educational programs. For sale, the museum offers many prints reproduced from the collection and unique gifts to explore nature. The park is in Henderson on US 41 N.

John James Audubon State Park
PO Box 576 (3100 US Hwy 41 North)
Henderson KY 42419
270-826-2247
http://parks.ky.gov/stateparks/au/

LAKE MALONE STATE PARK

Spanning 788 lake acres, Lake Malone captures Kentucky's beauty in a small package. The lake is enclosed by dramatic 50-foot sandstone bluffs rising above the water's edge and surrounded by hardwood forests. The park has a campground, marina, beach and hiking trail. From Greenville, take US 431 south to KY 973.

Lake Malone State Park
PO Box 93, 331 State Route 8001
Dunmore KY 42339
270-657-2111
http://parks.ky.gov/stateparks/lm/

RECREATION & TRAVEL
State Parks, Resort Parks & Historic Sites

South Central Region

Caves, Lakes & Corvettes Region

Cordell Hull Scenic Byway is called a
"Roller Coaster Highway."
Source: Sid Webb

BARREN RIVER LAKE STATE RESORT PARK

After a day exploring the area's caves, enjoy the aboveground delights to be found at Barren River Lake. The lodge and cottages curve 'round the 10,000-acre lake, providing spectacular views of sunsets. In addition to boating and fishing, the resort has an 18-hole golf course, horseback riding, tennis courts, beach, pool and a paved trail for hiking and biking. The resort is 44 miles southeast of Bowling Green. Take I-65 to the Cumberland Parkway, then US 31E south.

Barren River Lake State Resort Park
1149 State Park Road, Lucas KY 42156
270-646-2151 Reservations: 800-325- 0057
Marina: 270-646-2357
Golf Pro Shop: 800-295-1876
http://parks.ky.gov/resortparks/br/

NOLIN LAKE STATE PARK

"Top off" your visit to Mammoth Cave National Park with a trip to Nolin Lake. A campground and a 5,795 acre lake make Nolin the site for aboveground recreation. Nolin is north of Mammoth Cave from KY 728 and KY 1827; or 45 miles southeast of Rough River Dam State Resort from KY 259 to KY 728 and KY 1827.

Nolin Lake State Park
PO Box 340, Bee Spring KY 42207
270-286-4240
http://parks.ky.gov/stateparks/nl/

OLD MULKEY MEETINGHOUSE STATE HISTORIC SITE

The oldest log meetinghouse in Kentucky was built in 1804 during a period of religious revival. Many Revolutionary War soldiers and pioneers, including Daniel Boone's sister, Hannah, are buried here. The structure has twelve corners in the shape of a cross and three doors, symbolic of the Holy Trinity. From Glasgow, take scenic KY 63 to KY 163 south.

Old Mulkey Meetinghouse State Historic Site
38 Old Mulkey Park Road
Tompkinsville KY 42167
270-487-8481
http://parks.ky.gov/statehistoricsites/om/

Southern Lakes & Rivers Region

DALE HOLLOW LAKE STATE RESORT PARK

Overlooking a 28,000-acre lake, this lodge offers unsurpassed comforts amid a backdrop of unspoiled wilderness. A conference center adjoining the lodge is the perfect venue for business retreats. The new 18-hole golf course is ranked by Golf Digest as one of the nation's best. There's also fishing, boating, scuba diving, swimming and multi-use trails for hiking, horseback riding and mountain biking. The campground has sites for horse owners adjacent to riding trails. From Glasgow or Burnside, take KY 90 to KY 449 & KY 1206.

Dale Hollow Lake State Resort Park
6371 State Park Road, Burkesville KY 42717
Lodge: 270-433-7431
Reservations: 800-325-2282
Golf Pro Shop: toll-free 866-903-7888 (PUTT)
http://parks.ky.gov/resortparks/dh/

GENERAL BURNSIDE ISLAND STATE PARK

During the Civil War, Union General Ambrose Burnside patrolled what was then the Cumberland River surrounding this 400-acre island to keep watch for the Confederates. Today, the waters of Lake Cumberland are more placid, a peaceful retreat for campers, boaters, golfers and fishermen. A marina near the park has all the supplies for a great day on the lake and the campground is the perfect home base for outdoor adventure. The only challenge to modern day visitors may be the 18-hole golf course, fun but certainly not hazard-free! The park is 8 miles south of Somerset on US 27.

General Burnside Island State Park
PO Box 488, 8801 S. Highway 27
Burnside KY 42519
606-561-4104 or 606-561- 4192
http://parks.ky.gov/stateparks/ge/

GREEN RIVER LAKE STATE PARK

Enjoy lakeside fun at the campground on the shores of this 8,200 acre lake; with a beach, tie-ups for boats, miniature golf and multi-use trails for hiking, horseback riding and mountain biking. A marina near the park offers supplies and rental boats. The park is south of Campbellsville on KY 55.

Green River Lake State Park
179 Park Office Road, Campbellsville KY 42718
270-465-8255
http://parks.ky.gov/stateparks/ge/

LAKE CUMBERLAND STATE RESORT PARK

With more than 60,000 acres of water and 1,225 miles of shoreline, Lake Cumberland is considered to be one of the finest fishing and boating areas in the Eastern United States. Perched high above this watery expanse, Lure Lodge offers the water-lover panoramic views of the lake and an indoor pool complex. The resort has a 9-hole, par-3 golf course, nature trails and horseback riding. From I-65, take the Cumberland Pkwy to US 127. From I-75, exit on KY 80 west.

Lake Cumberland State Resort Park
5465 State Park Road, Jamestown KY 42629
270-343-3111 Reservations: 800-325-1709
Marina: 888-782-8336
http://parks.ky.gov/resortparks/lc/

**American Cave and
Karst Center, Horse Cave**
Source: Kentucky Department of Tourism

RECREATION & TRAVEL

State Parks, Resort Parks & Historic Sites

North Central Region

Kentucky Derby Region

E.P. "TOM" SAWYER STATE PARK

This park is a mecca for indoor and outdoor recreation enthusiasts. Sign up for a summer aquatics program or one of the team sports scheduled year-round in the park's gymnasium. The park has an outstanding BMX track where the BMX Nationals are held annually. In Louisville, take the Gene Snyder Freeway northeast to the westbound Westport Rd exit.

E.P. "Tom" Sawyer State Park
3000 Freys Hill Road, Louisville KY 40241
502-426-8950
http://parks.ky.gov/stateparks/gr/

LINCOLN HOMESTEAD STATE PARK

The same spirit of adventure that brought other pioneers to Kentucky led Abraham Lincoln's grandparents to the knolls of Kentucky near the Beech Fork River. The park features the original home of Lincoln's mother, replicas of the 1782 cabin and blacksmith shop where his father was reared and learned his trade, and the home of Mordecai Lincoln, the favorite uncle of the President. Thomas Lincoln and Nancy Hanks, Abraham Lincoln's parents, were married here in June 1806. Split-rail fences and pioneer furniture portray the rugged pioneer life. An 18-hole golf course accents the rolling hills of this historic setting and offers visitors

quite a different set of challenges than those faced by the pioneers. Take the Bluegrass Parkway to US 150 east or KY 555 south.

Lincoln Homestead State Park
5079 Lincoln Park Road, Springfield KY 40069
859-336-7461 (Golf Pro Shop)
http://parks.ky.gov/stateparks/lh/

MY OLD KENTUCKY HOME STATE PARK

Federal Hill was the inspiration for Stephen Foster's famous ballad, My Old Kentucky Home. Today, this Georgian-style mansion is as endearing to visitors as it was in 1852, the year Foster wrote what has become the official state song while visiting his cousins, the Rowan family. Step into the days of the

My Old Kentucky Home
Source: Sid Webb

antebellum South as costumed guides escort you through the stately mansion and formal gardens. During summer months, the outdoor drama "Stephen Foster -The Musical" is performed under the stars in the park's amphitheater. Christmas candlelight tours highlight the holidays when the mansion is adorned with holly, pine and fruit garlands. The park is in Bardstown on US 150.

My Old Kentucky Home State Park
P O Box 323, 501 East Stephen Foster Avenue
Bardstown KY 40004
502-348-3502
Golf Pro Shop: 502-349-6542
Stephen Foster - The Musical: 800-626–1563
http://parks.ky.gov/stateparks/mk/

ROUGH RIVER DAM STATE RESORT PARK
Rough River Dam is surrounded by rolling countryside overlooking a 5,000 acre lake. Some of the finest fishing in the state is to be found in the deep waters of Rough River. Non-anglers can enjoy the lake on a pontoon, or scurry across quickly on water skis or jet skis. The resort has a 9-hole, par-three golf course and the beautiful Lafayette 18-hole Golf Course is just a couple miles from the park. Enjoy the history and folklore of the area with a trip to the Pine Knob Theatre, offering outdoor dramas from June to September. The park is located off the Western Kentucky Parkway. Take KY 79 north at Caneyville.

Rough River Dam State Resort Park
450 Lodge Road, Falls of Rough KY 40119
Lodge: 270-257-2311

Reservations: 800-325-1713
http://parks.ky.gov/resortparks/rr/

TAYLORSVILLE LAKE STATE PARK
The campground at this park is a home base from which anglers vie for bass, bluegill and crappie in the 3,050 acre lake. The park has horse campsites and trails for hiking, horseback riding and biking. The park is 20 miles southeast of I-64, exit 32. Take KY 55 south to KY 44 east and KY 248.

Taylorsville Lake State Park
PO Box 205, 1320 Park Road
Taylorsville KY 40071
502-477-8713
Campground: 502-477-0086
Marina: 502-477-8766
http://parks.ky.gov/stateparks/tl/index.htm

Barren River State Resort
Source: Sid Webb

Bluegrass Region

BLUE LICKS BATTLEFIELD
STATE RESORT PARK
Throughout history, the salt springs at Blue Licks attracted prehistoric animals, Indians, pioneers and 19th-century Southerners who came for the therapeutic waters. Blue Licks was also the site of the last Revolutionary War battle in Kentucky, in 1782. Visit the Pioneer Museum to learn more about the fascinating history of Blue Licks. The park is 48 miles northeast of Lexington on US 68.

Blue Licks Battlefield State Resort Park
(Mail Address)
PO Box 66, Mount Olivet KY 41064
(Resort Location)
10299 Maysville Road, Carlisle KY 40311
859-289-5507 Reservations: 800-443-7008
http://parks.ky.gov/resortparks/bl/

BOONE STATION STATE HISTORIC SITE
Ever restless for new frontier, Daniel Boone left Fort Boonesborough and established a pioneer station on this site in 1779. Located north of the Kentucky River, near what is today the town of Athens, the settlement was home to 15 or 20 families in the early 1780s. However, the Boone family suffered many hardships during the three years they lived

Blue Lick Soldiers
Source: Sid Webb

here, including the deaths of their son Israel and their nephew Thomas at the Battle of Blue Licks. Daniel Boone's brother, Samuel, is buried at Boone Station. To reach the site, take I-75, exit 104 to KY 418 East (Athens-Boonesborough Rd) then turn left on KY 1973, then turn right on Gentry Road.

Boone Station State Historic Site
240 Gentry Road
Lexington, KY 40502
859-263-1073
http://parks.ky.gov/statehistoricsites/bs/

Shelby, (1750-1826) Kentucky's esteemed first and fifth governor. Shelby is buried at his estate, Traveller's Rest. The cemetery and picnic area are 5 miles south of Danville off US 127.

Constitution Square State Historic Site
134 South Second Street, Danville KY 40422
859-239-7089
http://parks.ky.gov/statehistoricsites/cs/

FORT BOONESBOROUGH STATE PARK
Daniel Boone and his men reached the Kentucky

Fort Boonesborough
Source: Sid Webb

CONSTITUTION SQUARE & ISAAC SHELBY CEMETERY STATE HISTORIC SITES

Constitution Square preserves the constitutional conventions that preceded statehood. For eight years the frontier statesmen who lived in what was the Kentucky County of Virginia struggled for independence. Finally, on June 1, 1792 Kentucky became the fifteenth state in the Union and Isaac Shelby, a Revolutionary War hero and convention delegate, was named the first governor of the new Commonwealth. Visit Grayson's Tavern and the first post office west of the Alleghenies; and replicas of the jail, courthouse and meeting house. From Lexington, take US 27 south to KY 34 west. From Louisville, take I-64 east to US 127 south.

While in Danville, also visit the grave of Isaac

River on April 1, 1775, and established Kentucky's second settlement. Fort Boonesborough has been reconstructed as a working fort complete with cabins, blockhouses and furnishings. Resident artisans, in period clothing, perform craft demonstrations and impart pioneer experiences to modern-day visitors. The Kentucky River Museum in the historic Lockmaster's House on Lock and Dam 10 provides personal glimpses into the lives of families who lived on the river and worked the locks and dams in the 1900s. Camp on the Kentucky River as Daniel Boone did and enjoy the modern-day fun of a pool complex with a water slide. From I-75, take exit 95. On I-64, exit at Winchester.

Fort Boonesborough State Park
4375 Boonesborough Road, Richmond KY 40475

859-527-3131
http://parks.ky.gov/stateparks/fb/

WAVELAND STATE HISTORIC SITE

This beautiful Greek Revival home was built in 1847 by Joseph Bryan, a grandnephew of Daniel Boone. Tours of Waveland focus on the Bryan family and life on a 19th-century Kentucky plantation. Waveland is south of Lexington off US 27.

Waveland State Historic Site
225 Waveland Museum Lane
Lexington KY 40514
859-272-3611
http://parks.ky.gov/statehistoricsites/wv/

WHITE HALL STATE HISTORIC SITE

Near Fort Boonesborough is another historic treasure, the home of Cassius Marcellus Clay: emancipationist, newspaper publisher, Minister to Russia, and friend to Abraham Lincoln. Clay's daughter, Laura Clay, was born at White Hall in 1849 and was politically active for women's suffrage and states' rights. In 1920, Laura Clay became the first woman to be nominated for U.S. President by a major political party. This restored 44-room Italianate mansion was built in 1799 and remodeled in the 1860s. In addition to the heirloom and period furnishings, White Hall has many unique features for its day, including indoor running water and central heating. The park is off I -75 at Exit 95.

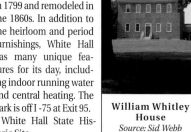

William Whitley House
Source: Sid Webb

White Hall State Historic Site
500 White Hall Shrine Road, Richmond KY 40475
859-623-9178
http://parks.ky.gov/statehistoricsites/wh/

WILLIAM WHITLEY HOUSE STATE HISTORIC SITE

This is the first brick home and circular racetrack in Kentucky, completed in 1794 by William Whitley and his wife Esther. The estate, known as Sportsman's Hill, is a monument to pioneer ingenuity and resourcefulness. The brick house was built in the Flemish bond pattern for greater strength and has a secret chamber for hiding in the event of an Indian attack. Dubbed the "Guardian of Wilderness Road," the house was a gathering spot for early Kentuckians, including George Rogers Clark and Daniel Boone. Take US 27 south from Lexington to US 150 east.

William Whitley House State Historic Site
625 William Whitley Road, Stanford KY 40484
606-355-2881
http://parks.ky.gov/statehistoricsites/ww/

OLD FORT HARROD STATE PARK

In 1774, James Harrod established the first permanent settlement west of the Alleghenies in what would become Central Kentucky. Preserving Kentucky's pioneer history, the fort has been reconstructed near the site of the original. Heavy timbers form stockade walls and enclose the cabins and blockhouses. Craftspeople, dressed in period clothing, perform pioneer tasks such as woodworking, weaving, basketry and blacksmithing and tend the farm animals and gardens. The Lincoln Marriage Temple shelters the original log cabin where Abraham Lincoln's parents were married on June 12, 1806. The cabin was originally built in Washington County. It was recently moved to the present site. The Mansion Museum houses Civil War artifacts, an outstanding historical gun display, Native American artifacts and a Lincoln collection. The park is 32 miles southwest of Lexington on US 68 in Harrodsburg.

Old Fort Harrod State Park
PO Box 156, 100 South College St.
Harrodsburg KY 40330
859-734-3314
http://parks.ky.gov/stateparks/fh/

PERRYVILLE BATTLEFIELD STATE HISTORIC SITE

On October 8, 1862, the rural peace of this tranquil countryside was shattered by cannon explosions and the death moans of young soldiers. Perryville became the site of the most destructive Civil War battle in the state which left more than 6,000 killed, wounded or missing. The park museum tells of the battle that was the South's last serious attempt to gain possession of Kentucky. The battlefield is one of the most unaltered Civil War sites in the nation; vistas visible today are virtually those the soldiers saw on that fateful day in 1862. A self-guided walking tour on the battlefield interprets battle events. From Lexington, take US 68 west to US 150 west.

Perryville Battlefield State Historic Site
PO Box 296, 1825 Battlefield Road
Perryville KY 40468
859-332-8631
http://parks.ky.gov/statehistoricsites/pb/

Northern Kentucky Region

Big Bone Lick
Source: Sid Webb

BIG BONE LICK STATE PARK

Fifteen to twenty-thousand years ago, during a period known as the Pleistocene Epoch, a great ice sheet covered an area from Canada to the Ohio River. On the edges of this ice sheet, great herds of giant mastodons, wooly mammoths and bison were attracted to the warm salt springs that still bubble from the earth at Big Bone Lick. The salty marsh that attracted the prehistoric visitors also proved to be a fatal attraction. Some of the giant creatures became trapped and perished in what the early pioneers called "jelly ground," leaving skeletons and clues about life in prehistoric Kentucky. Discovered by European explorers in 1739, fossils from Big Bone Lick were sent to museums throughout the world and examined by Benjamin Franklin and President Thomas Jefferson. The extensive fossil collection excavated from this site recognizes Big Bone Lick as the birthplace of American vertebrate paleontology. Visitors to the museum and Discovery Trail can witness a scene in Kentucky long before the arrival of man and walk along a boardwalk through a rec-reated marsh and savannah. The park is also home

to modern-day Ice Age descendants, a buffalo herd! Exit I-75 at KY 338.

Big Bone Lick State Park
3380 Beaver Road, Union KY 41091
859-384–3522
http://parks.ky.gov/stateparks/bb/

GENERAL BUTLER STATE RESORT PARK

This hilltop resort at the confluence of the Ohio and Kentucky Rivers, honors a prominent military family. Named for Gen.William Orlando Butler, the family's military fame spanned from Colonial times through the American Revolution, the War of 1812, the Mexican War and the Civil War. The Butler-Tur-pin House, built in 1859, offers a glimpse of the family history with 18th- and 19th-century heir-looms. Capture some of the area's river town charm in the resort's hilltop lodge and enjoy golf, hiking, swimming and tennis. A spacious conference center makes this resort a destination for business as well as pleasure. The park also features an excit-ing new dining concept, "Two Rivers Restaurant" spotlighting Kentucky cuisine. The park is 44 miles northeast of Louisville, off I-71 at Carrollton.

General Butler State Resort Park
PO Box 325, 1608 Highway 227
Carrollton KY 41008
502-732-4384
Reservations: 866-462-8853 (866-GOBUTLER)
http://parks.ky.gov/resortparks/gb/

KINCAID LAKE STATE PARK

A campground, a 183-acre lake, hiking trails, mini-golf and a new 9-hole golf course are all the ingredients that make Kincaid Lake a popular retreat for campers, fishermen, boaters and golf-ers. The golf course is set in wooded, rolling ter-rain and features undulating fairways. Explore the lake in a rental boat from the marina, or soak up the summer sunshine at the lakeside swimming pool. Surrounded by open woodland, the camp-ground offers quiet seclusion with all the modern conveniences campers expect. The park is 48 miles southeast of Covington and 61 miles northeast of Lexington. Take US 27 to Falmouth and KY 159 to the park.

Kincaid Lake State Park
565 Kincaid Park Road, Falmouth KY 41040
859-654-3531 Pro Shop: 859-654-8555
http://parks.ky.gov/stateparks/kn/

RECREATION & TRAVEL
State Parks, Resort Parks & Historic Sites

Eastern Region

Eastern Highlands North Region

BREAKS INTERSTATE PARK
The Russell Fork River has carved a 250-million year-old masterpiece, a canyon 5 miles long and 1,600 feet deep! Considered the "Grand Canyon of the South," the beauty of Breaks Interstate is showcased along hiking trail and overlooks. The park has a lodge, cottages and campground. Located 30 miles southeast of Pikeville on KY/VA 80.

Breaks Interstate Park
PO Box 100, Breaks VA 24607
276-865-4413 Reservations: 800-982-5122
http://parks.ky.gov/stateparks/bi/

CARTER CAVES STATE RESORT PARK
Beneath the forested hills of this resort, nature has hidden more than 20 twisting caverns. Visit Cascade Cave, with a 30-foot underground waterfall or X Cave, where, for millions of years, nature has formed luminous stone fans, pipes and spirals. Above ground, enjoy golf, canoeing, hiking, horseback riding and mountain biking on 20 miles of single and multi-use trails. In addition to the beautiful fieldstone lodge, the resort offers cottages in a wooded setting. Carter Caves is 30 miles west of Ashland, off I-64 west to KY 182 north.

Carter Caves State Resort Park

344 Caveland Drive, Olive Hill KY 41164
606-286 -4411 Reservations: 800-325- 0059
http://parks.ky.gov/resortparks/cc/

FISHTRAP LAKE STATE PARK
Fishtrap Lake is 7 miles south of Pikeville in Pike County, home of the legendary Hatfield-McCoy feud. The feud lasted from the Civil War to the 1890s, a result of war conflicts, romantic entanglements and property disputes. Feuds are less likely these days since the Levisa Fork of the Big Sandy River was impounded in 1969, creating the calming waters of Fishtrap Lake. Enclosed by the highest dam in Kentucky (195 feet) and guarded by the Appalachia Mountains, the 1,130 acre lake is narrow and deep. The lake draws its name from the pioneers who noticed the fish traps used by the Native Americans. To this day, the lake has a great reputation for fishing; bass, bluegill, catfish and hybrid stripers. A privately operated marina and a Corps of Engineers campground provide the means to explore a lake that's the "real McCoy." For infor-

Fishing the Kentucky River
Source: Sid Webb

mation on Fishtrap Lake & the Hatfield-McCoy feud contact the Pikeville -Pike County Tourism Commission

PO Box 1497 (150 Huffman Lane)
Pikeville KY 41502
800-844-7453
http://www.kystateparks.com/stateparks/ft/

GRAYSON LAKE STATE PARK

Sheer sandstone canyons and gentle slopes contain the 1,512 acres of Grayson Lake. The land was a favorite camping site for Shawnee and Cherokee Indians, and you will discover why with a visit to the park's spacious campground. Enjoy a picnic meal cooked over the grill and relax under the stars in a tent or camper. The 18-hole golf course, Hidden Cove, was ranked among the best of its type in 2005 by Golf Digest. The park is 25 miles southwest of Ashland. Take I -64 west to KY 7 south.

Thomas Walker Cabin
Source: Sid Webb

Grayson Lake State Park
314 Grayson Lake Park Road, Olive Hill KY 41164
606-474 -9727
Golf Pro Shop: toll-free 866-905-7888 (PUTT)
http://parks.ky.gov/stateparks/gl/

GREENBO LAKE STATE RESORT PARK

The fieldstone lodge at this resort is named in honor of Jesse Hilton Stuart, (1906-1984) Poet Laureate and native of Greenup County. Enjoy Stuart's writing in the lodge's reading room. Dive into adventure at the pool waterslide, spend a day on the lake in a rental pontoon or enjoy hiking, horseback riding and mountain biking on the resort's 30 miles of multi-use trails. The resort is located on KY 1, 18 miles north of I- 64 from the Grayson exit.

Greenbo Lake State Resort Park
965 Lodge Road, Greenup KY 41144
606-473 -7324 Reservations: 800-325- 0083
http://parks.ky.gov/resortparks/go/

JENNY WILEY STATE RESORT PARK

This mountain resort is named for a brave pioneer woman, Jenny Wiley. Taken captive by Indians in 1789, Wiley endured the slaying of her brother and children and escaped after 11 months of captivity. Imagine our heroine eluding her captors as you hike the trails that weave through the wilderness. During the summer, the hills ring with the sounds of popular Broadway musicals in the Jenny Wiley Theatre. The resort is in Prestonsburg off US 23/460 on KY 3.

Jenny Wiley State Resort Park
75 Theatre Court, Prestonsburg KY 41653
606-886-2711 Reservations: 800-325-0142
Jenny Wiley Theatre: 606-886-9274
http://parks.ky.gov/resortparks/jw/

PAINTSVILLE LAKE STATE PARK

Paintsville Lake gleams like a jewel in the crown of the mountains of Eastern Kentucky. With steep cliffs and wooded coves along the shoreline, this lake provides 1,140 acres of boating, skiing and fishing. After a day on the lake, relax in the campground, featuring 32 developed sites with restrooms, showers, laundry and sewer hookups. A full-service marina is located near the campground, offering rental houseboats, pontoons and fishing boats. For a glimpse into a vanished way of life, visit the nearby Mountain Homeplace. This living history farm recreates Appalachian farm life in the mid-1800s. Located 4 miles west of Paintsville, off KY 40 from US 460.

Paintsville Lake State Park
PO Box 920, 1151 KY Route 2275
Staffordsville KY 41256
Office: 606-297-8486
Campground: 606-297-8488
Paintsville Lake Marina & Grill: 606-297-LAKE
http://parks.ky.gov/stateparks/pl/

YATESVILLE LAKE STATE PARK

This park has a variety of campsites to suit anyone's idea of "roughing it," including double-wide sites for two RVs and boat-in, primitive sites. The 2,300-acre lake offers good bluegill, bass and crappie fishing. On shore, enjoy challenging play on the park's new Eagle Ridge Golf Course, an Arthur Hills designed "Mountain Masterpiece". To reach the park take US 23 to Louisa and follow the signs .

Yatesville Lake State Park, Louisa KY 41230
Campground: 2667 Pleasant Ridge Road
    606-673-1490
Marina: 26762 Hwy. 1185, 606-686-2361
Golf Course: 1410 Golf Course Rd
    866-906-7888(PUTT)
http://parks.ky.gov/stateparks/yl/

Eastern Highlands South Region

BUCKHORN LAKE STATE RESORT PARK

Tucked away in the mountains, Buckhorn is truly the "Great Escape." The resort is a mecca for nature-lovers and folks who want to get away from it all. Curl up next to the lodge's fireplace or enjoy the mountain air from your private balcony. Surrounded by mist-ringed mountains marching down to the lake's edge, every view from this resort

Cumberland Falls
Source: Sid Webb

is inspiring. The lodge also features a Conference Center, with all the guest services under one roof. Delicious catered meals are served fresh from the kitchen and guest rooms are only a few steps away. The resort is 124 miles southeast of Lexing-

ton. Take I-64 east to the Mountain Parkway. Exit at Campton and take KY 15 south to KY 28 west, then KY 1833 to the park.

Buckhorn Lake State Resort Park
4441 KY Highway 1833, Buckhorn KY 41721
606-398-7510 Reservations: 800-325-0058
http://parks.ky.gov/resortparks/bk/

CARR CREEK STATE PARK

Enjoy a variety of activities at this park on Carr Fork Lake. Park your RV or pitch your tent and relax in one of the best campgrounds in southeastern Kentucky. Conveniently located off KY 15, the campground offers all the camper comforts surrounded by mountain scenery. The park also features the longest lakefront sand beach in the Kentucky State Park system. A full-service marina near the park provides lake access as well as fishing and boating supplies. Pleasure boaters and fishermen can explore the 750-acre lake with miles of shoreline and good bass, crappie and walleye fishing. The park is 15 miles southeast of Hazard on KY 15 south.

Carr Creek State Park
2086 Smithboro Road, PO Box 249
Sassafras KY 41759
606-642-4050
http://parks.ky.gov/stateparks/ck/

CUMBERLAND FALLS
STATE RESORT PARK

Imagine a wall of water falling 60 feet into a boulder-strewn gorge, a whispering mist that kisses the face and a magical moonbow visible on a clear night under a full moon. Known as the "Niagara of the South," the 125-foot wide curtain of water is dramatic day or night. But it is only at night during a full moon that you can see the moonbow, a phenomenon not found anywhere else in the Western Hemisphere! Feel the excitement of the river on a rafting or canoe trip. A professional outfitter is located 5 miles east of the resort. As spectacular as the setting that surrounds it, the historic Dupont Lodge, built of massive hemlock beams and knotty pine, offers a spectacular view of the Cumberland River Valley. The lodge is a perfect retreat after a day of hiking, rafting, swimming or horseback riding. From I-75, take the Corbin exit and US 25W to KY 90.

Cumberland Falls State Resort Park
7351 Highway 90, Corbin KY 40701
606-528-4121 Reservations: 800-325- 0063
http://parks.ky.gov/resortparks/cf/

Source: Sid Webb

DR. THOMAS WALKER STATE HISTORIC SITE

Although Daniel Boone is often remembered as Kentucky's most famous pioneer, Dr. Thomas Walker was actually the first frontiersman in Kentucky, preceding Boone by 17 years. A physician and surveyor, Walker led the first expedition through Cumberland Gap in 1750. Dr. Walker was an agent for the Loyal Land Company of Virginia and was exploring the western wilderness seeking land for settlement. Near the river, which he named the Cumberland, Dr. Walker built the first cabin in Kentucky, a replica of which stands on the site today. Dr. Walker's journal, recorded during his four-month exploration, described plentiful

wildlife, thickly tangled woods and rugged terrain. That same rugged beauty discovered years before the era of Daniel Boone still sits in wait for your discovery today. Come visit the Dr. Thomas Walker State Historic Site and follow in the footsteps of the famous--and not so famous--Kentucky pioneers.

4929 KY 459
Barbourville, KY 40906-9603
606-546-4400
http://parks.ky.gov/statehistoricsites/dt/

KINGDOM COME STATE RESORT PARK

Kentucky's newest resort park combines the breathtaking beauty of Eastern Kentucky with the exploration of its coal heritage. With an elevation of 2,700 feet, Kingdom Come is Kentucky's highest state park. Resting near the Kentucky-Virginia border on the crest of Pine Mountain, the park offers scenic vistas second to none. Extraordinary rock formations are featured at this park, including Log Rock, a natural sandstone bridge, and Raven Rock, a giant monolith that soars 290-feet into the air at a 45-degree angle. Many visitors flock to the park during mild weather to view the park's growing population of black bears. Others come to explore Kentucky's coal heritage at the Kentucky Coal Mining Museum and nearby Portal 31. The peaceful atmosphere of the School House Inn encourages visitors to linger and enjoy the area.

Kingdom Come State Park
PO Box M, 502 Park Road
Cumberland KY 40823
606-589 –2479
http://parks.ky.gov/stateparks/kc/

LEVI JACKSON WILDERNESS ROAD STATE PARK

Hike in the footsteps of pioneers on two historic trails, the Wilderness Road and Boone's Trace. These thoroughfares carried more than 200,000 settlers from the eastern colonies into the western frontier between 1774 and 1796. But danger lurked along the way; McNitt's Defeat, Kentucky's worst Indian massacre, occurred here in 1786. Visit the Mountain Life Museum and the 19th-century McHargue's Mill. The park is south of London, off I-75 at exit 38.

Levi Jackson Wilderness Road State Park
998 Levi Jackson Mill Road, London KY 40744
606-878-8000
http://parks.ky.gov/stateparks/lj/

NATURAL BRIDGE STATE RESORT PARK

It has taken nature millions of years to form the natural sandstone arch from which this park takes its name. Located adjacent to the Daniel Boone National Forest, near the Red River Gorge Geological Area, the bridge spans 78 feet and is 65 feet high. At Natural Bridge, each season has a unique charm. Hikers are drawn to this rugged, scenic area of high stone cliffs and stone arches, but tenderfoots can also enjoy the scenic, ridge-top views from the park's sky lift. Hemlock Lodge is nestled in the mountainside, overlooking a pool complex and Hoedown Island. The resort is 52 miles southeast of Lexington, off the Mountain Parkway on KY 11.

Natural Bridge State Resort Park
2135 Natural Bridge Road, Slade KY 40376
606-663 -2214 Reservations: 800-325-1710
http://parks.ky.gov/resortparks/nb/

PINE MOUNTAIN STATE RESORT PARK

Overlooking the Kentucky Ridge State Forest, this mountaintop resort became Kentucky's first state park in 1924. The Mountain Laurel Festival is celebrated here the last weekend in May. Experience the beauty of each season at Pine Mountain on hiking trails named Hemlock Garden, Honeymoon Falls, Living Stairway and Rock Hotel. Relax in the lodge with private balconies overlooking the forest or in one of the cozy cottages. This resort is home of the championship 18-hole golf course Wasioto Winds, recently ranked by Golf Digest as the fourth best new public course in the nation. Designed by Michael Hurdzan, Ph.D., it is a links-style course in a valley between two mountains. Wasioto Winds offers a pro shop with clubs and apparel, all-weather golf carts and an indoor training center. Golf packages are offered year round. Wasioto Winds proudly hosts the First Tee of Pine Mountain, a youth development program. The resort is 15 miles north of Middlesboro off US 25E in Pineville.

Pine Mountain State Resort Park
1050 State Park Road, Pineville KY 40977
606-337-3066 Reservations: 800-325-1712
Wasioto Winds Pro Shop (Information
& Tee Times): 800-814-8002 or 606-337-1066
http://parks.ky.gov/resortparks/pm/

PINE MOUNTAIN TRAIL
(Under Development)

The Pine Mountain Trail project is the brainchild of many government and private groups to showcase the geology, history and spectacular scenery of the central Appalachian Mountains. Ultimately, the trail will be 120 miles long and link Breaks Interstate Park with Cumberland Gap National Park. The trail will traverse the crest of Pine Mountain on the Kentucky-Virginia border, and cross terrain replete with pioneer homesteads, water-

Natural Bridge
Source: Sid Webb

falls, cliffs, rock shelters, caves, upland bogs and scenic overlooks. Currently, 28 miles of the trail is available for hiking and non-motorized vehicles. Trail guides, maps and gear are available at www.pinemountaintrail.com For information on the Pine Mountain Trail, contact:

Letcher County Cooperative Extension Service
ATTN: Pine Mountain Trail Conference
PO Box 784, Whitesburg KY 41858
606-633-2362
http://www.kystateparks.com/stateparks/pt/

OUR ATTRACTIONS GROW BETTER WITH AGE

Kentucky has always been a great place to explore and now it's never been easier. We've mapped out unique heritage trails for you, featuring pioneer history in Daniel Boone country, colorful outdoor theater, tasty barbeque, bluegrass and country music, genuine working bourbon distilleries and, of course, beautiful horses. So bring your family to Kentucky and experience our unbridled spirit. Call today for an official copy of the Kentucky Visitors Guide.

Kentucky
UNBRIDLED SPIRIT

1-800-225-TRIP ext.KYA
www.KentuckyTourism.com

RECREATION & TRAVEL
Tourist Attractions

Western Lakes Region

BARDWELL AREA: Carlisle County Chamber of Commerce (270-628-5459); **Westvaco Wildlife ManagmentArea**—Bottomland hardwood, swamp area and Great Blue Heron Rookery (270-335-3151); **Winford Public Wildlife Area**—237 acres. Waterfowl, rabbit, deer, raccoon, fishing

BENTON AREA: Marshall County Tourist Commission (270-527-3128); (Benton) **Forgotten Past Museum**—Attraction with gift shop, go carts, bumper cars, mini golf, antique steam engine, museum, and arcade (270-527-9244); (*Calvert City*) **Kentucky Lake**

Buffalo, Land Between the Lakes
Source: Sid Webb

Motor Speedway—Race super late models and open wheel modified and limited sportsmen (270-395-3600); (*Draffenville*) **Kentucky Opry Show**—Wholesome entertainment for the entire family, featuring country, gospel and bluegrass music (888-459-8704); (*Gilbertsville*) **Henry's Golf Range**—Golf driving range, mini-golf, batting cages, go-carts (270-362-8170); **Henry's Race Place**—Western Kentucky's longest go-kart track (270-362-8170); **Maggie's Jungle Golf and Jungle Run**—Miniature golf, nature trail and petting zoo (270-362-8933); **Mike Wells 4 Rivers Outdoors**—Fishing guide service (270-362-4278); (*Hardin*) **Hardin Southern Railroad**—A delightful two-hour eighteen-mile round trip nostalgic rail adventure authentically reviving an experience from the past (270-437-4555); **Kenlake State Resort Parks**—See State Parks; **Mid-**

South Rail Heritage Foundation—Displaying a collection of historic railroad equipment adjacent to the Hardin Southern Railroad (270-898-8722); **Weakley's Guide Service**—Licensed fishing guides on Kentucky Lake. Sport fishing specialist: largemouth and smallmouth bass, crappie, bluegill, white bass and catfish (877-547-3474)

CADIZ AREA: Cadiz/Trigg County Tourist Commission (270-522-6343); **Canal Loop Trail**—Hiking and biking in the northern part of Land Between the Lakes (270-924-2000); **Elk & Bison Prairie**—Watch for elk and bison, or listen as the wind rustles through Indian Grass, as the prairie comes back to life (800-LBL-7077); **Janice Mason Art Museum**—A mix of local and regional artists is featured with mediums ranging from metal sculpture to watercolor (270-522-9056); **Kentucky Lake**—See State Parks; **Lake Barkley State Resort Park**—See State Parks; **Land Between the Lakes (LBL)**—Located in Western Kentucky and Tennessee, LBL offers 170,000 acres of wildlife, history and outdoor recreation opportunties, wrapped by 300 miles of undeveloped shoreline (800-LBL-7077); **Log House Antiques** (270-522-0610); **Whitetail Creek Outfitters**—Guided whitetail deer hunting (270-924-9639); **Sinking Fork Pay Lake and Fun Park**—swimming, horseshoes, volleyball, picnic area badminton, croquet and fishing (270-235-9677);

The Homeplace—This living history farm, with 16 original log structures, re-creates the life of a rural farm family before the Civil War. Demonstrations of butter making, tobacco firing, weaving, and plowing (800-LBL-7077); **Woodlands Nature Sta-**

Wooldridge Monuments Maplewood
Cemetery, Mayfield
Source: Kentucky Department of Tourism

tion—Hands-on encounter with the natural world the environmental education center nestled in the woods between Honker and Hematite Lakes (800-LBL-7077); **Wrangler's Riding Stables**—Scenic trails at Land Between The Lakes National Recreation Park (270-752-8266)

CLINTON AREA: Clinton Co. Judge's Office (270-653-4369); **Hickman County Museum**—1870s home of Captain Henry Watson of the Confederate Army. Local household, farm, business, government, medical & military items (270-653-6948); **Columbus-Belmont State Park**—See State Parks

EDDYVILLE/KUTTAWA AREA: **Lyon County Joint Tourism Commission** (800-355-3885); **Amaze'n Mazes Fort Venture**—Wild and crazy two-level labyrinth of twists and turns (270-388-8050); **Anderson Woodland Trail**—Beautiful hiking trail with view of Lake Barkley (800-355-3885); **Black Barn Herbs**—Grows pesticide free, hard to find herbs, beautiful perennials and fresh produce (270-365-5023); **Campbell's Orchard**—Peaches

and several different kinds of apples during season. Gift Shop has preserves, molasses, etc. Fried peach and apple pies (270-388-2738); **Eddyville Fun Park**—Go-karts, inflatables, lazer tag, miniature train, jump shot. pizza, snacks & arcade (270-388-9188); **Happy Trails Riding Stables**—Guided horse-back riding through wilderness/nature trails (270-871-4370); **Hook Line & Sinker Guide Service**—Fishing on Kentucky and Barkley Lakes, experienced guides and boats (270-388-0525); **Mineral Mound State Park**—See State Parks; **Rose Hill/Lyon County Museum**—Oldest standing structure in Old Eddyville. Home is on the National Register (270-388-9986); **Venture River Water Park**—Wave pool, 10 exciting slides and kiddie pool (270-388-7999)

ELKTON AREA: **City of Elkton** (270-265-9877); **Guthrie Railroad Museum**—Renovated caboose from the L&N Railroad (270-483-2683); **Milliken Memorial Community House**—Georgian mansion built in 1927, rare books and fine antiques. On the National Register of Historic Places (270-265-5816); **Robert Penn Warren Home**—The nation's first poet laureate and three-time Pultizer Prize winner is remembered here at his home (270-483-2683)

GRAND RIVERS/SMITHLAND AREA: **Livingston County Tourist Commission** (800-977-0325); **Grand Rivers Tourist Commission** (888-493-01520); **Belle of Grand Rivers**—A 55-foot replica of a turn of the century riverboat that tours Kentucky and Barkley Lake (800-498-0428); **Morris Toy Museum**—Museum displaying toys from the 1800s to the present (270-988-3591); **Grand Rivers Jetty and Walking Trail**—The concrete walkway is identified by its red border, has benches at the lakefront and on the jetty and is lighted at night. Public beach area (270-362-0152); **Kentucky Kayak Kountry**—Paddle sports, recreation, sales and rental of canoes and kayaks. Guided whitewater trips (270-362-0081); **Kentucky Lock and Dam**—Longest dam on the Tennessee River. A major generating plant in the TVA power system (800-467-1388); **Lake Barkley**—Bordering TVA's Land Between the Lakes Recreation Area in the rolling hills of southwest Kentucky and north central Tennessee, this lake offers waterfowl hunting, fishing, nature trails, a national battlefield, and a national waterfowl refuge (270-362-8430); **Lake Barkley Lock and Dam**—The Cheatham Lock and Dam enables river vessels to travel easily from Nashville, Tennessee, to the mouth of the Cumberland River. Lake Barkley connects to Kentucky Lake by a canal (270-362-4236); **Ohio River Public Wildlife Area**—

Waterfowl hunting area (502-564-7863); **Patti's 1880s Settlement**—Relaxed dining in 1880s atmosphere featuring homemade pies and 2" thick pork chops. Historic log cabin settlement with unique shops, miniature golf and animal park (888-736-2515); **Shawnee Queen River Taxi**—A 48-passenger river taxi that plies the Ohio River between Golconda, Rosiclare, Elizabethtown, Cave-in-Rock, Illinois and Carrsville, Kentucky with stops at each town (877-667-6123); **Vulcan Limestone Quarry** (270-362-4266)

HICKMAN AREA: Hickman Chamber of Commerce (270-236-2902); **Dorena, Mo - Hickman, Ky Toll Ferry**—Toll Ferry across the Mississippi River (731-285-0390); **R N Henson Broommaker's Museum**—1930s working broom shop. Museum with original equipment, photos, and historical mementos (270-236-2360); **Reelfoot Lake Public Wildlife Area**—Adequate trails through flat-bottomed riverland with 2,500 acres (901-538-2481); **The Olde House**—The oldest brick house in Hickman probably built as a slave house (731-885-3314); **Warren Thomas Museum**—A century-old church, highlights the history of the area's black community (270-236-2423)

HOPKINSVILLE/OAK GROVE AREA/FORT CAMPBELL: Hopkinsville/ Christian County CVB (800-842-9959); **Amazing Acres**—(270-881-2445); **Bravard Vineyards & Winery**—A small, farm/family winery (270-269-2583); **Brushy Fork Creek**—Paul and Patricia Ferrell are both self-taught artisans, Paul Ferrell is a woodturner and Patricia is a potter with a greenhouse of ferns and orchids (270-424-5988); **Christian Way Farm**—Experience planting, tending or harvesting the crops and feeding the animals (270-269-2434); **Copper Canyon Ranch**—Recreated 1880s mining town, live entertainment, comedy, music, stunts, live reenacted western gunfights, picnic area (270-269-2416); **Dan Cayce Guide Service**—Lake Barkley and Kentucky Lake adjoining the Land Between The Lakes National Park (LBL) offers Crappie and White Bass (Stripe) fishing (800-456-2952); **Don F. Pratt Memorial Museum**—History of the 101st Airborne Division Air Assault the "Screaming Eagles." (270-798-3215); **Fort Campbell Memorial Park**—Commemorates the 248 soldiers who died in a plane crash in Newfoundland (800-842-9959); **Fort Campbell Public Wildlife Area**—85,000 acres with a variety of forest wildlife and farm habitat, sinkholes and beaver lakes which attract wood ducks and shore birds. Trout streams available and 2 lakes with warm water fish species (270-789-2175); **Jefferson Davis State Historic Site**—See State Parks; **Oak Grove War Memorial Walking Trail**—One-mile walking trail lined with markers of all of the United States' wars and conflicts from the French and Indian War to Desert Storm (270-439-5675); **Pennyrile Forest State Resort Park**—See State Parks; **Pennyrile State Forest**—14,669 acres, native pine, hardwood trees. Kentucky's largest state forest. Hiking, picnicking. Restricted deer hunting; **Pennyroyal Area Museum**—Travel back in time to see the Night Riders lighting up the sky during the tobacco war...the Cherokee Indians' travails along the Trail of Tears...and clairvoyant Edgar Cayce performing his miracles (270-887-4270); **Trail of Tears Commemorative Park**—The Trail of Tears Commemorative Park used by the Cherokees on the infamous Trail of Tears and includes the gravesites of Chiefs White Path and Fly Smith (270-886-8033)

MARION AREA: Marion Tourism Commission (270-965-5015); **Amish Community**—A thriving Amish community of over 400 residents includes six Amish schools and four church districts. Many homes and farms have shops that sell their wares (800-755-0361); **Ben E. Clement Mineral Museum**—Fluorite crystal and other minerals, photographs, letters, records, mining equipment, and other memorbilia (888-965-4263); **Cave-In Rock Ferry**—Free riverboat ferry crosses the Ohio River to Cave-In Rock in Illinois (800-755-0361); **Crittenden County Historical Museum**—Authentic memorabilia from early pioneers (270-965-9257); **Fohs Hall Community Arts Foundation**—National Registry art gallery (270-965-5983); **Mantle Rock Native Education and Cultural Center**—Classes in Native American arts and culture, guides for walking tours of neighboring Mantle Rock, the mid-point

Eagle feather bonnet
Source: Kentucky Department of Tourism

on the "Trail of Tears," where hundreds of victims of the Indian Removal Act perished in the winter of 1838–39 (270-965-5882); **Paddy's Bluff Retreat (ATV Park)**—650 acres of forested land along the beautiful Cumberland River. Primitive trails for all terrain vehicles and primitive campsites (270-988-1822); **Paula Collins China Shoppe**—Internationally known china artist displays her work and gives lessons in china painting (270-965-9210)

MAYFIELD AREA: Mayfield Tourism Commission (270-247-6101); **Edana Locus House**—Built by multi-millionaire banker Ed Gardner, this circa 1928 home houses the visitor center. six acre estate, 11 room mansion (270-247-6101); **Icehouse Art Gallery & Western Kentucky Museum**—Hand crafted items and artwork by well known regional artists will interest collectors. Museum displays early industries of Mayfield and Graves County (270-247-6971); **Kaler Bottoms Public Wildlife Area**—Cypress swamps with low-lying wet terrain, swamp, great blue heron rookery, black vulture roost (502-564-4336); **Twilight Cabaret Productions**—Seasonal theatre events. Dinner theatre mystery-comedy (270-436-2399); **Wooldridge Monuments**—18 figure group of sandstone and Italian marble monuments, "The Strange Procession That Never Moves." Henry G. Wooldridge, a horse trader who moved to Mayfield around 1840 chose to commemorate his family, pets and himself with life-sized statues grouped around his tomb (270-247-6101)

MURRAY AREA: Murray Tourism Commission (800-651-1603); **Clara M. Eagle Gallery**—Display of all different media from canvas to performance, art classics to contemporary (270-762-3052); **Hazel Antique Shopping District**—12 shops and antique malls and 500 antique dealers (270-492-8175); **John Morgan's Guide Service**—Crappie fishing on Kentucky Lake (270-436-2810); **Murray Art Guild**—Visual Arts Organization that provides exhibitions, workshops and demonstrations housed in the Linn House which is on the National Register of Historic Places (270-753-4059); **Playhouse in the Park** (270-759-1752); **Wrather West Kentucky Museum**—Social, cultural and economic development of western Kentucky and the Jackson Purchase.(270-762-4771)

PADUCAH AREA: Paducah/McCracken County Convention and Visitors Bureau (800-PADUCAH);

Alben W. Barkley Museum—Captain William Smedley's 1852 home, listed in the National Register of Historic Places, showcases memorabilia of Alben W. Barkley (270-534-8264); **Annie's Horse-drawn Carriage Rides**—Tour downtown Paducah from a horse-drawn carriage (270-210-6095);

Iron Horse Locomotive, Paducah
Source: Kentucky Department of Tourism

Hotel Metropolitan—Opening 2006 as an African-American Heritage Museum. Save America's Treasures project, the 1908 hotel housed famous African-American entertainers and sports figures during segregation; **Legendary Chief Paduke Statue**—Chief of Sub-tribe of Chickasaw Indians, who lived and hunted in the area until Jackson Purchase, 1818. General William Clark, who founded Paducah, named it in honor of the chief. Sculptured by Lorado Taft in 1909; **Lower Town Arts District**—Studios and galleries of resident artists, including potters, painters, jewelry makers, printmakers and bookbinders (270-444-9191); **Luther F. Carson Four Rivers Center**—Performing arts center hosts Broadway hits, theatre, dance and a musical series with well-known entertainers (270-450-4444); **Maiden Alley Cinema**—International & domestic art films, created by individuals working outside the mainstream industry (888-442-7007); **Market House Theatre**—Nationally recognized, award winning community theatre producing plays and musicals (888-648-7529); **Metropolis Lake State Nature Preserve**—Natural lake ringed with bald cypress and swamp tupelo. Five species of rare fish, beaver, wintering place for bald eagles, hiking, birding and nature sudy; **Museum of the American Quilter's Society**—Quilts and the stories they tell at this national museum. Displays the vigorous rebirth of quiltmaking internationally since the 1970s (270-442-8856); **Paducah International Raceway**—5/8 mile, high bank dirt track. Racing, late model, modified, pre-stock and street stock autos (270-898-7469); **Paducah Raiload Museum**—Contains a model train layout and local and national history exhibits (270-519-7377); **Paducah Wall to Wall Murals**—Renowned artist Robert Dafford captures Paducah's rich history in lifesized paintings on the city's floodwall (800-723-8224); **Players Bluegrass Downs**—Live racing (270-444-7117); **River Heritage Museum**—This Save America's Treasures project, housed in downtown's oldest standing structure, has interactive exhibits that tell the story of the Four Rivers Region (800-PADUCAH); **Steam Locomotive No.1518**—A Mikado steam engine, the last "Iron Horse" used by the Illinois Central Railroad (800-PADUCAH); **West Kentucky Wildlife Management Area**—Deer, squirrels, rabbits, dove, racoons, ducks. Seven fishing ponds, picnic areas, hiking, primitive camping, horseback riding (270-488-3233); **Whitehaven Mansion/Welcome Center**—This landmark, once destined for destruction, was built in the 1860s (270-554-2077); **William Clark Market House Museum**—Story of a town that has survived tremendous challenges, including the Battle of Paducah and the 1937 flood. Features entire gingerbread woodwork interior of the 1877 List Drug Store (270-443-7759); **Yeiser Art Center**—Contemporary art by regional, and national artists. 19th & 20th century American and European art (270-442-2453)

PRINCETON AREA: Princeton/Caldwell County Chamber of Commerce (270-365-5393); **Adsmore House Museum and Ratliff Gunshop**—Circa 1857 Greek Revival home restored to late Victorian grandeur and filled with the Smith-Garrett family's personal belongings. Gunshop restored to early 1840 (270-365-3114); **Big Springs Park on the Trail of Tears**—City park situated on the camping site of the Cherokee Indians in 1838 while they were on the "Trail of Tears" march (270-365-9575);

Caldwell Railroad Museum—Railroad memorabilia and caboose exhibits (270-365-0582); **Donaldson Creek Hunting Camp**—Offering whitetail deer and turkey hunting (270-365-5118); **Jones-Keeney Public Wildlife Area**—Nature preserve and a few trails. Scenic overlooks. Bow and rifle ranges wildlife viewing (502-564-4336); **Princeton Art Guild**—Regional artists featured in a historic building (constructed 1817) that was on the "Trail of Tears." (270-365-3959)

WICKLIFFE AREA: Ballard County Chamber of Commerce (270-335-5999); **Barlow House**—11 room house built by local patriarch Clifton Jesse Barlow (270-334-3010); **Ballard County Wildlife Management Area**—Sloughs with some hardwoods stands, fishing lakes, and hunting. Eagles can be seen in winter. Primitive camping (270-224-2244); **Fort Jefferson Memorial Cross**—View three states from this 95-foot memorial that stands high upon a bluff at the confluence of the Ohio and Mississippi Rivers (270-335-3438); **Swan Lake Wildlife Management Area**—Near the confluence of the Ohio and Mississippi rivers, this prime wintering area for migratory waterfowl contains numerous sloughs, oxbow lakes and Kentucky's largest natural lake, Swan Lake (270-224-2244); **Wickliffe Mounds State Historic Site**—See State Parks

Bluegrass, Blues & Barbeque

CENTRAL CITY/GREENVILLE AREA: Central City Touris Commission (270-338-5422); Greenville/Muhlenberg County Chamber of Commerce (270-338-5422); **Brewco Motorsports**—Kentucky's only top level professional sports team (270-754-2264); **Everly Brothers Monument**—Town tribute to Don and Phil Everly, international singing stars; **House of Onyx**—One of the world's largest gemstone dealers, mineral hall and warehouse of Mexican onyx carvings (800-844-3100); **Lake Malone State Park**—See State Parks; **Rails to Trails**—six-mile multi-use trails which connect Central City and Greenville (270-338-5422)

DIXON AREA: Webster County Economic Development Corp (270-639-7015); **Parker Warner Historic Museum**—Historic photography, memorabilia, written and oral history (270-667-5022); **Webster County Civil War Driving Tour**—Several Civil War battlesites and the campsite of General Nathan B. Forrest (270-667-5022)

HARTFORD/ROSINE AREA: Ohio County Tourism Commission (270-274-1090); **Bill Monroe's Birthplace**—Boyhood home of Bill Monroe, the "Father of Bluegrass Music." (888-987-6444); **Bluegrass Motorcycle Museum**—20 Vintage Ameri-

can-made motorcycles and 30 years of memorabilia (270-298-7764); **Fordsville Historical Society and Depot Museum**—A restored depot built in 1916 and discontinued in 1942, includes relics of Kentucky rural life (270-276-5656); **Ohio County Museum**—Two-story historic home built 1880, on National Historic Register. Includes a small country store, relocated one-room schoolhouse, and, L&N caboose on a track. 1838 log cabin (270-298-3444); **Ohio County Park**—A replica of Old Fort Harrod and nature trails (270-298-4466); **Peabody Public Wildlife Area**—Reclaimed coal mines, many of which are water-filled, provide excellent fishing and birding opportunities (502-564-4336); **Rosine Barn Jamboree**—Live jam sessions of Bluegrass, Country and Gospel music (270-274-9744); **Rosine Cemetery**—Early 1860s cemetery. Bill Monroe, known internationally as the "Father of Bluegrass," and most of his family are buried here, including Birch & Charlie Monroe and Pendleton (Uncle Pen) Vandiver (270-274-5552); **Washburn Lake**—Fishing, launching area, boat rentals (502-564-4336)

Bill Monroe
Source: Kentucky Department of Tourism

HAWESVILLE AREA: Hancock County Tourism (270-927-8137); **Hancock County Museum**—located in the old Railroad Depot (270-295-6637); **Hancock County Farm Museum**—See tools and transportation from the past (270-295-3653); **Pate House**—Built in 1822, the scene of Abraham Lincoln's first trial in which he defended himself against charges of operating a ferry across the Ohio River without a license

HENDERSON AREA: Henderson County Tourist Commission (800-648-3128); **Ellis Park Race Course Inc**—Year-round simulcasting from all major N. America racetracks

Interior view of Bill Monroe's birthplace near Owensboro
Source: Kentucky Department of Tourism

(800-333-8110); **Henderson Fine Arts Center** (270-831-9800); **John James Audubon State Park**—See State Parks; **Sloughs Wildlife Management Area**—10,000 acres of Kentucky's finest hunting grounds and wetlands is home to 30,000 Canada geese and 10,000 ducks in winter (270-827-2673)

MADISONVILLE AREA: Madisonville/Hopkins County Chamber of Commerce (270-821-3435); **Dawson Springs Museum & Art Center** (270-797-3891); **Glema Mahr Center for the Arts** (270-824-8685); **Governor Ruby Laffoon Log Cabin**—Birthplace of Kentucky Governor Ruby Laffoon (270-821-3986); **Historical Society of Hopkins Co. Library & Museum; Lake Beshear**—760 acres, fishing and boat ramp; **Madisonville Kart World**—Go-kart slick track, formula one go-karts road course, batting cages and large arcade room (270-824-1116); **Sport Shooters**—Indoor shooting range (270-825-1733); **Tradewater Public Wildlife Area**—724 acres, deer, squirrel, raccoon, hiking and birding; **White City Wildlife Management Area**—5,472 acres, rabbit, quail, deer, dove, turkey, waterfowl, fishing, ramp and primitive camping

MORGANFIELD AREA: Union County Economic Development Foundation (270-389-9600); **James D. Veatch Camp Breckinridge Museum & Arts Center**—U.S. Military training center in 1942. Old officer's club has over 40 murals painted on the wall by German POW Daniel Mayer (270-389-4420)

OWENSBORO AREA: Owensboro/ Daviess County Tourist Commission (800-489-1131); *(Maceo)* **Carpenter Lake**—Fishing, ramp, dock, boat rentals and tackle; **Kingfisher Lakes**—Fishing and ramps; *(Owensboro)* **Ben Hawes State Park**—See State Parks; **Cowboy's of Kentucky, Inc.**—IPRA Rodeo in September, Pro Bullriders in May, music and dancing on the second Saturday throughout the summer (877-686-7433); **Executive Inn Rivermont Showroom Lounge**—Riverfront showroom with Las Vegas-style headliner entertainment (800-626-1936); **Goldie's Best Little Opryhouse in Kentucky**—Live family entertainment every Friday and Saturday night, featuring some of the most talented musicians, singers and comedians (270-926-0254); **Hall of Fame**—"Hometown Hero" Hall of Fame showcases the celebrities that have reached national or international acclaim, from the Owensboro area (800-489-1131); **International Bluegrass Music Museum**—State of the art, interactive museum dedicated to perserving and encouraging the growth of Bluegrass music (888-692-2656); **Lambert Land Maize & Pumpkin Patch LLC**—15 acre interactive corn maize & pumpkin patch (270-764-1448); **Owensboro Area Museum of Science and History**—Exhibits on natural, cultural and regional history, Wendell Ford Government Education Center, a SpeedZeum, a permanent motor sports gallery (270-687-2732); **Owensboro Museum of Fine Art**—The permanent collection includes American, European and Asian fine arts and decorative arts dating back to the 14th century (270-685-3181); **Owensboro Symphony Orchestra** (270-684-0661); **Panther Creek Park**—7 pavilions, a 6-acre stocked lake, gazebo and butterfly gardens, and 1876 refurbished one-room school house, a fire tower, a swinging bridge (270-685-6142); **Reid's Orchard**—An Orchard Apple Festival is held the third weekend in October (270-685-2444); **River City Trolley**—Route circles through the historic downtown area (270-687-8570); River Park Center—Premiere arts and cultural center for the Western Kentucky Region (270-687-2787); **Shelton Memorial**—Colonel Charles Shelton was the last POW from the Vietnam War (800-489-1131); **Theatre Workshop of Owensboro**—Known as "The Longest Running Show in Town" (270-683-5003); **Western Kentucky Botanical Gardens** (270-852-8925)

Caves, Lakes & Corvettes Region

BOWLING GREEN AREA: **Bowling Green Area CVB** (800-326-7465); *(Bowling Green)* **Barren River Imaginative Museum of Science** (270-843-9779); **Beech Bend Raceway Park**—Campground, amusement park, drag strip, and an oval track (270-781-7634); **Bowling Green Assembly Plant** (270-745-8019); **Bowling Green Chamber Orchestra, Inc.**—Kentucky's only fully professional chamber orchestra (270-846-2426); **Bowling Green Western Symphony Orchestra** (270-745-7681); **Chaney's Dairy Barn**—Specially selected Kentucky crafts and foods (270-843-5567); **Civil War Driving Tour**—Confederate Gen. Simon Bolivar Buckner quickly moved a detachment of troops to occupy Bowling Green on Sept. 18, 1861 (800-326-7465); **College Hill Historic Neighborhood Walking Tour**—Styles, forms and construction methods are mixed freely throughout the district (800-326-7465); **Duncan Hines Scenic Byway**—This 82-mile route begins at the former home and office of author Duncan Hines in Bowling Green, it crosses the Green River by ferry (800-326-7465); **Eloise B. Houchens Center**—Greek Revival mansion built in 1904 by Francis Kister, one-time Mayor of Bowling Green and co-builder of St. Joseph Catholic Church (270-842-6761); **Fountain Square Park**—Built between 1871 and 1872 according to plans of John Cox Underwood. The original stone fountain was replaced in 1881 by the present cast iron fountain (270-782-0222); **Greenwood Park, Inc**—36 holes of unique and challenging mini golf. Go-kart track, bumper boat pool, and batting cage; **Historic L & N Depot & Railpark**—Passenger Depot made of local limestone (270-745-0090); **Jacksons Orchard and Nursery**—Apples, peaches, honey, pumpkins and freshly made apple cider (270-781-5303); **Kentucky Library and Museum**—History, arts and crafts, Felts House, an 1830s log structure (270-745-2592); **Lost River Cave and Valley**—Kentucky's only underground boat tour (866-274-2283); **National Corvette Museum**—The 68,000 sq. ft. showcase to America's sports car features more than 75 Corvettes (800-538-3883); **Public Theatre of Kentucky, Phoenix Theatre** (270-781-6233); **Raceworld**—Two race tracks featuring scale NASCAR cars for true racing excite-

ment, a game room with rock climbing wall, a 360 degree motion theater simulator and Fun Zone Kiddie area (270-781-7223); **Riverview at Hobson Grove**—Built by Atwood and Juliet VanMeter Hobson and listed on the National Register. An official site of the Civil War Discovery Trail, as it was used for storage of Confederate munitions when the Confederate forces held Bowling Green (270-843-5565); **ShakeRag Historic District Walking Tour**—Bowling Green's first National Register District recognized for its significance to African American history (800-326-7465); **St. Joseph Catholic Church**—On the National Register of Historic Places because of its artistic and historic significance. The Gothic style church was constructed in three stages over a 30 year period (270-842-2525); **Upper East Main Street Historic Walking Tour**—Residences built between 1870 and 1930 (800-326-7465); *(Woodburn)* **Triple H Stables**—Guided trail rides (270-529-0061)

EDMONTON AREA: **Edmonton/Metcalfe County Chamber of Commerce** (270-432-3222); **Barn Lot Theater** (270-432-2276); **Historic Metcalfe County Courthouse**—One of the oldest courthouses in Kentucky (888-826-3181)

FRANKLIN AREA: **Franklin/Simpson County Tourism Commission** (866-531-2040); **African American Heritage Center** (270-586-0099); **Franklin Drive In** (877-586-1905); **Gallery on the Square** (270-586-8055); **Kentucky Downs Race Course**—Year 'round simulcast wagering (270-586-7778);

Mammoth Cave
Source: Kentucky Department of Tourism

Octagon Hall—A unique octagon shaped house (occupied during Civil War by Confederate and also Federal troops) and is on National Register of Historic Places (270-586-9343); **Old Stone Jail and Simpson County Archives**—Built in 1879 and used until 1986. The buildings house a museum and genealogical archives (270-586-4228)

GLASGOW AREA: **Glasgow/Barren County Tourist & Convention Center** (866-531-2040); *(Glasgow)* **Barren River Lake State Resort Park**—See State Parks; **Fort Williams**—In October 1863, Confederate forces raided Fort Williams. Union losses were 9 KIA, 26 WIA and 226 POWs. The fort stands today as a well-preserved "Earthen Fortification." (800-264-3161); **Plaza Theatre**—The 1934 theatre is a center for cultural events such as music, performing arts and movies (270-361-2101); **Brigadoon State Nature Preserve**—181 acres of rich protected woodlands containing wildflowers and rare species; **South Central Kentucky Cultural Center**—Preservation of the unique history and culture of "the Barrens." (888-256-6941); *(Lucas)* **Barren River Lake Public Wildlife Area**—20,000 acres in and around the lake. Hiking, picnicking, fishing and hunting (270-646-5167)

MAMMOTH CAVE AREA/ CAVE CITY: Cave City Tourist Commission (800-346-8908); **Edmonson County Tourist Commission** (800-624-8687); *(Cave City)* **Big Mike's Mystery House**—Guided tour through Mistifying gravity rooms, optical illusions and different oddities (270-773-5144); **Cave Country Go-Carts** (270-773-2299); **Crystal Onyx Cave and Campground**—Beautiful formations such as delicate crystalline draperies, rimstone pools and a pre-historic burial site (270-773-2359); **Dinosaur World**—More than 100 life sized dinosaurs in a beautiful natural setting; dig for authentic fossils in the fossil dig; and learn in the prehistoric dinosaur museum, work a giant dinosaur-themed jigsaw puzzle and dinosaur movies (270-773-4345); **Double J Stables & Horsemans Camp**—Guided trail rides through Mammoth Cave National Park and wildlife viewing (800-730-HRSE); **Floyd Collins Museum**—Tells the bizarre and tragic story of Floyd Collins, the explorer who died in Sand Cave (270-773-3366); **Guntown Mountain**—A Wild West town, amusement rides and onyx cave (270-773-3530); **Hillbilly Hound Fun Park**—18 hole miniature golf, go-kart track, family game room, kiddie rides, and snack bar (270-773-4249); **Kentucky Action Park/ Jesse James Stables**—alpine slide, guided scenic trail rides on horseback, go-carts, trampoline, rock wall, old time photos, game room, bumper cars, bumper boats, 18 hole western themed mini-gold, and 30 min. cave tours in Poutlaw Cave (800-798-0560); **Mammoth Cave Canoe and Kayak**—Canoeing outfitter on the Green River (270-773-3366); **Mammoth Cave Wax Museum**—American history and contributions made by each famous person (270-773-3010); **Mammoth Cave Wildlife Museum**—Kentucky's first and largest wildlife museum including big animals from all over the world (270-773-2255); **Miss Green River Boat Excursion**—A 63-foot twin diesel-powered riverboat for trips on the Green River within Mammoth Cave National Park (270-758-2243); **Onxy Cave**—1/2 hour tour through this unique underground world of columns, stalactites, stalagmites, and other cave formation (270-773-3530); **Outlaw Cave**—Beautiful stalactites, stalagmites, huge column formations from ceiling to floor (800-798-0560); **Rock-n-Roll Bumper Boats**—Includes a miniature golf course (270-773-6027); **Yogi Bear's Jellystone Park Waterslide** (800-523-1854); *(Mammoth Cave)* **Mammoth Cave National Park**—Established to preserve the cave system, including Mammoth Cave, the scenic river valleys of the Green and Nolin Rivers, and a portion of the hilly country of south central Kentucky. This is the longest recorded cave system in the world with more than 365 miles explored and mapped (800-967-2283); **Nolin Lake State Park**—See State Parks; *(Park City)* **Diamond Caverns**—Tours for over 143 years features intricate drapery deposits lining the halls in cascades of naturally colorful calcite with thousands of stalactites, stalagmites and flowstone deposits throughout the entire tour (270-749-2233); **Green River Canoe Outfitters**—Canoeing outpost, full livery service, and self-guided trips (270-749-2041); *(Roundhill)*, **Lazy Acres Trails & Paylake**—Over 1,000 acres available for horseback riding and camping, fully-stocked paylake (270-286-4189).

MORGANTOWN AREA: **Morgantown/Butler County Chamber of Commerce** (270-526-6827); **Green River Museum** (270-526-5342)

MUNFORDVILLE/HORSE CAVE: **Munfordville Tourism Commission** (888-686-3673); **Hart County Tourist Commission** (800-762-2869); *(Horse Cave)* **American Cave Museum / Hidden**

Kentucky Repertory Theatre in Horse Cave
Source: Kentucky Department of Tourism

River Cave—Descend 150 feet underneath the streets of historic downtown Horse Cave to the underground river that flows thrugh Hidden River Cave (270-786-1466); **Kentucky Caverns**—Tour features stalactites, stalagmites, and other formation created by water and time (800-762-2869); **Kentucky Down Under**—Kangaroos snakes colorful Rainbow Lorikeets in the Aviary and learn about Aboriginal culture (800-762-2869); **Kentucky Repertory Theatre at Horse Cave**—Kentucky's Professional Festival Theatre, is nationally known for its excellence (800-342-2177); *(Munfordville)* **Battle for the Bridge Historic Preserve**—219 acres of the Munfordville Battlefield and site of three Civil War battles including the most strategically important battle in Kentucky's Civil War history (270-524-0101); **Big Buffalo Crossing Canoe & Kayak Rental** (866-233-2690); **Hart County Historical Museum**—Pre-columbian Native Americans and the earliest settlements to the mid-20th Century (270-524-0101)

RUSSELLVILLE AREA: **Logan County Chamber of Commerce** (270-726-2206); *(Adairville)* **Red River Meeting House and Cemetery**—Site of the beginning of the Great Revival of 1800 and of the First Camp Meeting in the World on the third Sunday in June, 1800; listed on the National Register of Historic Places (270-539-6528); *(Auburn)* **Auburn History Museum** (270-542-4677); *(Lewisburg)* **Century House Winery & Vineyards** (270-755-2807); *(Russellville)* **Bibb House Museum** (270-726-4181); **1817 Saddle Factory Museum**—In 1820 there were 44 workers, mainly indentured servants and slaves, living on the site making saddles, bridles, shoes, and a variety of other leather goods. Early Kentucky saddles, primitive tools, and living quarters for the workers were located in the attic, where they drew and wrote on the plaster walls (270-726-4181); *(South Union)* **Shaker Museum at South Union**—The Shakers were a communal religious organization that flourished in America during the 19th century. The Shaker Museum, in a the 40-room 1824 Centre House, is filled with scores of original artifacts exemplifying the Shakers' fine craftmanship (800-811-8379)

SCOTTSVILLE AREA: Scottsville/Adair County Chamber of Commerce (270-237-4782); **Allen County Historical Museum**—Early 1900s structure includes Civil War memorabilia (270-237-3026); **Mennonite Community** (270-237-4782); **The Tabernacle**—Built in 1897, and the seat of early revivals and gospel singing held in Allen County

TOMPKINSVILLE AREA: Tompkinsville/Monroe County Chamber of Commerce (270-487-1314)**;** (*Gamaliel*) **Free-Town Church**—Built in 1846 by freed slaves of William Howard, who gave them 400 acres on which to build homes, known as Free-Town. Albert Martin gave them the land for the church. The logs are held together by wooden pegs and chinked with clay (270-487-1314);

(*Tompkinsville*) **Clover Hill Trap Club**—Three field courses for ATA registered birds (270-487-5418); **Cumberland River Ferry**—One of the last remaining free-floating ferries (270-487-1314); **Fisherman's Paradise-Kettle Creek Pay Lake** (270-487-1020); **McFarland Creek Outdoors**—4-wheeler nature rides, paint ball games, horseback rides, historic bus tours, nature hikes, carriage rides, petting zoo, water tubing and go cart rides (270-487-5563); **Monroe County Marble Dome**—A wooden structure that covers a 20x40-foot marble yard. The game of Rolley-Hole marbles is native to Monroe County, KY and Clay County, TN (270-487-1314); **Old Mulkey Meetinghouse State Historic Site**—See State Parks

Southern Lakes & Rivers Region

BURKESVILLE AREA: Cumberland County Tourist & Convention Commission (270-433-5133); *(Bakerton)* **Kentucky Trophy Fishing**—Trophy Striped Bass fishing (270-433-6333); *(Burkesville)* **Dale Hollow Lake State Resort Park**—See State Parks; **Dale Hollow Public Wildlife Area**—Shoreline provides habitat for deer, raccoon, and other small mammals (615-736-5181); **Mud Camp Creek Public Wildlife Area**—Steep, narrow forested ridges to narrow valleys for fishing, primitive camping and hiking (270-465-5039)

CAMPBELLS-VILLE AREA: Taylor County Tourist Commission (800-738-4719); **Friendship One-Room School House**—A museum that contains historic school memorabilia from 1918-1955 (270-465-5410); **Green River Lake State Park**—See State Parks; **Green River Public Wildlife Area**—20,500

acres (270-465-5039); **Hiestand House Museum**—1823 dwelling is one of 12 German stone houses in Kentucky (270-789-4343); **Tebbs Bend Battlefield Association**—Tebbs Bend Green River Bridge Civil War Battlefield is located adjacent to Green River Lake where the Atkinson-Griffon House, Confederate Hospital is located (270-465-8726); **The Homeplace on Green River**—1803 house, 1850s bank, barn, corn crib, feedlot, 227 acres (270-465-4511); **U.S. Army Corps of Engineers Visitor Center**—Office/Visitor Center for U.S. Army Corp of Engineers at Green River Lake (270-465-4463)

Big South Fork Scenic Railway
Source: Kentucky Department of Tourism

COLUMBIA AREA: Columbia/Adair County Tourism Commission (270-384-6020); *(Columbia)* **John B. Begley Chapel**—Neo-Gothic chapel designed by F. Fay Jones, the world's foremost chapel architect (800-

264-0138); *(Kinfley)* **Janice Holt & Henry Giles Home**—The log home of Janice Holt & Henry Giles; listed on the National Register of Historic Places

GREENSBURG AREA: Greensburg/Green County Chamber of Commerce (270-932-4298); **Canoe Kentucky Livery**—Canoeing and outfitter (800-Kcanoe-1); **Green River Paddle Trail Park**—Cabins, canoe, and kayak rentals are available (270-932-4298); **Greensburg Walking Tour**—Greensburg 's National Register Historic District and John Hunt Morgan Trail (270-932-4298); **Old Green County Courthouse**—Limestone buildings on the Square, built in 1803, is a museum listed on National Register. Oldest courthouse west of the Alleghenies (270-932-4298)

JAMESTOWN AREA: Russell County Tourist Commission (888-833-4220); *(Jamestown)* **Kentucky Off-Track**—Live horse race simulcasts (270-343-3939); **Lake Cumberland State Resort Park**—See State Parks; **Shell's Wolf Creek Outfitter** (270-343-2510); **Wolf Creek National Fish Hatchery**—Produce 1,000,000 fish per year (270-343-3797); *(Russell Springs)* **AJ Guide Service**—Specializing in catching striped bass (270-866-6207); **Bates Guide Service**—Specializes in year round trophy striper fishing (270-866-8703); **Striper Mania Guide Service** (270-866-6717)

LIBERTY AREA: Economic Dev. Authority of Casey County (606-787-9973); **Clementsville Motorsports**—Mud racing at its finest, truck and tractor pulling (606-787-5541)

MONTICELLO AREA: Monticello/Wayne County Chamber of Commerce (606-348-3064); **Mill Springs Mill**—Constructed in 1877, a historic grist mill, listed on the National Register of Historic Places (606-348-3064); **Victor's Striper Fishing Charter** (800-505-6447)

SOMERSET AREA: Somerset/Pulaski County CVB (800-642-6287); *(Burnside)* **General Burnside Island State Park**—See State Parks; **Lake Cumberland Speedway**—3/8 mile dirt round track (606-561-8994); *(Nancy)* **Haney's Appledale Farm** (606-636-6148); *(Somerset)* **Beaver Creek Public Wildlife Area**—Fishing, hunting, hiking trails, and wildlife viewing, 17,347 acres (606-376-8083); **D.C. Guide Service**—Fishing boats with the latest fishing equipment (800-804-5819); **Lake Cumberland**—Lake Cumberland is the second largest lake

Cumberland River
Source: Sid Webb

in the Cumberland River system (606-679-6337); **Mill Springs Battlefield** (606-679-1859); **POW/MIA Memorial Garden**—Dedicated to the American servicemen/women listed as Prisoners of War and/or Missing in Action since World War I (606-679-1079); **The Center for Rural Development**—Performing arts and meeting/convention facility (606-677-6000)

STEARNS/WHITLEY CITY AREA: McCreary County Tourist Commission (888-284-3718); *(Stearns)* **Big South Fork National River and Recreation Area**—Pristine natural setting panoramic views, hiking, fishing and white water rafting (606-376-5073); **Big South Fork Scenic Railway**—13-mile round trip scenic train ride in enclosed or open air cars through the heart of the Big South Fork National Recreation Area (800-462-5664) *See Coupon below;* **Blue Heron Mining Community**—Coal town tours exhibits & recorded messages. Oral history recordings in ghost structures, mining artifacts (606-376-5073); **Koger Barthell Mining Camp**—Reconstructed 1910 mining camp, company store, 12 miner's houses, schoolhouse and 1909-34 antique cars (888-550-5748); **McCreary County Museum**—The 1907 Stearns Coal & Lumber Company office building highlights history from the Indian and Pioneer era through the "Boom" times of the coal and lumber industries (606-376-5730); *(Whitley City)* **Natural Arch Scenic Area**—Magnificent sandstone arch, picnicking and hiking. 50'x 90'arch (606-679-2010); **Yahoo Falls-Big South Fork NRRA**—State's tallest waterfall with hiking trails, overlooks, picnic area (606-376-5073)

Kentucky Derby Region

BARDSTOWN AREA: Bardstown/Nelson County Tourist Commission (800-638-4877); **Around the Town Carriage**—Narrated tour through historic Bardstown on horse-drawn carriages (502-348-0331); **Bardstown Walking Tour** (800-638-4877); **Basilica of St. Joseph Proto-Cathedral**—First Catholic Diocese west of the Allegheny Mountains (502-348-3126); **Civil War Museum/Old Bardstown Village**—State's largest collection of artifacts featuring the war's Western Theatre (502-349-0291); **Four Roses Distillery Warehouse Operations**—Bottling

Visitors stroll near the lake in
Bernheim Forest, near Louisville
Source: Sid Webb

done by hand, sweet aging Bourbon in white oak barrels (502-543-2264); **Guided Craft Tours**—Kentucky craft artists in their homes and studios (502-349-1777); **Heaven Hill Distilleries Bourbon Heritage Center**—High-tech interactive exhibits and theater (502-337-1000); **Heaven Hill Distilleries Trolley**—A narrated, introductory tour of historic Bardstown and its attractions (800-638-4877); **My Old Kentucky Dinner Train**—Vintage 1940s dining cars carry passengers through scenic Kentucky countryside for lunch and dinner excursions (502-348-7300); **My Old**

Kentucky Home State Park—Visit the Bardstown mansion, Federal Hill, inspiration for Stephen Foster's "My Old Kentucky Home" (502-348-3502); **Old Bardstown Village**—Authentic village of nine log cabins 150-200 years old (502-349-0291); **Old County Jail**—Original 1874 jail and restored Jailer's Inn (800-948-5551); **Oscar Getz Museum of Whiskey History**—Artifacts relating to distilleries, stills, cooperage, antique bottles and advertising art (502-348-2999); **Stephen Foster, The Musical**—Outdoor musical based on the life of America's first great composer. Features many of Foster's most popular songs including "Oh Susanna" and "My Old Kentucky Home" (800-626-1563); **War Memorial of Mid-America**—Historic buildings feature artifacts from the Revolutionary War through Desert Storm (502-349-0291); **Wildlife/Natural History Museum**—North American animals in natural habitat, fossils and minerals from around the world (502-349-0291); **Women of the Civil War Museum**—Contributions of women during the Civil War (502-349-0291); *(Bloomfield)* **Springhill Winery & Plantation Bed and Breakfast**—Kentucky's Wine Heritage and tasting room or patio overlooking the Vineyards (502-252-9463); *(Nazareth)* **Sisters of Charity of Nazareth**—Exhibits illustrate the role of this order in education, healthcare and social services (502-331-4529); (New Haven) **Kentucky Railway Museum**—Ride through the scenic and historic Rolling Fork River Valley on a restored passenger train (800-272-0152); *(Trappist)* **Abbey of Gethsemani**—The largest and America's oldest order of Cistercian Monks was founded in 1848. The monastery also produces cheese, fruitcake and bourbon fudge; burial site of Thomas Merton. (502-549-4406)

BEDFORD AREA: **Trimble County Tourist Commission** (502-255-7196); **Bray Orchards & Roadside Market**—Since 1910 (502-255-3607)

BRANDENBURG AREA: Meade County Tourism (270-422-3967); **Buttermilk Falls**—Historic hiking trail in a beautiful natural setting (270-422-3626);

John Hunt Morgan Civil War Driving Trail—Gen. John Hunt Morgan's ride through Meade County (270-422-3626); **Otter Creek Park**—2,600 acres of forest next to the Ohio River (502-574-4583)

ELIZABETHTOWN/RADCLIFF AREA / FORT KNOX: Elizabethtown Tourism & Convention Bureau (800-437-0092); **Radcliff/Ft. Knox Convention & Tourism Commission** (800-834-7540); *(Elizabethtown)* **Black History Gallery**—Emma Reno Connor collection of the accomplishments and events pertinent to the Black American experience (270-769-5204); **Brown Pusey House**—Built in 1825, example of rural Federal architecture. Known as "The Hill House," a boarding house and inn. It once housed General George Custer and his wife in the 1870s (270-765-2515); **Costumed Historic Downtown Walking Tour**—Tour covers 25 historic sites with actors as characters like Sarah Bush Lincoln, Carry Nation, and General George Custer (800-437-0092); **Elizabethtown Historic Driving Tour**—Covering 36 historical sites (800-437-0092); **Hardin County History Museum**—Story of Hardin County from early Indian inhabitants to modern times (270-737-4126); **Hardin County Schools Performing Arts Center** (270-769-8837); **Lincoln Heritage House**—Double log house crafted in part by Abraham Lincoln's father, Thomas Lincoln (270-765-2175); **Sarah Bush Johnston Lincoln Cabin**—Replica of Sarah Bush Johnston's cabin she lived in when she married Thomas Lincoln (270-765-2175); **Schmidt Museum of Coca-Cola Memorabilia**—World's largest privately owned collection of Coca-Cola memorabilia (270-234-1100); **Swope's Cars of Yesteryear Museum**—50 antique and classic cars (270-765-2181); *(Fort Knox)* **Patton Museum of Cavalry & Armor**—World-class U.S. Military Museum featuring the history of the Cavalry-Armor Forces including General George S. Patton Jr.'s personal belongings, a section of the Berlin Wall and display on U.S. Gold Vault (800-334-7540); *(Glendale)* **Antiques & Crafts in Historic Glendale**—Carriage rides (270-369-6188);

Speed Art Museum, Louisville
Source: Kentucky Department of Tourism

(Radcliff) **Hardin County Playhouse**—Comedy's, mystery's musical's and old favorites (270-351-0577); **Saunders Springs Nature Preserve**—26 acres of hiking, biking and walking trails (800-334-7540); *(West Point)* **Bridges To The Past**—Walking trail over 3 stone bridges built prior to the Civil War (800-334-7540); **Fort Duffield**—Built in 1861 Kentucky's largest and best preserved Civil War earthen fortification with living history programs (502-922-4574); **Knob Creek Gun Range**—Recreational shooting year 'round, bi-annual Machine Gun Shoot draws 8-10 thousand visitors from across the states and abroad (502-922-4457); **Music Ranch USA**—Country jamboree old time Rock, Blues, some Bluegrass and Gospel (502-922-9393); **Tioga Falls National Recreation Trail**—A scenic and historic two-mile hike winding over Muldraugh Hill (800-334-7540)

HODGENVILLE AREA: Larue County Chamber of Commerce (270-358-3411); **Abraham Lincoln Birthplace National Historic Site**—Built at the location of Lincoln's birth, the solid marble, neoclassical monument houses the symbolic cabin of Lincoln's birth (270-358-3137); **Abraham Lincoln Boyhood Home**—Located in Knob Creek and now part of the National Park System as a unit of Abraham Lincoln

Abraham Lincoln Boyhood Home, National Historic Site, Hodgenville
Source: Sid Webb

Birthplace National Historic Site, the Lincoln family residence from 1811 to 1816 (270-358-3137); **Lincoln Jamboree**—Country music showplace (270-358-3545); **Lincoln Museum, Inc.**—Dioramas featuring wax figures trace Lincoln's life from birth to death (270-358-3163)

IRVINGTON/HARDINSBURG AREA: Breckinridge County Tourism (270-756-0268); *(Cloverport)* **Cloverport Community Museum**—Historic riverport town in Breckinridge County (270-788-3811); *(Hardinsburg)* **Breckinridge Co. Historical Society Museum**—Historic Taylor House (270-756-0268); *(Irvington)* **Broadmoor Gardens and Conservatory**—Kukenhoff Gardens in Holland was the inspiration for this garden, which includes water gardens, a tropical plant conservatory, a rock garden, animal topiaries, an iris garden, a lily garden, an all-white moon garden and a two-mile trail through wildflower meadows (270-547-4200)

LAGRANGE AREA: Oldham County Tourist & Convention Commssion (800-813-9953); *(Crestwood)* **Duncan Memorial Chapel**—English Gothic Chapel is built of native stone and located in one of Kentucky's oldest cemeteries (502-241-8392); **Harrods Creek Baptist Church**—Organized in 1797; registered on the National Historic Register of His-

toric Places (502-241-4983); **Yew Dell Gardens—** Rare garden plants and display gardens are one of only 12 American gardens designated as Partnership Gardens by the Garden Conservancy (502-241-4788); *(Goshen)* **Creasey Mahan Nature Preserve—**Encompasses 100 acres nature trails, wildlife exhibits, and old springhouse and birds in the avian rehab program (502-228-4362); *(La Grange)* Crawford **Hot Air Balloons—**Scenic hot air balloon rides; **D W Griffith Site—** David Wark Griffith, an Oldham County native, is buried at Mt. Tabor Cemetery in Centerfield. The pioneer filmaker's Civil War epic, Birth of a Nation, set a new standard for Hollywood in 1915; **Historic District of LaGrange—**Shops are housed in storefronts and homes circa 1840-1930. CSX working railroad runs down the middle of Main Street (502-222-5293); **Little Big Horse Trails** (502-222-1842); **Oldham County History Cen-**

Tank at Patton Museum, Fort Knox
Source: Kentucky Department of Tourism

ter (502-222-0826); **Rob Morris Home—**Stately white frame house is the home of the founder of the Order of the Eastern Star, Dr. Robert Morris (502-222-0248);

(Pewee Valley) **Confederate Cemetery—**Site of the only state burial ground for Southern veterans of the Civil War; **Little Colonel Playhouse** (502-241-9906)

It's a
Kentucky thing...
The Sheltowee Trace, a National Recreation Trail, runs for 268-miles through the length of the Daniel Boone National Forest. It is aptly named — Sheltowee means "Big Turtle" and was the name given to Daniel Boone when he was adopted into the Shawnee tribe. Hikers, retracing the steps of Daniel Boone, can see landmarks along the trail marked with the sign of the turtle.

LEBANON AREA: Lebanon Tourist & Convention Commission *(270-692-9594); (Bradfordsville)* **William Clark Quantrill Civil War Driving Tour**—Posing as a Union soldier at times, Quantrill murdered and pillaged along with the James Brothers. In Bradfordsville he burned the community for revenge (270-337-3796); *(Lebanon)* **Cecil L. Gorley Trail**—3.2 mile naturalist walking trail around Fagan Branch Reservoir (270-692-2491); **Goodin View Farm Store and Maze**—Fresh produce, farm raised shrimp, catfish, hybrid striped bass (270-692-0165); **Historic Homes & Landmarks Tour**—Homes with Civil War history (270-692-0021); **Lebanon Aquatic Center**—34 acre park featuring outdoor tennis and basketball courts, fitness trail, indoor pool, Outdoor 100' slide pool (270-692-6272); **Lebanon Civil War Park**—Major General George H. Thomas (Rock of Chickamauga) led Union forces from Lebanon to Mill Springs in January 1862, first major battle in Kentucky (270-692-6272); **Lebanon National Cemetery**—Built in 1863 to bury the Union soldiers killed in battle at Perryville, also veterans of WWI, WWII, Korean Conflict and Vietnam (270-692-3390); **Scenic Hwy & Byway US 68**—Historic trail used by notables like Andrew Jackson, Jane Todd Crawford and General Lafayette (270-692-

**Copper Still,
Maker's Mark Distillery**
Source: Kentucky Department of Tourism

0021); *(Loretto)* **Holy Cross Church**—Site of first Mass in Kentucky and first Catholic Church west of the Allegheny Mountains (270-865-2521); **Maker's Mark Distillery,** National Historic Landmark— Tour bourbon-making process (270-865-2099); *(Nerinx)* **Loretto Motherhouse**—One of the first religious orders of women west of the Allegheny Mountains. 1860 church, 1812 log cabin of founder Fr. Charles Nerinckx (270-865-5811)

LEITCHFIELD AREA: Grayson County Tourism Commission (888-624-9951*); (Caneyville)* **Pine Knob Theatre**—Outdoor live 500-seat theatre (270-879-8190); *(Clarkson)* **Buck Country Outfitters**—Trophy deer and turkey outfitter offering guided hunts and lodging (270-242-9639*); (Falls of Rough)* **Rough River Dam State Resort Park**—See State Parks; **Rough River Lake**—Rocky cliffs add to the beauty of the shoreline of this 5,100 acre lake (270-257-2061); *(Leitchfield)* **Blackrock Motor Sports Park**—A statewide natural trained race track with national competitions (270-259-5960); **Calvin Ray's Live Music-Family Entertainment**—Live entertainment with major headliners (270-879-0582); **Jack Thomas House/Grayson Co Historical Society**—Earliest brick house in Grayson County constructed circa 1814 by Jack Thomas (270-230-8989*)*

LOUISVILLLE AREA: Greater Louisville CVB (888-LOUISVILLE); *(Fairdale)* **Jefferson County Memorial Forest**—Designated as a National Audubon Society Wildlife Refuge, the forest offers environmental education, adventure programs, hiking, climbing and wildlife watching (502-368-5404); *(Harrods Creek)* **C Q Princess**—85 foot luxury dinner yacht (502-228-1651); *(Louisville)* **Actors Theatre of Louisville**—Award-winning professional stage company performing comedies, dramas, musicals and the internationally-celebrated Humana Festival of New American Plays (800-4-ATL-TIX); **American Printing House for the Blind**—World's largest company devoted solely to producing products for people who are blind or visually impaired. Founded in 1858, it is the oldest institution of its kind in the United States (800-223-1839); **Art Sparks Interactive Gallery**—Hands-on gallery dedicated to visual arts (502-634-2700); **Art! Art! Barking Dog Dance Company**—Professional modern dance reperatory company (502-893-9966); **Belle of Louisville/Spirit of Jefferson**—The Belle of Louisville, built in 1914, is the oldest operating steam-driven paddlewheeler in the country. This beautiful national historic landmark offers sightseeing excursions Cruises originate at the downtown Louisville Wharf (866-832-0011); **Brennan**

Historic House and Medical Office Museum—c. 1912 medical office museum, extensive collection of victorian furniture, art, sculpture, china and silver in a restored Italianate brick and limestone residence (502-540-5145); **Broad Run Vineyards**—Operated by three generations of the Kushner-Hyatt family (502-231-0372); **Buena Vista Carriage**—Horse drawn carriage rides through downtown Louisville and Ohio River waterfront (502-417-7109) **Callahan Museum**—Located at the American Printing House for the Blind tells the story of the history of the education of people who are blind (800-223-1839); **Cathedral of the Assumption**—Recently restored 1852 Cathedral (502-582-2971); **Center-Stage Theatre at Jewish Community Center** (502-238-2720); **Churchill Downs**—Officially opened in 1875, became the World's Most Legendary Racetrack and "Home of the Kentucky Derby" (800-283-3729); **Comedy Caravan**—Award winning comedy theater featuring national touring professional comedians (502-459-0022); **Conrad-Caldwell House Museum**—1895 mansion is among the most ornate in the Old Louisville area

George Rogers Clark bust at Locust Grove, Louisville
Source: Sid Webb

(502-636-5023); **Creative Diversity Art Studio**—A venue where artists with disabilities can express, expand and nurtue their artisic potential in collaboration with other artists (502-767-4723); **E. P. Tom**

Sawyer State Park—See State Parks; **Embroiders' Guild of America, Inc.**—The Margaret Parshall Gallery features exhibits of needlework, library and antique tool display (502-589-6956); **Farmington Historic Home**—Designed from a

Locust Grove
Source: Sid Webb

plan by Thomas Jefferson and completed in 1816 using slave labor, the 14-room house is furnished with antiques from the period. A summer kitchen, springhouse, stone barn, and a recreated early 19th century garden are located on the 18-acre grounds. Abraham Lincoln, a close friend of Speed's son Joshua, spent about three weeks at Farmington in 1841 (502-452-9920); **Filson Historical Society**—Offering an extensive library, museum and a special collections department, the Society is headquartered in the Ferguson Mansion (502-635-5083); **Frazier Historical Arms Museum**—1000 years of history (866-886-7103); **Gheens Science Hall and Rauch Planetarium**—Public astronomy programs, a star show and three different laser light shows (502-852-6664); **Glassworks**—Glass artists and galleries, providing visitors with a rich portrayal of the magic, mystery and

beauty of glass (502-584-4510); **Historic Locust Grove**—The ca.1790 Georgian house was the last home of Revolutionary War hero General George Rogers Clark, whose campaign doubled the size of the United States. The site features nine outbuildings, restored gardens, a museum gallery and museum store (502-897-9845) *(See Coupon below)*; **Hite Art Institue Galleries**—University gallery (502-852-4483); **Iroquois Amphitheater**—Open-air, state-of-the-art proscenium theater on a hillside (502-368-5865); **Kentucky Center for African-American Heritage**—The theme "One More River to Cross" is the state's pre-eminent black history museum and educational center (502-583-4100); **Kentucky Derby Museum**—Located at Gate 1 of historic Churchill Downs, the museum presents the traditions and excitement of the "greatest two minutes in sports." (502-637-1111); **Little Loom House**—Keeping the art of hand-weaving and its history alive and is housed in three century-old cabins that are listed on the National Register of Historic Places (502-367-4792); **Louisville Bats Professional Baseball**—See advertisement in Sports—Professional baseball. Triple A affiliate of the Cincinnati Reds (502-212-2287); **Louisville Extreme Park**—Bikes and Blades extreme park (502-456-8100); **Louisville Free Public Library Galleries**—Free exhibitions and programs on art, culture, books, communications, social and cultural issues (502-574-1600); **Louisville Horse Trams**—Horse and carriage rides in downtown Louisville (502-581-0100); **Louisville Orchestra**—Classical Concert Series, Coffee Concert Series, NightLites Concert Series, Pops Series, Family Concert Series and Summer Concert Series (800-775-7777); **Louisville Science Center & IMAX Theatre**—Engaging hands-on exhibits and an incredible film in the four-story IMAX Theatre (800-591-2203); **Louisville Slugger Museum**—Home of the World's Biggest Baseball Bat (877-775-8443); **Louisville Visual Art Association**—Contemporary visual art center (502-896-2146); **Louisville Zoo**—Over 1300 exotic animals in natural exhibits with exotic plants throughout the 134-acre zoo, nestled amid rolling hills in the heart of Louisville (502-459-2181); **McAlpine Locks and Dam**—Constructed in 1961-64 by the U.S. Army Corps of Engineers, the dam is 8,627 ft. long and has 9 gates, 22 ft. x 100 ft (502-774-3517); **Muhammad Ali Center**—See advertisement in Sports—An education and cultural center designed to preserve and share the legacy of Muhammad Ali, and further promote respect, hope and understanding across cultural and geographic borders (800-626-5646); **Music Theatre Louisville** (502-589-4060); **Pleiades Theatre Company**—Louisville's premiere Women's Theatre Company (502-637-3064); **Portland Museum**—Portland and Louisville's river history with an animatronic robot of the first female steamboat captain Mary Miller (502-776-7678); **Riverside, The Farnsley-Moremen Landing**—300-acre historic site is an 1837 Kentucky "I-House" (502-935-6809); **S.A.R. Historical Museum**—National headquarters of the Sons of the American Revolution Historical Museum (502-589-1776); **Six Flags Kentucky Kingdom**—Theme and water park located in the heart of Louisville features more than 110 rides and attractions (800-727-3267); **Speed Art Museum**—Holdings include 17th century Dutch and Flemish paintings, European tapestries and contemporary art (502-634-2700); **Squallis Puppeteers**—Offers arts opportunities (502-544-1299); **Stage One**—Entertaining and professional theatre for the young (800-775-7777); **The Kentucky Center**—Performances in the grand Whitney Hall, the intimate Bomhard Theater, the ever-changing Boyd Martin Experimental Theater

or the restored W.L. Lyons Brown Theatre (800-775-7777); **The Spirit**—A replica of the fabled river boats of by-gone days (866-832-0011); **Thomas Edison House**—A museum located in an 1850s house where Edison boarded while working as telegrapher in 1866-1867 (502-585-5247); **Whitehall Historic Home**—Built in 1855 and situated on 8.5 acres of grounds and gardens (502-897-2944); **Zachary Taylor National Cemetery**—National Historic Landmark includes the graves of President and Mrs. Zachary Taylor (1784-1850), 12th president of the U.S. (502-893-3852)

NEW CASTLE AREA: Henry County Chamber of Commerce (502-845-0806); *(New Castle)* **Lake Jericho Recreation Area**—137 acre lake with picnic aand camping (502-743-5205); **Smith-Berry Vineyard and Winery** (502-845-7091); *(Smithfield)* **Our Best Restaurant**—Traditional southern items (502-845-7682)

SHELBYVILLE AREA: **Shelbyville/Shelby County Visitors Bureau** (800-680-6388); **American Saddlebred Horse Farm Tours**—Shelby County has been called "The Saddlebred Capital of the World," with American Saddlebred breeding and training facilities (502-633-6388);

The Horse Experience
There's a little something for everyone...

www.shelbyvilleky.com

Visit Shelbyville, the American Saddlebred Capital of the world, and experience an authentic horse farm tour as well as unique shopping and restaurants, golf, boating and fishing

Just off I-64 between Louisville & Frankfort
To plan your horse experience call
1-800-680-6388

Kentucky

Guist Creek
MARINA & CAMPGROUND

• Fishing & Boating
• RV & Tent Camping
• Live Bait & Tackle
• Fishing Boat Rentals
• Boat / Pontoon Slip Rentals

Guist Creek Marina & Campground
11990 Boat Dock Road
Shelbyville, Kentucky 40065
(502) 647-5359
www.guistcreek.com *Kentucky*

Buffalo Crossing Restaurant and Fun Ranch—A 1,000-acre working bison farm and attraction with petting zoo, lakes and playgrounds (877-700-0047); **Clear Creek Family Activity Center**—Indoor competition and children's splash pool, walking/running track, gymnasium, game room and outdoor splash pool with water slide (502-633-5059); **Lake Shelby**—Restored authentic log cabin homestead. Near historic site of Squire Boone's Painted Stone Station (502-633-5059)

SHEPHERDSVILLE AREA: **Shepherdsville/Bullitt Co. Tourist & Convention Commission** (800-526-2068); *(Clermont)* **Bernheim Arboretum and Research Forest**—14,000 acres including a 250-acre arboretum with over 2800 trees and shrubs labeled, a fishing lake, biking and over 50 miles of hiking trails (502-955-8512); **Jim Beam American Outpost**—World-famous Jim Beam Distillery (502-543-9877); *(Lebanon Junction)* **Junction Jamboree**—Rated the Number One Country Music stage show in Kentucky (502-833-0800); *(Shepherdsville)* **Bullitt County History Museum**—Located in the century-old front portion of the county courthouse (502-921-0161); **C.R. Wilson Bluegrass Friday Night**—Bluegrass music for the entire family (502-239-8004); **Hawks View Gallery**—Watch as artists create exquist glass-blown art from start to finish (502-955-1010); **Kart Kountry**—The longest go-kart track in the United States is over 1.5 miles long, miniature golf course, batting cages and bumper boats (502-543-9588); **Old Stone Bank**—

Glassworks, Louisville
Source: Kentucky Department of Tourism

Built in 1830, this bank is believed to be the first west of the Alleghenies (800-526-2068); **Old Stone Jail**—Built in 1891 and used until 1947 (800-526-2068); **Woodsdale One-Room Schoolhouse**—Built in 1808, the Schoolhouse represents 145 years of continuous teaching (800-526-2068)

Covered bridge near Springfield
Source: Sid Webb

SPRINGFIELD AREA: **Springfield/Washington County Chamber of Commerce** (859-336-3810); *(Mt. Zion)* **Mt. Zion Covered Bridge**—One of the longest multi-span bridges in Kentucky, built 1871-72; *(Springfield)* **1851 Historic Maple Hill Manor B&B, Alpaca Farm and Handcrafted Gift Shop**—14 acres includes an orchard of 100+ fruit trees, 200+ raspberry bushes, a nature preserve, alpacas, llamas and pygmy goats (800-886-7546); **Lincoln Homestead State Park**—See State Parks; **Rolling Hills Vineyard and Winery**—(859-262-6154); **St. Catherine Motherhouse**—Home of the first U.S. community of Dominican Sisters (859-336-9303); **St. Rose Proto-Priory**—The first Catholic educational institution west of the Alleghenies (859-336-3121); **Washington County Courthouse**—Completed in 1816, it houses the marriage documents of Abraham Lincoln's parents, Nancy Hanks and Thomas Lincoln. This is the oldest courthouse still in continuous use in Kentucky (859-336-5425); *(Willisburg)* **Willisburg Lake/Captain Bob's Boat Dock**—Man-made fishing with launching ramp, boat rentals and camping (859-375-0093)

TAYLORSVILLE AREA: **Taylorsville/Spencer County Economic Development Authority** (502-477-3246); **Taylorsville Lake**—Fishing, picnicking and hiking with historic log structures (502-477-8882); **Taylorsville Lake State Park**—See State Parks

Bluegrass Region

BEREA/RICHMOND AREA: Berea Tourist Commission (800-598-5263); **Richmond Tourism Commission** (800-866-3705); *(Berea)* **Berea Welcome Center**—A must-see stop in the arts and crafts capital of the Commonwealth (800-598-5263); *(Richmond)* **Acres of Land Winery, Inc** (866-714-WINE); **Battle of Richmond Driving Tour**—Part of the National Trust Civil War Discovery Trail and the Civil War Battle of Richmond (800-866-3705); **Berea Trail**—A driving trail that highlights the cultural heritage and craftsmanship of the artisans in the area (859-622-8439); **Central Kentucky Wildlife Management Area**—1,688 acres with three lakes with regulated hunting and fishing, skeet shooting, field trail and trap shooting (800-858-1549); **Deer Run Stables L.L.C.**—Horseback riding, trail rides, pony rides, hayrides, bonfires, picnics, and rustic camping.

Reenactment of the Civil War
Battle of Richmond
Source: Sid Webb

Riding lessons (859-527-6339); **Eastern Kentucky University Hummel Planetarium**—Experience the wonders that await us at the center of the galaxy or simply view the beauty of the sky above us (800-465-9191); **Estill Trail**—Highlights the cultural heritage and craftsmanship of the artisans in the area (859-622-8439); **Fort Boonesborough State Park**—See State Parks; **Historic Downtown Richmond**—Over 100 buildings on the National Register of Historic Places and three National Register Historic Districts (800-866-3705); **Irvinton House Museum** (859-626-1422); **Kentucky Artisan Center**—Showcases and sells Kentucky's outstanding arts, crafts, music, publications and more, and provides travel information about cultural heritage sites (859-985-5448); **Kentucky Artisan Heritage Trails**—The trails include local culture and scenic

beauty. Explore quaint towns and rural byways, shop in artisan Studios (859-622-8439); **Lake Reba Recreational Complex**—Golf course, fishing, biking, boating, gold and nature trails (859-623-8753); **Richmond Area Arts Center** (859-624-4242); **Richmond Cemetery**—Graves of U.S.Representative

Re-enactment of the Battle of Richmond
Source: Sid Webb

Daniel Breck, Cassius M. Clay and tombstones of Civil War Battle of Richmond soldiers (859-623-2529); **Richmond Raceway**—Stock car racing; **Valley View Ferry**—Kentucky's oldest continuous business, dating back to 1785 (859-258-3611); **White Hall State Historic Site**—See State Parks

CARLISLE AREA: Carlisle/Nicholas County Tourism (859-289-5174); **Blue Licks Battlefield State Resort Park**—See State Parks; **Carnico Lake**—Beautiful man-made lake with beach, fishing and boating (859-289-2577); **Jailer's Home & Dungeon**—Home built in 1820-24, dungeon cells built 1857 and housed prisoners in the 1850-1890s; **Nicholas County Depot & Museum**—built 1910 (859-289-4720); **The Mercury Building**—Restored 1820s house began as a saddlery shop and home of the Carlisle Mercury newspaper (859-289-4720)

CYNTHIANA AREA: Cynthiana/Harrison County Chamber of Commerce (859-234-5236); **Cynthiana County Museum**—Historical museum includes items from the Civil War particularly Battles of Cynthiana (859-234-7179); **Quiet Trails State Nature Preserve** (859-234-5382)

DANVILLE AREA: Danville/ County CVB (800-755-0076); **Amish/Mennonite Shops**—Farm landscapes, and shops with produce and handmade roducts (800-755-0076); **Chateau du Vieux Corbeau Winery/Elements Pottery**—Wine tasting and retail purchase. Elements Pottery Studio produces hand-made functional stoneware as well as candlees, hand-painted folk art pottery and other crafts. Hiking trails and the Crow-Barbee House, circa 1780, which now serves as a Bed & Breakfast (859-236-1808); **Central Kentucky Wildlife Refuge**—Six trails for hiking, photography, painting, and nature Study enriching to individuals or groups (800-755-0076); **Community Arts Center** (859-236-4054); **Constitution Square State Historic Site** See State Parks; **Historic Penn's Store**—A store site since 1845, in the Penn family since 1850. America's oldest country store still in ownership and operation by the same family (800-755-0076); **JFC Museum**—Collections of fossils, rocks, minerals and war memorabilia (800-755-0076); **John W.D. Bowling Model Railroad Museum**—Train layout contains 2,100 linear feet of track and 1.5 miles of wiring. Built in HO scale of 1 to 87. With 6,000 handmade trees 1,200 figures, and 160 Structures, it is the largest privately-held permanent layout in Kentucky (859-236-8954); **Kentucky School for the Deaf**—Opened in 1823, Jacobs Hall is the oldest surviving building, constructed in 1855-57 of Italianate design by architect Thomas Lewinski (859-239-7017); **Lightning Valley Motor Sports Park**—Go-Karts (800-755-0076); **McDowell House and Apothecary Shop**—On Christmas Day 1809, the first abdominal surgery was performed by Dr. Ephraim McDowell removing a tumor without anesthetic, from Jane Todd Crawford (859-236-2804); **Norton Center for the Arts**—Designed by a member of the Frank Lloyd Wright Foundation (877-448-7469); **Pioneer Playhouse Outdoor Dinner Theatre**—Kentucky's original outdoor dinner theater with a New York-based cast (859-236-2747); **Perryville Battlefield State Historic Site**—See State Parks; **The Wilderness Trace Art League Gallery**—Original arts & crafts, created by local artists in a historical building; **West T. Hill Community Theatre**—community theatre, with musicals, dramas, comedies and children workshops

FRANKFORT AREA: Frankfort/County Tourism & Convention Commission (800-960-7200); **A Little Bit Of Heaven Riding Stables**—Trail rides and lessons (502-223-8925); **Bluegrass Theatre Guild**—Community theatre (502-223-7529); **Buffalo Trace Distillery**—Distilling began two centuries ago making it the oldest distilling site in the United States; set on 110 acres Buffalo Trace Distillery provides for the complete production of whiskeys (800-654-8471); **Canoe Kentucky**—Water adventures and training on kayaks and canoes (888-226-6359); **Capital City Museum** (502-696-0607); **Country Place Jamboree**—Country music both new and old (502-223-3776); **Daniel Boone's Grave, Frankfort Cemetery**—Gravesite of Daniel and Rebecca Boone, Paul Sawyier, Joel T. Hart, Theodore O'Hara, Vice President Richard M. Johnson, and 17 Kentucky Governors (502-227-2403); **Downtown Frankfort Walking Tour**—Over 70 sites in historic downtown (502-875-8687); **Floral Clock**—Planted with thousands of colorful flowering plants, the face of this clock is 34 feet in diameter and located on the historic Capitol grounds (502-564-3449); **Frank Lloyd Wright's Zeigler House**—Designed for Reverend Jesse R. Zeigler in 1910. National Register (502-875-8687); **Governor's Mansion**—The official governor's residence since 1914, the Beaux Arts mansion, constructed of native limestone, was modeled after the Petit Trianon, Marie Antoinette's summer villa (502-564-8004); **Kentucky Department for Libraries & Archives**—Past and present meet in the Cooper Building, which houses the Kentucky Department for Libraries and Archives (502-564-8300); **Kentucky Department of Fish & Wildlife Game Farm**—132-acre recreational/education complex with two fishing lakes, songbird area, small wet-

Inside Switzer Covered Bridge, Franklin County
Source: Sid Webb

land, and Salato Wildlife Education Center (502-564-7863); **Kentucky Military History Museum**—Located in the Old State Arsenal, with Historic firearms, edged weapons, artillery, uniforms, flags and personal equipment (502-564-3265); **Kentucky State Capitol**—Completed in 1910 in the Beaux Arts design contains the First Lady Doll Collection (502-564-3449); **Kentucky Vietnam Veteran's Memorial**—The names of the Kentuckians killed in Vietnam are etched in granite beneath the memorial sundial, with the point of the gnomon's shadow actually touching the veteran's name of the anniversary of his death. Recognized as one of the most original and unusual memorials in the nation; **Liberty Hall Historic Site**—Georgian house built in 1796 by John Brown, one of Ky.'s first two U.S. Senators (888-516-5101); **Lt. Governor's Mansion**—The oldest official executive residence in the United States still in use. The federal-style mansion was home to 33 Kentucky governors from 1798-1914. Seven U.S. presidents have visited (502-564-8004); **Old State Capitol**—This national landmark was Kentucky's seat of government from 1831-1910. Greek Revival structure includes a unique, self-supporting staircase held together by precision and pressure (502-564-1792); **Orlando Brown House**—The Greek-Revival Orlando Brown House (1835) is a residence designed by Kentucky's most famous architect, Gideon Shryock. Part of Liberty Hall Historic Site (888-516-5101); **Rebecca Ruth Candy Factory Tours**—"Inventors of Bourbon Candy," began nearly a century ago in 1919 by two women, Rebecca and Ruth (800-444-3766); **Salato Wildlife Education Center**—An educational center with interactive and interpretive exhibits featuring native plants and animals (800-858-1549); **Starway Family Fun Park**—Miniature golf course features waterfalls, streams and bridges and New Rookie karts for younger driver (502-227-1864); **Switzer Covered Bridge**—One of Kentucky's few covered bridges, was built in 1855. Totally restored after floodwaters destroyed bridge; **Thomas D. Clark Center for Kentucky History**—Hands-on activities, interactive exhibits and dynamic collections. Research library contains unique genealogical records for tracing Kentucky ancestors (502-564-1792); **Vest-Lindsey House—**Early 19th century Federal house was home to U.S. Senator George Graham Vest (502-564-6980)

GEORGETOWN AREA: Georgetown/Scott County Tourist Commission (888-863-8600); **Amerson Farm Orchard & Winery—**Produce farm, and orchard with garden center and greenhouses offers delicious seasonal fruits and vegetables, garden plants, and crafts (502-863-3799); **Bi-Water Farm—**seasonal fruits and vegetables and crafts (502-863-3676); **Cardome Centre—**Divided into four basic phases: the earliest years, the Chambers/Robinson years, the Academy years, and the present (502-863-1575); **Cincinnati Bengals Partnership/Georgetown College—**NFL's Cincinnati Bengal's Summer Training Camp at Georgetown College. The only NFL Training Camp in Kentucky (502-868-6300); **Doublestink Hog Farm—**Kids activities on the farm (502-868-9703); **Evans Orchard & Cider Mill, LLC—**Gourmet apples, corn maze, fresh cider and homegrown products (502-863-2255); **Factory Stores of America—**Outlet Mall in Georgetown. with over 20 Stores (502-868-0682); **Georgetown & Scott Co Museum—**Located in the former U.S. Post Office (502-863-6201); **Georgetown College—**Founded in 1829 and the oldest Baptist college west of the Alleghenies. The

Stone fence in the Bluegrass
Source: Sid Webb

Anne Wright Wilson Fine Arts Building houses one of Central Kentucky's largest galleries (800-788-9985); **Toyota Motor Manufacturing—**Watch Toyota vehicles from stamping to final inspection (800-866-4485); **Ward Hall—**The largest Greek Revival house in Kentucky and the finest example of Greek Revival Architecture in the south. Prior to 1884, the Kentucky Legislature considered using this great house for the State Capitol (888-863-8600); **Whispering Woods Riding Stables—**12 wonderful horses, 250 acres of woods, creeks and ponds (502-570-9663)

HARRODS-BURG AREA: Har-rodsburg/Mercer County Tourist Commission (800-355-9192); **Big Red Stables—**Horseback riding on 1,000 acres of lush bluegrass farmlands (859-734-3118); **Canaan Land Farm—**A working sheep farm, this 18th century homestead has a historic wagon road and one of the earliest brick homes in the state (888-734-3984); **Dixie Belle Riverboat @ Shaker Village—**The Dixie Belle Riverboat offers public excursions on the Kentucky River along the scenic palisades (800-734-5611); **Downtown Historic District—**Most of the preserved buildings within this National Register of Historic Places District date back to the 1880s and 1890s (859-734-2364); **Harrodsburg Historical Society Morgan Row—**Oldest row house in Kentucky (859-734-5985); **Old Fort Harrod State Park—**See State Parks; **Olde Towne Park—**Includes a unique sculptured 14 x 32 foot cascading fountain, inspired by the dramatic limestone gorge of the Kentucky River known as the "Palisades" (800-355-9192); **Shaker Village of Pleasant Hill—**A premier living history site with 2,900 acres where costumed interpreters chronicle Shaker life and the village has 34 restored buildings. Skilled artisans work at 19th-century trades and historic farming brings the past to life. Riverboat excursions and horse-drawn carriage rides (800-734-5611)

LANCASTER AREA: Garrard County Chamber of Commerce (859-792-2282); **Garrard County Jail Museum** (859-792-3065); **Pleasant Retreat Governor William Owsley House—**Ca. 1804, the restored and furnished home of Ky.'s 16th gover-

A Distinct Destination
in the Bluegrass

SHAKER VILLAGE OF PLEASANT HILL
1-800-734-5611 I www.shakervillageky.org
3501 Lexington Rd., Harrodsburg, KY 40330

nor, William Owsley

LAWRENCEBURG AREA: **Anderson County Chamber of Commerce** (502-839-5564); **Four Roses Distillery LLC**—was built in the Spanish architectural style (502-839-3436); **Fair Winds At Beaver Lake Inc**—Lake fishing, camping and a bait and tackle shop (502-839-4402); **Kavanaugh House B&B and Antique Mall** (502-839-9880); **Lover's Leap Vineyard and Winery**—Largest vineyard in the state with national award winning wines (502-839-1299); **Wild Turkey - Austin Nichols Distillery**—Well-known 101 proof bourbon (502-839-4544)

LEXINGTON AREA: Lexington Convention and Visitors Bureau (800-845-3959); **Actors' Guild of Lexington**—Contemporary theatre (859-233-7330); **American Saddlebred Museum**—Dedicated to Kentucky's oldest native breed of horse, the American Saddlebred (800-829-4438); **Ashland, The Henry Clay Estate**—This National Historic Landmark houses the Henry Clay Memorial Foundation with a rare collection comprised almost exclusively of original Clay family items (859-266-8581); **Aviation Museum of**

Public art in Lexington
Source: Sid Webb

Paddock area at Keeneland, Lexington
Source: Sid Webb

Kentucky—Various historical aircraft and interactive displays (859-231-1219); **Blue Grass Tours**—Visit historic Calumet Farm, Keeneland Race Course, Kentucky Horse Park and the famous Man O'War Statue, Thoroughbred Park and historic highlights in downtown Lexington (800-755-6956); **Boone Station Historic Site**—See State Parks; **Center for Old Music in the New World**—Performance of early music mostly pre-1750 (859-269-2908); **Chrisman Mill Winery & Friends**—Wines, jewelry, gourmet foods, gifts and many Kentucky-made products (859-276-0032); **Explorium of Lexington**—Nine discovery zones with interactive exhibits designed to inspire imagination and curiosity, kids of all ages (859-258-3253); **Flag Fork Herb Farm, Inc**—Restaurant, gourmet food items, crafted items and herbal gardening supplies (859-233-7381); **Gratz Park**—Historic park in downtown Lexington. and surrounded by historic homes; **Headley-Whitney Museum**—Features a diverse collection of objects and hosts international and regional exhibitions (859-255-6653); **Hunt Morgan House & Civil War Museum**—Federal home built in 1814 by John Wesley Hunt, the first millionaire of the new West. John Hunt Morgan, "The Thunderbolt of the Confederacy," and Nobel Prize-winner Thomas Hunt Morgan also resided here; includes local Civil War memorabilia (859-233-3290); **Keeneland Race Course**—Thoroughbred horse racing (800-456-3412); **Kentucky Horse Park**—See State Parks; **Kentucky Theater**—Historic restored theater shows classic, modern and foreign films (859-231-6997); **Latrobe's Pope Villa**—One of three remaining examples of domestic design by B. H. Latrobe, one of the architects of our nation's capitol (859-253-0362); **Lexington Art League**—The Loudoun House is the home for promoting the visual arts (800-914-7990); **Lexington Cemetery**—Historic cemetery (859-255-5522); **Lexington Center/Rupp Arena**—Downtown complex with hotel, retail center, convention halls, and Rupp Arena, home of UK Men's Basketball (859-233-4567); **Lexington Children's Theatre**—Nationally recognized professional theatre (800-928-4545); **Lexington History Museum**—Regional history museum featuring changing exhibits with

Ashland, Henry Clay's Estate
Source: Kentucky Department of Tourism

emphasis on Bluegrass history, equine, early African-American life and technology (859-254-0530); **Lexington Legends**—Lexington's professional baseball team, a Class A affiliate of the Houston Astros; includes the Kentucky Baseball Hall of Fame Museum (859-252-4487); **Lexington Livery Horse Drawn Carriage Tours** (859-259-0000); **Lexington Opera House**—Built in 1886, offers national touring productions, local music & theatre performances (859-233-4567); **Lexington Philharmonic**—Music Director George Zack (888-494-4226); **Lexington Public Library**—The world's largest ceiling clock, a 74-foot-long Foucault pendulum (859-231-5500); **Loudoun House**—Art Gallery (800-914-7990); **Mary Todd House**—The girlhood home of Mary Todd Lincoln, America's First Lady (859-233-9999); **Raven Run Nature Sanctuary**—A 470+ acre nature sanctuary with 10 miles of trails (859-272-6105); **Red Mile Harness Track**—The oldest (1875) harness track in Kentucky. Site of the Kentucky Futurity, final jewel of trotting triple crown (859-255-0752); **Talon Winery and Vineyards**—Located at historic Fair View Farm in the original 18th century farmhouse (859-971-3214); **The Arboretum**—Features a one-and-a-half acre home demonstration garden (859-257-6955); **The Thoroughbred Center**—Observe trainers

with their horses (859-293-1853); **Thoroughbred Park**—2.5 acre park dedicated to the Thoroughbred industry. Seven life-size bronze horses racing to the finish line (859-288-2900); **University of Kentucky Art Museum**—Permanent collection of more than 3,800 European and American paintings, sculptures, prints, drawings, photographs and decorative arts (859-257-5716); **University of Kentucky Basketball Museum**—Relive moments of UK basketball history (800-269-1953); **Waveland State Historic Site**—See State Parks; **Woodsongs Old Time Radio Hour**—Featuring grassroots independent artists from Appalachia and around the world; broadcasts across the USA and internationally (859-252-8888)

NICHOLASVILLE AREA: Nicholasville Tourism Commission (859-887-7091); **Camp Nelson Civil War Heritage Park**—Union Army Civil War supply depot & training camp. White House, c. 1850, used as the officers' quarters by Union troops during the Civil War, 10,000 African American men gained their freedom at Camp Nelson. Camp Nelson National Cemetery begun 1867 with over 2,200 Civil War soldiers buried (859-881-5716); **Chrisman Mill Vineyards & Winery** (859-881-5007); **Harry C. Miller Lock Collection**—America's most comprehensive collection of safe locks (866-LSI-TRAIN); **High Bridge Park**—Eleven-acre park with reconstructed 1879 pavilion and overlook. Site overlooks Kentucky River, Palisades and historic railroad trestle (859-881-9126); **Hickman Creek Nature and Conference Center**—Historic site on Hickman Creek and palisades with log cabins (859-881-9126); **Jim Beam Nature Preserve** (859-259-9655); **Kentucky River Palisades**—Dramatic cliffs of the palisades is home to at least 25 mammal species and 35 reptile species.

two endangered bats, the Gray bat and Indiana bat. It also has the largest concentration of rare plant species (859-881-9126); **Oliver Perry House**—Circa 1850 building constructed by Oliver Perry. Confiscated by Union Army for Civil War 1863-1866 (859-885-3126); **Sugar Creek Resort**—Horseback riding, hiking, tubing, canoeing, rafting, kayaking, birding, picnicking and camping (859-885-9359); **Taylor Made Farm**—Thoroughbred Breeding Farm (859-885-3345); **Valley View Ferry**—Oldest continuously running business, in Kentucky, since 1785 (859-885-4500); **Wilmore Railroad Museum** (859-858-4411); **Wolf Run Wildlife Refuge**—Refuge for wild, domesticated and exotic animals (859-887-2256)

PARIS AREA: Paris/County Tourism Commission (888-987-3205); **Birthplace of African-American Inventor-Garrett Morgan**—Garrett Morgan invented the gas mask in 1912 and the tri-color traffic signal in 1923 (888-987-3205); **Bourbon County Courthouse**—Completed in 1905 with marble hallways and staircase and murals near the large dome (888-987-3205); **Cane Ridge Meeting House & Barton Warren Stowe Museum**—Said to be the largest one-room log structure standing in North America. Scene of August 1801 "Great Revival", largest on the Kentucky frontier (859-987-5350); **Claiborne Horse Farm**—Gravesite of the great Secretariat, 1973 Triple Crown winner and Derby winner Go for Gin (1994) (859-987-2330); **Colville Covered Bridge**—One of 13 covered bridges left in the State, the Colville bridge was built in 1877 (888-987-3205); **Duncan Tavern**—This three-story Stone tavern was built in 1788 on the courthouse square in Paris was a gathering place for pioneers such as Daniel Boone and Simon Kenton (859-987-1788); **Hopewell Musuem** (859-987-7274); **John Fox, Jr. Genealogical Library**—Duncan Tavern Historical Center (859-987-1788); **Nannine Clay Wallis Home & Arboretum**—Headquarters of the Garden Club of Kentucky, Inc. Seven-acre grounds contains an arboretum (859-987-6158); **Reed Valley Orchard** (859-987-6480)

STANFORD AREA: Standford/County Chamber of Commerce (606-365-4118); **Cedar Creek Lake**—780 acre sportsman fishing lake (606-365-2533); **Isaac Shelby Cemetery State Historic Site**—See State Parks; **Lincoln County Courthouse**—Some of the state's oldest records some on sheep skin (606-365-2533); **Stanford Historic L & N Depot**—Railroad depot museum of Louisville and Nashville (606-365-0207); **William Whitley House State Historic Site**—See State Parks

VERSAILLES/MIDWAY AREA: Woodford County

Tourism Commission (859-873-5122); **Bluegrass Scenic Railroad and Museum** (800-755-2476); **Boyd Orchards** (859-873-3097); **Buckley Wildlife Sanctuary**—National Audubon Sanctuary with 374 acres with hiking trails, nature center, and bird blind (859-873-5711); **Castle Hill Farm Winery & Vineyard** (859-879-6282); **Equus Run Vineyards**—Small boutique winery in horse country (877-905-2675); **Good Ol' Days Restaurant and Catering**—Hickory smoked meats, catfish jumpin' on the lake and legendary bluegrass music (877-793-FARM); **Jack Jouett**

Pisgah Presbyterian Church
Source: Sid Webb

House—Federal cottage built in 1793 by Captain Jack Jouett, a prominent leader for Kentucky Statehood, and one of the state's first importers of purebred horses and cattle (859-873-7902); Nostalgia Station Toy & Train Museum (859-873-2497); **Pisgah Presbyterian Church**—Established in 1784 as the first Presbyterian church west of the Allegheny Mountains on National Register (859-873-4161); **Thoroughbred Theatre** (859-846-9652); **Woodford Co. Historical Society Library & Museum**—It is housed in the former Big Spring Church, built circa 1819 (859-873-6786) **Woodford Reserve**—A National Historic Landmark established on the banks of Glenn's Creek in 1812. The only distiller using the traditional copper pot still method (859-879-1812)

WINCHESTER AREA: Winchester/County Tourism Commission (800-298-9105); Bluegrass Heritage Museum—History of the Bluegrass, America's first western frontier (859-745-1358); **Holly Rood Historic Home**—Started 1813 by James Clark (12th governor of Kentucky) was completed in 1814 (859-744-5062); **Leeds Center for the Arts**—Movie theatre built in 1926 (888-772-6985); **Lower Howard's Creek Nature and Heritage Preserve**—Area of settlement outside Fort Boonesborough features a pristine creek with small waterfalls, cliff areas, stone fences and gristmill (800-298-9105)

Northern Kentucky Region

AUGUSTA AREA: Augusta Welcome Center (606-756-2183); **Augusta Boatdock and Marina—**Food service and boat launch (606-756-2183); **Bracken Berry Farm—**U-pick blackberries and raspberries and pre-picked berries. Farm fresh honey (606-728-5419); **Bradford/Payne House—**Site of Underground Railroad activity according to oral traditions and newspaper accounts (606-756-

Bridge at Maysville
Source: Sid Webb

2183); **Historic Augusta—**Beautiful 18th century rivertown with restored homes and business fronts (606-756-2183)

CARROLLTON AREA: Carrollton/Carroll County Tourism & Convention Commission (800-325-4290); **Carroll County Courthouse—**Built in

1884, this historic building has a brass plaque on the interior wall marking the high water level mark during the famous 1937 Flood; **General Butler State Resort Park—**See State Parks; **Historic Masterson House—**Historic home c.1790 is the oldest two story brick structure built between Cincinnati & Louisville (800-325-4290); **Kentucky Veterans Memorial** (866-462-8853); **Point Park—**Located at the confluence of the Ohio and Kentucky Rivers with boat ramp, gazebo and playground; **The Old Stone Jail—**Built in 1880 (800-325-4290)

COVINGTON/NEWPORT   AREA: Northern Kentucky CVB (800-STAYNKY); *(Alexandria)* **Campbell County Log Cabin Museum** (859-635-5913); *(Burlington)* **Boone County Cliffs State Nature Preserve—**Steep wooded ridges and gentle rolling hills with picturesque creeks and valley. Hiking, birding and nature study (800-628-6800); **Dinsmore Homestead—**A unique historic site where visitors can learn what rural life was like in the 19th and early 20th centuries. Nature enthusiasts can enjoy the hiking trails (859-586-6117); *(Covington)* **BB Riverboats—**Riverboat rides on the Ohio River with lunch, dinner, sightseeing, and private charter cruises (800-261-8586); **Behringer/Crawford Museum—**Native American Prehistory (859-491-4003); **Carnegie Visual & Performing Arts Center** (859-491-2030); **Carroll Chimes Bell Tower—**The 100-foot bell tower contains one of the two American-made animated clocks in the world with 21 figures performing "The Pied Piper of Hamelin"(859-655-4159); **MainStrasse Village—**A restored 19th-century German neighborhood with shoppes and restaurants joined by cobblestone walkways (859-491-0458); **Mother of God Church—**Built in 1871 of Italian Renaissance basilica design (859-291-2288); **Railway Museum of Greater Cincinnati—**Interiors of railroad cars, railroad memorabilia and locomotives (859-491-7245); **St. Mary's Cathedral Basilica of**

the Assumption—The 100-year-old cathedral is of French-Gothic architecture and resembles Notre Dame in Paris. 80 stained glass windows and the second largest stained glass church window in the world (859-431-2060); **Totter's Otterville**—Educational entertainment center for children 10 and under (859-491-1441); *(Dayton)* **Queen City Riverboats**—Public cruises lunch and dinner (859-292-8687); *(Florence)* **Turfway Park Race Course**—Thoroughbred race track featurung live racing (800-733-0200); *(Ft. Mitchell)* **Morning Star Pottery Painting Studio** (859-581-3900); **Vent Haven Museum**—World's largest collection of ventriloquist memorabilia (859-341-0461); *(Highland Heights)* **Museum of Anthropology**—Northern Kentucky University (859-572-5259); *(Newport)* **East Row Historic District**—Kentucky's second largest his-

Art show in Maysville
Source: Sid Webb

Tower Clocks of Mother of God Church, Covington
Source: Kentucky Department of Tourism

toric district is distinguished by 1100 buildings built from 1870 to 1920 (859-292-3666); **Gameworks** (859-581-PLAY); **Hofbrauhaus Newport**—First authentic Hofbrauhaus outside of Munich Germany with traditional beer hall, and microbrewery (859-491-7200); **Kentucky Symphony Orchestra** (859-431-6216); **Newport Aquarium**—A water wonderland awaits you with thousands of aquatic creatures from around the world (800-538-3359); **Newport on the Levee**—An exciting riverfront Town Square with more than 12 restaurants, unique specialty shops, the clubs, theatres, game room, and the Newport Aquarium (866-538-3359); **Quiet Road Tours, Inc** (859-431-1300); **Shadowbox Cabaret** (888-887-4236); **The District of Newport**—A quirky, unusual, revitaliz-

ing historic main street area (859-292-3666); **World Peace Bell Exhibit Center**—The world's largest free swinging bell, weighs 66,000 lbs., is 12 feet in diameter and 12 feet high. The clapper weighs an amazing 6,878 pounds (800-543-0488); *(Union)* **Big Bone Lick State Park**—Presence of Ice Age mammals that traveled to the area in search of salt springs (859-384-3522); **Jane's Saddlebag Big Bone Lick Kentucky**—The "Saddlebag" houses, which were popular as tenant houses on larger farms in Kentucky. The Spirit of Boone County Flatboat replica of a 1700 flatboat (877-724-4266); *(Villa Hills)* **River-City Charter**—Private 40' river yacht on the Ohio River (859-341-8221); *(Walton)* **Benton Farms U-Pick**—Animals and straw maze (859-485-7000); *(Wilder)* **Fredericks Landing Rd. Wilder**—Park and boat dock (859-581-8884)

Maysville, Kentucky

From dusk to dawn... one of the prettiest little cities on the Ohio River.

www.cityofmaysville.com

Kentucky UNBRIDLED SPIRIT

FALMOUTH AREA: Pendleton County Chamber of Commerce (859-654-4189); **Kincaid Lake State Park**—See State Parks; **Kincaid Regional Theatre**—Professional summer theatre (800-647-7469); **Thaxton's Licking River Canoe Rental**—Canoe, kayak, raft and tube the historic Licking River. Riverside cabins and camping (877-643-8762)

FLEMINGSBURG AREA: Fleming County Chamber of Commerce (606-845-1223); **Brownings Orchard**—Fruit, berries and vegetables at beautiful Park Lake Mountain orchard. The Apple festival, held every weekend mid-September through October features apple cider, a corn maze, and lots of other home-grown Kentucky foods (606-849-2881); **DH Resorts, Inc.**—1200-acre "Dude Ranch" featuring the Mountain Lake Manor & Western Villages. They offer horseback riding, horse riding adventure packages, lodge, cabins, camping, 27-acre lake, pool, restaurant and group programs (800-737-7433); **Franklin Sousley Monument, Elizaville Cemetery**—Sousley was a PFC in the USMCR and helped to raise the flag at Iwo Jima in 1945. Immortalized in the famous photo by AP photographer Joe Rosenthal (606-845-1223); **Flemingsburg Historic District**—Nearly 200 homes and commercial buildings are included on the National Historic Register. Union soldiers occupied the Baptist Church and burned pews and fences for heat (606-845-1223); **Fleming County Public Wildlife Area**—A 2070-acre wildlife area full of a wide range of animals. Fishing and hiking (606-636-3312); **Goddard Covered Bridge**—The only surviving example of Ithiel Town Lattice design in Kentucky. Timbers are joined with wooden pegs. 60 feet long. National Register of Historic Places (606-845-1223); **Grange City Covered Bridge**—86-foot span. National Register of Historic Places (606-845-1223); **Ringo Mills Cov-**ered Bridge—Built in 1867, is a single span, Burr truss, without arches. Served as gristmill operation during the 1800s. National Register of Historic Places (606-845-1223)

MAYSVILLE AREA: Maysville-Mason County Tourism Commission (606-564-9419); (*Maysville*) Big Rock ATV & Dirtbike Park—2,000 acre ATV & dirtbike park (606-759-9106); **Carriage Museum**—Showcases transportation before the automobile: from a basic farmers wagon to an elegant four-seat carriages complete with fringe (606-759-7305); **Downtown Maysville Historic District** (606-564-9419); **Herb Farm @ Strodes Run**—A working, 63 acre Organic Herb Farm (606-742-2000); **Maysville Flood Wall Murals**—History of the Maysville spanning four centuries, from the time of Buffalo Hunting Grounds to 20th Century Market Street (606-564-9419); **Mefford's Fort**—Authentic 1787 log cabin (606-759-7411); **Museum Center**—An 1881 building that allows visitors to experience pioneer life through dioramas, artifacts, and timelines (606-564-5865); **National Underground Railroad Museum**—Slavery artifacts, documents and memorabilia documenting Maysville's role in the abolitionist movement and the role of slavery in America (606-564-9419); **Paradise Breeze Family Entertainment Complex**—Lap pool, arcade, batting cage, slides, paradise pavilion, go-karts, Rainbow Café (606-759-9416); **"R" Farm & More LLC**—A 130 acre pre-school and lower elementary children (606-742-2429); **Underground Railroad Driving Tour**—Unique driving tour allows you to retrace the footsteps of "Eliza" and countless other African slaves (606-564-9419); (*Mays Lick*) **Mays Lick Corn Maze** (606-763-6706)*; (Washington)* **Albert Sidney Johnston House**—Confederate Civil War General Albert Sidney Johnston's home (606-759-7411); **Harriet Beecher Stowe Slavery To Freedom Museum**—The early antebellum home where Harriet Beecher visited and witnessed a slave auction in 1833, which is said to have influenced her writing "Uncle Tom's Cabin" (606-759-4860); **Old Church Museum** (606-759-7411); **Old Washington Historic District & Visitors Center**—Established in 1786, is home to several authentic log cabins and early 1800s buildings this pioneer settlement is America's Northern Gateway to the West and early Kentucky architecture (606-759-7411); **Paxton Inn**—Built around 1810 by James A. Paxton, a local attorney and ardent abolitionist, thought to be a safe house for escaping slaves (606-759-7411)**; Simon Kenton Shrine**—Housed in an authentic log cabin built as a pioneer store in the 1780s (606-759-7411) **Mt. Olivet Area Visitor Information**

(859-289-5507); **Johnson Creek Covered Bridge**—Built in 1874, this 131 foot Smith truss-designed bridge; **Sunflower Sundries**—An herbal soap factory, a commercial kitchen producing jam, mustard and pickled aspargus, and organic gardens (606-763-6827)

OWENTON AREA: Owen County Chamber of Commerce (502-484-9900); **Elk Creek Hunt Club** (502-484-4569); **Elmer Davis Lake**—149 acres. Fishing, dock, ramp (502-484-5805); **John A. Kleber Wildlife Management Area**—Steep hillsides, narrow ridge tops and floodplains with a combination of woods, brush, grasslands and wildlife food plots (502-535-6335); **Larkspur Press**—See the art of making books the old-fashioned way (502-484-5390); **Twin Eagle Wildlife Management Area** (502-535-6335)

VANCEBURG AREA: Lewis County Tourism (606-796-2732); **Cabin Creek Covered Bridge**—Built in 1867, 114 feet long, burr truss design (606-796-2722); **Sand Hill Christian Church**—Built in 1860, pews facing double entry. Patterned after Alexander Campbell's home church,The Old Meeting House at Bethany WV (606-796-2722); **Union Soldier Monument**—The Monument honoring Union soldiers is said to be the only one of its kind south of the Mason-Dixon Line was built in 1884 (606-796-2722); **Veterans Memorial Park** (606-796-2722); **Victorian Rose & Restaurant/ Antique Pub** (606-796-2069)

WARSAW/SPARTA AREA: Gallatin County Tourism Commission (859-867-5691); **Craig's Creek Lake**—Over 1,000-acres of water on the Ohio River; **Hawkins-Kirby House**—House was built circa 1845 by Edmond Waller Hawkins, who was appointed by President Lincoln, Judge Advocate of the Northern Kentucky District during the Civil War (859-567-4591); **Kentucky Speedway**—"America's home of championship motorsports" featuring NASCAR, IRL, ARCA, ASA. (888-652-7223); **Markland Dam**—Viewing tower and picnic area (859-597-7661)

WILLIAMSTOWN/DRY RIDGE AREA: Grant County Visitor's Center (800-382-7117); **Barkers Blackberry Hill Winery** (859-428-0377); **Corinth Lake**—96-acre lake with fishing, boating, ramp (859-824-5922); **Curtis Gates Wildlife Refuge**—4 miles of dirt roads and trails for hiking, bird watching and a small fishing lake (800-858-1949); **Farmer Bill's**—A working farm with petting zoo and children's playground (859-823-1058); **House of Reptiles LLC**—90 species of reptiles and amphibians (859-824-4577); **Kentucky Cowtown, LLC**—A 52 acre complex (859-824-9236); **Pickin Patch, LLC**—Locally-grown Kentucky produce along with Amish specialty products (859-824-1265); **Williamstown Lake**—A 305-acre water reservoir for fishing, boating, and water skiing.

Eastern Highlands North Region

ASHLAND AREA: Ashland Area Convention & Visitors Bureau (800-377-6249); *(Ashland)* **Ashland Area Art Gallery** (606-329-1826); **Ashland Historical Tours** (800-377-6249); **Bar W Rodeo Productions**—Bull riding at its best (606-928-9334); **Clinton Furnace**—Iron furnace built in 1833 by Poage brothers; **Highlands Museum & Discovery Center** (606-329-8888); **Jesse Stuart Foundation**—A non-profit publishing house dedicated to preserving Jesse Stuart's literary works and promoting the culture and literature of Appalachia (606-

Exploring Kentucky
Source: Sid Webb

326-1667); **Paramount Arts Center**—The theatre is listed as on the National Register of Historic Places. The theatre has a resident ghost "Paramount Joe" and fans still come to see the location of Billy Ray Cyrus' famed "Achey Breaky Heart" video shoot (606-324-3175); *(Cattlesburg)* **Catlettsburg Flood-wall Murals** (606-739-4533); *(Princess)*; Princess Furnace—Iron furnace put into operation in 1864

Natural Bridge
Source: Kentucky Department of Tourism

by John Means; *(Summitt)* **Boyd County World War II Memorial** (606-928-9551)

FRENCHBURG AREA: **Frenchburg/Menifee County Chamber of Commerce** (606-768-9000); Broke Leg Falls—A gorgeous natural waterfall of over 60 feet (606-768-9000); **Clifty Wilderness Area**—Red River Gorge—12,600 acres, features arches, rock shelters, cliffs and back-country camping (606-663-2852)

GRAYSON AREA: **Grayson Tourism & Convention Commission** (606-474-8740); *(Grayson)* **Carter Caves State Resort Park**–See State Parks; **Grayson Lake**—Vertical rock cliffs rim the lake's 40 miles of shoreline (606-474-5815); **Grayson Lake State Park**—See State Parks; **Grayson Lake Wildlife Management Area** (502-564-4336); *(Olive Hill)* **Northeastern Kentucky Museum**—Tracing the area's heritage from the Indians to Vietnam (606-286-6012); **Tygarts State Forest**—Hiking, picnick-

ing and hunting (606-286-4411)

GREENUP AREA: **Ashland Area Convention & Visitors Bureau** (800-377-6249); *(Beechy)* **Serenity Acres Christian Outreach**—Retreat house, camping, family reunions, fishing and covered bridge nearby, walking trails, hayrides, playgrounds, wildlife watching (606-932-6698); *(Greenup)* **Jesse Stuart State Nature Preserve**—733 acres of woods and fields known as W-Hollow (502-573-2886); **Oldtown Covered Bridge**—Built in 1880 on Burr's Patented Design. Two-Span Bridge, 192 Ft Long, on National Register (877-868-7473); *(Maloneton)* **Bennett's Mill Covered Bridge**—Built 1855, Rare Wheeler Truss Covered Bridge, 155 Feet Long. It has been reported that the bridge was the oldest, longest, single span covered bridge in the world (800-377-6249); **Greenbo Lake State Resort Park**—See State Parks; *(Wurtland)* **Greenup County War Memorial** (606-836-3012); **Mcconnell House And School**—Georgian architecture built in 1833 (606-833-9098)

LOUISA AREA: **Lawrence County Tourism Commission** (606-920-9119); **Kentucky's Paveillon**—Five-story tall, 100 feet high paveillon serves as a welcome center of Country Music Highway (606-638-9998); **Yatesville Lake State Park**-See State Parks

MOREHEAD AREA: **Morehead Tourism Commission** (606-784-6221); **Cave Run Bicycle and Outdoor Center** (606-784-1818); **Cave Run Lake**—8,300 acres surface area. Known as the "Muskie Fishing Capitol of the South." (606-784-5624); **Claypool-Young Art Gallery** (606-783-5446); **Cora Wilson Stewart Moonlight School**—One-room school used for adult education in the late 1800s (800-654-1944); **Kentucky Folk Art Center** (606-783-2204); **Minor E. Clark Fish Hatchery**—One of the largest state-owned, warm-water fish hatcheries in the U.S. (606-784-6872); **Shallow Flats Wild-**

life **Observation Area**—Self-guided loop interpretive trail passes near restored wetlands with two observation decks and an observation scope (606-784-5624); **Sheltowee Trace National Recreation Trail**—A 269-Mile multiple-use national recreation trail (606-784-6428); **U.S. Forest Service Visitor Center**—The forest stretches over 694,985 acres and 21 counties south to Tennessee (606-784-5624)

MT. STERLING AREA: Mt. Sterling/Montgomery County Tourism Commission (866-415-7439); **Gallery For The Arts** (859-498-6264); **Main Cross**—Renovated historic block of buildings (859-498-8725); **Ruth Hunt Candy Company**—Started in 1921, produces high quality traditional Kentucky candies (800-927-0302); **The Bramble Ridge Orchard**—U-pick or purchase bagged apples (859-498-9123)

OWINGSVILLE AREA: Owingsville/Bath County Chamber of Commerce (606-674-2266); **Bath County Memorial Library**—Works by regional artists and craftsmen (606-674-2531); *(Salt Lick)* **Tater Knob Fire Tower**—First Fire Tower in the forest is 35 ft. tall (606-784-6428); **White Sulphur ATV Trail** (606-784-6428); **Zilpo Road National Forest Scenic Byway**—11-mile byway tour through the Daniel Boone National Forest (606-784-6428)

Loretta Lynn's Birthplace
Source: Kentucky Department of Tourism

PAINTSVILLE AREA: Paintsville Tourism Commission (800-542-5790); *(Oil Springs)* **Oil Springs Cultural Arts and Recreation Center/Oscar**—Antiques, artifacts collections, pottery, a history study room, arts and crafts library, recycle shop, woodshop, woodshop and music room (606-789-8108); *(Paintsville)* **Mayo Mansion**—This 43 room mansion was built by John CC Mayo in 1910. Mayo was the first eastern Kentucky coal baron (800-542-5790); **Mayo Memorial United Methodist Church**—Built by John CC Mayo from limestone that was lifted out of the area's mountains. The Pilcher Organ was donated by Andrew Carnegie (606-789-3296); **US 23 Country Music Highway Museum**—Entertainers featured in the museum are: Billy Ray Cyrus, The Judds, Ricky Skaggs, Hylo Brown, Loretta Lynn, Crystal Gayle, Dwight Yoakam, Patty Loveless, Tom T. Hall, Keith Whitley, Gary Stewart and Rebecca Lynn Howard (800-542-5790); *(River)* **Jenny Wiley Gravesite**—Cemetery where pioneer heroine Jenny Wiley is buried (800-542-5790); *(Staffordsville)* **Mountain Homeplace**—Actual working farm as it was in eastern Kentucky in the 1850s (800-542-5790); **Paintsville Lake State Park**—See State Parks; **Paintsville Lake Wildlife Management** (606-297-6312); *(Van Lear)* **Butcher Hollow**—Home of Country Music Divas Loretta Lynn and Crystal Gayle (606-789-3397); **Coal Miners' Museum**—Displays include Coal Mining Tools, a diorama, of the town as it was

in the 1930s, Old Town Jail, Van Lear Schools Collection (606-789-8540); **Dewey Dam Recreation Area/Day Use** (606-789-4521)

PIKEVILLE AREA: Pikeville/Pike County Tourism Commission (800-844-7453); *(Elkhorn City)* **Artists Collaborative Theatre, Inc** (606-754-5137); **Elkhorn Adventures White Water Rafting**—Russell Fork River (Class IV-Class VI Rapids) (800-982-5122); **Elkhorn City Railroad Museum**—Photos, tools, uniforms, and instruments used on the railroad (606-754-8300); *(Pikeville)* **Big Sandy Heritage Museum**—Preserves the history of the Hatfield & McCoy Feud and listed on the National Register of Historic Places (606-218-6050); **Fishtrap Lake State Park**—See State Parks; **Hatfield & Mccoy Feud Driving Tour**—Ten actual historic sites where the feud took place (800-844-7453); **Historic Dils Cemetery & Gardens**—Final resting place of the Hatfield

Mary Todd Lincoln House, Lexington
Source: Sid Webb

& McCoy feud chieftain Randolph McCoy and family members, botanical gardens, walking trail and overlook (800-844-7453); **Historic Downtown Pikeville Walking Tour**—53 historic buildings and homes listed on the National Register of Historic Places (800-844-7453); **Pikeville 'Cut-Thru Project'**— The project created over 400 acres of usable land by the removal of 18 million cubic yards of earth and is to date the second largest earth moving project in the world (800-844-7453)

PRESTONSBURG AREA: Prestonsburg Tourism Commission (800-844-4704); **Dewey Lake**—Wooded hills rise some 700 feet above the lake (606-789-4521)**; East Kentucky Science Center**—85-seat Planetarium (877-889-0303); **Jenny Wiley State Resort Park**—See State Parks; **Jenny Wiley Theatre** (877-225-5598); **Kentucky Opry**—Country, Bluegrass, Oldies (888-Mac-Arts); **Middle Creek National Battlefield**—The site of the larg-

est and most significant Civil War Battle in Eastern Kentucky (800-844-4704); **Mountain Arts Center**—Country, Bluegrass, Gospel, Pop, Orchestra and Classic (888-622-2787); **Prince Albert Stables**—Displaying the Rocky Mountain horse, a breed preserved in the eastern Kentucky mountains for over 150 years (606-874-9219); **Samuel May House**—Restored 1817 brick home (606-889-9608); **Thunder Ridge Racing & Entertainment Complex**—Stock car racing and live harness racing (606-886-7223)

SALYERSVILLE AREA: Salyersville Tourism Commission (606-349-2409); **Magoffin County Historical Society Log Village** (606-349-1607)

WEST LIBERTY AREA: West Liberty Tourism Commission (606-743-3330); **Morgan County Courthouse**—National Register of Historic Places (606-743-3763); **Morgan County Genealogy Center**—Genealogy and Historical Society located in a renovated WRA Jail (606-743-7491); **Old Mill Park**—Historic site of the Well's Grist Mill (606-743-2300); **Paint Creek Log School House** (606-743-2300); **Wrigley Arch And Falls**—features a waterfall and a natural arch (606-743-2300)

Eastern Highlands South Region

BARBOURVILLE AREA: Barbourville Tourism & Recreation Commission (606-546-6197); *(Gray)* **Dizney Mountain Arena & Rodeo** (606-546-3210); **Dr. Thomas Walker State Historic Site**—See State Parks; **Knox Historical Museum** (606-546-4300)

BEATTYVILLE AREA: Lee County Tourism (606-464-2888); **Three Forks Historical Museum** (606-464-2888)

Hensley Settlement at Cumberland Gap
Source: Sid Webb

BOONEVILLE AREA: Owsley County Tourism (606-593-7296); **Old Drive In** (606-593-5370)

CAMPTION AREA: Wolfe County Tourism (606-668-6475); **Old Campton Burial Grounds** (606-668-3040); **Torrent Falls Family Climbing Adventure**—the first climbing adventure park in the U.S. (606-668-6613); **Wolfe County Historical Museum** (606-668-6650); **Swift Creek Arts and Crafts Gallery** (606-725-4860)

HARLAN AREA: Harlan Tourist & Convention Commission (606-573-4156); **Cumberland Tour**ist & Convention Commission (606-589-5812); *(Baxton)* **Mountain Outdoors** (606-573-6260); *(Benham)* **Kentucky Coal Mining Museum** — Exhibits on the miners' home, hospital, commissary, engineering, coal sampling, a mock mine tour and the Loretta Lynn "Coal Miner's Daughter" exhibit (606-848-1530); *(Cumberland)* **Big Black Mountain**—Kentucky's highest point atop Black Mountain, 4,145 ft (606-848-1530); **Blanton Forest State Nature Preserve**—Kentucky's largest and most diverse old-growth forest. Over 400 different species of plants (502-573-2886); **Godbey Appalachian Cultural & Fine Arts Center**—Appalachian artifacts, oral histories, photographs, art collections, pottery, dulcimer making, and music (606-589-2145); **Kingdom Come State Park**—See State Parks; *(Evarts)* **Cloverfork Museum and Highsplint Reunion** (606-837-3220); **Kentucky Mountain Trails of Harlan County** (606-573-4156); *(Harlan)* **Cranks Creek Public Wildlife Management Area** (606-549-2305); **Harlan County Coal Miners Memorial Monument**—Commemorates memory of Harlan County miners that have lost their lives (800-216-2022); **Kentenia State Forest** (606-573-1460); **Portal 31 Mine Tour** (606-848-1530); **USS Harlan County Archives**—Artifacts of decommissioned US Navy amphibious tank landing ship. (606-573-4156); *(Pine Mountain)* **Pine Mountain Settlement School**—A National Historic Landmark with weekend nature classes during the spring and

Broom Corn in Window at Shaker Village, Harrodsburg
Source: Kentucky Department of Tourism

fall to students of all ages (606-558-3571); *(Smith)* **Cumberland Shadow Trail** (606-573-7655); **Martins Fork Lake** (606-573-7655); **Smith Recreation Area**—Picnic tables, shelters, white sand beach, basketball and more (606-573-7655)

HAZARD AREA: Perry County Tourism Commission (606-439-2659); *(Buckhorn)* **Buckhorn Lake**—Beautiful, mountainous terrain with a historic log structure (606-398-7251); **Buckhorn Lake State Resort Park**—See State Parks; **Buck-**

horn Log Cathedral Church—Made of white oak from the surrounding mountains and is listed on the National Register of Historic Places (606-398-7382); *(Hazard)* **Bobby Davis Museum and Park** (606-439-4325); **Greater Hazard Area Performing Arts** (800-246-7521)

HINDMAN AREA: Knott County Tourism Commission (606-785-5881); *(Hindman)* **Hindman Settlement School/Marie Stewart Crafts**—Founded in 1902 provides evening folk dances and a crafts shop dedicated to preserving the rich, traditional crafts of the area (606-785-5475); **Kentucky Appalachian Artisan Center**—An art gallery with exhibit changing every 4-8 weeks and a retail

Lincoln Homestead
Source: Sid Webb

sales outlet to market Artisan wares from Eastern Kentucky (606-785-9855); **Kentucky School of Craft** (800-246-7521); **Knott County Historical and Genealogical Society** (606-785-5751); *(Sassafras)* **Carr Creek State Park**—See State Parks

HYDEN AREA: Leslie County Tourism Commission (606-672-2154); *(Wendover)* **Frontier Nursing Service**—The oldest American school of nurse-midwifery in existence (1925) Includes the National Historic Landmark home of founder Mary Breckinridge (606-672-2317); *(Whitesburg)* **Appalshop**—Nationally renowed arts, media, & education center, includes Appalshop Film & Video and Roadside Theater (606-633-0108); **Bad Branch State Nature Preserve** (606-663-0362); **Saint Christopher Chapel**—houses a 15th-century stained glass window (606-672-2317)

INEZ AREA: Martin County Economic Development (606-298-2800)

IRVINE AREA: Estill Development Alliance **(606-732-2450);** *(Irvine)* **Soggy Bottom Farm** (606-723-4568); *(Ravena)* **Cottage Furnace**—Iron production site during mid to late 1800s; **Fitchburg Furnace**—Built by masons from Ravenna, Italy in 1869, the twin stacks went into operation in 1870 and became the largest charcoal-burning furnace in the world. This is the only double furnace in Kentucky (606-723-2450)

JACKSON AREA: Jackson/Breathitt County **Chamber of Commerce** (606-666-4159); **Breathitt County Museum** (606-666-4159)

LONDON/CORBIN AREA: London/Laurel **County Tourism Commission** (800-348-0095); *(Corbin)* **Sanders Cafe & Museum**—Colonel Sanders' original restaurant, birthplace of Kentucky Fried Chicken with artifacts and memorabilia from early KFC (606-528-2163); *(East Bernstadt)* **Kinlee Stables**; *(London)* **Camp Wildcat Civil War Battlefield**—Recognized as the first Union victory of the Civil War (800-348-0095); **Daniel Boone Motocross Park** (606-877-1364); **Laurel River Lake** (606-864-6412); **Levi Jackson State Park**—See State Parks; **London Community Orchestra** (606-864-4194); **London Dragway** (606-878-8883); **London Go Karts** (606-864-0761); **McNitt Cemetery** (606-878-8000); **Mountain Life Museum** (606-878-8000); **Rockcastle Adventures Canoe Livery** (606-864-9407);

MANCHESTER AREA: Manchester/Clay County Chamber of Commerce (606-598-1754)

MCKEE AREA: Jackson County Tourism Commission (606-287-8395)**; Mill Creek Wildlife Management Area** (606-287-7832); **Horse Lick Creek Biosphere**—This 62-sqaure mile watershed area designated the "Last Great Places" by the Nature Conservancy (606-878-7664)

MT. VERNON/RENFRO VALLEY AREA: Mt. Vernon/Rockcastle County Tourist Commission (800-252-6685); **BitterSweet Cabin Museum** (800-

Constitution Square, Danville
Source: Sid Webb

252-6685); **Brush Arbor Appalachian Pioneer Log Village** (859-433-3208); **Kentucky Music Hall of Fame and Museum**—Honors Kentucky performers, songwriters, publishers, promoters, managers, broadcasters, comedians and other music professionals who have made significant contributions to the music industry in Kentucky and around the world (877-356-3263); **Renfro Valley Entertainment Center**—Music, singing and comedy where visitors can enjoy some of the best live entertainment in the country (800-765-7464)

PINEVILLE/MIDDLESBORO AREA: Bell County Tourism Commission (800-988-1075); *(Frakes)*

Henderson Settlement (606-337-3613); *(Middlesboro)* Bell County Historical Society Museum (606-242-0005); **Coal House Museum** (800-988-1075); **Cumberland Gap National Historical Park**—An 800 ft. deep natural break in the Cumberland Mountains. One of the largest National Historical Parks in the country with

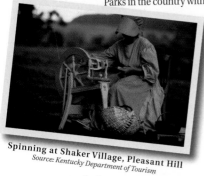

Spinning at Shaker Village, Pleasant Hill
Source: Kentucky Department of Tourism

20,305 acres. Overlooks three states (606-248-2817); **Cumberland Gap Tunnel** (606-248-1075); **Hensley Settlement**—The restored isolated Appalachian farmstead flourished during the first half of the 20th century and is on the National Register of Historic Places (606-248-2817); **The Lost Squadron/P-38 Museum**—home of the "Glacier Girl", a World War II P-38 Lightening (606-248-1149); **Wilderness Road Tours** (606-248-2626); *(Pineville)* **Chained Rock** (800-325-1712); **Kentucky Ridge State Forest** (606-337-3011); **Pine Mountain State Resort Park**—See State Parks; **The Bell Theatre** (606-337-3806);

STANTON/RED RIVER GORGE AREA: **Powell County Tourism Commission** (606-663-1161); *(Clay City)* **Meadowgreen Park Bluegrass Music Hall** (606-663-9008); **Pilot Knob State Nature Preserve**—Considered to be the place where Daniel Boone first stood and looked out over the Bluegrass region of Kentucky (502-573-2886); **Red River His-**torical **Museum** (606-663-2555); **Red River Outdoors** (606-663-ROCK); *(Slade)* **Kentucky Reptile Zoo**—Over 100 species of reptiles such as mambas, cobras, rattlesnakes, anacondas, lizards, turtles and alligators (606-663-9160); **Natural Bridge Sky Lift Inc.**—Sky lift to the top of Natural Bridge (606-663-2922); **Natural Bridge State Resort Park**—See State Parks; *(Stanton)* **Red River Gorge National Geological Area**—Back-country camping, hiking with more than 80 natural arches, hundreds of miles of hiking trails, a 36-mile looping driving tour, and the Red River (Kentucky's only National Wild and Scenic River) (606-663-2852)

WHITESBURG AREA: Letcher County Tourism Commission (606-632-1200); *(Blackey)* **C.B. Caudill Store & History Center** (606-633-3281); *(Seco)* **Seco Company Store & Winery**—Restored commissary and camp houses of the South East Coal Company. (606-855-7968); *(Whitesburg)* **Lilley Cornett Woods**—National natural landmark and state wildlife refuge is one of Kentucky's few remaining tracts of virgin forest. (606-633-5828); **Little Shepherd Trail** (606-573-4156); **Roadside Theater** (606-633-0108)

WILLIAMSBURG/CORBIN AREA: Williamsburg Tourist & Convention Commission (606-549-0530); *(Corbin)* **Betty Hamilton Center for the Performing Arts**; **Bill's Riding Stables** (606-528-2066); **Corbin Speedway** (606-526-8899); **Cumberland Falls Rainbow Mist Ride** (800-541-7238); **Cumberland Falls State Resort Park**—See State Parks; **Cumberland Star Riverboat**—Offers sight-seeing, lunch and charter cruises on the Cumberland River and upper Lake Cumberland (800-541-7238); **Sheltowee Trace Outfitters** (800-541-7238); **The Depot on Main**—Laugh Tracks Comedy Club (606-523-1117); *(Williamsburg)* **Cumberland Museum** (800-315-3100); **R/C Speedway** (606-521-5343); **Hal Rogers Family Entertainment Center**—water park, miniature golf (866-812-1860)

Stephanie Durst

RECREATION & TRAVEL
State Fair

On Sept. 22, 1902, the first Kentucky State Fair opened at Churchill Downs in Louisville. The event was designed to boost the state's declining livestock industry, and the legislature provided a $15,000 appropriation, designated solely for premiums to the top livestock, horse and domestic entries.

The State Fair was modeled after Kentucky's many agricultural fairs, the first on Col. Lewis Sanders' Fayette County farm in 1816. These early fairs were stock shows and horse shows, often combined with seed exchanges and lectures to benefit the progressive farmer. Manufacturers of farm implements arranged displays, and competitions were held for "women's work," domestic and culinary classes. Once industrial expositions and world fairs became popular after the Civil War, all of the latest inventions were revealed at the fair.

Kentucky State Fair
Source: Kentucky Department of Tourism

That first State Fair drew 75,000 people to see races of steam automobiles, demonstrations of dynamo-powered farm implements and the head-on collision of two locomotives. For the next few years Kentucky communities submitted competitive bids to host the fair. The 1903 Fair occupied the Daviess County Fairgrounds in Owensboro, but very few people attended. The resulting debt, coupled with a lawsuit testing the state's premium appropriation, caused the fair to be cancelled in 1904.

Lexington won the bid in 1905, and large crowds flocked to the fairgrounds later known as the Red Mile, but Louisville's bid was highest in 1906, sending the event back to Churchill Downs. That same year the first official State Fair Board was named, and Louisville was selected as the permanent site

for the Kentucky State Fair.

In September 1908 the Kentucky State Fairgrounds opened in western Louisville. The new facility included a grandstand, half-mile race-track and livestock pavilion. The Midway featured games of chance, exotic shows, food vendors and the earliest amusement rides, the Ferris wheel and the carousel. The Merchants and Manufacturers Building – the most modern exposition building in America – was dedicated in 1921.

Events at the Kentucky State Fair reflected the trends and happenings of the time, introducing transportation milestones such as airplanes and automobiles and communications advancements from radio to television. The State Fair became the live showcase for new music genres and the largest venue for public education.

The original fairgrounds grew gradually, surviving the Great Depression and benefiting from the New Deal. During World War II, however, the fairgrounds were converted to wartime manufacturing industries, and the 1942 and 1943 State Fairs were cancelled. The State Fair returned to Churchill Downs in 1944 and 1945, but, after the war, plans were drawn up for a brand new year-round, multipurpose facility. The opening of the state-of-the-art Kentucky Fair & Exposition Center was covered live on national television during the 1956 State Fair.

The State Fair has continued to grow and change with the times, showcasing traditional and modern exhibits and entertainment at a site that now ranks as the eighth-largest exposition facility in the United States. In 2004 the 100th Kentucky State Fair was commemorated with a major history exhibition and the publication of a 200-page book.

RECREATION & TRAVEL
The Belle of Louisville   Kadie Engstrom

When the first steamboat, the *New Orleans*, came down the Ohio River in 1811, it began a chain reaction that led to the development of the country. Before there were railroads and traversable roads, the rivers were the highways, and steamboats were the semitrailers of the 19th century.

Thousands of packet (freight) boats and towboats traveled every navigable waterway in Kentucky, bringing people to settle the towns and cities and work the farms and factories. They carried goods of all kinds – farm products, livestock, tools, grain, tobacco, coal, cotton, wagons, cloth, household supplies – everything needed to advance the commerce of the Commonwealth.

The major rivers – the Kentucky, Big Sandy, Cumberland, Tennessee, Licking, Green, Barren,

Source: Belle of Louisville

Ohio – all saw the advent and the progress of the steamboat era. The peak time in history for the hard-working steam-powered vessels was from the 1820s to 1880s, though packets and towboats were still built well into the 20th century.

By the 1960s nearly all the steamboats were gone, lost to fires, snags, ice and explosions, and replaced by diesel-powered towboats. The last of the packet boats is the sternwheel steamer *Belle of Louisville*. Built in 1914 as the *Idlewild* (renamed the *Avalon* in 1948, then the *Belle of Louisville* in 1962), it is the oldest operating steamboat in the country. It is the only steamboat in the United States to ever reach the ripe old age of 90, and the *Belle* will turn 91 on October 18, 2005. The *Belle of Louisville* is a National Historic Landmark and is on the Register of Historic Places. The *Belle*, like many steamboats before it, is an important link to Kentucky's past.

RECREATION & TRAVEL

Major Festivals & Special Events

William E. Matthews

All year long, Kentucky is alive with more than 700 festivals, several world-class sporting championships, major concerts and many more events too numerous to list. Whether it's a Bluegrass jam session or a symphony orchestra concert, an apple festival or an art opening, Kentucky can fill your calendar of weekend celebrations in a heartbeat. The festivals and events feature arts, culture and celebrations of Kentucky heritage. Listed events in this chapter have been recognized by the Kentucky Tourism Council, Southeast Tourism Society and more than 100 festivals prepared by the Kentucky Festivals & Events Association.

KENTUCKY TOURISM COUNCIL'S FALL 2005 TOP 10 FESTIVALS & EVENTS

The Kentucky Tourism Council recognizes the Top 10 Festivals four times each year. The Fall 2005 picks include: **MainStrasse Village Maifest** *(Covington)*—Maifest is based on the German tradition of welcoming the first spring wines, but visitors also feel welcome as they stroll down cobblestone walkways in this restored 19th century German neighborhood. **Roots & Heritage Festival** *(Lexington)*—This three-day street fair recreates the powerful spirit of the African-American culture and history with live entertainment, vendors and delicious food. **National Quartet Convention** *(Louisville)*—Features over 60 premier artists performing Southern Gospel music along with over 400 exhibitors. **Kentucky Bourbon Festival** *(Bardstown)*—Five-day international festival celebrating the history, passion and art of making Kentucky bourbon. **Horse Cave Heritage Festival** *(Horse Cave)*—

Lincoln Days Festival, Hodgenville
Source: Kentucky Department of Tourism

Celebration of the area's rich cultural heritage, featuring a quilt show, live music, car show and activities for the entire family. **World Chicken Festival** *(London)*—Tribute to Col. Harland Sanders of Kentucky Fried Chicken with the world's largest skillet, frying-up delicious chicken. **Marion County Country Ham Days** *(Lebanon)*—Family-oriented community festival serving-up country ham with all the trimmings, a Pegasus parade and live entertainment. **St. James Court Art Show** *(Louisville)*—700+ artists and craftspeople exhibiting their creations in Old Louisville. **Reid's Orchard Apple Festival** *(Owensboro)*—Apples galore and vendors, hay rides, carnival rides, arts and crafts booths and much more make this a true autumn festival. **North American International Livestock Exposition** *(Louisville)*—Largest all-breed, purebred livestock show in the world.

ADDITIONAL 2005 SPRING, SUMMER AND WINTER/HOLIDAY TOP 10 WINNERS

Hillbilly Days Festival *(Pikeville)*—This festival provides a taste of Appalachian culture with bluegrass and country music, square dancing and clogging. Sample authentic southern cooking and find treasures from local artisans and crafters, as toe-tapping tunes dominate the square.

Kentucky Derby Festival *(Louisville)*—The Derby Festival consists of more than 70 events over a two-week period leading up to the legendary annual running of the Kentucky Derby "Run for the Roses." Includes the Pegasus Parade, the Great Steamboat Race, the Great Balloon Race, Thunder

Over Louisville and more.

International Bar-B-Q Festival *(Owensboro)*— Barbeque at its best! Cooking teams compete in this world famous festival with its more than 10 tons of mutton, 5,000 chickens and 1,500 gallons of burgoo, plus live concerts, arts and crafts, games and rides.

Hatfield-McCoy Reunion Festival *(Pikeville)*— More than 100 years ago, the Hatfield & McCoy families took up arms against each other in one of the most publicized feuds of all times. In 2000, the two families came together for a reunion and this gathering has evolved into an annual festival.

Great American Brass Band Festival *(Danville)*—An old-time brass band concert in the park that recaptures the nostalgia of peaceful, turn-of-the-century America. Features military, ragtime, Civil War and international bands, a band history conference and decorator picnic.

Southern Lights: Spectacular Sights on Holiday Nights *(Lexington)*—Nearly 4-mile drive starting at Ky. Horse Park Campground and proceeding through a dreamland of dazzling lighted and often moving displays.

Kentucky Crafted: The Market *(Louisville)*— Features 300 of Kentucky's finest contemporary and traditional crafts. Stage activities include musicians, actors, demonstrators. Also performing artists featuring Folk, Bluegrass, Jazz, thumbpicking guitar and Gospel.

Ky. Mountain Laurel Festival *(Pineville)*—Touted as Ky.'s oldest running festival, it showcases beautiful girls vying for the title of "Mountain Laurel Festival Queen."

KENTUCKY FESTIVALS & EVENTS ASSOCIATION'S TOP 100 LIST

Anderson County Burgoo Festival (Lawrenceburg), (502) 680-0453

A Taste of Harrison County (Cynthiana), (859) 234-5236

Aurora Country Festival, (270) 703-6060

Battle of Cynthiana-Civil War Days (859) 234-5236

Battle of Sutherland's Hill (Owensboro), (800) 489-1131

Beaver Creek Bluegrass Festival, (800) 264-3161

Black Gold Festival (Hazard), (606) 436-0161

Bourbon & Bluegrass Festival (Frankfort), (502) 647-0377

Brass Band Festival (Danville), (800) 755-0076

Buffalo Crossing Fall Craft Show (Shelbyville), (502) 647-0377

Bullitt Co. Derby Days, (502) 543-6727

Catfish Festival (Morgantown), (270) 526-6827

Casey County Apple Festival, (606) 787-6747

Central City Music Festival, (270) 754-2360

Chocolate Festival (Washington), (606) 759-7074

Civil War Days (Columbus-Belmont State Park), (270) 677-2327

Civil War Days (Paducah), (800) 723-8224

Civil War Living History Weekend (Washington), (606) 759-7411

Coffee Cup Concert Series (Covington), (859) 781-3094

Constitution Square Festival (Danville), (859) 239-7089

Court Days (Mt. Sterling), (859) 498-8732

Creative Arts Festival (Henderson), (270) 826-9531

Cumberland River Festival (Burkesville), (270) 864-4190

Daniel Boone Festival (Barbourville), (606) 564-4300

Daniel Boone Pioneer Festival (Winchester), (859) 744-0556

Day Out with Thomas (New Haven), (502) 549-5470

Duncan Hines Festival (Bowling Green), (270) 782-0800

Eddyville Founder's Festival, (800) 355-3885

Festival of Mountain Masters (Harlan), (606) 573-2900

Fleur de Lis Festival (Louisville), (502) 244-8086

Founder's Day (Salyersville), (606) 349-1607

Freedom Fest (Murray), (800) 715-5004

Fleming County Covered Bridge Festival, (606) 845-1223

Forkland Heritage Festival & Revue (Gravel Switch), (859) 332-7606

Glasgow Highland Games, (270) 651-3141

Glendale Crossing Festival, (800) 437-0092

Great American Pottery Festival (Richmond), (800) 866-3705

Guthrie Yard Sale & Bazaar (270) 483-2511

Hardin County Civil War Days, (270) 737-4126

Hart County Civil War Days, (270) 524-2892

HarvestFest (Elkton), (270) 265-9877

Hatfield & McCoy Festival (Pikeville), (800) 844-7453

Herbfest (Carrsville), (270) 988-3132

Hillbilly Days (Pikeville), (800) 844-7453

Hoofprints on the Stairs (Lebanon), (270) 692-0021

International BBQ Festival (Owensboro), (800) 489-1131

Irvington Railroad Festival, (270)547-3835

Janice & Henry Giles Arts & Crafts Festival (Knifely), (270) 384-5906

Jeffersontown Gaslight Festival, (502) 267-2070

Kaleidoscope of Culture (Elizabethtown), (270) 737-4126

Kentucky Apple Festival (Paintsville), (800) 542-5790

Kentucky Book Fair (Frankfort), (502) 695-3477

Kentucky Bourbon Festival (Bardstown), (800) 638-4877

Kentucky Crafted: The Market (Louisville), (888) 833-ARTS

Kentucky Deer Festival (Greenville), (270) 338-5422

Kentucky Derby Festival (Louisville), (502) 584-6383

Kentucky Heartland Festival (Elizabethtown), (270) 765-4334

Kentucky Lake Bluegrass Festival (Aurora), (800) 467-7145

Kentucky State Fair (Louisville), (502) 367-5180

Kid's Fishing Derby (Jamestown), (270) 434-3797

Lawrence County Septemberfest, (606) 638-9775

Little River Days (Hopkinsville), (270) 887-4290

Lincoln's Days (Hodgenville), (270) 358-4910

Little Green Men Festival (Hopkinsville), (800) 842-9959

Logan Co. Auburn Autumn Days, (270) 542-4149

Logan Co. Heritage & Tobacco Festival, (270) 726-2206

Heart of Trenton Main Street Festival (Trenton), (270) 466-3332.

Marion County Country Ham Days, (270) 692-9594

Master Musicians Festival (Somerset), (606) 678-2225

Mayfest (Lexington), (859) 231-7335

Morgan County Sorghum Festival, (606) 743-3330

Morgan's Raid (Georgetown), (502) 863-1575

Mountain Laurel Festival (Pineville), (800) 988-1075

Multicultural Festival (Owensboro), (800) 489-1131

Nibroc Festival (Corbin), (606) 528-6390

Ohio Valley Harvest Festival (Louisville), (502) 495-5106

Old Time Fiddlers Contest (Leitchfield), (270) 259-3578

Owensboro-Daviess County Motorsports Festival, (800) 489-1131

Paducah Summer Festival, (800) 723-8224

Pennington Folk Festival (Princeton), (270) 365-3959

Pioneer Days/Civil War Living History (Bardstown), (502) 349-0291

Poage Landing Days (Ashland), (606) 329-1056

Poppy Mountain Bluegrass Festival (Morehead), (606) 784-2277

River Heritage Bluegrass Festival (Brandenburg), (270) 422-4225

Sacajawea Festival (Cloverport), 270-788-6632

Sadieville Railroad Festival, (502) 587-4576

Shakespeare Festival (Lexington), (859) 257-4929

Shelbyville Horse Show Jubilee, (502) 633-6388

Simon Kenton Frontier Festival (Washington), (800) 575-7302

Southern Kentucky Festival of Books (Bowling Green), (270) 745-5016

Springbean Memorial Mountain Music Festival (Tyner), (877) 800-7344

Summer Motion (Ashland), (606) 327-4424

Trigg County Country Ham Festival, (270) 522-3892

Van Lear Town Celebration, (606) 789-8540

Waterfront Festival (Carrsville), (270) 988-3632

Watermelon Festival (Tompkinsville), (270) 487-5504

West Kentucky Book Expo (Sturgis), (270) 333-9316

Western Kentucky Highland Festival (Paducah), (270) 443-2064

Woodcarver's Day (Washington), (606) 564-3559

Bourbon Festival, Bardstown
Source: Kentucky Department of Tourism

For more information on these and hundreds of additional festivals and special events in Kentucky, visit Kentucky Festivals and Events Association, http://www. kyfestivals.com; Kentucky Department of Tourism, / www.kentuckytourism.com/events.aspx; and Southeast Tourism Society; http://www.escapetothesoutheast.com

RECREATION & TRAVEL

National Parks & Historic Sites

ABRAHAM LINCOLN BIRTHPLACE NATIONAL HISTORIC SITE

In the fall of 1808, Thomas and Nancy Lincoln settled on the 348 acre Sinking Spring Farm. Two months later on February 12, 1809, Abraham Lincoln was born in a one-room log cabin near the Sinking Spring. Here the Lincolns lived and farmed before moving to land a few miles away at Knob Creek. The area was established by Congress on July 17, 1916. An early 19th century Kentucky cabin, symbolic of the one in which Lincoln was born, is preserved in a memorial building at the site of his birth.

    2995 Lincoln Farm Road
    Hodgenville, KY 42748
    (270) 358-3137, (270) 358-3138
    www.nps.gov/abli

BIG SOUTH FORK NATIONAL RIVER & RECREATION AREA

The free-flowing Big South Fork of the Cumberland River and its tributaries pass through 90 miles of scenic gorges and valleys containing a wide range of natural and historic features. The area offers a broad range of recreational opportunities including camping, whitewater rafting, kayaking, canoeing, hiking, horseback riding, mountain biking, hunting and fishing. The U.S. Army Corps of Engineers, with its experience in managing river basins, was charged with land acquisition, planning and development of facilities. Now completed, these lands and facilities are operated and maintained by the National Park Service for the benefit and use of the public.

    4564 Leatherwood Road
    Oneida, TN 37841
    (423) 286-7275, (606) 376-5073
    www.nps.gov/biso

CUMBERLAND GAP NATIONAL HISTORIC PARK

The story of the first doorway to the west is commemorated at the national park, located where the borders of Tennessee, Kentucky and Virginia meet. Carved by wind and water, Cumberland Gap forms a major break in the formidable Appalachian Mountain chain. First used by large game animals in their migratory journeys, followed by Native Americans, the Cumberland Gap was the first and best avenue for the settlement of the interior of this nation. From 1775 to 1810, the Gap's heyday, between 200,000 and 300,000 men, women and children from all walks of life, crossed the Gap into "Kentuckee."

    US 25E South
    P.O. Box 1848
    Middlesboro, KY 40965-1848
    (606) 248-2817

MAMMOTH CAVE NATIONAL PARK

Mammoth Cave National Park was established to preserve the cave system, including Mammoth Cave, the scenic river valleys of the Green and Nolin rivers, and a section of south central Kentucky. This is the longest recorded cave system in the world with more than 360 miles explored and mapped.

    P.O. Box 7
    Mammoth Cave, KY 42259
    (270) 758-2180
    www.nps.gov/maca/

TRAIL OF TEARS NATIONAL HISTORIC TRAIL

See Trail of Tears article on page 122.

RECREATION & TRAVEL

Dr. Gary O'Dell *Cave Exploration*

Snow-covered mountain peaks. Verdant tropical jungles. The deep ocean abyss. The polar icecaps. The limitless depths of space. These are some of the last frontiers of human endeavor. Most of us can only vicariously experience such exploits through

Pushing a tight lead in a Rockcastle County cave
Source: Gary O'Dell

television documentaries and magazine accounts. There is in Kentucky, however, a frontier that remains accessible to the ordinary person. Explorations in the underground wilderness of caves generally require only minimal investment in equipment and the application of plain common sense along with informal training in safety and methods. Kentucky is home to Mammoth Cave, the world's longest, and thousands of other caverns large and small. Here, sometimes, it is possible to walk in places where no human foot has ever tread.

Caving can be hazardous, because caves have many slippery slopes, abrupt drop-offs, loose rocks, deep holes, or may be prone to rapid flooding. Among the most serious risks to the cave explorer are head injuries, injuries sustained from falling, drowning and hypothermia. To reduce the risk of a serious accident, anyone entering a non-commer-cial cave should follow these basic safety rules:

- Never go caving alone; preferably go in the company of experienced explorers. Always tell someone where you are going, and when you expect to return.
- Always carry at least three separate sources of light, along with extra bulbs and batteries.
- Wear head protection: a hardhat or helmet with a chinstrap to keep your helmet on your head during a fall.
- Dress appropriately for the environment; caves in Kentucky have an average interior temperature of about 54 F, but some sections of a cave may be colder in winter. If entering a wet cave, layered clothing will help to conserve body heat.
- Wear boots with an aggressive tread that provides ankle protection (never slick-soled shoes).
- Watch the weather closely. Many caves contain active underground streams. An innocuous ankle-deep trickle can become a roaring torrent after a heavy rain. Sticks or leaves stuck to the walls or ceiling can indicate the cave floods completely.

The best way not to be the victim in a cave rescue is to have the proper equipment, experience and training before venturing into a cave on your own.

Stalactite meets stalagmite in a Breckinridge County cave
Source: Chris Anderson, Darklight Imagery

The flip side is that caves are fragile environments that can be easily damaged by the explorer. Heavy visitor traffic through a cave can disrupt the ecosystem; many of the animal species dwelling in caves are threatened or endangered. Mineral deposits such as stalactites and stalagmites are delicate and can be harmed just by touching, since the oils of human skin can stop its growth. These formations are very slow growing and, if broken off, may take centuries to regenerate if at all. Nothing is more disturbing than to enter a cave, once beautifully decorated, and find only broken stubs and piles of litter and trash. The guiding principle of the explorer is to "cave softly." The motto of the National Speleological Society is, "Take nothing but pictures, leave nothing but footprints, kill nothing but time."

Source: Chris Anderson, Darklight Imagery

For those interested in cave exploration, a good first step might be to visit one of Kentucky's many commercial show caves to test one's comfort level in an underground environment. Carter Caves State Park, in addition to regular tours, also offers self-guided tours for two of the "wild" caves in the park; visitors must obtain a permit before entering one of these caves and demonstrate that they are properly equipped.

Local chapters of the National Speleological Society (www.caves.org) can help provide the training necessary for safe and responsible exploration of wild caves in Kentucky.

Large trunk passage in a Breckinridge County cave
Source: Chris Anderson, Darklight Imagery

Mineral deposits built these rimstone dams in a Breckinridge County cave
Source: Chris Anderson, Darklight Imagery

Cave entrance in Pulaski County
Source: Robert Coomer

Floyd Collins

Floyd Collins died while trapped in Sand Cave in 1925. His death became a national sensation.

Sheet music for a traditional ballad called "The Death of Floyd Collins," written by the Rev. Andrew Jenkins and Mrs. Irene Spain, was published in 1925 and sold thousands of copies.

Kentucky Travel Time Radio Show

Super Talk Radio Show 96.1 FM
www.kytraveltime.com

Super Talk 96.1 WLXO in Lexington has a new talk radio program, "Kentucky Travel Time." The program is produced by Kentucky's Eastern Highlands North and Eastern Highlands South tourism regions. and airs each Saturday from 12:00 noon to 1:00 pm. The program hosts deliver a week-to-week travel guide to listeners interested in entertainment, historical sites, heritage and cultural sites, out-of-the-way restaurants, modern lodging facilities, nature-based tourism locations, campgrounds, fall festivals and a host of other under-recognized places to visit, all located in the beautiful mountain area of Kentucky known as the "Kentucky Highlands."

 Show Sponsors

Kentucky Dept. of Tourism, www.kytourism.com
Kentucky Dept. of Parks, www.kyparks.gov
Eastern Highlands North, Kentucky Appalachians, www.kyappalachians.com
Eastern Highlands South, Daniel Boone Country, www.danielboonecountry.com
511/Tour Southern & Eastern Kentucky, www.tourseky.com
Kentucky Artisan Heritage Trail, www.kaht.com
The Clark Group Clark's Kentucky Almanac, www.kyalmanac.com

Eastern Highlands Region - North
Bath County: Big K's Campsites, bigkscamping@yahoo.com; Super 8 Motel, 606-674-2200; Clear Creek Grocery and Restaurant, rjjohson@adelphia.net; Artie's Antiques, 606-674-2528; **Boyd County:** Ashland Area Convention & Visitors Bureau, www.visitashlandky.com; **Elliott County:** Laurel Gorge Inn, www.laurelgorgeinn; Tobacco Festival, 606-736489; **Floyd County:** Mountain Arts Center, www.macarts.com; Comfort Suites, www.hwhotels.com; Holiday Inn, 606-886-0001; Jenny Wiley Theatre, www.jtheatre.com; Prestonsburg Tourism Commission, www.prestonsburgky.org; East Kentucky Science Center, www.wedoscience.org; Country At Heart, 606-886-8957; StoneCrest Golf Course, www.stonecrestprestonsburg.com; Kentucky Highland Folk Festival, www.prestonsburgky.org; Honda of Prestonsburg, 606-886-9261; **Greenup County:** Greenup County Tourism & Convention Commission, www.greenupcountytourism.com; **Johnson County:** Paintsville Tourism Commission,www.paintsville.org Ramada Inn of Paintsville, ramadapaintsville.com; Paintsville Lake Marina, 606-297-LAKE; **Lawrence County:** Lawrence County Tourism Commission, www.lawrencecokytourism.com; **Martin County:** Inez Tourism, "Roy F. Collier Community Center," www.rccenter.com; **Menifee County:** Frenchburg/Menifee County Chamber of Commerce, www.frenchburgmenifee.com; **Morgan County:** West Liberty Tourism Commission, www.cityofwestliberty.com; **Pike County:** Pikeville-Pike County Tourism Commission, www.tourpikecounty.com; **Rowan County:** Morehead Tourist & Convention Commission, www.moreheadtourism.com;

Knott County: Alice Lloyd College. www.alc.edu; Knott County Tourism Commission, 606-758-5881; Hindman Settlement School, www.hindmansettlement.org; Bank of Hindman, 606-785-3158; Jerry Slone, Attorney, 606-785-9222; Kentucky Appalachian Artisan Center, www.artisancenter.net; **Magoffin County:** Salyersville Tourism, 606-349-2409; The Keeping Room, 606-349-3358; Kozy Korner Restaurant, 606-349-8601; **Montgomery County:** Mt. Sterling-Montgomery Tourism Commission, www.mtsterlingtourism,com; Ruth Hunt Candies, www.ruthhuntcandy.com; Mt. Sterling Arts Council, www.gatewayarts center.com

Eastern Highlands Region - South
Bell County: Bell County Tourism Commission, www.mountaingateway.com; **Breathitt County:** Jackson/Breathitt County Chamber of Commerce, 606-666-4159; **Clay County:** Manchester/Clay County Tourist Commission, 606-598-1754; **Estill County:** Estill Development Alliance, www.estillcountyky.net; **Harlan County:** Cumberland Tourism Commission, www.kingdomcome.org; Harlan Tourist Commission, www.harlanonline.net/tourism; **Jackson County:** Jackson County Tourism, www.eastky.net/jacksonco; **Knox County:** Barbourville Tourist & Recreation Commission, www.barbourville.com; **Laurel County:** London/Laurel County Tourist Commission, www.laurelkytourism.com Dog Patch Trading Post, www.dogpatchtradingpost.com Lee County; Lee County Tourism Committee, 606-464-2888; **Leslie County:** Leslie County Tourism Commission, 606-672-2154; **Letcher County:** Letcher County Tourism & Convention Commission, 606-632-1200; Courthouse Café, chcafe@aol.com; **Rockcastle County:** Mt. Vernon-Rockcastle Co. Tourist Commission, www.rockcastlecokytourism.com; Kentucky Music Hall of Fame & Museum, www.kymusichalloffame; Red Hill Horse Camp, Livingston, www.redhillhorsecamp.com; **Owsley County:** Owsley County Tourist Commission; **Perry County:** Perry County Tourism Commission, 606-439-2659; **Powell County :** Powell County Tourism Commission, www.powellcountytourism.com; **Whitley County:** Williamsburg Tourist Commission, www.williamsburgky.com; Corbin Tourist & Convention Commission, www.corbinkentucky.us; **Wolfe County** Wolfe County Tourism, 606-668-6475

Kentucky Bed & Breakfasts

- Overnight Bed & Breakfast Accommodations

- Bed & Breakfast Gift Certificates Available

- B&B Cookbook for Sale

- Weddings/Special Events

- Meetings/Socials

BED & BREAKFAST ASSOCIATION OF KENTUCKY
233 Rose Hill
Versailles, KY 40383-1223
www.kentuckybb.com,
email: info@kentuckybb.com

Bed & Breakfasts

The Bed and Breakfast Association of Kentucky is a statewide professional association of nearly 100 member B&Bs pledged to provide guests with exceptional hospitality, comfort, safety and satisfaction. All member inns are inspected and approved using the highest quality principles to meet state and local requirements and standards. BBAK offers accommodations ranging from small quaint log cabins and unique farm settings to classic mansions and historic inns.

Members are grouped into seven regions. Please access the website, www.kentuckybb.com for more information and a listing of BBAK members throughout the state.

Source: Kentucky Bed & Breakfast Association

BLUE GRASS REGION

1823 Historic Rose Hill Inn in Versailles is a 180-year-old restored mansion, with elegant surroundings. Guests can walk on a 3-acre property visiting gardens, or pet the golden retrievers, goats and miniature donkey. Rooms have a queen or king bed, with private bath, some with jacuzzis. A delicious breakfast is served in the dining room and leisure time can be spent in the parlor, on the front porch, or visiting the wonderful horse farms nearby.

Lyndon House Bed & Breakfast in Lexington offers Victorian style furnishings, wireless Internet and private baths. Located downtown, it is in walking distance to many fine restaurants, shops, and theatres. Historic sites and beautiful gardens are part of the Lyndon House neighborhood. In the morning, guests are treated to made-to-order breakfast in the Solarium with the local newspaper, fine Columbian coffee and southern style biscuits.

Swann's Nest at Cygnet Farm in Lexington has luxury bed and breakfast accommodations in the heart of Thoroughbred country and is tucked into the rolling countryside less than a mile from Keeneland Racecourse and only five minutes from Blue Grass Airport.

EASTERN REGION

The Bennett House in Richmond offers hospitality when you step through the double oversize entry doors into the historic Queen Anne, Romanesque home. Guests receive a complimentary breakfast, express check-out. The historic home built in 1889 has meeting and banquet facilities for up to 70.

The Presidents' House Bed & Breakfast in Catlettsburg is just minutes away from Ashland, KY, and Huntington, WV, and is especially convenient for visitors to Marshall University events.

A large collection of authentic Presidential memorabilia and autographs add special interest to guest rooms, each named for a President of the United States and decorated according to his period in history. All rooms have queen-size beds and private baths

HEARTLAND REGION

1851 Historic Maple Hill Manor in Springfield is a nationally recognized Bed & Breakfast, Wedding / Special Events Showplace, Alpaca & Llama Farm, and Handcrafted Gift Gallery & Alpaca Fiber Studio set on 14 tranquil acres. Each of the seven guest rooms has air conditioning and private baths. Awaken to the delightful strains of chamber music and a full country 'gourmet' breakfast.

1879 Merriman Manor Bed & Breakfast in Harrodsburg offers a complimentary full country breakfast with their special Key Lime Parfait. The Manor is designated a Kentucky landmark and listed on the National Register of Historic Places.

WESTERN REGION

Victorian Quarters B&B in Henderson offers all suites with private baths and full kitchens and snacks. They serve a full or continental breakfast and offer an above ground swimming pool with a location across from the Ohio River.

Featured Bed & Breakfast Inns

Bennett House, The
419 W Main St
Richmond, KY 40475
Phone: 859 623-7876
Phone: 877 204-3436
Fax: 859-623-5229
Email: smart@bennetthousebb.com
Website: www.bennetthousebb.com

1851 Historic Maple Hill Manor
2941 Perryville Rd
U.S. 150 EAST
Springfield, KY 40069
Phone: 859-336-3075,
800-886-7546
Fax: 859-336-3076
Email: stay@maplehillmanor.com
Website: www.maplehillmanor.com

1823 Historic Rose Hill Inn
233 Rose Hill
Versailles, KY 40383
Phone: 859-873-5957, 800-307-0460
Fax: 859-873-1813
Email: Innkeepers@rosehillinn.com
Website: www.rosehillinn.com

Presidents' House Bed & Breakfast
2206 Walnut St. (US 23)
Catlettsburg, KY 41129
Phone: 606-739-8118,
877-500-3452
Email: presidentshouse@gmail.com
Website: www.thepresidentshouse.com

Lyndon House Bed & Breakfast
507 North Broadway
Lexington, KY 40508
Phone: 859-225-3631
800-494-9597
Fax: 859-281-1167
Email: Innkeeper@lyndonhouse.com
Website: www.lyndonhouse.com

1879 Merriman Manor Bed & Breakfast
362 N. College St.
Harrodsburg, KY 40330
Phone: 859-734-6289,
877-734-6289
Email: merrimanmanor@bellsouth.net
Website: www.1879merrimanmanor.com

Swann's Nest at Cygnet Farm
3463 Rosalie Lane
Lexington, KY 40510
Phone: 859-226-0095
Fax: 859-252-4499
Email: swannsnest@alltel.net
Website: www.swannsnest.com

Victorian Quarters B&B
109 Clay Street
Henderson, KY 42420
Phone: 270-831-2778
Email: rosannacoy@aol.com
Website:
www.victorianquartersbb.com

Campgrounds

CITY	CAMPGROUND	SITES	PHONE
Albany	Grider Hill Dock & Indian Creek Lodge	20	(606) 387-5501
Albany	Wolf River Resort	87	(606) 387-5841
Alexandria	A J Jolly Golf Course & Campground	25	(859) 635-4423
Bardstown	Holt's Campground	32	(502) 348-6717
Bardstown	White Acres Campground	100	(502) 348-9677
Beattyville	Lago Linda	35	(606) 464-2876
Bee Spring	Moutardier Campground CE	172	(270) 286-4511
Beechburg	Fleming County Wildlife Area		(800) 858-1549
Benton	Bee Spring Lodge and Marina	15	(800) 732-0088
Benton	Big Bear Resort and Marina	75	(800) 922-2327
Benton	Birmingham Point RV Park		(270) 354-8482
Benton	King Creek Resort and Marina		(800) 733-6710
Benton	Lakeside Campground & Marina Inc.	55	(270) 354-8157
Benton	Lakewood Camping Resort		(270) 354-9122
Benton	Malcolm Creek Resort	42	(800) 733-6713
Benton	Sportsman's Anchor Resort	53	(800) 326-3625
Benton	Town & Country Resort	31	(800) 347-1470
Berea	Oh! Ky Campground	70	(859) 986-1150
Bowling Green	Beech Bend Park	500	(270) 781-7634
Bowling Green	Bowling Green KOA	120	(800) 562-2458
Brandenburg	Otter Creek Park	250	(502) 574-4583
Bronston	Lake Cumberland RV Park & Golf Driving Range	60	(877) 461-2404
Buckhorn	Buckhorn Tailwater Campground CE	30	(606) 398-7220
Burkesville	Sulphur Creek Resort	22	(270) 433-7272
Burlington	River Ridge Park	75	(859) 586-7282
Cadiz	Boat Haven Resort & Marina	12	(888) 557-7638
Cadiz	Devils Elbow Campground C.E.	20	(270) 924-5878
Cadiz	Goose Hollow Campround & RV Park	44	(270) 522-2267
Cadiz	Kamptown RV Resort	93	(270) 522-7976
Cadiz	Lake Barkley Public Wildlife Area		(615) 736-5181
Cadiz	Prizer Point Marina & Resort	50	(800) 548-2048
Cadiz	Willow Creek Campground & Restaurant		(270) 522-0808
Calvert City	Cypress Lakes Campground	125	(270) 395-4267
Calvert City	Kentucky Lake KOA	90	(800) KOA-8540
Campbellsville	Cedarcrest Lodging and Entertainment	101	(877) 822-8552
Campbellsville	Pikes Ridge Campground Green River Lake	30	(877) 444-6777
Campbellsville	Smith Ridge Campground	80	(877) 444-6777
Carlisle	Clay Wildlife Area		(859) 289-2564
Cave City	Crystal Onyx Cave and Campground	25	(270) 773-2359
Cave City	Oakes Cabins and Campground	9	(270) 773-4740
Cave City	Singin Hills RV & Camping Park	24	(270) 773-3789
Cave City	Yogi Bear's Jellystone Park Camp-Resort	200	(800) 523-1854
Central City	Western Kentucky RV Park	50	(270) 757-0345
Clarkson	Ponderosa Boat Dock	70	(270) 242-7215
Clarkson	Wax Campground CE		(270) 286-4511
Columbia	Holmes Bend Marina-Resort	105	(800) 801-8154
Corbin	Corbin KOA Campground	87	(800) 562-8132
Corbin	Sheltowee Trace Outfitters		(800) 541-7238
Corinth	Three Springs Campground	18	(859) 806-3030
Crittenden	Cincinnati South Campground (KOA)	88	(800) 562-9151
Cub Run	Dog Creek Campground CE	24	(270) 286-4511
Danville	Pioneer Playhouse	50	(859) 236-2747

CITY	CAMPGROUND	SITES	PHONE
Drakesboro	Gregory Lake RV Park	103	(270) 476-9223
Dry Ridge	Campers Village	40	(859) 824-5836
Dunmor	Dogwood Lake Camping Resort	144	(270) 657-8380
Eddyville	Dryden Bay Campground	37	(270) 388-0289
Eddyville	Eddy Creek Marina Resort	16	(800) 626-2300
Eddyville	Holiday Hills Resort	100	(800) 337-8550
Eddyville	Hurricane Creek	51	(270) 522-8821
Eddyville	Indian Point RV Park	200	(800) 605-8562
Eddyville	Lake Barkley RV Resort	121	(800) 910-PARK
Elizabethtown	Elizabethtown KOA	78	(800) 562-7605
Falls Of Rough	Cave Creek CE	86	(877) 444-6777
Falls Of Rough	Peter Cave		(270) 257-8376
Frankfort	Kentucky River Campground	105	(866) 227-2465
Franklin	KOA Franklin	104	(800) 562-5631
Frenchburg	Lost Hound Campground	30	(606) 768-6095
Gilbertsville	Moors Resort and Marina	117	(800) 626-5472
Glasgow	Beaver Creek Campground	12	(270) 646-2055
Glendale	Glendale Campground	91	(270) 369-7755
Golden Pond	5 Various Campgrounds	29	(270) 924-2000
Golden Pond	Turkey Bay		(270) 924-5602
Grand Rivers	Canal Campground	84	(877) 444-6777
Grand Rivers	Lighthouse Landing	60	(800) 491-7245
Grayson	Valley Breeze RV Campground	17	(606) 474-6779
Hardin	Aurora Oaks Campground	50	(888) 886-8704
Harlan	Camp Blanton		(606) 573-6811
Harrodsburg	Chimney Rock RV Park	65	(859) 748-5252
Harrodsburg	Cummins Ferry Campground & Marina	105	(859) 865-2003
Hartford	Ohio County Park	75	(270) 298-4466
Hawesville	Vastwood Park of Hancock County	12	(270) 927-8778
Hillsboro	DH Resorts, Inc.	10	(800) 737-7433
Horse Cave	Horse Cave KOA Kampground	65	(800) 562-2809
Hyden	Trace Branch Campground/Rec Area CE	15	(606) 398-7251
Jamestown	Kendall Recreation Area	83	(877) 444-6777
Kuttawa	Eureka Recreational Area	27	(877) 444-6777
Lancaster	Riverview RV	53	(606) 548-2113
Lawrenceburg	Fair Winds At Beaver Lake Inc	10	(502) 839-4402
Lewisburg	Shady Cliff Resort & Marina	8	(270) 657-9580
Lexington	Kentucky Horse Park Campground	260	(800) 678-8813
Littcarr	Littcarr Campground	35	(606) 642-3052
Livermore	Livermore RV Park	33	(270) 278-2113
Livingston	Rockcastle River Outpost		(606) 864-9407
London	London Dock and Rockcastle Campground	27	(606) 864-5225
London	Westgate R.V. Camping	14	(606) 878-7330
London, Corbin, Mckee	Various Campgrounds		(877) 444-6777
Louisa	Falls Campground	60	(606) 686-3398
Lucas	Narrows Campground CE	90	(877) 444-6777
Lynch	Portal 31 RV Park	12	(606) 848-1530
Mammoth Cave	Mammoth Cave National Park		(800) 967-2283
Mammoth Cave Nat'l Park	Double J Stables & Horsemans Camp		(800) 730-HRSE
Marion	Paddy's Bluff Retreat		(270) 836-4297
Marion	S&J RV Park	10	(270) 965-3338
Mayfield	Kaler Bottoms Public Wildlife Area		(502) 564-4336
Maysville	Maysville River Park Marina	33	(606) 564-2520
Mc Daniels	Axtel CE	158	(877) 444-6777
Mc Daniels	Laurel Branch CE	77	(877) 444-6777
Mc Daniels	North Fork CE	107	(877) 444-6777
Middlesboro	Ridge Trail Backcountry	20	(606) 298-2817
Milton	Helton Camping	100	(502) 268-3241
Monticello	Conley Bottom Resort, Inc.	120	(606) 348-6351
Monticello	Cumberland Camping	40	(606) 348-5253
Monticello	Fall Creek Campground	10	(606) 348-6042
Morehead	Clay Lick Campground		(606) 784-5624
Morehead	Twin Knobs Campground and Recreation Area	216	(877) 444-6777
Morganfield	Moffitt Lake Recreation Area	85	(270) 333-4845

CITY	CAMPGROUND	SITES	PHONE
Morgantown	Steamboat Landing Marina		(270) 662-0019
Mortons Gap	Best Western Pennyrile Inn and Campground	16	(270) 258-5201
Mount Vernon	Nicely Campground	50	(606) 256-5637
Murray	Bullfrog Campground	25	(270) 474-1144
Murray	Holly Green RV Park	36	(270) 753-5652
Murray	Water's Edge RV Park & Marina	55	(888) 651-3084
Murray	Wildcat Creek Recreation Area	50	(270) 436-5628
Nancy	Pulaski County Park	45	(606) 636-6450
New Concord	Lakeview Cottages & Marina	8	(270) 436-5876
Nicholasville	River Otter Outfitters/Sugar Creek Resort		(859) 885-9359
Owensboro	Windy Hollow Campground	250	(270) 785-4150
Paducah	Duck Creek RV Park	75	(270) 415-0404
Paducah	Fern Lake Campground	70	(270) 444-7939
Parkers Lake	Eagle Falls Resort	40	(888) 318-2658
Ravenna	Aldersgate Camp & Retreat Center	10	(606) 723-5078
Renfro Valley	Lake Linville Marina and Campgrounds	36	(606) 256-9696
Renfro Valley	Renfro Valley KOA	101	(800) 562-2475
Renfro Valley	Renfro Valley RV Park	79	(800) 765-7464
Richmond	Deer Run Stables L.L.C.		(859) 527-6339
Roundhill	Lazy Acres Trails & Paylake		(270) 286-4189
Russell Springs	Indian Hills Resort & KOA	170	(800) 562-5617
Russell Springs	Pine Crest RV Park and Cabins	58	(270) 866-5615
Salt Lick	Clear Creek Campground	21	(606) 784-6428
Salt Lick	Outpost Campground	52	(606) 683-2311
Salt Lick	White Sulphur Horse Camp		(606) 784-6428
Salt Lick	Zilpo Campgrounds	172	(606) 768-2722
Sanders	Eagle Valley Campground	200	(859) 347-9361
Sawyer	Sawyer Lake, Bee Rock & Little Lick	6	(606) 679-2010
Scottsville	Bailey's Point Campground	215	(877) 444-6777
Scottsville	Dam & Tailwater Campground CE	48	(877) 444-6777
Scottsville	Walnut Creek Marina	30	(270) 622-5858
Shelbyville	Guist Creek Marina and Campground	26	(502) 647-5359
Shelbyville	Lake Shelby Campground		(502) 633-5069
Shepherdsville	Grand-ma's RV Camping	38	(502) 543-7023
Shepherdsville	Louisville South KOA	175	(800) 562-1880
Slade	Bee Rock Campground	10	(606) 663-9199
Slade	Koomer Ridge	54	(606) 663-2852
Slade	Pumpkin Bottom in the Red River Gorge		(859) 663-9701
Smith	Martins Fork Lake and Recreation Area		(606) 573-1468
Smith	Smith Recreation Area		(606) 573-7655
Smithfield	Lake Jericho Recreation Area	62	(502) 743-5205
Smithland	Birdsville RV Park	34	(270) 928-2820
Somerset	Cumberland Point Campground	30	(877) 444-6777
Somerset	Fishing Creek Recreation Area	48	(877) 444-6777
Somerset	Waitsboro Recreation Area	25	(606) 561-5513
Sparta	Sparta Campground	80	(859) 356-9859
Stearns	Bear Creek Horse Camp	23	(423) 569-3321
Stearns	Big South Fork - Blue Heron Campground	45	(800) 365-CAMP
Taylorsville	Rolling Hills Camping Resort	71	(502) 477-1291
Tiline	Cumberland River Farm Campground	13	(270) 928-2180
Union	Big Bone Landing Marina & Campground	62	(859) 384-1713
Versailles	Lakeside Arena	60	(859) 873-9155
Wallingford	Fox Valley Recreation Area	100	(606) 849-2143
Wallins Creek	Camp O Cumberland		(606) 664-2909
Walton	Oak Creek Campground	100	(877) 604-3503
West Liberty	Gamble's Campground and Stable	28	(606) 522-3400
West Point	Salt River Recreation Area		(502) 922-4065
Whitley City	Alum Ford	8	(423) 569-9778
Whitley City	Barren Fork & Bell Farm Horse & Great Meadows	41	(606) 376-5323
Whitley City	Sand Hill Recreation Park	32	(606) 376-9333
Whitley City	Stampede Run Horse Camp	15	(606) 376-9666
Williamsburg	Williamsburg RV Park	30	(800) 426-3267
Willisburg	Captain Bobs Boat Dock	12	(859) 375-0093

Source: Kentucky Department of Tourism

RECREATION & TRAVEL

Hiking

Jerrell Goodpaster

Source: Sid Webb

There's no better way to experience the natural beauty of Kentucky than by hiking one of the state's numerous trails. The trails provide access to wildflowers, wildlife and geologic wonders. They can be used for bird watching, backpacking and more. From casual strolls along the Green River, in Mammoth Cave National Park, to exposed ridge top traverses in the Red River Gorge — it can be found in the Bluegrass State. The possibilities are endless.

A visiting hiker might begin a hiking vacation in the east-central part of Kentucky, at Cave Run Lake. The 100 miles of hiking trails near the lake should provide an adequate warm-up for even the most seasoned hiker. Bald eagles, Canada geese, herons and other avian delights can be spotted in this area. The Sheltowee Trace, a 270-mile trail, which follows the Daniel Boone National Forest south to Tennessee, passes through this area and intersects many of the Cave Run trails.

After a few days at Cave Run Lake, the curious hiker can move south a few miles to the Red River Gorge region. This area, combined with the Natural Bridge State Resort Park and the Clifty Wilderness Area, is home to some of the finest trails in the state. The Auxier Ridge Trail exposes hikers to rugged sandstone cliffs and provides good views of the surrounding topography. The Rock Bridge Trail twists between and beneath giant hemlocks on its way to Creation Falls, which is located just a few feet away from one of the most unique natural arches on the planet. Trails to Natural Bridge, Sky Bridge, Gray's Arch, or one of the other magnificent arches, are sure to please even the most discriminating trail lover.

Visitors who follow the Daniel Boone National

Forest south will find more trails near Yahoo Falls, Cumberland Falls and the Natural Arch Scenic Area. If these fail to satisfy, one can keep traveling south to the Big South Fork National River and Recreation Area. The 50-mile long John Muir Trail will hold anyone's attention for a day or two, but it is only a sample of what the Big South Fork has to offer.

From the Big South Fork, hikers can either move east to more trails and the amazing overlooks of Cumberland Gap National Historical Park and Breaks Interstate Park, or west to the 60 miles of fascinating trails in Mammoth Cave National Park. If the 15 stream crossings on the Wet Prong Loop Trail fail to provide relief from summer heat, a cave tour might do the trick. While visitors are cruising along the extraordinary Cedar Sink Trail, members of the Pine Mountain Trail Conference will be putting the finishing touches on the hundred-mile long Pine Mountain Trail. Hikers who can't wait for its completion can hop further west to the Land Between the Lakes. The 60-mile long North-South Trail is a great place to watch the sun set over Kentucky Lake, or perhaps bring a Kentucky hiking vacation to a close. Of course, a hiker with more time could backtrack and hike the hundreds of miles of trail we skipped over. So many trails, so little time.

Source: Sid Webb

Well, what about that?

"Many people seem concerned about snakes . . . copperheads and rattlesnakes inhabit the [Red River Gorge]. However . . . they pose only a small statistical risk to hikers. . . . I would confidently suspect that the average person is more likely to be seriously harmed in the Red by hornets, or in a traffic accident."

("Red River Gorge Trail Guide," Jerrell Goodpaster, Lost Branch Publications, Owingsville: 2005)

RECREATION & TRAVEL

Ghosts
& Haunted Places

Lynwood Montell

"Across the centuries, people have passed along from one generation to the next their cherished heirlooms, such as beliefs, traditions, and historically significant family and community stories. Sitting around fires, or under a shade tree at night, older men and women told stories to entertain, also to explain the unexplainable. Children have always looked to parents, and especially grandparents, for insights into the mysteries of the world about them. Adults told stories about the things they had witnessed or experienced. They often embellished them with their own interpretation of the events described, perhaps even simply to make a good story better.

Kentucky was settled by people with a myriad of social and cultural backgrounds. They were mostly Americans by birth, but of various nationalities and races, being chiefly of English, Scottish, Irish, Scots-Irish, French, German, and African descent. Many of these early ancestors, who moved across the mountains onto the western frontier, preferred the soon-to-be comforts of towns and villages, while others became primarily backwoods people by choice. They fondly accepted the wild freedom of the frontier rural landscape. 'A lonely house in the middle of a great farm was their ideal, and they attained it even before it could be done with safety,' according to geologist Nathan S. Shaler. All of these groups brought with them the folk heritage of their geographical origin. Folk beliefs and narratives of all varieties, told and retold in any given area, reflect the ethnic makeup of the people who live there. Thus it is that the wealth of the stories and beliefs brought to an area by immigrants are translated, and sometimes modified, as they are passed along

The John Hunt family plot, Lexington Cemetery
Source: Sam Stephens

from generation to generation.

All across the state, Kentuckians have produced a great body of supernatural beliefs, stories, and historical legends. From the pioneer times down to the present, Kentucky has always been rich in ghost legends or personal accounts of ghostly visitations. Traditional stories that tell of ghostly sightings and felt presences of spirits and other supernatural creatures still persists as a vestige of the past, as they help to describe life and times of a bygone era. ...

Back then, it was common practice for a particular member of the family to assume the role as storyteller and tell 'those old scary tales' until the youngsters were often afraid to go to bed at night. In 1976, a resident of Urbana, Illinois, who had grown up in a logging camp in Henderson County, Kentucky, shared the following description of family ghost-telling sessions: 'We lived in this little shack-like house there on the Ohio River when I was a little fellow. It had cracks between the planks in the floor. When my dad would tell them old scary stories of a night, I would sit there, just scared to death. Every now and then, I would look down at the floor, afraid that something would reach up through one of them cracks in the floor and grab me by the leg!

Well, after he had told so many of them old tales, we'd all be scared to death. So me and my brothers would hop up out of our chairs and head for bed. We'd jump into bed, pull the quilts over our heads and stay there that way 'til the next morning. I mean, we was too afraid to get out of bed!'"

Reprinted with permission from the University Press of Kentucky, "Ghosts Across Kentucky," William Lynwood Montell, pages xii-xiii (Lexington: 2000).

RECREATION & TRAVEL
Planetariums & Observatories

The **Arnim D. Hummel Planetarium**, located on the campus of Eastern Kentucky University in Richmond, is open each week for school programs, public programs and special events. Opened in 1988, it contains a Spitz Space Voyager projection system under a 67.5 feet dome. One of the largest and most sophisticated planetariums in the U.S., the Hummel Planetarium has seating for 164 people. Ph. (606) 622-1547, http://www.eku.edu/planetarium/

The **Gheens Science Hall and Rauch Planetarium** in Louisville is designed primarily for astronomy and space science education. The original planetarium, the Rauch Memorial Planetarium, was built in 1962 in honor of Rabbi Joseph Rauch. At the time, it was the first planetarium built in Kentucky. Razed in 1998, it reopened in 2001 as the new Gheens Science Hall and Rauch Planetarium with a 55 foot diameter hemispherical dome. The installation of the Spitz Electric Sky Immersavision technology is only the fourth such installation in the world. Ph. (502) 852-6664, http://www.louisville.edu/planetarium/

The **Weatherford Planetarium** at Berea College in Berea offers students a guided tour through the current sky to discover what's up right now. Using sky mythology, sky imagery and music, students work their way from the North Star to the paths of the planets. Ph: (859) 985-3301, http://physics.berea.edu

The **Hardin Planetarium** at Western Kentucky University in Bowling Green serves university students, the community and the state. Programs at the planetarium are designed to be entertaining and educational. Closed to the public in the summer. Ph. (270) 745-4044 or 3817, www.wku.edu/Dept/Academic/Ogden/Phyast/p4_.htm

The **Golden Pond Planetarium and Observatory**, located in Cadiz at the Land Between the Lakes Visitor's Center, offers a 40-foot dome. Novice astronomers can learn to identify the constellations on a simulated night sky, or visitors can observe the stars through one of four telescopes. Ph. (800) 455-5897 toll-free, http://www.lbl.org/PLGate.html

The **East Kentucky Science Center**, located in Prestonsburg, allows the night sky to capture the imaginations of young and old alike. On a dark

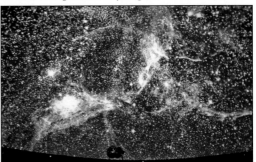

Gheens Science Hall & Rauch Planetarium located on the University of Louisville campus
Source: Kentucky Department of Tourism

moonless night, the sky is so filled with stars it's hard to tell one from another. Ph. (606) 889-0303, www.wedosience.org

The **Morehead State University Space Science Center,** Morehead, has been established to provide a research and educational facility with state-of-the art laboratories for undergraduate students in space science. The center originated from a joint NASA-Morehead State venture to develop a large aperture radiotelescope, satellite tracking station and associated laboratories and degree programs. Ph. (606) 783-2381, www.moreheadstate.edu

The **StarLab Planetarium**, at the Living Arts & Science Center in Lexington has a 16' x 11' dome with a projector that can display the night sky as it looks from anywhere on the Earth at anytime of the night or year. Open on Thursdays and Fridays in the school year on a first-come, first-served basis. Ph. (859) 252-5222 or 255-2284, www.livingartsandscience.org/science_discovery_field_trips.htm

RECREATION & TRAVEL
Hotels & Motels

Amerisuites (800) 833-1516
www.amerisuites.com
Florence, Louisville

Baymont Inn and Suites (800) 301-0200
www.baymontinns.com
Corbin, Shepherdsville

Best Western (800) 937-8376
www.bestwestern.com
Cave City, Elizabethtown, Florence,
Louisville, Morehead, Paris, Russellville,
Somerset, Winchester

Best Western (800) 528-1234
www.bestwestern.com
Frankfort, Harrodsburg, Hopkinsville,
Lexington, London, Louisa, Maysville,
Paducah, Russell

Comfort Inn (800) 221-2222
Bowling Green, Cave City

Comfort Inn (800) 228-5150
www.comfortinn.com
Bardstown, Brooks, Corbin, Danville,
Erlanger, Franklin, Henderson, La Grange,
Lexington, London, Louisville, Morehead,
Oak Grove, Paducah, Somerset, Winchester

Country Hearth Inn (888) 443-2784
www.countryhearth.com/hotels
Danville, Eddyville, Elizabethtown,
Shelbyville

Country Inn and Suites (800) 456-4000
www.countryinns.com
Corbin, Georgetown, Lexington, Louisville,
Paducah, Shepherdsville

Courtyard by Marriott (800) 321-2211
www.marriott.com
Bowling Green, Covington, Erlanger,
Florence, Lexington, Louisville, Paducah

Days Inn (800) 329-7466
www.daysinn.com
Beaver Dam, Berea, Bowling Green,
Carrollton, Cave City, Corbin, Elizabethtown,

Days Inn (cont.) (800) 329-7466
Fort Wright, Frankfort, Franklin,
Georgetown, Glasgow, Grayson, La Grange,
Lexington, London, Louisville, Morehead,
Mount Sterling, Murray, Oak Grove,
Owensboro, Paducah, Paintsville, Richmond,
Shelbyville, Shepherdsville, Springfield,
Williamstown

Days Inn (800) 325-2525
www.daysinn.com
Hazard, Kuttawa, Somerset

Drury Inn (800) 378-7946
www.druryhotels.com
Bowling Green, Louisville, Paducah

Econo Lodge (800) 553-2226
www.econolodge.com
Georgetown, Berea, Bowling Green,
Hopkinsville, Lexington, Richwood

Embassy Suites Hotel (800) 362-2779
Covington, Lexington

Extended Stay America (800) 398-7829
www.extstay.com
Florence, Lexington, Louisville

Fairfield Inn by Marriott (800) 228-2800
www.fairfieldinn.com
Ashland, Bowling Green, Brooks, Corbin,
Frankfort, Georgetown, Hopkinsville,
Lexington, Owensboro

Hampton Inn (800) HAMPTON
www.hamptoninn.com
Florence, Louisville

Hampton Inn (800) 426-7866
www.hamptoninn.com
Ashland, Bardstown, Bowling Green, Brooks,
Carrollton, Corbin, Covington, Danville, Dry
Ridge, Elizabethtown, Frankfort, Franklin,
Georgetown, Hazard, Hebron, Horse Cave,
Kuttawa, Lebanon, Lexington, Louisville,
Owensboro, Paducah, Richmond, Somerset,
Winchester

Hilton Garden Inn (800) 445-8667
Lexington, Louisville

Holiday Inn Express (800) 465-4329
www.holiday-inn.com
Berea, Brooks, Carrollton, Covington,
Danville, Dry Ridge, Elizabethtown, Erlanger,
Fort Mitchell, Frankfort, Harlan, Henderson,
Hopkinsville, La Grange, Lexington, ,
Lexington, London, Louisville, Middlesboro,
Monticello, Morehead, Oak Grove,
Owensboro, Paducah, Richmond, Richwood,
Somerset, Whitley City, Winchester

Hotel Ivy (866) IVY-3171
www.ivyhotels.com
Georgetown, Walton

Howard Johnson (800) 446-4656
Elizabethtown, Florence, Lexington

Hyatt Regency (800) 233-1234
Lexington, Louisville

Knights Inn (800) 843-5644
Berea, Corbin, Lexington, Paducah

LaQuinta Inn (800) 531-5900
www.laquinta.com
Elizabethtown, Lexington, Richmond

Marriott (800) 228-9290
www.marriott.com
Lexington, Louisville

Microtel Inn (888) 771-7171
www.microtelinn.com
Bowling Green, Georgetown, Lexington,
Prestonsburg

Microtel Inns & Suites (800) 771-7171
www.microtelinn.com
Dry Ridge, Louisville

Motel 6 (800) 466-8356
www.motel6.com
Bowling Green, Georgetown, Lexington,
Louisville, Morgantown, Owensboro,
Paducah, Shepherdsville, Elizabethtown

National Heritage Inn & Suites
(877) 256-8600
www.renfrovalleyheritageinn.com
Mount Vernon, Renfro Valley

Quality Inn (800) 228-5151
www.qualityinn.com
Bowling Green, Brooks, Cave City, Corbin,
Louisville, Paducah

Quality Inn & Suites (800) 424-6423
www.choicehotels.com
Elizabethtown, Lexington, Louisville,
Owensboro, Radcliff, Richmond, Russellville

Radisson (800) 333-3333
www.radisson.com
Covington, Lexington, Louisville

Ramada Inn (800) 272-6232
www.ramada.com
Bardstown, Catlettsburg, Elizabethtown,
Fort Wright, Lexington, Lexington, London,
Louisville, Maysville, Morehead, Owensboro

Red Carpet Inn (800) 251-1962
Bardstown, Frankfort, Paducah,
Williamstown

Red Roof Inn (800) 733-7663
www.redroof.com
Bowling Green, Lexington, Louisville,
Richmond

Residence Inn (800) 331-3131
www.residenceinn.com
Erlanger, Lexington, Louisville

Sleep Inn (800) 753-3746
London, Louisville

SpringHill Suites by Marriott (888) 287-9400
www.marriott.com
Lexington, Louisville

Super 8 Motel (800) 800-8000
www.super8.com
Berea, Brandenburg, Campbellsville,
Carrollton, Cave City, Central City,
Corbin, Danville, Dry Ridge, Dry Ridge,
Elizabethtown, Florence, Fort Mitchell,
Georgetown, Hazard, La Grange, London,
Louisa, Louisville, Mayfield, Maysville,
Morehead, Munfordville, Owensboro,
Owingsville, Prestonsburg, Radcliff,
Richmond, Shepherdsville, Somerset,
Whitesburg, Williamsburg

Travelodge (800) 578-7878
www.travelodge.com
Florence, Newport

Sports

J ust as the sun defines the day and the moon puts its signature on the night, it is a sphere that comes to mind when sports in Kentucky is the subject. This particular orb also rises and sets, though rapidly—a dribble, you might say. And few would question its relentless influence on the state's psyche.

Kentucky is, indeed, Planet Basketball. It is the land where glass backboards line the driveways of the well-to-do and rusty hoops are nailed to the sides of barns, where pools of light on late summer nights bathe the baskets in angelic glow as youngsters play

John A. McGill

Photo Sources:
Kentucky Department of Tourism
Lexington Herald-Leader
Sid Webb

another game of pick-up in city parks throughout the state. Say amen.

It's where the Baron of the Bluegrass ruled, where Uncle Ed and the red towel-waving faithful thrived in Bowling Green, where Peck Hickman put the University of Louisville on the map. It's where Joe B. and Denny C. carried on, building their own traditions. It's the place to which Eddie Sutton said he'd crawl, only to eventually limp away under a dark NCAA cloud.

It's where Ricky P. ego tripped all the way from New York to Lexington and later from Boston to Louisville, becoming a Benedict Arnold to many in blue, but the Genius Savior to those in red and black. And it's where a fellow named Tubby established a consistent standard of success while also winning folks over with his admirable character and easygoing ways off the court. It's also where Kentucky Wesleyan, Kentucky State and Georgetown College have made significant contributions to the college basketball landscape, winning national titles in various divisions.

Perhaps most of all, it's where true believers of the bouncing ball reside just this side of Battyville. If the University of Kentucky fails to make it to the Final Four in any given year, for instance, it is wise to keep all sharp objects away from UK followers—who are either mouthing off or in deep mourning over the Shakespearean tragedy of it all. *Et tu, Big Blue?* Still, even though hoops prompt the most hosannas in Kentucky, it is noteworthy to remember that several individuals and teams have had a significant national impact in a number of other sports. A short list would include:

- In horse racing, we find the state's other signature sport, a result n ot only of having the world's most famous horse race in the Kentucky Derby at Churchill Downs in Louisville, but also by having the world's most lucrative horse sales at Keeneland in Lexington – an unrivaled collection of magnificent horse farms that, appropriately enough, take the approximate shape of a horseshoe around the city.
- In golf, Lexington's Gay Brewer winning the 1967 Masters, Louisville's Bobby Nichols winning the 1964 PGA Championship, and Louisville's Frank Beard becoming the PGA's leading money winner and named player of the year in 1969.
- In auto racing, Louisville's Danny Sullivan winning the 1985 Indianapolis 500 and the CART Indy Car national championship in 1988; Owensboro's Darrell Waltrip winning the 1989 Daytona 500 and ranked third on the all-time list for career wins in NASCAR with 84; and brother Michael Waltrip winning the Daytona 500 in 2001 and 2003.
- In swimming, Louisville's Mary T. Meagher Plant winning three gold medals in the 1984 Olympics. In 1981 she set a world record in the 100-meter butterfly at 57.93 seconds—a mark that Sports Illustrated has called "the fifth-greatest, single event record of all time in any sport." SI also ranked Mary T. 17th on the list of the 100 greatest female athletes of all time. She was a 14-year-old eighth grader when she set her first world record, beating the previous 200-meter butterfly mark by one-tenth of a second at the 1979 Pan Am Games.
- In football, for all its history of woe, the University of Kentucky having head coaches go into the record books: Paul "Bear" Bryant, whose greater fame came while winning national championships at Alabama, and Blanton Collier, Bryant's successor at UK who later coached the Cleveland Browns to an NFL title.
- Centre College shocking Harvard 6-0 in football in 1921, a game that the New York Times would later call the biggest upset in sports in the first half of the 20th century.
- In National Association of Intercollegiate Athletics football, Georgetown College setting an NAIA record by appearing in four consecutive national championship games from 1999-2002, winning back-to-back titles in 2000 and 2001 to add to a previous championship in 1991.
- And in baseball, Pee Wee Reese, born in Ekron, and later residing in Louisville, becoming a Hall of Fame shortstop with the Brooklyn Dodgers. Meanwhile, back in 1884, Louisville's "Bud" Hillerich turned a wooden bat for Pete "The Old Gladiator" Browning of the Louisville Eclipse baseball team. They called it the Louisville Slugger. It's kind of caught on since.

What follows, then, is a look at Kentuckians who have excelled in a number of sports at every level. While some of the lists cited here can doubtless have more names added to them, we leave that to the day when an almanac devoted exclusively to sports in Kentucky is created—when more categories can be explored and current ones expanded.

In the meantime, we trust the anecdotes and historical data cited here bring you a measure of the diversity of accomplishment to be found in Kentucky's sports history—worthy accompaniment to the ubiquitous bounce of the basketball that remains at the heart of its identity.

Muhammad Ali's Boxing Record

Total bouts: 61
Knockouts: 37
Won by Decision: 19
Loss by Decision: 4
Knocked Out: 1

ALI'S YEAR-BY-YEAR FIGHT RESULTS

(*** = Heavyweight Title bouts)

Date	Opponent	Site	Result
1960			
29-Oct	Tunney Hunsaker	Louisville	W6
27-Dec	Herb Siler	Miami Beach	KO4
1961			
17-Jan	Anthony Sperti	Miami Beach	KO3
7-Feb	Jim Robinson	Miami Beach	KO1
21-Feb	Donnie Fleeman	Miami Beach	KO7
19-Apr	Lamar Clark	Louisville	KO2
26-Jun	Duke Sabedong	Las Vegas	W10
22-Jul	Alonzo Johnson	Louisville	W10
7-Oct	Alex Miteff	Louisville	KO6
29-Nov	Willie Besmanoff	Louisville	KO7
1962			
10-Feb	Sonny Banks	New York City	KO4
28-Feb	Don Warner	Miami Beach	KO4
23-Apr	George Logan	Los Angeles	KO6
19-May	Billy Daniels	New York City	KO7
20-Jul	Alejandro Lavorante	Los Angeles	KO5
15-Nov	Archie Moore	Los Angeles	KO4
1963			
24-Jan	Charlie Powell	Pittsburgh	KO3
13-Mar	Doug Jones	New York	W10
18-Jun	Henry Cooper	London, England	KO5
1964			
25-Feb	Sonny Liston	Miami Beach	TKO7***
1965			
25-May	Sonny Liston	Lewiston, Maine	KO1***
22-Nov	Floyd Patterson	Las Vegas	KO12***
1966			
29-Mar	George Chuvalo	Toronto, Canada	W15***
21-May	Henry Cooper	London, England	KO6***
6-Aug	Brian London	London, England	KO3***
10-Sep	Karl Mildenberger	Frankfurt, Germany	KO12***
14-Nov	Cleveland Williams	Houston	KO3***
1967			
6-Feb	Ernie Terrell	Houston	W15***
22-Mar	Zora Folley	New York City	KO7***

1970			
26-Oct	Jerry Quarry	Atlanta	KO3
7-Dec	Oscar Bonavena	New York City	KO15
1971			
8-Mar	Joe Frazier	New York City	L15***
26-Jul	Jimmy Ellis	Houston	KO12
17-Nov	Buster Mathis	Houston	W12
26-Dec	Jurgen Blin	Zurich, Switzerland	KO7
1972			
1-Apr	Mac Foster	Tokyo, Japan	W15
1-May	George Chuvalo	Vancouver, Canada	W12
27-Jun	Jerry Quarry	Las Vegas	KO7
19-Jul	Alvin Lewis	Dublin, Ireland	KO11
20-Sep	Floyd Patterson	New York City	KO8
21-Nov	Bob Foster	Stateline, Nevada	KO8
1973			
14-Feb	Joe Bugner	Las Vegas	W12 31-
Mar	Ken Norton	San Diego	L12
10-Sep	Ken Norton	Los Angeles	W12 20-
Oct	Rudy Lubbers	Jakarta, Indonesia	W12
1974			
28-Jan	Joe Frazier	New York City	W12
30-Oct	George Foreman	Kinshasa, Zaire	KO8***
1975			
24-Mar	Chuck Wepner	Cleveland	KO15***
16-May	Ron Lyle	Las Vegas	KO11***
30-Jun	Joe Bugner	Kuala Lampur, Malaysia	W15***
1-Oct	Joe Frazier	Quezon City, Phillipines	KO14***
1976			
20-Feb	Jean-Pierre Coopman	Hato Rey, Puerto Rico	KO5***
30-Apr	Jimmy Young	Landover, Md.	W15***
24-May	Richard Dunn	Munich, Germany	KO5***
28-Sep	Ken Norton	New York City	W15***
1977			
16-May	Alfredo Evangelista	Landover, Md.	W15***
29-Sep	Earnie Shavers	New York City	W15***
1978			
15-Feb	Leon Spinks	Las Vegas	L15***
15-Sep	Leon Spinks	New Orleans	W15***
1980			
2-Oct	Larry Holmes	Las Vegas	KO'd11***
1981			
11-Dec	Trevor Berbick	Nassau, Bahamas	L10

SPORTS

Horse Racing

Ed Bowen

THE INDUSTRY

*As Kentucky cash crops go,
nothing tops the horse.*

The horse is the leading cash crop in Kentucky. Its sales of more than $1 billion exceeds the individual totals from the poultry, tobacco and cattle industries. The economic impact on Kentucky has been placed at more than $4 billion annually. The thoroughbred is the leading breed in the horse industry in terms of economic impact.

The industry is concerned with three major areas: breeding, racing and sales. Here is a closer look at each element.

BREEDING

Kentucky produces more than 25 percent of all thoroughbreds born in North America. The foal crop of 2003 was 8,674 out of a national total of 33,110. There are more than 350 thoroughbred stallions standing in the state and they are bred to more than 20,000 mares. Although fewer than 10 percent of thoroughbred stallions in the nation stand in Kentucky, they account for 35 percent of all breedings—a result of the concentration in the state of the best and therefore most utilized stallions.

Source: Sid Webb

Another indicator of Kentucky's prominence in breeding is found in the concentration of mares that are stabled permanently in the state or are brought into the state to be bred. (Artificial insemination is not allowed in the registration of thoroughbreds, so mares mated with Kentucky stallions have to be physically present.) One of many statistics underscoring Kentucky's leadership among breeding states is the fact that 98 of the 131 Kentucky Derby winners (75 percent) and eight of the 11 Triple Crown winners were foaled (born) in the state.

Kentucky's 450 thoroughbred farms maintain green space covering approximately 1,350,000 acres devoted to breeding and raising horses. The state's horse industry provides 100,000 jobs, directly and indirectly. A vast network of supporting industries includes feed, tack, veterinary services and supplies, fencing, barn building, painting, landscaping, tree trimming, horse van hauling, advertising and publicity, purchasing and selling agent services, printing, signage, sale companies and distribution of news via printed and electronic media. At the race track, trainers, grooms, exercise riders, mutuel clerks, and various other occupations swell the number of those employed because of the thoroughbred industry.

In addition, the equine industry has an $8.8 billion impact on state tourism, accounting for an additional 14,600 jobs. The Kentucky Horse Park in Lexington is devoted solely to the horse. It covers 200 acres and attracts nearly a million visitors annually.

RACING

A total of 7,125 horses participated in 2,649 races in Kentucky in 2004. Total purses amounted to $87,057,315. The majority of purse distribution comes from the "takeout" from the total amounts bet on the races, including on-site wagering and simulcast wagering from other sites around the country. Takeout is set by the state. Specific percentages are earmarked for the purse account, the operation of the track and the state. In addition, another $9 million is offered in purse supplements from the Kentucky Thoroughbred Development Fund. The KTDF was established by state statute in 1978 and receives three-quarters of 1 percent of money wagered at Kentucky tracks and 2 percent of simulcast wagering from elsewhere. The fund provides premiums to owners of Kentucky-breds that win races in the state. As of 2005, approximately $12 million from the 6 percent sales tax on stallion services will be held out of the state's general coffers and will fund an additional program offering additional incentives to be developed by industry and government.

SALES

Two major thoroughbred auction companies are headquartered in Kentucky: Keeneland and Fasig-Tipton Co. Both are located in Lexington.

For many years, Kentucky breeders tended to send their yearlings to market in New York, but during World War II, restrictions on train travel prompted the formation of Breeders' Sales Company, a cooperative that began conducting sales on the grounds of Keeneland's race course. Later, Breeders' Sales was folded into the Keeneland Association and Keeneland's yearling sales became the most fashionable thoroughbred auction in the world.

The success of Keeneland sale graduates around the world bring leading buyers from Europe, Japan, and Dubai as well as from across North America. Sixteen Kentucky Derby winners and five Epsom Derby winners have been sold at Keeneland. The record price for a thoroughbred sold at auction is $13,100,000—paid for Seattle Dancer as a Keeneland yearling in 1985. By contrast, Kentucky Derby and Preakness winner Canonero II brought only $1,200 as a yearling in 1969.

Keeneland currently conducts four separate sales annually—for yearlings, weanlings, 2-year-olds and breeding stock. In 2004, these sales required a total of 32 days and saw 7,609 horses sell for a total of $677,966,400, an average of $89,101.

Fasig-Tipton Co., centered in New York, has conducted auctions throughout North America. It had a presence in Kentucky prior to the emergence of Breeders' Sales, and Fasig-Tipton returned to the state to establish a permanent division in the 1970s. Triple Crown winner Seattle Slew, Kentucky Derby and Belmont winner Bold Forbes and filly Derby winner Genuine Risk quickly established Fasig-Tipton's Lexington sale ring as another prime source of thoroughbreds. In 2004, Fasig-Tipton conducted five separate auctions, during which 1,510 horses were sold for a total of $86,867,700, averaging $57,528.

Regulation & Organizations of the Industry

KENTUCKY HORSE RACING AUTHORITY

Gov. Ernie Fletcher abolished the Kentucky State Racing Commission in 2004 and replaced it with the Kentucky Horse Racing Authority. The new authority has the regulatory roles traditionally in the hands of the old commissions, along with a responsibility to promote the industry. Members of the old commission and the new authority are appointed by the governor. The authority is responsible for the integrity of racing and licenses those involved in the day-to-day jobs of the race track. The testing of horses for illegal medication is an example of its responsibilities. Other states and provinces in North America have similar racing commissions. Thus there is no central government authority controlling the industry nationwide.

THE JOCKEY CLUB

Organized in New York in 1894, The Jockey Club originally had a regulatory position in several states, and its rules of racing were widely recognized. Over the years, however, state racing commissions were assigned the responsibility of racing oversight in their individual purviews.

The Jockey Club remains an important organization, however, in another way. In the late 19th Century, the club acquired the rights to the fledgling American Stud Book, a breed registry. Ever since, the club has fulfilled the role of registering North American thoroughbreds and ensuring the integrity of the Stud Book. All states and provinces in North

Source: Sid Webb

America recognize The Jockey Club as the sole source of registration in order for a thoroughbred to be permitted to participate in a pari-mutuel race.

The Jockey Club maintains offices in New York City and Lexington. The Jockey Club family of companies now includes The Jockey Club Information Systems, which provides some 27,000 catalogue pages for thoroughbred auctions throughout North America; Equineline, which provides racing and breeding information to more than 15,000 customers from 60 countries; Equibase, the official database of the racing industry, which is a partnership with the Thoroughbred Racing Association and collects, produces and stores statistics on all races at North American tracks; InCompass, which provides computerized accounting/management systems to race tracks; and The Jockey Club Technology Services, which provides technical support for all the other companies.

NATIONAL THOROUGHBRED ASSOCIATION/ BREEDERS' CUP LIMITED, LEXINGTON

The first running of the Breeders' Cup, the "Super Bowl" of thoroughbred racing, was held in 1984. The series first involved seven races and now has eight—each with a purse of $1 million or more. The Breeders' Cup, held near the end of the year, has a large bearing on which horses are named champions of their various age/gender divisions. The Breeders' Cup, whose officers live in Lexington, is joined organizationally with the National Thoroughbred Association, which undertakes many of the industry's promotional roles, including television and lobbying efforts in Washington, D. C.

GRAYSON-JOCKEY CLUB RESEARCH FOUNDATION, LEXINGTON

An affiliate of The Jockey Club, the foundation has financial headquarters in New York and staff offices in Kentucky. The foundation's membership is open to all who care for horses, and its sole role is to raise funds to support veterinary research—specifically to promote the health and soundness of the horse.

In 2004, the foundation supplied $825,000 to university researchers throughout North America and in England for 20 specific projects addressing diseases and injuries, including state of the art techniques such as DNA vaccination, gene therapy and adult stem cell treatment. Over the last 25 years, the Grayson-Jockey Club has provided more than $12 million to conduct more than 200 projects at 32 institutions. Among the key institutions receiving funds is the Maxwell Gluck Equine Research Center at the University of Kentucky, which was founded by a joint funding effort involving the estate of breeder/owner Gluck, the Commonwealth of Kentucky and the thoroughbred industry.

THOROUGHBRED OWNERS AND BREEDERS ASSOCIATION, LEXINGTON

TOBA was formed in 1961 and is a national trade organization of leading thoroughbred horse breeders and owners. It has approximately 3,000 members and seven employees. TOBA's mission is to "improve the economics, integrity and pleasure of the sport on behalf of thoroughbred owners and breeders." Projects managed by TOBA include the American Graded Stakes Committee, The Greatest Game LLC, Sales Integrity Program, and Claiming Crown. TOBA is also represented on the board of directors of the National Thoroughbred Racing Association as a founding member and on the American Horse Council. TOBA is the owner of The Blood-Horse magazine.

AMERICAN ASSOCIATION OF EQUINE PRACTITIONERS, LEXINGTON

Founded by a small group of equine specialists in 1954 during a meeting in Louisville, the American Association of Equine Practitioners has grown into an international organization of more than 8,500 members. Offices are located in Lexington. Kentucky resident membership totaled 284 in 2005. Despite the rural nature of the state, this number ranks Kentucky within the top five states in AAEP membership, illustrating the concentration of expertise in the commonwealth. The AAEP holds an annual meeting in different American cities, presenting papers on state of the art aspects of veterinary care for horses, as well as sponsoring continuing education seminars for members.

KENTUCKY THOROUGHBRED ASSOCIATION AND KENTUCKY THOROUGHBRED OWNERS AND BREEDERS, LEXINGTON

A conjoined organization of some 1,000 members, the KTA-KTOB supports and promotes the industry through various programs and lobbying efforts in the state capital of Frankfort. The KTA also is responsible of administering the Kentucky Thoroughbred Development Fund. One of the KTA's most important functions is its role, in conjunction with the Kentucky Horsemen's Benevolent and Protective Association, in representing horsemen (owners) in negotiating purse contracts with two of the state's tracks, Keeneland and Churchill Downs.

THE KENTUCKY HORSEMEN'S BENEVOLENT AND PROTECTIVE ASSOCIATION, LOUISVILLE

With 6,000 members, the KHBPA focuses on representing horsemen (owners) in negotiating purse contracts with the state's race tracks. (In the cases of Keeneland and Churchill Downs, the KHBPA shares this function with the KTA.) The KHBPA, like sister organizations in other states and the national umbrella HBPA organization, provides various benevolent services to members of the thoroughbred racing community.

Ed Bowen

Horse Racing
Thoroughbreds

HISTORY

The thoroughbred horse was developed in England and the first horse regarded as a thoroughbred to come to the Colonies was Bulle Rock, imported to Virginia in 1730. In Kentucky, racing originally was conducted through the streets. As early as 1791, three-day meetings were held over what was known as the Lexington Course, and during that decade race meetings were also held in Georgetown, Danville, Versailles, Bardstown and Shelbyville.

Henry Clay was among the original members of the first Kentucky Jockey Club, which was established in 1979 in a meeting at John Postlethwait's

Tavern in Lexington. This organization conducted race meetings in Maysville, Winchester, Paris, Versailles, Flemingsburg, Harrodsburg and Richmond, in addition to Lexington.

(In those days, the phrase Jockey Club described an organization of men involved in the sport rather than a group of jockeys, as the word is used today. England's Jockey Club had been established several decades earlier, and the phrase was adopted by many organizations, including both ruling bodies and companies owning racetracks.)

Kentucky racing was originally a sport of short dashes, more like quarter horse racing than the thoroughbred racing of today. The rising popular-

Source: Sid Webb

ity of four-mile heat races gave rise to the need for improved and more established stock. The first thoroughbred stallion known to have been brought to Kentucky was Benjamin Wharton's Blaze, which was advertised at stud in Georgetown in 1797.

During the 19th century, racing was conducted in several locations, including Louisville's handsome Woodlawn Course. In 1832, the Kentucky Association track in Lexington was renovated and became the second track "stripped" of grass, as the Union Course in New York had been a decade earlier. The

hills and flowing creeks in Central Kentucky.

Bluegrass, which gives its name to the area (officially *poa pratensis*) was not native to the region, but was used as lush pasture grass as the area was cleared.

Another element that made Kentucky inviting was the fact that the area was less ravaged during the Civil War than was the horse country of Tennessee, which had been another burgeoning center of successful racehorse breeding.

The concentration of breeding in Central Kentucky in the aftermath of the Civil War gave rise to an increased degree of professionalism among horsemen in the area, which further strengthened the Bluegrass region's status. The state became a supplier not only for local horsemen but for non-resident owners—as it is to this day.

A. J. Alexander (see "Noted Kentucky Breeders") raised his horses in Kentucky at Woodburn Stud and was among the first to be a commercial breeder, producing horses specifically for the market rather than racing them himself.

Man O'War (Kentucky Horse Park)
Source: Sid Webb

Kentucky Association had been formed in 1828.

Racing on dirt ovals became common and was instrumental in determining the shape of racing in this country. While English racing continued to be conducted in short three- or four-day meetings, the use of dirt surfaces rather than more delicate grass made possible the extended race meetings that still prevail in the United States.

Long race meetings also meant that stables were provided at various racetracks, whereas in England horses were trained in private yards and had to be transported to the racecourse for each start.

The breeding of thoroughbreds was established in the Upper Atlantic and Tidewater regions and spread south and west. The Bluegrass became the leading area for thoroughbred breeding, one key reason being the mineral-providing Ordovician limestone that is the undergirding of the rolling

Many Kentucky horses were sent as yearlings to where the buyers were. For example, the great Domino was bred in Kentucky by Maj. Barak Thomas and sent to be sold at the Tattersall's annual auction in New York City, where he was purchased by Wall Street tycoon James R. Keene for $3,000 in 1892.

At the same time, out-of-state sportsmen also supported the development of Kentucky breeding by purchasing farms in the Commonwealth. Keene established Castleton Stud (see "Historic Farms"), and such other major New York industrialists as August Belmont I, August Belmont II, members of the Whitney family and Walter Salmon—along with Pennsylvanians Samuel D. Riddle and Joseph E. Widener—bought or leased farms in Kentucky.

Chicago tycoons William Monroe Wright and John D. Hertz also purchased farms—Calumet and Stoner Creek, respectively. More recently, the list includes Texan Nelson Bunker Hunt, South African minerals tycoon Graham Beck, Gulfstream Jet founder Allen Paulson, Khaled Abdullah of Saudi Arabia, and the Maktoums, the ruling family of Dubai. All of them have purchased Kentucky farms

Kentucky Gov. Brereton C. Jones and Mrs. Jones, a descendant of the Alexanders.

Runnymede Farm: Established near Paris by Col. Ezekiel Clay Runnymede following the Civil War, the farm was owned by Col. Clay and his brother-in-law, Col. Catesby Woodford. They bred several major Kentucky racehorses and breeding animals. The best included Ben Brush, winner of the 1896

Source: Sid Webb

and hired professional managers to run them.

Other major businessmen prefer to breed in Kentucky by sending their mares to be boarded on the professional, commercial farms. They have included William Woodward Sr., Marshall Field, Charles Engelhard, Mrs. Henry Carnegie Phipps and her son and grandson, Ogden and Ogden Mills Phipps.

All of these patterns continue into the present, although the number of Kentucky-raised horses sent to be sold outside the state is far fewer than those that are auctioned at the sales held in Lexington by both Keeneland and Fasig-Tipton.

SOME HISTORIC KENTUCKY FARMS

Woodburn Stud (see A. J. Alexander): Now called Airdrie Stud, the old property is owned by former

Kentucky Derby and many other races. Ben Brush later became the sire of leading stallions Broomstick and Sweep.

Another Runnymede-bred was Hanover, a champion of the 1880s which returned to Kentucky and was the nation's leading sire four times. Clay and Woodford were not the official breeders of record of Miss Woodford, but they raised her, the first Thoroughbred to earn $100,000. The farm has remained in the family and today is run by Catesby Woodford Clay, a grandson of Ezekiel Clay. Recent horses bred by Runnymede include the 2005 Illinois Derby winner, Greeley's Galaxy.

Hamburg Place (see John E. Madden)

Castleton Stud: Established by James R. Keene

in 1893. Keene, a Wall Street tycoon, became a dominant breeder and owner although he was said to visit the farm only rarely. He entrusted its care to his brother-in-law, Maj. Foxhall Daingerfield. Keene bred 13 champion horses in addition to buying and racing the great horse Domino. Commando, a champion son of Domino, sired Colin, which was an unbeaten in 15 races. Sysonby, another Keene champion, was so revered that after his death in 1906, it was estimated that a crowd of 4,000 attended his funeral. He was later exhumed and his skeleton placed in the American Museum of Natural History in New York City.

Idle Hour Stock Farm/Darby Dan Farm: Established by Col. E. R. Bradley (see above), Idle Hour was home to major stallions such as Black Toney, Blue Larkspur, and North Star III during the 1920s and 1930s. Col. Bradley also imported the foundation French-bred mare La Troienne. Col. Bradley won the Kentucky Derby four times. He died in

teaugay (1963) and Proud Clarion (1967), Preakness/Belmont Stakes winner Little Current (1974) and English Derby winner Roberto (1972). Darby Dan is now operated by a daughter and grandson of Galbreath, Mrs. Jody Phillips and her son, John Phillips.

Calumet Farm: The Lexington property purchased in 1924 by William Monroe Wright of Chicago was renamed Calumet Farm for the baking powder company that Wright owned. He turned it into a successful standardbred farm. After his death in 1931, his son, Warren Wright Sr., converted the operation to thoroughbreds.

Throughout the rest of Warren Wright's life (which ended in 1950) and continuing with his widow (later Mrs. Gene Markey), Calumet dominated American racing as no other farm has ever done. From 1941-1958, Calumet bred and raced a record seven Kentucky Derby winners: Whirlaway (1941), Pensive (1944), Citation (1948), Ponder

Source: Esther Webb

1946 and the core of the farm later was acquired by John W. Galbreath and renamed Darby Dan Farm. Galbreath, a real estate developer and builder from Columbus, Ohio, imported European champions Ribot and Sea-Bird II to stand at stud there, as well as acquiring the champion Swaps and other top-level stallions. Under Galbreath's direction, Darby Dan bred and raised Kentucky Derby winners Cha-

(1949), Hill Gail (1952), Iron Liege (1957), and Tim Tam (1958). A large measure of that success could be attributed to Calumet's famed trainers, Ben and Jimmy Jones.

Whirlaway and Citation were also Triple Crown winners. Calumet was the nation's leading breeder 14 times and the leading owner 12 times between 1941 and 1961. Wright and Mrs. Wright/Markey bred 17 champions, including Horse of the Year designees Whirlaway, Twilight Tear, Armed, Citation and Coaltown. In 1968, Mrs. Wright's Forward Pass became Calumet's eighth homebred Derby winner, but the farm's fortunes declined after that.

It was not until the late 1970s—when Alydar, Our Mims, Davona Dale and other outstanding runners emerged—that Calumet regained a measure of its former prestige. After Mrs. Markey's death in 1982, the farm was managed by a relative, J. T. Lundy, until it was sold due to insolvency in 1992. During that time, Calumet added another Derby winner, Strike the Gold (1991), as breeder, bringing the total to nine, and also bred and raced another Horse of the Year, Criminal Type (1990). The farm was sold at auction for $17 million to Henryk de Kwiatkowski. It has been run by his widow and children ever since his death in 2003.

Faraway Farm: Located outside Lexington, Faraway enjoyed it greatest fame as the home of Man o' War as a stallion. Man o' War stood most of his stud career (1920-47) at the farm and was an enormous attraction to tourists from around the world. Will Harbut, his groom, became famous for his eloquent spiel about what he called the "mostest hoss that ever was."

Faraway was owned for many years by Man o' War's owner, the eastern sportsman Samuel R. Riddle, along with Mr. and Mrs. Walter M. Jeffords Sr. (Mrs. Jeffords was Mrs. Riddle's niece.) Today, the barn where Man o' War stood has been renovated and that portion of the old Faraway is now part of Greg Goodman's Mt. Brilliant Farm.

Claiborne Farm: (See Arthur Hancock Sr. et al)
Spendthrift Farm: (See Leslie Combs II)
The Whitney Studs: Harry Payne Whitney followed his father, W. C. Whitney, into racing. He leased a farm in New Jersey as he was establishing a leading stable in the East. Whitney then purchased property in Lexington. He bred champions Equipoise, Top Flight and others among a record (for the time) 191 stakes winners. After his death in 1930, his son, C. V. Whitney, took over the stable and farm. He had a similar and lengthy career as a leading breeder and owner.

Whitney's Fisherman was the first American

Source: Sid Webb

horse to win the Washington, D. C., International, a pioneering international race run in Maryland. Adjacent to the Harry Payne Whitney and C. V. Whitney property was Greentree Stud, established by Harry Payne Whitney's sister-in-law, Mrs. Helen Hay Whitney.

Mrs. Whitney won the Kentucky Derby with

Twenty Grand in 1931 and Shut Out in 1942. After her death in 1944, Greentree passed to her children, New York *Herald-Tribune* publisher John Hay (Jock) Whitney and Mrs. Charles S. Payson. The farm's success continued under their management. Greentree bred the champion Capot and purchased and raced the 1953 Horse of the Year, Tom Fool, who later became an important sire.

C. V. Whitney's widow, Marylou Whitney, resumed the breeding and racing operation after his death and won the 2004 Belmont Stakes with homebred Birdtown. Part of the old Whitney complex is now known as Payson Stud and is operated by Mrs. Virginia Kraft Payson, who had married Charles S. Payson after his first wife's death. Most of the Whitney property was sold in various parcels to Gainesway Farm, first owned by founder John R. Gaines and later purchased by Graham Beck.

The Maktoum Studs: Beginning in the early 1980s, the ruling family of Dubai became a major presence in sales, racing and breeding, both in this country and abroad. Sheikhs Maktoum al Maktoum, Mohammed al Maktoum and Hamdan al Maktoum established elaborate, highly professional and successful farms in Kentucky: Gainsborough, Shadwell and Darley at Jonabell.

The *Blood-Horse* magazine estimated in 2005 that the family had invested about $7 billion in horses, farms, a racetrack in Dubai, veterinary centers and racing-related items. The family has been so active in the yearling market that in 1989 and 1990, the Maktoums accounted for more than 40 percent of gross sales at the Keeneland summer sale.

Sheikh Mohammed alone has purchased more than $650 million worth of horses at public auction. The best go into the various breeding operations owned by the family in Kentucky and elsewhere. Among the champions bred in Kentucky by the Maktoums and exported to race abroad were Epsom Derby winners

Source: Sid Webb

Erhaab, Nashwan and Lammtarra.

Juddmonte Farm: Just as the Maktoums did, Prince Khaled Abdullah of Saudi Arabia established a superb Kentucky farm as one of his bases for an international breeding operation. In addition to its many major victories in Europe, Juddmonte also has raced a strong division in this country. Its more than 100 grade/group 1 winners, including Empire Maker, the Belmont Stakes winner of 2003.

Lane's End Farm: (See William S. Farish)

Overbrook Farm: (See W. T. Young)

Well, what about that...?

Although the world may remember Henry Clay as a significant and effective politicians and statesmen, few realize he was equally a progressive stockman. Clay had a keen eye for fine horses, in particular Thoroughbreds, and was one of the leaders in establishing the Bluegrass region of Kentucky as the nation's premier Thoroughbred breeding center. Successful in his own time, the blood of his two foundation mares and his foundation stallion pulsed through the veins of not less than 11 Kentucky Derby winners, three of which were foaled on his farm.

Source: Kentucky Horse Park

Famous Kentucky-bred Horses
Ed Bowen

*Kentucky-breds have a rich
and famous history*

Here are thumbnail portraits of famous horses bred (born) in Kentucky. Names in parentheses indicate the sire (father), dam (mother), and maternal grandsire.

ALYDAR, foaled 1975 (Raise a Native-Sweet Tooth, by On-and-On) Bred and raced by Calumet Farm. Raced 1977-79. Won 14 of 26 races, earned $957,195.

ALYSHEBA, foaled 1984 (Alydar-Bel Sheba, by Lt. Stevens) Bred by Preston Madden, raced by Dorothy and Pam Scharbauer. Raced 1986-88. Won 11 of 26 races, earned $6,679,242.

A.P. INDY, foaled 1989 (Seattle Slew-Weekend Surprise, by Secretariat) Bred by William S. Farish & Partners, raced by Tomonori Tsurumaki. Raced 1991-92. Won 8 of 11 races, earned $2,979,815.

AZERI, foaled 1998 (Jade Hunter-Zodiac Miss, by Ahonoora) Bred by Allen Paulson, raced by Paulson's Living Trust. Raced 2001-2004. Won 17 of 24 races, earned $4,079,820. Azeri was the champion older female for three consecutive years (2002-04) and was also overall Horse of the Year in 2002. During that first championship season, she won eight of nine races, culminating with a dominant performance in the Breeders' Cup Distaff. Her many other major triumphs included three consecutive victories in the Apple Blossom Handicap at Oaklawn Park in Arkansas. She is the all time leading earning female in North American racing.

BOLD RULER, foaled 1954 (Nasrullah-Miss Disco, by Discovery) Bred and raced by Mrs. Henry Carnegie Phipps (Wheatley Stable). Raced 1956-58. Won 23 of 33 races, earned $764,204. Eight time leading sire.

BROOMSTICK, foaled 1901 (Ben Brush-Elf, by Galliard) Bred by Col. Milton Young, raced by Capt. Samuel S. Brown. Raced 1903-1905. Won 14 of 39 races, earned $74,730. Leading sire.

BUCKPASSER, foaled 1963 (Tom Fool-Busanda, by War Admiral) Bred and raced by Ogden Phipps. Raced 1965-67. Won 25 of 31 races, earned $1,462,014.

BULL LEA, foaled 1935 (Bull Dog-Rose Leaves, by Ballot) Bred by Coldstream Stud, raced by Calumet Farm. Raced 1937-39. Won 10 of 27 races, earned $94,825. Leading sire.

CITATION, foaled 1945 (Bull Lea-Hydroplane II, by Hyperion) Bred and raced by Calumet Farm. Raced 1947-1951. Won 32 of 45 races, earned $1,085,760. Triple Crown winner.

COLIN, foaled 1905 (Commando-Pastorella, by Springfield) Bred and raced by James R. Keene. Raced 1907-08. Won 15 of 15 races, earned 178,110.

COUNT FLEET, foaled 1940 (Reigh Count-Quickly, by Haste) Bred and raced by Mrs. John D. Hertz. Raced 1943-44. Won 16 of 21 races, earned $250,300.

DAMASCUS, foaled 1964 (Sword Dancer-Kerala, by My Babu) Bred and raced by Mrs. Edith W. Bancroft. Raced 1966-68. Won 21 of 32 races, earned $1,176,781.

Calumet Farm
Source: Sid Webb

DANZIG, foaled 1977 (Northern Dancer-Pas de Nom, by Admiral's Voyage). Bred by Derry Meeting Farm and William S. Farish, raced by Henry de Kwiatkowski. Raced in 1980. Won 3 of 3 races, earned $32,400. Leading sire.

DISCOVERY, foaled 1931 (Display-Ariadne, by Light Brigade). Bred by Walter Salmon's Mereworth Farm, raced by Alfred G. Vanderbilt. Raced 1933-36. Won 27 of 63 races, earned $195,287.

DOMINO, foaled 1891 (Himyar-Mannie Gray, by Enquirer) Bred by Maj. Barak Thomas, raced by James R. Keene and Foxhall Keene. Raced 1893-95. Won 19 of 25 races, earned $193,500.

EASY GOER, foaled 1986 (Alydar-Relaxing, by Buckpasser) Bred and raced by Ogden Phipps. Raced 1988-90. Won 14 of 20 races, earned $4,873,770.

EQUIPOISE, foaled 1928 (Pennant-Swinging, by Broomstick) Bred by Harry Payne Whitney, raced by C. V. Whitney. Raced 1930-35. Won 29 of 51 races, earned $338,610.

EXTERMINATOR, foaled 1915 (McGee-Fair Empress, by Jim Gore) Bred by F. D. (Dixie) Knight, raced primarily by Willis Sharpe Kilmer. Raced 1917-1924, won 50 of 100 races, earned $252,996.

FAIR PLAY, foaled 1905 (Hastings-Fairy Gold, by Bend Or) Bred and raced by August Belmont II. Raced 1907-1909. Won 10 of 32 races, earned $86,950. Sire of Man o' War.

FOREGO, foaled 1970 (Forli-Lady Golconda, by Hasty Road) Bred and raced by Lazy F. Ranch. Raced 1973-78. Won 34 of 57 races, earned $1,938,957.

GALLANT FOX, foaled 1927 (Sir Gallahad III-Marguerite, by Celt) Bred and raced by William Woodward Sr.'s Belair Stud. Raced 1929-30. Won 11 of 17 races, earned $328,165. Triple Crown winner.

HAIL TO REASON, foaled 1958 (Turn-to-Nothirdchance, by Blue Swords) Bred by Bieber-Jacobs Stable, raced by Patrice Jacobs. Raced in 1960. Won 9 of 18 races, earned $328,434.

HANOVER, foaled 1884 (Hindoo-Bourbon Belle, by Bonnie Scotland) Bred by Catesby Woodford and Ezekiel F. Clay, raced by Mike and Phil Dwyer. Raced 1886-87. Won 32 of 50 races, earned $118,887.

HINDOO, foaled 1878 (Virgil-Florence, by Lexington) Bred by Daniel Swigert, raced by Mike and Phil Dwyer. Raced 1880-82. Won 30 of 35 races, earned $71,875.

JOHN HENRY, foaled 1975 (Ole Bob Bowers-Once Double, by Double Jay) Bred by Robert Lehman, raced by Sam Rubin. Raced 1977-84. Won 39 of 83 races, earned $6,597,947.

KELSO, foaled 1957 (Your Host-Maid of Flight, by Count Fleet) Bred and raced by Mrs. Richard C. du Pont Jr. Raced 1959-66. Won 39 of 63 races, earned $1,977,896. Five-time Horse of the Year.

LEXINGTON, foaled 1850 (Boston-Alice Carneal, by Sarpedon) Bred by Dr. Elisha Warfield, raced by Richard Ten Broeck. Raced 1852-55. Won 6 of 7 races, earned $56,600. Sixteen-time leading sire.

MAN O' WAR, foaled 1917 (Fair Play-Mahubah, by Rock Sand) Bred by August Belmont II, raced by Samuel D. Riddle. Raced 1919-20. Won 20 of 21 races, earned $249,465.

MISS WOODFORD, foaled 1882 (Billet-Fancy Jane, by Neil Robinson) Bred by George Bowen, raced primarily by Mike and Phil Dwyer. Raced

John Henry
Source: Ky. Department of Tourism

1882-86. Won 37 of 48 races, earned $118,270. Miss Woodford was the first American race horse of either gender to earn as much as $100,000.

MR. PROSPECTOR, foaled 1970 (Raise a Native-Gold Digger, by Nashua) Bred by Spenthrift Farm, raced by A. I. Savin. Raced 1973-74. Won 7 of 14 races, earned $121,171. Leading sire.

NASHUA, foaled 1952 (Nasrullah-Segula, by Johnstown) Bred by William Woodward Sr. Raced by William Woodward Jr. and Leslie Combs II. Raced 1952-56. Won 22 of 30 races, earned $1,288,565.

NATIVE DANCER, foaled 1952 (Polynesian-Geisha, by Discovery) Bred and raced by Alfred G. Vanderbilt. Raced 1952-53. Won 21 of 22 races, earned $785,240. First Thoroughbred TV hero.

OMAHA, foaled 1932 (Gallant Fox-Flambino, by Wrack) Bred and raced by William Woodward Sr.'s Belair Stud. Raced 1934-36. Won nine of 22 races, earned $154,755. Triple Crown winner.

PERSONAL ENSIGN, foaled 1984 (Private Terms-Grecian Banner, by Hoist the Flag). Bred and raced by Ogden Phipps. Raced 1986-88. Won 13 of 13 races, earned $1,679,880.

ROUND TABLE, foaled 1954 (Princequillo-Knight's Daughter, by Sir Cosmo) Bred by Claiborne Farm, raced by Travis M. Kerr. Raced 1956-59. Won 43 of 66 races, earned $1,749,869.

RUFFIAN, 1972 (Reviewer-Shenanigans, Native Dancer) Bred and raced by Mr. and Mrs. Stuart Janney Jr. Raced 1974-75. Won 10 of 11 races, earned $313,429.

SEABISCUIT, foaled 1933 (Hard Tack-Swing On, by Whisk Broom) Bred by Mrs. Henry Carnegie Phipps, raced primarily by Charles S. Howard. Raced 1935-40. Won 33 of 89 races, earned $437,730.

SEATTLE SLEW, foaled 1974 (Boldnesian-My Charmer, by Poker) Bred by Ben Castleman, raced by Jim and Sally Hill and Karen and Mickey Taylor. Raced 1976-78. Won 14 of 17 races, earned $1,208,726. Triple Crown winner.

SIR BARTON, foaled 1916 (Star Shoot-Lady Sterling, by Hanover) Bred by John E. Madden and Vivian Gooch, raced by Comdr. J. K. L. Ross. Raced 1918-20. Won 13 of 31 races, earned $116,857. First

Triple Crown winner.

SPECTACULAR BID, foaled 1976 (Bold Bidder-Spectacular, by Promised Land) Bred by Mrs. William Jason and Mrs. William Gilmore, raced by Harry Meyerhoff and family. Raced 1978-80. Won 26 of 30 races, earned $2,781,608.

SUNDAY SILENCE, foaled 1986 (Halo-Wishing Well, by Understanding) Bred by Oak Cliff Thoroughbreds, raced by Arthur Hancock III and partners. Raced 1988-90. Won 9 of 14 races, earned $4,968,554.

SYSONBY, foaled 1902 (Melton-Optime, by Orme) Bred and raced by James R. Keene. Raced 1904-05. Won 14 of 15 races, earned $184,438.

TOM FOOL, foaled 1949 (Menow-Gaga, by Bull Dog). Bred by Duval Headley, raced by Greentree Stable. Raced 1951-53. Won 21 of 30 races, earned $570,165.

TWILIGHT TEAR, foaled 1941 (Bull Lea-Lady Lark, by Blue Larkspur) Bred and raced by Calumet Farm. Raced 1943-45. Won 18 of 24 races, earned $202,165.

WAR ADMIRAL, foaled 1934 (Man o' War-Brushup, by Sweep) Bred and raced by Samuel D. Riddle. Raced 1936-39. Won 21 of 26 races, earned $273,240. Triple Crown winner.

WHIRLAWAY, foaled 1938 (Blenheim II-Dustwhirl, by Sweep) Bred and raced by Calumet Farm. Raced 1940-43. Won 32 of 60 races, earned $561,161. Triple Crown winner.

Renowned Breeders
Ed Bowen

R. A. ALEXANDER (1819-1867)—With an inheritance from an uncle in Scotland, Alexander established Woodburn Stud in Woodford County (now known as Airdrie Stud and still an operating thoroughbred farm). Alexander helped shape the thoroughbred industry along modern lines with professional management and annual auctions of his yearlings.

COL. E. R. BRADLEY (1859-1946)—Legend places Col. Bradley as a steel worker in his native Pittsburgh, then a cowboy, prospector and miner. But when he testified in Congress he described himself as a gambler. Bradley developed gambling halls in various cities, most fashionably in Palm Beach, Fla. He also took a great interest in thoroughbred breeding and racing and won four runnings of the Kentucky Derby with Behave Yourself (1921), Bubbling Over (1926), Burgoo King (1932) and Broker's Tip (1933).

HENRY CLAY (1777-1852)—Known in world affairs for the Treaty of Ghent and for his four attempts to be elected president, Henry Clay was also an avid agriculturalist. Among animals raised at his home, Ashland, in Lexington, were thoroughbreds. Some of his stock became ancestors to important horses still found in the thoroughbred gene pool. A total of 11 Kentucky Derby winners trace to Clay's mares Magnolia and Margaret Wood.

LESLIE COMBS II (1901-1990) — Combs took the concept of syndication of stallions to a new level and launched an era in which ownership of virtually all highly commercial stallions was divided into 32 to 40 shares. The most noteworthy of these transactions included his syndication of Nashua, the 1955 Horse of the Year, for $1,252,100, making him the first horse sold for as much as $1 million.

WILLIAM S. FARISH (1939-)—William S. Farish was born in Texas, where his family had launched Humble Oil, but he moved to Kentucky and established Lane's End Farm in Versailles as one of the world's leading thoroughbred operations. In partnerships, he has bred and sold winners of each of the Triple Crown races: Kentucky Derby winner Charismatic, Preakness winner Summer Squall and Belmont Stakes winners A.P. Indy and Lemon Drop Kid.

JOHN R. GAINES (1928-2005)—John R. Gaines established two versions of Gainesway Farm in Lexington and created a highly successful commercial breeding and selling operation. He was instrumental in establishing the Breeders' Cup, the Kentucky State Horse Park and the National Thoroughbred Racing Association.

JAMES BEN ALI HAGGIN (1821-1914)—A grandson of a Turkish Army officer, Haggin was born in Kentucky but roamed the West and South America, mining gold, copper and silver. He raised horses on the 44,000-acre tract he acquired in California and then came back to Kentucky, where he acquired Elmendorf Farm and increased it to some 9,000 acres. Part of the property still carries the name Elmendorf, while other parcels became separate — and important — breeding farms, including Spendthrift, Gainesway, Greentree, Normandy, Payson Stud and C. V. Whitney Farms.

ARTHUR B. HANCOCK SR. (1875-1957)—Hancock expanded his family's Virginia breeding operation into Kentucky with the establishment of Claiborne Farm near Paris on land inherited by his wife. Claiborne became one of the world's renowned farms both in breeding its own horses and in standing stallions and boarding mares and raising foals for many prestigious clients. During Hancock's lifetime, Claiborne's important sire acquisitions included Celt, Wrack, Sir Gallahad III, Double Jay, Princequillo and Blenheim II. Sir Gallahad was purchased in France in partnership with key Claiborne client William Woodward Sr., Marshall Field and R. A. Fairbairn.

ARTHUR B. HANCOCK JR. (1910-1972)—Claiborne Farm's status in the thoroughbred world was maintained and perhaps enhanced by Arthur B. (Bull) Hancock Jr., who ran it from 1947 when his father became ill until his own death in 1972. Bull Hancock continued the pattern of acquisition of top stallions, including five-time leading sire Nasrullah and English Triple Crown winner Nijinsky II.

SETH W. HANCOCK (1949-)—He was only 23 when his father passed away, and he soon found himself running Claiborne far earlier than he had anticipated. Hancock proved himself early on by syndicating Secretariat for more than $6 million, a record at the time. The great horse came to stand at Claiborne after winning the Triple Crown in 1973. Hancock has continued the tradition of his father and grandfather, both as a breeder and in acquiring stallions and raising horses for clients. During his tenure, Claiborne was the leading breeder in 1984 when homebred Swale won the Kentucky Derby and Belmont Stakes.

HAL PRICE HEADLEY (1888-1962)—An exemplar of the versatile agriculturist and businessman, Kentucky native Headley was the breeder and owner of champion filly and producer Alcibiades and importer of English-bred stallion Pharamond II. The latter sired Headley's champion, Menow. Headley was the prime inspiration and initial leader in creation of Keeneland Race Course, which returned racing to Lexington in 1936 after the old Kentucky Association track had closed.

WARNER L. JONES JR. (1916-1994)—Warner Jones Jr. was involved in virtually every aspect of racing and breeding. He was on the board of Churchill Downs for more than 50 years and was chairman for a dozen years. At the same time, he ran a commercial operation at his Hermitage Farm in Louisville, where he bred 1953 Kentucky Derby winner Dark Star and more than 130 other stakes winners. Jones also stood leading sire Raja Baba and he twice consigned world-record priced yearlings to the Keeneland summer sale in vastly different eras.

JOHN E. MADDEN (1856-1929)—Born in Pennsylvania, Madden moved to Lexington and established Hamburg Place, part of which is still a farm owned by grandson Preston Madden. The other part has become a major shopping development carrying the same name. Madden converted from a successful career with standardbreds and became a leading thoroughbred breeder, owner and seller. He also was a trainer and adviser to some of the most successful owners in the East. Madden was the nation's leading breeder in races won annually from 1917-1927 and the leader in earnings from 1917-1923. He bred five Kentucky Derby winners — Old Rosebud (1914), Sir Barton (1919), Paul Jones (1920), Zev (1923) and Flying Ebony (1925). Sir Barton became the first Triple Crown winner. Years later, grandson Preston Madden added to that legacy by breeding the 1987 Derby winner, Alysheba.

H. P. McGRATH (1814-1881)—Born near Lexington but lured to the life of gambling clubs in New Orleans and the East, McGrath returned to his roots to establish McGrathiana as a thoroughbred farm. He bred and raced Aristides, which in 1875 won the first Kentucky Derby.

DANIEL SWIGERT (1833-1912)—Once the manager of Woodburn, Daniel Swigert acquired his own farms—first Stockwood and then Preakness Stud, which he renamed Elmendorf. Among the many champions he bred was Kentucky Derby winner Hindoo, later the sire of Domino. Swigert bred two other Derby winners, Apollo and Ben Ali. He also owned Derby winner Baden-Baden. The unbeaten 2-year-old Tremont and the champion mare Firenze were also among the horses he bred.

MAJ. BARAK THOMAS (1826-1906)—Maj. Thomas had various jobs before launching into thoroughbred breeding. He was one of the first to approach it as a full-time occupation, and this emphasis on professionalism had a role in establishing Kentucky as the center of the industry. He established Dixiana Farm and Hira Villa Stud in Lexington and was the breeder of both Himyar and his bellwether son, Domino.

W. T. YOUNG (1918-2004)—W. T. Young was a prominent businessman, philanthropist and leader in Kentucky. Among his major gifts was $5 million to help build the University of Kentucky library that is named for him. Young did not venture into the thoroughbred industry until the 1970s, but he developed Overbrook Farm and quickly made a mark. He bred and raced Storm Cat and returned the horse to stand at stud at Overbrook. Storm Cat became the leading sire of 1999 and 2000 and has been the leading sire of 2-year-olds seven times. Young won the Kentucky Derby in 1996 with his homebred, Grindstone. Tabasco Cat, which he bred and raced in partnership, won the Preakness and Belmont Stakes in 1994.

Thoroughbred Race Tracks
Ed Bowen

CHURCHILL DOWNS
Louisville

Home of the Kentucky Derby, Churchill Downs was established as the Louisville Jockey Club in 1875. Churchill Downs is the oldest track in the United States to have had racing annually, without interruption. While the Derby is the track's centerpiece, several other important stakes races are held—including the **Kentucky Oaks**, companion piece to the Derby which was also inaugurated in 1875. Now run on the day before the Derby, the Oaks is a 1 1/8 mile race for 3-year-old fillies.

Churchill Downs
Source: Department of Commerce,
Creative Services

The **Kentucky Jockey Club Stakes** is a 1 1/16-mile race for 2-year-olds that serves as a test of each horse's prospects of becoming a Derby entrant the following spring. The **Clark Handicap** is for 3-year-olds and older. The **Stephen Foster Handicap** is for 3-year-olds and up. **The Breeders' Cup** has been hosted by Churchill Downs in 1988, 1991, 1994, 1998 and 2000. In 2005, Churchill Downs

unveiled a massive expansion and renovation that cost $121million. Adjacent to the grandstand and clubhouse is the Kentucky Derby Museum.

KEENELAND
Lexington

The Kentucky Association track in Lexington closed in 1933, ending its run as the oldest racetrack in America (dating from 1828). Hal Price Headley and other horsemen worked with business leaders to found a new racing association and Keeneland was born in 1936. Beginning in the World War II era, thoroughbred auctions were held on the grounds. Keeneland subsequently rose to the top of the world's horse sales. The **Blue Grass Stakes** was first run in 1911 and immediately was regarded

Churchill Downs
Source: Department of Commerce,
Creative Services

as a Kentucky Derby prep. The race was revived at Keeneland in 1937 and now has a $750,000 purse.

The **Phoenix Breeders' Cup,** first contested in 1831, is the oldest race in America still being run, but not continuously. The **Ashland Stakes** for 3-year-old fillies has a purse of $500,000. **The Spinster**, open to fillies and mares 3 years old and up, is run at 1 1/8 miles with a purse of $500,000. The **Queen Elizabeth II Challenge Cup** began in 1984 and its first running was viewed by the woman it was named after, Queen Elizabeth II of England. **The Royal Chase for the Sport of Kings** is a steeplechase that has played host to Her Majesty Princess Anne. A number of Keeneland's races are sponsored by companies and horse farms, including the Blue Grass Stakes, supported by Toyota.

TURFWAY PARK
Florence

Turfway was known as Latonia when it opened in 1959. The spring meeting's signature has long been the **Lane's End Stakes. The Kentucky Cup Day of Champions** presents five stakes races and is an annual feature of late summer/early autumn.

ELLIS PARK
Henderson

The track opened in 1922 as Dade Park and was operated by James C. Ellis for most of its first 30 years. The track's **Gardenia Stakes** is a graded race for fillies and mares and carries a purse of $200,000.

KENTUCKY DOWNS, Franklin: Kentucky Downs has year-round simulcast wagering. There is a short live race meeting each September. Key race is the $200,000 **Kentucky Cup Turf Handicap**, run in conjunction with Kentucky Cup Day at Turfway Park.

Keeneland
Sources: Sid Webb

The Kentucky Derby
Ed Bowen

*They run for roses,
and a page in racing history.*

Widely regarded as the most famous horse race in the country and one of the great races of the world, the Kentucky Derby is the goal of virtually all horsemen. In fact, the mating patterns of thousands of thoroughbreds are made with the Derby in mind. Of the 131 Derby winners, 98 were bred (born) in Kentucky.

The Derby is run at Churchill Downs in Louisville on the first Saturday in May. At 1 1/4 miles, it almost always represents the longest test its entrants have yet faced. The Derby is exclusively for 3-year-olds and is the first race in the Triple Crown series, followed by the Preakness Stakes in Maryland and the Belmont Stakes in New York.

The Derby has been an annual event ever since its inaugural race in 1875. Col. M. Lewis Clark formed the Louisville Jockey Club and envisioned the Derby to be a counterpart of the famous Epsom Derby in England. The track had become known as Churchill Downs after the family from which the property was acquired.

The race rose to regional fame, but the track's health and the race's importance waned over the years. By 1902 a local tailor, Col. Matt Winn, was induced to take over management in an attempt to save the track and the race.

Col. Winn promoted the Derby by catering to the New York media and by convincing railroad lines to take blocks of tickets and schedule extra cars to Louisville. By 1915, when Harry Payne Whitney, a major Eastern owner, won the race with the filly Regret, he proclaimed the race the greatest in America. With that seal of approval from a nationally renowned horseman, the Derby was secure.

By 1946, Churchill Downs boasted a crowd of 100,000 annually. That figure was not actually reached according to Kentucky Racing Commission records until 1969, but it has been far surpassed since. The record crowd is 163,628, which attended the 100th running of the event in 1974. The 2005 running, won by 50-1 longshot Giacomo, attracted the second-largest crowd, 156,435. In 2005, parimutuel betting on the Derby at Churchill Downs and at simulcasting locations totaled $103,325,518.

KENTUCKY DERBY FACTS

- **Fastest time:** Secretariat, 1:59 2/5 in 1973
- **Longest odds of a winner:** 91.45-1, Donerail, 1913
- **Shortest odds of a winner:** 2-5, Calumet Farm entry (Citation & Coaltown), 1948; and Count Fleet, 1943
- **Percentage of winning favorites:** 38% (50 of 131)
- **Most wins, breeder:** Calumet Farm, 9
- **Most wins, owner:** Calumet Farm, 8
- **Most wins, trainer:** Ben A. Jones, 6
- **Jockey, most wins:** Eddie Arcaro and Bill Hartack, 5 each
- **Stallion, most winners sired:** Falsetto, Virgil, Sir Gallahad III, and Bull Lea, 3 each
- **Largest field:** 23, in 1974 (the field is now limited to 20)
- **Smallest field:** 3, in 1892 and 1905
- **Filly winners:** Regret, 1915; Genunie Risk, 1980; Winning Colors, 1988
- **Largest winning margin:** 8 lengths (Old Rosebud, 1914; Johnstown, 1939; Whirlaway, 1941; Assault, 1946)
- **Largest winner's purse:** Giacomo, $1,639,600 in 2005
- **Triple Crown winners:** 11 (Sir Barton, 1919; Gallant Fox, 1930; Omaha, 1935; War Admiral, 1937; Whirlaway, 1941; Count Fleet, 1943; Assault, 1946; Citation, 1948; Secretariat, 1973; Seattle Slew, 1977; Affirmed, 1978)

Source: Churchill Downs

Infield at the Kentucky Derby
Source: Lexington Herald-Leader

Kentucky Derby Winners

YR	WINNER	OWNER	TRAINER	JOCKEY	SECOND	THIRD	TIME	MONEY
2005	Giacomo, gr/ro. c.	Mr. & Mrs. Jerome S. Moss	John Shirreffs	M. Smith	Closing Argument	Afleet Alex	02:02.8	$1,639,600
2004	Smarty Jones, ch. c.	Someday Farm	John Servis	S. Elliott	Lion Heart	Imperialism	02:04.1	†5,854,800
2003	Funny Cide, ch. g.	Sackatoga Stable	Barclay Tagg	J. Santos	Empire Maker	Peace Rules	02:01.2	800,200
2002	War Emblem, dkb/br. c.	The Thoroughbred Corp.	Bob Baffert	V. Espinoza	Proud Citizen	Perfect Drift	02:01.1	†1,875,000
2001	Monarchos, gr/ro. c.	John C. Oxley	John T. Ward Jr.	J. Chavez	Invisible Ink	Congaree	02:00.0	812,000
2000	Fusaichi Pegasus, b. c.	Fusao Sekiguchi	Neil Drysdale	K. Desormeaux	Aptitude	Impeachment	02:01.1	1,038,400
1999	Charismatic, ch. c.	Robert & Beverly Lewis	D. Wayne Lukas	C. Antley	Menifee	Cat Thief	02:03.3	886,200
1998	Real Quiet, b. c.	Mike Pegram	Bob Baffert	K. Desormeaux	Victory Gallop	Indian Charlie	02:02.4	738,800
1997	Silver Charm, gr/ro. c.	Robert & Beverly Lewis	Bob Baffert	G. Stevens	Captain Bodgit	Free House	02:02.4	700,000
1996	Grindstone, dkb/br. c.	Overbrook Farm	D. Wayne Lukas	J. Bailey	Cavonnier	Prince of Thieves	02:01.1	869,800
1995	Thunder Gulch, ch. c.	Michael Tabor	D. Wayne Lukas	G. Stevens	Tejano Run	Timber Country	02:01.3	707,400
1994	Go for Gin, b. c.	W. Condren-J. Cornacchia	Nicholas P. Zito	C. McCarron	Strodes Creek	Blumin Affair	02:03.7	628,800
1993	Sea Hero, b. c.	Rokeby Stable	MacKenzie Miller	J. Bailey	Prairie Bayou	Wild Gale	02:02.4	735,900
1992	Lil E. Tee, b. c.	W. Cal Partee	Lynn S. Whiting	P. Day	Casual Lies	Dance Floor	02:03.0	724,800
1991	Strike the Gold, ch. c.	Brophy-Condren-Cornacchia	Nicholas P. Zito	C. Antley	Best Pal	Mane Minister	02:03.1	655,800
1990	Unbridled, b. c.	Frances A. Genter Stable	Carl A. Nafzger	C. Perret	Summer Squall	Pleasant Tap	2:02	581,000
1989	Sunday Silence, dkb/br. c.	Gaillard-Hancock-Whittingham	Charles Whittingham	P. Valenzuela	Easy Goer	Awe Inspiring	2:05	574,200
1988	Winning Colors, ro. f.	Mr. & Mrs. Eugene Klein	D. Wayne Lukas	G. Stevens	Forty Niner	Risen Star	2:021/5	611,000
1987	Alysheba, b. c.	Dorothy & Pamela Scharbauer	Jack Van Berg	C. McCarron	Bet Twice	Avies Copy	2:032/5	618,600
1986	Ferdinand, ch. c.	Mrs. Howard B. Keck	Charles Whittingham	W. Shoemaker	Bold Arrangement	Broad Brush	2:024/5	609,400
1985	Spend a Buck, b. c.	Hunter Farm	Cam Gambolati	A. Cordero Jr.	Stephan's Odyssey	Chief's Crown	2:001/5	406,800
1984	Swale, dkb/br. c.	Claiborne Farm	W.C. Stephens	L. Pincay Jr.	Coax Me Chad	At the Threshold	2:022/5	537,400
1983	Sunny's Halo, ch. c.	David J. Foster Racing Stable	David C. Cross Jr.	E. Delahoussaye	Desert Wine	Caveat	2:021/5	426,000
1982	Gato Del Sol, gr. c.	Hancock III & Peters	Edwin Gregson	E. Delahoussaye	Laser Light	Reinvested	2:022/5	428,850
1981	Pleasant Colony, dkb/br. c.	Buckland Farm	John P. Campo	J. Velasquez	Woodchopper	Partez	2:02	317,200
1980	Genuine Risk, ch. f.	Mrs. B.R. Firestone	LeRoy Jolley	J. Vasquez	Rumbo	Jaklin Klugman	2:02	250,550
1979	Spectacular Bid, gr. c.	Hawksworth Farm	Grover G. Delp	R. Franklin	General Assembly	Golden Act	2:022/5	228,650
1978	**Affirmed, ch. c.**	Harbor View Farm	Lazaro Barrera	S. Cauthen	Alydar	Believe It	2:011/5	186,900
1977	**Seattle Slew, dkb/br. c.**	Karen L. Taylor	W.H. Turner Jr.	J. Cruguet	Run Dusty Run	Sanhedrin	2:021/5	214,700
1976	Bold Forbes, dkb/br. c.	E. Rodriguez Tizol	Lazaro Barrera	A. Cordero Jr.	Honest Pleasure	Elocutionist	2:013/5	165,200
1975	Foolish Pleasure, b. c.	John L. Greer	LeRoy Jolley	J. Vasquez	Avatar	Diabolo	2:02	209,600
1974	Cannonade, b. c.	John M. Olin	W.C. Stephens	A. Cordero Jr.	Hudson County	Agitate	2:04	274,000
1973	**Secretariat, ch. c.**	Meadow Stable	Lucien Laurin	R. Turcotte	Sham	Our Native	1:592/5	155,050
1972	Riva Ridge, b. c.	Meadow Stable	Lucien Laurin	R. Turcotte	No Le Hace	Hold Your Peace	2:014/5	140,300
1971	Canonero II, b. c.	Edgar Caibett	Juan Arias	G. Avila	Jim French	Bold Reason	2:031/5	145,500
1970	Dust Commander, ch. c.	Robert Lehmann	Don Combs	M. Manganello	My Dad George	High Echelon	2:032/5	127,800
1969	Majestic Prince, ch. c.	Frank McMahon	John Longden	W. Hartack	Arts and Letters	Dike	2:014/5	113,200
1968	#Forward Pass, b c.	Calumet Farm	Henry Forrest	I. Valenzuela	Francie's Hat	T. V. Commercial	2:021/5	122,600
1967	Proud Clarion, b. c.	Darby Dan Farm	Loyd Gentry	R. Ussery	Barbs Delight	Damascus	2:003/5	119,700
1966	Kauai King, dkb/br. c.	Michael J. Ford	Henry Forrest	D. Brumfield	Advocator	Blue Skyer	2:02	120,500
1965	Lucky Debonair, b. c.	Mrs. Ada L. Rice	Frank Catrone	W. Shoemaker	Dapper Dan	Tom Rolfe	2:011/5	112,000
1964	Northern Dancer, b. c.	Windfields Farm	Horatio Luro	W. Hartack	Hill Rise	The Scoundrel	2:00	114,300
1963	Chateaugay, ch. c.	Darby Dan Farm	James Conway	B. Baeza	Never Bend	Candy Spots	2:014/5	108,900
1962	Decidedly, gr. c.	El Peco Ranch	Horatio Luro	W. Hartack	Roman Line	Ridan	2:002/5	119,650
1961	Carry Back, br. c.	Mrs. J.A. Price	J.A. Price	J. Sellers	Crozier	Bass Clef	2:04	120,500
1960	Venetian Way, ch. c.	Sunny Blue Farm	Vic Sovinski	W. Hartack	Bally Ache	Victoria Park	2:022/5	114,850
1959	Tomy Lee, b. c.	Fred Turner Jr.	Frank Childs	W. Shoemaker	Sword Dancer	First Landing	2:021/5	119,650
1958	Tim Tam, dk. b. c.	Calumet Farm	H.A. Jones	I. Valenzuela	Lincoln Road	Noureddin	2:05	116,400
1957	Iron Liege, b. c.	Calumet Farm	H.A. Jones	W. Hartack	Gallant Man	Round Table	2:021/5	107,950
1956	Needles, b. c.	D & H Stable	H.L. Fontaine	D. Erb	Fabius	Come On Red	2:032/5	123,450
1955	Swaps, ch. c.	R.C. Ellsworth	M.A. Tenney	W. Shoemaker	Nashua	Summer Tan	2:014/5	108,400
1954	Determine, gr. c.	A.J. Crevolin	Willie Molter	R. York	Hasty Road	Hasseyampa	2:03	102,050
1953	Dark Star, br. c.	Cain Hoy Stable	Edward Hayward	H. Moreno	Native Dancer	Invigorator	2:02	90,050
1952	Hill Gail, dk. b. c.	Calumet Farm	B.A. Jones	E. Arcaro	Sub Fleet	Blue Man	2:013/5	96,300
1951	Count Turf, b. c.	J.J. Amiel	Sol Rutchick	C. McCreary	Royal Mustang	Ruhe	2:023/5	98,050
1950	Middleground, ch. c.	King Ranch	Max Hirsch	W. Boland	Hill Prince	Mr. Trouble	2:013/5	92,650
1949	Ponder, dk. b. c.	Calumet Farm	B.A. Jones	S. Brooks	Capot	Palestinian	2:041/5	91,600
1948	**Citation, b. c.**	Calumet Farm	B.A. Jones	E. Arcaro	Coaltown	My Request	2:052/5	83,400

YR	WINNER	OWNER	TRAINER	JOCKEY	SECOND	THIRD	TIME	MONEY
1947	Jet Pilot, ch. c.	Maine Chance Farm	Tom Smith	E. Guerin	Phalanx	Faultless	2:06 4/5	92,160
1946	**Assault, ch. c.**	King Ranch	Max Hirsch	W. Mehrtens	Spy Song	Hampden	2:06 3/5	96,400
1945	Hoop, Jr., b. c.	F.W. Hooper	Ivan H. Parke	E. Arcaro	Pot o' Luck	Darby Dieppe	2:07	64,850
1944	Pensive, ch. c.	Calumet Farm	B.A. Jones	C. McCreary	Broadcloth	Stir Up	2:04 1/5	64,675
1943	**Count Fleet, br. c.**	Mrs. John Hertz	G.D. Cameron	J. Longden	Blue Swords	Slide Rule	2:04	60,725
1942	Shut Out, ch. c.	Greentree Stable	John M. Gaver	W.D. Wright	Alsab	Valdina Orphan	2:04 2/5	64,225
1941	**Whirlaway, br. c.**	Calumet Farm	B.A. Jones	E. Arcaro	Staretor	Market Wise	2:01 2/5	61,275
1940	Gallahadion, b. c.	Milky Way Farm	Roy Waldron	C. Bierman	Bimelech	Dit	2:05	60,150
1939	Johnstown, b. c.	Belair Stud	James Fitzsimmons	J. Stout	Challedon	Heather Broom	2:03 2/5	46,350
1938	Lawrin, br. c.	Woolford Farm	B.A. Jones	E. Arcaro	Dauber	Can't Wait	2:04 4/5	47,050
1937	**War Admiral, br. c**	Glen Riddle Farms	George Conway	C. Kurtsinger	Pompoon	Reaping Reward	2:03 1/5	52,050
1936	Bold Venture, ch. c.	M.L. Schwartz	Max Hirsch	I. Hanford	Brevity	Indian Broom	2:03 3/5	37,725
1935	**Omaha, ch. c.**	Belair Stud Stable	James Fitzsimmons	W. Saunders	Roman Soldier	Whiskolo	2:05	39,525
1934	Cavalcade, br. c.	Brookmeade Stable	R.A. Smith	M. Garner	Discovery	Agrarian	2:04	28,175
1933	Brokers Tip, br. c.	E.R. Bradley	H.J. Thompson	D. Meade	Head Play	Charley O.	2:06 4/5	48,925
1932	Burgoo King, ch. c.	E.R. Bradley	H.J. Thompson	E. James	Economic	Stepenfetchit	2:05 1/5	52,350
1931	Twenty Grand, b. c.	Greentree Stable	James Rowe Jr.	C. Kurtsinger	Sweep All	Mate	2:01 4/5	48,725
1930	**Gallant Fox, b. c.**	Belair Stud Stable	James Fitzsimmons	E. Sande	Gallant Knight	Ned O.	2:07 3/5	50,725
1929	Clyde Van Dusen, ch. g.	H.P. Gardner	Clyde Van Dusen	L. McAtee	Naishapur	Panchio	2:10 4/5	53,950
1928	Reigh Count, ch. c.	Mrs. John Hertz	B.S. Mitchell	C. Lang	Misstep	Toro	2:10 2/5	55,375
1927	Whiskery, b. c.	H.P. Whitney	Fred Hopkins	L. McAtee	Osmand	Jock	2:06	51,000
1926	Bubbling Over, ch. c.	E.R. Bradley	H.J. Thompson	A. Johnson	Bagenbaggage	Rock Man	2:03 4/5	50,075
1925	Flying Ebony, blk. c.	G.A. Cochran	W.B. Duke	E. Sande	Captain Hal	Son of John	2:07 3/5	52,950
1924	Black Gold, blk. c.	Mrs. R. M. Hoots	Hanley Webb	J. D. Mooney	Chilhowee	Beau Butler	2:05 1/5	52,775
1923	Zev, b. c.	Rancocas Stable	D.J. Leary	E. Sande	Martingale	Vigil	2:05 2/5	53,000
1922	Morvich, b. c.	Benjamin Block	Fred Burlew	A. Johnson	Bet Mosie	John Finn	2:04 3/5	46,775
1921	Behave Yourself, b. c.	E.R. Bradley	H.J. Thompson	C. Thompson	Black Servant	Prudery	2:04 1/5	38,450
1920	Paul Jones, br. g.	Ral Parr	Wm. Garth	T. Rice	Upset	On Watch	2:09	30,375
1919	**Sir Barton, ch. c.**	J.K.L. Ross	H.G. Bedwell	J. Loftus	Billy Kelly	Under Fire	2:09 4/5	20,825
1918	Exterminator, ch. g.	Willis Sharpe Kilmer	Henry McDaniel	W. Knapp	Escoba	Viva America	2:10 4/5	14,700
1917	Omar Khayyam, ch c.	Billings & Johnson	C.T. Paterson	C. Borel	Ticket	Midway	2:04 3/5	16,600
1916	George Smith, blk. c.	John Sanford	Hollie Hughes	J. Loftus	Star Hawk	Franklin	2:04	9,750
1915	Regret, ch. f.	H.P. Whitney	James Rowe Sr.	J. Notter	Pebbles	Sharpshooter	2:05 2/5	11,450
1914	Old Rosebud, b. c.	H.C. Applegate	F.D. Weir	J. McCabe	Hodge	Bronzewing	2:03 2/5	9,125
1913	Donerail, b. c.	T.P. Hayes	T.P. Hayes	R. Goose	Ten Point	Gowell	2:04 4/5	5,475
1912	Worth, br. c.	H.C. Hallenbeck	Frank M. Taylor	C. H. Shilling	Duval	Flamma	2:09 2/5	4,850
1911	Meridian, b. c.	R.F. Carman	A. Ewing	G. Archibald	Governor Gray	Colston	2:05	4,850
1910	Donau, b. c.	William Gerst	George Ham	F. Herbert	Joe Morris	Fighting Bob	2:06 2/5	4,850
1909	Wintergreen, b. c.	J.B. Respess	C. Mack	W. Powers	Miami	Dr. Barkley	2:08 1/5	4,850
1908	Stone Street, b. c.	C.E. Hamilton	J.W. Hall	A. Pickens	Sir Cleges	Dunvegan	2:15 1/5	4,850
1907	Pink Star, b. c.	J. Hal Woodford	W.H. Fizer	A. Minder	Zal	Ovelando	2:12 3/5	4,850
1906	Sir Huon, b. c.	George J. Long	Peter Coyne	R. Troxler	Lady Navarre	James Reddick	2:08 4/5	4,850
1905	Agile, b.c.	S.S. Brown	Robert Tucker	J. Martin	Ram's Horn	Layson	2:10 3/4	4,850
1904	Elwood, b. c.	Mrs. C.E. Durnell	C.E. Durnell	F. Pryor	Ed Tierney	Brancas	2:08 1/2	4,850
1903	Judge Himes, b. c.	C.R. Ellison	J.P. Mayberry	H. Booker	Early	Bourbon	2:09	4,850
1902	Alan-a-Dale, b. c.	T.C. McDowell	T.C. McDowell	J. Winkfield	Inventor	The Rival	2:08 3/4	4,850
1901	His Eminence, b. c.	F.B. VanMeter	F.B. VanMeter	J. Winkfield	Sannazarro	Driscoll	2:07 3/4	4,850
1900	Lieut. Gibson, b. c.	Charles H. Smith	Charles H. Hughes	J. Boland	Florizar	Thrive	2:06 1/4	4,850
1899	Manuel, b. c.	A.H. & D.H. Morris	Robert J. Walden	F. Taral	Corsini	Mazo	2:12	4,850
1898	Plaudit, br. c.	J.E. Madden	J.E. Madden	W. Simms	Lieber Karl	Isabey	2:09	4,850
1897	Typhoon II, ch. c.	J.C. Cahn	J.C. Cahn	F. Garner	Ornament	Dr. Catlett	2:12 1/2	4,850
1896	Ben Brush, b. c.	M.F. Dwyer	Hardy Campbell	W. Simms	Ben Eder	Semper Ego	2:07 3/4	4,850
1895	Halma, blk. c.	Byron McClelland	Byron McClelland	J. Perkins	Basso	Laureate	2:37 1/2	2,970
1894	Chant, b. c.	Leigh & Rose	Eugene Leigh	F. Goodale	Pearl Song	Sigurd	2:41	4,020
1893	Lookout, ch. c.	Cushing & Orth	Will McDaniel	E. Kunze	Plutus	Boundless	2:39 1/4	3,840
1892	Azra, b. c.	Bashford Manor	John H. Morris	A. Clayton	Huron	Phil Dwyer	2:41 1/2	4,230
1891	Kingman, b. c.	Jacobin Stable	Dud Allen	I. Murphy	Balgowan	High Tariff	2:52 1/4	4,550
1890	Riley, b. c.	Edward Corrigan	Edward Corrigan	I. Murphy	Bill Letcher	Robespierre	2:45	5,460
1889	Spokane, ch. c.	Noah Armstrong	John Rodegap	T. Kiley	Proctor Knott	Once Again	2:34 1/2	4,880
1888	Macbeth II, b. g.	Chicago Stable	John Campbell	G. Covington	Gallifet	White	2:38 1/4	4,740
1887	Montrose, b. c.	Labold Brothers	John McGinty	I. Lewis	Jim Gore	Jacobin	2:39 1/4	4,200
1886	Ben Ali, br. c.	J.B.A. Haggin	Jim Murphy	P. Duffy	Blue Wing	Free Knight	2:36 1/2	4,890
1885	Joe Cotton, ch. c.	J.T. Williams	Alex Perry	E. Henderson	Bersan	Ten Booker	2:37 1/4	4,630
1884	Buchanan, ch. c.	W. Cottrill	William Bird	I. Murphy	Loftin	Audrain	2:40 1/4	3,990
1883	Leonatus, b. c.	Chinn & Morgan	Raleigh Colston	W. Donahue	Drake Carter	Lord Raglan	2:43	3,760
1882	Apollo, ch. g.	Morris & Patton	Green B. Morris	B. Hurd	Runnymede	Bengal	2:40 1/2	4,560
1881	Hindoo, b. c.	Dwyer Brothers	James Rowe Sr.	J. McLaughlin	Lelex	Alhambra	2:40	4,410
1880	Fonso, ch. c.	J.S. Shawhan	Tice Hutsell	G. Lewis	Kimball	Bancroft	2:37 1/2	3,800
1879	Lord Murphy, b. c.	Geo. W. Darden & Co.	George Rice	C. Shauer	Falsetto	Strathmore	2:37	3,550
1878	Day Star, ch. c.	T.J. Nichols	Lee Paul	J. Carter	Himyar	Leveler	2:37 1/4	4,050
1877	Baden Baden, ch. c.	Daniel Swigert	Ed Brown	W. Walker	Leonard	King William	2:38	3,300
1876	Vagrant, br. g.	William Astor	James Williams	R. Swim	Creedmoor	Harry Hill	2:38 1/4	2,950
1875	Aristides, ch. c.	H.P. McGrath	Ansel Williamson	O. Lewis	Volcano	Verdigris	2:37 3/4	2,850

(Triple Crown winners in bold.)

SPORTS

The chance of a lifetime... Billy Reed

Four springs ago, two men, not now identified, laid plans which are about to come to fruition. One was planning the mating which led to the winner of the Kentucky Derby. The other was lighting a fire under the mash at the Brown-Forman Distillery. Strength to them both.

—Joe Palmer, Spring, 1952

As legend has it, thoroughbred racing and bourbon whiskey both came to prosper in Kentucky as nowhere else because of the rich limestone soil and the minerals in the water, particularly in the central part of the commonwealth. The soil and the water produced a strain of grass that, it was said, looked blue if held to a flame. And thus did Kentucky become the Bluegrass State, known internationally for its horse farms, race tracks and distilleries.

The proximity of the horses and the bourbon led to the invention of a drink known as the mint julep, which was served at the most prestigious breeding farms to buyers who had come to inspect the young horses that were for sale. And thus did Kentucky develop its own brand of Southern hospitality.

A decade after the Civil War, when the Old South was deep in the throes of reconstruction, a couple of Louisville businessmen opened a racetrack in the city's South End. It was named Churchill Downs, after the family who owned the property, and it had a couple of spires — twin spires, as they came to be known — atop the grandstand to give it a touch of class.

In the spring of 1875, the track sponsored a stakes race known as the Kentucky Derby, modeled after the Epsom Derby in England, in order to give the state's breeders a showcase for their best young horses. The first Derby was won by a little red colt named Aristides, who saved the day for owner H.P. McGrath when his stablemate, the favored Chesapeake, faltered and "spit out the bit," as horsemen put it.

Among the crowd that day was a youngster named Matt Winn, who watched the Derby from his father's wagon parked in the track infield. He grew up loving Churchill Downs and the Derby to the point that, when the track was on the brink of bankruptcy in the early 1900s, Winn put together a group of investors to save it.

From that time until his death in 1948, Winn lived and breathed the Kentucky Derby. Far ahead of his time in the areas of marketing and promotion, Winn personally built the Derby into the world's best-known and most-coveted race. At some point, he adopted the honorary title of "Colonel," which enhanced his image as a Southern gentlemen.

While Winn was building the Derby and Churchill Downs, racing also prospered in other parts of the state. In Northern Kentucky, Latonia (now Turfway) provided the legal gambling action for guys and dolls who patronized the area's nightclubs, casinos and gin joints. And in Central Kentucky, the breeders, weary of the trouble and expense of sending their sales yearlings to Saratoga in upstate New York, founded a combination race track and sales company in 1936. Named Keeneland, in honor of founder Jack Keene, the picturesque plant outside Lexington represented "racing as it was meant to be," and sales yearlings that were literally the cream of the international crop.

Every year, more than 35,000 thoroughbreds are born throughout the world. Only one can win the Kentucky Derby in the spring of his 3-year-old year, which is why the singer Dan Fogelberg called it "the chance of a lifetime in a lifetime of chance" in his song, "Run for the Roses."

Virtually next door to Keeneland on the Versailles Pike, just across from the Blue Grass Field airport, lies Calumet Farm, which still is the home of more Kentucky Derby winners (eight) than any other owner. Of the 11 horses that have won racing's Triple Crown (Derby, Preakness and Belmont Stakes), two carried Calumet's devil's red-and-blue silks — Whirlaway in 1941 and Citation in 1948.

Through the years, as tobacco, coal and bourbon have fallen out of favor with many, horse racing has become Kentucky's signature industry. It's what separates Kentucky from, say, Ohio or West Virginia. And a virtual cottage industry has grown around the Derby.

Although the race itself generally lasts only a couple of minutes (Secretariat's 1973 time of 1:59 2/5 for the mile and a quarter still is the Derby record), the festival celebrating it begins two weeks earlier and includes a hot-air balloon race, a steamboat race, a parade, a fireworks display that draws 400,000 to the banks of the Ohio River and some of the most celebrated parties this side of Hollywood.

On Derby Day, it's *de rigeur* for women to wear outlandish hats. For the men, it's ties and sports jackets in colors and patterns that seldom are seen away from the golf course. And it's expected that everyone will knock back a mint julep or two, make many trips to the betting windows and shed a tear when Stephen Foster's melancholy "My Old Kentucky Home" is played as the Derby horses come on the track.

The owner, trainer, and jockey who are lucky enough to win the Derby — and, make no mistake, luck is every bit as important as pedigree and talent — win more than a gold trophy. They win a little slice of immortality. Have you ever won the Kentucky Derby? Inevitably, that's the first question a horseman gets asked when he or she meets a stranger.

In 2005, longshot Giacomo won the Derby and paid $102.60 for a $2 win bet, second highest in Derby history. The superfecta, which requires picking the top four horses in order, was worth more than $1 million.

Out in Arizona, a bettor had a winning superfecta ticket, but couldn't find it. He looked everywhere, going through bags and bags of trash. No luck. Finally he shared his plight with the pari-mutuel clerk who had sold him the ticket. She looked around her work area and found the ticket. The new millionaire gave her a generous tip. He might even have bought her a mint julep or two.

Strength to them both.

y'know what?

1943 SIX-MAN FOOTBALL STATE CHAMPIONS

Perryville High School won the Six-Man Football Kentucky State Championship in 1943 against Chaplin at University of Kentucky's Stoll Field. During WWII, smaller schools in Kentucky reverted to six-man teams because students were either drafted or volunteered for service.
Pictured above are, First row L to R: Sam Stephens , Chester Shepperson, Kamos Carpenter, K.W. Sinkhorn, Frances Seltsam, Boyd Crain, Oscar Gibson,
Ralph Thompson (killed first day of combat during Vietnam War);
Second row L to R: Robert C. "Soupy" Campbell (Centre College), Principal and Coach Garland Young, James Moss, Harlie Lanham, Jr., Robert Bottoms, Berry Preston.
Those still living are: Sam Stephens, Harlie Lanham, Jr., Frances Seltsam, Oscar Gibson and Garland Young

SPORTS

Horse Racing
Saddlebreds

Tolley Graves,
American Saddlebred Museum

Kentucky is home to America's only native breed of horse, the American Saddlebred. A very special breed of horse – beautiful, intelligent, fun to ride or drive and adaptable to any use – this is a horse for every horse person.

The American Saddlebred is easily recognized in a backyard or in a show ring. His proud head and tail carriage, combined with size and substance,

Kentucky Horse Park
Source: Sid Webb

clearly distinguish this elegant horse from any other light horse breed.

The conformation of the breed is striking and enables him to perform well at many endeavors. With his long legs and sloping pasterns, the ideal Saddlebred has high stepping action along with a ground-covering stride. A long, arching neck and large expressive eye complete the picture of beauty and refinement.

By the initial publication of the Kentucky Almanac in 1788, the foundation had begun for the horse known as the Kentucky Saddler through most of the 1800s. The name American Saddle Horse became official in 1891 with the formation of the registry. Common usage prompted another change in the latter half of the twentieth century,

and this popular and versatile breed is now known as the American Saddlebred.

The Saddlebred was developed by eighteenth century colonists who sought a good-looking, sensible, adaptable and comfortable animal to ride and drive. The American Saddlebred is a composite of several breeds, including the Narragansett Pacer, the Thoroughbred, the Morgan, the Hackney and the Canadian Pacer.

Early breeders took care to maintain the easy gaits of the first Saddlers, and added quality, size and strength. A utility horse of beauty, high intelligence and good disposition these horses were the mainstay of the Confederate cavalry during the Civil War and the choice mount of many generals on both sides of the war. Some noted "Saddlers" serving in the war were Robert E. Lee's Traveller, Ulysses S. Grant's Cincinnati, Sherman's Lexington, Stonewall Jackson's Little Sorrel, John Hunt Morgan's Black Bess and General Meade's Baldy. After the war, General Grant allowed the Southerners to take their horses home, thus ensuring their breeding programs would continue.

Kentucky has always been the center of the Saddlebred industry. The first known horse show was held just north of Lexington in 1816. With the invention of the steam engine, many people switched their horses from work to recreational activities and horse shows grew in popularity. As the Saddlebreds' favorite thing to do is show off, many spectators were attracted to their proud carriage, lively expression and high leg action. From their ancestors Saddlebreds inherited the ability to perform at the slow gait and rack, distinct four-beat gaits where only one hoof hits the ground at a time.

The characteristics that have contributed to the Saddlebred's reputation as the "peacock of the show ring" also make him an excellent sport horse. Smoothness of gaits, speed coupled with intelligence, powerful muscling plus an innate desire to please, enable him to do whatever is asked of him. Saddlebreds compete successfully in a variety of disciplines including jumping, barrel racing, driving, dressage, endurance riding, etc. A Saddlebred is capable of almost any task he is asked to perform and will do it with extraordinary style.

Saddlebreds have even attained celebrity status. Buffalo Bill Cody's mount, Columbus, was a star in his 1890s Wild West Show. Mr. Ed and Fury became television stars will long-running hit shows. William Shatner, an owner and exhibitor of American Saddlebreds, had some of his horses appear in scenes from Star Trek Generations. Other Saddlebreds have been cast as Black Beauty and Toronado, Zorro's dashing mount.

The first Kentucky State Fair was held in 1902, with the Saddle Horse Show a prime attraction. Louisville is still the location every August for the World's Grand Championship Horse Show. If you visit Kentucky in the summer, chances are there will be a Saddlebred horse show near you. County fairs featuring Saddlebreds are held every weekend throughout the state. Louisville's prestigious Rock Creek Show is held in June, followed by the largest outdoor Saddle Horse show in the world at Lexington's Red Mile in July.

Visitors to the area seeking more Saddlebred information should stop at the beautiful Kentucky Horse Park in Lexington. The American Saddlebred Museum is located on the Horse Park grounds and also houses the offices of the American Saddlebred Registry and Association. The museum features permanent, special and interactive exhibits. An award winning feature movie on the breed plays in the theater along with various videos stationed throughout the museum. If you are looking for Saddlebreds in your home location you may find them on the computer-based locator program that prints out a list of farms. A child-friendly area of the museum features a touch screen question and answer game and two large Saddlebred rocking horses, a favorite ride for visitors of all ages.

Many of the legendary Saddlebred show horses lived in Kentucky, and many are buried here in the Bluegrass, including six-time Five-Gaited World's Champions Wing Commander and My-My. Five-Gaited World's Grand Champions Imperator, Sky Watch and Wild-Eyed And Wicked are buried at the Horse Park's Hall of Champions. The remains of Rex Peavine, Five-Gaited Grand Champion at the Kentucky State Fair in 1903, are also located at the American Saddlebred Museum.

A thrilling show horse, a true and loyal companion, the American Saddlebred is the horse for everyone. More than one hundred years of careful development through selective breeding have produced a horse that is as uniform in its style and conformation today as the saddle horses of Civil War times. A bit more polished and refined, but still the same hard-working, intelligent and graceful breed that deserves the title "The Horse America Made."

I wish you'd look...

BREEDS OF HORSES IN KENTUCKY

Yes, we love Thoroughbreds, Standardbreds, Quarter Horses...and many other horse breeds that Kentuckians adore for their beauty, gait, temperament, style and personality. These breeds include: American Gaited Pony, American Miniature, American Paint, American Saddle Horse, American Shetland Pony, American Walking Pony, American Warmblood, Appaloosa, Arabian, Barb, Belgian, BelgianWarmblood, Buckskin, Donkey, Clydesdale, Dutch Warmblood, Friesian, Hackney Horse, Half Arabian, Highland Pony, Irish Hunter, Lipizzaner, Lusitano, Missouri Fox Trotter, Morgan Horse, Mountain Pleasure Horse, Mule, Mustang, National Show Horse, National Spotted Saddle Horse, New Forest Pony, Paint, Palamino, Peruvian Paso, QuArab Horse, Racking Horse, Rocky Mountain Horse, Tarpan, Tennessee Walking Horse, Shetland Pony, Spanish Barb, Welsh pony and ... Zebra.

Source: Kentucky Horse Park and http://cowboyfrank.com

SPORTS

Horse Racing
Standardbreds

Origins of the Standardbred trace back to Messenger, an English Thoroughbred foaled in 1780, and later exported to the U.S. Messenger was the great-grandsire of Hambletonian 10, to whom every Standardbred can trace its heritage. The name "Standardbred" originated because the early trotters (pacers would not come into favor until much later) were required to reach a certain standard for the mile distance in order to be registered. The mile is still the standard distance covered in nearly every harness race.

The first Standardbred races were contested along roads, with men challenging their friends to see who had the swifter horse. Often the streets of cities were cleared for racing — that's why so many cities have a Race Street.

In many respects, the Standardbred resembles its ancestor the Thoroughbred. It does not stand as tall, averaging 15.2 hands, although it has a longer body. The head is refined, set on a medium-sized neck. The quarters are muscular yet sleek. The clean hind legs are set well back. This breed appears in varying colors, although bay, brown and black are predominant; weight varies between 800 and 1000 pounds.

Standardbred racing is contested on two gaits, the trot and the pace. Trotters move with a diagonal gait; the left front and right rear legs move in unison, as to the right front and left rear. It requires much skill by the trainer to get a trotter to move perfectly at high speeds, even though the trotting gait is a natural one in the animal world.

Pacers, on the other hand, move the legs on one side of their body in tandem: left front and rear, and right front and rear. This action shows why pacers are often called "sidewheelers." Pacers, which account for about 80 percent of the performers in harness racing, are aided in maintaining their gait by plastic loops called hobbles, which keep their legs moving in synchronization.

The Red Mile

The date was Tuesday, Sept. 28, 1875, and it was the inaugural opening day of the Great Fall Trots at The Red Mile, sponsored by the newly reorganized Kentucky Trotting Horse Breeders Association. The Red Mile, located just one mile from downtown Lexington and well-known for its fast, red clay and one-mile track, is the second oldest harness track in the world.

The Red Mile offers showcase horse racing each year plus full-card simulcasting 365 days a year from top harness outlets such as Meadowlands, Mohawk and Woodbine (including simulcasts of quarter horse racing from Los Alamitos, Sunland Park and other tracks).

In 2004, the Red Mile hosted its inaugural Quarter Horse meet, which marked the first time that breed had raced in the Bluegrass in more than a decade. The Red Mile hosts numerous other events, such as horse sales, wedding receptions, holiday parties, concerts, circuses, reunions, corporate meetings and many more events.

The Round Barn, a picturesque building listed on the National Register of Historic Places, offers a charm all its own. It is available for a host of events and can accommodate up to 200 guests; for non-seated events it will easily hold more.

Leading drivers at the Red Mile are: Wins: Josh Sutton (Spring) – 31; David Miller (Grand Circuit) – 37; UDR: Mike Zeller (Spring) - .387; John Patterson, Jr. (Grand Circuit) - .0379; Purses: John Meittinis (Spring) - $84,680; and David Miller (Grand Circuit) - $1,280,060. Leading trainers are: Clint Binkley (Spring) – 16 and Brett Pelling and Charles Sylverster (Grand Circuit) – 11.

Reprinted with permission from The Red Mile (www. theredmile.com) and the U.S. Trotting Association (www.ustrotting.com).

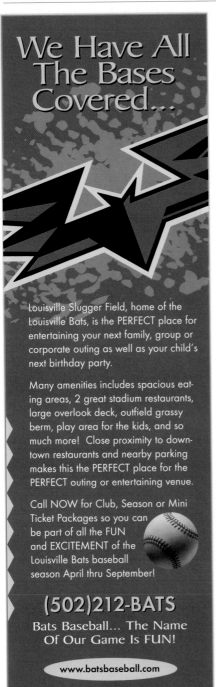
HISTORY OF
RIVER CITY BASEBALL

Baseball has some of its deepest roots embedded in Louisville as the River City was an original member of the National League. Hall of Famers such as Honus Wagner and Carlton Fisk played here as well as Kentucky native Pee Wee Reese.

The relationship between Louisville and the national pastime dates back over 130 years to 1874 when professional baseball was first played in Louisville and has been in town for all but 19 years.

The Louisville Redbirds became the first Minor League team in history to have one miilion fans in one season, accomplishing the feat in 1983. By being the first franchise to break the one million mark in attendance, Louisville set the stage for the renaissance of Minor League baseball's popularity which continues to escalate today.

Much has transpired in regards to professional baseball in Louisville since the early days of the 1980s. Cardinal Stadium was vacated for the state-of-the-art Louisville Slugger Field which opened in 2000. After a 16-year working agreement with the St. Louis Cardinals, the franchise became the top farm club of the Milwaukee Brewers in 1998 followed by the Cincinnati Reds in 2000. The team name has changed from the Redbirds to the RiverBats and then to the Bats since the franchise's inception in 1982. Though the team has experienced a number of changes, one thing that remains constant is this area's affinity for professional baseball.

An affiliation with the Cincinnati Reds complemented the opening of Louisville Slugger Field perfectly in that the interest generated was not limited to a local level. Fans frequently travel from all over Kentucky, Indiana and Ohio to see the future stars of the Cincinnati Reds. Whereas Louisville baseball is an affordable family entertainment option, Louisville Slugger Field is one reason fans keep coming back for more.

Louisville Slugger Field has a charisma all its own as it blends the aura of baseball's storied past with modern-day amenities. If numbers are any indication, the fans certainly agree; Louisville won the attendance title in Slugger Field's first season as 685,863 fans came through the turnstiles. The team has won the attendance title every year since Slugger Field opened, including 2001 when the Bats won the Governors' Cup Championship as the best team in the International League.

Contributed by Megan Dimond, Assistant Director of Media & PR, Louisville Bats.

Minor League Baseball is an organization that has endured more than a century of social, political and cultural changes. Through the pioneering spirit of its membership and leaders, minor league baseball has evolved and remains a vital component of the American landscape. Today, minor league baseball touches the lives of people and cultures throughout the world.

In 2005, a record-setting 40 million fans attended regular season games, breaking the attendance record that had stood since 1949. Total regular season attendance has increased in 20 of the last 24 seasons and has surpassed 33 million in each of the last twelve seasons. This enormous fan base, drawing more fans than the NBA, the NFL and the NHL combined, is centered on minor league baseball's attractiveness to all spectrums of our communities – the young and the young-at-heart, families of all sizes and varieties and diverse economic sectors — all coming together for America's favorite game.

In Lexington, the Lexington Legends are drawing people from all over the Bluegrass region and surrounding states to Applebee's Park. It's the entire family that is coming, and businesses, too, because Lexington Legends baseball is fun. It has something for the young and the young at heart.

Kids can play in the Kid Zone and ride the carousel; families can sit down to eat in the Maker's Mark club restaurant and watch the field on our in-house television feed, or visitors can spread out a picnic blanket along the outfield line catching foul balls; and businesses can entertain their clients in a corporate suite surrounded by the glamour and ambience of baseball. All can watch the antics of mascots and fans alike as they enjoy their days and their evenings watching America's game.

The Lexington Legends are about entertainment and our commitment to customer service is unparalleled. From beginning to end of the fan's experience, we make sure everything is done to make your visit to Applebee's Park fun and entertaining. We invest - along with our sponsors and advertisers - in your experience because we have learned that you will return.

Our philosophy is simple. We focus on you, the fans—we know what you want and what you like. We strive to bring clean, safe entertainment to Kentucky where fans get great value for their discretionary dollar, and, more importantly, their discretionary leisure time.

Come join us during the 2006 Lexington Legends season. Together, we'll make it fun!

SPORTS
Baseball

John A. McGill

*Four Kentuckians
have made it to Cooperstown,
but many others have made their mark.*

It wasn't that easy for Jackie Robinson to break the color barrier in baseball in 1947, and it was a pair of Kentuckians who played significant roles in helping him make history.

Gov. Albert B. "Happy" Chandler, born near Corydon, was the commissioner of major league baseball at the time and worked behind the scenes to pave the way for Robinson to be signed to a major league contract. And Pee Wee Reese, the Brooklyn Dodgers shortstop and team captain, was the player who refused to sign a petition by his teammates threatening a boycott if Robinson joined the team.

Robinson joined the Dodgers, and on his first road trip, which was to Cincinnati, fans began to heckle him. Reese, however, walked over to Robinson and put his arm across Robinson's shoulder. It silenced the crowd.

Reese, who some regard as being from Louisville but actually was born in Ekron, was as good at playing baseball as he was at doing the right thing. He was an All-Star selection 10 times during a career that stretched from 1940 to 1958. The Dodgers won the National League pennant seven times in that period.

Both Chandler and Reese are in baseball's Hall of Fame. Two other Kentuckians have joined them in Cooperstown: U.S. Sen. Jim Bunning of Southgate and Earle Combs of Pebworth.

Bunning is the only pitcher to throw no-hitters in both the American and National Leagues—and one of them was a perfect game, coming while pitching for Philadelphia in a 6-0 win over the New York Mets in Shea Stadium on June 21, 1964. Bunning had a career record of 224-184 with a 3.27 ERA. He was a minor league manager for several years before entering politics.

Combs was the leadoff hitter for the 1927 New York Yankees, the team that was dubbed "Murderers' Row." Joining Combs were talents such as

Babe Ruth and Lou Gehrig. The 1927 Yankees are still regarded as one of the greatest teams in history. Combs batted .356 that year with 231 hits, a club record that held until 1986 when Don Mattingly topped it. Combs had a career batting average of .325, and although he attempted a come-

Ronnie Martinez was the starting pitcher for the Legends,
Lexington Legends vs Greensboro Grasshoppers baseball
game, Applebee's Park, Lexington, KY
Source: Lexington Herald-Leader

back after fracturing his skull crashing into an outfield wall (they weren't padded back then), he retired after a comeback attempt in 1935. Combs, who had a 29-game hitting streak in 1931, was replaced by none other than Joe DiMaggio.

Others from the Bluegrass State have had significant major league careers.

Don Gullett of South Shore was a 19-year-old rookie when he was hastily called in to pitch for Cincinnati after the Reds' ace, Jim Maloney, hurt himself running the bases. In his first major league appearance in April of 1970, Gullett pitched five scoreless innings and picked up the decision. It wasn't long after that that manager Sparky Anderson was saying that Gullett would become a sure Hall of Fame pick one day.

Gullett had a 16-6 record with an impressive 2.64 ERA and led the National League in winning percentage at .727. He had a 61-26 record with the Reds over a four-year period that included the Reds' world championship years of 1975 and 1976, where he started Game One in both World Series. He became a free agent in 1977 and went to the Yankees, going 14-4 in a year when New York won the World Series. Chronic shoulder problems led to severe rotator cuff damage and cut short his career. Gullett would become the longtime pitching coach for the Reds.

Gus Bell of Louisville started with the Pittsburgh Pirates in 1950 but made his mark after being traded to Cincinnati, where he hit a career-high 30 home runs in 1953. Bell was with the Reds for nine years and had more than 100 RBI four times. Gus, the father of Buddy Bell, was a four-time All-Star.

Lou Johnson of Lexington played a key role for the Los Angeles Dodgers when they won the World Series in 1965, hitting the decisive home run in Game 7. Earlier in the season, he scored the lone run in Sandy Koufax's perfect game—earning the nickname "Sweet Lou."

Woodie Fryman, the tobacco farmer from Ewing, was slow to make it to professional baseball, not signing until he was 25. But his career went into hyperspeed after that. With only 12 minor league appearances, the lefthander was called up for the 1966 season by the Pittsburgh Pirates and threw three straight shutouts. It was the start of an 18-year career that saw him throw four one-hitters and twice be named an All-Star.

Doug Flynn of Lexington was a reserve infielder on The Big Red Machine, the nickname given to the Cincinnati Reds of the 1970s, who won back-to-back World Series championships in 1975 and 1976 and are regarded along with the 1927 New York Yankees as one of the greatest teams in baseball history. Even though he was known far more for his glove work than his batting, Flynn tied the modern major league record with three triples in a single game against Montreal on Aug. 5, 1980.

Joe Cowley of Lexington set an American League pitching record by striking out the first seven Texas Rangers batters to open a game on May 28, 1986, and in September of that year threw a no-hitter against the California Angels despite issuing seven walks. Cowley did this with the Chicago White Sox, but his major league debut came with the Yankees. After eight years in the minors, he was named a starter by New York in July of 1984. He won eight straight decisions and finished 9-2.

There are many more, including: Clint Johnson, an Ashland native who was a star in the old Negro leagues and was elected to the Kentucky Athletic Hall of Fame. Others who were standouts in the old Negro leagues included Louisville's John Beckwith, who played seven positions and hit 54 home runs for the Homestead Grays in 1928, and Greenup's Clinton (Hawk) Thomas, who hit .407 for the Philadelphia team in 1924.

Steve Hamilton, the Morehead native who pitched 11 years in the major leagues, mostly for the Yankees, is one of only three men who played on both a World Series and an NBA championship team. Paul Derringer was a 20-game winner for the Reds in the late 1930s and early 1940s. John Shelby Sr. of Lexington played for the Dodgers, including when L.A. won the World Series over Oakland in 1998.

Few may recall that Cotton Nash, one of the most popular and productive players in UK basketball history, also briefly played in the majors (with the White Sox and Twins from 1967-70). Steve Finley of Paducah first made it to the majors in 1989, played for the 2001 World Series champion Arizona Diamondbacks and is now with the L.A. Angels. He came into 2005 with 293 career home runs. Austin Kearns of Lexington, Terry Shumpert of Paducah, Brad Wilkerson of Owensboro, pitcher Paul Byrd of Louisville and pitcher Brandon Webb Wright of Ashland are among other Kentuckians currently playing.

Unfortunately, two Kentucky natives also were involved in one of the most tragic incidents in baseball history.

In 1920, Cleveland Indians shortstop Ray Chapman, a native of Beaver Dam, was hit in the temple by a pitch and died in the hospital 12 hours later, the only modern era major league player to be fatally injured in a game. Chapman was a talented player, stealing 52 bases in 1917—a record that wasn't broken until 1980. The Yankees pitcher who threw the fateful pitch was Carl Mays of Liberty.

Little League Baseball

VALLEY SPORTS AMERICAN
2002 Little League World Series Champion

When Louisville's Valley Sports American all-star team reached the championship game of the Little League World Series in 2002, it became the first Kentucky team to accomplish the feat in the then 56-year history of the event.

But Valley Sports was just warming up. They went on to beat Japan 1-0 for the championship to become the first United States team to win it all since 1998—and only the 10th U.S. cham-

pion over a 35-year span.

Valley's triumph produced only the third 1-0 score in the history of Little League World Series championship games as the team closed out with a 24-game winning streak.

Members of the team: Aaron Alvey, Justin Elkins, Ethan Henry, Alex Hornback, Wes Jenkins, Casey Jordan, Shane Logsdon, Blaine Madden, Zach Osborne, Jake Remines, Josh Robinson, Wes Walden.

Coaches: Troy Osbourne, Keith Elkins, Dan Roach.

KHSAA Boys Baseball

MOST STATE CHAMPIONSHIPS

School	Titles
Louisville Manual	6
Owensboro	6
Louisville St. Xavier	5
Newport Catholic	4
Ashland Blazer	3
Harrison Co.	3
Lexington Lafayette	3
Lexington Tates Creek	3
Lou. Pleasure Ridge Park	3

PAST STATE CHAMPIONS

Year	Champion
1940	Newport
1941	Newport
1942	Louiville St. Xavier
1943	Louisville Male
1944	(no tournament held)
1945	Louisville St. Xavier
1946	Newport Catholic
1947	Louisville Manual
1948	Prestonsburg
1949	Louisville St. Xavier
1950	Newport Catholic
1951	Louisville St. Xavier
1952	Louisville Manual
1953	St. Joseph
1954	Newport Catholic
1955	Louisville Manual
1956	Newport Catholic
1957	Louisville Manual
1958	Maysville
1959	Louisville Manual
1960	Paducah Tilghman
1961	Caverna
1962	Louisville Manual
1963	Covington Holmes
1964	Owensboro
1965	Bowling Green
1966	Ashland
1967	Ashland
1968	Ashland
1969	Owensboro
1970	Elizabethtown
1971	Daviess Co.
1972	Caverna
1973	Lexington Henry Clay
1974	Somerset
1975	Elizabethtown
1976	Owensboro
1977	Owensboro
1978	Lexington Tates Creek
1979	Shelby Co.
1980	Lexington Tates Creek
1981	Louisville St. Xavier
1982	Madison Central
1983	Owensboro
1984	East Carter
1985	Owensboro Catholic
1986	Lexington Tates Creek
1987	Owensboro
1988	Lexington Lafayette
1989	Lexington Lafayette
1990	Paintsville
1991	Franklin-Simpson
1992	Lexington Lafayette
1993	Harrison Co.
1994	Lou. Pleasure Ridge Park
1995	Lou. Pleasure Ridge Park
1996	Lou. Pleasure Ridge Park
1997	Harrison Co.
1998	Harrison Co.
1999	Lexington Catholic
2000	Henderson Co.
2001	Boyd Co.
2002	Covington Catholic
2003	Lexington Paul Dunbar
2004	Christian Co.
2005	Lexington Christian

MOST HITS (CAREER)

No.	Player	School	Years	Hits
1.	J.B. Schmidt	Harrison Co.	1994-00	275
2.	B.J. Foley	Corbin	1995-02	236
3.	Scott Fryman	Harrison Co.	1990-94	228
4.	Brent Hampton	Harrison Co.	1990-95	227
5.	Will Renaker	Harrison Co.	1994-98	226
6.	Noochie Varner	Harrison Co.	1995-99	223
7.	Brad Wilkerson	Apollo	1991-95	221
8.	Derrick Alfonso	Warren Central	1999-04	220
9.	Jeff Derrickson	Bryan Station	1997-01	204
10.	Ryan Cox	Taylor Co.	1997-00	202

MOST HOME RUNS (CAREER)

No.	Player	School	Years	Home Runs
1.	Paul Morse	Danville	1989-92	62
2.	Shon Walker	Harrison Co.	1989-92	52
3.	Corey Hart	Greenwood	1998-00	48
3.	Kendall Withers	Harrison Co.	1995-99	48
5.	Dion Newby	Harrison Co.	1990-93	46
6.	Glen McDonald	Middlesboro	1993-96	45
7.	Will Renaker	Harrison Co.	1994-98	43
7.	Brad Allison	Harrison Co.	1988-92	43
7.	Chris Snopek	Harrison Co.	1986-89	43
10.	Noochie Varner	Harrison Co.	1995-99	37

MOST RUNS BATTED IN (CAREER)

No.	Player	School	Years	RBI
1.	Will Renaker	Harrison Co.	1994-98	253
2.	Paul Morse	Danville	1989-92	230
3.	B.J. Foley	Corbin	1995-02	220
4.	Noochie Varner	Harrison Co.	1995-99	207
5.	J.B. Schmidt	Harrison Co.	1994-00	202
6.	Brad Wilkerson	Apollo	1991-95	198
7.	Kendall Withers	Harrison Co.	1995-99	195
7.	Scott Fryman	Harrison Co.	1990-94	195
9.	Brandon Gupton	Taylor Co.	1998-01	191
10.	Brian Coffman	Bullitt Central	1997-00	186

HIGHEST BATTING AVERAGE (CAREER)

No.	Player	School	Years	Avg.
1.	David Owens	Rockcastle Co.	1975-78	.584
2.	Noah Welte	St. Patrick	1997-00	.568
3.	Soren Wolf	Monticello	1998-01	.526
4.	Brandon Coffey	Walton-Verona	1997-00	.502
5.	Aaron McClure	Hickman Co.	1997-01	.486
6.	Will Renaker	Harrison Co.	1994-98	.464
7.	David Goodwin	Powell Co.	1977-80	.458
8.	Matt Durham	Scott Co.	1997-99	.444
9.	Michael Evans	Hickman Co.	1997-00	.443
9.	Brad Wilkerson	Apollo	1991-95	.443

MOST PITCHING WINS (CAREER)

No.	Player	School	Years	Wins
1.	Mark Galvin	Elizabethtown	1996-00	42
2.	Mike Blakeman	Green Co.	1965-68	41
3.	Daniel Carrender	Pulaski Co.	1995-99	37
3.	Eric Asbury	Harrison Co.	1992-96	37
3.	Brad Wilkerson	Apollo	1991-95	37
6.	Jon Kirby	Estill Co.	1999-02	33
7.	Shane Smith	Nicholas Co.	1999-01	32
8.	Jeremy Sowers	Ballard	1998-01	31
8.	Andy Baldwin	Taylor Co.	1997-00	31
8.	John Smith	Middlesboro	1988-92	31

LOWEST EARNED RUN AVERAGE (CAREER)

No.	Player	School	Years	ERA
1.	David Slovak	Eastern	2002-04	.085
2.	Jimmy Osting	Trinity	1993-95	1.09
3.	Mark Galvin	Elizabethtown	1996-00	1.36
4.	Brad Wilkerson	Apollo	1991-95	1.58
5.	Clint Brodsky	Boone Co.	2001-03	1.59

MOST SHUTOUTS (CAREER)

No.	Player	School	Years	Total
1.	Mike Blakeman	Green Co.	1965-68	18
2.	Jeremy Sowers	Ballard	1998-01	17
3.	Mark Galvin	Elizabethtown	1996-00	13
4.	Jon Kirby	Estill Co.	1999-02	12
4.	Jimmy Osting	Trinity	1993-95	12

ALL-TIME WINNINGEST COACHES

No.	Coach	Schools	Wins
1.	Larry Gumm*	Green Co.	974
2.	Don Richardson	Madison Central	952
3.	Charlie Adkins*	Paintsville	785
4.	Mac Whitaker*	Harrison Co.	730
5.	Charlie Taylor	Somerset	702
6.	G.J. Smith*	South Laurel	696
7.	Bill Tom Wayne*	Henderson Co.	665
8.	Greg Shelton	Franklin-Simpson	643
9.	Ron Myers	Elizabethtown	613
10.	Jack Hicks	Owensboro	606

KENTUCKY MR. BASEBALL WINNERS

Year	Player	School
1989	Tab Brown	St. Xavier
1990	Darren Burton	Pulaski Co.
1991	Trever Miller	Trinity
1992	Shon Walker	Harrison Co.
1993	Dion Newby	Harrison Co.
1994	Scott Downs	Pleasure Ridge Park
1995	Brad Wilkerson	Apollo
1996	Aaron McGlone	Greenup Co.
1997	Scott Hodges	Henry Clay
1998	Austin Kearns	Lafayette
1999	Joseph Blanton	Franklin-Simpson
2000	Spencer Graeter	Ballard
2001	Jeremy Sowers	Ballard
2002	Brad Corley	Pleasure Ridge Park
2003	Josh Ellis	Paul Dunbar
2004	Collin Cowgill	Henry Clay
2005	Chaz Roe	Lafayette

(Source: KHSAA Sports Information)

Source: Lexington Herald-Leader

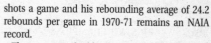

SPORTS

Basketball

John A. McGill

Kentucky teams have generated enough stories of national championships and All America players – even a pro title – to fill any almanac on their own— but none more intriguing than Kentucky State's.

At the start of the 1970s decade, the Thorobreds won three consecutive National Association of Intercollegiate Athletics, or NAIA, championships with talent that many observers felt might well be capable of defeating the University of Kentucky.

There's certainly cause to dispute that claim—at least in the 1969-70 season, when Adolph Rupp's Wildcats, led by Dan Issel, were ranked No. 1 in the nation much of the year before losing in a regional final to Jacksonville and 7-foot Artis Gilmore.

That same season, Kentucky State was fashioning the first of its three straight NAIA titles—and rapidly gaining a national reputation that went far beyond the norm for a small college team.

That's because the Frankfort-based school had a pair of remarkable players: Travis "The Machine" Grant and Elmore Smith, both of whom would later become first round NBA draft picks.

Grant, a 6-foot-7 forward, was also sometimes called "Machine Gun," an apt description of his ability to shoot up an opponent at will. Grant had an incredible career field goal accuracy of 63.8 percent.

Smith, a 7-foot center, averaged nine blocked shots a game and his rebounding average of 24.2 rebounds per game in 1970-71 remains an NAIA record.

They were coached by Lucias Mitchell, who later would become coach at Norfolk State but before leaving gave Kentucky State its most illustrious era in basketball, by far.

Smith and Grant played together when Kentucky State won national titles in 1970 and 1971, but Smith declared hardship to enter the NBA draft and missed his senior season. Not that it mattered. Grant led the Thorobreds to yet another championship in 1972. It is worth noting that to win these titles, Kentucky State had to survive the NAIA's 32-team tournament played over six days in Kansas City.

Smith was the first pick of the Buffalo Braves in the 1971 NBA draft (and third pick overall). A year later, Grant was chosen by the Los Angeles Lakers as their first pick (and 13th overall).

Kentucky's rich basketball tradition is reflected in many ways—not the least of which being UK's seven NCAA titles, Louisville's two NCAA titles, Kentucky Wesleyan's eight NCAA Division II titles, and Georgetown's one NAIA crown. Add to that the American Basketball Association crown that the Kentucky Colonels won in 1975.

But for sheer audacity, it is hard to top Kentucky State's brief but golden era of basketball excellence.

Patrick Sparks' attempt on the basket is blocked by Morgan Sylvester
Source: Lexington Herald-Leader

KHSAA Boys Basketball

ALL-TIME WINNINGEST SCHOOLS

Rank	School	Wins
1.	Ashland Blazer	1,737
2.	Paducah Tilghman	1,656
3.	Central City	1,578
4.	Monticello	1,234
5.	Paris	1,195
6.	Lexington Lafayette	1,187
7.	Wayne Co.	1,149
8.	Newport Central Catholic	1,149
9.	Paintsville	1,201

BOYS' SWEET 16 STATE CHAMPIONS

Year	Champion	Score	Runner-Up
1918	Lexington	16-15	Somerset
1919	Lexington	21-17	Somerset
1920	Lexington	56-13	Ashland
1921	Louisville Manual	32-17	Union Academy
1922	Lexington	55-27	Frankfort
1923	Louisville Manual	41-17	Clark County
1924	Lexington	15-10	Ft. Thomas
1925	Louisville Manual	40-11	Winchester
1926	Louisville St. Xavier	26-13	Danville
1927	M.M.I.	34-25	London
1928	Ashland	13-11	Carr Creek
1929	Heath	21-16	Corinth
1930	Corinth	22-20	Kavanaugh
1931	Louisville Manual	34-23	Tolu
1932	Hazard	15-13	Louisville Male
1933	Ashland	33-25	Horse Cave
1934	Ashland	26-13	Danville
1935	Louisville St. Xavier	32-18	Newport
1936	Corbin	24-18	Nebo
1937	Midway	30-22	Inez
1938	Sharpe	36-27	Maysville
1939	Brooksville	42-39	Hindman
1940	Hazel Green	35-29	Ashland
1941	Inez	35-27	Louisville St. Xavier
1942	Lexington Lafayette	44-32	Harlan
1943	Hindman	29-26	Louisville St. Xavier
1944	Harlan	40-28	Dayton
1945	Louisville Male	68-42	Central City
1946	Breckinridge Training	68-36	Dawson Springs
1947	Maysville	54-40	Brewers
1948	Brewers	65-48	Maysville
1949	Owensboro	65-47	Lexington Lafayette
1950	Lexington Lafayette	55-51	Clark County
1951	Clark County	69-44	Cuba
1952	Cuba	58-52	Louisville Manual
1953	Lexington Lafayette	84-53	Paducah Tilghman
1954	Inez	63-55	Newport
1955	Hazard	74-66	Adair County
1956	Carr Creek	72-68	Henderson
1957	Lexington Lafayette	55-52	Louisville Eastern
1958	Louisville St. Xavier	60-49	Daviess County
1959	North Marshall	64-63	Louisville Manual
1960	Louisville Flaget	65-56	Monticello
1961	Ashland	69-50	Lexington Dunbar
1962	Louisville St. Xavier	62-58	Ashland
1963	Louisville Seneca	72-66	Lexington Dunbar
1964	Louisville Seneca	66-56	Breckinridge County
1965	Breckinridge Co.	95-73	Covington Holy Cross
1966	Shelby County	62-57	Male
1967	Earlington	54-53	Covington Catholic
1968	Glasgow	77-68	Louisville Seneca
1969	Louisville Central	101-72	Ohio County
1970	Louisville Male	70-69	Madison
1971	Louisville Male	83-66	Anderson County
1972	Owensboro	71-63	Elizabethtown
1973	Louisville Shawnee	81-68	Louisville Male
1974	Louisville Central	59-54	Louisville Male
1975	Louisville Male	74-59	Lexington Henry Clay
1976	Edmonson County	74-52	Christian County
1977	Louisville Ballard	68-59	Louisville Valley
1978	Shelby County	68-66	Covington Holmes
1979	Lexington Lafayette	62-52	Christian County
1980	Owensboro	57-56	Louisville Doss
1981	Simon Kenton	70-63	Mason County
1982	Laurel County	53-51	North Hardin
1983	Lexington Henry Clay	35-33	Carlisle County
1984	Logan County	83-70	Bourbon County
1985	Hopkinsville	65-64	Clay County
1986	Pulaski County	47-45	Pleasure Ridge Park
1987	Clay County	76-73	Louisville Ballard
1988	Louisville Ballard	88-79	Clay County
1989	Pleasure Ridge Park	75-73	Wayne County
1990	Louisville Fairdale	77-73	Covington Holmes
1991	Louisville Fairdale	67-63	Lexington Tates Creek
1992	University Heights	59-57	Lexington Catholic
1993	Marion County	85-77	Lexington Paul Dunbar
1994	Louisville Fairdale	59-56	Lexington Paul Dunbar
1995	Breckinridge Co.	70-63	Pleasure Ridge Park
1996	Paintsville	71-53	Ashland Blazer
1997	Louisville Eastern	71-59	Ft. Thomas Highlands
1998	Scott County	89-78	Paintsville
1999	Louisville Ballard	71-47	Scott County
2000	Elizabethtown	79-69	Lexington Catholic
2001	Lexington Lafayette	54-49	Louisville Male
2002	Lexington Catholic	83-53	Paducah Tilghman
2003	Mason County	86-65	Louisville Ballard
2004	Warren Central	66-56	Mason County
2005	South Laurel	72-59	Warren Central

ALL-TIME LEADING SCORERS (CAREER)

Rank	Player	School	Points
1.	Kelly Coleman	Wayland	4,337
2.	Charlie Osborne	Flat Gap	3,647
3.	Harry Todd	Earlington	3,567
4.	Chris Harrison	Tollesboro	3,542
5.	Charles Thomas	Harlan	3,365
6.	Clem Haskins	Taylor Co.	3,325
7.	Ty Rogers	Lyon Co.	3,300
8.	Fred Hale	Williamstown	3,233
9.	Ervin Stepp	Phelps	3,228
10.	Manual Forrest	Lou. Moore	3,226

MOST POINTS SCORED (GAME)

No.	Player	School	Year	Points
1.	Wayne Oakley	Hanson	1954	114
2.	Danny Cornett	Breck.Training	1964	87
3.	Wayne Golden	Lou. Shawnee	1970	84
3.	Jack Winders	Morton's Gap	1954	84
5.	Bob Slusher	Lone Jack	1957	83
5.	Bill Burnett	Paris	1916	83
7.	Roger Bolton	Lynn Camp	1968	78
8.	Ervin Stepp	Phelps	1980	75
8.	Kelly Coleman	Wayland	1956	75
10.	Chris Harrison	Tollesboro	1991	73

ALL-TIME LEADING REBOUNDERS (CAREER)

No.	Player	School	Rebounds
1.	Harry Todd	Earlington	2,188
2.	Tim Stephens	McCreary Co.	2,157
3.	J.R. VanHoose	Paintsville	2,069
4.	Brian Saylor	Red Bird	1,558
5.	Keith Blackburn	Eminence	1,506
6.	Charles Thomas	Harlan	1,441
7.	Edward Congleton	Lee Co.	1,388
8.	Dennis Johnson	Harrodsburg	1,347
9.	Chase Gibson	Pikeville	1,344
10.	Parke Congleton	Lee. Co.	1,323

ALL-TIME WINNINGEST COACHES

No.	Coach	Schools	Wins
1.	William Kean	Central	856
2.	Russ Williamson	Inez	793
3.	Bobby Keith	Clay Co.	767
4.	Pearl Combs	Vicco/Hindman	760
5.	Don Parsons	Madisonville	714
6.	John Bill Trivette	Pikeville	709
7.	Marvin Meredith	Russell	677
8.	Ron Bevars*	North Hardin	669
9.	Al Prewitt	Henry Co./Henry Clay	654
10.	David Fraley*	Powell Co./Pulaski Co.	630

* active

KENTUCKY MR. BASKETBALL WINNERS

Year	Player	School
1956	Kelly Coleman	Wayland
1957	Billy Ray Lickert	Lexington Lafayette
1958	Ralph Richardson	Russell Co.
	Harry Todd	Earlington
1959	Pat Doyle	North Marshall
1960	Jeff Mullins	Lexington Lafayette
1961	Randy Embry	Owensboro
1962	Mike Silliman	Louisville St. Xavier
1963	Mike Redd	Louisville Seneca
1964	Wes Unseld	Louisville Seneca
1965	Butch Beard	Breckinridge Co.
1966	Mike Casey	Shelby Co.
1967	Jim McDaniels	Allen Co.
1968	Terry Davis	Shelby Co.
1969	Ron King	Louisville Central
1970	Robert Brooks	Richmond Madison
1971	Jimmy Dan Conner	Anderson Co.
1972	Jerry Thurston	Owensboro
1973	Wesley Cox	Louisville Male
1974	Jack Givens	Lexington Bryan Station
1975	Dom Fucci	Lexington Tates Creek
1976	Darrell Griffith	Louisville Male
1977	Jeff Lamp	Louisville Ballard
1978	Doug Schloemer	Covington Holmes
1979	Dirk Minniefield	Lexington Lafayette
1980	Ervin Stepp	Phelps
1981	Phil Cox	Cawood
1982	Todd May	Virgie
1983	Winston Bennett	Louisville Male
1984	Steve Miller	Lexington Henry Clay
1985	Tony Kimbro	Louisville Seneca
1986	Rex Chapman	Owensboro Apollo
1987	John Pelphrey	Paintsville
1988	Richie Farmer	Clay Co.
1989	Allan Houston	Louisville Ballard
1990	Dwayne Morton	Louisville Central
1991	Jermaine Brown	Louisville Fairdale
1992	Tick Rogers	Hart Co.
1993	Jason Osborne	Louisville Male
1994	Elton Scott	Marion Co.
1995	Charles Thomas	Harlan
1996	Daymeon Fishback	Greenwood
1997	Brandon Davenport	Owensboro
1998	J.R. VanHoose	Paintsville
1999	Rick Jones	Scott Co.
2000	Scott Hundley	Scott Co.
2001	Josh Carrier	Bowling Green
2002	Brandon Stockton	Glasgow
2003	Ross Neltner	Fort Thomas Highlands
2004	Chris Lofton	Mason Co.
2005	Dominic Tilford	Jeffersontown

KHSAA Girls Basketball

ALL-TIME WINNINGEST SCHOOLS

No.	School	Wins
1.	George Rogers Clark	575
2.	Paris	504
3.	Henderson Co.	500

GIRLS' SWEET 16 STATE CHAMPIONS

Year	Champion	Score	Runner-Up
1920	Paris	32-10	Nicholasville
1921	Ashland	22-11	Clark Co.
1922	Ashland	39-7	Sardis
1923	West Louisville	8-5	Cresent Springs
1924	Ashland	13-11	Georgetown
1925	Georgetown	40-0	Hardyville Memorial
1926	Maysville	23-16	Henderson
1927	West Louisville	19-18	Georgetown
1928	Ashland	27-11	Oddville
1929	Ashland	23-10	Oddville
1930	Hazard	23-18	Woodburn
1931	Woodburn	24-19	Ashland
1932	Woodburn	25-20	Paintsville
1975	Louisville Butler	60-43	Barren Co.
1976	Lou. Sacred Heart	68-55	Butler
1977	Laurel Co.	48-46	Paris
1978	Laurel Co.	63-48	Breathitt Co.
1979	Laurel Co.	43-36	Lafayette
1980	Louisville Butler	65-49	Franklin Co.
1981	Pulaski Co.	50-42	Marshall Co.
1982	Marshall Co.	48-44	Mercy
1983	Warren Central	57-49	Whitesburg
1984	Marshall Co.	55-53	Belfry
1985	Whitley Co.	38-37	Atherton
1986	Oldham Co.	49-48	Franklin-Simpson
1987	Laurel Co.	50-48	Doss
1988	Louisville Southern	57-34	Oldham Co.
1989	Clay Co.	48-44	Clark Co.
1990	Henry Clay	62-50	Southern
1991	Laurel Co.	33-31	Clark Co.
1992	Louisville Mercy	44-38	Clay Co.
1993	Nicholas Co.	48-46	Warren East
1994	M.C. Napier	88-56	Highlands
1995	Scott Co.	68-45	Pulaski Co.
1996	Union Co.	44-37	Central Hardin
1997	Hazard	54-38	Elizabethtown
1998	Elizabethtown	45-37	Montgomery Co.
1999	Lexington Catholic	57-42	Assumption
2000	West Carter	58-50	Shelby Co.
2001	Lexington Catholic	36-34	Manual
2002	Lou. Sacred Heart	57-46	Jackson Co.
2003	Lou. Sacred Heart	42-40	Lexington Catholic
2004	Lou. Sacred Heart	43-34	Lexington Catholic
2005	Lexington Catholic	59-54	Clinton Co.

ALL-TIME LEADING SCORERS (CAREER)

No.	Player	School	Points
1.	Jaime Walz	Ft. Thomas Highlands	4,948
2.	Geri Grigsby	McDowell	4,385
3.	Kim Mays	Knox Central	3,952
4.	Carolyn Alexander	Hazard	3,726
5.	Lisa Harrison	Louisville Southern	3,469
6.	Mandy Harmon	Sheldon Clark	3,280
7.	Marialice Jenkins	Fordsville	3,266
8.	Erica Hallman	Covington Holmes	3,187
9.	Sherry Mitchell	Muhlenberg Central	3,155
10.	SeSe Helm	Warren Central	3,144

MOST POINTS SCORED (GAME)

No.	Player	School	Year	Points
1.	Geri Grigsby	McDowell	1975	81
2.	Beverly Smallwood	Dorton	1987	71
3.	Heather Benton	Leslie Co.	2004	66
3.	Melissa Brandon	Oneida Baptist	1996	66
5.	Jody Sizemore	Leslie Co.	1999	63
5.	Sondra Miller	M.C. Napier	1983	63
7.	Heather Benton	Leslie Co.	2004	60
7.	Jaime Walz	Ft. Thomas Highlands	1995	60
9.	Jody Sizemore	Leslie Co.	1998	58

ALL-TIME LEADING REBOUNDERS (CAREER)

No.	Player	School	Rebounds
1.	Sarah Elliott	Jackson Co.	1,843
2.	Jaime Walz	Ft. Thomas Highlands	1,762
3.	Megan Gray	Harrison Co.	1,754
4.	Lisa Harrison	Louisville Southern	1,716
5.	Kyra Elzy	Oldham Co.	1,703
6.	Jessica Schmidt	Walton-Verona	1,674
7.	Jade Perry	Muhlenberg North	1,647
8.	Angela Brown	Clinton Co.	1,569
9.	Amanda Collins	Pike Co. Central	1,491
10.	Jenni Benningfield	Louisville Assumption	1,480

ALL-TIME WINNINGEST COACHES

No.	Coach	Schools	Wins
1.	Howard Beth*	Marshall Co.	678
2.	Randy Napier*	M.C. Napier/Perry Co. Central	594
3.	John High*	Whitesburg/Breathitt Co. /Montgomery Co.	559

4.	Wendell Wilson*	Leslie Co.	550
5.	John "Hop" Brown	West Carter	514
6.	Bill Goller	Holy Cross	512
7.	Doug & Sue Kincer	Fleming-Neon	484
8.	Roy Bowling	Laurel Co./Lou. Mercy	483
9.	Bill Brown	Lou. Southern/Lou. Ballard	475
9.	Willis McClure	Owensboro Apollo	475

* active

KENTUCKY MISS BASKETBALL WINNERS

Year	Player	School
1976	Donna Murphy	Newport
1977	Geri Grigsby	McDowell
1978	Irene Moore	Breathitt Co.
1979	Beth Wilkerson	Paris
1980	Lisa Collins	Laurel Co.
1981	Lillie Mason	Olmstead
1982	Connie Goins	Frankfort Western Hills
1983	Clemette Haskins	Warren Central
1984	Carol Parker	Marshall Co.
1985	Brigette Combs	Whitesburg
1986	Kris Miller	Owensboro Catholic
1987	Mary Taylor	Marshall Co.
1988	Kim Pehlke	Louisville Doss
1989	Lisa Harrison	Louisville Southern
1990	Kim Mays	Knox Central
1991	Ida Bowen	Sheldon Clark
1992	Becky McKinley	Bullitt East
1993	Brandi Ashby	Webster Co.
1994	Laurie Townsend	Owensboro Apollo
1995	Ukari Figgs	Scott Co.
1996	Jaime Walz	Fort Thomas Highlands
1997	Rachel Byars	Union Co.
1998	Beth Vice	Montgomery Co.
1999	Jody Sizemore	Leslie Co.
2000	Jenni Benningfield	Louisville Assumption
2001	Katie Schweggman	Louisville Bishop Brossart
2002	Erica Hallman	Covington Holmes
2003	Megen Gearhart	West Carter
2004	Crystal Kelly	Louisville Sacred Heart
2005	Carly Omerod	Louisville Sacred Heart

(Source: KHSAA Sports Information)

University of Kentucky women's basketball coach, Mickie DeMoss, answers questions on media day in Lexington, Nov. 3, 2004
Source: Lexington Herald-Leader

Colleges & Universities

CUMBERLAND COLLEGE
MEN'S BASKETBALL

CUMBERLAND COLLEGE BY THE NUMBERS
- Overall record: 915-467
- 5 30-win seasons
- 20 20-win seasons

ALL-TIME LEADING SCORERS

No.	Player	Years	Games	Pts.	Avg.
1.	Roger Richardson	1980-84	138	2,068	15.0
2.	Wilford Jackson	1960-64	107	1,945	18.1
3.	Bob Long	1967-70	65	1,830	28.1
4.	Ivan Johnson	1998-03	134	1,815	13.5
5.	Maurice Byrd	1970-74	106	1,809	17.1
6.	Garrett Gregory	1983-87	135	1,782	13.2
7.	Brian Key	1992-96	129	1,690	13.1
8.	Brad Gover	1994-97	99	1,573	15.9
9.	Larry Gorman	1977-79	73	1,501	20.6
10.	Larry Hurt	1971-74	83	1,475	17.7

ALL-TIME CAREER SCORING AVERAGES

No.	Player	Years	Games	Pts.	Avg.
1.	Bob Long	1967-70	65	1,830	28.1
2.	Larry Gorman	1977-79	73	1,501	20.6
3.	Wilford Jackson	1960-64	107	1,945	18.1
4.	Larry Hurt	1971-74	83	1,475	17.7
5.	Maurice Byrd	1970-74	106	1,809	17.1

ALL-TIME LEADING REBOUNDERS

No.	Player	Years	Rebounds	Avg.
1.	Maurice Byrd	1970-74	1,281	11.9
2.	Wiley Brown	1960-64	1,054	10.0
3.	Melvin Harris	1971-75	1,033	9.2
4.	Garrett Gregory	1983-87	962	7.1
5.	Steve Banks	1975-78	920	10.8
6.	Raymond Cox	1966-70	911	9.3
7.	Jerry Brown	1964-67	864	10.2
8.	Jim Rollins	1964-67	859	11.5
9.	Bob Long	1967-70	832	12.8
10.	Joe Dallas	1977-80	808	10.9

ALL-TIME ASSISTS LEADERS

No.	Player	Years	Assists	Avg.
1.	Tony Pietrowski	1994-99	654	3.9
2.	John McCoy	1982-86	625	4.6
3.	Larry Gorman	1977-79	624	8.6
4.	Junie Hemphill	1984-88	585	4.4
5.	Ivan Johnson	1998-03	451	3.4
6.	Brian Key	1990-94	378	3.3
7.	Garry Patton	1975-78	358	5.0
8.	Scott Thomas	1982-86	327	2.7
9.	Ed Bowen	1980-82	273	7.4
9.	Doug Oak	1990-94	273	2.2

ALL-TIME STEALS LEADERS

No.	Player	Years	Steals
1.	Ivan Johnson	1998-03	229
2.	Tony Pietrowski	1994-99	214
3.	Brian Key	1990-94	176
4.	Don Skipper	1988-90	128
4.	Steve Glenn	1989-91	128
6.	Jerry Williams	1999-01	106

7.	Doug Garth	1993-97	99
8.	Mark Vernon	1998-02	94
9.	Demorrius Thomas	2001-	91
10.	Eric Bailey	1996-98	74

(Source: Cumberland College Sports Information)

CUMBERLAND COLLEGE
WOMEN'S BASKETBALL

CUMBERLAND COLLEGE BY THE NUMBERS
- Overall record: 473-389
- 10 20-win seasons

ALL-TIME LEADING SCORERS

No.	Player	Years	Games	Pts.	Avg.
1.	Soni Smith	1980-84	101	2,015	19.9
2.	Hope Peace-Akins	1986-91	124	1,622	13.0
3.	Jamie Walker	1999-03	126	1,492	11.8
4.	Haven Aldridge	1994-98	120	1,490	12.4
5.	Jessie Holt	1998-02	123	1,404	11.4
6.	Lisa Barton Nantz	1982-86	108	1,394	12.9
7.	Candi Fannin	1990-94	117	1,358	11.6
8.	Missie Irvin	1989-94	123	1,356	11.0
9.	Charline Gibson	1990-94	125	1,353	10.7
10.	Betsy Rains	1982-86	110	1,315	11.9

ALL-TIME CAREER SCORING AVERAGES

No.	Player	Years	Games	Pts.	Avg.
1.	Soni Smith	1980-84	101	2,015	19.9
2.	Nicole LaVan	1999-01	54	902	19.3
3.	Barbara Spratling	1986-88	54	989	18.3
4.	Anita Ledbetter	1976-80	45	702	15.6
5.	Hope Peace-Akins	1986-91	124	1,622	13.0

ALL-TIME LEADING REBOUNDERS

No.	Player	Years	Rebounds	Avg.
1.	Rhonda Hodges	1979-83	861	7.4
2.	Mioshi Moore	1988-92	779	6.7
3.	Geri Antrobus	1991-95	767	6.7
4.	Susan Zellner	1976-80	755	8.2
5.	Lisa Barton Nantz	1982-86	741	6.9
6.	Carrie Dawson	1979-83	682	6.4
7.	Allison Wilburn	1981-84	643	7.9
8.	Jana Newman	1985-87	640	6.2
9.	Allison Smith	1985-87	634	11.3
10.	Kim Feistritzer	1990-94	627	5.0

ALL-TIME ASSISTS LEADERS

No.	Player	Years	Assists
1.	Missie Irvin	1989-94	634
2.	Jessie Holt	1998-02	474
3.	Konnie Irvin-Snyder	1985-89	414
4.	Hope Peace-Akins	1986-91	408
5.	Betsy Rains	1982-86	366
6.	Mandy Calihan	1994-98	354
7.	Candi Fannin	1990-93	345
8.	Monica Hang	2002-04	335
8.	Lisa Pflueger	1980-84	335
10.	Soni Smith	1980-84	327

ALL-TIME FREE THROW PERCENTAGE (CAREER)

No.	Player	Years	FTA	FTM	PCT.
1.	Betsy Rains	1982-86	292	241	.825
2.	Jessie Holt	1998-02	279	226	.810
3.	Christy Webster	1994-98	304	245	.806
4.	Lindsay Holder	1999-02	139	111	.799
5.	Konnie Irvin-Snyder	1985-89	116	92	.793
6.	Haven Aldridge	1994-98	351	278	.792
7.	Charline Gibson	1990-94	242	186	.769
8.	Barbara Spratling	1986-88	218	167	.766
9.	Missie Irvin	1990-94	321	245	.763
10.	Annette Wormsley	1987-90	273	207	.758

(Source: Cumberland College Sports Information)

EASTERN KENTUCKY UNIVERSITY
MEN'S BASKETBALL

EKU BY THE NUMBERS
- Overall record: 1,029-970
- 4 20-win seasons
- 6 NCAA Tournament appearances

ALL-TIME LEADING SCORERS

No.	Player	Years	Pts.	Avg.
1.	Antonio Parris	1983-87	1,723	16.9
2.	John Allen	1990-94	1,635	14.1
3.	Arlando Johnson	1991-95	1,617	14.1
4.	Carl Brown	1972-76	1,592	16.2
5.	Eddie Bodkin	1963-66	1,587	21.1
6.	James Tillman	1978-80	1,514	27.0
7.	Charles Mitchell	1970-73	1,507	20.6
8.	Jack Adams	1953-56	1,460	20.6
9.	DeMarkus Doss	1992-96	1,442	13.2
10.	Kenny Elliott	1975-79	1,353	13.3

ALL-TIME CAREER SCORING AVERAGES

No.	Player	Years	Pts.	Avg.
1.	James Tillman	1978-80	1,514	27.0
2.	Eddie Bodkin	1963-66	1,587	21.1
3.	Charles Mitchell	1970-73	1,507	20.6
4.	Jack Adams	1953-56	1,460	20.6
5.	George Bryant	1969-72	1,345	19.5

ALL-TIME LEADING REBOUNDERS

No.	Player	Years	Rebounds	Avg.
1.	Mike Smith	1988-92	977	8.6
2.	Jim Baechtold	1948-52	933	10.6
3.	Garfield Smith	1965-68	884	13.2
4.	Jack Adams	1953-56	870	12.3
5.	Mike Oliver	1974-78	859	8.9
6.	Eddie Bodkin	1963-66	812	11.0
7.	Carl Greenfield	1968-71	802	11.8
8.	Dave Bootcheck	1976-80	728	7.4
9.	Elmer Tolson	1949-53	716	8.2
10.	Willie Woods	1967-70	693	10.8

ALL-TIME WINNINGEST COACHES

Coach	Years	Record	Pct.
Paul McBrayer	16	219-144	.603
Max Good	8	96-129	.427
Guy Strong	6	78-65	.545
James E. Baechtold	5	70-57	.551
Ed Byhre	5	69-63	.523
Charles T. Hughes	6	68-40	.630

(Source: Eastern Kentucky University Sports Information)

EASTERN KENTUCKY UNIVERSITY
WOMEN'S BASKETBALL

EKU BY THE NUMBERS
- Overall record: 482-405
- 4 Ohio Valley Conference championships
- 1 NCAA Tournament appearance
- 6 20-win seasons
- 1 WNIT appearance

ALL-TIME LEADING SCORERS

No.	Player	Years	Pts.
1.	Lisa Goodin	1980-84	1,920
2.	Jaree Goodin	1989-93	1,679
3.	Peggy Gay	1975-79	1,674
4.	Katie Kelly	2000-04	1,626
5.	Kim Mays	1992-95	1,587
6.	Charlotte Sizemore	1997-02	1,561
7.	Kelly Cowan	1987-91	1,515
8.	Angie Cox	1988-92	1,425
9.	Tina Wermuth	1979-83	1,403
10.	Laphelia Doss	1994-98	1,378

ALL-TIME LEADING REBOUNDERS

No.	Player	Years	Rebounds
1.	Laphelia Doss	1994-98	1,027
2.	Sandra Mukes	1978-82	975
3.	Jaree Goodin	1989-93	914
4.	Tina Wermuth	1979-83	866
5.	Carla Coffey	1984-88	751
6.	Maisha Thomas-Blanton	1991-95	711
7.	Teresa McNair	1999-03	631
8.	Shannon Brady	1981-85	625
9.	Charlotte Sizemore	1997-02	611
10.	Tina Cottle	1983-85	577

ALL-TIME ASSISTS LEADERS

No.	Player	Years	Assists
1.	Angie Cox	1988-92	488
2.	Katie Kelly	2000-04	395
3.	Cheryl Jones	1989-92	394
4.	Mikki Bond	1998-02	389
5.	Lisa Goodin	1980-84	374
6.	Samantha Young	1991-96	350
7.	Charlotte Sizemore	1997-02	344
8.	Zoey Artist	1998-02	307
9.	Kim Mays	1992-95	297
10.	Maisha Thomas-Blanton	1991-95	270

ALL-TIME STEALS LEADERS

No.	Player	Years	Steals
1.	Teresa McNair	1999-03	406
2.	Angie Cox	1988-92	327
3.	Maisha Thomas-Blanton	1991-95	236
4.	Charlotte Sizemore	1997-02	228
5.	Mikki Bond	1998-02	227

ALL-TIME WINNINGEST COACHES

Coach	Years	Record	Pct.
Larry Joe Inman	17	286-192	.598
Dianne Murphy	7	96-101	.487
Shirley Duncan	4	41-59	.410

(Source: Eastern Kentucky University Sports Information)

GEORGETOWN COLLEGE
BASKETBALL

GEORGETOWN BY THE NUMBERS:
- Overall record: 1582-818
- One NAIA national title (1998)
- 3 first team All Americans
- 3 Coach of the Year awards

FIRST TEAM ALL AMERICANS
Kenny Davis
Dick Vories
Will Carlton

WINNINGEST COACHES
Jim Reid (529)
Bob Davis (415)
Happy Osborne (281)

ITEMS OF NOTE
- Georgetown holds the NAIA record for most consecutive trips to the national championship with 14 (1992-2005).
- Georgetown defeated Southern Nazarene (Okla.) 83-69 in the 1998 title game.
- Bob Davis was NAIA Coach of the Year in 1959, Jim Reid in 1994 and Happy Osborne in 1998.

(Source: Georgetown College Sports Information)

KENTUCKY STATE UNIVERSITY
MEN'S BASKETBALL

K-STATE BY THE NUMBERS
- Overall record: 889-705
- 1 NCAA Tournament appearance (1962)
- 3 NAIA national championships (1970, 1971, 1972)
- 10 NAIA district championships
- 1 SIAC Tournament championship (2001)
- 4 First Team All Americans (selected 8 times)
- 5 Coach of the Year awards

K-STATE FIRST TEAM ALL AMERICANS
Travis Grant, forward (1970, 1971, 1972)
Elmore Smith, center (1971)
Gerald Cunningham, forward (1975, 1976, 1977)
Billy Ray Bates, forward (1978)

ITEMS OF NOTE
- Coach Lucius Mitchell led the Thorobreds to NAIA championships in 1970, 1971 and 1972. His powerful 1970-71 team posted the school's best record, 31-2.
- Elmore Smith's 22.6 career rebounding average ranks among college basketball's all-time best. He pulled down 36 rebounds in a win over Lincoln.
- Legendary three-time All-American Travis "The Machine" Grant once scored 75 points in a single game, making good on 35 field goals. The total pints likely would have been considerably higher had the three-point field goal rule been established.) He finished his career with 4,045 points and a 33.4 scoring average.
- The Thorobreds scored 159 points in a game on two occasions.
- Harvey Carmichael handed out 21 assists in a win over Carson-Newman.

ALL-TIME LEADING SCORERS

No.	Player	Years	Games	Pts.	Avg.
1.	Travis Grant	1968-72	121	4,045	33.4
2.	Gerald Cunningham	1973-77	121	2,635	21.8
3.	Elmore Smith	1968-71	85	1,813	21.3
4.	Billy Ray Bates	1974-78	107	1,723	16.1
5.	Lewis Linder	1972-76	116	1,574	13.6
6.	Mike Busby	1977-81	111	1,483	13.0
7.	Harvey Carmichael	1971-75	123	1,318	10.7
8.	Fred Bowles	1981-85	95	1,309	13.8
9.	Tyrone Jordan	1978-82	106	1,246	11.8
10.	Alfred Smith	1978-82	88	1,238	14.1

ALL-TIME CAREER SCORING AVERAGES

No.	Player	Years	Games	Pts.	Avg.
1.	Travis Grant	1968-72	121	4,045	33.4
2.	Gerald Cunningham	1973-77	121	2,635	21.8
3.	Elmore Smith	1968-71	85	1,813	21.3
4.	Billy Ray Bates	1974-78	107	1,723	16.1
5.	Alfred Smith	1978-82	88	1,238	14.1

ALL-TIME LEADING REBOUNDERS

No.	Player	Years	Rebounds	Avg.
1.	Elmore Smith	1968-91	1,917	22.6
2.	Travis Grant	1968-72	1,121	9.4
3.	Gerald Cunningham	1973-77	1,023	10.3
3.	William Graham	1967-71	1,023	9.3
5.	Roy Smith	1974-77	910	11.7
6.	Andre Hampton	1971-75	847	11.7
7.	Billy Ray Bates	1974-78	784	7.3
8.	Charles Tyron	1977-80	758	6.5
9.	Arthur Box	1971-75	679	6.7
10.	Sam Sibert	1971-72	664	20.1

ALL-TIME ASSISTS LEADERS

No.	Player	Years	Assists
1.	Harvey Carmichael	1971-75	972
2.	Jerry Stafford	1969-73	909
3.	Lewis Linder	1972-76	687
4.	Johnny Mitchell	1975-78	456
5.	Jerome Brister	1976-81	449
6.	Leonard Williams	1978-80	381
7.	Michael Douglas	1993-97	358
8.	Toby Joseph	1989-93	302
9.	Travis Grant	1968-72	267
10.	Bruce Coles	1978-80	255

ALL-TIME WINNINGEST COACHES

Coach	Years	Record	Pct.
Lucias Mitchell	8	192-47	.803
Joseph G. Fletcher	10	149-85	.637
James B. Brown	7	93-70	.571

(Source: Kentucky State University Sports Information)

KENTUCKY WESLEYAN COLLEGE
MEN'S BASKETBALL

KWC BY THE NUMBERS
- Overall record: 1,416-701
- 8 NCAA Division II national championships (1966, 1968, 1969, 1973, 1987, 1990, 1999, 2001)
- 18 Final Four appearances
- 20 Elite Eight appearances
- 91 NCAA Tournament wins
- 14 Great Lakes Valley Conference titles
- 5 GLVC Tournament championships

- 6 30-win seasons
- 27 Top 10 national poll finishes
- 3 National Player of the Year award winners
- 17 First Team All Americans
- 6 National Coach of the Year award winners

FIRST TEAM ALL AMERICANS

Mason Cope (1957)
Sam Smith (1967)
Dallas Thornton (1968)
George Tinsley (1969)
Jyronna Ralston (1974)
Rod Drake (1984)
Dwight Higgs (1984)
J.B. Brown (1988)
Corey Crowder (1990)
Willis Cheaney (1995)
Antonio Garcia (1998)
Dana Williams (1999)
Leroy John (2000)
Lorico Duncan (2001)
Tyrus Boswell (2002)
Ronald Evans (2002)
Marlon Parmer (2003)

OTHER KWC ALL AMERICANS

Fairce Woods (1946, 1949)
Joe Roop (1955)
Bill Bibb (1957)
Kelly Coleman (1959)
Gary Auten (1961)
Dick O'Neill (1969)
John Duncan (1970, 1971)
Jim Smith (1970)
Willie Johnson (1976)
Ray Harper (1985)
Dave Bennett (1985, 1986)
Sam L. Smith (1987)
Alex Kreps (1992)
Carlos Skinner (1993)

ITEMS OF NOTE

- Kentucky Wesleyan College is the all-time Division II winner with 1,416 victories.
- Fairce Woods was the first Panther to earn All-America recognition and the first to score 1,000 career points.
- KWC has won eight NCAA Division II national titles under five different coaches (Guy Strong, Bob Daniels, Bob Jones, Wayne Chapman and Ray Harper).
- Wayne Chapman won 82 percent of his games and two NCAA championships during his five-year tenure as head coach.
- KWC's eight national titles ranks second only to UCLA's 11 among all Division I, II, III programs.
- The Panthers notched their first victory by beating Eastern Kentucky 44-22 in 1908.
- The legendary "King" Kelly Coleman averaged 27.7 points per game during his three seasons at KWC, scoring 40 or more points on four occasions. Coleman averaged 30.3 ppg in 1960, third best in the nation.
- Corey Crowder (1991), Antonio Garcia (1999) and Marlon Parmer (2003) won National Division II Player of the Year awards.
- Thirty-six former Panthers have played at the professional level.

ALL-TIME LEADING SCORERS

No.	Player	Years	Games	Pts.	Avg.
1.	Corey Crowder	1988-91	118	2,282	19.3
2.	Dwight Higgs	1981-84	120	2,228	18.6
3.	Kelly Coleman	1958-60	75	2,077	27.7
4.	George Tinsley	1966-69	119	2,014	16.9
5.	Dallas Thornton	1965-68	112	1,929	17.5
6.	Gary Auten	1959-62	102	1,774	17.4
7.	Rod Drake	1981-84	120	1,664	13.9
8.	Mike Williams	1971-73	87	1,568	18.0
9.	Fairce Woods	1946-49	89	1,424	16.0
10.	Gino Bartolone	1998-01	133	1,361	10.1

ALL-TIME CAREER SCORING AVERAGES

No.	Player	Years	Games	Pts.	Avg.
1.	Kelly Coleman	1958-60	75	2,077	27.7
2.	Corey Crowder	1988-91	118	2,282	19.3
3.	Sam Smith	1966-67	58	1,102	19.0
4.	Dwight Higgs	1981-84	120	2,228	18.6
5.	Jyronna Ralston	1973-74	57	1,031	18.1
6.	Mike Williams	1971-73	87	1,568	18.0
7.	Dave Bennett	1985-86	61	1,083	17.8
8.	Sam L. Smith	1986-87	63	1,115	17.7
9.	Dallas Thornton	1965-68	112	1,929	17.5
9.	Lorico Duncan	2000-01	68	1,193	17.5

ALL-TIME LEADING REBOUNDERS

No.	Player	Years	Rebounds	Avg.
1.	George Tinsley	1966-69	1,115	9.4
2.	James Greene	1970-73	1,088	10.2
3.	Antonio Garcia	1998-99	997	14.2
4.	John Duncan	1968-71	974	10.1
5.	Larry Morris	1969-72	945	9.3
6.	Kelly Coleman	1958-60	904	12.1
7.	Dallas Thornton	1965-68	903	8.1
8.	Corey Crowder	1988-91	806	6.8
9.	J.B. Brown	1985-88	797	6.6
10.	Willie Johnson	1974-76	723	9.4

ALL-TIME ASSISTS LEADERS

No.	Player	Years	Assists	Avg.
1.	Willis Cheaney	1992-95	635	5.6
2.	Rod Drake	1981-84	458	3.8
3.	Patrick Critchelow	1996-99	454	3.6
4.	Ray Harper	1983-85	442	7.1
5.	Andra Whitlow	1984-87	438	3.7
6.	Junebug Rakes	1988-91	415	3.6
7.	Kim Clay	1986-89	411	3.8
8.	Steve Divine	1990-93	405	3.4
9.	Kris Kemp	1994-97	361	3.1
10.	Dwight Higgs	1981-84	328	2.7

ALL-TIME WINNINGEST COACHES

Coach	Years	Record	Pct.
Ray Harper	9	242-45	.843
Robert Wilson	15	204-141	.591
Wayne Boultinghouse	6	129-45	.741
Wayne Chapman	5	128-29	.815
Bob Jones	8	119-90	.569
Mike Pollio	5	117-35	.770
Bob Daniels	5	110-36	.753

(Source: Kentucky Wesleyan College Sports Information)

KENTUCKY WESLEYAN COLLEGE
WOMEN'S BASKETBALL

KWC BY THE NUMBERS

- Overall record: 279-455
- 3 All Americans
- 10 All Great Lakes Valley Conference players (selected 11 times)

KWC ALL AMERICANS

Stacy Calhoun (1989)
Octavia Dean (1992)
Jill Burness (1995 Academic)

ITEMS OF NOTE

- Ex-UK Wildcat Randy Embry led the Lady Panthers to a 17-1 record during his second (and final) season as head coach.
- In 1984, Margie Speaks led the nation in free throw shooting, making good on 89.2 percent of her attempts.
- The 1991-92 team is the school's only 20-game winner, finishing with a 21-7 record.
- The 1983-84 team led the nation in free throw accuracy by hitting 75.9 percent of its free throws.

ALL-TIME LEADING SCORERS

No.	Player	Years	Games	Pts.	Avg.
1.	Angie Johnson	1996-99	109	1,782	16.3
2.	Stacy Calhoun	1987-90	110	1,672	15.2
3.	Brenda Britt	1981-84	99	1,532	15.5
4.	Carrie Bridgeman	1996-99	110	1,373	12.5
5.	Kerrie Moore	1992-96	111	1,320	11.9
6.	Alice Shade	1988-91	111	1,312	11.8
7.	Janice Johnson	1979-82	84	1,232	14.7
8.	Leslie Warren	2000-03	105	1,156	11.0
9.	Margie Speaks	1982-85	97	1,064	11.0
10.	Amy Gruen	1988-91	83	1,029	12.4

ALL-TIME LEADING REBOUNDERS

No.	Player	Years	Rebounds	Avg.
1.	Jenny Boyd	1991-94	807	7.5
2.	Alice Shade	1988-91	708	6.4
3.	Kerrie Moore	1992-96	689	6.2
4.	Brenda Britt	1981-84	688	6.9
5.	Carrie Bridgeman	1996-99	649	5.9
6.	Janice Johnson	1979-82	642	7.7
7.	Angie Johnson	1996-99	627	5.8
8.	Willia Hayes	1985-88	578	5.8
9.	Amy Gruen	1988-91	572	6.8
10.	Jill Burness	1994-95	518	9.8

ALL-TIME ASSISTS LEADERS

No.	Player	Years	Assists	Avg.
1.	Kelly Brewer	1996-99	478	4.3
2.	Stacy Calhoun	1987-90	465	5.2
3.	Tracey Wilson	1988-91	403	4.0
4.	Brandy Reynolds	2001-04	376	3.5
5.	Tina Ashby	1979-82	368	4.4
6.	Brenda Britt	1981-84	360	3.6
7.	Amanda Peters	2001-03	334	4.2
8.	Kim Baughn	1993-95	314	4.3
9.	Angie Johnson	1996-99	306	2.8
10.	Margie Speaks	1982-85	272	2.8

ALL-TIME STEALS LEADERS

No.	Player	Years	Steals
1.	Stacy Calhoun	1987-90	303
2.	Kelly Brewer	1996-99	210
3.	Tracey Wilson	1988-91	190
4.	Angie Johnson	1996-99	185
5.	Brandy Reynolds	2001-04	178
6.	Jenny Boyd	1990-94	152
7.	Willia Hayes	1983-87	144
8.	Amanda Peters	2001-03	120
9.	Tracy Watson	1986-90	120
10.	Carrie Bridgeman	1996-99	114

ALL-TIME WINNINGEST COACHES

Coach	Years	Record	Pct.
Scott Lewis	3	48-33	.593
Brent Matthew	4	47-47	.500
Michele Rupe	4	38-72	.345
Gene Minton	3	31-52	.400
Mike Simpson	3	31-53	.369
Tandy Bradford	3	21-59	.263
Randy Embry	2	20-14	.588

(Source: Kentucky Wesleyan College Sports Information)

MIDWAY COLLEGE
WOMEN'S BASKETBALL

MIDWAY BY THE NUMBERS

- Overall record: 145-300
- The basketball program is the oldest athletic program at Midway College.
- 1 NAIA All American
- 2 NAIA All American Scholar-Athletes
- 2 National Small College All Americans
- 4 All Region XII athletes
- 14 KIAC All Conference selections

ALL-TIME LEADING SCORERS

No.	Player	Years	Pts.
1.	Michella Hopkins	1994-98	1,633
2.	Natalie Dial	2002-	1,232
3.	Amy Klein	1999-03	1,094
4.	Jill Potts	1993-97	1,029
5.	Karen Frasure	1992-96	1,023
6.	Jessica Eden	1997-02	1,016

ALL-TIME LEADING REBOUNDERS

No.	Player	Years	Rebounds
1.	Jill Potts	1993-97	836
2.	Michella Hopkins	1994-98	692
3.	Susan Sullins	1994-98	606
4.	Natalie Dial	2002-	597

ALL-TIME ASSISTS LEADERS

No.	Player	Years	Assists
1.	Amy Klein	1999-03	511
2.	Jenny Wiley	1993-96	343
3.	Courtney Kerr	1993-95	316
4.	Tia Garrett	2002-	277
5.	Whitney Allison	1996-99	263

ALL-TIME STEALS LEADERS

No.	Player	Years	Steals
1.	Jenny Wiley	1993-96	220
2.	Amy Klein	1999-03	201
3.	Jill Potts	1993-97	194
4.	LaChae Churn	2001-04	158
5.	Tia Garrett	2002-	138
6.	Jessica Eden	1997-02	137
7.	Michella Hopkins	1994-98	133

(Source: Midway College Sports Information)

MOREHEAD STATE UNIVERSITY
MEN'S BASKETBALL

MOREHEAD STATE BY THE NUMBERS
- Overall record: 940-884
- 5 NCAA Tournament appearances (1956, 1957, 1961, 1983, 1984)
- 7 All Americans (selected eight times)
- 9 Ohio Valley Conference titles (1956, 1957, 1961, 1963, 1969, 1972, 1974, 1984, 2003)
- 2 OVC Tournament championships (1983, 1984)
- 4 OVC Player of the Year selections
- 4 coaches voted OVC Coach of the Year (selected 5 times)
- 51 All OVC players (selected 84 times)
- 2 KIAC championships (1941, 1944)

MOREHEAD STATE ALL AMERICANS
Earl Duncan, forward (1943)
Warren Cooper, center (1945)
Sonny Allen, guard (1950)
Dan Swartz, center (1955, 1956)
Steve Hamilton, forward (1957)
Harold Sergent, guard (1963)
Leonard Coulter, forward (1972)

ITEMS OF NOTE
- The Eagles claimed their first win when they defeated Cumberland 37-25 in 1929.
- Ellis Johnson, Morehead State's all-time winningest coach, was an All American as a guard on Adolph Rupp's first University of Kentucky team. Johnson is still regarded as one of the greatest all-around athletes in UK history.
- Ex-Eagle player and athletics director Steve Hamilton played in a World Series with the New York Yankees and an NBA championship series with the Los Angeles Lakers. Hamilton once had 38 rebounds in a game against Florida State.
- Current Eagles coach Kyle Macy was an All-American at U.K. Macy later spent several seasons in the NBA.
- In the 2001-02 season, Morehead State led all NCAA Division I schools in free throw percentage (78.4).
- The 2003-04 Morehead State team led all Division I schools in field goal accuracy, hitting 51 percent.
- All-American guard Harold Sergent was a standout member of the powerful 1961 state champion Ashland Tomcats, a team many still rank as the best ever in Kentucky high school basketball history.

ALL-TIME LEADING SCORERS

No.	Player	Years	Games	Pts.	Avg.
1.	Ricky Minard	2000-04	114	2,381	20.9
2.	Herbie Stamper	1975-79	99	2,072	20.9
3.	Dan Swartz	1953-56	69	1,925	27.5
4.	Sonny Allen	1946-50	92	1,923	20.8
5.	Steve Hamilton	1954-58	102	1,829	17.8
6.	Brett Roberts	1988-92	107	1,788	16.7
7.	Leonard Coulter	1971-74	77	1,781	23.1
8.	Granny Williams	1959-62	76	1,637	21.5
9.	Harold Sergent	1962-65	63	1,469	23.2
10.	Ted Hundley	1973-77	100	1,450	14.5

ALL-TIME CAREER SCORING AVERAGES

No.	Player	Years	Games	Pts.	Avg.
1.	Dan Swartz	1953-56	69	1,925	27.5
2.	Harold Sergent	1962-65	63	1,469	23.2
3.	Leonard Coulter	1971-74	77	1,781	23.1
4.	Granny Williams	1959-62	76	1,637	21.5

5.	Ricky Minard	2000-04	114	2,381	20.9
6.	Herbie Stamper	1975-79	99	2,072	20.9
7.	Sonny Allen	1946-50	92	1,923	20.8
8.	Earl Duncan	1939-43	74	1,430	19.3
9.	Warren Cooper	1942-45	54	1,011	18.5
10.	Steve Hamilton	1954-58	102	1,829	17.8

ALL-TIME LEADING REBOUNDERS

No.	Player	Years	Rebounds	Avg.
1.	Steve Hamilton	1954-58	1,675	16.4
2.	Norm Pokley	1960-63	1,046	n/a
3.	Leonard Coulter	1971-74	961	12.5
4.	Lamar Green	1966-69	914	n/a
5.	Ted Hundley	1973-77	901	9.0
6.	Brett Roberts	1988-92	897	8.4
7.	Bob McCann	1984-87	862	10.5
8.	Doug Bentz	1989-93	808	7.2
9.	Willie Jackson	1966-69	793	11.3
10.	Thornton Hill	1956-59	781	n/a

ALL-TIME ASSISTS LEADERS

No.	Player	Years	Assists
1.	Marquis Sykes	1999-03	606
2.	Ricky Minard	2000-04	417
3.	Howard Wallen	1971-74	411
4.	Ted Docks	1995-99	356
5.	Jeff Fultz	1980-84	336
6.	Guy Minnifield	1981-84	284
7.	Pat Tubbs	1989-92	254
8.	Jeff Griffin	1985-87	249
9.	Marty Cline	1992-95	237
10.	Rocky Adkins	1978-82	231

ALL-TIME WINNINGEST COACHES

Coach	Years	Record	Pct.
Ellis Johnson	15	196-158	.553
Bobby Laughlin	12	166-120	.580
Wayne Martin	9	130-120	.520
Kyle Macy	8	102-121	.457

(Source: Morehead State University Sports Information)

MOREHEAD STATE UNIVERSITY
WOMEN'S BASKETBALL

MOREHEAD STATE BY THE NUMBERS
- Overall record: 160-240
- The 1978-79 Lady Eagles posted the program's best record at 28-4.
- Lady Eagle teams have topped the 100-point mark on 15 occasions.
- 11 First Team All-Ohio Valley Conference players (selected 16 times)
- 3 Lady Eagles named OVC Player of the Year
- 3 Lady Eagle coaches voted OVC Coach of the Year

FIRST TEAM ALL OVC PLAYERS
Donna Murphy (1978, 1979, 1980)
Donna Stephens (1979, 1980, 1981)
Michelle Stowers (1979)
Priscilla Blackford (1982, 1983)
Connie Appelman (1985)
Kelly Stamper (1987)
Julie Magrane (1992)
Bev Smith (1993)
Amy Kieckbusch (1997)
Tasha Gales (2002)
Travece Turner (2003)

ALL-TIME LEADING SCORERS

No.	Player	Years	Games	Pts.	Avg.
1.	Donna Murphy	1976-80	105	2,059	19.6
2.	Donna Stephens	1978-82	93	1,710	18.4
3.	Julie Magrane	1988-92	107	1,697	15.9
4.	Tasha Gales	1999-03	105	1,602	15.3
5.	Robin Harmon	1978-82	121	1,599	13.2
6.	Bev Smith	1988-03	111	1,592	14.3
7.	Kandi Brown	2000-04	114	1,583	13.9
8.	Priscilla Blackford	1980-84	94	1,481	15.8
9.	Michelle Stowers	1976-80	109	1,459	13.4
10.	Megan Hupfer	1992-96	106	1,444	13.6

ALL-TIME LEADING REBOUNDERS

No.	Player	Years	Rebounds	Avg.
1.	Donna Murphy	1976-80	1,442	13.7
2.	Priscilla Blackford	1980-84	1,075	11.4
3.	Donna Stephens	1978-82	1,044	11.2
4.	Julie Magrane	1988-92	1,034	9.7
5.	Bev Smith	1988-93	879	7.9
6.	Michelle Stowers	1976-80	846	7.8
7.	Tasha Gales	1999-03	822	7.8
8.	DeVonda Williams	2000-04	800	7.0
9.	Megan Hupfer	1992-96	792	7.5
10.	Kelly Stamper	1985-89	722	6.6

ALL-TIME ASSISTS LEADERS

No.	Player	Years	Assists
1.	Irene Moore	1978-82	499
2.	Susann Brown	1975-79	455
3.	Kelly Stamper	1985-89	454
4.	Rita Berry	1980-84	449
5.	Robin Harmon	1978-82	429
6.	Hilary Swisher	1993-98	425
7.	Stacey Spake	1990-94	379
8.	Kandi Brown	2000-04	363
9.	B.J. Bradford	1987-91	353
10.	Tiphanie Bates	1983-87	332

ALL-TIME STEALS LEADERS

No.	Player	Years	Steals
1.	B.J. Bradford	1987-91	198
2.	Kelly Stamper	1985-89	191
3.	Hilary Swisher	1993-98	181
3.	Stacey Spake	1990-94	181
5.	Kandi Brown	2000-04	177
6.	Sherita Joplin	1991-95	170
7.	DeVonda Williams	2000-04	153
8.	Tiphanie Bates	1983-87	148
9.	Shawne Marcum	1993-97	136
10.	Julie Magrane	1988-92	131

ALL-TIME WINNINGEST COACHES

Coach	Years	Record	Pct.
Mickey Wells	9	156-01	.632
Loretta Marlow	9	110-116	.487
Laura Litter	8	76-144	.345

(Source: Morehead State University Sports Information)

MURRAY STATE UNIVERSITY
MEN'S BASKETBALL

MSU BY THE NUMBERS
- Overall record: 1,316-764
- 12 NCAA Tournament appearances
- 19 Ohio Valley Conference titles (1951, 1964, 1968, 1969, 1980, 1982, 1983, 1988, 1989, 1990, 1991, 1992, 1994, 1995, 1996, 1997, 1998, 1999, 2000)
- 11 Racers named OVC Player of the Year
- 53 All OVC players (selected 97 times)
- 5 OVC Athletes of the Year (selected seven times)
- 7 OVC Coach of the Year awards (selected 11 times)

OVC PLAYERS OF THE YEAR
- Jim Jennings, center (1964) – led the team in scoring all three seasons. Finished career with 1,370 points and 1,147 rebounds and averaged 19.3 points per game.
- Claude Virden, forward (1969) – Averaged 23.5 ppg as a junior in 1969 and had 1,490 career points. Averaged 11 rebounds per game. Hit 86 percent of his free throws in 1967-68 season.
- Les Taylor, guard (1972, 1973) – MSU's first two-time OVC Player of the Year. Scored 1,477 points and averaged 21.1 ppg. Averaged 25.6 ppg in 1971-72 season.
- Gary Hooker, forward/center (1980) – Averaged 18.6 points and 12.3 rebounds while shooting 55 percent from the field in 1979-80 season.
- Glen Green, guard/forward (1983) – Ended his career with 1,557 points after twice leading the club in scoring. Had career marks of 49 percent shooting from the field and 77 percent free throw shooting. Also had 423 assists and 141 steals.
- Jeff Martin, forward (1988, 1989) – MSU's all-time leading scorer with 2,484 points. Career scoring average of 21.2 ppg. Averaged 26.0 in 1987-88. Made good on 52 percent of his field goal attempts. His 806 points during 1987-1988 campaign is an MSU record.
- Popeye Jones, forward (1990, 1991) – MSU was the only Division I school to offer him a scholarship. Became a superstar after shedding 40 pounds. Scored 2,057 points. MSU's all-time leading rebounder with 1,374. Led the nation with 469 rebounds in 1990-91.
- Marcus Brown, guard (1995, 1996) – MSU's third all-time leading scorer with 2,236 points. His 26.4 scoring average in 1995-96 is the school's best for a single season. Hit 85 percent of his free throws. Connected on 173 three-pointers during his career.
- De'Teri Mayes, forward (1998) – His 21.26 career scoring average is MSU's best. Only played 63 games but still managed to score 1,340 points. Holds the school record for three-point goals with 103. Hit 41 percent of his three-point attempts. Shot 80 percent from the free throw line.
- Aubrey Reese, guard (2000) – Ended his career with 1,291 points. Connected on 105 three-pointers, including 54 during the 1999-2000 season. Had 383 assists and 134 steals.
- Cuthbert Victor, forward (2004) – Twice led the club in scoring and had 1,485 career points and 935 rebounds. Averaged 10.2 rebounds as a senior. Shot a blistering 63 percent from the field in his final season, and 59 percent for his career. Had 167 steals and a MSU all-time best 160 blocked shots.

OTHER MSU PLAYERS WITH RETIRED JERSEYS
- Garrett Beshear, forward/center, three-time All-OVC selection; scored 1,716 points while twice leading the club in field goal percentage.
- Howie Crittenden, guard, a prep school legend at Cuba High School and still the holder of six MSU records; scored 2,019 points and averaged 19.4 ppg; made a school-best 731 free throws, including 19 in a single game on three different occasions.
- Johnny Reagan, forward, twice led the team in scoring.
- Bennie Purcell, guard, two-time All-OVC pick who finished his career with 1,054 points; averaged 18.3 as a senior in 1951-52; shot 77 percent from the charity stripe that season.
- Joe Fulks, forward, twice led the team in scoring; went on

to become an NBA legend; credited with introducing the jump shot into the game; once called the "Babe Ruth of basketball."
- Paul King, forward, All-OVC pick in 1990; scored 1,108 points; made 173 treys while shooting 40 percent from beyond the three-point line; finished with 99 blocked shots.

ITEMS OF NOTE
- MSU won nine OVC titles in the 1990s, tops among all Division I programs. In all, MSU has won 19 OVC championships, the most by any conference school.
- Prior to taking over at MSU, Mick Cronin served as an assistant to Cincinnati's Bob Huggins and Louisville's Rick Pitino.
- Three generations of the Goheen family excelled at college hoops. Robert and Bennie played for MSU, while Bennie's son, Barry, was a standout at Vanderbilt.
- Ex-Racer Bennie Purcell's son, Mel, is a former pro tennis champion. Mel is now MSU's men's tennis coach.

ALL-TIME LEADING SCORERS

No.	Player	Years	Games	Pts.	Avg.
1.	Jeff Martin	1985-89	117	2,484	21.2
2.	Isaac Spencer	1997-01	127	2,248	17.7
3.	Marcus Brown	1993-96	118	2,236	18.9
4.	Popeye Jones	1988-92	123	2,057	16.7
5.	Howie Crittenden	1952-56	104	2,019	19.4
6.	Lamont Sleets	1079-84	111	1,902	17.1
7.	Vincent Rainey	1994-97	113	1,888	16.7
8.	Frank Allen	1989-93	116	1,811	15.6
9.	Garrett Beshear	1951-53	112	1,716	15.3
10.	Glen Green	1979-83	115	1,557	13.5

ALL-TIME LEADING REBOUNDERS

No.	Player	Years	Rebounds
1.	Popeye Jones	1988-92	1,374
2.	Dick Cunningham	1965-68	1,292
3.	Jim Jennings	1961-64	1,147
4.	Stewart Johnson	1963-66	981
5.	Isaac Spencer	1997-01	976
6.	Cuthbert Victor	2000-04	935
7.	Marcelous Starks	1971-74	875
8.	Ron Johnson	1968-71	837
9.	Quitman Sullins	1954-58	791
10.	Claude Virden	1967-70	778

ALL-TIME ASSISTS LEADERS

No.	Player	Years	Assists
1.	Don Mann	1985-89	531
2.	Lamont Sleets	1979-84	459
3.	Glen Green	1979-83	423
4.	Chad Townsend	1996-98	383
5.	Aubrey Reese	1997-00	383
6.	Frank Allen	1989-93	364
7.	Kevin Paschel	2000-04	363
8.	Isaac Spencer	1997-01	357
9.	Grover Woolard	1973-77	341
10.	Brian Stewart	1980-84	322

(Source: Murray State University Sports Information)

NORTHERN KENTUCKY UNIVERSITY
MEN'S BASKETBALL

NKU BY THE NUMBERS
- Men's overall record: 565-398
- Women's overall record: 645-256
- 1 NCAA Women's NCAA Division II national championship (2000)

- 2 National Player of the Year award winners (selected three times)
- 12 All Americans (selected 14 times)

NKU NATIONAL PLAYERS OF THE YEAR
Michelle Cottrell, basketball (2001, 2002)
Krystal Lewallen, softball (2004)

ALL AMERICANS
Michelle Cottrell, basketball (2000, 2001, 2002)
Derek Fields, basketball (1989)
Paul Cluxton, basketball (1997)
LaRon Moore, basketball (1997)
Craig Sanders, basketball (2002)
Brenden Stowers, basketball (2003)
Kristin Koralewski, volleyball (n/a)
Krystal Lewallen, softball (2004)
Ricki Rothbauer, softball (n/a)
Stephanie Leimbach, softball (n/a)
Curtis Phelps, golf (n/a)
Kim Keyer-Scott, golf (n/a)

NKU ATHLETIC HALL OF FAME MEMBERS
Richard Derkson, basketball (1971-75)
Peggy Vincent, basketball (1975-79)
Peggy Ludwig, volleyball (1975-78)
Gary Wall, baseball (1974-78)
Johnny Lott, cross country (1975-79)
Dan Doellman, basketball (1975-79)
Jeff Stowers, basketball (1972-76)
Russ Kerdolff, baseball (1975-79)
Julie Thomas Perry, volleyball (1976-79)
Marilyn Moore, basketball/volleyball coach (n/a)
Derek Fields, basketball (1985-89)
Melissa Wood-Fleming, basketball (1983-87)
Kevin Cieply, soccer (1981-84)
Gary Flowerdew, baseball (1985-88)
Brenda Ryan, basketball/softball (1978-82)
Roger Klein, tennis coach (1975-88)
Paul Steenken, tennis (1983-86)
Brady Jackson, basketball (1979-83)
Julee Hill, volleyball/basketball (1975-78)
Barbara Harkins, basketball (1978-82)
Dave Krebs, soccer (1981-82)
Bill Aker, baseball coach (1972-2000)
Dr. Jim Bilbo, team physician (1986-present)
Diane Redmond, basketball (1975-79)
J.T. Roberts, soccer (1993-96)
Amy Flaugher, basketball/softball (1978-82)
Tim Grogan, basketball (1975-79)
Nancy Berger, volleyball (1979-82)
Paul Cluxton, basketball (1993-97)
John Toebben, men's soccer coach (1990-2002)
2000 NCAA Division II women's basketball national champions

ITEMS OF NOTE
- Paul Cluxton set an NCAA all-time record in 1996-97 by connecting on 94 percent of his free throws. His career mark was 93.4 percent.
- Michelle Cottrell was a three-time NCAA Division II All-American and was twice named National Player of the Year. She was also named Most Outstanding Player of the 2000 Division II Elite Eight.
- The NKU women's team won the 2000 NCAA Division II national title by beating North Dakota State 71-62 in overtime. Nancy Winstel was the head coach.

- Peggy Vincent is the women's all-time leading scorer with 1,883 points and the all-time leading rebounder with 1,166.
- Bill Aker retired with 806 wins in 29 seasons as Norse baseball coach.

(Source: Northern Kentucky University Sports Information)

THOMAS MORE COLLEGE
MEN'S BASKETBALL

THOMAS MORE BY THE NUMBERS

- Overall record: 598-815
- 12 Intercollegiate athletic teams
- Winning percentage of .533 (96-74) in Connor Convocation Center

ALL-TIME LEADING SCORERS

No.	Player	Years	Pts.
1.	Rick Hughes	1992-92	2,605
2.	Brian O'Conner	1977-81	2,078
3.	Larry Staverman	1954-58	1,673
4.	Brian Clapp	1985-89	1,492
5.	Steve Butcher	1985-89	1,466
6.	Dan Tieman	1958-62	1,454
7.	John Wendefer	1968-72	1,404
8.	Dan Schmidt	1955-59	1,315
9.	Dave Faust	1977-81	1,285
10.	Frank Emmerich	1960-63	1,252

ALL-TIME LEADING REBOUNDERS

No.	Player	Years	Rebounds
1.	Brian O'Conner	1977-81	1,180
2.	Larry Staverman	1954-58	1,114
3.	Todd Bender	1974-78	1,010
4.	Gary Alhrich	1958-61	906
5.	Rick Hughes	1992-96	897
6.	John Wendefer	1968-72	895
7.	Steve Butcher	1985-89	803
8.	Dan Lenihan	1980-84	727
9.	Brian Clapp	1985-89	712
10.	Don Schmidt	1955-59	678

ALL-TIME ASSISTS LEADERS

No.	Player	Years	Assists
1.	Jim Nestheide	1978-82	454
2.	Jim Weyer	1954-58	435
3.	David Green	1995-99	399
4.	Ron Dawn	1974-78	375
5.	Billy Arthur	1989-92	362
6.	Dave Faust	1977-81	344
7.	Les Stewart	1959-62	331
8.	Bob Beck	1969-73	322
9.	Dan Tieman	1958-62	319
10.	Mark Klein	1999-03	311

ALL-TIME STEALS LEADERS

No.	Player	Years	Steals
1.	Billy Arthur	1989-92	223
2.	David Green	1995-99	191
3.	Mark Klein	1999-03	186
4.	Rick Hughes	1992-96	146
5.	Tim Cutter	1989-93	124
6.	Lath Kirk	1984-89	111
7.	Markel Snyder	1993-97	110
8.	Andrae Woodard	2002-	109
8.	Adam Gergen	1995-99	109
10.	Andy Helmers	1993-97	106

ALL-TIME WINNINGEST COACHES

Coach	Years	Record	Pct.
Charlie Wolf	5	81-67	.547
Larry Cox	8	96-95	.503
Jim Weyer	18	208-259	.445
Gerald Orosz	4	22-37	.373
Jim Connor	12	133-235	.361
Terry Connor	7	58-122	.322

(Source: Thomas More University Sports Information)

THOMAS MORE COLLEGE
WOMEN'S BASKETBALL

ALL-TIME LEADING SCORERS

No.	Player	Years	Pts.
1.	Amy Burk	1995-99	1,706
2.	Kim Prewitt	1992-95	1,501
3.	Sherry Clinkenbeard	1994-98	1,229
4.	Holly Roberts	1998-03	1,219
5.	Shawnta Neely	1990-94	1,188
6.	Jamie Boehl	1986-89	1,181
7.	Bridget New	1998-02	1,181
8.	Joanna Bess	2000-04	1,136
9.	Kim Byron	1988-92	1,134
10.	Brenda Simon	1983-87	1,051

ALL-TIME LEADING REBOUNDERS

No.	Player	Years	Rebounds
1.	Kim Byron	1988-92	917
2.	Brenda Simon	1983-87	784
3.	Bridget New	1998-02	757
4.	Amy Burk	1995-99	703
5.	Sherry Clinkenbeard	1994-98	610
6.	Rita Haneburg	1974-77	567
7.	Sue Lally	1981-85	511
8.	Laura Richter	1986-89	469
9.	Christy Hoffediz	1995-99	454
10.	Joanna Bess	2000-04	420

ALL-TIME ASSISTS LEADERS

No.	Player	Years	Assists
1.	Shannon Galbraith	1994-98	430
2.	Jamie Boehl	1986-89	354
3.	Joanna Bess	2000-04	276
4.	Shawna Kelly	1998-02	273
5.	Dawn Franzen	1993-95	199
6.	Nancy West	1989-91	176
7.	Jodi Schroeder	2000-04	169
8.	Chris Long	1988-92	167
9.	Kim Prewitt	1992-95	156
10.	Michelle Parnell	1988-91	151

ALL-TIME THREE-POINT GOALS (CAREER)

No.	Player	Years	FGM
1.	Kim Prewitt	1992-95	242
2.	Amy Burk	1995-99	144
3.	Allison Byars	2001-04	133
4.	Holly Roberts	1998-03	128
5.	Allison Ramsey	1994-96	105
6.	Joanna Bess	2000-04	96
7.	Ashley Will	1999-03	95
8.	Sherry Clinkenbeard	1994-98	87
9.	Jodi Schroeder	2000-04	86
10.	Bethany Vice	1998-02	80

(Source: Thomas More University Sports Information)

TRANSYLVANIA UNIVERSITY
MEN'S BASKETBALL

TRANSY BY THE NUMBERS
- Overall record: 1,088-906
- 2 first team All Americans
- 1 NAIA National Player of the Year
- 8 Academic All Americans

FIRST TEAM ALL AMERICANS
Vince Bingham (1998)
Collier Mills (2001)

ITEMS OF NOTE
- Transy finished its first season in 1903 with a 3-1 record. Among its victims were Georgetown and State College of Kentucky, later to become the University of Kentucky.
- Former governor and baseball commissioner Albert B. "Happy" Chandler captained the 1920-21 Transy team that had a 4-4 record.
- Former Transy head coaches include C.M. Newton and Lee Rose.
- Don Lane spent 26 years as Transy's head coach, retiring after the 2001 season with an all-time record of 509-241.
- Collier Mills was a first-team All-American and National Player of the Year in 2001. Collier's father, Terry, and older brother, Cameron, both played for the University of Kentucky.

ALL-TIME LEADING SCORERS

No.	Player	Years	Pts.
1.	Vince Bingham	1994-98	2,109
2.	Daniel Swintosky	1990-95	2,000
3.	Jeff Blandon	1985-88	1,906
4.	Dale Cosby	1971-74	1,881
5.	Everett Bass	1969-72	1,875
6.	Jennis Stidham	1958-61	1,867
7.	Collier Mills	1997-01	1,774
8.	Andre Flynn	1982-85	1,670
9.	Jim Hurley	1966-68	1,628
10.	Jack Lucas	1960-63	1,611

MISCELLANEOUS STATISTICAL LEADERS (CAREER)

Category	Player	Years	Total
Rebounds	Everett Bass	1969-72	1,308
Assists	James Clay	1961-65	560
Blocked Shots	John Tyler	1984-88	247
Field Goal Percent	Orbrey Gritton	1985-89	59.6
Three-point Percent	Rod Runyon	1987-91	49.1
Free Throw Percent	Larry Kopczyk	1977-80	85.7

ALL-TIME WINNINGEST COACHES

Coach	Years	Record	Pct.
Don Lane	26	509-241	.679
C.M. Newton	14	176-167	.513
Lee Rose	8	160-57	.737

(Source: Transylvania University Sports Information)

TRANSYLVANIA UNIVERSITY
WOMEN'S BASKETBALL

TRANSY BY THE NUMBERS
- Overall record: 495-336
- 6 20-win seasons
- 1 first team All American

FIRST TEAM ALL AMERICAN
Marcia Webb (1999)

ITEMS OF NOTE
- From 1902 to 1930, Transy's women's team had a 68-27 record, far superior to their male counterparts.
- The 1922-23 state champion women's team finished with an 8-0 record, allowing opponents only nine field goals the entire season.
- Pat Deacon coached for 17 seasons, guiding the school to its first 20-win season (21-6) in 1986-87.
- Current coach Mark Turner took the Pioneers to the NAIA national tournament for the first time in 1996-97.

ALL-TIME LEADING SCORERS

No.	Player	Years	Pts.
1.	Joretta Carney	1988-92	1,670
2.	Elaine Russell	1994-98	1,664
3.	Kathy Hill	1978-82	1,621
4.	Tari Young	1999-03	1,586
5.	Ashley Sanders	1995-99	1,574
6.	Marcia Webb	1996-99	1,570
7.	Mary Jean Rogers	1980-84	1,320
8.	Martha Bruner	1989-93	1,270
9.	Karen Server	1989-93	1,212
10.	Beth Lucas	1982-86	1,164

MISCELLANEOUS STATISTICAL LEADERS (CAREER)

Category	Player	Years	Total
Rebounds	Elaine Russell	1994-98	1,085
Assists	Lisa Doyle	1986-90	577
Blocked Shots	Marcia Webb	1996-99	139
Field Goal Percent	Joretta Carney	1988-92	54.8
Three-point Percent	Melissa Butcher	1991-94	43.2
Free Throw Percent	Amber Smith	1990-93	78.5

ALL-TIME WINNINGEST COACHES

Coach	Years	Record	Pct.
Mark Turner	18	312-175	.640
Pat Deacon	16	175-146	.545

(Source: Transylvania University Sports Information)

UNIVERSITY OF KENTUCKY
MEN'S BASKETBALL

UK BY THE NUMBERS
- Overall Record: 1,904-580-1
- 7 NCAA championships (1948, 1949, 1951, 1958, 1978, 1996, 1998)
- 2 National Invitation Tournament titles (1946, 1976)
- 43 Southeastern Conference titles (1933, 1935, 1937, 1939, 1940, 1942, 1944, 1945, 1946, 1947, 1948, 1949, 1950, 1951, 1952, 1954, 1955, 1957, 1958, 1962, 1964, 1966, 1968, 1969, 1970, 1971, 1972, 1973, 1975, 1977, 1978, 1980, 1982, 1983, 1984, 1986, 1995, 1996, 1998, 2000, 2001, 2003, 2005)
- 25 SEC Tournament championships (1933, 1937, 1939, 1940, 1942, 1944, 1945, 1946, 1947, 1948, 1949, 1950, 1952, 1984, 1986, 1992, 1993, 1994, 1995, 1997, 1998, 1999, 2001, 2003, 2004)
- 15 first team All Americans (selected 21 times)
- 87 All SEC players (selected 145 times)
- 8 Olympic Gold Medal winners
- 4 coaches named National Coach of the Year

FIRST TEAM ALL AMERICANS

- Aggie Sale, forward/center (1932, 1933) – National Player of the Year in 1933; scored the first two points for Adolph Rupp at UK; the Cats' first big-time scorer; Rupp always listed Sale among the best players he ever coached.

- Leroy Edwards, center (1935) – nicknamed "Cowboy," he only played one season at UK, earning National Player of the Year honors; extremely strong, physical player; his 16.3 scoring average was UK's best until Alex Groza showed up a decade later.

- Bob Brannum, center (1944) – only 17 when he earned All-America honors; another tough, bruising player; left UK after his freshman season, joined the military, then returned to UK, only to find himself on the bench; transferred to Michigan State.

- Ralph Beard, guard (1947, 1948, 1949) – fiery competitor and a brilliant player; still regarded as the yardstick by which all UK guards are measured; UK was 130-10 during the four years Beard and Wah Wah Jones played; graced the first cover of Sports Illustrated magazine.

- Alex Groza, center (1947, 1948, 1949) – quick agile center and the first UK player to average 20 points per game; two-time Final Four MVP; left UK as the all-time leading scorer with 1,744 points.

- Bill Spivey, center (1951) – UK's first seven-footer; only played two seasons, but scored 1,213 points and led the 1951 club to the NCAA title; ruled ineligible for his senior season and later banned from the NBA even though he was never found guilty of being involved in the point-shaving scandal of the late 1940s.

- Cliff Hagan, forward/center (1952, 1954) – two-time All-American and one of the few athletes to win championships at the high school, college and pro levels; very graceful, and the owner of a lethal hook shot; teamed with Frank Ramsey to give UK one of the greatest 1-2 combos in college basketball history.

- Johnny Cox, forward (1959) – lean and tough, he helped guide the "Fiddlin' Five" to the 1958 NCAA title; ended his career with 1,461 points and 1,004 rebounds, making him one of only four Wildcats to crack the 1,000 mark in those categories.

- Cotton Nash, forward/center (1964) – one of the most charismatic Wildcats of all-time; also, one of the greatest; three-time All-American, he left as UK's all-time leading scorer with 1,770 points; only Wildcat to average 20 points per game three times; reached the 1,000-point club faster than any other Wildcat, surpassing the mark in his 45th game.

- Dan Issel, center (1970) – UK's all-time leading scorer with 2,138 points; the only Wildcat to average more than 30 points per game for a season; averaged 33.9 points and 13.2 rebounds as a senior; hit for a school record 53 points against Ole Miss; went on to have a brilliant pro career.

- Kyle Macy, guard (1980) – arguably the most popular Wildcat of all-time; a smooth backcourt player with a deadly jumper and nerves of steel; averaged 12.5 points for the powerful 1978 NCAA title club; hit 89 percent of his free throws, a UK all-time best.

- Kenny Walker, forward/center (1986) – two-time All-American and second only to Issel in scoring with 2,080 points; known as "Sky," he was the leading scorer for Joe B. Hall's last UK team and Eddie Sutton's first; twice chosen SEC Player of the Year.

- Jamal Mashburn, forward (1993) – the single most important Wildcat in the post-probation era; could pass, score, rebound and defend; scored 1,843 points despite playing in only 98 games; turned pro after three seasons at UK.

- Tony Delk, guard (1996) – UK's fifth all-time leading scorer with 1,890 points and the school's all-time leader with 283 three-point buckets; had seven treys in UK's championship win over Syracuse in 1996; Final Four and SEC tourney MVP

in 1996; once scored 70 points in a high school game.

- Ron Mercer, forward/guard (1997) – easily ranks among the most gifted and multi-dimensional Wildcats of all-time; accounted for 1,013 points despite playing just two seasons; scored 20 points against Syracuse in the 1996 NCAA title game; SEC tourney MVP in 1997.

OTHER UK PLAYERS WITH RETIRED JERSEYS

- Basil Hayden (1920-22) – UK's first All-American (1921); later coached UK for one season.

- Burgess Carey (1925-26) – earned All-America recognition for his great defensive prowess; captain of the 1925-26 club.

- Carey Spicer (1929-31) – holds the distinction of being Rupp's first All-American player; also earned All-America recognition in 1929 under John Mauer; instrumental in helping bring success to Rupp's up-tempo, fast-breaking style.

- Adolph Rupp (1930-1972) – won 876 games, four NCAA titles, one NIT crown and 27 SEC championships during his 42 years at the helm; four-time National Coach of the Year; seven-time SEC Coach of the Year; inducted into Naismith Hall of Fame in 1969.

- Frenchy DeMoisey (1932-34) – Rupp's third All-American, a prolific scorer and one of the first players to shoot a hook shot; once scored 39 points in 39 minutes during a two-game span; one sportswriter called him a "whirling dervish."

- Mickey Rouse (1938-40) – three-year backcourt starter and the first U.K. player to have his jersey retired; earned All-SEC honors for his play during the 1939-40 season.

- Kenny Rollins (1943, 1947-48) – smooth, unselfish guard and captain of the great "Fabulous Five" club that won the 1948 NCAA title and, later, an Olympic gold medal in London games; once held high-scoring Bob Cousy to three points.

- Wah Wah Jones (1946-49) – Maybe the greatest all-around athlete to ever play at UK; an All-American in basketball and All-SEC in football; also excelled at baseball; a four-time All-SEC and All-SEC tourney selection; a genuine Kentucky legend.

- Cliff Barker (1947-49) – oldest member of the "Fabulous Five," he was a magician with the basketball; it was once said that he could do everything with a basketball except make it talk; spent time in a German POW camp during World War II.

- Frank Ramsey (1951, 1953-54) – probably the most-successful on-court Wildcat of all-time; won an NCAA title at UK and enough NBA championship rings with Boston to open a jewelry store; a slashing, driving player; Rupp once said, "if we win by 30, Frank gets three points; if we win by three, he gets 30."

- Lou Tsioropoulos (1951, 1953-54) – the super strong "Golden Greek" teamed with Hagan and Ramsey to lead UK to its only perfect season (25-0); superb rebound and defender, he once held LSU's Bob Pettit to 17 points, 13 below his average.

- Billy Evans 1952, 1954-55) – a much underrated player and a key contributing member of the unbeaten 1953-54 squad; a member of the 1956 U.S. team that captured the Olympic gold medal; also excelled at tennis.

- Gayle Rose (1952, 1954-55) – two-year backcourt starter, he averaged 6.7 points for the unbeaten 1953-54 team; came back as a senior to help lead UK to a 23-3 record and another SEC title.

- Cawood Ledford (1953-92) – the legendary "Voice of the Wildcats" for 39 years and one of the most-beloved figures in UK history; named Kentucky Sportscaster of the Year 22 times; elected to the Kentucky Athletic Hall of Fame and the Kentucky Journalism Hall of Fame.

- Jerry Bird (1954-56) – two-year starter, he averaged 16.2 points as a senior; the eldest brother in one of Kentucky's greatest sports families; brothers Calvin, Rodger and Billy played football at UK, while son Steve was a standout receiver at Eastern Kentucky University.
- Phil Grawmeyer (1954-56) – an outstanding performer whose career was hampered by injuries; a valuable member of that powerful 1953-54 team; grabbed 703 rebounds in just 71 games.
- Bob Burrow (1955-56) – Rupp's first JUCO player; scored 1,023 points and pulled down 823 rebounds in his two seasons at UK; scored 50 points against LSU; his 34 rebounds against Temple remains UK's single-game best.
- Vernon Hatton (1956-58) – will forever be remembered for hitting a last-second 47-footer in the first overtime to keep UK alive in its three-overtime win over Temple; later hit the game-winning bucket against Temple in the NCAA semifinal game; scored 30 against Seattle in the championship game; SEC Sophomore of the Year in 1956.
- Bill Keightley (1962-present) – the man known as "Mr. Wildcat" has been UK's equipment manager for more than 40 years; the last remaining connection to the Rupp Era.
- Louie Dampier (1965-67) – another extremely popular Wildcat, and arguably the finest long-range shooter in school history; averaged 21.1 points for "Rupp's Runts" during the memorable 1965-66 season; shot 50.8 percent from the field and 84.4 percent from the free throw line; went on to become the all-time leading scorer in ABA history.
- Pat Riley (1965-67) – averaged 22 points and 8.9 rebounds for the "Runts"; scored 1,464 points as a Wildcat; played several years in the NBA, then went on to coach the Lakers to four NBA titles in the 1980s; named NBA Coach of the Decade.
- Joe B. Hall (1973-85) – had the daunting task of following Rupp, the only coach most UK fans had ever known; had a record of 297-100 in 13 seasons; led the Cats to the 1978 NCAA title and the 1976 NIT crown; played at UK in the late 1940s.
- Kevin Grevey (1973-75) – two-time All-American, his 21.4 career scoring average trails only Issel and Nash; a lefty with a deadly outside jumper; scored 34 points in the 1975 NCAA title game loss to UCLA; played several years in the NBA.
- Jack Givens (1975-78) – another deadeye southpaw, "Goose" blistered Duke with a towering 41-point performance in the 1978 NCAA championship game; UK's third all-time leading scorer with 2,038 points; Final Four MVP in 1978.
- Rick Robey (1975-78) – scored 20 points and grabbed 11 rebounds in the 1978 title game win over Duke; shot 63.5 percent from the field as a senior; led the club in rebounding three times; shot 81 percent from the free throw line during the 1974-75 season.
- Richie Farmer (1989-92) – one of the "Unforgettables" who helped bring UK basketball back after NCAA probation; hit six crucial free throws to seal UK's stunning 100-95 upset of LSU; a true prep legend after leading Clay County High to five straight Sweet 16 appearances, including the 1987 championship.
- Deron Feldhaus (1989-92) – a rugged second-generation Wildcat who blended a hard-nosed inside game with a soft outside shooting touch; averaged 14.4 points on Rick Pitino's first UK team; had 13 rebounds against LSU and Shaquille O'Neal; his father, Allen, played at UK in the early 1960s.
- John Pelphrey (1989-92) – a remarkably intelligent and shrewd player who used his high basketball IQ to beat more naturally gifted players; scored 16 points in the classic loss against Duke in an NCAA regional final; hit 160 three-pointers during his career; also had 327 assists and 173 steals.

- Sean Woods (1990-92) – a fierce competitor best remembered for sinking a daring bank shot over Duke's Christian Laettner that gave UK a one-point lead with 2 seconds to play in the regional final; led the SEC in assists as a sophomore; had 21 points and nine assists in the classic against Duke; finished his career with 482 assists.
- Rick Pitino (1990-97) – brought UK out of the darkness imposed by NCAA sanctions; posted a 219-50 record at UK; led the powerful 1995-96 club to the NCAA title; came back the next year, and despite an injury to Derek Anderson, led UK to the title game, losing in overtime to Arizona; left UK to coach the Boston Celtics.

ITEMS OF NOTE

- UK (then State College) recorded its first win when it defeated Lexington YMCA 11-10 on Feb. 18, 1903.
- Athletic teams were officially christened "Wildcats" in 1909.
- UK claimed its first championship in 1921 by defeating Tulane, Mercer, Mississippi A&M and Georgia in the Southern Intercollegiate Athletic Association title game. That year, Basil Hayden became UK's first All-American.
- Alumni Gym opened on Dec. 13, 1924. Critics called it a "white elephant."
- Adolph Rupp is named UK coach on March 23, 1930.
- Ralph Beard's free throw gives UK a 46-45 victory over Rhode Island in the NIT championship game.
- Members of the 1947-48 NCAA title team are nicknamed the "Fabulous Five." They are Ralph Beard, Wah Wah Jones, Alex Groza, Kenny Rollins and Cliff Barker. That group would later help the U.S. win the gold medal in the 1948 Olympic Games held in London.
- In 1949, UK captures its second consecutive NCAA title by defeating Oklahoma A&M 46-36 in Seattle.
- Memorial Coliseum opens on Dec. 1, 1950. Critics call it a "white elephant."
- UK wins the 1951 NCAA title by stopping Kansas State 68-58 in the final game.
- UK is suspended by the NCAA for the 1952-53 season.
- Cawood Ledford broadcasts his first UK game on Dec. 5, 1953.
- UK wins the 1958 NCAA championship by beating Seattle 84-72 in Louisville.
- UK beats Tennessee 69-66 on Jan. 18, 1969 to become the first school to win 1,000 games.
- On June 9, 1969, Tom Payne becomes the first black player to sign with UK.
- Adolph Rupp coaches his last game at UK on March 18, 1972, a 73-54 loss to Florida State in the NCAA tournament.
- Joe B. Hall coaches his first game at UK, a 75-66 win at Michigan State.
- UK falls to UCLA 92-85 in the 1975 NCAA championship game.
- UK beats NC-Charlotte 71-67 to win the 1976 NIT title.
- On Dec. 10, 1977, as top-ranked UK is defeating Kansas on "Adolph Rupp Night" in Lawrence, Kansas, Rupp dies in Lexington.
- Jack "Goose" Givens erupts for 41 points to lead UK to a 94-88 victory over Duke in the 1978 NCAA championship game.
- Joe B. Hall announces his retirement on March 22, 1985.
- On Nov. 22, 1985, Eddie Sutton coaches his first game at UK, a 77-58 win over Northwestern (La.) State.
- On March 10, 1989, in the wake of an NCAA investigation, Eddie Sutton resigns as UK coach. Two months later, the NCAA places UK's basketball program on probation.
- Rick Pitino is named UK coach on June 2, 1989.
- On Nov. 28, 1989, Rick Pitino wins his first game at UK, a 76-73 victory over Ohio University.
- Rick Pitino makes history by naming Bernadette Locke an assistant on his coaching staff.
- On March 28, 1992, in what many call the greatest NCAA Tournament game ever played, UK loses to Duke on a

last-second shot by Christian Laettner. It is also Cawood Ledford's last game as "Voice of the Wildcats."
- UK clips Syracuse 76-67 to win the 1996 NCAA championship.
- UK returns to the NCAA championship game in 1997, losing to Arizona 84-79 in the final game. Two months later, Rick Pitino resigns as UK coach.
- On May 12, 1997, C.M. Newton introduces Orlando "Tubby" Smith as UK's new coach.
- Tubby Smith wins his first game at UK, defeating ex-Cat Kyle Macy's Morehead State squad 88-49.
- UK's "Comeback Cats" rally from a 10-point halftime deficit to defeat Utah 78-69 in the 1998 NCAA championship game.
- After a long illness, Cawood Ledford dies at his home in Harlan on Sept. 5, 2001.

ALL-TIME LEADING SCORERS

No.	Player	Years	Games	Pts.	Avg.
1.	Dan Issel	1968-70	83	2,138	25.8
2.	Kenny Walker	1983-86	132	2,080	15.8
3.	Jack Givens	1975-78	123	2,038	16.6
4.	Keith Bogans	2000-03	135	1,923	14.2
5.	Tony Delk	1993-96	133	1,890	14.2
6.	Jamal Mashburn	1991-93	98	1,843	18.8
7.	Kevin Grevey	1973-75	84	1,801	21.4
8.	Tayshaun Prince	1999-02	135	1,775	13.1
9.	Cotton Nash	1962-64	78	1,770	22.6
10.	Alex Groza	1945-49	120	1,744	14.4

ALL-TIME CAREER SCORING AVERAGES

No.	Player	Years	Games	Pts.	Avg.
1.	Dan Issel	1968-70	83	2,138	25.8
2.	Cotton Nash	1962-64	78	1,770	22.7
3.	Kevin Grevey	1973-75	84	1,801	21.4
4.	Bob Burrow	1955-56	51	1,023	20.1
5.	Louie Dampier	1965-67	80	1,575	19.7
6.	Bill Spivey	1950-51	63	1,213	19.3
7.	Cliff Hagan	1951-54	77	1,475	19.2
8.	Jamal Mashburn	1990-93	98	1,843	18.8
9.	Mike Casey	1968-71	82	1,535	18.7
10.	Pat Riley	1965-67	80	1,464	18.3

ALL-TIME LEADING REBOUNDERS

No.	Player	Years	Rebounds	Avg.
1.	Dan Issel	1968-70	1,078	12.9
2.	Frank Ramsey	1951-54	1,038	11.4
3.	Cliff Hagan	1951-54	1,035	13.4
4.	Johnny Cox	1957-59	1,004	12.0
5.	Cotton Nash	1962-64	962	12.3
6.	Kenny Walker	1983-86	942	7.1
7.	Sam Bowie	1980-84	843	8.8
8.	Rick Robey	1975-78	838	8.0
9.	Bob Burrow	1955-56	823	16.1
10.	Winston Bennett	1984-88	799	6.0

ALL-TIME ASSISTS LEADERS

No.	Player	Years	Assists	Avg.
1.	Dirk Minniefield	1980-83	646	5.3
2.	Anthony Epps	1994-97	544	3.9
3.	Roger Harden	1983-86	498	4.1
4.	Wayne Turner	1996-99	494	3.3
5.	Sean Woods	1990-92	482	5.3
6.	Kyle Macy	1978-80	470	4.8
7.	Cliff Hawkins	2001-04	468	3.7
8.	Ed Davender	1985-88	436	3.4
9.	Travis ford	1992-94	428	4.3
10.	Saul Smith	1998-01	363	2.5

ALL-TIME WINNINGEST COACHES

Coach	Years	Record	Pct.
Adolph Rupp	42	876-190	.822
Joe B. Hall	13	297-100	.748
Rick Pitino	8	219-50	.814
Tubby Smith	7	219-58	.791

UNIVERSITY OF KENTUCKY
WOMEN'S BASKETBALL

UK BY THE NUMBERS
- Overall record: 535-410
- 1 NWIT championship (1990)
- 1 Southeastern Conference championship (1982)
- 4 Top 20 finishes (1980, 1981, 1982, 1983)
- 5 All America players (selected 7 times)

UK ALL AMERICANS
- Pam Browning, center (1977) – scored 1,598 points; twice hit for a career high 35 points.
- Maria Donhoff, forward (1978) – ended with 1,187 points; scored 20 points in her first varsity game.
- Valerie Still, center (1981, 1982, 1983) – UK's all-time leading scorer (2,763 points), men or women; also the school's top rebounder with 1,525; scored more than 30 in a game on 23 occasions.
- Kristi Cushenberry, guard (1990) – ninth all-time leading scorer with 1,358 points; hit a school-best 39.7 percent of her three-point attempts.
- Vanessa Foster-Sutton, center (1990) – twice led the team in rebounding; shot 59 percent from the field in 1990.

ITEMS OF NOTE
- UK women played their first game on Feb. 21, 1903.
- The 1924 UK women went 10-0, winning the championship of the South.
- After a 50-year hiatus, women began playing again at UK in the 1970s, reaching varsity status in 1974. Sue Feamster was the first coach.
- Debbie Yow took over as coach in 1976.
- In 1979, UK upset second-ranked Tennessee 66-64 in front of 4,500 fans in Memorial Coliseum.
- Terry Hall was named head coach in 1980.
- UK broke the national attendance record for a women's collegiate game when 10,622 fans saw the Cats beat Old Dominion 80-66 in Memorial Coliseum on Feb. 5, 1983.
- Sharon Fanning became the new head coach in 1987.
- The 1990 club finished with a 23-8 record, winning three tournament titles, including the NWIT.
- In 1995, Bernadette Locke-Mattox became the fifth UK women's coach.
- In 2003, Valerie Still became the first Lady Cat to have her jersey retired. Still is married to ex-Wildcat Rob Lock. Her brother, Art, was an All-American for the football Wildcats; Long-time Tennessee assistant coach Mickie DeMoss named head coach at UK.
- Former Cat guard Stacey Reed is married to former UK guard Jeff Sheppard.

ALL-TIME LEADING SCORERS

No.	Player	Years	Games	Pts.	Avg.
1.	Valerie Still	1979-83	119	2,763	23.2
2.	Leslie Nichols	1982-86	111	1,797	18.2
3.	Pam Browning	1974-78	107	1,598	14.9
4.	Liz Lukschu	1977-81	119	1,488	12.5
5.	SeSe Helm	2000-04	108	1,487	13.8
6.	Stacey Reed	1991-95	114	1,482	13.0

7.	Tiffany Wait	1995-00	122	1,445	11.8
8.	Jodie Whitaker	1985-89	111	1,433	12.9
9.	Kristi Cushenberry	1988-92	118	1,358	11.5
10.	Belitta Croley	1984-88	94	1,339	14.2

ALL-TIME CAREER SCORING AVERAGES

No.	Player	Years	Games	Pts.	Avg.
1.	Valerie Still	1979-83	119	2,763	23.2
2.	Leslie Nichols	1982-86	111	1,797	18.2
3.	Pam Browning	1974-78	107	1,598	14.9
4.	Belitta Croley	1984-88	94	1,339	14.2
5.	SeSe Helm	2000-04	108	1,487	13.8

ALL-TIME LEADING REBOUNDERS

No.	Player	Years	Rebounds	Avg.
1.	Valerie Still	1979-83	1,525	12.8
2.	Leslie Nichols	1982-86	877	7.9
3.	Debra Oden	1976-80	785	7.2
4.	Kim Denkins	1994-98	762	7.1
5.	Liz Lukschu	1977-81	722	6.1
6.	LaTonya McDole	1998-02	711	6.1
7.	Jocelyn Mills	1989-93	703	6.8
8.	Maria Donhoff	1977-81	692	5.7
9.	SeSe Helm	2000-04	672	6.2
10.	Karen Mosely	1982-86	633	5.8

ALL-TIME ASSISTS LEADERS

No.	Player	Years	Assists	Avg.
1.	Patty Jo Hedges	1980-83	731	6.1
2.	Sandy Harding	1983-87	706	6.4
3.	Jodie Whitaker	1985-89	464	4.2
3.	Lea Wise	1979-83	464	3.7
5.	Stacey Reed	1991-95	442	3.9
6.	Rita Adams	1999-03	400	3.6
7.	Tracye Davis	1987-91	367	3.2
8.	Tiffany Wait	1995-00	339	2.8
9.	Lisa Collins	1980-84	325	2.8
10.	Leslie Nichols	1982-86	323	2.9

ALL-TIME WINNINGEST COACHES (BY PERCENTAGE)

Coach	Years	Record	Pct.
Terry Hall	7	138-66	.676
Debbie Yow	4	79-40	.664
Sue Feamster	5	64-39	.621
Sharon Fanning	8	134-97	.580
Bernadette Mattox	8	91-135	.402

(Source: University of Kentucky University Sports Information)

UNIVERSITY OF LOUISVILLE
MEN'S BASKETBALL

U OF L BY THE NUMBERS

- Overall record: 1,484-793
- 2 NCAA championships (1980, 1986)
- 1 NIT championship(1956)
- 32 NCAA appearances (1951, 1959, 1961, 1964, 1967, 1968, 1972, 1974, 1975, 1977, 1978, 1979, 1980, 1981, 1982, 1983, 1984, 1986, 1988, 1989, 1990, 1992, 1993, 1994, 1995, 1996, 1997, 1999, 2000, 2003, 2004, 2005)
- 1 NAIB title (1948)
- 1 Conference USA championship (2005)
- 5 first team All Americans
- 1 Final Four Most Valuable Player

FIRST TEAM ALL AMERICANS

- Charlie Tyra, center (1957) – scored 1,728 points and grabbed 1,617 rebounds; led the 1956 Cardinals to the NIT championship.
- Wes Unseld, center (1967, 1968) – earned All-America recognition all three years at U of L; twice had 30 rebounds in a game; only player to be named NBA MVP and Rookie of the Year in the same season.
- Darrell Griffith, guard (1980) – arguably the greatest U of L player of all-time; an incredible athlete with out-of-this-world leaping ability; carried the Cards to the 1980 NCAA title.
- Pervis Ellison, center (1989) – made his mark as a freshman by helping the Cards capture the 1986 NCAA crown; finished his career with 2,143 points.
- Clifford Rozier, center (1994) – averaged 17 points per game and 11 rebounds as a Cardinal.

OTHER U OF L ALL AMERICANS

Don Goldstein, forward (1959)
John Turner, forward (1961)
Butch Beard, guard (1969)
Jim Price, guard (1972)
Junior Bridgeman, guard (1975)
Allen Murphy, guard (1975)
Phil Bond, guard (1976)
Wesley Cox, forward (1977)
Rick Wilson, guard (1978)
Lancaster Gordon, guard (1984)
DeJuan Wheat, guard (1997)
Reece Gaines, guard (2003)

ALL-TIME LEADING SCORERS

No.	Player	Years	Games	Pts.	Avg.
1.	Darrell Griffith	1976-80	126	2,333	18.5
2.	DeJuan Wheat	1993-97	136	2,183	16.1
3.	Pervis Ellison	1985-89	136	2,143	15.8
4.	Reece Gaines	1999-03	125	1,945	15.6
5.	Milt Wagner	1981-86	144	1,836	12.8
6.	Derek Smith	1978-82	131	1,826	13.9
7.	LaBradford Smith	1987-91	133	1,806	13.6
8.	Charlie Tyra	1953-57	95	1,728	18.2
9.	Herbert Crook	1984-88	142	1,723	12.1
10.	Wes Unseld	1965-68	82	1,686	20.6

ALL-TIME CAREER SCORING AVERAGES

No.	Player	Years	Games	Pts.	Avg.
1.	Wes Unseld	1965-68	82	1,686	20.6
2.	Butch Beard	1966-69	83	1,580	19.0
3.	Darrell Griffith	1976-80	126	2,333	18.5
4.	Charlie Tyra	1953-57	95	1,728	18.2
5.	John Reuther	1962-67	74	1,346	18.2
6.	Jim Price	1969-72	87	1,490	17.1
7.	Clifford Rozier	1992-94	65	1,104	17.0
8.	John Turner	1958-61	86	1,451	16.9
9.	Allen Murphy	1972-75	89	1,453	16.4
10.	Mike Grosso	1968-70	59	958	16.2

ALL-TIME LEADING REBOUNDERS

No.	Player	Years	Rebounds	Avg.
1.	Charlie Tyra	1953-57	1,617	17.0
2.	Wes Unseld	1965-68	1,551	18.9
3.	Pervis Ellison	1985-89	1,149	8.4
4.	Fred Sawyer	1958-61	1,040	12.0
5.	Rodney McCray	1979-84	1,029	7.6
6.	Billy Thompson	1982-86	930	6.5
7.	John Turner	1958-61	919	10.6
8.	Derek Smith	1978-82	884	6.7
9.	Herbert Crook	1984-88	877	6.2
10.	Don Goldstein	1956-59	868	10.7

ALL-TIME ASSISTS LEADERS

No.	Player	Years	Assists	Avg.
1.	LaBradford Smith	1987-91	713	5.4
2.	Phil Bond	1972-77	528	n/a
3.	DeJuan Wheat	1993-97	498	3.7
4.	Keith Williams	1986-90	482	n/a
5.	Reece Gaines	1999-03	475	3.8
6.	Billy Thompson	1982-86	459	3.2
7.	Milt Wagner	1981-86	432	3.0
8.	Rick Wilson	1974-78	394	n/a
9.	Everick Sullivan	1988-92	393	n/a
10.	Darrell Griffith	1976-80	383	3.0

ALL-TIME DUNKS LEADERS

No.	Player	Years	Dunks
1.	Pervis Ellison	1985-89	162
2.	Alvin Sims	1993-96	123
3.	Darrell Griffith	1976-80	117
3.	Cornelius Holden	1988-92	117
5.	Rodney McCray	1979-83	103

ALL-TIME WINNINGEST COACHES

Coach	Years	Record	Pct.
Denny Crum	30	675-295	.696
Peck Hickman	23	443-183	.708
Rick Pitino	4	97-35	.735
John Dromo	4	68-23	.747

(Source: University of Louisville Sports Information)

WESTERN KENTUCKY UNIVERSITY
MEN'S BASKETBALL

WKU BY THE NUMBERS
- Overall record: 1,507-746
- 19 Ohio Valley Conference titles (1949, 1950, 1952, 1954, 1955, 1956, 1957, 1960, 1961, 1962, 1966, 1967, 1970, 1971, 1972, 1976, 1980, 1981, 1982)
- 9 OVC Tournament championships (1949, 1952, 1953, 1954, 1966, 1967, 1976, 1978, 1981)
- 6 Sun Belt Conference titles (1987, 1994, 1995, 2001, 2002, 2003)
- 5 Sun Belt Tournament championships (1993, 1995, 2001, 2002, 2003)
- 19 NCAA Tournament appearances (1940, 1960, 1962, 1966, 1967, 1970, 1971, 1976, 1978, 1980, 1981, 1986, 1987, 1993, 1994, 1995, 2001, 2002, 2003)
- 12 National Invitation Tournament appearances (1942, 1943, 1948, 1949, 1950, 1952, 1953, 1954, 1965, 1982, 1992, 2005)
- 27 All Americans (selected 35 times)

WKU ALL AMERICANS
William "Red" McCrocklin, center (1938)
Carlisle Towery, center (1940, 1941)
Oran McKinney, center (1943)
Dee Gibson, guard (1948)
Don Ray, forward (1948)
Odie Spears, forward (1948)
Bob Lavoy, center (1949, 1950)
John Oldham, guard (1949)
Buddy Cate, forward (1950)
Rip Gish, forward/center (1951)
Tom Marshall, forward (1953, 1954)
Art Spoelstra, center (1953)
Ralph Crosthwaite, center (1958)
Bobby Rascoe, guard (1962)
Darel Carrier, guard (1964)
Clem Haskins, forward (1965, 1966, 1967)
Jim McDaniels, center (1969, 1970, 1971)
Johnny Britt, guard (1976)
Craig McCormick, center (1982)
Kannard Johnson, forward (1984)
Tellis Frank, forward (1987)
Brett McNeal, guard (1989)
Darnell Mee, guard (1993)
Chris Robinson, forward/guard (1996)
Chris Marcus, center (2001, 2002)
Nigel Dixon, center (2004)
Mike Wells, guard (2004)

ITEMS OF NOTE
- Legendary coach Ed Diddle won his first game at WKU in 1922 when his Hilltoppers posted a 103-7 victory. Diddle also served as WKU football coach for seven seasons (1922-28), compiling a 38-24-2 won-loss record.
- The first Hilltoppers to have their jerseys retired were Ed Diddle, Clem Haskins, Tom Marshall, Jim McDaniels, John Oldham and Carlisle Towery.
- Dr. Kelly Thompson, Ed Diddle, L.T. Smith, Ted Hornback, Nick Denes, Dr. Dero Downing and John Oldham were elected to the Ohio Valley Conference Hall of Fame.
- Clem Haskins, Tom Marshall and Jim McDaniels were named to the Ohio Valley Conference Half-Century team.
- Clem Haskins, Wayne Chapman, Jim McDaniels and Johnny Britt were all chosen OVC Player of the Year.
- Were it not for a highly controversial officiating call that resulted in a loss to Michigan, the Hilltoppers would have met UK's Rupp's Runts in the Mideast Regional final of the 1966 NCAA Tournament. Western led Michigan by one point when the ball was tied up between Cazzie Russell and WKU's Greg Jones with one second to play. This was before the change of possession arrow rule, so a jump ball was called. Jones was whistled for a foul as he jumped for the tip and Russell hit both ends of a one-and-one with no time left on the clock to give Michigan a 79-78 win.
- Wayne Chapman transferred to WKU after playing on the University of Kentucky freshman team with Pat Riley and Louie Dampier.
- Led by Jim McDaniels' 35 points and 11 rebounds, the Hilltoppers ripped UK 107-83 when the two clubs finally clashed in the 1971 NCAA tourney.
- Wes Strader served as radio play-by-play man for Hilltopper basketball and football for 36 years (1964-2000).

ALL-TIME LEADING SCORERS

No.	Player	Years	Games	Pts.	Avg.
1.	Jim McDaniels	1968-71	81	2,238	27.6
2.	Ralph Crosthwaite	1955-59	103	2,076	20.1
3.	Tom Marshall	1950-54	100	1,909	19.1
4.	Brett McNeal	1985-89	120	1,856	15.5
5.	Johnny Britt	1972-76	103	1,765	17.1
6.	Kannard Johnson	1983-87	126	1,738	13.8
7.	Clem Haskins	1964-67	76	1,680	22.1
8.	Bobby Rascoe	1959-62	80	1,670	20.9
9.	Chris Robinson	1992-96	120	1,656	13.0
10.	Art Spoelstra	1951-54	92	1,510	16.4

ALL-TIME CAREER SCORING AVERAGES

No.	Player	Years	Games	Pts.	Avg.
1.	Jim McDaniels	1968-71	81	2,238	27.6
2.	Clem Haskins	1964-67	76	1,680	22.1
3.	Bobby Rascoe	1959-62	80	1,670	20.9
4.	Ralph Crosthwaite	1955-59	103	2,076	20.1
5.	Darel Carrier	1961-64	69	1,318	19.1
5.	Tom Marshall	1950-54	100	1,909	19.1
7.	Johnny Britt	1972-76	103	1,765	17.1
8.	Charlie Osborne	1958-61	80	1,359	17.0
9.	Art Spoelstra	1951-54	92	1,510	16.4
10.	Wayne Chapman	1965-68	79	1,292	16.3

ALL-TIME LEADING REBOUNDERS

No.	Player	Years	Rebounds	Avg.
1.	Ralph Crosthwaite	1954-58	1,309	12.7
2.	Tom Marshall	1950-54	1,225	12.3
3.	Jim McDaniels	1968-71	1,118	13.8
4.	Art Spoelstra	1951-54	1,043	11.3
5.	Bob Daniels	1953-57	964	9.9
6.	Greg Smith	1965-68	932	11.8
7.	Harry Todd	1959-62	924	11.6
8.	Dwight Smith	1964-67	856	11.0
9.	Kannard Johnson	1983-87	840	6.7
10.	Clem Haskins	1964-67	809	10.6

ALL-TIME STEALS LEADERS

No.	Player	Years	Steals
1.	Darnell Mee	1990-93	259
2.	Chris Robinson	1992-96	203
3.	Brett McNeal	1985-89	148
4.	Darius Hall	1991-95	146
5.	Darrin Horn	1991-95	139
6.	Mark Bell	1991-93	135
7.	Bobby Jones	1980-84	134
8.	Derek Robinson	1998-02	124
9.	Joe Harney	1995-99	121
10.	Patrick Sparks	2001-03	119

ALL-TIME WINNINGEST COACHES

Coach	Years	Record	Pct.
Ed Diddle	42	759-302	.715
John Oldham	7	146-41	.781
Jim Richards	7	102-84	.548
Clem Haskins	6	101-73	.580
Dennis Felton	5	100-54	.649

(Source: Western Kentucky University Sports Information)

WESTERN KENTUCKY UNIVERSITY
WOMEN'S BASKETBALL

WKU BY THE NUMBERS

- Overall record: 693-344
- 1 National Runner-Up (1992)
- 3 NCAA Final Fours (1985, 1986, 1992)
- 3 NCAA Sweet 16s (1991, 1993, 1995)
- 15 NCAA Tournament appearances (1985, 1986, 1987, 1988, 1989, 1990, 1991, 1992, 1993, 1994, 1995, 1997, 1998, 2000, 2003)
- 7 Sun Belt titles (1989, 1990, 1992, 1993, 1997, 2003, 2004)
- 8 Sun Belt Tournament championships
- 5 NWIT appearances
- 1 KWIC championship (1929)
- 3 First Team All Americans

WKU FIRST TEAM ALL AMERICANS

Lillie Mason, forward (1986)
Clemette Haskins, guard (1987)
Tandreia Green, forward (1989)

ITEMS OF NOTE

- The Lady Toppers appeared in 11 consecutive NCAA Tournaments (1985-1995).
- The Lady Toppers have appeared in 41 different invitational tournaments, winning 15 while posting a 63-27 record overall.
- In 2000, Lillie Mason became the first Lady Topper to have her jersey retired.
- The Lady Toppers won their first game in 1914, beating Logan College 12-8. Win number 600 came on Dec. 4, 2000 with a 99-80 win over Tennessee Tech.

- Hall of Fame men's coach Ed Diddle served as WKU women's coach for two seasons, finishing with an 11-6 record.
- Paul Sanderford posted a career record of 365-120, leading his teams to post-season play in 14 of his 15 years at the helm.
- The largest crowd to watch the Lady Toppers in E.A. Diddle Arena was 12,951. In that 1986 game, the Lady Toppers defeated Old Dominion 74-64.

ALL-TIME LEADING SCORERS

No.	Player	Years	Games	Pts.	Avg.
1.	Lillie Mason	1982-86	125	2,262	18.1
2.	ShaRae Mansfield	1998-01	127	1,804	14.2
3.	Kami Thomas	1983-86	128	1,796	14.0
4.	Tandreia Green	1987-90	125	1,781	14.2
5.	Clemette Haskins	1984-87	128	1,762	13.8
6.	Natalie Powers	1998-02	117	1,641	14.0
7.	Kim Pehlke	1989-92	127	1,487	11.7
8.	Beth (Lane) Blanton	1976-79	116	1,446	12.5
9.	Brenda Chapman	1975-78	94	1,436	15.3
10.	Shae Lunsford	1996-99	118	1,386	11.7

ALL-TIME CAREER SCORING AVERAGES

No.	Player	Years	Games	Pts.	Avg.
1.	Lillie Mason	1982-86	125	2,262	18.1
2.	Pam Hart	1976-79	83	1,325	16.6
3.	Leslie Logsdon	2001-	92	1,373	14.9
4.	ShaRae Mansfield	1998-01	127	1,804	14.2
4.	Tandreia Green	1987-90	125	1,781	14.2
6.	Natalie Powers	1998-02	117	1,641	14.0
6.	Kami Thomas	1983-86	128	1,796	14.0
8.	Clemette Haskins	1984-87	128	1,762	13.8
9.	Laurie Heltsley	1979-82	88	1,153	13.1
10.	Beth (Lane) Blanton	1976-79	116	1,446	12.5

ALL-TIME LEADING REBOUNDERS

No.	Player	Years	Rebounds	Avg.
1.	Lillie Mason	1982-86	1,012	8.1
2.	ShaRae Mansfield	1998-01	1,000	7.9
3.	Shea Lunsford	1996-99	883	7.5
4.	Tandreia Green	1987-90	875	7.0
5.	Donna Doellman	1976-79	823	8.4
6.	Alicia Polson	1978-81	747	6.6
7.	Traci Patton	1985-88	744	n/a
8.	Dianne Depp	1981-84	735	7.2
9.	Brigette Combs	1986-89	717	n/a
10.	Gina Brown	1982-85	712	5.8

ALL-TIME ASSISTS LEADERS

No.	Player	Years	Assists
1.	Clemette Haskins	1984-87	731
2.	Renee Westmoreland	1990-93	477
3.	Dawn Warner	1993-96	440
4.	Kelly Smith	1988-91	398
5.	Camryn Whitaker	2000-	388
6.	Kim Pehlke	1989-92	374
7.	Debbie O'Connell	1986-89	348
8.	Jaime Walz	1997-00	336
9.	Kami Thomas	1983-86	335
10.	Kristina Covington	1998-03	299

ALL-TIME WINNINGEST COACHES

Coach	Years	Record	Pct.
Paul Sanderford	15	365-120	.753
Steve Small	4	88-40	.688
Mary Taylor Cowles	3	62-33	.652
Eileen Canty	4	50-62	.446
Julia Yeater	2	44-18	.710

(Source: Western Kentucky University Sports Information)

John A. McGill

SPORTS

Football

For a state known for basketball, Kentucky has nevertheless produced a considerable amount of football buzz over the years. In fact, state schools have produced seven national championships.

Georgetown College has won three NAIA national titles, Eastern Kentucky University has won two NCAA Division I-AA titles (and was in the title game four straight years from 1979 to 1982), Western Kentucky won the NCAA Division I-AA title in 2002 and the University of Kentucky was recognized as the 1950 NCAA Division I-A champion in a recent rating system done by Jeff Sagarin.

Kentucky's football history doesn't stop there. For instance:

Centre College's win over Harvard in 1921 not only would later be deemed the biggest sports upset in the first 50 years of the 20th century by the *New York Times*, it also prompted one of the excited faithful in Danville to paint the side of a cow "C6 H0"—which wasn't some rudimentary chemistry equation but, rather, the game's final score.

Known as "The Praying Colonels" because they knelt on the field before each game in prayer, there was perhaps more than the usual need for prayer prior to the Harvard game. That's because many of the players reportedly placed large bets on themselves the night before in Boston pool halls. (It was, needless to say, a decidedly different world back then.)

Numerous other noteworthy individuals and events have spiced the state's football history, among them:

Paul "Bear" Bryant, the last coach to compile an overall winning record as the University of Kentucky football coach, going 60-23-5 and making four bowl appearances. Bryant left UK to coach at Texas A&M, then took over at Alabama, where he won a slew of national titles. Bryant's record in 38 years at Maryland, Kentucky, Texas A&M and Alabama was 323-85-17.

Louisville native **Paul Hornung**, aptly nicknamed "The Golden Boy," won the Heisman Trophy at Notre Dame in 1956 and became a star running back for Vince Lombardi's Green Bay Packers. His 176 points in 1960 still remains an NFL record for single-season scoring.

Howard Schnellenberger, another Louisville native, was an All America tight end at UK before launching a stellar coaching career. Schnellenberger revived programs at Miami, where he won a national title in his fourth year, and at Louisville, where he laid the groundwork for the school's current success. His U of L teams beat such teams as Texas, Michigan State, North Carolina, West Virginia and Virginia. But his biggest win at Louisville came in the 1990 Fiesta Bowl when the Cardinals beat Alabama 31-7. In 2001, he fielded the first-ever

Morehead
Source: Herald-Leader

team at Florida Atlantic University, which already has wins over Division I teams, the most notable an upset of Hawaii its only home loss in 2004.

Johnny Unitas starred at the University of Louisville before becoming one of the NFL's greatest quarterbacks in a 17-year career with the Baltimore Colts. Inducted into the pro football Hall of Fame in 1979, Unitas led the Colts to one Super Bowl title and three NFL championships. In the 1958 NFL title game, Unitas engineered a pair of 80-yard drives in a 23-17 win over the New York Giants that is still considered by many to be the greatest pro game ever played.

Quarterbacks in this state have been particularly impressive. UK quarterbacks **Babe Parilli** and **George Blanda** have been inducted into the College Football Hall of Fame and Pro Football Hall of Fame, respectively. UK quarterback **Tim Couch** was the No. 1 draft pick of the Cleveland Browns and Louisville has boasted such quarterbacks as **Johnny Unitas, Chris Redman, Jeff Brohm** and **Stefan LeFors**.

Quarterback **Phil Simms**, who grew up in Louisville and played college ball at Morehead State, was named the MVP of Super Bowl XXI after he completed 22 of 25 passes to lead the New York Giants to a 39-20 win over the Denver Broncos, giving the Giants their first-ever Super Bowl title. Simms, who played 15 years, is now a key analyst for network NFL telecasts.

Kentucky's Sugar Bowl win over top-ranked Oklahoma broke the Sooners' 31-game winning streak. That UK team was recently recognized as the 1950 national champion by Jeff Sagarin, whose college football rating index has been a staple of *USA Today* since 1985. Sagarin applied his rating system to the seasons that determined champions prior to bowl games and as a result named UK the 1950 champions—a designation that is now listed in the NCAA record book.

In addition to having UK tackle **Bob Gain** become the first SEC player to win the Outland Trophy as the nation's best lineman in 1950, Bear Bryant also had standouts such as All American quarterback **Babe Parilli**, **George Blanda** and **Jerry Claiborne**, who would become UK coach in 1982.

Eastern Kentucky coach **Roy Kidd** was inducted into the College Football Hall of Fame in 2003 after compiling a 315-123-8 record, including two national titles, in 39 years at the school. Kidd was a two-time Division I-AA national Coach of the Year.

Though not a native, **Buddy Ryan** lived on a 200-plus acre farm in Lawrenceburg when he was the architect of the Chicago Bears' "46" defense that helped produce a Super Bowl champion and later as head coach with the Philadelphia Eagles and Arizona Cardinals. **Twin sons Rex and Rob Ryan** got their coaching starts here, Rex at Morehead State and Eastern Kentucky and Rob at Western Kentucky. Both are now defensive coordinators in the NFL, Rex with the Baltimore Ravens and Rob with the Oakland Raiders.

KHSAA Football

ALL-TIME WINNINGEST SCHOOLS

Rank	School	Wins
1.	Louisville Male	750
2.	Ft. Thomas Highlands	736
3.	Mayfield	709
4.	Paducah Tilghman	680
5.	Danville	655
6.	Owensboro	625
7.	Hopkinsville	580
8.	Louisville Manual	579
9.	Middlesboro	577
10.	Ashland Blazer	576

MOST ALL-TIME CHAMPIONSHIPS

1.	Ft. Thomas Highlands	16
2.	Louisville Trinity	15
3.	Louisville St. Xavier	11
4.	Danville	10
5.	Beechwood	9
6.	Mayfield	7
7.	Louisville Male	6
8.	Boyle Co.	5
8.	Covington Catholic	5
10.	Bardstown	4
10.	Lynch	4

ALL-TIME LEADING SCORERS (CAREER)

No.	Player	School	Points
1.	Herbie Phelps	Old Kentucky Home	722
2.	Kelvin Turner	Danville	702
3.	Monquantae Gibson	Louisville Moore	696
4.	Derek Homer	Fort Knox	680
5.	Shaun Alexander	Boone Co.	662
6.	Josh Gross	Russell	632
7.	Mike Minix	Paintsville	618
8.	Jeremy Britt	Danville	602
9.	Jon Chapman	Pikeville	594
10.	Michael West	Lawrence Co.	584

ALL-TIME LEADING RUSHERS (CAREER)

No.	Player	School	Years	Yards
1.	Derek Homer	Fort Knox	1993-96	8,224
2.	Jeremy Britt	Danville	1995-98	7,839
3.	Michael West	Lawrence Co.	1998-01	7,725
4.	Kelvin Turner	Danville	2001-04	7,170
5.	Scott Russell	Evarts	1988-91	7,090
6.	Quinton Henson	Lynn Camp	1996-99	7,148
7.	Monquantae Gibson	Lou. Moore	1998-01	6,741
8.	Mark Higgs	Owensboro	1980-83	6,721
9.	Brent Coleman	Pikeville	1993-96	6,696
10.	Shaun Alexander	Boone Co.	1991-94	6,662

ALL-TIME LEADING PASSERS (CAREER)

No.	Player	School	Years	Yards
1.	Tim Couch	Leslie Co.	1991-95	12,167
2.	Brian Brohm	Lou. Trinity	2001-03	10,579
3.	Kyle Moore	Breathitt Co.	1995-98	10,026
4.	Brandon Smith	Boyle Co.	2001-04	8,796
5.	Andy Ahrens	Lou. Ballard	1998-01	8,686
6.	Ryan Jones	Madison Cent.	1996-99	8,662
7.	John W. Monin	Bardstown	1998-01	8,268
8.	Neil Warren	South Laurel	1996-99	8,138
9.	Zach Barnard	O'boro Catholic	2002-04	8,124
10.	Dustin Gruza	Mason Co.	2000-03	8,040

MOST TOUCHDOWN PASSES (CAREER)

No.	Player	School	Years	TDs
1.	Tim Couch	Leslie Co.	1991-95	133
2.	Brian Brohm	Lou. Trinity	2001-03	119
3.	Brandon Smith	Boyle Co.	2001-04	116
4.	Jeff Duggins	Boyle Co.	1998-01	112
4.	Jacob Doss	Lex. Catholic	1999-02	112
6.	Kyle Moore	Breathitt Co.	1995-98	111
7.	Neil Warren	South Laurel	1996-99	104
8.	Chris Redman	Lou. Male	1991-94	102
9.	John Wesley Monin	Bardstown	1998-01	99
10.	Allen Sperry	Breathitt Co.	1999-00	92
10.	Gino Guidugli	Ft. Thomas High.	1998-00	92

ALL-TIME LEADING RECEIVERS (CAREER)

No.	Player	School	Years	Rec.	Yards
1.	Montrell Jones	Lou. Male	1997-00	266	4,345
2.	Gerad Parker	Lawrence. Co.	1996-99	238	4,736

3.	Jason Reynolds	Bullitt East	1991-94	227	2,852
4.	Maurice Marchman	Lou. Ballard	1999-01	178	2,867
5.	Chris Lofton	Mason Co.	2001-03	175	3,511
6.	Ben Smith	Taylor Co.	1997-99	163	2,283
6.	Michael Bush	Lou. Male	1999-02	163	3,031
8.	Clay Wolford	Lex. Catholic	1997-00	155	2,586
9.	Neal Brown	Boyle Co.	1994-97	154	2,327
10.	Dan Baker	Leslie Co.	1991-94	149	2,410

ALL-TIME WINNINGEST COACHES

No.	Coach	Schools	Wins
1.	Joe Jaggers	North Hardin	292
2.	Bob Schneider*	Newport Central Catholic	289
3.	Mojo Hollowell	Henderson Co.	285
4.	Walter Brugh	Paintsville	280
5.	Dudley Hilton*	Bell Co.	273
6.	Garnis Martin	Bardstown	271
7.	Philip Haywood*	Belfry	270
8.	Bob Redman*	Lou. Male	267
9.	Owen Hauck	Boone Co.	258
10.	Jack Morris	Mayfield	254

KENTUCKY MR. FOOTBALL AWARD WINNERS

Year	Player	School
1986	Frank Jacobs	Newport Central Catholic
1987	Kurt Baber	Paducah Tilghman
1988	Jeff Brohm	Louisville Trinity
1989	Pookie Jones	Calloway Co.
1990	Damon Hood	Warren Central
1991	Scott Russell	Evarts
1992	Billy Jack Haskins	Paducah Tilghman
1993	Jeremy Simpson	Lincoln Co.
1994	Shaun Alexander	Boone Co.
1995	Tim Couch	Leslie Co.
1996	Derek Homer	Fort Knox
1997	Dennis Johnson	Harrodsburg
1998	Jared Lorenzen	Highlands
1999	Travis Atwell	Hancock Co.
2000	Montrell Jones	Louisville Male
2001	Jeff Duggins	Boyle Co.
2002	Michael Bush	Louisville Male
2003	Brian Brohm	Louisville Trinity
2004	Curtis Pulley	Hopkinsville

(Source: KHSAA Sports Information)

Colleges & Universities

EASTERN KENTUCKY UNIVERSITY
FOOTBALL

EKU BY THE NUMBERS:
- Overall record: 509-319-38
- 2 national championships (1979, 1982)
- 17 Division I-AA playoff appearances
- 1 bowl championship (1967)
- 18 Ohio Valley Conference titles
- 3 undefeated teams (1940, 1954, 1982)
- 56 All Americans
- 216 All OVC players
- 2 College Football Hall of Fame inductees
- 1 OVC Hall of Fame inductee

ITEMS OF NOTE:
- EKU won its first game in 1927, beating St. Mary's 32-6.
- Roy Kidd ended his career with a 315-123-8 record. He was a two-time National Coach of the Year award winner and a 10-time OVC Coach of the Year selection. He was inducted into the College Football Hall of Fame and the OVC Hall of Fame in 2003.
- Ex-Colonel defensive back George Floyd was inducted into the Divisional Class for the College Football Hall of Fame in 1999. Floyd was a first-team All-America pick and OVC Defensive Player of the Year in 1980.
- EKU ranks first in OVC history with a conference record of 263-104-7.
- Wally Chambers, a first-team All-America pick in 1972, was voted NFL Defensive Rookie of the Year in 1973 as a tackle with the Chicago Bears.
- Current coach Danny Hope, a 1981 EKU graduate, has participated in nine bowl games while serving as an assistant at Louisville, Wyoming and Purdue.
- Assistant coach and Corbin native Steve Bird, a first-team All-American receiver at EKU, comes from one of the most-celebrated athletic families in Kentucky sports history. His father, Jerry, played basketball at UK under Adolph Rupp while his uncles Calvin, Rodger and Billy all played football at UK.
- The Colonels have a 171-36-1 all-time record at Kidd Stadium.

INDIVIDUAL CAREER RECORDS

Category	Player	Years	Total
Scoring	Elroy Harris	1985-88	355
Rushing Yards	Markus Thomas	1989-92	5,552
Rushing Average	Markus Thomas	1989-92	6.6
Passing Yards	Jim Guice	1965-68	5,041
Touchdown Passes	Jim Guice	1965-68	46
Receptions	Bobby Washington	1994-97	154
Receiving Yards	Rondel Menendez	1995-98	2,990
TD Receptions	Rondel Menendez	1995-98	27
Total Offense	Markus Thomas	1989-92	5,552
Field Goals	Dale Dawson	1983-86	49
PATS	David Flores	1977-80	126
Interceptions	George Floyd	1978-81	22

ALL-TIME WINNINGEST COACH

Coach	Years	Record	Pct.
Roy Kidd	39	315-123-8	.716

(Source: Eastern Kentucky University Sports Information)

GEORGETOWN COLLEGE
FOOTBALL

GEORGETOWN BY THE NUMBERS
- Overall Record: 462-415-20
- Three NAIA national titles (1991, 2000, 2001)
- 2 First Team All Americans
- 2 Coach of the Year awards

FIRST TEAM ALL AMERICANS
- Eddie Eviston
- John Michael Sullivan

ITEMS OF NOTE
- Bill Cronin was named NAIA Coach of the Year in 2000 and 2001.
- Bill Cronin's overall coaching record at Georgetown is 88-14 (1999-present).

KENTUCKY STATE UNIVERSITY
FOOTBALL

K-STATE BY THE NUMBERS
- Overall record: 333-391-26
- 7 bowl appearances (1928, 1935, 1943, 1948, 1971, 1975, 1997)
- 2 perfect seasons (1934, 1937)
- 30 All Americans (selected 43 times)

ITEMS OF NOTE
- William Coleman and George "Big Bertha" Edwards both earned All-America recognition in each of the four years they played for the Thorobreds.
- Henry A. Kean posted a 73-17-6 record (.760 percent) during his 12 years as head coach. Kean also coached the basketball and baseball teams.
- The Thorobreds own a 4-3 record in bowl games.

K-STATE ALL AMERICANS
William Coleman, tackle (1932, 1933, 1934, 1935)
Alphonso Bumphas, guard (1934, 1935)
George "Big Bertha" Edwards, halfback (1934, 1935, 1936, 1937)
William "Bus" Davidson, tackle (1934, 1935)
Robert Hardin, end (1934)
Joe Kendell, quarterback (1934, 1935, 1936)
Eugene Toomer, tackle (1937, 1938)
William Scaife, tackle (1938)
Melvin Bailey, center (1938)
Asbury Rogers, guard (1938)
Redford Rogers, quarterback (1939)
Hoy Thurman, halfback (1941)
Herbert Trawick, guard (1940, 1941, 1942)
Warren George, center (1941)
Warren Cyrus, end (1942)
James Williamson, tackle (1946)
Pierre "Red" Jackson, center (1948)
Richard "Chick" Corbin, halfback (1948)
Alvin Hanley, halfback (1948)
Harry Daniels, tackle (1948)
D'Artagnan Martin (1970)
Wiley Epps (1972)
Frank Oliver (1974)
Marcus Dover (1997)
Michael Mason (1997)
Cletidus Hunt (1998)
Travis Hardin, offensive line (1998)
Seneca Gray, offensive line (1999)
Alvon Brown, running back (1999)
Lakunta Farmer, linebacker (1999)

ALL-TIME WINNINGEST COACHES

Coach	Years	Record	Pct.
Henry A. Kean	12	73-17-6	.760
LeRoy Smith	13	65-62-3	.512
George Small	6	33-40	.452
George Edwards	6	27-27-1	.500

(Source: Kentucky State University Sports Information)

MOREHEAD STATE UNIVERSITY
FOOTBALL

MOREHEAD STATE BY THE NUMBERS
- Overall record: 285-387-22
- 10 All Americans (selected 11 times)
- 2 Ohio Valley Conference Player of the Year selections
- 3 OVC Coach of the Year awards
- 5 Academic All Americans
- 62 All OVC players (selected 74 times)
- 2 All Pioneer Football League Coach of the Year awards

MOREHEAD STATE ALL AMERICANS
John "Buck" Horton, center (1938)
Stanley Radjunas, guard (1939)
Paul Adams, center (1940)
Vincent "Moose" Zachem, center (1942)
Joe Lustic, running back (1946)
Dave Haverdick, defensive tackle (1969)
John Christopher, punter (1981, 1982)
Billy Poe, offensive guard (1986)
Darrell Beavers, defensive back (1990)
David Dinkins, quarterback (2000)

ITEMS OF NOTE
- The 1941 Eagles routed Rio Grande, 104-0.
- Ellis Johnson, the school's winningest basketball coach, also coached football for 16 seasons, posting an overall record of 54-44-10.
- Quarterback Phil Simms, the 1977 OVC Player of the Year and eventual Super Bowl MVP with the New York Giants, threw for 5,545 yards during his four years at Morehead State.
- David Dinkins scored a school-record 32 points in a 2000 win over Kentucky Wesleyan.

MOREHEAD STATE FOOTBALL RECORDS (CAREER)

Most Points	David Dinkins (384)
Most Yards Passing	Chris Swartz (9,028)
Most Touchdown	Passes: Chris Swartz (55)
Most Yards Rushing	David Dinkins (3,765)
Most Rushing Touchdowns	David Dinkins (63)
Most Pass Receptions	Jerome Williams (166)
Most Total Offense	David Dinkins (9,337)
Most Field Goals	Lenn Duff (18)
Longest Field Goal	Charlie Stepp (54 yards)
Best Punting Average	John Christopher (42.4)
Longest Punt	Don Rardin (78 yards)
Most Tackles	Tommy Warren (270)
Most Interceptions	Vic Williams (16)

ALL-TIME WINNINGEST COACHES

Coach	Years	Record	Pct.
Matt Ballard	11	64-53	.547
Ellis Johnson	16	54-44-10	.551
Guy Penny	8	39-39-2	.500
George D. Downing	8	28-32-3	.467
Jake Hallum	4	22-17-1	.546

(Source: Morehead State University Sports Information)

MURRAY STATE UNIVERSITY
FOOTBALL

MSU BY THE NUMBERS
- Overall Record: 421-332-36
- 8 Ohio Valley Conference titles (1948, 1950, 1951, 1979, 1986, 1995, 1996, 2002)
- 10 All America players
- 12 OVC Player of the Year selections
- 1 National Coach of the Year
- 4 OVC Coach of the Year selections
- 211 All OVC players

MSU ALL AMERICANS

- Al Giordano, guard/LB (1955) – tough, hard-nosed player who excelled on both offense and defense. Also played professional baseball.
- Gary Foltz, end (1962) – outstanding pass catcher. Led the team in receptions in 1960 and 1962.
- Don Clayton, TB (1973) – holds the MSU rushing record with 2,804 yards. Ran for 1,403 yards in 1973 and 1,257 yards in 1974.
- Eddie McFarland, DB (1977) – ranks eighth on the all-time tackles list with 332. Had his best year in 1977 with 94 tackles.
- Terry Love, DB, (1979) – excellent defender and team leader. Opposing quarterbacks rarely threw in his direction.
- Charlie Wiles, G (1986) - outstanding player who helped guide the Racers to a 6-1 league record and OVC title.
- Derrick Cullors, RB (1995) – holds MSU single-season records for rushing (1,765 yards), touchdowns (20) and scoring (120). Ran for 253 yards in 1995 game against Western Illinois.
- William Hampton, DB (1995, 1996) – Holds the school record for career interceptions with 19. Returned five for touchdowns. Had 115 interception return yards against Akron in 1984.
- Reggie Swinton, WR (1996) – Second all-time receiver with 2,346 career yards. Finished with 139 catches. Had career totals of 26 TDs and 156 points.
- Shane Andrus, PK (2001) – Kicked 26 field goals and holds the MSU record for longest field goal, a 52-yarder against Eastern Illinois in 2002.

MSU OVC PLAYERS OF THE YEAR

John Wheeler, Lineman (1964)
Larry Tillman, QB (1968)
Rick Fisher, RB (1971)
George Greenfield, RB (1972)
Danny Lee Johnson, RB (1978)
Terry Love, DB (1979)
Gino Gibbs, QB (1981)
Michael Proctor, QB (1989)
Derrick Cullors, RB (1995)
William Hampton, DB (1995)
Mike Cherry, QB (1996)
Justin Fuente, QB (1999)

WINNINGEST COACHES BY PERCENTAGE

Coach	Years	Record	Pct.
Carlisle Cutchin	6	37-11-4	.771
Mike Gottfried	3	22-11-1	.667
Houston Nutt	4	31-16-0	.660
Frank Beamer	6	42-23-2	.646
Roy Stewart	12	60-33-11	.645

ITEMS OF NOTE

- Each spring, Racer players wrap up their off-season conditioning with the Iron Horse Challenge, a three-day competition that tests strength, speed, desire and teamwork. The Iron Horse Challenge was the brainchild of MSU strength and conditioning coach Mike Vinson.
- Three MSU coaches have been voted OVC Coach of the Year: Bill Furgerson (1968), Mike Gottfried (1979) and Houston Nutt (1995, 1996).
- Houston Nutt won the Eddie Robinson Award as National Coach of the Year in 1995.
- A thoroughbred runs a 400-meter lap around the Stewart Stadium track every time the Racers score.
- Brien Bivens holds the MSU record for longest punt, 90 yards in a 2002 game against Southeast Missouri.
- In 1928, MSU defeated Will-Mayfield by the score of 119-6.
- MSU won its first game in 1924, beating Lambuth 7-0. Win number 400 came in 1999 when the Racers beat Kentucky Wesleyan 53-0.

ALL-TIME LEADING SCORERS

No.	Player	Years	Pts.
1.	Paul Hickert	1984-87	263
2.	Greg Miller	1997-00	212
3.	Chris Dill	1991-95	206
4.	Rob Hart	1996-97	183
5.	Willie Cannon	1983-87	174
6.	Reggie Swinton	1994-97	156
6.	Terrence Tillman	1998-00	156
8.	Jeff Lancaster	1980-83	153
9.	Greg Duncan	1988-90	145
10.	Stan Watts	1968-71	141

ALL-TIME LEADING RUSHERS

No.	Player	Years	Yards
1.	Don Clayton	1972-74	2,804
2.	Danny Lee Johnson	1977-81	2,522
3.	Willie Cannon	1983-87	2,370
4.	Rick Fisher	1969-71	2,297
5.	Rodney Payne	1985-87	2,189
6.	Waynee McGowan	1991-94	2,099
7.	Anthony Downs	1996-97	2,037
8.	Ron Lane	2002-04	2,011
9.	Nick Nance	1978-81	1,928
10.	Billy Blanchard	2001-02	1,796

ALL-TIME LEADING PASSERS

No.	Player	Years	Yards
1.	Michael Proctor	1986-89	8,632
2.	Stewart Childress	2000-03	7,581
3.	Justin Fuente	1998-99	6,392
4.	Larry Tillman	1965-68	5,037
5.	Kevin Sisk	1983-85	4,917
6.	Mike Cherry	1995-96	4,490
7.	Tony Fioravanti	1960-63	3,449
8.	Matt Haug	1967-70	3,407
9.	Tom Pandolfi	1972-74	2,970
10.	Mike Dickens	1976-78	2,677

ALL-TIME LEADING RECEIVERS

No.	Player	Years	Rec.
1.	Terrence Tillman	1998-00	146
2.	Reggie Swinton	1994-97	139
3.	Deandre Green	2002-03	126
4.	Lee McCormick	1982-85	122
5.	Shaun Boykins	1998-00	111
6.	James Huff	1987-90	107
7.	Jack Wolf	1967-70	101
8.	Joe Perez	1998-99	100
9.	Billy Hess	1967-70	96
10.	Glen Arterburn	1986-89	95

(Source: Murray State University Sports Information)

MURRAY STATE UNIVERSITY
FOOTBALL

MSU BY THE NUMBERS

- Overall Record: 421-332-36
- 8 Ohio Valley Conference titles (1948, 1950, 1951, 1979, 1986, 1995, 1996, 2002)
- 10 All America players
- 12 OVC Player of the Year selections
- 1 National Coach of the Year
- 4 OVC Coach of the Year selections
- 211 All OVC players

MSU ALL AMERICANS

- Al Giordano, guard/LB (1955) – tough, hard-nosed player who excelled on both offense and defense. Also played professional baseball.
- Gary Foltz, end (1962) – outstanding pass catcher. Led the team in receptions in 1960 and 1962.
- Don Clayton, TB (1973) – holds the MSU rushing record with 2,804 yards. Ran for 1,403 yards in 1973 and 1,257 yards in 1974.
- Eddie McFarland, DB (1977) – ranks eighth on the all-time tackles list with 332. Had his best year in 1977 with 94 tackles.
- Terry Love, DB, (1979) – excellent defender and team leader. Opposing quarterbacks rarely threw in his direction.
- Charlie Wiles, G (1986) - outstanding player who helped guide the Racers to a 6-1 league record and OVC title.
- Derrick Cullors, RB (1995) – holds MSU single-season records for rushing (1,765 yards), touchdowns (20) and scoring (120). Ran for 253 yards in 1995 game against Western Illinois.
- William Hampton, DB (1995, 1996) – Holds the school record for career interceptions with 19. Returned five for touchdowns. Had 115 interception return yards against Akron in 1984.
- Reggie Swinton, WR (1996) – Second all-time receiver with 2,346 career yards. Finished with 139 catches. Had career totals of 26 TDs and 156 points.
- Shane Andrus, PK (2001) – Kicked 26 field goals and holds the MSU record for longest field goal, a 52-yarder against Eastern Illinois in 2002.

MSU OVC PLAYERS OF THE YEAR

John Wheeler, Lineman (1964)
Larry Tillman, QB (1968)
Rick Fisher, RB (1971)
George Greenfield, RB (1972)
Danny Lee Johnson, RB (1978)
Terry Love, DB (1979)
Gino Gibbs, QB (1981)
Michael Proctor, QB (1989)
Derrick Cullors, RB (1995)
William Hampton, DB (1995)
Mike Cherry, QB (1996)
Justin Fuente, QB (1999)

WINNINGEST COACHES BY PERCENTAGE

Coach	Years	Record	Pct.
Carlisle Cutchin	6	37-11-4	.771
Mike Gottfried	3	22-11-1	.667
Houston Nutt	4	31-16-0	.660
Frank Beamer	6	42-23-2	.646
Roy Stewart	12	60-33-11	.645

ITEMS OF NOTE

- Each spring, Racer players wrap up their off-season conditioning with the Iron Horse Challenge, a three-day competition that tests strength, speed, desire and teamwork. The Iron Horse Challenge was the brainchild of MSU strength and conditioning coach Mike Vinson.
- Three MSU coaches have been voted OVC Coach of the Year: Bill Furgerson (1968), Mike Gottfried (1979) and Houston Nutt (1995, 1996).
- Houston Nutt won the Eddie Robinson Award as National Coach of the Year in 1995.
- A thoroughbred runs a 400-meter lap around the Stewart Stadium track every time the Racers score.
- Brien Bivens holds the MSU record for longest punt, 90 yards in a 2002 game against Southeast Missouri.
- In 1928, MSU defeated Will-Mayfield by the score of 119-6.
- MSU won its first game in 1924, beating Lambuth 7-0. Win number 400 came in 1999 when the Racers beat Kentucky Wesleyan 53-0.

ALL-TIME LEADING SCORERS

No.	Player	Years	Pts.
1.	Paul Hickert	1984-87	263
2.	Greg Miller	1997-00	212
3.	Chris Dill	1991-95	206
4.	Rob Hart	1996-97	183
5.	Willie Cannon	1983-87	174
6.	Reggie Swinton	1994-97	156
6.	Terrence Tillman	1998-00	156
8.	Jeff Lancaster	1980-83	153
9.	Greg Duncan	1988-90	145
10.	Stan Watts	1968-71	141

ALL-TIME LEADING RUSHERS

No.	Player	Years	Yards
1.	Don Clayton	1972-74	2,804
2.	Danny Lee Johnson	1977-81	2,522
3.	Willie Cannon	1983-87	2,370
4.	Rick Fisher	1969-71	2,297
5.	Rodney Payne	1985-87	2,189
6.	Waynee McGowan	1991-94	2,099
7.	Anthony Downs	1996-97	2,037
8.	Ron Lane	2002-04	2,011
9.	Nick Nance	1978-81	1,928
10.	Billy Blanchard	2001-02	1,796

ALL-TIME LEADING PASSERS

No.	Player	Years	Yards
1.	Michael Proctor	1986-89	8,632
2.	Stewart Childress	2000-03	7,581
3.	Justin Fuente	1998-99	6,392
4.	Larry Tillman	1965-68	5,037
5.	Kevin Sisk	1983-85	4,917
6.	Mike Cherry	1995-96	4,490
7.	Tony Fioravanti	1960-63	3,449
8.	Matt Haug	1967-70	3,407
9.	Tom Pandolfi	1972-74	2,970
10.	Mike Dickens	1976-78	2,677

ALL-TIME LEADING RECEIVERS

No.	Player	Years	Rec.
1.	Terrence Tillman	1998-00	146
2.	Reggie Swinton	1994-97	139
3.	Deandre Green	2002-03	126
4.	Lee McCormick	1982-85	122
5.	Shaun Boykins	1998-00	111
6.	James Huff	1987-90	107
7.	Jack Wolf	1967-70	101
8.	Joe Perez	1998-99	100
9.	Billy Hess	1967-70	96
10.	Glen Arterburn	1986-89	95

(Source: Murray State University Sports Information)

THOMAS MORE COLLEGE
FOOTBALL

THOMAS MORE BY THE NUMBERS

- Overall record: 103-44
- Second fastest Division III school to reach 100 wins
- 3 undefeated regular season records (1991, 1995, 2001)
- 2 NCAA Division III championship playoff appearances (1992, 2001)

ALL-TIME LEADING SCORERS

No.	Player	Years	PTS
1.	Will Castleberry	1997-00	296
2.	Derrick Jett	1991-94	222
3.	Ryan Reynolds	1991-94	210

4.	Carlton Carter	1992-95	198
5.	Jeff Runion	2000-03	189
6.	Erik Ward	1993-95	160
7.	Justin Frisk	2001-02	156
8.	Curtis Williams	1998-01	152
8.	Dan Calhoun	1992-96	152
10.	Tyran Thompson	2002-	102

ALL-TIME LEADING RUSHERS

No.	Player	Years	Att.	Yards	TDs
1.	Will Castleberry	1997-00	944	4,546	45
2.	Ryan Reynolds	1991-94	669	3,666	31
3.	Derrick Jett	1991-93	563	2,686	37
4.	Dan Calhoun	1992-96	493	2,386	24
5.	Carlton Carter	1992-95	448	2,289	31
6.	Curtis Williams	1998-01	419	2,218	22
7.	Tyran Thompson	2002-	433	1,938	22
8.	Justin Frisk	2001-02	330	1,888	23

ALL-TIME LEADING PASSERS

No.	Player	Years	Com.	Att.	Int.	Yards	TD
1.	Dustin Hicks	1995-98	442	868	36	5,745	35
2.	Jesse Lowery	1999-01	304	647	n/a	4,357	38
3.	Larry Hutson	1992-95	346	620	22	4,042	40
4.	John Paul Case	1990-93	326	620	24	3,757	32
5.	Nate Berkley	2003-	170	345	26	2,780	26

ALL-TIME LEADING RECEIVERS

No.	Player	Years	Rec.	Yards	Avg.
1.	Todd Newman	1991-94	108	1,741	16.1
2.	Andy Shields	1995-98	98	1,262	12.9
3.	Chris Kent	1994-97	86	1,201	14.0
4.	Will Castleberry	1997-00	69	716	10.4
5.	Chris Wagner	1990-93	66	n/a	n/a
6.	Craig Rieck	1996-99	65	1,501	23.1
7.	Jeff Krohmer	1997-99	60	973	16.2
8.	Greg Stofko	1990-93	59	722	12.2
9.	Lee Turner	1995-96	57	860	15.1
10.	Ryan Reynolds	1991-94	52	n/a	n/a

ALL-TIME WINNINGEST COACHES

Coach	Years	Record	Pct.
Vic Clark	9	61-29	.678
Dean Paul	5	40-12	.769
Mike Hallett	1	4-6	.400

(Source: Thomas More University Sports Information)

UNIVERSITY OF KENTUCKY
FOOTBALL

UK BY THE NUMBERS

- Overall Record: 534-528-44
- One national title (1950)
- Eight Bowl Appearances
- Two Southeastern Conference titles (1950, 1976)
- 15 first-round NFL draft choices
- 22 first team All Americans (selected 26 times)
- 9 Academic All Americans
- 65 first team All SEC players (selected 87 times)

FIRST TEAM ALL AMERICANS

- Derek Abney, kick returner (2002) – set six NCAA records, 11 SEC records and 14 school records, including NCAA marks for most kick return touchdowns in a season (6, four on punts and two on kickoffs) and in a career (8, 6 on punts and 2 on kickoffs).
- Sam Ball, tackle (1965) – three-year letterman at offensive tackle and first-round NFL draft choice by Baltimore Colts

- Rodger Bird, halfback (1965) – also a two-time All-SEC player who had 646 yards rushing and 12 touchdowns in 1965 and had a career-high 157 yards rushing against Virginia Tech in 1963
- Warren Bryant, tackle (1976) – Also won the Jacobs Award in 1976 as the outstanding SEC blocker; named to the Lakeland (Fla.) Ledger 25-year All-SEC team (1961-85)
- Ray Correll, guard (1953) – Named defensive most valuable player in UK's 20-7 win over TCU in the 1952 Cotton Bowl and named to the All-Time Cotton Bowl team.
- Tim Couch, quarterback (1998) – Led the nation in pass completions while second in completion percentage, passing yardage and touchdown passes; fourth in Heisman Trophy voting; Gave up senior year of eligibility and was No. 1 NFL draft pick (by Cleveland) in 1999.
- Bob Gain, tackle (1949, 1950) – Four-year letterman who, in addition to winning the 1950 Outland Trophy, was a three-time All-SEC selection.
- Irv Goode, center and linebacker (1961) – While primarily recognized for his ability at center, Goode had 23 tackles against national champion Ole Miss in 1960. Thirteen-year NFL veteran and two-time Pro Bowl selection.
- Clyde Johnson, tackle (1942) – UK's first All American; played two years in the NFL with the Los Angeles Rams.
- Lou Michaels, tackle (1956, 1957) – Named the SEC's Outstanding Lineman in 1956 by Birmingham TD Club and the SEC's Outstanding Player by the Nashville Banner in 1957; also averaged 39.8 yards as a punter; inducted into the College Football Hall of Fame in 1992
- Steve Meilinger, end (1952, 1953) – Named to Quarter Century All-SEC team by Birmingham QB Club (1950-74); had 75 career catches for 1,210 yards (16.1 average) while also rushing for 714 yards and intercepting six passes.
- Doug Moseley, center (1951) – Also played linebacker on Bear Bryant teams that went 28-8 and won an SEC title; Co-captain of the 1951 team that went 8-4 and beat TCU 20-7 in the Cotton Bowl
- Rick Norton, quarterback (1965) – Held UK season record for passing with 1,823 yards and 11 TDs in 1965; threw for 373 yards against Houston in 1965; first round draft pick of the Miami Dolphins in 1966
- Rick Nuzum, center (1974) – Was named UK's MVP in 1974 and played three seasons in the NFL
- Glenn Pakulak, punter (2002) – Holds UK modern era records for best average yards per punt in a season (45.58 in 2002) and in a career (44.43, 2000-2002)
- Babe Parilli, quarterback (1950, 1951) – Finished fourth and third in Heisman Trophy voting as a junior and senior; held school record for career TD passes with 50; completed 331 of 592 passes for 4,351 yards in three years as UK went 28-8, won an SEC title, and played in the Orange, Sugar and Cotton Bowls.
- Mike Pfeifer, offensive tackle (1989) – Strong offensive lineman who was also a first-team All SEC selection
- Howard Schnellenberger, end (1955) – Won four varsity letters at both offensive and defensive end; co-captain of 1955 team; 44 career receptions for 618 yards (14 average) and 11 touchdowns; Caught a 22-yard TD pass from Bob Hardy for a 14-13 win over Tennessee in 1954; later coached Baltimore Colts, then returned to college ball to revive University of Miami football and win the national championship in 1983; laid the groundwork for University of Louisville's rise in football, including a win over Alabama in the Fiesta Bowl.
- Elmore Stephens, tight end (1974) – A Time magazine selection, but was not picked to All-SEC first or second teams
- Art Still, end (1977) – Set school single-season record for tackles behind the line with 22 in 1977; Named SEC Outstanding Senior Player in 1977 by the Birmingham TD Club and to the 25-year All-SEC Team (1961-75) by the Lakeland (Fla.) Ledger; played 12 years in the NFL with

Kansas City and Buffalo.
- Herschel Turner, tackle (1963) – Played both offensive and defensive tackle and also was a first-team All-SEC pick. Played two years with St. Louis in the NFL.
- James Whalen, tight end (1999) – Originally a walk-on player, set UK single-season record for receptions with 90 (for 1,019 yards) in1999 and is fifth in career receptions with 120 (for 1,324 yards)

OTHER UK PLAYERS WITH RETIRED JERSEYS

- George Adams, running back, first team All-SEC 1984
- Ermal Allen, quarterback (1939-41), also played basketball; 22 years with the Dallas Cowboys as an assistant coach and director of research and development
- Calvin Bird, do-everything player (running back, defensive back, receiver and returner) named SEC Sophomore of the Year in 1958
- George Blanda, quarterback and punter/kicker, four-year letterman (1945-48) and first player in pro football to score 2,000 career points (2,002 total). Member of Pro Football Hall of Fame
- Paul (Bear) Bryant (honorary), coach, led UK to its first national and SEC championships in 1950 and went 60-23-5 in eight years; In addition to consecutive appearances in the Orange, Sugar and Cotton Bowls from 1950-52, led UK to its first-ever bowl game, the Great Lakes Bowl in 1947; coached eight first-team All Americans
- Jerry Claiborne, end and defensive back, holds the UK single-season record for interceptions with nine for 130 yards in 1949; named Coach of the Year in three different conferences (Southern in 1963, ACC in 1973-75-76 and SEC in 1983); 179-122-8 in 28 years as a coach at Virginia Tech, Maryland and UK, where he went 41-46-3 despite an 0-10-1 start; elected to the College Football Hall of Fame in 1999
- Blanton Collier (honorary), coach, went 41-36-3 in eight seasons, including a 7-3 record in his first year (1954) as successor to Bear Bryant, winning SEC Coach of the Year award by the Nashville Banner; hailed for his 5-2-1 record against arch-rival Tennessee; played at Paris High School, where he also began his head coaching career in 1927; left job as Cleveland Browns assistant to take UK position, returned to Browns as head coach and went 76-34-2 from 1963-1970 with an NFL title in 1964 and four division titles
- Sonny Collins, halfback, first team All-SEC for three seasons (1973-75) and the Nashville Banner's SEC Player of the Year in1974
- Bob Davis, halfback, 2083 yards rushing from 1935-37
- Dermontti Dawson, offensive line, All-SEC in 1987, seven-time Pro Bowl selection while playing with Pittsburgh Steelers
- Joe Federspiel, linebacker, first-team All-SEC and team MVP in 1971, named to SEC All-Decade Team for the 1970s by the Atlanta Journal-Constitution
- Mark Higgs, running back, third in UK history with 2,892 rushing yards who averaged school records of 6.6 yards per carry (one season) and 5.43 yards (career)
- Tom Hutchinson, split end, all-time leading receiver until 1977 with 94 catches for 1,483 yards, first team All-SEC 1960-61-62
- Wallace "Wah Wah" Jones, end, first team All-SEC in 1948 who is the only UK athlete to have his jersey retired in both football and basketball. Four-year lettermen in both sports, plus baseball
- Ralph Kercheval, all-around athlete in 1931-33 who is still regarded as perhaps the finest punter in SEC history. Still holds several UK records including single-game punting average (52.0 average with minimum of 10 punts). Second longest punt in UK history (78 yards) and career average of 44.8 yards per punt
- Rick Kestner, first-team All-SEC offensive end in 1964-65. Caught nine pases for 185 yards and three touchdowns in

UK's 27-21 upset of top-ranked Ole Miss in 1964.
- Jim Kovach, linebacker, all-time leading UK tackler, first team All-SEC 1978
- Dicky Lyons, do-everything player, first-team All-SEC 1967-68; first player in SEC history to have 1,000 yards in rushing, punt returns and kickoff returns; career punt return average of 15.4 yards per return still a UK record
- Charlie McClendon, defensive end, cornerback and tight end; helped lead Bear Bryant's 1949 team to the Orange Bowl and 1950 team to the Sugar Bowl. As head coach at LSU for 18 years, had a 137-59-7 record and went to 13 bowl games.
- Derrick Ramsey, quarterback, first-team All-SEC and third team All-American in 1977; and named Outstanding SEC Quarterback by the Birmingham Touchdown Club. Led UK to 9-3 and 10-1 records his last two seasons.
- Jay Rhodemyre, center and linebacker, first-team All-SEC in 1947; named to UK's All-Time Team by both the Lexington Herald-Leader and Louisville Courier-Journal
- Dave Roller, defensive lineman, first-team All-SEC in 1969-70. Ten-year NFL career.
- Larry Seiple, runner, receiver, returner and punter; holds UK records for everage reception in a season (23.5 yards in 1965) and career (19.8); famous for his fake punt and run on fourth-and-41 yards to go that went 70 yards for a touchdown against Ole Miss and keyed a 16-7 win.
- Washington "Wash" Serini, center, earned four varsity letters while playing for three different coaches (A.D. Kirwan, Bernie Shively, Paul Bryant); first-team All-SEC in 1944
- Bernie A. Shively (honorary), head coach for one season (1945) and athletics director for 30 years (1938-67); credited with the construction of 11,000-seat Memorial Coliseum in 1950 when many regarded it as a "white elephant" that would rarely if ever see capacity attendance.
- Harry Ulinski, center and linebacker; four-year letterman undr Paul Bear Bryant and captain of the 1949 team that went 9-3; first-team All-SEC in 1949.
- Jeff Van Note, defensive end, team's MVP as a senior in 1968; played 18 years with the Atlanta Falcons as a center and a six-time Pro Bowl selection

ITEMS OF NOTE:

- The first college football game in the South was at UK's Stoll Field when Centre played Kentucky University (now Transylvania) in 1880.
- In 1881, UK became the first Southeastern Conference team to introduce football. The school was then known by a variety of names: A&M College, Kentucky State College and/or State University of Kentucky.
- "The Immortals" were the only undefeated, untied and unscored upon team in UK history. They went 7-0-0 in 1898.
- Shipwreck Kelly rushed for a then school record 280 yards in 57-0 win over Maryville in 1930. He also was first team All Name.
- UK tackle Bob Gain won the 1950 Outland Trophy as the nation's best lineman, becoming the first SEC player to be so honored.
- Kentucky's Nat Northington was the first African American player to sign with an SEC team and the first to play in a league game, versus Ole Miss in 1967.
- In 1983, UK became the first school in NCAA history to go to a bowl game after being winless the previous season as Jerry Claiborne's team earned a spot in the Hall of Fame Bowl in Birmingham.
- In 1989, UK became the first SEC school to win the College Football Association Academic Achievement Award with a graduation rate of 90 percent (18 of 20 of their 1983 freshman signees earning diplomas).
- Bear Bryant's UK record: 60-23-5 in eight seasons (1946-1953).

- Successor Blanton Collier's UK record: 41-36-3 in eight seasons and a 5-2-1 record against arch-rival Tennessee. (Collier would go on to coach the Cleveland Browns to an NFL title.)

ALL-TIME LEADING SCORERS

No.	Player	Years	TD	FG	PAT	PTS
1.	Joey Worley	1984-87	0	57	75	246
2.	Seth Hanson	1997-2001	0	35	127	232
3.	Craig Yeast	1995-98	32	0	0	192
4.	Doug Pelfrey	1990-92	0	34	65	167
5.	George Adams	1981-84	27	0	2	166
6.	Moe Williams	1993-95	27	0	1	164
7.	Dicky Lyons	1966-68	26	1	4	163
7.	Taylor Begley	2002-04	0	24	91	163
9.	Rodger Bird	1963-65	27	0	0	162
10.	Sonny Collins	1972-75	26	0	2	160

ALL-TIME LEADING RUSHERS

No.	Player	Years	Att.	Yards	Avg.	TD
1.	Sonny Collins	1972-75	777	3835	4.9	26
2.	Moe Williams	1993-95	618	3333	5.4	26
3.	Mark Higgs	1984-87	532	2892	5.4	25
4.	George Adams	1981-84	638	2648	4.2	25
5.	Artose Spinner	1999-2002	438	2105	4.8	17
6.	Marc Logan	1983-86	389	1769	4.5	11
7.	Derrick Ramsey	1975-77	446	1764	3.9	25
8.	Anthony White	1996-99	364	1758	4.8	11
9.	Rodger Bird	1963-65	397	1699	4.2	21
10.	Derek Homer	1997-2000	353	1689	4.8	11

ALL-TIME LEADING PASSERS

No.	Player	Years	Com.	Att.	Int.	Pct.	Yards	TD
1.	Jared Lorenzen	2000-03	862	1514	41	.569	10,354	78
2.	Tim Couch	1996-98	795	1184	35	.671	8435	74
3.	Bill Ransdell	1983-86	469	816	29	.575	5564	22
4.	Rick Norton	1963-65	298	598	44	.498	4514	26
5.	Babe Parilli	1949-51	331	592	37	.559	4351	50
6.	Randy Jenkins	1979-83	363	699	53	.519	4148	24
7.	Pookie Jones	1991-93	263	504	19	.522	3459	16
8.	Dusty Bonner	1997, 99	313	479	13	.653	3380	26
9.	Jerry Woolum	1960-62	216	407	24	.531	2759	11
10.	Bernie Scruggs	1969-71	239	493	31	.485	2704	13

ALL-TIME LEADING RECEIVERS

No.	Player	Years	Rec.	Yards	Avg.	TD
1.	Craig Yeast	1995-98	208	2899	13.9	28
2.	Derek Abney	2000-03	197	2339	11.9	18
3.	Anthony White	1996-99	194	1520	7.8	8
4.	Derek Homer	1997-2000	129	1052	8.2	2
5.	James Whalen	1997-99	120	1324	11.0	13
6.	Quentin McCord	1996-2000	112	1743	15.6	15
7.	Kevin Coleman	1995-98	107	1428	13.3	13
8.	Tom Hutchinson	1960-62	94	1483	15.7	9
9.	Felix Wilson	1977-79	90	1508	16.8	10
10.	Derek Smith	1999-2001	89	1224	13.8	9

(Source: University of Kentucky Sports Information)

UNIVERSITY OF LOUISVILLE
FOOTBALL

U OF L BY THE NUMBERS

- Overall record: 405-401-17
- 10 first team All Americans
- 8 USA Conference Player of the Year award winners (selected 12 times)
- 12 bowl appearances (1958, 1970, 1977, 1991, 1993, 1998, 1999, 2000, 2001, 2002, 2003, 2004).

FIRST TEAM ALL AMERICANS

Tom Lucia (1949)
Lenny Lyles (1957)
Ken Kortas (1963)
Tom Jackson (1972)
Otis Wilson (1979)
Roman Oben (1994)
Jamie Asher (1995)
Sam Madison (1996)
Ibn Green (1999)
Anthony Floyd (2000)

ITEMS OF NOTE

- Ex-Cardinal Johnny Unitas went on to become one of the greatest NFL quarterbacks of all-time with the Baltimore Colts. Unitas is a member of the NFL Hall of Fame.
- Lenny Lyles, a 1957 All-American, also had a long and successful career in the NFL.
- The 1991 Cardinals scored what is arguably the greatest win in school history by topping Alabama 34-7 in the 1991 Fiesta Bowl. Quarterback Browning Nagle threw for three touchdowns in the lopsided upset win.
- Former U of L coach Howard Schnellenberger is generally credited with being the driving force that led to the annual Louisville-Kentucky game.

ALL-TIME LEADING SCORERS

No.	Player	Years	TD	FG	PAT	PTS
1.	Lenny Lyles	1954-57	49	0	6	300
2.	Nate Smith	2000-03	0	44	143	275
3.	David Akers	1993-96	0	35	111	216
4.	Ibn Green	1996-99	33	0	0	198
5.	Arnold Jackson	1997-00	32	0	2	196
6.	Ron Bell	1987-90	0	36	82	190
7.	Eric Shelton	2003-04	30	0	0	180
7.	Jon Hilbert	1996-99	0	22	114	180
7.	Howard Stevens	1971-72	30	0	0	180
10.	Ralph Dawkins	1990-93	29	0	0	174

ALL-TIME LEADING RUSHERS

No.	Player	Years	Att.	Yards	Avg.
1.	Walter Peacock	1972-75	811	3,204	4.0
2.	Nathan Poole	1975-78	517	2,903	5.6
3.	Lenny Lyles	1954-57	394	2,786	7.1
4.	Howard Stevens	1971-72	509	2,723	5.3
5.	Frank Moreau	1995-99	499	2,599	5.2
6.	Tom Lucia	1947-50	n/a	2,542	n/a
7.	Deon Booker	1985-88	n/a	2,363	n/a
8.	Ralph Dawkins	1990-93	525	2,159	4.1
9.	Anthony Shelman	1991-94	459	2,114	4.6
10.	Calvin Prince	1976-77	431	2,078	4.8

ALL-TIME LEADING PASSERS

No.	Player	Years	Com.	Att.	Pct.	Yards	TD
1.	Chris Redman	1996-99	1,031	1,679	.614	12,541	84
2.	Dave Ragone	1999-02	685	1,180	.581	8,596	74
3.	Jay Gruden	1985-88	572	1,049	.545	7,024	44
4.	Stefan LeFors	2001-04	416	630	.660	5,853	38
5.	Ed Rubbert	1983-86	430	873	.493	5,496	28
6.	Jeff Brohm	1989-93	402	715	.562	5,451	38
7.	Marty Lowe	1991-95	416	767	.542	4,861	27
8.	Browning Nagle	1989-90	333	597	.558	4,653	32
9.	John Madeya	1970-72	364	746	.488	4,504	34
10.	Dean May	1980-83	328	602	.545	4,359	29

ALL-TIME LEADING RECEIVERS

No.	Player	Years	Rec.	Yards	Avg.	TD
1.	Arnold Jackson	1997-00	299	3,670	12.3	31
2.	Ibn Green	1996-99	217	2,830	13.0	33

3.	J.R. Russell	2001-04 187	2,619	14.0	19
4.	Miguel Montano	1994-97 175	2,305	13.2	5
5.	Jamie Asher	1991-94 153	1,741	11.4	5
6.	Ralph Dawkins	1990-93 151	1,667	11.0	12
7.	Deion Branch	2000-01 143	2,204	15.4	18
8.	Lavell Boyd	1997-99 135	1,775	13.1	10
9.	Zek Parker	1998-01 128	1,804	14.1	13
9.	Jim Zamberlan	1965-67 128	n/a	n/a	11

ALL-TIME WINNINGEST COACHES

Coach	Years	Record	Pct.
Frank Camp	23	118-95-2	.556
Howard Schnellenberger	10	54-56-2	.491
John L. Smith	5	41-21-0	.661
Lee Corso	4	28-11-3	.690
Tom King	6	27-21-0	.563

(Source: University of Louisville Sports Information)

WESTERN KENTUCKY
FOOTBALL

WKU BY THE NUMBERS

- Overall record: 490-312-30
- 1 NCAA Division I-AA national championship (2002)
- 8 NCAA I-AA playoff appearances
- 8 Ohio Valley Conference championships (1952, 1963, 1970, 1971, 1973, 1978, 1980, 2000)
- 2 bowl appearances (1952, 1963)
- 16 first team All Americans
- 3 OVC Coach of the Year award winners (selected five times)
- 97 All OVC players (selected 128 times)

WKU FIRST TEAM ALL AMERICANS

Jimmy Feix, quarterback (1952)
Jim Hardin, guard (1957)
John Mutchler, End (1963)
Dale Lindsey, linebacker (1964)
Lawrence Brame, defensive end (1970)
Jim Barber, linebacker/academic (1971)
Virgil Livers, defensive back (1974)
John Bushong, defensive tackle (1974)
Dave Carter, center (1976)
Chip Carpenter, guard (1977)
Pete Walters, guard (1980)
Tim Ford, defensive end (1980)
Donnie Evans, defensive end (1980)
Patrick Goodman, center (1999)
Melvin Wisham, linebacker (2000)
Bobby Sippio, defensive back (2000)

ITEMS OF NOTE

- Western defeated McNeese State, 34-14, to win the NCAA Division I-AA national championship in 2002.
- Ex-Hilltopper standout Romeo Crennel is currently the head coach of the Cleveland Browns. Crennel served as assistant coach for 24 years with the New England Patriots, including the position of defensive coordinator since 2001.
- Jimmy Feix, Virgil Livers and Willie Taggart were the first WKU players to have their uniform jerseys retired. Feix would later become one of the school's most successful coaches.
- Wes Strader was the Hilltoppers' radio play-by-play announcer for 36 years (1964-2000).
- Legendary WKU basketball coach Ed Diddle was the head football coach for seven seasons (1922-28), compiling a 38-24-2 won-loss mark.
- WKU has participated in two bowl games, winning both. In the 1952 Refrigerator Bowl, the Hilltoppers beat Arkansas State 34-19. Quarterback Jimmy Feix was named the game's MVP. In the 1963 Tangerine Bowl, the powerful Hilltoppers, led by MVP quarterback Sharon Miller, blanked the Coast Guard Academy 27-0.
- John Mutchler, Dickie Moore, Lawrence Brame, Lonnie Shuster, Virgil Livers, Rick Green, Biff Madon and John Hall all earned OVC Player of the Year recognition.

ALL-TIME LEADING SCORERS

No.	Player	Years	Pts.
1.	Willie Taggart	1995-98	286
2.	Peter Martinez	2000-02	279
3.	Jeff Poisel	1996-99	265
4.	Clarence Jackson	1970-73	252
5.	Dan Maher	1985-88	250
6.	Dickie Moore	1965-68	206
7.	Joe Arnold	1985-88	192
8.	Antwan Floyd	1993-96	166
9.	Jim Vorhees	1966-69	164
10.	Max Stevens	1950-53	162

ALL-TIME LEADING RUSHERS

No.	Player	Years	Att.	Yards
1.	Willie Taggart	1995-1998	721	3,997
2.	Antwan Floyd	1993-96	697	3,775
3.	Joe Arnold	1985-88	642	3,570
4.	Dickie Moore	1965-68	607	3,560
5.	Clarence Jackson	1970-73	563	2,707

ALL-TIME LEADING PASSERS

No.	Player	Years	Com.	Att.	Yards
1.	Jeff Cesarone	1984-87	735	1379	8,566
2.	Johnny Vance	1966-69	289	592	4,046
3.	John Hall	1977-80	286	571	3,876
4.	Justin Haddix	2003-present	239	438	3,851
5.	Jimmy Feix	1949-52	272	554	3,780

ALL-TIME LEADING RECEIVERS

No.	Player	Years	Rec.	Yards
1.	Jay Davis	1968-71	131	2,236
2.	Alan Mullins	1982-85	124	1,866
3.	Keith Paskett	1983-86	123	2,117
4.	Robert Coates	1986-89	119	1,445
5.	Cedric Jones	1984-88	117	1,632

ALL-TIME WINNINGEST COACHES

Coach	Years	Record	Pct.
Jimmy Feix	16	106-56-6	.649
Jack Harbaugh	14	91-68-0	.572
Nick Denes	11	57-39-7	.587
Jack Clayton	9	50-33-2	.602

(Source: Western Kentucky University Sports Information)

Louisville's Brian Brohm
Source: Lexington Herald-Leader

John A. McGill

Motorsports

In 1982 when he was a rookie at the Indianapolis Motor Speedway, Louisville's Danny Sullivan was on a practice lap when the fiberglass cowling surrounding his cockpit flew off and sent the car into a spin. He crashed hard into the third turn wall. Later, while being looked over in the track's infield hospital, Sullivan, who was unhurt, said from behind the examining curtain: "You know what? You really DO know you're going 200 miles an hour when it's backwards."

Three years later, Sullivan would become a part of Indy 500 lore when he again went backwards. This time it was while attempting to pass Mario Andretti for the race lead and launching into a full 360-degree spin. But he emerged unscathed and pointed in the right direction. Later, Sullivan tried an identical pass on Andretti, again for the lead and this time succeeded. For a guy with Hollywood looks, it was a Hollywood script. They called Sullivan's 1985 Indy 500 victory the "Spin and Win" race. He would also win the CART Indy Car national title in 1988. Sullivan is the only prominent driver from Kentucky in the ultra-fast world of open wheel, open cockpit racing (he also drove in Formula One), but a number of other drivers—most notably Owensboro brothers Darrell and Michael Waltrip—have been major forces in NASCAR stock car racing.

Owensboro's Darrell Waltrip won three national titles and the 1989 Daytona 500 when the series was known as the Winston Cup. His 84 career wins are the most by any driver in the modern NASCAR era, which began in 1971. And younger brother Michael is a two-time Daytona 500 winner. They are the most famous of drivers from Owensboro, but hardly the only ones. In fact, this city of only 54,076 has produced an astounding number of world-class drivers in several forms of racing.

Owensboro had six drivers in the 2003 Daytona 500, a number that no other city could come close to matching. Six still compete in various NASCAR series, most of them in the Nextel Cup, the sanctioning body's highest level. Bill Sterrett, Sr. won three world championships

Dario Franchetti's pit crew looks over the car during practice for the Belterra Casino Indy 300 at the Kentucky Speedway in Sparta
Source: Lexington Herald-Leader

in hydroplane racing, and his son Bill Jr. was also a prominent racer. Brother Terry Sterrett also competed in the Miss Owensboro hydroplane, while Jim McCormick was one of the sports most dominant drivers in the 1960s and 1970s.

Owensboro's Cooper Hayden, meanwhile, won a top fuel national drag racing championship in 1968. Owensboro also has produced three world class motorcycle racers: brothers Nicky, Tommy and Roger Lee Hayden. Jeremy Mayfield and the Green brothers (Jeff, David and Mark) also have made names for themselves in NASCAR. But the man who preceded them all was Owensboro native G.C. Spencer, who dominated small tracks throughout the Midwest in the 1940s and 1950s with his "Flying Saucer" car. Spencer eventually made it to NASCAR, finishing fourth in the 1965 point standings.

SPORTS

Golf

John A. McGill

The 1960s were the golden era for Kentucky professional golfers. Louisville's Bobby Nichols won the PGA championship in 1964, Lexington's Gay Brewer won the Masters in 1967 and Louisville's Frank Beard was the PGA's leading money winner and winner of the PGA Player of the Year award in 1969.

No decade has seen as many Kentucky golfers record as many important victories since, but oth-

Justin Mullannax at the Kentucky Open
Source: Lexington Herald-Leader

ers have made significant accomplishments.

Topping the list is **Kenny Perry** of Franklin, who remains a prominent PGA tour regular and has earned more than $18 million with nine career wins—six of which have come since he turned 40.

Perry, who played high school golf in Paducah and college golf at Western Kentucky University, was a member of the U.S. Ryder Cup team in 2004.

Perhaps his most compelling tournament was one he lost—the 1996 PGA Championship at Louisville's Valhalla Golf Club. Then a relative unknown, Perry led the event despite a bogey on the 72nd hole. It proved costly, however, when Mark Brooks birdied the final hole to force a playoff. Perry lost on the first extra hole.

Larry Gilbert of Lexington was, as Sports Illustrated called him, "a hero to the nation's club pros." Gilbert won three National Club Pro Championships and played in several U.S. Opens and PGA Championships, but opted to stay close to his family rather than join the PGA tour.

In 1993 he and his wife Brenda took the last $4,000 out of their bank account to have a go at the Senior PGA tour. Gilbert won $516,000 as a rookie and in July of 1997 won his first major, the Senior Players Championship. By then his career earnings had crossed $3.2 million. Six months later, Gilbert, 55, died of lung cancer.

Lexington's **Myra VanHoose Blackwelder**, became the first woman to earn a full sports scholarship at the University of Kentucky, went on to become LPGA Rookie of the Year in 1980. She won more than $90,000 in 1988 and finished on the top 10 money list three times.

Jodie Mudd of Louisville won four PGA events and finished fifth on the PGA money list in 1990. He had a seventh-place finish in the 1989 Masters and tied for fourth in the 1990 British Open.

Others who have made their mark on the national stage include Paducah's **Russ Cochran**, Middlesboro's **George Cadle**, Lexington's **Jim O'Hern,** Louisville's **Ted Schulz**, Madisonville's **Brad Fabel**, Pikeville's **Robert Damron** and Union's **Steve Flesch**, who ranks 47th in all-time PGA career earnings.

WOMEN'S STATE AMATEUR
Golf Champions

Year	Champion	Tournament Site
1923	Mrs. Charles McCraw	Audubon CC
1924	Mrs. Charles McCraw	Lexington CC
1925	Emma Peffer	Twin Oaks CC
1926	Mrs. Charles McCraw	Louisville CC
1927	Mrs. Walter Hopkins	Paris CC
1928	Emma Peffer	Middleboro CC
1929	Mrs. Harvey Meyers	Lexington CC
1930	Mrs. Elvina LeBus	Fort Mitchell CC
1931	Marion Miley	Big Spring CC
1932	Marion Miley	Ashland CC
1933	Mrs. Willard Johnson	Owensboro CC
1934	Marion Miley	Winchester CC
1935	Marion Miley	Audubon CC
1936	Mrs. Willard Johnson	Owensboro CC
1937	Marion Miley	Ashland CC
1938	Marion Miley	Louisville CC
1939	B. Little	Bellefonte CC
1940	B. Little	Lexington CC
1941	Mrs. Willard Johnson	Ft. Mitchell CC
1946	Miss Verna Lee Stone	Winchester CC
1947	Mrs. Willard Johnson	Big Spring CC
1948	Verna Lee Stone	Idle House CC
1949	Betty Rowland	Bellefonte CC
1950	Mrs. S. D. W. Seaver	Audubon CC
1951	Betty Rowland	Owensboro CC
1952	Betty Rowland	Summit Hills CC
1953	Betty Rowland	Lexington CC
1954	Charlene Cross	Boiling Springs CC
1955	Charlene Cross	Owensboro CC
1956	Katty Wylie	Paintsville CC
1957	Mrs. Charlene C. Baumgarten	Louisville CC
1958	Mrs. Gaines Wilson, Jr.	Hopkinsville CC
1959	Mrs. Gaines Wilson, Jr.	Idle Hour CC
1960	Mrs. Gaines Wilson, Jr.	Paxton Park CC
1961	Mrs. Gaines Wilson, Jr.	Bellefonte CC
1962	Margaret Jones	Big Springs CC
1963	Mrs. Gaines Wilson, Jr.	Village Green CC
1964	Brenda High	Owensboro CC
1965	Mary Lou Daniel	Summit Hills CC
1966	Kaye Beard	Paintsville CC
1967	Anne M. Combs	Tates Creek CC
1968	Margaret Jones	Mayfield CC
1969	Kaye Beard	Wildwood CC
1970	Margaret Jones	Big Elm CC
1971	Margaret Jones	Owensboro CC
1972	Brenda High	Hopkinsville CC
1973	Mrs. Ronald C. Hacker	Bellefonte CC
1974	Anne M. Combs	Winchester CC
1975	Myra Van Hoose	Indian Hills CC
1976	Myra Van Hoose	London CC
1977	Anne M. Combs	Lone Oak CC
1978	Anne M. Combs	Paintsville CC
1979	Anne Rush	Spring Lake CC
1980	Mrs. Kaye Beard Potter	Wildwood CC
1981	Julie Zembrodt	Calvert City CC
1982	Julie Zembrodt	Lincoln Homestead CC
1983	Anne M. Combs	Bellefonte CC
1984	Mrs. Jessica Cornelius	Eagle's Nest CC
1985	Mrs. Gaines Wilson, Jr.	Owensboro CC
1986	Sandy Byron	Arlington CC
1987	Debbie Blank	Glenwood Hall CC
1988	Joan Rizer	Paintsville CC
1989	Joan Rizer	Big Elm CC
1990	Joan Rizer	Madisonville CC
1991	Joan Rizer	Lincoln Homestead CC
1992	Laurie Goodlett	Fox Run CC
1993	Laurie Goodlett	Calvert City CC
1994	Joan Rizer	Gibson Bay CC
1995	Christine Ridenour	Summit CC
1996	Cynthia Powell	Crooked Creek CC
1997	Jenny Throgmorten	Henderson CC
1998	Heather Kraus	Kearney Hill Golf Links
1999	Whitney Wade	Eagle Trace CC
2000	Whitney Wade	Perry Park CC
2001	Whitney Wade	Mayfield G & CC
2002	Mandy Goins	Woodson Bend Golf Resort
2003	Katie Fraley	Stone Crest Golf Course
2004	Lauren Scholl	Lafayette Golf Club
2005	Taryn Durham	Shelbyville Country Club

(Source: Women's Kentucky State Golf Association, www. wksga.org)

You Go Girl!

EMILY WOLFF (FLORENCE), 2005 WINNER

Dorothy Waters Junior Girls' Golf Award
WOMEN'S KENTUCKY STATE GOLF ASSOCIATION

The purpose of the Dorothy Waters Junior Girls' Golf Award is to promote participation in tournament golf among Kentucky junior girl golfers in the hope that they will discover the lifetime of challenge, enjoyment and friendships that the game offers.

www.wksga.org/2005dorothywaters.html

SPORTS

Olympics

Mark Maloney

Deciding on the most significant contributions to the Olympic Games made by athletes with Kentucky connections is a debate of—appropriately enough—Olympic proportions.

Kentucky's first Olympic medalists, in the 1904 St. Louis Games, were a pair of track and field athletes from Louisville, Ralph Waldo Rose and Nate Cartmell.

Rose, the first man ever to break the 50-foot barrier in the shot put, won the gold in his specialty and also won a silver (discus) and bronze (hammer throw). Cartmell earned silvers in the 100- and 200-meter dashes.

Cartmell returned to add an individual bronze and two relay golds while Rose earned his second gold in the shot put in London in 1908. Rose would also win gold and silver medals at the 1912 Stockholm Games.

What Rose is best remembered for, though, is for carrying the United States flag during opening ceremonies of the 1908 Games. Of 18 nations participating, only the U.S. – Rose – failed to dip the flag as it passed England's King Edward VII.

UK's Aronda Primault during her uneven bars routine
Source: Lexington Herald-Leader

The American flag has dipped only once at an Olympics since, at the 1932 Winter Games in Lake Placid, N.Y., Billy Fiske, a bobsledder, dipped to then-New York Gov. Franklin D. Roosevelt. Since 1942, it has been national law that the U.S. flag should not be dipped "to any person or thing."

Any "Kentucky Olympic" debate would also have to include the Fabulous Five and A Great Eight.

The University of Kentucky basketball team's Fab Five, which had won the NCAA title, combined with the Phillips Oilers to win the 1948 gold in London. Cliff Barker, Alex Groza and native sons Ralph Beard Jr. (Hardinsburg), Wallace "Wah Wah" Jones (Harlan) and Kenny Rollins (Wickliffe) represented U.K., along with coach, Adolph Rupp, who served as an assistant.

The U.S. Naval Academy fielded A Great Eight, the name given to the 1952 eight-oared shell with coxswain rowing team that won by the largest margin ever at Helsinki. Wayne Frye of Trinity rowed in the seven seat for a squad that also won a record three national championships and 29 races in a row.

Dr. Dot Richardson, a University of Louisville medical school graduate, hit a two-run home run in the first-ever gold-medal softball game (Atlanta, 1996), leading the U.S. to a 3-1 win over China. She also helped the team rebound from three straight defeats – to Japan, China and Australia – in the 2000 Sydney Games to successfully defend the gold. In the medal round, the Americans beat the same three teams they had lost to earlier.

But was Richardson more significant than Louisville's Mary T. Meagher? "Madame Butterfly" swam to three golds in three days at the 1984 Los Angeles Games.

Still, a case can be made that the greatest contribution by a Kentuckian to the Olympics was The Greatest himself—Muhammad Ali.

He first excelled as Cassius Clay, winning the light heavyweight gold medal at the 1960 Rome Games just one year out of Louisville Central High School. He would become the three-time heavyweight champion of the world. The story goes that Clay, dismayed after being hassled and refused service at an all-white Louisville restaurant following his accomplishment, threw his gold medal into the Ohio River.

The International Olympic Committee presented Ali with a replacement medal at the 1996 Atlanta Games—but that was only prelude to one of the Games' most touching moments.

The final person to light the fire at opening ceremonies is always a well-kept secret. In Atlanta, it turned out to be Ali. Even though a physical shell of his former self, even though his body was shaking from Parkinson's syndrome, Ali appeared and took the Olympic flame from swimmer Janet Evans, ascending the steps with the torch to light the cauldron as thousands cheered and millions more watched worldwide.

It was, without question, one of most touching and inspiring moments the Games have ever produced.

Kentucky has a rich history in the Olympic Games. Along with the medalists and moments listed here, many other non-medal winners have represented their state and country with grace and true sportsmanship.

The most significant contribution? The choice is yours.

OLYMPIC MEDAL WINNERS

SUMMER GAMES

Athletics: Track and Field (*demonstration sport)

1904 -- Nate Cartmell, Louisville (100-meter dash SILVER, 200 SILVER); Ralph Rose, Louisville (shot put GOLD, discus SILVER and hammer throw BRONZE)

1908 -- Nate Cartmell, Louisville (4x400 relay GOLD, 200-meter dash BRONZE, sprint medley relay GOLD*); Ralph Rose, Louisville (shot put GOLD)

1912 -- Ralph Rose, Louisville shot put, both hands GOLD and shot put SILVER)

1924 -- Eugene Oberst, Owensboro (javelin BRONZE)

1932 -- Percy Beard, Hardinsburg (110-meter high hurdles SILVER)

1972 -- Ralph Mann, University of Kentucky faculty (400-meter hurdles SILVER)

1992 -- LaVonna Martin, former Lexington resident (100-meter hurdles SILVER)

1996 -- Tim Harden, University of Kentucky (4-x-100 relay SILVER)

2000 -- Passion Richardson, University of Kentucky (4-x-100 relay BRONZE)

2004 -- Dwight Phillips, University of Kentucky (long jump GOLD)

Baseball

1988 -- Ty Griffin, Fort Campbell (GOLD*)

1996 -- Chad Green, University of Kentucky (BRONZE)

2000 -- Jon Rauch, Westport, Morehead State; and Brad Wilkerson, Owensboro (GOLD)

Basketball

1948 -- Cliff Barker; Ralph Beard Jr., Hardinsburg; Alex Groza; Wallace Jones, Harlan; Kenny Rollins, Wickliffe; all University of Kentucky (GOLD, with Adolph Rupp, assistant coach)

1956 -- Bill Evans, University of Kentucky (GOLD)

1960 -- Adrian Smith, Farmington, University of Kentucky (GOLD)

1964 -- Jeff Mullins, Lexington (GOLD)

1968 -- Mike Silliman, Louisville (GOLD)

1972 -- Kenny Davis, Georgetown College (SILVER). (USA team refused medals because of disputed finish loss to the Soviet Union in the gold-medal game)

1984 -- C.M. Newton (manager, gold-medal team)

1996 -- Ceal Barry (women's team leader, gold-medal team); Clem Haskins (men's assistant coach, gold-medal team)

2000 -- Alan Houston, Louisville (GOLD); Tubby Smith, University of Kentucky, and Gene Keady, Western Kentucky, (assistant coaches, gold-medal team)

Boxing

1952 -- Norvel Lee, Covington (light heavyweight GOLD)

1960 -- Muhammad Ali (then known as Cassius Clay), Louisville (light heavyweight GOLD)

Diving

1972 -- Micki King, University of Kentucky administrator (women's 3-meter springboard GOLD)

Gymnastics

2004 -- Jason Gatson, Winchester (team SILVER)

Judo

1984 -- Ed Liddie, Cumberland College (extra-lightweight BRONZE)

Rowing

1952 -- Wayne Frye, Trinity (Eight-oared shell with coxswain GOLD)

1964 -- Thomas Amlong, Fort Knox (Eight-oared shell with coxswain GOLD)

Sailing

1932 -- Temple Ashbrook (6-meter class individual SILVER)

Shooting

1920 -- Willis "Ching" Lee, Natlee (Military rifle 300+600 team GOLD, 300-meter prone team GOLD, 300-meter standing team SILVER, 600-meter prone team GOLD; Miniature rifle 50-meter team GOLD, team free rifle GOLD, Running deer, single shot BRONZE)

1984 -- Patty Spurgin, Murray State (air rifle GOLD)

2000 -- Nancy Napolski Johnson, University of Kentucky (air rifle GOLD)

Softball

1996 -- Dot Richardson, University of Louisville Medical School (GOLD)

2000 -- Dot Richardson, University of Louisville Medical School (GOLD)

Swimming

1972 -- Gary Conelly, University of Kentucky coach (4-x-100 freestyle relay GOLD, 4-x-200 freestyle relay GOLD)

1976-2004 -- Mark Schubert, University of Kentucky graduate (coach of multiple medal winners)

1984 -- Mary T. Meagher, Louisville (100-meter butterfly GOLD, 200-meter butterfly GOLD, 4-x-100 medley relay GOLD)

1988 -- Mary T. Meagher, Louisville (200-meter butterfly BRONZE, 4-x-100 medley relay SILVER)

1992 -- Megan Kleine, Lexington (4-x-100 medley relay GOLD; coached by John Brucato, Lexington)

2000 -- Nate Dusing, Covington (4 x 200 freestyle relay SILVER)

2004 -- Nate Dusing, Covington (4-x-100 freestyle relay BRONZE); Rachel Komisarz, University of Kentucky (women's 4-x-200 freestyle relay GOLD); Annabel Kosten, University of Kentucky (Netherlands' women's 4-x-100 freestyle relay, BRONZE)

Volleyball

1984 -- Rich Duwelius, Benton (GOLD)

WINTER GAMES

1980 -- Warren Strelow, Kentucky Thoroughblades (GOLD-medal hockey team goalie coach)

1994 -- Ville Peltonen, Kentucky Thoroughblades (hockey BRONZE, Finland)

1998 -- Jan Caloun, Kentucky Thoroughblades (hockey GOLD, Czech Republic); Ville Peltonen, Kentucky Thoroughblades, (hockey BRONZE, Finland)

2002 -- Brian Shimer, Morehead State (four-man bobsled driver) BRONZE; Doug Sharp, University of Louisville track staff (four-man bobsled side-pusher), BRONZE; Warren Strelow, Kentucky Thoroughblades (silver-medal hockey team goalie coach); Walter Bush, Kentucky Thoroughblades owner, recipient of the Olympic Order

MEDIA

An Interview with J.T. Whitlock

J.T. Whitlock says there aren't any secrets anymore.

Media is all encompassing — it is print and electronic broadcasting, according to Mr. Whitlock. It's newspapers, radio, television and even merchant handbills with local news included. His point of clarification: a reader is going to get all of them to get the news. One supplements the other. Print can't get the message out as quickly as the electronic media; but, due to the time restrictions, radio and television can just give highlights. Public interest and necessity — that's what the media is all about.

Radio and TV can give news straight from the scene, what's "hot as a firecracker." That's what whets the appetite. Then, a person will buy a newspaper for the details; to get the rest of the story. Here's what Whitlock used to tell journalism classes: "The local news report on the radio is that Aunt Susie fell and hurt herself. That's it, no other details cause there's not enough time. You might get a bit more detail on the television news. But, the newspaper will print the story with the details, describing how badly she was hurt, who helped her up and how it all happened."

At 81 J.T. Whitlock is still flying his airplane and riding his motorcycle. Whitlock credits his longevity to family heredity and a lesson his mother, who lived to 102, taught him. Her key to a long and well-lived life was "doing what you want to do."

The Executive Director Emeritus of the Kentucky Broadcasters Association, J.T. Whitlock is a lifetime board member and lifetime executive committee member of the association. He has high praise for the staff and board members of the association and speaks with pride about the great strides the association has made from its beginning.

Henry Watterson (1840-1921), influential editor of *The Courier-Journal* for over 50 yrs
Source: *Kentucky Department of Libraries & Archives*

Living within eight miles of the home where he was born, Whitlock is a resident of Lebanon, Marion County. He fell into his life-long career in broadcasting when he was asked to help with the electrical wiring on a brand new radio station in Lebanon. Two gentlemen, Charles Shuffett and Pete Hulse, had decided to construct a radio station, which Mr. Whitlock describes as a novelty in those days (the late 1940s). Apparently Shuffett and Hulse were typical entrepreneurs with "no money, but lots of ambition." When they approached him to help wire the station, Whitlock says he felt sorry for them and decided to help out — he had learned his electrician's skills during service in the military during WWII. He helped with the wiring and the station went on the air in 1953.

Whitlock agreed to "help out" again when he was asked to sell advertising for the station. Two years passed and the owners decided to sell; the new stockholders said they'd buy it if "J.T." would run it. Although he knew nothing about running a station, he found it to be one in the same as selling advertising: talk to people and find out what they want. Eight years later, he and two other men bought the station and he ran it for 47 years, broadcasting as WLBN 1590-AM and WLSK 100.9-FM.

Hand-picked by then KBA president Alex Temple, Whitlock served the association in varying titles for 37 years. The part of the free labor he liked the best was going to Washington D.C. He says, "Politicians want to be seen and heard — they have to have good media or they won't stay in office."

In reflecting upon the broadcasting industry, Mr. Whitlock pointed out two areas in which major progress has been made: integration and the overhaul by the Federal Communications Commission. Now, operators, managers and air talent are completely integrated: male and female, black and white are integrated "nicely."

Local radio and television is all about serving the local needs. No one has to be isolated anymore; rural America has access to knowledge that is equal to what would be available in a metro area or even the world.

"Some people and even old-timers sensational-

ize the news," Whitlock said, "News must be accurate, it must be the facts. If it turns out to be sensational, that's okay; let the reader draw his own conclusion. If the owner puts personal thoughts in, better to call it an editorial; because it's not the news, it's just someone else's opinion of the facts."

A firm believer in talk shows, Mr. Whitlock laughs and describes good talk show hosts as "good entertainers." He even enjoys listening to people he doesn't agree with because it's provocative and makes you stop and think. In 1955 he had a two-hour morning talk show, BackTalk. "Controversy is best because it gets people to disagree and both sides of the subject can be brought out. No one person is smart enough — a cross-section of ideas is needed. Then it's a good composite when you finish with the show." Whitlock said that he listens to Rush Limbaugh, "He's quite a good entertainer and makes me think."

Pioneer Radio & Television Stations

In "Towers over Kentucky, A History of Radio and Television in the Bluegrass State," Frances M. Nash, author and veteran radio station owner, describes the advent of broadcasting and the changes wireless transmissions brought to Kentucky. Published in 1995, the book celebrates the 75th anniversary of the radio broadcasting industry and the 50th anniversary of the Kentucky Broadcasters Association. Although much experimentation with "radiocasts" had been ongoing around the U.S. and within Kentucky since before 1920, the official "first" licensed radio station was WHAS in Louisville. Broadcasting as the "station of the Courier-Journal and Louisville Times," the first show went on the air on July 18, 1922. Both the newspaper and radio station were owned by Robert Worth Bingham.

As anyone who has lived through it, everyday life in America changed dramatically after WWII. "Radios with pictures" was an idea that had been around since experiments in the early 1900s. Kentucky's first television broadcast was a variety show on WAVE-TV in Louisville — it was the evening before Thanksgiving, November 24, 1948. The owner, George Norton, Jr., also owned WAVE radio. It seems that radio station owners had been given early advice by an NBC radio official to obtain a TV license as soon as possible. WAVE-TV was the 41st TV station in the U.S. WHAS-TV went on the air on March 27,

> "I want to reach to the farthest confines of the state, where a man can string an aerial from his cabin to the nearest pine tree, and setting before the fire, have a pew in church, a seat at the opera, or a desk at the university."
> - Robert Worth Bingham

1950 — both WHAS radio and WHAS-TV were owned by Barry Bingham. Estimates indicate that about 25,000 TV sets, which sold for $300-$400 (with five- to seven-inch screens), were being used in the Louisville metropolitan area.

Source: "Towers over Kentucky, A History of Radio and Television in the Bluegrass State," Frances M. Nash, Host Communications, Inc. (Lexington:1995).

History of Newspapers

Jerry Gibson

Kentucky's history of the printed news actually began five years before it became a state. It was conceived as a result of the major political issue of the time — separation from Virginia. It was decided at the second constitutional convention, assembled in Danville, that some publicity was needed for this important topic and that a printing press would be required, primarily to generate public favor. The year was 1785. A special committee was formed to find a printer willing to move to the Kentucky frontier. Looking first to Philadelphia, then Virginia, the committee faced the disappointing reality — no established printer wanted to risk the move. John Bradford, a young Virginian who had settled in Lexington, learned of the plan and approached Gen. James Wilkinson, a member of the special search committee, and offered to establish a newspaper in Kentucky. The committee, meeting again in Danville, accepted Bradford's offer and promised to provide as much public patronage as they could offer. According to a history published by the Kentucky Press Association, the citizens of Danville had expected the paper to be established in their community. However, the trustees of Lexington offered Bradford a location and assistance in setting up the printing shop there.

The first issue of the *Kentucke Gazette* was published in Lexington on Saturday, August 11, 1787 and was distributed to 180 subscribers. Subscribers paid 18 shillings a year for the service. The Gazette was four pages and measured 7 by 8-1/2 inches. No copy of the first edition has survived; however, an original of the second issue, published a week later on August 18, 1787, may be found in the Lexington Public Library. There is evidence that early publications were printed on paper manufactured in Kentucky.

Bradford died at home in Lexington on March 20, 1830, at the age of 80. The *Kentucke Gazette*, operated at times by his sons and others, lasted a total of 60 years ending publication in 1848.

Historic headline from the Park City Daily News
Source: Sid Webb

The first competitor to the *Kentucke Gazette* was the *Kentucky Herald*, which began printing in Lexington in 1795. By 1811 several dozen publications had been established. Two papers, *The Mirror* (1806) and *Farmer's Friend* (1809), that started up in Russellville may have been the first publications in the western part of the new state.

Louisville did not have its own paper until 1801 when the *Farmer's Library* was launched. It ceased publication in 1808, after being eclipsed by competition from the new *Louisville Gazette*.

The first daily newspaper appeared in Louisville in 1826 was the *Public Advertiser*, which had begun as a weekly in 1818. It is credited as the first daily newspaper west of the Alleghenies. Publisher Shadrach Penn became one of the most influential men in the state until his paper lost out in very public battles with the new *Louisville Journal*, founded in 1830 by George Prentice. Prentice, who was 21 years old, had come to Kentucky to write a biography of statesman Henry Clay when Clay was running for the office of U.S. president. He engaged in a fiery war of words with Penn and the *Public Advertiser*. Prentice eventually triumphed and became the dominant voice in Louisville and a very strong influence throughout the state.

In western Kentucky the community of Paducah read its first hometown newspaper in 1830. Since then 50 different newspapers have been published there. Many other Kentucky communities can boast of long-established and influential newspapers and strong editors; however, print space herein restricts further elaboration.

One short-lived but historic paper was the *True American*, published by abolitionist Cassius M. Clay of Madison County from offices in Lexington. The paper lasted only three months in 1845, but helped to bring attention to the deprivations of slaves in Kentucky. Published from a shop on North Mill Street, it had 240 subscribers for the first issue and grew to 500 by the second issue.

(See story about Cassius Clay below.)

While George Prentice's *Louisville Journal* continued to gain influence, a former employee, Walter N. Haldeman, began a competing newspaper, *The Morning Courier*, in 1844. While the *Journal* was a strong Union advocate during the Civil War, the *Courier* was run out of Louisville by federal authorities because of its strong support of Confederate causes. Haldeman moved his offices to Nashville and published the paper with a Bowling Green dateline during the war. After the war, the *Courier* was relocated back to Louisville. Meanwhile, Prentice had hired prominent Nashville journalist Henry Watterson to run the *Journal*. Watterson, then 28, approached Haldeman about joining forces. On November 8, 1868, the public was surprised to see the first edition of the *Louisville Courier-Journal*, the merger having been kept quiet. In its history, especially under the influence of the Bingham family, which owned the paper from 1918 to 1987, the newspaper became a predominant publication in Kentucky.

The origins of the *Lexington Herald-Leader*, Lexington's only major newspaper today, can be traced back over 130 years to the *Lexington Daily Press*. Its descendant, the *Morning Herald*, was first published January 1, 1895 and became known as the *Lexington Herald* in 1905. Another large circulating newspaper during this time was the *Kentucky Leader* (formed by a group of Fayette County Republicans in 1888) which eventually became known as the *Lexington Leader* in 1901. In 1937 the owner of the *Leader*, John G. Stoll, bought the *Herald*, and both daily papers were published concurrently (the *Herald* in the morning and the *Leader* in the afternoon) for the next 46 years. The newspapers had a combined Sunday edition, but their editorial policies were quite different. The *Leader* was a Republican, society-based evening edition, and the *Herald* a more political, heavily Democratic morning edition. In 1973 the Herald-Leader Co. was purchased by the Knight Newspapers, Inc., now the Knight-Ridder Corp. The papers were merged in 1983 into a single, morning newspaper that is still published as *The Lexington Herald-Leader*.

Cassius Marcellus Clay (1810-1903)

PASSIONATE. COMMITTED. DEDICATED. These are words that describe Cassius Marcellus Clay (1810-1903), a politician, ambassador to Russia under the Lincoln administration, and passionate newspaper editor. The cousin of Kentucky statesman, Henry Clay, he was born near Richmond.

Cassius Clay
Source: White Hall

Clay attended Transylvania University and Yale. Like many young Kentuckians he found his lifelong passion during college when he was impressed by an anti-slavery speech by the abolitionist William Lloyd Garrison in 1832.

Clay, like his cousin Henry, was an emancipationist who sought to eliminate slavery by peaceful, legal means over time.

Clay completed a law degree at Transylvania and embarked on a political career: Clay, elected state representative from Madison County in 1835, was defeated the next year, but was then elected again in 1837.

His newspaper, *The True American*, was issued at Lexington on June 4, 1845. The vehicle for delivering his emancipationist agenda to the public, Clay's intent was persuasion — to convince the common person that all men should be emancipated, free from restraint, control or the power of another; especially, free from bondage. Although Cassius Clay won accolades for his oratory, the subject matter and his passionate presentation made him many enemies in Central Kentucky, which was considered a center of the Southern slave trade. He was threatened often, fought many duels and once was attacked by a hired assassin. At one point, Clay fortified the print shop against attack with a cannon and a supply of weapons. A mob, empowered with a court injunction, entered the offices, boxed up the press and shipped it by rail to Cincinnati. Clay continued to print from Cincinnati with a Lexington dateline for a short time. He published *The Examiner* from Louisville, again arguing for emancipation.

Source: Kentucky Educational Television, KET Electronic Field Trip, White Hall, and http://www.ket.org/trips/whitehall/clay_2.htm and The Kentucky Encyclopedia (University Press:1992).

NEWSPAPERS

COMPANY	ADD1	ADD2	CITY	ZIP	PHONE	FAX
Adair County Community Voice	316 Public Sq	PO Box 159	Columbia	42728	(270) 384-9454	(270) 384-9343
Adair Progress	98 Grant Ln	PO Box 595	Columbia	42728	(270) 384-6471	(270) 384-6474
Advocate Messenger (The)	330 S 4th St		Danville	40422	(859) 236-2551	(859) 236-9566
American Baptist Newspaper	1715 W Chestnut St		Louisville	40203	(502) 587-8714	(502) 585-4840
American Classifieds	4312 Bishop Ln		Louisville	40218	(502) 458-5400	(502) 458-5596
Anderson News (The)	133 S Main St		Lawrenceburg	40342	(502) 839-6906	(502) 839-3118
Appalachian News-Express	129 Caroline Ave	PO Box 410	Pikeville	41502	(606) 437-4054	(606) 437-4246
Banner (The)		PO Box 802	Mt Vernon	40456	(606) 256-9150	(606) 256-9155
Barbourville Mountain Advocate	214 Knox St	PO Box 1288	Barbourville	40906	(606) 546-9225	(606) 546-3175
Barren County Progress		PO Box 190	Glasgow	42142	(270) 651-2274	(270) 651-2274
Bear Facts (The)	Pikeville College	PO Box 453	Pikeville	41501	(606) 218-5265	(606) 218-5269
Beattyville Enterprise (The)	149 E Main St	PO Box 126	Beattyville	41311	(606) 464-2444	(606) 464-8858
Berea Citizen (The)	711 Chestnut St Ste 2	147 Sycamore St	Berea	40403	(859) 986-0959	(859) 986-0960
Better Living	3804 Dixie Hwy	PO Box 207	Erlanger	41018	(859) 727-2970	(859) 727-2663
Big Sandy News (The)	115 Louisa Plz Ste 4	PO Box 766	Louisa	41230	(606) 638-4581	(606) 638-9949
Boone County Recorder	6948 Oakwood Dr	PO Box 129	Florence	41042	(859) 283-0404	(859) 283-7285
Booneville Sentinel (The)	Old Hwy 11 No 202	PO Box 158	Booneville	41314	(606) 593-6627	(606) 593-6638
Bourbon County Citizen	123 W 8th St		Paris	40362	(859) 987-1870	(859) 987-3729
Bourbon Times (The)	419 Main St	PO Box 777	Paris	40362	(859) 987-6397	(859) 987-6399
Bracken County News	216 Frankfort St	PO Box 68	Brooksville	41004	(606) 735-2198	(606) 735-2199
Breathitt County News (The)		PO Box 816	Jackson	41339	(606) 666-8067	(606) 666-8069
Breckinridge Herald-News Inc	120 Old Hwy 60 E	PO Box 6	Hardinsburg	40143	(270) 756-2109	(270) 756-1003
Bridge (The)	Somerset Community College	808 Monticello St	Somerset	42501	(606) 679-8501	(606) 677-4027
Business First Louisville Inc	501 S 4th St Ste 130	PO Box 249	Louisville	40201	(502) 583-1731	(502) 587-1703
Butler County Banner	120 E Ohio St	PO Box 219	Morgantown	42261	(270) 526-4151	(270) 526-3111
Cadiz Record (The)	58 Nunn Blvd	PO Box 1670	Cadiz	42211	(270) 522-6605	(270) 522-3001
Campbell County Recorder	6948 Oakwood Dr		Florence	41042	(859) 283-0404	(859) 283-0404
Campus Times	Campbellsville Univ	1 University Dr	Campbellsville	42718	(270) 789-5035	(270) 789-5035
Carlisle County News	422 Main St	PO Box 309	Bardwell	42023	(270) 628-5490	(270) 628-3167
Carrollton News Democrat	124B Dennis Dr	PO Box 60	Carrollton	41008	(502) 732-4261	(502) 732-0453
Casey County News	428 Woodlawn Ave	PO Box 40	Liberty	42539	(606) 787-7171	(606) 787-8306
Cats' Pause			Lexington	40503	(859) 278-3474	(859) 278-3477
Central Kentucky News-Journal		PO Box 1138	Campbellsville	42719	(270) 465-8111	(270) 465-2500
Central Record (The)	106 Richmond St	PO Box 800	Lancaster	40444	(859) 792-2831	(859) 792-3448
Centre College Cento (The)	Centre College	Box 43	Danville	40422	(859) 238-5533	(859) 236-7925
Chevy Chaser Magazine	434 Old Vine	PO Box 22731	Lexington	40522	(859) 266-6537	(859) 255-0672
Citizen Advertiser (The)	123 W 8th St	PO Box 158	Paris	40362	(859) 987-1870	(859) 987-3729
Citizen Times (The)	611 E Main St	PO Box 310	Scottsville	42164	(270) 237-3441	(270) 237-4943
Citizen Voice & Times	108 Court St	PO Box 660	Irvine	40336	(606) 723-5161	(606) 723-5509
Clay City Times (The)	209 N Main St	PO Box 547	Stanton	40380	(606) 663-5540	(606) 663-6397
Clinton County News	116 Washington St	PO Box 360	Albany	42602	(606) 387-5144	(606) 387-7949
College Heights Herald	Western KY Univ	122 Garrett Ctr	Bowling Green	42101	(270) 745-2653	(270) 745-2697
Columbia News	98 Grant Ln	PO Box 595	Columbia	42728	(270) 384-6471	(270) 384-6474
Commonwealth Journal	110-112 E Mt Vernon St		Somerset	42501	(606) 678-8191	(606) 679-4866
Community	3630 Dutchmans Ln		Louisville	40205	(502) 451-8840	(502) 458-0702
Concord (The)	Bellarmine College	2201 Newburg Rd	Louisville	40201	(502) 452-8157	(502) 452-8050
Courier-Journal (The)	525 W Broadway	PO Box 740031	Louisville	40202	(800) 765-4011	(502) 582-3601
Crittenden Press (The)	125 E Bellville St	PO Box 191	Marion	42064	(270) 965-3191	(270) 965-2516
Cumberland County News	412 Cthse Sq	PO Box 307	Burkesville	42717	(270) 864-3891	(270) 864-3497
Cynthiana Democrat	302 Webster Ave	PO Box 160	Cynthiana	41031	(859) 234-1035	(859) 234-8096
Daily News (The)	813 College St	PO Box 90012	Bowling Green	42102	(270) 781-1700	(270) 783-3237
Daily News (The)	120 N 11th St	PO Box 579	Middlesboro	40965	(606) 248-1010	(606) 248-7614
Dawson Springs Progress	131 S Main St	PO Box 460	Dawson Springs	42408	(270) 797-3271	(270) 797-3273

NEWSPAPERS

COMPANY	ADD1	ADD2	CITY	ZIP	PHONE	FAX
Eastern Progress	117 Donovan Annex	Eastern KY Univ	Richmond	40475	(859) 622-1881	(859) 622-2354
Echo (The)	Pikeville College	147 Sycamore St	Pikeville	41501	(606) 218-5250	(606) 432-9328
Edmonson News Inc	101 S Main St	PO Box 69	Brownsville	42210	(270) 597-3115	(270) 597-3115
Elliott County News		PO Box 222	Sandy Hook	41171	(606) 743-3551	(606) 743-3565
Estill County Tribune	6135 Winchester Rd		Irvine	40336	(606) 723-5012	(606) 723-5012
Falmouth Outlook (The)	210 Main St	PO Box 111	Falmouth	41040	(859) 654-3332	(859) 654-4365
Flemingsburg Gazette	140 Electric St	PO Box 32	Flemingsburg	41041	(606) 845-9211	(606) 845-3299
Florence Recorder	6948 Oakwood Dr		Florence	41042	(859) 283-0404	(859) 283-7285
Floyd County Times	263 S Central Ave	PO Box 390	Prestonsburg	41653	(606) 886-8506	(606) 886-3603
Foothills Courier	379 Walnut St		Frenchburg	40322	(606) 768-6134	(606) 768-6134
Fort Campbell Courier	15095 Ft Campbell Blvd		Oak Grove	42262	(270) 798-9969	(270) 798-6247
Franklin Favorite	103 N High	PO Box 309	Franklin	42135	(270) 586-4481	(270) 586-6031
Fulton Leader (The)	304 E State Line	PO Box 1200	Fulton	42041	(270) 472-1121	(270) 472-1129
Gallatin County News	211 3rd St	PO Box 435	Warsaw	41095	(859) 567-5051	(859) 567-6397
Georgetonian (The)	Georgetown College		Georgetown	40324	(502) 863-8150	(502) 868-8888
Georgetown News & Graphic	1481 Cherry Blossom Way	400 E College St	Georgetown	40324	(502) 863-1111	(502) 863-6296
Glasgow Daily Times	100 Commerce Dr	PO Box 1179	Glasgow	42142	(270) 678-5171	(270) 678-5052
Gleaner (The)	455 Klutey Park Plz	PO Box 4	Henderson	42420	(270) 827-2000	(270) 827-2765
Grant County News	151 N Main St	PO Box 247	Williamstown	41097	(859) 824-3343	(859) 824-5888
Grayson County News-Gazette	307 W Market St	PO Box 305	Leitchfield	42755	(270) 259-9622	(270) 259-5537
Grayson Journal-Enquirer	240 E Main St		Grayson	41143	(606) 474-5101	(606) 474-0013
Green River Republican	120 E Ohio St	PO Box 219	Morgantown	42261	(270) 526-4151	(270) 526-3111
Greensburg Record-Herald	102 W Court St	PO Box 130	Greensburg	42743	(270) 932-4381	(270) 932-4441
Hancock Clarion (The)	230 Main St	PO Box 39	Hawesville	42348	(270) 927-6945	(270) 927-6947
Hardin County Independent	318 N Mulberry St		Elizabethtown	42701	(270) 737-5585	(270) 737-6634
Harlan Daily Enterprise (The)	1548 S US Hwy 421	PO Box Drawer E	Harlan	40831	(606) 573-4510	(606) 573-0042
Harrodsburg Herald (The)	101 W Broadway	PO Box 68	Harrodsburg	40330	(859) 734-2726	(859) 734-0737
Hart County News-Herald	570 S Dixie St	PO Box 340	Horse Cave	42749	(270) 786-2676	(270) 786-4470
Hazard Herald (The)	439 High St	PO Box 869	Hazard	41702	(606) 436-5771	(606) 436-3140
Henry County Local	1378 Eminence Rd	PO Box 209	New Castle	40050	(502) 845-2858	(502) 845-2921
Herald News	118 S Main St	PO Box 87	Edmonton	42129	(270) 432-3291	(270) 432-4414
Herald-Ledger	143 Main St	PO Box 747	Eddyville	42038	(270) 388-2269	(270) 388-5540
Hickman County Gazette	308 S Washington St	PO Box 200	Clinton	42031	(270) 653-3381	(270) 653-3322
Hickman Courier	1232 Moscow Ave	PO Box 70	Hickman	42050	(270) 236-2726	(270) 236-2726
Independent (The)	226 17th St	PO Box 311	Ashland	41105	(800) 955-5860	(606) 326-2678
Inside the Turret	408 W Dixie Ave		Ft Knox	40121	(502) 624-1211	(502) 624-2095
Interior Journal (The)	111 E Main St	PO Box 995	Stanford	40484	(606) 365-2104	(606) 365-2105
Intermountain Publishing		PO Box 999	Jackson	41339	(606) 666-2451	(606) 666-5757
Jackson County Sun	101 Main St	PO Box 130	McKee	40447	(606) 287-7197	(606) 287-7196
Jackson Times (The)	1001 College Ave	PO Box 999	Jackson	41339	(606) 666-2451	(606) 666-5757
Jessamine Journal (The)	507 N Main St	PO Box 8	Nicholasville	40340	(859) 885-5381	(859) 887-2966
Journal Enterprise (The)	100 Walnut St	PO Box 190	Providence	42450	(270) 667-2068	(270) 667-9160
Kenton Community Recorder	6948 Oakwood Dr		Florence	41042	(859) 283-0404	(859) 283-7285
Kentucky Coal Journal	226 Grandview Dr	PO Box 3068	Pikeville	41502	(606) 432-0206	(606) 432-2162
Kentucky Enquirer (The)	311 W Main St		Ft Mitchell	41017	(859) 578-5500	(859) 578-5515
Kentucky Gazette (The)		PO Box 778	Frankfort	40602	(800) 462-6204	(502) 875-8330
Kentucky Journal of Commerce & Industry	2303 Greene Way		Louisville	40220	(859) 491-4737	(502) 491-5322
Kentucky Kernel	Univ of KY	Journalism Bldg	Lexington	40506	(859) 257-2871	(859) 323-1906
Kentucky Living	4515 Bishop Ln	PO Box 32170	Louisville	40232	(800) 595-4846	(502) 459-1611
Kentucky Monthly	213 St Clair St		Frankfort	40601	(888) 329-0053	(502) 227-5009
Kentucky New Era	1618 E 9th St		Hopkinsville	42241	(270) 886-4444	(270) 887-3222
Kentucky Post (The)	421 Madison Ave	PO Box 729	Covington	41011	(859) 292-2600	(859) 291-2525
Kentucky Standard (The)	110 W Stephen Foster Ave	PO Box 639	Bardstown	40004	(502) 348-9003	(502) 348-1971

NEWSPAPERS

COMPANY	ADD1	ADD2	CITY	ZIP	PHONE	FAX
La Voz de Kentucky	La Voz Inc	PO Box 54516	Lexington	40555	(859) 621-2108	(859) 231-0197
Lake News (The)	205 5th Ave	PO Box 498	Calvert City	42029	(270) 395-5858	(270) 395-5858
Landmark Community Newspaper	601 Taylorsville Rd	PO Box 549	Shelbyville	40066	(502) 633-4334	(502) 633-4447
LaRue County Herald News	40 Shawnee Dr		Hodgenville	42748	(270) 358-3118	(270) 358-4852
Laurel News Journal	115 CVB Ln	PO Box 2108	London	40743	(606) 877-2595	(606) 877-9565
Leader-News	1730 W Everly Brothers Blvd	PO Box 471	Central City	42330	(270) 754-3000	(270) 754-9484
Lebanon Enterprise (The)	119 S Proctor Knott Ave	PO Box 679	Lebanon	40033	(270) 692-6026	(270) 692-2118
Ledger-Independent (The)	121 Limestone Ave	PO Box 518	Maysville	41056	(606) 564-9091	(606) 564-6693
Leo-Louisville Eccentric Observer	640 S 4th St No 100		Louisville	40202	(502) 895-9770	(502) 895-9779
Leslie County News	2009 Main St	PO Box 967	Hyden	41749	(606) 672-2841	(606) 672-7409
Letcher County Community News Press		PO Box 217	Cromona	41810	(606) 855-4541	(606) 855-9290
Lewis County Herald	206 Main St		Vanceburg	41179	(606) 796-2331	(606) 796-3110
Lexington Herald-Leader (The)	100 Midland Ave		Lexington	40508	(859) 231-3200	(859) 254-9738
Licking Valley Courier	142 Prestonsburg St	PO Box 187	West Liberty	41472	(606) 743-3551	(606) 743-3565
Livingston Ledger	US 60	PO Box 129	Smithland	42081	(270) 928-2128	(270) 928-2907
Louisville Cardinal (The)	Univ of Louisville	Miller-IT Ctr	Louisville	40292	(502) 852-8727	(502) 857-0700
Louisville Daily Sports	325 E Breckinridge St		Louisville	40203	(502) 582-2050	
Louisville Defender	1720 Dixie Hwy	PO Box 2557	Louisville	40201	(502) 772-2591	(502) 775-8665
Louisville Magazine	137 W Muhammad Ali Blvd		Louisville	40202	(502) 625-0100	(502) 625-0109
Manchester Enterprise	103 3rd St	PO Box 449	Manchester	40962	(606) 598-8174	(606) 598-2330
Mayfield Messenger (The)	201 N 8th St	PO Box 709	Mayfield	42066	(270) 247-1515	(270) 247-6336
McCreary County Record	61 Geary Ave	PO Box 9	Whitley City	42653	(606) 376-5356	(606) 376-9565
McLean County News		PO Box 266	Calhoun	42327	(270) 273-3287	(270) 273-3544
Meade County Messenger	235 Main St	PO Box 678	Brandenburg	40108	(270) 422-2155	(270) 422-2110
Messenger (The)	947 Donaldson Hwy		Erlanger	41018	(859) 283-5270	(859) 283-6226
Messenger-Inquirer	221 S Main St	PO Box 529	Madisonville	42431	(270) 824-3300	(270) 821-6855
Metcalfe County Light (The)	1401 Frederica St	PO Box 1480	Owensboro	42302	(270) 926-0123	(270) 686-7868
Monroe County Citizen	113 E Stockton	PO Box 58	Edmonton	42129	(270) 432-5511	(270) 432-5511
Morehead News	301 N Main St		Tompkinsville	42167	(270) 487-8666	(270) 487-8666
Mountain Citizen (The)	722 W 1st St	PO Box 1029	Morehead	40351	(606) 784-4116	(606) 784-7337
Mountain Eagle (The)	Main St Cain Bldg	PO Box 808	Inez	41224	(606) 298-7570	(606) 298-3711
Mt Sterling Advocate	41 N Webb Ave	PO Box 406	Whitesburg	41858	(606) 633-2252	(606) 633-2843
Mt Vernon Signal	219 Midland Trl	PO Box 185	Mt Sterling	40353	(859) 498-2222	(859) 498-2228
Mt Washington Pioneer News Bureau	115 E Main St	PO Box 269	Mt Vernon	40456	(606) 256-2244	(606) 256-9526
Murray Ledger & Times	611 Bardstown Rd	PO Box 1040	Mt Washington	40047	(502) 538-7398	(502) 538-4049
Murray State News	1001 Whitnell Ave		Murray	42071	(270) 753-1916	(270) 753-1927
News Democrat & Leader	2609 University Station		Murray	42071	(270) 762-4468	(270) 762-3175
News Herald (The)	120 Public Sq	PO Box 270	Russellville	42276	(270) 726-8394	(270) 726-8398
News Journal	152 W Bryan St	PO Box 219	Owenton	40359	(502) 484-3431	(502) 484-3221
News Journal	105 S 2nd St	PO Box 418	Williamsburg	40769	(606) 549-0643	(606) 528-9779
News Outlook	215 N Main St	PO Box 1524	Corbin	40702	(606) 528-9767	(606) 528-9779
News-Enterprise (The)	18 Water St	PO Box 377	Owingsville	40360	(606) 674-2181	(606) 674-9994
Northerner (The)	408 W Dixie Ave		Elizabethtown	42701	(270) 769-1200	(270) 769-7318
Nicholas Countian & Carlisle Mercury (The)	218 N Locust St		Carlisle	40311	(800) 566-8068	(859) 288-6947
Ohio County Times News (The)	Northern KY Univ	203 University Ctr	Highland Heights	41076	(859) 572-5260	(859) 572-5772
Oldham Era (The)	314 Main St	PO Box 226	Hartford	42347	(270) 298-7100	(270) 298-9572
Paducah Sun (The)	204 S 1st St	PO Box 5	LaGrange	40031	(502) 222-2183	(502) 222-7194
Paintsville Herald (The)	408 Kentucky Ave	PO Box 2300	Paducah	42002	(270) 575-8600	(270) 442-7859
Pangram (The)	209 Main St	PO Box 1547	Paintsville	41240	(606) 789-5315	(606) 789-9717
Pineville Sun	KY Wesleyan College	PO Box 529	Owensboro	42302	(270) 852-3607	(270) 852-3597
Pioneer News (The)	210 Virginia Ave	PO Box 250	Pineville	40977	(606) 337-2333	(606) 337-2360
Progress (The)	455 Buckman	PO Box 98	Shepherdsville	40165	(502) 955-6348	(502) 955-9704
	101 N Public Sq		Glasgow	42141	(270) 659-2146	(270) 651-2274

NEWSPAPERS

COMPANY	ADD1	ADD2	CITY	ZIP	PHONE	FAX
Quadrangle	Jefferson Community College	109 E Broadway	Louisville	40202	(502) 213-2287	
Rambler (The)	Transylvania College		Lexington	40507	(859) 233-3315	
Record (The)	209C W White Oak St		Leitchfield	42754	(270) 259-6061	(270) 230-8405
Record (The)	1200 S Shelby St		Louisville	40203	(502) 636-0296	(502) 636-2379
Richmond Register (The)	380 Big Hill Ave.	PO Box 190	Richmond	40475	(859) 623-1669	(859) 623-2337
Russell County News (The)	120 Wilson St	PO Box 5	Russell Springs	42642	(270) 866-3191	(270) 866-3198
Russell Register (The)		PO Box 5	Jamestown	42629	(270) 343-6397	(270) 343-6363
Salyersville Independent	W Maple St	PO Box 29	Salyersville	41465	(606) 349-2915	(606) 349-8609
Sebree Banner (The)	7128 St Rt 56 E	PO Box 36	Sebree	42455	(270) 835-7521	(270) 835-9521
Seminary Times	Louisville Presbyterian Theological Seminary	1044 Alta Vista Rd	Louisville	40205	(502) 895-3411	(502) 895-1096
Sentinel (The)	1558 Hill St		Radcliff	40160	(270) 351-4407	(270) 351-4407
Sentinel Echo (The)	123 W 5th St	PO Box 830	London	40743	(606) 878-7400	(606) 878-7404
Sentinel-News	703 Taylorsville Rd	PO Box 399	Shelbyville	40066	(502) 633-2526	(502) 633-2618
Somerset Pulaski News Journal	675 Monticello St	PO Box 1565	Somerset	42502	(606) 678-0161	(606) 678-9032
Southsider Magazine	434 Old Vine St	PO Box 22731	Lexington	40622	(859) 281-2379	(859) 255-0672
Spectrum	Spalding Univ	851 S 4th St	Louisville	40203	(502) 585-9911	(502) 588-7170
Spencer Magnet (The)	51 W Main St	PO Box 219	Taylorsville	40071	(502) 477-2239	(502) 477-2110
Springfield Sun (The)	108 Progress Ave	PO Box 31	Springfield	40069	(859) 336-3716	(859) 336-7718
State Journal (The)	1216 Wilkinson Blvd	PO Box 368	Frankfort	40602	(502) 227-4556	(502) 227-2831
Sturgis News (The)	617 N Adams St	PO Box 218	Sturgis	42459	(270) 333-5545	(270) 333-9943
Thoroughbred News (The)	KY State Univ		Frankfort	40601	(502) 597-7377	(502) 597-6764
Thousandsticks News	2009 Main St	PO Box 917	Hyden	41749	(606) 672-3399	(606) 672-7409
Three Forks Tradition	87 Main St	PO Box 557	Beattyville	41311	(606) 464-2888	(606) 464-2388
Times Argus (The)	202 W Broad St	PO Box 31	Central City	42330	(270) 754-2331	(270) 754-1805
Times Journal (The)	120 Wilson St	PO Box 190	Russell Springs	42642	(270) 866-3191	(270) 866-3198
Times Leader	607 W Washington St	PO Box 439	Princeton	42445	(270) 365-5588	(270) 365-7299
Timea Tribune	201 N Kentucky Ave	PO Box 516	Corbin	40701	(270) 528-2464	(606) 528-9850
Todd County Standard Inc		PO Box 308	Elkton	42220	(270) 265-2439	(270) 265-2571
Tompkinsville News	105 N Main St		Tompkinsville	42167	(270) 487-5576	(270) 487-8639
Towers	Southern Baptist Theological Seminary	2825 Lexington Rd	Louisville	40280	(502) 897-4310	(502) 897-4880
Trail Blazer (The)	Morehead State Univ	102 Breckinridge	Morehead	40351	(606) 783-5312	(606) 783-9113
Tribune-Courier	100 W 11th St	PO Box 410	Benton	42025	(270) 527-3162	(270) 527-4567
Tri-City News (The)	805 E Main St		Cumberland	40823	(606) 589-2588	(606) 589-2689
Trimble Banner	12216 US Hwy 42	PO Box 289	Bedford	40006	(502) 255-3205	(502) 255-7797
Troublesome Creek Times (The)	27 E Main St	PO Box 1500	Hindman	41822	(606) 785-5134	(606) 785-0105
T-Ville News Trader (The)	105 N Main St		Tompkinsville	42167	(270) 487-5576	(270) 487-8639
Union County Advocate (The)	214 W Main St	PO Box 370	Morganfield	42437	(270) 389-1833	(270) 389-3926
Union Express (The)	Union College	C/M Box 841	Barbourville	40906	(606) 546-1251	
Utopian	Thomas More College		Crestview Hills	41017	(859) 344-3605	(859) 344-3345
Voice Tribune (The)	3818 Shelbyville Rd	PO Box 7129	Louisville	40257	(502) 897-8900	(502) 897-8915
Wayne County Outlook	109 E Columbia Ave	PO Box 432	Monticello	42633	(606) 348-3338	(606) 348-8848
West Kentucky News		PO Box 1135	Paducah	42002	(270) 442-7389	(270) 442-5220
Winchester Sun (The)	20 Wall St	PO Box 4300	Winchester	40392	(859) 744-3123	(859) 745-0638
Wolfe County News		PO Box 129	Campton	41301	(606) 668-3595	(606) 662-4010
Woodford Sun	184 S Main St	PO Box 29	Versailles	40383	(859) 873-4131	(859) 873-0300

Source: The Kentucky Directory Gold Book 2005-2006

RADIO & TELEVISION STATIONS

CITY	COMPANY	PHONE
Albany	WANY 1390-AM/106.3-FM	(606) 387-5186
Albany	WSBI 1250-AM	(606) 387-8126
Ashland	Daystar WTSF-TV 61	(606) 329-2700
Ashland	WLGC 1520-AM/105.7-FM	(606) 920-9565
Ashland	WOKT 1040-AM/WOKO 1060-AM	(606) 928-3778
Barbourville	TV4	
Barbourville	WYWY 950-AM/WKKQ 96.1-FM	(606) 546-4128
Bardstown	WAKY 102.7-FM	(502) 348-3943
Bardstown	WBRT 1320-AM	(502) 348-3943
Beattyville	WLJC-TV (Channel 65)	(606) 464-3600
Beattyville	WLJC 102.1-FM	(606) 464-3600
Benton	WCBL 1290-AM/99.1-FM	(270) 527-3102
Bowling Green	WBKO/WBWG-TV (Channel 13)	(270) 781-1313
Bowling Green	WKYU-PBS	(270) 745-2400
Bowling Green	WNKY-TV (Channel 40)	(270) 781-2140
Bowling Green	WBGN 1340-AM/WUHU 107.1-FM	(270) 843-0107
Bowling Green	WCVK 90.7-FM/WJVK 91.7-FM	(270) 781-7326
Bowling Green	WGGC 95.1-FM	(800) 275-9442
Bowling Green	WKCT 930-AM/WDNS 93.3-FM	(270) 781-2121
Bowling Green	WKYU 88.9-FM/WDCL 89.7-FM/WKPB 89.5-FM/WKUE-FM	(270) 745-5489
Bowling Green	WLYE 94.1-FM	(270) 843-3333
Bowling Green	WRUS 610-AM/WBVR 96.7-FM	(270) 843-3333
Bowling Green	WWHR 91.7-FM	(270) 745-5439
Brandenburg	WMMG 1140-AM/93.5-FM	(270) 422-4440
Burkesville	WKYR 107.9-FM	(270) 433-7191
Cadiz	WHVO 1480-AM	(270) 886-1480
Cadiz	WKDZ 1110-AM/106.5-FM	(270) 522-3232
Calvert City	WCCK 95.7-FM	(270) 395-5133
Campbellsville	WOBP-TV 4	(270) 789-5210
Campbellsville	WAKY 1540-AM/WGRK 103.1-FM	(270) 789-1464
Campbellsville	WGRK 103.1-FM	(270) 932-7401
Campbellsville	WTCO 1450-AM/WCKQ 104.1-FM	(270) 789-2401
Campbellsville	WVLC 99.9-FM	(270) 789-0099
Catlettsburg	WTCR 1420-AM/103.3-FM	(606) 739-8427
Central City	WMTA 1380-AM	(270) 754-1380
Central City	WNES 1050-AM/WQXQ 101.9-FM	(270) 754-3000
Columbia	WAIN 1270-AM/93.5-FM	(270) 384-2135
Columbia	WHVE 92.7-FM	(270) 384-7979
Corbin	WCTT 680-AM/107.3-FM	(606) 528-4717
Corbin	WKDP 1330-AM/99.5-FM	(606) 528-8617
Cumberland	WCPM 1280-AM/WSEH 102.7-FM	(606) 589-4623
Cynthiana	WCYN 1400-AM	(859) 234-1400
Danville	WDFB 1170-AM/88.1-FM	(859) 236-9333
Danville	WHBN 1420-AM	(859) 236-2711
Danville	WHIR 1230-AM/WHIR 107.1-FM/WRNZ 105.1-FM	(859) 236-2711
Dry Ridge	WNKR 106.5-FM	(859) 824-9106
East Bernstadt	WJJA 98.5-FM	(606) 843-9999
East Bernstadt	WOBZ-TV (Channel 9)	(606) 843-9999
Eddyville	WWLK 900-AM	(270) 388-9726
Edmonton	WKNK 99.1-FM	(270) 432-0990
Elizabethtown	WASE 103.5-FM	(270) 766-1035
Elizabethtown	WIEL 1400-AM/WTHX 107.3-FM	(270) 763-0800
Elizabethtown	WKMO 106.3-FM	(270) 763-0800
Elizabethtown	WLVK 105.5-FM	(270) 766-1035
Elizabethtown	WQXE 98.3-FM	(270) 737-8000
Elizabethtown	WRZI 101.5-FM	(270) 763-0800
Elizabethtown	WULF 94.3-FM	(270) 765-0943
Elkton	WEKT 1070-AM	(270) 265-5636
Falmouth	WIOK 107.5-FM	(859) 472-1075
Falmouth	WYGH 1440-AM	(859) 472-1075
Flemingsburg	WFLE 1060-AM/95.1-FM	(606) 849-4433
Florence	ICN6-TV	(859) 392-7685
Frankfort	Kentucky Broadcasters Association	(888) 843-5221
Frankfort	KY Afield	
Frankfort	WKYT-TV (Bureau)	(502) 564-3400
Frankfort	WLKY-TV (Bureau)	(502) 875-5151
Frankfort	Kentucky Public Radio Capitol Bureau	(502) 641-3404
Frankfort	WFKY 1490-AM/WKYW 104.9-FM/WKED 103.7-FM	(502) 223-6924
Frankfort	WKYL 102.1-FM	(502) 875-1130
Franklin	WFKN 1220-AM	(502) 696-9595
Frenchburg	WUPX-TV (Channel 67)	(606) 586-4481
Fulton	WKZT 1270-AM	(606) 768-9282
Georgetown	WRVG 89.9-FM	(270) 472-1270
Glasgow	WCDS 1440-AM/WHHT 106.7-FM	(270) 651-6050
Glasgow	WCDS 1440-AM/WOVO 105.3-FM	(270) 651-6050
Glasgow	WCLU 1490-AM/WCLU 102.3-FM	(270) 651-9149
Glasgow	WKLX 100.7-FM	(270) 651-6050
Glasgow	WPTQ 103.7-FM/WHHT 106.7-FM	(270) 651-6050

RADIO & TELEVISION STATIONS

CITY	COMPANY	PHONE
Grayson	WGOH 1370-AM/WUGO 102.3-FM	(606) 474-5144
Greenville	WKYA 105.5-FM	(270) 338-6655
Hardin	WAAJ 89.7-FM	(270) 437-4095
Hardin	WVHM 90.5-FM	(270) 437-4095
Hardinsburg	WXBC 104.3-FM	(270) 756-1043
Hardinsburg	WFSR 970-AM/WTUK 105.1-FM	(606) 573-1470
Harlan	WHLN 1410-AM	(606) 573-2540
Harold	WPRG-TV (Channel 5)	(606) 478-4200
Harold	WYMT-TV (Bureau)	(606) 478-5711
Harold	WXLR 104.9-FM/WXHZ 105.3-FM	(606) 478-1040
Hartford	WAJA 1600-AM/WXMZ 106.3-FM	(270) 298-3268
Hartford	WAJA 1600-AM/WXMZ 106.3-FM	(270) 298-3268
Hartford	WSNR 1600-AM/WKHB 106.3-FM	(270) 298-3268
Hartford	WWHK 105.5-FM	(270) 338-2815
Hazard	WYMT-TV (Channel 57)	(606) 436-5757
Hazard	WJMD 104.7-FM	(606) 439-3358
Hazard	WKIC 1390-AM/WSGS 101.1-FM751	(606) 436-2121
Hazard	WZQQ 97.9-FM	(606) 436-9898
Henderson	WEHT-TV (Channel 25)	(800) 879-8542
Henderson	WSON 860-AM	(270) 826-3923
Highland Heights	WNKU 89.7-FM	(859) 572-6500
Hindman	WKCB 1340-AM/107.1-FM	(606) 785-3129
Hindman	WQXY 1560-AM	(606) 785-3129
Hodgenville	WXAM 430-AM	(270) 358-4707
Hopkinsville	WKAG-TV (Channel 43)	(270) 885-4300
Hopkinsville	WHOP 1230-AM/98.7-FM	(270) 885-5331
Hopkinsville	WNKJ 89.3-FM	(270) 886-9655
Irvine	WIRV 1550-AM	(606) 723-5138
Jackson	WEKG 810-AM/WJSN 106.5-FM	(606) 666-7531
Jamestown	WJRS 104.9-FM	(270) 343-4444
Jenkins	WKYG 1000-AM	(606) 832-4655
Keavy	WVCT 91.5-FM	(606) 528-4671
Lebanon	WQ6AY-TV	(270) 692-0237
Lebanon	WLBN 1590-AM/WLSK 100.9-FM	(270) 692-3126
Leitchfield	WMTL 870-AM/WKHG 104.9-FM	(270) 259-3165
Lexington	KET-TV (Channels 1-8)	(859) 258-7000
Lexington	WDKY-TV (Channel 56)	(859) 269-5656
Lexington	WKMJ-TV (Channel 15)	(859) 258-7000
Lexington	WKYT-TV (Channel 27)	(859) 299-0411
Lexington	WLEX-TV (Channel 18)	(859) 259-1818
Lexington	WTVQ-TV (Channel 36)	(859) 294-3836
Lexington	Radio Vida WYGH 1440-AM	(859) 420-5544
Lexington	WBTF 107.9-FM	(859) 233-1515
Lexington	WBUL 98.1-FM	(859) 422-1000
Lexington	WBVX 92.1-FM	(859) 233-1515
Lexington	WCYN 102.3-FM	(859) 253-5900
Lexington	WKQQ 100.1-FM/WLKT 104.5-FM	(859) 422-1000
Lexington	WLAP 630-AM/WXRA 1580-AM	(859) 422-1000
Lexington	WLRO 101.5-FM/WXZZ 103.3-FM/WLTO 102.5-FM	(859) 253-5900
Lexington	WLXG 1300-AM/WGKS 96.9-FM/WCDA 106.3-FM	(859) 233-1515
Lexington	WLXO 96.1-FM	(859) 233-1515
Lexington	WMJK 105.5-FM	(859) 422-1000
Lexington	WMJR 1380-AM	(859) 278-0894
Lexington	WMKJ 105.5-FM/WMXL 94.5-FM/WXRA 105.5-FM	(859) 422-1000
Lexington	WRFL 88.1-FM	(859) 257-4636
Lexington	WUKY 91.3-FM	(859) 257-3221
Lexington	WVLK 590-AM/WVLK 92.9-FM	(859) 253-5900
Liberty	WWFT 1250-AM	(859) 245-1000
Liberty	WKDO 1560-AM/98.7-FM	(606) 787-7331
London	WFTG 1400-AM/WWEL 103.9-FM	(606) 864-2148
London	WGWL 980-AM	(606) 878-0980
London	WGWM 980-AM	(606) 878-0980
London	WWLT 103.1-FM	(859) 885-7109
Louisa	WYGE 92.3-FM	(606) 877-1326
Louisa	WSAC 92.3-FM	(606) 638-9203
Louisa	WZAQ 92.3-FM	(606) 638-9203
Louisville	WAVE-TV (Channel 3)	(502) 561-4150
Louisville	WBKI-TV (Channel 34)	(502) 809-3400
Louisville	WBNA-TV 21	(502) 964-2121
Louisville	WDRB-TV (Channel 41)	(502) 584-6441
Louisville	WHAS-TV (Bureau)	(502) 582-7220
Louisville	WHAS-TV (Channel 11)	(502) 582-7711
Louisville	WLKY-TV (Channel 32)	(502) 893-3671
Louisville	WYCS-TV 24	(502) 966-0624
Louisville	Kentucky News Network	(888) 566-0001
Louisville	WAMZ 97.5-FM	(502) 479-2222
Louisville	WDJX 99.7-FM/WLRS 105.1-FM/WXMA 102.3-FM	(502) 625-1200
Louisville	WEGK 104.3-FM/WGZB 96.5-FM/WMJM 101.3-FM	(502) 625-1220

RADIO & TELEVISION STATIONS

CITY	COMPANY	PHONE
Louisville	WFIA 900-AM/WGTK 970-AM/WFIA 94.7-FM/WRVI 105.9-FM	(502) 339-9470
Louisville	WFPL 89.3-FM/WFPK 91.9-FM/WUOL 90.5-FM	(502) 814-6500
Louisville	WGTK 970-AM/WRVI 105.9-FM	(502) 339-9470
Louisville	WHAS 840-AM/WKJK 1080-AM	(502) 479-2222
Louisville	WJIE 88.5-FM/93.9-FM	(502) 968-1220
Louisville	WJZL 93.1-FM	(502) 479-2222
Louisville	WLCR 1040-AM	(502) 451-9527
Louisville	WLLV 1240-AM/WLLU 1350-AM	(502) 776-1240
Louisville	WPTI 103.9FM/WSFR 107.7-FM	(502) 589-4800
Louisville	WQMF 95.7-FM/WTFX 100.5-FM/WZKF KISS 98.9-FM	(502) 479-2222
Louisville	WRKA 103.1-FM/WVEZ 106.9-FM	(502) 589-4800
Louisville	WTMT 620-AM/WTSZ 105.7-FM	(502) 583-6200
Louisville	WTSZ 1600-AM/105.7-FM	
Louisville	WUOL 90.5-FM	(502) 814-6513
Louisville	WXLN 105.1-FM	(502) 777-9956
Louisville	WXXA 790-AM	(502) 927-8121
Madisonville	WFMW 730-AM/WKTG 93.9-FM	(270) 821-4096
Madisonville	WKTG 93.9-FM	(270) 821-1156
Madisonville	WSOF 89.9-FM	(270) 825-3004
Madisonville	WTTL 1310-AM/WYMV 106.9-FM/WWKY 97.9-FM	(270) 821-1310
Manchester	WKLB 1290-AM	(606) 598-2445
Manchester	WTBK 105.7-FM	(606) 598-7588
Marion	WMJL 1500-AM/102.7-FM	(270) 965-2271
Martin	WMDJ 100.1-FM	(606) 874-8005
Mayfield	WDXR 1450-AM/WLIE 94.3-FM	(270) 443-1000
Mayfield	WKBG 102.1-FM	(270) 247-5122
Mayfield	WLLE 94.7-FM	(270) 247-5122
Mayfield	WQGR 94.7-FM	(270) 247-5122
Mayfield	WYMC 1430-AM	(270) 247-1430
Maysling	WTOW 920-AM/WXKQ 103.9-FM	(606) 633-2711
Maysville	WFTM 1240-AM/95.9-FM	(606) 564-3361
McDaniels	WBFI 91.5-FM/WBFI 99.9-FM	(270) 257-2689
Middlesboro	WYMT-TV (Bureau)	(606) 248-5702
Middlesboro	WFXY 1490-AM/WXJB 96.5-FM/WANO 1230-AM	(606) 248-1560
Middlesboro	WMIK 560-AM/92.7-FM	(606) 248-5842
Monticello	WFLW 1360-AM/WKYM 101.7-FM	(606) 348-7083
Monticello	WMKZ 93.1-FM	(606) 348-3393
Morehead	WIOBM-5	(606) 784-7515
Morehead	WIVY 96.3-FM	(606) 784-9966

CITY	COMPANY	PHONE
Morehead	WMKY 90.3-FM	(606) 783-2001
Morganfield	WMSK 1550-AM/95.3-FM	(270) 389-1550
Morgantown	WLBQ 1570-AM	(270) 526-3321
Mt Sterling	WMST 1150-AM	(859) 498-1150
Munfordville	WLOC 1150-AM	(270) 786-1000
Murray	WQTV-TV	
Murray	WKMS 91.3-FM	(800) 599-4737
Murray	WNBS 1340-AM/WRKY 1130-AM/WFGE 103.7-FM	(270) 753-2400
Nicholasville	WVRB 95.3-FM	(859) 885-7109
Nortonville	WKMA-TV 35	(270) 669-4016
Owensboro	Brescia Broadcast	(270) 685-3131
Owensboro	WKCM 1160-AM/WBIO 94.7-FM	(270) 927-8121
Owensboro	WKWC 90.3-FM	(270) 852-3601
Owensboro	WOMI 1490-AM/WBKR 92.5-FM	(270) 683-1558
Owensboro	WTCJ 105.7-FM/WLME 102.9-FM/WXCM 97.1-FM	(270) 927-8121
Owingsville	WVJS 1420-AM	(270) 927-8121
Owingsville	WKCA-107.7 FM	(606) 674-2266
Paducah	WPSD-TV (Channel 6)	(270) 415-1900
Paducah	WGCF 89.3-FM	(270) 462-3020
Paducah	WKYX 570-AM/WKYQ 93-FM/WDDJ 96.9-FM/WPAD-AM	(270) 534-9690
Paducah	WLIE 94.3-FM	(270) 247-5122
Paducah	WLLE 102.1-FM	(270) 247-5122
Paducah	WREZ 105.5-FM	(270) 442-1055
Paducah	WZZL 106.7-FM/WREZ 105.5-FM	(270) 554-1067
Paintsville	WKLW 94.7-FM	(606) 789-6664
Paintsville	WKYH 600-AM	(606) 789-3333
Paintsville	WSIP 1490-AM/98.9-FM	(606) 789-5311
Paris	WPTJ 90.7-FM	(859) 484-9691
Pikeville	WBPA 1460-AM	(606) 754-5044
Pikeville	WJSO 90.1-FM	(606) 478-2969
Pikeville	WLSI 1240-AM/WZLK 107.5-FM	(606) 437-4051
Pikeville	WPKE 1240-AM/WPKE 103.1-FM/WDHR 93.1-FM/WBPA 1460-AM	(606) 437-4051
Pineville	WRPT 960-AM	(606) 432-8103
Pineville	WRIL 106.3-FM	(606) 337-5200
Pippa Passes	WWJD 91.7-FM	(606) 368-6131
Prestonsburg	WDOC 1310-AM/WQHY 95.5-FM	(606) 886-8409
Princeton	WPKY 1580-AM/WAVJ 104.9-FM	(270) 365-2072
Renfro Valley	WRVK 1460-AM	(606) 256-2146

RADIO & TELEVISION STATIONS

CITY	COMPANY	PHONE
Richmond	WCBR 1110-AM	(859) 623-1235
Richmond	WEKU 88.9-FM 96.9-FM 95.1-FM/WEKH 90.9-FM/WEKF 88.5-FM	(800) 621-8890
Richmond	WEKY 1340-AM/WCYO 100.7-FM/WKXO 1500-AM/WLFX 106.7-FM/WIRV 1550-AM	(859) 623-1340
Richmond	WXII (Channel 60)	(859) 622-1885
Russell Springs	WIDS 570-AM	(270) 866-8800
Russell Springs	WJKY 1060-AM	(270) 866-3487
Salyersville	WRLV 1140-AM/WRLV 97.3-FM	(606) 349-6125
Scottsville	WPBM-TV 31	(270) 618-8831
Scottsville	WLCK 1250-AM/WVLE 99.3-FM	(270) 237-3149
Shelbyville	WJZO 101.7-FM	(502) 479-2222
Somerset	WHMJ 102.3-FM	(606) 679-5151
Somerset	WKEQ 910-AM/WLLK 93.9-FM	(606) 678-5151
Somerset	WSFC 1240-AM/WSEK 97.1-FM	(606) 678-5151
Somerset	WTHL 90.5-FM	(606) 679-6300
Somerset	WTLO 1480-AM	(606) 678-8151
Stanford	WRSL 1520-AM/WXKY 96.3-FM	(606) 365-2126
Stanton	WXKY 96.3-FM	(859) 885-7109
Stanton	WBFC 1470-AM	(606) 663-6631
Stanton	WSKV 104.9-FM	(606) 663-2811
Tompkinsville	WTKY 1370-AM/92.1-FM/WKWY 102.7-FM	(270) 487-6119
Tyner	WWAG 107.9-FM	(606) 287-9924
Upton	WJCR 90.1-FM	(270) 369-8614
Vanceburg	WKKS 1570-AM/104.9-FM	(606) 796-3031
Vancleve	WMTC 730-AM/99.9-FM	(606) 666-5006
Versailles	WCGW 770-AM	(859) 873-8844
Versailles	WWFT 1250-AM/WCGW 770-AM/WJMM 99.1-FM	(859) 873-8096
West Liberty	WCBJ-FM 103.7	(606) 668-9225
West Liberty	WLKS 1450-AM/WLKS 102.9-FM	(606) 743-1029
West Liberty	WMOR 1330-AM/WQXX 106.1-FM	(606) 784-4141
Whitesburg	WEZC 1480-AM	(606) 855-7888
Whitesburg	WIFX 94.3-FM	(606) 633-9430
Whitesburg	WMMT 88.7-FM	(606) 633-0108
Whitley City	WHAY 98.3-FM	(606) 376-2218
Wickliffe	WBCE 1200-AM	(270) 335-5171
Wickliffe	WGKY 95.9-FM	(270) 335-3896
Williamsburg	WEKC 710-AM	(606) 549-3000
Williamsburg	WEZJ 1440-AM/WEZJ 104.3-FM/WEKX 102.7-FM	(606) 549-2285

Clark's Kentucky Almanac 2006

Source: The Kentucky Directory Gold Book 2005-2006

It's a Kentucky Thing

Renfro Valley Barn Dance — From downtown Chicago to Cincinnati, and finally home to Kentucky — Radio pioneer, John Lee Lair was instrumental in discovering and promoting the talents of many country music performers. His Cumberland Ridge Runners (the first string-band on radio to feature Kentucky mountain music) was a mainstay on Chicago's WLS "National Barn Dance" in the 1930s. To further his dream of moving his radio show closer to home, Lair and many of his entertainers went to station WLW in Cincinnati, Ohio. John Lair felt that radio needed a little more realism and more heart-felt sincerity. So there, at the Cincinnati Music Hall, the Renfro Valley Barn Dance was born in 1937. Within two years, the show finally went home — to Renfro Valley.

On opening night, November 4, 1939, Lair stepped to the microphone on the stage of the big barn and said: "This is the Renfro Valley Barn Dance, coming to you direct from a real barn in Renfro Valley, Kentucky — the first and only barn dance on the air presented by the actual residents of an actual community. ..." A Kentucky tradition was born; a tradition that lives on today in Renfro Valley.

Source: Kentucky Music Hall of Fame and Museum, www.kentuckymusicmuseum.com

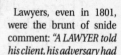

History of the Kentucky Almanac

Although John Bradford preserved much of the history of Central Kentucky in the *Kentucky Gazette*, we know little about his educational background, except that he "demonstrated as an adult a proficiency in both writing and mathematics" and was gifted with considerable mechanical ingenuity. Born June 6, 1749, in Prince County, Virginia, he was a descendant of William Bradford, a young man who sailed with his wife Dorothy for America in 1620 aboard the "Mayflower." William Bradford later became governor of the Plymouth Colony.

It 1775 Bradford came to Kentucky to be an assistant to George May, the official surveyor in the future Virginia county, Kentucky County. Like many, he crossed the mountainous barrier between Virginia and the "west" into mostly unexplored and untamed territory without his wife and children — they stayed behind in the safety of Fauquier County, Va. It would be 10 years (1785 or 1785) before he brought his family to Fayette County.

After a decade of intervening adventures, Bradford established the *Kentucky Gazette*, the first newspaper west of the Allegheny Mountains. The first issue was Aug. 11, 1787. Soon, the press of the *Gazette* was used in printing other pamphlets and books. Starting in 1788 Bradford also published a yearly booklet he called The Kentucky Almanac. Usually containing 30-40 pages, it may have been the first pamphlet printed in the West. Bradford eventually published over 100 books and pamphlets.

The Kentucky Almanac was a combination religious newspaper, short story magazine, scientific journal, farm paper, government bulletin and

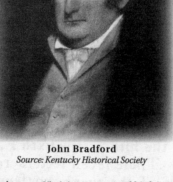

John Bradford
Source: Kentucky Historical Society

humor sheet. The price of the almanac was 12-1/2 cents per copy, one dollar per dozen, eight dollars per gross (Jan. 4, 1803) and available for sale in Lexington.

Bradford peppered his almanac with tidbits from Benjamin Franklin, reports from Europe, cures, anecdotes and comic stories. *Note* — Modern-day readers of the old almanac texts must be forewarned: until the late 1780s, American publishers practiced the English method of typesetting the letter "s" as an "f." Benjamin Franklin disapproved of this practice in the late 1780s.

Lawyers, even in 1801, were the brunt of snide comment: *"A LAWYER told his client, his adversary had removed his fuit out of one court into another; to which his client replied, "Let him remove it to the devil if he pleases; I am fure my attorney, for money, will follow it."*

Family advice was frequent: *"There fhould be methinks, as little merit in loving a woman for her beauty, as in loving a man for his profperity; both being equally subject to change."*

The publication of the Kentucky Almanac was, for the most part, continuous from 1794 until 1856. Although it remained in the Bradford family for many decades, the management changed a number of times in later years.

Sources: "The Voice of the Frontier, John Bradford's Notes on Kentucky," Thomas D. Clark, Ed., University Press of Kentucky (Lexington:1993) and http://www.mayflowerfamilies.com/mayflower/william_bradford.htm.

THE ALMANAC.

THE utility of the Almanac, is so well known, that few house-keepers fail to procure one every year. To enable professional men to know on what day of the week any day in any month would happen, various kinds of perpetual almanacs have been invented, and some of them applied to a ring, a seal, a watch, and even a watch paper; but in order to have at all times the benefit of such invention, it is necessary to carry it constantly with you. As the most portable of these were liable to be lost or mislaid, attempts to form and commit to memory a perpetual almanac, have completely succeeded. The following is descriptive of one of the best that has been published, and is founded on the Gregorian Calendar, as adopted in the Prayer Book of the Church of England.

In the Calendar, opposite the first day of January is the letter A, and opposite the second day, the letter B, the third C, the fourth D, the fifth E, the sixth F, and the seventh G. These seven letters represent the seven days of the week, consequently opposite the eighth day of January is the Letter A again, and so on in the same succession throughout the year. Now if the first day of January should be Sunday the letter A will stand against every Sunday in the year; the letter B will stand against every monday in the year; &c. In order therefore to remember what letter stands opposite to the first day of every month in the Calendar, commit the following to memory.

Note — until the late 1780s, American publishers practiced the English method of typesetting the letter "s" as an "f".

Source: The Kentucky Almanac 1808, published by Dan Bradford, Lexington, Ky.

MAXIMS.
Time, Business and Recreation.

For every thing you buy or sell, let or hire, make an exact bargain at first; and be not put off to a here-after by one that says to you we shan't disagree about trifles.

Rather pay wages to a servant, than accept the offered help of occasional attendants—such are never paid.

He that followeth his recreation when he should be minding his business, is likely in a little time to have no business to follow.

It is the greatest art and philosophy of life to make the best of the present, whether it be good or bad; and to bear the one with resignation and patience, and enjoy the other with thankfulness and moderation.

How unthinking must those unhappy persons be, who make it a common excuse for idle and pernicious amusement, that they do it to kill time.

After you have used faithful diligence in your lawful calling, perplex not your thoughts about the issue and success of your endeavors but labor to compose your mind to all conditions of life, to a quiet and steady dependance on God's providence, being anxiously careful for nothing.

Diligence alone is a fair fortune, and industry a good estate; Idleness doth waste a man as insensibly as industry doth approve him: You may be a younger brother for your own fortune, but industry will make you an heir.

Leisure, without learning, is death, and idleness the grave of a living man.

Rise early to your business—learn good things, and oblige good men; these are the things you never shall repent of.

Time is the most precious, and yet the most brittle jewel we have: it is what every man bids largely for, when he wants it, and throws it away most lavishly when he has it.

Source: The Kentucky Farmer's Almanac 1817, published by T. Henderson, Georgetown, Ky.

UNIQUELY KENTUCKY

Place Names

Robert Rennick

People have often asked how did something get its name? When enough have asked this of places in a certain area, some enterprising scholar, who calls himself an onomastician, produces a book (perhaps in dictionary form) that explains the name derivations in that area.

Some of the more discerning readers of these

> If the entry simply states that the place bears the name of so-and-so, it may, or may not, mean that it was actually named for so-and-so. Couldn't it have been named for another so-and-so or even another place called such-and-such?

dictionaries, however, may be confused about some of the derivations included, depending on how the derivations are worded. For instance, if the entry states that a certain place was named for so-and-so, then it's obvious that so-and-so was the name source. Or maybe not so obvious. Jonesville was named after Sam Jones can be taken at face value, but what if it turns out that Jonesville was named in 1850 and Sam Jones was born, in obscurity, only six months before?

If the entry simply states that the place bears the name of so-and-so, it may, or may not, mean that it was actually named for so-and-so. Couldn't it have been named for another so-and-so or even another place called such-and-such?

Even if the onomastician has zeroed in on the name source he may say nothing about why that name was given to the place. And isn't this what many of us who use a dictionary want to know: Why was the place called such-and-such instead of some other name? The onomastician, however, seldom obliges us. For one thing, the identities of few namers are even known; fewer still left for posterity their reasons for the names they gave. So we readers can only guess the reasons (or assume then on the basis of what we'd have done if we were the namers). And we'll never know if we've guessed right.

Sometimes an onomastician's name explanation is based on the assumption that the name of the place is the name that was actually intended for it. But what if it wasn't? In olden days people usually communicated by long hand, and handwriting then, as now, was undecipherable. Such was the case with several Kentucky post office petitions. The clerks in Washington receiving these petitions and acting upon them were under the usual time pressure of federal bureaucrats, and lacking any interest in seeking clarification would simply record what they thought they saw.

And thus Eveline Britton's request in 1902 for post office in her name to serve her Red River neighborhood in Clay County was recorded as **Eriline**. When she and her husband Van, who would operate it, learned how much trouble it would be to change it, they just let it go.

To serve their store near the head of the Right

Fork of Lawrence County's Blaine Creek, the Hay brothers submitted the name of a neighbor, Britt Maxie, for their new office. But in April 1899 the office was authorized as Mazie. When Britt himself became postmaster over twenty years later he too didn't bother to change the name.

So the dictionary complier will spend a lot of time seeking the source of Eriline and the identity of Mazie. I'm afraid I did when I first got into this business and was rushing to meet a deadline. Later, when I allowed myself to investigate name origins more carefully, I came up with the right derivations.

I also learned enough to correct other gross errors. For instance, I learned that **Helechawa** was not named for Delancey Walbridge's daughter but for his mother. And that **Gulnare** (in Pike County) was not the name of a character in a Sir Walter Scott novel, but rather one on *The Corsair*, an epic poem by Lord Byron.

The accurate onomastician must constantly be alert to errors and be ever more vigilant in seeking truer name derivations. But, more importantly, he should qualify what he thinks he knows. If he's not 100 percent sure of something he should say so, qualifying his attempted explanations with something like "it's believed that" or "some say that" or "according to local tradition." Until recently few of us have done this, probably because we don't want our readers to think we don't know our subject. But in many cases, at this point in our investigations, we really don't.

To serve the L&Ns Siler (formerly Dewey) Station in Knox County, three miles east of Corbin, a post office was established in 1899 to be called Peace for the local family of Simon and Sarah Peace. But the application for it was misread by postal clerk as **Place** and never corrected. While the post office was Place till it closed in November 1963, local folks have always called the vicinity Siler for the station. You can imagine how many times I've asked the derivation of the Place name. I have to explain to members of several Place families all over the country that this place was not named for any of their relatives.

Peace (or Place) be with you.

Reprinted with written permission of the Kentucky Humanities Council.

Oddsville, Kentucky

Helechawa (Wolfe County): W. Delancey Walbridge of New York, president of the Ohio and Kentucky Railroad, honored his mother, Helen Chase Walbridge, by basing the name of a new railroad station and post office on her name.

Thealka (Johnson County): This post office was named after a steamboat which honored the owner's daughter, Alka. The boat was meant to be The Alka, but the sign painter ran the letters together, and the rest is history.

Oddsville (Harrison County): Rejecting all of this community's preferred names because they were too common, the U.S. Post Office Department in Washington advised choosing an "odd" name. They know how to follow directions in Harrison County.

Mazie (Lawrence County): This post office was probably named for Britt Maxie, who submitted his own name to the U.S. Post Office Department, only to find that some clerk couldn't read his handwriting.

Blind Tiger: In the Upper South, this name usually describes a place that straddles two political jurisdictions, one wet and the other dry. There have been many Blind Tigers on the Kentucky-Tennessee line.

Battletown (Meade County): After a daylong fight between Nathan Hubbard and Jimmy Bennett over a disagreement long lost in the mists of history, someone suggested the obvious name for this community, where fisticuffs were not uncommon.

Eastern, Kentucky (Floyd County): Yes, there really is a post office named Eastern, Kentucky, and it's on the Right Fork of Beaver Creek some four miles above Martin.

Dogtown (Whitley County): The name was unofficial, but it stuck because of the mutts who chased the local mail carrier in this area near Williamsburg.

Disputanta (Rockcastle County): Suggested by a mediator, this was the perfect name for a community that had argued endlessly over the name of a new post office.

Pippa Passes (Knott County): Alice Lloyd, Boston-born founder of Alice Lloyd College, named the college community after the Robert Browning poem. Its heroine, Pippa, sings a song that famously ends, "God's in his heaven—All's right with the world!"

Contributed by The Kentucky Humanities Council.

Sponsors & Advertisers Index
(Sponsors are indicated in bold)

General Index

Note: Due to space constraints many of the remarkable individuals named in the various charts in the Sports section are not listed in this index. Also, for Sponsors and Advertisers, see index on page 784.

We invite you to join us in the continuation of a historical publication — the **Kentucky Almanac and Book of Facts.**

Granted, our adventure in publishing the first Kentucky Almanac since 1856 doesn't reach the challenges Dr. Thomas Walker or Christopher Gist faced as they entered the Kentucky wilderness. But, publishing an almanac is an enormous job. We suspected it from the beginning. Now we know for certain.

Would we have published the Kentucky Almanac and Book of Facts if we had known all the challenges, time and effort it would take? The answer is an unequivocal and resounding, YES. Admittedly we would do some things differently. But, we feel quite satisfied with our accomplishment. We are very proud of our new almanac and hope you find it informative, enlightening and enjoyable to read.

Despite all our efforts, we know it isn't perfect. Certainly, we want it to be perfect — an almanac that every Kentuckian will be proud of and turn to often for entertainment and the assurance that the content is accurate. We acknowledge that inadvertent mistakes have been made, important events and people unintentionally omitted. Send us corrections, additions, opinions, helpful hints and obscure, but significant facts, covering any topic pertinent to our understanding of Kentucky — where we've been and where we're going.

Call us with your comments at 1-800-944-3995; email us at info@theclarkgroupinfo. com; or visit our web site: www.kyalmanac.com/comments. Keep in mind we will use our web site to make corrections throughout the year. We will use your suggestions and guidance as we prepare for the 2007 edition and other publications.

Again, we wish to extend our deepest thanks to the many contributors who worked so hard, spending long hours researching, compiling, writing and editing the professional and scholarly essays contained within the almanac. We owe a similar debt of gratitude to the many community historians, librarians and officials who assisted us by submitting essays on their counties and cities. We trust that all of these contributors will be pleased and proud to have played such an important part in this truly historic accomplishment.

Finally, we want to acknowledge our eternal gratitude for our friend and supporter, Thomas D. Clark, who died June 28, 2005, just weeks before his 102nd birthday. Dr. Clark's early advice, encouragement and his outstanding Foreword were always leading us over these last few months to keep going and to make sure we did our best. We hope Dr. Clark would have been as proud of the Kentucky Almanac as he was of his chosen state, Kentucky.

Sincerely,
The Staff of The Clark Group
Lexington, Kentucky
Publishers of Clark's Kentucky Almanac and Book of Facts 2006

The **Clark** Group